Lecture Notes in Computer Science 6996

Commenced Publication in 1973
Founding and Former Series Editors:
Gerhard Goos, Juris Hartmanis, and Jan van Leeuwen

Tevfik Bultan   Pao-Ann Hsiung (Eds.)

Automated Technology for Verification and Analysis

9th International Symposium, ATVA 2011
Taipei, Taiwan, October 11-14, 2011
Proceedings

 Springer

Volume Editors

Tevfik Bultan
University of California, Department of Computer Science
Santa Barbara, CA 93106-5110, USA
E-mail: bultan@cs.ucsb.edu

Pao-Ann Hsiung
National Chung Cheng University
Department of Computer Science and Information Engineering
168 University Road, Min-Hsiung, Chiayi, Taiwan–62102, ROC
E-mail: pahsiung@cs.ccu.edu.tw

ISSN 0302-9743   e-ISSN 1611-3349
ISBN 978-3-642-24371-4   ISBN 978-3-642-24372-1 (eBook)
DOI 10.1007/978-3-642-24372-1
Springer Heidelberg Dordrecht London New York

Library of Congress Control Number: 2011936735

CR Subject Classification (1998): D.2, D.1, F.3, C.2, D.3, C.2.4

LNCS Sublibrary: SL 2 – Programming and Software Engineering

Typesetting: Camera-ready by author, data conversion by Scientific Publishing Services, Chennai, India

Printed on acid-free paper

Springer is part of Springer Science+Business Media (www.springer.com)

Preface

This volume contains the proceedings of the 9th International Symposium on Automated Technology for Verification and Analysis (ATVA) held during October 11–14, 2011 in Taipei, Taiwan. The goal of the ATVA conferences is to promote research on theoretical and practical aspects of automated analysis, verification and synthesis by providing a forum for interaction between the regional and the international research communities and industry in the field.

There were 75 papers submitted to ATVA 2011, and among these the Program Committee accepted 23 regular papers, 2 tool papers and 11 short papers. Each paper received at least three reviews which was followed by an online discussion conducted using the EasyChair system. In addition to the presentation of the accepted papers, the ATVA 2011 program included three keynote talks and tutorials by Edmund M. Clarke (Carnegie Mellon University, USA), Orna Kupferman (Hebrew University, Israel) and Daniel Kroening (Oxford University, UK), as well as two invited talks by Masahiro Fujita (University of Tokyo, Japan) and Moonzoo Kim (KAIST, Korea), resulting in an exceptionally strong technical program of the highest quality.

ATVA 2011 was co-located with the Infinity Workshop (co-chaired by Fang Yu and Chao Wang) and the Embedded Systems Week which consisted of three leading conferences: International Conference on Compilers, Architectures and Synthesis of Embedded Systems (CASES), International Conference on Hardware/Software Codesign and System Synthesis (CODES+ISSS), and the International Conference on Embedded Software (EMSOFT). The co-location of these events created a unique environment for interaction among many researchers from a variety of areas which contributed to the success of ATVA 2011.

We would like to acknowledge the contributions that made ATVA 2011 a successful event. First, we would like to thank all the authors who submitted their work to ATVA and we hope that they continue to submit their high-quality work to ATVA in future years. We thank the Program Committee members and the external reviewers for their hard work in providing a rigorous and fair evaluation of each submission, and providing detailed comments and feedback to help authors improve their work. We are very grateful to the keynote and invited speakers for enriching the symposium by presenting their distinguished and internationally recognized research. We would like to thank the Steering Committee members for their guidance. We would like to thank the ATVA 2011

General Chair Hsu-Chun Yen and ATVA 2011 Local Arrangements Chair Farn Wang. Their contributions were crucial in making ATVA 2011 a successful event. Finally, we would like to thank the institutions that sponsored ATVA 2011.

We are proud of the quality of the ATVA 2011 proceedings and we sincerely hope that the readers find them informative and rewarding.

July 2011   Tevfik Bultan
                                                              Pao-Ann Hsiung

Organization

General Chair

Hsu-Chun Yen   National Taiwan University, Taiwan

Program Chairs

Tevfik Bultan   University of California at Santa Barbara, USA
Pao-Ann Hsiung   National Chung Cheng University, Taiwan

Program Committee

Parosh Abdulla	Uppsala University, Sweden
Samik Basu	Iowa State University, USA
Bernard Boigelot	University of Liege, Belgium
Ahmed Bouajjani	University of Paris Diderot, France
Swarat Chaudhuri	Pennsylvania State University, USA
Alessandro Cimatti	FBK-IRST, Italy
E. Allen Emerson	University of Texas at Austin, USA
Xiang Fu	Hofstra University, USA
Masahiro Fujita	University of Tokyo, Japan
Patrice Godefroid	Microsoft Research, USA
Susanne Graf	Verimag Laboratory, France
Holger Hermanns	Saarland University, Germany
Franjo Ivancic	NEC Laboratories, USA
Jie-Hong Roland Jiang	National Taiwan University, Taiwan
Sarfraz Khurshid	University of Texas at Austin, USA
Daniel Kroening	Oxford University, UK
Orna Kupferman	Hebrew University, Israel
Insup Lee	University of Pennsylvania, USA
Jerome Leroux	CNRS, France
Rupak Majumdar	Max Planck Institute, Germany
Darko Marinov	University of Illinois at Urbana-Champaign, USA
Kedar Namjoshi	Bell Labs, USA
Madhu Parthasarathy	University of Illinois at Urbana-Champaign, USA
Corina Pasareanu	NASA Ames Research Center, USA
Doron Peled	Bar Ilan University, Israel
Abhik Roychoudhury	National University of Singapore, Singapore
Andrey Rybalchenko	Technische Universität München, Germany
Sven Schewe	University of Liverpool, UK

Prasad Sistla	University of Illinois at Chicago, USA
Yih-Kuen Tsay	National Taiwan University, Taiwan
Tomas Vojnar	Brno University of Technology, Czech Republic
Bow-Yaw Wang	Academia Sinica, Taiwan
Chao Wang	NEC Laboratories, USA
Farn Wang	National Taiwan University, Taiwan
Hsu-Chun Yen	National Taiwan University, Taiwan
Fang Yu	National Chengchi University, Taiwan
Wenhui Zhang	Chinese Academy of Sciences, China

Local Arrangements Chair

Farn Wang	National Taiwan University, Taiwan

Steering Committee

E. Allen Emerson	University of Texas at Austin, USA
Insup Lee	University of Pennsylvania, USA
Doron Peled	Bar Ilan University, Israel
Teruo Higashino	Osaka University, Japan
Farn Wang	National Taiwan University, Taiwan
Hsu-Chun Yen	National Taiwan University, Taiwan

Sponsoring Institutions

National Taiwan University, College of EE and CS, Taiwan
Academia Sinica, Institute of Information Science, Taiwan
Academia Sinica, Research Center for Information Technology Innovation,
    Taiwan
National Science Council, Taiwan
Ministry of Education, Taiwan

External Reviewers

Jade Alglave	Marsha Chechik
Mohamed Faouzi Atig	Sanjian Chen
Anaheed Ayoub	Yu-Fang Chen
Gogul Balakrishnan	Misty Davies
Hernan Baro Graf	Laurent Doyen
Benedikt Bollig	Michael Emmi
Marco Bozzano	Constantin Enea
David Bushnell	John Fearnley
Chia-Wei Chang	Luis María Ferrer Fioriti
Sudipta Chattopadhyay	Emmanuel Fleury

Khalil Ghorbal
Hugo Gimbert
Alberto Griggio
Olga Grinchtein
Peter Habermehl
Cheng-Shen Han
Arnd Hartmanns
Nannan He
Alexander Heussner
Lukas Holik
Chung-Hao Huang
Geng-Dian Huang
Lei Ju
Lukasz Kaiser
Andrew King
Anvesh Komuravelli
David Landsberg
Adonis Lin
Michel Ludwig
Antoine Miné
Sergio Mover
Aniello Murano
O. Olivo
Hans-Jörg Peter
Dawei Qi

Markus Rabe
Ahmed Rezine
Alexander Roederer
Kristin Rozier
Indranil Saha
Roopsha Samanta
Sriram Sankaranarayanan
Wendelin Serwe
Junaid Siddiqui
Mihaela Sighireanu
Jiri Simacek
Ales Smrcka
Michael Tautschnig
Stefano Tonetta
Ming-Hsien Tsai
Andrea Turrini
Vincent Wang
Ralf Wimmer
Jung-Hsuan Wu
Zhilin Wu
Guowei Yang
Shun-Ching Yang
Yu Yang
Lingming Zhang

Table of Contents

Tool Papers

Short Papers

Statistical Model Checking
for Cyber-Physical Systems*

Edmund M. Clarke and Paolo Zuliani

Computer Science Department
Carnegie Mellon University
Pittsburgh, PA, USA
{emc,pzuliani}@cs.cmu.edu

Abstract. Statistical Model Checking is useful in situations where it is either inconvenient or impossible to build a concise representation of the global transition relation. This happens frequently with cyber-physical systems: Two examples are verifying Stateflow-Simulink models and in reasoning about biochemical reactions in Systems Biology. The main problem with Statistical Model Checking is caused by rare events. We describe how Statistical Model Checking works and demonstrate the problem with rare events. We then describe how Importance Sampling with the Cross-Entropy Technique can be used to address this problem.

1 Introduction

Cyber-Physical Systems are characterized by the tight interaction between a digital computing component (the Cyber part) and a continuous-time dynamical system (the Physical part). The concept is better explained by examples. A modern airliner governed by the autopilot is a typical Cyber-Physical System (CPS). The autopilot is a software which provides inputs to the aircraft's engines and flight control surfaces (*e.g.*, rudder, flaps, *etc.*) on the basis of various sensor readings and an appropriate control law. The autopilot greatly reduces the pilot's workload and can improve the aircraft's fuel economy. Another example of CPS is a car equipped with an Anti-lock Braking System. The ABS modulates braking power to avoid a complete lock-up of the car's wheels in hard braking or low adherence situations. In this way, the friction between the tires and the road surface is maintained, thereby allowing the driver to keep control of the vehicle and improving safety.

Cyber-Physical Systems enjoy wide adoption in our society, even in safety-critical applications, but are difficult to reason about. In particular, to automatically prove behavioral properties of a CPS is exceedingly difficult. One of the

* This research was sponsored by the National Science Foundation under contracts no. CNS0926181 and no. CNS0931985, the SRC under contract no. 2005TJ1366, General Motors under contract no. GMCMUCRLNV301, the Air Force (Vanderbilt University) under contract no. 18727S3, the GSRC under contract no. 1041377 (Princeton University), the Office of Naval Research under award no. N000141010188, and DARPA under contract FA8650-10-C-7077.

T. Bultan and P.-A. Hsiung (Eds.): ATVA 2011, LNCS 6996, pp. 1–12, 2011.

obstacles is due to the fact that currently we do not know how to interface formal verification techniques for the cyber part with the well-established engineering techniques used to design the physical part of the system [12]. Another obstacle is that most CPSs feature stochastic effects, because of uncertainties present in the system components or the environment. For example, a flight control system needs to be able to cope with (possibly) unreliable readings from sensors, or to recognize and react appropriately when hit by "random" cosmic radiation at high altitudes. As a result, fully formal verification of a CPS is currently not possible, while validation boils down to extensive system simulations and bench/live tests. However, in the past decade there has been progress towards formal verification for CPSs.

In this paper we single out one particular verification technique that aims at tackling both obstacles above: Statistical Model Checking [22,21,16,5]. This technique addresses the verification problem for general stochastic systems, *i.e.*, to compute the probability that a stochastic model satisfies a given temporal logic property. For example, we would like to know the probability of a fuel-control system failing to ensure an optimal air-fuel flow ratio, given unreliable readings from the engine's sensors. We express such properties in Bounded Linear Temporal Logic (BLTL), a variant of LTL [13] in which the temporal operators are equipped with time bounds. As CPS models, we use a stochastic version of control systems modeled in Stateflow/Simulink - the *de facto* standard tool for embedded system design.

Numerical methods [1,2,3,4,7] have been developed to compute with high precision the probability that a stochastic system satisfies a temporal logic formula, but they are generally only feasible for systems with up to $10^8 - 10^9$ states [10,18]. The state space of modern CPSs very often exceeds this limit (or is infinite), hence the need for methods such as Statistical Model Checking, which solve the verification problem for stochastic systems in a less precise, yet rigorous and more efficient way.

Statistical model checking addresses the verification problem as a statistical inference problem: it samples behaviors (simulations) of the system model, checks their conformance with respect to the temporal formula, and finally applies a *statistical estimation* technique to compute an approximate value for the probability that the formula is satisfied. The returned value will be, with high probability, close to the true probability that the formula holds. The key observation behind statistical model checking's efficiency is that for large, complex systems, simulation is generally easier and faster than building a concise representation of the global transition relation of the system.

Statistical model checking was introduced by Younes [20], and phrased as a hypothesis testing problem. In that setting, the task is to decide whether the temporal formula is satisfied with a probability greater than a given threshold. Later work [6,16] generalized statistical model checking using statistical estimation techniques (*e.g.*, the Chernoff bound). Hypothesis-testing methods are more efficient than estimation techniques when the probability that the formula holds is distant from the user-specified threshold [19]. Sequential Bayesian techniques for both hypothesis testing and estimation were introduced in [8,23] and shown to perform very well.

The main problem with statistical model checking is caused by rare events, *i.e.*, temporal formulae whose satisfaction probability is very small. When estimating the probability of such formulae, the number of simulations needed to ensure a good estimate becomes unfeasible. In this paper we show that Importance Sampling and the Cross-Entropy method can efficiently address this problem.

2   Background

Statistical model checking is essentially a Monte Carlo technique, since it is based on randomized sampling of simulations of a stochastic model. In this Section, we first describe the temporal logic used to express properties and how statistical model checking works. Next, we give a summary of the Monte Carlo method and the rare-event problem.

2.1   Statistical Model Checking

We start by defining the Bounded Linear Temporal Logic (BLTL) [11,8]. For a model $\mathcal{M}$, we denote by SV the finite set of real-valued state variables. An Atomic Proposition (AP) over SV is a Boolean predicate of the form $y \sim v$, where $y \in SV$, $\sim$ is one of $\{\geq, \leq, =\}$, and $v \in \mathbb{R}$. A BLTL property is built on a finite set of Boolean predicates over SV using Boolean connectives and temporal operators. The syntax of the logic is given by the following grammar:

$$\phi ::= y \sim v \,|\, (\phi_1 \vee \phi_2) \,|\, (\phi_1 \wedge \phi_2) \,|\, \neg\phi_1 \,|\, (\phi_1 \mathbf{U}^t \phi_2),$$

where $\sim \in \{\geq, \leq, =\}$, $y \in SV$, $v \in \mathbb{Q}$, and $t \in \mathbb{Q}_{\geq 0}$.

The formula $\phi_1 \mathbf{U}^t \phi_2$ holds true if and only if, *within* time t, ϕ_2 will be true and ϕ_1 will hold until then. Bounded versions of the usual $\mathbf{F}$ and $\mathbf{G}$ operators are easily defined: $\mathbf{F}^t \phi = true \; \mathbf{U}^t \phi$ requires ϕ to hold true within time t; $\mathbf{G}^t \phi = \neg \mathbf{F}^t \neg \phi$ requires ϕ to hold true up to time t. Also, BLTL can be seen as a sublogic of Metric Temporal Logic [9].

The semantics of BLTL is defined with respect to executions (traces) of $\mathcal{M}$. A trace σ is a sequence $(s_0, t_0), (s_1, t_1), \ldots$, with the meaning that the system moved to state s_{i+1} after having sojourned for time t_i in state s_i. We assume non-Zeno behavior about $\mathcal{M}$, *i.e.*, for any trace σ it must be $\sum_{i=0}^{\infty} t_i = \infty$. In other words, the system cannot make an infinite number of transitions in a finite amount of time. This assumption is necessary for ensuring termination of statistical model checking.

The fact that a trace σ satisfies the BLTL property ϕ is denoted by $\sigma \models \phi$. We denote the trace suffix starting at step i by σ^i, where σ^0 denotes the full trace σ.

Definition 1. *The semantics of BLTL for a trace σ^k $(k \in \mathbb{N})$ is:*

- $\sigma^k \models AP$ iff AP holds true in state s_k;
- $\sigma^k \models \phi_1 \vee \phi_2$ iff $\sigma^k \models \phi_1$ or $\sigma^k \models \phi_2$;
- $\sigma^k \models \phi_1 \wedge \phi_2$ iff $\sigma^k \models \phi_1$ and $\sigma^k \models \phi_2$;
- $\sigma^k \models \neg\phi_1$ iff $\sigma^k \models \phi_1$ does not hold;
- $\sigma^k \models \phi_1 \mathbf{U}^t \phi_2$ iff $\exists i \geq 0$ such that

    a) $\sum_{l=0}^{i-1} t_{k+l} \leq t$, and

    b) $\sigma^{k+i} \models \phi_2$, and

    c) $\forall\, 0 \leq j < i,\ \sigma^{k+j} \models \phi_1$.

Statistical model checking is based on checking system simulations, *i.e.*, *finite* traces (naturally, simulations need to be finite in length). Therefore, one has to prove that $\sigma \models \phi$ has a well-defined semantics and will not change its truth-value by continuing the simulation. In [23] we proved well-definedness and the fact that a finite prefix of the trace is sufficient for BLTL model checking, which is crucial for termination.

Definition 2. *[11,23] The sampling bound $\#(\phi) \in \mathbb{Q}_{\geq 0}$ of a BLTL formula ϕ is defined as:*

$$\#(y \sim v) = 0$$
$$\#(\neg\phi_1) = \#(\phi_1)$$
$$\#(\phi_1 \vee \phi_2) = \max(\#(\phi_1), \#(\phi_2))$$
$$\#(\phi_1 \wedge \phi_2) = \max(\#(\phi_1), \#(\phi_2))$$
$$\#(\phi_1 \mathbf{U}^t \phi_2) = t + \max(\#(\phi_1), \#(\phi_2))$$

Since we assumed non-zenoness, any trace will reach the sampling bound with a finite prefix (not necessarily of the same length). We have the following lemma.

Lemma 1. *[23] For any BLTL formula ϕ and trace σ, the relation $\sigma \models \phi$ is well-defined and can be checked using only a finite prefix of σ of duration $\#(\phi)$.*

The verification problem for a stochastic system $\mathcal{M}$ and a BLTL formula ϕ is the following: to compute the probability that $\mathcal{M}$ satisfies ϕ. We are in particular interested in discrete-time stochastic systems, since statistical model checking is based on simulation. The problem is well-posed, as it can be shown that the set of traces of $\mathcal{M}$ satisfying ϕ is measurable, thereby defining the probability p that $\mathcal{M}$ satisfies ϕ [22].

    Suppose now that the stochastic system $\mathcal{M}$ satisfies the BLTL formula ϕ with some (unknown) probability $p = \mathrm{Prob}\{\sigma \mid \sigma \models \phi\}$. The key idea behind statistical model checking [22] is that the behavior of $\mathcal{M}$ (with respect to property ϕ) can be modeled by a Bernoulli random variable with success parameter p. This random variable can be repeatedly evaluated via system simulation in the following way. Let σ be a trace of $\mathcal{M}$, then one can define the Bernoulli random variable B that returns 1 if $\sigma \models \phi$ and 0 otherwise. In other words, the probability mass function of B is

$$\mathrm{Prob}(B(\sigma) = 1) = p \qquad\qquad (\sigma \models \phi) \qquad\qquad (1)$$

$$\mathrm{Prob}(B(\sigma) = 0) = 1 - p \qquad\qquad (\sigma \models \neg\phi)$$

Therefore, by running a simulation of $\mathcal{M}$ and by checking ϕ on the resulting trace we can obtain a sample of B.

2.2 The Monte Carlo Method

We consider the problem of estimating the probability of rare events in a stochastic CPS by means of randomized (*i.e.*, Monte Carlo) techniques. An event is said to be *rare* when its probability of occurrence is very low, say 10^{-8}. The Monte Carlo approach for estimating probabilities is by means of relative frequencies. Let X be a random variable defined over a probability space $(\Omega, \mathcal{F}, \mathrm{P})$. Suppose we want to estimate $p = \mathrm{P}(X \in B)$, the probability that X belongs to a given Borel set B. We first obtain a number of independent realizations of $I_B(X)$, the indicator function of B — $I_B(x)$ is 1 if $x \in B$ ("$X \in B$ has occurred"), 0 otherwise — and then compute their average to estimate p.

The theoretical justification of the Monte Carlo method is the strong law of large numbers. It states that if $X_1, X_2, \ldots$ is a sequence of independent and identically distributed (iid) random variables with $\mathrm{E}[\|X_1\|] < \infty$, then

$$\mathrm{P}\left(\lim_{n \to \infty} \frac{S_n}{n} = \mu\right) = 1$$

where $S_n = X_1 + \cdots + X_n$ and $\mu = \mathrm{E}[X_1]$. This means that the measure of the set of sample points for which $\frac{S_n}{n}$ converges to μ is 1. Therefore, we can approximate μ by taking the average of a *finite* number of realizations (samples) of X_1, since we know that the average will not converge to μ only for a negligible subset of realizations (a set of measure 0).

Returning to our problem of estimating $\mathrm{P}(X \in B) = p$ for a given random variable X and Borel set B, note that the random variable $I_B(X)$ is a Bernoulli of success parameter p, that is, $\mathrm{P}(I_B(X) = 1) = p$. Also, note that $p = \mathrm{E}[I_B(X)]$. Now, given a finite sequence $X_1, \ldots, X_N$ of random variables iid as X, the *crude Monte Carlo estimator* $\hat{p} = \frac{1}{N} \sum_{i=1}^{N} I_B(X_i)$ will converge to p as $N \to \infty$ (with probability 1) by the strong law of large numbers. The estimator $\hat{p}$ is readily shown to be *unbiased* (*i.e.*, $\mathrm{E}[\hat{p}] = p$) and its variance is:

$$\mathrm{Var}(\hat{p}) = \frac{\mathrm{Var}(I_B(X))}{N} \ .$$

Also, from the central limit theorem it follows that for large N the distribution of $\hat{p}$ is approximately a normal distribution of mean $\hat{p}$ and variance $\mathrm{Var}(I_B(X))/N$. The variance of $\hat{p}$ will thus tends to 0 as we increase the sample size N, leading to more precise estimates. However, a small variance does not necessarily imply a good estimate.

The *relative error* associated with the estimate $\hat{p}$ is an important quantity for assessing the quality of an estimator, especially in the rare-event case ($p \ll 1$). It is defined as the ratio

$$\mathrm{RE}(\hat{p}) = \frac{\sqrt{\mathrm{Var}(\hat{p})}}{\mathrm{E}[\hat{p}]}$$

and intuitively it is a "measure" of the accuracy of the estimator $\hat{p}$ with respect to its standard deviation. Since the crude Monte Carlo estimator is unbiased, the sample $X_1, \ldots, X_N$ is iid, and $p \ll 1$, it follows that

$$\mathrm{RE}(\hat{p}) = \frac{\sqrt{\mathrm{Var}(I_B(X))/N}}{p} = \frac{\sqrt{p(1-p)}}{p\sqrt{N}} \approx \sqrt{\frac{1}{Np}} \; .$$

Now, if N is kept constant and $p \to 0$, it follows that $\mathrm{RE}(\hat{p}) \to \infty$. For example, to estimate $p = 10^{-8}$ with a relative error of 0.01 we would need about $N \approx \frac{1}{p\mathrm{RE}^2(\hat{p})} = 10^{12}$ samples — an unfeasible quantity. Therefore, in order to keep the relative error low as $X \in B$ becomes rarer, we need to increase the sample size, thereby meaning that crude Monte Carlo is not an efficient technique for estimating very low probabilities. Alternatively, one can try to find another estimator whose variance is smaller than $\mathrm{Var}(\hat{p})$, for a given sample size. Importance sampling is a technique for devising estimators with reduced variance, and thus with low relative error.

3   Importance Sampling

Importance Sampling is a variance-reduction technique for the Monte Carlo method, developed in the late 1940s. Here we present a brief overview of Importance Sampling — more details and applications can be found, for example, in Srinivasan's book [17].

3.1   Basics

We consider the more general case of estimating $c = \mathrm{E}[g(X)] < \infty$ for a random variable X and a measurable function $g{:}\mathbb{R} \to \mathbb{R}^{\geq 0}$. (By defining $g(X) = I_B(X)$ we recover the previous case.) We assume that the distribution of X is absolutely continuous with respect to the Lebesgue measure, and denote by f the corresponding density. The *crude Monte Carlo* (MC) estimator is

$$\hat{c} = \frac{1}{N} \sum_{i=1}^{N} g(X_i)$$

where $X_1, \ldots, X_N$ be random variables iid with density f. By the strong law of large numbers, $\hat{c}$ converges to c with probability 1. Also, it is unbiased, and its variance is

$$\mathrm{Var}(\hat{c}) = \frac{1}{N} (\mathrm{E}[g^2(X)] - c^2) \; . \tag{2}$$

In our statistical model checking setting, we are interested in determining the probability that a stochastic system satisfies a certain temporal logic formula ϕ. In this setting, the random variables $X_1, \ldots, X_N$ are independent executions (simulations) $\sigma_1, \ldots, \sigma_N$ of the system, represented by time series of the system variables (traces). The function g is just the model checker that verifies whether a trace satisfies ϕ. Therefore, given a trace σ the random variable $g(\sigma)$ is again a Bernoulli — 1 if the trace σ satisfies ϕ, and 0 otherwise. Also, it is the random variable previously defined in (1).

We now introduce Importance Sampling. Suppose we had another (absolutely continuous) distribution for X, with corresponding density f_*, such that the ratio f/f_* is well-defined. The entire theory of importance sampling rests upon the following fundamental identity:

$$c = \mathrm{E}[g(X)]$$
$$= \int_{\mathbb{R}} g(x)f(x)\,dx$$
$$= \int_{\mathbb{R}} g(x)\frac{f(x)}{f_*(x)}f_*(x)\,dx$$
$$= \int_{\mathbb{R}} g(x)W(x)f_*(x)\,dx$$
$$= \mathrm{E}_*[g(X)W(X)] \tag{3}$$

where $\mathrm{E}_*[\cdot]$ denotes expectation with respect to the density f_*. The term $W(x) = \frac{f(x)}{f_*(x)}$ is the *weighting* function, or *likelihood ratio*. Naturally, for all x such that $g(x)f(x) > 0$, it must be $f_*(x) > 0$. The density f_* is known as the *biasing* (or *proposal*) density.

The *Importance Sampling* (IS) estimator is

$$\hat{c}_{\mathrm{IS}} = \frac{1}{N}\sum_{i=1}^{N} g(X_i)W(X_i)$$

where $W(x) = f(x)/f_*(x)$ is the likelihood ratio and $X_1, \ldots, X_N$ are random variables iid with density f_* (the biasing density). The IS estimator is unbiased by (3), and its variance is:

$$\mathrm{Var}(\hat{c}_{\mathrm{IS}}) = \frac{1}{N}(\mathrm{E}_*[g^2(X)W^2(X)] - c^2) . \tag{4}$$

The crucial problem in importance sampling is to find a biasing density such that the variance (4) of the IS estimator is smaller than the variance (2) of the crude MC estimator.

It turns out that there exists a biasing density which can minimize the variance (4) of the IS estimator. In particular, it is easy to verify that when the function g is non-negative the following *optimal biasing* density actually results in a zero-variance estimator:

$$f_*(x) = \frac{g(x)f(x)}{c} .$$

But in practice it is difficult to sample from f_*, since it depends on $c = \mathrm{E}[g(X)]$, the (unknown) quantity we are trying to estimate. Therefore, instead of trying to come up with the optimal density, it may be preferable to search in a parametrized family of densities for a biasing density "close" to the optimal one. This is exactly the approach taken by the cross-entropy method.

4   The Cross-Entropy Method

The cross-entropy method was introduced in 1999 by Rubinstein [14]. Assume that the original (or nominal) density f of X belongs to a parametric family $\{f(\cdot, u) \mid u \in \mathcal{U}\}$, and in particular $f(\cdot) = f(\cdot, v)$ for some fixed $v \in \mathcal{U}$. (For example, a common family is the *natural exponential family*.) The method chooses the biasing density from the family such that the Kullback-Leibler divergence between the optimal biasing density and the chosen density is minimal.

The cross-entropy method has two basic steps:

1. find a density with minimal Kullback-Leibler divergence with respect to the optimal biasing density;
2. perform importance sampling with the biasing density computed in step 1 to estimate $\mathrm{E}[g(X)]$.

We will see that step 1 actually requires to sample X. In practice, the number of samples generated for step 2 will be larger than for step 1.

Definition 3. *The* Kullback-Leibler *divergence of two densities f, h is*

$$\mathcal{D}(f, h) = \int_{\mathbb{R}} f(x) \ln \frac{f(x)}{h(x)} \, dx.$$

The Kullback-Leibler divergence is also known as the *cross-entropy* (CE). Formally, $\mathcal{D}$ is not a distance, since it is not symmetric, *i.e.*, $\mathcal{D}(f, h) \neq \mathcal{D}(h, f)$ in general. However, it can be shown that $\mathcal{D}$ is always non-negative, and that $\mathcal{D}(f, h) = 0$ iff $f = h$. Therefore, the CE can be useful in assessing how close two densities are.

We recall that our task is to estimate $c = \mathrm{E}[g(X)]$, where X is a random variable with density f and g is a non-negative, measurable function. We want to find a density in the parametric family such that the CE with the optimal biasing density f_* is minimal. Therefore, we need to solve the minimization problem:

$$u^* = \operatorname*{argmin}_{u \in \mathcal{U}} \ \mathcal{D}(f_*(\cdot), f(\cdot, u))$$

where $f_*(x) = g(x) f(x, v)/c$ is the optimal biasing density. This can be turned into a maximization problem as follows:

$$
\begin{aligned}
\operatorname*{argmin}_{u \in \mathcal{U}} \ \mathcal{D}(f_*(\cdot), f(\cdot, u)) &= \operatorname*{argmin}_{u \in \mathcal{U}} \ \mathrm{E}_* \left[\ln \frac{f_*(X)}{f(X, u)} \right] \\
&= \operatorname*{argmin}_{u \in \mathcal{U}} \int_{\mathbb{R}} f_*(x) \ln f_*(x) \, dx - \int_{\mathbb{R}} f_*(x) \ln f(x, u) \, dx \\
&= \operatorname*{argmax}_{u \in \mathcal{U}} \int_{\mathbb{R}} f_*(x) \ln f(x, u) \, dx \\
&= \operatorname*{argmax}_{u \in \mathcal{U}} \int_{\mathbb{R}} g(x) f(x, v) \ln f(x, u) \, dx \\
&= \operatorname*{argmax}_{u \in \mathcal{U}} \ \mathrm{E}[g(X) \ln f(X, u)]
\end{aligned}
$$

where in the second step we used the fact is $\mathcal{D}$ is non-negative and that the first integral does not depend on u. It turns out that for certain families of densities the maximization problem can be solved *analytically* [15, Chapter 3].

We now assume that $\mathbf{X}$ is a random vector, *i.e.*, $\mathbf{X}\colon\Omega \to \mathbb{R}^n$, which implies that function g must be defined over $\mathbb{R}^n$. Note that this does not change what we obtained so far. The optimal parameter $\mathbf{u}^* = \operatorname{argmax}_{u\in\mathcal{U}} \mathrm{E}[g(\mathbf{X}) \ln f(\mathbf{X}, u)]$ when $\mathbf{X}$ is in an exponential family of distributions is:

$$u_j^* = \frac{\mathrm{E}[g(\mathbf{X})X_j]}{\mathrm{E}[g(\mathbf{X})]}$$

where $\mathbf{u}^* = (u_1^*, \ldots, u_n^*)$ and X_j is the j-th component of $\mathbf{X}$.

The optimal parameter thus depends on the quantity we wish to estimate, *i.e.*, $\mathrm{E}[g(\mathbf{X})]$, and therefore u^* needs itself to be estimated by MC simulation. In the one-dimensional case we have that

$$u^* = \frac{\mathrm{E}[g(X)X]}{\mathrm{E}[g(X)]}$$

and u^* may be estimated from a sample $X_1, \ldots, X_N$ iid with density f (the nominal density) as:

$$\hat{u}^* = \frac{\sum_{i=1}^N g(X_i)X_i}{\sum_{i=1}^N g(X_i)} . \tag{5}$$

However, in statistical model checking $g(X_i)$ is either 1 or 0 — a sample trace either satisfies a temporal logic property or it does not. Furthermore, in the rare event case it will be very unlikely to "see" a sample trace that satisfies the temporal logic property, which means that for reasonable sample sizes Eq.(5) would just give $\frac{0}{0}$.

The problem can be circumvented by noting that

$$u^* = \frac{\mathrm{E}[g(X)X]}{\mathrm{E}[g(X)]} = \frac{\mathrm{E}_w[g(X)W(X,w)X]}{\mathrm{E}_w[g(X)W(X,w)]}$$

where $W(x,w) = f(x)/f(x,w)$ and $w \in \mathcal{U}$ is an arbitrary parameter (recall that $f(x) = f(x,v)$ is the nominal density of X). Note that the expectation is computed with respect to the biased density $f(\cdot, w)$. Again, u^* can be estimated by

$$\hat{u}^* = \frac{\sum_{i=1}^N g(X_i)W(X_i, w)X_i}{\sum_{i=1}^N g(X_i)W(X_i, w)} \tag{6}$$

where each X_i is distributed as $f(\cdot, w)$. Basically, we use importance sampling with a biasing density given by the parameter w. Intuitively, w would have to be chosen in such a way that the estimator (6) is well-defined. This means that w should substantially increase the probability of the event $g(X) = 1$. In the literature w is know as the *tilting parameter*.

In the random vector case, we have samples $\mathbf{X}_1, \ldots, \mathbf{X}_N$ iid as $f(\cdot, w)$ and the j-th component of the optimal parameter $\mathbf{u}^*$ is estimated by

$$\hat{u}_j^* = \frac{\sum_{i=1}^N g(\mathbf{X}_i) W(\mathbf{X}_i, w) X_{ij}}{\sum_{i=1}^N g(\mathbf{X}_i) W(\mathbf{X}_i, w)}$$

where X_{ij} is the j-th component of $\mathbf{X}_i$.

5   Experiments

We report preliminary results showing that our technique can be utilized to efficiently address the rare-event problem in statistical model checking. We have considered an example of CPS that is part of the Stateflow/Simulink package demos. The model[1] describes a fault-tolerant fuel control system for a gasoline engine. It detects sensor failures, and dynamically adjusts the control law to provide seamless operation. The system aims at keeping the air-fuel ratio close to the *stoichiometric* ratio of 14.6. The "correct" fuel rate is estimated by taking into account sensor readings for the amount of oxygen present in the exhaust gas (EGO), for the engine speed, throttle command and manifold absolute pressure. In the event of a single sensor fault, *e.g.*, the EGO sensor, the system detects the situation, computes an estimate for the sensor's reading, and operates the engine with a higher fuel flow rate. If two or more sensors fail, the engine is shut down, since the system cannot reliably control the air-fuel ratio.

The Stateflow control logic of the system has a total of 24 locations, grouped in 6 parallel states. The Simulink part of the system is described by several nonlinear equations and a linear differential equation with a switching condition. Overall, this model provides a representative summary of the important features of a CPS.

Our stochastic system is obtained by introducing random faults in the EGO, speed and manifold pressure sensors. We model the faults by three independent Poisson processes with different arrival rates. When a fault occurs, it is "repaired" with a fixed service time of one second (*i.e.*, the sensor remains in fault condition for one second, then it resumes normal operation). The model has no free inputs, since the throttle command provides a periodic triangular input, and the nominal speed is never changed. This ensures that, once we set the three fault rates, for any given temporal logic property ϕ the probability that the model satisfies ϕ does not change.

For our experiments we model checked the following BLTL formula ϕ:

$$\phi = \mathbf{F}^{100}\mathbf{G}^1(FuelFlowRate = 0)).$$

Informally, we would like to estimate the probability that within 100 seconds the fuel flow rate stays at zero for one second. The nominal fault rates for the

---

[1] More information on the model is available at `http://mathworks.com/products/` `simulink/demos.html?file=/products/demos/shipping/simulink/sldemo_` `fuelsys.html`

three sensors are all equal to $1/3600$. Since engine shutdown occurs when two or more sensors are faulty, the probability that the system satisfies ϕ is likely to be very close to 0. To compute the optimal biasing density we used tilting rates all equal to $1/10$.

In the table below we report our preliminary results. We performed two experiments, depending on the number of samples used to compute the optimal CE rates (step 1) and in the importance sampling phase (step 2). In the table we report the estimate for the probability that ϕ holds, the (approximate) relative error, and the total computation time (*i.e.*, simulation, model checking, and CE method). The experiments have been performed on a 2.2GHz Opteron 6174 computer running Matlab R2010b on Linux (64-bit).

		Estimate	RE	Time (h)
Samples	step 1 : 1,000 step 2 : 10,000	5.1×10^{-15}	0.47	1.7
	step 1 : 10,000 step 2 : 100,000	2.17×10^{-14}	0.13	17.8

From the magnitude of the probability estimates, we see that a crude Monte Carlo estimation would require about 10^{14} samples just to obtain one "success" sample. With feasible sample sizes of the order of 10^5, the Monte Carlo estimator would most likely return 0, thus incurring in a high error. Techniques based on confidence interval computation (*e.g.*, Chernoff bound) would require even larger sample sizes.

6   Conclusions

Statistical model checking efficiently addresses verification by combining the Monte Carlo method with temporal logic model checking. The technique is especially useful for verifying systems with very large state spaces, such as cyber-physical systems. The main problem with statistical model checking is caused by rare events. We have showed that Importance Sampling and the Cross-Entropy method can address this problem. In particular, we have successfully verified a representative example of cyber-physical system coded as a Stateflow-Simulink model, for which traditional verification techniques are not feasible.

References

1. Baier, C., Clarke, E.M., Hartonas-Garmhausen, V., Kwiatkowska, M.Z., Ryan, M.: Symbolic model checking for probabilistic processes. In: Degano, P., Gorrieri, R., Marchetti-Spaccamela, A. (eds.) ICALP 1997. LNCS, vol. 1256, pp. 430–440. Springer, Heidelberg (1997)
2. Baier, C., Haverkort, B.R., Hermanns, H., Katoen, J.-P.: Model-checking algorithms for continuous-time Markov chains. IEEE Trans. Software Eng. 29(6), 524–541 (2003)

3. Ciesinski, F., Größer, M.: On probabilistic computation tree logic. In: Baier, C., Haverkort, B.R., Hermanns, H., Katoen, J.-P., Siegle, M. (eds.) Validation of Stochastic Systems. LNCS, vol. 2925, pp. 147–188. Springer, Heidelberg (2004)
4. Courcoubetis, C., Yannakakis, M.: The complexity of probabilistic verification. Journal of the ACM 42(4), 857–907 (1995)
5. Grosu, R., Smolka, S.A.: Carlo Model Checking. In: Halbwachs, N., Zuck, L.D. (eds.) TACAS 2005. LNCS, vol. 3440, pp. 271–286. Springer, Heidelberg (2005)
6. Hérault, T., Lassaigne, R., Magniette, F., Peyronnet, S.: Approximate probabilistic model checking. In: Steffen, B., Levi, G. (eds.) VMCAI 2004. LNCS, vol. 2937, pp. 73–84. Springer, Heidelberg (2004)
7. Hinton, A., Kwiatkowska, M.Z., Norman, G., Parker, D.: PRISM: A tool for automatic verification of probabilistic systems. In: Hermanns, H. (ed.) TACAS 2006. LNCS, vol. 3920, pp. 441–444. Springer, Heidelberg (2006)
8. Jha, S.K., Clarke, E.M., Langmead, C.J., Legay, A., Platzer, A., Zuliani, P.: A Bayesian approach to Model Checking biological systems. In: Degano, P., Gorrieri, R. (eds.) CMSB 2009. LNCS, vol. 5688, pp. 218–234. Springer, Heidelberg (2009)
9. Koymans, R.: Specifying real-time properties with metric temporal logic. Real-time Systems 2(4), 255–299 (1990)
10. Kwiatkowska, M.Z., Norman, G., Parker, D.: Symmetry reduction for probabilistic model checking. In: Ball, T., Jones, R.B. (eds.) CAV 2006. LNCS, vol. 4144, pp. 234–248. Springer, Heidelberg (2006)
11. Maler, O., Nickovic, D.: Monitoring temporal properties of continuous signals. In: Lakhnech, Y., Yovine, S. (eds.) FORMATS 2004 and FTRTFT 2004. LNCS, vol. 3253, pp. 152–166. Springer, Heidelberg (2004)
12. Parnas, D.L.: Really rethinking 'Formal Methods'. IEEE Computer 43(1), 28–34 (2010)
13. Pnueli, A.: The temporal logic of programs. In: FOCS, pp. 46–57. IEEE, Los Alamitos (1977)
14. Rubinstein, R.Y.: The cross-entropy method for combinatorial and continuous optimization. Methodology and Computing in Applied Probability 2, 127–190 (1999)
15. Rubinstein, R.Y., Kroese, D.P.: The Cross-Entropy Method. Springer, Heidelberg (2004)
16. Sen, K., Viswanathan, M., Agha, G.: Statistical model checking of black-box probabilistic systems. In: Alur, R., Peled, D.A. (eds.) CAV 2004. LNCS, vol. 3114, pp. 202–215. Springer, Heidelberg (2004)
17. Srinivasan, R.: Importance Sampling. Springer, Heidelberg (2002)
18. Younes, H.L.S., Clarke, E.M., Zuliani, P.: Statistical verification of probabilistic properties with unbounded until. In: Davies, J. (ed.) SBMF 2010. LNCS, vol. 6527, pp. 144–160. Springer, Heidelberg (2011)
19. Younes, H.L.S., Kwiatkowska, M.Z., Norman, G., Parker, D.: Numerical vs. statistical probabilistic model checking. STTT 8(3), 216–228 (2006)
20. Younes, H.L.S., Musliner, D.J.: Probabilistic plan verification through acceptance sampling. In: AIPS Workshop on Planning via Model Checking, pp. 81–88 (2002)
21. Younes, H.L.S., Simmons, R.G.: Probabilistic verification of discrete event systems using acceptance sampling. In: Brinksma, E., Larsen, K.G. (eds.) CAV 2002. LNCS, vol. 2404, pp. 223–235. Springer, Heidelberg (2002)
22. Younes, H.L.S., Simmons, R.G.: Statistical probabilistic model checking with a focus on time-bounded properties. Inf. Comput. 204(9), 1368–1409 (2006)
23. Zuliani, P., Platzer, A., Clarke, E.M.: Bayesian statistical model checking with application to Stateflow/Simulink verification. In: HSCC, pp. 243–252 (2010)

Max and Sum Semantics
for Alternating Weighted Automata

Shaull Almagor and Orna Kupferman

Hebrew University, School of Engineering and Computer Science, Jerusalem, Israel

Abstract. In the traditional Boolean setting of formal verification, alternating automata are the key to many algorithms and tools. In this setting, the correspondence between disjunctions/conjunctions in the specification and nondeterministic/universal transitions in the automaton for the specification is straightforward. A recent exciting research direction aims at adding a quality measure to the satisfaction of specifications of reactive systems. The corresponding automata-theoretic framework is based on *weighted automata*, which map input words to numerical values. In the weighted setting, nondeterminism has a minimum semantics – the weight that an automaton assigns to a word is the cost of the cheapest run on it. For universal branches, researchers have studied a (dual) *maximum* semantics. We argue that a *summation* semantics is of interest too, as it captures the intuition that one has to pay for the cost of all conjuncts.

We introduce and study alternating weighted automata on finite words in both the max and sum semantics. We study the duality between the min and max semantics, closure under max and sum, the added power of universality and alternation, and arithmetic operations on automata. In particular, we show that universal weighted automata in the sum semantics can represent all polynomials.

1 Introduction

Formal verification is the study of algorithms and tools for the development of correct hardware and software systems. Traditional formal verification is Boolean: the system may either satisfy its specification or not satisfy it. A recent exciting research direction aims at adding a quality measure to the satisfaction of specifications of reactive systems, and using it in order to formally define and reason about quality of systems and in order to improve the quality of automatically synthesized systems.

The *automata-theoretic* approach uses the theory of automata as a unifying paradigm for system specification, verification, and synthesis [17,19]. By viewing computations as words (over the alphabet of possible assignments to variables of the system), we can view both the system and its specification as languages, and reduce problems like model checking, satisfiability, and synthesis, to questions about automata. The automata-theoretic approach has proven to be very versatile and fruitful.

T. Bultan and P.-A. Hsiung (Eds.): ATVA 2011, LNCS 6996, pp. 13–27, 2011.

Traditional automata accept or reject their input, and are therefore Boolean. A *weighted automaton* maps each word to a value from some semiring [13]. We focus on the *tropical* semiring. There, each transition of the automaton has a *cost* in $\mathbb{R}$, and the value of a run is the sum of the costs of the transitions taken along the run. A nondeterministic automaton $\mathcal{A}$ may have several runs on a word, and the *weight* of a word w in $\mathcal{A}$ is the value of the cheapest run on it. Applications of weighted automata over the tropical semiring include formal verification, where WFAs are used for the verification of quantitative properties [3,4,6,9,15] for reasoning about probabilistic systems [2], and for reasoning about the competitive ratio of on-line algorithms [1], as well as text, speech, and image processing, where the costs of the automaton are used in order to account for the variability of the data and to rank alternative hypotheses [5,14].

The rich structure of weighted automata makes them intriguing mathematical objects. Fundamental problems that have been solved decades ago for Boolean automata are still open or known to be undecidable in the weighted setting. This includes the problem of deciding whether a given nondeterministic weighted automaton can be determinized, and the problem of deciding whether the language of one automaton is contained (in the weighted sense) in the language of another automaton [8].

In the Boolean setting, the model of *alternating* automata has proven to be especially useful in the context of formal verification. While in a nondeterministic automaton the transition function specifies only existential requirements on the run, in an alternating automaton it specifies both existential and universal requirements. The universal requirements correspond to conjunctions in the specifications, making the translation of temporal-logic formulas to alternating automata simple and linear [7,18], as opposed to the exponential translation to nondeterministic automata [19]. The linear translation of temporal logic to alternating automata is essential in automata-based algorithms for model checking of branching temporal logic formulas [12], and is useful for further minimization of the automata [16], for handling of incomplete information [11], for algorithms that avoid determinization [10], and more.

In the Boolean setting, the semantics of both disjunctions and conjunctions is straightforward. Recall that in a nondeterministic weighted automaton, the weight of a word is the value of the cheapest run on it. This meets our intuition of a "minimum semantics" for disjunctions in the weighted setting. It is less clear what the semantics of conjunctions should be. If we want to maintain the traditional helpful dualization between disjunctions and conjunctions, then an appropriate semantics for conjunction is a *maximum* semantics. The maximum semantics is also suitable for an analysis in which the weights correspond to a confidence or a truth-level indication. However, if the analysis is used in order to study the *cost* of the satisfaction, then an appropriate semantics is a *summation* semantics, in which the cost of satisfying a conjunction $\varphi_1 \wedge \varphi_2$ is not the maximal cost of satisfying φ_1 or φ_2, but rather the sum of these costs. Note that for the motivation of quantitative specifications, where one wants to replace Boolean satisfaction by a quantitative value that describes the quality of the satisfaction, both the maximum and the summation semantics are of interest. The two possible semantics for conjunctions in the weighted setting induce two different semantics for universal branches in alternating weighted automata.

We study alternating weighted automata on finite words, in both the maximum and summation semantics. We refer to the automata by MAX-AWAs and SUM-AWAs, respectively. We start with the max semantics. We study the expressive power of MAX-AWAs, their closure properties with respect to the operators min, max, and negation of weighted languages, the power of alternation with respect to nondeterminism, and arithmetics with MAX-AWAs. We also formalize the duality between the min semantics of existential transitions and the max semantics of universal transitions by means of a negation operator on weighted languages. Alternating automata with the max semantics are studied in [4]. The automata there are on infinite words.[1] The fact we work with finite words, where the value of a sequence of costs follows the tropical semiring, enables us to get a clear picture on the effect of adding alternation on top of nondeterminism. Indeed, in the case of infinite words, several max semantics are possible for an infinite sequence of costs (c.f., limit average, discounted sum, and more). This makes the setting more involved and yields a less uniform picture [4]. Nevertheless, the picture we obtain, and in particular the fact alternation cannot be removed, are similar to the general picture obtained for the different variants of the max semantics in the setting of infinite words.

We continue and study the sum semantics. A key difference between MAX-AWAs and SUM-AWAs is the fact that in the sum semantics the weight of a word may be exponentially larger than its length (even when all costs in the automaton are bounded by a constant). One immediate implication of this is that alternation cannot be removed in SUM-AWA. We also study closure properties for SUM-AWA, and the added expressive power of alternation even in languages in which the weight of a word does not go beyond its length.

An interesting feature of SUM-AWA is their ability to represent polynomials. We say an automaton $\mathcal{A}$ over a singleton alphabet $\{a\}$ represents a function $f : \mathbb{N} \setminus \{0\} \rightarrow \mathbb{R}$, if for all $n \in \mathbb{N} \setminus \{0\}$, we have that $L_{\mathcal{A}}(a^n) = f(n)$. We show that SUM-AWA (in fact, we even do not need nondeterminism) can represent all polynomials. Moreover, when the coefficients of the polynomial are non-negative, we can construct $\mathcal{A}$ so that it has only non-negative costs. It is interesting to compare these results with the fact that regular automata on finite words cannot recognize polynomials (for example, the language of all words of the form a^{n^2} is not regular).

Due to the lack of space, some proofs are omitted and can be found in the full version, in the authors' home pages.

---

[1] More work on weighted automata on infinite words, all in the nondeterministic setting, include different semantics of the value of a run (for example, in B-automata [9], the value depends on counters whose values are manipulated during the run), and the relation to quantitative variants of LTL or MSO [6].

2   Alternating Weighted Automata

For a finite alphabet Σ, a word $w = \sigma_1 \cdot \sigma_2 \cdots \sigma_n$ is a finite sequence of letters from Σ. We use Σ^* to denote the set of all finite words over the alphabet Σ. A *nondeterministic finite weighted automaton* (NWA) is a tuple $\mathcal{A} = \langle \Sigma, Q, Q_0, \delta \rangle$, where Σ is a finite non-empty alphabet, Q is a finite non-empty set of *states*, $Q_0 \subseteq Q$ is a non-empty set of *initial states*, and $\delta : Q \times \Sigma \to 2^{Q \times \mathbb{R}}$ is a *weighted transition function*. Intuitively, when the automaton is in state q and it reads the letter σ, it moves to state q' at *cost* c, for some $\langle q', c \rangle \in \delta(q, \sigma)$.

A *run* r of $\mathcal{A}$ on a finite word $w = \sigma_1 \cdots \sigma_n \in \Sigma^*$ is a sequence $r = (q_0, c_0), (q_1, c_1), \ldots, (q_n, c_n)$ of $n + 1$ pairs in $Q \times \mathbb{R}$ such that $q_0 \in Q_0$, $c_0 = 0$, and for all $0 \leq i < n$, we have $(q_{i+1}, c_{i+1}) \in \delta(q_i, \sigma_{i+1})$. We associate the run r with the two sequences $S(r) = q_0, \ldots, q_n$ and $C(r) = c_0, \ldots, c_n$. We define $val(r) = c_0 + c_1 + \ldots + c_n$ to be the *value* of the run r. Thus, the costs of the transitions taken along the run are accumulated, and induce the value of the run.[2]

A weighted automaton $\mathcal{A}$ assigns weights to words in Σ^*. The weight of $w \in \Sigma^*$, denoted $L_{\mathcal{A}}(w)$, is the value of the cheapest run of $\mathcal{A}$ on w. Formally, $L_{\mathcal{A}}(w) = \min\{val(r) : r \text{ is a run of } \mathcal{A} \text{ on } w\}$. If there are no runs of $\mathcal{A}$ on w, then $L_{\mathcal{A}}(w)$ is undefined. The function $L_{\mathcal{A}}$ is called the *(weighted) language* of $\mathcal{A}$, and we say that $\mathcal{A}$ *recognizes* $L_{\mathcal{A}}$. We use $dom(L_{\mathcal{A}})$ to denote the domain of $L_{\mathcal{A}}$.

In an *alternating* automaton, the transition function may specify not only existential choices, but also *universal* ones. Below we define alternating weighted automata formally. For a given set X, let $\mathcal{B}^+(X)$ be the set of positive Boolean formulas over X (i.e., Boolean formulas built from elements in X using $\wedge$ and $\vee$), where we also allow the formulas **true** and **false**. For $Y \subseteq X$, we say that Y *satisfies* a formula $\theta \in \mathcal{B}^+(X)$ iff the truth assignment that assigns *true* to the members of Y and assigns *false* to the members of $X \setminus Y$ satisfies θ. The set Y *minimally satisfies* θ if Y satisfies θ and no set that is contained in Y satisfies θ. For example, the sets $\{x_1, x_3\}$ and $\{x_2, x_3\}$ both minimally satisfy the formula $(x_1 \vee x_2) \wedge x_3$, while the set $\{x_1, x_2\}$ does not satisfy this formula, and the set $\{x_1, x_2, x_3\}$ satisfies it but not minimally.

A *weighted alternating automaton* (AWA, for short) is a tuple $\mathcal{A} = \langle \Sigma, Q, q_0, \delta \rangle$, where Σ and Q are as in nondeterministic automata, $q_0 \in Q$ is an initial state[3] and $\delta : Q \times \Sigma \to \mathcal{B}^+(Q \times \mathbb{R})$ is a weighted transition function. In order to define runs of alternating automata, we first have to define trees and weighted labeled trees.

---

[2] Other common models for weighted automata include initial and final costs on states, transitions with an infinite cost, and accepting/non-accepting states. Our model here is simpler, yet our results can be easily extended to other models. Also, in general, an NWA may be defined with respect to any semiring $\langle \mathbb{K}, \oplus, \otimes, \bar{0}, \bar{1} \rangle$. The value of a run is then the semiring product of the costs along the run. The weight of a word is the semiring sum over the costs of all accepting runs on it. In this work, we focus on weighted automata defined with respect to the *min-sum semiring*, $\langle \mathbb{R} \cup \{\infty\}, \min, +, \infty, 0 \rangle$ (sometimes called the *tropical* semiring), as defined above.

[3] We could have assumed an initial foruma in $\mathcal{B}^+(Q)$ instead.

A *tree* is a prefix closed set $T \subseteq \mathbb{N}^*$ (i.e., if $x \cdot c \in T$, where $x \in \mathbb{N}^*$ and $c \in \mathbb{N}$, then also $x \in T$). The elements of T are called *nodes*. For every $x \in T$, the nodes $x \cdot c$, with $c \in \mathbb{N}$, are the *successors* of x. A node is a *leaf* if it has no successors. We sometimes refer to the length $|x|$ of x as its *level* in the tree. A *path* π of a tree T is a prefix-closed set $\pi \subseteq T$ such that $\varepsilon \in \pi$ and for every $x \in \pi$, either x is a leaf or there exists a unique $c \in \mathbb{N}$ such that $x \cdot c \in \pi$. A path is *full* if it contains a leaf.

An *edge* in T is a pair $\langle x, x \cdot c \rangle \in T \times T$. The set of edges in T is denoted $Edge(T)$. We sometimes refer to a path π as a sequence of edges. Then, we say that an edge $\langle x, x \cdot c \rangle$ is in π iff both x and $x \cdot c$ are in π. Given an alphabet Σ, a *weighted Σ-labeled tree* is a triple $\langle T, V, C \rangle$, where T is a tree, $V : T \to \Sigma$ maps each node of T to a letter in Σ, and $C : Edge(T) \to \mathbb{R}$ maps each edge of T to a cost in $\mathbb{R}$.

A run of a nondeterministic weighted automaton on a word can be thought of as a Q-labeled weighted tree with branching degree 1. Extending this notion, a run of an alternating automaton is a "real" Q-labeled weighted tree. Formally, given a word $w = \sigma_1 \cdot \sigma_2 \cdots \sigma_n$, a run of $\mathcal{A}$ on w is a Q-labeled weighted tree $\tau = \langle T_r, r, \rho \rangle$, such that the following hold:

- $\varepsilon \in T_r$ and $r(\varepsilon) = q_0$.
- Consider a node $x \in T_r$ with $r(x) = q$ and $\delta(q, \sigma_{|x|+1}) = \theta$. There is a (possibly empty) set $S = \{(q_1, c_1), \ldots, (q_k, c_k)\} \subseteq 2^{Q \times \mathbb{R}}$ such that S minimally satisfies θ and for all $1 \leq d \leq k$, we have that $x \cdot d \in T_r$, $r(x \cdot d) = q_d$, and $\rho(x, x \cdot d) = c_d$.

For example, if $\delta(q_0, \sigma_1) = ((q_1, 2) \vee (q_2, 3)) \wedge ((q_3, 0) \vee (q_4, -2))$, then possible runs of $\mathcal{A}$ on σ_1 have a root labeled q_0, have one node in level 1 labeled q_1 (and the weight of the edge to it is 2) or q_2 (with edge weight 3), and have another node in level 1 labeled q_3 (with edge weight 0) or q_4 (with edge weight -2). Note that if $\theta = \mathbf{true}$, then x need not have children. This is the reason why T_r may have leaves before level n. Also, since there exists no set S as required for $\theta = \mathbf{false}$, we cannot have a run that takes a transition with $\theta = \mathbf{false}$.

An AWA in which all the transitions are disjunctions is simply an NWA. An automaton in which all the transitions are conjunction is *universal*. An automaton that is both universal and nondeterministic (that is, $\delta(q, \sigma) \in Q \times \mathbb{R}$ for all q and σ) is *deterministic*.

As in the nondeterministic case, we want to define $L_\mathcal{A}$ to assign weights to words in Σ^*. To be consistent with the nondeterministic case, we want to define $L_\mathcal{A}(w) = \min\{(val(\tau)) : \tau \text{ is a run of } \mathcal{A} \text{ on } w\}$. If $\mathcal{A}$ does not have runs on w, then w is not in the domain of $L_\mathcal{A}$. For this definition to be complete, we need to define $val(\tau)$ for a run τ. As discussed in Section 1, we suggest and study two semantics for val. Let $\tau = \langle T, r, \rho \rangle$.

- In the *max* semantics, the value of every path in the tree is the sum of costs along the path, and the value of a run is the maximal value of a full path. Formally, $\text{MAX-}val(\tau) = \max\{\sum_{e \in \pi}(\rho(e)) : \pi \text{ is a path in } T\}$.
- In the *sum* semantics, the value of a run is the sum over all the costs in the edges of τ. Formally, $\text{SUM-}val(\tau) = \sum_{e \in Edge(T)} \rho(e)$.

Note that the two semantics are relevant only for universal transitions (that is, for transitions with $\wedge$). Note also that the sum semantics involves some nontrivial technical issues. To see this, note for example our requirement for the set S in the definition of a run tree to minimally satisfy the transition function. In the Boolean setting, as well as in the max semantics, we can remove the minimality requirement, as runs are monotonic: the more branches we have in the run tree, the more difficult it is for the run to be accepting or to have a minimal value. On the other hand, in the sum semantics, since $\mathcal{A}$ may have transitions with negative costs, sending more copies may actually reduce the value of a run. Moreover, even when all costs are positive, in the Boolean or the max semantics, it is clear that we have no reason to have multiple copies of the same state in the same level of the run tree. This is why S is a set of states, and no multiple occurrences of the same state are possible. In the sum semantics, one could argue that such multiple occurrences should be allowed, as they reflect the fact that some mission has to be fulfilled (and payed for) several times. We preferred not to proceed with this multiple-occurrence semantics, as it can be simulated by our sum semantics (by duplicating states).

We abbreviate the different types of automata by acronyms in $\{\text{MAX-}, \text{SUM-}\} \times \{A, U, N, D\} \times \{WA\}$. For example, MAX-UWA refers to a universal weighted automaton in the max semantics. For nondeterministic or deterministic automata we omit the semantics prefix and simply use NWA and DWA, respectively.

For two weighted languages L_1 and L_2, and $c \in \mathbb{R}$, we use $-L_1$, $L_1 + L_2$, $\max\{L_1, L_2\}$, and $c \cdot L_1$ to denote the weighted languages that negate L_1, sum L_1 and L_2, take their maximum, and multiply L_1 by c. Thus, for every word $w \in \Sigma^*$, we have that $(-L_1)(w) = -L_1(w)$, $(L_1 + L_2)(w) = L_1(w) + L_2(w)$, $\max\{L_1, L_2\}(w) = \max\{L_1(w), L_2(w)\}$, and $(c \cdot L_1)(w) = c \cdot L_1(w)$. Note that $(L_1 + L_2)(w)$ and $\max\{L_1, L_2\}(w)$ are defined only if both $L_1(w)$ and $L_2(w)$ are defined.

We say that two AWAs $\mathcal{A}_1$ and $\mathcal{A}_2$ are *equivalent* if for all $w \in \Sigma^*$ it holds that $L_{\mathcal{A}_1}(w) = L_{\mathcal{A}_2}(w)$. For two classes of automata γ_1 and γ_2, we say that γ_2 is *more expressive* than γ_1, denoted $\gamma_1 \leq \gamma_2$, if every language L that is recognized by an automaton in γ_1 can also be recognized by an automaton in γ_2. We also use the notations $\gamma_1 \not\leq \gamma_2$, $\gamma_1 < \gamma_2$, and $\gamma_1 \neq \gamma_2$, derived as expected from $\gamma_1 \leq \gamma_2$.

3   The Max Semantics

In this section we study the max semantics. As we mentioned above, one motivation for the max semantics is the duality with the min semantics of nondeterminism. We first formalize this duality and then study other properties of the max semantics.

3.1   The Duality between the Min and the Max Semantics

For a formula $\theta \in \mathcal{B}^+(Q \times \mathbb{R})$, let $\widetilde{\theta}$ be the formula obtained from θ by switching $\wedge$'s and $\vee$'s, switching **true**'s and **false**'s, and negating all the costs in the atoms of θ. If, for example, $\theta = (p, 3) \vee (\textbf{true} \wedge (q, -5))$, then $\widetilde{\theta} = (p, -3) \wedge (\textbf{false} \vee (q, 5))$.

For a transition function δ, let $\widetilde{\delta}$ be the transition function obtained from by dualizing δ. That is, for all $q \in Q$ and $\sigma \in \Sigma$, we have that $\widetilde{\delta}(q, \sigma) = \widetilde{\delta(q, \sigma)}$. Given an AWA $\mathcal{A} = \langle Q, \Sigma, q_0, \delta \rangle$, its *dual* AWA is $\widetilde{\mathcal{A}} = \langle Q, \Sigma, q_0, \widetilde{\delta} \rangle$.

Dualizing an alternating automaton in the unweighted setting complements the language of the automaton. Intuitively, it follows from the fact dualization amounts to switching the roles between the two players in the two-player game that the automaton models. In the case of MAX-AWAs, dualization is more involved and corresponds to negating the language of the automaton. Formally, we have the following.

Lemma 1. *Let $\mathcal{A}$ be a MAX-AWA. Then, $L(\widetilde{\mathcal{A}}) = -L(\mathcal{A})$.*

Proof. We first prove that for every word $w \in \Sigma^*$, we have that $L_{\widetilde{\mathcal{A}}}(w)$ is the maximal value of a minimal path in a run of $-\mathcal{A}$ on w, where $-\mathcal{A}$ is the MAX-AWA obtained from $\mathcal{A}$ by multiplying all the costs by -1. Proofs of duality claims such as this are usually technical. We give the main idea of the proof. The value of a word w in $L_{\mathcal{A}}$ can be thought of as the outcome of the following two-player game. The set of states in the game is Q. The game starts in the state q_0. In every round, Player 1 (the *maximizer*) chooses a set $E \subseteq Q$ that satisfies $\delta(q_i, w_i)$. Player 2 (the *minimizer*) then chooses a state $q_{i+1} \in E$, and the game continues in the same manner from q_{i+1}, reading w_{i+1}, and so on. The game ends when the last letter in w is read, and the value of the game is the sum of values along the selected transitions. The goal of Player 1 is to maximize the value, and the goal of Player 2 is to minimize it.

When the same game is played on $\widetilde{\mathcal{A}}$, the roles of the players are interchanged. Thus, Player 1 is now the minimizer, and Player 2 is the maximizer. The path induced by this game corresponds to a minimal path in a maximal run of $\mathcal{A}$ on w. Indeed, Player 1 determines which path is taken in every run of $\mathcal{A}$, and Player 2 determines which run is taken. This implies that the value of every $w \in \Sigma^*$ in $L_{\widetilde{\mathcal{A}}}$ is the value of the minimal path in a maximal run of $\mathcal{A}$ on w.

Now, for every word $w \in \Sigma^*$, we have that $L_{\widetilde{\mathcal{A}}}(w) = \max\{\min\{\sum_{e \in \pi}(-\rho(e)) : \pi$ is a path in $\tau\} : \tau$ is a run of $\mathcal{A}$ on $w\} = \max\{\min\{-\sum_{e \in \pi}(\rho(e)) : \pi$ is a path in $\tau\} : \tau$ is a run of $\mathcal{A}$ on $w\} = \max\{-\max\{\sum_{e \in \pi}(\rho(e)) : \pi$ is a path in $\tau\} : \tau$ is a run of $\mathcal{A}$ on $w\} = -\min\{\max\{\sum_{e \in \pi}(\rho(e)) : \pi$ is a path in $\tau\} : \tau$ is a run of $\mathcal{A}$ on $w\} = -L_{\mathcal{A}}(w)$.

A special case of Lemma 1 is when the automaton $\mathcal{A}$ is an NWA, in which case $\widetilde{\mathcal{A}}$ is a MAX-UWA. We then have the following.

Corollary 1. *A weighted language L is recognizable by an NWA iff $-L$ is recognizable by a MAX-UWA.*

3.2 Expressive Power

In the Boolean setting, natural questions to ask in the context of expressive power include closure to Boolean operators, and the added power of each of the branching modes. It is well known that in the Boolean setting, alternation and nondeterminism do not add to the expressive power of deterministic automata, and the latter are closed under union, intersection, and complementation. In the weighted setting, the operators that correspond to the Boolean ones are min, max, and negation. As we have seen above, MAX-AWAs are closed under negation. As in the Boolean setting, closure under min and max is easy, and follows from the semantics of the transitions of MAX-AWAs. Likewise, MAX-UWAs are closed under max.

In the Boolean setting, nondeterministic automata are closed under intersection. Indeed, the "product construction" enables us to trace several automata in parallel. Moreover, the "subset construction" enables us to trace even an unbounded type of intersection. Consequently, in the Boolean setting, alternation can be removed. We now turn to study the added expressive power of universal branches in the max semantics. We show that NWAs are not closed under max, and conclude that alternation in MAX-AWAs cannot be removed.

Let $\Sigma = \{a, b\}$. For $\sigma \in \Sigma$, let L_σ be the language that maps $w \in \Sigma^*$ to the number of occurrences of σ in w. In [4], the languages L_a and L_b are used in order to show that DWAs are not closed under min. Here we follow similar ideas and use them in the study of closure under max.

Theorem 1. NWAs *and* DWAs *are not closed under* max.

Proof. Consider the language $L = \max\{L_a, L_b\}$. The language L_a can be defined by a DWA with a single self loop that has cost 1 to a and cost 0 to b, and similarly for L_b. In the full version, we prove that no NWA can recognizes L. Essentially, it follows from the fact that all the reachable a-cycles in an NWA for L must have a strictly positive cost, which implies that runs on the word $a^{n+1}b^{n+1}$, where n is the number of states in the NWA, suggest runs with value strictly smaller than $n + 1$ to words of the form $a^j b^{n+1}$, for $j < n + 1$.

Since MAX-UWAs dualize NWAs, we can dualize Theorem 1 as follows.

Theorem 2. MAX-UWAs *and* DWAs *are not closed under* min.

Proof. We start with MAX-UWAs. Assume by way of contradiction that $\mathcal{A}$ is a MAX-UWA that recognizes $L = \min\{L_a, L_b\}$. From Lemma 1, we get that $\widetilde{\mathcal{A}}$ is an NWA such that $L_{\widetilde{\mathcal{A}}} = -L_{\mathcal{A}}$. Consider the NWA $\mathcal{B}$ obtained from $\widetilde{\mathcal{A}}$ by adding 1 to the cost of every transition. It is easy to verify that for every word w, we have that $L_{\mathcal{B}}(w) = |w| - L_{\mathcal{A}}(w)$. On the other hand, $\max\{L_a(w), L_b(w)\} = |w| - \min\{L_a(w), L_b(w)\} = |w| - L_{\mathcal{A}}(w)$. It follows that $\mathcal{B}$ is an NWA that recognizes $\max\{L_a, L_b\}$, which contradicts the proof of Theorem 1. Finally, observe that if $\mathcal{A}$ is a DWA, then $\mathcal{B}$ is a DWA as well, again contradicting the proof of Theorem 1.

Since MAX-UWAs are closed under max (in particular, Fig. 1 describes a MAX-UWA for $\max\{L_a, L_b\}$), Theorem 1 implies that alternation cannot be removed in the weighted setting with the max semantics. Combining this with dualization, we conclude with the following.

Corollary 2. MAX-UWA $\neq$ NWA, MAX-AWA $>$ NWA, *and* MAX-AWA $>$ MAX-UWA.

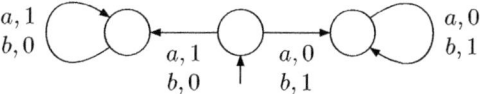

Fig. 1. A MAX-UWA for $\max\{L_a, L_b\}$

3.3   Arithmetics

In the weighted setting, additional interesting properties of automata are related to the fact they manipulate real values. In this section we consider the closure of max automata under addition and multiplication by a scalar.

Theorem 3. *DWAs, NWAs, MAX-UWAs, and MAX-AWAs are closed under addition.*

Proof. The proof is by construction: Given automata $\mathcal{A}_1$ and $\mathcal{A}_2$, we construct an automaton $\mathcal{A}$ of the same class such that $L_\mathcal{A} = L_{\mathcal{A}_1} + L_{\mathcal{A}_2}$. We describe the construction in detail in the full version. Essentially, the state space of $\mathcal{A}$ is the product of the state spaces of $\mathcal{A}_1$ and $\mathcal{A}_2$, and the transitions from $\langle q_1, q_2 \rangle$ sum the corresponding transitions from q_1 and q_2.

Next, we consider scalar multiplication. Clearly, multiplying all the costs of an AWA by a scalar c causes the value of every run to be multiplied by c (since the costs are summed along a path in the run tree). If $c \geq 0$, then multiplying by c is a monotonic (increasing) function. That is, if r_1 and r_2 are two runs, and $val(r_1) \leq val(r_2)$, then $c \cdot val(r_1) \leq c \cdot val(r_2)$. Therefore, the cheapest run stays the cheapest run, implying the following theorem.

Theorem 4. *MAX-AWAs, MAX-UWAs, NWAs and DWAs are closed under multiplication by a positive scalar.*

The case of a negative scalar is different, as multiplication is an anti-monotonic (decreasing) function. Dualization, together with Th. 4, imply that MAX-AWAs are closed under multiplication by a negative scalar. For the other classes, the fact that such a multiplication causes the cheapest run to become the most expensive run is crucial:

Theorem 5. *NWAs and MAX-UWAs are not closed under multiplication by a negative scalar.*

Proof. In the proof of Theorem 1, we saw that there is no NWA for $\max\{L_a, L_b\}$. On the other hand, there is an NWA $\mathcal{A}$ for $\min\{L_a, L_b\}$. Assume by way of contradiction that NWAs are closed under multiplication by a negative scalar. Then, by multiplying $\mathcal{A}$ by -1 we can obtain an NWA $\mathcal{A}'$ for $-\min\{L_a, L_b\}$. For every word w, we have that $\max\{L_a(w), L_b(w)\} = |w| - \min\{L_a(w), L_b(w)\}$. It is easy to construct an automaton $\mathcal{B}$ the recognizes the language $L(w) = |w|$. By Lemma 3, NWAs are closed under addition. By adding $\mathcal{A}'$ and $\mathcal{B}$ we obtain an NWA $\mathcal{C}$ such that $L_\mathcal{C}(w) = |w| - \min\{L_a(w), L_b(w)\} = \max\{L_a(w), L_b(w)\}$. So, $\mathcal{C}$ is an NWA that recognizes $\max\{L_a, L_b\}$, contradicting the fact that no such NWA exists. The proof for MAX-UWAs is dual.

4   The Sum Semantics

Recall that in a SUM-AWA $\mathcal{A}$, the value of a run is the sum of all the costs in the run tree. This corresponds to the intuition that $\mathcal{A}$ spawns copies that fulfill different tasks and has to pay for the costs of all tasks. The first observation we make about SUM-AWAs, which makes them an interesting arithmetic tool, is that they can recognize languages in which the weight of a word is not linear in its length.

4.1   Exponential Weights

In NWAs, and in fact even in MAX-AWAs, the value of a run of $\mathcal{A}$ on a word w of length n is bounded from above by $c_{\max} \cdot n$, where $c_{\max}$ is the maximal cost in $\mathcal{A}$. Indeed, even if several copies of the automaton run on the same prefix of the word, only one copy contributes to the value of the run, which is therefore linear in the length of the word. When we allow summing over all the weights in a tree, this is no longer true, and the weight of a word may become exponential. Consider for example the automaton $\mathcal{A}_{\exp}$ in Fig. 2 (we draw UWAs the same way we draw NWAs. but keep in mind that in UWAs, transitions with the same label are conjunctively related). The single run tree of $\mathcal{A}_{\exp}$ on the word a^n is a complete binary tree of depth n. Each level doubles the number accumulated so far (starting with 2), and so $L_{\mathcal{A}_{\exp}}(a^n) = 2^n$.

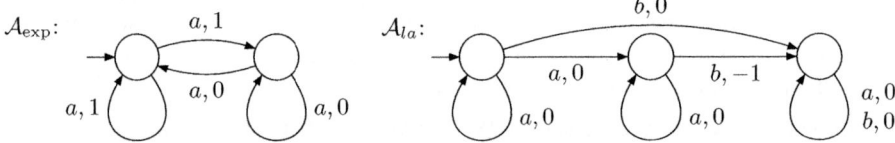

Fig. 2. The SUM-UWAs $\mathcal{A}_{exp}$ and $\mathcal{A}_{la}$

Since the number of edges in a run tree on a word w is bounded by $d^{|w|+1}$, where d is the branching degree of the tree, and d is bounded by the number of states of the automaton, we cannot go beyond an exponential weight, either positive of negative:

Lemma 2. *Let $\mathcal{A}$ be a SUM-AWA with n states. For every word $w \in \Sigma^*$, we have that $\min\{0, c_{min} \cdot n^{|w|+1}\} \leq L_{\mathcal{A}}(w) \leq c_{max} \cdot n^{|w|+1}$, where c_{min} and c_{max} are the minimal and maximal costs in $\mathcal{A}$, respectively.*

4.2   Expressive Power

One could argue that it is not "fair" to compare SUM-AWAs with NWA, due to the ability of the first to assign super-linear weights. As we show now, alternation cannot be removed even if we restrict attention to SUM-UWAs with linear-bounded language. To see this, consider the "leading a's" SUM-UWA $\mathcal{A}_{la}$ in Fig. 2. One can verify that for all $w \in \{a, b\}^*$, we have that

$$L_{\mathcal{A}_{l_a}}(w) = \begin{cases} -k & \text{if } w \in a^k \cdot b \cdot (a+b)^* \text{ for } k \geq 0, \\ 0 & \text{otherwise.} \end{cases}$$

It is not hard to prove that there is no NWA for $L_{\mathcal{A}_{l_a}}$. Thus, the power of SUM-AWAs goes beyond the ability to assign super-linear weights.

We now turn to study closure properties for SUM-AWAs. As in the Boolean setting, closure under min and summation is straightforward, as they correspond to existential and universal transitions.

Also, as has been the case in the max semantics, closure under multiplication by a positive scalar c is easy, as we only have to multiply the costs of $\mathcal{A}$ by c. Such a multiplication would work also with a negative scalar in case the automaton is universal. Indeed, all the costs in the single run are multiplied by the scalar. The general case, of a negative scalar and SUM-AWAs is less clear, and is related to the problem of closure under max. For this problem, we have examples to the lack of closure for following two fragments of SUM-AWAs.

Theorem 6. SUM-UWAs *and* SUM-AWAs *with non-negative costs are not closed under* max.

Proof. Consider the language $L = \max\{L_a, L_b\}$. Recall that L_a and L_b are recognized by DWAs with non-negative costs, which are a special case of SUM-AWAs. We prove that there is no SUM-UWA nor SUM-AWA with non-negative costs for L.

Consider a SUM-UWA $\mathcal{A}$ with n states, and consider the run τ of $\mathcal{A}$ on $w = a^{n+1}b^{n+1}$. Each level of τ consists of states of $\mathcal{A}$, where every state appears 0 or more times. We characterize the levels by vectors in $\mathbb{N}^Q$, which we represent as $\mathbb{N}^n$. For example, the vector $(2,0,1)$ means that in this level there are 2 copies of q_0, 1 copy of q_2 and no copies of q_1. Thus, τ can be thought of as a sequence of vectors. We say that a vector β is a *configuration* of $\mathcal{A}$.

Let β be a configuration, and consider what $\mathcal{A}$ does when it reads b. Every state $q_i \in Q$ sends out β_i copies of states in $\delta(q_i, b)$. That is, there are $d_1^i, ..., d_n^i$ such that q_i moves to the vector $(d_1^i, ..., d_n^i)$. Intuitively, q_i sends d_j^i copies of q_j. Let D be the $\mathbb{N}_{n \times n}$ matrix whose entries are $D_{ij} = d_j^i$. It is easy to verify that when $\mathcal{A}$ reads b in configuration β, it moves to the vector $D\beta$ (where β is considered as a column vector). Furthermore, when $\mathcal{A}$ is in configuration β and reads b, every state q_i accumulates w_i cost in the transition. Thus, the total cost accumulated in the transition is $\sum_{i=1}^n \beta_i w_i = \langle \beta, w \rangle$ (where $w = (w_1, ..., w_n)$ and $\langle \cdot, \cdot \rangle$ denotes the standard inner product).

Let $\alpha_0, ..., \alpha_n, \beta_0, ..., \beta_n$ be the levels of τ. For all $0 < i \leq n$ it holds that $\beta_i = D\beta_{i-1}$. Observe that $\beta_0, ..., \beta_n$ are $n+1$ vectors in $\mathbb{Q}^n$. Thus, there exists an index $1 \leq k \leq n$ such that β_k is linearly dependent on $\beta_0, ..., \beta_{k-1}$, so we can write $\beta_k = \sum_{j=0}^{k-1} c_j \beta_j$ for some $c_0, ..., c_{k-1} \in \mathbb{Q}$. Consider what happens when $\mathcal{A}$ reads b from β_k. The new configuration is

$$D\beta_k = D\sum_{j=0}^{k-1} c_k \beta_j = \sum_{j=0}^{k-1} c_j D\beta_j = \sum_{j=0}^{k-1} c_j \beta_{j+1} = \sum_{j=1}^{k-1} c_{j-1}\beta_j + c_{k-1}\sum_{j=0}^{k-1} c_k \beta_j$$

In particular, β_{k+1} is also linearly dependent on $\beta_0, ..., \beta_{k-1}$. It is easy to prove by induction that for all $t \geq k$ it holds that β_t is linearly dependent on $\beta_0, ..., \beta_{k-1}$.

Next, observe that since $\mathcal{A}$ has a single run, then the run must accumulate the cost $n + 1$ by configuration α_{n+1}, and must stay 0 through $\beta_0, ..., \beta_{n+1}$. Let $w = (w_0, ..., w_n)$ denote the cost vector accumulated at a b-transition, then for all $0 \leq i \leq n+1$ it holds that $\langle \beta_i, w \rangle = 0$. Let $\gamma = \sum_{j=0}^{k-1} e_j \beta_j$ for $e_1, ..., e_{k-1} \in \mathbb{Q}$, then the cost accumulated from γ when reading b is

$$\langle \gamma, w \rangle = \sum_{j=0}^{k-1} e_j \langle \beta_j, w \rangle = \sum_{j=0}^{k-1} e_j \cdot 0 = 0$$

We conclude that when $\mathcal{A}$ reads to $a^{n+1}b^{n+2}$ it accumulates cost 0 in all the transitions on the b-block. Hence, the weight assigned by $\mathcal{A}$ to $a^{n+1}b^{n+2}$ is $n+1$, which is a contradiction.

We proceed to SUM-AWA with non-negative costs. Let $\mathcal{A}$ be a SUM-AWA with n states and non-negative costs. Consider the cheapest run τ of $\mathcal{A}$ on $w = a^{2^n+1}b^{2^n+1}$. Since every prefix of this run is also a run of $\mathcal{A}$ on a prefix of w, we get that after reading a^{2^n+1}, the accumulated cost must be exactly $2^n + 1$. Indeed, a lower cost would imply that the value of a^{2^n+1} in $\mathcal{A}$ is less than $2^n + 1$, and, since accumulated costs are nonnegative, a higher cost implies that the weight of w is greater than $2^n + 1$. As we show in the full version, it follows that we can pump w to a word $w' = a^{2^n+1}b^k$, with $k > 2^n + 1$, such that $\mathcal{A}$ assigns to w' a weight smaller than k.

Since SUM-AWAs are closed under multiplication by a negative scalar, the fact they cannot recognize $\max\{L_a, L_b\}$ implies they also cannot recognize $\min\{L_a, L_b\}$, which can be recognized by an NWA.[4] Thus, keeping in mind the ability of SUM-AWA to assign super-linear weights, we can conclude with the following.

Corollary 3. SUM-UWA $\neq$ NWA, SUM-AWA $> NWA$, *and* SUM-AWA $>$ SUM-UWA.

4.3   SUM-UWA **and Polynomials**

For an automaton $\mathcal{A}$ over a singleton alphabet $\{a\}$ and a function $f : \mathbb{N} \setminus \{0\} \rightarrow \mathbb{R}$, we say that $\mathcal{A}$ *represents* f if for all $n \in \mathbb{N} \setminus \{0\}$, we have that $L_{\mathcal{A}}(a^n) = f(n)$. In this section, we study the presentation of polynomials by SUM-UWAs. Note that this study is not interesting in the context of NWAs or MAX-AWAs, as the latter can only represent linear functions.

Since we restrict attention to the alphabet $\{a\}$, all the words are of the form a^n for some n, and we abbreviate $L_{\mathcal{A}}(a^n)$ by $L_{\mathcal{A}}(n)$. Observe that for every AWA

---

[4] A popular example for the added power of NWA with respect to DWA is the language that maps $a \cdot b^i \cdot c$ to i and $a \cdot b^i \cdot d$ to $2i$ [13]. Interestingly, this language can be recognized by a SUM-UWA.

$\mathcal{A}$ we have $L_{\mathcal{A}}(0) = 0$, which is why we consider the domain $\mathbb{N} \setminus \{0\}$. By adding ϵ-transitions, we can easily extend the results to functions $f : \mathbb{N} \to \mathbb{R}$.

We start by describing our basic "building blocks". Consider the sequence of SUM-UWAs $\mathcal{A}_1, \mathcal{A}_2, \mathcal{A}_3, \ldots$ appearing in Fig. 3. It is easy to see that $\mathcal{A}_1$ defines the polynomial $f_1(n) = n$. As for $\mathcal{A}_d$, for $d \geq 2$, note that a run of $\mathcal{A}_d$ on a^n sends a copy of $\mathcal{A}_d$ and a copy of $\mathcal{A}_{d-1}$ to read a^{n-1}. Accordingly, a copy of $\mathcal{A}_{d-1}$ is sent to read a^i for all $0 \leq i \leq n - 1$. Thus, $L_{\mathcal{A}_d}(n) = \sum_{i=0}^{n} L_{\mathcal{A}_{d-1}}(n - i) = \sum_{i=0}^{n-1} L_{\mathcal{A}_{d-1}}(i)$. Let $f_d(n) = L_{\mathcal{A}_d}(n)$.

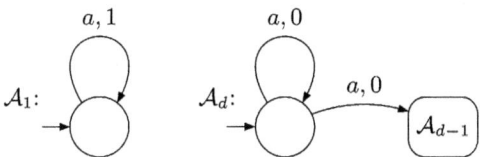

Fig. 3. The automata $\mathcal{A}_d$

Lemma 3. *For all $n \geq 1$ and $d \geq 1$, we have that* $f_d(n) = \begin{cases} \binom{n}{d} & \text{if } d \leq n \\ 0 & \text{otherwise.} \end{cases}$

Since $\binom{n}{d}$ is a polynomial of degree d, the set $\{\mathcal{A}_1, \ldots, \mathcal{A}_d\}$ of SUM-UWAs represents a set of polynomials of degrees $\{1, \ldots, d\}$. It is easy to construct a DWA $\mathcal{A}_0$ such that $L_{\mathcal{A}_0}(n) = 1$. Thus, the set $\{\mathcal{A}_0, \mathcal{A}_1, \ldots, \mathcal{A}_d\}$ represents a set of polynomials with degrees $\{0, 1, \ldots, d\}$. We claim that this set allows us to represent every polynomial. To prove this, we use the following lemma (the proof is a basic exercise in linear algebra).

Lemma 4. *Let $\{p_0, \ldots, p_d\}$ be polynomials over a commutative ring $\mathcal{R}$ such that p_i is of degree i. The set $\{p_0, \ldots, p_d\}$ forms a basis to the space of polynomials of degree at most d.*

By Lemma 4, and by the closure of SUM-UWAs under addition and scalar multiplication, we conclude that SUM-UWAs can span the entire space of polynomials of degree at most d. Note that according to Lemma 4, spanning the space requires coefficients from the ring $\mathcal{R}$. On the positive side, in order to span a polynomial with coefficients in $\mathbb{Z}$ or $\mathbb{Q}$, we only need costs in $\mathbb{Z}$ or $\mathbb{Q}$, respectively. On the negative side, this implies that for coefficients in $\mathbb{N}$ we may need costs from $\mathbb{Z}$ (which is the minimal ring containing $\mathbb{N}$). Note that while we only proved existence, it is easy to make the proof explicit and construct, given a polynomial p, a SUM-UWA that represents it. In order to do it, one simply multiplies $\mathcal{A}_d$ by the desired coefficient for n^d, then multiplies $\mathcal{A}_{d-1}$ by a proper scalar so as to fix the coefficient for n^{d-1}, and so on.

The fact that in order to represent a polynomial with coefficients in $\mathbb{N}$ we may need negative costs is disturbing. We now proceed to show that it is indeed not necessary: for every polynomial p with non-negative coefficients, we can construct a SUM-UWA $\mathcal{A}_p$ with non-negative costs such that $L_{\mathcal{A}_p}(n) = p(n)$. We also give an explicit construction of $\mathcal{A}_p$. As above, it is enough to show that we can construct a SUM-UWA for every monomial n^d.

Recall that $f_d(n)$ is $\binom{n}{d}$ for $d \leq n$, and is 0 otherwise. The following lemma shows how to define n^d using $\{f_1(n), ..., f_d(n)\}$. It is a well known result and we give the proof in the full version. The lemma and the proof refer to $S(n, k)$ – the *Stirling number of the second kind*, which is the number of ways to partition a set of size n into k subsets.

Lemma 5. $n^d = \sum_{k=1}^{d} k! S(d, k) f_k(n)$.

By Lemma 5, we can define n^d using $\{f_1(n), ..., f_d(n)\}$, and the coefficients are non-negative. By adding $1 = n^0$ to the set $\{n^1, ..., n^d\}$ we conclude that we can span any polynomial with non-negative coefficients using SUM-UWAs with non-negative costs. Moreover, we observe that all our constructions are of SUM-UWAs with self loops only. This follows from the definition of the basic blocks and the constructions proving the closure of SUM-UWA to addition and multiplication by a scalar, which preserve this property.

We can thus conclude with the following (the result about non-positive coefficients follows from the closure under multiplication by a negative scalar).

Theorem 7. *For every polynomial p with coefficients in a ring $\mathcal{R} \in \{\mathbb{R}, \mathbb{Q}, \mathbb{Z}\}$, we can construct a SUM-UWA $\mathcal{A}$ that defines p (with cost in $\mathbb{R}, \mathbb{Q}$ or $\mathbb{Z}$, respectively). Moreover, if the coefficients of p are all non-negative (non-positive), then we can construct $\mathcal{A}$ with non-negative (non-positive, resp.) costs only.*

5   Discussion

We introduced and studied two semantics – max and sum, for universal transitions of alternating weighted automata on finite words. The two semantics correspond to different interpretations of conjunctions in a weighted setting, and are of interest in quantitative formal reasoning. We showed that in both semantics, alternation strictly increases the expressive power of the automata. Also, in the sum semantics, it enables the automaton to represent super-linear functions, making universal transitions more significant then their dual nondeterministic transitions.

We plan to continue our study in several directions. In the theoretical front, we find the ability to represent polynomial by automata very interesting. In particular, it is interesting to see which operations on polynomials can be performed on the SUM-AWAs that represent them. Our results here already include addition of two polynomials and their multiplication by a scalar. It is a nice exercise to see that given a SUM-AWA that represents a polynomial p, we can easily construct a SUM-AWA for the derivative of p, or its integration. More challenging are constructions that correspond to multiplication of polynomials, decision procedures about their roots, and so on. In the more practical front, we are developing a weighted version of LTL that can specify quality of satisfaction. Conjunctions in the new logic can be interpreted in both semantics, and the translation to AWAs is a basic procedure in reasoning about specifications in the logic. Problems like membership (that is, finding weights) are easily decidable, and we are studying fragments for which language containment (that is, its weighted variant) is decidable. We are also studying an extension to automata on infinite words.

References

1. Aminof, B., Kupferman, O., Lampert, R.: Reasoning about online algorithms with weighted automata. ACM Transactions on Algorithms 6(2) (2010)
2. Baier, C., Bertrand, N., Grösser, M.: Probabilistic automata over infinite words: Expressiveness, efficiency, and decidability. In: Proc. 11th International Workshop on Descriptional Complexity of Formal Systems, pp. 3–16 (2006)
3. Chatterjee, K., Doyen, L., Henzinger, T.: Quantitative languages. In: Kaminski, M., Martini, S. (eds.) CSL 2008. LNCS, vol. 5213, pp. 385–400. Springer, Heidelberg (2008)
4. Chatterjee, K., Doyen, L., Henzinger, T.: Alternating weighted automata. In: Kutyłowski, M., Charatonik, W., Gębala, M. (eds.) FCT 2009. LNCS, vol. 5699, pp. 3–13. Springer, Heidelberg (2009)
5. Culik, K., Kari, J.: Digital images and formal languages. In: Handbook of Formal Languages. beyond words, vol. 3, pp. 599–616 (1997)
6. Droste, M., Gastin, P.: Weighted automata and weighted logics. In: Caires, L., Italiano, G.F., Monteiro, L., Palamidessi, C., Yung, M. (eds.) ICALP 2005. LNCS, vol. 3580, pp. 513–525. Springer, Heidelberg (2005)
7. Emerson, E.A., Jutla, C.: Tree automata, μ-calculus and determinacy. In: Proc. 32nd FOCS, pp. 368–377 (1991)
8. Krob, D.: The equality problem for rational series with multiplicities in the tropical semiring is undecidable. Int. J. of Algebra and Computation 4(3), 405–425 (1994)
9. Kuperberg, D.: Linear temporal logic for regular cost functions. In: Proc. 28th STACS, pp. 627–636 (2011)
10. Kupferman, O.: Avoiding determinization. In: Proc. 21st LICS, pp. 243–254 (2006)
11. Kupferman, O., Vardi, M.Y.: Synthesis with incomplete information. In: Advances in Temporal Logic, pp. 109–127. Kluwer Academic Publishers, Dordrecht (2000)
12. Kupferman, O., Vardi, M.Y., Wolper, P.: An automata-theoretic approach to branching-time model checking. Journal of the ACM 47(2), 312–360 (2000)
13. Mohri, M.: Finite-state transducers in language and speech processing. Computational Linguistics 23(2), 269–311 (1997)
14. Mohri, M., Pereira, F.C.N., Riley, M.: Weighted finite-state transducers in speech recognition. Computer Speech and Language 16(1), 69–88 (2002)
15. Schützenberger, M.P.: On the definition of a family of automata. Information and Control 4(2-3), 245–270 (1961)
16. Somenzi, F., Bloem, R.: Efficient Büchi automata from LTL formulae. In: Emerson, E.A., Sistla, A.P. (eds.) CAV 2000. LNCS, vol. 1855, pp. 248–263. Springer, Heidelberg (2000)
17. Thomas, W.: Automata on infinite objects. In: Handbook of Theoretical Computer Science, pp. 133–191 (1990)
18. Vardi, M.Y.: Nontraditional applications of automata theory. In: Hagiya, M., Mitchell, J.C. (eds.) TACS 1994. LNCS, vol. 789, pp. 575–597. Springer, Heidelberg (1994)
19. Vardi, M.Y., Wolper, P.: Reasoning about infinite computations. Information and Computation 115(1), 1–37 (1994)

Making Software Verification Tools Really Work[*]

Jade Alglave, Alastair F. Donaldson, Daniel Kroening, and Michael Tautschnig

Department of Computer Science, University of Oxford, Oxford, UK

Abstract. We discuss problems and barriers which stand in the way of producing verification tools that are robust, scalable and integrated in the software development cycle. Our analysis is that these barriers span a spectrum from theoretical, through practical and even logistical issues. Theoretical issues are the inherent complexity of program verification and the absence of a common, accepted semantic model in tools. Practical hurdles include the challenges arising from real-world systems features, such as floating-point arithmetic and weak memory. Logistical obstacles we identify are the lack of standard benchmarks to drive tool quality and efficiency, and the difficulty for academic research institutions of allocating resources to tool development. We propose simple measures which we, as a community, could adopt to make the design of serious verification tools easier and more credible. Our long-term vision is for the community to produce tools that are indispensable for a developer but so seamlessly integrated into a development environment, as to be invisible.

1 Introduction

The sophistication and scalability of practical software verification tools has increased dramatically over the last decade. In particular, semi-automatic analysis of moderate-sized software using *model checking* has become viable due to the development of two primary methods: counterexample-guided abstraction refinement (CEGAR) [19] and bounded model checking (BMC) [15]. Counterexample-guided abstraction refinement, realised via predicate abstraction [30] and symbolic model checking [17] of Boolean programs [2], lies at the heart of Microsoft's Static Driver Verifier [4], which is now routinely used by developers of Windows device drivers. Other software model checkers, including BLAST [12], SATABS [21] and CPACHECKER [13] have followed this model and had impact within the research community. Bounded model checking was conceived as a hardware verification technique based on a natural encoding of circuits in propositional logic. Dramatic advances in the performance of SAT and SMT solvers have allowed this technique to be lifted to analyse the behaviour of programs, through a bit-level encoding of variables and operations. Bounded model checking tools such as CBMC [20] and F-SOFT [35] are effective at finding bugs in system-level software, and have been applied in the automotive domain [41]. Recent applications of the k-induction method [43] to software verification [25] have facilitated the use of BMC for verification, not just falsification, of race-freedom properties in software for the Cell BE processor [27].

---

[*] Supported by the Engineering and Physical Sciences Research Council (EPSRC) under grants no. EP/G051100/1 and EP/H017585/1.

T. Bultan and P.-A. Hsiung (Eds.): ATVA 2011, LNCS 6996, pp. 28–42, 2011.

We believe that a long-term vision for the field is to produce verification tools that are a necessary component of any serious development environment. Despite current success stories, formal verification using model checking based techniques is a long way from such mainstream adoption. Our analysis is that this is due to the following barriers, amongst others:

1. the difficulty of justifying the allocation of resources to tool development in an academic environment;
2. a lack of consensus on what software verification tools should handle, and as a consequence a lack of comparability;
3. a lack of guidance during the software development process, e.g., via unified benchmarks to drive quality and efficiency.

Past articles and discussions have addressed the topic of making verification technology practical, focusing on technology transfer of verification techniques [36] and the role of formal methods in software engineering [44]. The ambitious *Verified Software Initiative* [32] aims to exactly address the problem of practical verification tools, stating as one of its goals "[the construction of] a coherent toolset that automates the theory and scales up to the analysis of industrial-strength software".

In this position paper, we add our voices to the discussion. We believe the above challenges can be addressed via three means: *investment in tools*, encouraged by more stringent requirements for experimental repeatability when submitting verification papers, and a new category of "experimental validation" papers at verification conferences; a *standardisation process* to allow commonality in the way tools are designed and operated; and *challenge benchmarks* to allow tools to be easily tested, improved and compared, thus driving quality.

2   Community Support for Tool Development

Numerous technical problems have to be solved when designing software verification tools, and there is a need for robust tools in order to conduct proper scientific investigation in verification. We briefly discuss ways in which the verification community can support tool development efforts.

2.1   Allocating Resources to Tool Development

A significant portion of research in software verification is carried out by academics, but there are significant barriers for tool development in this community:

It is difficult to obtain research funding for tool development. Proposals for academic funding usually focus on a "big idea" – something novel, seriously challenging, and perhaps a little bit crazy. Without centering on the big idea, a funding proposal will likely be rejected as tame. This sort of blue-sky thinking is important for the development of ground-breaking, non-incremental ideas, but provides no means to develop serious tools over a long period of time. Crucially, resources for long-term tool maintenance and regression testing are usually not requested in a funding proposal.

The priorities of publication venues are a disincentive to building robust tools. Getting a paper accepted to a prestigious venue in automatic verification tends to require a new, deep theoretical idea. While some experimental evaluation is also usually expected, putting together a minimal prototype and concentrating on the theoretical side of a piece of work is a better short-term strategy for getting a paper accepted than painstakingly conducting a rigorous experimental evaluation on a large benchmark set, comparing with a range of other tools. Little or no credit will be given for ensuring that the tool being presented is robust and usable *beyond* the benchmark set used for evaluation. Understandably, time-pressured reviewers tend to scrutinise the theoretical detail of a novel technique readily available in the text of the paper, rather than investing time downloading, installing and experimenting with the associated implementation. They will often not clock whether a reported implementation is a minimal prototype, or a serious piece of software.

In today's environment, two of the main factors used to measure academic success are amount of research money raised, and number of high-quality publications. In this light, the above barriers suggest that an academic who pushes their research group to knock together a series of minimal prototype tools in the run up to major conference deadlines will have greater short-term success than an academic who invests significant time and effort in building robust tools.

2.2 The Need for Robust Tools

One might argue that it is not the responsibility of academics to build robust tools: instead, the job of an academic researcher is to push the boundaries of science by developing novel algorithms, investigating their theoretical properties, and providing proof-of-concept experimental demonstrations. For such proofs-of-concept, aren't minimal prototypes OK? Of course, we are not arguing that academic researchers should be responsible for building industrial-strength tools. But basing research solely on minimal prototypes can be a barrier to scientific progress.

Non-robust tools can lead to vacuous verification. The SLAM verification engine is at the absolute opposite end of the spectrum from being a minimal prototype tool: it is a serious collection of software developed over several years by a dedicated team of researchers, and has led to major uptake of verification technology by industry. This long-term effort has resulted in new insights not possible with the early prototypes: recent work describing the version 2 of the SLAM engine identifies device driver benchmarks where verification using SLAM 2 takes longer than with the original engine, despite a wealth of new optimisations [3]. The reason is that the original version of SLAM is less accurate, and as a result sometimes reported "verification successful" without having established a complete correctness argument. This report on a mature tool suggests that we should be skeptical of experimental results reported for quick prototypes, and illustrates the added value of long-term tool maintenance for research.

Without solid tools, we cannot really do science. Natural sciences hinge upon repeatability of experiments, and the ability to compare complementary or competing techniques in a controlled way. With verification tools, repeatability is often not possible: tools are sometimes to immature to be made available, or snapshots of the versions used to generate experimental results for a given paper are not taken. Tool comparison is also a challenge. Reviewers quite reasonably expect an implementation of a new method to be compared with prior implementations of competing techniques, but it is hard for authors to conduct such a comparison when prior implementations are not available or no longer work.

3   Program Semantics: Minimum Requirements

Designing software verification tools is hindered by the inherent difficulty of the task in general, and the complexity of real-world languages. The inherent difficulty of verification leads to no clear minimum bar for the sorts of input programs that all tools should be capable of handling. The complexity of real-world languages leads to pragmatic decisions related to the handling of semantic features, which are not usually documented and often differ from tool to tool. We now discuss a selection of these issues in some detail.

The specification for a compiler is relatively simple: given semantics for languages A and B, an $A \rightarrow B$ compiler should take any valid program in language A and transform it into a semantically equivalent program in language B. The time taken for transformation should be roughly linear in the size of A. Of course, implementing compilers is challenging, due to the lack of formal specifications for source and target languages, but it is clear that the task of building a compiler is achievable (barring pathological examples [45]).

In contrast, we know from basic undecidability results in computer science that we will never be able to build a verifier that takes an arbitrary program in a Turing-complete language, and decides whether that program is correct (under some appropriate notion of correctness) within some reasonable time bound.

3.1   What Should All Software Verification Tools Handle, *a minima*?

Because of this inherent difficulty, it is clear that a given software verification tool will not be capable of handling certain input programs. But we would expect that there should be large classes of very simple programs which any respectable software verification tool should be able to cope with. For instance, although loops are hard to analyse in general, a simple program involving loops with a fixed-and-small number of iterations should not be problematic to handle. While pointer-manipulating programs can be tough to analyse, support for straightforward parameter passing by reference via pointers should be non-negotiable. In particular, any verifier should be capable of correctly processing a program with a small and finite state-space (say with fewer than 10,000 states).

In practice, this is often not the case: a prototype verification tool may implement sophisticated algorithms geared towards solving a particular class of problems, but may diverge or crash when invoked on some trivial example program that does not fall within this class. Our viewpoint is that the difficulty of program verification *in general* is not an excuse for tools to perform abysmally, or produce unsound or incomplete results, on simple examples. We need to set the bar somewhere.

3.2   The Challenges of Semantic Features in Real-World Languages

Research dealing with full-scale languages with complex semantics cannot realistically handle all of their features in all cases. However, it is important that tool designers identify those features which are not handled, and clearly document what the limitations of their tool are. We briefly consider some examples of semantically challenging issues faced by verification tools for C programs:

Bit-level accuracy. Languages in the C family represent numeric types by fixed-width bit-vectors. Thus arithmetic operations may overflow, breaking standard mathematical identities such as $x + 1 > x$. Because arithmetic over/underflow can be the source of subtle bugs, especially in system-level software, it is vital that software verifiers for C-like languages reason with bit-level accuracy. This means parametrising the verifier by a given machine word-size. While early software verifiers tended to use a mathematical model of integers with infinite range, advances in bit-vector solvers led to bit-level accurate tools such as CBMC [20] and F-SOFT [35]. Nowadays, bit-level accurate reasoning is commonplace and widely accepted, primarily owing to the progress modern SAT and SMT solvers have made.

Floating point. Reasoning directly about floating point arithmetic can in principle be achieved by bit-blasting, following the IEEE 754 standard. While this approach is implemented, e.g., by the CBMC tool, it does not scale well due to the immense complexity of floating point circuits. Pragmatic alternatives to supporting floating-point reasoning include treating floating point variables as *fixed* point, or as intervals of *real* numbers, in which case a real arithmetic solver can be exploited. The difficulty with such approaches are that they do not provide accurate results for real programs. While for some users this may be acceptable, for others it may not be, thus such decisions should be clearly documented. Alternative approaches avoid direct reasoning by soundly approximating floating-point computation, either through abstraction [16] or expression canonization [22]. An important open problem is to design fast SMT solvers for floating-point arithmetic [42].

Weak memory models. Analysis tools for *concurrent* programs need to consider the problem of weak memory models exhibited by all modern multicore architectures (e.g., x86 or Power), where the model of computation is not *sequentially consistent* (SC) [38]. Soundness in the presence of weak memory involves considering all possible ways in which memory accesses could be resolved by the hardware, greatly increasing the (already high) complexity of concurrent software analysis. As a result, it is understandable that practical concurrent software verifiers may pragmatically assume an unrealistically strong memory model.

If a tool that aims at handling concurrent programs running on modern multicores supposes SC to be the execution model [26], the tool is strictly unsound, yet perhaps practically useful in finding concurrency bugs or increasing confidence in the correctness of concurrent software. Some programming disciplines such as the *data race free guarantee* (DRF) [1] allow the tool to ignore the details of the memory model, for the discipline enforces the illusion of SC. Hence, tools that assume their input programs to be DRF and SC to be the execution model, e.g., [23], are sound. However, this means that they cannot handle *lock-free synchronisation* [29], a programming style favoured by engineers for its performance, such as for example in the Linux kernel [40].

Again, whether a concurrent software verifier handles weak memory in a sound or restricted manner should be a clearly stated design decision.

System-level features. When applying verification tools to embedded systems software, users typically require support for low-level features such as interrupts, inline assembly and DMA. Correctness for this sort of software often requires careful layout of memory according to machine-specific alignment constraints. These kinds of features are platform-specific, and therefore we do not anticipate a general solution. However, at present, system-level features tend to be modelled in an ad hoc manner for individual applications. A generic framework for describing system-level characteristics relevant to verification, which could then be customised by users for specific needs, does not currently exist and would be be a major step beyond the current state of the art.

Handling source code which is not standard-compliant. While a compiler is typically free to generate arbitrary code where an input program does not conform to the language standard, software verifiers cannot be free to assign specific, arbitrary semantics in such cases. Because bug-finding is an important goal of a software verifier and bugs often arise from lack of adherence to language standards, strictly speaking a verifier should consider *every possible* effect for a statement whose semantics are undefined. Naturally, this strict requirement may not be achievable in practice, and the way to handle or implement certain language features can be controversial. In the absence of a consensus, we believe that developers should state explicitly, and as precisely as possible, how they handle a certain underspecified feature. As an instance, program verifiers may use a fixed order of evaluation of expressions with side effects, while the language standard permits any ordering.

4   The Lack of Guidance in the Process of Writing Tools

Given an input language with well-defined semantics, the question about how to proceed to arrive at a practically useful software verification tool arises. As it is impossible to solve all technical problems in a single step, a suitable form of incremental development must be found. The realization of a research idea, which often involves novel algorithms, effectively results in a conflict of interest: both the novel algorithm must be implemented as efficiently as possible, and several technical hurdles must be overcome. The latter will in parts be well known, whereas other technical challenges might only become visible once the tool has evolved far enough to be applied in verification of real software systems.

To date, we are still in the unfortunate situation that there is only very little preexisting code that offers both high quality and comprehensive documentation to cover all those fundamental technical issues. Such a code base would need to provide a formally defined intermediate representation for at least one major programming language. Furthermore, standard program analyses, as available in compilers, would be expected.

The development of decision procedures, in particular SAT and SMT solvers, has made a lot more progress in the last decade than the development of software verification tools has. Despite continuing evolution and improvement, gritty technical issues tend not to hinder the integration of new algorithms with existing solvers. We identify some of the key advantages in the history of the development of decision procedures, compared with software verifiers:

Publication of technical aspects of decision procedures. Both algorithmic and technical challenges are acknowledged, well documented (in terms of scientific publications – cf. [28,14] for prime examples), and hence technical aspects relevant to tool development are well-understood by the community at large, and easily available to outsiders. Compare this situation to software verification, where entire tools (implemented in hundreds of thousands of lines of code) are often documented in no more than a single conference or journal publication, usually focussing on the tool's core algorithms, presented at a high level of abstraction. It seems that researchers in software verification tools are reluctant to write up technical details, perhaps due to the perception that highly technical papers will be considered engineering, not research, and rejected.

SAT/SMT software architectures have become mature. As a consequence of sharing knowledge about algorithms and problems, in terms of publications and often also source code, developers of decision procedures benefit from lessons learned in other tools [14], hence avoiding redundant re-invention.

Well-defined input languages. Decision procedures benefit from simpler and more formally defined input languages [24,10], compared with software verifiers. The standardisation of programming languages such as C or C++ still leaves many aspects intentionally undefined. A sound software verification tool must thus consider all possible interpretations or offer controllable parameters to the user.

Comparability and competitions. An essential part of any scientific work is a fair and comprehensive comparison to related work. For software verification tools, this is – at present – largely impossible. As such, we are unable to assess progress.

Again, decision procedures have done much better. First, publicly available standard benchmark sets exist to perform comparisons. Second, well established competitions[1,2,3] provide additional incentive to adhere to common input languages, and provide reward for technical improvements. Third, theories and benchmark categories provide precise guidance to users of the technologies, enabling them to select the most suitable tool for their needs [9]. All these measurable facts (performance on standard benchmark sets and supported theories) permit precise, scientific assessment of progress.

We cannot (and should not) change the fact that software verification tools have to deal with complex general-purpose input languages. Yet many such problems could be offloaded to a front end that builds a formally defined intermediate representation. For the reasons laid out in Sec. 2, however, it is challenging for research groups to invest in building such a front end. As an alternative, software verification tool developers could team up to define a subset of a widely used programming language the support of which can be expected from any tool claiming to perform software verification.

Any such standardisation effort will foster comparability; yet two further problems need to be addressed to fully enable comparability: a) for performance comparison, a

---

[1] http://www.satcompetition.org/

[2] http://www.smtcomp.org/

[3] http://www.cs.miami.edu/~tptp/CASC/

publicly available set of benchmarks in the standardised language must be made available; b) a categorisation similar to theories, as found in SMT, must be established.

5 Proposals for Supporting the Development of Software Verification Tools

Based on the critical assessment of the present situation we propose a way forward. We first discuss possible evolutions in our community, and note the long-term benefits that can be associated with building recognised tools. We then steer towards solutions of technical problems.

5.1 Publication Incentives

As discussed in Sec. 2, serious development of tools is not rewarded by the evaluation criteria of publication venues. We propose two strategies for improving this situation:

Repeatability requirements. Publication venues in formal verification should require authors to make implementations of novel algorithms available for inspection and validation by reviewers. To avoid reviewer anonymity being compromised by IP address logging, publication venues should make use of secure means for implementations and benchmarks to be uploaded as part of a paper submission. Such features are already available in submission management systems such as EasyChair. Authors should also provide comprehensive instructions on how to operate the provided software in order to reproduce the paper's results. Reviewers should be encouraged to try to reproduce a selection of results using the provided implementation, and should be encouraged to comment explicitly on whether they have attempted to do so. Review reports should discuss the experience of using the reported implementation, and it should be reasonable to suggest rejecting a paper because the implementation does not work, fails on reasonable examples beyond the benchmark set reported in the paper, or cannot be used due to a lack of comprehensible operating instructions. Working towards standardised interfaces, as proposed in Sec. 5.3, will considerably simplify such evaluations, both for authors and reviewers.

There are two immediate thorny issues associated with such a scheme. First, it relies on reviewers and authors having a common working environment (e.g., using the same operating system and machine word size), and some papers may report experiments on hardware or software which is not universal, or even proprietary. Second, it makes it difficult for industrial practitioners to publish research results where it is not possible to release associated implementations. Reasonable measures would need to be taken to work around these issues, without discouraging valuable contributions from industry. Possible solutions include:

- Requesting that implementations target a specific, widely available OS (virtual machine images may be an option as well).
- Where this is not possible, or where implementations are proprietary, requiring authors to build a web interface through which reviewers can interact with a tool without actually downloading the tool executable.

Also concerned by the problem of experimental repeatability, the databases community has taken exemplary steps to address this at least four years ago [39]. The Call for Papers of the 2008 ACM SIGMOD/PODS Conference includes Experimental Repeatability Requirements in its guidelines for research papers,[4] which are summarised as follows:

> *"To help published papers achieve an impact and stand as reliable reference-able works for future research, the SIGMOD 2008 reviewing process includes an assessment of the extent to which the presented experiments are repeatable by someone with access to all the required hardware, software, and test data. Thus, we attempt to establish that the code developed by the authors exists, runs correctly on well-defined inputs, and performs in a manner compatible with that presented in the paper."*

We strongly believe that the verification community should take a similar stand.

Encouraging experimental validation papers. The databases and systems community also encourages validation of previously published techniques via independent experiments to the extent that it is possible to have a paper accepted by a top databases conference or journal merely by re-implementing and comprehensively evaluating a technique reported previously by a different research group. For example, the Call for Papers of the VLDB 2012 conference includes an *Experiments and Analysis Track*, which "seeks papers that focus on the experimental evaluation of existing algorithms and data structures". This includes explicitly the category of *Result Verification*, for "papers that verify or refute results published in the past and that, through the renewed analysis, help to advance the state of the art".[5]

This publication model allows serious implementation work to be rewarded by prestigious publications, reducing the problem discussed in Sec. 2.1 of implementation work being at odds with short-term goals.

Currently, Calls for Papers at top verification conferences include no such encouragement of result verification, and it is not clear whether a *Result Verification*-style paper would be taken seriously, or rejected due to lack of novelty. We recommend that active steps should be taken to change this situation. The HCI community also discussed the issue of result replication recently via a panel at the 2011 ACM CHI Conference [46].

A note on tool demonstration papers. One might ask at this stage whether tool demonstration papers, which are common in Calls for Papers at verification conferences, serve the goal of encouraging serious implementation. We do not believe this to be the case; tool demonstration papers can often only provide a bite-sized overview of a particular technique.

5.2   Benefits from Building Tools

The benefits of robust tools to the verification community and beyond are clear but, as discussed in Sec. 2.1, there is little short-term reward for tool development in an academic environment. However, there are longer-term benefits to serious tool development. We illustrate this by considering three well-known verification tools:

---

[4] http://www.sigmod08.org/sigmod_research.shtml
[5] http://www.vldb2012.org/call-for-contributions/experiments-and-analysis-track/

- SPIN, an explicit-state model checker designed at Bell Labs, and now maintained by the NASA/JPL laboratory for reliable software
- SLAM, a CEGAR-based software model checker, designed at Microsoft Research
- PRISM, a probabilistic symbolic model checker designed at the University of Birmingham, and now maintained at the University of Oxford.

Serious software tools can be highly cited. We consider citation counts for the two most highly cited papers on each of these tools:[6]

- SPIN [33,34]: cited 5323 times
- SLAM [6,5]: cited 929 times
- PRISM [37,31]: cited 735 times

These large citation counts indicate significant recognition for the efforts that have gone into development of these tools.

Serious software tools boost research. A robust tool can be used as the basis for a great deal of further research. Looking at the publication records of the key designers of the above tools, we find that each tool has led to tens of further high-quality publications. In the long term, the effort expended in producing a high-quality verification tool pays off, since one does not need to repeatedly construct throw-away prototypes for individual paper deadlines.

5.3   Standards for Tool Interfaces

In order for a software verification tool to be used (either to reproduce experimental results, or simply to be applied by a practitioner), it is important that the user a) knows how to operate the tool from the command-line or via a GUI, and b) is aware of "magic" keywords and syntactic constructs used in input programs for property specification and/or environment modelling.

To compare two software verification tools geared towards the same input language, one must understand equivalences between command-line or GUI options of both tools, and how equivalent properties and/or environmental assumptions can be specified/modelled using the respective syntactic constructs provided by the tools.

Tool options together with syntax for modelling and specification, together with the language which a verification tool targets, comprise the *interface* of the tool. Clearly the tasks of using an unfamiliar tool and making comparisons between two tools would be eased by *standards* for tool interfaces.

We make the following recommendations in this area:

Focus first on ANSI-C. Given the wide range of programming languages being used today, we cannot expect a long-term convergence on a single language to be supported by all software verification tools. If more front ends for input language processing were available, possibly a convergence towards some intermediate representation could be sought. At present, however, the best we can do is focus on the single programming

---

[6] Citation counts are taken from Google Scholar on 11 July 2011. For each tool, we have summed the citation count for its key papers. Self-citations have not been excluded.

language most widely supported by the community: ANSI-C. We propose working out a standard interface for ANSI-C verifiers, as discussed below, then using this interface as a basis for tool operation and comparison. If successful, a similar process could be followed for other languages.

Focusing on ANSI-C still requires tools to agree on, or at least identify differences between the precise way in which features that are left undefined in the standard are modelled. We propose a benchmark-based solution to this in Sec. 5.4.

Property specification and environment modelling. In current software verification tools we find a wide range of techniques and assumptions used both in property specification and environment modelling. For example, the BLAST model checker uses the magic variable __BLAST_NONDET to specify a nondeterministic value, while with CBMC one obtains a nondeterministic value of type T by calling a function declared with return value of type T but the body of the function being unavailable. A common verification-level construct is the *assume* statement, which restricts verification to consider only paths on which, when executed, the *assume* statement's guard ϕ evaluates to *true*. Individual tools tend to provide bespoke syntax for *assume* statements (e.g., CBMC uses __CPROVER_assume(ϕ)). Most verifiers unsoundly but pragmatically agree that the effect of calling a function whose body is unavailable should be a no-op, but that the function should return a nondeterministic result; however, this is rarely a documented feature. Correctness properties may be expressed in some tools via external specification languages [7,11], language extensions [8], or may be embedded in comments using a tool-specific syntax [18].

Given input programs that deviate from the ANSI-C standard, e.g., by reading from invalid memory, or depending on the order in which side-effecting actual parameter expressions are passed, distinct verification tools tend to explore specific behaviours decided upon by the tool implementers. While it is fine for a *compiler* to behave arbitrarily on non-compliant programs, this is not the case for a *verifier*, which should a) detect and report non-compliance, and ideally b) explore all possible ways in which the non-compliant feature could be implemented, in order to catch potential bugs in an implementation-independent manner.

As a result of this variety of approaches, it is currently in general impossible to run the same input program, without modification, through different software verification tools and obtain consistent results. We propose:

- the design of a standard set of syntactic constructs for property specification and environment modelling in C programs. This would be derived from a careful study of the constructs used by existing tools, and possibly also building upon the advances made in other programming languages, such as Spec# [8] or JML [18]. The adoption of such a standard would allow C benchmarks to be evaluated, without modification, by a range of tools.
- the construction of benchmarks to categorise the ways in which verifiers handle non-standard ANSI-C programs. This would allow tool users to understand the sorts of bugs a verifier will find, and whether two distinct tools will behave similarly when given non-compliant programs.

A standard command-line interface. A much more straightforward proposal is that a standard command-line interface for C verifiers be agreed on. The standard would specify arguments to indicate files to be checked, the main function or functions to be analysed, and possibly even the sorts of generic properties (such as division-by-zero or buffer overflows) to be analysed. We recommend that specification of preprocessor macros, include directories, and other commands shared with compilers, should follow the interface of the widely used GNU C compiler. This standard interface would make it easy to write generic scripts to invoke C verifiers, further easing comparison between tools. Furthermore, the standard would make it possible to build user interfaces in a tool-independent manner, allowing at least simple input programs to be verified with the press of a single button.

5.4   Benchmarks to Drive Quality, Comparability, and Competition

The possibility of comparability afforded by a common interface will enable building standard benchmark sets that serve as a basis for fair and scientific comparison. Benchmarks and fair comparison lead towards measurements of progress, and will ultimately enable setting up competitions. We acknowledge that deriving a fair and representative benchmark suite will clearly be even more challenging than, e.g., in case of SAT solvers. Random programs are likely not useful. Different input languages, such as C or Java will require separate benchmark suites. Even if common interfaces are established, different verification tools will remain geared towards different tasks, thus fair comparisons on benchmarks are hard to achieve. We do expect, however, that *branding*, described below, will help to categorise different verification tools according to their strengths.

We expect the design of such a benchmark suite to have several further benefits:

Setting a minimum bar for verification tools. Software model checkers have been available for more than a decade, thus users should reasonably expect them to perform sensibly on small input programs. A set of small benchmark programs will therefore permit to label a given analysis tool a true *software verification tool*. This set of benchmarks will only define *minimal standards*, as discussed in Sec. 3.1. Yet these standard benchmarks will help make tool development easier – one immediately has tests to work towards.

Semantic foundations. A set of benchmarks with precisely defined semantics and independently validated verification results can serve as test whether a tool matches expected semantics for particular language features. As discussed in Sec. 3.2, we acknowledge that not all tools will faithfully handle all semantic aspects of real-world programming languages, and may treat challenging features (e.g., floating-point arithmetic and weak memory) in an unsound but pragmatic way. The proposed benchmark suite will serve as litmus test for verification tools, determining whether a tool faithfully treats a particular language feature, and when this is not the case perhaps even inferring that the tool conforms to a specific known deviation in the way this feature is handled (e.g., determining that fixed-point or real number semantics are used for what should be floating-point reasoning). The benchmarks will allow *branding* of software verification tools, allowing users to quickly get a feeling for whether a tool will be applicable to their particular problem. Our hope is that designers of verification tools will strive for a high-quality branding by the benchmark suite, spurring them on to build robust and usable software.

Driving quality and scalability. If the verification community widely adopts such a benchmark suite, a new verification technique will be taken seriously only if it operates correctly and reasonably efficiently on these benchamrks. This will drive competitiveness, as was observed in the case of decision procedures. If a sufficient level of interface compatibility is achieved, we will be able to run automated competitions, which will provide an incentive to work towards better scalability.

Competition. A competition event with high visibility would foster the transfer of theoretical and conceptual advancements in software verification into practical tools, and would also give credit and benefits to students who spend considerable amounts of time developing verification algorithms and software packages. The first such competition event will compare state-of-the-art software verifiers with respect to effectiveness and efficiency, and the results will be represented at TACAS 2012. [7]

6 Summary

We have discussed the barriers we currently perceive to advancing of the state of the art in software verification tools. We have proposed a number of simple measures which we believe could seriously help this situation: encouragement from the community in the form of a new category of paper and more stringent requirements for experimental reproducibility (inspired by similar measures within the databases and systems community); a common interface for ANSI-C verifiers to enable benchmark compatibility and tool comparison; and a suite of benchmarks which will set a minimum bar for the sophistication of verification tools, provide litmus tests to automatically infer whether and how particular semantic features are handled, and drive the quality and scalability of tools through competitions (inspired by the dramatic competition-driven success in the field of decision procedures).

Technology transfer of hardware verification techniques into practical use proceeded via a sequence of "small steps" [36]. We hope that our proposed measures will act as small steps to continue the transfer of *software* verification techniques into mainstream practice, which has been gaining more and more momentum over the last decade.

Acknowledgments. We thank Vijay D'Silva for stimulating discussion during the writing of this paper, and for useful pointers to related work. We are also grateful to Dragan Bošnački for insightful comments on an earlier draft of this work.

References

1. Adve, S., Hill, M.: Weak Ordering – A New Definition. In: ISCA (1990)
2. Ball, T., Rajamani, S.: Boolean programs: A model and process for software analysis. Tech. Rep. 2000-14, Microsoft Research (February 2000)

---

[7] Dirk Beyer, Competition on Software Verification, http://www.sosy-lab.org/~dbeyer/smc-comp/

3. Ball, T., Bounimova, E., Kumar, R., Levin, V.: SLAM2: Static driver verification with under 4% false alarms. In: FMCAD, pp. 35–42. IEEE, Los Alamitos (2010)

4. Ball, T., Bounimova, E., Levin, V., Kumar, R., Lichtenberg, J.: The static driver verifier research platform. In: Touili, T., Cook, B., Jackson, P. (eds.) CAV 2010. LNCS, vol. 6174, pp. 119–122. Springer, Heidelberg (2010)

5. Ball, T., Rajamani, S.: The SLAM project: debugging system software via static analysis. In: Principles of Programming Languages (POPL), pp. 1–3. ACM, New York (2002)

6. Ball, T., Rajamani, S.K.: The SLAM toolkit. In: Berry, G., Comon, H., Finkel, A. (eds.) CAV 2001. LNCS, vol. 2102, pp. 260–264. Springer, Heidelberg (2001)

7. Ball, T., Rajamani, S.K.: SLIC: a specification language for interface checking (of C). Tech. Rep. MSR-TR-2001-21, Microsoft Research (2001)

8. Barnett, M., DeLine, R., Fähndrich, M., Jacobs, B., Leino, K.R.M., Schulte, W., Venter, H.: The Spec# programming system: Challenges and directions. In: Meyer, B., Woodcock, J. (eds.) VSTTE 2005. LNCS, vol. 4171, pp. 144–152. Springer, Heidelberg (2008)

9. Barrett, C., Stump, A., Tinelli, C.: The Satisfiability Modulo Theories Library (SMT-LIB) (2010), http://www.smt-lib.org

10. Barrett, C., Stump, A., Tinelli, C.: The SMT-LIB Standard: Version 2.0. In: Proceedings of the 8th International Workshop on Satisfiability Modulo Theories (2010)

11. Beyer, D., Henzinger, T.A., Jhala, R., Majumdar, R.: BLAST documentation, http://www.sosy-lab.org/~dbeyer/blast_doc/ (retrieved July 11, 2011)

12. Beyer, D., Henzinger, T.A., Jhala, R., Majumdar, R.: The software model checker BLAST. STTT 9(5-6), 505–525 (2007)

13. Beyer, D., Keremoglu, M.E.: CPACHECKER: A tool for configurable software verification. In: Gopalakrishnan, G., Qadeer, S. (eds.) CAV 2011. LNCS, vol. 6806, pp. 184–190. Springer, Heidelberg (2011)

14. Biere, A.: Picosat essentials. JSAT 4(2-4), 75–97 (2008)

15. Biere, A., Cimatti, A., Clarke, E., Strichman, O., Zhu, Y.: Bounded model checking. In: Advances in Computers (2003)

16. Brillout, A., Kroening, D., Wahl, T.: Mixed abstractions for floating-point arithmetic. In: FMCAD, pp. 69–76. IEEE, Los Alamitos (2009)

17. Burch, J., Clarke, E., McMillan, K., Dill, D., Hwang, L.J.: Symbolic model checking: 10^{20} states and beyond. In: Information and Computation (1992)

18. Chalin, P., Kiniry, J.R., Leavens, G.T., Poll, E.: Beyond assertions: Advanced specification and verification with JML and ESC/Java2. In: de Boer, F.S., Bonsangue, M.M., Graf, S., de Roever, W.-P. (eds.) FMCO 2005. LNCS, vol. 4111, pp. 342–363. Springer, Heidelberg (2006)

19. Clarke, E., Grumberg, O., Jha, S., Lu, Y., Veith, H.: Counterexample-guided abstraction refinement for symbolic model checking. Journal of the ACM (JACM) (2003)

20. Clarke, E., Kröning, D., Lerda, F.: A tool for checking ANSI-C programs. In: Jensen, K., Podelski, A. (eds.) TACAS 2004. LNCS, vol. 2988, pp. 168–176. Springer, Heidelberg (2004)

21. Clarke, E., Kroening, D., Sharygina, N., Yorav, K.: Predicate abstraction of ANSI-C programs using SAT. Formal Methods in System Design (FMSD), 105–127 (2004)

22. Collingbourne, P., Cadar, C., Kelly, P.H.J.: Symbolic crosschecking of floating-point and SIMD code. In: EuroSys. ACM, New York (2011)

23. Calcagno, C., Distefano, D., O'Hearn, P., Yang, H.: Compositional shape analysis by means of bi-abduction. In: POPL 2009, pp. 289–300 (2009)

24. Satisfiability: Suggested Format (1993), ftp://dimacs.rutgers.edu/pub/challenge/satisfiability/

25. Donaldson, A., Haller, L., Kroening, D., Rümmer, P.: Software verification using k-induction. In: Yahav, E. (ed.) SAS 2011. LNCS, vol. 6887, pp. 351–368. Springer, Heidelberg (2011)

26. Donaldson, A., Kaiser, A., Kroening, D., Wahl, T.: Symmetry-aware predicate abstraction for shared-variable concurrent programs. In: Gopalakrishnan, G., Qadeer, S. (eds.) CAV 2011. LNCS, vol. 6806, pp. 356–371. Springer, Heidelberg (2011)

27. Donaldson, A.F., Kroening, D., Ruemmer, P.: Automatic analysis of DMA races using model checking and k-induction. Formal Methods in System Design 39(1), 83–113 (2011)

28. Eén, N., Sörensson, N.: An extensible SAT-solver. In: Giunchiglia, E., Tacchella, A. (eds.) SAT 2003. LNCS, vol. 2919, pp. 502–518. Springer, Heidelberg (2004)

29. Fraser, K., Harris, T.: Concurrent Programming Without Locks. ACM Trans. Comput. Syst. 25(2) (2007)

30. Graf, S., Saïdi, H.: Construction of abstract state graphs with PVS. In: Grumberg, O. (ed.) CAV 1997. LNCS, vol. 1254, pp. 72–83. Springer, Heidelberg (1997)

31. Hinton, A., Kwiatkowska, M.Z., Norman, G., Parker, D.: PRISM: A tool for automatic verification of probabilistic systems. In: Hermanns, H. (ed.) TACAS 2006. LNCS, vol. 3920, pp. 441–444. Springer, Heidelberg (2006)

32. Hoare, C., Misra, J., Leavens, G.T., Shankar, N.: The verified software initiative: A manifesto. ACM Comput. Surv. 41, article 22 (October 2009)

33. Holzmann, G.: Design and Validation of Computer Protocols. Prentice Hall, Englewood Cliffs (1991)

34. Holzmann, G.J.: The model checker SPIN. IEEE Trans. Software Eng. 23(5), 279–295 (1997)

35. Ivancic, F., Yang, Z., Ganai, M.K., Gupta, A., Shlyakhter, I., Ashar, P.: F-Soft: Software verification platform. In: Etessami, K., Rajamani, S.K. (eds.) CAV 2005. LNCS, vol. 3576, pp. 301–306. Springer, Heidelberg (2005)

36. Kurshan, R.P.: Verification technology transfer. In: Grumberg, O., Veith, H. (eds.) 25 Years of Model Checking. LNCS, vol. 5000, pp. 46–64. Springer, Heidelberg (2008)

37. Kwiatkowska, M.Z., Norman, G., Parker, D.: PRISM: Probabilistic symbolic model checker. In: Field, T., Harrison, P.G., Bradley, J., Harder, U. (eds.) TOOLS 2002. LNCS, vol. 2324, pp. 200–204. Springer, Heidelberg (2002)

38. Lamport, L.: How to Make a Correct Multiprocess Program Execute Correctly on a Multiprocessor. IEEE Trans. Comput. 46(7), 779–782 (1979)

39. Manolescu, I., Manegold, S.: Performance evaluation and experimental assessment – conscience or curse of database research? In: VLDB, pp. 1441–1442. ACM, New York (2007)

40. McKenney, P.: http://www.rdrop.com/users/paulmck/RCU/

41. Post, H., Sinz, C., Merz, F., Gorges, T., Kropf, T.: Linking functional requirements and software verification. In: RE, pp. 295–302. IEEE Computer Society, Los Alamitos (2009)

42. Rümmer, P., Wahl, T.: An SMT-LIB theory of binary floating-point arithmetic. In: International Workshop on Satisfiability Modulo Theories (SMT) (2010)

43. Sheeran, M., Singh, S., Stålmarck, G.: Checking safety properties using induction and a SAT-solver. In: Johnson, S.D., Hunt Jr., W.A. (eds.) FMCAD 2000. LNCS, vol. 1954, pp. 108–125. Springer, Heidelberg (2000)

44. Steffen, B.: Major threat: From formal methods without tools to tools without formal methods. In: ICECCS, p. 15. IEEE Computer Society, Los Alamitos (2004), panel discussion

45. Veldhuizen, T.L.: C++ templates are Turing complete. Tech. rep. (2003), http://citeseerx.ist.psu.edu/viewdoc/summary?doi=10.1.1.14.3670 (retrieved July 11, 2011)

46. Wilson, M.L., Mackay, W., Chi, E., Bernstein, M., Russell, D., Thimbleby, H.: RepliCHI – CHI should be replicating and validating results more: discuss. In: CHI Extended Abstracts, pp. 463–466. ACM, New York (2011)

Synthesizing, Verifying, and Debugging SoC with FSM-Based Specification of On-Chip Communication Protocols

Masahiro Fujita

VLSI Design and Education Center,The University of Tokyo
fujita@ee.t.u-tokyo.ac.jp

Abstract. In general on-chip communication protocols, such as OCP[1], can be specified and represented with finite state machines (FSM). Such communication protocols are basically collections of individual transactions or commands, such as simple read/write and bust read/write, and each transaction or command can be specified with a FSM. So a given communication protocol can be represented with a set of FSMs which work jointly. Based on these FSM-based specifications, we have been developing not only pure formal and semi-formal verification techniques using FSMs as specifications, but also synthesis and debugging techniques, such as automatic generation of protocol converters and post-silicon verification/debugging supports. In this paper, we show first how FSM-based specifications can describe sate-of-the-art on-chip communication protocols, and then their application to such synthesis and verification/debug for SoC designs are presented.

1   Introduction

Generally speaking, it is good if we can have clear separation between communication and computation when designing large and complicated systems, such as SoC designs. Reuses of IP cores would become much simpler, and verification of entire systems would become much easier. One way to realize such separation is to introduce formal specifications for communication protocols to be used for synthesis and verification in pre- and post-silicon stages as shown in Figure 1. In this paper, first we define on-chip communication protocols with FSM (Finite State Machine) oriented descriptions, and then they are used for various synthesis and verification problems found in SoC designs. FSM oriented representations are commonly used when specifying communication protocols both in software and hardware. By specifying them with formal methods, reasoning about communication can be separated from their computations, which makes the design process much more clear. Here FSM-based specifications targeting state-of-the-art on-chip communication protocols, such as OCP[1] and AXI[2], are introduced. Those FSM can immediately be used as properties for simulation-based and formal verification through inclusion/equivalence checking of communication parts of the designs and/or model checking with properties

T. Bultan and P.-A. Hsiung (Eds.): ATVA 2011, LNCS 6996, pp. 43–50, 2011.

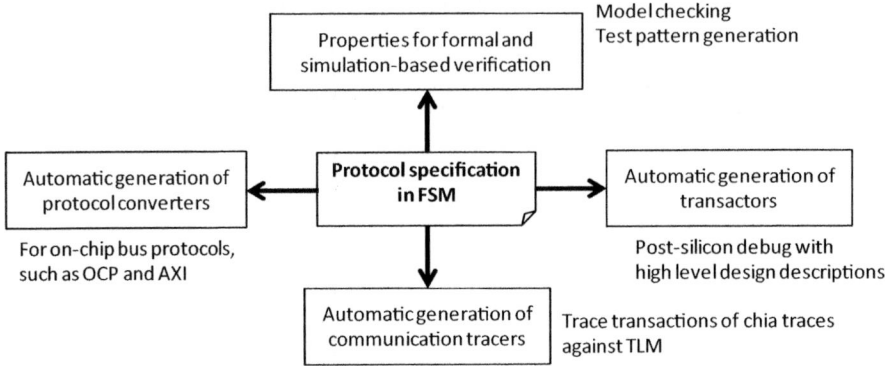

Fig. 1. Synthesis and verification using protocol specification in FSM

generated by decomposition from FSMs. Besides direct verification of designs with FSM representations, various problems relating to SoC designs can be processed with them. In the following sections, after showing how state-of-the-art on-chip communication protocols can be specified with FSMs, two of their applications, automatic generation of protocol converters and automatic mapping of simulation/chip traces among different levels of design descriptions are shown.

2   FSM-Based Specification of On-Chip Communication Protocols

As shown in [3], simple blocking protocols can be specified with regular expressions which are practically equivalent to FSMs. Each *blocking* command/transaction in the given protocol, where the next command must wait until a response of the current command has been received, is specified with one FSM. Modern communication protocols, however, use *non-blocking* protocols, where the next command can be issued before receiving a response for the current command. In order to specify such non-blocking protocols, two separated FSMs are required [4], one for request and the other for response. Such FSM representation for "simple read" command of OCP is shown is Figure 2. The FSM for request is in charge of issuing request, and the one for response is in charge of receiving response. As they are running in parallel, non-blocking protocols can be processed.

State-of-the-art protocols also have "burst mode" where multiple data are sent with a single command. In [4], a multi-level FSM has been introduced to deal with various bust modes in communication. Example FSM representations for "burst read" command in AXI protocol are shown in Figure 3. Here a super state is introduced which represents a FSM in lower level as shown in the figure. By repeatedly visiting such super states, multiple data transfers in burst modes can be described with FSM in a uniform way.

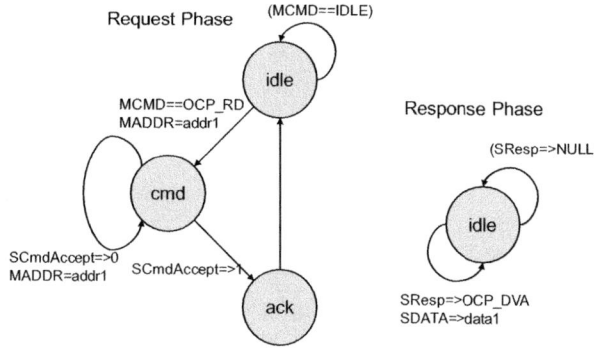

Fig. 2. Automaton for OCP simple read transaction

Real-life protocols can be defined as collections of individual commands. This naturally introduces a hierarchical model of protocols as shown in Figure 4, where a protocol is modelled as a set of sequences [4]. Sequences correspond to command and are mutually exclusive transactions sharing the same initial state. Also, a sequence have at most two FSMs to represent behavior of request and response separately.

3   Automatic Generation of On-Chip Communication Protocol Converters

Protocol converters interpret the given two protocols and realize the communication between them by applying appropriate transformations to control as well as data signals. In other words, a protocol converter follow both protocols, and basically it can be realized by computing the cross product of the two protocols. As protocols are represented as collections of sequences or FSMs, a protocol converter is a collection of FSMs that are the products of two sets of corresponding FSM for each sequence. For the synthesis of each product, basically cross producing two FSMs [3] is computed by taking care of "dependency" among data variable, i.e., a protocol converter can send out data to slave sides only after it received it from master sides. As state-of-the-art on-chip communication protocols need both of request and response FSMs as well as multi-level ones, this cross product computation has been extended [4]. With the hierarchical protocol representations, size of exploration space, when computing cross product, is reduced and becomes manageable. Parallelism between request and response FSMs, which is essential for non-blocking protocols, is realized by synthesizing transducer FSMs for request and response separately.

[4] also gave ideas to hide loops in FSM, so that explosions of exploration spaces are avoided. Two kinds of edges, returning ones and loop transition ones, which make a loop are defined as shown in Figure 5. Returning edges are the

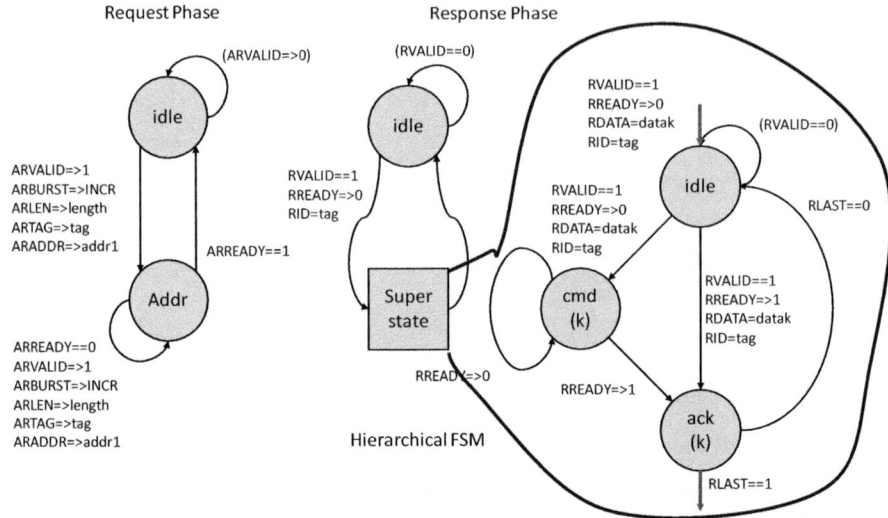

Fig. 3. Automaton for AXI burst read transaction

Fig. 4. Hierarchical model of protocol

edges whose destinations are the initial states. Before computing the cross product, returning edges are removed by adding the end state. The destination of returning edges are replaced to the end state. On the other hand, loop transition edges are the ones heading to the already visited states when traversing a FSM. Loop transition edges are removed by replacing Subgraphs containing loop transition edges with superstates. A Subgraph corresponding to the superstate is called KernelGraph, while the owner of the superstate is called ShellGraph. The cross product computation is applied to a pair of KernelGraphs and a pair of ShellGraphs separately. After that, a pair of superstates in the FSM resulting from ShellGraphs is replaced with the FSM resulting from KernelGraphs.

The synthesis flow of partial transducers with datapaths (shown in Figure 6) consists of the following 4 steps, assuming that FSMs for both protocols and specification of data words are given. As step1, a datapath to handle incompatibility of data words/behaviors is designed by hand. A datapath can be either combinational or sequential circuit. For semantical incompatibilities, combinational circuits such as adders and tables are used. To realize behaviors depending on the values of data words, sequential circuits such as counters and accumulator are used. As step2, a FSM to drive the datapath is designed manually. Activities of the driver FSM includes setting initial values, waiting for data-ready signal,

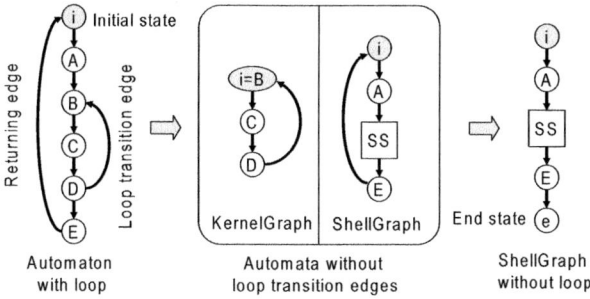

Fig. 5. Definition and removal of loop edges within an automaton

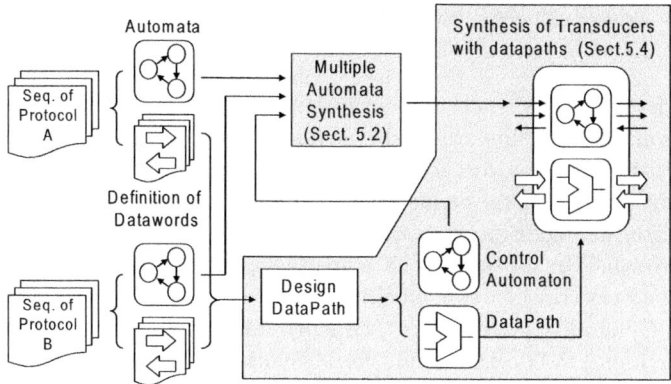

Fig. 6. Overview of the proposed method

and getting resulting values. As step3, cross product computation is applied to protocol FSM and the driver FSM. After synthesis, a partial transducer FSM is obtained which connects the master, the slave and the datapath. Finally as step4, a partial transducer is obtained by putting the datapath and the partial transducer FSM together. For protocols with multiple sequences, partial transducers are concatenated to make a whole transducer. Datapaths can be shared among partial transducer FSMs when internal state of datapaths can be shared.

Please note that by supplying customized datapath for the synthesis processes, some sorts of computation, such as bit-width conversions and error correction, can also be included in the protocol converters generated.

4   Post-Silicon Verification and Debugging of SoC with FSM-Based Specifications of On-Chip Communication Protocols

One of the most important issues, when verifying and debugging SoC designs, is how to convert and translate test vectors and execution traces among different

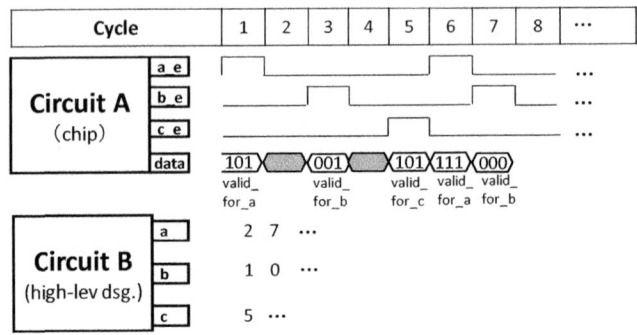

Fig. 7. An interface of chip A that transfers data in handshake protocol and that of the corresponding high-level design B

levels of design stages, such as system level in C/C++, RTL, gate and actual implementations on chips. Manual conversion is time consuming and can easily introduce errors. Moreover, for long traces, such as the ones generated from actual chip runs, manual conversion is simply impossible. We have proposed a post-silicon debugging framework utilizing high-level designs instead of low-level designs [5,6] by automatically translating chip traces into the ones for high level designs referring to the specification in FSM for on-chip communication protocols. Generally speaking, I/O sequences of chip execution cannot be used as they are in high-level design simulation, because (1) the signal values on the chip I/O sequences are not *valid* at every cycle, (2) data can be transferred in various ways through on chip interfaces, (3) there is also variation in the structures of interface ports. Therefore, a *mapping* method to convert the I/O sequences of chip execution to the corresponding ones in high-level design simulation is prerequisite to realize such post-silicon debugging approach first introduced in [5]. For a simple example, consider the two circuits shown in Figure 7, where Circuit A is a chip implementation and Circuit B is the corresponding high-level design. In A, when the signal value of the port **a_e** is high, the signals on the port **data** is *valid for* the value of the port **a** of B. In the same way, the port **data** is *valid for* **b** and **c**, when the signal values of ports **b_e** and **c_e** are high, respectively. Intuitively, the expected I/O sequence mapping for this example is to generate the I/O sequence for each port of B, that is, $< 2, 7, \cdots >$ for **a**, $< 1, 0, \cdots >$ for **b**, $< 5, \cdots >$ for **c**, from the sequence $< 101, xxx, 001, xxx, 101, 111, 000, \cdots >$ of **data**, where x is a *don't care* value. This kind of conversions can be made automatically once protocol specification in FSM for the chip implementation are given, as this is sort of automatic conversion of protocols in different levels and the techniques shown in the previous section can be used.

Figure 8 shows the post-silicon debugging framework based on automatic trace conversion with FSM-based protocol specifications. When an error is detected in a chip execution, the erroneous I/O sequence revealing the error is obtained as

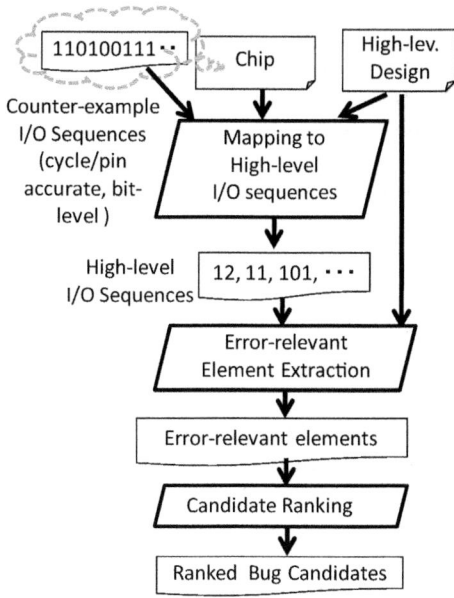

Fig. 8. A post-silicon debugging framework using high-level design description[5]

a counter-example. Such erroneous I/O sequences of the chip execution should be converted to the I/O sequences of the corresponding high-level design. Then, debugging is conducted using the high-level design simulation with the converted I/O sequences.

Let us discuss with an example shown in Figure 9(a) where Module A is a chip implementation and Module B is a corresponding high-level design. Here, we assume that A has a 12-bit output port **data**, and that B has three output ports, **a**, **b**, and **c**, declared as integers. Module A is designed to transfer consecutive three output values at each clock cycle at a port **data** and each output value occupies four bits. Whereas, module B generates the corresponding three output values from the three different ports at the same time. For example, the upper

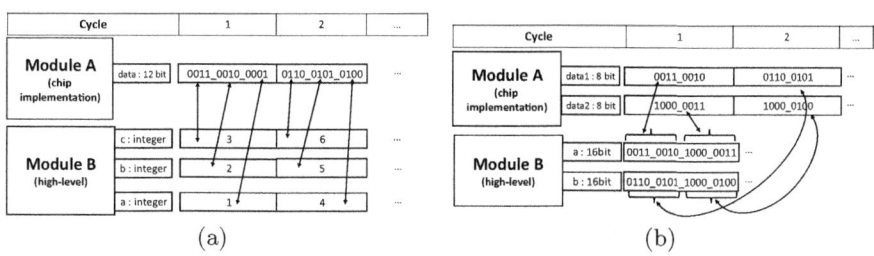

Fig. 9. Pairs of I/O sequences of a chip and a high-level design

four bits of data at the first clock cycle in A corresponds to the value of **a** at the first cycle in B, and the next four bits at the first clock cycle in A corresponds to the value of **b** at the first cycle in B.

Clearly this is a problem of protocol conversions with some data manipulations, and so the techniques shown in the previous section can be utilized. That is, referring to the two protocols that correspond to the two levels of designs, a sort of protocol converters are generated and executed in order to convert the chip traces into the ones for high level. As reserve protocol converters can also be automatically generated, high level simulation vectors can be translated into the ones for lower levels as well.

5   Concluding Remarks

In this paper synthesis and verification/debugging techniques based on FSM-based protocol specification targeting SoC designs are summarized. Their details can be found in the literatures. FSM-based specifications can also be applied to hardware supports for post-silicon debugging, such as [7,8], where hardware which traces communication among blocks/cores in SoC can be automatically generated from FSM-based specifications of communication protocols.

As a summary it can be concluded that the FSM-based specification for on-chip communication protocol can take the central roles in SoC designs where their communication and computation can be separately analyzed.

References

1. Open Core Protocol International Partnership: Open Core Protocol Specification version 2.1
2. ARM: AMBA 3 AXI Specification v1.0
3. Passerone, R., Rowson, J.A., Vincentelli, A.S.: Automatic Synthesis of Interfaces between Incompatible Protocols. In: Proceedings of Design Automation Conference, pp. 8–13 (1998)
4. Watanabe, S., Seto, K., Ishikawa, Y., Komatsu, S., Fujita, M.: Protocol Transducer Synthesis using Divide and Conquer Approach. In: Proceedings of 12th Asia and South Pacific Design Automation Conference, pp. 280–285 (2007)
5. Lee, Y., Nishihara, T., Matsumoto, T., Fujita, M.: A Post-Silicon Debug Support Using High-level Design Description. In: Proc. of The 18th Asian Test Symposium, pp. 141–147 (November 2009)
6. Lee, Y., Matsumoto, T., Fujita, M.: Generation of I/O sequences for a high-level design from those in post-silicon for efficient post-silicon debugging. In: Proc. of International Conference on Computer Design, pp. 402–408 (October 2010)
7. Gharehbaghi, A.M., Fujita, M.: Transaction-Based Debugging of System-on-Chips with Patterns. In: Proc. of 27th IEEE International Conference on Computer Design, pp. 186–192 (October 2009)
8. Gharehbaghi, A.M., Fujita, M.: Global transaction ordering in Network-on-Chips for post-silicon validation. In: Proc. of International Symposium on Quality Electronic Design, pp. 284–289 (March 2011)

Automated Analysis of Industrial Embedded Software

Moonzoo Kim and Yunho Kim

Computer Science Department
Korea Advanced Institute of Science and Technology (KAIST)
Daejeon, South Korea
moonzoo@cs.kaist.ac.kr, kimyunho@kaist.ac.kr

Abstract. For the last few decades, automated software analysis techniques such as software model checking and concolic testing have advanced in a large degree. However, such techniques are not frequently applied to industrial software due to steep learning curve and hidden costs to apply these techniques to industrial software in practice. Therefore, to enable technology transfer to industry, it is essential to conduct concrete case studies applying automated techniques to real-world industrial software. These studies can serve as references for field engineers who want to improve quality of software by adopting automated analysis techniques. Furthermore, concrete applications of such techniques can guide new research goals and directions to solve practical limitations observed in the studies. In this paper, we describe our experience of applying various automated software analysis techniques to industrial embedded software such as flash memory storage platform and smartphone platform.

1 Introduction

Manual testing is a de-facto standard method to improve the quality of software in industry. However, conventional testing methods frequently fail to detect faults in target programs, since it is infeasible for a test engineer to manually create test cases sufficient to detect subtle errors in specific/exceptional execution paths among an enormous number of different execution paths. These limitations are serious issues in many industrial projects, particularly in embedded system domains where high reliability is required and product recall for bug-fixing incurs significant economic loss.

To solve such limitations, many researchers have worked to develop automated software analysis techniques such as model checking [5], software model checking [8], and concolic testing (a.k.a., dynamic symbolic execution) [13,6]. However, such techniques are not frequently applied to industrial software due to steep learning curve and hidden costs to apply these techniques to industrial software in practice. For example, although model checking is a fully automated technique, model creation/extraction is a mostly manual process which causes large cost in an industrial setting. In addition, for software model checking, a user does not have to make a target model unlike model checking, but still he/she has to build a valid environment model to obtain meaningful verification results. Furthermore, to achieve effective and efficient analysis results, a user has to understand the limitations of automated techniques, which are not clearly described in related technical papers. Consequently, field engineers often hesitate to adopt automated analysis techniques in their projects.

T. Bultan and P.-A. Hsiung (Eds.): ATVA 2011, LNCS 6996, pp. 51–59, 2011.

To realize the benefits of automated software analysis techniques in practical settings, our group has worked to apply automated analysis techniques such as software model checking and concolic testing (a.k.a. dynamic symbolic execution) to industrial software by collaborating with consumer electronics companies such as Samsung Electronics. Through the collaboration, we realized that it is essential to conduct concrete case studies of applying automated techniques to real-world industrial software. These studies can serve as references for field engineers who want to improve quality of software by adopting automated analysis techniques. Furthermore, concrete applications of such techniques can guide new research directions to solve practical limitations observed in the studies. In this paper, we share our experience of applying various tools of model checking, software model checking, and concolic testing to flash memory storage platform [9,11,10] and smartphone platform [12].

2   Unified Storage Platform for OneNAND Flash Memory

2.1   Overview of the Unified Storage Platform

The unified storage platform (USP) is a software solution for OneNAND based embedded systems. Figure 1 presents an overview of the USP: it manages both code storage and data storage. USP allows processes to store and retrieve data on OneNAND through a file system. USP contains a flash translation layer (FTL) through which data and programs in the OneNAND device are accessed. FTL is a core part of the storage platform for flash memory, since logical data can be mapped to separated physical sectors due to the physical characteristics of flash memory (see Section 2.2). FTL consists of the three layers: a sector translation layer (STL), a block management layer (BML), and a low-level device driver layer (LLD).

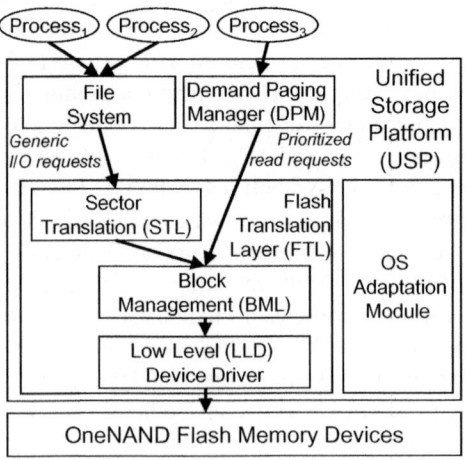

Fig. 1. Overview of the USP

Generic I/O requests from processes are fulfilled through the file system, STL, BML, and LLD, in that order. Although the USP allows concurrent I/O requests from multiple processes through the STL, the BML operations must be executed sequentially, not concurrently. For this purpose, the BML uses a binary semaphore to coordinate concurrent I/O requests from the STL. In addition to generic I/O requests, a process can make a *prioritized read request* for executing a program through the demand paging manager (DPM) and this request goes directly to the BML. A prioritized read request from the DPM can preempt generic I/O operations requested by STL. After the prioritized read request is completed, the preempted generic I/O operations should be resumed again.

2.2   Logical-to-Physical Sector Translation

A NAND flash device consists of a set of *pages* that are grouped into *blocks*. A *unit* can be equal to a block or multiple blocks. Each page contains a set of *sectors*. Operations are either read/write operations on a page, or erase operations on a block. NAND can write data only on an empty page and the page can be emptied by erasing the block containing the page. Therefore, when new data is written to the flash memory, rather than directly overwriting old data, the data is written on empty physical sectors and the physical sectors that contain the old data are marked as invalid. Since the empty physical sectors may reside in separate physical units, one logical unit (LU) containing data is mapped to a linked list of physical units (PU). STL manages the mapping from the logical sectors (LS) to the physical sectors (PS). This mapping information is stored in a sector allocation map (SAM), which returns the corresponding PS offset from a given LS offset. Each PU has its own SAM. Figure 2 illustrates the mapping from logical sectors to physical sectors where one unit contains one block and a block consists of four pages, each of which has one sector.

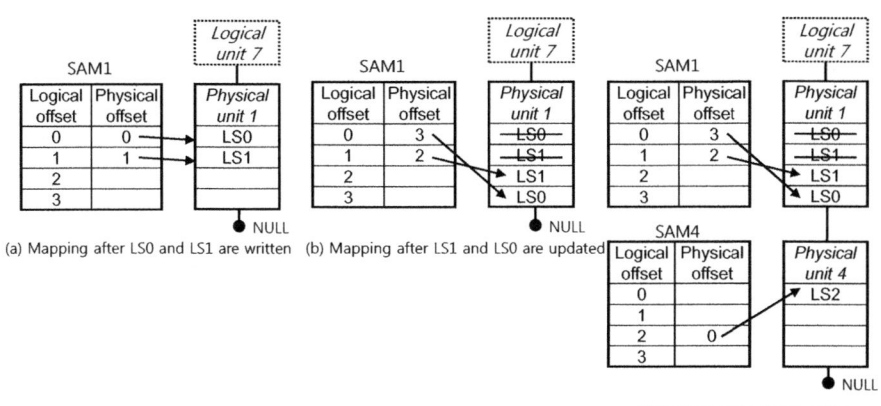

Fig. 2. Mapping from logical sectors to physical sectors

2.3   Analysis Results and Discussions

Multi-sector Read Function. We began by analyzing a multi-sector read (MSR) function in STL (see Section 2.2) that reads multiple physical sectors that correspond to logical sectors specified by a user. We selected MSR as it is a core function of USP and relatively small (157 lines of C code) but with complex control (i.e., four-level nested loops) and data structure (i.e., LU, PU, and SAM). The requirement property we checked is that the read buffer of MSR should contain corresponding data in physical sectors at the end of MSR. In addition, to obtain valid verification results, we had to provide an operational environment of MSR such as following:

1. For each logical sector, at least one physical sector that has the same value exists.
2. If the i_{th} LS is written in the k_{th} sector of the j_{th} PU, then the $(i \bmod m)_{th}$ offset of the j_{th} SAM is valid and indicates the PS number k, where m is the number of sectors per unit.
3. The PS number of the i_{th} LS must be written in *only* one of the $(i \bmod m)_{th}$ offsets of the SAM tables for the PUs mapped to the $\lfloor \frac{i}{m} \rfloor_{th}$ LU.

We applied model checking techniques to MSR through a symbolic model checker NuSMV [3], an explicit model checker Spin [7], and C-bounded model checker CBMC [4] (more detail can be found in [9]) using 64 bit Linux machine equipped with 3 Ghz Xeon dual-core cpu. For NuSMV and Spin, we built a model for MSR manually. We found that it was a highly challenging task to build a NuSMV model for a C program with complex control and data structure (a corresponding MSR model is 1000 lines long). The above model checkers did not detect a violation of the requirement property in problem instances up to 10 physical units and 6 logical sectors. Figure 3 shows the verification performances of the above model checkers in terms of time and memory. NuSMV spent more than 90% of time in dynamic reordering of BDD variables due to hard-to-abstract SAMs and showed an order-of-magnitude slower speed than Spin. For memory consumption, NuSMV showed better performance than Spin. CBMC showed better performance in terms of both time and memory than Spin and NuSMV. Note that CBMC demonstrated relatively slow increases of time/memory cost as the problem size grows up (i.e., scalability of CBMC is better than NuSMV and Spin due to the underlying industrial-strength SAT solver). Though the verification was conducted on a small-scale, this exhaustive result provided good confidence on the correctness of MSR. Thus, we found that a software model checker could be used as an effective unit-testing tool for embedded software.

BML and LLD Layers. We applied software model checkers Blast [1] and CBMC to several components in the BML and LLD layers (we could not apply Spin and NuSMV, since translation from BML/LLD C code to formal models would require large human effort). In these experiments, we had to build valid environment models for target units as we did for MSR. We found several bugs including a preemption error caused by a prioritized read operation and an error that does not propagate a BML semaphore exception to STL, which is required to reset USP (Section 2.1). Figure 4 shows a call graph of the topmost STL functions toward BML functions. When a BML function such as BML_GetVolInfo raises a semaphore exception for any reason, that exception

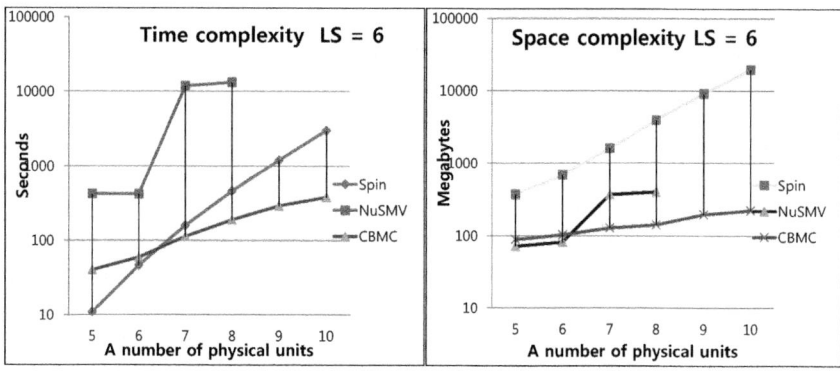

Fig. 3. Comparison of verification performance among NuSMV, Spin, and CBMC

should be handled by STL functions, but `_GetSInfo` does not pass the exception to its caller in some cases. Total size of all functions from STL to BML is around 2500 lines of C code on average. Blast failed to detect the error and raised false alarms due to its limitations on handling bitwise operators and nested data structures. CBMC detected this error in 12 minutes with consuming 3 Gbyte of memory on average (details of the experiments can be found in [11]).

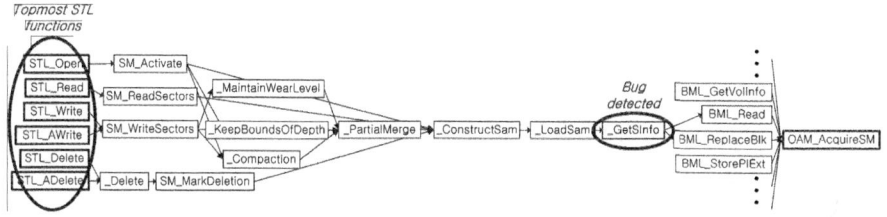

Fig. 4. Call graph of the topmost STL functions using the BML semaphore

In these analyses, however, we found that both Blast and CBMC had limitations for complex embedded C programs. For example, Blast often analyzed array operations incorrectly and its result could not be trusted. In contrast, CBMC did not suffer accuracy problems, but due to its loop unwinding scheme, extensive loop analysis (i.e., unwinding many times) was infeasible. In addition, when a target code invokes external libraries, the analysis accuracy decreases unless a user makes an environment model for such libraries. Consequently, we decided to focus on more scalable and automated analysis techniques and concentrated on concolic testing techniques (see Section 3).

3   Concolic Testing Technique

Concolic (CONCrete + symbOLIC) testing [13,6] combines both a concrete dynamic analysis and a symbolic static analysis to automatically explore all possible execution paths of a target program by negating every branching decision in execution paths. Thus, concolic testing aims to overcome the limitation of conventional testing as well as software model checking. Concolic testing can analyze a target program with less memory than state model checking, since it does not store the entire state space, but analyzes each execution path one by one in a systematic manner (i.e., through depth first search strategy). In addition, concolic testing can analyze a target program faster than state model checking, since search space of concolic testing (i.e., explicit path model checking) is usually smaller than that of state model checking. Although concolic testing may fail to detect bugs which can be discovered by state model checkers, concolic testing techniques can be a good trade-off between effectiveness and efficiency. In addition, unlike model checking, external library calls can be handled using concrete input and output values, thus achieving better applicability. Lastly, concolic testing generates concrete test cases, which are invaluable assets for industrial software projects (i.e., through conventional testing, regression testing, and product line testing, etc.).

It is, however, still necessary to check the effectiveness and efficiency of concolic testing on industrial software through concrete case studies, since this technique is relatively new and depends on many other static and dynamic components. These components potentially include SMT solvers, virtual machines, code instrumenters, compilers, etc. In addition, in our experience we found that successful application of concolic testing depends on the expertise of a human engineer, as they must determine what should be declared as symbolic input and what should be the initial input from which symbolic analysis begins, which search strategy should be chosen, etc.

4   Samsung Linux Platform (SLP) for Smartphones

4.1   File Manager

The SLP file manager (FM) monitors a file system and notifies corresponding applications of events in the file system. FM uses an `inotify` system call to register directories/files to monitor. When the directories and files that are being monitored change, the Linux kernel generates `inotify` events and adds these events to an `inotify` queue. FM reads an event from the queue and notifies corresponding programs of the event through a D-BUS inter-process communication interface. For example, when a user adds an MP3 file to a file system, FM notifies a music player to update its playlist automatically. A fault in FM can cause serious problems in SLP, since many applications depend on FM. FM is written in C and around 10,000 lines long.

Symbolic Inputs. To apply concolic testing, we must specify symbolic variables in a target program, based on which symbolic path formulas are generated at runtime. We specified `inotify_event` as a symbolic input, whose fields are defined as follows:

```
struct inotify_event {
    int wd;        /*Watch descriptor */
    uint32_t mask;   /*Event */
    uint32_t cookie;/*Unique cookie associating events*/
    char     name[];/*Optional null-terminated name */};
    uint32_t len;    /*Size of 'name' field */
```

wd indicates the watch for which this event occurs. mask contains bits that describe the type of an event. cookie is a unique integer that connects related events. name[] represents a file/directory path name for which the current event occurs and len indicates a length of the file/directory path name. Among the five fields, we specified wd, mask, and cookie as symbolic variables, since name and len are optional fields. We built a symbolic environment to provide an inotify_event queue that contains up to two symbolic inotify_events.

Analysis Results. By using a concolic testing tool CREST [2], we detected an infinite loop fault in FM in one second. After FM reads an inotify_event in the queue, the event should be removed from the queue to process the other events in the queue. For a normal event, the wd field of the event is positive. Otherwise, the event is abnormal. We found that FM did not remove an abnormal event from the queue and caused an infinite loop when an abnormal event was added to the queue. This bug had not been detected before because original developers did not make test cases that contained abnormal events, which were hard to trigger. Note that external SLP libraries used by FM could be handled by CREST without difficulty (but with decreased path coverage), since CREST simply used concrete values for library calls without building a corresponding symbolic path formula.

4.2 Security Library

The security library in SLP provides API functions for various security applications on mobile platforms such as SSH (secure shell) and DRM (digital right management). The security library consists of security function layer (security APIs such as AES or SHA), complex math function layer (elliptic curve, large prime number generators, etc), and a large integer function layer. Most functions in the library are well documented and its input/output behaviors are clearly defined based on mathematical semantics. We analyzed a large integer function layer (around 2500 lines long) using CREST.

Symbolic Inputs. A large integer is represented by the L_INT data structure:
```
struct L_INT {
unsigned int size;//Allocated mem size in 32 bits
unsigned int len; //# of valid 32 bit elements
unsigned int *da; //Pointer to the dynamically allocated data array.
unsigned int sign;//0:non-negative, 1: negative }
```
To test large integer functions, we built a symbolic large integer generator that returns a symbolic large integer n (line 12) as shown in Figure 5. Lines 3-5 allocate memory for n (line 5). Line 3 declares the size of n as a symbolic variable of unsigned char type. Note that line 4 enforces a constraint on size such that min≤size≤max. Without this constraint, size can be 255, which will generate unnecessarily many large integers, since the number of generated large integers increases as the size increases. Line 5 allocates memory for n using L_INT_Init(). For simple analysis, we assume that len==size (line 6). Lines 8-9 fill out a data array of n, if necessary (line 7). Since we assume that size==len, we do not allow the most-significant bytes to be 0 (line 10). Using gen_s_int(), we developed test drivers for all 14 large integer functions to checks their basic mathematical properties such as $(n1 + n2)\%m ==$ $(n2 + n1)\%m$ for L_INT_ModAdd$(n1, n2, m)$.

Analysis Results. We inserted 40 assertions in the 14 large integer functions and found that all 14 large integer functions violated some assertions. CREST running on a Linux machine (3.6Ghz Core2Duo) generates 7537 test cases for the 14 large integer functions in five minutes. For example, test_L_INT_ModAdd() generated 831 test cases

```
01:L_INT* gen_s_int(int min,int max,int to_fill) {
02:  unsigned char size, i;
03:  CREST_unsigned_char(size); //symbolic variable
04:  if(size> max  || size< min) exit(0);
05:  L_INT  *n=L_INT_Init(size);
06:  n->len=size;
07:  if(to_fill){// sym. value assignment
08:    for(i=0; i < size; i++) {
09:      CREST_unsigned_int(n->da[i]);}
10:    if(n->da[size-1]==0) exit(0);   }
11:  return n;}
```

Fig. 5. Symbolic large integer generator

to test L_INT_ModAdd(). 17 of the 831 test cases violated $(n1 + n2)\%m == (n2 + n1)\%m$. We analyzed L_INT_ModAdd(L_INT d,L_INT n1,L_INT n2,L_INT m) and found that this function did not check the size of d (destination). Thus, if the size of d is smaller than (n1+n2)%m, this function writes beyond the allocated memory for d, which may corrupt d later by other memory writes. This bug had not been caught before, since high level security functions invoked L_INT_ModAdd() with m that is smaller than n1 and n2, thus escaping from exceptional error-triggering scenarios. Automated analysis techniques are very effective to explore such corner case scenarios and detect hidden bugs.

5   Conclusion and Future Work

We have shown that difficult verification problems in industrial software can be handled successfully using automated formal analysis tools. Though the projects were conducted on a small-scale, Samsung Electronics highly valued the analysis results. At the same time, the experience gained in these projects led the authors to realize the practical limitations on the scalability and applicability of software model checking and the necessity of conducting further research to develop an advanced concolic testing technique for complex embedded software such as smartphone platforms. Currently, we are working with University of Nebraska to develop a hybrid concolic testing technique that utilizes a genetic algorithm to cover the weaknesses of pure concolic testing. In addition, Samsung Elctronics and KAIST continue collaboration to analyze Android 2.3 platform using concolic testing techniques.

Acknowledgements. This research was partially supported by the ERC of Excellence Program of Korea Ministry of Education, Science and Technology(MEST) / National Research Foundation of Korea) (Grant 2011-0000978).

References

1. Beyer, D., Henzinger, T., Jhala, R., Majumdar, R.: The software model checker Blast: Applications to software engineering. In: Software Tools for Technology Transfer (2007)
2. Burnim, J.: CREST - automatic test generation tool for C,
   http://code.google.com/p/crest/

3. Cimatti, A., Clarke, E., Giunchiglia, E., Giunchiglia, F., Pistore, M., Roveri, M., Sebastiani, R., Tacchella, A.: NuSMV 2: An opensource tool for symbolic model checking. In: Brinksma, E., Larsen, K.G. (eds.) CAV 2002. LNCS, vol. 2404, pp. 359–364. Springer, Heidelberg (2002)

4. Clarke, E., Kröning, D., Lerda, F.: A tool for checking ANSI-C programs. In: Jensen, K., Podelski, A. (eds.) TACAS 2004. LNCS, vol. 2988, pp. 168–176. Springer, Heidelberg (2004)

5. Clarke, E., Grumberg, O., Peled, D.A.: Model Checking. MIT Press, Cambridge (2000)

6. Godefroid, P., Klarlund, N., Sen, K.: DART: Directed automated random testing. In: Programming Language Design and Implementation (2005)

7. Holzmann, G.: The Spin Model Checker. Wiley, New York (2003)

8. Jhala, R., Majumdar, R.: Software model checking. ACM Computing Surveys 41(4), 21–74 (2009)

9. Kim, M., Choi, Y., Kim, Y., Kim, H.: Formal verification of a flash memory device driver - an experience report. In: Havelund, K., Majumdar, R. (eds.) SPIN 2008. LNCS, vol. 5156, pp. 144–159. Springer, Heidelberg (2008)

10. Kim, M., Kim, Y., Choi, Y.: Concolic testing of the multi-sector read operation for flash storage platform software. In: Formal Aspects of Computing (to be published)

11. Kim, M., Kim, Y., Kim, H.: A comparative study of software model checkers as unit testing tools: An industrial case study. IEEE Transactions on Software Engineering (TSE) 37(2) (2011)

12. Kim, Y., Kim, M., Jang, Y.: Concolic testing on embedded software - case studies on mobile platform programs. In: European Software Engineering Conference/Foundations of Software Engineering (ESEC/FSE) Industrial Track (2011)

13. Sen, K., Marinov, D., Agha, G.: CUTE: A concolic unit testing engine for C. In: European Software Engineering Conference/Foundations of Software Engineering, ESEC/FSE (2005)

Nondeterministic Update of CTL Models by Preserving Satisfaction through Protections

Miguel Carrillo and David A. Rosenblueth

Instituto de Investigaciones en Matemáticas Aplicadas y en Sistemas
Universidad Nacional Autónoma de México
Apdo. 20-726, 01000 México D.F., México
drosenbl@servidor.unam.mx, miguel.mcb@gmail.com

Abstract. We present a recursive algorithm to update a Kripke model so as to satisfy a formula of the Computation-Tree Logic (CTL). Recursive algorithms for model update face a difficulty: deleting (adding) transitions from (to) a Kripke model to satisfy a universal (an existential) subformula may dissatisfy some existential (universal) subformulas. Our method employs protected models to overcome this difficulty. We demonstrate our algorithm with a classical example of automatic synthesis described by Emerson and Clarke in 1982. From a dummy model, where the accessibility relation is the identity relation, our algorithm can efficiently generate a model to satisfy a specification of mutual exclusion in a variant of CTL. Such a variant extends CTL with an operator that limits the out-degree of states. We compare our method with a generate-and-test algorithm and outline a proof of soundness and completeness for our method.

1 Introduction

A Computation-Tree Logic (CTL) model checker is an automated tool that has as input (1) a Kripke model formalizing a system, (2) a CTL formula expressing a desirable property of this system, and (3) a set of distinguished initial states of the model. The output is either a confirmation or a denial that the model satisfies the formula at all the initial states, meaning that the system respectively has, or does not have, the required property. In case of denial, the model checker often produces a *counterexample*, consisting of an error trace. This counterexample is intended as a guide for manually updating or repairing the model, or high-level description of the model, so that the unsatisfied property is fulfilled. We believe that even a partial automation of such a repairing process could have a big impact on the use of the model checking technique.

In spite of its relevance, the problem of mechanically updating a Kripke model has been little studied. As far as we know, Buccafurri et al. [1] proposed the first work on CTL model update by using abduction to repair Kripke models with the addition and removal of transitions. In a later work, Calzone et al. [2] gave

T. Bultan and P.-A. Hsiung (Eds.): ATVA 2011, LNCS 6996, pp. 60–74, 2011.

a method for updating Kripke models with the addition and removal not only of transitions, but of labels as well, dependent on biases determined by the application domain (biochemical networks). More recently, Zhang and Ding [7] have devised a generate-and-test model-repair algorithm.

Model update methods based on counterexamples produced by a model checker have a drawback. The model repair focused on invalidating one particular counterexample to a universal property does not guarantee that the repaired model satisfies this property, because there may be more than one counterexample, and all counterexamples must be treated simultaneously. Furthermore, if the defective model does not satisfy an *existential* property, the model checker does not provide a useful counterexample. Hence, this drawback invites considering a method based on a concept other than that of counterexamples.

We present a recursive method for repairing models in a nondeterministic way, based on the preservation of the satisfaction of subformulas via a mechanism of *protections*. To update a model with respect to a formula φ, our method recursively updates the model with respect to the subformulas of φ. Every time our method updates a model to satisfy a subformula α, the satisfaction of α is *protected*. This protection ensures that if α is a proper subformula of β, and β is a subformula of φ, then an update to satisfy β causes no loss of the satisfaction of α achieved with a previous update. To facilitate the treatment of negation, our algorithm requires that CTL formulas be in *negation normal form* and written with a set of operators *closed under duality*.

Emerson and Clarke [5] anticipated the problem of CTL model update when they gave an automated method for a closely related problem: synthesizing a model from a specification in a variant of CTL. Emerson and Clarke [5] ask themselves whether their method can be developed into a practical software tool and encourage further research:

> Similarly [to SAT solvers and model checkers], the average case performance of the decision procedure used by the synthesis method may be substantially better than the potentially exponential time worst case [...] We therefore believe that this approach may in the long run turn out to be quite practical.

Supporting this belief, we show that a software tool that implements our algorithm can efficiently synthesize a model from a specification of the mutual exclusion problem written in CTL augmented with an operator to limit the out-degree of states. We carry out such a synthesis by repairing a dummy model (where the accessibility relation is the identity relation) to satisfy the given CTL specification. A comparison with the execution time of a direct algorithm, based on generation and testing, exhibits the advantages of our algorithm.

After fixing the notation in Section 2, we treat CTL model update in Section 3. Next, we show in Section 4 the performance of our algorithm through an application to faulty models of mutual exclusion. Section 5 compares our algorithm with others and summarizes some conclusions.

2   Technical Preliminaries

This section gives some introductory definitions and fixes the notation. We assume some familiarity with CTL model checking and refer the reader to [4] for a more thorough treatment.

A *signature* $\Sigma = \langle S, V \rangle$ consists of a pair of nonempty finite sets. We call the elements of S and V, *states*, and *(propositional) variables*, respectively. Unless otherwise stated, we assume that $\Sigma = \langle S, V \rangle$ is *an arbitrary fixed signature*. The set of *literals* over V is $\mathrm{Lit}(V) = V \cup \{\neg p \mid p \in V\}$. The *complement* of literals is defined by $\overline{p} = \neg p$ and $\overline{\neg p} = p$, $\forall p \in V$. If $X \subseteq \mathrm{Lit}(V)$ then: $\overline{X} = \{\overline{\ell} \mid \ell \in X\}$; X is *consistent* iff $\forall\ \ell \in X$, $\overline{\ell} \notin X$; and X is *V-maximal* iff $\forall\ p \in V$, $p \in X$ or $\neg p \in X$. If $R \subseteq S^2$ then R is *total* iff $\forall\ s \in S$, $\exists\ t \in S$ such that $(s,t) \in R$. The set of *successors of s* under R is $R[s] = \{t \mid (s,t) \in R\}$. If C and D are sets then: I_D is *the identity on* D, $I_D = \{(t,t) \mid t \in D\}$; and C_D is *the constant C on* D, $C_D \colon D \to \{C\}$, $C_D(t) = C\ \forall t \in D$. If $A \cap B = \emptyset$, $f \colon A \to C$, and $g \colon B \to D$, $f \cup g$ is the function $f \cup g \colon A \cup B \to C \cup D$, $f \cup g(t) = f(t)$ if $t \in A$ and $f \cup g(t) = g(t)$ if $t \in B$.

Definition 1 (Kripke Σ-models). *We say that $\mathcal{M} = \langle S^{\mathcal{M}}, R^{\mathcal{M}}, L^{\mathcal{M}} \rangle$ is a Kripke Σ-model iff: $S^{\mathcal{M}} = S$, $R^{\mathcal{M}} \subseteq S^2$ is total, and $L^{\mathcal{M}} \colon S^{\mathcal{M}} \to 2^{\mathrm{Lit}(V)}$ is such that $\forall\ t \in S^{\mathcal{M}}$, $L^{\mathcal{M}}(t)$ is consistent and V-maximal.*

If $(s,t) \in R$ we call (s,t) a *transition from s to t* and we abbreviate this to sRt. We call L the *labeling function* of $\mathcal{M}$. If $\ell \in \mathrm{Lit}(V)$ and $s \in S$, then $L[s \oplus \ell]$ denotes the labeling function such that $L[s \oplus \ell](s) = (L(s) \cup \{\ell\}) - \{\overline{\ell}\}$ and $L[s \oplus \ell](t) = L(t)$ for $t \neq s$. $\mathbf{K}_\Sigma$ denotes the *set of Σ-models*.

Models are often represented graphically as in Section 4, writing only positive literals as labels of the states. We identify the components of Σ-models and signatures by using superscripts: $\mathcal{M} = \langle S^{\mathcal{M}}, R^{\mathcal{M}}, L^{\mathcal{M}} \rangle$, $\Sigma = \langle S^\Sigma, V^\Sigma \rangle$.

Next, we define an extension of CTL [4]. We use a base of operators *closed under duality*. The following pairs are *dual operators*: $(\bot, \top)$, $(\vee, \wedge)$, $(\mathbf{EX}, \mathbf{AX})$, $(\mathbf{EU}, \mathbf{AR})$, and $(\mathbf{AU}, \mathbf{ER})$. We restrict formulas to a *negation normal form* (**NNF**), by limiting the application of negation to variables. However, since we use a base of operators closed under duality, other instances of negation may be considered as shorthand. We add to CTL *out-degree formulas* $\mathbf{OD} \leq n$, and their duals $\mathbf{OD} > n$, to limit the number of transitions going out of a state.

Definition 2 (Σ-CTL and Σ-XCTL). *Formulas of signature Σ of the Computation-Tree Logic, Σ-CTL (abbreviated Φ), have the following syntax:*

$$\Phi ::= \bot \mid \top \mid \ell \mid (\Phi \vee \Phi) \mid (\Phi \wedge \Phi) \mid (\mathbf{EX}\,\Phi) \mid (\mathbf{AX}\,\Phi) \mid$$
$$\mathbf{E}[\Phi\,\mathbf{U}\,\Phi] \mid \mathbf{A}[\Phi\,\mathbf{R}\,\Phi] \mid \mathbf{A}[\Phi\,\mathbf{U}\,\Phi] \mid \mathbf{E}[\Phi\,\mathbf{R}\,\Phi] \mid (\mathbf{OD} \leq n) \mid (\mathbf{OD} > n)$$

where ℓ stands for any literal in $\mathrm{Lit}(V)$ and $n \in \mathbb{N}$.

We will single out the modal fragment of Σ-CTL. Σ-XCTL formulas (abbreviated Ψ) have the following syntax:

$$\Psi ::= \bot \mid \top \mid \ell \mid (\Psi \vee \Psi) \mid (\Psi \wedge \Psi) \mid (\mathbf{EX}\,\Psi) \mid (\mathbf{AX}\,\Psi)$$

We use $\varphi \in \Sigma$-CTL to indicate that φ is a Σ-CTL formula. The size of φ, written $|\varphi|$, is the number of operators occurring in φ. We view other temporal operators ($\mathbf{EF}$, $\mathbf{AF}$, $\mathbf{EG}$, $\mathbf{AG}$) and propositional operators ($\rightarrow$, $\leftrightarrow$, exclusive or $\veebar$) as abbreviations.

The above CTL syntax is a key point in the simplicity of our model update algorithm. Any syntax that has a base of operators similar to those used in model checking [4], e.g. $\{\neg, \wedge, \mathbf{EX}, \mathbf{AF}, \mathbf{EU}\}$, complicates model update w.r.t. formulas $\neg \alpha$, $\mathbf{AF}\,\alpha$, and $\mathbf{E}[\alpha\,\mathbf{U}\,\beta]$ (e.g. [7]). Another key point is that our algorithm focuses on Σ-XCTL formulas, and more complex operators $\mathbf{EU}$, $\mathbf{AR}$, $\mathbf{AU}$, and $\mathbf{ER}$, are treated by means of their fixed-point characterizations [4].

Next, we provide basic definitions for the protection mechanism.

Definition 3 (Σ-Protections). $P = \langle E, A, L \rangle$ is a Σ-protection iff

1. $E \subseteq A \subseteq S^2$, and
2. $L \colon S \to 2^{\mathrm{Lit}(V)}$ is such that $\forall t \in S$, $L(t)$ is consistent.

We call states in $E[s]$ ($A[s]$) successors of s existentially (universally) protected. We will use $\mathbf{P}_\Sigma$ to denote the set of Σ-protections.

Definition 4 (Protected models, $P_{\mathcal{M}}$, and $P_\perp$). Let $\mathcal{M} \in \mathbf{K}_\Sigma$ be a model and $P \in \mathbf{P}_\Sigma$. We say that $\mathcal{M}$ is protected by P, and we write $\mathcal{M} \rhd P$ iff:

1. $E^P \subseteq R^{\mathcal{M}} \subseteq A^P$, and
2. $\forall t \in S^{\mathcal{M}} : L^{\mathcal{M}}(t) \supseteq L^P(t)$.

We say that $(\mathcal{M}, P)$ is a protected Σ-model iff $\mathcal{M} \rhd P$, and we use $\mathbf{KP}_\Sigma$ to denote the set of protected Σ-models. The full protection for $\mathcal{M}$ is $P_{\mathcal{M}} = (R^{\mathcal{M}}, R^{\mathcal{M}}, L^{\mathcal{M}})$. The empty protection for any $\mathcal{M} \in \mathbf{K}_\Sigma$ is $P_\perp = (\emptyset, S^\Sigma \times S^\Sigma, L_\perp)$, where $L_\perp(s) = \emptyset$ for all $s \in S^\Sigma$.

If $R \subseteq S^2$ and $s \in S$, a path in R beginning at s, is a sequence $\pi \colon \mathbb{N} \to S$, such that $\pi(0) = s$ and $\forall\, n \in \mathbb{N}$, $\pi(n)R\pi(n+1)$. We write π_n instead of $\pi(n)$ and we use $\Pi_{R,s}$ to denote the set of paths in R beginning at s.

Definition 5 (Σ-CTL protected semantics). If $(\mathcal{M}, P) \in \mathbf{KP}_\Sigma$ is a protected Σ-model, $s \in S^{\mathcal{M}}$ and $\varphi \in \Sigma$-CTL, then we say that $(\mathcal{M}, P)$ satisfies φ at s, and we write $(\mathcal{M}, P), s \models \varphi$, according to:

1. $(\mathcal{M}, P), s \not\models \bot$. $(\mathcal{M}, P), s \models \top$. $(\mathcal{M}, P), s \models \ell$ iff $\ell \in L^P(s)$.
2. $(\mathcal{M}, P), s \models \alpha \vee \beta$ iff $(\mathcal{M}, P), s \models \alpha$ or $(\mathcal{M}, P), s \models \beta$.
3. $(\mathcal{M}, P), s \models \alpha \wedge \beta$ iff $(\mathcal{M}, P), s \models \alpha$ and $(\mathcal{M}, P), s \models \beta$.
4. $(\mathcal{M}, P), s \models \mathbf{EX}\,\alpha$ iff $\exists t \in E^P[s]$ such that $(\mathcal{M}, P), t \models \alpha$.
5. $(\mathcal{M}, P), s \models \mathbf{AX}\,\alpha$ iff $\forall t \in A^P[s]$, $(\mathcal{M}, P), t \models \alpha$.
6. $(\mathcal{M}, P), s \models \mathbf{E}[\alpha\,\mathbf{U}\,\beta]$ iff $\exists \pi \in \Pi_{E^P,s}$, and $\exists j \in \mathbb{N}$ such that $(\mathcal{M}, P), \pi_j \models \beta$ and $\forall i \in \mathbb{N}$, $i < j \to (\mathcal{M}, P), \pi_i \models \alpha$.
7. $(\mathcal{M}, P), s \models \mathbf{A}[\alpha\,\mathbf{U}\,\beta]$ iff $\forall \pi \in \Pi_{A^P,s}$, $\exists j \in \mathbb{N}$ such that $(\mathcal{M}, P), \pi_j \models \beta$ and $\forall i \in \mathbb{N}$, $i < j \to (\mathcal{M}, P), \pi_i \models \alpha$.

8. $(\mathcal{M}, P), s \models \mathbf{E}[\alpha \mathbf{R} \beta]$ iff $\exists \pi \in \Pi_{E^P, s}$ *such that either*
   (a) $\forall k \in \mathbb{N}, (\mathcal{M}, P), \pi_k \models \beta$, *or*
   (b) $\exists j \in \mathbb{N}$ *such that* $(\mathcal{M}, P), \pi_j \models \alpha$ *and* $\forall i \in \mathbb{N}, i \leq j \rightarrow (\mathcal{M}, P), \pi_i \models \beta$.
9. $(\mathcal{M}, P), s \models \mathbf{A}[\alpha \mathbf{R} \beta]$ iff $\forall \pi \in \Pi_{A^P, s}$, *either*
   (a) $\forall k \in \mathbb{N}, (\mathcal{M}, P), \pi_k \models \beta$, *or*
   (b) $\exists j \in \mathbb{N}$ *such that* $(\mathcal{M}, P), \pi_j \models \alpha$ *and* $\forall i \in \mathbb{N}, i \leq j \rightarrow (\mathcal{M}, P), \pi_i \models \beta$.
10. $(\mathcal{M}, P), s \models \mathbf{OD} \leq n$ *iff* $|A^P[s]| \leq n$.
11. $(\mathcal{M}, P), s \models \mathbf{OD} > n$ *iff* $|E^P[s]| > n$.

Definition 6 (Σ-CTL semantics). *If $\mathcal{M}$ is a Σ-model, $s \in S^{\mathcal{M}}$ and $\varphi \in \Sigma$-CTL, we say that $\mathcal{M}$ satisfies φ at s, $\mathcal{M}, s \models \varphi$, iff $(\mathcal{M}, P_{\mathcal{M}}), s \models \varphi$.*

We extend Σ-CTL protected semantics to sets of states and sets of formulas. If $S \subseteq S^{\mathcal{M}}$ then $(\mathcal{M}, P), S \models \varphi$ iff for all $s \in S$, $(\mathcal{M}, P), s \models \varphi$. If $\Gamma \subseteq \Sigma$-CTL then $(\mathcal{M}, P), s \models \Gamma$ iff for all $\varphi \in \Gamma$, $(\mathcal{M}, P), s \models \varphi$. If φ_1, φ_2 are two Σ-CTL formulas, we say that φ_1 and φ_2 are *logically equivalent*, and we write $\varphi_1 \equiv \varphi_2$, iff for all $\mathcal{M} \in \mathbf{K}_\Sigma$ and all $s \in S^{\mathcal{M}}$: $\mathcal{M}, s \models \varphi_1$ iff $\mathcal{M}, s \models \varphi_2$.

We use the following equivalences, known as fixed-point characterizations, to recursively compute a model update w.r.t. **EU**, **AU**, **ER**, and **AR** formulas:

$$\mathbf{E}[\alpha \mathbf{U} \beta] \equiv \beta \vee (\alpha \wedge \mathbf{EX} \, \mathbf{E}[\alpha \mathbf{U} \beta]) \qquad \mathbf{E}[\alpha \mathbf{R} \beta] \equiv \beta \wedge (\alpha \vee \mathbf{EX} \, \mathbf{E}[\alpha \mathbf{R} \beta])$$
$$\mathbf{A}[\alpha \mathbf{U} \beta] \equiv \beta \vee (\alpha \wedge \mathbf{AX} \, \mathbf{A}[\alpha \mathbf{U} \beta]) \qquad \mathbf{A}[\alpha \mathbf{R} \beta] \equiv \beta \wedge (\alpha \vee \mathbf{AX} \, \mathbf{A}[\alpha \mathbf{R} \beta])$$

A model update w.r.t. **EU** and **AU** formulas can be computed with a least fixed-point (lfp) operator, while a model update w.r.t. **ER** and **AR** can be computed with a greatest fixed-point (gfp) operator [4, page 63].

3   CTL Update Algorithms

In this section, we describe an algorithm that uses protected models for model update w.r.t. Σ-CTL formulas. After a brief explanation of the pseudo-code and basic update operations, we describe two model update algorithms for Σ-XCTL formulas. The first one is a *direct* algorithm that we include here with the sole purpose of emphasizing the main features of the model-update problem. The second one implements our method for model update using protected models. After this, we describe how to extend our method for considering all Σ-CTL formulas, and an operation to add states in the update process. Finally, we state the main theorems of soundness and completeness for our algorithm.

3.1   Nondeterministic Pseudo-Code

We use a high level *nondeterministic pseudo-code*. If A is a finite set, the command "**guess** $x \in A$" computes the *nondeterministic choice* of an element u from A and assigns u to x; if $A = \emptyset$, *the computation fails*. The command "$x \leftarrow e$" is a *nondeterministic assignment* equivalent to "**guess** $x \in A_e$", where A_e is the set of values produced by the nondeterministic computation of e; if A_e is a singleton we write "$x := e$" instead of "$x \leftarrow e$".

If P is a *nondeterministic procedure*, i.e. P has some occurrence of **guess**, and $P(a_1, \ldots, a_n)$ is *a call to P* with arguments $a_1, \ldots, a_n$, the *computation of* $P(a_1, \ldots, a_n)$ consists of a set of computation paths. Each occurrence of a command **guess** $x \in A$ allows to continue a computation on different *computation paths*, one path for each element of A.

We use two commands to indicate the *end of a computation path* in a nondeterministic procedure P: "**return** r" expresses that r is one of the results computed by P; and **fail** halts the computation of a path without returning any result. Computation paths ending with **return** are *successful paths*, and those ending with **fail** are *unsuccessful paths*. The *set of results computed by* $P(a_1, \ldots, a_n)$, is denoted by $P[a_1, \ldots, a_n]$. Thus, $P[a_1, \ldots, a_n] = \emptyset$ means that, for the given arguments, all the computation paths of P are unsuccessful; in this case we say that P *fails*.

3.2   Modification of Models

We build our algorithm for model update by using a few basic operations to gradually change the input model.

Definition 7 (Update operations). *Let $\mathcal{M} \in \mathbf{K}_\Sigma$, $s, s' \in S^\mathcal{M}$, $\ell \in \mathrm{Lit}(V)$, $S' \subseteq S^\mathcal{M}$, and S'' a finite set, such that $S' \neq \emptyset$ and $S'' \cap S^\mathcal{M} = \emptyset$. The* update operations *on Kripke models are:*

1. $\mathbf{L}^u(\mathcal{M}, s, \ell) = \langle S^\mathcal{M}, R^\mathcal{M}, L^\mathcal{M}[s \oplus \ell] \rangle$. *Add ℓ to $L^\mathcal{M}(s)$, and remove $\bar{\ell}$.*
2. $\mathbf{T}^+(\mathcal{M}, s, s') = \langle S^\mathcal{M}, R^\mathcal{M} \cup \{(s, s')\}, L^\mathcal{M} \rangle$. *Add (s, s') to $R^\mathcal{M}$.*
3. $\mathbf{T}^u(\mathcal{M}, s, S') = \langle S^\mathcal{M}, (R^\mathcal{M} - (\{s\} \times R^\mathcal{M}[s])) \cup (\{s\} \times S'), L^\mathcal{M} \rangle$.
   Set $R^\mathcal{M}[s] = S'$.
4. $\mathbf{S}^+(\mathcal{M}, S'') = \langle S^\mathcal{M} \cup S'', R^\mathcal{M} \cup I_{S''}, L^\mathcal{M} \cup \overline{V}_{S''} \rangle$.
   Add S'' to $S^\mathcal{M}$, add $I_{S''}$ to $R^\mathcal{M}$, and label all $t \in S''$ with negative literals.

The above operations are sufficient to transform a given Σ-model into any other Σ-model. Besides, the operations $\mathbf{L}^u$, $\mathbf{T}^+$ and $\mathbf{T}^u$ make the modification of a model satisfy literals, **EX** formulas, and **AX** formulas, respectively. Note that $\mathbf{S}^+(\mathcal{M}, S'')$ has additional states and therefore does not preserve Σ.

Below, we give a precise definition of what we regard as an acceptable modification of a model $\mathcal{M}$ w.r.t. a formula φ.

Definition 8 (Modifications of $\mathcal{M}$ w.r.t. φ). *If $\mathcal{M}$ is a Σ-model, $s \in S^\mathcal{M}$ and $\varphi \in \Sigma\text{-}XCTL$, we define, by recursion on φ, the set of modifications of $\mathcal{M}$ w.r.t. φ at s, Modif $(\mathcal{M}, s, \varphi)$:*

1. $Modif(\mathcal{M}, s, \bot) = \emptyset \quad and \quad Modif(\mathcal{M}, s, \top) = \{\mathcal{M}\}$
2. $Modif(\mathcal{M}, s, \ell) = \{\mathbf{L}^u(\mathcal{M}, s, \ell)\}$
3. $Modif(\mathcal{M}, s, \alpha \vee \beta) = Modif(\mathcal{M}, s, \alpha) \cup Modif(\mathcal{M}, s, \beta)$
4. $Modif(\mathcal{M}, s, \alpha \wedge \beta) = \{\mathcal{M}' \in \mathbf{K}_\Sigma \mid \mathcal{M}' \in Modif^F(\mathcal{M}, s, \{\alpha, \beta\})$
   $\& \ \mathcal{M}', s \models \{\alpha, \beta\}\}$
5. $Modif(\mathcal{M}, s, \mathbf{EX}\,\alpha) = \{\mathcal{M}' \in \mathbf{K}_\Sigma \mid \exists s' \in S^\mathcal{M}.$
   $\mathcal{M}' \in Modif(\mathbf{T}^+(\mathcal{M}, s, s'), s', \alpha) \ \& \ \mathcal{M}', s \models \mathbf{EX}\,\alpha\}$

6. $Modif(\mathcal{M}, s, \mathbf{AX}\,\alpha) = \{\mathcal{M}' \in \mathbf{K}_\Sigma \mid \exists S' \in 2^{S^{\mathcal{M}}} - \{\emptyset\}.$
$\mathcal{M}' \in Modif^*(\mathbf{T}^u(\mathcal{M}, s, S'), S', \alpha)$
$\&\ \mathcal{M}', s \models \mathbf{AX}\,\alpha\}$

Where $Modif^F(\mathcal{M}, s, \Gamma)$ is the extension of $Modif(\mathcal{M}, s, \varphi)$ to $\Gamma \subseteq \Sigma\text{-XCTL}$:

$$Modif^F(\mathcal{M}, s, \Gamma) = \begin{cases} \{\mathcal{M}\} & \text{if } \Gamma = \emptyset \\ \{\mathcal{M}' \in \mathbf{K}_\Sigma \mid \exists \psi \in \Gamma.\ \exists \mathcal{M}'' \in Modif(\mathcal{M}, s, \psi). \\ \quad \mathcal{M}' \in Modif^F(\mathcal{M}'', s, \Gamma - \{\psi\})\} & \text{if } \Gamma \neq \emptyset \end{cases}$$

and $Modif^*(\mathcal{M}, S, \varphi)$ is the extension of $Modif(\mathcal{M}, s, \varphi)$ to $S \subseteq S^{\mathcal{M}}$:

$$Modif^*(\mathcal{M}, S, \varphi) = \begin{cases} \{\mathcal{M}\} & \text{if } S = \emptyset \\ \{\mathcal{M}' \in \mathbf{K}_\Sigma \mid \exists t \in S.\ \exists \mathcal{M}'' \in Modif(\mathcal{M}, t, \varphi). \\ \quad \mathcal{M}' \in Modif^*(\mathcal{M}'', S - \{t\}, \varphi)\} & \text{if } S \neq \emptyset \end{cases}$$

Observe that for all $\mathcal{M}' \in Modif(\mathcal{M}, s, \varphi)$, $\mathcal{M}', s \models \varphi$.

3.3   A Direct Update Algorithm for Σ-XCTL

We now define a direct algorithm, XUPD_1, that we use as reference to compare our algorithm that updates protected models. For simplicity, we temporarily ignore some concerns that will be considered in the following sections. We now focus on Σ-XCTL, we do not include an operation for adding states, and we are not concerned about efficiency. XUPD_1 is an algorithm similar to generate-and-test methods. First, using basic update operations, XUPD_1 generates models to satisfy the simplest subformulas of the given formula. Then, XUPD_1 modifies these models to satisfy more complex subformulas. Finally, the produced models are tested to verify whether or not they satisfy the whole formula.

$\mathrm{XUPD}_1(\mathcal{M}, s, \varphi)$ % Find models for φ at state s modifying $\mathcal{M}$.
INPUT: $\mathcal{M} \in \mathbf{K}_\Sigma$, $s \in S^{\mathcal{M}}$, $\varphi \in \Sigma\text{-XCTL}$
OUTPUT: $Modif(\mathcal{M}, s, \varphi)$
1   **if** $\mathcal{M}, s \models \varphi$ **then** $\mathcal{M}' := \mathcal{M}$
2   **else case** φ **of**
3       $\bot$: **fail**
4       $\top$: $\mathcal{M}' := \mathcal{M}$
5   ℓ : $\mathcal{M}' := \mathbf{L}^u(\mathcal{M}, s, \ell)$
6       $\alpha \vee \beta$: $\{$**guess** $\delta \in \{\alpha, \beta\}$; $\mathcal{M}' \leftarrow \mathrm{XUPD}_1(\mathcal{M}, s, \delta\,)\}$
7       $\alpha \wedge \beta$: $\mathcal{M}' \leftarrow \mathrm{XUPD}_1^F(\mathcal{M}, s, \{\alpha, \beta\})$
8       $\mathbf{EX}\,\alpha$: $\{$**guess** $s' \in S^{\mathcal{M}}$; $\mathcal{M}' \leftarrow \mathrm{XUPD}_1(\mathbf{T}^+(\mathcal{M}, s, s'), s', \alpha)\}$
9       $\mathbf{AX}\,\alpha$: $\{$**guess** $S' \in 2^{S^{\mathcal{M}}} - \{\emptyset\}$; $\mathcal{M}' \leftarrow \mathrm{XUPD}_1^*(\mathbf{T}^u(\mathcal{M}, s, S'), S', \alpha)\}$
10 **if** $\mathcal{M}', s \models \varphi$ **then return** $\mathcal{M}'$ **else fail**

where $\mathrm{XUPD}_1^F(\mathcal{M}, s, \Gamma)$ and $\mathrm{XUPD}_1^*(\mathcal{M}, S, \varphi)$ are procedures that implement $Modif^F(\mathcal{M}, s, \Gamma)$ and $Modif^*(\mathcal{M}, S, \varphi)$, respectively. I.e., $\mathrm{XUPD}_1^F(\mathcal{M}, s, \Gamma)$ updates a model $\mathcal{M}$ w.r.t. a set of formulas Γ at s and $\mathrm{XUPD}_1^*(\mathcal{M}, S, \varphi)$ updates a model $\mathcal{M}$ w.r.t. φ at a set of states S.

Line (10) of XUPD_1 is necessary to guarantee that the returned model, $\mathcal{M}'$, meets the requirement $\mathcal{M}', s \models \varphi$ in three cases of φ: *(i)* if $\varphi = \alpha \wedge \beta$, and at line (7) XUPD_1^F applies a first update to satisfy α and a second update to satisfy β, then α may be dissatisfied by the second update, e.g. $\varphi = (\mathbf{EX}\, p) \wedge (\mathbf{EX}\, \neg p)$; *(ii)* if $\varphi = \mathbf{EX}\, \alpha$, the update of XUPD_1 at line (8) may remove the transition (s, s') and dissatisfy $\mathbf{EX}\, \alpha$ at s, e.g. $\varphi = \mathbf{EX}\, (p \wedge \mathbf{AX}\, q)$; *(iii)* if $\varphi = \mathbf{AX}\, \alpha$, the update of XUPD_1^* at line (9) may add a transition (s, s') such that α is not true at s' and dissatisfy $\mathbf{AX}\, \alpha$ at s, e.g. $\varphi = \mathbf{AX}\, (p \wedge \mathbf{EX}\, q)$.

We illustrate the need for line (10) in XUPD_1 for case *(ii)*. Let $\mathcal{M}_0$ be the model in Fig. 1(a). First, $\mathrm{XUPD}_1(\mathcal{M}_0, s0, \mathbf{EX}\, (p \wedge \mathbf{AX}\, q))$ guesses $s0$ and calls $\mathrm{XUPD}_1(\mathbf{T}^+(\mathcal{M}_0, s0, s0), s0, p \wedge \mathbf{AX}\, q)$. Then, $\mathrm{XUPD}_1(\mathbf{T}^+(\mathcal{M}_0, s0, s0), s0, p)$ produces $\mathcal{M}'_1$ (Fig. 1(b)). Finally, $\mathrm{XUPD}_1(\mathcal{M}'_1, s0, \mathbf{AX}\, q)$ guesses $\{s1\}$ and calls $\mathrm{XUPD}_1^*(\mathbf{T}^u(\mathcal{M}'_1, s0, \{s1\}), \{s1\}, q)$ that produces $\mathcal{M}'_2$ (Fig. 1(c)). Transition $(s0, s0)$ was removed and $\mathcal{M}'_2, s0 \not\models \mathbf{EX}\, (p \wedge \mathbf{AX}\, q)$, but line (10) prevents XUPD_1 from returning $\mathcal{M}'_2$.

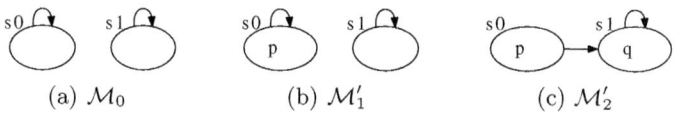

(a) $\mathcal{M}_0$ (b) $\mathcal{M}'_1$ (c) $\mathcal{M}'_2$

Fig. 1. The need for line (10) in $\mathrm{XUPD}_1(\mathcal{M}_0, s0, \mathbf{EX}\, (p \wedge \mathbf{AX}\, q))$

3.4   An Algorithm for Updating Protected Models

Intuitively, a call to $\mathrm{XUPD}_{prot}((\mathcal{M}, P), s, \varphi)$ gradually transforms $\mathcal{M}$ attempting to satisfy the subformulas of φ. Models $\mathcal{M}'$ produced by XUPD_{prot} to satisfy a subformula ψ are accompanied by a "protection" P' containing a part of $\mathcal{M}'$ sufficient to satisfy ψ. In this case, we will say that "$\mathcal{M}'$ is protected by P'". A key feature of XUPD_{prot} is that if $\mathcal{M}$ is protected by P and $\mathrm{XUPD}_{prot}((\mathcal{M}, P), s, \psi)$ produces $(\mathcal{M}', P')$, then $\mathcal{M}'$ is protected by P' and P' is a protection "no smaller" than P (Definition 11). Hence, XUPD_{prot} preserves satisfaction of previously treated subformulas.

Definition 9 (Update operations on protected models). *Let* $(\mathcal{M}, P) \in \mathbf{KP}_\Sigma$, $s \in S^{\mathcal{M}}$, $\ell \in \mathrm{Lit}(V)$, $s' \in A^P[s]$, $S' \subseteq A^P[s]$, *and* S'' *a finite set, such that* $E^P[s] \subseteq S' \neq \emptyset$ *and* $S'' \cap S^{\mathcal{M}} = \emptyset$. *The* update operations on protected models *are:*

1. $\mathbf{L}^u((\mathcal{M}, P), s, \ell) = (\mathbf{L}^u(\mathcal{M}, s, \ell), \langle E^P, A^P, L^P[s \oplus \ell] \rangle)$.
   Update label ℓ *of state* s *and protect* ℓ *in* $L^P(s)$.
2. $\mathbf{T}_\exists^+((\mathcal{M}, P), s, s') = (\mathbf{T}^+(\mathcal{M}, s, s'), \langle E^P \cup \{(s, s')\}, A^P, L^P \rangle)$.
   Add transition (s, s') *and existentially protect* (s, s') *in* E^P.
3. $\mathbf{T}_\forall^u((\mathcal{M}, P), s, S') = (\mathbf{T}^u(\mathcal{M}, s, S'), \langle E^P, A^P - (\{s\} \times (A^P[s] - S')), L^P \rangle)$.
   Update $R^{\mathcal{M}}[s]$ *to* S' *and set the universal protection of* s *to* S'.

4. $\mathbf{S}_\forall^+((\mathcal{M},P),S'') = (\mathbf{S}^+(\mathcal{M},S''),\langle E^P, A^P \cup S'' \times (S^{\mathcal{M}} \cup S''), L^P \cup \emptyset_{S''}\rangle).$
   Add states S'' to $\mathcal{M}$ and $\forall t \in S''$, set $A^P[t]$ to $S^{\mathcal{M}} \cup S''$ and $L^P[t]$ to $\emptyset$.

Note that all the above operations, except $\mathbf{S}_\forall^+$, preserve the signature.

We extend to protected models our definition of modification of a model.

Definition 10 (Modifications of $(\mathcal{M},P)$ w.r.t. φ). *If $(\mathcal{M},P) \in \mathbf{KP}_\Sigma$ is a protected model, $s \in S^{\mathcal{M}}$ and $\varphi \in \Sigma$-XCTL, we define, by recursion on φ, the set of modifications of $(\mathcal{M},P)$ w.r.t. φ at s, $\mathit{Modif}((\mathcal{M},P),s,\varphi)$:*

1. $\mathit{Modif}((\mathcal{M},P),s,\bot) = \emptyset$ and $\mathit{Modif}((\mathcal{M},P),s,\top) = \{(\mathcal{M},P)\}$
2. $\mathit{Modif}((\mathcal{M},P),s,\ell) = \begin{cases} \emptyset & \text{if } \bar{\ell} \in L^P(s) \\ \{\mathbf{L}^u((\mathcal{M},P),s,\ell)\} & \text{if } \bar{\ell} \notin L^P(s) \end{cases}$
3. $\mathit{Modif}((\mathcal{M},P),s,\alpha \vee \beta) = \mathit{Modif}((\mathcal{M},P),s,\alpha) \cup \mathit{Modif}((\mathcal{M},P),s,\beta)$
4. $\mathit{Modif}((\mathcal{M},P),s,\alpha \wedge \beta) = \mathit{Modif}^F((\mathcal{M},P),s,\{\alpha,\beta\})$
5. $\mathit{Modif}((\mathcal{M},P),s,\mathbf{EX}\,\alpha) = \{(\mathcal{M}',P') \in \mathbf{KP}_\Sigma \mid \exists s' \in A^P[s].$
   $(\mathcal{M}',P') \in \mathit{Modif}(\mathbf{T}_\exists^+((\mathcal{M},P),s,s'),s',\alpha)\}$
6. $\mathit{Modif}((\mathcal{M},P),s,\mathbf{AX}\,\alpha) = \{(\mathcal{M}',P') \in \mathbf{KP}_\Sigma \mid \exists S' \subseteq A^P[s].$
   $E^P[s] \subseteq S' \neq \emptyset \,\&$
   $(\mathcal{M}',P') \in \mathit{Modif}^*(\mathbf{T}_\forall^u((\mathcal{M},P),s,S'),S',\alpha)\}$

where $\mathit{Modif}^F((\mathcal{M},P),s,\Gamma)$ and $\mathit{Modif}^*((\mathcal{M},P),S,\varphi)$ are defined analogously to $\mathit{Modif}^F(\mathcal{M},s,\Gamma)$ and $\mathit{Modif}^*(\mathcal{M},S,\varphi)$, respectively.

Next, we define an algorithm for updating protected models. $\mathrm{XUPD}_{prot}((\mathcal{M},P),s,\varphi)$ finds models for φ at state s by modifying $\mathcal{M}$ and respecting the protection P. The initial call to XUPD_{prot} may use the empty protection $P_\bot$.

$\mathrm{XUPD}_{prot}((\mathcal{M},P),s,\varphi)$ % Find $(\mathcal{M}',P')$ w.r.t. φ at s.
INPUT: $(\mathcal{M},P) \in \mathbf{KP}_\Sigma$, $s \in S^{\mathcal{M}}$, and $\varphi \in \Sigma$-XCTL
OUTPUT: $\mathit{Modif}((\mathcal{M},P),s,\varphi)$

```
 1 if (M, P), s ⊨ φ then  (M′, P′) := (M, P)
 2 else case φ of
 3              ⊥       : fail
 4              ⊤       : (M′, P′) := (M, P)
 5              ℓ       : if ℓ̄ ∈ L^P(s) then fail
 6                        else (M′, P′) := L^u((M, P), s, ℓ)
 7        α ∨ β  : {guess δ ∈ {α, β};
 8                        (M′, P′) ← XUPD_prot((M, P), s, δ )}
 9        α ∧ β  : (M′, P′) ← XUPD^F_prot((M, P), s, {α, β})
10        EX α   : {guess s′ ∈ A^P[s];
11                        (M′, P′) ← XUPD_prot(T_∃^+((M, P), s, s′), s′, α)}
12        AX α   : {guess S′ ∈ {X ⊆ A^P[s] | E^P[s] ⊆ X  &  X ≠ ∅};
13                        (M′, P′) ← XUPD*_prot(T_∀^u((M, P), s, S′), S′, α)}
14 return (M′, P′)
```

where $\mathrm{XUPD}^F_{prot}((\mathcal{M},P),s,\Gamma)$ and $\mathrm{XUPD}^*_{prot}((\mathcal{M},P),S,\varphi)$ are procedures that implement $\mathit{Modif}^F((\mathcal{M},P),s,\Gamma)$ and $\mathit{Modif}^*((\mathcal{M},P),S,\varphi)$, respectively.

Observe that XUPD_{prot} does not need a verification similar to the verification in line (10) of XUPD_1. Protections guarantee that the returned model, $(\mathcal{M}', P')$, meets the requirement $(\mathcal{M}', P'), s \models \varphi$. For basic formulas $(\top, \ell)$, XUPD_{prot} meets such a requirement. Besides, when XUPD_{prot} modifies the labeling, or adds or removes transitions, XUPD_{prot} uses the current protection to preserve the satisfaction of previously treated subformulas.

3.5 Model Update for Σ-CTL and Addition of States

We extend XUPD_{prot} to formulas that use the operators **EU**, **AR**, **AU**, and **ER**. These operators are replaced by their fixed-point characterizations and then treated by a mechanism for detecting loops. For this loop-detecting mechanism we add to the parameters a set of visited states $W \subseteq S \times \Sigma\text{-CTL}$. We illustrate how to modify the pseudo-code in the cases of **EU** and **AR**; the modifications for **AU** and **ER** are similar.

$\text{UPD}_{prot}((\mathcal{M}, P, W), s, \varphi)$ % Find $(\mathcal{M}', P', W')$ w.r.t. φ at s.
INPUT: $(\mathcal{M}, P) \in \mathbf{KP}_\Sigma$, $W \subseteq S \times \Sigma\text{-CTL}$, $s \in S^\mathcal{M}$, and $\varphi \in \Sigma\text{-CTL}$.
OUTPUT: $\textit{Modif}((\mathcal{M}, P, W), s, \varphi)$
  1   **if** $(\mathcal{M}, P), s \models \varphi$ **then** $(\mathcal{M}', P', W') := (\mathcal{M}, P, W)$
  2   **else case** φ **of**
        ⋮
14         $\mathbf{E}[\alpha\,\mathbf{U}\,\beta]$: **if** $(s, \varphi) \in W$ **then** **fail** % default for lfp
15   **else** $(\mathcal{M}', P', W') \leftarrow \text{UPD}_{prot}((\mathcal{M}, P, \{(s, \varphi)\} \cup W), s,$
                                         $\beta \vee (\alpha \wedge \mathbf{EX}\,\varphi))$
16         $\mathbf{A}[\alpha\,\mathbf{R}\,\beta]$: **if** $(s, \varphi) \in W$
             then $(\mathcal{M}', P', W') := (\mathcal{M}, P, W)$ % default for gfp
17   **else** $(\mathcal{M}', P', W') \leftarrow \text{UPD}_{prot}((\mathcal{M}, P, \{(s, \varphi)\} \cup W), s,$
                                          $\beta \wedge (\alpha \vee \mathbf{AX}\,\varphi))$
18   **return** $(\mathcal{M}', P', W')$

State addition is only necessary when a model update fails to find a model with a given signature. For example, if $\varphi = \mathbf{EX}\,p \wedge \mathbf{EX}\,\neg p$, $\Sigma = (\{s_0\}, \{p\})$, and $(\mathcal{M}, P)$ is a protected Σ-model, then $\text{XUPD}_{prot}[(\mathcal{M}, P), s_0, \mathbf{EX}\,p \wedge \mathbf{EX}\,\neg p] = \emptyset$. Assuming that $n = |\varphi|$, we can extend our model update procedure for adding states to $\mathcal{M}$ until $\text{XUPD}_{prot}[(\mathcal{M}, P), s, \varphi] \neq \emptyset$ or $|S^\mathcal{M}| > n8^n$. This bound on the number of states is justified by a *small model theorem for CTL* [6]: if φ is satisfiable then φ is satisfiable in a model of size less than or equal to $n8^n$.

$\text{XUPD}_{S+}((\mathcal{M}, P), s, \varphi)$ % Add states until $\text{XUPD}_{prot}[(\mathcal{M}, P), s, \varphi] \neq \emptyset$.
INPUT: $(\mathcal{M}, P) \in \mathbf{KP}_\Sigma$, $s \in S^\mathcal{M}$, $\varphi \in \Sigma\text{-XCTL}$
OUTPUT: $\textit{Modif}(\mathbf{S}_\forall^+((\mathcal{M}, P), S^{\Sigma'} - S^\Sigma), s, \varphi)$
Where, assuming $n = |\varphi|$, Σ' is the minimal signature such that: $\Sigma' \supseteq \Sigma$
and $(\textit{Modif}(\mathbf{S}_\forall^+((\mathcal{M}, P), S^{\Sigma'} - S^\Sigma), s, \varphi) \neq \emptyset$ or $|S^{\Sigma'}| > n8^n$).
  1   $n := |\varphi|$; $m := n8^n$;
  2   **while** $\text{XUPD}_{prot}[(\mathcal{M}, P), s, \varphi] = \emptyset$ **and** $|S^\mathcal{M}| \leq m$ **do**

3   {Let $s'' \notin S^{\mathcal{M}}$;   % s'' is a new state
4             $(\mathcal{M}, P) := \mathbf{S}_\forall^+((\mathcal{M}, P), \{s''\})\}$
5 $(\mathcal{M}', P') \leftarrow \text{XUPD}_{prot}((\mathcal{M}, P), s, \varphi)$ % "$\leftarrow$" fails if XUPD_{prot} fails
6 **return** $(\mathcal{M}', P')$

3.6   Soundness and Completeness of XUPD_{prot}

We outline here a proof of soundness and completeness for XUPD_{prot}.

First, the application of XUPD_{prot} to a protected model $(\mathcal{M}, P)$ should produce protected models $(\mathcal{M}', P')$ such that P' is not "smaller" than P. Therefore, we define a partial order on protections suitable for model update.

Definition 11 (Partial order on protections). *If* $P, P' \in \mathbf{P}_\Sigma$ *are two protections, then we say that* P' *is* not smaller than P, *and we write* $P' \succeq P$ *iff:* $E^{P'} \supseteq E^P$, $A^{P'} \subseteq A^P$, *and* $\forall t \in S : L^{P'}(t) \supseteq L^P(t)$.

Second, observe that XUPD_{prot} implements *Modif*. Models computed by XUPD_{prot} are exactly modifications of the input model.

Theorem 1 ($\text{XUPD}_{prot} = Modif$). *For all* $(\mathcal{M}, P) \in \mathbf{KP}_\Sigma$, $s \in S^{\mathcal{M}}$, *and* $\varphi \in \Sigma\text{-}XCTL$: $\text{XUPD}_{prot}[(\mathcal{M}, P), s, \varphi] = Modif((\mathcal{M}, P), s, \varphi)$.

Hence, soundness of XUPD_{prot} is a consequence of the following theorem.

Theorem 2 (Modifications w.r.t. φ **satisfy** φ**).** *If* $(\mathcal{M}, P) \in \mathbf{KP}_\Sigma$, $s \in S^{\mathcal{M}}$, *and* $\varphi \in \Sigma\text{-}XCTL$, *then:* $(\mathcal{M}', P') \in Modif((\mathcal{M}, P), s, \varphi) \Rightarrow (\mathcal{M}', P'), s \models \varphi$.

To prove completeness of XUPD_{prot}, it is important to know whether there is a modification of $(\mathcal{M}, P)$ for φ, i.e. whether $(\mathcal{M}, P)$ is "φ-modifiable".

Definition 12 (φ**-modifiable**). *Let* $(\mathcal{M}, P) \in \mathbf{KP}_\Sigma$, $s \in S$, *and* $\varphi \in \Sigma\text{-}CTL$. *We say that* $(\mathcal{M}, P)$ *is* φ-modifiable *at* s *iff* $Modif((\mathcal{M}, P), s, \varphi) \neq \emptyset$.

In addition, we need to prove that if φ is "satisfiable" then XUPD_{prot} produces at least one result. Thus, we need to clarify the notion of "satisfiable".

Definition 13 (Satisfiable). *Let* $\varphi \in \Sigma\text{-}CTL$, $P \in \mathbf{P}_\Sigma$, *and* $s \in S$.
(1) φ *is* P-satisfiable *at* s *iff* $\exists (\mathcal{M}', P') \in \mathbf{KP}_\Sigma. (\mathcal{M}', P'), s \models \varphi \ \& \ P' \succeq P$.
(2) φ *is* $\mathbf{K}_\Sigma$-satisfiable *at* s *iff* $\exists \mathcal{M}' \in \mathbf{K}_\Sigma. \mathcal{M}', s \models \varphi$.

Fortunately, P-satisfiable and φ-modifiable have a nice relationship.

Theorem 3 (P**-satisfiable** $\approx$ φ**-modifiable**). *For all* $(\mathcal{M}, P) \in \mathbf{KP}_\Sigma$, $s \in S^{\mathcal{M}}$, $\varphi \in \Sigma\text{-}XCTL$: φ *is* P-satisfiable *at* s *iff* $(\mathcal{M}, P)$ *is* φ-modifiable *at* s.

Finally, completeness of XUPD_{prot} is a consequence of the following Corollary.

Corollary 1 ($\mathbf{K}_\Sigma$**-satisfiable** $\approx$ φ**-modifiable**). *For all* $\mathcal{M} \in \mathbf{K}_\Sigma$, $s \in S^{\mathcal{M}}$, *and* $\varphi \in \Sigma\text{-}XCTL$: φ *is* $\mathbf{K}_\Sigma$-satisfiable *at* s *iff* $(\mathcal{M}, P_\bot)$ *is* φ-modifiable *at* s.

Proof. ($\Rightarrow$). Let $\mathcal{M}' \in \mathbf{K}_\Sigma$ such that $\mathcal{M}', s \models \varphi$. Then, $(\mathcal{M}', P_{\mathcal{M}'}), s \models \varphi$ and $P_{\mathcal{M}'} \succeq P_\bot$. Therefore, by Theorem 3, $Modif((\mathcal{M}, P_\bot), s, \varphi) \neq \emptyset$.

($\Leftarrow$). If $(\mathcal{M}', P') \in Modif((\mathcal{M}, P_\bot), s, \varphi)$ then $(\mathcal{M}', P'), s \models \varphi$ and $P_{\mathcal{M}'} \succeq P'$. Hence, $(\mathcal{M}', P_{\mathcal{M}'}), s \models \varphi$ and $\mathcal{M}', s \models \varphi$. □

In summary, we have that XUPD$_{prot}$ is sound and complete:

Theorem 4 (XUPD$_{prot}$ is sound and complete). *For all $\mathcal{M} \in \mathbf{K}_\Sigma$, $s \in S^\mathcal{M}$, and $\varphi \in \Sigma$-XCTL:*

1. *If $(\mathcal{M}', P') \in$ XUPD$_{prot}[(\mathcal{M}, P_\bot), s, \varphi]$ then $(\mathcal{M}', P'), s \models \varphi$.*
2. *If φ is $\mathbf{K}_\Sigma$-satisfiable at s then XUPD$_{prot}[(\mathcal{M}, P_\bot), s, \varphi] \neq \emptyset$.*

4 Synthesizing a Model of the Mutual Exclusion Problem

We illustrate our model update method with an application to a mutual exclusion problem described by Emerson and Clarke [5] (we show other examples at the web site of UPD$_{prot}$, http://turing.iimas.unam.mx/ctl_upd3/form1.prl). Emerson and Clarke present a method to automatically synthesize *synchronization skeletons*, from a CTL specification, through the synthesis of a model of the specification. In the conclusions, Emerson and Clarke wonder if their synthesis method can be developed into a *practical* software tool. With this example, we contribute to the belief in a positive answer to this question.

The specification of the mutual exclusion problem by Emerson and Clarke uses a variant of CTL *with processes* [5]. We adapt such a specification to our definition of Σ-CTL. Thus, our specification of the mutual exclusion problem is the conjunction of the following formulas, where $i, j \in \{1, 2\}$ and $i \neq j$ (in tests of our prototype, we factorized the occurrences of the **AG** operator):

1. Start state. Both processes are in their noncritical region: $(n_1 \wedge n_2)$
2. Each process i is always exactly in one of the three code regions:
   $\mathbf{AG}\,((n_i \vee t_i \vee c_i) \wedge (n_i \rightarrow \neg(t_i \vee c_i)) \wedge (t_i \rightarrow \neg(n_i \vee c_i)) \wedge (c_i \rightarrow \neg(n_i \vee t_i)))$
3. Any move that process i makes from its noncritical (critical) region is into its trying (noncritical) region, and such a move is always possible:
   $\mathbf{AG}\,((n_i \rightarrow ((\mathbf{AX}\,(t_i \vee n_i)) \wedge (\mathbf{EX}\,t_i))) \wedge (c_i \rightarrow ((\mathbf{AX}\,(n_i \vee c_i)) \wedge (\mathbf{EX}\,n_i))))$
4. Any move that process i makes from its trying region is into its critical region and such a move is possible when it is the turn of process i:
   $\mathbf{AG}\,((t_i \rightarrow (\mathbf{AX}\,(c_i \vee n_i))) \wedge ((t_i \wedge turn_i) \rightarrow (\mathbf{EX}\,c_i)))$
5. A transition by one process cannot cause a move by the other. If process i is in region $r_i \in \{n_i, t_i, c_i\}$ and process j moves, then i remains in r_i:
   $\mathbf{AG}\,(\,((r_i \wedge n_j) \rightarrow (\mathbf{AX}\,(t_j \rightarrow r_i))) \wedge ((r_i \wedge t_j) \rightarrow (\mathbf{AX}\,(c_j \rightarrow r_i))) \wedge$
   $((r_i \wedge c_j) \rightarrow (\mathbf{AX}\,(n_j \rightarrow r_i)))\,)$
6. Some process can always move. If some process is in its noncritical region then both processes can move; otherwise only one process can move:
   $\mathbf{AG}\,(((n_1 \vee n_2) \rightarrow (turn_1 \wedge turn_2)) \wedge ((\neg n_1 \wedge \neg n_2) \rightarrow (turn_1 \veebar turn_2))\,)$

7. Each transition is due to the movement of exactly one process:
   AG $(((turn_1 \wedge turn_2) \rightarrow (\mathbf{OD} \leq 2)) \wedge ((\neg turn_1 \vee \neg turn_2) \rightarrow (\mathbf{OD} \leq 1)))$.
8. Split state $s = (t_1, t_2, turn_1, turn_2)$ into states $(t_1, t_2, turn_1, \neg turn_2)$ and
   $(t_1, t_2, \neg turn_1, turn_2)$ and separate the transitions going towards s. This requirement reflects a preference of Emerson and Clarke to distinguish all
   states by their propositional labels [5, p. 258]:
   AG $((t_i \wedge n_j) \rightarrow (\mathbf{EX}\,(t_j \wedge turn_i)))$

We tested UPD_{prot} by updating the dummy model in Fig. 2 w.r.t. the above
specification of the mutual exclusion problem. The first solution generated by
UPD_{prot} is the model in Fig. 3 having the expected structure [5, Fig. 11, p. 259].

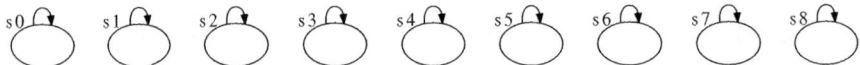

Fig. 2. A dummy model of nine states

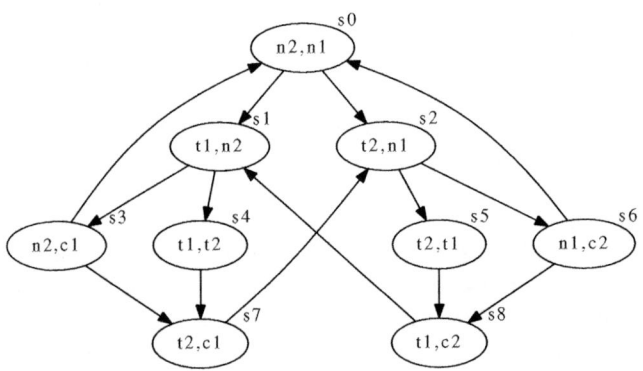

Fig. 3. Model produced by UPD_{prot} (variables $turn_i$ are omitted)

In the above specification, we include only formulas to specify the *local structure* of the system, through the operators **AX** and **EX** and an outermost
operator **AG**. We do not include formulas to specify *global behavior* of the
system by using operators **F, G, U**, or **R**. Global behavior formulas, for ex-
ample **AG** $(t_i \rightarrow \mathbf{EF}\,c_i)$ and **AG** $\neg\mathbf{EF}\,(c_1 \wedge c_2)$, are generally expected to be a
consequence of formulas for local structure. Intuitively, it is relatively easier to
synthesize a model to satisfy formulas specifying local structure than to synthesize a model to satisfy formulas specifying global behavior. Global behavior
formulas can be used instead to update a faulty model, presumably close to a
correct model. A difference between model synthesis and model update is related
to the difference between these two kinds of formula.

By using the non-trivial specification above, UPD_{prot} produces the model in
Fig. 3 from the dummy model in Fig. 2 after 16.43 seconds (Table 1).

Table 1. UPD_1 vs. UPD_{prot} in the repair of a faulty model of mutual exclusion. N indicates the number of changes needed to repair the model. Input models are obtained by removing, according to the marks ✗, transitions (s_i, s_j) and labels n_i in s_j, from the model of Fig. 3. A mark ✗ in the column "all" means that the input model is that of Fig. 2. Option -cN restricts the search to a maximum of N changes. Entries "—" mean "no answer after 1 hour". Times reported are those required to produce the first solution by using a PC with a dual-core processor at 2.0 GHz and 2 GB of RAM.

N	s_0s_1	s_1s_3	s_3s_7	s_2s_5	n_1s_0	n_2s_1	all	UPD_1 -cN	UPD_{prot} -cN	UPD_1	UPD_{prot}
1	✗							1.91	0.61	—	1.79
2	✗	✗						5.72	0.66	—	1.81
3	✗	✗	✗					67.00	0.80	—	1.83
4	✗	✗	✗	✗				1161.49	0.94	—	8.98
5	✗	✗	✗	✗	✗			1274.80	0.95	—	8.99
6	✗	✗	✗	✗	✗	✗		—	1.22	—	9.16
55	✗	✗	✗	✗	✗	✗	✗	—	14.96	—	16.43

The header spans: "Removed parts (✗)" over columns s_0s_1 through all; "Time (seconds)" over the four rightmost columns.

5 Related Work and Conclusions

We compare our work with other CTL updaters and give concluding remarks.

Calzone et al. [2] present a modeling system, Biocham, that can translate a biochemical network N into a Kripke model $\mathcal{M}_N$. If φ is a CTL formula expressing a property of N, and $\mathcal{M}_N$ does not satisfies φ, then, for some instances of φ, Biocham can generate an update of N, N', such that $\mathcal{M}_{N'}$ does satisfy φ.

Biocham's update algorithm classifies CTL formulas into three classes: *universal* (*existential*) formulas contain only non-negated universal (existential) operators; *unclassified* formulas contain both universal and existential operators.

If φ is universal, Biocham uses NuSMV [3] to compute a *counterexample*, i.e. a path π that makes φ false. Then, Biocham generates and tests models by *deleting transitions* occurring in π. If φ is existential, Biocham generates and tests models by *adding transitions with a bias* taken from the application domain. If φ is unclassified, then Biocham treats φ by deleting and adding transitions. However, the deletions (additions) for satisfying universal (existential) formulas may dissatisfy some existential (universal) or unclassified formulas. Therefore, trying to satisfy the three kinds of formulas, Biocham *uses a heuristic*: it first treats the existential formulas, then the unclassified ones, and finally the universal ones. If some formulas are dissatisfied by the last step, the process repeats.

Compared with our method, a drawback of Biocham is that the use of biases and heuristics makes it incomplete. Another disadvantage is that the use of domain-dependent biases makes it a non-general method.

Zhang and Ding [7] propose a model-update method w.r.t. CTL formulas, that employs "constraints" when updating formulas containing a conjunction $\alpha \wedge \beta$ of two nonpropositional formulas. Once the first conjunct α is treated, producing a model $\mathcal{M}'$ satisfying α, the second conjunct β is dealt with, using α as a constraint as follows. The model $\mathcal{M}'$ is updated so as to obtain a model $\mathcal{M}''$

satisfying β. Next, a model checker is called to determine whether or not $\mathcal{M}''$ satisfies α also. Models satisfying β are repetitively computed until one is found that does satisfy α [7, pp. 141, 143]. Therefore, Zhang and Ding's algorithm, as UPD_1, is similar to methods based on generation and testing.

Compared with UPD_{prot}, an implementation of Zhang and Ding's algorithm would be as inefficient as UPD_1 (Table 1). Another disadvantage of Zhang and Ding's algorithm is that, because it uses an operator base ($\{\mathbf{EX}, \mathbf{AF}, \mathbf{EU}\}$) more appropriate for model checking than for model update, it is less clear than UPD_{prot}. For example, it is not clear how Zhang and Ding's algorithm updates a model to satisfy any of the formulas $\mathbf{AX}\,\alpha$, $\mathbf{EF}\,\alpha$, or $\mathbf{A}[\alpha\,\mathbf{U}\,\beta]$.

We have shown that, by using protected models, UPD_{prot} overcomes inherent difficulties in the update of CTL formulas having universal and existential quantifiers, and preserves the satisfaction of subformulas through the updating process. We showed that UPD_{prot} can efficiently update a dummy model w.r.t. a specification of the mutual exclusion problem in a variant of CTL, and we outlined a proof of soundness and completeness for UPD_{prot}. Future work includes formalizing an order on protected models, using selection strategies in the implementation of nondeterministic choices, and experimental comparison with other CTL updaters.

References

1. Buccafurri, F., Eiter, T., Gottlob, G., Leone, N.: Enhancing model checking in verification by AI techniques. Artificial Intelligence 112(1-2), 57–104 (1999)
2. Calzone, L., Chabrier-Rivier, N., Fages, F., Soliman, S.: Machine learning biochemical networks from temporal logic properties. In: Priami, C., Plotkin, G.D. (eds.) Transactions on Computational Systems Biology VI. LNCS (LNBI), vol. 4220, pp. 68–94. Springer, Heidelberg (2006)
3. Cimatti, A., Clarke, E.M., Giunchiglia, F., Roveri, M.: NuSMV: a new Symbolic Model Verifier. In: Halbwachs, N., Peled, D. (eds.) CAV 1999. LNCS, vol. 1633, pp. 495–499. Springer, Heidelberg (1999)
4. Clarke, E.M., Grumberg, O., Peled, D.A.: Model Checking. MIT Press, Cambridge (1999)
5. Emerson, E.A., Clarke, E.M.: Using branching time temporal logic to synthesize synchronization skeletons. Science of Computer Programming 2, 241–266 (1982)
6. Emerson, E.A., Halpern, J.Y.: Decision procedures and expressiveness in the temporal logic of branching time. JCSS 30(1), 1–24 (1985)
7. Zhang, Y., Ding, Y.: CTL model update for system modifications. Journal of Artificial Intelligence Research 31, 113–155 (2008)

Type-Based Automated Verification of Authenticity in Asymmetric Cryptographic Protocols

Morten Dahl[2], Naoki Kobayashi[1], Yunde Sun[1], and Hans Hüttel[2]

[1] Tohoku University
[2] Aalborg University

Abstract. Gordon and Jeffrey developed a type system for verification of asymmetric and symmetric cryptographic protocols. We propose a modified version of Gordon and Jeffrey's type system and develop a type inference algorithm for it, so that protocols can be verified automatically as they are, without any type annotations or explicit type casts. We have implemented a protocol verifier SPICA2 based on the algorithm, and confirmed its effectiveness.

1 Introduction

Security protocols play a crucial role in today's Internet technologies including electronic commerce and voting. Formal verification of security protocols is thus an important, active research topic, and a variety of approaches to (semi-)automated verification have been proposed [8,5,15]. Among others, type-based approaches [1,14,15] have advantages that protocols can be verified in a modular manner, and that it is relatively easy to extend them to verify protocols at the source code level [4]. They have however a disadvantage that users have to provide complex type annotations, which require expertise in both security protocols and type theories. Kikuchi and Kobayashi [18] developed a type inference algorithm but it works only for symmetric cryptographic protocols.

To overcome the limitation of the type-based approaches and enable fully automated protocol verification, we integrate and extend the two lines of work – Gordon and Jeffrey's work [15] for verifying protocols using both symmetric and asymmetric cryptographic protocols, and Kikuchi and Kobayashi's work. The outcome is an algorithm for automated verification of authenticity in symmetric and asymmetric cryptographic protocols. The key technical novelty lies in the symmetric notion of *obligations* and *capabilities* attached to name types, which allows us to reason about causalities between actions of protocol participants in a general and uniform manner in the type system. It not only enables automated type inference, but also brings a more expressive power, enabling, e.g., verification of multi-party cryptographic protocols. We have developed a type inference algorithm for the new type system, and implemented a protocol verification tool SPICA2 based on the algorithm. According to experiments, SPICA2 is very fast; it could successfully verify a number of protocols in less than a second.

The rest of this paper is structured as follows. Section 2 introduces spi-calculus [2] extended with correspondence assertions as a protocol description language. Sections 3 and 4 present our type system and sketches a type inference algorithm. Section 5 reports implementation and experiments. Sections 6 and 7 discuss extensions and related work respectively. Proofs are found in the full version of this paper [10].

T. Bultan and P.-A. Hsiung (Eds.): ATVA 2011, LNCS 6996, pp. 75–89, 2011.

2   Processes

This section defines the syntax and operational semantics of the spi-calculus extended with correspondence assertions, which we call spi_{CA}. The calculus is essentially the same as that of Gordon and Jeffrey [15], except (i) there are no type annotations or casts (as they can be automatically inferred by our type inference algorithm), and (ii) there are no primitives for witness and trust; supporting them is left for future work.

We assume that there is a countable set of *names*, ranged over by $m, n, k, x, y, z, \ldots$. By convention, we often use $k, m, n, \ldots$ for free names and $x, y, z, \ldots$ for bound names.

The set of messages, ranged over by M, is given by:

$$M ::= x \mid (M_1, M_2) \mid \{M_1\}_{M_2} \mid \{\!|M_1|\!\}_{M_2}$$

(M_1, M_2) is a pair consisting of M_1 and M_2. The message $\{M_1\}_{M_2}$ ($\{\!|M_1|\!\}_{M_2}$, resp.) represents the ciphertext obtained by encrypting M_1 with the symmetric (asymmetric, resp.) key M_2. For the asymmetric encryption, we do not distinguish between encryption and signing; $\{\!|M_1|\!\}_{M_2}$ denotes an encryption if M_2 is a public key, while it denotes signing if M_2 is a private key.

The set of processes, ranged over by P, is given by:

$$P ::= \mathbf{0} \mid M_1!M_2 \mid M?x.P \mid (P_1 \mid P_2) \mid *P \mid (\nu x)P \mid (\nu_{sym}x)P \mid (\nu_{asym}x, y)P$$
$$\mid \mathbf{check}\ M_1\ \mathbf{is}\ M_2.P \mid \mathbf{split}\ M\ \mathbf{is}\ (x, y).P \mid \mathbf{match}\ M_1\ \mathbf{is}\ (M_2, y).P$$
$$\mid \mathbf{decrypt}\ M_1\ \mathbf{is}\ \{x\}_{M_2}.P \mid \mathbf{decrypt}\ M_1\ \mathbf{is}\ \{\!|x|\!\}_{M_2^{-1}}.P$$
$$\mid \mathbf{begin}\ M.P \mid \mathbf{end}\ M$$

The names denoted by x, y are *bound* in P. We write $[M_1/x_1, \ldots, M_n/x_n]P$ for the process obtained by replacing every free occurrence of $x_1, \ldots, x_n$ in P with $M_1, \ldots, M_n$. We write $\mathbf{FN}(P)$ for the set of free (i.e. non-bounded) names in P.

Process $\mathbf{0}$ does nothing, $M_1!M_2$ sends M_2 over the channel M_1, and $M_1?x.P$ waits to receive a message on channel M_1, and then binds x to it and behaves like P. $P_1 \mid P_2$ executes P_1 and P_2 in parallel, and $*P$ executes infinitely many copies of P in parallel.

We have three kinds of name generation primitives: (νx) for ordinary names, $(\nu_{sym}x)$ for symmetric keys, and $(\nu_{asym}x_1, x_2,)$ for asymmetric keys. $(\nu_{asym}x_1, x_2, P)$ creates a fresh key pair (k_1, k_2) (where k_1 and k_2 are encryption and decryption keys respectively), and behaves like $[k_1/x_1, k_2/x_2]P$. The process $\mathbf{check}\ M_1\ \mathbf{is}\ M_2.P$ behaves like P if M_1 and M_2 are the same name, and otherwise behaves like $\mathbf{0}$. The process $\mathbf{split}\ M\ \mathbf{is}\ (x, y).P$ behaves like $[M_1/x, M_2/y]P$ if M is a pair (M_1, M_2); otherwise it behaves like $\mathbf{0}$. $\mathbf{match}\ M_1\ \mathbf{is}\ (M_2, y).P$ behaves like $[M_3/y]P$ if M_1 is a pair of the form (M_2, M_3); otherwise it behaves like $\mathbf{0}$. Process $\mathbf{decrypt}\ M_1\ \mathbf{is}\ \{x\}_{M_2}.P$ ($\mathbf{decrypt}\ M_1\ \mathbf{is}\ \{\!|x|\!\}_{M_2^{-1}}.P$, resp.) decrypts ciphertext M_1 with symmetric (asymmetric, resp.) key M_2, binds x to the result and behaves like P; if M_1 is not an encryption, or an encryption with a key not matching M_2, then it behaves like $\mathbf{0}$. The process $\mathbf{begin}\ M.P$ raise an event $\mathbf{begin}\ M$ and behaves like P, while $\mathbf{end}\ M$ just raises an event $\mathbf{end}\ M$; they are used to express expected authenticity properties.

Example 1. We use the three protocols in Figure 1, taken from [15], as running examples. POSH and SOSH protocols aim to pass a new message msg from B to A, so

POSH:	**SOPH**	**SOSH**
A->B: n	A->B: $\{\| (\text{msg},\text{n}) \|\}_{pk_B}$	A->B: $\{\|\text{n}\|\}_{pk_B}$
B begins msg	B begins msg	B begins msg
B->A: $\{\| (\text{msg},\text{n}) \|\}_{sk_B}$	B->A: n	B->A: $\{\|\text{msg},\text{n}\|\}_{pk_A}$
A ends msg	A ends msg	A ends msg

Fig. 1. Informal Description of Three Protocols

$(\nu_{asym} sk_B, pk_B)(net!pk_B \mid$ (* create asymmetric keys for B and make pk_B public *)
$(\nu non)(net!non \mid$ (* A creates a nonce and sends it *)
$net?ctext.\textbf{decrypt } ctext \textbf{ is } \{\|x\|\}_{pk_B^{-1}}.$ (* receive a cypertext and decrypt it*)
$\textbf{split } x \textbf{ is } (m, non').\textbf{check } non \textbf{ is } non'.$ (* decompose pair x and check nonce *)
$\textbf{end } m) \mid$ (* believe that m came from B *)
$net?n.$ (* B receives a nonce *)
$(\nu msg)\textbf{begin } msg.$ (* create a message and declare that it is going to be sent*)
$net!\{\|(msg, n)\|\}_{sk_B})$ (* encrypt and send (msg, n) *)

Fig. 2. Public-Out-Secret-Home (POSH) protocol in spi$_{CA}$

that A can confirm that msg indeed comes from B, while SOPH protocol aims to pass msg from A to B, so that A can confirm that msg has been received by B. The second and fourth lines of each protocol expresses the required authenticity by using Woo and Lam's correspondence assertions [20]. "B begins msg" on the second line of POSH means "B is going to send msg", and "A ends msg" on the fourth line means "A believes that B has sent msg". The required authenticity is then expressed as a correspondence between begin- and end-events: whenever an end-event ("A ends msg" in this example) occurs, the corresponding begin-event ("B begins msg") must have occurred.[1] In the three protocols, the correspondence between begin- and end-events is guaranteed in different ways. In POSH, the correspondence is guaranteed by the signing of the second message with B's secret key, so that A can verify that B has created the pair (msg, n). In SOPH, it is guaranteed by encrypting the first message with B's public key, so that the nonce n, used as an acknowledgment, cannot be forged by an attacker. SOSH is similar to POSH, but keeps n secret by using A and B's public keys.

Figure 2 gives a formal description of POSH protocol, represented as a process in spi$_{CA}$. The first line is an initial set-up for the protocol. An asymmetric key pair for B is created and the decryption key pk_B is sent on a public channel net, on which an attacker can send and receive messages. The next four lines describe the behavior of A. On the second line, a nonce non is created and sent along net. On the third line, a ciphertext $ctext$ is received and decrypted (or verified) with B's public key. On the fourth line, the pair is decomposed and it is checked that the second component coincides with the nonce sent before. On the fifth line, an end-event is raised, meaning that A believes that

---

[1] There are two types of correspondence assertions in the literature: non-injective (or one-to-many) and injective (or one-to-one) correspondence. Throughout the paper we consider the latter.

msg came from B. The last three lines describe the behavior of B. On the sixth line, a nonce n is received from *net*. On the seventh line, a new message *msg* is created and a begin-event is raised, meaning that B is going to send *msg*. On the last line, the pair (msg, n) is encrypted (or signed) with B's secret key and sent on *net*.   □

Following Gordon and Jeffrey, we call a process *safe* if it satisfies correspondence assertions (i.e. for each end-event, a corresponding begin-event has occurred before), and *robustly safe* if a process is safe in the presence of arbitrary attackers (representable in spi_{CA}). Proving robust safety automatically is the goal of protocol verification in the present paper. To formalize the robust safety, we use the operational semantics shown in Figure 3. A runtime state is a quadruple $\langle \Psi, E, N, \mathcal{K} \rangle$, where Ψ is a multiset of processes, and E is the set of messages on which begin-events have occurred but the matching end-events have not. N is the set of names (including keys) created so far, and $\mathcal{K}$ is the set of key pairs. The special runtime state **Error** denotes that correspondence assertions have been violated. Note that a reduction gets stuck when a process does not match a rule. For example, **split** M **is** $(x, y).P$ is reducible only if M is of the form (M_1, M_2). Using the operational semantics, the robust safety is defined as follows.

$$\langle \Psi \uplus \{n?y.P, n!M\}, E, N, \mathcal{K} \rangle \longrightarrow \langle \Psi \uplus \{[M/y]P\}, E, N, \mathcal{K} \rangle \quad \text{(R-COM)}$$

$$\langle \Psi \uplus \{P \mid Q\}, E, N, \mathcal{K} \rangle \longrightarrow \langle \Psi \uplus \{P, Q\}, E, N, \mathcal{K} \rangle \quad \text{(R-PAR)}$$

$$\langle \Psi \uplus \{*P\}, E, N, \mathcal{K} \rangle \longrightarrow \langle \Psi \uplus \{*P, P\}, E, N, \mathcal{K} \rangle \quad \text{(R-REP)}$$

$$\langle \Psi \uplus \{(\nu x)P\}, E, N, \mathcal{K} \rangle \longrightarrow \langle \Psi \uplus \{[n/x]P\}, E, N \cup \{n\}, \mathcal{K} \rangle \ (n \notin N) \quad \text{(R-NEW)}$$

$$\langle \Psi \uplus \{(\nu_{sym} x)P\}, E, N, \mathcal{K} \rangle \longrightarrow \langle \Psi \uplus \{[k/x]P\}, E, N \cup \{k\}, \mathcal{K} \rangle \ (k \notin N) \quad \text{(R-NEWSK)}$$

$$\langle \Psi \uplus \{(\nu_{asym} x, y)P\}, E, N, \mathcal{K} \rangle$$
$$\longrightarrow \langle \Psi \uplus \{[k_1/x, k_2/y]P\}, E, N \cup \{k_1, k_2\}, \mathcal{K} \cup \{(k_1, k_2)\} \rangle \ (k_1, k_2 \notin N)$$
$$\text{(R-NEWAK)}$$

$$\langle \Psi \uplus \{\textbf{check } n \text{ is } n.P\}, E, N, \mathcal{K} \rangle \longrightarrow \langle \Psi \uplus \{P\}, E, N, \mathcal{K} \rangle \quad \text{(R-CHK)}$$

$$\langle \Psi \uplus \{\textbf{split } (M, N) \text{ is } (x, y).P\}, E, N, \mathcal{K} \rangle \longrightarrow \langle \Psi \uplus \{[M/x, N/y]P\}, E, N, \mathcal{K} \rangle$$
$$\text{(R-SPLT)}$$

$$\langle \Psi \uplus \{\textbf{match } (M, N) \text{ is } (M, z).P\}, E, N, \mathcal{K} \rangle \longrightarrow \langle \Psi \uplus \{[N/z]P\}, E, N, \mathcal{K} \rangle$$
$$\text{(R-MTCH)}$$

$$\langle \Psi \uplus \{\textbf{decrypt } \{M\}_k \text{ is } \{x\}_k.P\}, E, N, \mathcal{K} \rangle \longrightarrow \langle \Psi \uplus \{[M/x]P\}, E, N, \mathcal{K} \rangle \quad \text{(R-DECS)}$$

$$\langle \Psi \uplus \{\textbf{decrypt } \{\!|M|\!\}_{k_1} \text{ is } \{\!|x|\!\}_{k_2-1}.P\}, E, N, \mathcal{K} \rangle$$
$$\longrightarrow \langle \Psi \uplus \{[M/x]P\}, E, N, \mathcal{K} \rangle \ (\text{if } (k_1, k_2) \in \mathcal{K}) \quad \text{(R-DECA)}$$

$$\langle \Psi \uplus \{\textbf{begin } M.P\}, E, N, \mathcal{K} \rangle \longrightarrow \langle \Psi \uplus \{P\}, E \uplus \{M\}, N, \mathcal{K} \rangle \quad \text{(R-BGN)}$$

$$\langle \Psi \uplus \{\textbf{end } M\}, E \uplus \{M\}, N, \mathcal{K} \rangle \longrightarrow \langle \Psi, E, N, \mathcal{K} \rangle \quad \text{(R-END)}$$

$$\langle \Psi \uplus \{\textbf{end } M\}, E, N, \mathcal{K} \rangle \longrightarrow \textbf{Error} \quad (\text{if } M \notin E) \quad \text{(R-ERR)}$$

Fig. 3. Operational Semantics

Definition 21 (safety, robust safety) *A process P is safe if $\langle \{P\}, \emptyset, \mathbf{FN}(P), \emptyset \rangle \not\longmapsto^*$* **Error***. A process P is robustly safe if $P|O$ is safe for every spi$_{CA}$ process O that contains no begin/end/check operations.*[2]

3 Type System

This section presents a type system such that well-typed processes are robustly safe. This allows us to reduce protocol verification to type inference.

3.1 Basic Ideas

Following the previous work [14,15,18], we use the notion of *capabilities* (called effects in [14,15]) in order to statically guarantee that end-events can be raised only after the corresponding begin-events. A capability φ is a multiset of *atomic capabilities* of the form $\mathbf{end}(M)$, which expresses a permission to raise "end M" event. The robust safety of processes is guaranteed by enforcing the following conditions on capabilities: (i) to raise an "end M" event, a process must possess and consume an atomic $\mathbf{end}(M)$ capability; and (ii) an atomic $\mathbf{end}(M)$ capability is generated only by raising a "begin M" event. Those conditions can be statically enforced by using a type judgment of the form: $\Gamma; \varphi \vdash P$, which means that P can be safely executed under the type environment Γ and the capabilities described by φ. For example, $x : T; \{\mathbf{end}(x)\} \vdash \mathbf{end}\, x$ is a valid judgment, but $x : T; \emptyset \vdash \mathbf{end}\, x$ is not. The two conditions above can be locally enforced by the following typing rules for begin and end events:

$$\frac{\Gamma; \varphi + \{\mathbf{end}(M)\} \vdash P}{\Gamma; \varphi \vdash \mathbf{begin}\, M.P} \qquad \frac{}{\Gamma; \varphi + \{\mathbf{end}(M)\} \vdash \mathbf{end}\, M}$$

The left rule ensures that the new capability $\mathbf{end}(M)$ is available after the begin-event, and the right rule for end ensures that the capability $\mathbf{end}(M)$ must be present.

The main difficulty lies in how to pass capabilities between processes. For example, recall the POSH protocol in Figure 2, where begin- and end-events are raised by different protocol participants. The safety of this protocol can be understood as follows: B obtains the capability $\mathbf{end}(msg)$ by raising the begin event, and then passes the capability to A by attaching it to the nonce n. A then extracts the capability and safely executes the end event. As n is signed with B's private key, there is no way for an attacker to forge the capability. For another example, consider the SOPH protocol in the middle of Figure 1. In this case, the nonce n is sent in clear text, so that B cannot pass the capability to A through the second message. Instead, the safety of the SOPH protocol is understood as follows: A attaches to n (in the first message) an *obligation* to raise the begin-event. B then discharges the obligation by raising the begin-event, and notifies of it by sending back n. Here, note that an attacker cannot forge n, as it is encrypted by B's public key in the first message.

---

[2] Having no check operations is not a limitation, as an attacker process can check the equality of n_1 and n_2 by **match** (n_1, n_1) **is** $(n_2, x).P$.

To capture the above reasoning by using types, we introduce types of the form $\mathbf{N}(\varphi_1, \varphi_2)$, which describes names carrying an obligation φ_1 and a capability φ_2. In the examples above, n is given the type $\mathbf{N}(\emptyset, \{\mathbf{end}(msg)\})$ in the second message of POSH protocol, and the type $\mathbf{N}(\{\mathbf{end}(msg)\}, \emptyset)$ in the first message of SOPH protocol.

The above types $\mathbf{N}(\emptyset, \{\mathbf{end}(msg)\})$ and $\mathbf{N}(\{\mathbf{end}(msg)\}, \emptyset)$ respectively correspond to *response* and *challenge types* in Gordon and Jeffrey's type system [15]. Thanks to the uniform treatment of name types, type inference for our type system reduces to a problem of solving constraints on capabilities and obligations, which can further be reduced to linear programming problems by using the technique of [18]. The uniform treatment also allows us to express a wider range of protocols (such as multi-party cryptographic protocols). Note that neither obligations nor asymmetric cryptography are supported by the previous type system for automated verification [18]; handling them requires non-trivial extensions of the type system and the inference algorithm.

3.2 Types

Definition 31 *The syntax of types, ranged over by τ, is given by:*

$$
\begin{aligned}
\tau &::= \mathbf{N}_\ell(\varphi_1, \varphi_2) \mid \mathbf{SKey}(\tau) \mid \mathbf{DKey}(\tau) \mid \mathbf{EKey}(\tau) \mid \tau_1 \times \tau_2 \\
\varphi &::= \{A_1 \mapsto r_1, \dots, A_m \mapsto r_m\} && \textit{capabilities} \\
A &::= \mathbf{end}(M) \mid \mathbf{chk}_\ell(M, \varphi) && \textit{atomic cap.} \\
\iota &::= x \mid 0 \mid 1 \mid 2 \mid \cdots && \textit{extended names} \\
\ell &::= \mathbf{Pub} \mid \mathbf{Pr} && \textit{name qualifiers}
\end{aligned}
$$

Here, r_i ranges over non-negative rational numbers.

The type $\mathbf{N}_\ell(\varphi_1, \varphi_2)$ is assigned to names carrying obligations φ_1 and capabilities φ_2. Here, obligations and capabilities are mappings from atomic capabilities to rational numbers. For example, $\mathbf{N}_\ell(\{\mathbf{end}(a) \mapsto 1.0\}, \{\mathbf{end}(b) \mapsto 2.0\})$ describes a name that carries the obligation to raise $\mathbf{begin}\, a$ once, and the capability to raise $\mathbf{end}\, b$ twice. Fractional values are possible: $\mathbf{N}_\ell(\emptyset, \{\mathbf{end}(b) \mapsto 0.5\})$ means that the name carries a half of the capability to raise $\mathbf{end}\, b$, so that if combined with another half of the capability, it is allowed to raise $\mathbf{end}\, b$. The introduction of fractions slightly increases the expressive power of the type system, but the main motivation for it is rather to enable efficient type inference as in [18]. When the ranges of obligations and capabilities are integers, we often use multiset notations; for example, we write $\{\mathbf{end}(a), \mathbf{end}(a), \mathbf{end}(b)\}$ for $\{\mathbf{end}(a) \mapsto 2, \mathbf{end}(b) \mapsto 1\}$. The atomic capability $\mathbf{chk}_\ell(M, \varphi)$ expresses the capability to check equality on M by $\mathbf{check}\, M\, \mathbf{is}\, M'.P$: since nonce checking releases capabilities this atomic effect is used to ensure that each nonce can only be checked once. The component φ expresses the capability that can be extracted by the check operation (see the typing rule for check operations given later).

Qualifier ℓ attached to name types are essentially the same as the **Public/Private** qualifiers in Gordon and Jeffrey's type system and express whether a name can be made public or not. We often write $\mathbf{Un}$ for $\mathbf{N}_{\mathbf{Pub}}(\emptyset, \emptyset)$.

The type $\mathbf{SKey}(\tau)$ describes symmetric keys used for decrypting and encrypting values of type τ. The type $\mathbf{EKey}(\tau)$ ($\mathbf{DKey}(\tau)$, resp.) describes asymmetric keys used for encrypting (decrypting, resp.) values of type τ. The type $\tau_1 \times \tau_2$ describes pairs of values of types τ_1 and τ_2. As in [18], we express the dependency of types on names by using indices. For example, the type $\mathbf{Un} \times \mathbf{N}_\ell(\emptyset, \{\mathbf{end}(0)\})$ denotes a pair (M_1, M_2) where M_1 has type $\mathbf{Un}$ and M_2 has type $\mathbf{N}_\ell(\emptyset, \{\mathbf{end}(M_1)\})$. The type $\mathbf{Un} \times (\mathbf{Un} \times \mathbf{N}_{\mathbf{Pub}}(\emptyset, \{\mathbf{end}(0, 1) \mapsto r\}))$ describes triples of the form $(M_1, (M_2, M_3))$, where M_1 and M_2 have type $\mathbf{Un}$, and M_3 has type $\mathbf{N}_{\mathbf{Pub}}(\emptyset, \{\mathbf{end}(M_2, M_1) \mapsto r\})$. In general, an index i is a natural number referring to the i-th closest first component of pairs. In the syntax of atomic capabilities $\mathbf{end}(M)$, M is an extended message that may contain indices. We use the same metavariable M for the sake of simplicity.

Predicates on types. Following Gordon and Jeffrey, we introduce two predicates $\mathbf{Pub}$ and $\mathbf{Taint}$ on types, inductively defined by the rules in Figure 4. $\mathbf{Pub}(\tau)$ means that a value of type τ can safely be made public by e.g. sending it through a public channel. $\mathbf{Taint}(\tau)$ means that a value of type τ may have come from an untrusted principal and hence cannot be trusted. It may for instance have been received through a public channel or have been extracted from a ciphertext encrypted with a public key.

The first rule says that for $\mathbf{N}_\ell(\varphi_1, \varphi_2)$ to be public, the obligation φ_1 must be empty, as there is no guarantee that an attacker fulfills the obligation. Contrary, for $\mathbf{N}_\ell(\varphi_1, \varphi_2)$ to be tainted, the capability φ_2 must be empty if $\ell = \mathbf{Pub}$, as the name may come from an attacker and the capability cannot be trusted.[3]

$\mathbf{Pub}$ and $\mathbf{Taint}$ are a sort of dual, flipped by the type constructor $\mathbf{EKey}$. In terms of subtyping, $\mathbf{Pub}(\tau)$ and $\mathbf{Taint}(\tau)$ may be understood as $\tau \leq \mathbf{Un}$ and $\mathbf{Un} \leq \tau$ respectively, where $\mathbf{Un}$ is the type of untrusted, non-secret data. Note that $\mathbf{DKey}$ is co-variant, $\mathbf{EKey}$ is contra-variant, and $\mathbf{SKey}$ is invariant; this is analogous to Pierce and Sangiorgi's IO types with subtyping [19].

$$\frac{\ell = \mathbf{Pub} \qquad \varphi_1 = \emptyset}{\mathbf{Pub}(\mathbf{N}_\ell(\varphi_1, \varphi_2))} \qquad \frac{\ell = \mathbf{Pub} \Rightarrow \varphi_2 = \emptyset}{\mathbf{Taint}(\mathbf{N}_\ell(\varphi_1, \varphi_2))} \qquad \frac{\mathbf{Pub}(\tau_1) \qquad \mathbf{Pub}(\tau_2)}{\mathbf{Pub}(\tau_1 \times \tau_2)}$$

$$\frac{\mathbf{Taint}(\tau_1) \qquad \mathbf{Taint}(\tau_2)}{\mathbf{Taint}(\tau_1 \times \tau_2)} \qquad \frac{\mathbf{Pub}(\tau) \qquad \mathbf{Taint}(\tau)}{\mathbf{Pub}(\mathbf{SKey}(\tau))} \qquad \frac{\mathbf{Pub}(\tau) \qquad \mathbf{Taint}(\tau)}{\mathbf{Taint}(\mathbf{SKey}(\tau))}$$

$$\frac{\mathbf{Taint}(\tau)}{\mathbf{Pub}(\mathbf{EKey}(\tau))} \qquad \frac{\mathbf{Pub}(\tau)}{\mathbf{Taint}(\mathbf{EKey}(\tau))} \qquad \frac{\mathbf{Pub}(\tau)}{\mathbf{Pub}(\mathbf{DKey}(\tau))} \qquad \frac{\mathbf{Taint}(\tau)}{\mathbf{Taint}(\mathbf{DKey}(\tau))}$$

Fig. 4. Predicates $\mathbf{Pub}$ and $\mathbf{Taint}$

Operations and relations on capabilities and types. We write $dom(\varphi)$ for the set $\{A \mid \varphi(A) > 0\}$. We identify capabilities up to the following equality $\approx$:

$$\varphi_1 \approx \varphi_2 \iff (dom(\varphi_1) = dom(\varphi_2) \land \forall A \in dom(\varphi_1).\varphi_1(A) = \varphi_2(A)).$$

We write $\varphi \leq \varphi'$ if $\varphi(A) \leq \varphi'(A)$ holds for every $A \in dom(\varphi)$ and we define the summation of two capabilities by: $(\varphi_1 + \varphi_2)(A) = \varphi_1(A) + \varphi_2(A)$. This is a natural extension of the multiset union. We write $\varphi_1 - \varphi_2$ for the least φ such that $\varphi_1 \leq \varphi + \varphi_2$.

---

[3] These conditions are more liberal than the corresponding conditions in Gordon and Jeffrey's type system. In their type system, for Public Challenge φ_1 (which corresponds to $\mathbf{N}_{\mathbf{Pub}}(\varphi_1, \emptyset)$ in our type system) to be tainted, φ_1 must also be empty.

As we use indices to express dependent types, messages may be substituted in types. Let i be an index and M a message. The substitution $[M/i]\tau$ is defined inductively in the straight-forward manner, except for pair types where

$$[M/i](\tau_1 \times \tau_2) = ([M/i]\tau_1) \times ([M/(i+1)]\tau),$$

such that the index is shifted for the second component.

3.3 Typing

We introduce two forms of type judgments: $\Gamma; \varphi \vdash M : \tau$ for messages, and $\Gamma; \varphi \vdash P$ for processes, where Γ, called a type environment, is a sequence of type bindings of the form $x_1 : \tau_1, \ldots, x_n : \tau_n$. Judgment $\Gamma; \varphi \vdash M : \tau$ means that M evaluates to a value of type τ under the assumption that each name has the type described by Γ and that capability φ is available. $\Gamma; \varphi \vdash P$ means that P can be safely executed (i.e. without violation of correspondence assertions) if each free name has the type described by Γ and the capability φ is available. For example, $x : \mathbf{Un}; \{\mathbf{end}(x)\} \vdash \mathbf{end}\,x$ is valid but $x : \mathbf{Un}; \emptyset \vdash \mathbf{end}\,x$ is not.

We consider only the judgements that are *well-formed* in the sense that (i) φ refers to only the names bound in Γ, and (ii) Γ must be well-formed, i.e., if Γ is of the form $\Gamma_1, x : \tau, \Gamma_2$ then τ only refers to the names bound in Γ_1 and x is not bound in neither Γ_1 nor Γ_2. See [10] for the formal definition of the well-formedness of type environments and judgments. We freely permute bindings in type environments as long as they are well-formed; for example, we do not distinguish between $x : \mathbf{Un}, y : \mathbf{Un}$ and $y : \mathbf{Un}, x : \mathbf{Un}$.

Typing. The typing rules are shown in Figure 5. The rule T-CAST says that the current capability can be used for discharging obligations and increasing capabilities of the name. T-CAST plays a role similar to the typing rule for cast processes in Gordon and Jeffrey's type system, but our cast is implicit and changes only the capabilities and obligations, not the shape of types. This difference is important for automated type inference. The other rules for messages are standard; T-PAIR is the standard rule for dependent sum types (except for the use of indices).

In the rules for processes, the capabilities shown by _ can be any capabilities. The rules are also similar to those of Gordon and Jeffrey, except for the rules T-OUT, T-IN, T-NEWN, and T-CHK. In rule T-OUT, we require that the type of message M_2 is public as it can be received by any process, including the attacker. Similarly, in rule T-IN we require that the type of the received value x is tainted, as it may come from any process. This is different from Gordon and Jeffrey's type system where the type of messages sent or received from public channels must be $\mathbf{Un}$, and a subsumption rule allows any value of a public type to be typed as $\mathbf{Un}$ and a value of type $\mathbf{Un}$ to be typed as any tainted type. In effect, our type system can be considered a restriction of Gordon and Jeffrey's such that the subsumption rule is only allowed for messages sent or received via public channels. This point is important for automated type inference.

In rule T-NEWN, the obligation φ_1 is attached to the fresh name x and recorded in the atomic check capability. Capabilities corresponding to φ_1 can then later be extracted by a check operation if the obligation has been fulfilled. In rule T-CHK, $\mathbf{chk}_\ell(M_1, \varphi_4)$

$$\frac{}{\Gamma, x : \tau; \varphi \vdash x : \tau} \text{ (T-VAR)}$$

$$\frac{\Gamma; \varphi_1 \vdash M_1 : \tau_1 \quad \Gamma; \varphi_2 \vdash M_2 : [M_1/0]\tau_2}{\Gamma; \varphi_1 + \varphi_2 \vdash (M_1, M_2) : \tau_1 \times \tau_2} \text{ (T-PAIR)}$$

$$\frac{\Gamma; \varphi_1 \vdash M_1 : \tau_1 \quad \Gamma; \varphi_2 \vdash M_2 : \mathbf{SKey}(\tau_1)}{\Gamma; \varphi_1 + \varphi_2 \vdash \{M_1\}_{M_2} : \mathbf{N}_\ell(\emptyset, \emptyset)} \text{ (T-SENC)}$$
$$\frac{\Gamma; \varphi_1 \vdash M_1 : \tau \quad \Gamma; \varphi_2 \vdash M_2 : \mathbf{EKey}(\tau)}{\Gamma; \varphi_1 + \varphi_2 \vdash \{\!|M_1|\!\}_{M_2} : \mathbf{N}_\ell(\emptyset, \emptyset)} \text{ (T-AENC)}$$

$$\frac{\Gamma; \varphi_1 \vdash M : \mathbf{N}_\ell(\varphi_2, \varphi_3)}{\Gamma; \varphi_1 + \varphi_2' + \varphi_3' \vdash M : \mathbf{N}_\ell(\varphi_2 - \varphi_2', \varphi_3 + \varphi_3')} \text{ (T-CAST)}$$

$$\frac{}{\Gamma; \emptyset \vdash \mathbf{0}} \text{ (T-ZERO)} \qquad \frac{\Gamma; \varphi_1 \vdash P_1 \quad \Gamma; \varphi_2 \vdash P_2}{\Gamma; \varphi_1 + \varphi_2 \vdash P_1 \mid P_2} \text{ (T-PAR)} \qquad \frac{\Gamma; \emptyset \vdash P}{\Gamma; \emptyset \vdash *P} \text{ (T-REP)} \qquad \frac{\Gamma; \varphi' \vdash P \quad \varphi' \leq \varphi}{\Gamma; \varphi \vdash P} \text{ (T-CSUB)}$$

$$\frac{\Gamma; \varphi_1 \vdash M_1 : \mathbf{N}_\ell(\emptyset, \emptyset) \quad \Gamma; \varphi_2 \vdash M_2 : \tau \quad \mathbf{Pub}(\tau)}{\Gamma; \varphi_1 + \varphi_2 \vdash M_1 ! M_2} \text{ (T-OUT)}$$
$$\frac{\Gamma; \varphi_1 \vdash M : \mathbf{N}_\ell(\emptyset, \emptyset) \quad \Gamma, x : \tau; \varphi_2 \vdash P \quad \mathbf{Taint}(\tau)}{\Gamma; \varphi_1 + \varphi_2 \vdash M?x.P} \text{ (T-IN)}$$
$$\frac{\Gamma, x : \mathbf{SKey}(\tau); \varphi \vdash P}{\Gamma; \varphi \vdash (\nu_{sym} x)P} \text{ (T-NEWSK)}$$

$$\frac{\Gamma, x : \mathbf{N}_\ell(\varphi_1, \emptyset), \varphi + \{\mathbf{chk}_\ell(x, \varphi_1)\} \vdash P}{\Gamma; \varphi \vdash (\nu x)P} \text{ (T-NEWN)} \qquad \frac{\Gamma, k_1 : \mathbf{EKey}(\tau), k_2 : \mathbf{DKey}(\tau); \varphi \vdash P}{\Gamma; \varphi \vdash (\nu_{asym} k_1, k_2)P} \text{ (T-NEWAK)}$$

$$\frac{\Gamma; \varphi_1 \vdash M_1 : \mathbf{N}_\ell(\_, \_) \quad \Gamma; \varphi_2 \vdash M_2 : \mathbf{SKey}(\tau) \quad \Gamma, x : \tau; \varphi_3 \vdash P}{\Gamma; \varphi_1 + \varphi_2 + \varphi_3 \vdash \mathbf{decrypt}\ M_1\ \mathbf{is}\ \{x\}_{M_2}.P} \text{ (T-SDEC)}$$

$$\frac{\Gamma; \varphi_1 \vdash M_1 : \mathbf{N}_\ell(\_, \_) \quad \Gamma; \varphi_2 \vdash M_2 : \mathbf{DKey}(\tau) \quad \Gamma, x : \tau; \varphi_3 \vdash P}{\Gamma; \varphi_1 + \varphi_2 + \varphi_3 \vdash \mathbf{decrypt}\ M_1\ \mathbf{is}\ \{\!|x|\!\}_{M_2^{-1}}.P} \text{ (T-ADEC)}$$

$$\frac{\Gamma; \varphi_1 \vdash M_1 : \mathbf{N}_\ell(\_, \_) \quad \Gamma; \varphi_2 \vdash M_2 : \mathbf{N}_\ell(\emptyset, \varphi_5) \quad \Gamma; \varphi_3 + \varphi_4 + \varphi_5 \vdash P}{\Gamma; \varphi_1 + \varphi_2 + \varphi_3 + \{\mathbf{chk}_\ell(M_1, \varphi_4)\} \vdash \mathbf{check}\ M_1\ \mathbf{is}\ M_2.P} \text{ (T-CHK)}$$

$$\frac{\Gamma; \varphi_1 \vdash M : \tau_1 \times \tau_2 \quad \Gamma, y : \tau_1, z : [y/0]\tau_2; \varphi_2 \vdash P}{\Gamma; \varphi_1 + \varphi_2 \vdash \mathbf{split}\ M\ \mathbf{is}\ (y, z).P} \text{ (T-SPLIT)}$$

$$\frac{\Gamma; \varphi_1 \vdash M_1 : \tau_1 \times \tau_2 \quad \Gamma; \varphi_2 \vdash M_2 : \tau_1 \quad \Gamma, z : [M_2/0]\tau_2; \varphi_3 \vdash P}{\Gamma; \varphi_1 + \varphi_2 + \varphi_3 \vdash \mathbf{match}\ M_1\ \mathbf{is}\ (M_2, z).P} \text{ (T-MATCH)}$$

$$\frac{\Gamma; \varphi + \{\mathbf{end}(M)\} \vdash P}{\Gamma; \varphi \vdash \mathbf{begin}\ M.P} \text{ (T-BEGIN)} \qquad \frac{}{\Gamma; \varphi + \{\mathbf{end}(M)\} \vdash \mathbf{end}\ M} \text{ (T-END)}$$

Fig. 5. Typing Rules

in the conclusion means that the capability to check M_1 must be present. If the check succeeds, the capability φ_5 attached to M_2 can be extracted and used in P. In addition, the obligations attached to M_2 must be empty, i.e. all obligations initially attached to the name must have been fulfilled, and hence the capability φ_4 can be extracted and used in P. The above mechanism for extracting capabilities through obligations is different from Gordon and Jeffrey's type system in a subtle but important way, and provides more expressive power: see [10]. The remaining rules should be self-explanatory.

The following theorem guarantees the soundness of the type system. The proof is given in the full version [10].

Theorem 1 (soundness). *If* $x_1 : \mathbf{Un}, \ldots, x_m : \mathbf{Un}; \emptyset \vdash P$, *then* P *is robustly safe.*

Example 2. Recall the POSH protocol in Figure 2. Let τ be $\mathbf{Un} \times \mathbf{N_{Pub}}(\emptyset, \{\mathbf{end}(0)\})$. Then the process describing the behavior of B ($net?n. \cdots$ in the last five lines) is typed as the upper part of Figure 6. Here, $\Gamma = net : \mathbf{Un}, sk_B : \mathbf{EKey}(\tau), n : \mathbf{Un}, msg : \mathbf{Un}$.

$$
\cfrac{\Gamma; \emptyset \vdash msg : \mathbf{Un} \quad \cfrac{\Gamma; \emptyset \vdash n : \mathbf{N_{Pub}}(\emptyset, \emptyset)}{\Gamma; \{\mathbf{end}(msg)\} \vdash n : \mathbf{N_{Pub}}(\emptyset, \{\mathbf{end}(msg)\})}}{\cfrac{\Gamma; \{\mathbf{end}(msg)\} \vdash (msg, n) : \tau}{\cdots}}
$$

$$
\cfrac{\cfrac{\cfrac{\Gamma; \{\mathbf{end}(msg), \mathbf{chk_{Pub}}(msg, \emptyset)\} \vdash net!\{|(msg, n)|\}_{sk_B}}{\Gamma; \{\mathbf{chk_{Pub}}(msg, \emptyset)\} \vdash \mathbf{begin}\, msg. \cdots}}{net : \mathbf{Un}, sk_B : \mathbf{EKey}(\tau), n : \mathbf{Un}; \emptyset \vdash (\nu msg) \cdots}}{net : \mathbf{Un}, sk_B : \mathbf{EKey}(\tau); \emptyset \vdash net?n. \cdots}
$$

$$
\cfrac{\cfrac{\cfrac{\Gamma_3; \{\mathbf{end}(m)\} \vdash \mathbf{end}\, m}{\Gamma_3; \{\mathbf{chk_{Pub}}(non, \emptyset)\} \vdash \mathbf{check}\, non\, \mathbf{is}\, non'. \cdots}}{\Gamma_2, x : \tau; \{\mathbf{chk_{Pub}}(non, \emptyset)\} \vdash \mathbf{split}\, x\, \mathbf{is}\, (m, non). \cdots}}{\Gamma_2; \{\mathbf{chk_{Pub}}(non, \emptyset)\} \vdash \mathbf{decrypt}\, ctext\, \mathbf{is}\, \{|x|\}_{pk_B^{-1}}. \cdots}
$$

Fig. 6. Partial Typing of the POSH Protocol

Similarly, the part $\mathbf{decrypt}\, ctext\, \mathbf{is}\, \{|x|\}_{pk_B^{-1}}. \cdots$ of process A is typed as the lower part of Figure 6. Here, $\Gamma_2 = net : \mathbf{Un}, pk_B : \mathbf{DKey}(\tau), non : \mathbf{Un}, ctext : \mathbf{Un}$ and $\Gamma_3 = \Gamma_2, x : \tau, m : \mathbf{Un}, non' : \mathbf{N_{Pub}}(\emptyset, \{\mathbf{end}(m)\})$. Let P_1 be the entire process of the POSH protocol. It is typed by $net : \mathbf{Un}; \emptyset \vdash P_1$.

The SOPH and SOSH protocols in Figure 1 are typed in a similar manner. We show here only key types:

SOPH

$pk_B : \mathbf{EKey}(\mathbf{Un} \times \mathbf{N_{Pub}}(\{\mathbf{end}(0)\}, \emptyset)), sk_B : \mathbf{DKey}(\mathbf{Un} \times \mathbf{N_{Pub}}(\{\mathbf{end}(0)\}, \emptyset))$

SOSH

$pk_A : \mathbf{EKey}(\mathbf{Un} \times \mathbf{N_{Pr}}(\emptyset, \{\mathbf{end}(0)\})), sk_A : \mathbf{DKey}(\mathbf{Un} \times \mathbf{N_{Pr}}(\emptyset, \{\mathbf{end}(0)\}))$
$pk_B : \mathbf{EKey}(\mathbf{Un} \times \mathbf{N_{Pr}}(\emptyset, \emptyset)), \quad sk_B : \mathbf{DKey}(\mathbf{Un} \times \mathbf{N_{Pr}}(\emptyset, \emptyset))$

Note that for POSH and SOPH the name qualifier must be $\mathbf{Pub}$, and only for the SOSH protocol may it be $\mathbf{Pr}$. □

4 Type Inference

We now briefly discuss type inference. For this we impose a minor restriction to the type system, namely that in rule T-PAIR, if M_1 is not a name then the indice 0 cannot occur in τ_2. Similarly, in rule T-MATCH we require that index 0 does not occur unless M_2 is a name. These restrictions prevent the size of types and capabilities from blowing up. Given as input a process P with free names $x_1, \ldots, x_n$, the algorithm to decide $x_1 : \mathbf{Un}, \ldots, x_n : \mathbf{Un}; \emptyset \vdash P$ proceeds as follows:

1. Determine the *shape of the type* (or simple type) of each term via a standard unification algorithm, and construct a template of a type derivation tree by introducing qualifier and capability variables.
2. Generate a set C of constraints on qualifier and capability variables based on the typing rules such that C is satisfiable if and only if $x_1 : \mathbf{Un}, \ldots, x_n : \mathbf{Un}; \emptyset \vdash P$.
3. Solve the qualifier constraints.
4. Transform the capability constraints to linear inequalities over the rational numbers.
5. Use linear programming to determine if the linear inequalities are satisfiable.

In step 1, we can assume that there are no consecutive applications of T-CAST and T-CSUB. Thus, the template of a type derivation tree can be uniquely determined: for each process and message constructor there is an application of the rule matching the constructor followed by at most one application of T-CAST or T-CSUB.

At step 3 we have a set of constraints C of the form:

$$\{\ell_i = \ell_i' \mid i \in I\} \cup \{(\ell_j'' = \mathbf{Pub}) \Rightarrow (\varphi_j = \emptyset) \mid j \in J\} \cup C_1$$

where I and J are finite sets, $\ell_i, \ell_i', \ell_j''$ are qualifier variables or constants, and C_1 is a set of effect constraints (like $\varphi_1 \leq \varphi_2$). Here, constraints on qualifiers come from equality constraints on types and conditions $\mathbf{Pub}(\tau)$ and $\mathbf{Taint}(\tau)$. In particular, $(\ell_j'' = \mathbf{Pub}) \Rightarrow (\varphi_j = \emptyset)$ comes from the rule for $\mathbf{Taint}(\mathbf{N}_{\ell_j''}(\varphi, \varphi_j))$. By obtaining the most general unifier θ of the first set of constraints $\{\ell_i = \ell_i' \mid i \in I\}$ we obtain the constraint set $C' \equiv \{(\theta\ell_j'' = \mathbf{Pub}) \Rightarrow (\theta\varphi_j = \emptyset) \mid j \in J\} \cup \theta C_1$. Let $\gamma_1, \ldots, \gamma_k$ be the remaining qualifier variables, and let $\theta' = [\mathbf{Pr}/\gamma_1, \ldots, \mathbf{Pr}/\gamma_k]$. Then C is satisfiable if and only if $\theta' C'$ is satisfiable. Thus, we obtain the set $\theta' C'$ of effect constraints that is satisfiable if and only if $x_1 : \mathbf{Un}, \ldots, x_n : \mathbf{Un}; \emptyset \vdash P$ holds.

Except for step 3, the above algorithm is almost the same as our previous work and we refer the interested reader to [17,18]. By a similar argument to that given in [18] we can show that under the assumptions that the size of each begin/end assertion occurring in the protocol is bounded by a constant and that the size of simple types is polynomial in the size of the protocol, the type inference algorithm runs in polynomial time.

Example 3. Recall the POSH protocol in Figure 2. By the simple type inference in step 1 we get the following types for names:

$$non, non' : \mathbf{N}, pk_B : \mathbf{DKey}(\mathbf{N} \times \mathbf{N}), \ldots$$

By preparing qualifier and capability variables we get the following elaborated types and constraints on those variables:

$$non : \mathbf{N}_{\gamma_1}(\xi_{0,o}, \xi_{0,c}), non' : \mathbf{N}_{\gamma_1'}(\xi_{0,o}', \xi_{0,c}'), \ldots$$
$$\mathbf{Pub}(\mathbf{N}_{\gamma_1}(\xi_{0,o}, \xi_{0,c})) \quad \gamma_1 = \gamma_1' \quad \xi_6 \leq \xi_3 + \xi_4 + \xi_5$$
$$\xi_2 \geq \xi_{0,o}' + (\xi_5 - \xi_{0,c}') \quad \xi_7 \geq \xi_1 + \xi_2 + \xi_3 + \{\mathbf{chk}_{\gamma_1}(non, \xi_4)\} \quad \cdots$$

Here, the constraint $\mathbf{Pub}(\mathbf{N}_{\gamma_1}(\xi_{0,o}, \xi_{0,c}))$ comes from *net!non*, and the other constraints from **check** *non* is *non*. $\cdots$. By solving the qualifier constraints, we get $\gamma_1 = \gamma_1' = \mathbf{Pub}, \ldots$, and are left with constraints on capability variables. By computing (an over-approximation of) the domain of each capability, we can reduce it to constraints on linear inequalities. For example, by letting $\xi_i = \{\mathbf{chk_{Pub}}(non, \xi_4) \mapsto x_i, \mathbf{end}(m) \mapsto y_i, \ldots\}$, the last constraint is reduced to:

$$x_7 \geq x_1 + x_2 + x_3 + 1 \quad y_7 \geq y_1 + y_2 + y_3 + 0 \quad \cdots$$

5   Implementation and Experiments

We have implemented a protocol verifier SPICA2 based on the type system and inference algorithm discussed above. The implementation is mostly based on the formalization in the paper, except for a few extensions such as sum types and private channels to securely distribute initial keys. The implementation can be tested at http://www.kb.ecei.tohoku.ac.jp/~koba/spica2/.

We have tested SPICA2 on several protocols with the results of the experiments shown in Table 1. Experiments were conducted using a machine with a 3GHz CPU and 2GB of memory.

The descriptions of the protocols used in the experiments are available at the above URL. POSH, SOPH, and SOSH are (spi$_{CA}$-notations of) the protocols given in Figure 1. GNSL is the generalized Needham-Schroeder-Lowe protocol [9]: see [10] for details. Otway-Ree is Otway-Ree protocol using symmetric keys. Iso-two-pass is from [15], and the remaining protocols are the Needham-Schroeder-Lowe protocol and its variants, taken from the sample programs of Cryptyc [16] (but with type annotations and casts removed). ns-flawed is the original flawed version, nsl-3 and nsl-7 are 3- and 7-message versions of Lowe's fix, respectively. See [16] for the other three. As the table shows, all the protocols have been correctly verified or rejected. Furthermore, verification succeeded in less than a second except for GNSL. For GNSL, the slow-down is caused by the explosion of the number of atomic capabilities to be considered, which blows up the number of linear inequalities obtained from capability constraints.

Table 1. Experimental results

Protocols	Typing	Time (sec.)	Protocols	Typing	Time (sec.)
POSH	yes	0.001	ns-flawed	no	0.007
SOPH	yes	0.001	nsl-3	yes	0.015
SOSH	yes	0.001	nsl-7	yes	0.049
GNSL	yes	7.40	nsl-optimized	yes	0.012
Otway-Ree	yes	0.019	nsl-with-secret	yes	0.023
Iso-two-pass	yes	0.004	nsl-with-secret-optimized	yes	0.016

6 Extensions

In this section, we hint on how to modify our type system and type inference algorithm to deal with other features. Formalization and implementation of the extensions are left for future work.

Our type system can be easily adopted to deal with non-injective correspondence [13], which allows multiple end-events to be matched by a single begin-event. It suffices to relax the typing rules, for example, by changing the rules for begin- and end-events to:

$$\frac{\Gamma; \varphi + \{\mathbf{end}(M) \mapsto r\} \vdash P \qquad r > 0}{\Gamma; \varphi \vdash \mathbf{begin}\, M.P} \qquad\qquad \frac{r > 0}{\Gamma; \varphi + \{\mathbf{end}(M) \mapsto r\} \vdash \mathbf{end}\, M}$$

Fournet et al. [12] generalized begin- and end-events by allowing predicates to be defined by Datalog programs. For example, the process:

$$\mathbf{assume}\ employee(a); \mathbf{expect}\ canRead(a, handbook)$$

is safe in the presence of the clause "canRead(X,handbook) :- employee(X)". Here, the primitives **assume** and **expect** are like non-injective versions of **begin** and **end**. A similar type system can be obtained by extending our capabilities to mappings from ground atomic formulas to rational numbers (where $\varphi(L) > 0$ means L holds), and introducing rules for assume and expect similar to the rules above for begin and end-events. To handle clauses like "canRead(X,handbook) :- employee(X)", we can add the following rule:

$$\frac{\Gamma; \varphi + \{L \mapsto r\} \vdash P \qquad \text{There is an (instance of) clause } L : - L_1, \ldots, L_k}{\Gamma; \varphi \vdash P}$$
$$r \le \varphi(L_i) \text{ for each } i \in \{1, \ldots, k\}$$

This allows us to derive a capability for L whenever there are capabilities for $L_1, \ldots, L_k$. To reduce capability constraints to linear programming problems, it suffices to extend the algorithm to obtain the domain of each effect [18], taking clauses into account (more precisely, if there is a clause $L : - L_1, \ldots, L_k$ and $\theta L_1, \ldots, \theta L_k$ are in the domain of φ, we add θL to the domain of φ).

To deal with trust and witness in [15], we need to mix type environments and capabilities, so that type environments can also be attached to names and passed around. The resulting type system is rather complex, so that we leave the details to another paper.

7 Related Work

The present work extends two lines of previous work: Gordon and Jeffrey's type systems for authenticity [14,15], and Kikuchi and Kobayashi's work to enable type inference for symmetric cryptographic protocols [18]. In our opinion the extension is non-trivial, requiring the generalization of name types and a redesign of the type system. This has yielded a fully-automated and efficient protocol verifier. As for the expressive power, the fragment of Gordon and Jeffrey's type system (subject to minor restrictions) without trust and witness can be easily embedded into our type system. On the other hand, thanks to the uniform treatment of name types in terms of capabilities and obligations, our type system can express protocols that are not typable in Gordon and Jeffrey's type system, like the GNSL multi-party protocol [9]. See [10] for more details.

Gordon et al. [3,4] extended their work to verify source code-level implementation of cryptographic protocols by using refinement types. Their type systems still require refinement type annotations. We plan to extend the ideas of the present work to enable partial type inference for their type system. Bugliesi, Focardi, and Maffei [6,11,7] have proposed a protocol verification method that is closely related to Gordon and Jeffrey's type systems. They [11] developed an algorithm for automatically inferring *tags* (which roughly correspond to Gordon and Jeffrey's types in [14,15]). Their inference algorithm is based on exhaustive search of taggings by backtracking, hence our type inference would be more efficient. As in Gordon and Jeffrey type system, their tagging and typing system is specialized for the typical usage of nonces in two-party protocols, and appears to be inapplicable to multi-party protocols like GNSL.

There are automated protocol verification tools based on other approaches, such as ProVerif [5] and Scyther [8]. Advantages of our type-based approach are: (i) it allows modular verification of protocols[4]; (ii) it sets up a basis for studies of partial or full type inference for more advanced type systems for protocol verification [4] (for an evidence, recall Section 6); and (iii) upon successful verification, it generates types as a certificate, which explains why the protocol is safe, and can be independently checked by other type-based verifiers [15,4]. On the other hand, ProVerif [5] and Scyther [8] have an advantage that they can generate an attack scenario given a flawed protocol. Thus, we think that our type-based tool is complementary to existing tools.

Acknowledgment. This work was partially supported by the Mitsubishi Foundation.

References

1. Abadi, M.: Secrecy by typing in security protocols. JACM 46(5), 749–786 (1999)
2. Abadi, M., Gordon, A.D.: A Calculus for Cryptographic Protocols: The Spi Calculus. Information and Computation 148(1), 1–70 (1999)
3. Bengtson, J., Bhargavan, K., Fournet, C., Gordon, A.D., Maffeis, S.: Refinement types for secure implementations. In: Proceedings of the 21st IEEE Computer Security Foundations Symposium (CSF 2008), pp. 17–32 (2008)
4. Bhargavan, K., Fournet, C., Gordon, A.D.: Modular verification of security protocol code by typing. In: Proceedings of POPL 2010, pp. 445–456 (2010)
5. Blanchet, B.: From Secrecy to Authenticity in Security Protocols. In: Hermenegildo, M.V., Puebla, G. (eds.) SAS 2002. LNCS, vol. 2477, pp. 342–359. Springer, Heidelberg (2002)
6. Bugliesi, M., Focardi, R., Maffei, M.: Analysis of typed analyses of authentication protocols. In: 18th IEEE Computer Security Foundations Workshop (CSFW-18 2005), pp. 112–125 (2005)

---

[4] Although the current implementation of SPICA2 only supports whole protocol analysis, it is easy to extend it to support partial type annotations to enable modular verification. For that purpose, it suffices to allow bound variables to be annotated with types, and generate the corresponding constraints during type inference. For example, for a type-annotated input $M?(x : \tau_1).P$, we just need to add the subtype constraint $\tau_1 \leq \tau$ to rule T-IN.

7. Bugliesi, M., Focardi, R., Maffei, M.: Dynamic types for authentication. Journal of Computer Security 15(6), 563–617 (2007)
8. Cremers, C.J.F.: Unbounded verification, falsification, and characterization of security protocols by pattern refinement. In: Proceedings of ACM Conference on Computer and Communications Security (CCS 2008), pp. 119–128 (2008)
9. Cremers, C.J.F., Mauw, S.: A family of multi-party authentication protocols - extended abstract. In: Proceedings of WISSEC 2006 (2006)
10. Dahl, M., Kobayashi, N., Sun, Y., Hüttel, H.: Type-based automated verification of authenticity in asymmetric cryptographic protocols (2011), full version
    http://www.kb.ecei.tohoku.ac.jp/~koba/papers/protocol-full.pdf
11. Focardi, R., Maffei, M., Placella, F.: Inferring authentication tags. In: Proceedings of the Workshop on Issues in the Theory of Security (WITS 2005). pp. 41–49 (2005)
12. Fournet, C., Gordon, A.D., Maffeis, S.: A type discipline for authorization policies. ACM Trans. Prog. Lang. Syst. 29(5) (2007)
13. Gordon, A.D., Jeffrey, A.: Typing one-to-one and one-to-many correspondences in security protocols. In: Okada, M., Babu, C. S., Scedrov, A., Tokuda, H. (eds.) ISSS 2002. LNCS, vol. 2609, pp. 263–282. Springer, Heidelberg (2003)
14. Gordon, A.D., Jeffrey, A.: Authenticity by typing for security protocols. Journal of Computer Security 11(4), 451–520 (2003)
15. Gordon, A.D., Jeffrey, A.: Types and effects for asymmetric cryptographic protocols. Journal of Computer Security 12(3-4), 435–483 (2004)
16. Haack, C., Jeffrey, A.: Cryptyc (2004), http://www.cryptyc.org/
17. Kikuchi, D., Kobayashi, N.: Type-based verification of correspondence assertions for communication protocols. In: Shao, Z. (ed.) APLAS 2007. LNCS, vol. 4807, pp. 191–205. Springer, Heidelberg (2007)
18. Kikuchi, D., Kobayashi, N.: Type-based automated verification of authenticity in cryptographic protocols. In: Castagna, G. (ed.) ESOP 2009. LNCS, vol. 5502, pp. 222–236. Springer, Heidelberg (2009)
19. Pierce, B., Sangiorgi, D.: Typing and subtyping for mobile processes. Mathematical Structures in Computer Science 6(5), 409–454 (1996)
20. Woo, T.Y., Lam, S.S.: A semantic model for authentication protocols. In: RSP: IEEE Computer Society Symposium on Research in Security and Privacy, pp. 178–193 (1993)

Formalization of Finite-State Discrete-Time Markov Chains in HOL

Liya Liu, Osman Hasan, and Sofiène Tahar

Dept. of Electrical & Computer Engineering, Concordia University
1455 de Maisonneuve W., Montreal, Quebec, H3G 1M8, Canada
{liy_liu,o_hasan,tahar}@ece.concordia.ca

Abstract. The mathematical concept of Markov chains is widely used to model and analyze many engineering and scientific problems. Markovian models are usually analyzed using computer simulation, and more recently using probabilistic model-checking but these methods either do not guarantee accurate analysis or are not scalable. As an alternative, we propose to use higher-order-logic theorem proving to reason about properties of systems that can be described as Markov chains. As the first step towards this goal, this paper presents a formalization of time homogeneous finite-state Discrete-time Markov chains and the formal verification of some of their fundamental properties, such as Joint probabilities, Chapman-Kolmogorov equation and steady state probabilities, using the HOL theorem prover. For illustration purposes, we utilize our formalization to analyze a simplified binary communication channel.

1   Introduction

In probability theory, Markov chains are used to model time varying random phenomena that exhibit the memoryless property [3]. In fact, most of the randomness that we encounter in engineering and scientific domains has some sort of time-dependency. For example, noise signals vary with time, duration of a telephone call is somehow related to the time it is made, population growth is time dependant and so is the case with chemical reactions. Therefore, Markov chains have been extensively investigated and applied for designing systems in many branches of science and engineering. Some of their important applications include functional correctness and performance analysis of telecommunication and security protocols, reliability analysis of hardware circuits, software testing, internet page ranking and statistical mechanics.

Traditionally, simulation has been the most commonly used computer-based analysis technique for Markovian models. The approximate nature of simulation poses a serious problem in highly sensitive and safety critical applications, such as, nuclear reactor control and aerospace software engineering. To improve the accuracy of the simulation results, Markov Chain Monte Carlo (MCMC) methods [16], which involve sampling from desired probability distributions by constructing a Markov chain with the desired distribution, are frequently applied. The major limitation of MCMC is that it generally requires hundreds of

T. Bultan and P.-A. Hsiung (Eds.): ATVA 2011, LNCS 6996, pp. 90–104, 2011.

thousands of simulations to evaluate the desired probabilistic quantities and becomes impractical when each simulation step involves extensive computations. Other state-based approaches to analyze Markovian models include software packages, such as Markov analyzers and reliability or performance evaluation tools, which are all based on numerical methods [27]. Although these software packages can be successfully applied to analyze large scale Markovian models, the results cannot be guaranteed to be accurate because the underlying iterative methods are not 100% precise. Another technique, *Stochastic Petri Nets (SPN)* [9], has been found as a powerful method for modeling and analyzing Markovian systems because it allows local state modeling instead of global modeling. The key limiting factor of the application of SPN models using this approach is the complexity of their analysis.

Formal methods are able to conduct precise system analysis and thus overcome the inaccuracies of the above mentioned techniques. Due to the extensive usage of Markov chains in analyzing safety-critical systems, probabilistic model checking [24] has been recently proposed for analyzing Markov chains. It offers exact solutions but is limited by the state-space explosion problem [2] and the time of analyzing a system is largely dependent on the convergence speed of the underlying algorithms. Similarly, we cannot verify generic mathematical properties using probabilistic model checking due to the inherent state-based nature of the approach. Thus, the probabilistic model checking approach, even though is capable of providing exact solutions automatically, is quite limited in terms of handling a variety of systems and properties.

In this paper, we propose to use higher-order-logic theorem proving [7] as a complementary technique for analyzing Markovian models and thus overcome the limitations of the above mentioned techniques. Time-homogeneousity is an important concept in analyzing Markovian models. In particular, we formalize a time-homogeneous Discrete-Time Markov Chain (DTMC) with finite state space in higher-order logic and then, building upon this definition, formally verify some of the fundamental properties of a DTMC, such as, *Joint Probability Distribution, Chapman-Kolmogorov Equation*, and *Steady-state Probabilities* [3]. These properties play a vital role in reasoning about many interesting characteristics while analyzing the Markovian models of real-world systems as well as pave the path to the verification of more advanced properties related to DTMC. In order to illustrate the effectiveness of our work and demonstrate its utilization, we present the formal analysis of a simplified binary communication channel.

2   Related Work

As described above, Markov Analyzers, such as *MARCA* [17] and *DNAmaca* [15], which contain numerous matrix manipulation and numerical solution procedures, are powerful autonomous tools for analyzing large-scale Markovian models. Unfortunately, most of their algorithms are based on iterative methods that begin from some initial approximation and end at some convergent point, which is the main source of inaccuracy in such methods.

Many reliability evaluation software tools integrate simulation and numerical analyzers for modeling and analyzing the reliability, maintainability or safety of systems using Markov methods, which offer simplistic modeling approaches and are more flexible compared to traditional approaches, such as Fault Tree [14]. Some prevalent tool examples are *Möbius* [19] and *Relex Markov* [23]. Some other software tools for evaluating performance, e.g. *MACOM* [25] and *HYDRA* [6], take the advantages of a popular Markovian algebra, i.e., *PEPA* [21], to model systems and efficiently compute passage time densities and quantities in large-scale Markov chains. However, the algorithms used to solve the models are based on approximations, which leads to inaccuracies.

Stochastic Petri Nets provide a versatile modeling technique for stochastic systems. The most popular softwares are *SPNP* [4] and *GreatSPN* [8]. These tools can model, validate, and evaluate the distributed systems and analyze the dynamic events of the models using something other than the exponential distribution. Although they can easily manage the size of the system model, the iterative methods employed to compute the stationary distribution or transient probabilities of a model result in inaccurate analysis.

Probabilistic model checking [1,24] is the state-of-the-art formal Markov chain analysis technique. Numerous probabilistic model checking algorithms and methodologies have been proposed in the open literature, e.g., [5,20], and based on these algorithms, a number of tools, e.g., *PRISM* [22] and *VESTA* [26] have been developed. They support the analysis of probabilistic properties of DTMC, Continuous-Time Markov chains, Markov decision processes and Semi-Markov Process and have been used to analyze many real-world systems including communication and multimedia protocols. But they suffer from state-space explosion as well as do not support the verification of generic mathematical expressions. Also, because of numerical methods implemented in the tools, the final results cannot be termed 100% accurate. The proposed HOL theorem proving based approach provides another way to specify larger systems and accurate results.

HOL theorem proving has also been used for conducting formal probabilistic analysis. Hurd [13] formalized some measure theory in higher-order logic and proposed an infrastructure to formalize discrete random variables in HOL. Then, Hasan [10] extended Hurd's work by providing the support to formalize continuous random variables [10] and verify the statistical properties, such as, expectation and variance, for both discrete and continuous random variables [10,11]. Recently, Mhamdi [18] proposed a significant formalization of measure theory and proved Lebesgue integral properties and convergence theorems for arbitrary functions. But, to the best of our knowledge, the current state-of-the-art high-order-logic theorem proving based probabilistic analysis do not provide any theory to model and verify Markov systems and reasoning about their corresponding probabilistic properties. The main contribution of the current paper is to bridge this gap. We mainly build upon Hurd's work to formalize DTMC and verify some of their basic probabilistic properties. The main reason behind choosing Hurd's formalization of probability theory for our work is the availability of formalized discrete and continuous random variables in this framework, as described above. These random variables can be utilized along with our formalization of DTMC to formally represent real-world systems by their corresponding Markovian models in higher-order logic and reason about these models in a higher-order-logic theorem prover.

3 Probability Theory and Random Variables in HOL

A *measure space* is defined as a triple (Ω, Σ, μ) where Ω is a set, called the *sample space*, Σ represents a σ-algebra of subsets of Ω and the subsets are usually referred to as *measurable sets*, and μ is a *measure* with domain Σ. A *probability space* is a measure space $(\Omega, \Sigma, \mathcal{P}r)$ such that the measure, referred to as the probability and denoted by $\mathcal{P}r$, of the sample space is 1.

The measure theory developed by Hurd [13] defines a measure space as a pair (Σ, μ). Whereas the sample space, on which this pair is defined, is implicitly implied from the higher-order-logic definitions to be equal to the universal set of the appropriate data-type. Building upon this formalization, the probability space was also defined in HOL as a pair $(\mathcal{E}, \mathbb{P})$, where the domain of $\mathbb{P}$ is the set $\mathcal{E}$, which is a set of subsets of infinite Boolean sequences $\mathbb{B}^{\infty}$. Both $\mathbb{P}$ and $\mathcal{E}$ are defined using the Carathéodory's Extension theorem, which ensures that $\mathcal{E}$ is a σ-algebra: closed under complements and countable unions.

Now, a random variable, which is one of the core concepts in probabilistic analysis, is a fundamental probabilistic function and thus can be modeled in higher-order logic as a deterministic function, which accepts the infinite Boolean sequence as an argument. These deterministic functions make random choices based on the result of popping the top most bit in the infinite Boolean sequence and may pop as many random bits as they need for their computation. When the functions terminate, they return the result along with the remaining portion of the infinite Boolean sequence to be used by other programs. Thus, a random variable which takes a parameter of type α and ranges over values of type β can be represented in HOL by the following function.

$$\mathcal{F} : \alpha \to B^{\infty} \to \beta \times B^{\infty}$$

As an example, consider a Bernoulli($\frac{1}{2}$) random variable that returns 1 or 0 with equal probability $\frac{1}{2}$. It has been formalized in higher-order logic as follows

```
∀ s. bit s = if shd s then 1 else 0, stl s
```

where the functions shd and stl are the sequence equivalents of the list operations 'head' and 'tail', respectively. The function bit accepts the infinite Boolean sequence s and returns a pair. The first element of the returned pair is a random number that is either 0 or 1, depending on the Boolean value of the top most element of s. Whereas, the second element of the pair is the unused portion of the infinite Boolean sequence, which in this case is the tail of the sequence.

Once random variables are formalized, as mentioned above, we can utilize the formalized probability theory infrastructure to reason about their probabilistic properties. For example, the following Probability Mass Function (PMF) property can be verified for the function bit using the HOL theorem prover.

$\vdash \mathbb{P} \{s \mid \text{FST (bit s)} = 1\} = \frac{1}{2}$

where the function FST selects the first component of a pair and $\{x|C(x)\}$ represents a set of all x that satisfy the condition C.

The above approach has been successfully used to formally verify most basic probability theorems [13], such as the law of additivity, and conditional probability related properties [12]. For instance, the conditional probability has been formalized as:

Definition: *Conditional Probability*
$\vdash \forall$ A B.
    cond_prob A B = $\mathbb{P}(A \cap B) / \mathbb{P}(B)$

which plays a vital role in our work. Another frequently used formally verified theorem, in our work, is the *Total Probability Theorem* [12], which is described, for a finite, mutually exclusive, and exhaustive sequence B_i of events and an event A, as follows

$$Pr(A) = \sum_{i=0}^{n-1} Pr(B_i)Pr(A|B_i). \tag{1}$$

We also verified the following closely related property in HOL

$$Pr(B)Pr(A|B) = Pr(A)Pr(B|A) \tag{2}$$

where events A and B are measurable. This property will be used in verifying some important Markov chain properties later.

4   Formal Modeling of Discrete-Time Markov Chains

Given a probability space, a stochastic process $\{X_t : \Omega \to S\}$ represents a sequence of random variables X, where t represents the time that can be discrete (represented by non-negative integers) or continuous (represented by real numbers) [3]. The set of values taken by each X_t, commonly called states, is referred to as the *state space*. The *sample space* Ω of the process consists of all the possible sequences based on a given state space S. Now, based on these definitions, a *Markov process* can be defined as a stochastic process with Markov property. If a Markov process has finite or countably infinite state space, then it is called a *Markov chain* and satisfies the following Markov property.

For all k and p, if $p < t$, $k < p$ and x_{t+1} and all the states x_i ($i \in [k, t)$) are in the state space, then

$$Pr\{X_{t+1} = x_{t+1}|X_t = x_t, \ldots, X_p = x_p \ldots, X_k = x_k\} = \\ Pr\{X_{t+1} = x_{t+1}|X_t = x_t\}. \tag{3}$$

Additionally, if t ranges over nonnegative integers or, in other words, the time is a discrete quantity, and the states are in a finite state space, then such a Markov chain is called a *Finite-state Discrete-Time Markov Chain*. A Markov chain, if with the same conditional probabilities $\mathcal{P}r(X_{n+1} = a \mid X_n = b)$, is referred to as the *time-homogeneous Markov chain* [3]. Time-homogeneousity is an important concept in analyzing Markovian models and therefore, in our development, we focus on formalizing Time-homogeneous Discrete-Time Markov Chain with finite space, which we refer to in this paper as DTMC. A DTMC is usually expressed by specifying:

- an initial distribution defined by $\pi_0(s) = \mathcal{P}r(X_0 = s)$, $\pi_0(s) \geq 0 (\forall s \in S)$, and $\sum_{s \in S} \pi_0(s) = 1$.
- transition probabilities p_{ij} defined as $\forall i, j \in S$, $p_{ij} = \mathcal{P}r\{X_{t+1} = j | X_t = i\}$, $p_{ij} \geq 0$ and $\sum_{j \in S} p_{ij} = 1$

Based on the above mentioned definitions, we formalize the notion of a DTMC in HOL as the following predicate:

Definition 1:
Time_homogeneous Discrete-Time Markov Chain with Finite state space
⊢ ∀ f l x Linit Ltrans.
  Time_homo_mc f l x Linit Ltrans =
  (∀ i. (i < l) ⇒
    ($\mathbb{P}$\{s | FST (f 0 s) = x_i\} = EL i Linit) ∧
    ($\sum_{k=0}^{l-1}$(EL i Linit = 1))) ∧
  (∀ t i j. (i < l) ∧ (j < l) ⇒
    ($\mathbb{P}$\{s | FST (f (t + 1) s) = x_j\}|\{s | FST (f t s) = x_i\} =
         (EL (i * l + j) Ltrans)) ∧
    ($\sum_{k=0}^{l-1}$(EL (i * l + k) Ltrans = 1))) ∧
  (∀ t k. (k < l) ⇒ measurable \{s | FST (f t s) = x_k\}) ∧
  (∀ t. $\bigcup_{k=0}^{l-1}$ \{s | FST (f t s) = x_k\} = UNIV) ∧
  (∀ t u v. (u < l) ∧ (v < l) ∧ (u ≠ v) ⇒
    disjoint (\{s | FST (f t s) = x_u\} \{s | FST (f t s) = x_v\})) ∧
  (∀ i j m r t w L Lt.
    ((∀ k. (k ≤ r) ⇒ (EL k L < l)) ∧ (i < l) ∧ (j < l) ∧
    (Lt ⊆ [m, r]) ∧ (m ≤ r) ∧ (w + r < t)) ⇒
    ($\mathbb{P}$(\{s | FST (f (t + 1) s) = x_j\}|\{\{s | FST (f t s) = x_i\} ∩
      ($\bigcap_{k \in Lt}$ \{s | FST (f (w + k) s) = $x_{(EL\ k\ L)}$\})\}) =
    $\mathbb{P}$(\{s | FST (f (t + 1) s) = x_j\}|\{s | FST (f t s)= x_i\}))) ∧
  (∀ t n i j.
    (i < l) ∧ (j < l) ⇒
    ($\mathbb{P}$(\{s | FST (f (t + 1) s) = x_j\}|\{s | FST (f t s) = x_i\}) =
    $\mathbb{P}$(\{s | FST (f (n + 1) s) = x_j\}|\{s | FST (f n s) = x_i\})))

The function Time_homo_mc accepts a sequence of random variables f, the cardinality of the set of their possible states l, a function x that accepts the index and returns the state corresponding to the given DTMC, and two real lists: the initial states probability distribution Linit and the transition probabilities Ltrans.

The predicate `Time_homo_mc` adheres to following five conditions:

- the DTMC must follow the given initial distribution `Linit`, in which the summation of all the elements is 1. The transition probabilities `Ltrans`, in which the summation of each l elements is 1, is an intrinsic characteristic of a stochastic matrix.
- all events involving the Markov chain random variables are measurable ($\forall$ t k. (k < l) ⇒ measurable {s | FST (f t s) = x_k}).
- the union of all states forms the state space as a universal set `UNIV` ($\forall$ t. $\bigcup_{k=0}^{l-1}$ {s | FST (f t s) = x_k} = UNIV).
- the fifth condition ensures that the states in the state space of a given Markov chain are mutually exclusive ($\forall$ t u v. (u < l) ∧ (v < l) ∧ (u ≠ v) ⇒ disjoint ({s | FST (f t s) = x_u} {s | FST (f t s) = x_v})).
- the sixth condition corresponds to the memoryless property in Equation (3). Mathematically, if x_{t+1}, x_t, x_i and x_j are the states in the state space, and $w + k < t$, then the following equation holds

$$
\begin{aligned}
Pr\{X_{t+1} = x_{t+1} | X_t = x_t, \ldots, X_{w+k} = x_i, X_k = x_j, \ldots\} = \\
Pr\{X_{t+1} = x_{t+1} | X_t = x_t\}.
\end{aligned}
\tag{4}
$$

  We model history of states in our formalization by a list L, which contains the state elements ranging from 0 to $l-1$. Thus, the list L, with $r + 1$ elements or less, represents the indices of passed states and its elements have to be less than l ($\forall$ k. (k $\leq$ r) ⇒ (EL k L < l)). In ($\bigcap_{k \in Lt}$ {s | FST (f (w + k) s) = $x_{(EL \; k \; L)}$}), where the function (EL k L) returns the kth element of the list L, it gives a general time index of every event and a flexible length of the event sequence. (k ϵ Lt) makes sure that the passed states can be freely chosen from a set `Lt`, which includes natural numbers and is a subset of the interval [m, r] (Lt $\subseteq$ [m, r]). Condition (w + r < t) ensures that the states in this intersection set are passed states.
- the last condition represents the time homogeneousity of a discrete-time Markov chain f.

It is important to note that for generality our definition can work with discrete-time random variables of any data type.

5   Verification of Discrete-Time Markov Chain Properties

In this section, we present the formal verification of the most important properties of discrete-time Markov Chain.

5.1   Joint Probability of a Markov Chain

The joint probability of a Markov chain defines the probability of events involving two or more random variables associated with a chain. Joint probability is very useful in analyzing multi-stage experiments when an event chain happens, and reversible stochastic processes. Also, this concept is the basis for joint probability generating function, which is used in many different fields. Mathematically, the joint probability of $n + 1$ discrete random variables $X_0, X_1, \ldots, X_n$ in a Markov chain can be expressed as [3]:

$$Pr\{X_t = x_0, \cdots, X_{t+n} = x_n\} =$$
$$\prod_{k=0}^{n-1} Pr\{X_{t+k+1} = x_{k+1}|X_{t+k} = x_k\}Pr\{X_t = x_0\}. \tag{5}$$

In Equation (5), $Pr\{X_{t+k+1} = x_{k+1}|X_{t+k} = x_k\}$ can be found in the given one-step transition probabilities.

We formalize this property in HOL as following theorem:

Theorem 1: *Joint Probability*
```
⊢ ∀ f l x t n L Linit Ltrans.
    (Time_homo_mc f l x Linit Ltrans) ∧
    (EVERY (λa. a < l) L) ∧ (n + 1 ≤ LENGTH L) ⇒
    P(⋂ⁿ_{k=0}{s | FST (f (t + k) s) = x_(EL k L)}) =
    ∏ⁿ⁻¹_{k=0}P({s | FST (f (t + k + 1) s) = x_(EL (k+1) L)}|
        {s | FST (f (t + k) s) = x_(EL k L)})
    P{s | FST (f t s) = x_(EL 0 L)}
```

The variables above are used in the same context as Definition 1. The first assumption ensures that f is a Markov chain. All the elements of the indices sequence L are less than l and the length of L is larger than or equal to the length of the segment considered in the joint events. The conclusion of the theorem represents Equation (5) in higher-order logic based on the probability theory formalization, presented in Section 3. The proof of Theorem 1 is based on induction on the variable n, Equation (1) and some arithmetic reasoning.

5.2 Chapman-Kolmogorov Equation

The well-known Chapman-Kolmogorov equation [3] is a widely used property of time homogeneous Markov chains as it facilitates the use of a matrix theory for analyzing large Markov chains. It basically gives the probability of going from state i to j in $m+n$ steps. Assuming the first m steps take the system from state i to some intermediate state k, which is in the state space Ω and the remaining n steps then take the system from state k to j, we can obtain the desired probability by adding the probabilities associated with all the intermediate steps.

$$p_{ij}(m + n) = \sum_{k \in \Omega} p_{kj}(n)p_{ik}(m) \tag{6}$$

The notation $p_{ij}(n)$ denotes the n-step transition probabilities from state i to j.

$$p_{ij}(n) = Pr\{X_{t+n} = x_j|X_t = x_i\} \tag{7}$$

Based on Equation (6), and Definition 1, the Chapman-Kolmogorov equation is formalized as follows

Theorem 2: *Chapman-Kolmogorov Equation*
⊢ ∀ f i j x l m n Linit Ltrans.
  (Time_homo_mc f l x Linit Ltrans) ∧ (i < 1) ∧ (j < 1) ∧
  (∀ r. (r < 1) ⇒ (0 < ℙ{s | FST (f 0 s) = x_r})) ⇒
  ℙ({s | FST (f (m + n) s) = x_j}|{s | FST (f 0 s) = x_i}) =
  $\sum_{k=0}^{l-1}$(ℙ({s | FST (f n s) = x_j}|{s | FST (f 0 s) = x_k})
      ℙ({s | FST (f m s) = x_k}|{s | FST (f 0 s) = x_i}))

The variables m and n denote the steps between two states and both of them represent time. The first assumption ensures that the random process f is a time homogeneous DTMC, using Definition 1. The following two assumptions, $i < l$ and $j < l$, define the allowable bounds for the index variables. The last assumption is used to exclude the case when $Pr\{X_0 = x_j\} = 0$. Because it makes no sense to analyze the conditional probability when the probability of a state existing is 0. The conclusion of the theorem formally represents Equation (6).

The proof of Theorem 2 again involves induction on the variable n and both of the base and step cases are discharged using the following lemma.

Lemma 1: *Multistep Transition Probability*
⊢ ∀ f i j x n Linit Ltrans.
  (Time_homo_mc f l x Linit Ltrans) ∧ (i < 1) ∧ (j < 1) ∧
  (0 < ℙ{s | FST (f 0 s) = x_i}) ⇒
  ℙ({s | FST (f (n + 1) s) = x_j}|{s | FST (f 0 s) = x_i}) =
  $\sum_{k=0}^{l-1}$ℙ({s | FST (f 1 s) = x_j}|{s | FST (f 0 s) = x_k})
      ℙ({s | FST (f n s) = x_k}|{s | FST (f 0 s) = x_i})

The proof of Lemma 1 is primarily based on the Total Probability theorem (1).

5.3   Absolute Probabilities

The unconditional probabilities associated with a Markov chain are referred to as the absolute probabilities [3]. If the initial probability distribution of the system being in a state, which has index k is given by $Pr\{X_0 = x_k\}$, then the absolute probability of the system being in state j is given by

$$p_j(n) = Pr\{X_n = x_j\} = \sum_{k=0}^{l-1} Pr\{X_0 = x_k\}Pr\{X_n = x_j | X_0 = x_k\}. \qquad (8)$$

This shows that, given an initial probability distribution and the n-step transition probabilities, the absolute probabilities in the state j after n step from the start time 0 can be obtained by using this equation.

Based on our formal Markov chain definition, this property has been formalized as the following theorem:

Theorem 3: *Absolute Probability*

⊢ ∀ f j x l n t Linit Ltrans.
(Time_homo_mc f l x Linit Ltrans) ∧ (j < l) ∧
(∀ r. (r < l) ⇒ (0 < $\mathbb{P}$\{s | FST (f 0 s) = x_r\})) ⇒
$\mathbb{P}$\{s | FST (f n s) = x_j\} =
$\sum_{k=0}^{l-1}\mathbb{P}$\{s | FST (f 0 s) = x_k\}
$\mathbb{P}$(\{s | FST (f n s) = x_j\}|\{s | FST (f 0 s) = x_k\})

The proof of Theorem 3 is based on the Total Probability theorem along with some basic arithmetic and probability theoretic reasoning.

5.4   Steady State Probabilities

In many applications, analyzing the stability of Markovian models is of prime importance. For example, we are interested in the probability of states as time tends to infinity under certain conditions, like irreducibility and aperiodicity.

Let X_n, $n \geq 0$, be a Markov chain having state space Ω and one-step transition probability $P(x, y)$ for going from state with value x to a state with value y. If $\pi(x)$, $x \in \Omega$, are nonnegative numbers summing to one, and if

$$\pi(y) = \sum_{x\in\Omega} \pi(x)P(x,y), y \in \Omega \qquad (9)$$

then π is called a *stationary distribution*. The corresponding HOL definition is as follows. In this definition, x_k and x_i represent the variables x and y of Equation (9), respectively.

Definition 2: *Stationary Distribution*

⊢ ∀ p f n x l. stationary_dist p f n x l =
∀ i.
(0 ≤ (p x_i)) ∧($\sum_{k=0}^{l-1}$ (p x_k) = 1) ∧
(p x_i = $\sum_{k=0}^{l-1}$(p x_k)$\mathbb{P}$(\{s | FST (f (n + 1) s) = x_i\}|
\{s | FST (f n s) = x_k\}))

As a finite Markov chain, the steady state probabilities are defined to be a vector $V_j = \lim_{n\to\infty}\mathbb{P}(n)$. For a time homogeneous finite Markov chain with one-step transition probability $P(x, y)$, if V_j exists for all $j \in \Omega$, then V_j is known as the stationary probability vector of that Markov chain. In other words, V_j is a stationary distribution of a Markov chain if

- $\lim_{n\to\infty}p_j(n) = \sum_{i=0}^{l-1}\lim_{n\to\infty}p_i(n)p_{ij}$, $j = 0, 1, 2, \cdots$, (1 - 1)
- $\sum_{i=0}^{l-1} \lim_{n\to\infty} p_i(n) = 1$
- $0 \leq \lim_{n\to\infty} p_j(n)$

The steady state probability is formalized in HOL as follows

Theorem 4: *Steady State Probability*

⊢ ∀ f n x l Linit Ltrans.

```
(Time_homo_mc f l x Linit Ltrans) ∧
(∀ x j. ∃u. ℙ{s | FST (f n s) = xⱼ} → u) ⇒
(stationary_dist (λx k. limₙ→∞ℙ{s | FST (f n s) = xₖ}) f n x l)
```

The proof of Theorem 4 is primarily based on the linearity of limit of a sequence and the linearity of real summation.

5.5   Generalized Stationary Distribution

If a Markov chain with state space Ω and one-step transition probability $P(x, y)$ has a probability π that satisfies the detailed balance equations, given below, then this distribution π is stationary for $P(x, y)$. This theorem is called a *generalized stationary theorem* and can be mathematically described as follows:

$$\pi(x)P(x, y) = \pi(y)P(y, x), \forall x, y \in \Omega \tag{10}$$

The detailed balance equations can be formalized as follows, where x_i and x_j represent variables x and y of Equations (10), respectively.

Definition 3: *Detailed Balance Equations*
```
⊢ ∀ p f l. db_equations p f l =
  ∀ x i j n.
    (i < l) ∧ (j < l) ∧
    ((p xᵢ)ℙ({s | FST (f (n + 1) s) = xⱼ}|{s | FST (f n s) = xᵢ}) =
    (p xⱼ)ℙ({s | FST (f (n + 1) s) = xᵢ}|{s | FST (f n s) = xⱼ}))
```

The first input variable p in the above predicate is a function that accepts the state as the parameter and returns the probability given in Equation (10). Based on this definition, the stationary theorem can be defined as follows:

Theorem 5: *Generalized Stationary Distribution*
```
⊢ ∀ f x l n Linit Ltrans.
  (db_equations (λx i. ℙ{s | FST (f n s) = xᵢ}) f l) ∧
  (Time_homo_mc f l x Linit Ltrans) ⇒
  (stationary_dist (λx k. ℙ{s | FST (f n s) = xₖ}) f n x l)
```

Here, $\pi(x)$ is specified as a function $\lambda x\ i.\ \mathbb{P}\{s\ |\ FST\ (f\ n\ s) = x_i\}$. The proof of Theorem 5 is based on the Total Probability theorem, given in Equation (1), and the following Lemma:

Lemma 3: *Summation of Transition Probability*
```
⊢ ∀ f x l i n Linit Ltrans.
  (Time_homo_mc f l x Linit Ltrans) ∧ (i < l) ⇒
  ∑ⱼ₌₀^{l−1}ℙ({s | FST (f n s) = xⱼ}|{s | FST (f 0 s) = xᵢ} = 1
```

The proof script[1] for the formalization of Markov chain, presented in this section, consists of approximately 2600 lines of HOL code. These results not only ensure the correctness of our formal Markov chain definitions, presented in Section 4, but also play a vital role in analyzing real-world systems that are modeled by DTMC, as will be demonstrated in the next section.

---
[1] Available at http://users.encs.concordia.ca/~liy_liu/code.html

6   Application: Binary Communication Channel

In order to illustrate the usefulness of the proposed approach, we use our results to analyze a simplified binary communication channel model [28]. Also, we compare the analysis of the same example using probabilistic model checking.

A binary communication channel is a channel with binary inputs and outputs. The transmission channel is assumed to be noisy or imperfect, i.e., it is likely that the receiver gets the wrong digit. This channel can be modeled as a two-state time homogenous DTMC with the following state transition probabilities.

$$\mathcal{P}r\{X_{n+1} = 0 \mid X_n = 0\} = 1 - a; \qquad \mathcal{P}r\{X_{n+1} = 1 \mid X_n = 0\} = a;$$
$$\mathcal{P}r\{X_{n+1} = 0 \mid X_n = 1\} = b; \qquad \mathcal{P}r\{X_{n+1} = 1 \mid X_n = 1\} = 1 - b$$

The corresponding state diagram and channel diagram are given in Fig. 1. The binary communication channel is widely used in telecommunication theory as more complicated channels are modeled by cascading several of them. Here, variables X_{n-1} and X_n denote the digits leaving the systems $(n-1)^{th}$ stage and entering the nth one, respectively. a and b are the crossover bit error probabilities. Because variables X_0 is also a random variable, the initial state is not determined, $\mathcal{P}r\,(X_0 = 0)$ and $\mathcal{P}r\,(X_0 = 1)$ could not be 0 or 1.

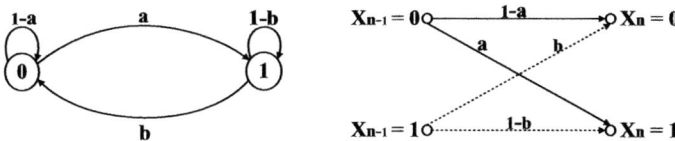

Fig. 1. State Diagram and Channel Diagram of the Binary Channel Model

Although the initial distribution is unknown, the given binary communication channel has been formalized in HOL as a generic model, using Definition 2.

Definition 4: *Binary Communication Channel Model*
⊢ ∀ f x a b p q.
   (binary_communication_channel_model f a b p q) =
     (Time_homo_mc f (2:num) x [p; q] [1 - a; a; b; 1 - b]) ∧
     (|1 - a - b| < 1) ∧ (0 ≤ a ≤ 1) ∧ (0 ≤ b ≤ 1) ∧
     (p + q = 1) ∧ (0 < p < 1) ∧ (0 < q < 1)

In this formal model, variable f represents the Markov chain and variables a, b, p and q are parameters of the functions of initial distribution and transition probabilities. The variable x represents a function that provides the state at a given index.

The first condition ensures that f is a time-homogeneous DTMC, with which the number of states 1 is 2, because there are only two states in the state space. List [p; q] corresponds to Linit in Definition 1 and another list [1 - a; a; b; 1 - b] gives the one-step transition probability matrix by combining all the rows into a list and corresponds to `Ltrans` in Definition 1. The next three conditions define the allowable intervals for parameters a and b to restrict the probability terms in [0,1]. It is important to note that, $|1 - a - b| < 1$ ensures that both a and b cannot be equal to 0 and 1 at the same time and thus avoids the zero transition probabilities. The remaining conditions correspond to one-step transition probabilities.

Next, we use our formal model to reason about the following properties.

Theorem 6: n^{th} *step Transition Probabilities*
$\vdash \forall$ f x a b n p q.
`(binary_communication_channel_model f x a b p q)` $\Rightarrow$
$(\mathbb{P}(\{s|\text{FST (f n s)}=x_0\}|\{s|\text{FST (f 0 s))}=x_0\}) = \frac{b+a(1-a-b)^n}{a+b}) \land$
$(\mathbb{P}(\{s|\text{FST (f n s)}=x_1\}|\{s|\text{FST (f 0 s))}=x_0\}) = \frac{a-a(1-a-b)^n}{a+b}) \land$
$(\mathbb{P}(\{s|\text{FST (f n s)}=x_0\}|\{s|\text{FST (f 0 s))}=x_1\}) = \frac{b-b(1-a-b)^n}{a+b}) \land$
$(\mathbb{P}(\{s|\text{FST (f n s)}=x_1\}|\{s|\text{FST (f 0 s))}=x_1\}) = \frac{a+b(1-a-b)^n}{a+b})$

Theorem 7: *Limiting State Probabilities*
$\vdash \forall$ f x a b p q.
`(binary_communication_channel_model f x a b p q)` $\Rightarrow$
$(\lim_{n\to\infty}\mathbb{P}(\{s|\text{FST (f n s)}=x_0\}|\{s|\text{FST (f 0 s))}=x_0\}) = \frac{b}{a+b}) \land$
$(\lim_{n\to\infty}\mathbb{P}(\{s|\text{FST (f n s)}=x_1\}|\{s|\text{FST (f 0 s))}=x_0\}) = \frac{a}{a+b}) \land$
$(\lim_{n\to\infty}\mathbb{P}(\{s|\text{FST (f n s)}=x_0\}|\{s|\text{FST (f 0 s))}=x_1\}) = \frac{b}{a+b}) \land$
$(\lim_{n\to\infty}\mathbb{P}(\{s|\text{FST (f n s)}=x_1\}|\{s|\text{FST (f 0 s))}=x_1\}) = \frac{a}{a+b})$

Theorem 6 has been verified by performing induction on n and then applying Theorem 2 and Lemma 3 and along with some arithmetic reasoning. Theorem 6 is then used to verify Theorem 7 along with limit of real sequence principles.

This small 2-state Markov chain case study clearly illustrates the main strength of the proposed theorem proving based technique against the probabilistic model checking approach, where we verified the desired probabilistic characteristics as generic theorems that are universally quantified for all allowable values of variables a, b and n. These variables can also be specialized to specific values to obtain corresponding precise conditional probabilistic values.

7   Conclusions

This paper presents a higher-order-logic formalization of time homogeneous DTMC. We built upon this formalization and verified fundamental DTMC properties using the HOL theorem prover. This infrastructure can be used to formally model systems, which can be expressed as DTMC and formally reason about their probabilistic properties. Due to the inherent soundness of this approach, it is guaranteed to provide exact answers, which is a very useful feature while analyzing the Markovian models associated with safety or mission-critical systems.

For illustration, we analyzed a binary communication channel. Our results exactly matched the corresponding paper-and-pencil based analysis, which ascertains the precise nature of the proposed approach.

To the best of our knowledge, the proposed work is the first of its kind and opens the doors of a new but very promising research direction, i.e., integrating HOL theorem proving in the domain of analyzing Markov chain based system models. We are currently working on extending the set of formally verified properties regarding DTMCs and applying a matrix theory on this set of properties, which will enable us to target a wider set of systems. We also plan to build upon the formalization of continuous random variables [10] and statistical properties [10,11] to formalize Continuous-Time Markov chains to be able to formally reason about statistical characteristics of a wider range of Markovian models.

Acknowledgment. We would like to thank Dr. Shengzhen Jin from the Chinese Academy of Sciences and Dr. Dongyu Qiu from Concordia University, for the useful discussions on Markov Chain theory and their feedback on the reported formalization.

References

1. Baier, C., Haverkort, B., Hermanns, H., Katoen, J.P.: Model Checking Algorithms for Continuous time Markov Chains. IEEE Transactions on Software Engineering 29(4), 524–541 (2003)
2. Baier, C., Katoen, J.: Principles of Model Checking. MIT Press, Cambridge (2008)
3. Bhattacharya, R.N., Waymire, E.C.: Stochastic Processes with Applications. John Wiley & Sons, Chichester (1990)
4. Ciardo, G., Muppala, J.K., Trivedi, K.S.: SPNP: Stochastic Petri Net Package. In: Workshop on Petri Nets and Performance Models, pp. 142–151 (1989)
5. de Alfaro, L.: Formal Verification of Probabilistic Systems. PhD Thesis, Stanford University, Stanford, USA (1997)
6. Dingle, N.J., Knottenbelt, W.J., Harrison, P.G.: HYDRA - Hypergraph-based Distributed Response-time Analyser. In: International Conference on Parallel and Distributed Processing Technique and Applications, pp. 215–219 (2003)
7. Gordon, M.J.C.: Mechanizing Programming Logics in Higher-Order Logic. In: Current Trends in Hardware Verification and Automated Theorem Proving, pp. 387–439. Springer, Heidelberg (1989)
8. GreatSPN (2011), http://www.di.unito.it/~greatspn/index.html
9. Haas, P.J.: Stochastic Petri Nets: Modelling, Stability, Simulation. Springer, Heidelberg (2002)
10. Hasan, O.: Formal Probabilistic Analysis using Theorem Proving. PhD Thesis, Concordia University, Montreal, QC, Canada (2008)
11. Hasan, O., Abbasi, N., Akbarpour, B., Tahar, S., Akbarpour, R.: Formal Reasoning about Expectation Properties for Continuous Random Variables. In: Cavalcanti, A., Dams, D.R. (eds.) FM 2009. LNCS, vol. 5850, pp. 435–450. Springer, Heidelberg (2009)
12. Hasan, O., Tahar, S.: Reasoning about Conditional Probabilities in a Higher-Order-Logic Theorem Prover. Journal of Applied Logic 9(1), 23–40 (2011)
13. Hurd, J.: Formal Verification of Probabilistic Algorithms. PhD Thesis, University of Cambridge, UK (2002)
14. Jonassen, D.H., Tessmer, M., Hannum, W.H.: Task Analysis Methods for Instructional Design. Lawrence Erlbaum, Mahwah (1999)

15. Knottenbelt, W.J.: Generalised Markovian Analysis of Timed Transition Systems. Master's thesis, Department of Computer Science, University of Cape Town, South Africa (1996)
16. MacKay, D.J.C.: Introduction to Monte Carlo Methods. In: Learning in Graphical Models. NATO Science Series, pp. 175–204. Kluwer Academic Press, Dordrecht (1998)
17. MARCA (2011), http://www4.ncsu.edu/~billy/marca/marca.html
18. Mhamdi, T., Hasan, O., Tahar, S.: On the Formalization of the Lebesgue Integration Theory in HOL. In: Kaufmann, M., Paulson, L.C. (eds.) ITP 2010. LNCS, vol. 6172, pp. 387–402. Springer, Heidelberg (2010)
19. Mobius (2011), http://www.mobius.illinois.edu/
20. Parker, D.: Implementation of Symbolic Model Checking for Probabilistic System. PhD Thesis, University of Birmingham, UK (2001)
21. PEPA (2011), http://www.dcs.ed.ac.uk/pepa/
22. PRISM (2011), http://www.prismmodelchecker.org/
23. RELEX (2011), http://www.ptc.com/products/relex/markov
24. Rutten, J., Kwaiatkowska, M., Normal, G., Parker, D.: Mathematical Techniques for Analyzing Concurrent and Probabilisitc Systems. CRM Monograph Series, vol. 23. American Mathematical Society, Providence (2004)
25. Sczittnick, M.: MACOM - A Tool for Evaluating Communication Systems. In: International Conference on Modelling Techniques and Tools for Computer Performance Evaluation, pp. 7–10 (1994)
26. Sen, K., Viswanathan, M., Agha, G.: VESTA: A Statistical Model-Checker and Analyzer for Probabilistic Systems. In: IEEE International Conference on the Quantitative Evaluation of Systems, pp. 251–252 (2005)
27. Steward, W.J.: Introduction to the Numerical Solution of Markov Chain. Princeton University Press, Princeton (1994)
28. Trivedi, K.S.: Probability and Statistics with Reliability, Queuing, and Computer Science Applications. John Wiley & Sons, Chichester (2002)

An Alternative Definition for Timed Automata Composition

Jean-Paul Bodeveix, Abdeldjalil Boudjadar, and Mamoun Filali

IRIT, University of Toulouse, France
{firstname.lastname}@irit.fr

Abstract. Due to the complexity and time-based aspects of modern systems, compositional verification and abstraction-based verification techniques have been proposed to deal with these issues by considering the verification of system components separately (composition) and working on more abstract structures (refinement). In this paper, we propose a revised definition of the product of timed automata (TA) and give a compositional semantics based on individual timed transition system (TTS) semantics. Moreover, we establish a new compositional refinement property where the refinement of timed systems composition is given by the refinement of each component. For this purpose, starting from the basic timed transition systems, we introduce an original composition operator endowed with good properties (associativity, trace inclusion, etc) and supporting communications via shared variables and synchronization of actions. Thereafter, we instantiate this framework for timed automata where we show how to associate such a TTS with two-levels static priority (committedness) to a TA and establish the compositionality theorem introduced by [5] with the mentioned refinement property.

Keywords: composition, refinement, timed automata.

1 Introduction

Timed automata have been studied for a long time now. However, a compositional framework is lacking. Until recently, the semantics of networks of timed automata were given in a monolithic way (vs a compositional way). Recently, [5] have analyzed thoroughly the problem and criticized existing solutions.

During the last two decades, software design has been known a surge of progress which leads to build complex systems through assemblies of components. In order to make the verification of such systems more efficient, compositional verification has been introduced. In fact, compositional verification [9] reduces the problem of checking whether a system $S = S_1 \parallel \ldots \parallel S_n$ satisfies a property P to the simple problem of checking whether each component S_i satisfies a property P_i where P is a composition of P_i. It is important to note that S is not actually constructed. If we consider the refinement property, this method can be reformulated as $A = A_1 \parallel \ldots \parallel A_n$ is refined by S if each component S_i refines A_i. Defining such a composition and finding a

T. Bultan and P.-A. Hsiung (Eds.): ATVA 2011, LNCS 6996, pp. 105–119, 2011.

suitable refinement relation for more complex models, such as timed automata
with invariants, communication and shared variables, became more sophisticated. In this paper, we are interested in setting a formal framework for reasoning
about timed automata. Thus, we can summarize our proposal in the following:

- A compositional product of extended
  symbolic timed transition systems with
  communication via shared variables
  and synchronization of actions where
  the associativity and trace inclusion
  properties hold.
- A refinement relation depending on the
  semantics of the former parallel composition operator and stating that the
  refinement of timed systems composition is given by the refinement of each
  component.
- An instantiation of the former compositional framework for timed automata
  composition.

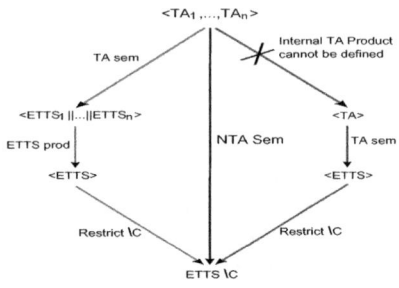

Fig. 1. TA product semantics

On a synchronization, to enable the receiver component to consider the updates
made by the sender action on shared variables, we define a new semantics for
the composition where the input transition guard is only checked after taking
into account the effect of the output transition action. It comes to applying the
join operator of relational algebra to compose send and receive actions.

Finally, thanks to this framework, a network of timed automata N satisfies a
property P on a global space if the network of timed automata N' corresponding
to the refinement of all TA of N satisfies P. Also, we revisit the results proposed
by [5]. The rest of the paper is organized as follows. Section 2 presents related
work. In Section 3, we state the problem of the interaction of communicating
timed automata and motivate our proposal. Section 4 presents the formal basis of
our work by introducing timed extensions of Labelled Transition Systems (LTS),
sufficient conditions for bisimilarity and define associative products. Section 5
introduces Timed Automata (TA) and Networks of Timed Automata (NTA),
their different ETTS (Extended Timed Transition Systems) semantics and establish relations between them as illustrated by Fig.1. Section 6 gathers some
important theorems established within our framework.

2   Related Work

Composition and refinement of extended timed systems, particularly timed automata, have been studied [7,2,11,5,4] during the last decade. However, a compositional framework is lacking. About this subject, we are only interested in
work [2,5] focusing on the composition of extended timed systems with communication, committedness and variables.

The authors of [2] define a framework with a non compositional semantics for UPPAAL timed automata product with a naive composition of send/receive actions. On a synchronization, such a model checks the guards of the involved transitions before applying any action. Moreover, the resulting transition action is the composition of send and receive actions.

[5] describes a framework for compositional abstraction and defines a parallel composition operator for UPPAAL timed automata. To establish their results, the authors of [5] restrict both TA and TTS structures so that their input transition guards and location invariant do not refer to shared variables. Furthermore, in TA a committed location should have an outgoing transition.

In this paper, we propose a new composition approach where the input transition guard is checked after taking into account the effect of the output transition action. Otherwise stated, the output transition action is simulated, it becomes effective if the guard evaluates to true. In fact, we consider a more abstract notion of timed transition systems. These changes solve the previous restrictions. Thus, our result is in fact independent of the way the pairs (guard/action) of the two timed automata are composed.

3   A New Composition of Timed Automata

This section motivates our work informally. We explain our proposal and compare it with [2,5]. Then, we present a synchronization pattern implemented thanks to our proposal.

3.1   Differences with Existing Approaches

Defining the product of timed automata is not an easy task because of the interaction of communicating processes through global variables. We illustrate this problem in Fig.2 that shows two timed automata where e is a shared variable initialized to 0. By now, the notation $g/l/a$ states a transition guarded by g, labelled by l and with an action a. Moreover, $c!$ (*output*) and $c?$ (*input*) are corresponding to a send/receive handshake communication over a channel c.

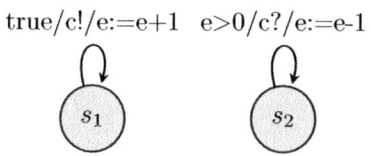

Fig. 2. Synchronization skeleton

1. When submitting this model (Fig.2.) to the UPPAAL tool, it blocks because UPPAAL checks that the guards of all involved transitions hold which is not the case in s_2 when $e = 0$. To sum up, Uppaal synchronization can be described by: $g_s/c!/a_s \parallel g_r/c?/a_r = g_s \wedge g_r/\tau/a_s; a_r$
2. [5] does not allow the skeleton of Fig.2. because the guard of the input transition ($e > 0$) depends on the shared variable e. The (guard/action) tuples are composable if $[a_s]g_r \equiv g_r$ as $g_s/c!/a_s \parallel g_r/c?/a_r = g_s \wedge [a_s]g_r/\tau/a_s; a_r$. Under this condition, this definition is equivalent to that of Uppaal.

We propose an alternative approach which changes the UPPAAL semantics: the input transition guard is checked after the execution of the output transition action, (here e:=e+1) which updates the value of the variable e to 1. Therefore, the guard $e > 0$ of the input transition will be satisfied. This proposal can be written as $g_s/c!/a_s \parallel g_r/c?/a_r = g_s \wedge [a_s]g_r/\tau/a_s; a_r$ where restrictions of [5] have been suppressed.

3.2   Benefits of the Proposal

Thanks to this new definition of timed automata composition, which consists in evaluating the guard of the receive event only after the assignment of the corresponding send event has been performed, we establish genuine composition and refinement results (Theorems 5 and 6). Moreover, the implementation of a conditional reception through shared variables becomes easy.

Conditional reception. Currently Uppaal offers pure synchronization only. We consider here the extension which consists in superposing message exchange to synchronization. Moreover, thanks to the proposed semantics, *conditional reception* where reception is enabled only if a condition over the received message is true, can be implemented easily. The following table, proposes a syntax and a translation for this construction, where v is a local variable, $C(v)$ is a boolean expression depending on v and local variables of the receiver, sh_c is a fresh shared

syntax	translation using our proposal
$\circ \xrightarrow{g/c!e/a} \circ$	$\circ \xrightarrow{g/c!/sh_c:=e;a} \circ$
$\circ \xrightarrow{g/c?v/a \text{ where } C(v)} \circ$	$\circ \xrightarrow{g \wedge C(sh_c)/c?/v:=sh_c;a} \circ$

variable dedicated to the communication over the synchronization channel c and e is an expression. We remark that such a feature is especially interesting for implementing resource allocators where requests are accepted according to the resources currently available. Actually, this synchronization pattern requires a guard depending on the local state but also a condition depending on the request. The following transitions illustrate such a pattern[1] .

client requests	allocator
$\circ \xrightarrow{R!100} \circ$ $\circ \xrightarrow{R!c} \circ$	$\circ \xrightarrow{R?g \text{ where } g\leq a/a:=a-g} \circ$

3.3   Transformation to Basic Uppaal

In order to reuse the Uppaal model checker, we outline a model transformation converting our proposal to Uppaal. The basic idea of such a transformation is to move the "late" reception guards evaluations to the sending point. We consider three steps:

---

[1] We use the conventions that an omitted guard defines a $\top$ guard and an omitted action defines a skip action.

Step 1 local variables occurring in guards of receptions become global. This transformation allows to evaluate guards out of their local initial context.

Step 2 distinguishing receptions. This transformation allows to retrieve the succeeding reception. Each reception is distinguished by a dedicated channel.

Step 3 moving reception conditions. The reception condition is moved to the sender side after calculating the effect of the sender command.

We summarize the preceding steps by the following table[2].

Step 1		
i: $\begin{array}{c}\text{int } l;\\ \circ \xrightarrow{g_r(l)/c?/a_r(l)} \circ\end{array}$	$\rightarrow$	i: $\begin{array}{c}\text{int } i\_l;\\ \circ \xrightarrow{g_r(i\_l)/c?/a_r(i\_l)} \circ\end{array}$

Step 2		Step 3	
$g/c!/a_s$ $\rightarrow$ $[\![_i g/c_i!/a_s$		$g/c_i!/a$ $\rightarrow$ $g \wedge [a]g_i/c_i!/a$	
$g_i/c?/a_i$ $\quad$ $g_i/c_i?/a_i$		$g_i/c_i?/a_i$ $\quad$ $\top/c_i?/a_i$	

Remark. The semantics of the conditional reception (3.2) as a translation to basic Uppaal would be much more complicated than the one relying on our semantics. Furthermore, we envision to formally validate these translations in a future work. We give them as a justification for modifying Uppaal semantics.

4 Transition System Extensions

Transition systems are an elegant model to represent behavioral aspects of active systems. They are essentially composed of states and transitions. States correspond to the configurations reached by the modeled system whereas transitions link these states through the actions made by such a system. Here, we introduce composable symbolic transition systems and define their associative product.

4.1 Labelled Transition Systems

Labelled transition systems [1] are the reference model used to express and to compare behaviors.

Definition 1 (LTS). *A labelled transition system (LTS) over an alphabet Σ is a triple $\langle Q, Q^0 \subseteq Q, \rightarrow \subseteq Q \times \Sigma \times Q \rangle$ where Q is the state space, Q^0 is the set of initial states and $\rightarrow$ the transition relation. We note $q \xrightarrow{l} q'$ for $(q, l, q') \in \rightarrow$.*

Definition 2 (Simulation). *Given two transition systems $T_c = \langle Q_c, Q_c^0, \rightarrow_c \rangle$ (concrete) and $T_a = \langle Q_a, Q_a^0, \rightarrow_a \rangle$ (abstract), T_a simulates T_c through a relation R, denoted by $T_a \preceq_R T_c$, if:*

- $\forall q_c \in Q_c^0$, *there exists* $q_a \in Q_a^0$ *such that* $R(q_c, q_a)$,

---

[2] $[\![]\!]$ denotes the non deterministic choice operator.

- $\forall q_c\ q_c'\ q_a\ l$, if $q_c \xrightarrow{l}_c q_c'$ and $R(q_c, q_a)$ there exists $q_a' \in Q_a$ such that $q_a \xrightarrow{l}_a q_a'$ and $R(q_c', q_a')$.

Two LTSs T and T' are bisimilar through a relation $R \subseteq Q \times Q'$ which we note $T \sim_R T'$, if $T \preceq_R T'$ and $T' \preceq_{R^{-1}} T$.

4.2   Composable Labelled Transition Systems

In order to make transition systems communicate, we specialize the state space and the alphabet to allow several communication protocols:

- via a shared space: we distinguish a local and a global state space and we introduce abstract actions that update the global state space. These actions may be non-deterministic and blocking.
- via CCS-like channels: we introduce a set C of send-receive channels where two transitions synchronize if their actions are complementary. The resulting transition of such a synchronization corresponds to an internal transition in the composition.
- via CSP-like synchronization: we introduce a set S of many-to-many synchronization events. Such a synchronization is used to model a system transition where all processes make a lock-step [13]. Here, we will use such a synchronization to model the evolution of time.

Furthermore, the concept of Committedness is a high level mechanism to express that committed transitions are given priority. Committedness-based hiding is supposed to be static: a non firable committed transition due to a blocking action can hide a firable non committed transition. A location q is said to be committed ($Comm(q) = \top$) if at least one of its outgoing transitions is committed.

Definition 3 (CLTS). *A composable LTS (CLTS) over a shared space $\mathcal{G}$, an action language[3] $\mathcal{A}$, a set of one-to-one channels C and a set of synchronization events S is a tuple $\langle Q, q^0, G^0 \subseteq \mathcal{G}, \to \rangle$ where:*

- *Q is the set of locations (local states) and $q^0 \in Q$ is the initial location,*
- *G^0 is the set of initial global states,*
- *$\to \subseteq Q \times \mathcal{L} \times \mathcal{A} \times \mathbb{B} \times Q$ is the transition relation where $\mathcal{L} = C? \cup C! \cup S \cup \{\tau\}$ is the set of labels, $C!$, resp $C?$, is the set of sending, resp receiving, events through channels of C and τ is the internal event. The boolean component specifies the transition committedness.*

Furthermore, a CLTS must satisfy a wellformedness condition: synchronization transitions (with a label in S) are supposed to be non committed.

We note $q \xrightarrow{l/a}_b q'$ for $(q, l, a, b, q') \in \to$. If absent, b is considered to be false. Therefore, we define formally the predicate $Comm$ by:

$$Comm(q) = \begin{cases} \top & \text{if } \exists\ l\ a\ q' \mid q \xrightarrow{l/a}_\top q' \\ \bot & \text{else} \end{cases}$$

---

[3] The action language $\mathcal{A}$ will be defined in section 5.4.

The semantics of a CLTS is specified by its associated LTS defined below. It allows comparing CLTSs through simulation and bisimulation.

Definition 4 (Semantics of a CLTS). *Given a global state space $\mathcal{G}$ and the semantics of the action language $[\![.]\!] : \mathcal{A} \to 2^{\mathcal{G} \times \mathcal{G}}$, the semantics of the CLTS $\langle Q, q^0, G^0, \to \rangle$ is the LTS $\langle \ Q \times \mathcal{G}, \ \{q^0\} \times G^0, \ \{((q,g), l, (q', g')) \mid \exists \ a \in \mathcal{A}, \exists \ b,$ $q \xrightarrow{l/a}_b q'$ and $(g, g') \in [\![a]\!]$ and $\neg b \Rightarrow q \not\xrightarrow{\cdot/\cdot}_\top \} \ \rangle$ where $q \not\xrightarrow{\cdot/\cdot}_\top$ means that there is no outgoing committed transition from q.*

The presence of the committed flag makes the semantics of CLTSs rather complex. In order to avoid managing priorities during simulation proofs, we consider a sufficient condition expressed as the simulation of the corresponding LTSs where the committed flag is considered as part of the label. The negated condition appearing in CLTSs semantics is replaced by a condition over committed states.

Definition 5 (Sufficient simulation condition). *Given two CLTSs T_c (concrete) and T_a (abstract) and refinement relations $R_l \subseteq Q_c \times Q_a$, $R_g \subseteq \mathcal{G}_c \times \mathcal{G}_a$ where $\mathcal{G}_c$, resp $\mathcal{G}_a$, is the global space of T_c, resp T_a. T_a simulates T_c, we note $T_a \preceq_{R_g, R_l} T_c$, if*

1. *The associated LTSs satisfy the sufficient condition for simulation, i.e:*
   - $R_l(q_c^0, q_a^0)$,
   - $\forall x \in G_c^0, \exists y \in G_a^0 \mid R_g(x, y)$,
   - $\forall q_c, q_c', q_a, l, a_1 \in A, b, x, x', y,$ if $q_c \xrightarrow{l/a_1}_b^c q_c'$ and $(x, x') \in [\![a_1]\!]$, $R_l(q_c, q_a), R_g(x, y)$ there exist $q_a' \in Q_a, a_2 \in A, y'$ such that $q_a \xrightarrow{l/a_2}_b^a q_a'$
     $\land \ (y, y') \in [\![a_2]\!] \land R_l(q_c', q_a') \land R_g(x', y')$
2. $\forall q_c \ q_a, R_l(q_c, q_a) \Rightarrow Comm(q_a) \Rightarrow Comm(q_c)$.

Theorem 1. *If $T_a \preceq_{R_g, R_l} T_c$ then T_a and T_c are similar, i.e. their associated LTSs are similar.*

Proof (sketch). Given a concrete LTS transition labeled (l, b), a concrete CLTS transition with label l and committedness b starts from the same state and is not hidden. The sufficient condition (1) ensures the existence of an abstract CLTS transition with the same label and committedness. If it is not hidden, it is present in the LTS, which establishes the refinement property. Otherwise, it is not committed ($b = \bot$) and a committed transition hides it. Thus, the abstract state is committed which implies the committedness of the concrete state (condition 2). It means that some concrete outgoing transition is committed which would hide the given concrete transition. □

4.3 Product of Composable Labelled Transition Systems

The product of composable transition systems is parameterized by two internal operations defined on the action language:

- $a_1 \triangleright a_2$ is used to compose actions associated to send-receive communication.
- $a_1 \odot a_2$ is used to compose actions associated to global synchronizations (lock-step). This operation is supposed to be commutative (resp. associative) in order to establish the commutativity (resp. the associativity) of the product.

It follows that our definition of the product is a generalized version of that given in [5].

Definition 6 (N-ary product of a family of CLTSs). *Given an indexed family of CLTSs $T_i = \langle Q_i, q_i^0, G_i^0, \rightarrow_i \rangle_{i \in I}$ over the same shared space and action language, their product $\Pi_{i \in I} T_i$ is defined by the CLTS $\langle \bigotimes_i Q_i, (q_1^0, \ldots, q_n^0), \bigcap_i G_i^0, \rightarrow \rangle$ where $\rightarrow$ is the smallest relation such that:*

$$\frac{q_i \xrightarrow{l/a}_{i,b} q_i' \quad l \in C! \cup C?}{q \xrightarrow{l/a}_b q[i \leftarrow q_i']} \; (async_i) \qquad \frac{q_i \xrightarrow{\tau/a}_{i,b} q_i' \quad (\bigvee_{j \in I} Comm(q_j)) \Rightarrow b}{q \xrightarrow{\tau/a}_b q[i \leftarrow q_i']} \; (\tau_i)$$

$$\frac{q_i \xrightarrow{c!/a_i}_{i,b_i} q_i' \quad q_j \xrightarrow{c?/a_j}_{j,b_j} q_j' \quad i \neq j \quad (\bigvee_{k \in I} Comm(q_k)) \Rightarrow b_i \vee b_j}{q \xrightarrow{\tau/a_i \triangleright a_j}_{b_i \vee b_j} q[i \leftarrow q_i', j \leftarrow q_j']} \; (sr_{i,j})$$

$$\frac{(\forall i \in I) \; q_i \xrightarrow{s/a_i}_i q_i' \quad s \in S}{q \xrightarrow{s/\odot_i a_i} q'} \; (sync)$$

$I = \{1, .., n\}$ is the set of indices. The notation $q[i \leftarrow q_i']$ states the replacement of the ith location of the vector q^4 by location q_i'. Moreover, the condition $Comm(q) \Rightarrow b$ with $q_i \xrightarrow{l/a}_i {}_b q_i'$ means that this transition should be committed if there exists another outgoing committed transition from q. Otherwise stated: a priority transition cannot be hidden by a priority transition. The product rules are explained in the following:

- The rule $async_i$ allows a CLTS T_i to synchronize with another CLTS T_j ($j \notin I$) of the external environment, for a future composition.
- The rule τ_i corresponds to an internal transition τ of the CLTS T_i. The resulting transition is uncommitted if the elements of the source state vector are all uncommitted.
- The rule sr (for send/receive) states that both T_i and T_j will be synchronized as a sender/receiver on the same channel c. The resulting transition of such a synchronization is committed if either the send or the receive transition has priority over all the other transitions. Otherwise, sr provides that the elements of the source state vector are all uncommitted.
- The rule $sync$ defines a multiple synchronization of a set of uncommitted transitions on the same event s.

Lemma 1 (Committedness). *The committedness of a CLTSs product state is the disjunction of the committedness of locations that it contains.*
$$Comm(\langle q_1, \ldots, q_n \rangle) = \bigvee_i Comm(q_i)$$

The proof of this lemma is similar to the proof of [5] done for two processes.

---

[4] q is an element of the product $\bigotimes_i Q_i$.

Theorem 2 (Generalized associativity). *If $\odot$ is associative, i.e. $\odot_{i \in I} \odot_{j \in J_i} a_{i,j} = \odot_{i \in I, j \in J_i} a_{i,j}$, the product of CLTSs is associative, i.e.:*

$$\Pi_{i \in I} (\Pi_{j \in J_i} T_{i,j}) \sim \Pi_{i \in I, j \in J_i} T_{i,j}$$

Proof (sketch). Again, this (tedious) proof is similar to that of [5] except that it is generalized to n-ary product and it relies on weaker assumptions.

4.4   CLTS with Location Invariants

In this section, we introduce location invariants in CLTS to restrict the set of states by reducing the global space valuations.

Definition 7 (CLTSI). *Given a global space $\mathcal{G}$, a CLTS with location invariants is a tuple $\langle Q, q^0, G^0, I, \rightarrow \rangle$ where $\langle Q, q^0, G^0, \rightarrow \rangle$ is a CLTS over $\mathcal{G}$ and $I : Q \rightarrow 2^{\mathcal{G}}$ associates an invariant on global variables to each location.*

By now, we define the semantics of CLTSIs through LTS and CLTS structures.

Definition 8 (Semantics of a CLTSI). *Given the global space $\mathcal{G}$ and the action language semantics $[\![.]\!] : A \rightarrow 2^{\mathcal{G} \times \mathcal{G}}$. The semantics of the CLTSI $\langle Q, q^0, G^0, I, \xrightarrow{-/-}_- \rangle$ is the LTS $\langle Q \times \mathcal{G}, \{q^0\} \times (G^0 \cap I(q_0)), \rightarrow_{/G_{Inv}} \rangle$ where $G_{Inv} = \{(q, I(q)) | q \in Q\}$ and $\langle Q \times \mathcal{G}, \{q^0\} \times G^0, \rightarrow \rangle$ is the semantics of the associated CLTS.*

Theorem 3 (Sufficient simulation condition). *Given two CLTSIs T_c (concrete) and T_a (abstract) on the same global space and the refinement relation $R \subseteq Q_c \times Q_a$ then T_a simulates T_c through R if their associated CLTSs satisfy the sufficient condition for simulation and $\forall q_c \ q_a, R(q_c, q_a) \Rightarrow I(q_c) \subseteq I(q_a)$.*

Proof. It is straightforward.

Definition 9 (Product of CLTSIs). *The product of CLTSIs is the product of their associated CLTSs with for each composed location, an invariant defined as the conjunction of the invariants of each elementary location.*

Theorem 4 (CLTSI product associativity). *If $\odot$ is associative, the product of CLTSIs is associative.*

This theorem is a generalized version of Theorem 2, where the associativity of CLTSIs product is proved using the associativity of CLTSs product.

Restriction of a CLTSI. In networks of TA, unmatched synchronizing transitions are ignored. Here, we define the corresponding operation on CLTSI, which is called restriction: a restriction of a CLTSI over a set of channels is a CLTSI where transitions composable over these channels have been deleted.

Definition 10 (CLTSIs restriction). *Let $T = \langle Q, q_0, G^0, I, \longrightarrow \rangle$ be a CLTSI over a shared space $\mathcal{G}$, an action language A and a set of one-to-one channels C. Let $C' \subseteq C$, we define $T \backslash C'$ to be the CLTSI $\langle Q, q_0, G^0, I, \longrightarrow' \rangle$ where*

$$\longrightarrow' = \longrightarrow \backslash \{q \xrightarrow{l/a}_b q' \mid l \in C'! \cup C'?\} \ .$$

4.5   Timed Transition Systems Extensions

Timed transition systems (TTS) [12] are the reference model to define the semantics of real-time formalisms. Basically, a TTS is a labeled transition system
where labels are events or delays. In this section, we will consider actions as
tuples *(guard, assignment)* to define the ETTS structure. In fact, an extended
timed transition system (ETTS) is a CLTSI which synchronizes on time. Furthermore, we consider the global state space structured as valued variables.

Definition 11 (ETTS). *An Extended Timed Transition System (ETTS) on a
set of variables $\mathcal{V}$ valued over a domain $\mathcal{D}$ and a set of channels C is a CLTSI
over the global space $\mathcal{G} = \mathcal{D}^{\mathcal{V}}$ where the n-ary synchronization events S are time
instants of $\mathbb{T} = \mathbb{R}_{\geq 0}$. Its action language is defined as the set of tuples (guard,
assignment) where a guard is a predicate over $\mathcal{V}$ and an assignment maps some
variables to expressions built on $\mathcal{V}$.*

The semantics of an ETTS depends on its action language semantics. Here, we
have chosen the following definition for the (guard, assignment) tuple[5]:

Actionlanguage	Semantics
$a := \quad g/ \parallel_{v \in V} v := e_v$	$[\![g/ \parallel_{v \in V} v := e_v]\!](x, x') = g(x) \wedge \bigwedge_{v \in V} x'(v) = [\![e_v]\!](x)$
$\quad\quad \mid a \rhd a$	
$\quad\quad \mid \odot_{i \in I} a_i$	

The notation $g/ \parallel_{v \in V}$ states the parallel update of variables of V as an assignment guarded by g. Both action composition operators $\odot$ and $\rhd$ are still
left undefined. Their semantics will be chosen to conform with Timed Automata
composition semantics. Concerning verification, our refinement relation preserves
a class of properties (trace inclusion, system invariants, etc). Here, we are only
interested in timed traces.

4.6   ETTS Timed Traces

The trace concept is extensively used to study the behavioral equivalences of
timed transition systems and to define the language of properties to be checked.
Different definitions of timed traces have been established [8]. They define the
timed trace as a sequence of visible events, each one tagged by a date d corresponding to the sum of delays of all transitions preceding it. These definitions
cannot be used in our framework, because we consider time-transitions as visible,
they change the global space. Furthermore, $\tau-$transitions stating a change of the
ETTS global space are considered as visible too. In this section, we establish a
new definition of ETTSs (diverging) timed traces.

Definition 12 (ETTS executions). *Let $\mathcal{T} = \langle Q, q^0, G^0, I, \rightarrow \rangle$ be an ETTS
over a shared space $\mathcal{G}$, a set of channels C and an action language $\mathcal{A}$. An execution is an infinite sequence of tuples (q^i, l_i, G^i) where q^i is a location, l_i is a*

---

[5] x, x' are valuations of $\mathcal{G}$.

label of an outgoing transition from q^i and G^i is the shared space corresponding to q^i. The set of all executions of $\mathcal{T}$, denoted by $Exec(\mathcal{T})$, is formally given by:

$$Exec(\mathcal{T}) = \{(q^0, l_0, G^0).\langle(q^i, l_i, G^i)\rangle_{i\in\mathbb{N}^*} \mid \forall i\ q^i \xrightarrow{g_i/l_i/a_i}_b q^{i+1} \wedge (G^i, G^{i+1}) \in \llbracket a_i \rrbracket \wedge$$
$$\forall g'_i\ l'_i\ a'_i\ b'\ q^{i'} q^i \xrightarrow{g'_i/l'_i/a'_i}_{b'} q^{i'} \Rightarrow (b' \Rightarrow b)\}$$

Moreover, an execution $e = \langle(q_0, l_0, G_0).(q_1, l_1, G_1)..\rangle$ is said time-diverging if $\sum_{l_i\in\mathbb{T}} l_i$ is diverging (not bounded).

For an an execution sequence e, we denote by $(e_i.q, e_i.l, e_i.G)$ the ith element of e, and by $e_{i..\infty}$ the sub-sequence of e starting from the ith element.

Definition 13 (Diverging timed traces). *A timed trace is an infinite sequence of triplets $\langle l, d, G\rangle$ where l is a label, d is a date corresponding to the sum of all delay labels preceding the current triplet and G is a global state. Each triplet corresponds to a transition stating a change of the global space or labelled by an external event. Furthermore, a timed trace $e = (\langle l_0, d_0, G_0\rangle).\langle l_1, d_1, G_1\rangle...)$ is time-diverging if values d_i diverge $(lim_{i\to\infty} d_i = \infty)$.*

By now, we adapt the previous definition of timed traces for ETTSs where we associate a triplet to each transition labelled by an event (discrete ot timed) or stating a change of the global state.

Definition 14 (ETTS timed traces). *Let $\mathcal{T} = \langle Q, q^0, G^0, I, \rightarrow\rangle$ be an ETTS. A trace of $\mathcal{T}$ is the projection erasing local states and stuttering of a time-diverging execution of $\mathcal{T}$. The Tr function associates a trace to a time-diverging execution. It is defined by:* $\quad Tr(e) = Tr_0(e)$
$$Tr_d(e) = \langle(e_{i_0}.l, d, e_{i_0}.G).Tr_{d+|e_{i_0}.l|}(e_{(i_0+1)..\infty})\rangle$$
where $i_0 = \min\{i \mid (e_i.l = \tau \Rightarrow e_i.G \neq e_{i+1}.G) \vee e_i.l \neq 0\}$ and $|e_i.l| = e_i.l$ if $e_i.l \in \mathbb{T}$ or 0 otherwise. The set TR of timed traces of $\mathcal{T}$ is defined as $TR(\mathcal{T}) = \{Tr(e) | e \in Exec(\mathcal{T})\}$.

5   Networks of Timed Automata

In the literature, several semantics for TA composition have been studied [2,5,14] and various parallel composition operators have been proposed, the well known ones are those of CCS [16] and CSP [13]. The semantics of both TA and networks of TA are expressed using generalized timed transition systems.

5.1   Timed Automata

A timed automaton is an abstract model of a timed system where all clocks are initialized to zero and increased synchronously. Several notions of committedness have been considered in the literature:

- In Uppaal [2], committedness is associated to states.
- In order to define a compositional semantics of timed automata using products of TTS, [5] proposes a restriction on Uppaal so that a committed state has always a firable outgoing transition and both location invariants and input transition guards do not depend on global variables.

– Our proposal does not require such restrictions but uses a slightly modified definition of a TTS [12], where location invariants have been introduced and the input transition guard is checked after taking into account the effect of the output transition action.

Definition 15 (Timed Automaton). *A timed automaton on a set of clocks χ and a set of channels C is a tuple $\langle Q, q^0, K, I, \rightarrow \rangle$ where:*

– *Q is the set of locations with $q^0 \in Q$ the initial location,*
– *$K \subseteq Q$ is the set of committed locations,*
– *$I : Q \rightarrow 2^{\chi \rightarrow \mathbb{T}}$ associates a clock invariant to each location,*
– *$\rightarrow \subseteq Q \times 2^{\chi \rightarrow \mathbb{T}} \times 2^{\chi} \times \Sigma \times Q$ is the transition relation defined with a clock guard and a reset set. $\Sigma = C? \cup C! \cup \{\tau\}$ is the set of transition labels.*

We note $q \xrightarrow{g/l/r} q'$ for $(q, g, r, l, q') \in \rightarrow$.

5.2 Semantics of Timed Automata

Different definitions of TA semantics through TTS models have been proposed [5,3,14]. Here, we define the semantics of a TA over an ETTS.

Definition 16 (ETTS of a timed automaton). *Given a timed automaton $\langle Q, q^0, K, I, \rightarrow_{ta} \rangle$ over a set $\mathcal{X}$ of clocks, its semantics is defined as an ETTS over the variables $\mathcal{X}$ by $\langle Q, q^0, G^0, I, \rightarrow \rangle$ where $G^0 = \mathcal{X} \times \{0\}$ and $\rightarrow$ is the smallest relation such that:*

$$\frac{q \xrightarrow{g/l/r}_{ta} q'}{q \xrightarrow{g/l/\|_{x \in r} x := 0}_{q \in K} q'}(action) \qquad \frac{q \in K}{q \xrightarrow{\bot/\tau/skip}_{\top} q}(empty) \qquad \frac{q \notin K}{q \xrightarrow{\top/d/\|_{x \in \mathcal{X}} x := x+d} q}(time)$$

Remarks. The *empty* transition is not firable. It is used to hold the committed-ness information of TA locations. The time transitions do not update local states. Throughout this paper, we consider the semantics of the reset as an action.

Simulation. We say that a TA T_c refines another TA T_a if the simulation relation holds between their associated ETTSs: $T_a \preceq T_c \triangleq ETTS(T_a) \preceq ETTS(T_c)$.

5.3 Networks of Timed Automata

In order to model concurrency and communication of concurrent systems, timed automata have been extended with parallel composition, giving rise to networks of TA (NTA). The Uppaal language [15] has adopted the CCS parallel composition operator.

Definition 17 (Network of timed automata). *A network of timed automata is a finite collection of timed automata defined on the same sets of clocks $\mathcal{X}$ and channels C.*

5.4   Semantics of a NTA

Several definitions of NTA semantics through transition systems have been established [2,5]. Here, we define the semantics of a NTA as an extended timed transition system. It is parameterized by the way guarded actions are composed on a send/receive synchronization, i.e. $(g_s/a_s) \triangleright (g_r/a_r)$. First, let us choose the following action language and its underlying semantics for ETTSs:

Action language	Semantics
a:= $a \triangleright a$	
$\mid \odot_{i \in I} a_i$	$[\![\odot_i a_i]\!](x, x') = \bigwedge_i [\![a_i]\!](x, x')$
$\mid (g/r)$	$[\![g/r]\!](x, x') = g(x) \wedge \bigwedge_{c \in r} x'(c) = 0 \wedge \bigwedge_{c \notin r} x'(c) = x(c)$
$\mid (g/c := c + d)$	$[\![g/c := c + d]\!](x, x') = g(x) \wedge x'(c) = x(c) + d$
$\mid (g/skip)$	$[\![g/skip]\!](x, x') = g(x) \wedge (x' = x)$

The semantics $[\![a \triangleright a]\!]$ depends on the semantics chosen for TA composition, and is still unspecified.

Definition 18 (NTA semantics). *Given a network of timed automata* $\langle Q_j, q_j^0, K_j, I_j, \to_j \rangle_{j \in J}$, *its semantics is defined by the ETTS* $\langle \bigotimes_j Q_j, (q_1^0, \ldots, q_n^0),$ $\bigwedge_j G_j^0, I, \to \rangle$ *where* $I(q) = \bigwedge_j I_j(q_j)$ *and* $\to$ *is the smallest relation such that:*

$$\frac{q_j \xrightarrow{g/\tau/r}_j q_j' \quad (\bigvee_{i \in J} q_i \in K_i) \Rightarrow q_j \in K_j}{q \xrightarrow{g/\tau/\|_{x \in r} x := 0}_{q_j \in K_j} q[j \leftarrow q_j']} \ (\tau_j)$$

$$\frac{q_i \xrightarrow{g_i/c!/r_i}_i q_i' \quad q_j \xrightarrow{g_j/c?/r_j}_j q_j' \quad i \neq j \quad g/r = g_i/r_i \triangleright g_j/r_j}{(\bigvee_{k \in J} q_k \in K_k) \Rightarrow q_i \in K_i \vee q_j \in K_j}{q \xrightarrow{g/\tau/r}_{q_i \in K_i \vee q_j \in K_j} q[i \leftarrow q_i', j \leftarrow q_j']} \ (sr_{i,j})$$

$$\frac{q_j \in K_j}{q \xrightarrow{\perp/\tau/skip}_\tau q} \ (empty) \qquad \frac{\bigwedge_j q_j \notin K_j}{q \xrightarrow{\tau/d/\odot_j x_j := x_j + d} q} \ (time)$$

Remark. NTA semantics [2] is not compositional according to [5] because it is not clear how to define the committedness of product locations. Thus, the internal product of TA cannot be defined.

Consequence (NTA refinement). Refinement between networks of timed automata is defined as refinement between their associated ETTSs. Formally, given two NTA $\mathcal{N}_c$ and $\mathcal{N}_a$; then: $\mathcal{N}_a \preceq \mathcal{N}_c \triangleq ETTS(\mathcal{N}_a) \preceq ETTS(\mathcal{N}_c)$.

Theorem 5 (Compositionality). *The ETTS of a network of TA is bisimilar to the restriction to time and* τ-*transitions of the product of ETTSs associated to individual timed automata. Formally,* $ETTS(NTA) \sim \Pi_i ETTS(TA_i) \backslash C$.

Proof. It is direct because we have the same composition rules in both sides. The difference resides in the occurrence of unmatched communication transitions in the ETTSs product, but these transitions will be suppressed when applying the restriction.   □

6   Composition and Refinement

In this section, we propose some compositionality results. Given the following definition of the operator $\triangleright$ $(join^6)$: $[\![a_1 \triangleright a_2]\!](x, y) = \exists z, [\![a_1]\!](x, z) \wedge [\![a_2]\!](z, y)$.

Theorem 6 (Refinement and parallel composition).
    Let T_1, T_2, T_3, T_4 be ETTSs and $R_g, R_l^{1,2}, R_l^{3,4}$ refinement relations where R_g is supposed to be functional from the concrete system to the abstract one. Then, we have: $T_1 \preceq_{R_g, R_l^{1,2}} T_2 \wedge T_3 \preceq_{R_g, R_l^{3,4}} T_4 \Rightarrow T_1 \| T_3 \preceq_{R_g, R_l^{1,2} \otimes R_l^{3,4}} T_2 \| T_4$ where $R \otimes R'(q_1, q_3)(q_2, q_4) = R(q_1, q_2) \wedge R'(q_3, q_4)$.

Remark. Compared to [5], this theorem enables the refinement of both global spaces in one simulation step, whereas [5] requires that the variables shared by T_1 and T_3 be refined through the identity relation.

Theorem 7 (Refinement and restriction). *Let T_i, T_j be two ETTSs on the same set of channels C and R be a refinement relation. Then $\forall C' \subseteq C\ T_i \preceq_R T_j \Rightarrow T_i \backslash C' \preceq_R T_j \backslash C'$.*

Consequence . Let $\mathcal{N} = \langle T_1, .., T_n \rangle$, $\mathcal{N}' = \langle T_1', .., T_n' \rangle$ be two networks of timed automata. Then, we have $(\forall i\ T_i \preceq T_i') \Rightarrow \langle T_1, .., T_n \rangle \preceq \langle T_1', .., T_n' \rangle$.

Theorem 8 (Refinement and trace properties). *Let T_i, T_j be two ETTSs on the same global space $\mathcal{G}$, R_l be a refinement relation of local spaces and P be a property over timed traces TR, then $((T_i \preceq_{Id, R_l} T_j) \wedge (T_j \models P)) \Rightarrow T_i \models P$ where $T \models P \triangleq \forall t \in TR(T), P(t)$.*

Consequence. Let $\langle T_1, .., T_n \rangle$ and $\langle T_1', .., T_n' \rangle$ be two NTA on the same global space. $\langle T_1, .., T_n \rangle \models P \wedge (\forall i\ T_i \preceq T_i') \Rightarrow \langle T_1', .., T_n' \rangle \models P$.

7   Conclusion

In this paper, we have defined an alternative TA composition and justified it through the definition of communication patterns and compositionality results. For this parallel composition operator, we have defined a corresponding refinement relation. We can resume our framework by Fig.1. where we distinguish two ways to establish the TA product semantics, with an important refinement property showing that: if each individual TA of a NTA refines another individual TA of another NTA, then the semantics of the first NTA refines that of the second NTA. Furthermore, the theorems[7] established within our framework have been validated using the CoQ [10] theorem prover. We also intend to define formally synchronization patterns as the one proposed in section 3.2, compare their direct and translation-based semantics and validate such translations. We also wish to extend our framework to time Petri net based systems. This formal framework will be used as a basis for the extensions of the FIACRE language [6].

---

[6] The operator *join* of relational algebra.

[7] The proofs are available at: "*http://www.irit.fr/PERSONNEL/ACADIE/bodeveix/* COQ/NTA/". The detailed proofs will be published in a forthcoming paper.

References

1. Arnold, A.: Finite transition systems: semantics of communicating systems. Prentice Hall International Ltd., Hertfordshire (1994), Translator-Plaice, John
2. Behrmann, G., David, A., Larsen, K.G.: A Tutorial on Uppaal. Department of computer science, Aalborg university (2004)
3. Bengtsson, J., Wang, Y.: Timed automata: Semantics, algorithms and tools. In: Desel, J., Reisig, W., Rozenberg, G. (eds.) Lectures on Concurrency and Petri Nets. LNCS, vol. 3098, pp. 87–124. Springer, Heidelberg (2004)
4. Bensalem, S., Bozga, M., Sifakis, J., Nguyen, T.H.: Compositional verification for component-based systems and application. In: Cha, S(S.), Choi, J.-Y., Kim, M., Lee, I., Viswanathan, M. (eds.) ATVA 2008. LNCS, vol. 5311, pp. 64–79. Springer, Heidelberg (2008)
5. Berendsen, J., Vaandrager, F.: Compositional Abstraction in Real-Time Model Checking. In: 6th International Conference on Formal Modelling and Analysis of Timed Systems, Saint Malo, France, pp. 233–249 (September 2008)
6. Berthomieu, B., Bodeveix, J., Filali, M., Garavel, H., Lang, F., Peres, F., Saad, R., Stoecker, J., Vernadat, F., Gaufillet, P., Lang, F.: The syntax and semantics of FIACRE. LAAS Laboratory, University of Toulouse (2009)
7. Bornot, S., Gößler, G., Sifakis, J.: On the construction of live timed systems. In: Graf, S. (ed.) TACAS 2000. LNCS, vol. 1785, pp. 109–126. Springer, Heidelberg (2000)
8. Bouyer, P., Markey, N., Reynier, P.A.: Robust model-checking of linear-time properties in timed automata. In: Correa, J.R., Hevia, A., Kiwi, M. (eds.) LATIN 2006. LNCS, vol. 3887, pp. 238–249. Springer, Heidelberg (2006)
9. Clarke, E.M., Long, D.E., McMillan, K.L.: Compositional model checking. In: LICS 1989, pp. 353–362 (1989)
10. Coq, Technical report, INRIA, http://coq.inria.fr
11. David, A., Hakansson, J., Larsen, K.G., Pettersson, P.: Model checking Timed Automata with Priorities Using DBM Subtraction, pp. 128–142. Springer, Heidelberg (2006)
12. Henzinger, T.A., Manna, Z., Pnueli, A.: Timed transition systems (1992)
13. Hoare, C.A.R.: Communicating Sequential Processes. Prentice-Hall, Englewood Cliffs (1985)
14. Jensen, H.E., Larsen, K.G., Skou, A.: Scaling up UPPAAL:automatic verification of real-time systems using compositionality and abstraction. In: Joseph, M. (ed.) FTRTFT 2000. LNCS, vol. 1926, p. 19. Springer, Heidelberg (2000)
15. Larsen, K.G., Pettersson, P., Wang, Y.: UPPAAL in a nutshell. Journal on Software Tools for Technology Transfert (1997)
16. Milner, R.: Communication and Concurrency. Prentice Hall Ltd., Englewood Cliffs (1989)

Model Checking EGF
on Basic Parallel Processes*

Hongfei Fu

RWTH Aachen University, Ahornstraße 55, D-52074 Aachen, Germany
hongfeifu@informatik.rwth-aachen.de

Abstract. In this paper we study the problem of model checking the logic EGF over Basic Parallel Processes (BPP). The logic EGF is obtained by extending the logic EF with the CTL* notation EGF, which means that there exists an infinite path on which there are infinitely many entries satisfying certain property. We prove that this problem is PSPACE-complete, and Σ_d^p-complete for certain classes of fixed formula with the nesting depth d of modal operators.

Keywords: infinite-state systems, Basic Parallel Processes, model checking, EGF.

1 Introduction

Verification of infinite structures has been studied intensively in the past two decades [2]. An important subarea is model checking of infinite-state systems. A model checking problem takes two parameters: a state s and a logical formula Φ. The task is to check if s satisfies the property encoded by Φ, or formally if $s \models \Phi$. In this paper, we study the model-checking problem of the logic EGF over Basic Parallel Processes.

Basic Parallel Processes (BPP) [3] are elementary infinite models for parallelism. In a BPP, a component of a parallel system is modeled as a symbol, and a state as a parallel composition of symbols. A symbol can produce more symbols through transitions, thus typically a BPP generates an infinite-state system. However the transition semantics of BPP is asynchronous, thus a BPP can be viewed as a communication-free Petri Net.

In [4] Esparza proved that model checking the logic EG [4] over BPP is undecidable, where the logic EG is obtained by extending Hennessy-Milner Logic (HML) with the EG operator. Consequently, the model-checking problem for BPPs is undecidable under Computation Tree Logic (CTL) and modal μ-calculus. The only branching-time logic not covered by the Logic EG is the Logic EF, which is HML equipped with the EF operator. For this logic Esparza has shown in [4] that the model-checking problem is decidable, where the atomic formulae are allowed to be arbitrary semilinear sets. On the other hand, he also proved that the problem is PSPACE-hard and Σ_d^p-hard for fixed formula, where

---

* Supported by a CSC scholarship.

T. Bultan and P.-A. Hsiung (Eds.): ATVA 2011, LNCS 6996, pp. 120–134, 2011.

d is the nesting depth of modal operators. Later, Mayr [7] showed that the problem can be solved in PSPACE and in Σ_d^p for fixed formulae with nesting depth d that start with a modal operator. Thus model-checking the Logic EF over BPPs is PSPACE-complete, and Σ_d^p-complete for such classes of fixed formulae. Mayr's method relies on the analysis of finite transition sequences under a BPP.

EGF is a CTL* notation which means that "there exists a path such that a certain property holds infinitely often". In *regular model checking* [1], EGF corresponds to a kind of *liveness property* and *recurrent reachability*. By adding EGF to the Logic EF, we obtain the logic EGF, which is a meaningful fragment of CTL* that expresses reachability properties and certain kind of recurrent reachability properties. It is a natural study to investigate the decidability and complexity for the logic EGF. In the viewpoint of the author of this paper, the method in [7] is specific to EF which involves only one-stage satisfaction, and can not be extended to EGF which involves infinite stages of satisfaction. In [9], To showed that model checking the logic EGF over BPPs is decidable, where the atomic formulae are tree-regular sets closed under permutation. However the corresponding complexity is non-primitive, since it requires negation of tree-automaton at each iteration.

In this paper, we restrict to the atomic formulae as in [7]. We prove that model checking the logic EGF over BPPs lies in PSPACE, and Σ_d^p for certain classes of fixed formula with the nesting depth d of modal operators. We show that any satisfaction set of a given EGF-formulae can be characterized by a special semilinear structure, which is already used in [8] to tackle the state explosion problem of the model checking of Petri Net. Based on this symbolic representation, we prove our complexity results.

2 Preliminaries

Let $Var = \{X, Y, Z, ...\}$ and $Act = \{a, b, c, ...\}$ be a countable set of *symbols* and *actions*, respectively.

For any set C, we denote C^* resp. $C^\oplus$ to be the free monoid resp. the free commutative monoid generated by C. Given a word w of C^* or $C^\oplus$, we denote $\lfloor w \rfloor$ to be the set $\{u \in C \mid u \text{ appears in } w\}$ and $m_u(w)$ to be the number of occurrence of u in w. Elements of $Var^\oplus$ are indicated by α, β and γ.

Basic Parallel Processes (BPP)

A *BPP* is a tuple (V, Δ) where $V \subseteq Var$ is a finite set of symbols, and Δ is a finite set of *rules* where each rule has the form $X \xrightarrow{a} \alpha$ with $X \in V$, $a \in Act$ and $\alpha \in V^\oplus$. Each BPP (V, Δ) specifies a labeled transition system where the state space is $V^\oplus$ and the transition relation is generated by the following rule:

$$\frac{X \xrightarrow{a} \alpha \in \Delta}{\beta X \gamma \xrightarrow{a} \beta \alpha \gamma}$$

In this paper, elements of $V^\oplus$ are called *BPP expressions*.

Note that BPP expressions are considered modulo commutativity, e.g. XYZ, ZYX and YXZ are deemed as one element. Intuitively, BPP expressions are parallel compositions of symbols, where each symbol can perform transitions independently of others.

Below in this section we fix a BPP (V, Δ). We write $\rightarrow^*$ resp. $\rightarrow^+$ to be the reflexive transitive closure resp. transitive closure of the one-step transition relation $\{\xrightarrow{a}\}_{a \in Act}$, where actions are not relevant here. We use the predicate $\mathbf{Tr}(\{\alpha_i\}_{i \geq 0})$ to indicate that the infinite sequence $\{\alpha_i\}_{i \geq 0}$ satisfies the condition that $\alpha_i \rightarrow^+ \alpha_{i+1}$ for all $i \geq 0$.

For each $r \in \Delta$ (e.g. $X \xrightarrow{a} \alpha$), we define $^\bullet r$ to be the symbol at the left hand side (e.g. X), and $r^\bullet$ to be the expression at the right hand side (e.g. α). We write $\alpha \rightarrow_r \beta$ if $\alpha = \gamma^\bullet r$ and $\beta = \gamma r^\bullet$, for some γ. Given $\sigma \in \Delta^*$ a finite sequence of rules, we write $\alpha \rightarrow_\sigma \beta$ if either $\sigma = \epsilon$ and $\alpha = \beta$, or $\sigma = r_1 r_2 \ldots r_k$ and there is $\{\gamma_l\}_{1 \leq l \leq k-1}$ such that $\alpha \rightarrow_{r_1} \gamma_1 \rightarrow_{r_2} \gamma_2 \ldots \gamma_{k-1} \rightarrow_{r_k} \beta$.

We define the following size functions:

- $|\alpha|$: the length of α (where $|\epsilon| = 0$)
- $|V|$: the number of symbols of V
- $\|\Delta\|$: the number of rules of Δ
- $|r| := |r^\bullet| + 2$ (where $r \in \Delta$)
- $|\Delta| := \sum_{r \in \Delta} |r|$

By commutativity, we can represent α as a multiset $\{m_X(\alpha)\}_{X \in V}$, where $m_X(\alpha)$ (the number of occurrence of X in α) is represented in *binary* encoding. Further we can represent all expressions appearing in Δ in binary. In this way, a BPP (V, Δ) and a BPP expression α can be stored in $\mathcal{O}(|V| \|\Delta\| \log |\Delta|)$ and $\mathcal{O}(|V| \log |\alpha|)$ space, respectively.

We use the notation γ^k to denote the parallel composition of k copies of γ, e.g., γ^3 stands for the expression $\gamma\gamma\gamma$ and γ^0 stands for ϵ.

The Logic EGF

The logic EGF is obtained from the logic EF [4,7] by adding the CTL* notation EGF, which means that "there exists a path such that a certain property holds infinitely often". The syntax is as follows:

$$\phi ::= \lambda \mid \neg\phi \mid \phi \wedge \phi \mid \langle a \rangle \phi \mid \mathrm{EF}\phi \mid \mathrm{EGF}\phi$$

where $a \in Act$ and λ is an atomic formula specific to BPP. We will use ϕ, ψ, φ to range over formulae of this logic. The size of ϕ, i.e., the length of the word representation of ϕ, is denoted $|\phi|$ where the length of atomic formulae $|\lambda|$ is defined to be 1.

We follow the restriction on atomic formulae adopted in [7] that λ has the form $X \geq k$, where $X \in V$ and $k \in \mathbb{N}_0$ (where $\mathbb{N}_0$ is the set of nonnegative natural numbers). The number k is represented (in its syntax) in binary encoding. We denote k_ϕ to be the largest k that appears in ϕ.

Before defining the semantics of our logic, we first introduce some notations. For any set $\mathcal{R} \subseteq V^\oplus$, we define

- $[\![a]\!][\mathcal{R}] := \{\alpha \in V^{\oplus} \mid \exists \beta.(\alpha \xrightarrow{a} \beta \wedge \beta \in \mathcal{R})\}$
- $[\![EF]\!][\mathcal{R}] := \{\alpha \in V^{\oplus} \mid \exists \beta.(\alpha \rightarrow^* \beta \wedge \beta \in \mathcal{R})\}$
- $[\![EGF]\!][\mathcal{R}] := \{\alpha \in V^{\oplus} \mid \exists \{\alpha_i\}_{i\geq 0}.(\alpha = \alpha_0 \wedge \mathbf{Tr}(\{\alpha_i\}_{i\geq 0}) \wedge \forall i > 0.(\alpha_i \in \mathcal{R}))\}$

The semantics of the logic EGF over BPPs is inductively defined as follows, where $[\![\phi]\!]$ is the satisfaction set of ϕ (i.e. the set of all states that satisfy ϕ).

- $[\![X \geq k]\!] := \{\alpha \in V^{\oplus} \mid m_X(\alpha) \geq k\}$
- $[\![\neg\phi]\!] := V^{\oplus} - [\![\phi]\!]$
- $[\![\phi \wedge \psi]\!] := [\![\phi]\!] \cap [\![\psi]\!]$
- $[\![\langle a\rangle\phi]\!] := [\![a]\!][[\![\phi]\!]]$
- $[\![EF\phi]\!] := [\![EF]\!][[\![\phi]\!]]$
- $[\![EGF\phi]\!] := [\![EGF]\!][[\![\phi]\!]]$

Note that the semantics of $EGF\phi$ states that $\alpha \in [\![EGF\phi]\!]$ iff there is an infinite path starting from α along which there are infinitely many entries belonging to $[\![\phi]\!]$. Instead of $\alpha \in [\![\phi]\!]$ we also write $\alpha \models \phi$.

3   Model Checking the Logic EGF

In this section we present a PSPACE algorithm for the model-checking problem of the Logic EGF over BPPs. The model-checking problem is defined as follows:

- INPUT: a BPP (V, Δ), an BPP expression α and a formula ϕ
- OUTPUT: whether $\alpha \models \phi$ or not

The input size is defined as $|V| \log |\alpha| + |V| \|\Delta\| \log |\Delta| + |\phi| \log k_\phi$.

The General Approach. A core in our PSPACE algorithm is a special semilinear structure which will be called "semisegment" in this paper. Semisegments already appear in [8], which are used to tackle the state explosion problem of the model checking on Petri Net. Here we show that the set of BPP expressions that satisfy any given EGF-formula can be "effectively" represented by a semisegment. This effective representation allows us to model-check the Logic EGF over BPPs in PSPACE.

Below we fix a BPP (V, Δ). We use r to range over Δ. The following two definitions introduce the notions of "segment" and "semisegment".

Definition 1. *A* segment *is a pair* $\langle \alpha, U \rangle$ *where* $\alpha \in V^{\oplus}$ *and* $U \subseteq V$. *The set of BPP expressions* spanned *by* $\langle \alpha, U \rangle$, *denotation* $\mathcal{P}(\langle \alpha, U \rangle)$, *is defined by:*

$$\mathcal{P}(\langle \alpha, U \rangle) := \{\beta \in V^{\oplus} \mid \exists \gamma \in U^{\oplus}.\beta = \alpha\gamma\}$$

The width *of* $\langle \alpha, U \rangle$, *denotation* $\|\langle \alpha, U \rangle\|$, *is defined as* $\max_{X \in V}\{m_X(\alpha)\}$.

Definition 2. *A* semisegment *is a finite set of segments. For convenience, we represent a semisegment by* $\{\langle \alpha_i, U_i \rangle\}_{i \in I}$ *where* I *is a finite indexing set and*

$\langle \alpha_i, U_i \rangle$ for $i \in I$ are segments of the semisegment. The set of BPP expressions spanned by a semisegment $\mathcal{B} = \{\langle \alpha_i, U_i \rangle\}_{i \in I}$, denotation $\mathcal{P}(\mathcal{B})$, is defined by:

$$\mathcal{P}(\mathcal{B}) = \bigcup_{i \in I} \mathcal{P}(\langle \alpha_i, U_i \rangle)$$

By convention $\mathcal{P}(\mathcal{B}) = \emptyset$ if $I = \emptyset$. The width of $\mathcal{B}$, denotation $\|\mathcal{B}\|$, is defined as $\max_{i \in I}\{\|\langle \alpha_i, U_i \rangle\|\}$ if $I \neq \emptyset$, and zero if $I = \emptyset$.

For example, the set $\{\gamma \mid m_X(\gamma) > 2\}$ is spanned by the segment $\langle X^3, V \rangle$ with width 3; $\{\gamma \mid m_X(\gamma) > 2, m_Y(\gamma) = 5\}$ by the segment $\langle X^3 Y^5, V - \{Y\}\rangle$ with width 5; and $\{\gamma \mid m_X(\gamma) < 3\}$ by the semisegment $\{\langle X^i, V - \{X\}\rangle\}_{i \in \{0,1,2\}}$ with width 2.

Our aim is to prove that for every formula ϕ, the set $[\![\phi]\!]$ can be effectively spanned by a semisegment. For atomic formulae $X \geq k$ the situation is clear: the semisegment contains just one segment $\langle X^k, V \rangle$. We show that semisegments are effectively closed under all operators of our logic.

We introduce more notations related to $\rightarrow^*$ and $\rightarrow^+$. Let $U \subseteq V$. We write $\beta \rightarrow^* [\alpha]_U$ if there is $\gamma \in U^{\oplus}$ such that $\beta \rightarrow^* \alpha\gamma$. And we write $\beta \rightarrow^+ [\alpha]_U$ if there is $\gamma \in U^{\oplus}$ such that $\beta \rightarrow^+ \alpha\gamma$.

First we prove the effective closedness for boolean operators and one-step next operators. The closedness for these operators are already known (see e.g. [8]). However here we focus on the effectiveness which lies in the width of segments and semisegments.

Proposition 1. Let $\mathcal{B}_1$, $\mathcal{B}_2$ be two semisegments. Then there is a semisegment $\mathcal{B}$ with $\|\mathcal{B}\| \leq \max\{\|\mathcal{B}_1\|, \|\mathcal{B}_2\|\}$ such that $\mathcal{P}(\mathcal{B}) = \mathcal{P}(\mathcal{B}_1) \cap \mathcal{P}(\mathcal{B}_2)$.

Proof. Let $\mathcal{B}_1 = \{\langle \alpha_i, U_i \rangle\}_{i \in I}$ and $\mathcal{B}_2 = \{\langle \alpha_j, U_j \rangle\}_{j \in J}$ with I, J two disjoint indexing sets. For each $(i,j) \in I \times J$, we clarify three cases as follows:

1. There is $X \in V$ such that $X \notin U_i$ and $m_X(\alpha_i) < m_X(\alpha_j)$. Then
$$\mathcal{P}(\langle \alpha_i, U_i \rangle) \cap \mathcal{P}(\langle \alpha_j, U_j \rangle) = \emptyset$$
   because if there is $\alpha \in \mathcal{P}(\langle \alpha_i, U_i \rangle) \cap \mathcal{P}(\langle \alpha_j, U_j \rangle)$, then $m_X(\alpha) = m_X(\alpha_i)$ and $m_X(\alpha) \geq m_X(\alpha_j)$; contradiction.
2. There is $X \in V$ such that $X \notin U_j$ and $m_X(\alpha_j) < m_X(\alpha_i)$. Then similarly in this case $\mathcal{P}(\langle \alpha_i, U_i \rangle) \cap \mathcal{P}(\langle \alpha_j, U_j \rangle) = \emptyset$.
3. Both the previous two cases do not hold. Then we show that
$$\mathcal{P}(\langle \alpha_i, U_i \rangle) \cap \mathcal{P}(\langle \alpha_j, U_j \rangle) = \mathcal{P}(\langle \alpha_{(i,j)}, U_{(i,j)} \rangle)$$
   where $\alpha_{(i,j)}$ is determined by: $m_X(\alpha_{(i,j)}) = \max\{m_X(\alpha_i), m_X(\alpha_j)\}$ for all $X \in V$, and $U_{(i,j)} := U_i \cap U_j$. Suppose $\alpha \in \mathcal{P}(\langle \alpha_i, U_i \rangle) \cap \mathcal{P}(\langle \alpha_j, U_j \rangle)$. Then for any $X \in V, m_X(\alpha) \geq \max\{m_X(\alpha_i), m_X(\alpha_j)\}$ and further if $X \notin U_i \cap U_j$ then $m_X(\alpha) = \max\{m_X(\alpha_i), m_X(\alpha_j)\}$. Hence $\alpha \in \mathcal{P}(\langle \alpha_{(i,j)}, U_{(i,j)} \rangle)$. Suppose now $\alpha \in \mathcal{P}(\langle \alpha_{(i,j)}, U_{(i,j)} \rangle)$. For any $X \in V$, if $X \notin U_i$ then $m_X(\alpha_i) \geq m_X(\alpha_j)$ and hence $m_X(\alpha) = m_X(\alpha_i)$. Thus $\alpha \in \mathcal{P}(\langle \alpha_i, U_i \rangle)$. Similarly we have $\alpha \in \mathcal{P}(\langle \alpha_j, U_j \rangle)$. Thus $\alpha \in \mathcal{P}(\langle \alpha_i, U_i \rangle) \cap \mathcal{P}(\langle \alpha_j, U_j \rangle)$.

Then either $\mathcal{P}(\langle \alpha_i, U_i \rangle) \cap \mathcal{P}(\langle \alpha_j, U_j \rangle)$ is emptyset or can be spanned by a segment with width no greater than $\max\{\|\langle \alpha_i, U_i \rangle\|, \|\langle \alpha_j, U_j \rangle\|\}$. Then we form $\mathcal{B}$ by the following simple fact:

$$\mathcal{P}(\mathcal{B}_1) \cap \mathcal{P}(\mathcal{B}_2) = \bigcup_{(i,j)\in I\times J}(\mathcal{P}(\langle\alpha_i,U_i\rangle) \cap \mathcal{P}(\langle\alpha_j,U_j\rangle)).$$

From the construction one can see that $\|\mathcal{B}\| \le \max\{\|\mathcal{B}_1\|, \|\mathcal{B}_2\|\}$. □

Proposition 2. *Let $\mathcal{B}$ be a semisegment. Then there is a semisegment $\mathcal{B}'$ with $\|\mathcal{B}'\| \le \|\mathcal{B}\| + 1$ such that $\mathcal{P}(\mathcal{B}') = V^\oplus - \mathcal{P}(\mathcal{B})$.*

Proof. If $\mathcal{B} = \emptyset$, then $\mathcal{B}'$ is just $\langle\epsilon, V\rangle$ which spans $V^\oplus$. Suppose $\mathcal{B} \ne \emptyset$ and $\mathcal{B} = \{\langle\alpha_i, U_i\rangle\}_{i\in I}$. For any $i \in I$, we can directly obtain from the definition that $V^\oplus - \mathcal{P}(\langle\alpha_i, U_i\rangle)$ is the set of all α's such that either $m_X(\alpha) < m_X(\alpha_i)$ or $m_X(\alpha) > m_X(\alpha_i)$ with $X \notin U_i$, for some $X \in V$. Thus:

$$V^\oplus - \mathcal{P}(\langle\alpha_i, U_i\rangle) = \bigcup_{(X,k)\in K_i} \mathcal{P}(\langle X^k, V - \{X\}\rangle) \cup \bigcup_{X\in V-U_i} \mathcal{P}(\langle X^{m_X(\alpha_i)+1}, V\rangle)$$

where the index set $K_i = \{(X, k) \in V \times \mathbb{N}_0 \mid k < m_X(\alpha_i)\}$. Thus $V^\oplus - \mathcal{P}(\langle\alpha_i, U_i\rangle)$ can be spanned by a semisegment with width bounded by $\|\langle\alpha_i, U_i\rangle\| + 1$. Then the result follows from $V^\oplus - \mathcal{P}(\mathcal{B}) = \bigcap_{i\in I}(V^\oplus - \mathcal{P}(\langle\alpha_i, U_i\rangle))$ and Proposition 1. □

It is worth noting that after the negation, the space needed to store the semisegment may grow exponentially, however its width grows only linearly.

Proposition 3. *Let $\mathcal{B}$ be a semisegment. Then there is a semisegment $\mathcal{B}'$ with $\|\mathcal{B}'\| \le \|\mathcal{B}\| + 1$ such that $\mathcal{P}(\mathcal{B}') = [\![a]\!][\mathcal{P}(\mathcal{B})]$.*

Proof. Let $\mathcal{B} = \{\langle\alpha_i, U_i\rangle\}_{i\in I}$. It is clear that $[\![a]\!][\mathcal{P}(\mathcal{B})] = \bigcup_{i\in I} [\![a]\!][\mathcal{P}(\langle\alpha_i, U_i\rangle)]$. Thus we need only to prove the proposition for each $\langle\alpha_i, U_i\rangle$. Fix a $\langle\alpha_i, U_i\rangle$. By definition, $\alpha \in [\![a]\!][\mathcal{P}(\langle\alpha_i, U_i\rangle)]$ iff there are $X, \alpha', \beta', \beta, \gamma$ such that

1. $\alpha = \alpha' X \gamma$, $X \xrightarrow{a} \beta'\beta \in \Delta$ and $\alpha_i = \alpha'\beta'$;
2. both β and γ lies in $U_i^\oplus$.

Then it is not hard to verify that the set $[\![a]\!][\mathcal{P}(\langle\alpha_i, U_i\rangle)]$ is spanned by the semisegment $\{\langle\alpha' X, U_i\rangle\}_{(\alpha', X)\in K}$ where the index set $K \subseteq V^\oplus \times V$ is defined as follows: $(\alpha', X) \in K$ iff there is β', β such that $X \xrightarrow{a} \beta'\beta \in \Delta$, $\beta \in U_i^\oplus$ and $\alpha_i = \alpha'\beta'$. Moreover, $\|\{\langle\alpha' X, U_i\rangle\}_{(\alpha', X)\in K}\| \le \|\langle\alpha_i, U_i\rangle\| + 1$. □

Now we consider the operators EF and EGF. The case for the operator EF is covered by the following proposition.

Proposition 4. *Let $\mathcal{B}$ be a semisegment. Then there is a semisegment $\mathcal{B}'$ with $\|\mathcal{B}'\| \le |V| \cdot \|\mathcal{B}\|$ such that $\mathcal{P}(\mathcal{B}') = [\![\mathrm{EF}]\!][\mathcal{P}(\mathcal{B})]$.*

Proof. Let $\mathcal{B} = \{\langle\alpha_i, U_i\rangle\}_{i\in I}$. It suffices to show that $[\![\mathrm{EF}]\!][\mathcal{P}(\langle\alpha_i, U_i\rangle)]$ can be spanned by a semisegment with width bounded by $|V|\|\langle\alpha_i, U_i\rangle\|$ for each $i \in I$. Suppose $\alpha \in [\![\mathrm{EF}]\!][\mathcal{P}(\langle\alpha_i, U_i\rangle)]$, then we have $\alpha \to^* [\alpha_i]_{U_i}$. We prove that there is β, α' with $|\beta| \le |\alpha_i|$ such that $\alpha = \beta\alpha'$, $\beta \to^* [\alpha_i]_{U_i}$ and $\alpha' \to^* [\epsilon]_{U_i}$. For $\alpha = \epsilon$ the situation is clear. Now suppose $|\alpha| > 0$. Let $\alpha = X_1 \ldots X_k$ where $k = |\alpha|$. By the transition semantics of BPP, there are $\{\gamma_j\}_{1\le j\le k}$, $\{\gamma'_j\}_{1\le j\le k}$ such that $X_j \to^* \gamma_j\gamma'_j$ and $\gamma'_j \in U_i^\oplus$ for all $1 \le j \le k$, and $\alpha_i = \gamma_1 \ldots \gamma_k$. Note that $\sum_{j=1}^{k} |\gamma_j| = |\alpha_i|$, so there are at most $|\alpha_i|$ j's such that $\gamma_j \neq \epsilon$, which are listed as $j_1, \ldots, j_l$ (where $l \leq |\alpha_i|$). Let $\beta = X_{j_1} \ldots X_{j_l}$ and α' be the expression such that $\alpha = \beta\alpha'$. Then $|\beta| \leq |\alpha_i|$. Further $\beta \to^* [\alpha_i]_{U_i}$ and $\alpha' \to^* [\epsilon]_{U_i}$.

Then one can verify that the set $[\![EF]\!][\mathcal{P}(\langle\alpha_i, U_i\rangle)]$ is spanned by the semiseg-ment $\{\langle\beta, U'\rangle\}_{\beta\in K}$ where the index set $K \subseteq V^\oplus$ is defined as follows:

$$\beta \in K \text{ iff } |\beta| \leq |\alpha_i| \text{ and } \beta \to^* [\alpha_i]_{U_i},$$

and $U' = \{Y \in V \mid Y \to^* [\epsilon]_{U_i}\}$. Further the width of the semisegment is bounded by $|V| \|\langle\alpha_i, U_i\rangle\|$. $\square$

To tackle EGF, we need the following crucial lemma, which says that EGF can be effectively reduced to EF.

Lemma 1. *Let $\mathcal{S}$ be a segment. Then $\alpha \in [\![EGF]\!][\mathcal{P}(\mathcal{S})]$ iff there is $\alpha \to^* X\beta$ and $X \to^+ X\gamma$ such that $X\beta \in \mathcal{P}(\mathcal{S})$ and $X\beta\gamma \in \mathcal{P}(\mathcal{S})$.*

Proof. Let $\mathcal{S} = \langle\alpha'', U\rangle$. We prove the two directions.

"if": From $X\beta \in \mathcal{P}(\mathcal{S})$ and $X\beta\gamma \in \mathcal{P}(\mathcal{S})$, it follows from the definition of segments that $\gamma \in U^\oplus$. Thus $X\beta\gamma^n \in \mathcal{P}(\mathcal{S})$ for all $n \in \mathbb{N}_0$. Then we can con-struct the following infinite path: $X\beta\gamma^0 \to^+ X\beta\gamma^1 \to^+ X\beta\gamma^2 \ldots$. It follows that $\alpha \in [\![EGF]\!][\mathcal{P}(\mathcal{S})]$.

"only if": Since $\alpha \in [\![EGF]\!][\mathcal{P}(\mathcal{S})]$, there is an infinite path $\alpha \to^+ \alpha_1 \to^+ \alpha_2 \ldots$ such that $\alpha_n \in \mathcal{P}(\mathcal{S})$ for all $n \in \mathbb{N}$. By Dickson's Lemma, there is $n_1, n_2 \in \mathbb{N}$ with $n_1 < n_2$ such that $\alpha_{n_2} = \alpha_{n_1}\gamma''$ for some γ''. It follows from the definition that $\gamma'' \in U^\oplus$. Our task is to find an X in α_{n_1} such that $X \to^+ X\gamma$ with $\gamma \in U^\oplus$.

By decomposing the transition sequence $\alpha_{n_1} \to^+ \alpha_{n_1}\gamma''$ into transitions of single symbols, there is an expression α' and three finite sequences $\{X_l\}_{1\leq l\leq k}$, $\{\beta'_l\}_{1\leq l\leq k}$, $\{\gamma'_l\}_{1\leq l\leq k}$ (for some $k \in \mathbb{N}$) such that:

1. $\alpha_{n_1} = X_1 X_2 \ldots X_k \alpha'$ and $X_1 \ldots X_k = \beta'_1 \ldots \beta'_k$.
2. $X_l \to^+ \beta'_l\gamma'_l$ for all $1 \leq l \leq k$.
3. $\gamma'' = \gamma'_1 \ldots \gamma'_k$ (therefore $\gamma'_l \in U^\oplus$ for all $1 \leq l \leq k$).

Intuitively, the path from α_{n_1} to α_{n_2} is caused by transitions of $\{X_l\}_{1\leq l\leq k}$, while α' stays still and the "spin-offs" $\{\gamma'_l\}_{1\leq l\leq k}$ form γ''. Here we view $\{X_l\}_{1\leq l\leq k}$ as distinct symbols distinguished by their subscripts and denote $\mathcal{V}$ to be the set $\{X_1, \ldots, X_k\}$. Then from $X_1 \ldots X_k = \beta'_1 \ldots \beta'_k$ we can construct a partition $\pi = \{\pi_1, \ldots, \pi_k\}$ of $\mathcal{V}$ (where $\pi_l : 1 \leq l \leq k$ can be $\emptyset$) such that for all $1 \leq l \leq k$, $\beta'_l = Y_1 \ldots Y_{|\pi_l|}$ with $\pi_l = \{Y_1, \ldots, Y_{|\pi_l|}\}$ (here $\beta'_l = \epsilon$ corresponds to $\pi_l = \emptyset$).

Consider now a directed graph G where the vertex set is $\mathcal{V}$, and there is an edge from X_{l_1} to X_{l_2} iff $X_{l_2} \in \pi_{l_1}$. Two immediate observations are as follows:

1. (†) Each X_l has exactly one parent, i.e., there is exactly one edge into X_l;
2. (‡) If X_l has no children (i.e. $\pi_l = \emptyset$), then $\beta'_l = \epsilon$ (hence $X_l \to^+ \gamma'_l$).

By (†), there is a cycle (possibly a self-loop) in G. Let L be a cycle of G (chosen arbitrarily) which sequentially goes through distinct vertices $X'_1, \ldots, X'_{k'}$ then back to $X'_{k'+1}$ with $X'_{k'+1} = X'_1$. Further by (†), the only edges between vertices $\{X'_l\}_{1 \leq l \leq k'}$ are edges of L. Now consider any vertex Z such that $Z \notin L$ but the parent of Z lie on L. We prove that $Z \to^+ [\epsilon]_U$.

Let X'_l be the parent of Z on L. First we prove that any Z' reachable from Z cannot be on any cycle of G. Suppose not, let L' be a cycle that contains such a Z'. Using (†), we can prove inductively that $Z \in L'$ and $X'_l \in L'$ by back-tracing the walk from X'_l to Z and then to Z'. Moreover, the child of X'_l on L' is Z. We can also prove by induction that all vertices of L lie on L' by back-tracing L from X'_l. Since $Z \in L'$ we have $L \neq L'$. Let $X'_{l'}$ be the child of X'_l that lies on L. Then since $X'_{l'} \in L'$ and the child of X'_l on L' is Z, we have $X'_{l'}$ has another parent on L' different from X'_l. Contradiction to (†).

Then we define the set $\mathcal{U} \subseteq V$ as the least set satisfying the following conditions:

- For all $X_l \in V$, if X_l has no children then $X_l \in \mathcal{U}$ (i.e. $\mathcal{U}$ contains all X_l that has no children)
- For all $X_l \in V$, if all children of X_l belongs to $\mathcal{U}$, then $X_l \in \mathcal{U}$

It can be proved by induction that $X_l \to^+ [\epsilon]_U$ for all $X_l \in \mathcal{U}$, where (‡) is used for the base step. We show that $Z \in \mathcal{U}$. Suppose not, then Z has a child and there is a child Z_1 of Z with $Z_1 \notin \mathcal{U}$. Then from Z_1 we can find Z_2 by the same argument. Recursively we construct an infinite sequence $\{Z_l\}_{l \in \mathbb{N}}$ such that $Z_l \notin \mathcal{U}$ for all $l \in \mathbb{N}$. Then since V is finite, the infinite sequence must contain a cycle starting from some Z_l reachable from Z, contradiction.

Then for every $1 \leq l \leq k'$, we have $X'_l \to^+ [X'_{l+1}]_U$. Thus if we start from X'_1, then go through L and then back to X'_1, we obtain that $X'_1 \to^+ [X'_1]_U$, i.e., there is $\gamma \in U^\oplus$ such that $X'_1 \to^+ X'_1 \gamma$. Now let X be X'_1 and β be the expression satisfying $\alpha_{n_1} = X'_1 \beta$. By the definition of segments, it is clear that $X\beta \in \mathcal{P}(\mathcal{S})$ and $X\beta\gamma \in \mathcal{P}(\mathcal{S})$. □

Proposition 5. *Let $\mathcal{B}$ be a semisegment. Then there is a semisegment $\mathcal{B}'$ with $\|\mathcal{B}'\| \leq |V|(\|\mathcal{B}\| + 1)$ such that $\mathcal{P}(\mathcal{B}') = [\![EGF]\!][\mathcal{P}(\mathcal{B})]$.*

Proof. Let $\mathcal{B} = \{\langle \alpha_i, U_i \rangle\}_{i \in I}$. Since I is finite, we have:

$$[\![EGF]\!][\mathcal{P}(\mathcal{B})] = \bigcup_{i \in I} [\![EGF]\!][\mathcal{P}(\langle \alpha_i, U_i \rangle)]$$

Thus we need only to show that each $[\![EGF]\!][\mathcal{P}(\langle \alpha_i, U_i \rangle)]$ can be spanned by a semisegment with width bounded by $|V|(\|\langle \alpha_i, U_i \rangle\| + 1)$. By Lemma 1, we have $\alpha \in [\![EGF]\!][\mathcal{P}(\langle \alpha_i, U_i \rangle)]$ iff there is X, β, γ such that $\alpha \to^* X\beta \in \mathcal{P}(\langle \alpha_i, U_i \rangle)$, $X \to^+ X\gamma$ and $X\beta\gamma \in \mathcal{P}(\langle \alpha_i, U_i \rangle)$. The assertion $X\beta \in \mathcal{P}(\langle \alpha_i, U_i \rangle)$ further falls into two cases:

1. $\beta = \alpha_i \beta'$ and $X\beta'\gamma \in U_i^\oplus$.
2. $\beta = \alpha'_i \beta'$, $\alpha_i = X\alpha'_i$ and $\beta'\gamma \in U_i^\oplus$.

Then the set $[\![EGF]\!][\mathcal{P}(\langle\alpha_i, U_i\rangle)]$ is equal to $\bigcup_{\beta \in K}[\![EF]\!][\mathcal{P}(\langle\beta, U_i\rangle)]$ where the index set $K \subseteq V^\oplus$ is as follows: $\beta \in K$ iff

1. either $\beta = X\alpha_i$ for some X such that $X \in U_i$ and $X \rightarrow^+ [X]_{U_i}$; (this corresponds to the first case)
2. or $\beta = \alpha_i$ and there is X such that $m_X(\beta) > 0$ and $X \rightarrow^+ [X]_{U_i}$. (this corresponds to the second case)

By Proposition 4, $[\![EGF]\!][\mathcal{P}(\langle\alpha_i, U_i\rangle)]$ can be spanned by a semisegment with width bounded by $|V|(\|\langle\alpha_i, U_i\rangle\| + 1)$.   □

Through Proposition 1 – 5, we obtain the following theorem which can be proved by induction on the structure of ϕ.

Theorem 1. *For any formula ϕ, there exists a semisegment $\mathcal{B}_\phi$ with $\|\mathcal{B}_\phi\| \leq b(\phi)$ such that $\mathcal{P}(\mathcal{B}_\phi) = [\![\phi]\!]$, where the function $b(\phi)$ is inductively defined by:*

$$b(X \geq k) = k \qquad\qquad b(\langle a\rangle\phi) = b(\phi) + 1$$
$$b(\neg\phi) = b(\phi) + 1 \qquad\qquad b(EF\phi) = |V| \cdot b(\phi)$$
$$b(\phi \wedge \psi) = \max\{b(\phi), b(\psi)\} \qquad b(EGF\phi) = |V| \cdot (b(\phi) + 1)$$

Moreover, $b(\phi) = \mathcal{O}((k_\phi + |\phi|)|V|^{|\phi|})$.

Theorem 1 only illustrates the existence of a semisegment with well-controlled width. However in the proofs of Proposition 1 – 5 we do construct out explicitly a semisegment that fulfill the proposition. For example, In Proposition 3 "$\{\langle\alpha'X, U_i\rangle\}_{(\alpha',X)\in K}$" is constructed for each "$[\![a]\!][\mathcal{P}(\langle\alpha_i, U_i\rangle)]$", and then the target "$\mathcal{B}'$" can be constructed. And in Proposition 5, "$\bigcup_{\beta\in K}[\![EF]\!][\mathcal{P}(\langle\beta, U_i\rangle)]$" is constructed for each "$[\![EGF]\!][\mathcal{P}(\langle\alpha_i, U_i\rangle)]$"; then by further construction in the proof of Proposition 4, we can construct out the target "$\mathcal{B}'$". In Theorem 2, we will deal with the computational aspect of semisegments, where those constructions in the proofs of Proposition 1 – 5 correspond directly to our PSPACE algorithm.

We first prove some useful lemmas. Recall here that every expression α can be represented by its equivalent multiset. It follows that a segment $\mathcal{S}$ with $\|\mathcal{S}\| \leq k$ can be stored in $\mathcal{O}(|V| \log k)$ space.

Lemma 2. *For any two segments $\mathcal{S}_1$, $\mathcal{S}_2$, if $\mathcal{P}(\mathcal{S}_1) = \mathcal{P}(\mathcal{S}_2)$ then $\mathcal{S}_1 = \mathcal{S}_2$.*

Proof. Straightforward from Definition 1.   □

Lemma 3. *Let $U \subseteq V$. The problems if $\beta \rightarrow^+ [\alpha]_U$ and if $\beta \rightarrow^* [\alpha]_U$ can both be decided in NP in $\log(|\alpha| \cdot |\beta| \cdot |\Delta|)$ and $|V|, \|\Delta\|$.*

Proof. In [5, Theorem 3.1], Esparza proved that for β, β' and $\rho \in \Delta^\oplus$, there exists $\sigma \in \Delta^*$ such that the Parikh image of σ is ρ and $\beta \rightarrow_\sigma \beta'$ iff

1. $m_Z(\beta) + \sum_{r\in\Delta}(m_Z(r^\bullet) - m_Z(^\bullet r)) \cdot m_r(\rho) = m_Z(\beta')$ for all $Z \in V$.
2. for each $r \in \lfloor\rho\rfloor$, there is $\sigma' \in \lfloor\rho\rfloor^*$ and β'' such that $\beta \rightarrow_{\sigma'} \beta''$ and $m_{\bullet r}(\beta'') > 0$.

Based on this result, we proceed as follows. Let U, α, β be the input. We assign to each $Z \in V$ an integer variable v_Z, and to each rule r of Δ an integer variable v_r. Then we guess a set $\Delta' \subseteq \Delta$ (Δ' can be stored in $\mathcal{O}(|V|\|\Delta\|\log|\Delta|)$ space) and check if the following conditions hold:

1. the integer programming problem which contains the following restrictions
   (a) $v_Z + m_Z(\alpha) = m_Z(\beta) + \sum_{r \in \Delta}(m_Z(r^{\bullet}) - m_Z(^{\bullet}r)) \cdot v_r$, for all $Z \in V$;
   (b) $v_Z \geq 0$ and $v_r > 0$, for all $Z \in V$ and $r \in \Delta'$;
   (c) $v_Z = 0$ and $v_r = 0$, for all $Z \notin U$ and $r \in \Delta - \Delta'$.
   has an solution. This can be solved in NP (see [6, pp. 339]). Note that all numbers appeared above are stored in binary.
2. for each $r \in \Delta'$, there is $\sigma' \in \Delta'^*$ such that $\beta \to_{\sigma'} {}^{\bullet}r\beta'$ for some β'. This can be done by performing a reachability test on the directed graph whose vertex set is V and there is an edge from X to Y iff $X \to_{r'} Y\beta'$ for some $r' \in \Delta'$ and β'.

Then one can obtain that Δ' satisfies the conditions above iff there is $\sigma \in \Delta^*$ such that $\lfloor \sigma \rfloor = \Delta'$ and $\beta \to_\sigma \alpha\gamma$ for some $\gamma \in U^{\oplus}$. Thus $\beta \to^* [\alpha]_U$ iff there exists such Δ'; and $\beta \to^+ [\alpha]_U$ iff there exists such Δ' which is nonempty.   □

In the following theorem, we present our model checking algorithm.

Theorem 2. *The problem if $\alpha \models \phi$ is in PSPACE.*

Proof. In the proof we will use the important fact that for any formula ϕ, a semisegment $\mathcal{B}$ that spans the set $[\![\phi]\!]$ can have a width bounded by $b(\phi)$ (cf. Theorem 1). It follows that any segment $\langle \alpha, U \rangle \in \mathcal{B}$ can be stored in $\mathcal{O}(|\phi||V|(\log(|\phi||V|k_\phi)))$ space, which is polynomial in $|\phi|$, $\log k_\phi$ and $|V|$.

The core of the proof is a procedure $\text{Seg}(\phi, \mathcal{S})$ which takes as input a EGF-formula ϕ and a segment $\mathcal{S}$ with $\|\mathcal{S}\| \leq b(\phi)$. The procedure will have the following two properties:

1. $\text{Seg}(\phi, \mathcal{S})$ can be computed in PSPACE in $|V| \log b(\phi)$ and $\|\Delta\| \log |\Delta|$.
2. The semisegment $\{\mathcal{S} \mid \text{Seg}(\phi, \mathcal{S}) = 1\}$ spans the set $[\![\phi]\!]$, for any ϕ.

With these properties, we can decide in PSPACE if $\alpha \models \phi$ as follows: enumerate all segments $\mathcal{S}$ with $\|\mathcal{S}\| \leq b(\phi)$ and check if $\text{Seg}(\phi, \mathcal{S}) = 1$ and $\alpha \in \mathcal{P}(\mathcal{S})$; we answer 'yes' if there is such segment, and 'no' otherwise. Below we show the procedure, which is recursive on the structure of ϕ.

- $\text{Seg}(X \geq k, \mathcal{S}) = 1$ if $\mathcal{S} = \langle X^k, V \rangle$.
- $\text{Seg}(\neg\phi, \mathcal{S}) = 1$ if $\|\mathcal{S}\| \leq b(\phi) + 1$ and for all $\mathcal{S}'$ such that $\|\mathcal{S}'\| \leq b(\phi)$ and $\text{Seg}(\phi, \mathcal{S}') = 1$, $\mathcal{P}(\mathcal{S}) \cap \mathcal{P}(\mathcal{S}') = \emptyset$.
- $\text{Seg}(\phi \wedge \psi, \mathcal{S}) = 1$ if there are $\mathcal{S}_1, \mathcal{S}_2$ with $\|\mathcal{S}_1\| \leq b(\phi)$, $\|\mathcal{S}_2\| \leq b(\psi)$ such that $\text{Seg}(\phi, \mathcal{S}_1) = 1$, $\text{Seg}(\psi, \mathcal{S}_2) = 1$ and $\mathcal{P}(\mathcal{S}) = \mathcal{P}(\mathcal{S}_1) \cap \mathcal{P}(\mathcal{S}_2)$.
- $\text{Seg}(\langle a \rangle \phi, \langle \alpha, U \rangle) = 1$ if there is $\langle \alpha', U' \rangle$ and $X, \alpha'', \beta', \beta$ such that
  1. $\|\langle \alpha', U' \rangle\| \leq b(\phi)$ and $\text{Seg}(\phi, \langle \alpha', U' \rangle) = 1$
  2. $\alpha = \alpha''X$, $X \xrightarrow{a} \beta'\beta \in \Delta$ and $\alpha' = \alpha''\beta'$.
  3. $U = U'$ and $\beta \in U^{\oplus}$.

- $\text{Seg}(\text{EF}\phi, \langle \alpha, U \rangle) = 1$ if there is $\langle \beta, U' \rangle$ such that
  1. $\|\langle \beta, U' \rangle\| \leq b(\phi)$ and $\text{Seg}(\phi, \langle \beta, U' \rangle) = 1$
  2. $|\alpha| \leq |\beta|$ and $\alpha \rightarrow^* [\beta]_{U'}$.
  3. $Y \in U$ iff $Y \rightarrow^* [\epsilon]_{U'}$, for all $Y \in V$.
- $\text{Seg}(\text{EGF}\phi, \langle \alpha, U \rangle) = 1$ if there is $\langle \alpha', U' \rangle$ and $X \in V$ such that
  1. $\|\langle \alpha', U' \rangle\| \leq b(\phi)$ and $\text{Seg}(\phi, \langle \alpha', U' \rangle) = 1$.
  2. $X \rightarrow^+ [X]_{U'}$.
  3. either $X \in U'$, $|\alpha| \leq |X\alpha'|$ and $\alpha \rightarrow^* [X\alpha']_{U'}$,
     or $m_X(\alpha') > 0$, $|\alpha| \leq |\alpha'|$ and $\alpha \rightarrow^* [\alpha']_{U'}$.
  4. $Y \in U$ iff $Y \rightarrow^* [\epsilon]_{U'}$, for all $Y \in V$.
- In other cases $\text{Seg}(\phi, \mathcal{S}) = 0$.

Note that the problem if $\mathcal{P}(\mathcal{S}) = \mathcal{P}(\mathcal{S}_1) \cap \mathcal{P}(\mathcal{S}_2)$ is decidable in polynomial time in $\log \max\{|\mathcal{S}|, |\mathcal{S}_1|, |\mathcal{S}_2|\}$ and $|V|$ through the proof of Proposition 1 and Lemma 2. The problem if $\mathcal{P}(\mathcal{S}_1) \cap \mathcal{P}(\mathcal{S}_2) = \emptyset$ is similar. Then by Lemma 3, one can obtain that the space needed for computation at each recursion step of the procedure is polynomial in $\log k_\phi, \log |\Delta|$ and $|\phi|, |V|, \|\Delta\|$. Moreover, since the recursion depth of the procedure is at most $\mathcal{O}(|\phi|)$, the procedure can be implemented in polynomial space in $|\phi| \log k_\phi + |V| \|\Delta\| \log |\Delta|$.

Now we prove the second property of the procedure $\text{Seg}(\phi, \mathcal{S})$. The proof is by induction on the structure of ϕ. The base step where $\phi = X \geq k$ is clear. For the inductive step, the cases when $\phi = \psi \wedge \varphi$, $\phi = \langle a \rangle \psi$, $\phi = \text{EF}\psi$ and $\phi = \text{EGF}\psi$ correspond directly to the constructions in the proofs of Proposition 1 and Proposition 3 – 5, respectively. For example, the semisegment $\mathcal{B}' = \{\mathcal{S} \mid \text{Seg}(\text{EF}\phi, \mathcal{S}) = 1\}$ is exactly the result of the construction from $\mathcal{B} = \{\mathcal{S} \mid \text{Seg}(\phi, \mathcal{S}) = 1\}$ in the proof of Proposition 4. The situation for $\phi = \text{EGF}\psi$ is the same but a bit complicated, since we need to insert the construction in the proof of Proposition 4 into the one in the proof of Proposition 5.

The only exception is the case $\phi = \neg \psi$ which follows from the fact that for any semisegment $\mathcal{B}$ and natural number $k \geq \|\mathcal{B}\|$, $V^\oplus - \mathcal{P}(\mathcal{B})$ can be spanned by the semisegment:

$$\mathcal{B}' = \{\langle \alpha, U \rangle \mid \mathcal{P}(\langle \alpha, U \rangle) \cap \mathcal{P}(\mathcal{B}) = \emptyset \text{ and } \|\langle \alpha, U \rangle\| \leq k + 1\}$$

By definition, $\mathcal{P}(\mathcal{B}') \subseteq V^\oplus - \mathcal{P}(\mathcal{B})$. And by Proposition 2, there is a semisegment $\mathcal{B}''$ with $\|\mathcal{B}''\| \leq \|\mathcal{B}\| + 1$ such that $\mathcal{P}(\mathcal{B}'') = V^\oplus - \mathcal{P}(\mathcal{B})$ and $\mathcal{P}(\mathcal{B}'') \subseteq \mathcal{P}(\mathcal{B}')$. Thus $V^\oplus - \mathcal{P}(\mathcal{B}) = \mathcal{P}(\mathcal{B}')$. □

Remark 1. It is worth noting that from the proof of Theorem 2, we can compute a semisegment that spans the set $[\![\phi]\!]$ for any formula ϕ in PSPACE, except for the space for the output tape.

In [7], Mayr proved that model checking the logic EF (which is the logic EGF without the EGF operator) over BPPs is PSPACE-complete. Thus, we have the following theorem.

Theorem 3. *The model-checking problem for the logic EGF over Basic Parallel Processes is* PSPACE-complete.

4   Fixed Formula

In this section we consider the complexity of EGF model-checking problem over BPPs for fixed formula. The "fixed" case is formalized as follows.

Definition 3. *The* depth *of a formula ϕ is recursively defined as follows:*

- *$depth(X \geq k) = 0$*
- *$depth(\neg\phi) = depth(\phi)$*
- *$depth(\phi \wedge \psi) = \max\{depth(\phi), depth(\psi)\}$*
- *$depth(\Box\phi) = depth(\phi) + 1$ where $\Box \in \{\text{EF}, \text{EGF}, \langle a \rangle\}$.*

We define $\mathcal{F}_d$ as the set of all formulae of depth at most d, and $\mathcal{F}'_d$ as the set of all formulae of the form $\Box\phi$ where $\Box \in \{\text{EF}, \text{EGF}, \langle a \rangle\}$ and $\phi \in \mathcal{F}_d$. The model-checking problem for fixed formula is formally defined as follows:

- *PARAMETER: $d \in \mathbb{N}_0$, the depth of formula*
- *INPUT: BPP (V, Δ), expression α and formula $\phi \in \mathcal{F}'_d$.*
- *OUTPUT: if $\alpha \models \phi$.*

The input size is defined again as $|V| \log |\alpha| + |V| \|\Delta\| \log |\Delta| + |\phi| \log k_\phi$.

Below we fix a BPP (V, Δ). We prove by induction on d that the problem is in Σ^p_{d+1}, using oracle characterization of polynomial hierarchy. To this purpose, we need another two lemmas for EF and EGF, which are less dependent on segments and bases.

We introduce more notations. Let $U \subseteq V$, β and $k \in \mathbb{N}_0$. We define $\lceil\beta\rceil$ as $\max_{X \in V}\{m_X(\beta)\}$, $\lfloor\beta\rfloor_k$ as the set $\{Y \in V \mid m_Y(\beta) \geq k\}$, and θ_U as the expression satisfying: $m_Z(\theta_U) = 1$ if $Z \in U$, and $m_Z(\theta_U) = 0$ if $Z \notin U$, for all $Z \in V$.

Lemma 4. *Let $\mathcal{B}$ be a semisegment with $\|\mathcal{B}\| \leq k$. Then $\alpha \in [\![\text{EF}]\!][\mathcal{P}(\mathcal{B})]$ iff there is β such that $\beta \in \mathcal{P}(\mathcal{B})$, $\lceil\beta\rceil \leq k + 1$ and $\alpha \rightarrow^* [\beta]_{\lfloor\beta\rfloor_{k+1}}$.*

Proof. "if": Let $\langle\alpha', U'\rangle \in \mathcal{B}$ be a segment such that $\beta \in \mathcal{P}(\langle\alpha', U'\rangle)$. Since $\|\langle\alpha', U'\rangle\| \leq k$, we have $\lfloor\beta\rfloor_{k+1} \subseteq U'$. Thus $\alpha \rightarrow^* [\beta]_{\lfloor\beta\rfloor_{k+1}}$ implies $\alpha \rightarrow^* [\beta]_{U'}$. It follows that $\alpha \in [\![\text{EF}]\!][\mathcal{P}(\mathcal{B})]$.

"only if": Suppose that $\alpha \in [\![\text{EF}]\!][\mathcal{P}(\mathcal{B})]$. Then there is $\langle\alpha', U'\rangle \in \mathcal{B}$ and γ such that $\alpha \rightarrow^* \gamma$ and $\gamma \in \mathcal{P}(\langle\alpha', U'\rangle)$. Let β be given by: $m_Y(\beta) = \min\{m_Y(\gamma), k+1\}$ for all $Y \in V$. By $\|\langle\alpha', U'\rangle\| \leq k$, $\lfloor\gamma\rfloor_{k+1} \subseteq U'$. Thus $\beta \in \mathcal{P}(\mathcal{B})$. Then the result follows from the fact that $\alpha \rightarrow^* [\beta]_{\lfloor\beta\rfloor_{k+1}}$. $\qquad\square$

Lemma 5. *Let $\mathcal{B}$ be a semisegment with $\|\mathcal{B}\| \leq k$. Then $\alpha \in [\![\text{EGF}]\!][\mathcal{P}(\mathcal{B})]$ iff there is X, β and $U \subseteq V$ such that the following conditions hold:*

1. *$X \rightarrow^+ [X\theta_U]_U$, $m_X(\beta) > 0$ and $\lceil\beta\rceil \leq k + 1$;*
2. *$\beta\theta_U^{k+1} \in \mathcal{P}(\mathcal{B})$ and $\alpha \rightarrow^* [\beta\theta_U^{k+1}]_W$ where $W := \lfloor\beta\rfloor_{k+1} \cup U$.*

Proof. "if": Let $\langle\alpha',U'\rangle \in \mathcal{B}$ be a segment such that $\beta\theta_U^{k+1} \in \mathcal{P}(\langle\alpha',U'\rangle)$. By $\|\mathcal{B}\| \leq k$, we have $W \subseteq U'$. Then $\beta\theta_U^{k+n}\gamma' \in \mathcal{P}(\langle\alpha',U'\rangle)$ for any $n \in \mathbb{N}$ and any $\gamma' \in W^\oplus$. Since $X \to^+ [X\theta_U]_U$ and $U \subseteq W$, we have $\beta\theta_U^{k+n} \to^+ [\beta\theta_U^{k+n+1}]_W$ for all $n \in \mathbb{N}$. Then by $\alpha \to^* [\beta\theta_U^{k+1}]_W$, $\alpha \in [\![EGF]\!][\mathcal{P}(\langle\alpha',U'\rangle)]$.

"only if": Let $\langle\alpha',U'\rangle \in \mathcal{B}$ be a segment such that $\alpha \in [\![EGF]\!][\mathcal{P}(\langle\alpha',U'\rangle)]$. Then from the proof of Proposition 5, there must be $X, \beta', \gamma, \gamma'$ such that the following holds:

1. $\alpha \to^* \beta'\gamma \in \mathcal{P}(\langle\alpha',U'\rangle)$, $X \to^+ X\gamma'$ and $\gamma\gamma' \in U'^\oplus$;
2. either $X \in U'$ and $\beta' = X\alpha'$, or $m_X(\beta') > 0$ and $\beta' = \alpha'$.

Let β be given by: $m_Y(\beta) = \min\{m_Y(\beta'\gamma), k+1\}$ for all $Y \in V$ (note that $m_X(\beta) > 0$). And let $U = \lfloor\gamma'\rfloor$ (then $U \subseteq U'$). Then $X \to^+ [X\theta_U]_U$, $\alpha \to^* [\beta]_{\lfloor\beta\rfloor_{k+1}}$ and then $\alpha \to^* [\beta\theta_U^{k+1}]_W$ ($W = \lfloor\beta\rfloor_{k+1} \cup U$). From $\|\mathcal{B}\| \leq k$, we obtain that $W \subseteq U'$. Thus we have $\beta\theta_U^{k+1} \in \mathcal{P}(\langle\alpha',U'\rangle)$ by $\beta'\gamma \in \mathcal{P}(\langle\alpha',U'\rangle)$.   □

The main result for fixed formula is as follows.

Theorem 4. *Let* $\alpha \in V^\oplus$ *and* $\phi \in \mathcal{F}'_d$. *The problem if* $\alpha \models \phi$ *can be solved in* Σ_{d+1}^p.

Proof. Let $\phi = \square\psi$ with $\square \in \{EF, EGF, \langle a\rangle\}$ and $\psi \in \mathcal{F}_d$. The proof is by induction on d. Recall that every expression can be represented in its multiset form.

Base Step: $d = 0$. Then ψ contains only atomic formulae and boolean operators. For $\phi = \langle a\rangle\psi$, we guess a transition $\alpha \overset{a}{\to} \beta$ and check if $\beta \models \psi$ in polynomial time by a simple recursive procedure on the structure of ψ. For $\phi = EGF\psi$, we know that there is a semisegment $\mathcal{B}$ with $\|\mathcal{B}\| \leq b(\psi)$ such that $\mathcal{P}(\mathcal{B}) = \{\beta \mid \beta \models \psi\}$. Then by Lemma 5, we can check if $\alpha \models EGF\psi$ by checking if there is X, β and $U \subseteq V$ such that the following conditions hold:

1. $X \to^+ [X\theta_U]_U$, $m_X(\beta) > 0$ and $\lceil\beta\rceil \leq b(\psi) + 1$;
2. $\beta\theta_U^{b(\psi)+1} \models \psi$ and $\alpha \to^* [\beta\theta_U^{b(\psi)+1}]_W$ where $W := \lfloor\beta\rfloor_{b(\psi)+1} \cup U$.

Since $\lceil\beta\rceil \leq b(\psi)+1$, we can store $\beta\theta_U^{b(\psi)+1}$ in $\mathcal{O}(|V|\log b(\psi))$ space. By Lemma 3 and through deciding $\beta\theta_U^{b(\psi)+1} \models \psi$ in polynomial time, the checking can be solved in $\Sigma_1^p = NP$. For $\phi = EF\psi$, we proceed as for $EGF\psi$, however we use Lemma 4 instead.

Inductive Step: Let $\phi \in \mathcal{F}'_{d+1}$ and O be an oracle for $\mathcal{F}'_d$. We only clarify the case when $\phi = EGF\psi$ with $\psi \in \mathcal{F}_d$, the other cases are similar. We proceed much as the same as in the base step, however instead of checking $\beta\theta_U^{b(\psi)+1} \models \psi$ directly, we check if $\beta\theta_U^{b(\psi)+1} \models \psi$ recursively on the structure of ψ and we query O when we meet modal operators. Thus the problem can be solved in $NP^{\Sigma_{d+1}^p} = \Sigma_{d+2}^p$.   □

In [4], the following hardness result is shown.

Lemma 6. *For any $\alpha \in V^{\oplus}$ and $\psi \in \mathcal{F}_d$, the problem if $\alpha \models \mathrm{EF}\psi$ is Σ_{d+1}^p-hard.*

Combing this hardness result, we have the following theorem:

Theorem 5. *For any $\alpha \in V^{\oplus}$ and $\phi \in \mathcal{F}_d'$, the problem if $\alpha \models \phi$ is Σ_{d+1}^p-complete.*

5   Conclusion

We have shown that model checking the logic EGF is PSPACE-complete over BPPs, and Σ_d^p-complete for certain classes of fixed formula with nesting depth d of modal operators. These results coincide with the ones for the Logic EF obtained in [7]. Thus, adding EGF does not increase the complexity level.

Our method is different from and incorporates Mayr's for the Logic EF [7]. In general, we show that the set of expressions that satisfy a given formula can be "effectively" characterized by a simple semilinear structure called "semisegment" in this paper, which is already used in [8] to tackle the state explosion problem of the model checking of Petri Net. This symbolic representation also refines the semilinear sets used in [4]. The effectiveness of the representation lies in the "width" of the semisegment, which is a key factor in our PSPACE model checking algorithm.

The symbolic representation in our paper is syntactically simple. This simplicity provides a room for extension. A possible future work here is to study if this method can be extended to other meaningful CTL* fragments, e.g., other fairness fragments. It is also possible to extend this representation to quantitative verification such as verification of probabilistic properties.

References

1. Abdulla, P.A., Jonsson, B., Nilsson, M., Saksena, M.: A survey of regular model checking. In: Gardner, P., Yoshida, N. (eds.) CONCUR 2004. LNCS, vol. 3170, pp. 35–48. Springer, Heidelberg (2004)
2. Burkart, O., Caucal, D., Moller, F., Steffen, B.: Verification on infinite structures. In: Bergsta, J., Ponse, A., Smolka, S. (eds.) Handbook of Process Algebra, ch. 9, pp. 545–623. Elsevier Science, The Netherlands (2001)
3. Christensen, S.: Decidability and Decomposition in Process Algebras. Ph.D. thesis, The University of Edinburgh, Department of Computer Science, ECS-LFCS-93-278, Edinburgh, UK (1993)
4. Esparza, J.: Decidability of model checking for infinite-state concurrent systems. Acta Inf. 34(2), 85–107 (1997)
5. Esparza, J.: Petri nets, commutative context-free grammars, and basic parallel processes. Fundam. Inform. 31(1), 13–25 (1997)
6. Hopcroft, J., Ullman, J.: Introduction to Automata Theory, Languages, and Computation. Addison-Wesley, Reading (1979)

7. Mayr, R.: Weak bisimulation and model checking for basic parallel processes. In: Chandru, V., Vinay, V. (eds.) FSTTCS 1996. LNCS, vol. 1180, pp. 88–99. Springer, Heidelberg (1996)
8. Strehl, K., Thiele, L.: Interval diagram techniques for symbolic model checking of petri nets. In: DATE, pp. 756–757 (1999)
9. To, A.W., Libkin, L.: Recurrent reachability analysis in regular model checking. In: Cervesato, I., Veith, H., Voronkov, A. (eds.) LPAR 2008. LNCS (LNAI), vol. 5330, pp. 198–213. Springer, Heidelberg (2008)

Measuring Permissiveness in Parity Games: Mean-Payoff Parity Games Revisited[*]

Patricia Bouyer[1], Nicolas Markey[1], Jörg Olschewski[2], and Michael Ummels[1,3]

[1] LSV, CNRS & ENS Cachan, France
{bouyer,markey,ummels}@lsv.ens-cachan.fr
[2] Lehrstuhl Informatik 7, RWTH Aachen University, Germany
olschewski@automata.rwth-aachen.de
[3] LAMSADE, CNRS & Université Paris-Dauphine, France

Abstract. We study nondeterministic strategies in parity games with the aim of computing a *most permissive* winning strategy. Following earlier work, we measure permissiveness in terms of the *average* number/weight of transitions blocked by a strategy. Using a translation into mean-payoff parity games, we prove that deciding (the permissiveness of) a most permissive winning strategy is in NP ∩ coNP. Along the way, we provide a new study of mean-payoff parity games. In particular, we give a new algorithm for solving these games, which beats all previously known algorithms for this problem.

1 Introduction

Games extend the usual semantics of finite automata from one to several players, thus allowing to model interactions between agents acting on the progression of the automaton. This has proved very useful in computer science, especially for the formal verification of open systems interacting with their environment [20]. In this setting, the aim is to synthesise a controller under which the system behaves according to a given specification, whatever the environment does. Usually, this is modelled as a game between two players: Player 1 represents the controller and Player 2 represents the environment. The goal is then to find a *winning strategy* for Player 1, i.e. a recipe stating how the system should react to any possible action of the environment, in order to meet its specification.

In this paper, we consider *multi-strategies* (or *non-deterministic strategies,* cf. [1, 3]) as a generalisation of strategies: while strategies select only one possible action to be played in response to the behaviour of the environment, multi-strategies can retain several possible actions. Allowing several moves provides a way to cope with errors (e.g., actions being disabled for a short period, or timing imprecisions in timed games). Another quality of multi-strategies is their ability to be combined with other multi-strategies, yielding a refined multi-strategy, which is ideally winning for all of the original specifications. This offers a modular approach for solving games.

---

[*] Sponsored by ANR-06-SETI-003 DOTS, and by ESF-Eurocores LogICCC GASICS.

T. Bultan and P.-A. Hsiung (Eds.): ATVA 2011, LNCS 6996, pp. 135–149, 2011.

Classically, a strategy is more *permissive* than another one if it allows more behaviours. Under this notion, there does not need to exist a most permissive winning strategy [1]. Hence, we follow a different approach, which is of a quantitative nature: we provide a *measure* that specifies *how* permissive a given multi-strategy is. In order to do so, we consider *weighted games*, where each edge is equipped with a weight, which we treat as a *penalty* that is incurred when disallowing this edge. The penalty of a multi-strategy is then defined to be the average sum of penalties incurred in each step (in the limit). The lower this penalty is, the more permissive is the given multi-strategy. Our aim is to find one of the most permissive multi-strategies achieving a given objective.

We deal with multi-strategies by transforming a game with penalties into a *mean-payoff game* [11, 22] with classical (deterministic) strategies. A move in the latter game corresponds to a set of moves in the former, and is assigned a (negative) *reward* depending on the penalty of the original move. The penalty of a multi-strategy in the original game equals the opposite of the payoff achieved by the corresponding strategy in the mean-payoff game. In previous work, Bouyer et al. [3] introduced the notion of penalties and showed how to compute permissive strategies wrt. reachability objectives. We extend the study of [3] to parity objectives. This is a significant extension because parity objectives can express infinitary specifications. Using the above transformation, we reduce the problem of finding a most permissive strategy in a parity game with penalties to that of computing an optimal strategy in a *mean-payoff parity game*, which combines a mean-payoff objective with a parity objective.

While mean-payoff parity games have already been studied [9, 2, 7], we propose a new proof that these games are determined and that both players have optimal strategies. Moreover, we prove that the second player does not only have an optimal strategy with finite memory, but one that uses no memory at all. Finally, we provide a new algorithm for computing the values of a mean-payoff parity game, which is faster than the best known algorithms for this problem; the running time is exponential in the number of priorities and polynomial in the size of the game graph and the largest absolute weight.

In the second part of this paper, we present our results on parity games with penalties. In particular, we prove the existence of most permissive multi-strategies, and we show that the existence of a multi-strategy whose penalty is less than a given threshold can be decided in NP ∩ coNP. Finally, we adapt our deterministic algorithm for mean-payoff parity games to parity games with penalties. Our algorithm computes the penalties of a most permissive multi-strategy in time exponential in the number of priorities and polynomial in the size of the game graph and the largest penalty.

Due to space restrictions, most proofs are omitted in this extended abstract; they can be found in the full version of this paper [5].

Related Work. Penalties as we use them were defined in [3]. Other notions of permissiveness have been defined in [1, 19], but these notions have the drawback that a most permissive strategy might not exist. Multi-strategies have also been used for different purposes in [16].

The parity condition goes back to [12, 18] and is fundamental for verification. Parity games admit optimal memoryless strategies for both players, and the problem of deciding the winner is in NP ∩ coNP. As of this writing, it is not known whether parity games can be solved in polynomial time; the best known algorithms run in time polynomial in the size of the game graph but exponential in the number of priorities.

Another fundamental class of games are games with quantitative objectives. Mean-payoff games, where the aim is to maximise the average weight of the transitions taken in a play, are also in NP∩coNP and admit memoryless optimal strategies [11, 22]. The same is true for *energy games*, where the aim is to always keep the sum of the weights above a given threshold [6, 4]. In fact, parity games can easily be reduced to mean-payoff or energy games [13].

Finally, several game models mixing several qualitative or quantitative objectives have recently appeared in the literature: apart from mean-payoff parity games, these include generalised parity games [10], energy parity games [7] and lexicographic mean-payoff (parity) games [2] as well as generalised energy and mean-payoff games [8].

2   Preliminaries

A *weighted game graph* is a tuple $G = (Q_1, Q_2, E, \text{weight})$, where $Q := Q_1 \dot\cup Q_2$ is a finite set of *states*, $E \subseteq Q \times Q$ is the *edge* or *transition relation*, and weight: $E \rightarrow \mathbb{R}$ is a function assigning a *weight* to every transition. When weighted game graphs are subject to algorithmic processing, we assume that these weights are integers; in this case, we set $W := \max\{1, |\text{weight}(e)| \mid e \in E\}$.

For $q \in Q$, we write qE for the set $\{q' \in Q \mid (q, q') \in E\}$ of all successors of q. We require that $qE \neq \emptyset$ for all states $q \in Q$. A subset $S \subseteq Q$ is a *subarena* of G if $qE \cap S \neq \emptyset$ for all states $q \in S$. If $S \subseteq Q$ is a subarena of G, then we can restrict G to states in S, in which case we obtain the weighted game graph $G \upharpoonright S := (Q_1 \cap S, Q_2 \cap S, E \cap (S \times S), \text{weight} \upharpoonright S \times S)$.

A *play* of G is an infinite sequence $\rho = \rho(0)\rho(1)\cdots \in Q^\omega$ of states such that $(\rho(i), \rho(i+1)) \in E$ for all $i \in \mathbb{N}$. We denote by $\text{Out}^{\mathcal{G}}(q)$ the set of all plays ρ with $\rho(0) = q$ and by $\text{Inf}(\rho)$ the set of states occurring infinitely often in ρ.

A *play prefix* or a *history* $\gamma = \gamma(0)\gamma(1)\cdots\gamma(n) \in Q^+$ is a finite, nonempty prefix of a play. For a play or a history ρ and $j < k \in \mathbb{N}$, we denote by $\rho[j,k) := \rho[j, k-1] := \rho(j) \cdots \rho(k-1)$ its infix starting at position j and ending at position $k - 1$.

Strategies. A *(deterministic) strategy* for Player i in G is a function $\sigma : Q^* Q_i \rightarrow Q$ such that $\sigma(\gamma q) \in qE$ for all $\gamma \in Q^*$ and $q \in Q_i$. A strategy σ is *memoryless* if $\sigma(\gamma q) = \sigma(q)$ for all $\gamma \in Q^*$ and $q \in Q_i$. More generally, a strategy σ is *finite-memory* if the equivalence relation $\sim \subseteq Q^* \times Q^*$, defined by $\gamma_1 \sim \gamma_2$ if and only if $\sigma(\gamma_1 \cdot \gamma) = \sigma(\gamma_2 \cdot \gamma)$ for all $\gamma \in Q^* Q_i$, has finite index.

We say that a play ρ of G is *consistent* with a strategy σ for Player i if $\rho(k+1) = \sigma(\rho[0, k])$ for all $k \in \mathbb{N}$ with $\rho(k) \in Q_i$, and denote by $\text{Out}^G(\sigma, q_0)$ the set of all plays ρ of G that are consistent with σ and start in $\rho(0) = q_0$. Given a strategy σ of Player 1, a strategy τ of Player 2, and a state $q_0 \in Q$, there exists a unique play $\rho \in \mathrm{Out}^G(\sigma, q_0) \cap \mathrm{Out}^G(\tau, q_0)$, which we denote by $\rho^G(\sigma, \tau, q_0)$.

Traps and Attractors. Intuitively, a set $T \subseteq Q$ of states is a *trap* for one of the two players if the other player can enforce that the play stays in this set. Formally, a trap for Player 2 (or simply a 2-trap) is a subarena $T \subseteq Q$ such that $qE \subseteq T$ for all states $q \in T \cap Q_2$, and $qE \cap T \neq \emptyset$ for all $q \in T \cap Q_1$. A trap for Player 1 (or 1-trap) is defined analogously.

If $T \subseteq Q$ is not a trap for Player 1, then Player 1 has a strategy to reach a position in $Q \setminus T$. In general, given a subset $S \subseteq Q$, we denote by $\mathrm{Attr}_1^G(S)$ the set of states from where Player 1 can force a visit to S. From every state in $\mathrm{Attr}_1^G(S)$, Player 1 has a memoryless strategy σ that guarantees a visit to S in at most $|Q|$ steps. We call the set $\mathrm{Attr}_1^G(S)$ the 1-*attractor of S* and σ an *attractor strategy for S*. The 2-*attractor* of a set S, denoted by $\mathrm{Attr}_2^G(S)$, and attractor strategies for Player 2 are defined symmetrically. Notice that for any set S, the set $Q \setminus \mathrm{Attr}_1^G(S)$ is a 1-trap, and if S is a subarena (2-trap), then $\mathrm{Attr}_1^G(S)$ is also a subarena (2-trap). Analogously, $Q \setminus \mathrm{Attr}_2^G(S)$ is a 2-trap, and if S is a subarena (1-trap), then $\mathrm{Attr}_2^G(S)$ is also a subarena (1-trap).

Convention. We often drop the superscript G from the expressions defined above, if no confusion arises, e.g. by writing $\mathrm{Out}(\sigma, q_0)$ instead of $\mathrm{Out}^G(\sigma, q_0)$.

3   Mean-Payoff Parity Games

In this section, we establish that mean-payoff parity games are determined, that both players have optimal strategies, that for Player 2 even memoryless strategies suffice, and that the value problem for mean-payoff parity games is in $\mathrm{NP} \cap \mathrm{coNP}$. Furthermore, we present a deterministic algorithm which computes the values in time exponential in the number of priorities, and runs in pseudo-polynomial time when the number of priorities is bounded.

Formally, a *mean-payoff parity game* is a tuple $\mathcal{G} = (G, \chi)$, where G is a weighted game graph, and $\chi \colon Q \to \mathbb{N}$ is a priority function assigning a *priority* to every state. A play $\rho = \rho(0)\rho(1)\cdots$ is *parity-winning* if the minimal priority occurring infinitely often in ρ is even, i.e., if $\min\{\chi(q) \mid q \in \mathrm{Inf}(\rho)\} \equiv 0 \pmod 2$. All notions that we have defined for weighted game graphs carry over to mean-payoff parity games. In particular, a play of $\mathcal{G}$ is just a play of G and a strategy for Player i in $\mathcal{G}$ is nothing but a strategy for Player i in G. Hence, we write $\mathrm{Out}^{\mathcal{G}}(\sigma, q)$ for $\mathrm{Out}^G(\sigma, q)$, and so on. As for weighted games graphs, we often omit the superscript if $\mathcal{G}$ is clear from the context. Finally, for a mean-payoff parity game $\mathcal{G} = (G, \chi)$ and a subarena S of G, we write $\mathcal{G} \upharpoonright S$ for the mean-payoff parity game $(G \upharpoonright S, \chi \upharpoonright S)$.

We say that a mean-payoff parity game $\mathcal{G} = (G, \chi)$ is a *mean-payoff game* if $\chi(q)$ is even for all $q \in Q$. In particular, given a weighted game graph G, we obtain a mean-payoff game by assigning priority 0 to all states. We denote this game by $(G, 0)$.

For a play ρ of a mean-payoff parity game $\mathcal{G}$ that is parity-winning, its *payoff* is defined as

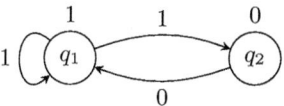

Fig. 1. A mean-payoff parity game for which infinite memory is necessary

$$\text{payoff}^{\mathcal{G}}(\rho) = \liminf_{n\to\infty} \frac{1}{n} \sum_{i=0}^{n-1} \text{weight}(\rho(i),\rho(i+1)) \,;$$

if ρ is not parity-winning, we set $\text{payoff}^{\mathcal{G}}(\rho) := -\infty$. If σ is a strategy for Player 1 in $\mathcal{G}$, we define its *value* from $q_0 \in Q$ as $\text{val}^{\mathcal{G}}(\sigma, q_0) = \inf_{\rho\in\text{Out}^{\mathcal{G}}(\sigma,q_0)} \text{payoff}^{\mathcal{G}}(\rho)$. Analogously, the value $\text{val}^{\mathcal{G}}(\tau, q_0)$ of a strategy τ for Player 2 is defined as the supremum of $\text{payoff}^{\mathcal{G}}(\rho)$ over all $\rho \in \text{Out}^{\mathcal{G}}(\tau, q_0)$. The *lower* and *upper value* of a state $q_0 \in Q$ are defined by $\underline{\text{val}}^{\mathcal{G}}(q_0) = \sup_\sigma \text{val}^{\mathcal{G}}(\sigma, q_0)$ and $\overline{\text{val}}^{\mathcal{G}}(q_0) = \inf_\tau \text{val}^{\mathcal{G}}(\tau, q_0)$, respectively. Intuitively, $\underline{\text{val}}^{\mathcal{G}}(q_0)$ and $\overline{\text{val}}^{\mathcal{G}}(q_0)$ are the maximal (respectively minimal) payoff that Player 1 (respectively Player 2) can ensure (in the limit). We say that a strategy σ of Player 1 is *optimal from* q_0 if $\text{val}^{\mathcal{G}}(\sigma, q_0) = \underline{\text{val}}^{\mathcal{G}}(q_0)$. Analogously, we call a strategy τ of Player 2 optimal from q_0 if $\text{val}^{\mathcal{G}}(\tau, q_0) = \overline{\text{val}}^{\mathcal{G}}(q_0)$. A strategy is *(globally) optimal* if it is optimal from every state $q \in Q$. It is easy to see that $\underline{\text{val}}^{\mathcal{G}}(q_0) \leq \overline{\text{val}}^{\mathcal{G}}(q_0)$. If $\underline{\text{val}}^{\mathcal{G}}(q_0) = \overline{\text{val}}^{\mathcal{G}}(q_0)$, we say that q_0 has a *value*, which we denote by $\text{val}^{\mathcal{G}}(q_0)$.

Example 1. Consider the mean-payoff parity game $\mathcal{G}$ depicted in Fig. 1, where a state or an edge is labelled with its priority, respectively weight; all states belong to Player 1. Note that $\text{val}^{\mathcal{G}}(q_1) = 1$ since Player 1 can delay visiting q_2 longer and longer while still ensuring that this vertex is seen infinitely often. However, there is no finite-memory strategy that achieves this value.

It follows from Martin's determinacy theorem [17] that mean-payoff parity games are determined, i.e., that every state has a value. Moreover, Chatterjee et al. [9] gave an algorithmic proof for the existence of optimal strategies. Finally, it can be shown that for every $x \in \mathbb{R} \cup \{-\infty\}$ the set $\{\rho \in Q^\omega \mid \text{payoff}(\rho) \geq x\}$ is closed under *combinations*. By Theorem 4 in [15], this property implies that Player 2 even has a memoryless optimal strategy. In the full version of this paper [5], we give a purely inductive proof of determinacy and the existence of (memoryless) optimal strategies. We thus have the following theorem.

Theorem 2. *Let $\mathcal{G}$ be a mean-payoff parity game.*

1. *$\mathcal{G}$ is determined;*
2. *Player 1 has an optimal strategy in $\mathcal{G}$;*
3. *Player 2 has a memoryless optimal strategy in $\mathcal{G}$.*

A consequence of the proof of Theorem 2 is that each value of a mean-payoff parity game is either $-\infty$ or equals one of the values of a mean-payoff game played on the same weighted graph (or a subarena of it). Since optimal memory-less strategies exist in mean-payoff games [11], the values of a mean-payoff game with integral weights are rational numbers of the form r/s with $|r| \leq |Q| \cdot W$ and $|s| \leq |Q|$. Consequently, this property holds for the (finite) values of a mean-payoff parity game as well.

We now turn towards the computational complexity of mean-payoff parity games. Formally, the *value problem* is the following decision problem: Given a mean-payoff parity game $\mathcal{G}$ (with integral weights), a designated state $q_0 \in Q$, and a number $x \in \mathbb{Q}$, decide whether $\mathrm{val}^{\mathcal{G}}(q_0) \geq x$. By Theorem 2, to decide whether $\mathrm{val}^{\mathcal{G}}(q_0) < x$, we can guess a memoryless strategy τ for Player 2 and check whether $\mathrm{val}^{\mathcal{G}}(\tau, q_0) < x$. It follows from a result of Karp [14] that the latter check can be carried out in polynomial time. Hence, the value problem belongs to coNP.

Corollary 3. *The value problem for mean-payoff parity games is in coNP.*

Via a reduction to *energy parity games*, Chatterjee and Doyen [7] recently proved that the value problem for mean-payoff parity games is in NP. Hence, these games do not seem harder than parity or mean-payoff games, which also come with a value problem in NP $\cap$ coNP.

Theorem 4 (Chatterjee-Doyen). *The value problem for mean-payoff parity games is in NP.*

A Deterministic Algorithm. We now present a deterministic algorithm for computing the values of a mean-payoff parity game, which runs faster than all known algorithms for solving these games. Algorithm SolveMPP

is based on the classical algorithm for solving parity games, due to Zielonka [21]. The algorithm employs as a subprocedure an algorithm SolveMP for solving mean-payoff games. By [22], such an algorithm can be implemented to run in time $\mathrm{O}(n^3 \cdot m \cdot W)$ for a game with n states and m edges. We denote by $f \sqcup g$ and $f \sqcap g$ the pointwise maximum, respectively minimum, of two (partial) functions $f, g \colon Q \to \mathbb{R} \cup \{\pm\infty\}$ (where $(f \sqcup g)(q) = (f \sqcap g)(q) = f(q)$ if $g(q)$ is undefined).

The algorithm works as follows: If the least priority p in $\mathcal{G}$ is even, the algorithm first identifies the least value of $\mathcal{G}$ by computing the values of the mean-payoff game $(G, 0)$ and (recursively) the values of the game $\mathcal{G} \upharpoonright Q \setminus \mathrm{Attr}_1(\chi^{-1}(p))$, and taking their minimum x. All states from where Player 2 can enforce a visit to a state with value x in one of these two games must have value x in $\mathcal{G}$. In the remaining subarena, the values can be computed by calling SolveMPP recursively. If the least priority is odd, we can similarly compute the greatest value of $\mathcal{G}$ and proceed by recursion. The correctness of the algorithm relies on the following two lemmas.

Lemma 5. *Let $\mathcal{G}$ be a mean-payoff parity game with least priority p even, $T = Q \setminus \mathrm{Attr}_1(\chi^{-1}(p))$, and $x \in \mathbb{R}$. If $\mathrm{val}^{(G,0)}(q) \geq x$ for all $q \in Q$ and $\mathrm{val}^{\mathcal{G} \upharpoonright T}(q) \geq x$ for all $q \in T$, then $\mathrm{val}^{\mathcal{G}}(q) \geq x$ for all $q \in Q$.*

Algorithm. SolveMPP($\mathcal{G}$)

Input: mean-payoff parity game $\mathcal{G} = (G, \chi)$
Output: val$^{\mathcal{G}}$

if $Q = \emptyset$ **then return** $\emptyset$
$p := \min\{\chi(q) \mid q \in Q\}$
if p is even **then**
    $g := \text{SolveMP}(G, 0)$
    if $\chi(q) = p$ for all $q \in Q$ **then return** g
    $T := Q \setminus \text{Attr}_1^{\mathcal{G}}(\chi^{-1}(p)); \ f := \text{SolveMPP}(\mathcal{G} \upharpoonright T)$
    $x := \min(f(T) \cup g(Q)); \ A := \text{Attr}_2^{\mathcal{G}}(f^{-1}(x) \cup g^{-1}(x))$
    return $(Q \to \mathbb{R} \cup \{-\infty\} \colon q \mapsto x) \sqcup \text{SolveMPP}(\mathcal{G} \upharpoonright Q \setminus A)$
else
    $T := Q \setminus \text{Attr}_2^{\mathcal{G}}(\chi^{-1}(p))$
    if $T = \emptyset$ **then return** $(Q \to \mathbb{R} \cup \{-\infty\} \colon q \mapsto -\infty)$
    $f := \text{SolveMPP}(\mathcal{G} \upharpoonright T); \ x := \max f(T); \ A := \text{Attr}_1^{\mathcal{G}}(f^{-1}(x))$
    return $(Q \to \mathbb{R} \cup \{-\infty\} \colon q \mapsto x) \sqcap \text{SolveMPP}(\mathcal{G} \upharpoonright Q \setminus A)$
end if

Lemma 6. *Let $\mathcal{G}$ be a mean-payoff parity game with least priority p odd, $T = Q \setminus \text{Attr}_2(\chi^{-1}(p))$, and $x \in \mathbb{R}$. If $\text{val}^{\mathcal{G}}(q) \geq x$ for some $q \in Q$, then $T \neq \emptyset$ and $\text{val}^{\mathcal{G} \upharpoonright T}(q) \geq x$ for some $q \in T$.*

Theorem 7. *The values of a mean-payoff parity game with d priorities can be computed in time $O(|Q|^{d+2} \cdot |E| \cdot W)$.*

Proof. We claim that SolveMPP computes, given a mean-payoff parity game $\mathcal{G}$, the function val$^{\mathcal{G}}$ in the given time bound. Denote by $T(n, m, d)$ the worst-case running time of the algorithm on a game with n states, m edges and d priorities. Note that, if $\mathcal{G}$ has only one priority, then there are no recursive calls to SolveMPP. Since attractors can be computed in time $O(n + m)$ and the running time of SolveMP is $O(n^3 \cdot m \cdot W)$, there exists a constant c such that the numbers $T(n, m, d)$ satisfy the following recurrence:

$$T(1, m, d) \leq c,$$
$$T(n, m, 1) \leq c \cdot n^3 \cdot m \cdot W,$$
$$T(n, m, d) \leq T(n - 1, m, d - 1) + T(n - 1, m, d) + c \cdot n^3 \cdot m \cdot W.$$

Solving this recurrence, we get that $T(n, m, d) \leq c \cdot (n + 1)^{d+2} \cdot m \cdot W$, which proves the claimed time bound.

    It remains to be proved that the algorithm is correct, i.e. that SolveMPP($\mathcal{G}$) = val$^{\mathcal{G}}$. We prove the claim by induction over the number of states. If there are no states, the claim is trivial. Hence, assume that $Q \neq \emptyset$ and that the claim is true for all games with less than $|Q|$ states. Let $p := \min\{\chi(q) \mid q \in Q\}$. We only consider the case that p is even. If p is odd, the proof is similar, but relies on Lemma 6 instead of Lemma 5.

Let T, f, g, x and A be defined as in the corresponding case of the algorithm, and let $f^* = \text{SolveMPP}(\mathcal{G})$. If $\chi(Q) = \{p\}$, then $f^* = g = \text{val}^{(G,0)} = \text{val}^{\mathcal{G}}$, and the claim is fulfilled. Otherwise, by the definition of x and applying the induction hypothesis to the game $\mathcal{G} \restriction T$, we have $\text{val}^{(G,0)}(q) \geq x$ for all $q \in Q$ and $\text{val}^{\mathcal{G} \restriction T}(q) = f(q) \geq x$ for all $q \in T$. Hence, Lemma 5 yields that $\text{val}^{\mathcal{G}}(q) \geq x$ for all $q \in Q$. On the other hand, from any state $q \in A$ Player 2 can play an attractor strategy to $f^{-1}(x) \cup g^{-1}(x)$, followed by an optimal strategy in the game $\mathcal{G} \restriction T$, respectively in the mean-payoff game $(G,0)$, which ensures that Player 1's payoff does not exceed x. Hence, $\text{val}^{\mathcal{G}}(q) = x = f^*(q)$ for all $q \in A$.

Now, let $q \in Q \setminus A$. We already know that $\text{val}^{\mathcal{G}}(q) \geq x$. Moreover, since $Q \setminus A$ is a 2-trap and applying the induction hypothesis to the game $\mathcal{G} \restriction Q \setminus A$, we have $\text{val}^{\mathcal{G}}(q) \geq \text{val}^{\mathcal{G} \restriction Q \setminus A}(q) = \text{SolveMPP}(\mathcal{G} \restriction Q \setminus A)(q)$. Hence, $\text{val}^{\mathcal{G}}(q) \geq f^*(q)$. To see that $\text{val}^{\mathcal{G}}(q) \leq f^*(q)$, consider the strategy τ of Player 2 that mimics an optimal strategy in $\mathcal{G} \restriction Q \setminus A$ as long as the play stays in $Q \setminus A$ and switches to an optimal strategy in $\mathcal{G}$ as soon as the play reaches A. We have $\text{val}^{\mathcal{G}}(\tau, q) \leq \max\{\text{val}^{\mathcal{G} \restriction Q \setminus A}(q), x\} = f^*(q)$. $\qquad\square$

Algorithm SolveMPP is faster and conceptually simpler than the original algorithm proposed for solving mean-payoff parity games [9]. Compared to the recent algorithm proposed by Chatterjee and Doyen [7], which uses a reduction to energy parity games and runs in time $O(|Q|^{d+4} \cdot |E| \cdot d \cdot W)$, our algorithm has three main advantages: 1. it is faster; 2. it operates directly on mean-payoff parity games, and 3. it is more flexible since it computes the values exactly instead of just comparing them to an integer threshold.

4   Mean-Penalty Parity Games

In this section, we define multi-strategies and *mean-penalty parity games*. We reduce these games to mean-payoff parity games, show that their value problem is in NP $\cap$ coNP, and propose a deterministic algorithm for computing the values, which runs in pseudo-polynomial time if the number of priorities is bounded.

Syntactically, a *mean-penalty parity game* is a mean-payoff parity game with non-negative weights, i.e. a tuple $\mathcal{G} = (G, \chi)$, where $G = (Q_1, Q_2, E, \text{weight})$ is a weighted game graph with $\text{weight} \colon E \to \mathbb{R}^{\geq 0}$ (or $\text{weight} \colon E \to \mathbb{N}$ for algorithmic purposes), and $\chi \colon Q \to \mathbb{N}$ is a priority function assigning a priority to every state. As for mean-payoff parity games, a play ρ is parity-winning if the minimal priority occurring infinitely often ($\min\{\chi(q) \mid q \in \text{Inf}(\rho)\}$) is even.

Since we are interested in controller synthesis, we define multi-strategies only for Player 1 (who represents the system). Formally, a *multi-strategy* (for Player 1) in $\mathcal{G}$ is a function $\sigma \colon Q^* Q_1 \to \mathcal{P}(Q) \setminus \{\emptyset\}$ such that $\sigma(\gamma q) \subseteq qE$ for all $\gamma \in Q^*$ and $q \in Q_1$. A play ρ of $\mathcal{G}$ is *consistent* with a multi-strategy σ if $\rho(k+1) \in \sigma(\rho[0, k])$ for all $k \in \mathbb{N}$ with $\rho(k) \in Q_1$, and we denote by $\text{Out}^{\mathcal{G}}(\sigma, q_0)$ the set of all plays ρ of $\mathcal{G}$ that are consistent with σ and start in $\rho(0) = q_0$.

Note that, unlike for deterministic strategies, there is, in general, no unique play consistent with a multi-strategy σ for Player 1 and a (deterministic)

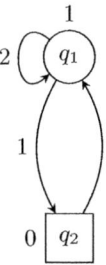

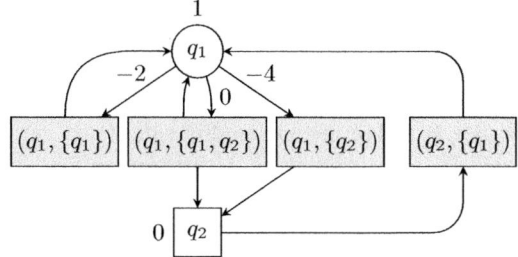

Fig. 2. A mean-penalty parity game

Fig. 3. The corresponding mean-payoff parity game

strategy τ for Player 2 from a given initial state. Additionally, note that every deterministic strategy can be viewed as a multi-strategy.

Let $\mathcal{G}$ be a mean-penalty parity game, and let σ be a multi-strategy. We inductively define $\mathrm{penalty}_\sigma^{\mathcal{G}}(\gamma)$ (the *total penalty* of γ wrt. σ) for all $\gamma \in Q^*$ by setting $\mathrm{penalty}_\sigma^{\mathcal{G}}(\varepsilon) = 0$ as well as $\mathrm{penalty}_\sigma^{\mathcal{G}}(\gamma q) = \mathrm{penalty}_\sigma^{\mathcal{G}}(\gamma)$ if $q \in Q_2$ and

$$\mathrm{penalty}_\sigma^{\mathcal{G}}(\gamma q) = \mathrm{penalty}_\sigma^{\mathcal{G}}(\gamma) + \sum_{q' \in qE \setminus \sigma(\gamma q)} \mathrm{weight}(q, q')$$

if $q \in Q_1$. Hence, $\mathrm{penalty}_\sigma^{\mathcal{G}}(\gamma)$ is the total weight of transitions blocked by σ along γ. The *mean penalty* of an infinite play ρ is then defined as the average penalty that is incurred along this play in the limit, i.e.

$$\mathrm{penalty}_\sigma^{\mathcal{G}}(\rho) = \begin{cases} \limsup\limits_{n \to \infty} \frac{1}{n}\, \mathrm{penalty}_\sigma^{\mathcal{G}}(\rho[0,n)) & \text{if } \rho \text{ is parity-winning,} \\ \infty & \text{otherwise.} \end{cases}$$

The mean penalty of a multi-strategy σ from a given initial state q_0 is defined as the supremum over the mean penalties of all plays that are consistent with σ, i.e.

$$\mathrm{penalty}^{\mathcal{G}}(\sigma, q_0) = \sup\{\mathrm{penalty}_\sigma^{\mathcal{G}}(\rho) \mid \rho \in \mathrm{Out}^{\mathcal{G}}(\sigma, q_0)\}.$$

The *value* of a state q_0 in a mean-penalty parity game $\mathcal{G}$ is the least mean penalty that a multi-strategy of Player 1 can achieve, i.e. $\mathrm{val}^{\mathcal{G}}(q_0) = \inf_\sigma \mathrm{penalty}^{\mathcal{G}}(\sigma, q_0)$, where σ ranges over all multi-strategies of Player 1. A multi-strategy σ is called *optimal* if $\mathrm{penalty}^{\mathcal{G}}(\sigma, q_0) = \mathrm{val}^{\mathcal{G}}(q_0)$ for all $q_0 \in Q$.

Finally, the *value problem for mean-penalty parity games* is the following decision problem: Given a mean-penalty parity game $\mathcal{G} = (G, \chi)$, an initial state $q_0 \in Q$, and a number $x \in \mathbb{Q}$, decide whether $\mathrm{val}^{\mathcal{G}}(q_0) \leq x$.

Example 8. Fig. 2 represents a mean-penalty parity game. Note that weights of transitions out of Player 2 states are not indicated as they are irrelevant for the mean penalty. In this game, Player 1 (controlling circle states) has to regularly *block* the self-loop if she wants to enforce infinitely many visits to the state with priority 0. This comes with a penalty of 2. However, the multi-strategy in which she blocks no transition can be played safely for an arbitrary number of times. Hence Player 1 can win with mean-penalty 0 (but infinite memory) by blocking the self-loop once every k moves, where k grows with the number of visits to q_2.

In order to solve mean-penalty games, we reduce them to mean-payoff parity games. We construct from a given mean-penalty parity game $\mathcal{G}$ an exponential-size mean-payoff parity game $\mathcal{G}'$, similar to [3] but with an added priority function. Formally, for a mean-penalty parity game $\mathcal{G} = (G, \chi)$ with game graph $G = (Q_1, Q_2, E, \text{weight})$, the game graph $G' = (Q'_1, Q'_2, E', \text{weight}')$ of the corresponding mean-payoff parity game $\mathcal{G}'$ is defined as follows:

- $Q'_1 = Q_1$ and $Q'_2 = Q_2 \cup \bar{Q}$, where $\bar{Q} := \{(q, F) \mid q \in Q, \emptyset \neq F \subseteq qE\}$;
- E' is the (disjoint) union of three kinds of transitions:
  (1) transitions of the form $(q, (q, F))$ for each $q \in Q_1$ and $\emptyset \neq F \subseteq qE$,
  (2) transitions of the form $(q, (q, \{q'\}))$ for each $q \in Q_2$ and $q' \in qE$,
  (3) transitions of the form $((q, F), q')$ for each $q' \in F$;
- the weight function weight' assigns 0 to transitions of type (2) and (3), but $\text{weight}'(q, (q, F)) = -2 \sum_{q' \in qE \setminus F} \text{weight}(q, q')$ to transitions of type (1).

Finally, the priority function χ' of $\mathcal{G}'$ coincides with χ on Q and assigns priority $M := \max\{\chi(q) \mid q \in Q\}$ to all states in $\bar{Q}$.

Example 9. Fig. 3 depicts the mean-payoff parity game obtained from the mean-penalty parity game from Example 8, depicted in Fig. 2.

The correspondence between $\mathcal{G}$ and $\mathcal{G}'$ is expressed in the following lemma.

Lemma 10. *Let $\mathcal{G}$ be a mean-penalty parity game, $\mathcal{G}'$ the corresponding mean-payoff parity game, and $q_0 \in Q$.*

1. *For every multi-strategy σ in $\mathcal{G}$ there exists a strategy σ' for Player 1 in $\mathcal{G}'$ such that $\text{val}(\sigma', q_0) \geq -\text{penalty}(\sigma, q_0)$.*
2. *For every strategy σ' for Player 1 in $\mathcal{G}'$ there exists a multi-strategy σ in $\mathcal{G}$ such that $\text{penalty}(\sigma, q_0) \leq -\text{val}(\sigma', q_0)$.*
3. *$\text{val}^{\mathcal{G}'}(q_0) = -\text{val}^{\mathcal{G}}(q_0)$.*

It follows from Theorem 2 and Lemma 10 that every mean-penalty parity game admits an optimal multi-strategy.

Corollary 11. *In every mean-penalty parity game, Player 1 has an optimal multi-strategy.*

We now show that Player 2 has a memoryless optimal strategy of a special kind in the mean-payoff parity game derived from a mean-penalty parity game. This puts the value problem for mean-penalty parity games into coNP, and is also a crucial point in the proof of Lemma 14 below.

Lemma 12. *Let $\mathcal{G}$ be a mean-penalty parity game and $\mathcal{G}'$ the corresponding mean-payoff parity game. Then in $\mathcal{G}'$ there is a memoryless optimal strategy τ' for Player 2 such that for every $q \in Q$ there exists a total order $\leq_q$ on the set qE with $\tau'((q, F)) = \min_{\leq_q} F$ for every state $(q, F) \in \bar{Q}$.*

Proof (Sketch). Let τ be a memoryless optimal strategy for Player 2 in $\mathcal{G}'$. For a state q, we consider the set qE and order it in the following way. We inductively define $F_1 = qE$, $q_i = \tau((q, F_i))$ and $F_{i+1} = F_i \setminus \{q_i\}$ for every $1 \leq i \leq |qE|$. Note that $\{q_1, \ldots, q_{|qE|}\} = qE$. We set $q_1 \leq_q q_2 \leq_q \cdots \leq_q q_{|qE|}$ and define a new memoryless strategy τ' for Player 2 in $\mathcal{G}'$ by $\tau'((q, F)) = \min_{\leq_q} F$ for $(q, F) \in \bar{Q}$ and $\tau'(q) = \tau(q)$ for all $q \in Q_2$. It can be shown that $\mathrm{val}(\tau', q_0) \leq \mathrm{val}(\tau, q_0)$ for all $q_0 \in Q$, which proves that τ' is optimal.   □

In order to put the value problem for mean-penalty parity games into $\mathrm{NP} \cap \mathrm{coNP}$, we propose a more sophisticated reduction from mean-penalty parity games to mean-payoff parity games, which results in a polynomial-size mean-payoff parity game. Intuitively, in a state $q \in Q_1$ we ask Player 1 *consecutively* for each outgoing transition whether he wants to block that transition. If he allows a transition, then Player 2 has to decide whether she wishes to explore this transition. Finally, after all transitions have been processed in this way, the play proceeds along the *last* transition that Player 2 has desired to explore.

Formally, let us fix a mean-penalty parity game $\mathcal{G} = (G, \chi)$ with game graph $G = (Q_1, Q_2, E, \text{weight})$, and denote by $k := \max\{|qE| \mid q \in Q\}$ the maximal out-degree of a state. Then the polynomial-size mean-payoff parity game $\mathcal{G}''$ has vertices of the form q and (q, a, i, m), where $q \in Q$, $a \in \{\text{choose}, \text{allow}, \text{block}\}$, $i \in \{1, \ldots, k+1\}$ and $m \in \{0, \ldots, k\}$; vertices of the form q and (q, choose, i, m) belong to Player 1, while vertices of the form (q, allow, i, m) or (q, block, i, m) belong to Player 2. To describe the transition structure of $\mathcal{G}$, let $q \in Q$ and assume that $qE = \{q_1, \ldots, q_k\}$ (a state may occur more than once in this list). Then the following transitions originate in a state of the form q or (q, a, i, m):

1. a transition from q to $(q, \text{choose}, 1, 0)$ with weight 0,
2. for all $1 \leq i \leq k$ and $0 \leq m \leq k$ a transition from (q, choose, i, m) to (q, allow, i, m) with weight 0,
3. if $q \in Q_1$ then for all $1 \leq i \leq k$ and $0 \leq m \leq k$ a transition from (q, choose, i, m) to (q, block, i, m) with weight 0, *except* if $i = k$ and $m = 0$;
4. for all $0 \leq m \leq k$ a transition from $(q, \text{choose}, k+1, m)$ to q_m with weight 0 (where q_0 can be chosen arbitrarily),
5. for all $1 \leq i \leq k$ and $0 \leq m \leq k$ a transition from (q, allow, i, m) to $(q, \text{choose}, i+1, i)$ with weight 0,
6. for all $1 \leq i \leq k$ and $1 \leq m \leq k$ a transition from (q, allow, i, m) to $(q, \text{choose}, i+1, m)$ with weight 0,
7. for all $1 \leq i \leq k$ and $0 \leq m \leq k$ a transition from (q, block, i, m) to $(q, \text{choose}, i+1, m)$ with weight $-2(k+1) \cdot \text{weight}(q, q_i)$.

Finally, the priority of a state $q \in Q$ equals the priority of the same state in $\mathcal{G}$, whereas all states of the form (q, a, i, m) have priority $M = \max\{\chi(q) \mid q \in Q\}$.

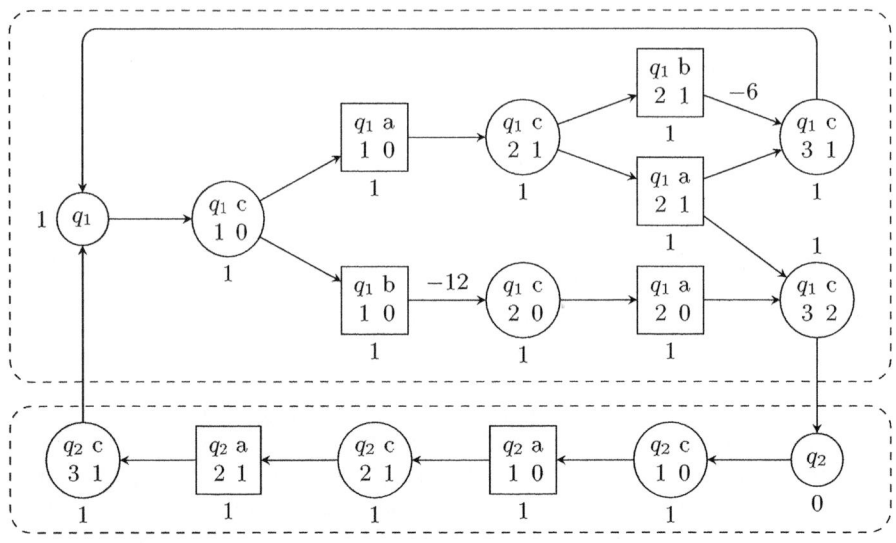

Fig. 4. The game $\mathcal{G}''$ associated with the game $\mathcal{G}$ of Fig. 2

Example 13. For the game of Fig. 2, this transformation would yield the game depicted in Fig. 4. In this picture, a, b and c stand for *allow*, *block* and *choose*, respectively; zero weights are omitted.

It is easy to see that the game $\mathcal{G}''$ has polynomial size and can, in fact, be constructed in polynomial time from the given mean-penalty parity game $\mathcal{G}$. The following lemma relates the game $\mathcal{G}''$ to the mean-payoff parity game $\mathcal{G}'$ of exponential size constructed earlier and to the original game $\mathcal{G}$.

Lemma 14. *Let $\mathcal{G}$ be a mean-penalty parity game, $\mathcal{G}'$ the corresponding mean-payoff parity game of exponential size, $\mathcal{G}''$ the corresponding mean-payoff parity game of polynomial size, and $q_0 \in Q$.*

1. *For every multi strategy σ in $\mathcal{G}$ there exists a strategy σ' for Player 1 in $\mathcal{G}''$ such that $\mathrm{val}(\sigma', q_0) \geq -\mathrm{penalty}(\sigma, q_0)$.*
2. *For every strategy τ for Player 2 in $\mathcal{G}'$ there exists a strategy τ' for Player 2 in $\mathcal{G}''$ such that $\mathrm{val}(\tau', q_0) \leq \mathrm{val}(\tau, q_0)$.*
3. *$\mathrm{val}^{\mathcal{G}''}(q_0) = -\mathrm{val}^{\mathcal{G}}(q_0)$.*

Since the mean-payoff game $\mathcal{G}''$ can be computed from $\mathcal{G}$ in polynomial time, we obtain a polynomial-time many-one reduction from the value problem for mean-penalty parity games to the value problem for mean-payoff parity games. By Corollary 3 and Theorem 4, the latter problem belongs to NP $\cap$ coNP.

Theorem 15. *The value problem for mean-penalty parity games belongs to NP $\cap$ coNP.*

Algorithm. SymbSolveMPP($\mathcal{G}$)

Input: mean-penalty parity game $\mathcal{G} = (G, \chi)$
Output: val$^{\mathcal{G}}$

if $Q = \emptyset$ **then return** $\emptyset$
$p := \min\{\chi(q) \mid q \in Q\}$
if p is even **then**
   $g := $ SymbSolveMP$(G, 0)$
   if $\chi(q) = p$ for all $q \in Q$ **then return** g
   $T := Q \setminus \text{Attr}_1^{\mathcal{G}}(\chi^{-1}(p))$; $f := $ SymbSolveMPP$(\mathcal{G} \upharpoonright T)$
   $x := \max(f(T) \cup g(Q))$; $A := \text{Attr}_2^{\mathcal{G}}(f^{-1}(x) \cup g^{-1}(x))$
   return $(Q \to \mathbb{R} \cup \{\infty\} : q \mapsto x) \sqcap$ SymbSolveMPP$(\mathcal{G} \upharpoonright Q \setminus A)$
else
   $T := Q \setminus \text{Attr}_2^{\mathcal{G}}(\chi^{-1}(p))$
   if $T = \emptyset$ **then return** $(Q \to \mathbb{R} \cup \{\infty\} : q \mapsto \infty)$
   $f := $ SymbSolveMPP$(\mathcal{G} \upharpoonright T)$; $x := \min f(T)$; $A := \text{Attr}_1^{\mathcal{G}}(f^{-1}(x))$
   return $(Q \to \mathbb{R} \cup \{\infty\} : q \mapsto x) \sqcup$ SymbSolveMPP$(\mathcal{G} \upharpoonright Q \setminus A)$
end if

A Deterministic Algorithm. Naturally, we can use the polynomial translation from mean-penalty parity games to mean-payoff parity games to solve mean-penalty parity games deterministically. Note that the mean-payoff parity game $\mathcal{G}''$ derived from a mean-penalty parity game has $O(|Q| \cdot k^2)$ states and $O(|Q| \cdot k^2)$ edges, where k is the maximum out-degree of a state in $\mathcal{G}$; the number of priorities remains constant. Moreover, if weights are given in integers and W is the highest absolute weight in $\mathcal{G}$, then the highest absolute weight in $\mathcal{G}''$ is $O(k \cdot W)$. Using Theorem 7, we thus obtain a deterministic algorithm for solving mean-penalty parity games that runs in time $O(|Q|^{d+3} \cdot k^{2d+7} \cdot W)$. If k is a constant, the running time is $O(|Q|^{d+3} \cdot W)$, which is acceptable. In the general case however, the best upper bound on k is the number of states, and we get an algorithm that runs in time $O(|Q|^{3d+10} \cdot W)$. Even if the numbers of priorities is small, this running time would not be acceptable in practical applications.

The goal of this section is to show that we can do better; namely we will give an algorithm that runs in time $O(|Q|^{d+3} \cdot |E| \cdot W)$, independently of the maximum out-degree. The idea is as follows: we use Algorithm SolveMPP on the mean-payoff parity game $\mathcal{G}'$ of exponential size, but we show that we can run it *on* $\mathcal{G}$, i.e., by handling the extra states of $\mathcal{G}'$ symbolically during the computation. As a first step, we adapt the pseudo-polynomial algorithm by Zwick and Paterson [22] to compute the values of a mean-penalty parity game with a trivial parity objective.

Lemma 16. *The values of a mean-penalty parity game with priority function $\chi \equiv 0$ can be computed in time $O(|Q|^4 \cdot |E| \cdot W)$.*

Algorithm SymbSolveMPP is our algorithm for computing the values of a mean-penalty parity game. The algorithm employs as a subroutine an algorithm

SymbSolveMP for computing the values of a mean-penalty parity with a trivial priority function (see Lemma 16). Since SymbSolveMP can be implemented to run in time $O(|Q|^4 \cdot |E| \cdot W)$, the running time of the procedure SymbSolveMPP is $O(|Q|^{d+3} \cdot |E| \cdot W)$. Notably, the algorithm runs in polynomial time if the number of priorities is bounded and we are only interested in the average *number* of edges blocked by a strategy in each step (i.e. if all weights are equal to 1).

Theorem 17. *The values of a mean-penalty parity game with d priorities can be computed in time $O(|Q|^{d+3} \cdot |E| \cdot W)$.*

Proof (Sketch). From Lemma 16 and with the same runtime analysis as in the proof of Theorem 7, we get that SymbSolveMPP runs in time $O(|Q|^{d+3} \cdot |E| \cdot W)$. To prove that the algorithm is correct, we show that there is a correspondence between the values the algorithm computes on a mean-penalty parity game $\mathcal{G}$ and the values computed by Algorithm SolveMPP on the mean-payoff parity game $\mathcal{G}'$. More precisely, we show that $\text{SolveMPP}(\mathcal{G}') \restriction Q = - \text{SymbSolveMPP}(\mathcal{G})$. The correctness of the algorithm thus follows from Lemma 10, which states that $\text{val}^{\mathcal{G}'} \restriction Q = - \text{val}^{\mathcal{G}}$.   □

5   Conclusion

In this paper, we have studied mean-payoff parity games, with an application to finding permissive strategies in parity games with penalties. In particular, we have established that mean-penalty parity games are not harder to solve than mean-payoff parity games: for both kinds of games, the value problem is in NP ∩ coNP and can be solved by an exponential algorithm that becomes pseudo-polynomial when the number of priorities is bounded.

One complication with both kinds of games is that optimal strategies for Player 1 require infinite memory, which makes it hard to synthesise these strategies. A suitable alternative to optimal strategies are ε-*optimal* strategies that achieve the value of the game by at most ε. Since finite-memory ε-optimal strategies are guaranteed to exist [2], a challenge for future work is to modify our algorithms so that they compute not only the values of the game but also a finite-memory ε-optimal (multi-)strategy for Player 1.

Acknowledgement. We thank an anonymous reviewer for pointing out the polynomial reduction from mean-penalty parity games to mean-payoff parity games, which has simplified the proof that mean-penalty parity games are in NP.

References

1. Bernet, J., Janin, D., Walukiewicz, I.: Permissive strategies: from parity games to safety games. RAIRO – ITA 36(3), 261–275 (2002)
2. Ioem, R., Chatterjee, K., Henzinger, T.A., Jobstmann, B.: Better quality in synthesis through quantitative objectives. In: Bouajjani, A., Maler, O. (eds.) CAV 2009. LNCS, vol. 5643, pp. 140–156. Springer, Heidelberg (2009)

3. Bouyer, P., Duflot, M., Markey, N., Renault, G.: Measuring permissivity in finite games. In: Bravetti, M., Zavattaro, G. (eds.) CONCUR 2009. LNCS, vol. 5710, pp. 196–210. Springer, Heidelberg (2009)

4. Bouyer, P., Fahrenberg, U., Larsen, K.G., Markey, N., Srba, J.: Infinite runs in weighted timed automata with energy constraints. In: Cassez, F., Jard, C. (eds.) FORMATS 2008. LNCS, vol. 5215, pp. 33–47. Springer, Heidelberg (2008)

5. Bouyer, P., Markey, N., Olschewski, J., Ummels, M.: Measuring permissiveness in parity games: Mean-payoff parity games revisited. Research Report LSV-11-17, Laboratoire Spécification et Vérification, ENS Cachan, France (2011)

6. Chakrabarti, A., de Alfaro, L., Henzinger, T.A., Stoelinga, M.: Resource interfaces. In: Alur, R., Lee, I. (eds.) EMSOFT 2003. LNCS, vol. 2855, pp. 117–133. Springer, Heidelberg (2003)

7. Chatterjee, K., Doyen, L.: Energy parity games. In: Abramsky, S., Gavoille, C., Kirchner, C., Meyer auf der Heide, F., Spirakis, P.G. (eds.) ICALP 2010, Part II. LNCS, vol. 6199, pp. 599–610. Springer, Heidelberg (2010)

8. Chatterjee, K., Doyen, L., Henzinger, T.A., Raskin, J.-F.: Generalized mean-payoff and energy games. In: FSTTCS 2010. LIPIcs, vol. 8, pp. 505–516. Schloss Dagstuhl - Leibniz-Zentrum fuer Informatik (2010)

9. Chatterjee, K., Henzinger, T.A., Jurdziński, M.: Mean-payoff parity games. In: LICS 2005, pp. 178–187. IEEE Computer Society Press, Los Alamitos (2005)

10. Chatterjee, K., Henzinger, T.A., Piterman, N.: Generalized parity games. In: Seidl, H. (ed.) FOSSACS 2007. LNCS, vol. 4423, pp. 153–167. Springer, Heidelberg (2007)

11. Ehrenfeucht, A., Mycielski, J.: Positional strategies for mean payoff games. Int. Journal of Game Theory 8(2), 109–113 (1979)

12. Emerson, E.A., Jutla, C.S.: Tree automata, mu-calculus and determinacy. In: FOCS 1991, pp. 368–377. IEEE Computer Society Press, Los Alamitos (1991)

13. Jurdziński, M.: Deciding the winner in parity games is in UP ∩ co-UP. Information Processing Letters 68(3), 119–124 (1998)

14. Karp, R.M.: A characterization of the minimum cycle mean in a digraph. Discrete Mathematics 23(3), 309–311 (1978)

15. Kopczyński, E.: Half-positional determinacy of infinite games. In: Bugliesi, M., Preneel, B., Sassone, V., Wegener, I. (eds.) ICALP 2006, Part II. LNCS, vol. 4052, pp. 336–347. Springer, Heidelberg (2006)

16. Luttenberger, M.: Strategy iteration using non-deterministic strategies for solving parity games. Research Report cs.GT/0806.2923, arXiv (2008)

17. Martin, D.A.: Borel determinacy. Annals of Mathematics 102, 363–371 (1975)

18. Mostowski, A.W.: Games with forbidden positions. Tech. Rep. 78, Instytut Matematyki, Uniwersytet Gdański, Poland (1991)

19. Pinchinat, S., Riedweg, S.: You can always compute maximally permissive controllers under partial observation when they exist. In: ACC 2005, pp. 2287–2292 (2005)

20. Thomas, W.: Infinite games and verification (extended abstract of a tutorial). In: Brinksma, E., Larsen, K.G. (eds.) CAV 2002. LNCS, vol. 2404, pp. 58–64. Springer, Heidelberg (2002)

21. Zielonka, W.: Infinite games on finitely coloured graphs with applications to automata on infinite trees. Theoretical Computer Science 200(1-2), 135–183 (1998)

22. Zwick, U., Paterson, M.: The complexity of mean payoff games on graphs. Theoretical Computer Science 158(1&2), 343–359 (1996)

Algorithms for Synthesizing Priorities
in Component-Based Systems

Chih-Hong Cheng[1], Saddek Bensalem[2], Yu-Fang Chen[3], Rongjie Yan[4],
Barbara Jobstmann[2], Harald Ruess[5], Christian Buckl[5], and Alois Knoll[1]

[1] Department of Informatics, Technischen Universität München, München, Germany
[2] Verimag Laboratory, Grenoble, France
[3] Institute of Information Science, Academia Sinica, Taipei, Taiwan
[4] State Key Laboratory of Computer Science, ISCAS, Beijing, China
[5] fortiss GmbH, München, Germany

Abstract. We present algorithms to synthesize component-based systems that
are safe and deadlock-free using priorities, which define stateless-precedence
between enabled actions. Our core method combines the concept of fault-
localization (using safety-game) and fault-repair (using SAT for conflict resolution). For complex systems, we propose three complementary methods as
preprocessing steps for priority synthesis, namely (a) data abstraction to reduce
component complexities, (b) alphabet abstraction and ♮-deadlock to ignore components, and (c) automated assumption learning for compositional priority
synthesis.

1 Introduction

Priorities [15] define *stateless-precedence relations between actions* available in
component-based systems. They can be used to restrict the behavior of a system in order
to avoid undesired states. They are particularly useful to avoid deadlock states (i.e., states
in which all actions are disabled), because they do not introduce new deadlock states and
therefore avoid creating new undesired states. Furthermore, due to their stateless property and the fact that they operate on the interface of a component, they are relatively
easy to implement in a distributed setting [17,9]. In a tool paper [11], we presented the
tool VISSBIP[1] together with a concept called *priority synthesis*, which aims to automatically generate a set of priorities such that the system constrained by the synthesized
priorities satisfies a given *safety property* or *deadlock freedom*. In this paper, we explain
the underlying algorithm and propose extensions for more complex systems.

Priority synthesis is expensive; we showed in [12] that synthesizing priorities for
safety properties (or deadlock-freedom) is NP-complete in the size of the state space of
the product graph. Therefore, we present an incomplete search framework for priority
synthesis, which mimics the process of *fault-localization* and *fault-repair* (Section 3).
Intuitively, a state is a fault location if it is the latest point from which there is a way to
avoid a failure, i.e., there exists (i) an outgoing action that leads to an *attracted state*, a

---

[1] Shortcut for **Vi**sualization and **s**ynthesis for **s**imple **BIP** systems.

T. Bultan and P.-A. Hsiung (Eds.): ATVA 2011, LNCS 6996, pp. 150–167, 2011.

state from which all paths unavoidably reach a bad state, and (ii) there exists an alternative action that avoids entering any of the attracted states. We compute fault locations using the algorithm for *safety games*. Given a set of fault locations, priority synthesis is achieved via fault-repair: an algorithm resolves potential conflicts in priorities generated via fault-localization and finds a satisfying subset of priorities as a solution for synthesis. Our symbolic encodings on the system, together with the new variable ordering heuristic and other optimizations, helps to solve problems much more efficiently compared to our preliminary implementation in [11]. Furthermore, it allows us to integrate an adversary environment model similar to the setting in Ramadge and Wonham's controller synthesis framework [22].

Abstraction or compositional techniques are widely used in verification of infinite state or complex systems for safety properties but *not all* techniques ensure that synthesizing an abstract system for deadlock-freeness guarantees deadlock-freeness in the concrete system (Section 4). Therefore, it is important to find appropriate techniques to assist synthesis on complex problems. We first revisit *data abstraction* (Section 4.1) for data domain such that priority synthesis works on an abstract system composed by components abstracted component-wise [7]. Second, we present a technique called *alphabet-abstraction* (Section 4.2), handling complexities induced by the composition of components. Lastly, for behavioral-safety properties (not applicable for deadlock-avoidance), we utilize automata-learning [3] to achieve *compositional priority synthesis* (Section 4.3).

We implemented the presented algorithms (except connection with the data abstraction module in D-Finder [8]) in the VISSBIP tool and performed experiments to evaluate them (Section 5). Our examples show that the process using fault-localization and fault-repair generates priorities that are highly desirable. Alphabet abstraction enables us to scale to arbitrary large problems. We also present a model for distributed communication. In this example, the priorities synthesized by our engine are completely local (i.e., each priority involves two local actions within a component). Therefore, they can be translated directly to distributed control. We summarize related work and conclude with an algorithmic flow in Section 6 and 7.

2   Component-Based Modeling and Priority Synthesis

2.1   Behavioral-Interaction-Priority Framework

The Behavior-Interaction-Priority (BIP) framework[2] provides a rigorous component-based design flow for heterogeneous systems. Rigorous design refers to the strict separation of three different layers (behaviors, interactions, and priorities) used to describe a system. A detailed description of the BIP language can be found in [6]. To simplify the explanations, we focus on *simple* systems, i.e., systems without hierarchies and finite data types. Intuitively, a simple BIP system consists of a set of automata (extended with data) that synchronize on joint labels.

Definition 1 (BIP System). *We define a (simple BIP) system as a tuple* $S = (C, \Sigma, \mathcal{P})$, *where*

---

[2] http://www-verimag.imag.fr/Rigorous-Design-of-Component-Based.html?lang=en

- Σ *is a finite set of* **events** *or interaction labels, called* **interaction alphabet**,
- $C = \bigcup_{i=1}^{m} C_i$ *is a finite set of* **components***. Each component C_i is a transition system extended with data. Formally, C_i is a tuple $(L_i, V_i, \Sigma_i, T_i, l_i^0, e_i^0)$:*

  - $L_i = \{l_{i_1}, \ldots, l_{i_n}\}$ *is a finite set of* control locations.
  - $V_i = \{v_{i_1}, \ldots, v_{i_p}\}$ *is a finite set of* (local) variables *with a finite domain. Wlog we assume that the domain is the Boolean domain* $\mathbb{B} = \{\texttt{True}, \texttt{False}\}$*. We use $|V_i|$ to denote the number of variables used in C_i. An* evaluation (or assignment) *of the variables in V_i is a functions $e : V_i \to \mathbb{B}$ mapping every variable to a value in the domain. We use $\mathcal{E}(V_i)$ to denote the set of all evaluations over the variables V_i. Given a Boolean formula $f \in \mathcal{B}(V_i)$ over the variables in V_i and an evaluation $e \in \mathcal{E}(V_i)$, we use $f(e)$ to refer to the truth value of f under the evaluation e.*
  - $\Sigma_i \subseteq \Sigma$ *is a subset of interaction labels used in C_i.*
  - T_i *is the set of* transitions*. A transition $t_i \in T_i$ is of the form (l, g, σ, f, l'), where $l, l' \in L_i$ are the* source and destination location*, $g \in \mathcal{B}(V_i)$ is called the* guard *and is a Boolean formula over the variables V_i. $\sigma \in \Sigma_i$ is an interaction label (specifying the event triggering the transition), and $f : V_i \to \mathcal{B}(V_i)$ is the* update function *mapping every variable to a Boolean formula encoding the change of its value.*
  - $l_i^0 \in L_i$ *is the* initial location *and $e_i^0 \in \mathcal{E}(V_i)$ is the initial evaluation of the variables.*

- $\mathcal{P}$ *is a finite set of interaction pairs (called* **priorities***) defining a relation $\prec \subseteq \Sigma \times \Sigma$ between the interaction labels. We require that $\prec$ is (1) transitive and (2) non-reflexive (i.e., there are no circular dependencies) [15]. For $(\sigma_1, \sigma_2) \in \mathcal{P}$, we sometimes write $\sigma_1 \prec \sigma_2$ to highlight the property of priority.*

Definition 2 (Configuration). *Given a system $\mathcal{S}$, a* configuration (or state) *c is a tuple $(l_1, e_1, \ldots, l_m, e_m)$ with $l_i \in L_i$ and $e_i \in \mathcal{E}(V_i)$ for all $i \in \{1, \ldots, m\}$. We use $\mathcal{C}_{\mathcal{S}}$ to denote the set of all reachable configurations. The configuration $(l_1^0, e_1^0, \ldots, l_m^0, e_m^0)$ is called the* initial configuration *of $\mathcal{S}$ and is denoted by c^0.*

Definition 3 (Enabled Interactions). *Given a system $\mathcal{S}$ and a configuration $c = (l_1, e_1, \ldots, l_m, e_m)$, we say an interaction $\sigma \in \Sigma$ is* **enabled** *(in c), if the following conditions hold:*

1. *(Joint participation) $\forall i \in \{1, \ldots, m\}$, if $\sigma \in \Sigma_i$, then $\exists g_i, f_i, l_i'$ such that $(l_i, g_i, \sigma, f_i, l_i') \in T_i$ and $g_i(e_i) = \texttt{True}$.*
2. *(No higher priorities enabled) For all other interaction $\bar{\sigma} \in \Sigma$ satisfying joint participation (i.e., $\forall i \in \{1, \ldots, m\}$, if $\bar{\sigma} \in \Sigma_i$, then $\exists (l_i, \bar{g}_i, \bar{\sigma}, \bar{f}_i, \bar{l}_i') \in T_i$ such that $\bar{g}_i(e_i) = \texttt{True}$), $(\sigma, \bar{\sigma}) \notin \mathcal{P}$ holds.*

Definition 4 (Behavior). *Given a system $\mathcal{S}$, two configurations $c = (l_1, e_1, \ldots, l_m, e_m)$, $c' = (l_1', e_1', \ldots, l_m', e_m')$, and an interaction $\sigma \in \Sigma$ enabled in c, we say c' is a σ-successor (configuration) of c, denoted $c \xrightarrow{\sigma} c'$, if the following two conditions hold for all components $C_i = (L_i, V_i, \Sigma_i, T_i, l_i^0, e_i^0)$:*

- *(Update for participated components) If $\sigma \in \Sigma_i$, then there exists a transition $(l_i, g_i, \sigma, f_i, l_i') \in T_i$ such that $g_i(e_i) = \mathtt{True}$ and for all variables $v \in V_i$, $e_i' = f_i(v)(e_i)$.*
- *(Stutter for idle components) Otherwise, $l_i' = l_i$ and $e_i' = e_i$.*

Given two configurations c and c', we say c' is reachable from c with the interaction *sequence $w = \sigma_1 \ldots \sigma_k$, denoted $c \xrightarrow{w} c'$, if there exist configurations $c_0, \ldots, c_k$ such that (i) $c_0 = c$, (ii) $c_k = c'$, and (iii) for all $i : 0 \leq i < k$, $c_i \xrightarrow{\sigma_{i+1}} c_{i+1}$. We denote the set of all configuration of S reachable from the initial configuration c^0 by $\mathcal{R}_S$. The* language *of a system S, denoted $\mathcal{L}(S)$, is the set $\{w \in \Sigma^* \mid \exists c' \in \mathcal{R}_S$ such that $c^0 \xrightarrow{w} c'\}$. Note that $\mathcal{L}(S)$ describes the behavior of S, starting from the initial configuration c^0.*

In this paper, we adapt the following simplifications:

- We do not consider uncontrollable events (of the environment), since the BIP language is currently not supporting them. However, our framework would allow us to do so. More precisely, we solve priority synthesis using a game-theoretic version of controller synthesis [22], in which uncontrollability can be modeled. Furthermore, since we consider only safety properties, our algorithms can be easily adapted to handle uncontrollable events.
- We do not consider data transfer during the interaction, as it is merely syntactic rewriting over variables between different components.

2.2   Priority Synthesis for Safety and Deadlock Freedom

Definition 5 (Risk-Configuration/Deadlock Safety). *Given a system $S = (C, \Sigma, \mathcal{P})$ and the set of* risk configuration *$\mathcal{C}_{risk} \subseteq \mathcal{C}_S$ (also called* bad states*), the system is* **safe** *if the following conditions hold. (A system that is not safe is called* **unsafe***.)*
- **(Deadlock-free)** $\forall c \in \mathcal{R}_S$, $\exists \sigma \in \Sigma$, $\exists c' \in \mathcal{R}_S : c \xrightarrow{\sigma} c'$
- **(Risk-state-free)** $\mathcal{C}_{risk} \cap \mathcal{R}_S = \emptyset$.

Definition 6 (Priority Synthesis). *Given a system $S = (C, \Sigma, \mathcal{P})$, and the set of risk configuration $\mathcal{C}_{risk} \subseteq \mathcal{C}_S$, priority synthesis searches for a set of priorities $\mathcal{P}_+$ such that*

- *For $\mathcal{P} \cup \mathcal{P}_+$, the defined relation $\prec_{\mathcal{P} \cup \mathcal{P}_+} \subseteq \Sigma \times \Sigma$ is also (1) transitive and (2) non-reflexive.*
- *$(C, \Sigma, \mathcal{P} \cup \mathcal{P}_+)$ is safe.*

Given a system S, we define the size of S as the size of the product graph induced by S, i.e, $|\mathcal{R}_S| + |\Sigma|$. Then, we have the following result.

Theorem 1 (Hardness of priority synthesis [12]) *Given a system $S = (C, \Sigma, \mathcal{P})$, finding a set $\mathcal{P}_+$ of priorities such that $(C, \Sigma, \mathcal{P} \cup \mathcal{P}_+)$ is safe is NP-complete in the size of S.*

We briefly mention the definition of **behavioral safety**, which is a powerful notion to capture erroneous behavioral-patterns for the system under design.

Definition 7 (Behavioral Safety). *Given a system $S = (C, \Sigma, \mathcal{P})$ and a regular language $\mathcal{L}_{\neg P} \subseteq \Sigma^*$ called the* risk specification*, the system is* **B-safe** *if $\mathcal{L}(S) \cap \mathcal{L}_{\neg P} = \emptyset$. A system that is not B-safe is called* **B-unsafe***.*

It is well-known that the problem of asking for behavioral safety can be reduced to the problem of risk-state freeness. More precisely, since $\mathcal{L}_{\neg P}$ can be represented by a finite automaton $\mathcal{A}_{\neg P}$ (the monitor), priority synthesis for behavioral safety can be reduced to priority synthesis in the synchronous product of the system $\mathcal{S}$ and $\mathcal{A}_{\neg P}$ with the goal to avoid any product state that has a final state of $\mathcal{A}_{\neg P}$ in the second component.

3   A Framework of Priority Synthesis Based on Fault-Localization and Fault-Repair

In this section, we describe our symbolic encoding scheme, followed by presenting our priority synthesis mechanism using a fault-localization and repair approach.

3.1   System Encoding

Our symbolic encoding is inspired by the execution semantics of the BIP engine, which during execution, selects one of the enabled interactions and executes the interaction. In our engine, we mimic the process and create a two-stage transition: For each iteration,

- (Stage 0) The *environment* raises all enabled interactions.
- (Stage 1) Based on the raised interactions, the *controller* selects one enabled interaction (if there exists one) while respecting the priority, and updates the state based on the enabled interaction.

Given a system $\mathcal{S} = (C, \Sigma, \mathcal{P})$, we use the following sets of Boolean variables to encode $\mathcal{S}$:

- $\{stg, stg'\}$ is the *stage indicator* and its primed version.
- $\bigcup_{\sigma \in \Sigma} \{\sigma, \sigma'\}$ are the variables representing interactions and their primed version. We use the same letter for an interaction and the corresponding variable, because there is a one-to-one correspondence between them.
- $\bigcup_{i=1...m} Y_i \cup Y_i'$, where $Y_i = \{y_{i1}, \ldots, y_{ik}\}$ and $Y_i' = \{y_{i1}', \ldots, y_{ik}'\}$ are the variables and their primed version, respectively, used to encode the locations L_i. (We use a binary encoding, i.e., $k = \lceil log|L_i| \rceil$). Given a location $l \in L_i$, we use $enc(l)$ and $enc'(l)$ to refer to the encoding of l using Y_i and Y_i', respectively.
- $\bigcup_{i=1...m} \bigcup_{v \in V_i} \{v, v'\}$ are the variables of the components and their primed version.

We use Algorithm 1 and 2 to create transition predicates $\mathcal{T}_{stage_0}$ and $\mathcal{T}_{stage_1}$ for Stage 0 and 1, respectively. Note that $\mathcal{T}_{stage_0}$ and $\mathcal{T}_{stage_1}$ can be merged but we keep them separately, in order to (1) have an easy and direct way to synthesize priorities, (2) allow expressing the freedom of the environment, and (3) follow the semantics of the BIP engine.

- In Algorithm 1, Line 2 computes for each interaction σ the predicate P_σ representing all the configurations in which σ is enabled in the current configuration. In Line 3, starting from the first interaction, $\mathcal{T}_{stage_0}$ is continuously refined by conjoining $\sigma' \leftrightarrow P_\sigma$ for each interaction σ, i.e., the variables σ' is true if and only if the interaction σ is enabled. Finally, Line 4 ensures that the system configuration does not change in stage 0.

Algorithm 1. Generate Stage-0 transitions

---

input : System $\mathcal{S} = (C, \Sigma, \mathcal{P})$
output: Stage-0 transition predicate $\mathcal{T}_{stage_0}$
begin

   for $\sigma \in \Sigma$ **do**

1   let predicate $P_\sigma :=$ True

   for $\sigma \in \Sigma$ **do**

      for $i = \{1, \ldots, m\}$ **do**

2   **if** $\sigma \in \Sigma_i$ **then** $P_\sigma := P_\sigma \wedge \bigvee_{(l,g,\sigma,f,l') \in T_i} (enc(l) \wedge g)$

   let predicate $\mathcal{T}_{stage_0} := stg \wedge \neg stg'$

   for $\sigma \in \Sigma$ **do**

3        $\mathcal{T}_{stage_0} := \mathcal{T}_{stage_0} \wedge (\sigma' \leftrightarrow P_\sigma)$

   for $i = \{1, \ldots, m\}$ **do**

4        $\mathcal{T}_{stage_0} := \mathcal{T}_{stage_0} \wedge \bigwedge_{y \in Y_i} y \leftrightarrow y' \wedge \bigwedge_{v \in V_i} v \leftrightarrow v'$

   return $\mathcal{T}_{stage_0}$

end

Algorithm 2. Generate Stage-1 transitions

---

input : System $\mathcal{S} = (C, \Sigma, \mathcal{P})$
output: Stage-1 transition predicate $\mathcal{T}_{stage_1}$
begin

   let predicate $\mathcal{T}_{stage_1} :=$ False

   for $\sigma \in \Sigma$ **do**

      let predicate $T_\sigma := \neg stg \wedge stg'$

      for $i = \{1, \ldots, m\}$ **do**

         if $\sigma \in \Sigma_i$ **then**

1           $T_\sigma := T_\sigma \wedge \bigvee_{(l,g,\sigma,f,l') \in T_i} (enc(l) \wedge g \wedge \sigma \wedge \sigma' \wedge enc'(l') \wedge \bigwedge_{v \in V_i} v' \leftrightarrow f(v))$

      for $\sigma' \in \Sigma, \sigma' \neq \sigma$ **do**

2           $T_\sigma := T_\sigma \wedge \sigma' =$ False

      for $i = \{1, \ldots, m\}$ **do**

3   **if** $\sigma \notin \Sigma_i$ **then** $T_\sigma := T_\sigma \wedge \bigwedge_{y \in Y_i} y \leftrightarrow y' \wedge \bigwedge_{v \in V_i} v \leftrightarrow v'$

      $\mathcal{T}_{stage_1} := \mathcal{T}_{stage_1} \vee T_\sigma$

   for $\sigma_1 \prec \sigma_2 \in \mathcal{P}$ **do**

4        $\mathcal{T}_{stage_1} := \mathcal{T}_{stage_1} \wedge ((\sigma_1 \wedge \sigma_2) \rightarrow \neg \sigma_1')$

   return $\mathcal{T}_{stage_1}$

end

- In Algorithm 2, Line 1, 2, 3 are used to create the transition in which interaction σ is executed (Line 2 ensures that only σ is executed; Line 3 ensures the stuttering move of unparticipated components). Given a priority $\sigma_1 \prec \sigma_2$, in configurations in which σ_1 and σ_2 are both enabled (i.e., $\sigma_1 \wedge \sigma_2$ holds), the conjunction with Line 4 removes the possibility to execute σ_1 when σ_2 is also available.

3.2 Step A. Finding Fix Candidates Using Fault-Localization

Synthesizing a set of priorities to make the system safe can be done in various ways, and we use Figure 1 to illustrate our underlying idea. Consider a system starting from state c_1. It has two risk configurations c_6 and c_7. In order to avoid risk using priorities, one method is to work on the initial configuration, i.e., to use the set of priorities $\{e \prec a, d \prec a\}$. Nevertheless, it can be observed that the synthesized result is not very desirable, as the behavior of the system has been greatly restricted.

Alternatively, our methodology works *backwards* from the set of risk states and finds states which is able to *escape from risk*. In Figure 1, as states c_3, c_4, c_5 unavoidably enter a risk state, they are within the *risk-attractor* (Attr(C_{risk})). For state c_2, c_8, and c_9, there exists an interaction which avoids risk. Thus, if a set of priorities P_+ can ensure

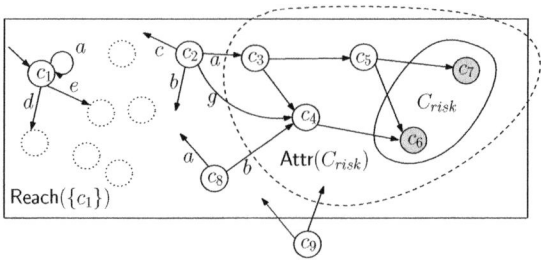

Fig. 1. Locating fix candidates

that from c_2, c_8, and c_9, the system can not enter the attractor, then P_+ is the result of synthesis. Furthermore, as c_9 is not within the set of reachable states from the initial configuration (Reach($\{c_1\}$) in Figure 1), then it can be eliminated without consideration. We call $\{c_2, c_8\}$ a **fault-set**, meaning that an erroneous interaction can be taken to reach the risk-attractor.

Under our formulation, we can directly utilize the result of **algorithmic game solving** [16] to compute the fault-set. Algorithm 3 explains the underlying computation: For conciseness, we use $\exists\varXi$ ($\exists\varXi'$) to represent existential quantification over all umprimed (primed) variables used in the system encoding. Also, we use the operator SUBS $(X, \varXi, \varXi')$ for variable swap (substitution) from unprimed to primed variables in X: the SUBS operator is common in most BDD packages.

- In the beginning, we create P_{ini} for initial configuration, P_{dead} for deadlock (no interaction is enabled), and P_{risk} for risk configurations.
- In Part A, adding a stage-0 configuration can be computed similar to adding the environment state in a safety game. In a safety game, for an environment configuration to be added, there exists a transition which leads to the attractor.
- In Part A, adding a stage-1 configuration follows the intuition described earlier. In a safety game, for a control configuration c to be added, all outgoing transitions of c should lead to the attractor. This is captured by the set difference operation PointTo \ Escape in Line 5.
- In Part B, Line 7 creates the transition predicate entering the attractor. Line 8 creates predicate OutsideAttr representing the set of stage-1 configuration outside the attractor. In Line 9, by conjuncting with OutsideAttr we ensure that the algorithm does not return a transition within the attractor.
- Part C removes transitions whose source is not within the set of reachable states.

3.3   Step B. Priority Synthesis via Conflict Resolution – From Stateful to Stateless

Due to our system encoding, in Algorithm 3, the return value $\mathcal{T}_f$ contains not only the risk interaction but also all possible interactions simultaneously available. Recall Figure 1, $\mathcal{T}_f$ returns three transitions, and we can extract **priority candidates** from each transition.

- On c_2, a enters the risk-attractor, while b, g, c are also available. We have the following candidates $\{a \prec b, a \prec g, a \prec c\}$.

Algorithm 3. Fault-localization

---

input : System $\mathcal{S} = (C, \Sigma, \mathcal{P})$, $\mathcal{T}_{stage_0}$, $\mathcal{T}_{stage_1}$
output: $\mathcal{T}_f \subseteq \mathcal{T}_{stage_1}$ as the set of stage-1 transitions starting from the fault-set but entering the risk attractor
begin

    let $P_{ini} := stg \wedge \bigwedge_{i=1\ldots m}(enc(l_i^0) \wedge \bigwedge_{v \in V_i} v \leftrightarrow e_i^0(v))$

    let $P_{dead} := \neg stg \wedge \bigwedge_{\sigma \in \Sigma} \neg \sigma$

    let $P_{risk} := \neg stg \wedge \bigvee_{(l_1,e_1,\ldots,l_m,e_m) \in C_{risk}}(enc(l_1) \wedge \bigwedge_{v \in V_1} v \leftrightarrow e_1(v) \wedge \ldots$
    $enc(l_m) \wedge \bigwedge_{v \in V_m} v \leftrightarrow e_m(v))$

    // Part A: solve safety game
    let Attr$_{pre}$:= $P_{dead} \vee P_{risk}$, Attr$_{post}$:= False

1   **while** True **do**

        // add stage-0 (environment) configurations
2   Attr$_{post,0}$:= $\exists \Xi' : (\mathcal{T}_{stage_0} \wedge$ SUBS$((\exists \Xi' : $ Attr$_{pre}), \Xi, \Xi'))$
        // add stage-1 (system) configurations
3   **let** PointTo := $\exists \Xi' : (\mathcal{T}_{stage_1} \wedge$ SUBS$((\exists \Xi' : $ Attr$_{pre}), \Xi, \Xi'))$
4   **let** Escape := $\exists \Xi' : (\mathcal{T}_{stage_1} \wedge$ SUBS$((\exists \Xi' : \neg$Attr$_{pre}), \Xi, \Xi'))$
5   Attr$_{post,1}$:= PointTo $\setminus$ Escape
6   Attr$_{post}$:= Attr$_{pre} \vee$ Attr$_{post,0} \vee$ Attr$_{post,1}$;   // Union the result
        if Attr$_{pre} \leftrightarrow$ Attr$_{post}$ **then** break;   // Break when the image saturates
        else Attr$_{pre}$:= Attr$_{post}$

    // Part B: extract $\mathcal{T}_f$
7   PointTo := $\mathcal{T}_{stage_1} \wedge$ SUBS$((\exists \Xi' : $ Attr$_{pre}), \Xi, \Xi'))$
8   OutsideAttr := $\neg$Attr$_{pre} \wedge (\exists \Xi' : \mathcal{T}_{stage_1})$
9    $\mathcal{T}_f$:= PointTo $\wedge$ OutsideAttr

    // Part C: eliminate unused transition using reachable states
    let Reach$_{pre}$:= P_{ini}, Reach$_{post}$:= False
10   **while** True **do**
        Reach$_{post}$:= Reach$_{pre} \vee$ SUBS$(\exists \Xi : ($Reach$_{pre} \wedge (\mathcal{T}_{stage_0} \vee \mathcal{T}_{stage_1})), \Xi', \Xi)$
        if Reach$_{pre} \leftrightarrow$ Reach$_{post}$ **then** break;   // Break when the image saturates
        else Reach$_{pre}$:= Reach$_{post}$
11   **return** $\mathcal{T}_f \wedge$ Reach$_{post}$
end

- On c_2, g enters the risk-attractor, while a, b, c are also available. We have the following candidates $\{g \prec b, g \prec c, g \prec a\}$[3].

- On c_8, b enters the risk-attractor, while a is also available. We have the following candidate $b \prec a$.

From these candidates, we can perform **conflict resolution** and generate a set of priorities that ensures avoiding the attractor. For example, $\{a \prec c, g \prec a, b \prec a\}$ is a set of satisfying priorities to ensure safety. Note that the set $\{a \prec b, g \prec b, b \prec a\}$ is not a legal priority set, because it creates circular dependencies. In our implementation, conflict resolution is performed using SAT solvers: In the SAT problem, any priority $\sigma_1 \prec \sigma_2$ is presented as a Boolean variable $\sigma_1 \prec \sigma_2$, which can be set to True or False. If the generated SAT problem is satisfiable, for all variables $\sigma_1 \prec \sigma_2$ which is evaluated to True, we add priority $\sigma_1 \prec \sigma_2$ to $\mathcal{P}_+$. The synthesis engine creates four types of clauses.

---

[3] Notice that at least one candidate is a true candidate for risk-escape. Otherwise, during the attractor computation, c_2 will be included within the attractor.

1. **[Priority candidates]** For each edge $t \in \mathcal{T}_f$ which enters the risk attractor using σ and having $\sigma_1, \ldots, \sigma_e$ available actions (excluding σ), create clause $(\bigvee_{i=1\ldots e} \underline{\sigma \prec \sigma_i})^4$.
2. **[Existing priorities]** For each priority $\sigma \prec \sigma' \in \mathcal{P}$, create clause $(\underline{\sigma \prec \sigma'})$.
3. **[Non-reflective]** For each interaction σ used in (1) and (2), create clause $(\neg \underline{\sigma \prec \sigma})$.
4. **[Transitive]** For any three interactions $\sigma_1, \sigma_2, \sigma_3$ used in (1) and (2), create clause $((\underline{\sigma_1 \prec \sigma_2} \wedge \underline{\sigma_2 \prec \sigma_3}) \Rightarrow \underline{\sigma_1 \prec \sigma_3})$.

When the problem is satisfiable, we only output the set of priorities within the priority candidates (as non-reflective and transitive clauses are inferred properties). Admittedly, here we still solve an NP-complete problem. Nevertheless,

- The number of interactions involved in the fault-set can be much smaller than Σ.
- As the translation does not involve complicated encoding, we observe from our experiment that solving the SAT problem does not occupy a large portion (less than 20% for all benchmarks) of the total execution time.

3.4   Optimization

Currently, we use the following optimization techniques compared to the preliminary implementation of [11].

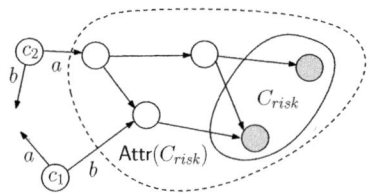

Fig. 2. A simple scenario where conflicts are unavoidable on the fault-set

(Handling Unsatisfiability). In the resolution scheme in Section 3.3, when the generated SAT problem is unsatisfiable, we can redo the process by moving some states in the fault-set to the attractor. This procedure is implemented by selecting a subset of priority candidates and annotate to the original system. We call this process **priority-repushing**. E.g., consider the system $\mathcal{S} = (C, \Sigma, \mathcal{P})$ in Figure 2. The fault-set $\{c_1, c_2\}$ is unable to resolve the conflict: For c_1 the priority candidate is $a \prec b$, and for c_2 the priority candidate is $b \prec a$. When we redo the analysis with $\mathcal{S} = (C, \Sigma, \mathcal{P} \cup \{a \prec b\})$, this time c_2 will be in the attractor, as now c_2 must respect the priority and is unable to escape using a. Currently in our implementation, we supports the repushing under fixed depth to increase the possibility of finding a fix.

(Variable Ordering Heuristics). As we use BDDs to compute the risk-attractor, a good initial variable ordering can greatly influence the total required time solving the game. We adapt the concept in the FORCE heuristic [2] where in the variable ordering, an interaction is placed approximately on the *center-of-gravity* of all participated components. This heuristic enables our solver to solve much larger problems. In addition, we allow the user to provide an initial variable ordering, such that FORCE heuristic can be applied more efficiently.

(Dense Variable Encoding). The encoding in Section 3.1 is *dense* compared to the encoding in [11]. In [11], for each component C_i participating interaction σ, one separate

---

^{4} In implementation, Algorithm 3 works symbolically on BDDs and proceeds on **cubes** of the risk-edges (a cube contains a set of states having the same enabled interactions and the same risk interaction), hence it avoids enumerating edges state-by-state.

variable σ_i is used. Then a joint action is done by an AND operation over all variables, i.e., $\bigwedge_i \sigma_i$. This eases the construction process but makes BDD-based game solving very inefficient: For a system $\mathcal{S}$, let $\Sigma_{use1} \subseteq \Sigma$ be the set of interactions where only one component participates within. Then the encoding in [11] uses at least $2|\Sigma \setminus \Sigma_{use1}|$ more BDD variables than the dense encoding.

4 Handling Complexities

In verification, it is standard to use *abstraction* and *modularity* to reduce the complexity of the analyzed systems. Abstraction is also useful in synthesis. However, note that if an abstract system is deadlock-free, it does not imply that the concrete system is as well (see the extended report [10] for examples). In the following, we propose three techniques.

4.1 Data Abstraction

Data abstraction techniques presented in the previous work [7] and implemented in the D-Finder tool kit [8] are *deadlock preserving*, i.e., synthesizing the abstract system to be deadlock free ensures that the concrete system is also deadlock free. Basically, the method works on an abstract system composed by components abstracted component-wise from concrete components. For example, if an abstraction preserves all control variables (i.e., all control variables are mapped by identity) and the mapping between the concrete and abstract system is precise with respect to all guards and updates (for control variables) on all transitions, then it is deadlock preserving. For further details, we refer interested readers to [7,8].

4.2 Alphabet Abstraction

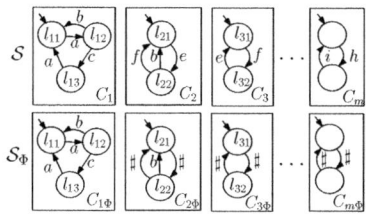

Second, we present *alphabet abstraction*, targeting to synthesize priorities to avoid deadlock (but also applicable for risk-freeness with extensions). The underlying intuition is to abstract concrete behavior of components out of concern. All proofs are listed in our extended report [10].

Fig. 3. A system $\mathcal{S}$ and its $\natural$-abstract system $\mathcal{S}_\Phi$, where $\Sigma_\Phi = \Sigma \setminus \{a, b, c\}$

Definition 8 (Alphabet Transformer). *Given a set Σ of interaction alphabet. Let $\Sigma_\Phi \subseteq \Sigma$ be **abstract alphabet**. Define $\alpha : \Sigma \to (\Sigma \setminus \Sigma_\Phi) \cup \{\natural\}$ as the alphabet transformer, such that for $\sigma \in \Sigma$,*

- *If $\sigma \in \Sigma_\Phi$, then $\alpha(\sigma) := \natural$.*
- *Otherwise, $\alpha(\sigma) := \sigma$.*

Definition 9 (Alphabet Abstraction: Syntax). *Given a system $\mathcal{S} = (C, \Sigma, \mathcal{P})$ and abstract alphabet $\Sigma_\Phi \subseteq \Sigma$, define the $\natural$-**abstract system** $\mathcal{S}_\Phi$ to be $(C_\Phi, (\Sigma \setminus \Sigma_\Phi) \cup \{\natural\}, \mathcal{P}_\Phi)$, where*

- *$C_\Phi = \bigcup_{i=1...m} C_{i\Phi}$, where $C_{i\Phi} = (L_i, V_i, \Sigma_{i\Phi}, T_{i\Phi}, l_i^0, e_i^0)$ changes from C_i by **syntactically** replacing every occurrence of $\sigma \in \Sigma_i$ to $\alpha(\sigma)$.*

– $\mathcal{P} = \bigcup_{i=1\ldots k} \sigma_i \prec \sigma_i'$ changes to $\mathcal{P}_\Phi = \bigcup_{i=1\ldots k} \alpha(\sigma_i) \prec \alpha(\sigma_i')$, and the relation defined by $\mathcal{P}_\Phi$ should be transitive and nonreflexive.

The definition for a configuration (state) of a $\natural$-abstract system follows Definition 2. Denote the set of all configuration of $\mathcal{S}_\Phi$ reachable from c_0 as $\mathcal{C}_{\mathcal{S}_\Phi}$. The update of configuration for an interaction $\sigma \in \Sigma \setminus \Sigma_\Phi$ follows Definition 3. The only difference is within the semantics of the $\natural$-interaction.

Definition 10 (Alphabet Abstraction: Semantics for $\natural$-interaction). *Given a configuration $c = (l_1, v_1, \ldots, l_m, v_m)$, the $\natural$-interaction is **enabled** if the following conditions hold.*

1. *(≥ 1 participants) **Exists** $i \in \{1, \ldots, m\}$ where $\natural \in \Sigma_{i\Phi}$, $\exists t_i = (l_i, g_i, \natural, f_i, l_i') \in T_{i\Phi}$ such that $g(v_i) = \texttt{True}$.*
2. *(No higher priorities enabled) There exists no other interaction $\sigma_b \in \Sigma$, $(\natural, \sigma_b) \in \mathcal{P}_\Phi$ such that $\forall i \in \{1, \ldots, m\}$ where $\sigma_b \in \Sigma_i$, $\exists t_{ib} = (l_i, g_{ib}, \sigma_{ib}, f_{ib}, l_i'') \in T_i$, $g_{ib}(v_i) = \texttt{True}$.*

Then for a configuration $c = (l_1, v_1, \ldots, l_m, v_m)$, the configuration after taking an enabled $\natural$-interaction changes to $c^\flat = (l_1^\flat, v_1^\flat, \ldots, l_m^\flat, v_m^\flat)$:

– *(**May-update** for participated components) If $\natural \in \Sigma_i$, then for transition $t_i = (l_i, g_i, \natural, f_i, l_i') \in T_{i\Phi}$ such that $g_i(v_i) = \texttt{True}$, either*
   1. *$l_i^\flat = l_i'$, $v_i^\flat = f_i(v_i)$, or*
   2. *$l_i^\flat = l_i$, $v_i^\flat = v_i$.*
   Furthermore, at least one component updates (i.e., select option 1).
– *(Stutter for unparticipated components) If $\natural \notin \Sigma_i$, $l_i^\flat = l_i$, $v_i^\flat = v_i$.*

Lastly, the behavior of a $\natural$-abstract system follows Definition 4. In summary, the above definitions indicate that in a $\natural$-abstract system, any local transitions having alphabet symbols within Σ_Φ can be executed in isolation or jointly. Thus, we have the following result.

Lemma 1 *Given a system $\mathcal{S}$ and its $\natural$-abstract system $\mathcal{S}_\Phi$, define $\mathcal{R}_\mathcal{S}$ ($\mathcal{R}_{\mathcal{S}_\Phi}$) be the reachable states of system $\mathcal{S}$ (corresponding $\natural$-abstract system) from from the initial configuration c^0. Then $\mathcal{R}_\mathcal{S} \subseteq \mathcal{R}_{\mathcal{S}_\Phi}$.*

As alphabet abstraction looses the execution condition by overlooking paired interactions, a $\natural$-abstract system is deadlock-free does not imply that the concrete system is deadlock free. E.g., consider a system $\mathcal{S}'$ composed only by C_2 and C_3 in Figure 3. When $\Phi = \Sigma \setminus \{b\}$, its $\natural$-abstract system $\mathcal{S}_\Phi'$ is shown below. In $\mathcal{S}'$, when C_2 is at location l_{21} and C_3 is at location l_{31}, interaction e and f are disabled, meaning that there exists a deadlock from the initial configuration. Nevertheless, in $\mathcal{S}_\Phi'$, as the $\natural$-interaction is always enabled, it is deadlock free.

In the following, we strengthen the deadlock condition by the notion of $\natural$-**deadlock**. Intuitively, a configuration is $\natural$-deadlocked, if it is deadlocked, or the only interaction available is the $\natural$-interaction.

Definition 11 ($\sharp$-deadlock). *Given a $\sharp$-abstract system $\mathcal{S}_\Phi$, a configuration $c \in \mathcal{C}_{\mathcal{S}_\Phi}$ is $\sharp$-deadlocked, if $\not\exists \sigma \in \Sigma \setminus \Sigma_\Phi, c' \in \mathcal{C}_{\mathcal{S}_\Phi}$ such that $c \xrightarrow{\sigma} c'$.*

In other words, a configuration c of $\mathcal{S}_\Phi$ is $\sharp$-deadlocked implies that all interactions labeled with $\Sigma \setminus \Sigma_\Phi$ are disabled at c.

Lemma 2 *Given a system $\mathcal{S}$ and its $\sharp$-abstract system $\mathcal{S}_\Phi$, define $\mathcal{D}$ as the set of deadlock states reachable from the initial state in $\mathcal{S}$, and $\mathcal{D}^\sharp$ as the set of $\sharp$-deadlock states reachable from the initial state in $\mathcal{S}_\Phi$. Then $\mathcal{D} \subseteq \mathcal{D}^\sharp$.*

Theorem 2 *Given a system $\mathcal{S}$ and its $\sharp$-abstract system $\mathcal{S}_\Phi$, if $\mathcal{S}_\Phi$ is $\sharp$-deadlock-free, then $\mathcal{S}$ is deadlock-free.*

(Algorithmic issues) Based on the above results, the use of alphabet abstraction and the notion of $\sharp$-deadlock offers a methodology for priority synthesis working on abstraction. Detailed steps are presented as follows.

1. Given a system $\mathcal{S}$, create its $\sharp$-abstract system $\mathcal{S}_\Phi$ by a user-defined $\Sigma_\Phi \subseteq \Sigma$. In our implementation, we let users select a subset of components $C_{s_1}, \ldots, C_{s_k} \in C$, and generate $\Sigma_\Phi = \Sigma \setminus (\Sigma_{s_1} \cup \ldots \cup \Sigma_{s_k})$.
   - E.g., consider system $\mathcal{S}$ in Figure 3 and its $\sharp$-abstract system $\mathcal{S}_\Phi$. The abstraction is done by looking at C_1 and maintaining $\Sigma_1 = \{a, b, c\}$.
   - When a system contains no variables, the algorithm proceeds by eliminateing components whose interaction are completely in the abstract alphabet. In Figure 3, as for $i = \{3 \ldots m\}$, $\Sigma_{i\Phi} = \{\sharp\}$, it is sufficient to eliminate all of them during the system encoding process.
2. If $\mathcal{S}_\Phi$ contains $\sharp$-deadlock states, we could obtain a $\sharp$-deadlock-free system by synthesizing a set of priorities $\mathcal{P}_+$, where the defined relation $\prec_+ \subseteq ((\Sigma \setminus \Sigma_\Phi) \cup \{\sharp\}) \times (\Sigma \setminus \Sigma_\Phi)$ using techniques presented in Section 3.
   - In the system encoding, the predicate $P_{\sharp dead}$ for $\sharp$-deadlock is defined as $stg = \texttt{False} \wedge \bigwedge_{\sigma \in \Sigma \setminus \Sigma_\Phi} \sigma = \texttt{False}$.
   - If the synthesized priority is having the form $\sharp \prec \sigma$, then translate it into a set of priorities $\bigcup_{\sigma' \in \Sigma_\Phi} \sigma' \prec \sigma$.

4.3   Assume-Guarantee Based Priority Synthesis

We use an assume-guarantee based compositional synthesis algorithm for behavior safety. Given a system $\mathcal{S} = (C_1 \cup C_2, \Sigma, \mathcal{P})$ and a risk specification described by a *deterministic finite state automaton* R, where $\mathcal{L}(R) \subseteq \Sigma^*$. We use $|\mathcal{S}|$ to denote the size of $\mathcal{S}$ and $|R|$ to denote the number of states of R. The synthesis task is to find a set of priority rules $\mathcal{P}_+$ such that adding $\mathcal{P}_+$ to the system $\mathcal{S}$ can make it B-Safe with respect to the risk specification $\mathcal{L}(R)$. This can be done using an *assume-guarantee* rule that we will describe in the next paragraph.

   We first define some notations needed for the rule. The system $\mathcal{S}_+ = (C_1 \cup C_2, \Sigma, \mathcal{P} \cup \mathcal{P}_+)$ is obtained by adding priority rules $\mathcal{P}_+$ to the system $\mathcal{S}$. We use $\mathcal{S}_1 = (C_1, \Sigma, \mathcal{P} \cap \Sigma \times \Sigma_1)$ and $\mathcal{S}_2 = (C_2, \Sigma, \mathcal{P} \cap \Sigma \times \Sigma_2)$ to denote two sub-systems of $\mathcal{S}$. We further partition the alphabet Σ into three parts Σ_{12}, Σ_1, and Σ_2, where Σ_{12} is the set of interactions appear both in the sets of components C_1 and C_2 (in words, the shared alphabet of C_1 and C_2), Σ_i is the set of interactions appear only in the set of components C_i (in words, the local alphabet of C_i) for $i = 1, 2$. Also, we require that the decomposition of the system must satisfy that $\mathcal{P} \subseteq \Sigma \times (\Sigma_1 \cup \Sigma_2)$, which means that we do not allow a shared interaction to have a higher priority than any other interaction. This is **required** for the soundness proof of the assume-guarantee rule, as we also explained in the extended report [10] that we will *immediately lose soundness by relaxing this restriction.* For $i = 1, 2$, the system $\mathcal{S}_{i+} = (C_i \cup \{d_i\}, \Sigma, (\mathcal{P} \cap \Sigma \times \Sigma_i) \cup \mathcal{P}_i)$ is obtained by (1) adding priority rules $\mathcal{P}_i \subseteq \Sigma \times \Sigma_i$ to $\mathcal{S}_i$ and, (2) in order to simulate stuttering transitions, adding a component d_i that contains only one location with self-loop transitions labeled with symbols in Σ_{3-i} (the local alphabet of the other set of components). Then the following assume-guarantee rule can be used to decompose the synthesis task into two smaller sub-tasks:

$$\frac{\mathcal{L}(\mathcal{S}_{1+}) \cap \mathcal{L}(R) \cap \mathcal{L}(A) = \emptyset \quad (a) \qquad \mathcal{L}(\mathcal{S}_{2+}) \cap \mathcal{L}(\overline{A}) = \emptyset \quad (b)}{\mathcal{L}(\mathcal{S}_+) \cap \mathcal{L}(R) = \emptyset \quad (c)}$$

The above assume-guarantee rule says that $\mathcal{S}_+$ is B-Safe with respect to $\mathcal{L}(R)$ iff there exists an assumption automaton A such that (1) $\mathcal{S}_{1+}$ is B-Safe with respect to $\mathcal{L}(R) \cap \mathcal{L}(A)$ and (2) $\mathcal{S}_{2+}$ is B-Safe with respect to $\mathcal{L}(\overline{A})$, where $\overline{A}$ is the complement of A, $\mathcal{P}_+ = \mathcal{P}_1 \cup \mathcal{P}_2$ and no conflict in $\mathcal{P}_1$ and $\mathcal{P}_2$. The above rule is both sound and complete for behavior safety verification (see [10]). However, it is unsound for deadlock freeness. An example can be found at the beginning of Section 4.

Notice that (1) the complexity of a synthesis task is NP-complete in the number of states in the risk specification automaton product with the size of the system and (2) $|\mathcal{S}|$ is approximately equals to $|\mathcal{S}_1| \times |\mathcal{S}_2|^5$. Consider the case that one decomposes the synthesis task of $\mathcal{S}$ with respect to $\mathcal{L}(R)$ into two subtasks using the above assume-guarantee rule. The complexity original synthesis task is NP-complete in $|\mathcal{S}| \times |R|$ and the complexity of the two sub-tasks are $|\mathcal{S}_1| \times |R| \times |A|$ and $|\mathcal{S}_2| \times |A|^6$, respectively. Therefore, if one managed to find a small assumption automaton A for the assume-guarantee rule, the complexity of synthesis can be greatly reduced. We propose to use the machine learning algorithm L* [3] to automatically find a small automaton that is suitable for compositional synthesis. Next, we will first briefly describe the L* algorithm and then explain how to use it for compositional synthesis.

The L* algorithm works iteratively to find a minimal deterministic automaton recognizing a target regular language U. It assumes a *teacher* that answers two types of queries: (a)*membership queries* on a string w, where the teacher returns *true* if w is in U and *false* otherwise, (b)*equivalence queries* on an automaton A, where the teacher returns *true* if $\mathcal{L}(A) = U$, otherwise it returns *false* together with a counterexample string in the difference of $\mathcal{L}(A)$ and U. In the i-th iteration of the algorithm, the L* algorithm acquires information of U by posing membership queries and guess a candidate automaton A_i. The correctness of the A_i is then verified using an equivalence query. If A_i is not a correct automaton (i.e., $\mathcal{L}(A) \neq U$), the counterexample returned from the teacher will be used to refine the conjecture automaton of the $(i + 1)$-th iteration. The learning algorithm is guaranteed to converge to the minimal deterministic finite state

---

[5] This is true only if the size of the alphabet is much smaller than the number of reachable configurations.

[6] Since A is deterministic, the sizes of A and its complement $\overline{A}$ are identical.

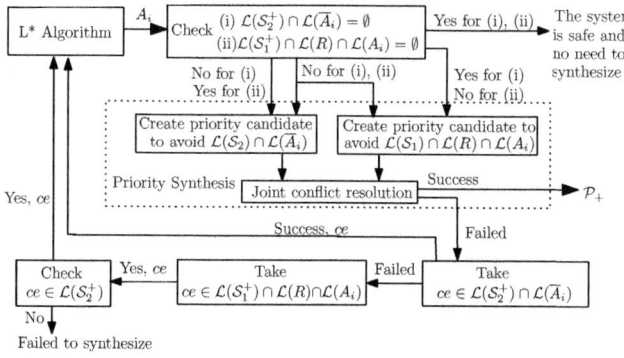

Fig. 4. The flow of the assume-guarantee priority synthesis

automaton of U in a polynomial number of iterations[7]. Also the sizes of conjecture automata increase strictly monotonically with respect to the number of iterations (i.e., $|A_{i+1}| > |A_i|$ for all $i > 0$).

The flow of our compositional synthesis is in Figure 4. Our idea of compositional synthesis via learning is the following. We use the notations S_i^+ to denote the system S_i equipped with a stuttering component. First we use L* to learn the language $\mathcal{L}(S_2^+)$. Since the transition system induced from the system S_2^+ has finitely many states, one can see that $\mathcal{L}(S_2^+)$ is regular. For a membership query on a word w, our algorithm simulates it symbolically on S_2^+ to see if it is in $\mathcal{L}(S_2^+)$. Once the L* algorithm poses an equivalence query on a deterministic finite automaton A_i, our algorithm tests conditions $\mathcal{L}(S_1^+) \cap \mathcal{L}(R) \cap \mathcal{L}(A_i) = \emptyset$ and $\mathcal{L}(S_2^+) \cap \mathcal{L}(\overline{A_i}) = \emptyset$ one after another. So far, our algorithm looks very similar to the compositional verification algorithm proposed in [14]. There are a few possible outcomes of the above test

1. Both condition holds and we proved the system is B-Safe with respect to $\mathcal{L}(R)$ and no synthesis is needed.
2. At least one of the two conditions does not hold. In such case, we try to synthesize priority rules to make the system B-Safe (see the details below).
3. If the algorithm fails to find usable priority rules, we have two cases:
   (a) The algorithm obtains a counterexample string ce in $\mathcal{L}(S_1^+) \cap \mathcal{L}(R) \setminus \mathcal{L}(\overline{A_i})$ from the first condition. This case is more complicated. We have to further test if $ce \in \mathcal{L}(S_2^+)$. A negative answer implies that ce is in $\mathcal{L}(A_i) \setminus \mathcal{L}(S_2^+)$. This follows that ce can be used by L* to refine the next conjecture. Otherwise, our algorithm terminates and reports not able to synthesize priority rules.
   (b) The algorithm obtains a counterexample string ce in $\mathcal{L}(S_2^+) \setminus \mathcal{L}(A_i)$ from the second condition, in such case, ce can be used by L* to refine the next conjecture.

The deterministic finite state automata R, A_i, and also its complement $\overline{A_i}$ can be treated as components without data and can be easily encoded symbolically using the approach

---

[7] In the size of the minimal deterministic finite state automaton of U and the longest counterexample returned from the teacher.

in Section 3.1. Also the two conditions can be tested using standard symbolic reachability algorithms.

Compositional Synthesis. Recall that our goal is to find a set of suitable priority rules via a small automaton A_i. Therefore, before using the ce to refine and obtain the next conjecture A_{i+1}, we first attempt to synthesis priority rules using A_i as the assumption automaton. Synthesis algorithms in previous sections can then be applied separately to the system composed of $\{S_1^+, R, A_i\}$ and the system composed of $\{S_2^+, \overline{A_i}\}$ to obtain two non-conflicting priority rules $\mathcal{P}_{1i} \subseteq (\Sigma_1 \cup \Sigma_{12}) \times \Sigma_1$ and $\mathcal{P}_{2i} \subseteq (\Sigma_2 \cup \Sigma_{12}) \times \Sigma_2$. Then $\mathcal{P}_{1i} \cup \mathcal{P}_{2i}$ is the desired priority for S to be B-Safe with respect to R. To be more specific, we first compute the CNF formulae f_1 and f_2 (that encode all possible priority rules that are *local*, i.e., we remove all non-local priority candidates) of the two systems separately using the algorithms in Section 3, and then check satisfiability of $f_1 \wedge f_2$. The priority rules $\mathcal{P}_{1i}$ and $\mathcal{P}_{2i}$ can be derived from the satisfying assignment of $f_1 \wedge f_2$.

5   Evaluation

We implemented the presented algorithms (except connection the data abstraction module in D-Finder [8]) in the VISSBIP[8] tool and performed experiments to evaluate them. To observe how our algorithm scales, in Table 1 we summarize results of synthesizing priorities for the dining philosophers problem[9]. Our preliminary result in [11] fails to synthesize priorities when the number of philosophers is greater than 15 (i.e., a total of 30 components), while currently we are able to solve problems of 50 within reasonable time. By analyzing the bottleneck, we found that 50% of the execution time are used to construct clauses for transitive closure, which can be easily parallelized. Also the synthesized result (i) does not starve any philosopher and (ii) ensures that each philosopher only needs to observe his left and right philosopher, making the resulting

Table 1. Experimental results

Problem	Time (seconds)				# of BDD variables				Remark
	NFM[1]	Opt.[2]	Ord.[3]	Abs.[4]	NFM	Opt.	Ord.	Abs.	
Phil. 10	0.813	0.303	0.291	0.169	202	122	122	38	[1] Engine based on [11]
Phil. 20	-	86.646	0.755	0.166	-	242	242	38	[2] Dense var. encoding
Phil. 25	-	-	1.407	0.183	-	-	302	38	[3] Initial var. ordering
Phil. 30	-	-	3.740	0.206	-	-	362	38	[4] Alphabet abstraction
Phil. 35	-	-	5.913	0.212	-	-	422	38	- Timeout/Not evaluated
Phil. 40	-	-	10.210	0.228	-	-	482	38	
Phil. 45	-	-	18.344	0.213	-	-	542	38	
Phil. 50	-	-	30.384	0.234	-	-	602	38	
DPU v1	5.335	0.299	x	x	168	116	x	x	[R] Priority repushing
DPU v2	4.174	0.537	1.134[R]	x	168	116	116[R]	x	x Not evaluated
Traffic	x	x	0.651	x	x	x	272	x	

[8] Available for download at http://www6.in.tum.de/~chengch/vissbip
[9] Evaluated under Intel 2.93GHz CPU with 2048Mb RAM for JVM.

priority very desirable. Contrarily, it is possible to select a subset of components and ask to synthesize priorities for deadlock freedom using alphabet abstraction. The execution time using alphabet abstraction depends on the number of selected components; in our case we select 4 components thus is executed extremely fast. Of course, the synthesized result is not very satisfactory, as it starves certain philosopher. Nevertheless, this is unavoidable when overlooking interactions done by other philosophers. Except the traditional dining philosophers problem, we have also evaluated on (i) a BIP model (5 components) for data processing in digital communication (DPU; See [10] for description) (i) a simplified protocol of automatic traffic control (Traffic). Our preliminary evaluation on compositional priority synthesis is listed in [10].

6   Related Work

For deadlock detection, well-known model checking tools such as SPIN [18] and NuSMV [13] support deadlock detection by given certain formulas to specify the property. D-Finder [8] applies compositional and incremental methods to compute invariants for an over-approximation of reachable states to verify deadlock-freedom automatically. Nevertheless, all the above tools do not provide any deadlock avoidance strategies when real deadlocks are detected.

Synthesizing priorities is subsumed by the framework of controller synthesis proposed by Ramadge and Wohnham [22], where the authors proposed an automata-theoretical approach to restrict the behavior of the system (the modeling of environment is also possible). Essentially, when the environment is modeled, the framework computes the risk attractor and creates a centralized controller. Similar results using centralized control can be dated back from [5] to the recent work by Autili et al [4] (the SYNTHESIS tool). Nevertheless, the centralized coordinator forms a major bottleneck for system execution. Transforming a centralized controller to distributed controllers is difficult, as within a centralized controller, the execution of a local interaction of a component might need to consider the configuration of all other components.

Priorities, as they are stateless, can be distributed much easier for performance and concurrency. E.g., the synthesized result of dining philosophers problem indicates that each philosopher only needs to watch his left and right philosophers without considering all others. We can continue with known results from the work of Graf et al. [17] to distribute priorities, or partition the set of priorities to multiple controllers under layered structure to increase concurrency (see work by Bonakdarpour et al. [9]). Our algorithm can be viewed as a step forward from centralized controllers to distributed controllers, as architectural constraints (i.e., visibility of other components) can be encoded during the creation of priority candidates. Therefore, we consider the work of Abujarad et al.[1] closest to ours, where they proceeds by performing distributed synthesis (known to be undecidable [21]) directly. In their model, they take into account the environment (which they refer it as faults), and consider handling deadlock states by either adding mechanisms to recover from them or preventing the system to reach it. It is difficult to compare two approaches directly, but we give hints concerning performance measure: (i) Our methodology and implementation works on game concept, so the complexity of introducing the environment does not change. (ii) In [1], for a problem of 10^{33} states,

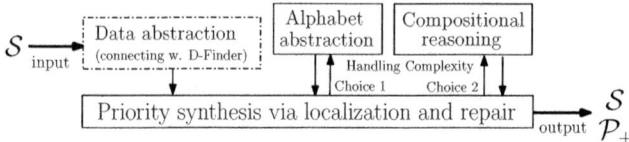

Fig. 5. The framework of priority synthesis presented in this paper, where the connection with the D-Finder tool [8] is left for future work

under 8-thread parallelization, the total execution time is 3837 seconds, while resolving the deadlock of the 50 dining philosophers problem (a problem of 10^{38} states) is solved within 31 seconds using our monolithic engine.

Lastly, the research of deadlock detection and mechanisms of deadlock avoidance is an important topic within the community of Petri nets (see survey paper [20] for details). Concerning synthesis, some theoretical results are available, e.g., [19], but efficient implementation efforts are, to our knowledge, lacking.

7   Conclusion

In this paper, we explain the underlying algorithm for priority synthesis and propose extensions to synthesize priorities for more complex systems. Figure 5 illustrates a potential flow of priority synthesis. A system can be first processed using data abstraction to create models suitable for our analysis framework. Besides the monolithic engine, two complementary techniques are available to further reduce the complexity of problem under analysis. Due to the stateless property and the fact that they preserve deadlock-freedom, priorities can be relatively easily implemented in a distributed setting.

References

1. Abujarad, F., Bonakdarpour, B., Kulkarni, S.: Parallelizing deadlock resolution in symbolic synthesis of distributed programs. In: PDMC 2009. EPTCS, vol. 14, pp. 92–106 (2009)
2. Aloul, F., Markov, I., Sakallah, K.: FORCE: a fast and easy-to-implement variable-ordering heuristic. In: GLSVLSI 2003, pp. 116–119. ACM, New York (2003)
3. Angluin, D.: Learning regular sets from queries and counterexamples. Information and Computation 75(2), 87–106 (1987)
4. Autili, M., Inverardi, P., Navarra, A., Tivoli, M.: SYNTHESIS: a tool for automatically assembling correct and distributed component-based systems. In: ICSE 2007, pp. 784–787. IEEE Computer Society, Los Alamitos (2007)
5. Balemi, S., Hoffmann, G., Gyugyi, P., Wong-Toi, H., Franklin, G.: Supervisory control of a rapid thermal multiprocessor. IEEE Transactions on Automatic Control 38(7), 1040–1059 (1993)
6. Basu, A., Bozga, M., Sifakis, J.: Modeling heterogeneous real-time components in BIP. In: SEFM 2006, pp. 3–12. IEEE, Los Alamitos (2006)
7. Bensalem, S., Bozga, M., Sifakis, J., Nguyen, T.: Compositional verification for component-based systems and application. In: Cha, S(S.), Choi, J.-Y., Kim, M., Lee, I., Viswanathan, M. (eds.) ATVA 2008. LNCS, vol. 5311, pp. 64–79. Springer, Heidelberg (2008)

8. Bensalem, S., Griesmayer, A., Legay, A., Nguyen, T.-H., Sifakis, J., Yan, R.-J.: D-Finder 2: Towards Efficient Correctness of Incremental Design. In: Bobaru, M., Havelund, K., Holzmann, G.J., Joshi, R. (eds.) NFM 2011. LNCS, vol. 6617, pp. 453–458. Springer, Heidelberg (2011)
9. Bonakdarpour, B., Bozga, M., Quilbeuf, J.: Automated distributed implementation of component-based models with priorities. In: EMSOFT 2011. ACM, New York (to appear, 2011)
10. Cheng, C.-H., Bensalem, S., Chen, Y.-F., Yan, R.-J., Jobstmann, B., Ruess, H., Buckl, C., Knoll, A.: Algorithms for synthesizing priorities in component-based systems (extended version), arXiv:1107.1383 [cs.LO] (2011)
11. Cheng, C.-H., Bensalem, S., Jobstmann, B., Yan, R.-J., Knoll, A., Ruess, H.: Model construction and priority synthesis for simple interaction systems. In: Bobaru, M., Havelund, K., Holzmann, G.J., Joshi, R. (eds.) NFM 2011. LNCS, vol. 6617, pp. 466–471. Springer, Heidelberg (2011)
12. Cheng, C.-H., Jobstmann, B., Buckl, C., Knoll, A.: On the hardness of priority synthesis. In: Bouchou-Markhoff, B., Caron, P., Champarnaud, J.-M., Maurel, D. (eds.) CIAA 2011. LNCS, vol. 6807, pp. 110–117. Springer, Heidelberg (2011)
13. Cimatti, A., Clarke, E., Giunchiglia, F., Roveri, M.: NuSMV: a new symbolic model verifier. In: Halbwachs, N., Peled, D.A. (eds.) CAV 1999. LNCS, vol. 1633, pp. 495–499. Springer, Heidelberg (1999)
14. Cobleigh, J., Giannakopoulou, D., Păsăreanu, C.: Learning assumptions for compositional verification. In: Garavel, H., Hatcliff, J. (eds.) TACAS 2003. LNCS, vol. 2619, pp. 331–346. Springer, Heidelberg (2003)
15. Gößler, G., Sifakis, J.: Priority systems. In: de Boer, F.S., Bonsangue, M.M., Graf, S., de Roever, W.-P. (eds.) FMCO 2003. LNCS, vol. 3188, pp. 314–329. Springer, Heidelberg (2004)
16. Grädel, E., Thomas, W., Wilke, T. (eds.): Automata, Logics, and Infinite Games. LNCS, vol. 2500. Springer, Heidelberg (2002)
17. Graf, S., Peled, D., Quinton, S.: Achieving distributed control through model checking. In: Touili, T., Cook, B., Jackson, P. (eds.) CAV 2010. LNCS, vol. 6174, pp. 396–409. Springer, Heidelberg (2010)
18. Holzmann, G.: The Spin Model Checker: Primer and Reference Manual. Addison-Wesley Professional, Reading (2004)
19. Iordache, M., Moody, J., Antsaklis, P.: Synthesis of deadlock prevention supervisors using Petri nets. IEEE Transactions on Robotics and Automation 18(1), 59–68 (2002)
20. Li, Z., Zhou, M., Wu, N.: A survey and comparison of Petri net-based deadlock prevention policies for flexible manufacturing systems. IEEE Transactions on Systems, Man, and Cybernetics 38(2), 173–188 (2008)
21. Pneuli, A., Rosner, R.: Distributed reactive systems are hard to synthesize. In: FOCS 1990, vol. 2, pp. 746–757. IEEE Computer Society, Los Alamitos (1990)
22. Ramadge, P., Wonham, W.: The control of discrete event systems. Proceedings of the IEEE 77(1), 81–98 (1989)

Trust Metrics for the SPKI/SDSI Authorisation Framework

Dominik Wojtczak

University of Liverpool, UK
d.k.wojtczak@liv.ac.uk

Abstract. SPKI/SDSI is a distributed Public Key Infrastructure (PKI) framework that allows for issuing authorisation certificates granting permissions to access selected parts of privileged data not only to single principals, but also to user-defined groups. The fact that the protocol is decentralised and there is no designated entity that verifies the identity of the users of the system makes the trustfulness vary significantly from one user to another. In order to tackle this problem in decentralised PKI systems many trust metrics were created for computing how much one user can trust another even if they have never interacted with each other before, e.g. the Web of Trust in PGP. We show how to apply two of these metrics in the SPKI/SDSI setting. Specifically, a metric that interprets these values as a probability of non-failure and a metric interpreting them as flows. The fact that SPKI/SDSI is essentially as powerful as pushdown systems makes computation of these trust metrics a lot harder in our setting than when the system can be represented as a finite graph. Actually, both of these problems are shown to be #P-complete, but at the same time we show a randomised approximation algorithm for the trust metric based on the probabilistic interpretation. Finally, to test how fast these values can be computed in practise, we implemented them in a tool called Spookey. Spookey allows for representing an arbitrary system of SPKI/SDSI certificates labelled with trust values. We present the performance results obtained by using our tool.

1 Introduction

Internet allows people around the globe to freely communicate with each other, share files and photos, engage in financial transactions, e.g. on eBay, or buy products online in shops. But such an open environment becomes an easy target for abuse and it is common to encounter agents fraudulently masquerading themselves as a person or an online shop that we trust. The two problems that we need to challenge in this setting are *authentication*, which is verifying that the entity we interact with is really the one that we think it is, and *authorisation*, which is verifying whether a given entity who was successfully authenticated has the rights to access some resource. Public Key Infrastructure (PKI) was developed to tackle the authentication problem. The currently widely adopted solution is defined by protocol X.509 that relies on the existence of so called Certification Authorities (CAs). A CA is an institution that is responsible for granting

T. Bultan and P.-A. Hsiung (Eds.): ATVA 2011, LNCS 6996, pp. 168–182, 2011.

certificates to trustworthy principals and whose responsibility is to check that the details specified in the issued certificate correspond to the valid information about that person or organisation. Only once this personal information is thoroughly verified, such a certificate can be signed by the CA's private key. The main assumption of this framework is that every user is in the possession of the valid public keys of all the CAs. Usually it is done by embedding these keys into the operating systems or the web browsers. The other underlying assumption is that each CA can be fully trusted. Any not fully trustworthy CA makes it easy to compromise the whole system and indeed there were cases when CAs signed fraudulent certificates. However, decentralised PKI systems emerged as an alternative to this approach. One of them is PGP [24] (Pretty Good Privacy), the most popular solution for confidential e-mail communication, another one is SPKI/SDSI [8] (Simple Public Key Infrastructure/Simple Distributed Security Infrastructure).

In PGP each user first generates his own private-public cryptographic key pair and then sends his public key bound together with his name and e-mail address to one of the *key servers* for storage and easy retrieval. To increase the reliability of these bindings, PGP introduced a security fault tolerance mechanism called *the Web of Trust* that works as follows. Each user can sign a public key that he trusts with his own private key. Such a signature is called a certificate and it can be easily verified whether it is valid and to which public key it corresponds to; such certificates are stored along the public keys at the key servers. Now, if someone trusts a given person and he possesses his valid public key then he should as well trust all the public keys that were certified correctly by that person's private key. This mechanism was later also used in other systems, e.g. the SSL certificates issued free of charge by CAcert.org [5] to the public have associated assurance points that increase with the number of times the identity of the owner of the certificate has been verified in person by the other users of the system. However, trusting equally all public keys that can be reached by such a *certificate chain* is problematic, because intuitively long certificate chains should be less trusted than short ones, while on the other hand, multiple independent certificate chains should increase our confidence. This was already pointed out in [24] and lead to the design of the first simple *trust metric* for the PGP's Web of Trust, i.e. a way of estimating how much confidence one should have in a given public key based on the information about the system. Since that time many more trust metrics were proposed. We will examine some of them later, after we define the SPKI/SDSI authorisation framework first.

SPKI/SDSI (pronounced "spooky-sudsy") is a distributed authorisation framework first specified in [8]. It was created by combining SPKI's style authorisation certificates and SDSI's S-expression naming schema and in short looks as follows. Any person, host or an organisation participating in the system is called a *principal* and it is identified with its public key. The public key of principal X will be denoted by $\mathcal{K}_X$. An identifier is any non-empty word over some fixed alphabet and is used to assign *roles* to principals. A *term* is a key followed by an arbitrary (and possibly empty) list of identifiers, i.e. *public_key*

<list of ids>. Each principal defines in his own namespace many-to-one connections between roles and principals by issuing *name certificates* (in short *name certs*). The SDSI specification allows for referring to principals by roles defined in other principal's namespaces. For instance $\mathcal{K}_{Alice}$ friend $\to \mathcal{K}_{Bob}$ specifies that Bob is a friend of Alice, $\mathcal{K}_{Alice}$ friend $\to \mathcal{K}_{Bob}$ friend specifies that all Bob's friends are also friends of Alice, and $\mathcal{K}_{Alice}$ friend friend $\to \mathcal{K}_{Alice}$ friend specifies that all friends of friends of Alice are also her friends. Formally, a name cert looks as follows: *public_key* id $\to t$, where t is an arbitrary term. Principals can also issue *authorisation certificates* (in short *auth certs*). Such certificates grant particular principals or user's specified roles, permission to operate on some of the resources the issuer owns. This allows the user to grant permission to a whole group of people not just individuals. For auth certs in SPKI/SDSI user can specify what resources he is granting the permission to and the validity period of the certificate. However, we will not consider these aspects in our analysis, because all expired auth certs can be easily removed at the very beginning of the analysis together with all auth certs that concern resources we are not interested in. Thanks to this assumption, an auth cert can simply be represented as: *public_key* id $\square \to t \ \square/\blacksquare$, where t is again an arbitrary term. The difference between an auth cert ending with $\square$ and one with $\blacksquare$ is the following: the principal granted access to a resource with $\square$ can delegate this authorisation further, while an authorisation with $\blacksquare$ does not allow for such a delegation. For any name or auth cert $x \to y$, x would be called its *head* and y would be called its *tail*. As pointed out in [6], certificates can be interpreted as prefix rewrite rules that can be composed iff they are *compatible with each other*, i.e. the prefix of the tail of the first one is the same as the head of the other. For instance, a name certs $\mathcal{K}_1$ id1 $\to \mathcal{K}_2$ id2 id3 can be composed with name cert $\mathcal{K}_2$ id2 $\to \mathcal{K}_3$ id4 to give a name cert $\mathcal{K}_1$ id1 $\to \mathcal{K}_3$ id4 id3 or an auth cert $\mathcal{K}_1 \square \to \mathcal{K}_2$ id1 $\square$ can be composed with a name cert $\mathcal{K}_2$ id1 $\to \mathcal{K}_3$ to give an auth cert $\mathcal{K}_1 \square \to \mathcal{K}_3 \square$. By repeating this procedure we can generate the *closure* of a given certificate set that can potentially contain infinitely many certificates. Now, a principal Y is allowed to access resources of principal X, denoted by $\mathcal{K}_X \hookrightarrow \mathcal{K}_Y$, iff this closure contains the certificate $\mathcal{K}_X \square \to \mathcal{K}_Y \square$ or $\mathcal{K}_X \square \to \mathcal{K}_Y \blacksquare$. The problem of deciding whether $\mathcal{K}_X \hookrightarrow \mathcal{K}_Y$ holds was already solved in [6], by computing the *name-reduction closure* of a certificate set; such a set of certificates is always finite.

Jha and Reps in [12] observed that any SPKI/SDSI certificate set is essentially a Pushdown System, where the set of control states is the same as the set of public keys and the stack alphabet contains the set of all identifiers plus the two special symbols $\square$ and $\blacksquare$. A state of such a Pushdown System is a pair (*public_key*, <a list/stack of ids>) and it was shown there that the state $(\mathcal{K}_Y, \square/\blacksquare)$ is reachable from $(\mathcal{K}_X, \square)$ in such a transition system iff $\mathcal{K}_X \hookrightarrow \mathcal{K}_Y$ holds in the original SPKI/SDSI certificate set. This algorithm has certain advantages over the name-reduction closure one as it allows to answer a lot more general authorisation problems using existing theory of pushdown systems.

Coming back to the Web of Trust in PGP, the problem with trusting equally all certificate chains of arbitrary length is that one cannot be always 100% sure that a given public key really belongs to the person he thinks it belongs to, i.e. how much he trusts that this *key binding* is correct. So the assigned trust to a certificate chain should intuitively decrease with its length. Moreover, even if the key binding to a given person is correct, we may have doubts how trustworthy she actually is when it comes to issuing certificates. Some people can be really careless when signing public keys while others take extra measures in order to verify the identity of the owner of a public key and will not sign it until they are absolutely sure that everything is right. In order to be on the safe side, we would need to remove all delegations to principals that we do not fully trust. An alternative solution is to allow the user to specify for each certificate how often, he thinks, the owner of the certified public key verifies her connections correctly. As in real-life trust values can vary between completely untrusted to completely trusted and all intermediate degrees are possible, so it is natural to represent the confidence by real numbers from 0 to 100%. Unlike the trust assigned to a key binding, the confidence of one person towards another should not be revealed publicly. A *trust metric* is a function that assigns a trust value to a given request or a public key from the perspective of another public key based on the full description of the trust network. A problem arises how can one compute the value of a trust metric without having to ask for the trust values that should be kept private. In our setting, we will simply assume that the user assigns just a single trust value to each of his certificates which in a way blends these private and public trust values together.

Every good trust metric should have the following set of intuitive properties. As pointed out in [19], one of them is that its value should have a clear intuitive meaningful interpretation. On top of that, trust should increase with the number of certificate chains that certify that a given public key is correct, but it should also take into consideration dependencies between such chains. If all of them depend on a single certificate then the assigned trust cannot be higher than the trust assigned to that crucial certificate. On the other hand, if there are multiple completely independent certification chains, the trust value should be higher than the maximum of the trust value assigned to any of them. It is simply because even if the certificate chain with the maximum trust value fails, there is still another chain that certifies that a given public key is valid.

A natural quantitative trust model for PGP's Web of Trust that captures all these phenomena was introduced by Maurer in [16]. Maurer considered the trust to range from marginal to ultimately trusted and so it can take any possible value between 0 (completely untrusted) and 1 (fully trusted). The trust assigned to a certificate is interpreted as the probability of that certificate being valid. In this model, the Web of Trust is represented by a finite graph where nodes correspond to the public keys and edges correspond to the certificates between them. Each edge is labelled with the probability of that edge actually existing in this graph. Now, the probability that there is a path from node u to node v in such a graph is the absolute trust the owner of the public key u should have in the public key v.

This model, in a natural way, also captures dependencies between certification chains and reinforcement of trust in the case of independent certification chains existing in a given system. Maurer also distinguished between the trust assigned to the key binding and the trust in the other person's reliability when it comes to signing other public keys. As pointed out before, we will not consider the distinction between these two values in our models, but we could quite easily extend them to handle it if necessary.

In exactly the same way we can assign and then interpret the trust values on the name and auth certs in SPKI/SDSI systems. In other words, a cert in such a system is valid with probability equal to the trust assigned to that rule. In this interpretation, the trust we should assign to the authorisation request $\mathcal{K} \hookrightarrow \mathcal{K}'$ is the probability that the closure of the certificate set, after all the invalid certificates were removed from it, contains $\mathcal{K} \square \rightarrow \mathcal{K}' \square$. Let us consider the following example, where each certificate is annotated with its trust value.

$$\mathcal{K}_{Alice} \square \xrightarrow{0.9} \mathcal{K}_{Alice} \text{ Dept\_of\_CS Bob } \square$$

$$\mathcal{K}_{Alice} \text{ Dept\_of\_CS } \xrightarrow{0.8} \mathcal{K}_{Alice} \text{ Uni\_of\_Liverpool Dept\_of\_CS}$$

$$\mathcal{K}_{Alice} \text{ Uni\_of\_Liverpool } \xrightarrow{0.9} \mathcal{K}_{UoL}$$

$$\mathcal{K}_{UoL} \text{ Dept\_of\_CS } \xrightarrow{0.9} \mathcal{K}_{DoCS}$$

$$\mathcal{K}_{DoCS} \text{ Bob } \xrightarrow{0.9} \mathcal{K}_{Bob}$$

$$\mathcal{K}_{Alice} \square \xrightarrow{0.9} \mathcal{K}_{Alice} \text{ Bob } \blacksquare$$

$$\mathcal{K}_{Alice} \text{ Bob } \xrightarrow{0.2} \mathcal{K}_{Bob}$$

We would like to know whether Bob can access Alice's computer. Alice requires a confidence of at least 60% in order to allow the access. In the Pushdown System interpretation of this example, we are looking for a path starting in $(\mathcal{K}_{Alice}, \square)$ and ending in $(\mathcal{K}_{Bob}, \square/\blacksquare)$. There are two such paths: $\mathcal{K}_{Alice} \square \xrightarrow{0.9} \mathcal{K}_{Alice} \text{ Dept\_of\_CS Bob } \square \xrightarrow{0.8} \mathcal{K}_{Alice} \text{ Uni\_of\_Liverpool Dept\_of\_CS Bob } \square \xrightarrow{0.9} \mathcal{K}_{UoL} \text{ Dept\_of\_CS Bob } \square \xrightarrow{0.9} \mathcal{K}_{DoCS} \text{ Bob } \square \xrightarrow{0.9} \mathcal{K}_{Bob} \square$ and $\mathcal{K}_{Alice} \square \xrightarrow{0.9} \mathcal{K}_{Alice} \text{ Bob } \blacksquare \xrightarrow{0.2} \mathcal{K}_{Bob} \blacksquare$. The assigned confidence would be the probability of both of these independent certification chains not failing which is equal to $1 - (1 - 0.8 \cdot 0.9^4) \cdot (1 - 0.9 \cdot 0.2) \approx 0.61$ and the access would be granted.

In the past ten years there was a substantial research in devising new more robust trust metrics for distributed PKI and many new trust metrics emerged, e.g. [19,15,14], the first such properly defined metric being [3]. These metrics were compared to each other in [15] in respect how strong they are against various possible attack scenarios. An attack of a malicious person whose public key is part of the system and who issues extra certificates in order to manipulate the other users' value of the trust metric, and also an attack where one of the trustworthy private keys in the system has been compromised were considered. It has turned out that a metric proposed in [15,19] based on interpreting the trust values as flows in a finite graph and computing the maximal flow from the source public key to the target public key is the most resistant one according to the suggested criteria. Moreover, such a metric in the setting of finite graphs has a big advantage of being computable in polynomial time using a classical algorithm for finding maximum flow in a graph [9]. The only undesirable property of this trust metric is that a long chain consisting of not fully trusted certificates, e.g. all having the trust value $p < 1$, will have the same trust assigned to it as a short chain with all certificates having the trust value p.

When we try to apply this trust metric to the SPKI/SDSI setting, we would like to keep the following intuition behind it: In the situation where the weights on all certificates are 1 (i.e. they are all fully trusted) the value of the metric for a given authorisation request is equal to the number of completely independent derivations of that request. Specifically, if the value of the metric is k, this means that we can find k disjoint certificate subsets $\mathcal{C}_1, \ldots, \mathcal{C}_k$ of the whole certificate set such that in each certificate set $\mathcal{C}_i$ the authorisation request succeeds. In the case when not all the trust values are equal to 1, then each set $\mathcal{C}_i$ comes with some weight $\in [0, 1]$ and a single certificate can be in multiple such sets as long as the total weight of the sets that contain it do not exceed the trust value of that certificate. This is similar to the situation in the flow networks where multiple flow carrying paths can use the same edge as long as they do not exceed its capacity. We will later formally define our trust metric based on the minimum cut of the certificate set, i.e. the minimum sum of the trust values among all subsets of certificates whose removal from the system causes a given authorisation request to fail. Therefore, we will call this metric the *mincut trust metric*. As it is well-known, for finite graphs the value of the minimum cut and the maximum flow coincide. Similarly here, the intuition behind the value of the just defined trust metric and the minimum cut formulation give the same value. For the same example presented before, the value of the mincut trust metric is $0.8 + 0.2 = 1$, because it suffices to remove the $\mathcal{K}_{Alice}$ Dept_of_CS $\overset{0.8}{\rightarrow}$ $\mathcal{K}_{Alice}$ Uni_of_Liverpool Dept_of_CS and $\mathcal{K}_{Alice}$ Bob $\overset{0.2}{\rightarrow}$ $\mathcal{K}_{Bob}$ certificates to invalidate both of the chains certifying $\mathcal{K}_{Alice} \hookrightarrow \mathcal{K}_{Bob}$. The value 1 of the mincut trust metric in this case is the same as if one fully trusted path connecting $\mathcal{K}_{Alice}$ with $\mathcal{K}_{Bob}$ existed in this system.

We think that our extension of SPKI/SDSI with trust values specification can be useful for constructing authorisation systems with an integrated trust management system. For an overview how to define trust and how trust management systems are being used in practice see [10,13,21].

Related Work: The first attempt to allow for assigning trust values to the certificates in the SPKI/SDSI system was already done in [12] where the connection between SPKI/SDSI and Pushdown Systems was established. The trust metric proposed there is based on labelling each certificate with a trust value from a bounded idempotent semiring and using this semiring's $\otimes$ operator to compute the value of the trust metric for a single path and this semiring's $\oplus$ operator to compute the trust metric for a set of paths in order to derive the final value of the trust metric for a given authorisation request. This effectively implies that there are only finitely many levels of trust, e.g. low, medium, high. Also, the value of the trust metric for several completely independent certificate chains is the same as the maximum trust value assigned to any of them, essentially as if the other certificate chains did not exist in the system. Another model that extends SPKI/SDSI certificates with trust values was given in [4]. An authorisation certificate in their setting is interpreted as recommendation rather than authorisation. The values assigned to the certificates are normalised so that they sum up to 1 for all certificates with the same head. These values are then interpreted as the probability of using a given certificate once it becomes applicable. One can then compute how often a given key occurs during such a random walk on this certificate set and use this value as a measure of reputation of the owner of this key when compared to the other principals. Notice, however, that this does not help in deciding whether a given principal should be allowed to access a given resource, because the relative trustworthiness of the principals is the same in the case where all of them are completely untrustworthy and in the case where they are all completely trustworthy.

2   Formal Definitions

As mentioned before, Pushdown Systems (PDSs) can directly encode arbitrary SPKI/SDSI certificate sets ([12]), and so we will formally define our trust metrics for PDSs only.

A Pushdown System (PDS), $\mathcal{P}$, is a 3-tuple (Q, Γ, Δ) consisting of a finite set of control states Q, a finite stack alphabet Γ, and a set of transition rules $\Delta \subseteq Q \times \Gamma \times Q \times \Gamma^*$. We will write $pX \to q\alpha$ to denote $(p, X, q, \alpha) \in \Delta$. When looking at a PDS as a SPKI/SDSI system, some of these rules will correspond to auth certs, some to name certs and some can make no sense in the SPKI/SDSI setting (e.g. $p\,\square \to q\,\square\,\square$). A configuration of a PDS is a pair $p\alpha \in Q \times \Gamma^*$ consisting of a control state and the content of the stack. The set of all configurations of a given PDS $\mathcal{P}$ will be denoted by conf($\mathcal{P}$). A PDS $\mathcal{P}$ generates in a natural way a transition system $\mathcal{S}_\mathcal{P} = (\text{conf}(\mathcal{P}), \to_\mathcal{P})$ on the set of configurations of $\mathcal{P}$ as follows. There is a transition in $\to_\mathcal{P}$ from the state $(u, X\alpha)$ to $(v, \beta\alpha)$, where $u, v \in Q$, $X \in \Gamma$ and $\alpha, \beta \in \Gamma^*$, iff $(u, X, v, \beta) \in \Delta$. We will write $\Rightarrow_\mathcal{P}$ for the reflexive transitive closure of $\to_\mathcal{P}$. We say that a given *request* $p\alpha \hookrightarrow q\beta$ holds in $\mathcal{P}$ iff $p\alpha \Rightarrow_\mathcal{P} q\beta$. Notice that this means that in the SPKI/SDSI setting $\mathcal{K} \hookrightarrow \mathcal{K}$ always succeeds for any $\mathcal{K}$ regardless of the set of the transition rules (i.e. the certificates present in the system).

A Labelled Pushdown System (LPDS) is a PDS that comes with a labelling function of the transition rules, $\Lambda : \Delta \to [0, 1]$, that assigns a real number between 0 and 1 to each rule. In general, the label could be taken from some arbitrary set, but for our purposes we restrict it to the $[0, 1]$ interval only.

The value of the probabilistic trust metric (PTM), for a given LPDS $\mathcal{P} = (Q, \Gamma, \Delta, \Lambda)$ and request $p\alpha \hookrightarrow q\beta$ is defined as follows. First, let us define an indicator function $\chi : 2^\Delta \to \{0, 1\}$, such that for any certificate set $\Delta' \subseteq \Delta$

we have $\chi(\Delta') = 1$ if $p\alpha \Rightarrow_{\mathcal{P}'} q\beta$ holds in the pushdown system $\mathcal{P}' = (Q, \Gamma, \Delta')$ and $\chi(\Delta') = 0$ otherwise. The value of the trust metric PTM is given by:

$$\text{PTM}(\mathcal{P}) = \sum_{\Delta' \subseteq \Delta} \chi(\Delta') \prod_{e \in \Delta'} \Lambda(e) \cdot \prod_{e \in \Delta \setminus \Delta'} (1 - \Lambda(e)).$$

Intuitively, this adds up the probability of all pushdown systems resulting from removing some of the rules from $\mathcal{P}$ and for which the given authorisation request succeeds. The probability of a given pushdown system occurring is equal to the product of trust values of the rules that it contains times the product of one minus the trust value of the rules that were removed.

On the other hand, the value of the mincut trust metric (MTM) for a given LPDS $\mathcal{P} = (Q, \Gamma, \Delta, \Lambda)$ and request $p\alpha \hookrightarrow q\beta$, where $p\alpha \neq q\beta$, is defined as follows.

$$\text{MTM}(\mathcal{P}) = \min_{\{\Delta' \subseteq \Delta \mid \chi(\Delta \setminus \Delta') = 0\}} \sum_{e \in \Delta'} \Lambda(e)$$

Intuitively, it is the minimum sum of the trust values of rules that once removed from Δ cause the given request to fail. For finite graphs this problem is equivalent to finding the maximum flow in a graph. When $p\alpha = q\beta$ we set $\text{MTM}(\mathcal{P}) = \infty$, because even if we remove all rules the request will succeed and such a request should be assigned the highest possible trust value; for this metric it is ∞, for PTM it would be 1.

Notice that we can transform any LPDS $\mathcal{P} = (Q, \Gamma, \Delta, \Lambda)$ into an LPDS $\mathcal{P}' = (Q', \Gamma, \Delta', \Lambda')$ such that $\text{PTM}(\mathcal{P}) = \text{PTM}(\mathcal{P}')$ and $\text{MTM}(\mathcal{P}) = \text{MTM}(\mathcal{P}')$ and all rules in Δ' have at most two stack symbols on the right-hand side, i.e. $\Delta' \subseteq Q \times \Gamma \times Q \times \Gamma^{\leq 2}$, in the following way. We start with $Q' = Q$ and for every rule $(p, X, q, Y_1 Y_2 \ldots Y_n) \in \Delta$ such that $n > 2$ we add new control states $q_1, q_2, \ldots, q_{n-2}$ to Q' and the following rules to Δ': $(p, X, q_{n-2}, Y_{n-1} Y_n)$, $(q_{n-2}, Y_{n-1}, q_{n-3}, Y_{n-2} Y_{n-1}), \ldots, (q_1, Y_2, q, Y_1 Y_2)$. Moreover, we set

$$\Lambda'((p, X, q_{n-2}, Y_{n-1} Y_n)) := \Lambda((p, X, q, Y_1 Y_2 \ldots Y_n))$$

and for all other newly added rules r we set $\Lambda'(r) := 1$. For rules $r = (p, X, q, \alpha) \in \Delta$ such that $|\alpha| \leq 2$ we just add r to Δ' and set $\Lambda'(r) := \Lambda(r)$. Such a LPDS is then said to be in a *normal form*.

3   Complexity of Computing the Trust Metrics

In the rest of the paper, whenever we say that we cannot *efficiently* compute something we mean that we cannot do it in polynomial time unless P = NP or some even stronger computational complexity assumption holds.

Probabilistic graphs are a standard model studied since the 1970s in the context of reliability estimation of telecommunication networks (see [1] for a survey). In such finite graphs an edge fails between two nodes with some given probability. Our Labelled Pushdown systems can obviously simulate all possible probabilistic graphs and so the problem of computing the value of the probabilistic trust metric for a given authorisation problem is at least as hard as computing the probability of connectedness of two particular nodes (called *s-t connectedness* problem) in a probabilistic graph. This problem was shown to be #P-complete in [17]. The complexity class #P was defined by Valiant in [22] as a class of function problems that output the number of accepting paths of a given nondeterministic polynomial time Turing machine. Clearly, any problem that is #P-hard is also NP-hard, because it is easier to check whether there is at least one accepting path than to count the number of them. Since then many other natural computational problems were shown to be #P-hard. We will now show that computing the mincut trust metric for a given authorisation request is also #P-hard. On the other hand, using the techniques from [22] one can check that computing the value of these two trust metrics is in #P, so both problems are #P-complete.

Theorem 1. *The problem of computing the mincut trust metric for weighted SPKI/SDSI certificate sets is #P-complete and even the problem of outputting a value that is no more than $\mathcal{O}(\log m)$ times bigger than the optimum value, where m is the number of name certs in the certificate set, is NP-hard.*

Proof. The proof is by reduction from the minimum set cover problem, which is #P-complete [22] and defined as follows: Given a set X of n elements and a family $\mathcal{S}$ of m subsets, $S_1, \ldots, S_m$, of X such that $\bigcup \mathcal{S} = X$, output a subfamily $\mathcal{C}$ of $\mathcal{S}$ with the minimum size such that $\bigcup \mathcal{C} = X$. The problem of approximating the minimum size of such a family $\mathcal{C}$ to within a $\mathcal{O}(\log m)$ relative factor (i.e. the problem of outputting for any given instance a number which is at most $\mathcal{O}(\log m)$ times bigger than the optimum value) is NP-hard [18].

In fact, we will show that the problem is #P-hard even if the weighted SPKI/SDSI certificate set, $\mathcal{D}$, have just two keys and all weights are equal to 1. The two keys will be denoted by $\mathcal{K}$ and $\mathcal{K}'$, and $\{S_1, \ldots, S_m\}$ will be the set of identifiers. For each $x \in X$ we add a single auth cert to $\mathcal{D}$. This auth cert looks as follows: let $S_{i_1}, S_{i_2}, \ldots, S_{i_l}$ be the list of all sets in the family $\mathcal{S}$ that contain x; the auth cert to add is $\mathcal{K} \,\square \to \mathcal{K}' \, S_{i_1} S_{i_2} \ldots S_{i_l}\square$. Moreover, for each set $S_i \in \mathcal{S}$ we add the following name cert: $\mathcal{K}' \, S_i \to \mathcal{K}'$. We show that the $(X, \mathcal{S})$ has a minimum set cover of size k iff the minimum number of certificates needed to be removed from $\mathcal{D}$ in order for the authorisation request $\mathcal{K} \hookrightarrow \mathcal{K}'$ to fail is k.

($\Rightarrow$) Take the minimum set cover $\mathcal{C}$ and for every $S \in \mathcal{C}$ remove all the name certs of the form $\mathcal{K}' \, S \to \mathcal{K}'$ from $\mathcal{D}$. Notice that, because $\mathcal{C}$ is a set cover, the tail of every auth cert in $\mathcal{D}$ will have at least one identifier whose corresponding name cert was removed and this will not let the rewriting of that auth cert to proceed. Therefore, $\mathcal{K} \hookrightarrow \mathcal{K}'$ will not hold in such a system.

($\Leftarrow$) Let $\mathcal{R}$ be a set of certificates such that $\mathcal{K} \hookrightarrow \mathcal{K}'$ does not to hold in $\mathcal{D} \setminus \mathcal{R}$ and whose cardinality is minimal and equals k. Notice that we can assume that $\mathcal{R}$ does not contain any auth cert of the form $\mathcal{K} \,\square \to \mathcal{K}' \, S_{i_1} \ldots S_{i_l}\square$, because removing the name cert $\mathcal{K}' \, S_{i_1} \to \mathcal{K}'$ instead would make it impossible for that auth cert to be rewritten and at the same time preserves the cardinality of $\mathcal{R}$. Therefore, let $\mathcal{R} = \{\mathcal{K} \, S_{i_1} \to \mathcal{K} \,, \ldots, \mathcal{K} \, S_{i_k} \to \mathcal{K} \}$. It is now easy to see that $\mathcal{C} = \{S_{i_1}, \ldots, S_{i_k}\}$ is a set cover of X, because otherwise the auth cert corresponding to any $x \in X \setminus \bigcup \mathcal{C}$ would prove that $\mathcal{K} \hookrightarrow \mathcal{K}'$.

We require two keys in this reduction only because of a technical issue that for any key $\mathcal{K}$, the authorisation $\mathcal{K} \hookrightarrow \mathcal{K}$ succeeds by default straight from the definition. Certificate sets with only one key can be seen as Context-Free Grammars and therefore we can easily obtain the following result of independent interest.

Corollary 2. *The following problem is #P-complete: Given a Context-Free Grammar G, a word w generated by G, output the minimum number of rewrite rules that have to be removed from G so that the word w is no longer generated by G.*

Moreover, it follows from the proof that not only we cannot efficiently compute the value of the mincut trust metric for $\mathcal{D}$, but also we cannot approximate it better than within $\mathcal{O}(\log n)$ relative factor, where n is the number of name certs in $\mathcal{D}$. If we require $\mathcal{D}$ to be in a normal form, then this inapproximability threshold will not hold anymore as transforming the auth certs used in the reduction to a normal form will introduce many new name certs into $\mathcal{D}$. However, even in that case we can show that it is NP-hard to approximate that value to a relative factor better than 1.3606 by reducing from the minimum vertex cover [7], which is defined as follows: Given a undirected graph (V, E), compute the minimum cardinality of a set $V' \subseteq V$ such that for all $(s, t) \in E$, we have $s \in V'$ or $t \in V'$. The reduction is given by the following certificate set $\mathcal{D}$: For each vertex $s \in V$ we have a symbol V_s and a name cert $\mathcal{K}' V_s \rightarrow \mathcal{K}'$. For each edge $(s, t) \in E$ we introduce a symbol $E_{s,t}$ together with a name cert $\mathcal{K}' E_{s,t} \rightarrow \mathcal{K}' V_s V_t$ and an auth cert $\mathcal{K} \square \rightarrow \mathcal{K}' E_{s,t}\square$. Using the same reasoning as before we can show that the minimum vertex cover of (V, E) is k iff the minimum number of rules needed to be removed from $\mathcal{D}$ for the authorisation request $\mathcal{K} \hookrightarrow \mathcal{K}'$ to fail is k.

4   Approximation of the Trust Metrics

Although computing the probabilistic trust metric is #P-complete, this does not rule out the possibility of efficiently approximating it for any given SPKI/SDSI certificate set. Unfortunately, it was shown in [17] that even approximation of the s-t connectedness of a probabilistic graph within a given $\epsilon > 0$ additive error (specified as a rational number in the binary notation) is #P-hard, so the same holds for the approximation of our metric. On the other hand, another option is a Monte Carlo algorithm (see, e.g. [20]), that basically randomly samples the state space and computes how often such a picked instance satisfies the property. When such an algorithm is run for a "long enough" time, the frequency of the property being satisfied by randomly chosen instances is a good approximation (but only with some probability less than 1) of the actual probability that the property is satisfied. The drawback of such a solution is that we cannot verify whether the returned value is a good approximation or not. In order to know what "long enough" is, we will make use of a special case of the Hoeffding's inequality when applied to the case where all the random variables are identically distributed and whose value can only be 0 or 1.

Theorem 3 (derivable from [11]). *If* $X_1, \ldots, X_n$ *are independent identically distributed random variables such that* $\mathrm{Prob}(X_i \in \{0, 1\}) = 1$, *then*

$$\mathrm{Prob}\left(\left|\frac{X_1 + \ldots + X_n}{n} - \mathbb{E}(X_1)\right| \geq \epsilon\right) \leq 2e^{-2\epsilon^2 n}.$$

For a given LPDS $\mathcal{P} = (Q, \Gamma, \Delta, \Lambda)$, notice that χ defined in Section 2 is a random variable over the sample space 2^Δ that takes only values from $\{0, 1\}$. Moreover, $\mathbb{E}\chi = \mathrm{PTM}(\mathcal{P})$, so we just need to define each X_j to be χ.

Assuming that no person assigns trust values with precision higher than, e.g. 10%, it does not make sense to approximate the value of the metric with precision much higher than that 10%. Therefore, we will simply set $\epsilon = 0.05$ in our calculations. Now, according to Theorem 3, in order to be 99.5% sure that the value our algorithm returns is within ϵ of the real value of the trust metric, we need $2e^{-2\epsilon^2 n}$ to be $\leq 0.5\%$. After simple calculations, we get that it suffices to set $n = 3/\epsilon^2 = 1200$ to achieve this. Our implementation of the Monte Carlo method in Spookey performs exactly that many random samplings from the sample space 2^Δ.

As for the mincut trust metric, the situation is a lot worse, because we already know that there is no efficient algorithm that could approximate its value to within any constant factor in general. Therefore, we will settle for a heuristic instead. Our algorithm provides an upper bound on the value of the mincut trust metric as follows. First, we perform a reachability analysis on the whole certificate set to check which authorisation requests fail even without removing any certificates from $\mathcal{D}$; these requests will have their trust value set to zero. Next, for any other authorisation request $\mathcal{K}_1 \hookrightarrow \mathcal{K}_2$ we compute the sum of all the trust values on the auth certs having $\mathcal{K}_1$ as their head. Clearly, by cutting all of them at once no authorisation request whose head's key is $\mathcal{K}_1$ can succeed. This is our first rough upper bound on the value of the mincut trust metric. Finally, we perform a number of random trials (in our algorithm set to one thousand) were we remove random certificates from $\mathcal{D}$. We stop a single trial once all the authorisation requests fail in the current certificate set or the cost of the current trial is already higher than the maximum currently assigned value to any authorisation request (and so no value can be improved with the current trial anymore). Unfortunately, we cannot provide any performance guarantee on the values return by this algorithm. However, we experimentally tested it against an algorithm that enumerates all possible cuts while pruning along the way the cuts that clearly cannot improve the current value of the trust metric. The dataset consisted of ten SPKI/SDSI certificate sets, each having three keys, each key having five auth certs and six name certs randomly generated for it. For some of them the enumeration algorithm needed more than twenty minutes to finish, despite the fact that it has successfully pruned most of the possible cuts along the way. We found that the trust value returned by our heuristic for this dataset was on the average only 22% higher than the optimal value, although it ran 2500 times faster.

5   Spookey and Experimental Results

In order to test for how large SPKI/SDSI certificate sets we can compute the approximations of these two metrics, we created a tool called Spookey. Spookey is implemented entirely in Java and allows for inputting arbitrary SPKI/SDSI certificate sets and computes the approximate value of the probabilistic trust metric by a Monte Carlo method and the min-cut trust metric using the proposed heuristic. The tool comes with a graphical user interface, but the performance results presented here were obtained by running it from the command line. Spookey can be downloaded from http://homepages.inf.ed.ac.uk/s0571094/spookey which also contains the description of the input format and example certificates sets.

We tested the performance of our implementation on randomly generated SPKI/SDSI certificate sets in normal form of various sizes; the tests were run using JVM version 1.6 with 1GB of available memory on Intel Core2 Duo 2.26GHz system. We considered three distinct random models. In the first one each key has exactly five auth certs and ten name certs randomly generated for it (the target key and all ids are picked uniformly at random). In the second, the expected number of auth certs and name certs is again five and ten, but their exact number is govern by a Poisson distribution. Finally, in the third model each key has again exactly five auth certs and ten name certs, but the target key is chosen using a *preferential attachment* method [2], i.e. the more incoming certs a key has the more likely it will be chosen as the target key for the next cert. This is meant to model scale-free properties of social networks that contain so-called *hub nodes*, nodes that have the number of connections many times higher than the average; such nodes are very unlikely to occur in uniformly random generated networks. Hubs in this case could be, e.g. institutions that contain name certificates for the public keys of all their employees; such a namespace is very likely to be linked to.

Table 1. The average running times of the probabilistic trust metric's approximation for each of the three random models: In the Constant model each key has five auth certs and ten name certs, in the Poisson model the number of auth certs and name certs is Poisson distributed with mean value five and ten, respectively, and in the Scale-free model each key has five auth certs and ten name certs, but the target key of a cert is chosen using a preferential attachment method; size denotes the number of keys in the set.

Type / Size	10	20	50	100	200
Constant	0.38	0.67	1.66	4.85	17.34
Poisson	0.38	0.68	1.66	4.84	17.27
Scale-free	0.38	0.67	1.66	4.85	17.37

Table 2. The average running times of the mincut trust metric's approximation for each of the three random models

Type / Size	10	20	50	100	200
Constant	1.25	2.16	7.38	22.96	91.93
Poisson	1.19	2.24	7.14	22.48	85.32
Scale-free	1.14	2.03	6.70	21.09	82.56

For each of these three random models, we generated fifty examples with 10, 20, 50, 100 keys and twenty examples with 200 keys. For each key used, $\mathcal{K}$, we generated exactly one authorisation request of the form $\mathcal{K} \hookrightarrow \mathcal{K}'$, where $\mathcal{K}'$ is chosen uniformly at random, so for a model with x keys we computed the value of the trust metric for x authorisation requests. Notice that this does not affect the running time significantly, because our approximation algorithms compute the outcome of every possible authorisation request at each step anyway, so the value of the trust metric for all the authorisations requests can be approximated at the same time in parallel. The average running times for the probabilistic trust metric are presented in Table 1 and for the mincut trust metric in Table 2. Notice that the computation of the probabilistic trust metric does not depend on the random model chosen, but the mincut trust metric does, although not significantly; it is just about 10% slower for the random model with target keys chosen uniformly at random than with target keys chosen using preferential attachment. The computation of the probabilistic trust metric is significantly faster and naturally more accurate than the mincut trust metric, but even for a relatively big certificate set with two hundred keys, the running time of one minute and a half for the approximation of the mincut trust metric may still be acceptable in practise. If we compare the running times given in [4] of approximating the metric proposed there for SPKI/SDSI certificate sets of size 50 with the running time of our approximation algorithms for certificate sets of that size, we can see that the approximation of our trust metrics is faster even though it was run on a computer with a slower processor and had less memory available to it. Also, let us note that our approximation algorithms are easily parallelisable and could be computed much faster when run on multiple computers at once.

6   Future Work

An important question to consider is whether there is a trust metric that could be efficiently computed for SPKI/SDSI certificate sets and that meets the intuitive criteria that we laid out in the introduction. Ideally, one that is resistant to the possible attacks considered in [15], and that could be computed in a decentralised manner. The presence of adversarial clients in our system can be modelled by a game extensions of our model; this would correspond to Pushdown Games [23], but with the type of winning conditions that were not studied for them before. Moreover, in practise, certificates would be added or removed from the SPKI/SDSI certificate set incrementally. Devising an efficient algorithm for computing the outcome of a single update to the certificate set would have a high practical value.

Acknowledgements. We would like to thank Kousha Etessami, Leslie Ann Goldberg and Merilin Miljan for the discussions concerning some aspects of this work as well as the anonymous reviewers whose comments helped to improve this paper. This research was supported by EPSRC grant EP/G050112/1.

References

1. Ball, M.O.: Computational Complexity of Network Reliability Analysis: An Overview. IEEE Transactions on Reliability 35(3), 230–239 (1986)
2. Barabási, A.: Emergence of Scaling in Random Networks. Science 286(5439), 509–512 (1999)
3. Beth, T., Borcherding, M., Klein, B.: Valuation of Trust in Open Networks. In: Gollmann, D. (ed.) ESORICS 1994. LNCS, vol. 875, pp. 3–18. Springer, Heidelberg (1994)
4. Bouajjani, A., Esparza, J., Schwoon, S., Suwimonteerabuth, D.: SDSIrep: A Reputation System Based on SDSI. In: Ramakrishnan, C.R., Rehof, J. (eds.) TACAS 2008. LNCS, vol. 4963, pp. 501–516. Springer, Heidelberg (2008)
5. CAcert certification Authority, http://www.cacert.org/
6. Clarke, D., Elien, J.-E., Ellison, C., Fredette, M., Morcos, A., Rivest, R.L.: Certificate chain discovery in SPKI/SDSI. Journal of Computer Security 9(4), 285–322 (2002)
7. Dinur, I., Safra, S.: On the Hardness of Approximating Minimum Vertex Cover. Annals of Mathematics 162, 439–485 (2005)
8. Ellison, C., Frantz, B., Lampson, B., Rivest, R., Thomas, B., Ylonen, T.: RFC 2693: SPKI Certificate theory (1999)
9. Ford Jr., L.R., Fulkerson, D.R.: Maximial flow through a newtork. Can. J. Math. 8, 399–404 (1956)
10. Grandison, T., Sloman, M.: A survey of trust in internet applications. IEEE Communications Surveys Tutorials 3(4), 2–16 (2000)
11. Hoeffding, W.: Probability Inequalities for Sums of Bounded Random Variables. Journal of the American Statistical Association 58(301), 13 (1963)
12. Jha, S., Reps, T.: Model checking SPKI / SDSI. Journal of Computer Security 12, 317–353 (2004)
13. Josang, A., Ismail, R., Boyd, C.: A survey of trust and reputation systems for online service provision. Decision Support Systems 43(2), 618–644 (2007)
14. Josang, A.: An algebra for assessing trust in certification chains. In: Proc. of the Network and Distributed Systems Security Symposium (1999)
15. Levien, R., Aiken, A.: Attack-Resistant Trust Metrics for Public Key Certification. In: Proceedings of the 7th USENIX Security, pp. 229–242 (1998)
16. Maurer, U.: Modelling a Public-Key Infrastructure. In: Martella, G., Kurth, H., Montolivo, E., Hwang, J. (eds.) ESORICS 1996. LNCS, vol. 1146, pp. 325–350. Springer, Heidelberg (1996)
17. Scott Provan, J., Ball, M.O.: The Complexity of Counting Cuts and of Computing the Probability that a Graph is Connected. SIAM Journal on Computing 12(4), 777 (1983)

18. Raz, R., Safra, S.: A Sub-Constant Error-Probability Low-Degree Test, and a Sub-Constant Error-Probability PCP Characterization of NP (1997)
19. Reiter, M.K., Stubblebine, S.G.: Authentication metric analysis and design. ACM Transactions on Information and System Security 2(2), 138–158 (1999)
20. Rubinstein, R.Y., Kroese, D.P.: Simulation and the Monte Carlo Method, 2nd edn. Wiley Series in Probability and Statistics, vol. 707. John Wiley & Sons, Chichester (2007)
21. Sabater, J., Sierra, C.: Review on Computational Trust and Reputation Models. Artificial Intelligence Review 24(1), 33–60 (2005)
22. Valiant, L.G.: The Complexity of Enumeration and Reliability Problems. SIAM Journal on Computing 8(3), 410 (1979)
23. Walukiewicz, I.: Pushdown Processes: Games and Model-Checking. Information and Computation 164(2), 234–263 (2001)
24. Zimmermann, P.R.: The Official PGP User's Guide. MIT Press, Cambridge (1995)

Antichain-Based QBF Solving

Thomas Brihaye[1], Véronique Bruyère[2], Laurent Doyen[3],
Marc Ducobu[1], and Jean-Francois Raskin[4]

[1] Institut de Mathématique – Université de Mons, Belgique
[2] Institut d'Informatique – Université de Mons, Belgique
[3] LSV, ENS Cachan & CNRS, France
[4] Département d'Informatique – Université Libre de Bruxelles, Belgique

Abstract. We consider the problem of QBF solving viewed as a reachability problem in an exponential And-Or graph. Antichain-based algorithms for reachability analysis in large graphs exploit certain subsumption relations to leverage the inherent structure of the explored graph in order to reduce the effect of state explosion, with high performance in practice.

In this paper, we propose simple notions of subsumption induced by the structural properties of the And-Or graphs for QBF solving. Subsumption is used to reduce the size of the search tree, and to define compact representations of certificates (in the form of antichains) both for positive and negative instances of QBF. We show that efficient exploration of the reduced search tree essentially relies on solving variants of Max-SAT and Min-SAT. Preliminary stand-alone experiments of this algorithm show that the antichain-based approach is promising.

1 Introduction

The problem of evaluating the truth value of a quantified Boolean formula (QBF) is one of the most popular PSPACE-complete problems, like SAT (the satisfiability problem for Boolean formulas) is the typical NP-complete problem. QBF is a simple and elegant formalism in which many problems of practical interest can be encoded, in a large number of areas such as automated planning, artificial intelligence, logic reasoning, and verification [14,6]. For instance, QBF can encode reachability problems more succinctly than SAT with a formula that is logarithmic in the diameter of the system when it can only be done linearly in the diameter with a SAT formula [18]. As another example, SAT and QBF can be integrated for bounded model-checking where the existence of a path is encoded by SAT, and termination is checked with QBF [10].

The simple form of QBF makes the problem appealing and accessible to a large community. However, despite its apparent simplicity, the design of efficient algorithmic solutions remains challenging. Recent progress has been observed in the practical approaches to this problem. In particular, generalizations of heuristics and optimizations used in SAT solving have been applied to QBF with some success [24,27].

Many algorithms have been proposed in the literature to solve QBF and competitive events like QBFEVAL aim at assessing the advances in reasoning about QBF [27,15]. Several leading QBF solvers are search-based. They typically use pruning techniques that extend the DPLL search strategy from SAT to QBF [8]. Common heuristics are unit

T. Bultan and P.-A. Hsiung (Eds.): ATVA 2011, LNCS 6996, pp. 183–197, 2011.

$$\psi = \underbrace{(x_1 \vee y_4 \vee y_7)}_{c_1} \wedge \underbrace{(x_2 \vee \bar{y}_4 \vee x_6)}_{c_2} \wedge \underbrace{(x_1 \vee x_3 \vee y_5 \vee \bar{y}_7)}_{c_3} \wedge$$

$$\underbrace{(\bar{x}_3 \vee \bar{y}_5 \vee \bar{x}_6 \vee y_7)}_{c_4} \wedge \underbrace{(\bar{x}_1 \vee x_2 \vee y_4)}_{c_5} \wedge \underbrace{(\bar{x}_2 \vee \bar{y}_7)}_{c_6} \wedge \underbrace{(x_1 \vee x_2 \vee x_3 \vee y_7)}_{c_7}$$

Fig. 1. The CNF formula ψ for the QBF formula $f = \forall x_1 x_2 x_3 \cdot \exists y_4 y_5 \cdot \forall x_6 \cdot \exists y_7 \cdot \psi$

propagation, conflict learning and back-jumping, which are implemented in tools like QuBE [16,17] and DepQBF [22,23]. Recent works have focused on certifying (rather than just evaluating) QBF formulas, as certificates can help in extracting error traces in QBF-encoded problems. The tool suites ChEQ and sKizzo/ozziKs evaluate and certify QBF formulas [3,17,24].

In verification and automata theory, a typical PSPACE-complete problem is the universality problem for nondeterministic finite automata. Despite its worst-case exponential complexity, dramatic performance improvements have been obtained recently for this problem by *antichain algorithms* [11,12]. One key idea of antichain algorithms is to exploit the underlying structure of automata constructions (classically, powerset-based constructions) to define *subsumption relations*, yielding compact symbolic representations, as well as sound pruning of the search space. Although QBF is also a PSPACE-complete problem, this natural idea has never been used in QBF solving.

In this paper, we identify structural properties of QBF and we define pruning strategies to obtain antichain algorithms for QBF. The purpose is to define and evaluate antichain-based techniques for QBF solving, and to suggest that their integration in other search-based solvers could be valuable. We take the classical view of QBF as a reachability problem in an exponential And-Or graph, where the nodes represent subformulas (the And-nodes correspond to universal quantifications, and the Or-nodes to existential quantifications). We illustrate the main ideas of the algorithm on the following running example. Let $f = \forall x_1 x_2 x_3 \cdot \exists y_4 y_5 \cdot \forall x_6 \cdot \exists y_7 \cdot \psi$ where ψ (shown in Fig. 1) is a CNF formula viewed as the set of clauses $\{c_1, c_2, \ldots, c_7\}$. The And-Or graph for f is a DAG where each level corresponds to a block of quantifiers (see a partial expansion in Fig. 2 where each clause c_i is identified with its index i). Nodes of the DAG are subsets $\varphi \subseteq \psi$ of clauses which remain to be satisfied in the evaluation game. The root of the DAG is the set ψ of all clauses. The successors of a node at level i are the sets of clauses obtained by assigning the variables quantified in the ith block of the formula. In the game interpretation, two players $P_\forall$ and $P_\exists$ choose the successor of the nodes (player $P_\forall$ in And-nodes, and $P_\exists$ in Or-nodes) by assigning the variables quantified in the block of the level of the node. The goal of player $P_\exists$ is to reach a node $\varnothing$ where all clauses are satisfied, and to avoid nodes where all literals of a clause are false (denoted by $\bot$). The QBF formula is true if and only if $P_\exists$ has a winning strategy to reach $\varnothing$ from the initial node ψ in the game. A key observation is that *set inclusion* is a subsumption relation that can be used to substantially reduce the size of the search tree: if player $P_\exists$ has a winning strategy from a node ψ_1 at level i, then player $P_\exists$ also has a winning strategy from all nodes $\psi_2 \subseteq \psi_1$ at level i, because in ψ_2 less clauses remain

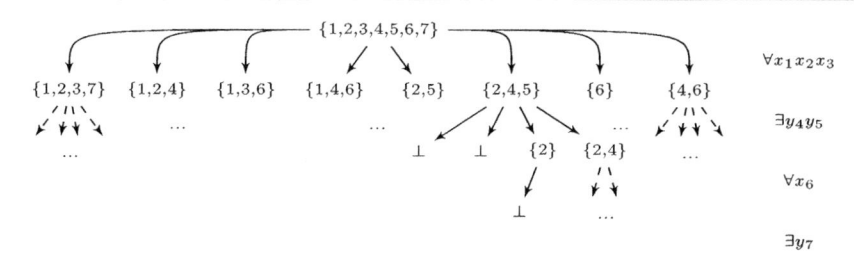

Fig. 2. Search tree for the formula of Fig. 1

to be satisfied. This has two implications in the search through the DAG. First, player $P_\exists$ should only consider valuations that make true a *maximal subset* of the remaining clauses, while player $P_\forall$ should make true a *minimal subset*. Computing such variable assignments reduces to solving variants of Max-SAT and Min-SAT problems [19,21]. Second, the set of winning nodes at level i is downward-closed, and the set of losing nodes at level i is upward-closed. Therefore, antichains of incomparable sets of clauses are the appropriate representation of winning and losing nodes. We exploit this structure when backward propagating the information collected during the exploration of the DAG, and we never explore a node which is smaller than a winning node (or greater than a losing node) at the same level. Finally, the information stored in the antichains at the end of the search is so rich that it immediately provides compact certificates for both positive and negative instances of QBF. Note that compact certificates represented by antichains is a new notion.

We propose an antichain algorithm which is search-based and reduces the search space using antichains of winning and losing nodes of the And-Or graph. Antichains can be viewed as compact symbolic representations which can be exponentially succinct, thus it also has the flavor of symbolic procedures. In contrast, traditional symbolic QBF solvers rely on binary decision diagrams (BDD) and they are based on quantifier elimination, such as Skolemization-based approaches [2] (with the aim at eliminating existentially quantified variables), or symbolic quantifier elimination by clause resolution or BDD algorithms [25]. The tool sKizzo falls in this category of solvers [5].

We have implemented the ideas presented in this paper in a stand-alone prototype in order to push and evaluate the approach, independently of the established heuristics commonly used in search-based QBF solvers. While some benchmarks are solved more efficiently with our prototype (e.g., see Fig. 5), the results are encouraging beyond the absolute performance. In particular the experiments and comparison with state-of-the-art solvers show that:

- the search trees constructed by our algorithm are generally much smaller (by orders of magnitude) as compared to the entire search space, thanks to subsumption (e.g., see Table 1);
- our algorithm automatically provides certificates with no additional cost, whereas in other approaches, additional computation is required to extract certificates after evaluation of the formula;

- difficult instances (several hundreds of variables, thousands of clauses) are solved by our prototype (e.g., see Table 1), and on several families of formulas, the overall behaviour of our algorithm scales better or similarly as the size of the formulas increases (e.g., see Figs. 5-8).

2   Preliminaries

2.1   Notations and QBF Problem

Let $V = \{x_1, x_2, \ldots, x_m\}$ be a set of m Boolean variables, we use $X, X_1, X_2, \ldots$ to denote subsets of V. A *literal* ℓ is either a variable $x \in V$ or the negation $\bar{x}$ of a variable $x \in V$, and a *clause* c is a disjunction of literals, or equivalently a set of literals. We use notations such as $\ell \in c$, $\bar{x} \in c$, etc. A CNF formula is a conjunction of clauses, or equivalently a set of clauses. The empty CNF formula is denoted by 1, and the empty clause by 0. In the figures we use the notations $\varnothing$ and $\perp$ instead of 1 and 0 respectively. Given a set $X \subseteq V$ and a CNF formula ψ over V, we denote by $\pi_X(\psi)$ the projection of ψ over X, with $\pi_X(\psi) = \{\pi_X(c) \mid c \in \psi\}$ and $\pi_X(c) = \{l \in c \mid (l = x \lor l = \bar{x})$ such that $x \in X\}$.

A *quantified Boolean formula* (QBF) is an expression $Q_1 X_1 \cdot Q_2 X_2 \cdots Q_n X_n \cdot \psi$ where each $Q_i \in \{\exists, \forall\}$ for $1 \le i \le n$, the sets $X_1, \ldots, X_n$ (called *blocks*) form a partition of V, and ψ is a CNF formula over V. We also write $Q_1 x_1 \cdot Q_2 x_2 \cdots Q_n x_n \cdot \psi$ when each block X_i contains one variable ($X_i = \{x_i\}$). Since ψ is in CNF we assume w.l.o.g. that the last block is *existential* (i.e., $Q_n = \exists$). The truth value of a QBF formula is defined as usual. The QBF *evaluation problem* is to decide whether a given QBF formula is true or false. This problem is PSPACE-complete [26].

A *valuation* for $X \subseteq V$ is a function $v : X \to \{0, 1\}$. The domain of v is $\mathrm{dom}(v) = X$. If $X = \{x_1, \ldots, x_k\}$, a valuation $v : X \to \{0, 1\}$ can be identified with a word $a_1 a_2 \cdots a_k \in \{0, 1\}^{|X|}$ such that $a_l = v(x_l)$ for all $1 \le l \le k$. The empty word ϵ corresponds to $\mathrm{dom}(v) = \varnothing$. Given a partition $P = X_1 \cup X_2 \cup \cdots \cup X_n$ of V, let $X_{\le i}$ be the set of variables $X_1 \cup X_2 \cdots \cup X_i$ (with $X_{\le 0} = \varnothing$), and let $X_{\ge i} = V \setminus X_{\le i-1}$. Given the valuations $v : X_{\le i-1} \to \{0, 1\}$ and $w : X_i \to \{0, 1\}$, let vw be the valuation identified with the concatenation of the words representing v and w.

A clause c is *satisfied* by a valuation v (written $v \models c$) if there exists $x \in \mathrm{dom}(v)$ such that either $x \in c$ and $v(x) = 1$, or $\bar{x} \in c$ and $v(x) = 0$. Given a CNF formula ψ, we denote by $\mathrm{sat}_v(\psi)$ the set of clauses $c \in \psi$ such that $v \models c$. We denote by $\psi[v]$ the CNF formula obtained by replacing in ψ each variable $x \in \mathrm{dom}(v)$ by its value $v(x)$. Formula $\psi[v]$ is supposed to be simplified using the laws $c \lor 1 = 1$, $c \lor 0 = c$ with c being a clause, and $\varphi \land 1 = \varphi$, $\varphi \land 0 = 0$ with φ being a CNF formula.

Let ψ be an unsatisfiable CNF formula. An *unsatisfiable core* ψ' of ψ is any subset of clauses of ψ, minimal for the inclusion, such that ψ' is still unsatisfiable.

2.2   QBF Problem as a Game

It is classical to view the QBF evaluation problem as reachability in an And-Or graph, or equivalently as a two-player reachability game [26]. For the formula $f = Q_1 x_1 \cdot$

$Q_2 x_2 \cdots Q_m x_m \cdot \psi$ over $V = \{x_1, x_2, \ldots, x_m\}$, the game is played in m rounds (numbered $1, \ldots, m$) by the existential player $P_\exists$ and the universal player $P_\forall$. In round i, the truth value of the variable x_i is chosen by player P_{Q_i}. After m rounds, the players have constructed a valuation $v : V \to \{0, 1\}$, and player $P_\exists$ wins if $\psi[v] = 1$ (all clauses are satisfied by v), otherwise player $P_\forall$ wins. It is easy to see that $P_\exists$ has a winning strategy in this game iff the formula f is true. Note that instead of having one round for each variable, we can also consider a game with one round for each block of variables, such that the blocks correspond to quantifier alternations in f. The players then choose a valuation for all the variables in the block at once, and the number of rounds is equal to the number of quantifier alternations in f. As the algorithms proposed in this paper are based on this game metaphor, we present the And-Or graph on which the game is played.

Let $P = X_1 \cup X_2 \cup \cdots \cup X_n$ be a partition of $V = \{x_1, x_2, \ldots, x_m\}$, and let $f = Q_1 X_1 \cdot Q_2 X_2 \cdots Q_n X_n \cdot \psi$ be a QBF formula over V. We define the *And-Or graph* $G_f = (S, S_\exists, S_\forall, s_0, E, F)$ where:

- $S = \{\psi[v] \mid \mathrm{dom}(v) = X_{\leq i-1}, \text{ for } i, 1 \leq i \leq n+1\}$;
- $S_\exists = \{\psi[v] \mid \mathrm{dom}(v) = X_{\leq i-1} \wedge Q_i = \exists, \text{ for } i, 1 \leq i \leq n\}$ is the set of $P_\exists$ nodes;
- $S_\forall = \{\psi[v] \mid \mathrm{dom}(v) = X_{\leq i-1} \wedge Q_i = \forall, \text{ for } i, 1 \leq i \leq n\}$ is the set of $P_\forall$ nodes;
- $s_0 = \psi$ is the initial node;
- $E = \{(\psi[v], \psi[vw]) \mid \mathrm{dom}(v) = X_{\leq i-1} \wedge \mathrm{dom}(w) = X_i, \text{ for } i, 1 \leq i \leq n\}$ is the set of edges;
- $F = \{\psi[v] \in S \mid \psi[v] = 1\}$ is the set of final nodes.

The set S is naturally partitioned into *levels* as follows: $S = \mathrm{Level}_1 \cup \mathrm{Level}_2 \cup \cdots \cup \mathrm{Level}_{n+1}$ where $\mathrm{Level}_i = \{\psi[v] \mid \mathrm{dom}(v) = X_{\leq i-1}\}$ for each $1 \leq i \leq n+1$. The objective of player $P_\exists$ is to reach the set F of nodes $\psi[v]$ such that all clauses of ψ are satisfied by v. The game starts in node s_0 and player P_Q ($Q \in \{\exists, \forall\}$) chooses the successor of node s if $s \in S_Q$. Thus if $s = \psi[v] \in S_\exists$ and $\mathrm{dom}(v) = X_{\leq i-1}$, then player $P_\exists$ chooses one of the $2^{|X_i|}$ possible successors of s in E, corresponding to a valuation $w : X_i \to \{0, 1\}$. A node s is *winning* for player $P_\exists$ if he has a strategy to force reaching a node in F from s, no matter the choices of $P_\forall$; otherwise it is *losing*. We denote by W the set of winning nodes for player $P_\exists$, and by $L = S \setminus W$ the set of losing nodes for $P_\exists$. We say that $P_\exists$ is *winning the game* if $s_0 \in W$. In the sequel, we use the notations W_i (resp. L_i) to denote $W \cap \mathrm{Level}_i$ (resp. $L \cap \mathrm{Level}_i$).

Proposition 1. *A QBF formula f is true iff player $P_\exists$ is winning the game G_f.*

Note that in the graph G_f, each node $\psi[v]$ with $\mathrm{dom}(v) = X_{\leq i-1}$ can be associated with the formula $\mathrm{Formula}(\psi[v]) \equiv Q_i X_i \cdots Q_n X_n \cdot \psi[v]$, and we can strengthen the previous proposition as follows.

Proposition 2. *Given a QBF formula f, the set of winning nodes in the graph G_f is $W = \{\psi[v] \in S \mid \mathrm{Formula}(\psi[v]) \text{ is true}\}$, and the set of losing nodes is $L = \{\psi[v] \in S \mid \mathrm{Formula}(\psi[v]) \text{ is false}\}$.*

2.3   Structure in the And-Or Graph and Antichains

We present in the next section an algorithm to solve the game played on G_f which exploits the following *subsumption* relation on QBF formulas. We write $f_1 \sqsubseteq f_2$ if

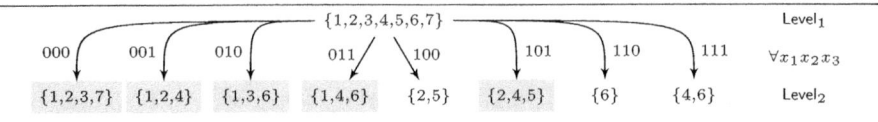

Fig. 3. Level_1 and Level_2 of G_f and the 5 minimal valuations of $P_\forall$

$f_1 = Q_i X_i \cdots Q_n X_n \cdot \psi_1$ and $f_2 = Q_i X_i \cdots Q_n X_n \cdot \psi_2$ are two QBF formulas with the same quantifier prefix, and $\psi_1 \subseteq \psi_2$. Intuitively, f_1 is more promising than f_2 for player $P_\exists$ because all strategies that are winning from ψ_2 are also winning from ψ_1.

Proposition 3. *Suppose that $f_1 \sqsubseteq f_2$. If f_2 is true, then f_1 is true; and if f_1 is false, then f_2 is false.*

As a direct consequence of Propositions 2 and 3, we obtain the next corollary.

Corollary 1. *In the graph G_f, for all nodes $s_1, s_2 \in \text{Level}_i$ such that $s_1 \subseteq s_2$, i.e. $\text{Formula}(s_1) \sqsubseteq \text{Formula}(s_2)$, if $s_2 \in W_i$, then $s_1 \in W_i$; and if $s_1 \in L_i$, then $s_2 \in L_i$.*

Hence, W_i is $\subseteq$-downward closed and L_i is $\subseteq$-upward closed. The set of $\subseteq$-maximal elements of W_i, noted $\lceil W_i \rceil$, is an *antichain* for the partial order $\subseteq$ (i.e., a set of pairwise incomparable elements) that canonically and compactly represents W_i. Similarly, the set of $\subseteq$-minimal elements of L_i, noted $\lfloor L_i \rfloor$, is an antichain that canonically and compactly represents L_i. Elements of these antichains are denoted α, β.

3   Algorithms

In Section 3.1, we discuss the computation of optimal valuations to explore only the most promising nodes, and in Section 3.2, we propose an antichain-based algorithm for solving the QBF evaluation game.

3.1   Maximal and Minimal Valuations

According to Corollary 1, when it is the turn for $P_\exists$ to play in node $s = \varphi$ in Level_i, he can restrict his choices among valuations $w : X_i \to \{0, 1\}$ that *maximize* the set of clauses of φ that are satisfied. Symmetrically, player $P_\forall$ can restrict his choices among valuations $w : X_i \to \{0, 1\}$ that *minimize* the set of clauses of φ that are satisfied.

We define the notion of maximal and minimal valuations as follows. Let φ be a CNF formula over $X_{\geq i}$. A valuation $w : X_i \to \{0, 1\}$ is φ-*maximal* if for all $w' : X_i \to \{0, 1\}$, $\text{sat}_w(\varphi) \subseteq \text{sat}_{w'}(\varphi)$ implies $\text{sat}_w(\varphi) = \text{sat}_{w'}(\varphi)$. Symmetrically, w is φ-*minimal* if for all $w' : X_i \to \{0, 1\}$, $\text{sat}_{w'}(\varphi) \subseteq \text{sat}_w(\varphi)$ implies $\text{sat}_w(\varphi) = \text{sat}_{w'}(\varphi)$.

Example 1. Consider the CNF formula ψ of Fig. 1, viewed as the set of clauses $\{c_1, c_2, \ldots, c_7\}$. In Level_1, we have $X_1 = \{x_1, x_2, x_3\}$ which are universal variables. Among the $2^3 = 8$ valuations, 5 are ψ-minimal (shaded in Fig. 3, where each clause c_i is identified with i). Remember that the nodes in the And-Or graph are the clauses that *remain* to be satisfied, thus maximal such sets correspond to minimal valuations. Note also that we may need to compute *all* maximal (or minimal) valuations in a node.

Maximal and minimal valuations can be computed by multiple calls to a SAT solver. Let us give the intuition for maximal valuations. Let φ be a set of clauses over $X_{\geq i}$. First notice that a valuation $w : X_i \to \{0, 1\}$ is φ-maximal if and only if it is $\pi_{X_i}(\varphi)$-maximal. Thus we can assume w.l.o.g. that φ is a set of clauses over X_i (instead of $X_{\geq i}$). Using a set of new variables $Y = \{y_c \mid c \in \varphi\}$, called selectors, we transform the set of clauses φ into a set of clauses φ' over $X_i \cup Y$ with the following property : if a valuation $w : X_i \cup Y \to \{0, 1\}$ satisfying φ' is such that $w(y_c) = 1$, then w satisfies c. By a first call to a SAT solver on φ', we get a valuation w and a subset C of clauses of φ that are satisfied by w. Then we modify φ' into φ'' by imposing the constraint that at least one of the variables y_c such that $w(y_c) = 0$ is true in φ, so that a second call to a SAT solver provides a subset of satisfied clauses of φ that strictly contains C. Iterating this procedure, we finally obtain a valuation that satisfies a maximal set of clauses in φ.

Computing maximal and minimal valuations can also be achieved thanks to solvers for variants of the *Maximum Satisfiability* (Max-SAT) and *Minimum Satisfiability* (Min-SAT) problems [19,21]. Given a CNF formula φ, the Max-Sat problem asks to compute a valuation that maximizes the *number* of satisfied clauses in φ (Min-Sat is defined symmetrically). Note that such a valuation is φ-maximal but the converse is not necessarily true. Given a CNF fomula $\varphi = \varphi_h \wedge \varphi_s$ where φ_h represents the *hard* clauses and φ_s represents the *soft* clauses, the *partial Max-SAT* problem consists in finding a valuation such that all hard clauses are satisfied and the number of satisfied soft clauses is maximized. This variant of Max-SAT can be used to generate *all* φ-maximal valuations as follows. The first φ-maximal valuation is computed by a call to a Max-SAT solver. The next ones are computed thanks to a partial Max-SAT solver, such that hard clauses with selectors impose that for each already computed φ-maximal valuation w, at least one new clause $c \notin \mathrm{sat}_w(\varphi)$ is satisfied.

3.2   Antichain-Based Algorithm

In this section we present an antichain-based algorithm to evaluate a QBF formula $f = Q_1 X_1 \cdots Q_n X_n \cdot \psi$. It is a search-based algorithm of the And-Or graph G_f with backward propagation of the information collected during the exploration. Such a forward-backward exploration was also used with success in timed games [9].

Our algorithm consists of two recursive procedures named $\mathsf{ATCSearch\exists}(\varphi, i)$ and $\mathsf{ATCSearch\forall}(\varphi, i)$ where φ is a node of G_f and i is the recursion level (see Algorithms 1 and 2). Initially, we make a call to $\mathsf{ATCSearch\exists}(\psi, 1)$ if $Q_1 = \exists$, and to $\mathsf{ATCSearch\forall}(\psi, 1)$ if $Q_1 = \forall$. These procedures determine whether a node φ is winning or losing for $P_\exists$, i.e. whether $\varphi \in W_i$ or $\varphi \in L_i$. The sets W_i and L_i are updated as global variables and compactly stored by antichains $\lceil W_i \rceil$ and $\lfloor L_i \rfloor$ respectively. They are used to prune the search by the *subsumption* checks (see lines 8, 11 in Algorithm 1).

The details of $\mathsf{ATCSearch\exists}(\varphi, i)$ are as follows. If φ is not even satisfiable, then it is a losing node; if φ is satisfiable and $i = n$, then it is winning since φ belongs to $S_\exists$; otherwise, the procedure enumerates the φ-*maximal* valuations w (line 7) and checks if $\varphi[w]$ is winning at level $i + 1$. For player $P_\exists$, maximal valuations are sufficient because the set of winning nodes is downward-closed (see Corollary 1). The recursive call to $\mathsf{ATCSearch\forall}(\varphi[w], i + 1)$ can be avoided if $\varphi[w]$ is in the downward-closure of $\lceil W_{i+1} \rceil$ (line 8), or if $\varphi[w]$ is in the upward-closure of $\lfloor L_{i+1} \rfloor$ (line 11). Finally, if all φ-maximal valuations have been explored, then φ is losing (line 17).

Algorithm 1. ATCSearch∃(φ, i)	**Algorithm 2.** ATCSearch∀(φ, i)
Require: node $\varphi \in S_\exists \cap$ Level$_i$, $i \leq n$.	**Require:** node $\varphi \in S_\forall \cap$ Level$_i$, $i < n$.
Ensure: Win if $\varphi \in W_i$, Lose if $\varphi \in L_i$.	**Ensure:** Win if $\varphi \in W_i$, Lose if $\varphi \in L_i$.

Algorithm 1. ATCSearch∃(φ, i)

1: **if** ¬IsSat(φ) **then**
2:     Add$(\varphi, \lfloor L_i \rfloor)$
3:     **return** Lose
4: **if** $i = n$ **then**
5:     Add$(\varphi, \lceil W_i \rceil)$
6:     **return** Win
7: **for** each φ-maximal valuation $w : X_i \rightarrow \{0,1\}$ **do**
8:     **if** $\exists \alpha \in \lceil W_{i+1} \rceil$ s.t. $\varphi[w] \subseteq \alpha$ **then**
9:         Add$(\varphi, \lceil W_i \rceil)$
10:        **return** Win
11:    **if** ¬$(\exists \alpha \in \lfloor L_{i+1} \rfloor$ s.t. $\alpha \subseteq \varphi[w])$ **then**
12:        R ← ATCSearch∀$(\varphi[w], i+1)$
13:        **if** R = Win **then**
14:            Add$(\varphi, \lceil W_i \rceil)$
15:            **return** Win
16: Add$(\varphi, \lfloor L_i \rfloor)$
17: **return** Lose

Algorithm 2. ATCSearch∀(φ, i)

1: **if** ¬IsSat(φ) **then**
2:     Add$(\varphi, \lfloor L_i \rfloor)$
3:     **return** Lose
4: **for** each φ-minimal valuation $w : X_i \rightarrow \{0,1\}$ **do**
5:     **if** $\exists \alpha \in \lfloor L_{i+1} \rfloor$ s.t. $\alpha \subseteq \varphi[w]$ **then**
6:         Add$(\varphi, \lfloor L_i \rfloor)$
7:         **return** Lose
8:     **if** ¬$(\exists \alpha \in \lceil W_{i+1} \rceil$ s.t. $\varphi[w] \subseteq \alpha)$ **then**
9:         R ← ATCSearch∃$(\varphi[w], i+1)$
10:        **if** R = Lose **then**
11:            Add$(\varphi, \lfloor L_i \rfloor)$
12:            **return** Lose
13: Add$(\varphi, \lceil W_i \rceil)$
14: **return** Win

The procedure ATCSearch∀(φ, i) for nodes $\varphi \in S_\forall$ is dual. Note that the case $i = n$ is not relevant since $Q_n = \exists$. By a symmetrical argument, $P_\forall$ needs to consider only the φ-minimal valuations.

In these two procedures, the φ-maximal and φ-minimal valuations are computed as explained in Section 3.1, by either using a SAT solver or a partial Max-SAT solver. Procedure IsSat(φ) tests whether formula φ is satisfiable by a call to a SAT solver. The antichains $\lceil W_i \rceil$ and $\lfloor L_i \rfloor$ (for $1 \leq i \leq n$) are initially empty. The antichain structure is maintained by the procedure Add which computes $\lceil \{\varphi\} \cup W_i \rceil$ and $\lfloor \{\varphi\} \cup L_i \rfloor$.

Example 2. Consider the CNF formula ψ of Fig. 1. Since $Q_1 = \forall$, the algorithm starts with ATCSearch∀$(\psi, 1)$ which needs to explore the 5 minimal valuations of Fig. 3. Assume that the first valuation is $(x_1 \mapsto 0, x_2 \mapsto 0, x_3 \mapsto 0)$, denoted 000, which satisfies clauses $4, 5, 6$. Then, the game proceeds to the node $\psi[w] = \psi[000] = \{1, 2, 3, 7\}$ of remaining clauses where the turn is to player $P_\exists$. The subgraph of G_f rooted at $\psi[000]$ is shown in the first tree of Fig. 4. Among the 4 possible valuations for player $P_\exists$, only 2 are maximal, namely 01 and 11. For valuation 01, only clauses 1 and 7 remain. At this point, all variables are instantiated except x_6 and y_7, and player $P_\exists$ wins by choosing $y_7 \mapsto 1$ which satisfies ψ no matter the value of x_6 chosen by player $P_\forall$.

Thus nodes $\{1, 7\}$ at Level$_3$, and $\{1, 2, 3, 7\}$ at Level$_2$ are winning, and the related antichains are updated as follows: $\lceil W_3 \rceil = \{\{1, 7\}\}$ and $\lceil W_2 \rceil = \{\{1, 2, 3, 7\}\}$.

At the root node of G_f, the valuation 000 is not a good choice for player $P_\forall$, and no conclusion can be drawn yet for this node (Fig. 3). We need to explore another choice for player $P_\forall$. The second tree of Fig. 4 shows the subgame rooted at node $\psi[001]$. In this case, with minimal valuation 00, player $P_\exists$ reaches node $\{1\}$ in Level$_3$. Since

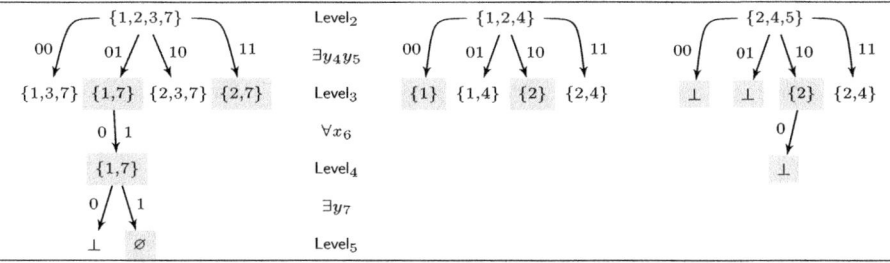

Fig. 4. Subgames rooted at $\psi[000]$, $\psi[001]$, and $\psi[101]$

$\{1\} \in W_3$ (indeed $\{1\} \subseteq \{1,7\} \in \lceil W_3 \rceil$, and W_3 is the downward-closure of $\lceil W_3 \rceil$), he knows immediately that he is winning without further exploring the graph. This situation illustrates the power of the subsumption which allows to prune the search for nodes smaller than previously visited winning ones. The antichain $\lceil W_2 \rceil$ is then updated to $\{\{1,2,3,7\}, \{1,2,4\}\}$. Valuation 001 is again a bad choice for $P_\forall$.

One can check that valuations 010 and 011 are bad choices for $P_\forall$ and their exploration leads to the following update of the antichains: $\lceil W_2 \rceil = \{\{1,2,3,7\}, \{1,2,4\}, \{1,3,6\}, \{1,4,6\}\}$ and $\lceil W_3 \rceil = \{\{1,7\}, \{6\}\}$. The last minimal valuation is 101 and for all choices of player $P_\exists$, there is a choice of player $P_\forall$ to falsify the formula (see the last tree in Fig. 4). Therefore $P_\exists$ is losing the game and the formula f is false.

The correctness of this algorithm is established using the notion of certificate presented in the next section.

Theorem 1. *Let f be a QBF formula. Applying Algorithms 1 and 2 on f returns* Win *if and only if f is true.*

4   Certificates

In the previous section we have described a search-based algorithm to evaluate a QBF formula f. This algorithm computes the sets of winning nodes and losing nodes for each level of the graph G_f, and these sets are compactly represented by antichains.

Our algorithm gathers enough information in these antichains to easily build *compact certificates* for both true and false QBF formulas. Intuitively, if f is true, that is, player $P_\exists$ is winning the game G_f, then a certificate is given by the antichains $\lceil W_i \rceil$, $1 \leq i \leq n$, and for each $\alpha \in W_i$ by the maximal valuation computed by Algorithm 1 when α has been declared winning. If f is false, a certificate is defined similarly from the antichains $\lfloor L_i \rfloor$. To the best of our knowledge these certificates are different from the ones considered in the literature [3,24].

We first define positive certificates as a witness for true QBF formulas. A *positive certificate* for a formula $f \equiv Q_1 X_1 \cdots Q_n X_n \cdot \psi$ is a pair $\langle (C_i^+)_{1 \leq i \leq n}, \mathsf{w} \rangle$ such that:

- each C_i^+ is a set of nodes at the ith level of the graph G_f, that is, $C_i^+ \subseteq \mathsf{Level}_i$;
- for each i such that $\mathsf{Level}_i \subseteq S_\exists$, w is a function that assigns a valuation $\mathsf{w}(\alpha)$: $X_i \rightarrow \{0,1\}$ to each $\alpha \in C_i^+$;
- and the following properties are verified:

1. $C_1^+ = \{\psi\}$.
2. for each $i < n$ such that $\mathsf{Level}_i \subseteq S_\exists$, for all $\alpha \in C_i^+$, there exists $\beta \in C_{i+1}^+$ such that $\alpha[\mathsf{w}(\alpha)] \subseteq \beta$.
3. for each $i < n$ such that $\mathsf{Level}_i \subseteq S_\forall$, for all $\alpha \in C_i^+$, for all $w : X_i \rightarrow \{0,1\}$, there exists $\beta \in C_{i+1}^+$ such that $\alpha[w] \subseteq \beta$.
4. for $i = n$, for all $\alpha \in C_i^+$, $\alpha[\mathsf{w}(\alpha)] = 1$.

Clearly, there exists a nondeterministic polynomial time algorithm to recognize pairs $\langle (C_i^+)_{1 \leq i \leq n}, \mathsf{w} \rangle$ that are not positive certificate. All the verification related to Conditions 1, 2 and 4 can be done in deterministic polynomial time while Condition 3 requires nondeterminism. Therefore, verifying the validity of a positive certificate is a problem in coNP.

Lemma 1. *If* $\langle (C_i^+)_{1 \leq i \leq n}, \mathsf{w} \rangle$ *is a positive certificate for a QBF formula* f, *then* f *is true.*

Lemma 2. *Let* $\lceil W_i \rceil$, $1 \leq i \leq n$, *be the antichains built by the execution of Algorithms 1 and 2 on formula* f. *For each* i *such that* $\mathsf{Level}_i \subseteq S_\exists$, *for all* $\alpha \in \lceil W_i \rceil$, *let* $\mathsf{w}(\alpha)$ *be the valuation used by Algorithms 1 when* α *has been declared winning. If* f *is true, then* $\langle (\lceil W_i \rceil)_{1 \leq i \leq n}, \mathsf{w} \rangle$ *is a positive certificate for* f.

The next theorem directly follows from the two previous lemmas.

Theorem 2. *Let* f *be a QBF formula. Then* f *is true if and only if there exists a positive certificate for* f.

Negative certificates are defined in a way similar to positive certificates; they are a witness for false formulas f.

5   Optimizations

5.1   Guiding the Search to Promising Valuations

We recall that in Algorithm 1, when φ is a satisfiable formula, and $i \leq n - 1$, player $P_\exists$ traverses all the maximal valuations $w : X_i \rightarrow \{0,1\}$ in the hope to find w such that $\varphi[w]$ is winning. The first optimization that we consider tries to guide the search to *promising* maximal valuations.

Improving ATCSearch∃. When considering all the maximal valuations $w : X_i \rightarrow \{0,1\}$, we observe that player $P_\exists$ is winning as soon as he can find a valuation w such that $\varphi[w] \subseteq \alpha$ for some $\alpha \in \lceil W_{i+1} \rceil$ (see Corollary 1). So, it is better for $P_\exists$ to first try to find such a valuation w. Suppose now that player $P_\exists$ cannot win by exploiting the elements of $\lceil W_{i+1} \rceil$. Then he should avoid considering maximal valuations w such that $\alpha \subseteq \varphi[w]$ for some $\alpha \in \lfloor L_{i+1} \rfloor$ as $\varphi[w]$ is losing (see Corollary 1). These two observations are exploited by the new algorithm.

Improving ATCSearch∀. We can improve the choice of minimal valuations for player $P_\forall$ in a symmetric manner. Indeed, $P_\forall$ should first look for a valuation w such that there exists $\alpha \in \lfloor L_{i+1} \rfloor$ with $\alpha \subseteq \varphi[w]$. If such a valuation does not exist, then he should only consider minimal valuations that avoid the set $\lceil W_{i+1} \rceil$ of winning nodes.

5.2 Improving the Information about Losing and Winning Nodes

Our algorithms can be seen as mixing a forward exploration of the And-Or graph G_f with a backward propagation of the information about the winning and losing nodes. We present below several ways of improving the propagation phase.

At initialization. Recall that the antichain $\lfloor L_i \rfloor$ is initially empty in Algorithms 1 and 2. We can add some useful information to $\lfloor L_i \rfloor$ in the following case. Consider the initial node ψ of G_f, and let i, $1 \le i \le n-1$. Suppose that the projection $d = \pi_{X_{\ge i}}(c)$ of a clause c in ψ on $X_{\ge i}$ has all its literals *universally quantified*. Then the clause d must be satisfied by a valuation generated before reaching Level$_i$ since otherwise player $P_\forall$ can falsify it. So, at initialization we can add $\{d\}$ to $\lfloor L_i \rfloor$ for any such d (all sets of clauses that contain d are losing at Level$_i$).

Some other information can be initially stored in the antichains $\lceil W_i \rceil$ and $\lfloor L_i \rfloor$ to better guide the search. Consider the initial node ψ of G_f, and its projection $\varphi = \pi_{X_{\ge i}}(\psi)$. If φ is unsatisfiable, then any unsatisfiable core of φ can be extracted and added to $\lfloor L_i \rfloor$. On the other hand, if φ is satisfiable and we further restrict φ to the existentially quantified variables, then we can compute a φ-maximal valuation w to get a maximal subset of satisfied clauses $\varphi' = \mathsf{sat}_w(\varphi)$. The set φ' can be added to $\lceil W_i \rceil$ because player $P_\exists$ has a winning strategy at Level$_i$ if the set of clauses not in φ' are satisfied when the game enters this level.

When updating $\lceil W_i \rceil$ *and* $\lfloor L_i \rfloor$. We now give an optimization that can be applied when updating the sets of winning and losing nodes during the search. We consider two scenarios. First, assume that node φ is declared winning by the algorithm ATCSearch$\exists$ in Level$_i$. This means that there exists a valuation $w : X_i \to \{0,1\}$ such that either $\varphi[w] \subseteq \alpha$ for some $\alpha \in \lceil W_{i+1} \rceil$, or $\varphi[w]$ is declared winning by the recursive call to ATCSearch$\forall$. Notice that φ is a subset of the set of clauses in the root ψ (projected on variables $X_{\ge i}$). It may happen that other clauses $c \in \psi$ are also satisfied by the valuation w. Thus, in a way to have bigger elements in $\lceil W_i \rceil$, it is preferable to add the set $\varphi' = \varphi \cup \{c \mid c \in \mathsf{sat}_w(\psi)\}$ instead of φ to $\lceil W_i \rceil$.

Second, assume that φ is declared losing by Algorithm ATCSearch$\exists$ in Level$_i$ with $i = n$. This means that φ is unsatisfiable. Instead of adding φ to $\lfloor L_i \rfloor$, we can add any unsatisfiable core $\varphi' \subseteq \varphi$ instead.

6 Experimental Results

Setting. We have implemented the algorithms of Section 3 with the optimizations of Section 5 in a stand-alone prototype in order to evaluate the impact of the antichain approach. Thus none of the classical heuristics used in search-based QBF solvers, like backjumping, unit propagation, and monotone literals elimination [8] has been integrated. The code is written partly in C for the low level operations on the data structures, and partly in Python to implement high level operations like the exploration of the And-Or graph, and for the construction of CNF formulas submitted to the SAT or partial Max-SAT solvers. We use Python to facilitate the fast evaluation of different ideas even if some price has to be paid at the performance level. We use the SAT solver MiniSat [13] and the partial Max-SAT solver Akmaxsat [20] to compute the maximal and minimal valuations as explained in Section 3.1, and PicoSAT [7] to compute unsatisfiable cores as described in Section 5.

In a preprocessing step, the formula is simplified with PreQuel [28] and then presented in a tree-like structure [4]. This is standard practice in QBF solving. The experiments were run on a PC equipped with a Intel i7 2.8GHz processor, 6 GB of RAM and running Linux Ubuntu 2.6.

Instances. We tested our algorithm on several instances proposed during the seventh QBF solvers evaluation (QBFEVAL'10) [27] and compared the results with the ones obtained with three state-of-the-art QBF solvers: QuBE-7.0, sKizzo-v0.8.2-beta and DepQBF-0.1 (winner of QBFEVAL'10). QuBE and DepQBF are search-based solvers, whereas sKizzo uses symbolic Skolemization.

The families k-* correspond to the encoding of the satisfiability problem for modal K formulas into QBF, and they are known to give difficult instances for search-based solvers. The families k-* have a deep level of quantifier alternations while the families Toilet* and aim-* have three quantifier alternations.

Results. In Table 1, **Var** (resp. **Cl, Blocs**) gives the number of variables (resp. clauses, blocs) of the instance and **Value** is its truth value. **Nodes** is the number of nodes of the And-Or graph that have been explored. The columns **ATC, QuBE, DepQBF**, and **sKizzo** present the execution times in seconds (with a timeout of 600 seconds) of our antichain-based solver and the three other solvers. The experimental results obtained with our solver are encouraging.

- According to pure performance, our prototype already performs better than the three state-of-the-art solvers for the families k-path-n and k-path-p.

  For other families in k-*, QuBE and DepQBF solvers (which are search-based) have often an execution time beyond 600 seconds.

  See Table 1, Fig. 5 and 6.
- The antichain approach leads to search trees that are *amazingly small* as compared to the size of the entire search space (see the **Nodes** entry in Table 1 as compared to the size of the entire search space in $O(2^{\mathbf{Var}})$); the antichains are thus also very small as they are composed of nodes of the search tree.
- For several families from the QBFLIB library [15] (including Toilet* and aim-*), the execution times of our solver follow the same shape of curve (at logarithmic scale, with a timeout of 600 seconds) as for the other three state-of-the-art solvers, see for instance the family aim-100 in Fig. 7 (true instances) and Fig. 8 (false instances).

Table 1. Family k-path-n

Instance	Var	Cl	Blocs	Value	Nodes	ATC	QuBE	DepQBF	sKizzo
k-path-n-01	108	275	7	1	14	0.22	0.01	0.005	0.01
k-path-n-02	180	481	9	1	43	0.93	0.01	0.02	0.05
k-path-n-05	384	1051	15	1	120	4.17	2.53	39.97	0.08
k-path-n-06	456	1257	17	1	142	7.54	13.74	/	0.26
k-path-n-10	732	2033	25	1	247	16.33	/	/	45.87
k-path-n-11	804	2234	27	1	269	27.36	/	/	445.71
k-path-n-20	1428	3992	45	1	503	95.19	/	/	/
k-path-n-21	1488	4155	47	1	452	88.81	/	/	/

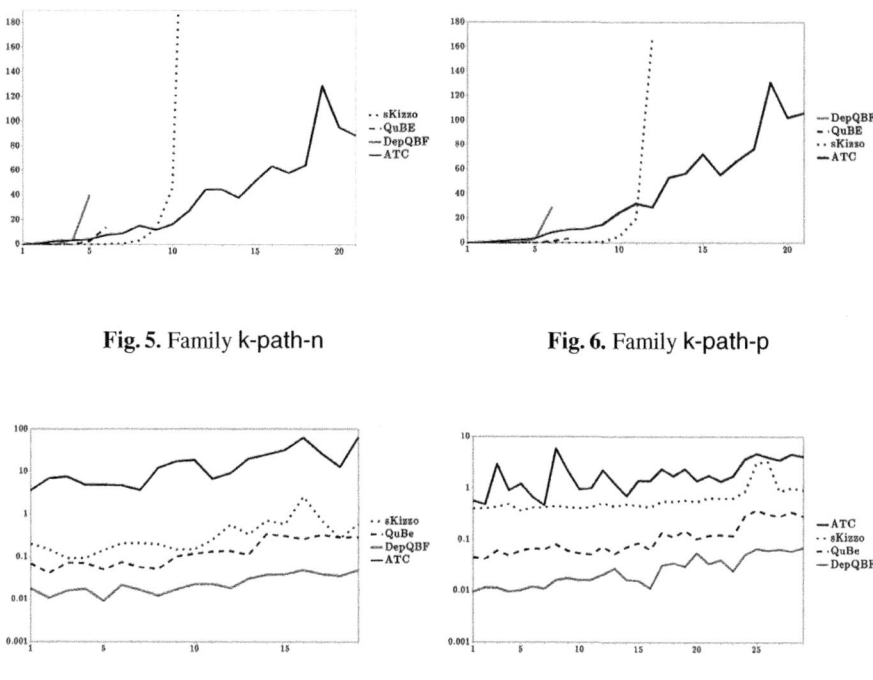

Fig. 5. Family k-path-n   **Fig. 6.** Family k-path-p

Fig. 7. Family aim-100 (true - log scale)   **Fig. 8.** Family aim-100 (false - log scale)

As explained in Section 3.1, the maximal and minimal valuations can be computed either with a SAT solver of with a partial Max-SAT solver. In Section 5.2, we described several ways to improve the information about losing and winning nodes in the antichains. These different approaches have been tested, and the experiments show the best approach can vary with the family of formulas that is tested (the table and figures always present the results for the best approach). For instance, depending on the family, the size of the search space can be either increased or decreased when using a partial MaxSAT solver instead of a SAT solver.

Along with deciding if a given QBF formula is true or false, our solver provides compact certificates in the form of antichains both for positive and negative instances of QBF, and *without any additional computation* (see Section 4). DepQBF solver does not construct certificates. For sKizzo and QuBE solvers, additional computation is required to extract certificates [3,17,24]. The log produced by sKizzo is evaluated by ozziKs to construct certificates (only for true instances); QuBE-cert (in the suite ChEQ) is an extension of QuBE that adds to QuBE the instrumentation required to generate certificates (for both true and false instances). In [3], experiments have been done with the family adder* with "*the surprising phenomenon that the time taken to reconstruct a model may overcome the time needed to solve the instance*".

7   Conclusion and Perspectives

The approach presented in this paper for QBF solving is inspired by previous works on effective antichain algorithms for PSPACE-complete problems in automata theory which are based on simple subsumption relations [11,12]. While the And-Or graph of QBF formulas enjoys such a subsumption relation, this idea has not been exploited in search-based QBF solvers. In a prototypical implementation, we have evaluated the feasibility of antichain-based algorithms for QBF. Experimental results show that on several benchmarks the size of the search tree is drastically reduced, and that some instances are solved more efficiently than by the leading QBF solvers. This shows that the antichain approach is promising and it provides a new research direction in the area. Its integration in standard search-based QBF solvers is worth investigating. On the other hand, our algorithm provides automatically compact certificates represented by antichains with no additional cost, and for both true and false instances.

We now plan to improve our algorithm with respect to the computation of the valuations. Indeed, we observed on the experiments that the execution time is partly spent when computing maximal and minimal valuations. Our current solver computes the *best* valuations since they are restricted to maximal/minimal ones, and exploit as much as possible the information stored in the antichains. We could instead compute *approximate* valuations in a way to decrease the execution time while keeping the advantages of the antichains [1].

Our work also provides a new application of the Max-SAT problem. We intend to submit instances coming from our experiments to the *Evaluation of Max-SAT Solvers* that is yearly organized as an affiliated event of the International Conference on Theory and Applications of Satisfiability Testing (SAT)[1]. We believe that the difficult instances we produce could be of interest to the Max-SAT community and that antichain-based QBF solving would benefit from their improvements.

Acknowledgements. We thank Marco Benedetti, the author of sKizzo, for his great help, Florian Lonsing for explanations about DepQBF, the QuBE's team for answers about their solver, and Nicolas Maquet for his guidance in the implementation.

References

1. Asano, T., Williamson, D.P.: Improved approximation algorithms for max sat. J. Algorithms 42(1), 173–202 (2002)
2. Benedetti, M.: Evaluating QBFs via Symbolic Skolemization. In: Baader, F., Voronkov, A. (eds.) LPAR 2004. LNCS (LNAI), vol. 3452, pp. 285–300. Springer, Heidelberg (2005)
3. Benedetti, M.: Extracting Certificates from Quantified Boolean Formulas. In: Kaelbling, L.P., Saffiotti, A. (eds.) IJCAI, pp. 47–53. Professional Book Center (2005)
4. Benedetti, M.: Quantifier Trees for QBFs. In: Bacchus, F., Walsh, T. (eds.) SAT 2005. LNCS, vol. 3569, pp. 378–385. Springer, Heidelberg (2005)
5. Benedetti, M.: sKizzo: A Suite to Evaluate and Certify QBFs. In: Nieuwenhuis, R. (ed.) CADE 2005. LNCS (LNAI), vol. 3632, pp. 369–376. Springer, Heidelberg (2005)

---

[1] See http://www.maxsat.udl.cat/

6. Benedetti, M., Mangassarian, H.: Qbf-based formal verification: Experience and perspectives. JSAT 5(1-4), 133–191 (2008)
7. Biere, A.: PicoSAT Essentials. JSAT 4(2-4), 75–97 (2008)
8. Cadoli, M., Giovanardi, A., Schaerf, M.: An algorithm to evaluate quantified Boolean formulae. In: Proc. of AAAI 1998/IAAI 1998, pp. 262–267. MIT Press, Cambridge (1998)
9. Cassez, F., David, A., Fleury, E., Larsen, K.G., Lime, D.: Efficient on-the-fly algorithms for the analysis of timed games. In: Abadi, M., de Alfaro, L. (eds.) CONCUR 2005. LNCS, vol. 3653, pp. 66–80. Springer, Heidelberg (2005)
10. Cook, B., Kroening, D., Sharygina, N.: Verification of boolean programs with unbounded thread creation. Theor. Comput. Sci. 388(1-3), 227–242 (2007)
11. De Wulf, M., Doyen, L., Henzinger, T.A., Raskin, J.-F.: Antichains: A New Algorithm for Checking Universality of Finite Automata. In: Ball, T., Jones, R.B. (eds.) CAV 2006. LNCS, vol. 4144, pp. 17–30. Springer, Heidelberg (2006)
12. Doyen, L., Raskin, J.-F.: Antichain Algorithms for Finite Automata. In: Esparza, J., Majumdar, R. (eds.) TACAS 2010. LNCS, vol. 6015, pp. 2–22. Springer, Heidelberg (2010)
13. Eén, N., Sörensson, N.: An extensible SAT-solver. In: Giunchiglia, E., Tacchella, A. (eds.) SAT 2003. LNCS, vol. 2919, pp. 502–518. Springer, Heidelberg (2004)
14. Egly, U., Eiter, T., Tompits, H., Woltran, S.: Solving Advanced Reasoning Tasks Using Quantified Boolean Formulas. In: Proc. of IAAI, pp. 417–422. AAAI Press, Menlo Park (2000)
15. Giunchiglia, E., Narizzano, M., Tacchella, A.: Quantified Boolean Formulas satisfiability library (QBFLIB) (2001), www.qbflib.org
16. Giunchiglia, E., Narizzano, M., Tacchella, A.: QuBE++: An Efficient QBF Solver. In: Hu, A.J., Martin, A.K. (eds.) FMCAD 2004. LNCS, vol. 3312, pp. 201–213. Springer, Heidelberg (2004)
17. Giunchiglia, E., Narizzano, M., Tacchella, A.: Clause/Term Resolution and Learning in the Evaluation of Quantified Boolean Formulas. J. Artif. Intell. Res. 26, 371–416 (2006)
18. Jussila, T., Biere, A.: Compressing BMC Encodings with QBF. Electron. Notes Theor. Comput. Sci. 174, 45–56 (2007)
19. Kohli, R., Krishnamurti, R., Mirchandani, P.: The Minimum Satisfiability Problem. SIAM J. Discrete Math. 7(2), 275–283 (1994)
20. Kügel, A.: Improved Exact Solver for the Weighted Max-SAT problem. Accepted at the workshop Pragmatics of SAT. To appear in easychair electronic proceedings (2011)
21. Li, C.M., Manyà, F.: MaxSAT, Hard and Soft Constraints. In: Handbook of Satisfiability. Frontiers in Artificial Intelligence and Applications, vol. 185, pp. 613–631. IOS Press, Amsterdam (2009)
22. Lonsing, F., Biere, A.: DepQBF: A dependency-aware QBF solver (System Description). Journal on Satisfiability, Boolean Modeling and Computation 7, 71–76 (2010)
23. Lonsing, F., Biere, A.: Integrating Dependency Schemes in Search-Based QBF Solvers. In: Strichman, O., Szeider, S. (eds.) SAT 2010. LNCS, vol. 6175, pp. 158–171. Springer, Heidelberg (2010)
24. Narizzano, M., Peschiera, C., Pulina, L., Tacchella, A.: Evaluating and certifying QBFs: A comparison of state-of-the-art tools. AI Commun. 22, 191–210 (2009)
25. Pan, G., Vardi, M.Y.: Symbolic Decision Procedures for QBF. In: Wallace, M. (ed.) CP 2004. LNCS, vol. 3258, pp. 453–467. Springer, Heidelberg (2004)
26. Papadimitriou, C.H.: Computational complexity. Addison-Wesley Publishing Company, Reading (1994)
27. Peschiera, C., Pulina, L., Tacchella, A., Bubeck, U., Kullmann, O., Lynce, I.: The Seventh QBF Solvers Evaluation (QBFEVAL 2010). In: Strichman, O., Szeider, S. (eds.) SAT 2010. LNCS, vol. 6175, pp. 237–250. Springer, Heidelberg (2010)
28. Samulowitz, H., Davies, J., Bacchus, F.: Preprocessing QBF. In: Benhamou, F. (ed.) CP 2006. LNCS, vol. 4204, pp. 514–529. Springer, Heidelberg (2006)

A Hierarchical Approach for the Synthesis of Stabilizing Controllers for Hybrid Systems*

Janusz Malinowski, Peter Niebert, and Pierre-Alain Reynier

LIF, Université de Provence & CNRS, UMR 6166, France

Abstract. We consider a discretization based approach to controller synthesis of hybrid systems that allows to handle non-linear dynamics. In such an approach, states are grouped together in a finite index partition at the price of a non-deterministic over approximation of the transition relation. The main contribution of this work is a technique to reduce the state explosion generated by the discretization: exploiting structural properties of ODE systems, we propose a hierarchical approach to the synthesis problem by solving it first for sub problems and using the results for state space reduction in the full problem. A secondary contribution concerns combined safety and liveness control objectives that approximate stabilization.

1 Introduction

The model of hybrid systems constitutes a very rich modeling framework as it allows the combination of continuous and discrete-event dynamics. It is used in numerous applications such as the control of physical or chemical processes by computer programs, avionics, etc. For such systems, except under strong restrictions on the continuous dynamics, the set of reachable configurations cannot be computed exactly. As a consequence, numerous approximation techniques have been devised, with the objective of building an abstract system for which analysis is possible. The basic setting of this work is the discretization in both time and (continuous) variables of the system. In particular, we allow arbitrary dynamics, and especially nonlinear ones. To simplify the presentation, we thus focus on the continuous dynamics, and do not consider general hybrid systems, but simply systems of ODEs.

Most works related to hybrid systems are concerned with verification, and especially focus on the approximate computation of the reachability set. We tackle here the (more difficult) problem of controller synthesis. The purpose of this work is to progress in the direction of realistic controller synthesis for nonlinear ODE systems. Given a plant (an open dynamical system), controller synthesis aims at designing a system which interacts with the plant in order to satisfy a given objective. A natural setting, which subsumes standard safety and reachability objectives, consists of the design of a feedback controller which allows to *stabilize* the system around a target configuration. There are two main contributions of this work. One concerns the formalisation and algorithmic handling of a pragmatic choice of control objectives that approximate the ideal of systems stabilized under control. The other, the main objective, concerns a state space reduction

---

* Partially supported by the ANR project ECSPER(ANR JC09_472677 ECSPER).

T. Bultan and P.-A. Hsiung (Eds.): ATVA 2011, LNCS 6996, pp. 198–212, 2011.

approach that helps render the synthesis problem feasible despite combinatory explosion in multi-variate nonlinear dynamics: a dedicated slicing technique is introduced for controller synthesis to rapidly eliminate « hopeless » states from the search space.

The most widespread notions of games found in control applications are safety games (such as Ramadge-Wonham games) where the controller is supposed to avoid something bad from happening (by forbidding some controllable transitions), and reachability games, where the controller is supposed to drive the system into a good state within a finite amount of time. Consider the objective of stabilizing an inverted pendulum in its vertical top position. With a game based approach, we would not know how to express convergence as a goal, but for a given distance ϵ, we can state that we want the pendulum to reach a neighbourhood of radius ϵ around the desired point and to stay forever within that region. We formalize these combined until and safety objectives, and provide an efficient, on-the-fly, linear algorithm for solving such stabilization games. This algorithm is derived from model-checking algorithms for the alternation-free fragment of the propositional μ-calculus [7,12].

State-space explosion in the number of variables is inherent in discretization techniques. To combat this problem, we propose an original hierarchical approach for the controller synthesis problem. It amounts to identifying subsets of variables of the ODE system whose dynamics is independent from all other variables. We formulize the induced relation as a bisimulation, and prove that it ensures the preservation of controllability in the subproblems w.r.t. stabilization objectives we consider. More precisely, winning states in the global problem are projected on winning states in the subproblems, which allows a strong reduction of the state space explored for the global problem. For simplicity, we only discuss ODE systems in the paper, but our work naturally applies to periodic controller synthesis for hybrid systems. A prototype implementation is presented, and experiments conducted on the inverted pendulum case study prove the vast improvement provided by this hierarchical approach.

Related work on hybrid systems in general and for the discretized approach in particular is vast. There is an obvious tradeoff between state explosion and non-determinism when discretizing hybrid systems for state space analysis. When the synthesis fails, it may not be clear whether this is due to the actual hybrid system or due to an overly coarse discretization. Discrete-state abstractions of nonlinear systems have been considered in [2,15], and the possibility of building as rough as possible abstractions by successive abstractions has been explored [6,1,13]. The problem of controller synthesis for nonlinear hybrid systems is also considered in [16], but only for safety objectives. Finally note that the notion of hierarchy we consider in ODE systems in our approach is not the same as hierarchical decomposition of controllers such as in [14].

Formalization of our notion of stabilization games is presented in Section 2. We present the discretization of a nonlinear ODE system in Section 3. Section 4 contains the presentation of our hierarchical approach, and Section 5 reports experiments.

2   Controller Synthesis for Stabilization Games

A standard way of modeling the control of synchronous systems is a two player game with alternating moves : for the duration of an interval, the controller can (deterministically) set the control parameters and the system replies at the end of the interval with a perturbed target, a non-deterministic response. The set of states thus decomposes into a bipartite graph of controllable and uncontrollable states. We fix finite sets of environment actions Σ_E, controller actions Σ_C, and atomic propositions Γ.

Definition 1 (Control Game Structure (CGS)). *A CGS over $(\Sigma_E, \Sigma_C, \Gamma)$ is a tuple $\mathcal{C} = \langle S_E, S_C, T, S_0, \lambda \rangle$ where S_C is the set of controller states, S_E the set of environment states, $S := S_E \uplus S_C$, a transition relation $T \subseteq (S_E \times \Sigma_E \times S_C) \cup (S_C \times \Sigma_C \times S_E)$, an initial state set $S_0 \subseteq S$, and $\lambda : S \to 2^\Gamma$ labels states by atomic propositions.*

We require the environment to be deadlock free, i.e. for every $s \in S_E$ there exists at least one $(s, a, s') \in T$ and we require controller actions to be deterministic, i.e. for every $s \in S_C$ and $a \in \Sigma_C$ there exists a unique $s' \in S_E$ such that $(s, a, s') \in T$. For a state $s \in S$, we let $\#Succ(s) = |\{s' \in S \mid (s, a, s') \in T \text{ for some } a \in \Sigma_E \cup \Sigma_C\}|$.

The game is turn-based and played as follows: starting from a controller state $s \in S_C$, the controller chooses an action $\sigma \in \Sigma_C$, which leads the system in a (single) environment state s' (as the controller actions are deterministic). Then, a turn of the environment in state $s' \in S_E$ consists of determining a state y such that $(s', \sigma', y) \in T$ for some $\sigma' \in \Sigma_E$. Such an interaction builds a *path* which is a finite or infinite sequence $\rho = (s_0, a_1, s_1, a_2, \ldots)$ such that $(s_k, a_{k+1}, s_{k+1}) \in T$ for every $k \geq 0$ (we do *not* require a path to begin with an initial state). To determine whether the controller or the environment wins, a *control objective* is given as a set W of (winning) paths, which defines which paths are winning for the controller.

Our work falls in the (well-studied) setting of parity games, which are memoryless determined (see for instance [9] for details). As a consequence, and to simplify the presentation, we directly focus on memoryless strategies (a.k.a controllers).

A (memoryless) *controller* is a mapping $c : S_C \to 2^{\Sigma_C}$ associating to a controller state $s \in S_C$ a non-empty set of controller actions $c(s)$. A path $s_0, a_1, s_1, a_2, \ldots$ is *controlled by* c iff for every $s_i \in S_C$ we have $a_{i+1} \in c(s_i)$. Given a state s, we say that a controller c *guarantees* a control objective W from s iff every path ρ beginning at s and controlled by c belongs to W. A state s is *winning* for control objective W iff there exists a controller c that guarantees W from s. Finally, a control game structure is winning for control objective W iff every initial state is winning for W.

We recall the widely used operator $\mathsf{CPre} : 2^S \longrightarrow 2^S$ (controllable predecessors). Intuitively, it aims at computing, given a set of target states X, the set of states from which the controller can guarantee to end up in X in one step. More formally, we define:

$$\mathsf{CPre}(X) = \{s \in S_C \mid \exists (s, a, s') \in T. s' \in X\} \cup \{s \in S_E \mid \forall (s, a, s') \in T. s' \in X\}$$

Note that if $s \in S_C$, there must exist a controllable action leading to X while if $s \in S_E$, we require that all possible successors for the environment must be in X.

2.1 Stabilization Games

Basic control objectives. We now consider more specific control objectives for hybrid systems with initial conditions. We define two basic control objectives:

STAY: Given a set of states $A \subseteq S$, stay forever in the set A. Formally, we define:

$$W_{\mathsf{Stay}(A)} = \{\rho = (s_0, a_1, s_1, a_2, \ldots) \mid \forall i \geq 0, s_i \in A\}$$

UNTIL: Given two sets of states $AB \subseteq S$, reach a state of B in a finite number of steps without leaving the set of allowed states A, where we require[1] that $B \subseteq A$. Formally:

$$W_{\mathsf{Until}(A,B)} = \{\rho = (s_0, a_1, s_1, a_2, \ldots) \mid \exists k \geq 0.s_k \in B \wedge \forall 0 \leq i < k, s_i \in A\}$$

$\mathsf{Stay}(\mathcal{C}, A)$ denotes the set of winning states of $\mathcal{C}$ w.r.t. the control objective $W_{\mathsf{Stay}(A)}$ and $\mathsf{Until}(\mathcal{C}, A, B)$ denotes the set of winning states w.r.t. $W_{\mathsf{Until}(A,B)}$. Intuitively, these objectives correspond to the linear time temporal logic properties GA and $A \mathcal{U} B$.

Fixpoint characterization. These winning sets can be defined in terms of fixpoints of operators over sets of states. Therefore, we define the two following operators:

$$O_{\mathsf{Stay}(A)}(X) = A \cap \mathsf{CPre}(X) \tag{1}$$
$$O_{\mathsf{Until}(A,B)}(X) = B \cup (A \cap \mathsf{CPre}(X)) \tag{2}$$

Intuitively, to stay forever in A, the controller should own an action which leads him to a winning state. This explains equation (1). To characterize $\mathsf{Until}(\mathcal{C}, A, B)$ (equation (2)), one starts from sets in B and computes the least fixpoint of states from which the controller can reach such states, using again the CPre operator. Then, we obtain the following fixpoint characterizations:

$$\mathsf{Stay}(\mathcal{C}, A) = \bigcap_{n \geq 0} O^n_{\mathsf{Stay}(A)}(S) \quad \text{and} \quad \mathsf{Until}(\mathcal{C}, A, B) = \bigcup_{n \geq 0} O^n_{\mathsf{Until}(A,B)}(\emptyset)$$

Here, we use the notation for the n-fold application of operators : $O^0(X) = X$ and $O^{n+1}(X) = O(O^n(X))$. Note, that for the (finite) set lattice over S the approximation $\bigcup_n O^n(\emptyset)$ is equal to the least fixpoint of O, i.e. the least set S' such that $O(S') = S'$ and similarly $\bigcap_n O^n(S)$ is equal to the greatest fixpoint.

Controllers' computation. For a state $s \in \mathsf{Until}(\mathcal{C}, A, B)$, we moreover define the *distance between s and B* as the least n such that $s \in O^{n+1}_{\mathsf{Until}(A,B)}(\emptyset)$. Notably, if $s \in B$ its distance from B is 0. We denote by $d(s, B)$ this value. In order to obtain controllers from these winning sets, one can proceed as follows. Let $A, B \subseteq S$. We distinguish the two objectives:

$\mathsf{Stay}(\mathcal{C}, A)$: for a state $s \in \mathsf{Stay}(\mathcal{C}, A) \cap S_C$, the controller has to choose any action $a \in \Sigma_C$ such that $s' \in \mathsf{Stay}(\mathcal{C}, A)$ for the unique triple (s, a, s').

$\mathsf{Until}(\mathcal{C}, A, B)$: for a state $s \in \mathsf{Until}(\mathcal{C}, A, B) \cap S_C$, if $s \in B$, then we do not need a strategy for this objective. Otherwise, if $s \notin B$, we must ensure progress towards the set B. This can be guaranteed if the controller chooses an action a such that the target state s' (i.e. such that $(s, a, s') \in T$) verifies $d(s', B) < d(s, B)$. By the fixpoint characterization of the set $\mathsf{Until}(\mathcal{C}, A, B)$, this is possible.

---

[1] The practically relevant objective is $\mathsf{Until}(A, A \cap B)$, which is equal to $\mathsf{Until}(A, B)$ under this assumption.

Stabilization objective. Recall that in our setting, our objective is to synthesize a controller for a dynamical system, which, starting from an intial configuration, leads the system towards a desirable configuration. To express our stabilization objective, we start from the two following properties: Goal is a set of goal states which describes a neigbourhood around the desirable configuration, Allow is a set of allowed states, which describes the legal configurations of the system. In the sequel, we assume that the inclusion Goal $\subseteq$ Allow holds.

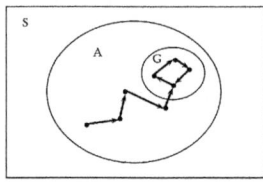

Intuitively, we are interested in synthesizing a controller which is able to guide the system from an initial state, while staying in the set Allow, towards a state from which it can stay in the set Goal forever. We will express formally this objective using the operators Stay and Until. In order to obtain efficient algorithms, we will use computations starting from initial configurations. We thus introduce some additional definitions. We formalize a subset of « reachable » states from the initial condition while respecting the description of « allowed » states. Formally, this set is defined as follows:

$$\mathsf{Acc}(\mathcal{C}, \mathsf{Allow}) = \{s \in S \mid \exists \rho = (s_0, a_1, \ldots, a_{n-1}, s_n) \text{ such that } s_0 \in S_0,$$
$$s_n = s \text{ and } \forall i \leq n, s_i \in \mathsf{Allow}\}$$

We are now equipped to formalize the sets of states we are interested in:

$$\mathsf{Stabilize}(\mathcal{C}, \mathsf{Allow}, \mathsf{Goal}) = \mathsf{Until}(\mathcal{C}, \mathsf{Acc}(\mathcal{C}, \mathsf{Allow}), \mathsf{Stay}(\mathcal{C}, \mathsf{Goal} \cap \mathsf{Acc}(\mathcal{C}, \mathsf{Allow})))$$

Intuitively, it reads as $\mathsf{Acc}(\mathcal{C}, \mathsf{Allow}) \; \mathcal{U} \; \mathsf{Stay}(\mathcal{C}, \mathsf{Goal} \cap \mathsf{Acc}(\mathcal{C}, \mathsf{Allow}))$. Note that the strategy for Stabilize is memoryless: it is a simple combination of the strategies for Stay (for states in Stay) and Until (for the other states) indicated above.

For the reader familiar with the μ-calculus, we note that Acc, Stay and Until can be characterized by the following formulae:

$$\mathsf{Post}(X) = \{s' \in S \mid \exists s \in X \text{ s.t. } s \to s' \in T\} \tag{3}$$
$$\mathsf{Acc}(\mathcal{C}, A) \; : \; \mu X. S_0 \vee (A \wedge \mathsf{Post}(X)) \tag{4}$$
$$\mathsf{Stay}(\mathcal{C}, A) \; : \; \nu X. A \wedge \mathsf{CPre}(X) \tag{5}$$
$$\mathsf{Until}(\mathcal{C}, A, B) \; : \; \mu X. B \vee (A \wedge \mathsf{CPre}(X)) \tag{6}$$

Note the identity $\mathsf{CPre}(X) = \langle \Sigma_C \rangle X \vee [\Sigma_E] X$. In particular, this allows to deduce a μ-calculus formula characterizing the states in $\mathsf{Stabilize}(\mathcal{C}, \mathsf{Allow}, \mathsf{Goal})$.

2.2 Algorithm for Stabilization Games

In the sequel, we present the (efficient) algorithm we used to solve the controller synthesis problem. This algorithm is used for each "level" in the hierarchical approach in Section 4.

This algorithm is derived from model checking algorithms for the alternation free μ-calculus, notably integrating concepts first published in [7,12]. In [5], the authors observe that these local algorithms can be used to decide reachability properties in (un)timed games. We extend this observation to the more complex specifications we consider here. This statement holds because the specification Stabilize can be expressed as a propsitional μ-calculus formula without alternation. This is a local algorithm, in the sense that the exploration of the transition system is started from initial states, and that the exploration of losing states is stopped.

The algorithm we consider is presented as Algorithm 1. Given a CGS $\mathcal{C}$, and two sets of states Goal, Allow such that Goal $\subseteq$ Allow, this algorithm returns a pair of sets of states, whose first component is Stabilize($\mathcal{C}$, Allow, Goal), and second component is Stay($\mathcal{C}$, Goal $\cap$ Acc($\mathcal{C}$, Allow)).

The algorithm consists of three phases:

1. the first while loop consists in a forward exploration of the reachability graph, restricted to states in Allow. At the end of this phase, the list *Passed* exactly contains the set Acc($\mathcal{C}$, Allow). In addition, the list NIG (standing for "Not In Goal") contains all the states outside Goal that can be reached from states in *Passed*. Finally, the dependance lists (elements $depend[s]$) contain, for each state $s \in Passed \cup NIG$, the set of predecessor states in *Passed*.

2. the second while loop aims at computing the set Stay($\mathcal{C}$, Goal $\cap$ Acc($\mathcal{C}$, Allow)), via variable $STAY$. Therefore, it proceeds in a backward propagation of states of NIG, by exploring the reachability graph (restricted to states in Allow) in a backward manner, using the dependency lists. States are added to the $Waiting$ list iff they are declared as losing. For environment states, this happens as soon as a successor is losing, while for controller states, it occurs when no successor is winning (a counter is used to check this).

3. the third while loop computes the set Stabilize($\mathcal{C}$, Allow, Goal), via variable $UNTIL$. As in the previous case, it proceeds in a backward propagation. However, the computation is dual: while for the computation of Stay (greatest fixpoint), the propagation concerns losing states, for the computation of Until (least fixpoint), it concerns winning states.

Note that the two first while loops can be merged, and thus performed simultaneously. In our implementation (see Section 5), we have given a higher priority to the backward propagation, thus avoiding the exploration of some losing states. The third loop must be performed once the second one has finished, as each edge will be explored only once, the status of the target state must be known when it is explored.

3 Nonlinear Systems and Discretizations

3.1 Nonlinear Systems with Inputs

We consider (possibly nonlinear) systems of ordinary differential equations:

Definition 2 (ODE system). *A system of ordinary differential equations (ODE system for short) is given by a triple $\mathcal{O} = (f, \mathcal{S}, U)$ where U is a finite set of input parameter values, $\mathcal{S} \subseteq \mathbb{R}^n$ denotes the state space of the system, and $f : \mathcal{S} \times U \to \mathbb{R}^n$ defines a parameterized system of differential equations [2]:*

$$\dot{x} = f(x, u), \qquad with\ x : \mathbb{R} \to \mathcal{S}, u \in U \tag{7}$$

---

[2] As usual, $\dot{x}$ denotes the first derivative of x.

Algorithm 1. Local Algorithm Local-Stabilize for a Stabilization Objective

---

Data: $\mathcal{C} = \langle S_E, S_C, T, S_0, \lambda \rangle$, Allow, Goal
Result: $UNTIL = $ Stabilize$(\mathcal{C}, $ Allow, Goal$); STAY = $ Stay$(\mathcal{C}, $ Goal $\cap$ Acc$(\mathcal{C}, $ Allow$))$

$Waiting \leftarrow S_0; NIG \leftarrow \emptyset; Passed \leftarrow \emptyset;$

while $Waiting \neq \emptyset$ **do**
    $s \leftarrow pop(Waiting); Passed \leftarrow Passed \cup \{s\};$
    foreach $(s, a, s') \in T$ **do**
        if $s' \notin$ Goal **then** $NIG \leftarrow NIG \cup \{s'\}$;
        $depend[s'] \leftarrow depend[s'] \cup \{s\};$
        if $s' \in$ Allow $\wedge s' \notin Passed$ **then** $Waiting \leftarrow Waiting \cup \{s'\};$
    end
end

$\forall s \in Passed \cap S_C; counter_C(s) \leftarrow \#Succ(s);$
$Waiting \leftarrow NIG; STAY \leftarrow Passed;$

while $Waiting \neq \emptyset$ **do**
    $s \leftarrow pop(Waiting);$
    $STAY \leftarrow STAY \setminus \{s\};$
    if $s \in S_C$ **then**
        foreach $s' \in depend[s]$ **do**
            if $s' \in STAY$ **then** $Waiting \leftarrow Waiting \cup \{s'\};$
        end
    else
        foreach $s' \in depend[s]$ **do**
            $counter_C(s') \leftarrow counter_C(s') - 1;$
            if $counter_C(s') = 0$ **then** $Waiting \leftarrow Waiting \cup \{s'\};$
        end
    end
end

$\forall s \in Passed \cap S_E, counter_E(s) \leftarrow \#Succ(s)$;
$Waiting \leftarrow STAY; UNTIL \leftarrow \emptyset$;
while $Waiting \neq \emptyset$ **do**
    $s \leftarrow pop(Waiting);$
    $UNTIL \leftarrow UNTIL \cup \{s\};$
    if $s \in S_C$ **then**
        foreach $s' \in depend[s]$ **do**
            $counter_E(s') \leftarrow counter_E(s') - 1;$
            if $counter_E(s') = 0$ **then** $Waiting \leftarrow Waiting \cup \{s'\};$
        end
    else
        foreach $s' \in depend[s]$ **do**
            if $s' \notin UNTIL$ **then** $Waiting \leftarrow Waiting \cup \{s'\};$
        end
    end
end

A configuration of $\mathcal{O}$ is a pair $c = (x, u) \in \mathcal{S} \times U$. *An* initial value problem (IVP for short) *is a pair* $\mathcal{E} = (\mathcal{O}, c_0)$ *composed of an ODE system $\mathcal{O}$ and a (initial) configuration* $c_0 = (x_0, u_0)$ *of $\mathcal{O}$.*

In the sequel, to ensure the existence of a unique solution to the IVP, we assume that for any $u \in U$, the function $f(\cdot, u)$ is locally Lipschitz.

Definition 3 (Trajectory). *Let $\mathcal{O} = (f, \mathcal{S}, U)$ be an ODE system. Given an initial configuration $c_0 = (x_0, u_0)$ of $\mathcal{O}$, a* trajectory *of an ODE system starting from c_0 is a triple $(\mathcal{I}, \sigma, \mathcal{X})$ where:*

- $\mathcal{I} = \{I_k \mid 0 \leq k \leq N\}$ *is a sequence of intervals such that:*
  - *if $N = +\infty$, then for all $k \in \mathbb{N}$, $I_k = [t_k, t'_k]$ with $t'_k = t_{k+1}$,*
  - *if $N < +\infty$, then $I_N = [t_N, t'_N]$ or $I_N = [t_N, +\infty)$ and for all $0 \leq k \leq N - 1$, $I_k = [t_k, t'_k]$ with $t'_k = t_{k+1}$,*
  - *in both cases, the initial time is $t_0 = 0$,*
- $\sigma = \{\sigma_k \mid 0 \leq k \leq N\}$ *is a sequence of elements of U such that $\sigma_0 = u_0$, and*
- $\mathcal{X} = \{x_k \mid 0 \leq k \leq N\}$ *is a sequence of continuous, piecewise differentiable functions. For all $0 \leq k \leq N$, $x_k : I_k \to \mathbb{R}^n$ is the solution of the IVP $(\mathcal{O}, c_k)$, where, for $k \geq 1$, $c_k = (x_{k-1}(t_k), \sigma_k)$.*

We say that a trajectory is finite (resp. infinite) if $N < +\infty$ (resp. $N = +\infty$).

Intuitively, the controller acts on the value of the input parameter u. It has to decide when to change this value (this defines the intervals $\mathcal{I}$) and which value has the input (this defines the sequence σ). Controller synthesis can thus be understood as the synthesis of a mapping which, given the history of the system (a finite trajectory), gives the timestamp of the next input change and the new value of the parameter.

Example 1 (An inverted pendulum). A cart of mass M carries an inverted pendulum of length l with a mass m at the end. The cart can be accelerated somehow by a horizontal force F. This classical control problem can be characterized by a system of four ODEs including as variables θ, the angle of the pendulum relative to the vertical axis, and x, its horizontal position relative to some origin :

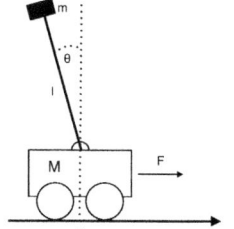

$$\begin{cases} \dot{x}_1 = x_2 \\ \dot{x}_2 = \dfrac{F + (l.x_4^2 - g.\cos x_3).m.\sin x_3}{M + m.\sin^2 x_3} \\ \dot{x}_3 = x_4 \\ \dot{x}_4 = \dfrac{g.\sin x_3.M - \cos x_3.F + (g - l.x_4^2.\cos x_3).m.\sin x_3}{l.M + l.m.\sin^2 x_3} \end{cases}$$

where $x_1 = x$ and $x_3 = \theta$

3.2 Discretizations

As nonlinear differential equations cannot be solved in general, we will approximate the system by a finite state system, which can be analyzed. Therefore, we first restrict the behaviour of the controller by considering a discrete-time controller, obtained by a sampling rate $\eta \in \mathbb{Q}_{>0}$. This means that discrete changes on the value of the input parameter u can only occur at timestamps in $\eta.\mathbb{N}$.

Then, it remains to approximate the infinite-state dynamics of the ODE system by a finite-state one. In the sequel, we fix an ODE system $\mathcal{O}$, together with an initial configuration $c_0 = (x_0, u_0)$ of $\mathcal{O}$ and let $\mathcal{E} = (\mathcal{O}, c_0)$ be the resulting IVP. We assume that the state-space $\mathcal{S}$ of the system is given by a hyper-rectangle $I_1 \times \cdots \times I_n$ of $\mathbb{R}^n$. This assumption is not restrictive for standard ODE systems. Then, we consider a mesh of the state-space obtained by the product of partitionings of each interval I_j, with $1 \le j \le n$. More precisely, we consider, for each $1 \le j \le n$, a partitioning $\mathcal{P}_j$ of I_j. This yields a finite state abstraction of the infinite state space of the system. Following definitions introduced in Section 2, we aim at obtaining a control game structure $\mathcal{C}(\mathcal{E}) = \langle S_E, S_C, T, S_0, \lambda \rangle$ over some alphabets $(\Sigma_E, \Sigma_C, \Gamma)$.

In this definition, the controller chooses the value of the input parameter, by choosing a letter in Σ_C. On the other side, the environment resolves the non-determinism associated with the ODE system. In particular, we do not need to label the transitions of the enviroment. This yields the following definitions:

$$
\begin{array}{ll}
S_C = \Pi_{j=1}^n \mathcal{P}_j & \Sigma_C = U \\
S_E = S_C \times U & \Sigma_E = \{e\}, \text{ for some letter } e \\
S_0 = \{(r_0, u_0)\} & \text{where } r_0 \text{ is such that } x_0 \in r_0
\end{array}
$$

Transitions of the controller are the following ones:

$$
T \cap S_C \times \Sigma_C \times S_E = \{s \xrightarrow{u} (s, u) \mid u \in U, s \in S_C\}
$$

Regarding transitions of the environment, we want to approximate, given a cell of the mesh (*i.e.* a partition of $\mathcal{S}$), and a value of the input, the reachable cells after a delay of η time units. Note that the assumption that for each value of u, the function $f(\cdot, u)$ is locally Lipschitz ensures the existence and the unicity of a solution to the IVP associated with the ODE system. However, as we consider here as possible initial values any value of a given cell (and a single value of u), there are infinitely many such problems. As a consequence, different cells can be reached from a single one. The problem of the computation of these successors has already been studied by several authors: interval numerical methods [10], standard mathematical techniques based on the evaluation of the Lipschitz constant [3], simulation of the system based on sensitivity analysis [8]... We do not detail here how such approximations can be obtained, as this is orthogonal to the purpose of this paper. However, to obtain a sound method, the transitions of the finite-state system should *over-approximate* the transitions of the ODE system:

Definition 4 (Sound over-approximation). *Let* $\mathcal{E} = (\mathcal{O}, c_0)$ *be an IVP. The CGS* $\mathcal{C} = \langle S_E, S_C, T, S_0, \lambda \rangle$ *is a sound over-approximation of* $\mathcal{E}$ *if it satisfies the following property:* $\forall (s, u) \in S_E, \forall x_0 \in s$, *let* $x(t)$ *be the unique solution to the IVP* (f, x_0, u). *Then for any* $s' \in S_C$ *such that* $x(\eta) \in s'$, *we have* $(s, u) \xrightarrow{e} s' \in T$.

Finally, we define the labelling function λ. Given a set of atomic propositions Γ, interpreted as subsets of $\mathcal{S}$ by a given mapping χ, we define λ as follows:

$$
\forall \gamma \in \Gamma, \forall s \in S_C, \gamma \in \lambda(s) \iff s \cap \chi(\gamma) \ne \emptyset
$$

We extend this mapping over S_E by letting $\lambda(s, u) = \lambda(s)$ for any $u \in U$. This is coherent as propositions in Γ are intended to express properties over states but not over parameter values. The above definitions ensure that the discretized CGS built from the partitionning of the state space simulates the behaviour of the ODE system:

Proposition 1 (Simulation). *Let $\mathcal{O} = (f, \mathcal{S}, U)$ be an ODE system, c_0 be a configuration of $\mathcal{O}$, and $\mathcal{C}$ be a CGS that is a sound over-approximation of $\mathcal{E} = (\mathcal{O}, c_0)$. Then, for any trajectory $(\mathcal{I}, \sigma, \mathcal{X})$ of $\mathcal{O}$ such that any interval $I \in \mathcal{I}$ is of the form $[k\eta, (k+1)\eta]$ for some $k \in \mathbb{N}$, there exists a path $\rho = (s_0, a_1, s_1, a_2, \ldots)$ in $\mathcal{C}$ such that $\sigma = (a_i)_i$, and for each i, we have $x_i(t_i) \in s_i$.*

Assume that the partitionings $\mathcal{P}_j$ are compatible with the properties labelings χ, in the sense that for any $s \in S_C$ and any $\gamma \in \Gamma$, we have $s \cap \chi(\gamma) \neq \emptyset$ if, and only if, $s \subseteq \chi(\gamma)$. Then the property of simulation entails that if we can synthesize a controller for the CGS $\mathcal{C}$ w.r.t. some control objective, then this controller can be used as a discrete-time controller for the ODE system $\mathcal{O}$ w.r.t. the same control objective. The only difference is that the atomic properties are ensured only at sampled timestamps.

4 Hierarchical Approach to Controller Synthesis

In this section, we present an original approach for the analysis of the discretizations of ODE systems. In principle, the discretization explodes with the number of variables. Our technique exploits dependencies between variables of the system to first solve smaller subsystems and then use the analysis results to dramatically reduce the size of the state space to explore with the full set of variables.

4.1 Abstractions Preserving Controllability

We present a particular abstraction used in the sequel, which is a bisimulation w.r.t. possible transitions, but only a simulation w.r.t. properties satisfaction. Within this setting, $\mathcal{C}_2$ can be seen as an abstraction of the system $\mathcal{C}_1$.

Definition 5. *Consider two CGS $\mathcal{C}_i = \langle S_E^i, S_C^i, T^i, S_0^i, \lambda^i \rangle$, and let $S^i = S_E^i \uplus S_C^i$ for $i = 1, 2$. We consider a surjective mapping $\alpha : S^1 \to S^2$, and the associated relation $R \subseteq S^1 \times S^2$ defined by $s_1 \, R \, s_2$ iff $\alpha(s_1) = s_2$.*

We say that α yields a property asymmetric bisimulation relation R if, and only if, for any pair $s_1 \, R \, s_2$:

1. *either $s_1 \in S_C^1$ and $s_2 \in S_C^2$, or $s_1 \in S_E^1$ and $s_2 \in S_E^2$,*
2. *if $s_1 \in S_0^1$, then also $s_2 \in S_0^2$,*
3. *for any $\gamma \in \Gamma$, if $\gamma \in \lambda_1(s_1)$, then also $\gamma \in \lambda_2(s_2)$,*
4. *for $(s_1, a, s_1') \in T^1$ there exists s_2' such that $(s_2, a, s_2') \in T^2$ and $s_1' \, R \, s_2'$, and*
5. *for $(s_2, a, s_2') \in T^2$ there exists s_1' such that $(s_1, a, s_1') \in T^1$ and $s_1' \, R \, s_2'$.*

The following proposition states that winning states of the abstract system cover the winning states of the concrete one. This property can be seen as a particular instance of the properties of zig-zags bisimulations, see e.g. [4].

Proposition 2. *Let C_i, $i = 1, 2$ be two **CGS**, and $\alpha : S^1 \to S^2$ be a mapping yielding a property asymmetric bisimulation relation. Let[3] $\gamma, \gamma' \in \Gamma$. Then we have:*

$$\mathsf{Stay}(C_1, \gamma) \subseteq \alpha^{-1}(\mathsf{Stay}(C_2, \gamma)) \ and \ \mathsf{Reach}(C_1, \gamma, \gamma') \subseteq \alpha^{-1}(\mathsf{Reach}(C_2, \gamma, \gamma'))$$

Proof (Sketch). We first prove the following property:

$$\forall X_1 \subseteq S_1, X_2 \subseteq S_2, \alpha(X_1) \subseteq X_2 \Rightarrow \begin{cases} \alpha(\mathsf{Post}_1(X_1)) \subseteq \mathsf{Post}_2(X_2) \\ \alpha(\mathsf{CPre}_1(X_1)) \subseteq \mathsf{CPre}_2(X_2) \end{cases}$$

where Post_i (resp. CPre_i) denotes the operator Post (resp. CPre) in the CGS C_i. These properties easily follow from points 1., 4. and 5. of Definition 5. As a consequence, this entails $\alpha(\mathsf{Acc}(C_1, \gamma)) \subseteq \mathsf{Acc}(C_2, \gamma)$. Indeed, the property holds for initial states (point 2. of Definition 5). Second, consider the characterization of sets $\mathsf{Stay}(C_i, \gamma)$ and $\mathsf{Reach}(C_i, \gamma, \gamma')$ by fixpoints presented in Section 2. We will prove the result by induction on the number of iterations of the fixpoint computation. Initially, the property holds for atomic properties by point 3. of Definition 5, and for the set of reachable states by the above result. The induction follows from the above property of CPre_i. $\quad\square$

4.2   Hierarchical Abstractions in ODE Systems

Formally, we consider an ODE system $\mathcal{O} = (f, \mathcal{S}, U)$ over real variables $x_1, \ldots, x_n$, to be as follows:

$$\begin{cases} \dot{x}_1 = f_1(x_1, \ldots, x_n, u) \\ \quad\vdots \\ \dot{x}_n = f_n(x_1, \ldots, x_n, u) \end{cases}$$

where for each $1 \le i \le n$, $f_i : \mathcal{S} \times U \to \mathbb{R}$ is supposed to be locally Lispchitz (notations are taken from Section 3).

Definition 6 (Dependency). *Let $i, j \in \{1, \ldots, n\}$. We say that mapping f_i does not depend on variable x_j iff for any $y, y' \in \mathbb{R}^n$ such that $y_k = y'_k$ for all $k \ne j$, we have $f_i(y) = f_i(y')$. Otherwise, we say that f_i depends on x_j.*

In particular, for standard ODE systems in which mappings f_i's are given by explicit expressions involving polynomials, sine, cosine, ..., the mapping does not depend on a variable as soon as it does not appear in this expression. For instance, regarding the inverted pendulum example, one can note that mappings f_3 and f_4 only depend on variables x_3 and x_4.

Definition 7 (Independent subset of variables). *Let $J \subset \{1, \ldots, n\}$. We say that the subset of variables J is independent if the subsystem obtained by the restriction to variables $\{x_j \mid j \in J\}$ constitutes an independent subsystem, i.e. iff for any $j \in J$, mapping f_j only depends on variables in the set $\{x_j \mid j \in J\}$.*

For the example of the inverted pendulum, there are four independent subsets of variables : $\emptyset$, $\{x_3, x_4\}$, $\{x_2, x_3, x_4\}$ and $\{x_1, x_2, x_3, x_4\}$.

---

[3] For readability, we shortcut $\lambda_i \gamma$ by simply γ in the expression $\mathsf{Stay}(C_i, \lambda_i(\gamma))$ and similarly for Reach.

Proposition 3. *The independent subsets of variables of an ODE system is a complete lattice.*

Definition 8. *Let $\mathcal{O}$ be an ODE system. We denote by $\mathcal{L}(\mathcal{O})$ the complete lattice of its independent subsets of variables. In addition, given $J, J' \in \mathcal{L}(\mathcal{O})$, we write $J' \prec J$ iff $J' \subsetneq J$, and there does not exist a set $J'' \in \mathcal{L}(\mathcal{O})$ such that $J' \subsetneq J''$ and $J'' \subsetneq J$.*

Definition 9. *Consider an IVP $\mathcal{E} = (\mathcal{O}, c_0)$, and a set of partitionings $\mathcal{P}_j$, for $1 \leq j \leq n$. For any set $J \in \mathcal{L}(\mathcal{O})$, we denote by $\mathcal{C}_J(\mathcal{E})$ the discretization of the subsystem of $\mathcal{O}$ restricted to J, w.r.t. partitionings $\mathcal{P}_j$, with $j \in J$.*

Let $J, J' \in \mathcal{L}(\mathcal{O})$ such that $J' \subseteq J$. We denote by $\pi_{J,J'}$ the projection from states of $\mathcal{C}_J(\mathcal{E})$ to states of $\mathcal{C}_{J'}(\mathcal{E})$ obtained by erasing components of J not in J'. We simply write π_J to denote the projection $\pi_{\{1,\ldots,n\},J}$.

The following Lemma states that independent subsets of variables can be used for hierarchical computations:

Lemma 1. *Let $J, J' \in \mathcal{L}(\mathcal{O})$ such that $J' \subseteq J$. The mapping $\pi_{J,J'}$ yields an asymmetric property bisimulation relation between $\mathcal{C}_J(\mathcal{E})$ and $\mathcal{C}_{J'}(\mathcal{E})$.*

Proof (Sketch). Let R denote the relation associated with $\pi_{J,J'}$. We have to prove that R satisfies point 1. to 5. of Definition 5. Points 1. to 4. easily follow by definition of a projection mapping, and would be true for any sets J, J' such that $J' \subseteq J$. Point 4 holds because J and J' are independent subset of variables. This implies that any trajectory $(\mathcal{I}', \sigma', \mathcal{X}')$ in the ODE system $\mathcal{O}$ restricted to J' can be extended into a trajectory $(\mathcal{I}, \sigma, \mathcal{X})$ in $\mathcal{O}$ restricted to J whose projection on J' coincides with $(\mathcal{I}', \sigma', \mathcal{X}')$. □

Algorithm 2. Hierarchical Algorithm for the Synthesis w.r.t. Stabilization Objectives

Data: $\mathcal{E} = (\mathcal{O}, c_0)$, Allow, Goal
Result: Stabilize$(\mathcal{C}(\mathcal{E}),$ Allow, Goal$)$

Compute the lattice $\mathcal{L}(\mathcal{O})$;
foreach $J \in \mathcal{L}(\mathcal{O})$, *ordered by increasing size* **do**
$\quad\quad A \leftarrow \pi_J(\text{Allow}) \cap \bigcap_{J' \prec J} \pi_{J,J'}^{-1}(U(J'))$;
$\quad\quad G \leftarrow \pi_J(\text{Goal}) \cap \bigcap_{J' \prec J} \pi_{J,J'}^{-1}(S(J'))$;
$\quad\quad (U(J), S(J)) \leftarrow$ Local-Stabilize$(\mathcal{C}_J(\mathcal{E}), A, G)$;
end
Return $U(\{1, \ldots, n\})$;

This allows us to derive Algorithm 2, which first solves the control problem for smaller sets of variables, and uses the results to limit the domain explored by further resolutions of the control problem: compute incrementally for all independent subsets bottom up the set of winning states for Stay and Until objectives, and exploit the asymmetric bisimulation and property inheritance (Proposition 2) to eliminate states from these two sets if they are not in Stay or Until in the projection.

This approach allows, based on the analysis on subsets of variables, to reduce the exploration space by observing what happens in the projection. To understand this intuitively, let us consider the independent subsets of the inverted pendulum. If the control objective is to go to a certain position and keep the pendulum close to the vertical position, three different problems have to be solved : first we solve the problem only for angular speed and position which means to solve the problem of balancing the pendulum independently of the vehicle movement. If, afterwards, the problem is extended to include vehicle speed and then vehicle position, states for which it is not possible to balance the pendulum are immediately removed from the sets of candidates with additional objectives for the position.

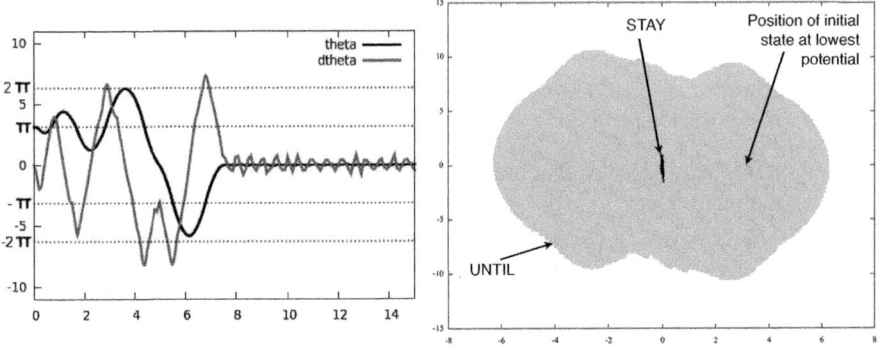

Fig. 1. A strategy simulation for a swing up and a representation of winning states

5   Experiments

We have realized a prototype implementation of the algorithms described in this paper and demonstrate its capacities using the example of the inverted pendulum.

As an illustration of what can be achieved with specifications, we consider the "swing up" problem: we suppose that the pendulum is initially hanging at its lowest potential energy (see image on the right) and we ask for a controller which lifts it to the vertical upright position. Figure 1 at left shows a simulated trajectory obtained from a synthetized controller which illustrates how the angle θ of the pendulum is raised from the lowest position (radiant angle π) with several swings before stabilizing with tiny oscillations at the vertical position (radiant 0). The image on the right shows the winning sets Stay (black) and Until (gray and black) for the stated swingup problem, a small box indicates the initial configuration.

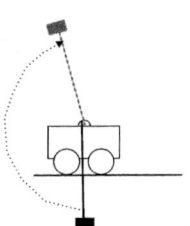

Concerning the reduction potential of the hierarchical algorithm, we give sample figures for the synthesis of a controller limiting all four variables of the pendulum. We count in particular the number of states explored with and without the hierarchical approach. The third line (exploration ratio, $\frac{explored}{|S_C|} * 100$) gives an impression of the advantage of the combined local and hierarchical approach over a global approach: for the biggest example, only 11% of the states are visited. The difference of the local approach with and without hierarchy is explored in the fourth and fifth line: using results from $\{x_3, x_4\}$ in the computation for $\{x_2, x_3, x_4\}$ allows a state space reduction of

48%. Data for $\{x_1, x_2, x_3, x_4\}$ without the hierarchical approach is not available since it was beyond our current implementation and available hardware.

	$\{x_3, x_4\}$	$\{x_2, x_3, x_4\}$	$\{x_1, x_2, x_3, x_4\}$
$\|S_E \cap \mathsf{Allow}\|$	1.049.600	136.448.000	6.822.400.000
$\|S_C \cap \mathsf{Allow}\|$	25.600	3.328.000	166.400.000
explored part of $S_C \cap \mathsf{Allow}$	17.616	815.643	18.261.684
exploration ratio	68%	24%	11%
explored without hierarchy	17.616	1.571.127	n/a
savings by hierachical approach	0%	48%	n/a
$\|S_C \cap \mathsf{Stay}\|$	1.683	50.787	1.305.059
$\|S_C \cap \mathsf{Until}\|$	10.121	432.547	9.678.467

Optimizations in the prototype. We discuss some of the optimizations we introduced in the prototype to make it work with case studies of the size of the pendulum.

The first two while loops of 1 can actually be merged and combined with a computation of $\mathsf{Stay}(\mathcal{C}, \mathsf{Allow} \cap \mathsf{Acc}(\mathcal{C}, \mathsf{Allow}))$. This combination has the advantage of avoiding the exploration of certain states and making the algorithm a bit more local.

It turned out that an explicit representation of $depend[s]$ by lists creates a major bottleneck in terms of memory usage: looking at the figures for S_E in the table, one can understand why, there are billions of transitions involved over which backward propagation may take place. The experiments shown here therefore add a symbolic overapproximation technique that allows to safely track supersets of the actual predecessors. Using these supersets in backward propagation is like adding non-determinism to the environment, thus, if a controller with this overapproximation exists, so does one for the case without.

In the future, we want to look into the possibility of optimizing memory usage of the algorithms by exploiting more knowledge about the structure of the state space.

6   Conclusions and Future Work

We have developped an approach for the synthesis of stabilizing controllers of hybrid systems that exploits the structure of differential equations for state reduction.

The combinatory explosion due to the non-deterministic overapproximation introduced by discretization is the big challenge and many techniques must be combined to make such approaches realistic. In our experiments, we found that the slicing approach helps in finding good abstractions for the independent variable subsets before going to more complex levels. This is orthogonal and complementary to compositional approaches such as [14] which are needed if one wants to synthesize controllers for complex systems: in hybrid systems there are limits to decomposition and this is where our slicing type approach can help. Another promising direction is the use of counterexample guided refinements for controller synthesis [11].

The reduction approach uses a notion of bisimulation for its correctness and the algorithms are fundamentally based on a certain fragment of the μ-calculus [4] : formulae without negation on the properties. The hierarchical reduction framework is thus open for extension to a much larger class of properties which can be expressed in the alternation free fragment of the μ-calculus, and it is not difficult to extend the proofs in Section 4 to a more general case.

In the future, we want to extend our work to the case of control objectives changing with time while preserving stabilization in the sense we use it here.

References

1. Alur, R., Dang, T., Ivancic, F.: Counterexample-guided predicate abstraction of hybrid systems. Theor. Comput. Sci. 354(2), 250–271 (2006)
2. Alur, R., Henzinger, T.A., Lafferriere, G., Pappas, G.J.: Discrete abstractions of hybrid systems. Proceedings of the IEEE (88), 971–984 (2000)
3. Asarin, E., Dang, T., Girard, A.: Hybridization methods for the analysis of nonlinear systems. Acta Inf. 43(7), 451–476 (2007)
4. Brandfield, J., Stirling, C.: Modal mu-calculi. In: The Handbook of Modal Logic, pp. 721–756. Elsevier, Amsterdam (2006)
5. Cassez, F., David, A., Fleury, E., Larsen, K., Lime, D.: Efficient on-the-fly algorithms for the analysis of timed games. In: Abadi, M., de Alfaro, L. (eds.) CONCUR 2005. LNCS, vol. 3653, pp. 66–80. Springer, Heidelberg (2005)
6. Clarke, E.M., Fehnker, A., Han, Z., Krogh, B.H., Ouaknine, J., Stursberg, O., Theobald, M.: Abstraction and counterexample-guided refinement in model checking of hybrid systems. Int. J. Found. Comput. Sci. 14(4), 583–604 (2003)
7. Cleaveland, R., Steffen, B.: A linear-time model-checking algorithm for the alternation-free modal mu-calculus. In: FMSD, pp. 48–58. Springer, Heidelberg (1993)
8. Donzé, A., Maler, O.: Systematic simulation using sensitivity analysis. In: Bemporad, A., Bicchi, A., Buttazzo, G. (eds.) HSCC 2007. LNCS, vol. 4416, pp. 174–189. Springer, Heidelberg (2007)
9. Grädel, E., Thomas, W., Wilke, T. (eds.): Automata, Logics, and Infinite Games: A Guide to Current Research. LNCS, vol. 2500. Springer, Heidelberg (2002)
10. Henzinger, T.A., Horowitz, B., Majumdar, R., Wong-Toi, H.: Beyond hytech: Hybrid systems analysis using interval numerical methods. In: Lynch, N.A., Krogh, B.H. (eds.) HSCC 2000. LNCS, vol. 1790, pp. 130–144. Springer, Heidelberg (2000)
11. Henzinger, T.A., Jhala, R., Majumdar, R.: Counterexample-guided control. In: Baeten, J.C.M., Lenstra, J.K., Parrow, J., Woeginger, G.J. (eds.) ICALP 2003. LNCS, vol. 2719, pp. 886–902. Springer, Heidelberg (2003)
12. Liu, X., Smolka, S.A.: Simple linear-time algorithms for minimal fixed points. In: Larsen, K.G., Skyum, S., Winskel, G. (eds.) ICALP 1998. LNCS, vol. 1443, pp. 53–66. Springer, Heidelberg (1998)
13. Moor, T., Davoren, J.M., Raisch, J.: Learning by doing systematic abstraction refinement for hybrid control synthesis. In: IEE Proc. Control Theory & Applications, Special issue on hybrid systems, vol. 153 (2006)
14. Perk, S., Moor, T., Schmidt, K.: Controller synthesis for an i/o-based hierarchical system architecture. In: International Workshop on Discrete Event Systems (WODES), pp. 474–479. IEEE, Los Alamitos (2008)
15. Tiwari, A., Khanna, G.: Series of abstractions for hybrid automata. In: Tomlin, C.J., Greenstreet, M.R. (eds.) HSCC 2002. LNCS, vol. 2289, pp. 465–478. Springer, Heidelberg (2002)
16. Tomlin, C., Lygeros, J., Sastry, S.: Computing controllers for nonlinear hybrid systems. In: Vaandrager, F.W., van Schuppen, J.H. (eds.) HSCC 1999. LNCS, vol. 1569, pp. 238–255. Springer, Heidelberg (1999)

Formal Analysis of Online Algorithms*

Benjamin Aminof[1], Orna Kupferman[1], and Robby Lampert[2]

[1] School of Computer Science and Engineering, Hebrew University, Jerusalem 91904, Israel
[2] Department of Computer Science, Weizmann Institute of Science, Rehovot 76100, Israel

Abstract. In [2], we showed how viewing online algorithms as reactive systems enables the application of ideas from formal verification to the competitive analysis of online algorithms. Our approach is based on weighted automata, which assign to each input word a cost in $\mathbb{R}^{\geq 0}$. By relating the "unbounded look ahead" of optimal offline algorithms with nondeterminism, and relating the "no look ahead" of online algorithms with determinism, we were able to solve problems about the competitive ratio of online algorithms and the memory they require.

In this paper we improve the application in three important and technically challenging aspects. First, we allow the competitive analysis to take into account assumptions about the environment. Second, we allow the online algorithm to have a bounded lookahead. Third, we describe a symbolic version of the model-checking algorithm and demonstrate its applicability. The first two contributions broaden the scope of our approach to settings in which the traditional analysis of online algorithms is particularly complicated. The third contribution improves the practicality of our approach and enables it to handle larger state spaces.

1 Introduction

In *formal verification*, we verify that a system has a desired property by checking whether a model of the system satisfies a formal specification of the property. An important feature of formal verification is that it enables reasoning about *reactive systems*, which maintain an on-going interaction with their environment [18].

Online algorithms for optimization problems can be viewed as reactive systems. An online algorithm processes requests in real-time: At each round, the environment issues a request, and the algorithm should process it. The sequence of requests is not known in advance, and the goal of the algorithm is to minimize the overall cost of processing all the requests in the sequence. For example, in the *paging* problem, we have a two-level memory hierarchy: A slow memory that contains n different pages, and a *cache* that contains at most k different pages (typically, $k \ll n$). Pages that are in the cache can be accessed at zero cost. If a request is made to access a page that is not in the cache, the page should be brought into the cache, at a cost of 1, and if the cache is full, some other page should first be evicted from the cache. The paging problem is, given a sequence of requested pages, to decide which page to evict whenever an eviction is needed. The goal is to minimize the total cost. Online algorithms for many problems have already been extensively studied for several decades, and have aroused much interest, both from a practical and a theoretical point of view [6].

* Supported in part by the Minerva Center at the Weizmann Institute, and by an Advanced Research Grant from the ERC under the European Community's 7th Framework Programme.

T. Bultan and P.-A. Hsiung (Eds.): ATVA 2011, LNCS 6996, pp. 213–227, 2011.

The interaction described above between an online algorithm and its environment is at the heart of formal verification. Still, the questions that are traditionally answered by formal-verification techniques are very different from those that are asked in the context of online algorithms. In formal verification, a system is checked with respect to a given specification. The specification can be qualitative (e.g., "whenever a request to a page is made, and this page is not in the cache, the page is brought into the cache") or quantitative (e.g., "what is the maximal number of page faults within a window of k rounds?") [11]. The most interesting question about an online algorithm, however, is of a different nature, and refers to its *competitive ratio*: the worst-case (with respect to all input sequences) ratio between the cost of the algorithm and the cost of an optimal solution (one that may be given by an *offline algorithm*, which knows the input sequence in advance). Thus, we can specify the model-checking problem of online algorithms as follows: Consider an optimization problem P. Given an algorithm g and a competitive ratio α, is g α-competitive with respect to an optimal offline algorithm for P?

Recently, we extended the scope of formal verification to reasoning about online algorithms [2]. The approach in [2] is based on *weighted finite automata* (WFAs, for short) [24,26]. A WFA $\mathcal{A}$ induces a partial *cost* function from Σ^* to $\mathbb{R}^{\geq 0}$. Technically, each transition of $\mathcal{A}$ has a cost associated with it. The cost of a run is the sum of the costs of the transitions taken along the run, and the cost of a word w, denoted $cost(\mathcal{A}, w)$, is the minimum cost over all accepting runs on it (the cost is undefined if no run on the word is accepting). Consider an optimization problem P with requests in Σ. An algorithm for P can be viewed as a mapping of words in Σ^+ to a set of actions available to the algorithm [5]. For a finite set S of configurations, we say that an algorithm uses memory S if there is a regular mapping of Σ^* into S such that the algorithm behaves in the same manner on identical continuations of words that are mapped to the same configuration.

The set of online algorithms for P that use memory S induces a WFA $\mathcal{A}_P$, with alphabet Σ and state space S, such that the transitions of $\mathcal{A}_P$ correspond to actions of the algorithms and the cost of each transition is the cost of the corresponding action. It is shown in [2] that many optimization problems have algorithms that use finite memory and can be modeled by weighted automata as described above. Moreover, the "unbounded look ahead" of the optimal offline algorithm corresponds to nondeterminism in $\mathcal{A}_P$, and the "no look ahead" of online algorithms corresponds to deterministic automata embedded in $\mathcal{A}_P$. Consequently, questions about the competitive ratio of online algorithms can be reduced to questions about *determinization* and *approximated determinization* of WFAs [3]. In particular, the model-checking problem for an online algorithm g can be reduced to the problem of deciding whether the pruning of $\mathcal{A}_P$ induced by g results in a deterministic automaton $\mathcal{A}_P^g$ that α-approximates $\mathcal{A}_P$ (that is, the automaton $\mathcal{A}_P^g$ accepts the same set of words as $\mathcal{A}_P$, and $cost(\mathcal{A}_P^g, w) \leq \alpha \cdot cost(\mathcal{A}_P, w)$ for all words w in this set). In addition, the synthesis problem for online algorithms can be reduced to the problem of deciding whether $\mathcal{A}_P$ contains an embedded deterministic automaton that α-approximates $\mathcal{A}_P$.

The competitive analysis of online algorithms takes into account the most hostile environment. Indeed, an online algorithm g is α-competitive if its cost with respect to every input sequences is at most α times the cost of an optimal solution. Quite often, however, the nature of the problem restricts the set of possible input sequences. Much research has been carried out in the online-algorithm community studying the competitive analysis of online algorithms under different assumptions about the environment [6]. For example, for the paging problem, Borodin et al. studied the *access graph model* [7], which takes into account the *locality of reference* principle. In the access graph model, the paging problem is equipped with a graph whose vertices are the pages, and two pages can be requested successively only if they are connected in the graph.

The first contribution of this paper is an extension of the framework in [2] to a setting in which assumptions about the environment can be taken into account. The issue of restricted environments is well studied in formal verification. Ideas like fairness [16], assume-guarantee reasoning [27], and synthesis under restricted environments [12], have been suggested in order to take assumptions about the environment into account. We study the competitive analysis of online algorithms in which assumptions about the environment are given by means of a *nondeterministic finite automaton* (NFA, for short). In this setting, the competitive ratio of an online algorithm is defined only with respect to input sequences that belong to the language of the assumption NFA. Our definition generalizes restrictions such as the one induced by the access graph — it supports all regular assumptions. In addition, it nicely combines with the automata-based approach initiated in [2]. Consider an online problem P, a set of configurations S for it, an approximation factor α, an online algorithm g that uses configurations in S, and an assumption NFA $\mathcal{U}$. We show that the problem of deciding whether g is α-competitive with respect to input sequences in $L(\mathcal{U})$ (*model checking with assumptions*) can be solved in polynomial time. On the other hand, the problem of deciding whether there is an online algorithm that uses configurations in S and is α-competitive with respect to input sequences in $L(\mathcal{U})$ (*synthesis with assumptions*) is NP-complete. We note that NP-hardness holds already for unweighted automata and $\alpha = 1$, and even when $\mathcal{U}$ is deterministic. This is in contrast to the setting with no assumptions studied in [2], in which synthesis with $\alpha = 1$ can be solved in polynomial time. Thus, interestingly, the addition of assumptions makes the problem substantially more complex.

The second contribution of this paper is an extension of the framework in [2] to a setting in which the online algorithm has a *bounded lookahead* on the requests yet to come. Since an offline algorithm can be viewed as an online algorithm with an unbounded lookahead, the setting of a bounded lookahead covers the "middle-ground" between onlineness and offlineness. However, considering online algorithms with lookahead is also interesting from a practical point of view. In practical applications, requests do not always arrive one by one, but sometimes naturally occur in bursts. Also, some applications benefit from delaying requests so that a block of requests can be served all at once, minimizing common overhead. Finally, in some applications requests are generated faster than they can be served, and thus the online algorithm has to maintain a buffer containing requests that are pending service. The challenges of manually analyzing online algorithms are even bigger in the setting of lookahead [1,8,31]. Indeed, the analysis has to take into an account the extended memory of the algorithm and the partition of the input stream to requests that are in the lookahead and those that are not. The automata-theoretic approach can be naturally extended to handle bounded lookahead in online algorithms by means of automata with a bounded lookahead. Such automata read, in each transition, a sequence of the next $l + 1$ letters, for a fixed parameter l (that is, the look ahead). We study the problems of determinization and approximated determinization of nondeterministic weighted automata with a bounded lookahead, and how questions about online algorithms can be reduced to them. Unfortunately, the analysis is exponential in the lookahead. A similar computational cost is needed in the analysis of lookahead in regular infinite games [19], and we prove that the cost indeed cannot be polynomial.

One of the main challenges in formal verification is the need to cope with very big, often infinite, state spaces. In our context, the state space often involves weights, and is thus very big. The third contribution of the paper is a description of a *symbolic algorithm* [10] for the problem of model-checking of online algorithms. In symbolic reasoning, the state space and the transitions of the system are given symbolically by characteristic functions over a set of variables that encode the state space of the system. The operations allowed to the verification algorithm correspond to manipulations of predicates over the set of variables. The fact a symbolic algorithm has to manipulate predicates over variables forces it to refer to sets of elements rather than to individual elements. The idea behind the algorithm is as follows. Consider a WFA $\mathcal{A}$. We say that a state q of $\mathcal{A}$, (α, i, t)-approximates a state q', for a competitive ratio α, an integer $i \geq 0$, and an additive factor t, if there is a deterministic automaton $\mathcal{A}^q$ with initial state q that is embedded in $\mathcal{A}$ and in which $cost(\mathcal{A}^q, w) \leq t + \alpha \cdot cost(\mathcal{A}^{q'}, w)$ for every word w of length at most i, where $\mathcal{A}^{q'}$ is $\mathcal{A}$ with initial state q'. We show that given a symbolic representation of pairs $\langle q, q' \rangle$ such that q (α, i, t)-approximates q', it is possible to generate a symbolic representation of pairs $\langle q, q' \rangle$ such that q $(\alpha, i+1, t')$-approximates q', for the minimal t' for which such an approximation exists. Note that $t' \geq t$. The symbolic algorithm then calculates a fixed-point of the above transformation. In the process, it detects cycles along which $\mathcal{A}^{q'}$ is "unboundedly better" than $\mathcal{A}^q$. The algorithm then concludes that t' should be increased to infinity. Finally, the answer to the model-checking problem is positive iff there is an initial state q such that q $(\alpha, i, 0)$-approximates q' for all the initial states q' of $\mathcal{A}$ and the iteration i in which a fixed-point was reached[1]. The symbolic implementation can handle also assumptions about the environment and algorithms with lookahead. We implemented our symbolic algorithm, and describe its application in reasoning about two online algorithms for the paging problem.

Due to the lack of space, some proofs and examples are omitted. The full version can be found in the authors' home pages.

2   Preliminaries

2.1   Weighted Automata

Standard automata map words in Σ^* to either "accept" or "reject". A weighted automaton can be viewed as a partial function (defined only for accepted words) from

---

[1] In [14], the authors use an iterative (non-symbolic) procedure that checks for α-competitive algorithms to the server problem. There, a fixed-point has been reached iff such an algorithm exists. By [2], the procedure can be terminated after two rounds of quadratically many iterations.

Σ^* to $\mathbb{R}^{\geq 0}$. Formally, a *weighted finite automaton* (WFA, for short) is a 6-tuple $\mathcal{A} = \langle \Sigma, Q, \Delta, c, Q_0, F \rangle$, where Σ is a finite input alphabet, Q is a finite set of states, $\Delta \subseteq Q \times \Sigma \times Q$ is a transition relation, $c : \Delta \to \mathbb{R}^{\geq 0}$ is a cost function, $Q_0 \subseteq Q$ is a set of initial states, and $F \subseteq Q$ is a set of final states. A transition $d = \langle q, a, p \rangle \in \Delta$ (also written as $\Delta(q, a, p)$) can be taken when $\mathcal{A}$ reads the input letter a, and it causes $\mathcal{A}$ to move from state q to state p with *cost* $c(d)$. The transition relation Δ induces a transition function $\delta : Q \times \Sigma \to 2^Q$ in the expected way. Thus, for a state $q \in Q$ and a letter $a \in \Sigma$, we have $\delta(q, a) := \{p : \Delta(q, a, p)\}$. A WFA $\mathcal{A}$ may be nondeterministic in the sense that it may have many initial states, and that for some $q \in Q$ and $a \in \Sigma$, it may have $\Delta(q, a, p_1)$ and $\Delta(q, a, p_2)$, with $p_1 \neq p_2$. If $|Q_0| = 1$ and for every state $q \in Q$ and letter $a \in \Sigma$ we have $|\delta(q, a)| \leq 1$, then $\mathcal{A}$ is a *deterministic* weighted finite automaton (DWFA, for short).

For a word $w = w_1 \ldots w_n \in \Sigma^*$, a *run* of $\mathcal{A}$ on w is a sequence $r = r_0 r_1 \ldots r_n \in Q^+$, where $r_0 \in Q_0$ and for every $1 \leq i \leq n$, we have $\langle r_{i-1}, w_i, r_i \rangle \in \Delta$. The run r is accepting if $r_n \in F$. The word w is accepted by $\mathcal{A}$ if there is an accepting run of $\mathcal{A}$ on w. The (unweighted) *language* of $\mathcal{A}$ is $L(\mathcal{A}) = \{w : w \text{ is accepted by } \mathcal{A}\}$. The cost of an accepting run is the sum of the weights of the transitions that constitute the run. Formally, let $r = r_0 r_1 \ldots r_n$ be an accepting run of $\mathcal{A}$ on w, and let $d = d_1 \ldots d_n \in \Delta^*$ be the corresponding sequence of transitions. The cost of r is $cost(\mathcal{A}, r) = \sum_{i=1}^{n} c(d_i)$. The cost of w, denoted $cost(\mathcal{A}, w)$, is the minimal cost over all accepting runs of $\mathcal{A}$ on w. Thus, $cost(\mathcal{A}, w) = \min\{cost(\mathcal{A}, r) : r \text{ is an accepting run of } \mathcal{A} \text{ on } w\}$.

For two WFAs $\mathcal{A}_1 = \langle \Sigma, Q_1, \Delta_1, c_1, Q_1^0, F_1 \rangle$ and $\mathcal{A}_2 = \langle \Sigma, Q_2, \Delta_2, c_2, Q_2^0, F_2 \rangle$, and $\alpha \geq 1$, we say that $\mathcal{A}_2$ *α-approximates* $\mathcal{A}_1$ if $L(\mathcal{A}_1) = L(\mathcal{A}_2)$ and for all words w in both languages, we have $cost(\mathcal{A}_2, w) \leq \alpha \cdot cost(\mathcal{A}_1, w)$. We say that $\mathcal{A}_2$ is *embedded* in $\mathcal{A}_1$ if $Q_2 = Q_1$, $Q_2^0 \subseteq Q_1^0$, $\Delta_2 \subseteq \Delta_1$, c_2 agrees with c_1 on Δ_2, and $F_1 = F_2$. Thus, $\mathcal{A}_2$ can be obtained from $\mathcal{A}_1$ by decreasing its nondeterminism. Finally, given an approximation factor $\alpha \geq 1$, we say that $\mathcal{A}$ is *α-determinizable by pruning* (α-DBP, for short) if $\mathcal{A}$ has an embedded DWFA that α-approximates $\mathcal{A}$.

2.2   Online Algorithms

A *problem* associates with each possible input I a set $F(I)$ of feasible solutions. In an *optimization problem* (of cost minimization), each solution in $F(I)$ has a cost in $\mathbb{R}^{\geq 0}$, and the goal is to find a feasible solution that minimizes the cost.

An *online algorithm* for an optimization problem P is an algorithm that gets as input a finite sequence of requests, and has to process each request (and end up in a feasible solution) without knowing the requests yet to come. In contrast, an *offline algorithm* for P gets the entire sequence in advance, and its decisions as to how to process a request may depend on the requests yet to come.

Formally, if we denote by Σ the set of requests, and denote by Γ the set of actions that are available to the algorithm, then an online algorithm corresponds to a function $g : \Sigma^+ \to \Gamma$. The processing of an input sequence $\sigma_1 \ldots \sigma_n$ by g is then $g(\sigma_1), g(\sigma_1 \sigma_2), g(\sigma_1 \sigma_2 \sigma_3), \ldots$. In typical optimization problems, there is a cost function $action\_cost : \Gamma \to \mathbb{R}^{\geq 0}$ that associates a cost with each action. The cost of processing an input sequence is the sum of the costs of the actions taken in order to process it. The performance of an online algorithm is typically worse than that of an offline algorithm for the same problem. For analyzing the performance of online algorithms we use *competitive analysis*, which compares the two performance values.

For an online algorithm g and an input $w \in \Sigma^+$, let $g(w)$ denote the cost of processing w by g, and let $\text{OPT}(w)$ denote the cost of processing w by the optimal offline algorithm. We say that an online algorithm g is α-*competitive* if there exists a constant β such that for all input sequences $w \in \Sigma^+$ we have that $g(w) \leq \alpha \cdot \text{OPT}(w) + \beta$. The *competitive ratio* of g is the smallest α for which g is α-competitive. In the rest of the paper we restrict attention to the multiplicative factor α and ignore the additive factor β, except for places where it is not immediately clear how to handle β.

2.3   An Automata-Theoretic Approach to Reasoning about Online Algorithms

Recall that an online algorithm corresponds to a function $g : \Sigma^+ \to \Gamma$ that maps sequences of requests (the history of the interaction so far) to an action to be taken. For a finite set S of configurations, we say that g *uses memory* S, if there is a regular mapping of Σ^* into S such that g behaves in the same manner on identical continuations of words that are mapped to the same configuration. We model the set of online algorithms that use memory S and solve an optimization problem P with requests in Σ and actions in Γ, by a WFA $\mathcal{A}_P = \langle \Sigma, S, \Delta, c, S_0, S \rangle$, where Δ and c describe transitions between configurations and their costs, and S_0 is a set of possible initial configurations. Formally, $\Delta(s, \sigma, s')$ if the set $\Gamma' \subseteq \Gamma$ of actions that process the request σ from configuration s by updating the configuration to s' is non-empty, in which case $c(\langle s, \sigma, s' \rangle) = \min_{\gamma \in \Gamma'} action\_cost(\gamma)$. Note that all the states of $\mathcal{A}_P$ are accepting. Thus, $\mathcal{A}_P$ assigns a cost to all sequences in Σ^*.

As demonstrated in [2], many optimization problems have online algorithms that require finite memory. Below we describe the modeling of the paging problem, presented in Section 1.

Example 1. [**The paging problem** [28]] A paging problem P with parameters n (number of pages) and k (size of the cache) induces a WFA $\mathcal{A}_P = \langle \Sigma, S, \Delta, c, S_0, S \rangle$, where $\Sigma = \{1, \ldots, n\}$ is the set of possible requests (page indices), $S = \{C \subseteq \{1, \ldots, n\} : |C| \leq k\}$ is a set of finite configurations, each describing the set of pages currently in the cache, Δ and c describe how (and at which cost) requests are served, and $S_0 = \{\emptyset\}$, indicating that the cache is initially empty. Thus, $\Delta(C, i, C')$ iff one of the following holds: (1) $i \in C$, in which case $C' = C$ and $c(\langle C, i, C' \rangle) = 0$, (2) $i \notin C$, $|C| < k$, and $C' = C \cup \{i\}$, in which case $c(\langle C, i, C' \rangle) = 1$, or (3) $i \notin C$, $|C| = k$, and there is $j \in C$ such that $C' = (C \setminus \{j\}) \cup \{i\}$, in which case $c(\langle C, i, C' \rangle) = 1$. Note that by the definition of S, a configuration stores only the set of pages currently in the cache, and there are no provisions for storing any extra information such as time-stamps, etc. A different automaton for the problem could have defined S in a way that allows the storage of such extra information. We will elaborate on this point in the sequel.

Note that the above modeling restricts attention to *lazy* (a.k.a. demand paging) algorithms, which minimize the change of configurations so that only the current request is served. By [25], for every non-lazy algorithm, there exists a lazy one that performs at least as well.

Let P be an optimization problem, and let $\mathcal{A}_P = \langle \Sigma, S, \Delta, c, S_0, S \rangle$ be a WFA for its algorithms that use memory S. Given a finite sequence of requests $w \in \Sigma^*$, each run of $\mathcal{A}_P$ on w corresponds to a way of serving the requests in w by an algorithm with configurations in S. The set of all runs includes all such algorithms, thus the cost of w in $\mathcal{A}_P$ is the cost of w in an optimal offline algorithm whose configurations are based on S (the configurations of the offline algorithm may also maintain the suffix of the input yet to be processed. This information, however, would be implicit in the nondeterminism of $\mathcal{A}_P$). On the other hand, an online algorithm has to process each request as soon as it arrives, without knowing the requests yet to arrive. Accordingly, an online algorithm that uses memory S corresponds to a DWFA embedded in $\mathcal{A}_P$ (note that this correspondence is lost if we consider unrestricted determinization of $\mathcal{A}_P$). Formally, given an online algorithm $g : \Sigma^+ \to \Gamma$ that uses memory S, let $h : \Sigma^* \to S$ be the regular mapping that witnesses that g uses memory S. Then, the DWFA embedded in $\mathcal{A}_P$ and induced by g is an automaton $\mathcal{A}_P^g$ in which, for all states $s \in S$ and requests $\sigma \in \Sigma$, we have $\delta(s, \sigma) = s'$, where s' is the configuration obtained by applying the action $g(w \cdot \sigma)$ from s, and w is such that $h(w) = s$. In other words, for all $w \in \Sigma^*$, we have $\delta(h(w), \sigma) = h(w \cdot \sigma)$.

Theorem 2. [2] *Given an online problem P and a set S of configurations, let $\mathcal{A}_P$ be a WFA, with state space S, that models online algorithms for P that use memory S. An online algorithm g, that uses memory S, is α-competitive iff $\mathcal{A}_P^g$ α-approximates $\mathcal{A}_P$.*

Note that the setting describes above forces the online algorithm to have the same state space as the offline one. In [2] we described how the framework can handle also online algorithms with a richer state space. The same idea can be applied to the extensions studied in the current paper.

3   Adding Assumptions on the Environment

As discussed in Section 1, an online algorithm can be viewed as a reactive system. The fact that a reactive system has to satisfy its specification with respect to all input sequences is analogous to the fact that an α-competitive online algorithm has to satisfy $g(w) \leq \alpha \cdot \mathrm{OPT}(w)$ for all input sequences $w \in \Sigma^+$. When reasoning about reactive systems, it is sometimes desirable to restrict the universal quantification over all input sequences to a subset of the possible inputs. The automata-theoretic approach naturally formalizes such assumptions in the context of online algorithms. We begin our study with unweighted automata, where things are typically simpler, and then move to weighted automata, which immediately translates to the context of online algorithms.

Given two NFAs, $\mathcal{A}$ and $\mathcal{U}$, we say that $\mathcal{A}$ is *determinizable by pruning with respect to assumptions in $\mathcal{U}$* ($\mathcal{U}$-DBP, for short), if $\mathcal{A}$ has an embedded DFA $\mathcal{A}'$ such that $L(\mathcal{A}) \cap L(\mathcal{U}) \subseteq L(\mathcal{A}')$. Thus, $\mathcal{A}$ is $\mathcal{U}$-DBP if it can be pruned to a deterministic automaton that accepts all the words in $L(\mathcal{A})$ that are also in $L(\mathcal{U})$. In this case we say that $\mathcal{A}'$ is a *witness* for $\mathcal{A}$ being $\mathcal{U}$-DBP. Similarly, for the weighted case, given a WFA $\mathcal{A}$, an NFA $\mathcal{U}$, and an approximation factor $\alpha \geq 1$, we say that $\mathcal{A}$ is α-$\mathcal{U}$-DBP if $\mathcal{A}$ has an embedded DWFA $\mathcal{A}'$ such that for all $w \in L(\mathcal{A}) \cap L(\mathcal{U})$ we have $cost(\mathcal{A}', w) \leq \alpha \cdot cost(\mathcal{A}, w)$. Intuitively, the NFA $\mathcal{U}$ specifies assumptions about the environment. In particular, usual determinization by pruning is a special case of the above, with $L(\mathcal{U}) = \Sigma^*$.

The *relaxed-α-DBP* problem is to decide, given a WFA $\mathcal{A}$, an approximation factor $\alpha \geq 1$, and an NFA $\mathcal{U}$, whether $\mathcal{A}$ is α-$\mathcal{U}$-DBP. The *relaxed-α-DBP witness-checking* problem is to decide, given a WFA $\mathcal{A}$, an NFA $\mathcal{U}$, $\alpha \geq 1$, and a DFA (DWFA) $\mathcal{A}'$ embedded in $\mathcal{A}$, whether $\mathcal{A}'$ is a witness for $\mathcal{A}$ being α-$\mathcal{U}$-DBP. When $\mathcal{A}$ and $\mathcal{A}'$ are NFAs (that is, unweighted), no approximation factor is given and we refer to the problems as the *relaxed-DBP* and the *relaxed-DBP witness-checking* problems.

The relaxed-α-DBP problem corresponds to the synthesis problem, whereas the witness-checking problem corresponds to model checking. In the setting with no assumptions about the environment, it was shown in [2] that the DBP-problem is polynomial for the unweighted case or for the weighted case with $\alpha = 1$, and is NP-complete for the weighted case with $\alpha > 1$. As the following theorem shows, adding assumptions makes the relaxed-DBP problem NP-complete already for the unweighted case, and thus significantly harder. On the positive side, adding assumptions does not make the problem harder in the weighted case with $\alpha > 1$, where it stays NP-complete, as in the setting with no assumptions.

Theorem 3. [Relaxed-DBP]

1. *The relaxed-DBP (relaxed-α-DBP) witness-checking problem is NLOGSPACE-complete (in* PTIME, *respectively).*
2. *The relaxed-DBP and the relaxed-α-DBP problems are NP-complete.*

Proof: For the witness-checking problem, the proof is based on reasoning about the product of $\mathcal{A}$ and $\mathcal{U}$, and can be found in the full version. For the relaxed-DBP and the relaxed-α-DBP problems, note that the problems are in NP since given $\mathcal{A}$ and $\mathcal{U}$, we can guess a DFA $\mathcal{A}'$ embedded in $\mathcal{A}$ and check whether it is a witness. By the above, this can be done in polynomial time.

In order to show that the problems are NP-hard, we describe a reduction from 3SAT to the relaxed-DBP problem. Let θ be a 3CNF formula with m clauses, $c_1, \ldots, c_m$, over the variables $x_1, \ldots, x_n$. We construct an NFA $\mathcal{A}^\theta$ and a DFA $\mathcal{U}^\theta$ over the alphabet $\{\#, 1, ..., m\}$, such that $\mathcal{A}^\theta$ is $\mathcal{U}^\theta$-DBP iff θ is satisfiable.

The NFA $\mathcal{A}^\theta$ has the form of a DAG with four levels. On the first level of the DAG there is a single initial state q_0. On the second level there are n states, $x_1, \ldots, x_n$, corresponding to the variables in θ. For each state x_i, there are m transitions, labeled $1, \ldots, m$ from q_0 to x_i. On the third level there are $2n$ states, $1_{true}, 1_{false}, \ldots, n_{true}, n_{false}$, corresponding to possible truth assignments to the variables. For every $1 \leq i \leq n$, there are transitions, labeled $\#$, from x_i to i_{true} and i_{false}. On the fourth level there is a single accepting state q_{acc}. For every $1 \leq i \leq n$, value $val \in \{true, false\}$, and letter $1 \leq j \leq m$, there is a transition labeled j from i_{val} to q_{acc} iff assigning val to variable i satisfies the clause c_j. For example, if the literal $\neg x_5$ appears in clause c_2, then there is a transition labeled 2 from the state 5_{false} to q_{acc}. It is easy to see that the language of $\mathcal{A}^\theta$ is $\{j\#k : 1 \leq j \leq m, 1 \leq k \leq m\}$. The DFA $\mathcal{U}^\theta$ is such that $L(\mathcal{U}^\theta) = \{j\#j : 1 \leq j \leq m\}$. It is easy to define $\mathcal{U}^\theta$ with $m + 2$ states. In the full version we prove that θ is satisfiable iff $\mathcal{A}^\theta$ is $\mathcal{U}^\theta$-DBP.   □

By Theorem 2, the application of our results to online algorithms is as follows.

Corollary 1. *Consider an optimization problem P with a set S of configurations, an approximation factor $\alpha \geq 1$, and an NFA $\mathcal{U}$.*

- **[model checking]** *Given an online algorithm g for P that uses configurations in S, deciding whether g is α-competitive with respect to environments restricted to input sequences in $L(\mathcal{U})$ can be solved in time polynomial in S and $\mathcal{U}$.*
- **[synthesis]** *Deciding whether there is an α-competitive online algorithm for P that uses configurations in S, with respect to environments restricted to input sequences in $L(\mathcal{U})$, is NP-complete.*

4   Reasoning about Online Algorithms with Look-Ahead

In this section we describe a framework for reasoning about online algorithms that have a *bounded lookahead* on the requests yet to come. We consider the case where the online algorithm can see not only the next request, but rather the next $l + 1$ requests for some constant $l \geq 0$. For several classes of optimization problems, like dynamic location and online graph problems, it was shown that online algorithms with a lookahead above a certain minimal length can achieve better competitive ratios than algorithms with a shorter (or no) lookahead [15,21]. To the best of our knowledge, there are also problems, like online bipartite matching [22], for which it is not fully known how beneficial a lookahead can be.

An *online algorithm with lookahead l* for an optimization problem P is an algorithm that at each point $i > 0$ in time, reads the next $l + 1$ requests $r_i, \ldots, r_{i+l}$ that need to be processed, and serves the request r_i. The requests $r_{i+1}, \ldots, r_{i+l}$ (i.e., the *lookahead*) are *not* served at time i, but rather when their respective times come. The use of the lookahead at time i is only to guide the algorithm in serving the request r_i. [2] Formally, given a set Σ of requests, and a set Γ of actions, let $\bot$ be a new symbol designating the end of the input. A word $x = x_1 \cdots x_n \in (\Sigma \cup \{\bot\})^+$ is *legal* if for all $1 \leq j < n$, if $x_j = \bot$ then $x_{j+1} = \bot$. For $n > 0$, we denote by $\Sigma_\bot^n = \{x \in (\Sigma \cup \{\bot\})^n : x$ is legal$\}$ the set of all legal lookahead words of length n, and by $\Sigma_\bot^+$ the set $\bigcup_{n>0} \Sigma_\bot^n$ of all legal words in $(\Sigma \cup \{\bot\})^+$. An online algorithm with lookahead l corresponds to a function $g : \Sigma^+ \times \Sigma_\bot^l \to \Gamma$. The processing of a sequence of requests $\sigma_1 \cdots \sigma_n \in \Sigma^n$ by g is then $g(\sigma_1, \sigma_2 \cdots \sigma_{l+1}), g(\sigma_1\sigma_2, \sigma_3 \ldots \sigma_{l+2}), \ldots, g(\sigma_1 \ldots \sigma_n, \sigma_{n+1} \ldots \sigma_{n+l})$, where $\sigma_i = \bot$ for every $i > n$. Note that at time $i > 0$ the lookahead is $\sigma_{i+1} \cdots \sigma_{i+l}$, and it contains the end-of-input symbol for every position after the last request σ_n. Similar to the case with no lookahead, we say that an online algorithm with lookahead of length l uses a finite memory S, if there is a regular mapping of $\Sigma^* \times \Sigma_\bot^l$ to S such that g behaves in the same manner on identical continuations of words that are mapped to the same configuration. The definitions of the cost of processing a sequence of requests, as well as the definitions of α-competitiveness and the competitive ratio of g, are carried over from the definitions given in Section 2 for online algorithms with no lookahead.

---

[2] Note that while this is perhaps the most natural kind of lookahead, other types of lookahead have also been considered in the literature. However, these (for example, the "strong lookahead" of [1] for paging) are usually specifically tailored for a specific class of optimization problems.

In order to handle algorithms with lookahead, we construct (instead of the automaton $\mathcal{A}_P$ of Section 2.3) an automaton $\mathcal{A}_{P,l}$ such that every online algorithm for P that uses memory S and lookahead of length l is embedded in $\mathcal{A}_{P,l}$. The construction of $\mathcal{A}_{P,l}$ is very similar to that of $\mathcal{A}_P$, the main difference being that now the alphabet of $\mathcal{A}_{P,l}$ is $\Sigma \times \Sigma_\perp^l$, to match the way requests are presented to an online algorithm with a lookahead of length l. Observe that not all sequences of letters in $\Sigma \times \Sigma_\perp^l$ need be considered. Indeed, if $(\sigma, y), (\sigma', y') \in \Sigma \times \Sigma_\perp^l$ are two consecutive blocks of requests presented to the online algorithm, then it must be that $y = \sigma' \cdot y_1' \cdots y_{l-1}'$, i.e., that the lookahead y indeed matches the following l requests. In order to make sure that irrelevant sequences have no influence, $\mathcal{A}_{P,l}$ does not accept such sequences (in fact, it simply crashes when reading such a sequence). To this end, $\mathcal{A}_{P,l}$ has to remember the lookahead in every input letter that it reads.

Formally, $\mathcal{A}_{P,l} = \langle \Sigma \times \Sigma_\perp^l, S_0 \cup (S \times \Sigma_\perp^l), \Delta, c, S_0, S \times \{\perp^l\}\rangle$, where $S_0 \subseteq S$ is the subset of initial configurations of S; For a source state u of the form $u = s \in S_0$ or $u = (s, x) \in S \times \Sigma_\perp^l$, an input $(\sigma, y) \in \Sigma \times \Sigma_\perp^l$, and a destination state $(s', x') \in S \times \Sigma_\perp^l$, we have that $\langle u, (\sigma, y), (s', x')\rangle \in \Delta$ iff *(i)* $y = x'$, and if u is of the form $u = (s, x)$ then $x_1 = \sigma$ and $x_2 \cdots x_l \cdot x_l' = y$, *(ii)* the set $\Gamma' \subseteq \Gamma$ of actions that process the request σ from configuration s, by updating the configuration to s', is non-empty; the cost of such a transition is $c(\langle u, (\sigma, y), (s', x')\rangle) = \min_{\gamma \in \Gamma'} action\_cost(\gamma)$; Note that the accepting states are all configurations that are coupled with a lookahead of $\perp^l$, which indicates that the input sequence has ended.

Let P be an optimization problem, and let $\mathcal{A}_{P,l}$ be a WFA for its algorithms that use memory S and lookahead of length l. Observe that, like $\mathcal{A}_P$, the automaton $\mathcal{A}_{P,l}$ represents the optimal offline algorithm for P in the sense that given a finite sequence of requests $w \in \Sigma^*$, the cost of w in $\mathcal{A}_P$ is the cost of w in an optimal offline algorithm whose configurations are in S. On the other hand, it is not hard to see that an online algorithm with lookahead of length l, that uses memory S, corresponds to a DWFA embedded in $\mathcal{A}_{P,l}$. Formally, given such an online algorithm $g : \Sigma^+ \times \Sigma_\perp^l \to \Gamma$, the DWFA embedded in $\mathcal{A}_{P,l}$ and induced by g is an automaton $\mathcal{A}_{P,l}^g$ in which, for every configuration $s \in S$, and every request (with lookahead) $(\sigma, y) \in \Sigma \times \Sigma_\perp^l$, we have that $\delta(s, (\sigma, y)) = (s', y)$ for every initial configuration $s \in S_0$, and $\delta(\langle(s, \sigma \cdot y_1 \cdots y_{l-1}), (\sigma, y)\rangle) = (s', y)$ for all $s \in S$; where s' is the configuration obtained by applying the action $g(w \cdot \sigma, y)$ from s, and w is such that $h(w, \sigma \cdot y_1 \cdots y_{l-1}) = s$.

Theorem 4. *Given an optimization problem P, a set S of configurations, and $l \geq 0$. Let $\mathcal{A}_{P,l}$ be a WFA that models online algorithms for P that use memory S and lookahead of length l. An online algorithm g that uses memory S and lookahead of length l is α-competitive iff $\mathcal{A}_{P,l}^g$ α-approximates $\mathcal{A}_{P,l}$.*

By [2], given $\mathcal{A}_{P,l}$, deciding if it has an embedded DWFA that α-approximates it (and also obtaining such DWFAs) can be done in time polynomial in the size of $\mathcal{A}_{P,l}$ if $\alpha = 1$, and is NP-complete for $\alpha > 1$; whereas given $\mathcal{A}_{P,l}^g$, deciding if it α-approximates $\mathcal{A}_{P,l}$ can be done in polynomial time for all values of α. Thus, Theorem 4 implies the following:

Corollary 2. *Consider an optimization problem P with a set S of configurations, an approximation factor $\alpha \geq 1$, and some $l \geq 0$.*

- [**model checking**] *Given an online algorithm g for P that uses configurations in S and lookahead of size l, deciding whether g is α-competitive can be solved in time polynomial in S and exponential in l.*
- [**synthesis**] *Deciding whether there is an α-competitive online algorithm for P that uses memory S and lookahead of length l, can be done in polynomial deterministic (nondeterministic) time in S for α = 1 (α > 1, respectively) and time exponential in l.*

Note that the model-checking and synthesis algorithms that we get are exponential in l. While we do not prove a matching lower bound, we were able to prove co-NP-hardness in l (by a reduction from the problem of deciding whether an NFW accepts all words of length l or less). Also, earlier work on lookahead in ω-regular games suggests that an exponential cost in the lookahead cannot be avoided [19].

5   Symbolic Model-Checking Algorithm

In this section we describe a symbolic model-checking algorithm for online algorithms. The explicit algorithm of [2] gets as input a WFA $\mathcal{A}_1 = \langle \Sigma, Q_1, \Delta_1, c_1, S_1, F_1 \rangle$, a DWFA $\mathcal{A}_2 = \langle \Sigma, Q_2, \Delta_2, c_2, s_2, F_2 \rangle$ embedded in $\mathcal{A}_1$, and an approximation factor α, and decides in polynomial time whether $\mathcal{A}_2$ α-approximates $\mathcal{A}_1$.

Let $m = |Q_1| = |Q_2|$. The algorithm is based on iteratively calculating functions $f_i : Q_1 \times Q_2 \to \mathbb{Z} \cup \{-\infty, \infty\}$. The dependency in m is reflected both in the size of the required data structure, and the number of iterations that the algorithm performs. A symbolic algorithm cannot avoid the time complexity that the iterative calculation involves, but it copes with the space complexity by working with a symbolic representation of all the components of the automata and of the functions f_i.

The data structures we work with are *Binary Decision Diagrams* (BDDs, for short) [9] and *multi-valued* BDDs (MVBDDs, for short). While a BDD represents a Boolean function, MVBDDs assign to each truth assignment of the variables a value in $\mathbb{Z} \cup \{-\infty, \infty\}$. We implement an MVBDD by an array of BDDs, each encoding a single bit of the value. Using b BDDs, the value of the MVBDD is then a b-bit signed two's complement integer. It has a minimum value of -2^{b-1} and a maximum value of $2^{b-1}-1$ (inclusive). In addition, we maintain two BDDs, for $-\infty$ and ∞.

We now move to a detailed description of the symbolic model-checking algorithm (Figure 1). In addition to α, the algorithm gets as input a symbolic representation of $\mathcal{A}_1$ and $\mathcal{A}_2$. The sets of variables X and W are used in order to encode Q_1 and Σ, respectively. Accordingly, the transition function Δ_1 is described by an MVBDD $trans_1 : X \times W \times X' \to \mathbb{N} \cup \infty$, where X' is a tagged copy of X. Formally, $trans_1(\langle q_1, a, q_1' \rangle)$ is $c(\langle q_1, a, q_1' \rangle)$ for $\langle q_1, a, q_1' \rangle \in \Delta_1$, and is ∞ otherwise. Note that the domain of $trans_1$ are truth assignments to the variables in X, W, and X', and not tuples in $Q_1 \times \Sigma \times Q_1$; since, however, the variables encode such triples, we abuse notation and refer to $trans_1(\langle q_1, a, q_1' \rangle)$. Note that we use weights in $\mathbb{N}$ rather than in $\mathbb{R}^{\geq 0}$. The sets S_1 and F_1 are described by the BDDs $init_1$ and fin_1 over X, respectively. The WFA $\mathcal{A}_2$ is described in a similar manner, with variables in Y and W. Let $V = X \cup X' \cup W \cup Y \cup Y'$. For convenience, we refer to all BDDs as functions from V (even though the function they maintain may be independent of some of the variables).

The algorithm uses the following operators.

- The functions **not** : $BDD \rightarrow BDD$ and **and** : $BDD \times BDD \rightarrow BDD$ operate as the corresponding logical operators of negation and conjunction, respectively.
- The operator **set_value** gets an MVBDD f, a BDD *cond*, and a value *val*, and sets the value of f to *val* for the inputs characterized by *cond*.
- The operator **prime** gets an MVBDD f whose function is independent of X' and Y' and turns it into an MVBDD that corresponds to the function obtained from f by replacing the variables in X and Y by their tagged copies in X' and Y'.
- The functions **add, sub, max** : $\text{MVBDD} \times \text{MVBDD} \rightarrow \text{MVBDD}$ return the MVBDD obtained by applying addition, subtraction, and maximum, respectively, on the given MVBDDs.
- The function **get_BDD** : $\text{MVBDD} \rightarrow BDD$ returns a BDD whose value is 1 exactly on the inputs on which the value of the given MVBDD is not ∞. In particular, **get_BDD**(*trans*) returns a BDD representing the (un-weighted) transitions.
- The function **less_than** : $\text{MVBDD} \times \text{MVBDD} \rightarrow BDD$ gets two MVBDDs, f and g, and returns a BDD h such that for all $v \in 2^V$, we have $h(v) = 1$ iff $f(v) \leq g(v)$.
- The function **var_max** : $2^V \times \text{MVBDD} \rightarrow \text{MVBDD}$ gets a set U of variables and an MVBDD g and returns an MVBDD f such that for all $v \in 2^V$, we have $f(v) = \max\{g(v') : v' \text{ agrees with } v \text{ on the variables not in } U\}$. Note that $f(v)$ is independent of the variables in U. The function **cond_max** : $2^V \times \text{BDD} \times \text{MVBDD} \rightarrow \text{MVBDD}$ is similar, but gets in addition a BDD s, and the maximum of the MVBDD g is taken only over v''s that agree with v on the variables not in U and satisfy $s(v') = 1$. If no such v' exists, then $f(v) = -\infty$.

The algorithm calculates functions $f_i : X \times Y \rightarrow \mathbb{Z} \cup \{-\infty, \infty\}$, for $0 \leq i \leq 2m^2$. The function f_i indicates the competitiveness of $\mathcal{A}_2$ with respect to words of length at most i. Formally, for every two states $q_1 \in Q_1$ and $q_2 \in Q_2$, the value $f_i(q_1, q_2)$, for $0 \leq i \leq m^2$, equals $-\infty$ if no word of length at most i is accepted from q_1, it equals ∞ if there exists a word of length at most i that is accepted from q_1 but not from q_2, and it equals $t \in \mathbb{Z}$ if t is the maximal value such that there exists a word of size at most i that is accepted from q_1 at a cost of c, and from q_2 at a cost of $\alpha \cdot c + t$. For $m^2 \leq i \leq 2m^2$, the algorithm takes into account cycles along which the performance of $\mathcal{A}_1$ is "unboundedly better" than that of $\mathcal{A}_2$, in which case the value of $f_i(q_1, q_2)$ is increased to ∞. As proved in [2], such cycles would be detected after at most m^2 iterations, and their influence on the ability of $\mathcal{A}_2$ to α-approximate $\mathcal{A}_1$ would be detected after another round of m^2 iterations. Thus, the algorithm needs not compute f_i for $i > 2m^2$.

The algorithm first defines f_0 so that $f_0(q_1, q_2)$ is $-\infty$ if $q_1 \notin F_1$, is 0 if $q_1 \in F_1$ and $q_2 \in F_2$, and is ∞ if $q_1 \in F_1$ and $q_2 \notin F_2$. Each loop iteration gets f_{i-1} and calculates f_i. For that, the algorithm calculates an MVBDD g. After executing Line 8, we have $g(\langle q_1, q_1', a, q_2, q_2' \rangle) = f_{i-1}(q_1', q_2') + c_2(q_2, a, q_2') - \alpha \cdot c_1(q_1, a, q_1')$. Thus, after Line 14, we have $f_i(q_1, q_2) = \max\{f_{i-1}(q_1, q_2), \max_{a \in \Sigma} f_a(q_1, q_2)\}$, where $f_a(q_1, q_2) = \max_{q_1' \in \delta_1(q_1, a)}[f_{i-1}(q_1', \delta_2(q_2, a)) + c_2(q_2, a, \delta_2(q_2, a)) - \alpha \cdot c_1(q_1, a, q_1')]$. If $i \geq m^2$ and $f_i(q_1, q_2) \geq f_{i-1}(q_1, q_2)$, then $f_i(q_1, q_2)$ is further increased, in Line 17, to ∞.

Finally, note that the fact we only care about embedded DWFA (only DWFA correspond to deterministic online algorithms) is crucial for the correctness of the algorithm.

Symbolic model-checking $(init_1, trans_1, fin_1, init_2, trans_2, fin_2, \alpha)$

1: $\mathbf{set\_value}(f_0, \mathbf{not}(fin_1), -\infty)$;
2: $\mathbf{set\_value}(f_0, \mathbf{and}(fin_1, fin_2), 0)$;
3: $\mathbf{set\_value}(f_0, \mathbf{and}(fin_1, \mathbf{not}(fin_2)), \infty)$;
4: $i := 0$;
5: **repeat**
6:    $i++$;
7:    $\mathbf{prime}(f_{i-1})$;
8:    **MVBDD** $g := \mathbf{sub}(\mathbf{add}(f_{i-1}, trans_2), \alpha \cdot trans_1)$;
9:    **BDD** $t_1 := \mathbf{get\_BDD}(trans_1)$;
10:   **BDD** $t_2 := \mathbf{get\_BDD}(trans_2)$;
11:   **BDD** $match\_trans := \mathbf{and}(t_1, t_2)$;
12:   **MVBDD** $f_a := \mathbf{cond\_max}(D, match\_trans, g)$;
13:   **MVBDD** $h := \mathbf{var\_max}(W, f_a)$;
14:   $f_i := \mathbf{max}\{f_{i-1}, h\}$;
15:   **if** $i \geq m^2$ **then**
16:      **BDD** $diff := \mathbf{less\_than}(f_{i-1}, h)$;
17:      $\mathbf{set\_value}(f_i, diff, \infty)$;
18:   **end if**
19: **until** $(f_i == f_{i-1})$ **or** $(i == 2m^2)$;
20: **BDD** $init\_states := \mathbf{and}(init_1, init_2)$;
21: **MVBDD** $approx := \mathbf{var\_max}(X \cup Y, init\_states, f_i)$;
22: **if** $(approx < \infty)$ **return true; else return false;**

Fig. 1. The symbolic model-checking algorithm

Indeed, the calculation of $f_a(q_1, q_2)$ makes use of the fact that in a DWFA, the state q_1 has only a single a-successor.

When implementing the symbolic algorithm, we have tried to minimize the maximal number of variables for a single MVBDD, but (as is the case with other symbolic algorithms that relate two systems) we could not avoid the construction of the MVBDD g that depends on all the variables in V.

We note here that the implementation of the symbolic algorithm is applicable also for the results appearing in the previous sections. The algorithm given in Section 3 for deciding whether a given online algorithm is α-competitive with respect to a given restriction on the environment actually uses the algorithm described above as a sub-routine. Before running the algorithm it should only compute a product of two automata. This can be easily implemented symbolically. As for the algorithm given in Section 4 for reasoning about online algorithms with lookahead, it simply uses the algorithm described above as a black-box.

Experimental Results. Before describing our experimental results, we would like to stress that the main contribution of the paper is the ideas behind the algorithm – our implementation is not a suggestion for a ready-to-run tool, but rather a justification for the argument that our algorithm can actually be implemented symbolically. It is very likely that researchers with more experience in implementations could have come up with a much better implementation. We still find it encouraging that even our naive implementation has led us to interesting and practical insights, as described below.

The most natural modeling of paging is by a WFA whose set of states corresponds to the configurations of the cache. Such a modeling corresponds to non-marking algorithms, as it does not allow the algorithm to use information beyond the set of pages that are currently in the cache. In the course of applying our implementation of the symbolic algorithm to paging, we have realized that the only non-marking competitive algorithm for paging we are aware of, Flush-when-Full (FWF) [6,23], is not lazy (also referred to as "demand paging" in [6]); that is, it may evict from the cache more than a single page in case an eviction is required. From a practical standpoint, such evictions are wasteful, and a reasonable implementation of FWF would keep the cache full at all times and only mark the pages spuriously evicted by FWF – thus treating FWF as a marking algorithm. This has led us to the development of an online algorithm that is both lazy and non-marking. Unfortunately for us, we later discovered that this algorithm already appears as ROTATE in [13], where it is proved to be k-competitive, by means of amortized analysis. The descriptions of both FWF and ROTATE can be found in the full version.

We have studied the k-competitiveness of ROTATE and FWF using an implementation of the symbolic algorithm written in Java, using JavaBDD [30] as a high level object oriented layer, on top of the BDD library CUDD [29]. As our test platform, we used a Pentium 4, 3.2Ghz Linux Machine with 4GB of RAM. Due to the limitations of the 32bit Java Virtual Machine we used, our program was limited to using at most 2GB of memory. A table with our experimental results can be found in the full version. The experimental results achieved with our naive implementation are not impressive, but we find them encouraging. First, they prove that formal reasoning about competitive ratios of online algorithms is feasible, both in theory and practice. Second, even though the instances we considered were very small, they have led us to rediscover the algorithm ROTATE, showing that a lot of insight can be gained even when working with small instances. Third, we discovered that while in the worst case the symbolic algorithm may run for $2m^2$ iterations, in practice it converges many orders of magnitude faster. For example, while some of our experiments have a value of $2m^2$ above 2^{50}, in all cases the algorithm converged to termination in at most 6 iterations! In fact, the main bottleneck seems to be the memory requirements of our BDD based implementation, and the associated time required to handle very big BDDs. It is our belief that representing MVBDDS not by arrays of BDDs, but rather by utilizing more efficient constructs such as *Multi Terminal BDDs (MTBDDs)* [17], or *Algebraic Decision Diagrams (ADDs)* [4], would enable much larger instances to be handled.

Acknowledgment. We thank Marek Chrobak for helpful discussions.

References

1. Albers, S.: On the influence of lookahead in competitive paging algorithms. Algorithmica 18, 283–305 (1997)
2. Aminof, B., Kupferman, O., Lampert, R.: Reasoning about online algorithms with weighted automata. ACM Transactions on Algorithms 6(2) (2010)
3. Aminof, B., Kupferman, O., Lampert, R.: Rigorous Approximated Determinization of Weighted Automata. In: Proc. 26th LICS, pp. 345–354 (2011)
4. Bahar, R.I., Frohm, E.A., Gaona, C.M., Hachtel, G.D., Macii, E., Pardo, A., Somenzi, F.: Algebraic decision diagrams and their applications. FMSD 10(2-3), 171–206 (1997)

5. Ben-David, S., Borodin, A., Karp, R.M., Tardos, G., Wigderson, A.: On the power of randomization in on-line algorithms. Algorithmica 11(2), 2–14 (1994)
6. Borodin, A., El-Yaniv, R.: Online Computation and Competitive Analysis. Cambridge Univ. Press, Cambridge (1998)
7. Borodin, A., Irani, S., Raghavan, P., Schieber, B.: Competitive Paging with Locality of Reference. J. Comput. Syst. Sci. 50(2), 244–258 (1995)
8. Breslauer, D.: On competitive on-line paging with lookahead. TCS 209(1-2), 365–375 (1998)
9. Bryant, R.E.: Graph-based algorithms for Boolean-function manipulation. IEEE Transactions on Computing C-35(8), 677–691 (1986)
10. Burch, J.R., Clarke, E.M., McMillan, K.L., Dill, D.L., Hwang, L.J.: Symbolic model checking: 10^{20} states and beyond. Information and Computation 98(2), 142–170 (1992)
11. Chakrabarti, A., Chatterjee, K., Henzinger, T.A., Kupferman, O., Majumdar, R.: Verifying quantitative properties using bound functions. In: Borrione, D., Paul, W. (eds.) CHARME 2005. LNCS, vol. 3725, pp. 50–64. Springer, Heidelberg (2005)
12. Chatterjee, K., Henzinger, T., Jobstmann, B.: Environment assumptions for synthesis. In: van Breugel, F., Chechik, M. (eds.) CONCUR 2008. LNCS, vol. 5201, pp. 147–161. Springer, Heidelberg (2008)
13. Chrobak, M., Karloff, H.J., Payne, T.H., Vishwanathan, S.: New Results on Server Problems. SIAM J. Discrete Math. 4(2), 172–181 (1991)
14. Chrobak, M., Larmore, L.L.: The server problem and on-line games. In: On-line Algorithms. DIMACS Series DMTCS, vol. 7, pp. 11–64 (1992)
15. Chung, F.R.K., Graham, R.L., Saks, M.E.: A dynamic location problem for graphs. Combinatorica 9(2), 111–131 (1989)
16. Francez, N.: Fairness. Texts and Monographs in Computer Science. Springer, Heidelberg (1986)
17. Fujita, M., McGeer, P.C., Yang, J.C.-Y.: Multi-Terminal Binary Decision Diagrams: An Efficient Data Structure for Matrix Representation. FMSD 10(2-3), 149–169 (1997)
18. Harel, D., Pnueli, A.: On the development of reactive systems. In: Logics and Models of Concurrent Systems. NATO ASI, vol. F-13, pp. 477–498 (1985)
19. Holtmann, M., Kaiser, Ł., Thomas, W.: Degrees of lookahead in regular infinite games. In: Ong, L. (ed.) FOSSACS 2010. LNCS, vol. 6014, pp. 252–266. Springer, Heidelberg (2010)
20. Immerman, N.: Nondeterministic space is closed under complement. I&C 17, 935–938 (1988)
21. Irani, S.: Coloring inductive graphs on-line. Algorithmica 11(1), 53–72 (1994)
22. Kao, M.-Y., Tate, S.R.: Online matching with blocked input. Inf. Process. Lett. 38(3), 113–116 (1991)
23. Karlin, A.R., Manasse, M.S., Rudolph, L., Sleator, D.D.: Competitive snoopy caching. Algorithmica 3(1), 79–119 (1988)
24. Kuich, W., Salomaa, A.: Semirings, Automata, Languages. Springer, Heidelberg (1986)
25. Manasse, M.S., McGeoch, L.A., Sleator, D.D.: Competitive algorithms for server problems. J. Algorithms 11(2), 208–230 (1990)
26. Mohri, M.: Finite-state transducers in language and speech processing. Computational Linguistics 23(2), 269–311 (1997)
27. Pnueli, A.: In transition from global to modular temporal reasoning about programs. In: Logics and Models of Concurrent Systems. NATO ASI, vol. F-13, pp. 123–144 (1985)
28. Sleator, D.D., Tarjan, R.E.: Amortized efficiency of list update and paging rules. Communications of the ACM 28(2), 202–208 (1985)
29. Somenzi, F.: CUDD package, 2.4.1., http://vlsi.colorado.edu/~fabio/CUDD/
30. Whaley, J.: JavaBDD package, 1.0b2., http://javabdd.sourceforge.net/
31. Young, N.: On-line caching as cache size varies. In: Proc. 2nd SODA, pp. 241–250 (1991)

Modal Transition Systems: Composition and LTL Model Checking

Nikola Beneš[1,*], Ivana Černá[1,**], and Jan Křetínský[1,2,***]

[1] Faculty of Informatics, Masaryk University, Brno, Czech Republic
[2] Institut für Informatik, Technische Universität München, Germany
{xbenes3, cerna, jan.kretinsky}@fi.muni.cz

Abstract. Modal transition systems (MTS) is a well established formalism used for specification and for abstract interpretation. We consider its disjunctive extension (DMTS) and we provide algorithms showing that refinement problems for DMTS are not harder than in the case of MTS. There are two main results in the paper. Firstly, we identify an error in a previous attempt at LTL model checking of MTS and provide algorithms for LTL model checking of MTS and DMTS. Moreover, we show how to apply this result to compositional verification and circumvent the general incompleteness of the MTS composition. Secondly, we give a solution to the common implementation and conjunctive composition problems lowering the complexity from EXPTIME to PTIME.

1 Introduction

Specification and verification of programs is a fundamental part of theoretical computer science and is nowadays regarded indispensable when designing and implementing safety critical systems. Therefore, many specification formalisms and verification methods have been introduced. There are two main approaches to this issue. The *behavioural* approach exploits various equivalence or refinement checking methods, provided the specifications are given in the same formalism as implementations. The *logical* approach makes use of specifications given as formulae of temporal or modal logics and relies on efficient model checking algorithms. In this paper, we combine these two methods.

The specifications are rarely complete, either due to incapability of capturing all the required behaviour in the early design phase, or due to leaving a bunch of possibilities for the implementations, such as in e.g. product lines [1]. One thus begins the design process with an underspecified system where some behaviour is already prescribed and some may or may not be present. The specification is

---

* The author has been supported by Czech Grant Agency, grant no. GD102/09/H042.
** The author has been supported by Czech Grant Agency, grant no. GAP202/11/0312.
*** The author is a holder of Brno PhD Talent Financial Aid and is supported by the Czech Science Foundation, grant No. P202/10/1469.

T. Bultan and P.-A. Hsiung (Eds.): ATVA 2011, LNCS 6996, pp. 228–242, 2011.

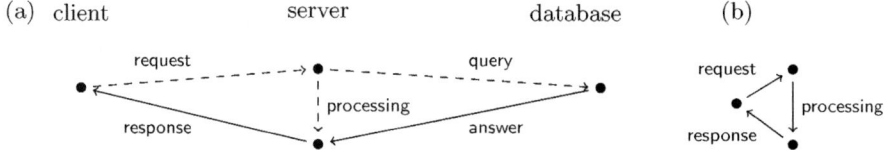

Fig. 1. An example of (a) a modal transition system (b) its implementation

then successively refined until a real implementation is obtained, where all the behaviour is completely determined. Of course, we require that our formalism allow for this *stepwise refinement*.

Furthermore, since supporting the *component based design* is becoming crucial, we need to allow also for the compositional verification. To illustrate this, let us consider a partial specification of a component that we design, and a third party component that comes with some guarantees, such as a formula of a temporal logic describing the most important behaviour. Based on these underspecified models of the systems we would like to prove that their interaction is correct, no matter what the hidden details of the particular third party component are. Also, we want to know if there is a way to implement our component specification so that the composition fulfills the requirements. Moreover, we would like to synthesize the respective implementation. We address all these problems.

Modal transition systems (MTS) is a specification formalism introduced by Larsen and Thomsen [2,3] allowing for stepwise refinement design of systems and their composition. A considerable attention has been recently paid to MTS due to many applications, e.g. component-based software development [4,5], interface theories [6,7], or modal abstractions and program analysis [8,9,10], to name just a few.

The MTS formalism is based on transparent and simple to understand model of *labelled transition systems* (LTS). While LTS has only one labelled transition relation between the states determining the behaviour of the system, MTS as a specification formalism is equipped with two types of transitions: the *must* transitions capture the required behaviour, which is present in all its implementations; the *may* transitions capture the allowed behaviour, which need not be present in all implementations. Figure 1 depicts an MTS that has arisen as a composition of three systems and specifies the following. A request from a client may arrive. Then we can process it directly or make a query to a database where we are guaranteed an answer. In both cases we send a response.

Such a system can be refined in two ways: a may transition is either implemented (and becomes a must transition) or omitted (and disappears as a transition). On the right there is an implementation of the system where the processing branch is implemented and the database query branch is omitted. Note that an implementation with both branches realized is also possible. This may model e.g. behaviour dependent on user input. Moreover, implementations may even be non-deterministic, thus allowing for modelling e.g. unspecified environment.

On the one hand, specifying may transitions brings guarantees on safety. On the other hand, liveness can be guaranteed to some extent using must transitions. Nevertheless, at an early stage of design we may not know which of several possible different ways to implement a particular functionality will later be chosen, although we know at least one of them has to be present. We want to specify e.g. that either **processing** or **query** will be implemented, otherwise we have no guarantee on receiving **response** eventually. However, MTS has no way to specify liveness in this setting. Therefore, *disjunctive modal transition systems* (DMTS) (introduced in [11] as solutions to process equations) are the desirable extension appropriate for specifying liveness. This has been advocated also in [12] where a slight modification of DMTS is investigated under the name *underspecified transition systems*. Instead of forcing a particular transition, the must transitions in DMTS specify a whole set of transitions at least one of which must be present. In our example, it would be the set consisting of **processing** and **query** transitions. DMTS turn out to be capable of forcing any positive Boolean combination of transitions, simply by turning it into the conjunctive normal form. Another possible solution to this issue is offered in [13] where one-selecting MTS are introduced with the property that *exactly* one transition from the set must be present.

As DMTS is a strict extension of MTS a question arises whether all fundamental problems decidable in the context of MTS remain decidable for DMTS, and if so, whether their complexities remain unchanged. We show that this is indeed the case. Therefore, using the more powerful DMTS is not more costly than using MTS.

There is also another good reason to employ the greater power of DMTS instead of using MTS. Often a set of requirements need to be satisfied at once. Therefore, we are interested in the *common implementation* (CI) problem, where one asks whether there is an implementation that refines all specifications in a given set, i.e. whether the specifications are consistent. (In accordance with the traditional usage, the states of (D)MTS specifications shall be called processes.) Moreover, we also want to construct the most general process refining all processes, i.e. the greatest lower bound with respect to the refinement. We call this process a *conjunction* as this composition is the analog of logical and. We show there may not be any process that is a conjunction of a given set of processes, when only considering MTS processes. However, we also show that there is always a DMTS process that is a conjunction of a given set of (D)MTS processes. This again shows that DMTS is a more appropriate framework than MTS.

As the first main result, we show a new perspective on these problems, namely we give a simple co-inductive characterization yielding a straightforward fixpoint algorithm. This characterization unifies the view not only (i) in the MTS vs. DMTS aspect, but also (ii) in the cases of number of specifications being fixed or a part of the input, and most importantly (iii) establishes connection between CI and the conjunction. Our new view provides a solution for DMTS and yields algorithms for the aforementioned cases with the respective complexities being the same as for CI over MTS as determined in [14,15]. So far, conjunction has been solved for MTS enriched with weights on transitions in [16], however, only for the deterministic case. Previous results on conjunction over DMTS [11] yield an algorithm that requires exponential time (even for only two processes on input). Our algorithm runs in polynomial time both for conjunction and CI for any fixed number of processes on input.

As the second main result, as already mentioned we would like to supplement the refinement based framework of (D)MTS with model checking methods. Since a specification induces a set of implementations, we apply the thorough approach of generalized model checking of Kripke structures with partial valuations [17,18] in our setting. Thus a specification either satisfies a formula φ if all its implementations satisfy φ; or refutes it if all implementations refute it; or neither of the previous holds, i.e. some of the implementations satisfy and some refute φ. This classification has also been adopted in [3] for CTL model checking MTS. Similarly, [19] provides a solution to LTL model checking over deadlock-free MTS, which was implemented in the tool support for MTS [20]. However, we identify an error in this LTL solution and provide correct model checking algorithms. The erroneous algorithm for the deadlock-free MTS was running in PSPACE, nevertheless, we show that this problem is 2-EXPTIME-complete by reduction to and from LTL games. The generalized model checking problem is equivalent to solving the problems (i) whether all implementations satisfy the given formula and if they do not then (ii) whether there exists an implementation satisfying the formula. We provide algorithms for both the universal and the existential case, and moreover, for the cases of MTS, deadlock-free MTS and DMTS, providing different complexities. Due to our reduction, the resulting algorithm can be also used for synthesis, i.e. if there is a satisfying implementation, we automatically receive it. Not only is the application in the specification area clear, but there is also an important application to abstract interpretation. End-users are usually more comfortable with linear time logic and the analysis of path properties requires to work with abstractions capturing over- and under-approximation of a system simultaneously. MTS are a perfect framework for this task, as may and must transitions can capture over- and under-approximations, respectively [8]. Our results thus allow for LTL model-checking of system abstractions, including counterexample generation.

Finally, we show how the model checking approach can help us getting around the fundamental problem with the parallel composition. There are MTS processes S and T, where the composed process $S \parallel T$ contains more implementations than what can be obtained by composing implementations of S and T. Hence the composition is not complete with respect to the semantic view. Some conditions to overcome this difficulty were identified in [15]. Here we show the general completeness of the composition with respect to the LTL formulae satisfaction, and generally to all linear time properties.

The rest of the paper is organized as follows. We provide basic definitions and results on refinements in Section 2. The results on LTL model checking and its relation to the parallel composition can be found in Section 3. The "logical and" composition is investigated in Section 4. Section 5 concludes and discusses future work. Due to space limitations the proofs are omitted and can be found in [21].

2   Preliminaries

In this section we define the specification formalism of disjunctive modal transition systems (DMTS). A DMTS can be gradually refined until we get a labelled transition system (LTS) where all the behaviour is fully determined. The semantics of a DMTS will thus be the set of its refining LTSs. The following definition is a slight modification of the original definition in [11].

Definition 2.1. *A* disjunctive modal transition system (DMTS) *over an action alphabet Σ and a set of propositions Ap is a tuple $(\mathcal{P}, \dashrightarrow, \longrightarrow, \nu)$ where $\mathcal{P}$ is a set of* processes, *$\dashrightarrow \; \subseteq \mathcal{P} \times \Sigma \times \mathcal{P}$ and $\longrightarrow \; \subseteq \mathcal{P} \times 2^{\Sigma \times \mathcal{P}}$ are* may *and* must *transition relations, respectively, and $\nu : \mathcal{P} \to 2^{Ap}$ is a valuation. We write $S \overset{a}{\dashrightarrow} T$ meaning $(S, a, T) \in \dashrightarrow$, and $S \longrightarrow T$ meaning $(S, T) \in \longrightarrow$. We require that whenever $S \longrightarrow T$ then (i) $T \neq \emptyset$ and (ii) for all $(a, T) \in T$ we also have $S \overset{a}{\dashrightarrow} T$.*

The original definition of DMTS does not include the two requirements, thus allowing for *inconsistent* DMTS, which have no implementations. Due to the requirements, our DMTS guarantee that all must obligations can be fulfilled. Hence, we do not have to expensively check for consistency[1] when working with our DMTS. And there is yet another difference to the original definition. Since one of our aims is model checking state *and* action based LTL, we not only have labelled transitions, but we also equip DMTS with a valuation over states.

Clearly, the must transitions of DMTS can be seen as a positive boolean formula in conjunctive normal form. Arbitrary requirements expressible as positive boolean formulae can be thus represented by DMTS, albeit at the cost of possible exponential blowup, as commented on in [22].

Example 2.2. Figure 2 depicts three DMTSs. The may transitions are drawn as dashed arrows, while each must transition of the form (S, T) is drawn as a solid arrow from S branching to all elements in T. Due to requirement (ii) it is redundant to draw the dashed arrow when there is a solid arrow and we never depict it explicitly.

While in DMTS we can specify that at least one of the selected transitions has to be present, in modal transition systems (MTS) we can only specify that a particular transition has to be present, i.e. we need to know from the beginning which one. Thus MTS is a special case of DMTS. Further, when the may and must transition relations coincide, we get labelled transition systems (with valuation).

Definition 2.3. *A DMTS $\mathfrak{S} = (\mathcal{P}, \dashrightarrow, \longrightarrow, \nu)$ is an* MTS (with valuation) *if $S \longrightarrow T$ implies that T is a singleton. We then write $S \overset{a}{\longrightarrow} T$ for $T = \{(a, T)\}$. If moreover $S \overset{a}{\dashrightarrow} T$ implies $S \overset{a}{\longrightarrow} T$, then $\mathfrak{S}$ is an* LTS. *Processes of an LTS are called* implementations.

---

[1] Checking consistency is an EXPTIME-complete problem. It is polynomial [11] only under an assumption that all "conjunctions" of processes are also present in the given DMTS which is very artificial in our setting. For more details, see [21].

A *DMTS* $\mathcal{G} = (\mathcal{P}, \dashrightarrow, \longrightarrow, \nu)$ is deterministic *if for every process S and action a there is at most one process T with* $S \overset{a}{\dashrightarrow} T$.

For the sake of readable notation, when speaking of a process, we often omit the underlying DMTS if it is clear from the context. Moreover, we say that S is deterministic (an MTS etc.) meaning that the DMTS on processes reachable from S is deterministic (MTS etc.). Further, when analyzing the complexity we assume we are given finite DMTSs.

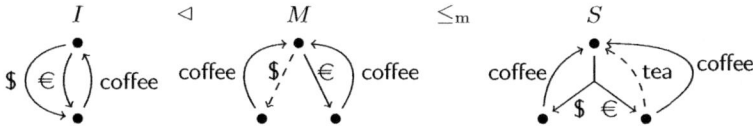

Fig. 2. An implementation I, a process M of an MTS, and a process S of a DMTS such that $I \lhd M \leq_m S$

When refining a process, we need to satisfy two conditions: (1) the respective refining process cannot allow any new behaviour not allowed earlier; and (2) if there is a requirement to implement an action by choosing among several options, the refining process can only have more restrictive set of these options.

Definition 2.4 (Modal refinement). *Let* $(\mathcal{P}, \dashrightarrow, \longrightarrow, \nu)$ *be a DMTS. Then* $R \subseteq \mathcal{P} \times \mathcal{P}$ *is called a* modal refinement relation *if for all* $(A, B) \in R$

- $\nu(A) = \nu(B)$, *and*
- *whenever* $A \overset{a}{\dashrightarrow} A'$ *then* $B \overset{a}{\dashrightarrow} B'$ *for some* B' *with* $(A', B') \in R$, *and*
- *whenever* $B \longrightarrow B'$ *then* $A \longrightarrow A'$ *for some* A' *such that for all* $(a, A') \in A'$ *there is* $(a, B') \in B'$ *with* $(A', B') \in R$.

We say that S modally refines T, denoted by $S \leq_m T$, *if there exists a modal refinement relation R with* $(S, T) \in R$.

Note that since a union of modal refinement relations is a modal refinement relation, the relation $\leq_m$ is the greatest modal refinement relation. Also note that on implementations the modal refinement coincides with bisimulation.

We now define the semantics of a process as a set of implementations that are refining it. The defined notion of thorough refinement is a semantic counterpart to the syntactic notion of modal refinement.

Definition 2.5 (Thorough refinement). *Let* I, S, T *be processes. We say that I is an* implementation of S, *denoted by* $I \lhd S$, *if I is an implementation and* $I \leq_m S$. *We say that S* thoroughly refines T, *denoted by* $S \leq_t T$, *if* $J \lhd S$ *implies* $J \lhd T$ *for every implementation J.*

While the syntactic characterization is sound, it is not complete since it is incomplete already for MTS. However, completeness can be achieved on a reasonable subclass.

Proposition 2.6. *Let S and T be processes. Then $S \leq_m T$ implies $S \leq_t T$. If T is deterministic then $S \leq_t T$ implies $S \leq_m T$.*

Next we show that both refinement problems are not harder for DMTS than for MTS. This allows for using more powerful DMTS instead of MTS. The following is proven similarly as in [15]. In order to prove the last claim significantly involved modifications of the approach of [23] are needed.

Theorem 2.7. *Deciding $\leq_m$ is PTIME-complete. Deciding $\leq_m$ when restricted to the refined (i.e. right-hand-side) process being deterministic is NLOGSPACE-complete. Deciding $\leq_t$ is EXPTIME-complete.*

3   LTL Model Checking

This section discusses the model checking problem for linear temporal logic (LTL) [24] and its application on compositional verification. The following definition of state and action based LTL is equivalent to that of [25], with a slight difference in syntax.

Definition 3.1 (LTL syntax). *The formulae of state and action based LTL (LTL in the following) are defined as follows.*

$$\varphi ::= \mathbf{tt} \mid p \mid \neg\varphi \mid \varphi \wedge \varphi \mid \varphi \, \mathbf{U} \, \varphi \mid \mathbf{X}\,\varphi \mid \mathbf{X}_a\,\varphi$$

where p ranges over Ap and a ranges over Σ.

We use the standard derived operators, such as $\mathbf{F}\,\varphi = \mathbf{tt}\,\mathbf{U}\,\varphi$ and $\mathbf{G}\,\varphi = \neg\,\mathbf{F}\,\neg\varphi$.

Definition 3.2 (LTL semantics). *Let I be an implementation. A run of I is a maximal (finite or infinite) alternating sequence of state valuations and actions $\pi = \nu(I_0), a_0, \nu(I_1), a_1, \ldots$ such that $I_0 = I$ and $I_{i-1} \xrightarrow{a_{i-1}} I_i$ for all $i > 0$. If a run π is finite, we denote by $|\pi|$ the number of state valuations in π, we set $|\pi| = \infty$ if π is infinite. We also define the ith subrun of π as $\pi^i = \nu(I_i), a_i, \nu(I_{i+1}), \ldots$ Note that this definition only makes sense when $i < |\pi|$. The set of all runs of I is denoted by $\mathcal{R}^\infty(I)$, the set of all infinite runs is denoted by $\mathcal{R}^\omega(I)$.*

The semantics of LTL on $\pi = \nu_0, a_0, \nu_1, a_1, \ldots$ is then defined as follows:

$$
\begin{aligned}
&\pi \models \mathbf{tt} &&\text{always} \\
&\pi \models p &&\Longleftrightarrow p \in \nu_0 \\
&\pi \models \neg\varphi &&\Longleftrightarrow \pi \not\models \varphi \\
&\pi \models \varphi \wedge \psi &&\Longleftrightarrow \pi \models \varphi \text{ and } \pi \models \psi \\
&\pi \models \varphi \, \mathbf{U} \, \psi &&\Longleftrightarrow \exists 0 \leq k < |\pi| : \pi^k \models \psi \text{ and } \forall 0 \leq j < k : \pi^j \models \varphi \\
&\pi \models \mathbf{X}\,\varphi &&\Longleftrightarrow |\pi| > 1 \text{ and } \pi^1 \models \varphi \\
&\pi \models \mathbf{X}_a\,\varphi &&\Longleftrightarrow |\pi| > 1, \, a_0 = a \text{ and } \pi^1 \models \varphi
\end{aligned}
$$

We say that an implementation I satisfies φ on infinite runs, denoted as $I \models^\omega \varphi$, if for all $\pi \in \mathcal{R}^\omega(I)$, $\pi \models \varphi$. We say that an implementation I satisfies φ on all runs, denoted as $I \models^\infty \varphi$, if for all $\pi \in \mathcal{R}^\infty(I)$, $\pi \models \varphi$.

The use of symbols ω and ∞ to distinguish between using only infinite runs or all runs is in accordance with standard usage in the field of infinite words.

It is common to define LTL over infinite runs only. In that respect, our definition of $\models^\omega$ matches the standard definition. In the following, we shall first talk about this satisfaction relation only, and comment on $\models^\infty$ afterwards.

The generalized LTL model checking problem for DMTS can be split into two subproblems – deciding whether all implementations satisfy a given formula, and deciding whether at least one implementation does. We therefore introduce the following notation: we write $S \models^\omega_\forall \varphi$ to mean $\forall I \lhd S : I \models^\omega \varphi$ and $S \models^\omega_\exists \varphi$ to mean $\exists I \lhd S : I \models^\omega \varphi$; similarly for $\models^\infty$.

Note that $\models^\omega_\exists$ contains a hidden alternation [26] of quantifiers, as it actually means $\exists I \lhd S : \forall \pi \in \mathcal{R}^\omega(I) : I \models^\omega \varphi$. No alternation is present in $\models^\omega_\forall$. This observation hints that the problem of deciding $\models^\omega_\forall$ is easier than deciding $\models^\omega_\exists$. Our first two results show that indeed, deciding $\models^\omega_\forall$ is not harder than the standard LTL model checking whereas deciding $\models^\omega_\exists$ is 2-EXPTIME-complete.

The only known correct result on LTL model checking of MTS is that deciding $MTS \models^\omega_\forall$ over MTS is PSPACE-complete [19]. This holds also for DMTS.

Theorem 3.3. *The problem of deciding $\models^\omega_\forall$ over DMTS is PSPACE-complete.*

Proof (Sketch). All implementations of S satisfy φ if and only if the may structure of S satisfies φ. □

In [18] the generalized model checking of LTL over partial Kripke structures (PKS) is shown to be 2-EXPTIME-hard. Further, [27] describes a reduction from generalized model checking of μ-calculus over PKS to μ-calculus over MTS. However, the hardness for *LTL* over MTS does not follow since the encoding of an LTL formula into μ-calculus includes an exponential blowup. There is thus no straightforward way to use the result of [27] to provide a polynomial reduction. Therefore, we prove the following theorem directly.

Theorem 3.4. *The problem of deciding $\models^\omega_\exists$ over DMTS is 2-EXPTIME-complete.*

Proof (Sketch). We show the reduction to and from the 2-EXPTIME-complete problem of deciding existence of a winning strategy in an LTL game [28]. An LTL game is a two player positional game over a finite Kripke structure. The winning condition is the set of all infinite plays (sequences of states) satisfying a given LTL formula.

Thus, an LTL game may be seen as a special kind of DMTS over unary action alphabet. Here the processes are the states of the Kripke structure, the may structure is the transition relation of the Kripke structure, and the must structure is built as follows. Every process corresponding to a state of Player I has one must transition spanning all may-successors; every process corresponding to a state of Player II has several must transitions, one to each may-successor. The implementations of such DMTS now correspond to strategies of Player I in the original LTL game. Thus follows the hardness part of the theorem.

For the containment part, we provide an algorithm that transforms the given DMTS into a Kripke structure with states assigned to the two players. This

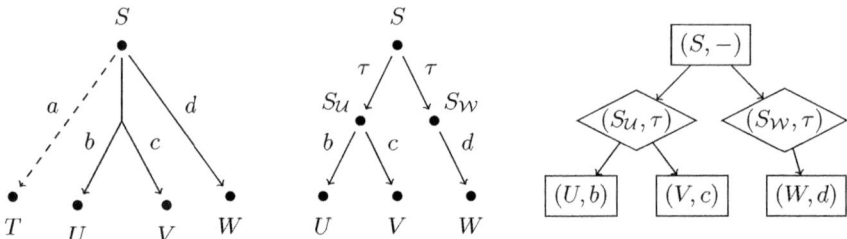

Fig. 3. Transformation from DMTS into a two player game

construction bears some similarities to the construction transforming Kripke MTS into alternating tree automata in [29].

The transformation from a DMTS into a two player game proceeds as follows. We first eliminate all may transitions that are not covered by any must transitions. We then modify the must transitions. For each $S \longrightarrow \mathcal{U}$ we create a unique new process $S_\mathcal{U}$ and set $S \xrightarrow{\tau} S_\mathcal{U}$ and $S_\mathcal{U} \xrightarrow{a} T$ for all $(a, T) \in \mathcal{U}$. We thus now have a labelled transition system, possibly with valuation. We then eliminate actions by encoding them into their target state, thus obtaining a Kripke structure. States that were created from processes of the original DMTS belong to Player II, states created from must transitions belong to Player I. The construction is illustrated in Fig. 3. We then modify the LTL formula in two steps. First, we add the possibility of a τ action in every odd step. Second, we transform the state-and-action LTL formula into a purely state-based one. The resulting game over the Kripke structure together with the modified LTL formula form the desired LTL game.   □

There are constructive algorithms for solving LTL games, i.e. not only do they decide whether a winning strategy exists, but they can also synthesize such a strategy. Furthermore, our reduction effectively transforms a winning strategy into an implementation satisfying the given formula. We can thus synthesize an implementation of a given DMTS satisfying a given formula in 2-EXPTIME.

Although the general complexity of the problem is very high, various subclasses of LTL have been identified in [30] for which the problem is computationally easier. These complexity results can be easily carried over to generalized model checking of DMTS.

Interestingly enough, deciding $\models_\exists^\omega$ is much easier over MTS.

Theorem 3.5. *The problem of deciding $\models_\exists^\omega$ over MTS is PSPACE-complete.*

Proof (Sketch). The proof is similar to the proof of Theorem 3.3, only instead of checking the may structure of S, we check the must structure of S.   □

However, despite its lower complexity, $\models_\exists^\omega$ over MTS is not a very useful satisfaction relation. As we only considered infinite runs, an MTS may (and frequently will) possess *trivial* implementations without infinite runs. The statement $S \models_\exists^\omega \varphi$ then holds vacuously for all φ. Two natural ways to cope with

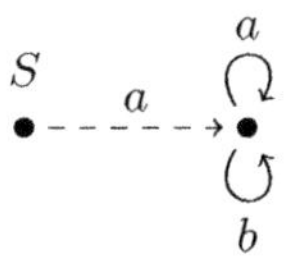

Fig. 4. No deadlock-free implementation of S satisfies $\mathbf{G}\,\mathbf{X}_a\,\mathbf{tt}$

this issue are (a) using $\models_\exists^\infty$ (see below) and (b) considering only deadlock-free implementations, i.e. with infinite runs only.

The deadlock-free approach has been studied in [19] and the proposed solution was implemented in the tool MTSA [20]. However, the solution given in [19] is incorrect. In particular, existence of a deadlock-free implementation satisfying a given formula is claimed even in some cases where no such implementation exists. A simple counterexample is given in Fig. 4. Clearly, S has no deadlock-free implementation with action a only, i.e. satisfying $\mathbf{G}\,\mathbf{X}_a\,\mathbf{tt}$. Yet the method of [19] as well as the tool [20] claim that such an implementation exists.

Furthermore, there is no chance that the approach of [19] could be easily fixed to provide correct results. The reason is that this approach leads to a PSPACE algorithm, whereas we prove again by reduction from LTL games that finding a deadlock-free implementation of a given MTS is 2-EXPTIME-hard. For more details see [21]. The containment in 2-EXPTIME is then proved by reduction to the problem of deciding $\models_\exists^\omega$ for DMTS. The basic idea is to modify all processes without must transitions, enhancing them with one must transition spanning all may-successors.

Proposition 3.6. *The problem of deciding the existence of a deadlock-free implementation of a given MTS satisfying a given LTL formula, is 2-EXPTIME-complete.*

We now turn our attention to the (a) option, i.e. all (possibly finite) runs, and investigate the $\models^\infty$ satisfaction. Checking properties even on finite runs is indeed desirable when considering (D)MTS used for modelling non-reactive systems. We show that deciding $\models_\exists^\infty$ and $\models_\forall^\infty$ over DMTS has the same complexity as deciding $\models_\exists^\omega$ and $\models_\forall^\omega$ over DMTS, respectively. We also show that contrary to the case of infinite runs, the problem of deciding $\models_\exists^\infty$ remains 2-EXPTIME-hard even for standard MTS.

Theorem 3.7. *The problem of deciding $\models_\exists^\infty$ over (D)MTS is 2-EXPTIME-complete, the problem of deciding $\models_\forall^\infty$ over (D)MTS is PSPACE-complete.*

Although we have so far considered the more general state and action based LTL, this costs no extra overhead when compared to state-based or action-based LTL.

Proposition 3.8. *The complexity of deciding $\models_\exists^\star$ and $\models_\forall^\star$ for $\star \in \{\omega, \infty\}$ remains the same if the formula φ is a purely state-based or a purely action-based formula.*

Table 1. Complexities of generalized LTL model checking

	$\models_\forall$	$\models_\exists$
MTS $\models^\omega$	PSPACE-complete	PSPACE-complete
MTS $\models^{df}$	PSPACE-complete	2-EXPTIME-complete
MTS $\models^\infty$	PSPACE-complete	2-EXPTIME-complete
DMTS	PSPACE-complete	2-EXPTIME-complete

The results of this section are summed up in Table 1. We use $\models^{df}$ to denote that only deadlock-free implementations are considered. Recall that the surprising result for $\models^\omega_\exists$ over MTS is due to the fact that the formula may hold vacuously.

The best known time complexity bounds with respect to the size of system $|S|$ and the size of LTL formula $|\varphi|$ are the following. In all PSPACE-complete cases the time complexity is $\mathcal{O}(|S| \cdot 2^{|\varphi|})$; in all 2-EXPTIME-complete cases the time complexity is $|S|^{2^{\mathcal{O}(|\varphi|)}} \cdot 2^{2^{\mathcal{O}(|\varphi| \log |\varphi|)}}$. The latter upper bound is achieved by translating the LTL formula into a deterministic Rabin automaton of size $2^{2^{\mathcal{O}(|\varphi| \log |\varphi|)}}$ with $2^{\mathcal{O}(|\varphi|)}$ accepting pairs, thus changing the LTL game into a Rabin game. State of the art algorithm for solving Rabin games can be found e.g. in [31].

3.1 Parallel Composition

We conclude this section with an application to compositional verification. In [3] the composition of MTS is shown to be incomplete, i.e. there are processes S_1, S_2 such that their composition $S_1 \parallel S_2$ has an implementation I that does *not* arise as a composition $I_1 \parallel I_2$ of any two implementations $I_1 \lhd S_1, I_2 \lhd S_2$. Completeness can be achieved only under some restrictive conditions [15]. Here we show that composition is sound and complete with respect to every logic of linear time, i.e. it preserves and reflects all linear time properties.

For the sake of readability, we present the results on MTS only. Nevertheless, the same holds for the straightforward extension of $\parallel$ to DMTS, see [21].

The composition operator used is based on synchronous message passing, since it is the most general one. Indeed, it encompasses the synchronous product as well as interleaving. It is defined as follows. Let $\Gamma \subseteq \Sigma$ be a *synchronizing alphabet*. Then

- for $a \in \Gamma$, we set $S_1 \parallel S_2 \overset{a}{\dashrightarrow} S_1' \parallel S_2'$ whenever $S_1 \overset{a}{\dashrightarrow} S_1'$ and $S_2 \overset{a}{\dashrightarrow} S_2'$;
- for $a \in \Sigma \setminus \Gamma$, we set $S_1 \parallel S_2 \overset{a}{\dashrightarrow} S_1' \parallel S_2$ whenever $S_1 \overset{a}{\dashrightarrow} S_1'$, and similarly $S_1 \parallel S_2 \overset{a}{\dashrightarrow} S_1 \parallel S_2'$ whenever $S_2 \overset{a}{\dashrightarrow} S_2'$;

and analogously for the must transition relation. As for valuations, we can consider any function $f : 2^{Ap} \times 2^{Ap} \to 2^{Ap}$ to define $\nu(S_1 \parallel S_2) = f(\nu(S_1), \nu(S_2))$, such as e.g. union.

The completeness of composition with respect to linear time logics holds for all discussed cases: both for MTS and DMTS, both for infinite and all runs, and both universally and existentially. We do not define linear properties formally here, see e.g. [32]. As a special case, one may consider LTL formulae.

Theorem 3.9. *Let S_1, S_2 be processes, φ a linear time property, and $\star \in \{\omega, \infty\}$. Then $S_1 \parallel S_2 \models^\star_\forall \varphi$ if and only if $I_1 \parallel I_2 \models^\star \varphi$ for all $I_1 \lhd S_1$ and $I_2 \lhd S_2$.*

Theorem 3.10. *Let S_1, S_2 be processes, φ a linear time property, and $\star \in \{\omega, \infty\}$. Then $S_1 \parallel S_2 \models^\star_\exists \varphi$ if and only if there exist $I_1 \lhd S_1$ and $I_2 \lhd S_2$ such that $I_1 \parallel I_2 \models^\star \varphi$.*

The idea of the proof is that the minimal (w.r.t. the set of runs) implementations of $S_1 \parallel S_2$ are decomposable, i.e. they can be written as $I_1 \parallel I_2$ where $I_1 \lhd S_1$ and $I_2 \lhd S_2$. The same holds for the maximal implementations of $S_1 \parallel S_2$. The results imply that although the composition is incomplete with respect to thorough refinement no new behaviour arises in the composition.

4   Common Implementation Problem and Conjunction

In the following, we study composing (D)MTS in the sense of logical conjunction. The *common implementation problem* (CI) is to decide whether there is an implementation refining all processes from a given set. Furthermore, we also want to construct the *conjunction*, i.e. the process that is the greatest lower bound for a given set of processes w.r.t. the modal refinement, if it exists. We show that although MTSs may not have an MTS conjunction, there is always a conjunction expressible as a DMTS. The complexity depends on the number of the input processes. We examine the complexity both for the case when it is fixed and when it is a part of the input.

Theorem 4.1. *For the number of input processes being a part of the input, the CI problem is EXPTIME-complete and conjunction can be computed in exponential time. For any fixed number of input processes, CI is PTIME-complete and conjunction can be computed in polynomial time.*

We first give a coinductive syntactic characterization of the problem and proceed by constructing the greatest lower bound.

Definition 4.2 (Consistency relation). *Let $(\mathcal{P}, \dashrightarrow, \longrightarrow, \nu)$ be a DMTS and $n \geq 2$. Then $C \subseteq \mathcal{P}^n$ is called a consistency relation if for all $(A_1, \ldots, A_n) \in C$*

- $\nu(A_1) = \nu(A_2) = \ldots = \nu(A_n)$, and
- *whenever there exists i such that $A_i \longrightarrow \mathcal{B}_i$, then there is some $(a, B_i) \in \mathcal{B}_i$ such that there exist B_j for all $j \neq i$ with $A_j \overset{a}{\dashrightarrow} B_j$ and $(B_1, \ldots, B_n) \in C$.*

In the following, we will assume an arbitrary, but fixed n. Clearly, arbitrary union of consistency relations is also a consistency relation, we may thus assume the existence of the greatest consistency relation for a given DMTS. We now show how to use this relation to construct a DMTS that is the greatest lower bound with regard to modal refinement (taken as a preorder).

Definition 4.3. *Let* $\mathfrak{S} = (\mathcal{P}, \dashrightarrow, \longrightarrow, \nu)$ *be a DMTS and* Con *its greatest consistency relation. We define a new DMTS* $\mathfrak{S}_{\mathsf{Con}} = (\mathsf{Con}, \dashrightarrow_{\mathsf{Con}}, \longrightarrow_{\mathsf{Con}}, \nu_{\mathsf{Con}})$, *where*

- $\nu_{\mathsf{Con}}((A_1, \ldots, A_n)) = \nu(A_1)$,
- $(A_1, \ldots, A_n) \overset{a}{\dashrightarrow}_{\mathsf{Con}} (B_1, \ldots, B_n)$ *whenever* $\forall i : A_i \overset{a}{\dashrightarrow} B_i$, *and*
- *whenever* $\exists j : A_j \longrightarrow \mathcal{B}_j$, *then* $(A_1, \ldots, A_n) \longrightarrow_{\mathsf{Con}} \mathcal{B}$ *where*
  $\mathcal{B} = \{(a, (B_1, \ldots, B_n)) \mid (a, B_j) \in \mathcal{B}_j \text{ and } (A_1, \ldots, A_n) \overset{a}{\dashrightarrow}_{\mathsf{Con}} (B_1, \ldots, B_n)\}$.

Clearly, the definition gives a correct DMTS due to the properties of Con, notably, $\mathcal{B}$ is never empty. The following two theorems state the results about the CI problem and conjunction construction, respectively. The second theorem also states that the actual result is stronger than originally intended.

Theorem 4.4. *Let* $S_1, \ldots, S_n$ *be processes. Then* $S_1, \ldots, S_n$ *have a common implementation if and only if* $(S_1, \ldots, S_n) \in$ Con.

Theorem 4.5. *Let* $(S_1, \ldots, S_n) \in$ Con. *Then the set of all implementations of* $(S_1, \ldots, S_n)$ *is exactly the intersection of the sets of all implementations of all* S_i. *In other words,* $I \lhd (S_1, \ldots, S_n)$ *if and only if* $I \lhd S_i$ *for all* i. *Therefore,* $(S_1, \ldots, S_n)$ *as a process of* $\mathfrak{S}_{\mathsf{Con}}$ *is the greatest lower bound of* $S_1, \ldots, S_n$ *with regard to the* modal *as well as the* thorough refinement.

The greatest consistency relation can be computed using standard greatest fixed point computation, i.e. we start with all $n$tuples of processes and eliminate those that violate the conditions. One elimination step can clearly be done in polynomial time. As the number of all $n$tuples is at most $|\mathcal{P}|^n$, this means that the common implementation problem may be solved in PTIME, if n is fixed; and in EXPTIME, if n is a part of the input. The problem is also PTIME/EXPTIME-hard, which follows from (a) PTIME-hardness of bisimulation of two LTSs and (b) EXPTIME-hardness of the common implementation problem for ordinary MTS [14]. The statement of Theorem 4.1 thus follows.

Note that even if $S_1, \ldots, S_n$ are MTSs, $(S_1, \ldots, S_n)$ may not be an MTS. Indeed, there exist MTSs without a greatest lower bound that is also an MTS; there may only be several maximal lower bounds, see Fig. 5. This gives another justification for using DMTS instead of MTS. However, if the MTSs are moreover *deterministic*, then the greatest lower bound is—as our algorithm computes it—also a deterministic MTS [16].

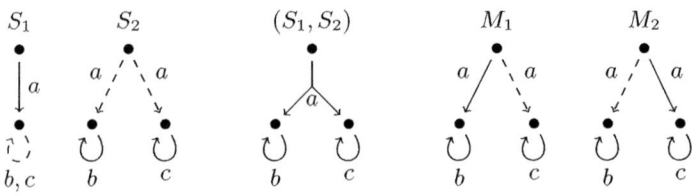

Fig. 5. MTSs S_1, S_2, their greatest lower bound (S_1, S_2), and their two maximal MTS lower bounds M_1, M_2

5   Conclusion and Future Work

Our generalization of the known algorithms has shown that refinement problems on DMTS are not harder than for MTS. As the first main result, we have solved the LTL model checking and synthesis problems and shown how the model checking approach helps overcoming difficulties with the parallel composition. We have implemented the algorithm in $\overrightarrow{\text{MoTraS}}$, our prototype tool available at http://anna.fi.muni.cz/~xbenes3/MoTraS/ (the site includes further details about the tool and its functionality). As the second main result, we have given a general solution to the common implementation problem and conjunctive composition.

There are several possible extensions of DMTS such as the mixed variant (where must transition need not be syntactically under the may transitions) or systems with partial valuation on states [3]. Yet another modification adds weights on transitions [16]. It is not clear whether all results of this paper can be extended to these systems and whether the respective complexities remain the same.

References

1. Larsen, K.G., Nyman, U., Wasowski, A.: Modeling software product lines using color-blind transition systems. STTT 9(5-6), 471–487 (2007)
2. Larsen, K.G., Thomsen, B.: A modal process logic. In: LICS, pp. 203–210. IEEE Computer Society, Los Alamitos (1988)
3. Antonik, A., Huth, M., Larsen, K.G., Nyman, U., Wasowski, A.: 20 years of modal and mixed specifications. Bulletin of the EATCS (95), 94–129 (2008)
4. Raclet, J.B.: Residual for component specifications. In: Proc. of the 4th International Workshop on Formal Aspects of Component Software (2007)
5. Bertrand, N., Pinchinat, S., Raclet, J.B.: Refinement and consistency of timed modal specifications. In: Dediu, A.H., Ionescu, A.M., Martín-Vide, C. (eds.) LATA 2009. LNCS, vol. 5457, pp. 152–163. Springer, Heidelberg (2009)
6. Raclet, J.B., Badouel, E., Benveniste, A., Caillaud, B., Passerone, R.: Why are modalities good for interface theories? In: ACSD, pp. 119–127. IEEE, Los Alamitos (2009)
7. Uchitel, S., Chechik, M.: Merging partial behavioural models. In: Proc. of FSE 2004, pp. 43–52. ACM, New York (2004)
8. Huth, M., Jagadeesan, R., Schmidt, D.A.: Modal transition systems: A foundation for three-valued program analysis. In: Sands, D. (ed.) ESOP 2001. LNCS, vol. 2028, pp. 155–169. Springer, Heidelberg (2001)
9. Godefroid, P., Huth, M., Jagadeesan, R.: Abstraction-based model checking using modal transition systems. In: Larsen, K.G., Nielsen, M. (eds.) CONCUR 2001. LNCS, vol. 2154, pp. 426–440. Springer, Heidelberg (2001)
10. Nanz, S., Nielson, F., Nielson, H.R.: Modal abstractions of concurrent behaviour. In: Alpuente, M., Vidal, G. (eds.) SAS 2008. LNCS, vol. 5079, pp. 159–173. Springer, Heidelberg (2008)
11. Larsen, K.G., Xinxin, L.: Equation solving using modal transition systems. In: LICS, pp. 108–117. IEEE Computer Society, Los Alamitos (1990)
12. Fecher, H., Steffen, M.: Characteristic mu-calculus formulas for underspecified transition systems. ENTCS 128(2), 103–116 (2005)

13. Fecher, H., Schmidt, H.: Comparing disjunctive modal transition systems with an one-selecting variant. J. of Logic and Alg. Program. 77(1-2), 20–39 (2008)
14. Antonik, A., Huth, M., Larsen, K.G., Nyman, U., Wasowski, A.: EXPTIME-complete decision problems for mixed and modal specifications. In: 15th International Workshop on Expressiveness in Concurrency (2008)
15. Beneš, N., Křetínský, J., Larsen, K., Srba, J.: On determinism in modal transition systems. Theoretical Computer Science 410(41), 4026–4043 (2009)
16. Juhl, L., Larsen, K.G., Srba, J.: Introducing modal transition systems with weight intervals (submitted)
17. Bruns, G., Godefroid, P.: Generalized model checking: Reasoning about partial state spaces. In: Palamidessi, C. (ed.) CONCUR 2000. LNCS, vol. 1877, pp. 168–182. Springer, Heidelberg (2000)
18. Godefroid, P., Piterman, N.: LTL generalized model checking revisited. In: Jones, N.D., Müller-Olm, M. (eds.) VMCAI 2009. LNCS, vol. 5403, pp. 89–104. Springer, Heidelberg (2009)
19. Uchitel, S., Brunet, G., Chechik, M.: Synthesis of partial behavior models from properties and scenarios. IEEE Trans. Software Eng. 35(3), 384–406 (2009)
20. D'Ippolito, N., Fischbein, D., Chechik, M., Uchitel, S.: MTSA: The modal transition system analyser. In: Proc. of ASE 2008, pp. 475–476. IEEE, Los Alamitos (2008)
21. Beneš, N., Černá. I., Křetínský, J.: Disjunctive modal transition systems and generalized LTL model checking. Technical report FIMU-RS-2010-12, Faculty of Informatics, Masaryk University, Brno (2010)
22. Beneš, N., Křetínský, J.: Process algebra for modal transition systemses. In: MEMICS. OASICS, vol. 16, pp. 9–18. Schloss Dagstuhl - Leibniz-Zentrum fuer Informatik, Germany (2010)
23. Beneš, N., Křetínský, J., Larsen, K.G., Srba, J.: Checking thorough refinement on modal transition systems is EXPTIME-complete. In: Leucker, M., Morgan, C. (eds.) ICTAC 2009. LNCS, vol. 5684, pp. 112–126. Springer, Heidelberg (2009)
24. Pnueli, A.: The temporal logic of programs. In: FOCS, pp. 46–57. IEEE, Los Alamitos (1977)
25. Chaki, S., Clarke, E.M., Ouaknine, J., Sharygina, N., Sinha, N.: State/event-based software model checking. In: Boiten, E.A., Derrick, J., Smith, G.P. (eds.) IFM 2004. LNCS, vol. 2999, pp. 128–147. Springer, Heidelberg (2004)
26. Godefroid, P., Jagadeesan, R.: Automatic abstraction using generalized model checking. In: Brinksma, E., Larsen, K.G. (eds.) CAV 2002. LNCS, vol. 2404, pp. 137–151. Springer, Heidelberg (2002)
27. Godefroid, P., Jagadeesan, R.: On the expressiveness of 3-valued models. In: Zuck, L.D., Attie, P.C., Cortesi, A., Mukhopadhyay, S. (eds.) VMCAI 2003. LNCS, vol. 2575, pp. 206–222. Springer, Heidelberg (2002)
28. Pnueli, A., Rosner, R.: On the synthesis of an asynchronous reactive module. In: Ronchi Della Rocca, S., Ausiello, G., Dezani-Ciancaglini, M. (eds.) ICALP 1989. LNCS, vol. 372, pp. 652–671. Springer, Heidelberg (1989)
29. Dams, D., Namjoshi, K.S.: Automata as abstractions. In: Cousot, R. (ed.) VMCAI 2005. LNCS, vol. 3385, pp. 216–232. Springer, Heidelberg (2005)
30. Alur, R., Torre, S.L.: Deterministic generators and games for LTL fragments. ACM Trans. Comput. Log. 5(1), 1–25 (2004)
31. Piterman, N., Pnueli, A.: Faster solution of rabin and streett games. In: Proceedings of LICS 2006, pp. 275–284. IEEE press, Los Alamitos (2006)
32. Baier, C., Katoen, J.P.: Principles of model checking. MIT Press, Cambridge (2008)

Efficient Inclusion Checking on Explicit and Semi-symbolic Tree Automata[*]

Lukáš Holík[1,2], Ondřej Lengál[1], Jiří Šimáček[1,3], and Tomáš Vojnar[1]

[1] FIT, Brno University of Technology, Czech Republic
[2] Uppsala University, Sweden
[3] VERIMAG, UJF/CNRS/INPG, Gières, France

Abstract. The paper considers several issues related to efficient use of tree automata in formal verification. First, a new efficient algorithm for inclusion checking on non-deterministic tree automata is proposed. The algorithm traverses the automaton downward, utilizing antichains and simulations to optimize its run. Results of a set of experiments are provided, showing that such an approach often very significantly outperforms the so far common upward inclusion checking. Next, a new semi-symbolic representation of non-deterministic tree automata, suitable for automata with huge alphabets, is proposed together with algorithms for upward as well as downward inclusion checking over this representation of tree automata. Results of a set of experiments comparing the performance of these algorithms are provided, again showing that the newly proposed downward inclusion is very often better than upward inclusion checking.

1 Introduction

Finite tree automata play a crucial role in several formal verification techniques, such as (abstract) regular tree model checking [3,5], verification of programs with complex dynamic data structures [6,11], analysis of network firewalls [7], and implementation of decision procedures of logics such as WS2S or MSO [15], which themselves have numerous applications (among the most recent and promising ones, let us mention at least verification of programs manipulating heap structures with data [16]).

Recently, there has been notable progress in the development of algorithms for efficient manipulation of non-deterministic finite tree automata (TA), more specifically, in solving the crucial problems of automata reduction [1] and of checking language inclusion [18,4,2]. As shown, e.g., in [4], replacing deterministic automata by non-deterministic ones can—in combination with the new methods for handling TA—lead to great efficiency gains. In this paper, we further advance the research on efficient algorithms for handling TA by (i) proposing a new algorithm for inclusion checking that turns out to significantly outperform the existing algorithms in most of our experiments and (ii) by presenting a semi-symbolic multi-terminal binary decision diagram (MTBDD) based representation of TA, together with various important algorithms for handling TA working over this representation.

---

[*] This work was supported by the Czech Science Foundation (projects P103/10/0306 and 102/09/H042), the Czech Ministry of Education (projects COST OC10009 and MSM 0021630528), the BUT FIT project FIT-S-11-1, and the Swedish UPMARC project.

T. Bultan and P.-A. Hsiung (Eds.): ATVA 2011, LNCS 6996, pp. 243–258, 2011.

The classic textbook algorithm for checking inclusion $L(\mathcal{A}_S) \subseteq L(\mathcal{A}_B)$ between two TA $\mathcal{A}_S$ (Small) and $\mathcal{A}_B$ (Big) first determinizes $\mathcal{A}_B$, computes the complement automaton $\overline{\mathcal{A}_B}$ of $\mathcal{A}_B$, and then checks language emptiness of the product automaton accepting $L(\mathcal{A}_S) \cap L(\overline{\mathcal{A}_B})$. This approach has been optimized in [18,4,2] which describe variants of this algorithm that try to avoid constructing the whole product automaton (which can be exponentially larger than $\mathcal{A}_B$ and which is indeed extremely large in many practical cases) by constructing its states and checking language emptiness on the fly. By employing the antichain principle [18,4], possibly combined with using upward simulation relations [2], the algorithm is often able to prove or refute inclusion by constructing a small part of the product automaton only[1]. We denote these algorithms as *upward* algorithms to reflect the direction in which they traverse automata $\mathcal{A}_S$ and $\mathcal{A}_B$.

The upward algorithms are sufficiently efficient in many practical cases. However, they have two drawbacks: (i) When generating the bottom-up post-image of a set S of sets of states, all possible n-tuples of states from all possible products $S_1 \times \ldots \times S_n, S_i \in S$ need to be enumerated. (ii) Moreover, these algorithms are known to be compatible with only upward simulations as a means of their possible optimization, which is a disadvantage since downward simulations are often richer and also cheaper to compute.

The alternative *downward* approach to checking TA language inclusion was first proposed in [13] in the context of subtyping of XML types. This algorithm is not derivable from the textbook approach and has a more complex structure with its own weak points; nevertheless, it does not suffer from the two issues of the upward algorithm mentioned above. We generalize the algorithm of [13] for automata over alphabets with an arbitrary rank ([13] considers rank at most two), and, most importantly, we improve it significantly by using the antichain principle, empowered by a use of the cheap and usually large downward simulation. In this way, we obtain an algorithm which is complementary to and highly competitive with the upward algorithm as shown by our experimental results (in which the newly proposed algorithm significantly dominates in most of the considered cases).

Certain important applications of TA such as formal verification of programs with complex dynamic data structures or decision procedures of logics such as WS2S or MSO require handling very large alphabets. Here, the common choice is to use the MONA tree automata library [15] which is based on representing transitions of TA symbolically using MTBDDs. However, the encoding used by MONA is restricted to *deterministic* automata only. This implies a necessity of immediate determinisation after each operation over TA that introduces nondeterminism, which very easily leads to a state space explosion. Despite the extensive engineering effort spent to optimize the implementation of MONA, this fact significantly limits its applicability.

As a way to overcome this difficulty, we propose a semi-symbolic representation of *non-deterministic* TA which generalises the one used by MONA, and we develop

---

[1] The work of [18] does, in fact, not use the terminology of antichains despite implementing them in a symbolic, BDD-based way. It specialises to binary tree automata only. A more general introduction of antichains within a lattice-theoretic framework appeared in the context of word automata in [19]. Subsequently, [4] has generalized [19] for explicit upward inclusion checking on TA and experimentally advocated its use within abstract regular tree model checking [4]. See also [10] for other combinations of antichains and simulations for word automata.

algorithms implementing the basic operations on TA (such as union, intersection, etc.) as well as more involved algorithms for computing simulations and for checking inclusion (using simulations and antichains to optimize it) over the proposed representation. We also report on experiments with a prototype implementation of our algorithms showing again a dominance of downward inclusion checking and justifying usefulness of our symbolic encoding for TA with large alphabets.

The rest of this paper is organised as follows. Section 2 contains basic definitions for tree automata, tree automata languages, and simulations. Section 3 describes our downward inclusion checking algorithm and its experimental comparison with the upward algorithms. Further, Section 4 presents our MTBDD-based TA encoding, the algorithms working over this encoding, and an experimental evaluation of these algorithms. Section 5 then concludes the paper.

2 Preliminaries

A *ranked alphabet* Σ is a set of symbols together with a ranking function $\# : \Sigma \to \mathbb{N}$. For $a \in \Sigma$, the value $\#a$ is called the *rank* of a. For any $n \geq 0$, we denote by Σ_n the set of all symbols of rank n from Σ. Let ε denote the empty sequence. A *tree* t over a ranked alphabet Σ is a partial mapping $t : \mathbb{N}^* \to \Sigma$ that satisfies the following conditions: (1) $dom(t)$ is a finite prefix-closed subset of $\mathbb{N}^*$ and (2) for each $v \in dom(t)$, if $\#t(v) = n \geq 0$, then $\{i \mid vi \in dom(t)\} = \{1, \dots, n\}$. Each sequence $v \in dom(t)$ is called a *node* of t. For a node v, we define the ith *child* of v to be the node vi, and the ith *subtree* of v to be the tree t' such that $t'(v') = t(viv')$ for all $v' \in \mathbb{N}^*$. A *leaf* of t is a node v which does not have any children, i.e., there is no $i \in \mathbb{N}$ with $vi \in dom(t)$. We denote by T_Σ the set of all trees over the alphabet Σ.

A (finite, non-deterministic) *tree automaton* (abbreviated sometimes as TA in the following) is a quadruple $\mathcal{A} = (Q, \Sigma, \Delta, F)$ where Q is a finite set of states, $F \subseteq Q$ is a set of final states, Σ is a ranked alphabet, and Δ is a set of transition rules. Each transition rule is a triple of the form $((q_1, \dots, q_n), a, q)$ where $q_1, \dots, q_n, q \in Q, a \in \Sigma$, and $\#a = n$. We use equivalently $(q_1, \dots, q_n) \xrightarrow{a} q$ and $q \xrightarrow{a} (q_1, \dots, q_n)$ to denote that $((q_1, \dots, q_n), a, q) \in \Delta$. The two notations correspond to the bottom-up and top-down representation of tree automata, respectively. (Note that we can afford to work interchangeably with both of them since we work with non-deterministic tree automata, which are known to have an equal expressive power in their bottom-up and top-down representations.) In the special case when $n = 0$, we speak about the so-called *leaf rules*, which we sometimes abbreviate as $\xrightarrow{a} q$ or $q \xrightarrow{a}$.

For an automaton $\mathcal{A} = (Q, \Sigma, \Delta, F)$, we use $Q^\#$ to denote the set of all tuples of states from Q with up to the maximum arity that some symbol in Σ has, i.e., if $r = max_{a \in \Sigma} \#a$, then $Q^\# = \bigcup_{0 \leq i \leq r} Q^i$. For $p \in Q$ and $a \in \Sigma$, we use $down_a(p)$ to denote the set of tuples accessible from p over a in the top-down manner; formally, $down_a(p) = \{(p_1, \dots, p_n) \mid p \xrightarrow{a} (p_1, \dots, p_n)\}$. For $a \in \Sigma$ and $(p_1, \dots, p_n) \in Q^{\#a}$, we denote by $up_a((p_1, \dots, p_n))$ the set of states accessible from $(p_1, \dots, p_n)$ over the symbol a in the bottom-up manner; formally, $up_a((p_1, \dots, p_n)) = \{p \mid (p_1, \dots, p_n) \xrightarrow{a} p\}$. We also extend these notions to sets in the usual way, i.e., for $a \in \Sigma$, $P \subseteq Q$, and $R \subseteq Q^{\#a}$, $down_a(P) = \bigcup_{p \in P} down_a(p)$ and $up_a(R) = \bigcup_{(p_1, \dots, p_n) \in R} up_a((p_1, \dots, p_n))$.

Let $\mathcal{A} = (Q, \Sigma, \Delta, F)$ be a TA. A *run* of $\mathcal{A}$ over a tree $t \in T_\Sigma$ is a mapping $\pi : dom(t) \to Q$ such that, for each node $v \in dom(t)$ of rank $\#t(v) = n$ where $q = \pi(v)$, if $q_i = \pi(vi)$ for $1 \le i \le n$, then Δ has a rule $(q_1, \ldots, q_n) \xrightarrow{t(v)} q$. We write $t \xRightarrow{\pi} q$ to denote that π is a run of $\mathcal{A}$ over t such that $\pi(\varepsilon) = q$. We use $t \Longrightarrow q$ to denote that $t \xRightarrow{\pi} q$ for some run π. The *language* accepted by a state q is defined by $\mathcal{L}_{\mathcal{A}}(q) = \{t \mid t \Longrightarrow q\}$, while the language of a set of states $S \subseteq Q$ is defined as $\mathcal{L}_{\mathcal{A}}(S) = \bigcup_{q \in S} \mathcal{L}_{\mathcal{A}}(q)$. When it is clear which TA $\mathcal{A}$ we refer to, we only write $L(q)$ or $L(S)$. The language of $\mathcal{A}$ is defined as $L(\mathcal{A}) = \mathcal{L}_{\mathcal{A}}(F)$. We also extend the notion of a language to a tuple of states $(q_1, \ldots, q_n) \in Q^n$ by letting $L((q_1, \ldots, q_n)) = L(q_1) \times \cdots \times L(q_n)$. The language of a set of n-tuples of sets of states $S \subseteq (2^Q)^n$ is the union of languages of elements of S, the set $L(S) = \bigcup_{E \in S} L(E)$. We say that X accepts y to express that $y \in L(X)$.

A *downward simulation* on TA $\mathcal{A} = (Q, \Sigma, \Delta, F)$ is a preorder relation $\preceq_D \subseteq Q \times Q$ such that if $q \preceq_D p$ and $(q_1, \ldots, q_n) \xrightarrow{a} q$, then there are states $p_1, \ldots, p_n$ such that $(p_1, \ldots, p_n) \xrightarrow{a} p$ and $q_i \preceq_D p_i$ for each $1 \le i \le n$. Given a TA $\mathcal{A} = (Q, \Sigma, \Delta, F)$ and a downward simulation $\preceq_D$, an *upward simulation* $\preceq_U \subseteq Q \times Q$ induced by $\preceq_D$ is a relation such that if $q \preceq_U p$ and $(q_1, \ldots, q_n) \xrightarrow{a} q'$ with $q_i = q$, $1 \le i \le n$, then there are states $p_1, \ldots, p_n, p'$ such that $(p_1, \ldots, p_n) \xrightarrow{a} p'$ where $p_i = p$, $q' \preceq_U p'$, and $q_j \preceq_D p_j$ for each j such that $1 \le j \ne i \le n$.

3   Downward Inclusion Checking

Let us fix two tree automata $\mathcal{A}_S = (Q_S, \Sigma, \Delta_S, F_S)$ and $\mathcal{A}_B = (Q_B, \Sigma, \Delta_B, F_B)$ for which we want to check whether $L(\mathcal{A}_S) \subseteq L(\mathcal{A}_B)$ holds. If we try to answer this query top-down and we proceed in a naïve way, we immediately realize that the fact that the top-down successors of particular states are *tuples* of states leads us to checking inclusion of the languages of tuples of states. Subsequently, the need to compare the languages of each corresponding pair of states in these tuples will again lead to comparing the languages of tuples of states, and hence, we end up comparing the languages of *tuples of tuples* of states, and the need to deal with more and more nested tuples of states never stops.

For instance, given a transition $q \xrightarrow{a} (p_1, p_2)$ in $\mathcal{A}_S$, transitions $r \xrightarrow{a} (s_1, s_2)$ and $r \xrightarrow{a} (t_1, t_2)$ in $\mathcal{A}_B$, and assuming that there are no further top-down transitions from q and r, it holds that $L(q) \subseteq L(r)$ if and only if $L((p_1, p_2)) \subseteq L((s_1, s_2)) \cup L((t_1, t_2))$. Note that the union $L((s_1, s_2)) \cup L((t_1, t_2))$ cannot be computed component-wise, this is, $L((s_1, s_2)) \cup L((t_1, t_2)) \ne (L(s_1) \cup L(t_1)) \times (L(s_2) \cup L(t_2))$. For instance, provided $L(s_1) = L(s_2) = \{b\}$ and $L(t_1) = L(t_2) = \{c\}$, it holds that $L((s_1, s_2)) \cup L((t_1, t_2)) = \{(b,b), (c,c)\}$, but the component-wise union is $(L(s_1) \cup L(t_1)) \times (L(s_2) \cup L(t_2)) = \{(b,b), (b,c), (c,b), (c,c)\}$. Hence, we cannot simply check whether $L(p_1) \subseteq L(s_1) \cup L(t_1)$ and $L(p_2) \subseteq L(s_2) \cup L(t_2)$ to answer the original query, and we have to proceed by checking inclusion on the obtained tuples of states. However, exploring the top-down transitions that lead from the states that appear in these tuples will lead us to dealing with tuples of tuples of states, etc.

Fortunately, there is a way out of the above trap. In particular, as first observed in [13] in the context of XML type checking, we can exploit the following property of the Cartesian product of sets $G, H \subseteq \mathcal{U}$: $G \times H = (G \times \mathcal{U}) \cap (\mathcal{U} \times H)$.

Hence, when we continue with our example, we get $L((p_1,p_2)) = L(p_1) \times L(p_2) \subseteq$ $L((s_1,s_2)) \cup L((t_1,t_2)) = (L(s_1) \times L(s_2)) \cup (L(t_1) \times L(t_2)) = ((L(s_1) \times T_\Sigma) \cap (T_\Sigma \times L(s_2))) \cup ((L(t_1) \times T_\Sigma) \cap (T_\Sigma \times L(t_2)))$. This can further be rewritten, using the distributive laws in the $(2^{T_\Sigma \times T_\Sigma}, \subseteq)$ lattice, as $L(p_1) \times L(p_2) \subseteq ((L(s_1) \times T_\Sigma) \cup (L(t_1) \times T_\Sigma)) \cap ((L(s_1) \times T_\Sigma) \cup (T_\Sigma \times L(t_2))) \cap ((T_\Sigma \times L(s_2)) \cup (L(t_1) \times T_\Sigma)) \cap ((T_\Sigma \times L(s_2)) \cup (T_\Sigma \times L(t_2)))$. It is easy to see that the inclusion holds exactly if it holds for all components of the intersection, i.e., if and only if $L(p_1) \times L(p_2) \subseteq ((L(s_1) \times T_\Sigma) \cup (L(t_1) \times T_\Sigma)) \wedge L(p_1) \times L(p_2) \subseteq ((L(s_1) \times T_\Sigma) \cup (T_\Sigma \times L(t_2))) \wedge L(p_1) \times L(p_2) \subseteq ((T_\Sigma \times L(s_2)) \cup (L(t_1) \times T_\Sigma)) \wedge L(p_1) \times L(p_2) \subseteq ((T_\Sigma \times L(s_2)) \cup (T_\Sigma \times L(t_2)))$.

Two things should be noted in the above condition: (1) If we are computing the union of languages of two tuples such that they have T_Σ at all indices other than some index i, we can compute it component-wise. For instance, $L(p_1) \times L(p_2) \subseteq ((L(s_1) \times T_\Sigma) \cup (L(t_1) \times T_\Sigma)) = (L(s_1) \cup L(t_1)) \times T_\Sigma$. This clearly holds iff $L(p_1) \subseteq L(s_1) \cup L(t_1)$. (2) If T_Σ does not appear at the same positions as in the inclusion $L(p_1) \times L(p_2) \subseteq ((L(s_1) \times T_\Sigma) \cup (T_\Sigma \times L(t_2)))$, it must hold that either $L(p_1) \subseteq L(s_1)$ or $L(p_2) \subseteq L(t_2)$.

Using the above observations, we can finally rewrite the equation $L(p_1) \times L(p_2) \subseteq L((s_1,s_2)) \cup L((t_1,t_2))$ into the following formula that does not contain languages of tuples but of single states only: $L(p_1) \subseteq L(s_1) \cup L(t_1) \wedge (L(p_1) \subseteq L(s_1) \vee L(p_2) \subseteq L(t_2)) \wedge (L(p_1) \subseteq L(t_1) \vee L(p_2) \subseteq L(s_2)) \wedge L(p_2) \subseteq L(s_2) \cup L(t_2)$.

The above reasoning can be generalized to dealing with transitions of any arity as shown in Theorem 1, proved in [12]. In the theorem, we conveniently exploit the notion of *choice functions*. Given $P_B \subseteq Q_B$ and $a \in \Sigma$, $\#a = n \geq 1$, we denote by $cf(P_B, a)$ the set of all choice functions f that assign an index i, $1 \leq i \leq n$, to all n-tuples $(q_1, \ldots, q_n) \in Q_B^n$ such that there exists a state in P_B that can make a transition over a to $(q_1, \ldots, q_n)$; formally, $cf(P_B, a) = \{f : down_a(P_B) \to \{1, \ldots, \#a\}\}$.

Theorem 1. *Let* $\mathcal{A}_S = (Q_S, \Sigma, \Delta_S, F_S)$ *and* $\mathcal{A}_B = (Q_B, \Sigma, \Delta_B, F_B)$ *be tree automata. For sets* $P_S \subseteq Q_S$ *and* $P_B \subseteq Q_B$ *it holds that* $L(P_S) \subseteq L(P_B)$ *if and only if* $\forall p_S \in P_S \ \forall a \in \Sigma :$ *if* $p_S \xrightarrow{a} (r_1, \ldots, r_{\#a})$,

$$
then \begin{cases} down_a(P_B) = \{()\} & if \#a = 0, \\[2mm] \forall f \in cf(P_B, a) \ \exists 1 \leq i \leq \#a : L(r_i) \subseteq \bigcup_{\substack{\overline{u} \in down_a(P_B) \\ f(\overline{u}) = i}} L(u_i) & if \#a > 0. \end{cases}
$$

3.1 Basic Algorithm of Downward Inclusion Checking

Next, we construct a basic algorithm for downward inclusion checking on tree automata $\mathcal{A}_S = (Q_S, \Sigma, \Delta_S, F_S)$ and $\mathcal{A}_B = (Q_B, \Sigma, \Delta_B, F_B)$. The algorithm is shown as Algorithm 1. Its main idea relies on a recursive application of Theorem 1 in function expand1. The function is given a pair $(p_S, P_B) \in Q_S \times 2^{Q_B}$ for which we want to prove that $L(p_S) \subseteq L(P_B)$—initially, the function is called for every pair (q_S, F_B) where $q_S \in F_S$. The function enumerates all possible top-down transitions that $\mathcal{A}_S$ can do from p_S (lines 3–8). For each such transition, the function either checks whether there is some transition $p_B \xrightarrow{a}$ for $p_B \in P_B$ if $\#a = 0$ (line 5), or it starts enumerating and recursively checking queries $L(p'_S) \subseteq L(P'_B)$ on which the result of $L(p_S) \subseteq L(P_B)$ depends according to Theorem 1 (lines 9–16).

The expand1 function keeps track of which inclusion queries are currently being evaluated in the set *workset* (line 2). Encountering a query $L(p'_S) \subseteq L(P'_B)$ with $(p'_S, P'_B) \in workset$ means that the result of $L(p'_S) \subseteq L(P'_B)$ depends on the result of $L(p'_S) \subseteq L(P'_B)$ itself. In this case, the function immediately successfully returns because the result of the query then depends only on the other branches of the call tree.

Algorithm 1. Downward inclusion

Input: Tree automata $\mathcal{A}_S = (Q_S, \Sigma, \Delta_S, F_S)$, $\mathcal{A}_B = (Q_B, \Sigma, \Delta_B, F_B)$
Output: *true* if $L(\mathcal{A}_S) \subseteq L(\mathcal{A}_B)$, *false* otherwise
1 **foreach** $q_S \in F_S$ **do**
2   **if** $\neg$expand1$(q_S, F_B, \emptyset)$ **then return** *false*;
3 **return** *true*;

Function. expand1 $(p_S, P_B, workset)$

     /* $p_S \in Q_S$, $P_B \subseteq Q_B$, and $workset \subseteq Q_S \times 2^{Q_B}$ */
1 **if** $(p_S, P_B) \in workset$ **then return** *true*;
2    $workset := workset \cup \{(p_S, P_B)\}$;
3 **foreach** $a \in \Sigma$ **do**
4   **if** $\#a = 0$ **then**
5   **if** $down_a(p_S) \neq \emptyset \wedge down_a(P_B) = \emptyset$ **then return** *false*;
6   **else**
7          $W := down_a(P_B)$;
8   **foreach** $(r_1, \ldots, r_{\#a}) \in down_a(p_S)$ **do**   /* $p_S \xrightarrow{a} (r_1, \ldots, r_{\#a})$ */
9   **foreach** $f \in \{W \to \{1, \ldots, \#a\}\}$ **do**
10              $found := false$;
11   **foreach** $1 \leq i \leq \#a$ **do**
12                  $S := \{q_i \mid (q_1, \ldots, q_{\#a}) \in W, f((q_1, \ldots, q_{\#a})) = i\}$;
13   **if** expand1$(r_i, S, workset)$ **then**
14                      $found := true$;
15   **break**;
16   **if** $\neg found$ **then return** *false*;
17 **return** *true*;

Using Theorem 1 and noting that Algorithm 1 necessarily terminates because all its loops are bounded, and the recursion in function expand1 is also bounded due to the use of *workset*, it is not difficult to see that the following theorem holds.

Theorem 2. *When applied on TA $\mathcal{A}_S = (Q_S, \Sigma, \Delta_S, F_S)$ and $\mathcal{A}_B = (Q_B, \Sigma, \Delta_B, F_B)$, Algorithm 1 terminates and returns true if and only if $L(\mathcal{A}_S) \subseteq L(\mathcal{A}_B)$.*

3.2 Optimized Algorithm of Downward Inclusion Checking

In this section, we propose several optimizations of the basic algorithm presented above that, according to our experiments, often have a huge impact on the efficiency of the algorithm—making it in many cases the most efficient algorithm for checking inclusion on tree automata that we are currently aware of. In general, the optimizations are based

---

Algorithm 2. Downward inclusion (antichains + preorder)

Input: TA $\mathcal{A}_S = (Q_S, \Sigma, \Delta_S, F_S), \mathcal{A}_B = (Q_B, \Sigma, \Delta_B, F_B), \preceq \subseteq (Q_S \cup Q_B)^2$
Output: *true* if $L(\mathcal{A}_S) \subseteq L(\mathcal{A}_B)$, *false* otherwise
Data: $NN := \emptyset$
1   **foreach** $q_S \in F_S$ **do**
2   **if** $\neg \text{expand2}(q_S, F_B, \emptyset)$ **then return** *false*;
3   **return** *true*;

Function. expand2 $(p_S, P_B, \textit{workset})$

/* $p_S \in Q_S$, $P_B \subseteq Q_B$, and $\textit{workset} \subseteq Q_S \times 2^{Q_B}$ */
1   **if** $\exists (p'_S, P'_B) \in \textit{workset} : p_S \preceq p'_S \wedge P'_B \preceq^{\forall\exists} P_B$ **then return** *true*;
2   **if** $\exists (p'_S, P'_B) \in NN : p'_S \preceq p_S \wedge P_B \preceq^{\forall\exists} P'_B$ **then return** *false* ;
3   **if** $\exists p \in P_B : p_S \preceq p$ **then return** *true*;
4   $\textit{workset} := \textit{workset} \cup \{(p_S, P_B)\}$;
5   **foreach** $a \in \Sigma$ **do**
6   **if** $\#a = 0$ **then**
7   **if** $down_a(p_S) \neq \emptyset \wedge down_a(P_B) = \emptyset$ **then return** *false*;
8   **else**
9          $W := down_a(P_B)$;
10   **foreach** $(r_1, \ldots, r_{\#a}) \in down_a(p_S)$ **do**   /* $p_S \xrightarrow{a} (r_1, \ldots, r_{\#a})$ */
11   **foreach** $f \in \{W \rightarrow \{1, \ldots, \#a\}\}$ **do**
12                $found := false$;
13   **foreach** $1 \leq i \leq \#a$ **do**
14                    $S := \{q_i \mid (q_1, \ldots, q_{\#a}) \in W, f((q_1, \ldots, q_{\#a})) = i\}$;
15   **if** expand2$(r_i, S, \textit{workset})$ **then**
16                       $found := true$;
17   **break**;
18   **if** $\nexists (r', H) \in NN : r' \preceq r_i \wedge S \preceq^{\forall\exists} H$ **then**
19                    $NN := (NN \setminus \{(r', H) \mid H \preceq^{\forall\exists} S, r_i \preceq r'\}) \cup \{(r_i, S)\}$;
20   **if** $\neg found$ **then return** *false*;
21   **return** *true*;

---

on an original use of simulations and antichains in a way suitable for the context of downward inclusion checking.

In what follows, we assume that there is available a preorder $\preceq \subseteq (Q_S \cup Q_B)^2$ compatible with language inclusion, i.e., such that $p \preceq q \implies L(p) \subseteq L(q)$, and we use $P \preceq^{\forall\exists} R$ where $P, R \subseteq (Q_S \cup Q_B)^2$ to denote that $\forall p \in P \exists r \in R : p \preceq r$. An example of such a preorder, which can be efficiently computed, is the (maximal) downward simulation $\preceq_D$. We propose the following concrete optimizations of the downward checking of $L(p_S) \subseteq L(P_B)$:

1. If there exists a state $p_B \in P_B$ such that $p_S \preceq p_B$, then the inclusion clearly holds (from the assumption made about $\preceq$), and no further checking is needed.
2. Next, it can be seen without any further computation that the inclusion does *not* hold if there exists some (p'_S, P'_B) such that $p'_S \preceq p_S$ and $P_B \preceq^{\forall\exists} P'_B$, and we have already established that $L(p'_S) \not\subseteq L(P'_B)$. Indeed, we have $L(P_B) \subseteq L(P'_B) \not\supseteq L(p'_S) \subseteq L(p_S)$, and therefore $L(p_S) \not\subseteq L(P_B)$.
3. Finally, we can stop evaluating the given inclusion query if there is some $(p'_S, P'_B) \in \textit{workset}$ such that $p_S \preceq p'_S$ and $P'_B \preceq^{\forall\exists} P_B$. Indeed, this means that the result of $L(p'_S) \subseteq L(P'_B)$ depends on the result of $L(p_S) \subseteq L(P_B)$. However, if $L(p_S) \subseteq L(P'_B)$ holds, then also $L(p_S) \subseteq L(P_B)$ holds because we have $L(p_S) \subseteq L(p'_S) \subseteq L(P'_B) \subseteq L(P_B)$.

Table 1. Percentages of cases in which the respective methods were the fastest

Size	Pairs	Timeout	Up	Up+s	Down	Down+s	Avg up speedup	Avg down speedup
50–250	323	20 s	31.21 %	0.00 %	53.50 %	15.29 %	1.71	3.55
400–600	64	60 s	9.38 %	0.00 %	39.06 %	51.56 %	0.34	46.56

The version of Algorithm 1 including all the above proposed optimizations is shown as Algorithm 2. The optimizations can be found in the function expand2 that replaces the function expand1. In particular, line 3 implements the first optimization, line 2 the second one, and line 1 the third one. In order to implement the second optimization, the algorithm maintains a new set NN. This set stores pairs (p_S, P_B) for which it has already been shown that the inclusion $L(p_S) \subseteq L(P_B)$ does *not* hold[2].

As a further optimization, the set NN is maintained as an antichain w.r.t. the pre-order that compares the pairs stored in NN such that the states from Q_S on the left are compared w.r.t. $\preceq$, and the sets from 2^{Q_B} on the right are compared w.r.t. $\succeq^{\exists\forall}$ (line 19). Clearly, there is no need to store a pair (p_S, P_B) that is bigger in the described sense than some other pair (p'_S, P'_B) since every time (p_S, P_B) can be used to prune the search, (p'_S, P'_B) can also be used.

Taking into account Theorem 2 and the above presented facts, it is not difficult to see that the following holds.

Theorem 3. *When applied on TA* $\mathcal{A}_S = (Q_S, \Sigma, \Delta_S, F_S)$ *and* $\mathcal{A}_B = (Q_B, \Sigma, \Delta_B, F_B)$, *Algorithm 2 terminates and returns true if and only if* $L(\mathcal{A}_S) \subseteq L(\mathcal{A}_B)$.

3.3   Experimental Results

We have implemented Algorithm 1 (which we mark as Down in what follows) as well as Algorithm 2 using the maximum downward simulation as the input preorder (which is marked as Down+s below). We have also implemented the algorithm of upward inclusion checking using antichains from [4] and its modification using upward simulation proposed in [2] (these algorithms are marked as Up and Up+s below). We tested our approach on 387 tree automata pairs of different sizes generated from the intermediate steps of abstract regular tree model checking of the algorithm for rebalancing red-black trees after insertion or deletion of a leaf node [4].

The results of the experiments are presented in the following tables. Table 1 compares the methods according to the percentage of the cases in which they were the fastest when checking inclusion on the same automata pair. The results are grouped into two sets according to the size of the automata measured in the number of states. The table also gives the average speedup of the fastest upward approach compared to the fastest downward approach in case the upward computation was faster than the downward one (and vice versa). Table 2 provides a comparison of the methods that

---

[2] In [12], a further optimization exploiting that $L(p_S) \subseteq L(P_B)$ has been shown to hold is proposed, but it is much more complicated in order to avoid memorizing possibly invalid assumptions made during the computation.

use simulation (either upward for Up+s or downward for Down+s) without counting the time for computing simulation (in such cases they were always faster than the methods not using simulations). This comparison is motivated by the observation that inclusion checking may be used as a part of a

Table 2. Percentages of cases in which the methods were the fastest when not counting the time for computing the simulation

Size	Pairs	Timeout	Up+s	Down+s	Avg up speedup	Avg down speedup
50–250	323	20 s	81.82 %	18.18 %	1.33	3.60
400–600	64	60 s	20.31 %	79.69 %	9.92	2116.29

Table 3. Percentages of successful runs that did not timeout

Size	Pairs	Timeout	Up	Up+s	Down	Down+s
50–250	323	20 s	100.00 %	100.00 %	74.92 %	99.07 %
400–600	64	60 s	51.56 %	51.56 %	39.06 %	90.62 %

bigger computation that anyway computes the simulation relations (which happens, e.g., in abstract regular model checking where the simulations are used for reducing the size of the encountered automata). Finally, Table 3 summarizes how often the particular methods were successful in our testing runs (i.e., how often they did not timeout.).

The results show that the overhead of computing upward simulation is too high in all the cases that we have considered, causing upward inclusion checking using simulation to be the slowest when the time for computing the simulation used by the algorithm is included[3]. Next, it can be seen that for each of the remaining approaches there are cases in which they win in a significant way. However, the downward approaches are clearly dominating in significantly more of our test cases (with the only exception being the case of small automata when the time of computing simulations is not included). Moreover, the dominance of the downward checking increases with the size of the automata that we considered in our test cases.

4   Semi-symbolic Representation of Tree Automata

We next consider a natural, semi-symbolic, MTBDD-based encoding of non-deterministic TA, suitable for handling automata with huge alphabets. We propose algorithms for computing downward simulations and for efficient downward inclusion checking on the considered representation. Due to space restrictions, we defer algorithms for further operations on the considered semi-symbolic representation of TA, including upward inclusion checking, to [12].

4.1   Binary Decision Diagrams

Let $\mathbb{B} = \{0, 1\}$ be the set of Boolean values. A *Boolean function* of *arity* k is a function of the form $f : \mathbb{B}^k \to \mathbb{B}$. We extend the notion of Boolean functions to an arbitrary

---

[3] Note that Up+s was winning over Up in the experiments of [2] even with the time for computing simulation included, which seems to be caused by a much less efficient implementation of the antichains in the original algorithm.

nonempty set S where a k-ary Boolean function extended to the domain set S is a function of the form $f : \mathbb{B}^k \to S$.

A *reduced ordered binary decision diagram* (ROBDD) [8] r over n Boolean variables $x_1, \ldots, x_n$ is a connected directed acyclic graph with a single *source node* (denoted as $r.root$) and at least one of the two *sink nodes* $\mathbf{0}$ and $\mathbf{1}$. We call *internal* the nodes which are not sink nodes. A function var assigns each internal node a Boolean variable from the set $X = \{x_1, \ldots, x_n\}$, which is assumed to be ordered by the ordering $x_1 < x_2 < \cdots < x_n$. For every internal node v there exist 2 outgoing edges labelled *low* and *high*. We denote by $v.low$ a node w and by $v.high$ a node z such that there exists a directed edge from v to w labelled by *low* and a directed edge from v to z labelled by *high*, respectively. For each internal node v, it must hold that $var(v) < var(v.low)$ and $var(v) < var(v.high)$ and also $v.low \neq v.high$. A node v represents an n-ary Boolean function $[\![v]\!] : \mathbb{B}^n \to \mathbb{B}$ that assigns to each assignment to the Boolean variables in X a corresponding Boolean value defined in the following way (using $\bar{x}$ as an abbreviation for $x_1 \ldots x_n$): $[\![\mathbf{0}]\!] = \lambda \bar{x} . \, 0$, $[\![\mathbf{1}]\!] = \lambda \bar{x} . \, 1$, and $[\![v]\!] = \lambda \bar{x} . \, (\neg x_i \wedge [\![v.low]\!]) \vee (x_i \wedge [\![v.high]\!])$ for $var(v) = x_i$. For every two nodes v and w, it holds that $v \neq w \implies [\![v]\!] \neq [\![w]\!]$. We say that an ROBDD r represents the Boolean function $[\![r]\!] = [\![r.root]\!]$. Dually, for a Boolean function f, we use $\langle f \rangle$ to denote the ROBDD representing f, i.e., $f = [\![\langle f \rangle]\!]$.

We generalise the standard *Apply* operation for manipulation of Boolean functions represented by ROBDDs in the following way: let op_1, op_2, and op_3 be in turn arbitrary unary, binary, and ternary Boolean functions. Then the functions $Apply_1$, $Apply_2$, and $Apply_3$ produce a new ROBDD which is defined as follows for ROBDDs f, g, and h: $Apply_1(f, op_1) = \langle \lambda \bar{x} . \, op_1([\![f(\bar{x})]\!]) \rangle$, $Apply_2(f, g, op_2) = \langle \lambda \bar{x} . \, op_2([\![f(\bar{x})]\!], [\![g(\bar{x})]\!]) \rangle$, and $Apply_3(f, g, h, op_3) = \langle \lambda \bar{x} . \, op_3([\![f(\bar{x})]\!], [\![g(\bar{x})]\!], [\![h(\bar{x})]\!]) \rangle$. In practice, one can also use *Apply* operations with side-effects.

The notion of ROBDDs is further generalized to *multi-terminal binary decision diagrams* (MTBDDs) [9]. MTBDDs are essentially the same data structures as ROBDDs, the only difference being the fact that the set of sink nodes is not restricted to two nodes. Instead, it can contain an arbitrary number of nodes labelled uniquely by elements of an arbitrary domain set S. All standard notions for ROBDDs can naturally be extended to MTBDDs. An MTBDD m then represents a Boolean function extended to S, i.e., $[\![m]\!] : \mathbb{B}^n \to S$. Further, the concept of *shared MTBDDs* is used. A shared MTBDD s is an MTBDD with multiple source nodes (or *roots*) that represents a mapping of every element of the set of roots R to a function induced by the MTBDD corresponding to the the given root, i.e., $[\![s]\!] : R \to (\mathbb{B}^n \to S)$.

4.2 Encoding the Transition Function of a TA Using Shared MTBDDs

We fix a tree automaton $\mathcal{A} = (Q, \Sigma, \Delta, F)$ for the rest of the section. We consider both a top-down and a bottom-up representation of its transition function. This is because some operations on $\mathcal{A}$ are easier to do on the former representation while others on the latter. We assume w.l.o.g. that the input alphabet Σ of $\mathcal{A}$ is represented in binary using n bits. We assign each bit in the binary encoding of Σ a Boolean variable from the set $\{x_1, \ldots, x_n\}$. We can then use shared MTBDDs with a set of roots R and a domain set S for encoding the various functions of the form $R \to (\Sigma \to S)$ that we will need.

Our *bottom-up* representation of the transition function Δ of the TA $\mathcal{A}$ uses a shared MTBDD Δ^{bu} over Σ where the set of root nodes is $Q^{\#}$, and the domain of labels of sink nodes is 2^Q. The MTBDD Δ^{bu} represents a function $[\![\Delta^{bu}]\!] : Q^\# \to (\Sigma \to 2^Q)$ defined as $[\![\Delta^{bu}]\!] = \lambda \, (q_1,\ldots,q_p) \, a \, . \, \{q \mid (q_1,\ldots,q_p) \xrightarrow{a} q\}$. It clearly holds that $[\![\Delta^{bu}((q_1,\ldots,q_p),a)]\!] = up_a((q_1,\ldots,q_p))$.

Our *top-down* representation of the transition function Δ of the TA $\mathcal{A}$ uses a shared MTBDD Δ^{td} over Σ where the set of root nodes is Q, and the domain of labels of sink nodes is $2^{Q^\#}$. The MTBDD Δ^{td} represents a function $[\![\Delta^{td}]\!] : Q \to (\Sigma \to 2^{Q^\#})$ defined as $[\![\Delta^{td}]\!] = \lambda \, q \, a \, . \, \{(q_1,\ldots,q_p) \mid q \xrightarrow{a} (q_1,\ldots,q_p)\}$. Clearly, $[\![\Delta^{td}(q,a)]\!] = down_a(q)$.

Sometimes it is necessary to convert between the bottom-up and top-down representation of a TA. For instance, when computing downward simulations (as explained below), one needs to switch between the bottom-up and top-down representation. Fortunately, the two representations are easy to convert (cf. [12]).

4.3   Downward Simulation on Semi-symbolically Encoded TA

We next give an algorithm for computing the maximum downward simulation relation on the states of the TA $\mathcal{A}$ whose transition function is encoded using our semi-symbolic representation. The algorithm is inspired by the algorithm from [14] proposed for computing simulations on finite (word) automata. For use in the algorithm, we extend the notion of downward simulation to tuples of states by defining $(q_1,\ldots,q_n) \preceq_D (r_1,\ldots,r_n)$ to hold iff $\forall 1 \leq i \leq n : q_i \preceq_D r_i$.

Our algorithm for computing downward simulations, shown as Algorithm 3, starts with a gross over-approximation of the maximum downward simulation, which is then pruned until the maximum downward simulation is obtained. The algorithm uses the following main data structures:

- For each $q \in Q$, $sim(q) \subseteq Q$ is the set of states that are considered to simulate q at the current step of the computation. Its value is gradually pruned during the computation. At the end, it encodes the maximum downward simulation being computed.
- The set $remove \subseteq Q^\# \times Q^\#$ contains pairs $((q_1,\ldots,q_n),(r_1,\ldots,r_n))$ of tuples of states, for which it is known that $(q_1,\ldots,q_n) \npreceq_D (r_1,\ldots,r_n)$, for processing.
- Finally, cnt is a shared MTBDD encoding a function $[\![cnt]\!] : Q^\# \to (\Sigma \to (Q \to \mathbb{N}))$ that for each $(q_1,\ldots,q_n) \in Q^\#$, $a \in \Sigma$, and $q \in Q$, gives a value $h \in \mathbb{N}$ such that $(q_1,\ldots,q_n)$ can make a bottom-up transition over a to h distinct states $r \in sim(q)$.

The algorithm works in two phases. We assume that we start with a TA whose transition function is represented bottom-up. In the *initialization* phase, the dual top-down representation of the transition function is first computed (note that we can also start with a top-down representation and compute the bottom-up representation as both are needed in the algorithm). The three main data structures are then initialized as follows:

- For each $q \in Q$, the set $sim(q)$ is initialized as the set of states that can make top-down transitions over the same symbols as q, which is determined using the *Apply* operation on line 9. This is, when starting the main computation loop on line 17, the value of sim for each state $q \in Q$ is $sim(q) = \{r \mid \forall a \in \Sigma : q \xrightarrow{a} (q_1,\ldots,q_n) \implies r \xrightarrow{a} (r_1,\ldots,r_n)\}$.
- The *remove* set is initialized to contain each pair of tuples of states $((q_1,\ldots,q_n), (r_1,\ldots,r_n))$ for which it holds that the relation $(q_1,\ldots,q_n) \preceq_D (r_1,\ldots,r_n)$ is broken

Algorithm 3. Computing downward simulation on semi-symbolic TA

Input: Tree automaton $\mathcal{A} = (Q, \Sigma, \Delta^{bu}, F)$
Output: Maximum downward simulation $\preceq_D \subseteq Q^2$
```
/* initialization */
```
1 $\Delta^{td} := \text{invertMTBDD}(\Delta^{bu})$;
2 $remove := \emptyset$;
3 $initCnt := \langle \lambda \, a \, . \, \emptyset \rangle$;   /* $[\![initCnt]\!] : \Sigma \to (Q \to \mathbb{N})$ */
4 **foreach** $q \in Q$ **do**
5      $sim(q) := \emptyset$;
6      $initCnt := Apply_2(\Delta^{td}(q), initCnt, (\lambda \, X \, Y \, . \, Y \cup \{(q, |X|)\}))$;
7   **foreach** $r \in Q$ **do**
8          $isSim := true$;
9          $Apply_2(\Delta^{td}(q), \Delta^{td}(r), (\lambda \, X \, Y \, . \, \textbf{if} \, (X \neq \emptyset \wedge Y = \emptyset) \, \textbf{then} \, isSim := false))$;
10   **if** $isSim$ **then**
11             $sim(q) := sim(q) \cup \{r\}$;
12   **else**
13   **foreach** $(q_1, \ldots, q_n) \in Q^\#, (r_1, \ldots, r_n) \in Q^\# : \exists 1 \leq i \leq n : q_i = q \wedge r_i = r$ **do**
14                 $remove := remove \cup \{((q_1, \ldots, q_n), (r_1, \ldots, r_n))\}$;
15 $cnt := \langle \lambda \, (q_1, \ldots, q_n) \, a \, . \, \emptyset \rangle$;   /* $[\![cnt]\!] : Q^\# \to (\Sigma \to (Q \to \mathbb{N}))$ */
16 **foreach** $(q_1, \ldots, q_n) \in Q^\#$ **do** $cnt((q_1, \ldots, q_n)) := initCnt$;
```
/* computation */
```
17 **while** $\exists((q_1, \ldots, q_n), (r_1, \ldots, r_n)) \in remove$ **do**
18     $remove := remove \setminus \{((q_1, \ldots, q_n), (r_1, \ldots, r_n))\}$;
19     $cnt((q_1, \ldots, q_n)) :=$
         $Apply_3(\Delta^{bu}((r_1, \ldots, r_n)), \Delta^{bu}((q_1, \ldots, q_n)), cnt((q_1, \ldots, q_n)), (\text{refine } sim \, remove))$;
20 **return** $\{(q, r) \mid q \in Q, r \in sim(q)\}$;

Function. $\text{refine}(\&sim, \&remove, up_a R, up_a Q, cnt_a Q)$

1 $newCnt_a Q := cnt_a Q$;
2 **foreach** $s \in up_a R$ **do**
3      $newCnt_a Q(s) := newCnt_a Q(s) - 1$;
4   **if** $newCnt_a Q(s) = 0$ **then**
5   **foreach** $p \in up_a Q : s \in sim(p)$ **do**
6   **foreach** $(p_1, \ldots, p_n) \in Q^\#, (s_1, \ldots, s_n) \in Q^\# : \exists 1 \leq i \leq n : p_i = p \wedge s_i = s$ **do**
7   **if** $\forall 1 \leq j \leq n : s_j \in sim(p_j)$ **then**
8                      $remove := remove \cup \{((p_1, \ldots, p_n), (s_1, \ldots, s_n))\}$;
9              $sim(p) := sim(p) \setminus \{s\}$;
10 **return** $newCnt_a Q$;

---

even for the initial approximation of $\preceq_D$, i.e., for some position $1 \leq i \leq n$ there is a pair $q_i, r_i \in Q$ such that $r_i \notin sim(q_i)$.

- To initialize the shared MTBDD cnt, the algorithm constructs an auxiliary MTBDD $initCnt$ representing a function $[\![initCnt]\!] : \Sigma \to (Q \to \mathbb{N})$. Via the *Apply* operation on line 6, this MTBDD gradually collects, for each symbol $a \in \Sigma$, the set of pairs (q, h) such that q can make a top-down transition to h distinct tuples over the symbol a. This MTBDD is then copied to the shared MTBDD cnt for each tuple of states $(q_1, \ldots, q_n) \in Q^\#$. This is justified by the fact that we start by assuming that the simulation relation is equal to $Q \times Q$, which for a symbol $a \in \Sigma$ and a pair $(q, h) \in cnt((q_1, \ldots, q_n))$ means that $(q_1, \ldots, q_n)$ can make a bottom-up transition over a to h distinct states $r \in sim(q)$.

The main *computation* phase gradually restricts the initial over-approximation of the maximum downward simulation being computed. As we have said, the *remove* set contains pairs $((q_1, \ldots, q_n), (r_1, \ldots, r_n))$ for which it holds that $(q_1, \ldots, q_n)$ cannot be simulated by $(r_1, \ldots, r_n)$, i.e., $(q_1, \ldots, q_n) \npreceq_D (r_1, \ldots, r_n)$. When such a pair is processed, the algorithm decrements the counter $[\![cnt((q_1, \ldots, q_n), a, s)]\!]$ for each state s for which there exists a bottom-up transition over a symbol $a \in \Sigma$ such that $(r_1, \ldots, r_n) \xrightarrow{a} s$. The meaning is that s can make one less top-down transition over a to some $(t_1, \ldots, t_n)$ such that $(q_1, \ldots, q_n) \preceq_D (t_1, \ldots, t_n)$. If $[\![cnt((q_1, \ldots, q_n), a, s)]\!]$ drops to zero, it means that s cannot make a top-down transition over a to any $(t_1, \ldots, t_n)$ such that $(q_1, \ldots, q_n) \preceq_D (t_1, \ldots, t_n)$. This means, for all $p \in Q$ such that p can make a top-down transition over a to $(q_1, \ldots, q_n)$, that s no longer simulates p, i.e., $p \npreceq_D s$. When the simulation relation between p and s, $p \preceq_D s$, is broken, then the simulation relation between all m-tuples $(p_1, \ldots, p_m)$ and $(s_1, \ldots, s_m)$ such that $\exists 1 \leq j \leq m : p_j = p \wedge s_j = s$ must also be broken, therefore the pair $((p_1, \ldots, p_m), (s_1, \ldots, s_m))$ is put to the *remove* set (unless the simulation relation between some other states in the tuples has already been broken before).

Correctness of the algorithm is summarised in the below theorem, which can be proven analogically as correctness of the algorithm proposed in [14], taking into account the meaning of the above described MTBDD-based structures and the operations performed on them.

Theorem 4. *When applied on a TA $\mathcal{A} = (Q, \Sigma, \Delta, F)$ whose transition function is encoded semi-symbolically in the bottom-up way as Δ^{bu}, Algorithm 3 terminates and returns the maximum downward simulation on Q.*

4.4 Downward Inclusion Checking on Semi-symbolically Encoded TA

We now proceed to an algorithm of efficient downward inclusion checking on semi-symbolically represented TA. The algorithm we propose for this purpose is derived from Algorithm 2 by plugging the expand3 function instead of the expand2 function. It is based on the same basic principle as expand2, but it has to cope with the symbolically encoded transition relation. In particular, in order to inspect whether for a pair (p_S, P_B) and all symbols $a \in \Sigma$ the inclusion between each tuple from $down_a(p_S)$ and the set of tuples $down_a(P_B)$ holds, the *doesInclusionHold* parameter initialized to *true* is passed to the *Apply* operation on line 9 of the expand3 function. If the algorithm finds out that the inclusion does not hold in some execution of the procDown function in the context of a single *Apply*, *doesInclusionHold* is assigned the *false* value, which is later returned by expand3. Otherwise expand3 returns its original *true* value.

4.5 Experimental Results

We have implemented a prototype of a library for working with TA encoded semi-symbolically as described above. We have used the CUDD library [17] as an implementation of shared MTBDDs. The prototype contains the algorithms presented in this section and some more presented in [12]. The results on downward inclusion checking that we have obtained with the explicitly represented TA encouraged us to also compare performance of the upward inclusion checking and downward inclusion checking on automata with large alphabets using our prototype.

Function. expand3 $(p_S, P_B, workset)$

/* $p_S \in Q_S$, $P_B \subseteq Q_B$, and $workset \subseteq Q_S \times 2^{Q_B}$ */

1 **if** $\exists (p'_S, P'_B) \in workset : p_S \preceq p'_S \wedge P'_B \preceq^{\forall\exists} P_B$ **then return** *true*;

2 **if** $\exists (p'_S, P'_B) \in NN : p'_S \preceq p_S \wedge P_B \preceq^{\forall\exists} P'_B$ **then return** *false* ;

3 **if** $\exists p \in P_B : p_S \preceq p$ **then return** *true*;

4 $workset := workset \cup \{(p_S, P_B)\}$;

5 $tmp := \langle \lambda a \,.\, \emptyset \rangle$;

6 **foreach** $p_B \in P_B$ **do**

7      $tmp := Apply_2(tmp, \Delta_B^{td}(p_B), (\lambda X Y \,.\, X \cup Y))$;

8 $doesInclusionHold := true$;

9 $Apply_2(\Delta_S^{td}(p_S), tmp, (\texttt{procDown}\ doesInclusionHold\ workset))$;

10 **return** $doesInclusionHold$;

Function. procDown $(\&doesInclusionHold, \&workset, down_a p_S, down_a P_B)$

1 **if** $() \in down_a p_S \wedge () \notin down_a P_B$ **then**

2      $doesInclusionHold := false$;

3 **else**

4      $W := down_a P_B$;

5   **foreach** $(r_1, \ldots, r_n) \in down_a p_S$ **do**   /* $p_S \xrightarrow{a} (r_1, \ldots, r_n)$ */

6   **foreach** $f \in \{W \to \{1, \ldots, n\}\}$ **do**

7              $found := false$;

8   **foreach** $1 \le i \le n$ **do**

9                  $S := \{q_i \mid (q_1, \ldots, q_n) \in W, f((q_1, \ldots, q_n)) = i\}$;

10   **if** expand3 $(r_i, S, workset)$ **then**

11                      $found := true$;

12   **break**;

13   **if** $\nexists (r', H) \in NN : r' \preceq r_i \wedge S \preceq^{\forall\exists} H$ **then**

14                  $NN := (NN \setminus \{(r', H) \mid H \preceq^{\forall\exists} S, r_i \preceq r'\}) \cup \{(r_i, S)\}$;

15   **if** $\neg found$ **then**

16              $doesInclusionHold := false$;

17   **return**;

We have compared the upward inclusion checking algorithm from [4] adapted for semi-symbolically represented tree automata, which is given in [12] (and marked as UpSym in the following), with the downward inclusion checking algorithm presented above. In the latter case, we let the algorithm use either the identity relation, which corresponds to downward inclusion checking without using any simulation (this case is marked as DownSym below), or the maximum downward simulation (which is marked as DownSym+s in the results). We have not considered upward inclusion checking with upward simulation due to its negative results in our experiments with explicitly encoded automata[4]. For the comparison, we used 97 pairs of tree automata with a large alphabet which we encoded into 12 bits. The size of the automata was between 50 and 150 states and the timeout was set to 300 s. The automata were obtained by taking the automata considered in Section 3.3 and labelling their transitions by randomly generated sets of symbols from the considered large alphabet.

The results that we have obtained are presented in the following tables. Table 4 compares the methods according to the percentage of the cases in which they were the

---

[4] We, however, note that possibilities of implementing upward inclusion checking combined with upward simulations over semi-symbolically encoded TA and a further evaluation of this algorithm are still interesting subjects for the future.

fastest when checking inclusion on the same automata pair. This table also presents the average speedup of the upward approach compared to the fastest downward approach in case the upward computation was faster than the downward one (and vice versa). Table 5 summarizes how often each of the methods was successful in the testing runs.

When we compare the above experimental results with the results obtained on the explicitly represented automata presented in Section 3.3, we may note that (1) downward inclusion checking is again significantly dominating, but (2) the advantage of exploiting downward simulation has decreased. According to the information we gathered from code profiling of our implementation, this

Table 4. Percentages of cases in which the respective methods were the fastest

UpSym	DownSym	DownSym+s	Avg up speedup	Avg down speedup
6.67%	90.67%	2.67%	24.39	4389.76

Table 5. Successful runs that did not timeout (in %)

UpSym	DownSym	DownSym+s
77.32%	77.32%	26.08%

is due to the overhead of the CUDD library which is used as the underlying layer for storage of shared MTBDDs of several data structures (which indicates a need of a different MTBDD library to be used or perhaps of a specialised MTBDD library to be developed).

We also evaluated performance of the implementation of the described algorithms using a semi-symbolic encoding of TA with performance of the algorithms using an explicit encoding of TA considered in Section 3 on the automata with the large alphabet. The symbolic version was in average 8676 times faster than the explicit one as expected when using a large alphabet.

5   Conclusion

We have proposed a new algorithm for checking language inclusion over non-deterministic TA (based on the one from [13]) that traverses automata in the downward manner and uses both antichains and simulations to optimize its computation. This algorithm is, according to our experimental results, mostly superior to the known upward algorithms. We have further presented a semi symbolic MTBDD-based representation of non-deterministic TA generalising the one used by MONA, together with important tree automata algorithms working over this representation, most notably an algorithm for computing downward simulations over TA inspired by [14] and the downward language inclusion algorithm improved by simulations and antichains proposed in this paper. We have experimentally justified usefulness of the symbolic encoding for non-deterministic TA with large alphabets.

Our experimental results suggest that the MTBDD package CUDD is not very efficient for our purposes and that better results could probably be achieved using a specialised MTBDD package whose design is an interesting subject for further work. Apart from that, it would be interesting to encode antichains used within the language inclusion checking algorithms symbolically as, e.g., in [18]. An interesting problem here is how to efficiently encode antichains based not on the subset inclusion but on a simulation relation. Finally, as a general target, we plan to continue in our work towards obtaining a really efficient TA library which could ultimately replace the one of MONA.

References

1. Abdulla, P.A., Bouajjani, A., Holík, L., Kaati, L., Vojnar, T.: Computing Simulations over Tree Automata: Efficient Techniques for Reducing Tree Automata. In: Ramakrishnan, C.R., Rehof, J. (eds.) TACAS 2008. LNCS, vol. 4963, pp. 93–108. Springer, Heidelberg (2008)
2. Abdulla, P.A., Holík, L., Chen, Y.-F., Mayr, R., Vojnar, T.: When Simulation Meets Antichains (On Checking Language Inclusion of Nondeterministic Finite (Tree) Automata). In: Esparza, J., Majumdar, R. (eds.) TACAS 2010. LNCS, vol. 6015, pp. 158–174. Springer, Heidelberg (2010)
3. Abdulla, P.A., Jonsson, B., Mahata, P., d'Orso, J.: Regular Tree Model Checking. In: Brinksma, E., Larsen, K.G. (eds.) CAV 2002. LNCS, vol. 2404, pp. 555–568. Springer, Heidelberg (2002)
4. Bouajjani, A., Habermehl, P., Holík, L., Touili, T., Vojnar, T.: Antichain-based Universality and Inclusion Testing over Nondeterministic Finite Tree Automata. In: Ibarra, O.H., Ravikumar, B. (eds.) CIAA 2008. LNCS, vol. 5148, pp. 57–67. Springer, Heidelberg (2008)
5. Bouajjani, A., Habermehl, P., Rogalewicz, A., Vojnar, T.: Abstract Regular Tree Model Checking. ENTCS, vol. 149. Elsevier, Amsterdam (2006)
6. Bouajjani, A., Habermehl, P., Rogalewicz, A., Vojnar, T.: Abstract Regular Tree Model Checking of Complex Dynamic Data Structures. In: Yi, K. (ed.) SAS 2006. LNCS, vol. 4134, pp. 52–70. Springer, Heidelberg (2006)
7. Bourdier, T.: Tree Automata-based Semantics of Firewalls. In: Proc. of SAR-SSI 2011. IEEE, Los Alamitos (2011)
8. Bryant, R.E.: Graph-based Algorithms for Boolean Function Manipulation. IEEE Trans. Computers (1986)
9. Clarke, E.M., McMillan, K.L., Zhao, X., Fujita, M., Yang, J.: Spectral Transforms for Large Boolean Functions with Applications to Technology Mapping. FMSD 10 (1997)
10. Doyen, L., Raskin, J.F.: Antichain Algorithms for Finite Automata. In: Esparza, J., Majumdar, R. (eds.) TACAS 2010. LNCS, vol. 6015, pp. 2–22. Springer, Heidelberg (2010)
11. Habermehl, P., Holík, L., Rogalewicz, A., Šimáček, J., Vojnar, T.: orest Automata for Verification of Heap Manipulation. In: Gopalakrishnan, G., Qadeer, S. (eds.) CAV 2011. LNCS, vol. 6806, pp. 424–440. Springer, Heidelberg (2011)
12. Holík, L., Lengál, O., Šimáček, J., Vojnar, T.: Efficient Inclusion Checking on Explicit and Semi-Symbolic Tree Automata. Tech. rep. FIT-TR-2011-04, FIT BUT, Czech Rep. (2011)
13. Hosoya, H., Vouillon, J., Pierce, B.C.: Regular Expression Types for XML. ACM Trans. Program. Lang. Syst. 27 (2005)
14. Ilie, L., Navarro, G., Yu, S.: On NFA Reductions. In: Karhumäki, J., Maurer, H., Păun, G., Rozenberg, G. (eds.) Theory Is Forever. LNCS, vol. 3113, pp. 112–124. Springer, Heidelberg (2004)
15. Klarlund, N., Møller, A., Schwartzbach, M.I.: MONA Implementation Secrets. International Journal of Foundations of Computer Science, 13(4) (2002)
16. Madhusudan, P., Parlato, G., Qiu, X.: Decidable Logics Combining Heap Structures and Data. SIGPLAN Not. 46 (2011)
17. Somenzi, F.: CUDD: CU Decision Diagram Package Release 2.4.2 (May 2011)
18. Tozawa, A., Hagiya, M.: XML Schema Containment Checking Based on Semi-implicit Techniques. In: Ibarra, O.H., Dang, Z. (eds.) CIAA 2003. LNCS, vol. 2759, pp. 213–225. Springer, Heidelberg (2003)
19. De Wulf, M., Doyen, L., Henzinger, T.A., Raskin, J.-F.: Antichains: A New Algorithm for Checking Universality of Finite Automata. In: Ball, T., Jones, R.B. (eds.) CAV 2006. LNCS, vol. 4144, pp. 17–30. Springer, Heidelberg (2006)

Assembling Sessions*

Philippe Darondeau[1], Loïc Hélouët[1], and Madhavan Mukund[2]

[1] IRISA, INRIA, Rennes, France
{philippe.darondeau,loic.helouet}@irisa.fr
[2] CMI, Chennai, India
madhavan@cmi.ac.in

Abstract. Sessions are a central paradigm in Web services to implement decentralized transactions with multiple participants. Sessions enable the cooperation of workflows while at the same time avoiding the mixing of workflows from distinct transactions. Languages such as BPEL, ORC, AXML that implement Web Services usually realize sessions by attaching unique identifiers to transactions. The expressive power of these languages makes the properties of the implemented services undecidable. In this paper, we propose a new formalism for modelling web services. Our model is session-based, but avoids using session identifiers. The model can be translated to a dialect of Petri nets that allows the verification of important properties of web services.

1 Introduction

Web services consist of interactions between multiple parties. In developing a formal model for web services, we have to consider two different points of view. The first focus is on the interactions themselves: they are typically structured using what we will call *sessions*. An example of a session could include sending an email or making an online payment. Informally, a session is a functionally coherent sequence of interactions between agents playing specific roles, such as server and client.

The second requirement is to capture the perspective of each agent. Typically, agents participate in more than one session at a time: while composing a mail, an agent may also participate in an online chat and, on the side, browse a catalogue to select an item to purchase from an online retailer. While some concurrent sessions may be independent of each other, there may also be non-trivial connections between sessions. For instance, to purchase an item online, one has to first participate in a session with the retailer to choose an item, then make the online payment in a session with the bank, which typically returns the agent to the shopping session with a confirmation of the transaction. Thus, we need a mechanism to describe how an agent moves between sessions, including the possibility of invoking multiple concurrent sessions.

* This work was partially funded by INRIA's DST Associated Team, and by the ARCUS program (Région Ile-de-France).

T. Bultan and P.-A. Hsiung (Eds.): ATVA 2011, LNCS 6996, pp. 259–274, 2011.

We propose a formal model for sessions to capture both these aspects. A guiding principle is that the model should support some formal verification. We base our approach on finite automata and model interaction through shared actions. These shared actions can update local variables of agents, which permits information to be transferred across agents. The local variables record the state of an agent across sessions to permit coordination between sessions.

Our model can be translated into a class of Petri nets called *Reset Post-G* nets [6] for which coverability is decidable. In terms of our model, this means, for instance, that asking whether a specific type of session occurs is decidable. The paper is organized as follows. After briefly discussing related work, we introduce our model through an example in the next section. This is followed by a formal definition of our model of session systems. Section 4 translates the semantics of session systems into Reset Post-G nets, and highlights decidability results for our model. We end with a brief conclusion. Due to lack of space, and also to improve readability, some proofs are only sketched.

Related Work. Several other frameworks propose sessions and mechanisms to *orchestrate* sessions into larger applications. The range of approaches includes agent-centric formalisms, such as BPEL [3], workflow-based formalisms such as ORC [8, 9], and declarative, rule-based formalisms such as AXML [1, 2]. Each approach has its advantages and drawbacks.

A BPEL specification describes a set of independent communicating agents equipped with a rich set of control structures. Coordination across agents is achieved through message-passing. Interactions are grouped into sessions implicitly by defining *correlations* which specify data values that uniquely identify a session—for instance, a purchase order number for an online retail transaction. This makes it difficult to identify the structure of sessions from the specification, and workflows are often implicit, known only at runtime. ORC is a programming language for the orchestration of services. It allows any kind of algorithmic manipulation of data, with an orchestration overlay that helps start new services and synchronize their results. ORC has better mechanisms to define workflows than BPEL, but lacks the notion of correlation that is essential to establish sessions among the participants in a service. AXML defines web services as a set of rules for transforming semi-structured documents described, for instance, in XML. However, it does not make workflows explicit, and does not have a native notion of session either. So, transactions must be defined using complex guards. A common feature of these formalisms is that they aim to describe *implementations* of web services or orchestrations. BPEL, ORC and AXML can easily simulate Turing Machines, hence rendering undecidable simple properties such as the termination of a service. In [4], the authors develop a model for *shared experience services* where multiple users participate in sessions by simultaneously accessing a shared communication interface—examples include conference calls and internet chat. Though this model has a superficial resemblance to our work—they define session data types and use finite automata to describe session behaviours—the main aim is to provide an event-driven programming language to describe such systems, without any support for verification, so their model has little in common with ours.

At a different level, Petri nets have often been used to specify workflows [10] or to serve as targets for translating high-level description languages such as BPEL [11, 7]. However, Petri nets are not expressive enough to model sessions with correlations as in BPEL, hence translations either are restricted to a subset of the workflow description language [11] or they are aimed at coloured extensions of Petri nets [7] for which many properties are undecidable. Our model can be translated to a less powerful class of Petri Nets which allows us to decide properties such as coverability and termination.

2   Motivational Example

To motivate the constructs that we incorporate into our model, we look at an example. We model an online retail system with three types of participants: clients (the buyers), servers (the sellers), and banks. The interactions between these entities can be broken up into two distinct phases: selecting and confirming the items to be purchased online, and paying for these items. The first phase, online sale, only concerns clients and servers while the second phase, online payment, involves all three types of entities.

In an online sale, a client logs in to a server and selects a set of items to buy. Selecting an item involves browsing the items on offer, choosing some of them, perhaps revoking some earlier choices and finally deciding to pay for the selected items. At this point, the client has to choose between several modes of payment. Once this choice is made, the online sale interaction is suspended and the second phase is triggered.

The second phase, online payment, involves the client and the server as well as a bank that is chosen by the server according to the mode of payment selected by the client. The server transfers the transaction amount to the bank. The bank then asks the client for credentials to authenticate itself and authorize this transaction. Based on the information provided by the client, the bank either accepts or rejects the transaction. This decision is based on several parameters, including the correctness of the authentication data provided and the client's credit limit. For simplicity, we can omit the details of how the bank arrives at this decision and model this as a nondeterministic choice between success and failure of the payment. When the payment phase ends, the client and server resume their interaction in the online sale. If the payment was successful, the server generates a receipt. Otherwise, the server generates an appropriate error notification. In case of a payment failure, the client can choose to abort the sale or retry the payment.

This example illustrates both aspects of web services identified in the Introduction. Online sale and online payment are examples of *sessions*—structured interactions involving multiple agents. On the other hand, the clients, servers and banks that participate in these sessions are examples of agents, each with its own control structure that determines how it evolves and moves from one session to another.

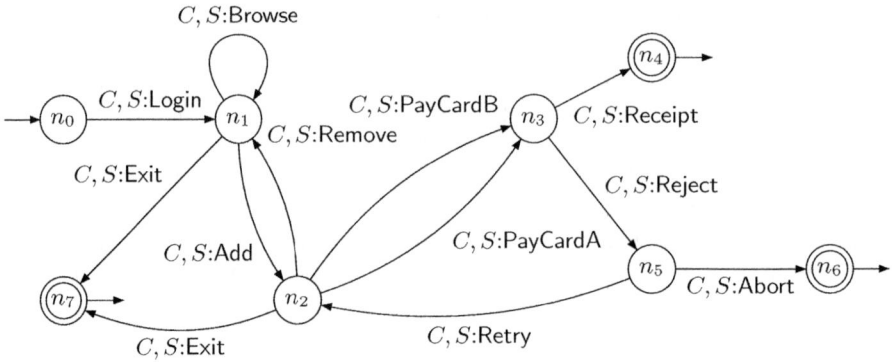

Fig. 1. Session template for Online Purchase

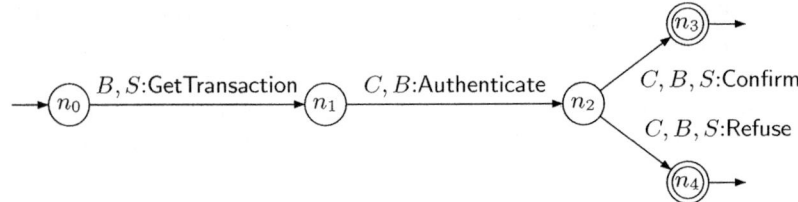

Fig. 2. Session template for Payment

We propose to use finite-state automata to describe *session schemes* and *agents*. These prescribe the underlying structure from which concrete sessions are instantiated. Figure 1 depicts a session scheme for online sale, while Figure 2 shows a scheme for online payment. In these automata, transitions are labelled by shared actions, such as PayCardA and Authenticate. Each shared action is annotated with the names of the participants: for instance, C, S : Login indicates that the action Login is shared by C and S. Here, C and S are not agents but abstract *roles*, to be played by actual agents when the scheme is instantiated as a concrete session.

Each session scheme has a start node, denoted by an incoming arrow and global final nodes marked by an outgoing arrow. Nodes with double circles are *return nodes* where one or more participants can exit the session without terminating the session itself. A session terminates when all participants have exited.

To ensure coordination between agents and across sessions, we need to equip the system with data. Each agent has a set of local variables that are updated as it evolves. In addition, each concrete session has variables to indicate its state, including the identities of the agents playing the various roles defined in the underlying session scheme. We will allow transitions to be guarded, so that a shared action may be enabled or disabled depending on the current state of the participating agents.

In a session system, several sessions that are active simultaneously may share agents—for instance, a customer may participate in online sales with two distinct retailers with the same bank. Sessions sharing an agent share the variables of this

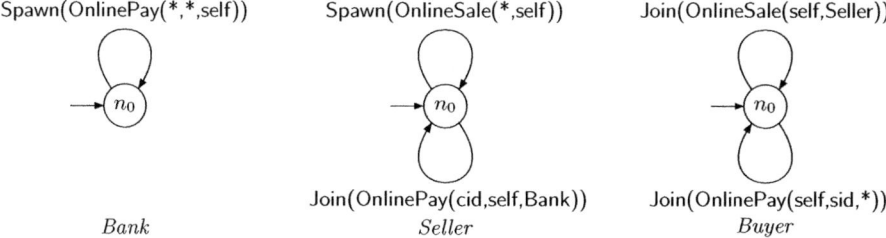

Fig. 3. Agents for Banks, Sellers and Buyers

agent, so one has to take care to avoid unwanted interferences across sessions. For example, if payment information pertaining to different sessions gets mixed, an authorization for a low-cost transaction may be misused to complete a high-cost purchase beyond the customer's credit limit. As we shall see, our model allows us to enforce controlled access to critical sections through variables and guards, and also verify that mutual exclusion is achieved through formal analysis of the model. For the sake of readability, we have not represented variables and guards in the examples here. Details can be found in the extended version of this work [5].

The other half of the system description consists of specifications for the agents. The agents *Bank*, *Seller* and *Client* are shown in Figure 3. There is one automaton for each agent: in this example, each agent has only a single state.

The typical actions of an agent are to spawn a new instance of a session scheme and to join an existing session. In this example, OnlinePay sessions are spawned by the bank and joined by the buyer and seller while OnlineSale sessions are spawned by the seller and joined by the buyer. The actions Spawn and Join refer to a session scheme with parameters that denote the association of agents to roles. For instance, the bank's action Spawn(OnlinePay(*,*,self)) spawns a new instance of the session scheme OnlinePay in which the current bank agent, self, plays the third role and the other two roles are left open for arbitrary agents. On the other hand, the buyer's action Join(OnlineSale(self,Seller)) says that the agent is willing to join any existing OnlineSale session in which the other participant is an instance of Seller, while Join(OnlinePay(self,sid,*)) says that the agent wants to join an OnlinePay session with a specific seller agent sid in the second role, but without any constraint on the bank playing the third role.

3   Session Systems

A *session system* has a finite set of *agents* identified by names. Each agent has a finite data store and a finite repository of links to other agents. Agents operate at two levels. Individually, an agent executes a sequence of commands that determine its interactions with the other agents. Collectively, interactions are grouped into sessions. Within sessions, sets of agents perform synchronized actions, updating their respective data stores and link repositories.

An agent can *spawn* sessions from predefined session schemes or *join* existing sessions. It can also *kill* sessions and *quit* them. Each agent has a set of local variables—the state of an agent is given by the current values of these variables.

Session schemes provide templates for interaction patterns involving an abstract set of roles. A *session* is an instance of such a scheme in which concrete agents are associated with the abstract roles. A session progresses through the execution of synchronized actions involving subsets of the participating agents. These actions are enabled through guards that depend on the identities and states of the participating agents.

There may be multiple instances of a given session scheme running at a given time. Agents cannot "name" or "address" individual sessions. However, agents can supply constraints when creating or joining sessions to filter out sessions from the collection of active sessions. Agents can join existing sessions synchronously or asynchronously. Agents that join a session synchronously are normally released just before the session *dies*.

Each session has a set of *role* variables that are used to describe the current mapping of abstract roles to concrete agents as well as to record constraints on the identity and type of agents that may join in the future to play roles that are currently unassociated.

In addition to sessions and agents, our model presupposes a global *scheduler* that manages sessions and serves requests for joining sessions. Agents can *query* this scheduler for the presence of a session of some kind. Queries are answered only if such session exists in the system.

3.1   Preliminaries

Let $\mathcal{A}$ denote a fixed, finite set of agents and $\mathbb{B} = \{\mathsf{tt}, \mathsf{ff}\}$ denote the set of boolean values. We assume the existence of two distinguished values $\bot$ and $\top$, whose interpretation will be explained later.

Each agent manipulates a set of local variables, organized as follows. There is a fixed set $X = X_A \uplus X_B$ of variable names, where X_A is the set of *agent variables*, including the distinguished variable *self*, and variables in X_B are boolean. A valuation of X is a pair of maps $V = (V_A, V_B)$ where $V_A : X_A \to \mathcal{A} \cup \{\bot\}$ and $V_B : X_B \to \mathbb{B} \cup \{\bot\}$. The variable *self* is a fixed read-only value: for agent a, $V_A(\mathit{self})$ always evaluates to a.

Each agent has a local copy of the set X. For $a \in \mathcal{A}$ and $x \in X$, $a.x$ denotes agent a's local copy of x. Though variables are local to agents, shared actions can observe and update local variables of all participating agents. When referring to variables and valuations of multiple agents simultaneously, we write $X^a = X_A^a \uplus X_B^a$ and $V^a = (V_A^a, V_B^a)$ to refer to the local variables and valuation of agent a, respectively.

In addition, session schemes are provided with a finite set Y of *role variables*, including a distinguished variable *owner*. Variables in Y are used to keep track of agents joining a session. A valuation of Y is a map $W : Y \to \mathcal{A} \cup \{\bot, \top\}$. The value $\top$ indicates that a role has been completed, so the corresponding agent is released from the session. When $W(y)$ is defined, we write $y.x$ as an abbreviation for $W(y).x$, the local copy of variable x in agent $W(y)$. In addition, we also equip each session with a *constraint map* $C : Y \to 2^{\mathcal{A}}$ that specifies constraints on the agents that can play each role. The set $C(y)$ indicates the set of agents that is compatible with the role y. We interpret $C(y) = \emptyset$ as an unconstrained role, rather than as a role that is impossible to fulfil.

3.2 Session Schemes

A session scheme is a finite automaton with guarded transitions labelled by shared actions. Formally, a *session scheme* over a set of role variables Y is a tuple $S = (N, n_0, \Sigma, \ell, \delta)$, where:

- N is a finite set of *session nodes*, with an initial node n_0.
- Σ is a finite alphabet of actions that includes the special action Die that prematurely kills a session.
- $\ell : \Sigma \times Y \to \{\perp, +, \top\}$ defines for each shared action $\sigma \in \Sigma$ and role $y \in Y$ the participation of y in σ.

  - If $\ell(\sigma, y) = \perp$, y is not involved in σ: σ can execute even if $W(y) = \perp$.
  - If $\ell(\sigma, y) \neq \perp$, y is involved in σ: we must have $W(y) \neq \perp$ for σ to occur.
  - If $\ell(\sigma, y) = \top$, y terminates with action σ, and then agent $W(y)$ is released if it joined the session synchronously.

- $\delta \subseteq N \times G \times \Sigma \times U \times N$, is a *transition relation* between nodes, where G is the set of *guards*, and U is the set of *update functions*.

A transition (n, g, σ, u, n') means that a session can move from node n to node n' when guard g holds with respect to W, the current valuations of Y and $\{V^a\}_{a \in \mathcal{A}}$, the current valuations of all the agents in the system. These valuations are then updated as specified by u. The guard g and update u can only read and modify values of variables for roles y such that $\ell(\sigma, y) \neq \perp$. A guard g is a boolean combination of assertions of the form $y.x_1$ and $y_1 = y_2.x_2$. The literal $y.x_1$ is true if $W(y) = a \in \mathcal{A}$ and $V_B^a(x_1) = \text{tt}$. The literal $y_1 = y_2.x_2$ is true if $W(y_1) \neq \top$, $W(y_2) = a \in \mathcal{A}$ and $W(y_1) = V_A^a(x_2)$. We lift this in the usual way to define the truth of the guard g.

3.3 Sessions

A session is an instance of a session template with roles assigned to agents in $\mathcal{A}$. Not all roles need to be defined in order for a session to be active—an action σ can be performed provided $W(y)$ is defined for every role that takes part in σ.

The constraint map C controls which agents can join the session in as yet undefined roles, as we shall see later.

We associate with each session a partial *return map* ρ from roles to states of agents. If $\rho(y)$ is defined, it means that the agent $W(y)$ is blocked and waiting for the session to end. Whenever $W(y)$ terminates in this session, or the session executes the action Die or it is killed by another agent, $W(y)$ resumes in the state $\rho(y)$.

3.4   Agents

The behaviour of an agent a is described by a tuple (Q, E, Δ, q_0) where

- Q is the set of control states, with initial state q_0.
- $\Delta \subseteq Q \times G \times E \times Q$ is the transition relation, where G is the set of *guards* over X^a. For simplicity, we define a guard as any function that maps each valuation $V^a = (V^a_A, V^a_B)$ of a to either tt or ff.
- E is a set of labels defining the *effect* of the transition, as described below.

Variable Assignment. $x := e$, where $x \in X$ and e is an expression over $\mathcal{A} \cup \mathbb{B} \cup \{\bot\} \cup X$ that is compatible with the type of x.

Asynchronous Session Creation. $ASpawn(s, l)$, where s is a session scheme, and l is a list of constraints of the form $y = x$ where $y \in Y$ and $x \in X_A$. The variables *self* and *owner* should not appear in the constraints. $ASpawn(s, l)$ does not execute if $V(x) = \bot$ for some variable x occurring in the constraints. The new session is created with a valuation W such that $W(owner) = V(self)$ and $W(y) = \bot$ for every other $y \in Y$. We also define the constraint map for the session as follows: $V(x) \in C(y)$ if and only if the constraint $y = x$ is in l.

Synchronous Session Creation. $SSpawn(s, l)$, like asynchronous session creation, with the difference that the agent gives up control. This action sets the return map $\rho(owner)$ to the target state of the transition carrying the spawn instruction to indicate where control returns when this agent's role terminates, when the session dies, or when the session is killed.

Asynchronous Join. $AJoin(s, y, l)$, where the variable y is the role of session scheme s that the process takes on joining the session and l specifies constraints of the form $y' = x'$, with $y' \in Y$ and $x' \in X_A$. $AJoin(s, y, l)$ does not execute if $V(x') = \bot$ for any variable x' occurring in the constraints. Otherwise, it produces a *pending join request* (a, s, y, ϕ) where $a = V(self)$. The map $\phi : Y \rightarrow 2^{\mathcal{A}}$ serves to filter out sessions from the collection of running sessions and is defined by $V(x') \in \phi(y')$ if and only if the constraint $y' = x'$ appears in l.

   The join request $AJoin(s, y, l)$ is granted with respect to a session of type s with valuation W and constraint C if $W(y) = \bot$ and $V(self) \in C(y)$ and also, for each y', $W(y') \in \phi(y')$. Pending requests are dealt with asynchonously: that is, control returns to the agent immediately, without waiting for the join request to be granted.

Plain Join. $PJoin(s, y, l)$ is like asynchronous join, except that this command can be executed only if and when a session of type s meeting contraint l exists. Thus, after the command, the agent has already a role in the joined session and proceeds in the target state of the transition with the join instruction.

Synchronous Join. $SJoin(s, y, l)$, like plain join, except that control returns to the agent only after the session that it joins ends: that is, this agent's role terminates, the session dies or the session is killed. This action sets the return map $\rho(y)$ to the target state of the transition carrying the join instruction to indicate where control returns.

Query. $Query(s, l)$, where list l specifies constraints of the form $x = y$ for $x \in X_A$ and $y \in Y$ (the variables *self* and *owner* may appear in these constraints). $Query(s, l)$ may execute even though $V(x) = \bot$ for some variable x occurring in the constraints. This command executes in an atomic step when some session with scheme s and valuation W satisfies all constraints $x = y$: that is, for every $x \in X_A$, if $V(x) \neq \bot$ then $V(x) = W(y)$ and if $V(x) = \bot$ then $W(y) \notin \{\bot, \top\}$. If the query succeeds, for each constraint $x = y$, $V(x)$ is updated to $W(y)$. In particular, if $V(x)$ was earlier $\bot$, x now acquires the value $W(y)$.

Kill. *Kill*, kills all sessions created by the agent $V(\textit{self})$. This has the same effect as when these sessions execute the action Die.

Quit. *Quit*, agent $V(\textit{self})$ leaves all sessions that it has entered. This has no effect other than removing this agent from all session environments.

A major difference between creating and joining a session is that the creator of a session owns the session and can kill it, whereas an agent that has joined a session can only quit, in which case the session stays active if some roles have not yet terminated.

Joining a session asynchronously is like thread creation: the agent that makes a join request does not have to wait for the completion of the activities resulting from the firing of the join transition.

On the other hand, joining a session synchronously is like a remote procedure call from the perspective of the joining agent since it loses control. From the perspective of the joined session, no new incarnation of a session scheme is produced. The calling agent recovers control when the session it has joined terminates—the return state of the calling agent is kept track of by the joined session in the return map ρ.

Let us now comment about plain joins, which are in between asynchronous and synchronous joins. Like a synchronous join, a plain join $PJoin(s, y, l')$ cannot be executed before there exists some session of the specified scheme s with role y free. Like an asynchronous join, an agent that executes a plain join does not have to wait for the completion of the activities resulting from the firing of the join transition. Thus, for an agent a, using a transition $PJoin(s, y, l')$ amounts to waiting for another agent a' to spawn a new session, if needed, before a moves to another state. With the three forms of joins, one can easily model synchronization mechanisms, remote procedure calls, or threading mechanisms.

Finally, we comment on the difference between quit and kill. An agent that *Quits* leaves all sessions it has entered—that is, it stops playing a role in each of them, but does not otherwise affect the continuation of these sessions for those agents still engaged in active roles. This is essential to model collaborative frameworks in which the number of participants is not fixed in advance—for example, consider chat sessions where participants can join and leave freely. Conversely, *Kill* allows the owner of a session to close it unilaterally, hence stopping the service (but without killing the participants ...)—note that, to ensure robustness, only the owner of a session can kill it.

3.5   Scheduling

The effect of agents' actions on sessions and session actions are handled by the scheduler. We do not give details about how this scheduler is implemented—for instance, it could be via a shared memory manager. We assume that the scheduler keeps track of all active sessions and pending session requests. Serving a session request just consists of finding a running session of type s whose valuation W is compatible with the constraint ϕ of a session demand $sd = (a, s, y, \phi)$ and assigning role y to agent a in this running session. We denote this by a specific action labelled *Serve*.

4   Semantics of Session Systems

Session Systems and Configurations

Let $\mathcal{A}$ be a set of agents, X a set of variables, Y a set of role variables and $\mathcal{S}$ a set of sessions defined over X and Y. The tuple $(\mathcal{A}, \mathcal{S}, X, Y)$ defines a *session system*. A *session configuration* is a tuple (s, n, W, C, ρ), where s is a session scheme name, n is a state of session scheme s, W is a valuation of Y, C is a constraint on roles and ρ is a return map.

An *agent configuration* for an agent $a \in \mathcal{A}$ is a pair (q, V) where q is a state of the agent, and V is a valuation for variables in X. A *session system configuration* is a triple (Ψ, Γ, P), where Ψ associates a configuration to each agent $a \in A$, Γ is a set of session configurations, and P is a set of pending demands to join sessions. The following proposition ensures that configurations can be represented as finitely indexed multisets, and encoded as vectors, or as markings of a Petri net.

Proposition 1. *Let $\mathcal{A}$ be a finite set of agents and $\mathcal{S}$ be a set of session schemes over finite sets of variables X and Y. If $\mathcal{A}$ and $\mathcal{S}$ are defined over finite sets of states Q_P and Q_S, respectively, then the set $\mathcal{C}$ of session systems configurations that are definable over $\mathcal{A}, \mathcal{S}, X, Y$ is isomorphic to $Q_P^{|\mathcal{A}|} \times 2^{|X_B| \cdot |\mathcal{A}|} \times \mathcal{A}^{|X_A| \cdot |\mathcal{A}|} \times \mathbb{N}^K$, where $K = |\mathcal{S}| \cdot |Q_S| \cdot |Y|^{2|\mathcal{A}|+|Q_P|+2} + |\mathcal{A}| \cdot |\mathcal{S}| \cdot |Y|^{|\mathcal{A}|+1}$*

A session system moves from one configuration to another by performing an action. The obvious actions are process moves from E (spawning a session, joining a session, query, kill, quit) and session moves from Σ (shared actions, including the special action Die). In addition, we have internal system moves that *serve* requests to join a session. We say that a configuration χ' is a *successor* of a configuration χ via action $\sigma \in E \cup \Sigma \cup \{Serve\}$, and write $\chi \xrightarrow{\sigma} \chi'$, if and only if starting from χ, the effect of applying σ produces configuration χ'.

Reset Post-G Nets

A *(labelled) Petri net* is a structure (P, T, λ, m_0, F) where P is a set of places, T is a set of transitions, λ is a function that associates a label to each transition of T, $m_0 : p \to \mathbb{N}$ associates a non-negative integer to each place of P, and $F : (P \times T) \cup (T \times P) \to \mathbb{N}$ is a weighted flow relation. A *marking* $m : P \to \mathbb{N}$

distributes tokens across the places. A transition t is enabled at m if each place p has at least $F(p,t)$ tokens. When t fires, the marking m is transformed to a new marking m' such that $m'(p) = m(p) - F(p,t) + F(t,p)$ for every place p.

In a *generalized self-modifying net* (G-net), the flow relation is enhanced to be of the form $F : (P \times T) \cup (T \times P) \to \mathbb{N}[P]$. In other words, the weights on the edges between places and transitions are polynomials over the contents of places in P. These polynomials are evaluated relative to the current marking to determine whether a transition is enabled and compute the effect of firing it.

In *Reset Post-G nets*, the input polynomials $F(p,t)$ are restricted so that $F(p,t) = \{p\}$ or $F(p,t) \in \mathbb{N}$. The term *reset* refers to the fact that every edge from a place p to a transition t weighted by a marking-dependent polynomial is in fact weighted by the monomial p, which corresponds to resetting place p. Reset Post-G nets are a very expressive class of Petri Nets, but yet several key properties of nets such as termination and coverability remain decidable for this class [6]. In the rest of the paper, we will only consider Reset Post-G nets such that $F(p,t) = p$ or $F(p,t) \in \{0,1\}$, and such that $F(t,p) \in \{0,1\}$ or $F(t,p)$ is a sum of places p' such that $F(p',t) = p'$.

Claim. Let $(\mathcal{A}, \mathcal{S}, X, Y)$ be a session system starting in a configuration χ_0. Then the transition system $(\mathcal{C}, \chi_0, \longrightarrow)$ is the marking graph of a Reset Post-G net.

We establish this claim by building a Reset Post-G net whose marking graph is isomorphic to the set of configurations of the session system, and whose transitions encode moves from one configuration to another. From $(\mathcal{A}, \mathcal{S}, X, Y)$, we build the following subsets of places:

- $P_{Q,\mathcal{A}} = \{p_{q,a}, \ldots\}$ associates a place to each pair (q, a) where $a \in \mathcal{A}$ is an agent and q is a state of a. Since the set of states Q_P of all agents is finite, the set $P_{Q,\mathcal{A}}$ is finite as well.
- $P_{V,\mathcal{A}} = \{p_{v,a}, \ldots\}$ associates a place to each pair (v, a) where $a \in \mathcal{A}$ is an agent and v is a valuation of X. Since X is finite and the variables in X range over finite domains, $P_{V,\mathcal{A}}$ is a finite set.
- $P_{SC} = \{p_{sc}, \ldots\}$ is a set of places indexed by session configurations—that is, there exists a place p_{sc} for every tuple $sc = (s, n, W, C, \rho)$ that describes a valid session configuration.
- Finally, $P_D = \{p_{sd}, \ldots\}$ is a set of places indexed by join requests—that is, we have one place for every tuple $sd = (a, s, y, \phi)$ representing a join action.

We can now define the transitions of the Reset Post-G net. As discussed earlier, each action that transforms a session configuration is either a process move, or a session move, or an internal system move that serves a pending join request. Each move of the session system is represented by a finite set of net transitions. This representation is not a bijection, because, for instance, a move of an agent can be enabled in more than one valuation and in more than one environment.

For each agent $a = (Q, E, \Delta, q_0)$, and transition $t = (q, g, e, q')$ in Δ, we build net transitions and flow relations as follows:

- When $t = (q, g, e, q')$ is a variable assignment, for every valuation v satisfying the guard g, we construct a transition $t_{e,v}$ such that $\lambda(t_{e,v}) = e$, with preset $\{p_{v,a}, p_{q,a}\}$, postset $\{p_{v',a}, p_{q',a}\}$, and flow relations $F(p_{v,a}, t) = F(p_{q,a}, t) = F(t, p_{v',a}) = F(t, p_{q',a}) = 1$, where $v' = e(v)$ is the result of applying e to v.

- When $t = (q, g, e, q')$ with $e = ASpawn(s, l)$, we construct one transition $t_{v,e}$ for each valuation v that satisfies the guard g, with preset $\{p_{v,a}, p_{q,a}\}$, postset $\{p_{v,a}, p_{q',a}, p_{sc}\}$, letting $sc = (s, n_0, W, C, \rho_\emptyset)$ where n_0 is the initial state of s, $W(\text{owner}) = a$ and $W(y) = \bot$ for all other roles y, C is generated by l and $\rho_\emptyset$ is the empty map. As for assignment transitions, we let $F(p_{v,a}, t) = F(p_{q,a}, t) = F(t, p_{v,a}) = F(t, p_{q',a}) = F(t, p_{sc}) = 1$.

- When $t = (q, g, e, q')$ with $e = SSpawn(s, l)$, we construct one transition $t_{v,e}$ for each valuation v that satisfies the guard g, with preset $\{p_{v,a}, p_{q,a}\}$ and postset $\{p_{v,a}, p_{sc}\}$, letting $sc = (s, n_0, W, C, \rho)$ where n_0 is the initial state of s, $W(\text{owner}) = a$ and $W(y) = \bot$ for all other roles y, C is generated by l and $\rho(\text{owner}) = q'$. We also let $F(p_{v,a}, t) = F(p_{q,a}, t) = F(t, p_{v,a}) = F(t, p_{sc}) = 1$. Note that with synchronous session creation, agent a loses control, and will resume in state q' after its role in s terminates. This information is kept in the return map ρ in sc.

- When $t = (q, g, e, q')$ with $e = AJoin(s, y, l)$, we construct a transition $t_{v,e}$ labelled by e for each valuation v that satisfies the guard g, with preset $\{p_{v,a}, p_{q,a}\}$ and postset $\{p_{v,a}, p_{q',a}, p_{sd}\}$, where $sd = (a, s, y, \phi)$ with map ϕ derived from the constraints in l. The flow relation is given by $F(p_{v,a}, t) = F(p_{q,a}, t) = F(t, p_{v,a}) = F(t, p_{q',a}) = F(t, p_{sd}) = 1$.

- When $t = (q, g, e, q')$ with $e = SJoin(s, y, l')$, we construct a transition $t_{v,e,sc}$ labelled by e for every valuation v that satisfies the guard g and for every session configuration $sc = (s, n, W, C, \rho)$ meeting constraint l' such that $W(y) = \bot$ and $a \in C(y)$. The preset of each transition is $\{p_{v,a}, p_{q,a}, p_{sc}\}$ and the postset is $\{p_{v,a}, p_{sc'}\}$, where $sc' = (s, n, W', C', \rho')$ is an updated session configuration in which $W'(y) = a$, $\rho'(y) = q'$, and C' is obtained by adding to C the constraints in l'. The flow relation is given by $F(p_{v,a}, t) = F(p_{q,a}, t) = F(p_{sc}, t) = F(t, p_{v,a}) = F(t, p_{sc'}) = 1$.

- When $t = (q, g, e, q')$ with $e = PJoin(s, y, l')$, we construct a transition $t_{v,e,sc}$ labelled by e for every valuation v satisfying the guard g and for every session configuration $sc = (s, n, W, C, \rho)$ meeting constraint l' such that $W(y) = \bot$ and $a \in C(y)$. The preset of each transition is $\{p_{v,a}, p_{q,a}, p_{sc}\}$ and the postset is $\{p_{v,a}, p_{q',a}, p_{sc'}\}$, where $sc' = (s, n, W', C', \rho)$ is an updated session configuration in which $W'(y) = a$ and C' is obtained by adding to C the constraints in l'. Unlike with synchronous join, the return map ρ is unchanged in sc' and control is returned via the output place $p_{q',a}$ to the agent executing the join instruction. The flow relation is given by $F(p_{v,a}, t) = F(p_{q,a}, t) = F(p_{sc}, t) = F(t, p_{v,a}) = F(t, p_{q',a}) = F(t, p_{sc'}) = 1$.

- When $t = (q, g, e, q')$ with $e = Query(s, l)$, we construct a transition $t_{v,e,v'}$ labelled by e for every valuation v satisfying the guard g, for every session configuration $sc = (s, n, W, C, \rho)$ meeting constraint l, and for every valuation v' computed from v by adding the bindings of agents induced by the constraints in l and the bindings of agents in W. The preset of each transition is $\{p_{v,a}, p_{q,a}, p_{sc}\}$ and the postset is $\{p_{v',a}, p_{q',a}, p_{sc}\}$. The flow relation is given by $F(p_{v,a}, t) = F(p_{q,a}, t) = F(p_{sc}, t) = F(t, p_{v',a}) = F(t, p_{q',a}) = F(t, p_{sc}) = 1$. Note that the transition does not consume any token from the place p_{sc}—it only tests the presence of a token.

- When $t = (q, g, e, q')$ with $e = Kill$, we construct a transition $t_{v,e}$ for every valuation v satisfying the guard g. Each of these transitions has as preset $\{p_{v,a}, p_{q,a}\} \cup \{p_{sc_i} \mid sc_i = (s, n, W, C, \rho) \wedge W(owner) = a\}$. The postset of the transition is the union of $\{p_{v,a}, p_{q',a}\}$ and the set of all places p_{q_j, b_j} such that b_j is a process which has issued a Synhronous Join with return state q_j. The flow relation is defined as follows: $F(p_{v,a}, t) = F(p_{q,a}, t) = F(t, p_{v,a}) = F(t, p_{q',a}) = 1$, $F(p_{sc_i}, t) = p_{sc_i}$ for every session configuration sc_i owned by agent a (the transition consumes all sessions created by a), and $F(t, p_{q_j, b_j}) = \sum \{p_{sc} \mid sc = (s', n', W', C', \rho') \wedge W'(y) = b_j \wedge \rho'(y) = q_j\}$. Note that an agent b_j can be blocked in at most one session, so $F(t, p_{q_j, b_j}) \leq 1$ and control is returned to agent b_j only when it was blocked.

- When $t = (q, g, e, q')$ with $e = Quit$, we construct a transition $t_{v,e}$ for every valuation v satisfying the guard g. Each of these transitions has preset $\{p_{v,a}, p_{q,a}\} \cup NT$, where $NT = \{p_{sc_i} \mid sc_i = (s, n, W, C, \rho) \wedge (\exists y)(W(y) = a)\}$. The postset of the transition is $\{p_{v,a}, p_{q',a}\} \cup NT'$, where NT' is the set of places $p_{sc_i'}$ representing session configurations $sc_i' = (s, n, W', C, \rho)$ such that, for some $sc_i = (s, n, W, C, \rho)$ in NT, $W(y) = a \Rightarrow W'(y) = \top$ and $W'(y) = W(y)$ otherwise for all y, and $W'(y) \neq \top$ for some y. The flow relation is defined as follows: $F(p_{v,a}, t) = F(p_{q,a}, t) = F(t, p_{v,a}) = F(t, p_{q',a}) = 1$, $F(p_{sc_i}, t) = p_{sc_i}$ for every session configuration sc_i appearing in NT (the transition consumes all sessions involving a), and $F(t, p_{sc_i'}) = p_{sc_i}$ for every session configuration sc_i' in NT'. This way, session configurations involving a, but still having other non-terminated roles, are transformed into session configurations without agent a.

The second part of the translation concerns the internal progress of sessions. We will distinguish two kinds of transitions, depending on whether the translated action brings the session to termination or not.

We consider first the non terminating actions $\sigma \neq Die$. Let $sc = (s, n, W, C, \rho)$ be a session configuration, and let $(n, g, \sigma, u, n') \in \delta$ with guard g and update u. Executing such an action in sc is conditioned to the satisfaction of guard g w.r.t. W and transforms sc into a configuration $sc' = (s, n', W', C', \rho)$, where $W'(y) = \top$ if $\ell(\sigma, y) = \top$ and $W'(y) = W(y)$ otherwise. Then for every valuation v that satisfies g, we construct a transistion $t_{sc,v}$ with preset $\{p_{v,a}, p_{sc}\}$ and postset $\{p_{sc'}, p_{v',a}\} \cup P_{\rho,\sigma}$, where $P_{\rho,\sigma} = \{p_{q'',a} \mid \exists y, W(y) \neq W'(y) \wedge \rho(y) = q'' \wedge W(y) = a\}$ and $v' = u(v)$ is the result of applying u to v. In other words, all agents that have joined the session synchronously and that leave the session by action σ resume their activity in the control state q'' specified at join time. The flow relation is $F(p_{v,a}, t_{sc,v}) = F(p_{sc}, t_{sc,v}) = F(t_{sc,v}, p_{sc'}) = F(t_{sc,v}, p_{v',a}) = 1$. Moreover, for every place $p_{q'',a}$ in $P_{\rho,\sigma}$, we let $F(t_{sc,v}, p_{q'',a}) = 1$.

We now consider the terminating action Die. For every session configuration $sc = (s, n, W, C, \rho)$, and for every $(n, g, \sigma, u, n') \in \delta$ such that $\sigma = $ Die and guard g is satisfied w.r.t. W, we construt a transition $t_{sc,die}$ labeled by action Die with the preset p_{sc} and the postset $P_\rho = \{p_{q'',a} \mid \exists y, \rho(y) = q'' \wedge W(y) = a\}$. The flow relation is $F(p_{sc}, t_{sc,die}) = 1$, and $F(t_{sc,die}, p) = 1$ for every p in P_ρ.

Finally, we have to translate into net transitions the system moves that serve pending join requests. Serving a request just consists of removing the request from the set of pending requests and modifying the configuration of a session compatible with this request in the set of session configurations.

For every Asynchronous Join pending demand $sd = (a, s, y, \phi)$ and for every session configuration $sc = (s, n, W, C, \rho)$ compatible with this request, we construct a transition $t_{sc,sd}$ labeled with the internal action $Serve$. The preset of $t_{sc,sd}$ is $\{p_{sc}, p_{sd}\}$ and its postset is $\{p_{sc'}\}$, where $sc' = (s, n, W', C', \rho)$ is obtained from sc by setting $W'(y) = a$ (and $W'(y') = W(y')$ for every $y' \neq y$) and letting C' be C augmented by the constraints in ϕ. The flow relation is given by $F(p_{sc}, t_{sc,sd}) = F(p_{sd}, t_{sc,sd}) = F(t_{sc,sd}, p_{sc'}) = 1$.

Note that for every transition of the global Petri net obtained in the end, the weight of the flow relation from a place p to a transition t is either 0 or 1 or $F(p, t) = p$, whereas the weight of the flow relation from a transition t to a place p is either 0 or 1 or a polynomial over the contents of a set of places. Hence, the semantic model for session systems corresponds to Reset Post-G nets.

Definition 1. *Let $\chi = (\Psi, \Gamma, P)$ and $\chi' = (\Psi', \Gamma', P')$ be two configurations of a session system. Configuration χ' is reachable from χ if and only if there exists a sequence of moves starting from χ that leads to configuration χ'. Configuration χ' covers χ, denoted by $\chi \sqsubseteq \chi'$, iff $\Psi' = \Psi$, and for every session configuration sc and session demand sd we have $\Gamma[sc] \leq \Gamma'[sc]$ and $P[sd] \leq P'[sd]$. Configuration χ' is coverable from χ iff there exists a sequence of moves starting from χ and leading to a configuration χ'' such that $\chi' \sqsubseteq \chi''$. A session system is bounded iff there exists some constant B such that $\Gamma[sc] \leq B$ and $P[sd] \leq B$ for every sc and sd in any reachable configuration $\chi = (\Psi, \Gamma, P)$.*

Proposition 2. *Given a session system $(\mathcal{A}, \mathcal{S}, X, Y)$ with initial configuration χ_0 and a configuration $\chi \in \mathcal{C}$, one can decide whether one can reach a marking χ' from χ_0 that covers χ. Termination—that is, the absence of infinite runs starting from χ_0—is also decidable.*

Proof: This proposition stems directly from the properties of Reset Post-G Nets, for which coverability of a given configuration and termination are decidable. □

Coverability is an important issue for the kind of services we want to model. To illustrate this, let us return to the example of Section 2, where we wanted to check that an agent a does not participate in two payments at the same time. This property may be expressed as follows: "There is no reachable configuration of the system in which agent a participates as a customer in at least two purchase sessions s, s' whose states are included in $\{n_3, n_5\}$". This property reduces to a coverability check in the Reset Post-G net modelling the session system.

Proposition 3. *Given a session system $(\mathcal{A}, \mathcal{S}, X, Y)$ with initial configuration χ_0, one can decide neither upon the reachability of a given configuration $\chi \in \mathcal{C}$ from χ_0 nor on the boundedness of the session system.*

Proof Sketch: One can simulate Reset Petri Nets with session systems. Now, boundedness and exact reachability are undecidable for Reset Petri Nets. □

5 Conclusion

We have proposed a session-based formalism for modeling distributed orchestrations. We voluntarily limited the expressiveness of the language to ensure decidability of some important practical properties. Indeed, many properties of session systems, such as the possibility for an agent or for a session to perform a given sequence of transitions, may be expressed as a coverability problem on Reset Post-G nets. As deadlock and exact reachability are undecidable in general, a natural question is how to restrict the model to enhance decidability.

A second issue to consider is the implementation of session systems. The natural implementation is a distributed architecture in which agents use only their local variables. However, agents share sessions that have to be managed globally, along with requests and queries. This means, in particular, that an implementation of session systems has to maintain a kind of shared memory that can be queried by agents. This can be costly, and a challenge is to provide implementations with the minimal synchronization.

A third issue is to consider session systems as descriptions of security protocols, and to see whether an environment can break security through legal use of the protocol. For instance, the well known session replay attack of the Needham-Schroeder protocol can apparently be modelled by a simple session type system, and the failure of the protocol (the existence of a session involving unexpected pairs of users) can be reduced to a coverability issue. Whether such an approach can be extended to more complex protocols for detecting unknown security failures is an open question.

References

1. Abiteboul, S., Benjelloun, O., Manolescu, I., Milo, T., Weber, R.: Active XML: A data-centric perspective on web services. In: BDA 2002 (2002)
2. Abiteboul, S., Segoufin, L., Vianu, V.: Static analysis of Active XML systems. In: PODS 2008, pp. 221–230 (2008)
3. Andrews, T., Curbera, F., Dholakia, H., Goland, Y., Klein, J., Leymann, F., Liu, K., Roller, D., Smith, D., Thatte, S., Trickovic, I., Weerawarana, S.: Business process execution language for web services (BPEL4WS). version 1.1 (2003)
4. Arlein, R.M., Dams, D., Hull, R.B., Letourneau, J.P., Namjoshi, K.S.: Telco meets the web: Programming shared-experience services. Bell Labs Technical Journal 14(3), 167–185 (2009)
5. Darondeau, P., Hélouët, L., Mukund, M.: Assembling sessions (long version). Technical report, Inria Rennes and Chennai Mathematical Institute (2011), http://www.irisa.fr/distribcom/DST09/DHM-ATVA-Long.pdf

6. Dufourd, C., Finkel, A., Schnoebelen, P.: Reset nets between decidability and un-decidability. In: Larsen, K.G., Skyum, S., Winskel, G. (eds.) ICALP 1998. LNCS, vol. 1443, pp. 103–115. Springer, Heidelberg (1998)
7. Hinz, S., Schmidt, K., Stahl, C.: Transforming BPEL to petri nets. In: van der Aalst, W.M.P., Benatallah, B., Casati, F., Curbera, F. (eds.) BPM 2005. LNCS, vol. 3649, pp. 220–235. Springer, Heidelberg (2005)
8. Kitchin, D., Cook, W.R., Misra, J.: A language for task orchestration and its semantic properties. In: Baier, C., Hermanns, H. (eds.) CONCUR 2006. LNCS, vol. 4137, pp. 477–491. Springer, Heidelberg (2006)
9. Misra, J., Cook, W.: Computation orchestration. Software and Systems Modeling 6(1), 83–110 (2007)
10. van der Aalst, W.M.P.: The application of Petri nets to workflow management. The Journal of Circuits, Systems and Computers 8(1), 21–66 (1998)
11. Verbeek, H.M.W., van der Aalst, W.M.P.: Analyzing BPEL processes using Petri nets. In: Second International Workshop on Applications of Petri Nets to Coordination, Workflow and Business Process Management, vol. 8(1), pp. 59–78 (2005)

Parametric Modal Transition Systems

Nikola Beneš[2,*], Jan Křetínský[2,3,**], Kim G. Larsen[1],
Mikael H. Møller[1], and Jiří Srba[1,***]

[1] Aalborg University, Denmark
[2] Masaryk University, Czech Republic
[3] Technische Universität München, Germany

Abstract. Modal transition systems (MTS) is a well-studied specification formalism of reactive systems supporting a step-wise refinement methodology. Despite its many advantages, the formalism as well as its currently known extensions are incapable of expressing some practically needed aspects in the refinement process like exclusive, conditional and persistent choices. We introduce a new model called parametric modal transition systems (PMTS) together with a general modal refinement notion that overcome many of the limitations and we investigate the computational complexity of modal refinement checking.

1 Introduction

The specification formalisms of Modal Transition Systems (MTS) [11,1] grew out of a series of attempts to achieve a flexible and easy-to-use compositional development methodology for reactive systems. In fact the formalism of MTS may be seen as a fragment of a temporal logic [5], while having a behavioural semantics allowing for an easy composition with respect to process constructs.

In short, MTS are labelled transition systems equipped with two types of transitions: *must* transitions which are mandatory for any implementation, and *may* transitions which are optional for an implementation. Refinement of an MTS now essentially consists of iteratively resolving the unsettled status of may transitions: either by removing them or by turning them into must transitions.

It is well admitted (see e.g. [15]) that MTS and their extensions like disjunctive MTS (DMTS) [12], 1-selecting MTS (1MTS) [6] and transition systems with obligations (OTS) [4] provide strong support for a specification formalism allowing for step-wise refinement process. Moreover, the MTS formalisms have applications in other contexts, which include verification of product lines [8,10], interface theories [17,15] and modal abstractions in program analysis [7,9,13].

Unfortunately, all of these formalisms lack the capability to express some intuitive specification requirements like exclusive, conditional and persistent choices.

---

* The author is supported by Czech Grant Agency, grant no. GAP202/11/0312.
** The author is a holder of Brno PhD Talent Financial Aid and is supported by the Czech Science Foundation, grant No. P202/10/1469.
*** The author is partially supported by Ministry of Education of The Czech Republic, grant no. MSM 0021622419.

T. Bultan and P.-A. Hsiung (Eds.): ATVA 2011, LNCS 6996, pp. 275–289, 2011.

In this paper we extend considerably the expressiveness of MTS and its variants so that it can model arbitrary Boolean conditions on transitions and also allows to instantiate persistent transitions. Our model, called *parametric modal transition systems* (PMTS), is equipped with a finite set of parameters that are fixed prior to the instantiation of the transitions in the specification. The generalized notion of modal refinement is designed to handle the parametric extension and it specializes to the well-studied modal refinements on all the subclasses of our model like MTS, disjunctive MTS and MTS with obligations.

To the best of our knowledge, this is the first sound attempt to introduce persistence into a specification formalism based on modal transition systems. The most related work is by Fecher and Schmidt on 1-selecting MTS [6] where the authors allow to model exclusive-or and briefly mention the desire to extend the formalism with persistence. However, as in detail explained in [3], their definition does not capture the notion of persistence. Our formalism is in several aspects semantically more general and handles persistence in a complete and uniform manner.

The main technical contribution, apart from the formalism itself, is a comprehensive complexity characterization of modal refinement checking on all of the practically relevant subclasses of PMTS. We show that the complexity ranges from P-completeness to Π_4^p-completeness, depending on the requested generality of the PMTS specifications on the left-hand and right-hand sides.

2 Parametric Modal Transition Systems

In this section we present the formalism of parametric modal transition systems (PMTS), starting with a motivating example and continuing with the formal definitions, followed by the general notion of modal refinement.

2.1 Motivation

Modal transition systems and their extensions described in the literature are lacking the capability to express several specification requirements like exclusive, conditional and persistent choices. We shall now discuss these limitations on an example as a motivation for the introduction of parametric MTS formalism with general Boolean conditions in specification requirements.

Consider a simple specification of a traffic light controller that can be at any moment in one of the four predefined states: *red*, *green*, *yellow* or *yellowRed*. The requirements of the specification are: when *green* is on the traffic light may either change to *red* or *yellow* and if it turned *yellow* it must go to *red* afterward; when *red* is on it may either turn to *green* or *yellowRed*, and if it turns *yellowRed* (as it is the case in some countries) it must go to *green* afterwords.

Figure 1a shows an obvious MTS specification (defined formally later on) of the proposed specification. The transitions in the standard MTS formalism are either of type may (optional transitions depicted as dashed lines) or must (required transitions depicted as solid lines). In Figure 1c, Figure 1d and Figure 1e we present three different implementations of the MTS specification where there

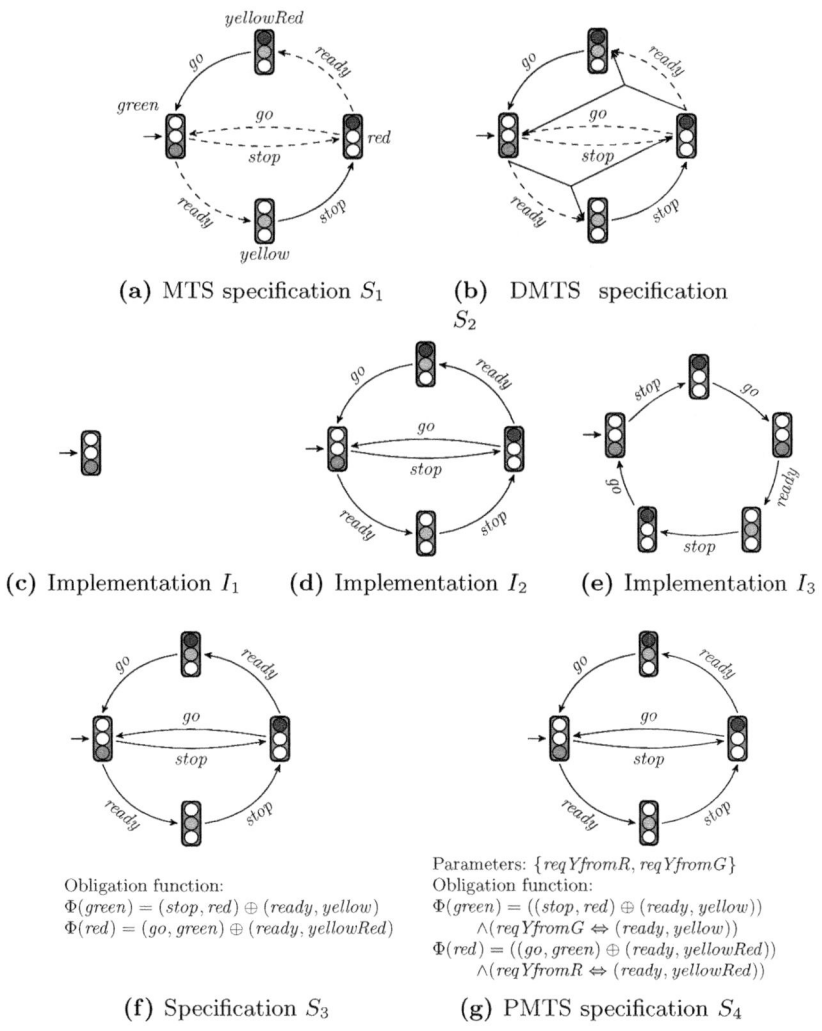

(a) MTS specification S_1

(b) DMTS specification S_2

(c) Implementation I_1 (d) Implementation I_2 (e) Implementation I_3

Obligation function:
$\Phi(green) = (stop, red) \oplus (ready, yellow)$
$\Phi(red) = (go, green) \oplus (ready, yellowRed)$

(f) Specification S_3

Parameters: $\{reqYfromR, reqYfromG\}$
Obligation function:
$\Phi(green) = ((stop, red) \oplus (ready, yellow))$
$\quad \wedge (reqYfromG \Leftrightarrow (ready, yellow))$
$\Phi(red) = ((go, green) \oplus (ready, yellowRed))$
$\quad \wedge (reqYfromR \Leftrightarrow (ready, yellowRed))$

(g) PMTS specification S_4

Fig. 1. Specifications and implementations of a traffic light controller

are no more optional transitions. The implementation I_1 does not implement any may transition as it is a valid possibility to satisfy the specification S_1. Of course, in our concrete example, this means that the light is constantly *green* and it is clearly an undesirable behaviour that cannot be, however, easily avoided. The second implementation I_2 on the other hand implements all may transitions, again a legal implementation in the MTS methodology but not a desirable implementation of a traffic light as the next action is not always deterministically given. Finally, the implementation I_3 of S_1 illustrates the third problem with the MTS specifications, namely that the choices made in each turn are not persistent and the implementation alternates between entering *yellow* or not. None of these problems can be avoided when using the MTS formalism.

A more expressive formalism of disjunctive modal transition systems (DMTS) can overcome some of the above mentioned problems. A possible DMTS specification S_2 is depicted in Figure 1b. Here the *ready* and *stop* transitions, as well as *ready* and *go* ones, are disjunctive, meaning that it is still optional which one is implemented but at least one of them must be present. Now the system I_1 in Figure 1c is not a valid implementation of S_2 any more. Nevertheless, the undesirable implementations I_2 and I_3 are still possible and the modelling power of DMTS is insufficient to eliminate them.

Inspired by the recent notion of transition systems with obligations [4], we can model the traffic light using specification as a transition system with arbitrary[1] obligation formulae. These formulae are Boolean propositions over the outgoing transitions from each state, whose satisfying assignments yield the allowed combinations of outgoing transitions. A possible specification called S_3 is given in Figure 1f and it uses the operation of exclusive-or. We will follow an agreement that whenever the obligation function for some node is not listed in the system description then it is implicitly understood as requiring all the available outgoing transitions to be be present. Due to the use of exclusive-or in the obligation function, the transition systems I_1 and I_2 are not valid implementation any more. Nevertheless, the implementation I_3 in Figure 1e cannot be avoided in this formalism either.

Finally, the problem with the alternating implementation I_3 is that we cannot enforce in any of the above mentioned formalisms a uniform (persistent) implementation of the same transitions in all its states. In order to overcome this problem, we propose the so-called parametric MTS where we can, moreover, choose persistently whether the transition to *yellow* is present or not via the use of parameters. The PMTS specification with two parameters *reqYfromR* and *reqYfromG* is shown in Figure 1g. Fixing a priori the (Boolean) values of the parameters makes the choices permanent in the whole implementation, hence we eliminate also the last problematic implementation I_3.

2.2   Definition of Parametric Modal Transition System

We shall now formally capture the intuition behind parametric MTS introduced above. First, we recall the standard propositional logic.

A Boolean formula over a set X of atomic propositions is given by the following abstract syntax

$$\varphi ::= \mathbf{tt} \mid x \mid \neg\varphi \mid \varphi \wedge \psi \mid \varphi \vee \psi$$

where x ranges over X. The set of all Boolean formulae over the set X is denoted by $\mathcal{B}(X)$. Let $\nu \subseteq X$ be a truth assignment, i.e. a set of variables with value true, then the satisfaction relation $\nu \models \varphi$ is given by $\nu \models \mathbf{tt}$, $\nu \models x$ iff $x \in \nu$, and the satisfaction of the remaining Boolean connectives is defined in the standard way. We also use the standard derived operators like exclusive-or $\varphi \oplus \psi = (\varphi \wedge \neg\psi) \vee (\neg\varphi \wedge \psi)$, implication $\varphi \Rightarrow \psi = \neg\varphi \vee \psi$ and equivalence $\varphi \Leftrightarrow \psi = (\neg\varphi \vee \psi) \wedge (\varphi \vee \neg\psi)$.

We can now proceed with the definition of parametric MTS.

---

[1] In the transition systems with obligations only positive Boolean formulae are allowed.

Definition 1. *A parametric MTS (PMTS) over an action alphabet Σ is a tuple (S, T, P, Φ) where S is a set of states, $T \subseteq S \times \Sigma \times S$ is a transition relation, P is a finite set of* parameters, *and $\Phi : S \to \mathcal{B}((\Sigma \times S) \cup P)$ is an obligation function over the atomic propositions containing outgoing transitions and parameters. We implicitly assume that whenever $(a, t) \in \Phi(s)$ then $(s, a, t) \in T$. By $T(s) = \{(a, t) \mid (s, a, t) \in T\}$ we denote the set of all outgoing transitions of s.*

We recall the agreement that whenever the obligation function for some node is not listed in the system description then it is implicitly understood as $\Phi(s) = \bigwedge T(s)$, with the empty conjunction being **tt**.

We call a PMTS *positive* if, for all $s \in S$, any negation occurring in $\Phi(s)$ is applied only to a parameter. A PMTS is called *parameter-free* if $P = \emptyset$. We can now instantiate the previously studied specification formalisms as subclasses of PMTS.

Definition 2. *A PMTS is called*

- *transition system with obligation (OTS) if it is parameter-free and positive,*
- *disjunctive modal transition system (DMTS) if it is an OTS and $\Phi(s)$ is in the conjunctive normal form for all $s \in S$,*
- *modal transition system (MTS) if it is a DMTS and $\Phi(s)$ is a conjunction of positive literals (transitions) for all $s \in S$, and*
- *implementation (or simply a labelled transition system) if it is an MTS and $\Phi(s) = \bigwedge T(s)$ for all $s \in S$.*

Note that positive PMTS, despite the absence of a general negation and the impossibility to define for example exclusive-or, can still express useful requirements like $\Phi(s) = p \Rightarrow (a, t) \wedge \neg p \Rightarrow (b, u)$ requiring in a state s a conditional presence of certain transitions. Even more interestingly, we can enforce binding of actions in different states, thus ensuring certain functionality. Take a simple two state-example: $\Phi(s) = p \Rightarrow (request, t)$ and $\Phi(t) = p \Rightarrow (response, s)$. We shall further study OTS with formulae in the disjunctive normal form that are dual to DMTS and whose complexity of parallel composition is lower [4] while still being as expressive as DMTS.

2.3   Modal Refinement

A fundamental advantage of MTS-based formalisms is the presence of *modal refinement* that allows for a step-wise system design (see e.g. [1]). We shall now provide such a refinement notion for our general PMTS model so that it will specialize to the well-studied refinement notions on its subclasses. In the definition, the parameters are fixed first (persistence) followed by all valid choices modulo the fixed parameters that now behave as constants.

First we set the following notation. Let (S, T, P, Φ) be a PMTS and $\nu \subseteq P$ be a truth assignment. For $s \in S$, we denote by $\mathrm{Tran}_\nu(s) = \{E \subseteq T(s) \mid E \cup \nu \models \Phi(s)\}$ the set of all admissible sets of transitions from s under the fixed truth values of the parameters. We can now define the notion of modal refinement between PMTS.

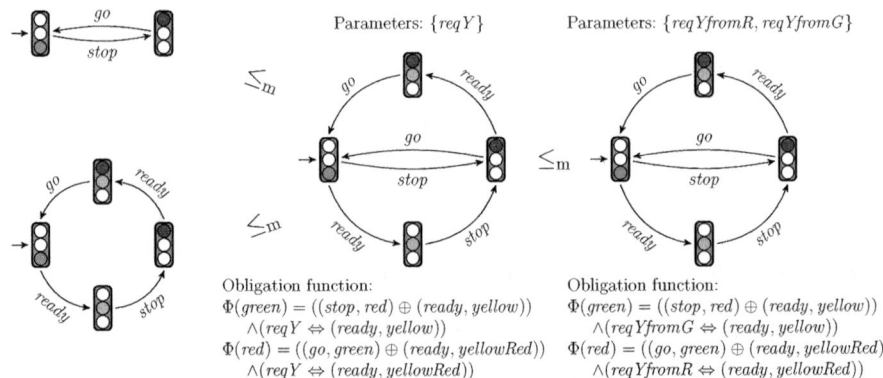

Fig. 2. Example of modal refinement

Definition 3 (Modal Refinement). *Let* (S_1, T_1, P_1, Φ_1) *and* (S_2, T_2, P_2, Φ_2) *be two PMTSs. A binary relation* $R \subseteq S_1 \times S_2$ *is a* modal refinement *if for each* $\mu \subseteq P_1$ *there exists* $\nu \subseteq P_2$ *such that for every* $(s, t) \in R$ *holds*

$$\forall M \in \mathrm{Tran}_\mu(s) : \exists N \in \mathrm{Tran}_\nu(t) : \ \forall(a, s') \in M : \exists(a, t') \in N : (s', t') \in R \ \wedge$$
$$\forall(a, t') \in N : \exists(a, s') \in M : (s', t') \in R \ .$$

We say that s *modally refines* t, *denoted by* $s \leq_m t$, *if there exists a modal refinement* R *such that* $(s, t) \in R$.

Example 4. Consider the rightmost PMTS in Figure 2. It has two parameters *reqYfromG* and *reqYfromR* whose values can be set independently and it can be refined by the system in the middle of the figure having only one parameter *reqY*. This single parameter simply binds the two original parameters to the same value. The PMTS in the middle can be further refined into the implementations where either *yellow* is always used in both cases, or never at all. Notice that there are in principle infinitely many implementations of the system in the middle, however, they are all bisimilar to either of the two implementations depicted in the left of Figure 2.

In the next section, we shall investigate the complexity of positive subclasses of PMTS. For this reason we prove the following lemma showing how the definition of modal refinement can be simplified in this particular case.

We shall first realize that in positive PMTS and for any truth assignment ν, $\mathrm{Tran}_\nu(s)$ is *upward closed*, meaning that if $M \in \mathrm{Tran}_\nu(s)$ and $M \subseteq M' \subseteq T(s)$ then $M' \in \mathrm{Tran}_\nu(s)$.

Lemma 5. *Consider Definition 3 where the right-hand side PMTS is positive. Now the condition in Definition 3 can be equivalently rewritten as a conjunction of conditions* (1) *and* (2)

$$\forall M \in \mathrm{Tran}_\mu(s) : \forall (a,s') \in M : \exists (a,t') \in T(t) : (s',t') \in R \qquad (1)$$

$$\forall M \in \mathrm{Tran}_\mu(s) : \mathrm{match}_t(M) \in \mathrm{Tran}_\nu(t) \qquad (2)$$

where $\mathrm{match}_t(M)$ *denotes the set* $\{(a,t') \in T(t) \mid \exists (a,s') \in M : (s',t') \in R\}$. *If the left-hand side PMTS is moreover positive too, Condition* (1) *is equivalent to*

$$\forall (a,s') \in T(s) : \exists (a,t') \in T(t) : (s',t') \in R . \qquad (3)$$

Proof. We shall first argue that the condition of modal refinement is equivalent to the conjunction of Conditions (4) and (5).

$$\forall M \in \mathrm{Tran}_\mu(s) : \exists N \in \mathrm{Tran}_\nu(t) : \forall (a,s') \in M : \exists (a,t') \in N : (s',t') \in R \quad (4)$$

$$\forall M \in \mathrm{Tran}_\mu(s) : \exists N \in \mathrm{Tran}_\nu(t) : \forall (a,t') \in N : \exists (a,s') \in M : (s',t') \in R \quad (5)$$

Let μ, ν, R, s and t be fixed. Definition 3 trivially implies both Conditions (4) and (5). We now prove that (4) and (5) imply the condition in Definition 3.

Let $M \in \mathrm{Tran}_\mu(s)$ be arbitrary. There is some $N_1 \in \mathrm{Tran}_\nu(t)$ satisfying (4) and some $N_2 \in \mathrm{Tran}_\nu(t)$ satisfying (5). Let now $N_1' = \{(a,t') \in N_1 \mid \exists (a,s') \in M : (s',t') \in R\}$. Consider $N = N_1' \cup N_2$. Clearly, as $\mathrm{Tran}_\nu(t)$ is upward closed, $N \in \mathrm{Tran}_\nu(t)$. Moreover, due to Condition (4) we have some $(a,t') \in N_1$ such that $(s',t') \in R$. Clearly, $(a,t') \in N_1'$ and thus also in N.

Now let $(a,t') \in N$ be arbitrary. If $(a,t') \in N_2$, due to Condition (5) we have some $(a,s') \in M$ such that $(s',t') \in R$. If $(a,t') \notin N_2$ then $(a,t') \in N_1'$. The existence of $(a,s') \in M$ such that $(s',t') \in R$ is then guaranteed by the definition of N_1'.

Let us now proceed with proving the claims of the lemma. Condition (4) is trivially equivalent to (1) since $\mathrm{Tran}_\nu(t)$ is upward closed. Condition (5) is equivalent to (2). Indeed, (2) clearly implies (5) and we show that also (5) implies (2). Let M be arbitrary. We then have some N satisfying (5). Clearly, $N \subseteq \mathrm{match}_t(M)$. Since $\mathrm{Tran}_\nu(t)$ is upward closed, $N \in \mathrm{Tran}_\nu(t)$ implies $\mathrm{match}_t(M) \in \mathrm{Tran}_\nu(t)$. Due to the upward closeness of both $\mathrm{Tran}_\mu(s)$ and $\mathrm{Tran}_\nu(t)$ in the case of a positive left-hand side, the equivalence of (1) and (3) follows.   □

Theorem 6. *Modal refinement as defined on PMTS coincides with the standard modal refinement notions on MTS, DMTS and OTS. On implementations it coincides with bisimulation.*

Proof. The fact that Definition 3 coincides with modal refinement on OTS as defined in [4] is a straightforward corollary of Lemma 5 and its proof. Indeed, the two conditions given in [4] are exactly conditions (3) and (5). As the definition of modal refinement on OTS coincides with modal refinement on DMTS (as shown in [4]) and thus also on MTS, the proof is done.

However, for the reader's convenience, we present a direct proof that Definition 3 coincides with modal refinement on MTS. Assume a parameter-free PMTS (S, T, P, Φ) where $\Phi(s)$ is a conjunction of transitions for all $s \in S$, in other words it is a standard MTS where the must transitions are listed in the conjunction and the may transitions are simply present in the underlying transition system

Table 1. Complexity of modal refinement checking of parameter-free systems

	Boolean	Positive	pCNF	pDNF	MTS
Boolean	Π_2^P-complete	coNP-complete	$\in$ coNP P-hard	coNP-complete	$\in$ coNP P-hard
Positive	Π_2^P-complete	coNP-complete	P-complete	coNP-complete	P-complete
pCNF	Π_2^P-complete	coNP-complete	P-complete	coNP-complete	P-complete
pDNF	Π_2^P-complete	P-complete	P-complete	P-complete	P-complete
MTS	Π_2^P-complete	P-complete	P-complete	P-complete	P-complete
Impl	NP-complete	P-complete	P-complete	P-complete	P-complete

but not a part of the conjunction. Observe that every transition $(s, a, t) \in T$ is contained in some $M \in \text{Tran}_\emptyset(s)$. Further, each must transition $(s, a, t) \in T$ is contained in all $M \in \text{Tran}_\emptyset(s)$. Therefore, the first conjunct in Definition 3 requires that for all may transition from s there be a corresponding one from t with the successors in the refinement relation. Similarly, the second conjunct now requires that for all must transitions from t there be a corresponding must transition from s. This is exactly the standard notion of modal refinement as introduced in [11].   □

3   Complexity of Modal Refinement Checking

We shall now investigate the complexity of refinement checking on PMTS and its relevant subclasses. Without explicitly mentioning it, we assume that all considered PMTS are now finite and the decision problems are hence well defined. The complexity bounds include classes from the polynomial hierarchy (see e.g. [14]) where for example $\Sigma_0^P = \Pi_0^P = P$, $\Pi_1^P = \text{coNP}$ and $\Sigma_1^P = \text{NP}$.

3.1   Parameter-Free Systems

Since even the parameter-free systems have interesting expressive power and the complexity of refinement on OTS has not been studied before, we first focus on parameter-free systems. Moreover, the results of this subsection are then applied to parametric systems in the next subsection. The results are summarized in Table 1. The rows in the table correspond to the restrictions on the left-hand side PMTS while the columns correspond to the restrictions on the right-hand side PMTS. Boolean denotes the general system with arbitrary negation. Positive denotes the positive systems, in this case exactly OTS. We use pCNF and pDNF to denote positive systems with formulae in conjunctive and disjunctive normal forms, respectively. In this case, pCNF coincides with DMTS. The special case of satisfaction relation, where the refining system is an implementation is denoted by Impl. We do not include Impl to the columns as it makes sense that an implementation is refined only to an implementation and here modal refinement corresponds to bisimilarity that is P-complete [2] (see also [16]). The P-hardness is hence the obvious lower bound for all the problems mentioned in the table.

We start with the simplest NP-completeness result.

Proposition 7. *Modal refinement between an implementation and a parameter-free PMTS is NP-complete.*

Proof. The containment part is straightforward. First we guess the relation R. As s is an implementation then the set $\mathrm{Tran}_\emptyset(s)$ is a singleton. We thus only need to further guess $N \in \mathrm{Tran}_\nu(t)$ and then in polynomial time verify the two conjuncts in Definition 3.

The hardness part is by a simple reduction from SAT. Let $\varphi(x_1, \ldots, x_n)$ be an given Boolean formula (instance of SAT). We construct two PMTSs (S, T, P, Φ) and (S', T', P', Φ') such that (i) $S = \{s, s'\}, T = (s, a, s'), P = \emptyset, \Phi(s) = (a, s')$ and $\Phi(s') = \mathbf{tt}$ and (ii) $S' = \{t, t_1, \ldots, t_n\}, T = \{(t, a, t_i) \mid 1 \leq i \leq n.\}, P' = \emptyset,$ $\Phi(t) = \varphi[(a, t_i)/x_i]$ and $\Phi(t_i) = \mathbf{tt}$ for all i, $1 \leq i \leq n$. Clearly, φ is satisfiable if and only if $s \leq_m t$. □

Next we show that modal refinement is Π_2^P-complete. The following lemma introduces a gadget used also later on in other hardness results. We will refer to it as the *-construction*.

Proposition 8. *Modal refinement between two parameter-free PMTS is Π_2^P-hard even if the left-hand side is an MTS.*

Proof. The proof is by polynomial time reduction from the validity of the quantified Boolean formula $\psi \equiv \forall x_1 \ldots \forall x_n \exists y_1 \ldots \exists y_m : \varphi(x_1, \ldots, x_n, y_1, \ldots, y_m)$ to the refinement checking problem $s \leq_m t$ where s and t are given as follows.

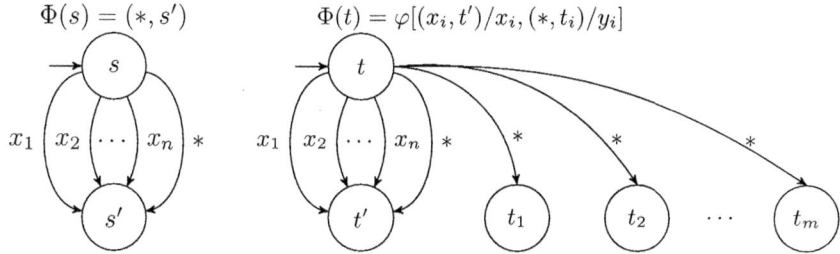

Assume that ψ is true. Let $M \in \mathrm{Tran}_\emptyset(s)$ (clearly $(*, s') \in M$) and we want to argue that there is $N \in \mathrm{Tran}_\emptyset(t)$ with $(*, t') \in N$ such that for all $(x_i, s') \in M$ there is $(x_i, t') \in N$ (clearly the states s', t' and t_i are in modal refinement) and for all $(x_i, t') \in N$ there is $(x_i, s') \in M$. Such an N can be found by simply including (x_i, t') whenever $(x_i, s') \in M$ and by adding also $(*, t')$ into N. As ψ is true, we include into N also all $(*, t_i)$ whenever y_i is set to true in ψ. Hence we get $s \leq_m t$.

On the other hand if ψ is false then we pick $M \in \mathrm{Tran}_\emptyset(s)$ such that M corresponds to the values of x_i's such that there are no values of $y_1, \ldots, y_m$ that make ψ true. This means that from t there will be no transitions as $\mathrm{Tran}_\emptyset(t) = \emptyset$ assuming that (x_i, t') have to be set to true whenever $(x_i, s') \in M$, otherwise the refinement between s and t will fail. However, now $(*, s') \in M$ cannot be matched from t and hence $s \not\leq_m t$. □

Proposition 9. *Modal refinement between two parameter-free PMTS is in Π_2^P.*

Proof. The containment follows directly from Definition 3 (note that the parameters are empty) and the fact that the last conjunction in Definition 3 is polynomially verifiable once the sets M and N were fixed. The relation R could be in principle guessed before it is verified, however, this would increase the complexity bound to Σ_3^p. Instead, we will initially include all pairs (polynomially many) into R and for each pair ask whether for every M there is N such that the two conjuncts are satisfied. If it fails, we remove the pair and continue until we reach (after polynomially many steps) the greatest fixed point. The complexity in this way remains in Π_2^p. We shall use this standard method also in further proofs and refer to it as a co-inductive computation of R.   □

Positive Right-Hand Side. We have now solved all the cases where the right-hand side is arbitrary. We now look at the cases where the right-hand side is positive. In the proofs that follow we shall use the alternative characterization of refinement from Lemma 5. The following proposition determines the subclasses on which modal refinement can be decided in polynomial time.

Proposition 10. *Modal refinement on parameter-free PMTS is in P, provided that both sides are positive and either the left-hand side is in pDNF or the right-hand side is in pCNF.*

Proof. Due to Lemma 5, the refinement is equivalent to the conjunction of (3) and (2). Clearly, (3) can be checked in P. We show that Condition (2) can be verified in P too. Recall that (2) says that

$$\forall M \in \mathrm{Tran}_\mu(s) : \mathrm{match}_t(M) \in \mathrm{Tran}_\nu(t)$$

where $\mathrm{match}_t(M) = \{(a, t') \in T(t) \mid \exists (a, s') \in M : (s', t') \in R\}$.

First assume that the left-hand side is in pDNF. If for some M the Condition (2) is satisfied then it is also satisfied for all $M' \supseteq M$, as $\mathrm{Tran}_\mu(s)$ is upwards closed. It it thus sufficient to verify the condition for all minimal elements (wrt. inclusion) of $\mathrm{Tran}_\mu(s)$. In this case it correspond to the clauses of $\Phi(s)$. Thus we get a polynomial time algorithm as shown in Algorithm 1.

Algorithm 1. Test for Condition (2) of modal refinement (pDNF)

Input   : states s and t such that $\Phi(s)$ is in positive DNF and $\Phi(t)$ is positive, relation R
Output: *true* if s, t satisfy the refinement condition, *false* otherwise
foreach *clause* $(a_1, s_1) \wedge \cdots \wedge (a_k, s_k)$ *in* $\Phi(s)$ **do**
> $N \leftarrow \{(a, t') \in T(t) \mid \exists i : a_i = a \wedge (s_i, t') \in R\}$;
> **if** $N \notin \mathrm{Tran}_\nu(t)$ **then return** false;

return true;

Second, assume that the right-hand side is in pCNF. Note that Condition (2) can be equivalently stated as

$$\forall M : \mathrm{match}_t(M) \notin \mathrm{Tran}_\nu(t) \Rightarrow M \notin \mathrm{Tran}_\mu(s) \tag{6}$$

As $\Phi(t)$ is in conjunctive normal form then $N \in \mathrm{Tran}_\nu(t)$ is equivalent to saying that N has nonempty intersection with each clause of $\Phi(t)$. We may thus enumerate all maximal $N \notin \mathrm{Tran}_\nu(t)$. Having a maximal $N \notin \mathrm{Tran}_\nu(t)$, we can easily construct M such that $N = \mathrm{match}_t(M)$. This leads to the polynomial time Algorithm 2.

Algorithm 2. Test for Condition (2) of modal refinement (pCNF)

Input   : states s and t such that $\Phi(s)$ is positive and $\Phi(t)$ is in positive CNF, relation R

Output: *true* if s, t satisfy the refinement condition, *false* otherwise

foreach *clause* $(a_1, t_1) \vee \cdots \vee (a_k, t_k)$ *in* $\Phi(t)$ **do**

$\quad\mid\quad M \leftarrow T(s) \setminus \{(a, s') \in T(s) \mid \exists i : a_i = a \wedge (s', t_i) \in R\};$

$\quad\mid\quad$ **if** $M \in \mathrm{Tran}_\mu(s)$ **then return** false;

return true;

The statement of the proposition thus follows. $\square$

Proposition 11. *Modal refinement on parameter-free PMTS is in coNP, if the right-hand side is positive.*

Proof. Due to Lemma 5 we can solve the two refinement conditions separately. Furthermore, both Condition (1) an (2) of Lemma 5 can be checked in coNP. The guessing of R is done co-inductively as described in the proof of Proposition 9.
$\square$

Proposition 12. *Modal refinement on parameter-free systems is coNP-hard, even if the left-hand side is in positive CNF and the right-hand side is in positive DNF.*

Proof. We reduce SAT into non-refinement. Let $\varphi(x_1, \ldots, x_n)$ be a formula in CNF. We modify φ into an equivalent formula φ' as follows: add new variables $\tilde{x}_1, \ldots, \tilde{x}_n$ and for all i change all occurrences of $\neg x_i$ into $\tilde{x}_i$ and add new clauses $(x_i \vee \tilde{x}_i)$ and $(\neg x_i \vee \neg \tilde{x}_i)$.

Observe now that all clauses contain either all positive literals or all negative literals. Let ψ^+ denote a CNF formula that contains all positive clauses of φ' and ψ^- denote a CNF formula that contains all negative clauses of φ'. As $\varphi' = \psi^+ \wedge \psi^-$ it is clear that φ' is satisfiable if and only if $(\psi^+ \Rightarrow \neg\psi^-)$ is not valid.

Now we construct two PMTSs (S, T, P, Φ) and (S', T', P', Φ') over $\Sigma = \{x_1, \ldots, x_n, \tilde{x}_1, \ldots, \tilde{x}_n\}$ as follows: (i) $S = \{s, s'\}$, $T = \{(s, x_i, s'), (s, \tilde{x}_i, s') \mid 1 \leq i \leq n\}$, $P = \emptyset$, $\Phi(s) = \psi^+[(x_i, s')/x_i, (\tilde{x}_i, s')/\tilde{x}_i]$ and $\Phi(s') = \mathbf{tt}$, and (ii) $S' = \{t, t'\}$, $T' = \{(t, x_i, t'), (t, \tilde{x}_i, t) \mid 1 \leq i \leq n\}$, $P' = \emptyset$, $\Phi(t) = \neg\psi^-[(x_i, t')/x_i, (\tilde{x}_i, t')/\tilde{x}_i]$ and $\Phi(t') = \mathbf{tt}$. Note that by pushing the negation of ψ^- inside, this formula can be written as pDNF. It is easy to see that now $s \leq_{\mathrm{m}} t$ if and only if $(\psi^+ \Rightarrow \neg\psi^-)$ is valid. Therefore, $s \not\leq_{\mathrm{m}} t$ if and only if φ is satisfiable. $\square$

Table 2. Complexity of modal refinement checking with parameters

	Boolean	positive	pCNF	pDNF
Boolean	Π_4^P-complete	Π_3^P-complete	$\in \Pi_3^P$ Π_2^P-hard	Π_3^P-complete
positive	Π_4^P-complete	Π_3^P-complete	Π_2^P-complete	Π_3^P-complete
pCNF	Π_4^P-complete	Π_3^P-complete	Π_2^P-complete	Π_3^P-complete
pDNF	Π_4^P-complete	Π_2^P-complete	Π_2^P-complete	Π_2^P-complete
MTS	Σ_3^P-complete	NP-complete	NP-complete	NP-complete
Impl	NP-complete	NP-complete	NP-complete	NP-complete

Note that the exact complexity of modal refinement with the right-hand side being in positive CNF or MTS and the left-hand side Boolean remains open.

3.2   Systems with Parameters

In the sequel we investigate the complexity of refinement checking in the general case of PMTS with parameters. The complexities are summarized in Table 2. We start with an observation of how the results on parameter-free systems can be applied to the parametric case.

Proposition 13. *The complexity upper bounds from Table 1 carry over to Table 2, as follows. If the modal refinement in the parameter-free case is in* NP, coNP *or* Π_2^P, *then the modal refinement with parameters is in* Π_2^P, Π_3^P *and* Π_4^P, *respectively. Moreover, if the left-hand side is an MTS, the complexity upper bounds shift from* NP *and* Π_2^P *to* NP *and* Σ_3^P, *respectively.*

Proof. In the first case, we first universally choose μ, we then existentially choose ν and modify the formulae $\Phi(s)$ and $\Phi(t)$ by evaluating the parameters. This does not change the normal form/positiveness of the formulae. We then perform the algorithm for the parameter-free refinement. For the second case note that implementations and MTS have no parameters and we may simply choose (existentially) ν and run the algorithm for the parameter-free refinement.   □

We now focus on the respective lower bounds (proof of Proposition 15 can be found in [3]).

Proposition 14. *Modal refinement between an implementation and a right-hand side in positive CNF or in DNF is NP-hard.*

Proof. The proof is by reduction from SAT. Let $\varphi(x_1, \ldots, x_n)$ be a formula in CNF and let $\varphi_1, \varphi_2, \ldots, \varphi_k$ be the clauses of φ. We construct two PMTSs (S, T, P, Φ) and (S', T', P', Φ') over the action alphabet $\Sigma = \{a_1, \ldots, a_k\}$ as follows: (i) $S = \{s, s'\}$, $T = \{(s, a_i, s') \mid 1 \le i \le k\}$, $P = \emptyset$, $\Phi(s) = \bigwedge_{1 \le i \le k}(a_i, s')$ and $\Phi(s') = \mathbf{tt}$ and (ii) $S' = \{t\} \cup \{t_i \mid 1 \le i \le k\}$, $T' = \{(t, a_i, t_i) \mid 1 \le i \le k\}$, $P' = \{x_1, \ldots, x_n\}$, $\Phi'(t) = \bigwedge_{1 \le i \le k}(a_i, t_i)$ and $\Phi'(t_i) = \varphi_i$ for all $1 \le i \le k$.

Notice that each φ_i in $\Phi'(t_i)$ is in positive form as we negate only the parameters x_i and every clause φ_i is trivially in DNF. Now we easily get that $s \leq_m t$ if and only if φ is satisfiable.   □

Proposition 15. *Modal refinement is Σ_3^P-hard even if the left-hand side is MTS.*

The following proof introduces a gadget used also later on in other hardness results. We refer to it as *CNF-binding*. Further, we use the $*$-construction here.

Proposition 16. *Modal refinement is Π_4^P-hard even if the left-hand side is in positive CNF.*

Proof (Sketch). Consider a Π_4^P-hard QSAT instance, a formula $\psi = \forall x \exists y \forall z \exists w :$ $\varphi(x, y, z, w)$ with φ is in CNF and x, y, z, w vectors of length n. We construct two system s and t and use the variables $\{x_1, \ldots, x_n\}$ as parameters for the left-hand side system s, and $\{y_1, \ldots, y_n\}$ as parameters for the right-hand side system t.

$$\Phi(s) = (*, s') \wedge \text{CNF-binding} \qquad \Phi(t) = (*, s') \wedge \varphi[(t_i, t')/x_i, (f_i, t')/\neg x_i,$$
$$(z_i, t')/z_i, (*, u_i)/w_i]$$

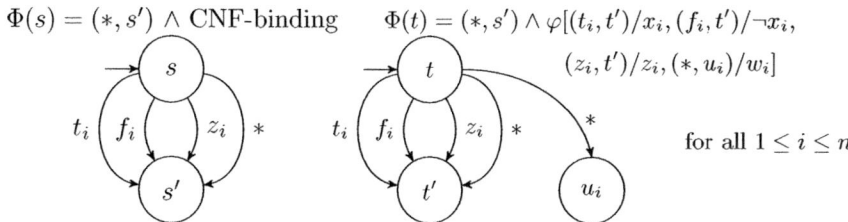

$$\text{for all } 1 \leq i \leq n$$

On the left we require $\Phi(s) = (*, s') \wedge \bigwedge_{1 \leq i \leq n} \big((x_i \Rightarrow (t_i, s')) \wedge (\neg x_i \Rightarrow (f_i, s'))\big)$ and call the latter conjunct *CNF-binding*. Thus the value of each parameter x_i is "saved" into transitions of the system. Note that although both t_i and f_i may be present, a "minimal" implementation contains exactly one of them. On the right-hand side the transitions look similar but we require $\Phi(t) = (*, t) \wedge \varphi'$ where φ' is created from φ by changing every positive literal x_i into (t_i, t'), every negative literal $\neg x_i$ into (f_i, t'), every z_i into (z_i, t'), and every w_i into $(*, u_i)$.

We show that ψ is true iff $s \leq_m t$. Assume first that ψ is true. Therefore, for every choice of parameters x_i there is a choice of parameters y_i so that $\forall z \exists w : \varphi(x, y, z, w)$ is true and, moreover, t_i or f_i is present on the left whenever x_i or $\neg x_i$ is true, respectively (and possibly even if it is false). We set exactly all these transitions t_i and f_i on the right, too. Further, for every choice of transitions z_i on the left there are w_i's so that $\varphi(x, y, z, w)$ holds. On the right, we implement a transition (z_i, t') for each z_i set to true and $(*, u_i)$ for each w_i set to true. Now φ' is satisfied as it has only positive occurrences of (t_i, t') and (f_i, t') and hence the extra t_i's and f_i's do not matter. Now for every implementation of s we obtained an implementation of t. Moreover, their transitions match. Indeed, t_i's and f_i's were set the same as on the left, similarly for z_i's. As for the $*$-transition, we use the same argumentation as in the original $*$-construction. On the left, there is always one. On the right, there can be more of them due to w_i's but at least one is also guaranteed by $\Phi(t)$.

Let now $s \leq_m t$. Then for every choice of x_i's—and thus also for every choice of *exactly* one transition of t_i, f_i for each i—there are y_i's so that every choice of transitions z_i can be matched on the right so that φ' is true with some transitions

$(*, u_i)$. Since choices of t_i/f_i correspond exactly to choices of x_i it only remains to set w_i true for each transition $(*, u_i)$ on the right, thus making φ true.   □

Based on the idea of CNF-binding, the following propositions are proved in [3].

Proposition 17. *Modal refinement is* Π_3^p*-hard for the left-hand side in positive CNF and the right-hand side in positive DNF.*

Proposition 18. *Modal refinement is* Π_2^p*-hard even if both sides are in positive CNF.*

The last three propositions use a modification of the CNF-binding idea called *DNF-binding*. Instead of $(x_i \Rightarrow (t_i, s')) \wedge (\neg x_i \Rightarrow (f_i, s'))$ we use $(x_i \wedge (t_i, s')) \vee (\neg x_i \wedge (f_i, s'))$ to bind parameters of the left-hand side system with transitions of the right-hand side system. Details are in [3].

Proposition 19. *Modal refinement is* Π_2^p*-hard even if left-hand side is in positive DNF and right-hand side is in positive CNF.*

Proposition 20. *Modal refinement is* Π_2^p*-hard even if left-hand side is in positive DNF and right-hand side is in positive DNF.*

Proposition 21. *Modal refinement is* Π_4^p*-hard even if the left-hand side is in positive DNF.*

Although the complexity may seem discouraging in many cases, there is an important remark to make. The refinement checking may be exponential, but only in the outdegree of each state and the number of parameters, while it is polynomial in the number of states. As one may expect the outdegree and the number of parameters to be much smaller than the number of states, this means that the refinement checking may still be done in a rather efficient way. This claim is furthermore supported by the existence of efficient SAT solvers that may be employed to check the inner conditions in the modal refinement.

4   Conclusion and Future Work

We have introduced an extension of modal transition systems called PMTS for parametric systems. The formalism is general enough to capture several features missing in the other extensions, while at the same time it offers an easy to understand semantics and a natural notion of modal refinement that specializes to the well-known refinements already studied on the subclasses of PMTS. Finally, we provided a comprehensive overview of complexity of refinement checking on PMTS and its subclasses.

We believe that our formalism is a step towards a more applicable notion of specification theories based on MTS. In the future work we will study logical characterizations of the refinement relation, investigate compositional properties and focus on introducing quantitative aspects into the model in order to further increase its applicability.

Acknowledgments. We would like to thank to Sebastian Bauer for suggesting the traffic light example and for allowing us to use his figure environments.

References

1. Antonik, A., Huth, M., Larsen, K.G., Nyman, U., Wasowski, A.: 20 years of modal and mixed specifications. Bulletin of the EATCS, vol. 95, pp. 94–129 (2008)
2. Balcazar, J.L., Gabarró, J., Santha, M.: Deciding bisimilarity is P-complete. Formal Aspects of Computing 4(6A), 638–648 (1992)
3. Beneš, N., Křetínský, J., Larsen, K.G., Møller, M.H., Srba, J.: Parametric modal transition systems. Technical report FIMU-RS-2011-03, Faculty of Informatics, Masaryk University, Brno (2011)
4. Beneš, N., Křetínský, J.: Process algebra for modal transition systemses. In: Matyska, L., Kozubek, M., Vojnar, T., Zemčík, P., Antos, D. (eds.) MEMICS. OASICS, vol. 16, pp. 9–18. Schloss Dagstuhl - Leibniz-Zentrum fuer Informatik, Germany (2010)
5. Boudol, G., Larsen, K.G.: Graphical versus logical specifications. Theor. Comput. Sci. 106(1), 3–20 (1992)
6. Fecher, H., Schmidt, H.: Comparing disjunctive modal transition systems with an one-selecting variant. J. of Logic and Alg. Program. 77(1-2), 20–39 (2008)
7. Godefroid, P., Huth, M., Jagadeesan, R.: Abstraction-based model checking using modal transition systems. In: Larsen, K.G., Nielsen, M. (eds.) CONCUR 2001. LNCS, vol. 2154, pp. 426–440. Springer, Heidelberg (2001)
8. Gruler, A., Leucker, M., Scheidemann, K.D.: Modeling and model checking software product lines. In: Barthe, G., de Boer, F.S. (eds.) FMOODS 2008. LNCS, vol. 5051, pp. 113–131. Springer, Heidelberg (2008)
9. Huth, M., Jagadeesan, R., Schmidt, D.A.: Modal transition systems: A foundation for three-valued program analysis. In: Sands, D. (ed.) ESOP 2001. LNCS, vol. 2028, pp. 155–169. Springer, Heidelberg (2001)
10. Larsen, K.G., Nyman, U., Wąsowski, A.: On modal refinement and consistency. In: Caires, L., Vasconcelos, V.T. (eds.) CONCUR 2007. LNCS, vol. 4703, pp. 105–119. Springer, Heidelberg (2007)
11. Larsen, K.G., Thomsen, B.: A modal process logic. In: LICS, pp. 203–210. IEEE Computer Society, Los Alamitos (1988)
12. Larsen, K.G., Xinxin, L.: Equation solving using modal transition systems. In: LICS, pp. 108–117. IEEE Computer Society, Los Alamitos (1990)
13. Nanz, S., Nielson, F., Riis Nielson, H.: Modal abstractions of concurrent behaviour. In: Alpuente, M., Vidal, G. (eds.) SAS 2008. LNCS, vol. 5079, pp. 159–173. Springer, Heidelberg (2008)
14. Papadimitriou, C.H.: Computational complexity. Addison-Wesley Publishing Co., Inc., Reading (1994)
15. Raclet, J.B., Badouel, E., Benveniste, A., Caillaud, B., Passerone, R.: Why are modalities good for interface theories? In: ACSD, pp. 119–127. IEEE, Los Alamitos (2009)
16. Sawa, Z., Jančar, P.: Behavioural equivalences on finite-state systems are PTIME-hard. Computing and Informatics 24(5), 513–528 (2005)
17. Uchitel, S., Chechik, M.: Merging partial behavioural models. In: FSE 2004, pp. 43–52. ACM, New York (2004)

Policy Iteration within Logico-Numerical Abstract Domains

Pascal Sotin[1], Bertrand Jeannet[1], Franck Védrine[2], and Eric Goubault[2]

[1] INRIA
{Pascal.Sotin,Bertrand.Jeannet}@inria.fr
[2] CEA-LIST LMeASI
{Frank.Vedrine,Eric.Goubault}@cea.fr

Abstract. Policy Iteration is an algorithm for the exact solving of optimization and game theory problems, formulated as equations on min max affine expressions. It has been shown that the problem of finding the least fixpoint of semantic equations on some abstract domains can be reduced to such optimization problems. This enables the use of Policy Iteration to solve such equations, instead of the traditional Kleene iteration that performs approximations to ensure convergence.

We first show in this paper that the concept of Policy Iteration can be integrated into numerical abstract domains in a generic way. This allows to widen considerably its applicability in static analysis. We then consider the verification of programs manipulating Boolean and numerical variables, and we provide an efficient method to integrate the concept of policy in a logico-numerical abstract domain that mixes Boolean and numerical properties. Our experiments show the benefit of our approach compared to a naive application of Policy Iteration to such programs.

1   Introduction

Kleene Iteration. Abstract Interpretation is a framework for solving verification problems expressed by semantic equations on a (concrete) lattice. Typically, it is used to compute an overapproximation of the reachable states of a program. The computation is performed by a *Kleene iteration* which starts at the bottom of an (abstract) lattice and applies the semantic equations until no new state is reached. In order to ensure and accelerate the termination of this process, an extrapolation operator (called *widening*) is used at the cost of additional approximations. Eventually, the result can be refined in a process called *narrowing*. We call the whole process *Kleene iteration with widening* (pictured on Fig. 3).

Running example. Consider the program of Fig. 1(a), taken from [1], with its Control Flow Graph (CFG), Fig. 1(b). It contains two nested loops and two integer variables. If the program reaches the program point ⑤, then $i = 100$. However, the *Kleene iteration with widening* on the boxes abstract domain fails to infer it: it infers only $i \geq 100$. The widening operator (applied at points ⓪ and ②) looses the constraint $i<100$ at point ②), and narrowing does not recover

T. Bultan and P.-A. Hsiung (Eds.): ATVA 2011, LNCS 6996, pp. 290–305, 2011.

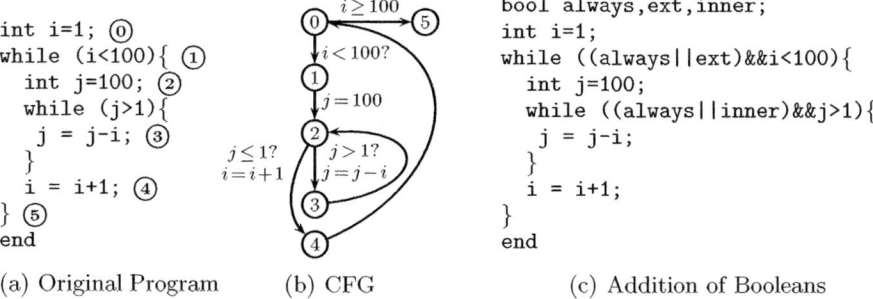

(a) Original Program   (b) CFG   (c) Addition of Booleans

Fig. 1. Two loops running example

it because of the back-edge ③ → ② of the inner loop. The problem we face here is not a weakness of the abstract domain, since the octagons or the polyhedra do not infer either i = 100, but a weakness of the Kleene Iteration with widening.

Policy Iteration. Introduced in [1], the use of *policy iteration* techniques for solving semantics equations with fixpoint allows to infer box-like invariants, among which the correct invariant at program point ⑤. This technique avoids the inaccuracy issues faced by the Kleene iteration with widening. The algorithm of [1] combines an iteration on a set of policies, that defines sound variations of the semantic equations, with a linear programming solver for solving them.

This approach is tailored to purely numerical (and linear) programs and cannot be applied directly to the program of Fig. 1(c), which is the program of Fig. 1(a) with additional Boolean variables.

- Policy iteration based on linear programming is precise but does not handle Boolean variables;
- Some abstract domains do handle the Boolean variables, but the use of Kleene iteration with widening for solving the abstract equations often delivers inaccurate results.

This article aims at taking the best of both worlds by performing *policy iteration on Kleene iterations with widening.* In particular we address the question of dealing with programs having both Boolean and numerical variables (eg. Fig. 1(c)).

Contributions. We first show how to integrate the concept of policy *inside* a numerical abstract domain (see Section 4). This was implemented in the generic abstract domain library APRON and enabled the precise analysis of Fig. 1(a) in the Abstract-Interpretation-based tool INTERPROC. We then show the advantage of this integration by implementing efficiently policies for logico-numerical abstract domains on top of our numerical policies. These policies have been implemented using MTBDDs and integrated in the BDDAPRON library (see Section 5). We could eventually perform the analysis of Fig. 1(c), for which Kleene iteration is not precise and for which policy iteration of [1] is not possible as is.

Outline. Section 2 recalls the basics of Abstract Interpretation, focusing on the abstract domains. Section 3 details the use of Kleene iteration and policy iteration for the resolution of semantic equations. Sections 4 and 5 present our contributions. Section 6 provides experiments which illustrate the questions of precision and efficiency. Section 7 will conclude and emphasize the interest in integrating the precision improvements due to policy iteration into traditional abstract interpretation frameworks.

2   Abstract Interpretation and Abstract Domains

Many static analysis problems come down to the computation of the least solution of a fixpoint equation $X = F(X), X \in C$ where C is a domain of concrete properties, and F a function derived from the semantics of the analysed program. Abstract Interpretation [2] provides a theoretical framework for reducing this problem to the solving of a simpler equation

$$Y = G(Y), Y \in A \tag{1}$$

in a domain A of *abstract properties*. Having performed this *static approximation*, one is left with the problem of solving Eqn. (1). The paper contributes to this problem, which is detailed in the next section.

We detail first how this general method will be instantiated (see also [2]).

- We consider simple programs without procedures that manipulate n scalar variables taking their values in a set D, as exemplified by the programs of Figs. 1(a) and 1(c). Their state-space has the structure $S = K \times D^n$, where K is the set of nodes of the control flow graph (CFG).
- We focus on the inference of invariants. The domain of concrete properties is $C = \mathcal{P}(S) = K \to \mathcal{P}(D^n)$: an invariance property is defined by the set of possible values for variables at each node.
- The equation to be solved is $X = F(X) = I \cup post(X)$, where I is the set of initial states and *post* is the successor-state function. The least solution $lfp(F)$ of this equation is the strongest inductive invariant of the program. This equation is actually partitioned along the nodes and edges of the CFG:

$$X^k = I^k \cup \bigcup_{(k',k)} [\![op^{(k',k)}]\!](X^{k'}) \, , \; X^k \in \mathcal{P}(D^n) \tag{2}$$

  $[\![op^{(k',k)}]\!] : \mathcal{P}(D^n) \to \mathcal{P}(D^n)$ reflects the semantics of the program instruction $op^{(k',k)}$ associated with the CFG edge (k', k). We consider here for *op* assignments $x := expr$ and tests $bexpr?$.
- Given an abstract domain A for $\mathcal{P}(D^n)$, abstracting Eqn. (2) in A consists in substituting $\cup$ and $[\![op]\!]$ functions in it with their abstract counterpart denoted with $\cup^\sharp$, $[\![op]\!]^\sharp$. We obtain a system

$$Y^k = I^{\sharp k} \cup^\sharp \bigcup_{(k',k)}^\sharp [\![op^{(k',k)}]\!]^\sharp(Y^{k'}) \, , \; Y^k \in A \tag{3}$$

Numerical abstract domains. If the considered program manipulates only numerical variables, $D = \mathbb{Q}$, and $C = K \rightarrow \mathcal{P}(\mathbb{Q}^n)$. Many *numerical* abstract domains have been designed for approximating subsets of $\mathbb{Q}^n$:

- The *box* domain [3] approximates such subsets by their bounding boxes. The abstract semantics of assignments and conditionals is based on classical interval arithmetic.
- The *octagons* domain [4] approximates such subsets by conjunction of $\mathcal{O}(n^2)$ inequalities of the form $a_i x_i + a_j x_j \geq b$ where $a_i, a_j \in \{-1, 0, 1\}$ and the bounds b's are inferred. The abstract semantics of octagons relies on a mixture of interval arithmetic and constraint propagation.
- These two domains are generalized by the *template polyhedra* domain [5] that considers conjunctions of M linear inequalities of the form $\boldsymbol{T}_m \cdot \boldsymbol{x} \geq b_m, 1 \leq m \leq M$, where the $\boldsymbol{T}_m$ are linear expressions provided by some external means and the bounds b_m are inferred. The abstract semantics is computed by linear programming.

Observe that some domains are more complex, like the *convex polyhedra* domain [6] that approximates numerical subsets by convex polyhedra: it infers not only bounds, but also the (unbounded) set of linear expressions to be bounded.

The APRON library [7] provides a common high-level API to such numerical domains, and defines a concrete semantics that should be correctly abstracted by the compliant abstract domains.

The BddApron logico-numerical abstract domain. The APRON concrete semantics and the abstract domains provided with it do not provide the adequate operations for programs that manipulate also Boolean and enumerated variables, which may contain instructions like

```
x := if b and x<=5 then x+1 else 0    or   b := b and x<=3
```

In this case $D = \mathbb{B} \uplus \mathbb{Q}$ and $\mathcal{P}(D^n) \simeq \mathcal{P}(\mathbb{B}^p \times \mathbb{Q}^q)$. A naive solution is to eliminate Boolean variables by encoding them in the control, so as to obtain a purely numerical program. However this solution (i) is neither efficient – the enumeration of Boolean valuations induces an exponential blow-up, (ii) nor it provides a high-level view on invariants and their manipulation. The BDDAPRON library [8] addresses issue (ii) by offering support for expressions and constraints that freely combine Boolean and numerical subexpressions and by leveraging any APRON-compliant numerical abstract domain to a *logico-numerical* abstract domain. Given a numerical abstract domain A_0 for $\mathcal{P}(\mathbb{Q}^q)$, it abstracts concrete properties in $\mathcal{P}(\mathbb{B}^p \times \mathbb{Q}^q) \simeq \mathbb{B}^p \rightarrow \mathcal{P}(\mathbb{Q}^q)$ with functions in $\mathbb{B}^p \rightarrow A_0$. The efficiency issue (i) is addressed by representing functions $f : \mathbb{B}^p \rightarrow A_0$ with MTBDDs [9], see Fig. 2. This representation does not improve the worst-case complexity in $\mathcal{O}(2^p)$, but the complexity of the representation and the operations becomes a function of the number of nodes of the BDDs/MTBDDs rather than a function of the number of (reachable) Boolean valuations. As in many applications the first number is is much smaller than the second one, the practical complexity is significantly improved.

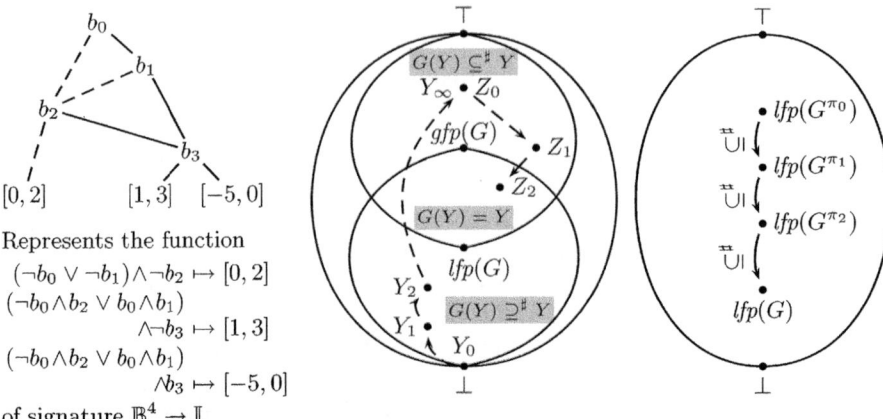

Fig. 2. Example of MTBDD   **Fig. 3.** Kleene iteration with   **Fig. 4.** Policy iteration
widening and narrowing

The contribution of this paper is to show how policy iteration solving techniques, which are described in the next section and currently apply to equations on numerical properties, can be *efficiently leveraged* to equations on logico-numerical properties by a generic integration to the abstract domain.

3   Abstract Equation Solving and Policy Iteration

The traditional way to solve the abstract semantic equation $Y = G(Y), Y \in A$ (*e.g.*, Eqn. (1)) is *Kleene iteration with widening and narrowing*. This consists in computing successively (*c.f.* Fig. 3)

- the ascending sequence $Y_0 = \bot$, $Y_{n+1} = Y_n \nabla G(Y_n)$, which converges in a finite number of steps to a post-fixpoint Y_∞;
- the descending sequence $Z_0 = Y_\infty$, $Z_{n+1} = G(Z_n)$, up to some rank N.

$\nabla : A \times A \to A$ is a *widening* operator that ensures convergence at the cost of additional *dynamic* approximations. The problem is that such approximations are often too strong, and that the descending sequence often fails to recover useful information, as discussed in the introduction. This is why this paper focuses on an alternative resolution method.

Policy iteration is an algorithm that has been developed originally in control and game theory. It has been introduced by Howard [10] and then extended by Hoffman and Karp [11] for stochastic games. It basically finds the value of a game, which is the unique fixpoint of the Shapley operator [12], which is the min of a max of certain affine functions.

Abstract semantic equations as min-max affine equations. As observed in [1], the abstract box semantics of programs with linear assignments and conditionals can be formulated as equations on lower and upper bounds, in which

```
int i=1; ⓪
while (i<100){ ①
  int j=100; ②
  while (j>1){
    j = j-i; ③
  }
  i = i+1; ④
} ⑤
end
```

(a) Program

(b) CFG

$$i_0 = [1,1] \cup^\sharp i_4$$
$$i_1 = [\![i < 100?]\!]^\sharp(i_0)$$
$$(i_2, j_2) = (i_1, [100, 100]) \cup^\sharp (i_3, j_3)$$
$$(i_3, j_3) = [\![j = j-i]\!]^\sharp \circ [\![j > 1?]\!]^\sharp(i_2, j_2)$$
$$(i_4, j_4) = [\![i = i+1]\!]^\sharp \circ [\![j \le 1?]\!]^\sharp(i_2, j_2)$$
$$i_5 = [\![i \ge 100?]\!]^\sharp(i_0)$$

$i_k = [i_k^-, i_k^+]$ and $j_k = [j_k^-, j_k^+]$ are the intervals associated with var. i and j at CFG node ⓚ

(c) Abstract Box Semantics

$i_0^- = \min(1, i_4^-)$	$i_0^+ = \max(1, i_4^+)$	$-i_0^- = \max(-1, -i_4^-)$
$i_1^- = i_0^-$	$i_1^+ = \min(99, i_0^+)$	$-i_1^- = -i_0^-$
$i_2^- = \min(i_1^-, i_3^-)$	$i_2^+ = \max(i_1^+, i_3^+)$	$-i_2^- = \max(-i_1^-, -i_3^-)$
$j_2^- = \min(100, j_3^-)$	$j_2^+ = \max(100, j_3^+)$	$-j_2^- = \max(-100, -j_3^-)$
$i_3^- = i_2^-$	$i_3^+ = i_2^+$	$-i_3^- = -i_2^-$
$j_3^- = \max(2, j_2^-) - i_2^+$	$j_3^+ = j_2^+ - i_2^-$	$-j_3^- = \min(-2, -j_2^-) + i_2^+$
$i_4^- = i_2^- + 1$	$i_4^+ = i_2^+ + 1$	$-i_4^- = -i_2^- - 1$
$j_4^- = j_2^-$	$j_4^+ = \min(1, j_2^+)$	$-j_4^- = -j_2^-$
$i_5^- = \max(100, i_0^-)$	$i_5^+ = i_0^+$	$-i_5^- = \min(-100, -i_0^-)$

(min and max are min max policies)

(d) Equivalent equations on bounds

(e) Normalizing equations on inf bounds

Fig. 5. Abstract Interpretation and Game Theory views of semantic equations on boxes

each bound is the min of a max of affine functions. Fig. 5 illustrates this point. Fig. 5(c) instantiates Eqn. (3) on the program of Fig. 5(a). Fig. 5(d) reformulates this as equations on bounds. Selecting the least solution in Fig. 5(c) is equivalent to maximizing lower and minimizing upper bounds in Fig. 5(d). In order to regularize this problem, we replace lower bounds of intervals with upper bounds by negating them, see Fig. 5(e), so as to manipulate only upper bounds subject to minimization. Such a formulation can be viewed a deterministic game problem between a min-player and a max-player. Several plays are possible, but we are interested in the optimal strategy (*i.e. policy*) of the min player that minimizes the bounds. Min policy iteration provides a solution to this problem.

Policy and policy iteration. In the context of an equation $Y = G(Y)$ where Y is a vector of upper bounds and G a min of max of affine functions, a *(min) policy* π is a choice of one argument per min in G, which results in a simpler function $G^\pi \sqsupseteq^\sharp G$ which is the max of affine functions. By observing that for any fixpoint of G and any min operator in G, the min will be reached by at least one argument, one deduces that the least fixpoint of G is also the least fixpoint of some G^π.

The policy iteration algorithm, illustrated by Fig. 4, works by
1. choosing an initial policy π_0;
2. at each step i, computing the least solution $Y_i = lfp(G^{\pi_i})$ of $Y = G^{\pi_i}(Y)$;

3. if Y_i is a solution of $Y = G(Y)$, the algorithm terminates, otherwise the *policy improvement step* consists in choosing a new policy π_{i+1} such that $lfp(G^{\pi_{i+1}}) \subseteq^{\sharp} lfp(G^{\pi_i})$, and to go back to step 2.

How is it done? As $G^{\pi_i} \supseteq^{\sharp} G$ and $Y \neq G(Y)$, $Y_i = G^{\pi_i}(Y_i) \supsetneq^{\sharp} G(Y_i)$. Therefore, for some p^{nth} component of the vector Y_i, we have

$$G(Y_i)^{(p)} = \min(e_1, \ldots, e_n) < Y_i^{(p)} = (G^{\pi_i}(Y_i))^{(p)} = e_j$$

where j results from the choice performed by the policy π_i, and $e_1, \ldots, e_n$ are the values of the max expressions evaluated on Y_i. The principle is to replace in π_{i+1} the choice j by a choice j' such that $e_{j'} = \min(e_1, \ldots, e_n)$. This ensures that $G^{\pi_{i+1}}(Y_i) \subsetneq^{\sharp} Y_i = lfp(G^{\pi_i})$, hence $lfp(G^{\pi_{i+1}}) \subsetneq^{\sharp} lfp(G^{\pi_i})$.

It is shown in [1] that for boxes, this method will terminate on a fixpoint of G, which is guaranteed to be the least fixpoint when G is not expansive for the sup norm. Some improvements of the original method of [1] have been made for dealing with degenerate cases in an efficient manner in [13]. Extensions of the method to deal with the zone, octagon, linear and quadratic templates are discussed in [14,15].

Policy iteration can also be seen as a Newton method for solving a system of min-max equation $Y = G(Y)$. Any of the expressions under the min operator can indeed be seen as a possible differential/linearization of G. A policy is the choice of such a differential, and solving $Y = G^{\pi}(Y)$ is akin to solving the linearization of G in one step in the classical Newton method.

Two methods for solving $Y = G^{\pi}(Y)$. Once a policy π is applied, one has to compute the least solution of a simpler equation $Y = G^{\pi}(Y)$ where G is the max of affine functions. This can be done either by linear programming as in [14], or by standard Kleene iteration as in [1].

1. Linear programming always computes the least solution, but presents some shortcomings:

    (a) It requires to write down the full equation system on bounds (whereas Kleene iteration works in practice by incremental exploration);
    (b) It does not allow to see the abstract domain (boxes, octagons, ...) and a policy linked to it as an abstract datatype (ADT).
    (c) If the program contains non-linear expressions, these must be linearized statically *before* the analysis (thus when no information is available...)

2. Kleene iteration with widening does not offer the guarantee of delivering the least solution (thus we loose theoretical results about policy improvement). However it exhibits better behaviour w.r.t. the points mentioned above:

    (a)(b) It integrates well in existing static analysers (such as INTERPROC, [7,16]) that manipulates abstract properties as abstract datatypes through normalized APIs (such as the APRON and the BDDAPRON APIs mentioned in Section 2).

(c) Linearization of non-linear expressions can be done dynamically as in [17], using the (under)approximations provided by the current Kleene iteration step.

One might object that as this technique still resorts to widening to ensure convergence, it should not improve on traditional Kleene iteration (without policies). The point is actually that here Kleene iteration is applied to simpler equations, with fewer dependency cycles (hence less widening points) and on which the descending sequence is likely to be more effective. The experiments in [1] and Section 6 confirms this conjecture.

For example, on Fig. 5, if one chooses the left policy for all min equations, like $i_1^+ = 99$ for the policy $i_1^+ = \min(99, i_0^+)$, the Kleene iteration solves the simpler equations in one iteration and finds $i_1 = [100, 100]$ to be compared to $i_1 = [100, +\infty]$ obtained by the global iteration without policies

In the next section, we show how the concept of policy can be integrated in an abstract domain and can be viewed as an ADT. This allows to leverage in Section 5 the use of policy iterations in logico-numerical domains.

4 Integrating Policies in Numerical Abstract Domains

Integrating policies in an abstract domain as described in Section 2 means in practice to "instrument" the equations of Fig. 5(c) with policies, in order to emulate the translation from these equations to the equations of Fig. 5(d) (in the case of the box abstract domain).

Instrumenting abstract operations with policies. The original semantic equations are made of the three operators described in Section 2: (i) $\sqcup^\sharp$, (ii) $[\![bexpr?]\!]^\sharp$, and (iii) $[\![x := expr]\!]^\sharp$. For all of the template-based numerical abstract domains for which policies have been used, min operators are introduced only by tests (ii) and assignments (iii). Hence only those two latter operations needs to be equipped with a policy. We thus introduced in the APRON API two new generic functions:

$$\begin{array}{ll} \text{meet\_cond\_apply\_policy}_0 : P_0 \times A_0 \times & Cond_0 \quad \to A_0 \\ \text{assign\_var\_apply\_policy}_0 : P_0 \times A_0 \times & Var \times Expr_0 \to A_0 \end{array} \quad (4)$$

where P_0 denotes the set of policies, A_0 the numerical abstract domain, $Expr_0$ the set of (linear) numerical expressions, and $Cond_0$ the set of Boolean formula on (linear) numerical constraints under disjunctive normal form (DNF).

The exact structure of policies depends on the considered abstract domain. We illustrate the case of the box abstract domain. In this domain, min expressions will be always decomposed into min expressions with two operands. Therefore, the domain of a *bound policy* is $\{l, r\}$, which stands for left and right: (l) if $\pi = l$, $\min^\pi(e_1, e_2) = e_1$, (r) if $\pi = r$, $\min^\pi(e_1, e_2) = e_2$. Consider now the intersection of an abstract property $a = \prod_{k=1}^n I_k$ with a single numerical constraint $c = \sum_{k' \in K'} \alpha_{k'} x_{k'} - \sum_{k'' \in K''} \alpha_{k''} x_{k''} + \beta \geq 0$ with $\alpha_{k'}, \alpha_{k''} > 0$ and $K' \cap K'' = \emptyset$. We want to express $a' = \text{meet\_cond\_apply\_policy}_0(\pi, a, c)$. The constraint c can be rewritten as

$$x_k \geq \frac{1}{\alpha_k}\left(\sum_{k' \in K' \setminus \{k\}} -\alpha_{k'} x_{k'} + \sum_{k'' \in K''} \alpha_{k''} x_{k''} + \beta \right) \qquad \text{if } k \in K'$$

$$x_k \leq \frac{1}{\alpha_k}\left(\sum_{k' \in K'} \alpha_{k'} x_{k'} - \sum_{k'' \in K'' \setminus \{k\}} \alpha_{k''} x_{k''} + \beta \right) \qquad \text{if } k \in K''$$

Hence $a' = \prod_{k=1}^{n} I'_k$ can be expressed as:

$$-(I'_k)^- = \begin{cases} \min^{\pi_{k,-}}\left(-I_k^-, \frac{1}{\alpha_k}\left(-\sum_{k' \in K' \setminus \{k\}} \alpha_{k'} I_{k'}^- + \sum_{k'' \in K''} \alpha_{k''} I_{k''}^+ + \beta \right) \right) & \text{if } k \in K' \\ -I_k^- & \text{otherwise} \end{cases}$$

$$(I'_k)^+ = \begin{cases} \min^{\pi_{k,+}}\left(I_k^+, \frac{1}{\alpha_k}\left(\sum_{k' \in K'} \alpha_{k'} I_{k'}^+ - \sum_{k'' \in K'' \setminus \{k\}} \alpha_{k''} I_{k''}^- + \beta \right) \right) & \text{if } k \in K'' \\ I_k^+ & \text{otherwise} \end{cases}$$

In practice, we associate a bound policy $\pi_{k,+/-}$ to each interval bound, hence $\pi \in \{l, r\}^{2q}$ for the intersection with a single linear inequality in q dimensions. Equalities are handled as the conjunction of two inequalities. This "instrumentation" with policies is generalized to conjunctions of m linear inequalities and equalities, which results in a policy in $\{l, r\}^{2qm}$. The meet of a with a general Boolean formula under DNF form $\bigvee_{i=1}^{p} \bigwedge_j c_{i,j}$ is handled as the disjunction of the meet of a with the p conjuncts $\bigwedge_j c_{i,j}$.

Assignments do not imply min operators in the box abstract domains. On octagons an assignment like $x_1 = 2x_2 + 4$ is performed by introducing a primed variable x'_1, intersecting the octagon with $x'_1 = 2x_2 + 4$ (*which implies min operators*), eliminating x_1 and renaming x'_1 in x_1. Still, ultimately only the meet_cond operation needs to be equipped with a policy. It is however not the case for more general linear templates.

Improving policies. Remind from Section 3 that given a solution $Y = G^\pi(Y)$, we need to improve the policy π if $G(Y) \subsetneq^\sharp Y$. We thus introduce in the API two new generic functions

$$\begin{aligned} \text{meet\_cond\_improve\_policy}_0 &: P_0 \times A_0 \times \quad Cond_0 \quad \to P_0 \\ \text{assign\_var\_improve\_policy}_0 &: P_0 \times A_0 \times Var \times Expr_0 \to P_0 \end{aligned} \qquad (5)$$

$\text{meet\_cond\_improve\_policy}(\pi, a, c)$ proceeds as follows ($\text{assign\_var\_improve\_policy}_0$ proceeds exactly in the same way).

– it computes $a' = \text{meet\_cond}_0(a, c)$ and $a'' = \text{meet\_cond\_apply\_policy}_0(\pi, a, c)$;
– if $a' = a''$, it returns π; otherwise, it chooses a new policy π' such that $a' = \text{meet\_cond\_apply\_policy}_0(\pi', a, c)$, following the principle explained in Section 3, and it returns it.

Integration in the policy iteration process. Once abstract operations are instrumented with policies, one parametrizes Eqn. (3) by associating to each operation $[\![op^{(k',k)}]\!]^{\sharp}$ a policy $\pi^{(k',k)}$:

$$Y^k = I^{\sharp k} \cup^{\sharp} \bigcup_{(k',k)}^{\sharp} \text{op\_apply}^{(k',k)}(\pi^{(k',k)}, Y^{k'}, args \ldots) \tag{6}$$

We apply the process described in Section 3. We fix an initial global policy π_0, and at each policy iteration step i,

1. We solve Eqn. (6) with $\pi = \pi_i$ using Kleene iteration with widening and narrowing; we obtain a solution Y_i.
2. We compute the new policy with $\pi_{i+1}^{(k',k)} = \text{op\_improve}(\pi_i^{(k',k)}, Y_i^{(k')}, args \ldots)$. If $\pi_{i+1} \neq \pi_i$, we iterate the process, otherwise we have a solution.

Implementation. Augmenting the APRON API with the 4 functions introduced by Eqns. (4)-(5) allowed us to integrate nicely policy iteration in the INTERPROC interprocedural analyser, based on the APRON numerical abstract domain libraries and the FIXPOINT equation solver [18]. Currently, we implemented these functions only for the box abstract domain. In the static analyser, we needed to add about 100 OCaml LOC to take care of the policy iteration process (creating policies, updating them and testing convergence). Once a policy π is fixed, we reuse the existing code for solving the equation $Y = G^{\pi}(Y)$.

As INTERPROC also addresses recursive programs, two additional abstract operations appear in the semantic equations: (i) procedure call, which involves projection and variable renaming, hence no policy; (ii) procedure returns, which involves the meet of two abstract values. We did not yet instrument the meet operation, but there is no theoretical problem to do it. Moreover, as we solve $Y = G^{\pi}(Y)$ by Kleene iteration, we can deal with more complex functions G^{π} than if we were tied to problems expressed as linear programs.

5   Policy for Logico-Numerical Abstract Domain

We showed in Section 4 how the concept of policy can be integrated into a numerical abstract domain in a generic way. The practical advantage was the ability to add the *boxpolicy* domain to the APRON library, and ultimately to the INTERPROC analyser, and to benefit for free from all the techniques it implements (*e.g.*, non-linear arithmetic and interprocedural analysis). In this section we show that this integration can be pushed further to the BDDAPRON logico-numerical abstract domain, which acts as a functor on top of an APRON domain, and that this can be done efficiently with MTBDDs.

BddApron abstract operation. As explained in Section 2, the BDDAPRON library proposes to abstract logico-numerical properties in $\mathcal{P}(\mathbb{B}^p \times \mathbb{Q}^q)$ by functions in $A = \mathbb{B}^p \to A_0$. Extending the conditional and assignment operations from A_0 to A is easy under the following conditions:

$$
\begin{aligned}
\mathsf{meet\_cond} &: A \times \quad Cond \quad \rightarrow A \\
\mathsf{assign\_var} &: A \times NVar \times Expr \rightarrow A \\
\mathsf{assign\_bvar} &: A \times BVar \times BExpr \rightarrow A
\end{aligned}
$$

$$
\mathsf{meet\_cond}(f, c) = \lambda \boldsymbol{b} \,.\, \mathsf{meet\_cond}_0\big(f(\boldsymbol{b}), c(\boldsymbol{b})\big)
$$

$$
\mathsf{assign\_var}(f, x_k, e) = \lambda \boldsymbol{b} \,.\, \mathsf{assign\_var}_0\big(f(\boldsymbol{b}), x_k, e(\boldsymbol{b})\big)
$$

$$
\mathsf{assign\_bvar}(f, b_k, \varphi) = \lambda \boldsymbol{b} \,.\, \left\{ \begin{array}{l} (\text{if } b_k \Leftrightarrow \varphi^+(\boldsymbol{b}) \text{ then } f^+(\boldsymbol{b}) \text{ else } \bot_0) \\ \cup_0^\sharp (\text{if } b_k \Leftrightarrow \varphi^-(\boldsymbol{b}) \text{ then } f^-(\boldsymbol{b}) \text{ else } \bot_0) \end{array} \right.
$$

$$
\text{where } f = ite(b_k, f^+, f^-) \text{ and } \varphi = ite(b_k, \varphi^+, \varphi^-)
$$

are decomposed into their cofactors w.r.t. b_k

Fig. 6. BDDAPRON abstract operations

- Conditions in tests are put under the form $Cond = \mathbb{B}^p \rightarrow Cond_0$.
- Assigned expressions are
  - either numerical expressions in $\quad Expr = \mathbb{B}^p \rightarrow Expr_0$;
  - or purely Boolean expressions in $BExpr = \mathbb{B}^p \rightarrow \mathbb{B}$.

In other words, they do not involve conditions on numerical variables. Examples are b0 = (b1 or (b2 and not b3)), x0 = (if b1 then x1+1 else x2-1).

Under these assumptions where the conditions and expressions are pointwise extensions of the conditions and expressions considered in A_0, tests and assignments in A can be defined as in Fig. 6. Notice that "forbidden" assignments like x = (if x>10 then 0 else x+1) or b = (x>=0) can be emulated by replacing conditional expressions with conditional assignments.

Boolean extension of numerical operations with policies. Observe the meet_cond operation in Fig. 6: it applies pointwise the meet_cond$_0$ operation to $f(\boldsymbol{b})$ and $c(\boldsymbol{b})$ for every $\boldsymbol{b} \in \mathbb{B}^p$. If we want to parameterize it with a policy, we need one policy $\pi(\boldsymbol{b}) \in P_0$ for each $\boldsymbol{b} \in \mathbb{B}^p$. If we have such a *logico-numerical policy* $\pi : \mathbb{B}^p \rightarrow P_0$, we apply meet_cond_apply_policy$_0$ pointwise to $\pi(\boldsymbol{b})$, $f(\boldsymbol{b})$ and $c(\boldsymbol{b})$ for each $\boldsymbol{b} \in \mathbb{B}^p$. We get the following definition.

Definition 1 (Logico-numerical policy). *If P_0 denotes the set of policies associated with the numerical abstract domain A_0, the set of policies associated with the logico-numerical domain $A = \mathbb{B}^p \rightarrow A_0$ is* $\boxed{P = \mathbb{B}^p \rightarrow P_0}$.

The op_apply_policy and op_improve_policy operations in A are defined in Fig. 7 by extending pointwise the corresponding operations in A_0. As the operation assign_bvar involves only the numerical operation $\cup_0^\sharp$, it does not need a policy.

We have set exactly the same framework than the one of Section 4. We can thus analyse logico-numerical programs with the BDDAPRON extension of any numerical domain equipped with policies (like the box domain). In this new context, the solution Y_i of $Y = G^{\pi_i}(Y)$ computed by Kleene iteration actually provides two kinds of information: the set of reachable Boolean valuations at a node, and the numerical invariant associated with each of them.

$$
\begin{aligned}
\text{meet\_cond\_apply\_policy} &: & P \times A \times && \textit{Cond} && \to A \\
\text{meet\_cond\_improve\_policy} &: & P \times A \times && \textit{Cond} && \to P \\
\text{assign\_var\_apply\_policy} &: & P \times A \times && \textit{Var} \times \textit{Expr} && \to A \\
\text{assign\_var\_improve\_policy} &: & P \times A \times && \textit{Var} \times \textit{Expr} && \to P
\end{aligned}
$$

$$
\begin{aligned}
\text{meet\_cond\_apply\_policy}(\pi, f, c) &= \lambda\boldsymbol{b} \,.\, \text{meet\_cond\_apply\_policy}_0\big(\pi(\boldsymbol{b}), f(\boldsymbol{b}), c(\boldsymbol{b})\big) \\
\text{meet\_cond\_improve\_policy}(\pi, f, c) &= \lambda\boldsymbol{b} \,.\, \text{meet\_cond\_improve\_policy}_0\big(\pi(\boldsymbol{b}), f(\boldsymbol{b}), c(\boldsymbol{b})\big) \\
\text{assign\_var\_apply\_policy}(\pi, f, x_k, e) &= \lambda\boldsymbol{b} \,.\, \text{assign\_var\_apply\_policy}_0\big(\pi(\boldsymbol{b}), f(\boldsymbol{b}), x_k, e(\boldsymbol{b})\big) \\
\text{assign\_var\_improve\_policy}(\pi, f, x_k, e) &= \lambda\boldsymbol{b} \,.\, \text{assign\_var\_improve\_policy}_0\big(\pi(\boldsymbol{b}), f(\boldsymbol{b}), x_k, e(\boldsymbol{b})\big)
\end{aligned}
$$

Fig. 7. Parametrization of logico-numerical operations with policies

Implementation with Mtbdds. Our operations involve functions of signature $\mathbb{B}^p \to T$. If they are represented with a tabulated representation, the complexity of abstract operations is in $\mathcal{O}(2^p)$. In particular we need 2^p numerical policies in P_0 at each edge of the program CFG.

The solution is to reuse the principle behind the BDDAPRON library, which is to represent functions of signature $\mathbb{B}^p \to T$ with MTBDDs [9]. As mentioned in Section 2, the complexity of an operation defined as

$$
\begin{aligned}
op : (\mathbb{B}^p \to T_1) \times (\mathbb{B}^p \to T_2) &\to (\mathbb{B}^p \to T) \\
(f_1, f_2) &\mapsto op(f_1, f_2) = \lambda\boldsymbol{b} \,.\, op_0\big(f_1(\boldsymbol{b}), f_2(\boldsymbol{b})\big) \\
&\text{with } op_0 : T_1 \times T_2 \to T
\end{aligned}
\tag{7}
$$

is $\mathcal{O}(2^p)$ with a tabulated representation of f_1 and f_2, and $\mathcal{O}(|f_1| \cdot |f_2|)$ with a MTBDD representation of f_1 and f_2 with $|f_1|$ and $|f_2|$ nodes. In the latter case the function op is implemented by a parallel, recursive descent of the MTBDDs f_1 and f_2, using memoization techniques to avoid exploring already explored pairs of subgraphs. As the functions of Fig. 7 follow the pattern of Eqn. (7), they benefit from such techniques.

The condition on a set T for representing functions in $\mathbb{B}^p \to T$ with MTBDDs is the ability (i) to test the equality of two elements in T, (ii) and to have a reasonably efficient hash function. In the case of the box domain, policies are elements of sets of the form $\{l, r\}^N$, as discussed in Section 4, and meet these requirements. It is also the case for policies for the octagon domain [14].

Concerning the initial policy, our (naive) tactic is to associate to each operation op of the CFG a constant policy $\pi_0^{(k', k)} = \lambda\boldsymbol{b} \,.\, p_0 \in P_0$.

6   Experiments

This section presents experimental results showing that policy iteration on logico-numerical abstract domains, as presented in Section 2, allows precise and tractable analysis of programs involving Boolean variables, numerical variables and even concurrency. The experiments were performed with the ConcurInterproc analyser, using BDDAPRON and logico-numerical policies.

Table 1. Experiments with modified examples of [1]

Program	Nesting	#$\mathbb{B}$	#$\mathbb{Q}$	Control points	Boxes only	Boxes+policies		Precision
						No sharing	Full sharing	
test1'	1	2	1	4	8ms	17ms	15ms (2 it.)	=
test2'	1	3	2	5	18ms	42ms	34ms (2 it.)	=
test3'	1	2	3	4	8ms	15ms	13ms (1 it.)	=
test4'	1	10	5	12	226ms	25 300ms	480ms (3 it.)	=
test5'	2	4	2	6	23ms	79ms	47ms (2 it.)	>
test6'	2	6	2	8	44ms	520ms	124ms (3 it.)	>
test7'	2	6	3	8	40ms	310ms	81ms (2 it.)	>
test8'	3	6	3	8	60ms	280ms	113ms (2 it.)	=
test9'	3	6	3	8	58ms	360ms	116ms (2 it.)	>

Table 2. Experiments with concurrent programs

Program	Threads, #$\mathbb{B}$, #$\mathbb{Q}$, control	Boxes only	Boxes+policies				Prec.
			No sharing	Full sharing	Disting.		
BlueTooth	$2T, 5\mathbb{B}, 3\mathbb{Q}, 87cpt$	0.21s	0.99s	0.84s (3 it.)	17%		=
Preemptive	$2T, 9\mathbb{B}, 1\mathbb{Q}, 352cpt$	0.83s	18.64s	1.37s (1 it.)	0.7%		=
Barrier	$2T, 5\mathbb{B}, 2\mathbb{Q}, 95cpt$	0.79s	3.05s	1.96s (2 it.)	9.5%		>
Loop2TML	$2T, 1\mathbb{B}, 6\mathbb{Q}, 37cpt$	0.10s	0.22s	0.21s (2 it.)	70%		>

Analysis of the running example. We perform the analysis of the programs shown on Figures 1(a) and 1(c). For these two programs, the analysis with boxes (only) does not infer the most precise bounds for i and j while the analysis with boxes and policies does. The use of policy iteration have little impact on the analysis times. Thanks to the MTBDDs, the analysis times for the program of Fig. 1(c) is of the same order of magnitude than the ones of Fig. 1(a), in spite of the eight possible Boolean valuations to consider.

Examples from [1] plus Booleans. We modify the programs experimented in [1] by introducing in a systematic way Boolean variables in order to demonstrate that:

1. Policy Iteration on boxes is more precise than boxes only.
2. Analysis time does not increase as fast as the number of boolean valuations.

We added a Boolean variable for each loop, each conditional and each variable modification. These Boolean variables are then used as additional condition to enter the loop, enter the then branch and perform the modification. For example, it introduces the uninitialized Boolean variables a and b in the following program:

```
while (x<100)          while (a && x<100)
    x=x+1;      ⟶          if (b) x=x+1;
```

The results are shown in Table 1. Column *program* gives the name of the original program with an additional ' to recall the transformation. Column *nesting* gives the maximum nesting depth of the loops. Column #$\mathbb{Q}$ and #$\mathbb{B}$ count respectively the number of numerical and Boolean variables (the latter being introduced by the transformation). The results obtained by our approach are shown in the column *boxes+policies, full sharing* and are to be compared with the ones without policies, taking into account whether the box abstract domain reach the same precision as policies (=) or not (>).

We also experimented the loss of efficiency that could be endured if we do not share the policies. The column *no sharing* indicates the analysis time when we take one policy per Boolean valuation instead of an MTBDD of policies.

All the analyses using policy iteration discover here the *best invariant* one could hope for boxes. The symbols > indicate cases where traditional boxes cannot infer this optimal invariant. The experiments show that for boxes with policy iteration timings tends to be proportional to the timings using the classical BDDAPRON boxes multiplied by the number of iterations. The idea of applying the method of [1] using one policy per boolean valuation does not scale (eg., test4' need to consider one thousand policies per meet operation).

Analysis of concurrent programs. Table 2 shows the results of experiments involving concurrent programs performing synchronisation using shared Boolean variables. The columns have to be interpreted like the ones of Tab. 1, with an additional column *disting.* containing the percentage of policies that truly need to be distinguished. Note that procedures have been inlined, and that the commutation between threads creates large control flow graphs with many cycles.

The results obtained by policy iterations can be far more precise than the ones obtained without, as it is the case for the program `Barrier` (which explains the increase of the analysis cost). The timings confirm that when both analyses are equally precise, our implementation is slower by a factor close to the number of policy explored. The experiments we have performed also showed that the iterations tend to be faster as the policies get improved.

7   Conclusion

We first showed in this paper how to integrate in a generic way the concept of policy into a numerical abstract domain. This is done at the cost of giving up the ability to solve *exactly* the equation $Y = G^\pi(Y)$ parametrized with the policy π using linear programming.However we believe that this shortcoming is largely counter-balanced by the gains, which are

  (i) the easy integration in existing static analysis tool, such as [18];
 (ii) the ability to build more complex abstract domains on top of such policy-equipped numerical domains and to address programs with other datatypes.

We demonstrated point (i) by equipping the box domain implemented in the APRON library with policies, and by integrating it in the INTERPROC tool. Our major contribution is however the demonstration of point (ii) in the case of programs manipulating Boolean and numerical variables. Instead of assigning a numerical policy to each Boolean valuation, we showed that we can use MTBDDS techniques to assign a single policy to a (potentially large) set of Boolean valuations. This efficient representation of *logico-numerical policies* was integrated in the BDDAPRON library.

Our experiments illustrated two points. They first showed that this latter technique improves in a spectacular way the efficiency of policies, compared to their naive application, even for simple programs with a dozen of Boolean variables. They also showed that despite the theoretical shortcoming of our approach mentioned above w.r.t. precision, in practice our combination of policy and Kleene iteration yields more precise results than the traditional approach that relies only on Kleene iteration.

A perspective opened by this work is the use of policy iteration in complex abstract domains that are parametrized by a numerical abstract domain, like the one proposed in [19] for dynamically allocated data-structures. Our approach enables the use of policies in this context, whereas the traditional approach based on translation to min-max equations as in Fig. 5(d) seems hardly feasible.

In some situations however, solving $Y = G^\pi(Y)$ by linear programming may be preferrable. Another perspective would be to apply the technique of this paper to obtain an initial overapproximation of the least solution of $Y = G^\pi(Y)$, and then to exploit the implicit partition of $\mathbb{B}^p$ provided by the MTBDDs of Y and/or π to generate a linear program without enumerating all Boolean valuations, and to solve it exactly.

References

1. Costan, A., Gaubert, S., Goubault, E., Martel, M., Putot, S.: A policy iteration algorithm for computing fixed points in static analysis of programs. In: Etessami, K., Rajamani, S.K. (eds.) CAV 2005. LNCS, vol. 3576, pp. 462–475. Springer, Heidelberg (2005)
2. Cousot, P., Cousot, R.: Abstract interpretation and application to logic programs. Journal of Logic Programming 13 (1992)
3. Cousot, P., Cousot, R.: Static determination of dynamic properties of programs. In: 2nd Int. Symp. on Programming, Dunod, Paris (1976)
4. Miné, A.: The octagon abstract domain. Higher-Order and Symbolic Computation 19 (2006)
5. Sankaranarayanan, S., Sipma, H.B., Manna, Z.: Scalable analysis of linear systems using mathematical programming. In: Cousot, R. (ed.) VMCAI 2005. LNCS, vol. 3385, pp. 25–41. Springer, Heidelberg (2005)
6. Halbwachs, N., Proy, Y., Roumanoff, P.: Verification of real-time systems using linear relation analysis. Formal Methods in System Design 11 (1997)
7. Jeannet, B., Miné, A.: APRON: A library of numerical abstract domains for static analysis. In: Bouajjani, A., Maler, O. (eds.) CAV 2009. LNCS, vol. 5643, pp. 661–667. Springer, Heidelberg (2009), http://apron.cri.ensmp.fr/library/
8. Jeannet, B.: The BDDAPRON logico-numerical abstract domains library, http://www.inrialpes.fr/pop-art/people/bjeannet/bjeannet-forge/bddapron/
9. Bryant, R.E.: Graph-based algorithms for boolean function manipulation. IEEE Trans. on Computers 35 (1986)
10. Howard, R.: Dynamic Programming and Markov Processes. Wiley, Chichester (1960)

11. Hoffman, A.J., Karp, R.M.: On nonterminating stochastic games. Management Sci. 12, 359–370 (1966)
12. Shapley, L.S.: Stochastic games. Proceedings of the National Academy of Sciences 39, 1095–1100 (1953)
13. Adjé, A., Gaubert, S., Goubault, E.: Computing the smallest fixpoint of nonexpansive mappings arising in game theory and static analysis of programs (2008)
14. Gaubert, S., Goubault, E., Taly, A., Zennou, S.: Static analysis by policy iteration on relational domains. In: De Nicola, R. (ed.) ESOP 2007. LNCS, vol. 4421, pp. 237–252. Springer, Heidelberg (2007)
15. Adjé, A., Gaubert, S., Goubault, E.: Coupling policy iteration with semi-definite relaxation to compute accurate numerical invariants in static analysis. In: Gordon, A.D. (ed.) ESOP 2010. LNCS, vol. 6012, pp. 23–42. Springer, Heidelberg (2010)
16. Jeannet, B., Argoud, M., Lalire, G.: The INTERPROC interprocedural analyzer, http://pop-art.inrialpes.fr/interproc/interprocweb.cgi
17. Miné, A.: Symbolic methods to enhance the precision of numerical abstract domains. In: Emerson, E.A., Namjoshi, K.S. (eds.) VMCAI 2006. LNCS, vol. 3855, pp. 348–363. Springer, Heidelberg (2005)
18. Jeannet, B.: Some experience on the software engineering of abstract interpretation tools. In: Int. Workshop on Tools for Automatic Program AnalysiS, TAPAS 2010. ENTCS, vol. 267. Elsevier, Amsterdam (2010)
19. Chang, B.Y.E., Rival, X.: Relational inductive shape analysis. In: Principles of Programming Languages, POPL 2008. ACM, New York (2008)

Small Strategies for Safety Games

Daniel Neider

Lehrstuhl für Informatik 7, RWTH Aachen University, Germany

Abstract. We consider safety games on finite, edge-labeled graphs and present an algorithm based on automata learning to compute small strategies. Our idea is as follows: we incrementally learn regular sets of winning plays until a winning strategy can be derived. For this purpose we develop a modified version of Kearns and Vazirani's learning algorithm. Since computing a minimal strategy in this setting is hard (we prove that the corresponding decision problem is NP-complete), our algorithm, which runs in polynomial time, is an interesting and effective heuristic that yields small strategies in our experiments.

1 Introduction

For the verification of soft- and hardware, especially for reactive systems, various techniques have been developed. The most important ones, such as testing [11] and model checking [2], have gained a wide industrial acceptance. All of these techniques have in common that they are naturally applied at the end of the developing process. Errors that are detected at this stage are often costly to fix.

A complementary approach is positioned earlier in the development process. Instead of implementing the whole system by hand, parts can be automatically synthesized from given specifications. This can be done in the following way: the specifications are translated into an infinite, two-person game on a finite graph in such a way that a winning strategy for one of the players corresponds to a system that satisfies the specifications.

During the last decades, much research has been spend on efficient algorithms to solve such infinite games, i.e., to determine the winner and to compute a winning strategy (see [7] for an overview). However, from a software engineering point of view it is less important how fast a winning strategy can be computed. More important is the question how much memory is needed to realize a winning strategy, i.e., how large the resulting system really is. In fact, this question seems to be hard to settle and untill today there is no satisfactory answer (although some approaches have been made, e.g., in [6], [3], and [8]). Even more intriguing is the task to compute winning strategies of small size or even minimal ones.

In this work we focus on the task of computing small strategies for safety games. A safety game is an infinite, two-person game played on a finite graph that is composed of safe and unsafe vertices. The objective is to stay inside the set of safe vertices no matter how the malevolent opponent plays. For this type of game there exist linear time algorithms that compute positional winning strategies, i.e., strategies that do only depend on the current position a play

T. Bultan and P.-A. Hsiung (Eds.): ATVA 2011, LNCS 6996, pp. 306–320, 2011.

has reached. However, a controller (or program) realizing a positional strategy can be large because it needs to keep track of the exact position of a play. Thus, although these algorithms are fast, they do not necessarily produce small results.

In the following we present a polynomial time algorithm that computes strategies for safety games, which often have a small representation. Our algorithm is based on automata learning in an active learning environment as it has been introduced by Angluin [1]. In this setting, a learner learns a regular language in interaction with a teacher. The idea of our approach is to interpret prefixes of winning plays as finite words and define winning strategies in terms of finite automata that have special structural properties (Section 2). Since we can solve safety games efficiently, we can easily determine which play prefix belongs to a winning play and which does not. Based on this knowledge we start learning regular sets of winning play prefixes until one of these sets realizes a winning strategy (Section 3). Since learning algorithms typically produce conjectures with increasing size, it is often possible to find small solutions. Moreover, a modified version of Kearns and Vazirani's learning algorithm [9], which we develop in Section 3.2, yields even better results than existing learning algorithms.

Unfortunately, in this setting computing minimal strategies is hard; we show that the corresponding decision problem "Given a safety game and $k \in \mathbb{N}$. Does an automaton with at most k states realizing a winning strategy exist?" is NP-complete (Section 2). Hence, our algorithm, which runs in polynomial time, is a heuristic, but it turns out that this heuristic produces good, i.e., small, results in our experiments (Section 4). In fact, these results are several times smaller than those derived from positional strategies.

2   Safety Games and Strategies

In this work, we consider safety games on deterministic edge-labeled arenas where the edge labels, or *actions*, are picked from some alphabet Σ. Formally, such an *arena* is a tuple $\mathcal{A} = (V_0, V_1, E)$ where the set V_0 of Player 0 vertices (drawn as circles) and the set V_1 of Player 1 vertices (drawn as squares) form a partition of the finite set $V = V_0 \uplus V_1$ of all vertices, and $E \subseteq V \times \Sigma \times V$ is a directed, deterministic, Σ-labeled edge relation such that $(v, a, v') \in E$ and $(v, a, v'') \in E$ implies $v' = v''$. Moreover, to avoid dealing with finite plays, we require that all vertices have at least one outgoing edge.

A *safety game* $\mathcal{G} = (\mathcal{A}, F)$ consists of an arena $\mathcal{A}$ and a set $F \subseteq V$ of *safe* vertices. It is played by two players, Player 0 and Player 1, as follows: a token is placed on some *initial vertex* v_0 and, depending on whether $v_0 \in V_0$ or $v_0 \in V_1$, the corresponding player chooses an edge $(v_0, a_0, v_1) \in E$ and the token is moved to vertex v_1. This process is then repeated ad infinitum and results in an infinite sequence $\rho_{v_0} = a_0 a_1 \ldots \in \Sigma^\omega$ of actions, which we call a *play*. Since $\mathcal{A}$ is deterministic, each play uniquely induces a path $\pi(\rho_{v_0}) = v_0 v_1 \ldots \in V^\omega$. However, the converse is not true: there may be distinct plays (even starting in the same initial vertex) that induce the same path. We write $\mathcal{G}: v_0 \xrightarrow{w} v$, if there exists a finite play prefix $w = a_0 \ldots a_n \in \Sigma^*$ such that $\pi(w) = v_0 \ldots v_{n+1}$ with

$v_{n+1} = v$. A play ρ_{v_0} is called *winning for Player 0* if $\pi(\rho_{v_0})$ stays inside the set of safe vertices, i.e., $v_i \in F$ for all $i \in \mathbb{N}$. If a play is not winning for Player 0, then it is winning for Player 1. Moreover, we define that a player loses if he picks in one of his vertices an action for which no outgoing edge exists. Note that a play itself does not carry the information in which vertex it starts. Hence, we write ρ_{v_0} to indicate that the play starts in v_0. If the initial vertex is clear from the context, we often omit the subscript v_0.

A strategy for Player i, $i \in \{0, 1\}$, is a partial mapping $f \colon \Sigma^* \dashrightarrow \Sigma$ that maps a finite play prefix $w \in \Sigma^*$ leading to a vertex $v \in V_i$ to an action $a \in \Sigma$ with $(v, a, v') \in E$. Intuitively, a strategy tells a player how to continue a play whenever it is his turn. A strategy is called a *winning strategy from vertex v_0* if all plays starting in v_0 and played according to f are winning for Player i. The set of all vertices from which Player i has a winning strategy is called the *winning region of Player i* and is denoted by $W_i \subseteq V$. Since safety games are determined, the winning region of Player $1 - i$ is $W_{1-i} = V \setminus W_i$ (cf. [7]).

Computing winning regions and winning strategies in safety games can be done using a straight-forward fixed-point computation: starting with the set $U_0 = F$, we remove from a set U_i all vertices $v \in V_0$ that do not have an edge $(v, a, v') \in E$ with $v' \in U_i$. Moreover, we remove all vertices $v \in V_1$ that have an edge $(v, a, v') \in E$ with $v' \notin U_i$. Since V is finite, this process terminates after at most $|V|$ steps and we obtain $W_0 = U_{|V|}$. A possible winning strategy for Player 0 simply picks for a vertex $v \in W_0 \cap V_0$ some action $a \in \Sigma$ such that there exists an edge $(v, a, v') \in E$ with $v' \in W_0$. The described fixed-point computation can be done efficiently in time and space linear in $|E|$. The winning region and a winning strategy for Player 1 can be computed using a similar fixed-point algorithm, e.g., as described in [7].

Since determining the winning region of both players can be done efficiently, and we are interested in finding small strategies, we concentrate on computing strategies for Player 0 and fix an initial vertex $v_0 \in W_0$ for the rest of this paper.

Representation of Strategies. The sketched fixed-point algorithm shows that both players can win (in their winning regions) using strategies that do not depend on the history of the play, but only on the current vertex the play has reached. Such strategies are called *positional* (or sometimes "memoryless"). However, a device (e.g., a controller or a program) that realizes a positional winning strategy needs to keep track of the current vertex a play has reached. A common way to do so is to use the arena $\mathcal{A}$ and delete all edges leaving Player 0 vertices that are not picked by the strategy. In fact, it is already enough to keep the part of this restricted arena that can still be reached from v_0. For a positional strategy f, we denote this part as $\mathcal{A}_f$ and call it a *representation of f*.

Our approach in this work is to encode winning strategies (not necessarily positional ones) differently in terms of finite automata. As we show later (cf. Section 4), this often allows us to find small representations. A deterministic finite automaton $\mathfrak{A} = (Q, \Sigma, q_0, \delta, F_{\mathfrak{A}})$ is defined in the usual way: Q is a finite set of states, Σ is the input alphabet, $q_0 \in Q$ is the initial state, $\delta \colon Q \times \Sigma \to Q$ is the transition function, and $F_{\mathfrak{A}} \subseteq Q$ is the set of final states. A run of $\mathfrak{A}$ on some input $w = a_0 \ldots a_n \in \Sigma^*$ is a sequence $q_0 \ldots q_{n+1}$ such that $\delta(q_i, a_i) = q_{i+1}$ for $i \in \{1, \ldots, n\}$; we then write $\mathfrak{A} \colon q_0 \xrightarrow{w} q_{n+1}$. A word w is accepted by $\mathfrak{A}$ if $\mathfrak{A} \colon q_0 \xrightarrow{w} q_{n+1}$ and $q_{n+1} \in F_{\mathfrak{A}}$. The language accepted by $\mathfrak{A}$ is defined as $L(\mathfrak{A}) = \{w \in \Sigma^* \mid w \text{ is accepted by } \mathfrak{A}\}$. A language L is called *regular* if there exists a deterministic finite automaton $\mathfrak{A}$ such that $L = L(\mathfrak{A})$. We define the *size* $|\mathfrak{A}|$ of an automaton $\mathfrak{A}$ as $|Q|$, i.e., the number of its states.

Our encoding of strategies works as follows: for a fixed initial vertex $v_0 \in W_0$, a strategy f induces a set of plays, which is generated by the different choices of Player 1. If f is positional (or a finite memory strategy, e.g., defined in [7]), then the corresponding set of finite play prefixes is regular. Conversely, the following definition characterizes when a regular language realizes a winning strategy.

Definition 1. *A finite automaton $\mathfrak{A} = (Q, \Sigma, q_0, \delta, F_{\mathfrak{A}})$ realizes a winning strategy for Player 0 in the safety game $\mathcal{G} = (\mathcal{A}, F)$ from vertex v_0 if it fulfills the following properties:*

1. *$L(\mathfrak{A})$ is prefix closed, i.e., for $a_0 \ldots a_n \in L(\mathfrak{A})$ also $a_0 \ldots a_{n-1} \in L(\mathfrak{A})$ holds, and $\varepsilon \in L(\mathfrak{A})$.*
2. *For all $w \in L(\mathfrak{A})$ with $\mathcal{G} \colon v_0 \xrightarrow{w} v$ the condition $v \in F$ holds.*
3. *For all $w \in L(\mathfrak{A})$ with $\mathcal{G} \colon v_0 \xrightarrow{w} v$, $v \in V_0$ there exists $(v, a, v') \in E$ such that $wa \in L(\mathfrak{A})$.*
4. *For all $w \in L(\mathfrak{A})$ with $\mathcal{G} \colon v_0 \xrightarrow{w} v$, $v \in V_0$ there exists no $a \in \Sigma$ such that $wa \in L(\mathfrak{A})$ and $(v, a, v') \notin E$ for all $v' \in V$.*
5. *For all $w \in L(\mathfrak{A})$ with $\mathcal{G} \colon v_0 \xrightarrow{w} v$, $v \in V_1$ and for all $(v, a, v') \in E$ the condition $wa \in L(\mathfrak{A})$ is satisfied.*

If a finite automaton $\mathfrak{A}$ satisfies Definition 1, we call $\mathfrak{A}$ a *strategy automaton*. In fact, a strategy automaton does not necessarily realize a unique strategy as it may allow more than one choice in Player 0 vertices. A derived strategy $f_{\mathfrak{A}}$ then looks as follows: let $w \in L(\mathfrak{A})$ such that $\mathcal{G} \colon v_0 \xrightarrow{w} v$, $v \in V_0$. Then, $f_{\mathfrak{A}}(w) = a$ for an arbitrary but fixed $a \in \Sigma$ such that $wa \in L(\mathfrak{A})$. Due to condition 3 of Definition 1, such a symbol always exists, but may not be unique. Let us show that $f_{\mathfrak{A}}$ is in fact a winning strategy for Player 0.

Proof. An induction over the length of a play prefix w using conditions 2 to 5 of Definition 1 shows that if w is played according to $f_{\mathfrak{A}}$, then $w \in L(\mathfrak{A})$. In particular, whenever a play reaches a vertex $v \in V_0$, Player 0 can pick an action $a \in \Sigma$ such that $wa \in L(\mathfrak{A})$. Since all finite plays $w \in L(\mathfrak{A})$ stay inside F (cf. condition 2) and $\varepsilon \in L(\mathfrak{A})$ (cf. condition 1), Player 0 can in fact win from v_0. □

Note that Definition 1 is sound: for any safety game $\mathcal{G}$ (with finitely many vertices) and an initial vertex $v_0 \in W_0$ one can construct an automaton realizing a winning strategy in $\mathcal{G}$ from v_0 in a straight-forward manner: we use the set W_0 itself as states of the automaton (together with a new sink state q_s) and the edges restricted to W_0 as transitions. The resulting automaton $\mathfrak{A}_{\mathcal{G}} = (Q, \Sigma, q_0, \delta, F_{\mathfrak{A}_{\mathcal{G}}})$ is called *canonical strategy automaton* and is defined as follows: $Q = W_0 \cup \{q_s\}$, $q_0 = v_0$, $F_{\mathfrak{A}_{\mathcal{G}}} = W_0$, and $\delta(v, a) = v' \Leftrightarrow v, v' \in W_0$ and $(v, a, v') \in E$ as well as $\delta(q, a) = q_s$ in any other case. It is not hard to verify that $\mathfrak{A}_{\mathcal{G}}$ is in fact a strategy automaton since it accepts exactly the finite prefixes of winning plays.

Size of Strategies. In order to compare positional strategies and strategies realized by strategy automata, we need a proper measure. For this purpose we define the *size* of a strategy in the following way.

Definition 2. *The size of a positional strategy f is the number of vertices in the restricted arena $\mathcal{A}_f$ (cf. page 308), denoted by $|\mathcal{A}_f|$. The size of a strategy realized by a strategy automaton $\mathfrak{A}$ is $|\mathfrak{A}|$, i.e., the number of $\mathfrak{A}$'s states.*

At this point we should note that for some special cases, e.g., if $V_0 = \emptyset$ or if the game has very few edges, Definition 2 may be too coarse. In the first case, $|\mathcal{A}_f|$ may be too large to correctly reflect the the amount of memory actually needed to realize a positional strategy. In the latter case, $\mathcal{A}_f$ also has very few edges, whereas in strategy automata for every action a transition is defined. However, besides these very special cases and for all experiments shown later, we claim that size as defined above is a reasonable measure to compare strategies.

In the sense of Definition 2, strategy automata can be very compact representations of strategies. For instance, consider the following family of safety games $(\mathcal{G}_n)_{n \in \mathbb{N}}$ over $\Sigma = \{a, b\}$, which is depicted in Figure 1: for $n \in \mathbb{N}$ let $\mathcal{G}_n = (V_0^n, V_1^n, E_n, F_n)$ be a safety game with $V_0^n = \{1, \dots, n\}$, $V_1^n = \emptyset$, $E_n = \{(i, a, (i+1 \mod n)+1) \mid 1 \le i \le n\} \cup \{(n, b, 1)\}$, and $F_n = V_0^n$. Since all vertices are safe, $W_0 = V_n^0$ holds.

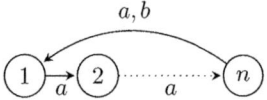

Fig. 1. The safety game $\mathcal{G}_n$

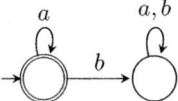

Fig. 2. A strategy automaton realizing a winning strategy in $\mathcal{G}_n$

Now, consider a positional strategy f. Such a strategy picks in every vertex an action that leads to the unique successor vertex. Hence, $\mathcal{A}_f$ covers the whole arena and we have $|\mathcal{A}_f| = |V_0^n| = n$. However, for all $n \in \mathbb{N}$, the automaton depicted in Figure 2 is a strategy automaton for any $v_0 \in V_0^n$. In contrast to $\mathcal{A}_f$, this automaton always has the same constant size. Clearly, in this example the realization of a positional strategy suffers from the fact that it exactly remembers which vertex a play has reached. This is of course superfluous in this example, and there are ways to minimize $\mathcal{A}_f$ once it is computed (cf. Section 4). However, it is unclear how a small positional strategy can be computed in general.

Minimal Strategy Automata. As we show later (cf. Section 3.1), checking whether a given automaton $\mathfrak{A}$ is a strategy automaton (i.e., satisfies Definition 1) can be done in polynomial time. However, the decision problem *"Given a safety game $\mathcal{G}$, $v_0 \in V$ and $k \in \mathbb{N}$. Does a strategy automaton with at most k states that realizes a winning strategy from v_0 exist?"* is NP-complete. Thus, constructing a minimal strategy automaton is a computationally hard task.

To prove the NP-hardness of this decision problem, we define a reduction from 3-SAT (satisfiability of Boolean formulae, cf. [12]), which is a simplified version of a reduction shown in [5]. In fact, the NP-hardness follows from results of an extended, but not published version of [5], but since this results are unavailable, we decided to show our reduction. Kupferman et al. [10] study a similar problem in the context of bounded synthesis, but their results cannot be transfered easily to our setting.

Our reduction works as follows: from a 3-SAT formula φ, we construct a polynomial-size safety game $\mathcal{G}_\varphi$ such that there exists a "small" strategy automaton realizing a winning strategy if and only if φ is satisfiable. Let us illustrate this with the example depicted in Figure 3. We consider the formula $\varphi := (\neg x_1 \vee \neg x_2 \vee x_3) \wedge (x_1 \vee \neg x_3 \vee x_4) \wedge (\neg x_1 \vee x_2 \vee \neg x_4)$, which consists of $m = 3$ clauses and $n = 4$ variables. The resulting safety game $\mathcal{G}_\varphi$ is shown in Figure 3. All but the gray-shaded vertices belong to F. The idea is as follows: the game consists of one sub-graph per clause. In each sub-graph, Player 0 can win by moving along a $\{0, 1\}$-labeled path (followed by $\perp^\omega$) that avoids the gray-shaded vertex. Such a path corresponds to an evaluation of the variables $x_1, \ldots, x_n$ that satisfies the clause: the first move assigns a value to x_1, the second to x_2, etc.

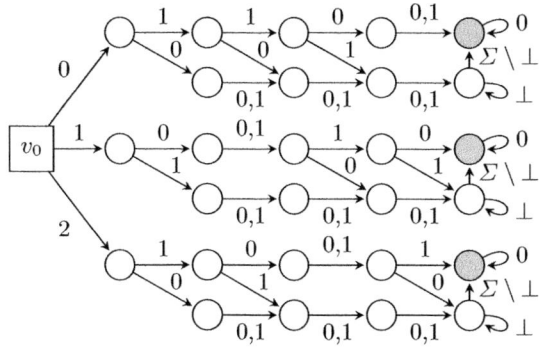 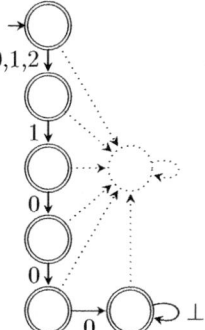

Fig. 3. Safety game $\mathcal{G}_\varphi$ for the formula $\varphi := (\neg x_1 \vee \neg x_2 \vee x_3) \wedge (x_1 \vee \neg x_3 \vee x_4) \wedge (\neg x_1 \vee x_2 \vee \neg x_4)$. All but the gray-shaded vertices belong to F.

Fig. 4. An automaton (with dotted sink state) realizing a winning strategy for Player 0 from v_0

Now, if φ is satisfiable, then there exists an interpretation of the variables that satisfies all clauses. From this interpretation we can derive a strategy automaton with at most $n + 3$ states (cf. Figure 4) that, no matter what edge Player 1 chooses in v_0, avoids the gray-shaded vertices. Contrary, if φ is unsatisfiable, then there are at least two sub-graphs in which Player 0 needs to follow distinct paths to avoid the gray-shaded vertices. However, an automaton realizing such a winning strategy needs strictly more than $n + 3$ states.

The following lemma states this idea formally and shows that the decision problem from above is NP-hard.

Lemma 1. *Let φ be a 3-SAT formula ranging over n variables. Then, there exists a strategy automaton $\mathfrak{A} = (Q, \Sigma, q_0, \delta, F_{\mathfrak{A}})$ with $|Q| = n+3$ states realizing a winning strategy for Player 0 in the safety game $\mathcal{G}_\varphi$ from vertex v_0 if φ is satisfiable. If φ is unsatisfiable, then any such strategy automaton has strictly more that $n + 3$ states.*

Beyond that, the results from the extended version of [5] show that the NP-hardness still holds for safety games with only one player (so-called solitary games) over an alphabet Σ with $|\Sigma| = 2$. A nondeterministic algorithm that guesses an automaton for a given safety game and verifies in polynomial time that the guessed automaton is a strategy automaton (cf. Section 3.1) proves that the decision problem is in fact NP-complete.

3 Learning Small Strategies

In the following we present our learning-based algorithm to compute strategy automata for safety games. Our algorithm is based on the active learning framework, which has been introduced by Angluin in [1]. In this setting, a *learner* wants to learn a regular *target language* $L \subseteq \Sigma^*$ over an a priori fixed alphabet Σ in interaction with a *teacher*. In order to do so, the learner is allowed to pose two different types of queries to the teacher. The first type is called a *membership query*, in which the learner presents the teacher an arbitrary word $w \in \Sigma^*$. The teacher then checks whether $w \in L$ and replies either "yes" or "no".

The second type of query is called *equivalence query*. There, the learner proposes a conjecture, typically given as an automaton $\mathfrak{A}$, and the teacher checks whether $L = L(\mathfrak{A})$. If $L(\mathfrak{A})$ equals L, then the teacher replies "yes". If this is not the case, the teacher has to provide a *counter-example* $w \in L \setminus L(\mathfrak{A}) \cup L(\mathfrak{A}) \setminus L$ as a witness that L and $L(\mathfrak{A})$ are different.

Angluin showed in [1] that every regular language can be learned efficiently, i.e., in time polynomial in the size of the minimal automaton accepting L and the length of the longest counter-example replied by the teacher. Afterwards, this result has been improved, e.g., in [13] and [9].

All these algorithms have in common that they produce conjectures of increasing size during the learning process. Our algorithm exploits this fact and works as shown in Algorithm 1.

At the latest, Algorithm 1 terminates once $L(\mathfrak{A}_\mathcal{G})$ has been learned. However, one of the conjectures produced during the learning process may already be a

---

Algorithm 1. Learning algorithm for strategy automata

---

1 For a given safety game $\mathcal{G}$ and initial vertex v_0 we compute W_0 (cf. Section 2) and construct the canonical strategy automaton $\mathfrak{A}_\mathcal{G}$.

2 We construct a teacher for the language $L(\mathfrak{A}_\mathcal{G})$.

3 We run a learning algorithm of our choice and terminate the learning process as soon as a conjecture realizes a winning strategy in $\mathcal{G}$ from v_0.

---

valid strategy automaton. In this case we terminate the learning process early and return this conjecture. Since the learning algorithm produces conjectures of increasing size, the resulting automaton has as most as many states as $\mathfrak{A}_G$ has but can be much smaller.

However, the quality of the results of our algorithm mainly depends on two aspects: the choice of the learning algorithm and how counter-examples are computed by the teacher. As it turns out in our experiments, the standard algorithms (i.e., the algorithms described in [1], [13] and [9]) often produce conjectures that are either large or do not satisfy Definition 1 (i.e., do not encode a winning strategy). Therefore, in Section 3.2 we develop an improved version of Kearns and Vazirani's learning algorithm [9], which circumvents some on the problems and yields better results in our experiments. The question how to compute "useful" counter-examples is beyond the scope of this paper since it largely depends on domain-specific characteristics of a game. However, in Section 3.1 we present a teacher capable of answering both types of queries in a generic way.

3.1   A Teacher for Strategy Automata

Our teacher is not designed to teach exactly the language $L(\mathfrak{A}_G)$. Instead, it uses $\mathfrak{A}_G$ only to answer membership queries, i.e., to "guide" the learner to come up with a conjecture realizing a winning strategy. The teacher answers equivalence queries by checking whether the proposed conjecture realizes a winning strategy. If this is not the case, it uses $\mathfrak{A}_G$ and the arena $\mathcal{A}$ to obtain a counter-example.

Answering Membership Queries. Based on the automaton $\mathfrak{A}_G$, answering membership queries is straight-forward. For a word $w \in \Sigma^*$ the teacher simulates the run of $\mathfrak{A}_G$ on w and returns "yes" or "no", depending on whether $w \in L(\mathfrak{A}_G)$.

Answering Equivalence Queries. On equivalence queries, the learner proposes a conjecture $\mathfrak{A} = (Q, \Sigma, q_0, \delta, F_{\mathfrak{A}})$ and the teacher needs to check whether $\mathfrak{A}$ is a strategy automaton, i.e., whether it satisfies Definition 1. First, we check for $\varepsilon \in L(\mathfrak{A})$ (cf. condition 1). If this is not the case, we return ε as counter-example.

Then, we verify that $L(\mathfrak{A})$ is prefix closed (cf. condition 1). $L(\mathfrak{A})$ is not prefix closed if there are words $w \notin L(\mathfrak{A})$ and $wa \in L(\mathfrak{A})$. We can find such words by searching for states $q, q' \in Q$ (both reachable from q_0) such that $\delta(q, a) = q'$ for some $a \in \Sigma$ and $q \notin F$, $q' \in F$. Since $L(\mathfrak{A}_G)$ is prefix closed, either w or wa is classified incorrectly by the conjecture. We can check which one by simulating $\mathfrak{A}_G$ on both w and wa and return the respective word as counter-example.

Finally, to verify conditions 2 to 5, we construct the product $\mathcal{A} \times \mathfrak{A}$ of the arena $\mathcal{A}$ and the conjecture $\mathfrak{A}$. The product $\mathcal{A} \times \mathfrak{A} = (Q', \Sigma, q'_0, \delta', F_{\mathcal{A} \times \mathfrak{A}})$ is again a finite automaton formally given as follows: $Q' = (V \cup \{v_s\}) \times Q$ (v_s is a new sink vertex), $F_{\mathcal{A} \times \mathfrak{A}}$ is unimportant and can be chosen arbitrarily, and for all $a \in \Sigma$ we define $\delta'((v, q), a) = (v', \delta(q, a))$ if a (unique) v' with $(v, a, v') \in E$ exists, or $\delta'((v, q), a) = (v_s, \delta(q, a))$ otherwise. Moreover, $\delta'((v_s, q), a) = (v_s, q)$ for all $a \in \Sigma$ and $q \in Q$. Note that whenever there is no edge (v, a, v') in E, the transition $\delta'((v, q), a)$ in the product points to a sink state (v_s, q).

Starting in q_0', we now perform a breadth-first search. For each state of the product reached during the search, we can check whether one of the conditions 2 to 5 is violated. Once a violation is detected, a word reaching the state in question is used to derive a counter-example, which is then returned. If no violation is found, the search terminates after visiting all states in the product. In this case, the conjecture realizes a winning strategy and we return "yes".

Runtime of the Teacher. To construct the teacher, we first need to construct the automaton $\mathfrak{A}_{\mathcal{G}}$. Using the fixed point algorithm described in Section 2, this can be done in time linear in $|E| \in \mathcal{O}(|V| \cdot |\Sigma|)$. The automaton $\mathfrak{A}_{\mathcal{G}}$ has size $|W_0| + 1 \in \mathcal{O}(V)$.

Once the teacher is constructed, answering membership queries can be done in time $|w|$ if w is the query asked.

The time needed to answer equivalence queries is dominated by the construction of $\mathcal{A} \times \mathfrak{A}$ and the following depth-first search. The product has size $|V| \cdot |Q|$ and a depth-first search is linear in the size of the product. If necessary, a counter-example can be computed on-the-fly and its length can be bounded by $|\mathcal{A} \times \mathfrak{A}|$. Hence, answering equivalence queries, i.e., checking whether an automaton is a strategy automaton, can be done in time $\mathcal{O}(|V| \cdot |Q|)$.

3.2   An Improved Learning Algorithm

The original learning algorithms (i.e., [1], [13] and [9]) have in common that, once a new state of the automaton to learn is discovered, all outgoing transitions of this state are examined. In our setting, this behavior is often undesirable. For instance, consider a finite prefix w of a winning play that reaches a vertex $v \in V_0$ and has the run $\mathfrak{A}\colon q_0 \xrightarrow{w} q$ on a conjecture. In this circumstance, one outgoing transition from q would suffice, but the original algorithms examine all transitions. This means that not only one way to successfully play on is considered, but all. As a result, often the automaton $\mathfrak{A}_{\mathcal{G}}$ is learned.

In order to circumvent this issue, we develop an improvement of Kearns and Vazirani's algorithm [9] that learns so-called *incompletely specified finite automata*. In such automata, not every transition needs to be defined, i.e., the transition function δ is a partial mapping $\delta\colon Q \times \Sigma \dashrightarrow Q$. If there is no run of $\mathfrak{A}$ on some input u, then we define that $\mathfrak{A}$ rejects u. In essence, our modification works as the original algorithm, but additionally maintains a set Δ of defined transitions along with the data gathered in the learning process. Every time a conjecture is produced, the algorithm only creates transitions contained in Δ.

For the remaining section, let L be a regular language (the *target language*) over a fixed alphabet Σ and $\mathfrak{A}_L = (Q_L, \Sigma, q_0^L, \delta_L, F_L)$ the minimal automaton accepting L. We assume $L \neq \emptyset$ and $L \neq \Sigma^*$ since both special cases can be covered by equivalence queries with the corresponding trivial one-state automata.

As the original algorithm, our algorithm organizes its data in sets $S, D \subseteq \Sigma^*$. Moreover, it maintains a set $\Delta \subseteq S \times \Sigma$. The set S consists of *access strings* that are used to identify the states of $\mathfrak{A}_L$: each $u \in S$ corresponds to the unique state $q \in Q_L$ that $\mathfrak{A}_L$ reaches on reading u. The learner makes sure that all access strings are distinct in the sense that there are no two access strings in S that lead to the same state of $\mathfrak{A}_L$, thus, preserving $|S| \leq |Q_L|$. The set D contains *distinguishing strings* that are used to witness that two access string in fact lead to different states. Formally, this means that for each two $u \neq u' \in S$ there is a $v \in D$ such that $uv \in L \Leftrightarrow u'v \notin L$. Finally, the set $\Delta \subseteq S \times \Sigma$ is the set of *defined transitions* and determines which transition are existing in a conjecture.

The learner organizes S and D in a binary tree called a *classification tree* $t(D, S)$. The inner nodes are the strings from D while the leaf nodes are the strings from S. The idea is to place some distinguishing string $v \in D$ at the root and partition all access string $u \in S$ depending on whether $uv \in L$ or not; the access string with $uv \in L$ are put in the right subtree while all others are put in the left subtree. This procedure is recursively repeated at each subtree until all access string are put in their own leaf node. In this way, each two access strings $u \neq u'$ are distinguished by their least common ancestor. Finally, the learner guarantees that ε is the root node, i.e., final and non-final states are distinguished, and that $\varepsilon \in S$, i.e., the initial state of $\mathfrak{A}_L$ is always accessible. Starting with an initial classification tree, the learner grows the tree in a non-trivial manner preserving the properties mentioned above.

From a given classification tree $t(D, S)$, we can derive a finite automaton $\mathfrak{A}_t = (Q_t, \Sigma, q_0^t, \delta_t, F_t)$. Since access strings are meant to identify states of $\mathfrak{A}_L$, we set $Q_t = S$. Final states are exactly those access strings $u \in S$ that are located in the right subtree of the root node ε, i.e., for which $u \cdot \varepsilon \in L$ holds. Finally, the initial state is $q_0^t = \varepsilon$.

In contrast to the original algorithm, in our modification a transition $\delta_t(u, a)$ of $\mathfrak{A}_t$ is only defined if $(u, a) \in \Delta$. If a transition is defined, then it is derived by a so-called *sifting* operation. Suppose that we want to know the destination of an a-transition from state $u \in S$. Clearly, this destination should have the same "behavior" (with respect to the distinguishing strings) as ua has. Such an access string can be derived by *sifting ua down t*: we start at the root node ε and at an inner node labeled with a distinguishing string v we descend either right or left depending on whether $uav \in L$ or not. This step is repeated recursively until a leaf node $u' \in S$ is reached. We can perform such a sifting operation efficiently using membership queries and write $\text{sift}(u) = u'$ if u' is the leaf node reached by sifting u down t. Then, the transitions of $\mathfrak{A}_t$ are defined by $\delta_t(u, a) = \text{sift}(ua)$ for all $(u, a) \in \Delta$. It may happen that not all access strings are reachable from ε. In this case, we drop all non-reachable states from Q_t.

Figure 5 sketches the learning algorithm. First, we initialize the tree t with $D = \{\varepsilon\}$ and $S = \{\varepsilon, w\}$ for some $w \in L \Leftrightarrow \varepsilon \notin L$. Since $L \neq \emptyset$ and $L \neq \Sigma^*$

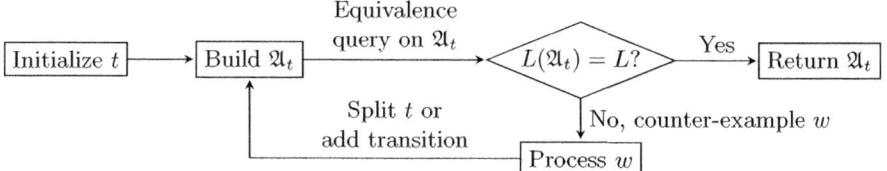

Fig. 5. The modified Kearns & Vazirani learning algorithm

such a word is returned on an equivalence query with an automaton accepting Σ^*. Then, we repeatedly build $\mathfrak{A}_t$, ask an equivalence query on $\mathfrak{A}_t$, and process a potential counter-example until an automaton accepting L is learned.

As long as $|S| < |Q_L|$ the automaton $\mathfrak{A}_t$ is necessarily different from $\mathfrak{A}_L$ and an equivalence query on $\mathfrak{A}_t$ will return a counter-example $w = a_1 \ldots a_n$ such that $w \in L \Leftrightarrow w \notin L(\mathfrak{A}_t)$. We can use this counter-example to identify either a new state of $\mathfrak{A}_L$ and, thus, a new access string, or a missing transition.

For a given counter-example $w = a_1 \ldots a_n$, we search for the smallest index $i \in \{1, \ldots, n\}$ such that either $\mathfrak{A}_t \colon q_0 \xrightarrow{a_1 \ldots a_i} u_i$ and $\mathrm{sift}(a_1 \ldots a_i) = u'_i$ with $u_i \neq u'_i$, or $\mathfrak{A}_t \colon q_0 \xrightarrow{a_1 \ldots a_i} u_i$ and $\delta_t(u_i, a_{i+1})$ is undefined. In the first case, by the choice of i, this means that the state $\mathfrak{A}_t$ reaches on reading $a_1 \ldots a_{i-1}$ is $\mathrm{sift}(a_1 \ldots a_{i-1}) = u_{i-1}$, but $a_1 \ldots a_{i-1}$ is in fact a new access string that should be distinguished from any other access string. Moreover, the string $a_i v$, where v is some distinguishing string for u_i and u'_i, distinguishes $a_1 \ldots a_{i-1}$ and u_{i-1}. To reflect this new knowledge, we update t and replace the leaf node u_{i-1} by an inner node $a_i v$ and two new leaf nodes u_{i-1} and $a_1 \ldots a_{i-1}$. This update is performed efficiently using membership queries. Finally, we set $\Delta := \emptyset$. In the second case, we add the pair (u_i, a_{i+1}) to Δ. Note that the transition $\delta_t(u_i, a_{i+1})$ is in fact needed, since $\mathfrak{A}_t$ rejects w, but w has to be accepted.

The learning terminates as soon as an equivalence query on $\mathfrak{A}_t$ indicates that $L(\mathfrak{A}_t) = L$. Hence, it is enough to show that our learner terminates eventually. Let us first argue that for every counter-example $w = a_1 \ldots a_n$ there is an index $i \in \{1, \ldots, n\}$ such that either $\mathfrak{A}_t \colon q_0 \xrightarrow{a_1 \ldots a_i} u_i$ and $\mathrm{sift}(a_1 \ldots a_i) = u'_i$ with $u_i \neq u'_i$, or $\mathfrak{A}_t \colon q_0 \xrightarrow{a_1 \ldots a_i} u_i$ and $\delta_t(u_i, a_{i+1})$ is undefined. To see that, suppose that no such index exists. Then, we have $\mathfrak{A}_t \colon q_0 \xrightarrow{w} u$ (since all transitions used are defined) and $\mathrm{sift}(w) = u$. In particular, this means that $u \cdot \varepsilon \in L \Leftrightarrow w \cdot \varepsilon \in L$. By definition of F_t, we know that $u \in F_t \Leftrightarrow u \cdot \varepsilon \in L \Leftrightarrow w = w \cdot \varepsilon \in L$. Hence, $w \in L(\mathfrak{A}_t) \Leftrightarrow w \in L$, which yields a contradiction since w is a counter-example.

Every time a counter-example is processed, the learner makes progress. Either a new access string is inserted into S, i.e., $|S|$ increases by one, or a new transition is added and $|\Delta|$ increases by one. Moreover, we know that $|S|$ is bounded by $|Q_L|$ and $|\Delta| \leq |S \times \Sigma|$. Hence, the learner terminates eventually and returns an automaton $\mathfrak{A}_t$ with $L(\mathfrak{A}_t) = L$. During the learning process the learner asks $\mathcal{O}(|Q_L|^2 \cdot |\Sigma|)$ equivalence queries and $\mathcal{O}(|Q_L| \cdot m \cdot \log|Q_L| + |\Sigma| \cdot |Q_L| \cdot \log|Q_L|)$ membership queries, where m is the length of the longest counter-example.

As in Kearns and Vazirani's original algorithm, on termination the automaton $\mathfrak{A}_t$ has the least number of states among all deterministic finite automata recognizing L. This is due to the fact that all deterministic finite automata recognizing L need at last $|Q_L|$ many states. Moreover, among all minimal automata it has the least number of transitions. Note that the presented algorithm not only works in our particular setting, but can be used to learn every regular languages.

3.3 Main Result

Let us conclude Section 3 by stating the main result of this work.

Theorem 1. *Let $\mathcal{G} = (\mathcal{A}, F)$ be a safety game with arena $\mathcal{A}$. Then, for each $v_0 \in W_0$ a strategy automaton $\mathfrak{A}$ realizing a winning strategy for Player 0 in $\mathcal{G}$ from v_0 can be learned in polynomial time such that $|\mathfrak{A}| \leq |W_0| + 1 \leq |V| + 1$.*

As described above, our algorithm terminates at the latest once the automaton $\mathfrak{A}_{\mathcal{G}}$ is learned. Thus, $|\mathfrak{A}| \leq |\mathfrak{A}_{\mathcal{G}}| \leq |W_0| + 1 \leq |V| + 1$. Moreover, if we plug in our modified learning algorithm, then the algorithm asks at most $\mathcal{O}(|V|^2 \cdot |\Sigma|)$ equivalence queries and $\mathcal{O}(|V| \cdot m \cdot \log |V| + |\Sigma| \cdot |V| \cdot \log |V|)$ membership queries; again m denotes the length of the longest counter-example returned on an equivalence query. If we use a breadth-first search to answer equivalence queries, then we can compute the shortest counter-example, whose length can be bounded by $|\mathcal{A} \times \mathfrak{A}_{\mathcal{G}}| \leq |V|^2$. Moreover, note that Theorem 1 still holds for any other learning algorithm that learns a regular language in polynomial time.

4   Experiments

We have implemented a proof-of-concept of Algorithm 1 in C++ using the `libalf` automata learning framework [4]. For general automata related operations, we use the `AMoRE(++)` library [4]. All experiments were run on an Intel Q9550 quad core processor with 4 GB of RAM. However, our implementation is not parallelized (hence, only uses one core) and no experiment consumed more than approximately 200 MB of RAM. Since almost all experiments finished within less than five minutes, we decided not to impose any timeout limit.

The general experimental setup was always the same: we constructed safety games $\mathcal{G}$ over $\Sigma = \{0, \dots, n\}$ and compared the size of the winning region W_0, the size of minimized automaton $\mathfrak{A}_{\mathcal{G}}$ (denoted by $\mathfrak{A}_{\mathcal{G}}^{\min}$), the size of the automaton $\mathfrak{A}_{\mathrm{KV}}^*$ learned using our modified version of Kearns and Vazirani's algorithm, and the size of a positional strategy $\mathcal{A}_f$. For the latter, we have implemented an algorithm that computes a positional strategy using a fixed-point computation and then picks for every Player 0 vertex the smallest action (for the natural order on Σ) that stays inside his winning region. Once this is done, we compute $\mathcal{A}_f$, interpret it as finite automaton, and minimize it. The result is denoted by $\mathcal{A}_f^{\min}$. In the following, results of Algorithm 1 using Kearns and Vazirani's original algorithm are not shown because in most cases the automaton $\mathfrak{A}_{\mathcal{G}}$ was learned.

An Artificial Example. Let us first present an example designed to show that our algorithm finds small solutions whereas all other described approaches necessarily produce larger ones. Hence, consider the safety game $\mathcal{G}^\star$ over $\Sigma = \{0, 1\}$ depicted in Figure 6. The idea of the game is as follows: starting from v_0, Player 1 chooses two bits $b_1, b_2 \in \{0, 1\}$. Afterwards, Player 0 needs to avoid the vertex v_s. He can do so by choosing the actions $a_0 = 1$, $a_1 \in \{b_1, 1\}$, and $a_2 \in \{b_2, 1\}$ one after the other ad infinitum. Hence, $W_0 = V \setminus \{v_s\}$.

Since Player 1 can decide which part of the arena a play reaches, all positional strategies f necessarily cover the whole arena (except for the vertex v_s). Thus, $|\mathcal{A}_f| = |V| - 1$. Moreover, the game is designed such that both $\mathcal{A}_f^{\min}$ and the minimal automaton $\mathfrak{A}_{\mathcal{G}^\star}^{\min}$ also have size $|V| - 1$. However, the result of our

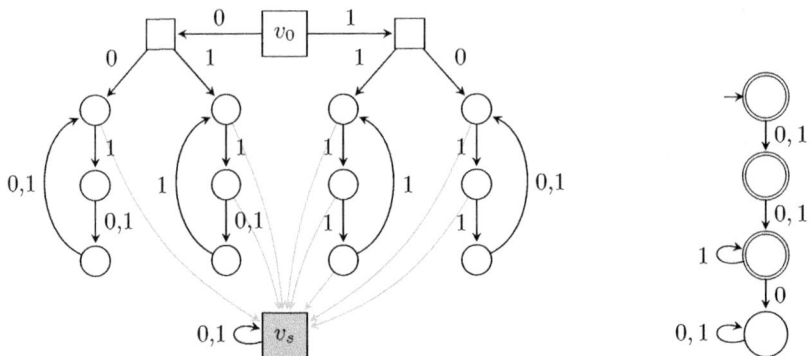

Fig. 6. The safety game $\mathcal{G}^\star$. All but the gray shaded vertices belong to F. All edges pointing to v_s are labeled with 0 and are for better readability gray shaded.

Fig. 7. The result $\mathfrak{A}_{\mathrm{KV}}^\star$ of our algorithm on $\mathcal{G}^\star$

algorithm using the improved version of Kearns and Vazirani's algorithm, which is depicted in Figure 7, has only size 4.

The idea of the game $\mathcal{G}^\star$ can be generalized: instead of only two bits, Player 1 chooses n bits $b_1, \ldots, b_n \in \{0, 1\}$ and in order to win, Player 0 needs to choose actions $a_0 = 1$, $a_1 \in \{b_1, 1\}$ to $a_n \in \{b_n, 1\}$ ad infinitum. Again, $\mathcal{A}_f^{\min}$ and $\mathfrak{A}_{\mathcal{G}^\star}^{\min}$ have size $|V| - 1$ whereas our experiments show that up to $n = 20$ the automaton $\mathfrak{A}_{\mathrm{KV}}^\star$ has the same structure as shown in Figure 7 and comprises $\mathcal{O}(\log |V|)$ states (note that the number of vertices of $\mathcal{G}^\star$ grows exponentially in n).

Experiments on Random Graphs. To benchmark our algorithm on more natural games, we implemented a random game generator. This generator produces safety games that are structurally similar to systems that arise when composing several subsystems. More precisely, our generator produces games over the alphabet $\Sigma = \{0, \ldots, m\}$ and works as follows. In the first step, it creates c "components", each of which consist of n vertices. In each component, the vertices have one outgoing edge pointing into their own component, and the generator makes sure that each component is strongly connected. All vertices belong to F, and with a probability of p_0 a vertex belongs to V_0. Then, the generator inserts a safe and an unsafe sink. In the second step, the generator creates additional edges. With a probability of a an edge points to a sink (to the unsafe sink if the source of the edge is a Player 0 vertex, or to the safe sink otherwise), and with a probability of b an edge points to a vertex that lies inside another component. In all other cases, an edge points to a vertex inside the same component. The initial vertex is chosen uniform randomly from all vertices inside W_0.

Figures 8 and 9 show the results of our experiments. In both cases, we fixed $\Sigma = \{0, 1, 2\}$, $p_0 = 0.5$, $a = 0.1$, and $b = 0.2$. For Series 1 of experiments (Figure 8), we fixed the number of component $c = 5$ and varied the size of the components n. For Series 2 (Figure 9), we fixed $n = 25$ and varied c. For each

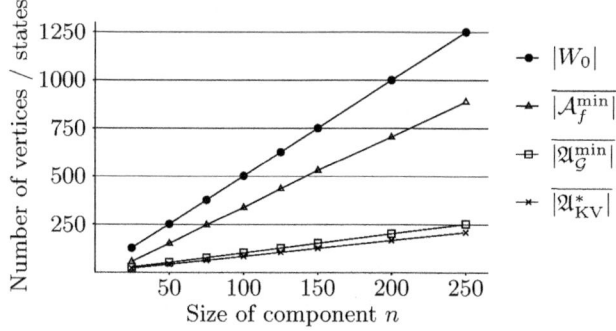

Fig. 8. Results of Series 1 (n varies; $c = 5$, $p_0 = 0.5$, $a = 0.1$, and $b = 0.2$)

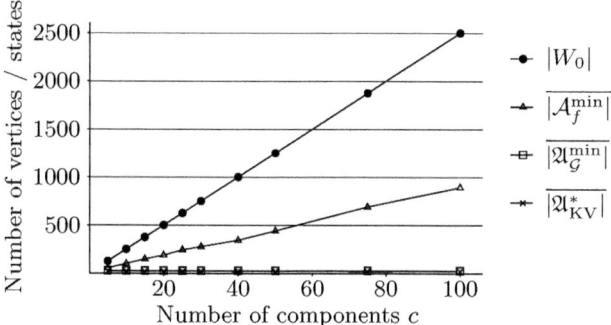

Fig. 9. Results of Series 2 (c varies; $n = 25$, $p_0 = 0.5$, $a = 0.1$, and $b = 0.2$)

combination, we generated 1000 games and averaged the results. Thus, each data point in the charts corresponds to the arithmetic mean of 1000 experiments.

The figures show $|W_0|$ as a point of reference. In both series, positional strategies do on average not cover the whole arena, but are larger than automata based strategies. In Series 1, positional strategies are approximately 4.2 times larger than automata based strategies. In Series 2, automata based strategies are even of constant size ($\overline{|\mathfrak{A}_\mathcal{G}^{\min}|} \approx 27$, $\overline{|\mathfrak{A}_{KV}^*|} \approx 21.5$) whereas positional strategies grow with the number of components. In both series, our algorithm often succeeded in learning strategy automata smaller than $\mathfrak{A}_\mathcal{G}^{\min}$

Finally, let us emphasize two observation: first, in both series automata based strategies outperform positional strategies significantly. Second, our learning based approach together with the modified Kearns and Vazirani's algorithm computes the smallest strategies in our experiments.

5   Conclusion

In this work we have considered the task of computing small winning strategies for safety games and have presented a polynomial time algorithm based on automata learning. Since computing minimal strategies in this setting is hard, our algorithm is a heuristic, which, however, yields good results compared to positional winning strategies. To improve the quality of our results, we have developed a domain-specific modification of Kearns and Vazirani's learning algorithm.

However, our modification does not yet exploit that the target languages in our setting are prefix-closed, and besides straight-forward filter operations on membership queries (e.g., do not ask queries for prefixes of accepting words), it is not clear how an intelligent learning algorithm for prefix-closed languages should be designed. Since prefix-closed languages occur not only in this particular setting, a an optimized learning algorithm would be of general interest.

Finally, we would like to apply the idea of learning winning strategies to games with more complex winning condition such as Büchi, Muller or parity conditions. Thereto, it would be necessary to develop efficient algorithms capable of learning languages of infinite words.

References

1. Angluin, D.: Learning regular sets from queries and counterexamples. Information and computation 75(2), 87–106 (1987)
2. Baier, C., Katoen, J.: Principles of model checking. The MIT Press, Cambridge (2008)
3. Bloem, R., Galler, S., Jobstmann, B., Piterman, N., Pnueli, A., Weiglhofer, M.: Specify, compile, run: Hardware from PSL. ENTCS 190(4), 3–16 (2007)
4. Bollig, B., Katoen, J.P., Kern, C., Leucker, M., Neider, D., Piegdon, D.R.: libalf: The automata learning framework. In: Touili, T., Cook, B., Jackson, P. (eds.) CAV 2010. LNCS, vol. 6174, pp. 360–364. Springer, Heidelberg (2010)
5. Ehlers, R.: Short witnesses and accepting lassos in ω-automata. In: Dediu, A.-H., Fernau, H., Martín-Vide, C. (eds.) LATA 2010. LNCS, vol. 6031, pp. 261–272. Springer, Heidelberg (2010)
6. Filiot, E., Jin, N., Raskin, J.F.: Compositional algorithms for LTL synthesis. In: Bouajjani, A., Chin, W.-N. (eds.) ATVA 2010. LNCS, vol. 6252, pp. 112–127. Springer, Heidelberg (2010)
7. Grädel, E., Thomas, W., Wilke, T. (eds.): Automata, Logics, and Infinite Games: A Guide to Research. LNCS, vol. 2500. Springer, Heidelberg (2002)
8. Holtmann, M., Löding, C.: Memory reduction for strategies in infinite games. In: Holub, J., Žďárek, J. (eds.) CIAA 2007. LNCS, vol. 4783, pp. 253–264. Springer, Heidelberg (2007)
9. Kearns, M., Vazirani, U.: An introduction to computational learning theory. The MIT Press, Cambridge (1994)
10. Kupferman, O., Lustig, Y., Vardi, M.Y., Yannakakis, M.: Temporal synthesis for bounded systems and environments. In: STACS. LIPIcs, vol. 9, pp. 615–626. Leibniz-Zentrum fuer Informatik (2011)
11. Myers, G., Badgett, T., Thomas, T., Sandler, C.: The art of software testing, vol. 28. John Wiley & Sons, Chichester (2004)
12. Papadimitriou, C.H.: Computational complexity. John Wiley and Sons Ltd., Chichester (1995)
13. Rivest, R.L., Schapire, R.E.: Inference of finite automata using homing sequences. In: Hanson, S.J., Rivest, R.L., Remmele, W. (eds.) MIT-Siemens 1993. LNCS, vol. 661, pp. 51–73. Springer, Heidelberg (1993)

Multi-core Nested Depth-First Search

Alfons Laarman[1], Rom Langerak[1], Jaco van de Pol[1],
Michael Weber[1], and Anton Wijs[2]

[1] Formal Methods and Tools, University of Twente, The Netherlands
{a.w.laarman,langerak,vdpol,michaelw}@cs.utwente.nl
[2] Eindhoven University of Technology, 5612 AZ Eindhoven, The Netherlands
a.j.wijs@tue.nl

Abstract. The LTL Model Checking problem is reducible to finding accepting cycles in a graph. The Nested Depth-First Search (NDFS) algorithm detects accepting cycles efficiently: on-the-fly, with linear-time complexity and negligible memory overhead. The only downside of the algorithm is that it relies on an inherently-sequential, depth-first search. It has not been parallelized beyond running the independent nested search in a separate thread (dual core).

In this paper, we introduce, for the first time, a multi-core NDFS algorithm that can scale beyond two threads, while maintaining exactly the same worst-case time complexity. We prove this algorithm correct, and present experimental results obtained with an implementation in the LTSmin tool set on the entire BEEM benchmark database. We measured considerable speedups compared to the current state of the art in parallel cycle detection algorithms.

1 Introduction

Moore's Law [18] states that the number of transistors that can be placed inexpensively on an integrated circuit doubles approximately every two years. Since several years, though, the law no longer relates to the processing speed, while it still relates to the memory capacity of computer hardware. In order to mitigate the declining increase of processing speed, hardware developers have opted for so-called *multi-core* architectures, where multiple cores exist on a processing unit. However, for many algorithms where the main bottleneck was traditionally memory related, a shift to speed related issues can be observed, since these algorithms do not automatically run faster on a multi-core machine. Instead, the introduction of multi-core machines demands a redesign of those algorithms.

This also holds for Model Checking (MC) algorithms; typically, in order to fully verify whether a system specification adheres to a given temporal property, an MC algorithm needs to store the entire so-called *state space* in memory. A state space is a directed graph which explicitly describes all potential behavior of the system specification. Recent observations [2] support that research should be focused on achieving faster MC; currently, memory capacity of the latest hardware allows the analysis of very large state spaces, but the required time to do so is often impractically long.

T. Bultan and P.-A. Hsiung (Eds.): ATVA 2011, LNCS 6996, pp. 321–335, 2011.

One advanced MC task is the verification of full Linear Temporal Logic (LTL) properties [1]. LTL can be subdivided into two classes of properties: safety properties, e.g. "nothing bad ever happens", and liveness properties, e.g. "eventually something good happens". While safety properties can be handled with so-called *reachability*, which entails visiting all states in the state space reachable from the initial state, liveness properties require a more complicated analysis.

An algorithm introduced by Courcoubetis et al. [5], often referred to as *Nested Depth-First Search* (NDFS), is particularly useful for checking liveness properties. It has a linear time-complexity and runs *on-the-fly*, i.e. without the need to generate the whole state space, and requires only two bits per state [21].

While reachability has been parallelized efficiently [16], a linear-time multi-core LTL MC algorithm was still unknown. NDFS cannot trivially be adapted to a multi-core setting, since it relies on depth-first search (DFS), which is inherently sequential [20]. And even though many other parallel LTL MC algorithms have been introduced over the course of years, none of them exhibits a worst-case linear-time complexity (or even $\mathcal{O}(n \times \log(n))$, with n the number of states) and the complete on-the-fly property [2, 3, 4].

Recent developments, which we group here under the term *Swarm Verification* (SV) [13, 14], have introduced new DFS-based techniques [6, 22] to perform MC tasks in parallel. Although mainly targeted at distributed-memory settings, in which multiple machines are employed, SV can trivially be used on a multi-core, i.e., shared-memory, machine as well. However, when doing so, the fact that the memory is shared is obviously not exploited.

In this paper, we first propose SV-based multi-core NDFS with shared state storage. While this speeds up cycle detection significantly, in the absence of accepting cycles each core still has to traverse the complete state space. Next, we introduce a fine-grained and basic sharing mechanism between threads. Even though parallel search may endanger the correctness of a multi-core NDFS by breaking the post-order, we prove that our algorithm is in fact correct. We subsequently add several known NDFS optimizations [21] to the new parallel setting. Finally, we demonstrate its usefulness in practice by comparing many experimental results obtained with an implementation of our algorithm with results obtained with existing parallel LTL MC algorithms.

Contributions. We present the first multi-core on-the-fly LTL model checking algorithm which is linear-time in the size of the input graph, and has a potential speedup greater than two. We provide a rigorous proof of its correctness and many benchmarks. Though the new algorithm does not scale perfectly for all inputs yet, we still believe to have come one step closer to solving the open question, put forth by Holzmann et al. and Barnat et al. [4, 12], of finding a time-optimal, scalable, parallel algorithm for accepting cycle detection.

Next, in Section 2, the preliminaries behind LTL MC are explained. Related work is discussed in Section 3. We propose a multi-core NDFS algorithm, prove its correctness and provide optimizations in Section 4. Section 5 contains a discussion on the experiments we conducted. Finally, in Section 6, considerations are addressed, conclusions are drawn and possibilities for future work are given.

2   Background (LTL Model Checking)

LTL MC entails checking that a system under verification $\mathcal{P}$ satisfies an LTL property ϕ, which may be a liveness property that reasons over infinite traces of the system ("eventually something good happens"). In order to reason about this, we first introduce the notion of a Büchi automaton:

Definition 1. *A Büchi automaton (BA) is a quadruple $\mathcal{B} = (\mathcal{S}, s_I, \text{post}, \mathcal{A})$, with $\mathcal{S}$ a finite set of states, s_I the initial state, $\text{post} : \mathcal{S} \to 2^{\mathcal{S}}$ the successor function, and $\mathcal{A} \subseteq \mathcal{S}$ a set of accepting states.*

If for $s, t \in \mathcal{S}$, we have $t \in \text{post}(s)$, then we can also write $s \to t$. The reflexive transitive closure of $\to$ is denoted by $\to^*$, and the transitive closure by $\to^+$. We call $s \to^* t$ and $s \to^+ t$ *paths* through $\mathcal{B}$, i.e. sequences of states connected by the successor function. Sometimes we interpret a path π as a set of states, and write $s \in \pi$, meaning that $s \in \mathcal{S}$ is included in the sequence of states of π. A *run* through $\mathcal{B}$ is an infinite path starting at s_I. Finally, we call a run π *accepting* if and only if for infinitely many $s \in \pi$, we have $s \in \mathcal{A}$. Checking the existence of such a run is called the *emptiness problem*.

To check an LTL property ϕ on $\mathcal{P}$, it suffices to solve the emptiness problem for the product of the state graph $\mathcal{G}_{\mathcal{P}}$ and the Büchi automaton $\mathcal{B}_{\neg\phi}$ (e.g. [23]). Here, $\mathcal{G}_{\mathcal{P}}$ is an explicit representation of all possible behavior of $\mathcal{P}$ in the form of a graph, and $\mathcal{B}_{\neg\phi}$ is the Büchi automaton accepting all infinite paths described by the negation of ϕ. A counterexample for ϕ in $\mathcal{B} = \mathcal{G}_{\mathcal{P}} \times \mathcal{B}_{\neg\phi}$ exists iff there exists some $a \in \mathcal{A}$ such that $s_I \to^* a$ and $a \to^+ a$ (i.e. there is an accepting run), where the latter is called an "accepting cycle". Hence, solving the emptiness problem corresponds with determining the reachability of an accepting cycle. The use of a successor function instead of a *transition relation* more closely corresponds with the setting for on-the-fly MC, where the graph structure is unknown in advance.

The first linear-time algorithm to detect accepting runs was proposed by Courcoubetis et al. [5] and, today, is often referred to as NDFS. Over the years, extensions to NDFS have been proposed in, e.g., [9, 15, 21]. In this paper, we propose a *multi-core* NDFS (MC-NDFS), which is based on NNDFS from [21]. Alg. 1 most closely resembles NNDFS from [21] with one minor modification: it does not include *early cycle detection* in dfs_blue, for this extension does not contribute to the understanding of MC-NDFS.

As in all NDFS algorithms, nndfs(s_I) initiates a DFS from state s_I, here called the *blue* DFS, since explored states are colored blue (note that initially, all states are white). As is usual, dfs_blue is performed with a stack, and a state is colored *cyan* if it is on the stack of dfs_blue. Hence, a newly visited state is first colored cyan, and after exploration, it is colored blue. At l.16, if the blue DFS backtracks over a state $s \in \mathcal{A}$, then dfs_red(s) is called, which is a secondary DFS to determine whether there exists a cycle containing s. As described in [21], on l.6, if a successor of s is colored cyan, then an accepting cycle is found, and the NNDFS exits. Otherwise, for each blue successor, dfs_red is called on l.10. Note that an accepting state s is colored red only after its red DFS is finished (l.18). During its red DFS it is cyan, hence it can be detected at l.6.

```
1  proc  nndfs(s_I)                  11  proc  dfs_blue(s)
2    dfs_blue(s_I)                   12    s.color := cyan
3    report no cycle                 13    for all t in post(s) do
                                      14      if t.color=white
4  proc dfs_red(s)                   15        dfs_blue(t)
5    for all t in post(s) do         16    if s ∈ A̅
6      if t.color=cyan               17      dfs_red(s)
7        report cycle & exit         18      s.color := red
8      else if t.color=blue          19    else
9        t.color := red              20      s.color := blue
10       dfs_red(t)
```

Alg. 1. An adapted New NDFS algorithm

NNDFS runs in linear time, since each reachable state is at most visited twice, once in the blue DFS and once in a red DFS. The algorithm is correct due to the fact that the red DFSs are initiated according to the post-order of the accepting states imposed by the blue DFS (i.e. the last visited accepting state is considered first, the last but one next, etc.), hence an already red state does not need to be re-explored later in another red DFS. This intuition is demonstrated with an abstract proof in [5]. In [9], a standalone correctness proof is given for NNDFS with early cycle detection and an extension called *allred* (both are explained in Section 3). In Section 4.4, we show how these extensions can be introduced in MC-NDFS in an elegant and correct way.

3   Related Work

Two prominent classes of linear-time algorithms to detect accepting runs are formed by the NDFS-*based* and the *Strongly Connected Component* (SCC)-*based* algorithms. The performance of both classes of algorithms is known to be similar, up to some exceptions: Algorithms in the NDFS class use less memory, while algorithms in the SCC class tend to find counter-examples faster [9, 10, 21]. Since we propose an NDFS-based algorithm, the emphasis here is on related work in the NDFS class. Finally, we also discuss breadth-first search (BFS)-*based* algorithms.

NDFS. As mentioned in Section 2, NDFS was introduced in [5]. There, a correctness proof is given based on the fact that red DFSs are initiated for accepting states based on the post-order enforced by the blue DFS. Holzmann et al. [15] observe that it suffices in a red DFS to check the reachability of a state currently on the stack of the blue DFS, i.e. a state colored cyan in NNDFS, since such a state can reach the accepting state which initiated the current red DFS, closing an accepting cycle.

Schwoon and Esparza [21] combine all of the above extensions and observe that some combinations of colors can never occur. This allows them to introduce a *two-bit color encoding*, also encoding a cyan color for states on the stack of the blue DFS. Finally, Gaiser and Schwoon [9] introduce the *allred* extension and give a standalone proof for their NNDFS. The *allred* extension incorporates an additional check in the blue DFS: if all successors of a state s are red, then s can be colored red as well. This avoids some calls of dfs_red. We will show later that for our MC-NDFS, this extension is very useful.

Parallel NDFS. Holzmann and Bošnački [11] proposed a dual-core NDFS based on the observation that a transition initiating a red DFS is an "irreversible state transition", i.e. it splits the state graph. A new thread is launched to handle the red DFS. Since both DFSs are still inherently sequential, the number of threads cannot exceed two, and both potentially have to search the entire state graph. Courcoubetis et al. already mentioned that the two DFSs could be interleaved.

Prominent model checking approaches primarily aimed at settings with distributed memory, e.g., when using a cluster or grid, are swarm verification (SV) [13, 14] and *Parallel Randomized DFS* [6, 22] (PRDFS). These are so-called *embarrassingly parallel* [8] techniques, since the individual workers operate fully independently, i.e. without communication with the other workers. From here on, when mentioning SV, we refer to existing SV and PRDFS techniques. Note that the search direction of a DFS is determined by the order in which states are selected for exploration from post(s) (for any $s \in \mathcal{S}$), e.g. on l.13 of Alg. 1. In SV, basically each worker performs a DFS with a unique ordering of the successor states. In this way, workers explore different parts of the reachable state graph first. This method has proven to be very successful for bug-hunting. In the absence of bugs, though, the graph will be explored N times, with N the number of workers, since the workers are unaware of each other's results. Although not explicitly mentioned before, SV can be performed in a multi-core setting as well with each worker performing the NDFS algorithm.

BFS-*based methods.* Several other LTL MC methods exists which are not DFS-based. Instead these algorithms rely on BFS techniques and are therefore easier to parallelize, even in a distributed setting. On the down side, the linear-time complexity and on-the-fly property is often lost.

Table 1. Multi-core BFS-based LTL MC algorithms and their worst-case time complexity and on-the-fly property. ($\mathcal{T}$ the set of reachable transitions, and h the height of the SCC quotient graph).

Algorithm	Time complexity	On-the-fly
MAP [2]	$\mathcal{O}(|\mathcal{A}|^2 \cdot |\mathcal{T}|)$	Heur.
OWCTY [4]	$\mathcal{O}(h \cdot |\mathcal{T}|)$	No
OTF_OWCTY [4]	$\mathcal{O}(h \cdot (|\mathcal{T}| + |\mathcal{S}|))$	Heur.

Tab. 1 gives a brief overview of those parallel LTL MC algorithms that have been found suitable for implementation in a multi-core setting [2, 3].

MAP preserves the on-the-fly property to the extent that it is heuristic: cycles can be detected early, but this is not guaranteed. By combining MAP with *One-Way-Catch-Them-Young* (OWCTY), the same property is transferred to the new on-the-fly OWCTY (OTF_OWCTY) algorithm. For the important class of weak LTL, the algorithm has been shown to be time-optimal [4], therefore it is the current state of the art in multi-core LTL MC.

4   Multi-core NDFS

4.1   A Basic Multi-core Swarmed NDFS

As already mentioned, SV is compatible with a shared-memory setting. However, the independence of workers in SV may result in duplicated states on the different machines, hence, when mapped naively to a multi-core machine, the shared memory is not exploited. Therefore, we store all states in a shared lockless hash table that has been shown to scale well for this purpose [16].

A basic SV NDFS algorithm executes an instance of Alg. 1 for each worker i with thread-local color variables. The two bits needed per state per worker are small compared to the state itself and for a dozen or so workers, memory usage is still lower than for SCC-based algorithms [21]. Local permutations of the post function direct workers to different regions of the state graph, resulting in fast bug-finding typical for SV. With $post_i^b$ ($post_i^r$) we denote the permutation of successors used in the blue (red) DFS by worker i. For inputs without accepting cycles this solution does not scale. In the next section, we attack this problem.

4.2   Multi-core NDFS with Global Coloring

A naive sharing of colors between multi-core workers is prone to influence the independent post-orders on which the correctness of the NDFS algorithm relies [5]. In the current section, we present a color-sharing approach which preserves correctness. The next section provides a correctness proof of this MC-NDFS algorithm.

The basic idea behind MC-NDFS in Alg. 2 is to share information in the backtrack of the red DFSs (dfs_red). A new (local) color *pink* is introduced to signify states on the stack of a red DFS, analogous to cyan for a blue DFS. When a red DFS backtracks, the states are globally colored red. These red states are now ignored by both *all* blue and red DFSs, thus pruning the search spaces for all workers i.

```
 1  proc mc-ndfs(s, N)                          13  proc dfs_red(s, i)
 2     dfs_blue(s, 1)‖..‖dfs_blue(s, N)         14     s.pink[i] := true
 3     report no cycle                          15     for all t in post_i^r(s) do
                                                 16        if t.color[i]=cyan
 4  proc dfs_blue(s, i)                          17           report cycle & exit all
 5     s.color[i] := cyan                        18        if ¬t.pink[i] ∧ ¬t.red
 6     for all t in post_i^b(s) do               19           dfs_red(t, i)
 7        if t.color[i]=white∧¬t.red             20     if s ∈ A
 8           dfs_blue(t, i)                      21        s.count := s.count − 1
 9     if s ∈ A                                  22        await s.count=0
10        s.count := s.count + 1                 23     s.red := true
11        dfs_red(s, i)                          24     s.pink[i] := false
12     s.color[i] := blue
```

Alg. 2. A Multi-core NDFS algorithm, coloring globally red in the backtrack

Additionally, we count the number of workers that initiate dfs_red in *s.count* (l.10) and wait with backtracking until this counter is 0 (l.21,22). This enforces that if multiple workers call dfs_red from the same accepting state, they will finish simultaneously. Fig. 3 illustrates the necessity of this synchronization by a simple counter example that could occur in absence of this synchronization.

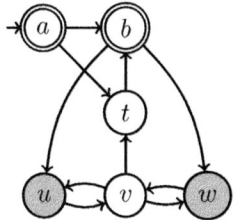

Fig. 3. Counter example to correctness of Mc-NDFS without **await** statement

A worker 1 could explore a, b, u, v, w, backtrack from w, explore t and backtrack all the way to the accepting state b where it will call a dfs_red at l.11. Then this dfs_red$(b, 1)$ could explore u, v, w and halt for a while. Now, a worker 2 could start dfs_red$(b, 2)$ in a similar fashion. Next, it could explore w, v, u, backtrack, mark u red and halt for a while. Then worker 1 continues to mark w red.

Note that the two accepting cycles contain red states, but both workers can still detect a cycle by continuing to explore v and t (b is cyan in the local coloring of both workers). However, a third worker can endanger this potential, while the first two workers halt for a while. After worker 3 searches a and subsequently t and b in a blue DFS, it will start a dfs_red at b, but because its successors are now red, worker 3 will backtrack and mark b red. Note that exactly this step is prevented by adding the **await** statement. Continuing with dfs_red$(a, 3)$, states t and a will also become red, obstructing workers 1 and 2 from finding a cycle.

No worker finds a cycle in this way, which thus constitutes a counter example for correctness. However, because worker 3 is forced to wait for the completion of the red DFSs of workers 1 and 2 before it can backtrack from state b in dfs_red$(b, 3)$, this counter example is invalid for Mc-NDFS.

Finally, we note that Mc-NDFS in Alg. 2 is presented in a form that eases analysis of correctness: without superfluous details. For example, the *pink* variable of states is separate from the *color* variable, which stores only the colors white, blue and cyan. The two-bit color encoding of [21] is thus dropped for a while. In the following section, we prove correctness of Mc-NDFS, after which we amend the algorithm in Section 4.4 with the extensions discussed in Section 3. The *allred* extension is shown to improve sharing between workers significantly.

4.3   Correctness Proof

In this section, we provide a correctness proof for Mc-NDFS. We assume that each line of the code above is executed atomically. The global state of the algorithm is the coloring of the input graph $\mathcal{B}$ and the program counter of each worker.

We use the following notations: The sets $White_i$, $Cyan_i$, $Blue_i$ and $Pink_i$ contain all the states colored white, cyan, blue, and pink by worker i, and Red contains all the red states. E.g., if $s.color[i] = blue$, we write $s \in Blue_i$. It follows from the assignments of the respective colors to the *color* variable that $White_i$, $Cyan_i$ and $Blue_i$ are disjoint. Also, we denote the state of one worker as dfs_red$(s, i)@X$, meaning that worker i is executing l.X in dfs_red for a state s. Finally, we use the modal operator $s \in \Box X$ to express that $\forall t \in \text{post}(s) : t \in X$.

Correctness of Mc-NDFS hinges on the fact that it will never miss all reachable accepting cycles, i.e. it will always find one if one exists. Recall from Section 2 that NDFS ensures that all reachable states are visited only once by both dfs_blue and dfs_red. Mc-NDFS ensures that each reachable state is visited *at least* once by both some dfs_blue and dfs_red, therefore for a reachable $a \in \mathcal{A}$, there is at least one dfs_red(a, i)@11 for some i, that initiates the recursion of the dfs_red.

This recursion continues at l.19, where it tries to find a $t \in Cyan_i$ at l.16 that would close the cycle. Now, if the cycle $a \to^+ a$ exists, worker i will either find a $t \in Cyan_i$, or is obstructed because it encounters a $t \in Red$ at l.18. Fig. 4 illustrates that workers can obstruct each other from finding cycles. For example, it is possible that a worker 1 initiates a dfs_red for a_1, marking r red. Then, a worker 2, with a different post$_i^b$, could start a dfs_red for a_2 and be obstructed from finding cycle $\{a_2, r, t, s\}$.

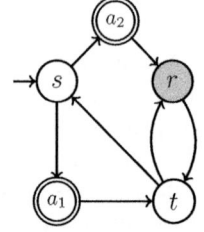

Fig. 4. An obstructed accepting cycle

We first state invariants that express basic relations between the colors in Mc-NDFS. Then, after Lemma 1, we prove the crucial insight (Thm. 1), termination (Thm. 2) and our main correctness result (Thm. 3).

L1. $\forall i : Blue_i \cup Pink_i \subseteq \Box(Blue_i \cup Cyan_i \cup Red)$
L2. $Red \subseteq \Box(Red \cup \bigcup_i(Pink_i \setminus Cyan_i))$
L3. $\forall i, a \in \mathcal{A} : a \in Blue_i \implies a \in Red$
L4. $\forall i, a \in \mathcal{A} : a \in Pink_i \implies a \in Cyan_i$
L5. $\forall i : Pink_i \subseteq (Blue_i \cup Cyan_i)$

Lemma 1. *The following invariant holds for* Mc-NDFS: $\forall s \in Red, a \in \mathcal{A} \setminus Red :$
$s \to^* a \implies (\exists i, p \in Pink_i, c \in Cyan_i : s \to^+ p \xrightarrow{\neg Red+} c \to^* a)$

Proof. We show that the property follows from the previous invariants L1-4. Assume $s \to^* a$ for some $s \in Red$ and $a \in Acc$ with $a \notin Red$. Let $s' \in Red$ be the *last* red state on the path $s \to^* a$. Then, since $s' \neq a$, it has a successor $t \notin Red$ in this path. By L2 we obtain $t \in Pink_i$ for some worker i, so let $p := t$.

Note that $t \neq a$, otherwise by L4 $t \in Cyan_i$ and by L2 $t \notin Cyan_i$. So we find another successor t' such that $s \to^* s' \to t \to t' \to^* a$. Assume towards a contradiction that no state on the path $t' \to^* a$ is in $Cyan_i$; recall that $t' \to^* a$ contains no Red states either. Then by L1, all states on $t' \to^* a$ are in $Blue_i$. But then also $a \in Blue_i$ and by L3, $a \in Red$, contradiction. So there exists a $c \in Cyan_i$ with $s \to^* p \to^+ c \to^* a$.

Theorem 1. Mc-NDFS *cannot miss all accepting cycles.*

Proof. Assume an Mc-NDFS run would miss all accepting cycles. Since there are only finitely many cycles, we can investigate the *last* "obstructed cycle" in this run, i.e., the last time that a dfs_red (which originated from some accepting state a on a cycle) encounters Red. That is, we are in dfs_red(s, i)@18 but we see $t \in Red$, although $s \to t \to^* a$.

Note that $a \notin Red$: Just before dfs_red(a, i)@11, $a.count$ was increased by l.10. Therefore, no other worker can make a red, because they are all forced to wait at l.22[1].

Hence we can apply Lemma 1, to obtain a path $p \xrightarrow{\neg Red+} c$ for some $p \in Pink_j$ and $c \in Cyan_j$. It follows that there is an $a' \in \mathcal{A}$ with $c \to^* a' \to^* p$ (property of DFS stacks). Fig. 5 provides an overview of the shape of the subgraph that we just discussed with the deduced colorings.

But now we have constructed a cycle for worker j which has not yet been obstructed. This contradicts the fact that we were

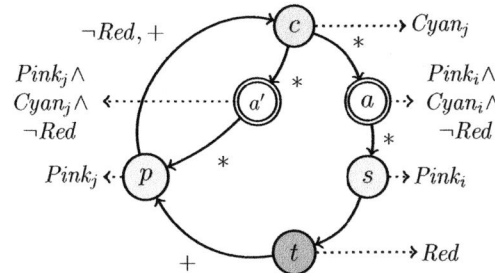

Fig. 5. Snapshot of the cycle in the *last* "obstructed cycle search". Edges with $*, +$ indicate paths of length ≥ 0 and > 0. Dotted arrows denote node colors and $\neg Red, +$ a path without red.

considering the *last* obstructed cycle. We conclude that there is no last obstructed cycle, hence there exists no run that misses all cycles. □

This proves partial correctness of MC-NDFS. In order to prove that an accepting cycle will eventually be reported, the algorithm is required to terminate.

Theorem 2. MC-NDFS *always terminates with some report at l.3 or l.17.*

Proof. Assuming dfs_red terminates, we can conclude termination of dfs_blue from the fact that for each worker i the set $Blue_i \cup Cyan_i$ grows monotonically (blue is never removed). Eventually, all the states are in the set and the blue search ends. Termination of the **await** statement at l.22 state follows from the basic observation that every worker i can have at most one counter increment on some accepting state, which is decremented at l.21 before waiting. Hence, when worker i is waiting, there can be no other worker waiting for i. Finally, all red DFSs terminate because also the set $Red \cup Pink_i$ grows monotonically. □

Theorem 3. MC-NDFS *reports* **cycle** *if there exists a reachable accepting cycle in the input graph $\mathcal{B}$ and it reports* **no cycle** *otherwise.*

Proof. By Theorem 2, the algorithm terminates with some report. If a cycle is reported at l.17 by worker i, we find an $s \in Pink_i$ and $t \in Cyan_i$ with $s \to t$. In that case there is a state $a \in Acc$ on the stack such that $t \to^* a \to^* s \to t$, so there is indeed an accepting cycle.

Otherwise, if no cycle is reported at l.3, all workers have terminated without reporting a cycle. By Theorem 1 there is no accepting cycle in the graph. □

---

[1] A race condition can occur here, because worker i could increase $a.count$ right after some worker j passed the check at l.22 in dfs_red(a, j). Next, worker i would start its dfs_red(a, i), and find that $a \in \Box(Red)$. So i will also make a red and return from dfs_red. It does not matter whether i or j makes a red first. Therefore, we can safely ignore such race conditions.

4.4   Extensions

We can improve MC-NDFS further. Alg. 3 presents MC-NNDFS, which is MC-NDFS with the extensions discussed in Section 3. First, we opted to extend MC-NDFS with *allred* [9] (l.16 and l.24–27). Since the parallel workload of the MC-NDFS algorithm depends entirely on the proportion of the state graph that can be marked red (see Section 5.2), *allred* can improve the scalability. Second, early cycle detection in dfs_blue (l.19–21) is needed to compete with SCC-based algorithms. Finally, the introduction of the two-bit color-encoding from [21] for each worker will eliminate the extra bit per worker used for the pink color.

Sketch of Correctness. The *allred* extension in dfs_blue introduces a new red coloring of a state s at l.27, affecting the proof of Lemma 1. But, since $s \in \Box(Red)$, the induction hypothesis can be applied for the successor t of s.

Due to the early cycle detection at l.19–21, some accepting cycles can be detected already in the blue search. The stack configuration of the blue search thus guarantees us that indeed a cycle with an accepting state exists that is reachable from s_I: $s_I \rightarrow^* t \rightarrow^* s \rightarrow t$ with $t \in \mathcal{A} \vee s \in \mathcal{A}$ (l.20).

The two-bit color encoding overwrites the value of the $s.color[i]$ at l.5. However, L5 shows that only $Cyan_i$ and $Blue_i$ are affected (not $White_i$). The removal of s from $Blue_i$ does not affect dfs_red, since it is insensitive to $Blue_i$. The removal of s from $Cyan_i$ seems more problematic, since cycle detection on l.7 depends on it. However, we also know that the only case where s is removed from $Cyan_i$, is in the initial dfs_red call from l.11 (recursive dfs_red calls are never made on $Cyan_i$ states, since a cycle would be detected at l.16 and l.19 would not have been reached). Hence, $s \in \mathcal{A}$. It turns out that if there exists a

```
 1  proc mc–ndfs(s,N)                      15  proc dfs_blue(s,i)
 2    dfs_blue(s,1)‖..‖dfs_blue(s,N)        16    allred := true
 3    report no cycle                       17    s.color[i] := cyan
                                            18    for all t in post_i^b(s) do
 4  proc dfs_red(s,i)                       19      if t.color[i]=cyan ∧
 5    s.color[i] := pink                    20      (s ∈ A ∨ t ∈ A)
 6    for all t in post_i^r(s) do           21        report cycle & exit all
 7      if t.color[i]=cyan                  22      if t.color[i]=white∧¬t.red
 8        report cycle & exit all           23        dfs_blue(t,i)
 9      if t.color[i]≠pink∧¬t.red           24      if ¬t.red
10        dfs_red(t,i)                      25        allred := false
11    if s ∈ A                              26    if allred
12      s.count := s.count − 1              27      s.red := true
13      await s.count=0                     28    else if s ∈ A
14    s.red := true                         29      s.count := s.count + 1
                                            30      dfs_red(s,i)
                                            31    s.color[i] := blue
```

Alg. 3. MC-NDFS with extensions (MC-NNDFS)

path $\pi \equiv s \to^* s$ with $(\pi \setminus s) \cap Cyan_i = \emptyset$, this accepting cycle would have been detected by early cycle detection in dfs_blue ($s_I \to^* s \to^* s' \to s$ with $s \in \mathcal{A}$). Hence, we do not need any provisions to *fix* the removal of s from $Cyan_i$. This fact was overlooked by Schwoon et al.[9, 21], leading them to complicate their NNDFS algorithm (Alg. 1) with delayed red coloring of accepting states.

5   Experiments

We implemented NNDFS, multi-core SV NNDFS and MC-NNDFS in the multi-core backend of the LTSmin model checking tool suite [17]. This enabled us to use the same input models (without translation) and the same language frontend (compiler). We also implemented randomized $post_i$ functions to direct threads to different regions of the state space, as discussed in Section 4.1.

We performed experiments on an AMD Opteron 8356 16-core (4×4 cores) server with 64 GB RAM, running a patched Linux 2.6.32 kernel. All tools were compiled using gcc 4.4.3 in 64-bit mode with high compiler optimizations (-O3). For comparison purposes, we used all 453 models with properties of the BEEM database [19]. To mitigate random effects in the benchmarks, runtimes are always averaged over 6 benchmark runs. We compared MC-NNDFS against multi-core SV NNDFS to answer the question whether a more integrated multi-core approach can win against an *embarrassingly parallel* algorithm. Furthermore, we compared with the best existing parallel LTL MC algorithm OTF_OWCTY, as implemented in DiVinE 2.5.1 [3].

Due to the *on-the-fly* nature of LTL algorithms, we distinguish models containing accepting cycles from models that do not contain them. On the former set, algorithms that build the state space *on-the-fly* and terminate early when a counter example can be found, are expected to perform very well.

5.1   Models with Accepting Cycles

We demonstrate the merits of multi-core SV NNDFS by comparing the runtimes with the sequential NNDFS. As expected, SV speeds up the detection of accepting cycles (crosses in Fig. 4) significantly compared to sequential NNDFS runs. We do not expect to see perfect speedups ($16 \times$ on 16 cores) across all benchmarks, since the search is undirected and some threads traverse parts of the state space which do not contribute to finding a cycle. However, for some models, multi-core SV NNDFS does exhibit perfect speedups, or even superlinear speedups. Due to randomization, multiple workers are more likely to find counter examples[6, 22].

Both multi-core SV NNDFS and MC-NNDFS find accepting cycles roughly within the same time (Fig. 5), there is only a small edge for MC-NNDFS (most crosses are in the upper half of the figure), due to work sharing effects. Apparently, the global red coloring does not cause much "obstruction" (see Section 4.3).

We isolated those runs of MC-NNDFS on models with cycles, that have a runtime longer than 0.1 sec, because only those yield meaningful scalability figures.

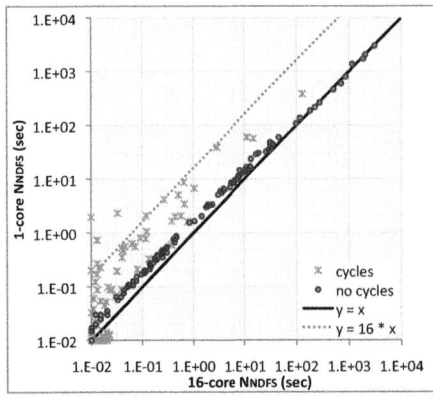
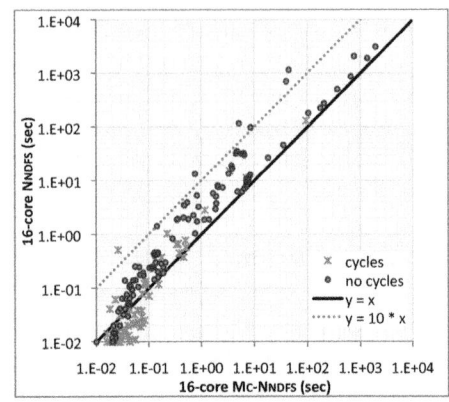

Fig. 4. Log-log scatter plot of multi-core SV NNDFS / sequential NNDFS runtimes

Fig. 5. Log-log scatter plot of MC-NNDFS / multi-core SV NNDFS runtimes

Fig. 7 on the next page shows that these models scale very well (the figure is cut off after a speedup of 20, but it extends well beyond speedups of 100). Out of 54 models with cycles (and runtimes $\geq$ 0.1 sec), $\approx$ 75 % exhibit at least eight-fold speedups and almost half exhibit superlinear speedups (factor > 16).

Finally, a comparison with OTF_OWCTY unsurprisingly shows that MC-NNDFS finds counter examples much faster (crosses in Fig. 6), due to its depth-first on-the-fly nature, while OTF_OWCTY is only heuristically on-the-fly.

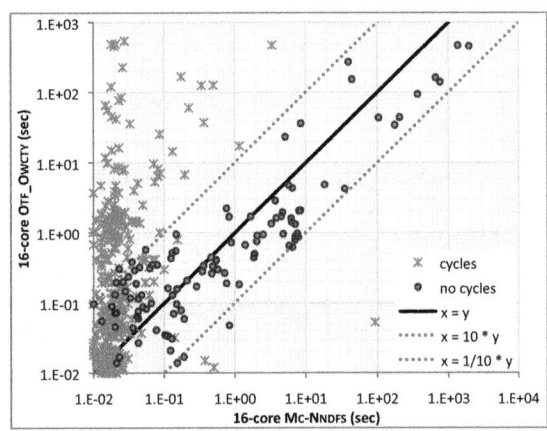

Fig. 6. Log-log scatter plot of MC-NNDFS / OTF_OWCTY runtimes

5.2   Models without Accepting Cycles

For models without accepting cycles, on-the-fly algorithms lose their edge over other algorithms, as the state space has to be traversed fully. We demonstrate this with our multi-core SV NNDFS benchmark runs, which degrade timewise to sequential NNDFS (dots in Fig. 4). We note that multi-core SV NNDFS causes little overhead compared to the sequential NNDFS version, hence it would be safe to run multi-core SV if the presence of a counter example is uncertain.

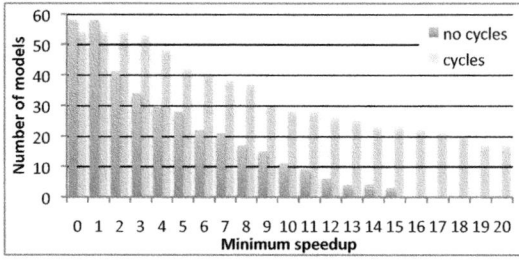

Fig. 7. Model counts of speedups with MC-NNDFS (base case: sequential NNDFS)

However, when comparing multi-core SV NNDFS against MC-NNDFS (Fig. 5), we observe significant speedups, in some cases more than ten-fold (dotted line) on 16 cores. Again, we isolated the runs of MC-NNDFS on models without cycles that run more than 1 sec (Fig. 7). We observed at least ten-fold speedups for 11 models out of 58 such models. In the BEEM database, we verified the nature of the 40 models that exhibit speedup greater than factor two. These include: *leader election* and other *communication protocols, hardware models, controllers, cache coherence protocols* and *mutual exclusion algorithms*.

Fig. 6 reveals that MC-NNDFS can mostly keep up with the performance of OTF_OWCTY. However, on some models without accepting cycles DiVinE is faster by a factor of 10 on 16 cores. Which algorithm performs best in these cases likely depends on model characteristics, which we have yet to investigate.

However, we did investigate the lack of MC-NNDFS scalability for some models without cycles in Fig. 7. All these cases lack states colored red by dfs_red. However, this does not hold the other way around: many models with few of these red states still exhibit speedups. This can be attributed to the red coloring by the *allred* extension. In fact, for all models without cycles, the proportion of states colored red by dfs_red turned out to be negligible, while *allred* accounts for the vast majority of the red colorings.

We found that the number of red colorings is strongly dependent on the exploration order ($post_i$). Fig. 8 illustrates that this is indeed possible. If a search advances first from s through t, then t cannot be colored red. This also holds for s, because one of its successors remains blue. However, if a is visited first, then u becomes red, hence later also t and s. It would be interesting to find a heuristic that maximizes red colorings.

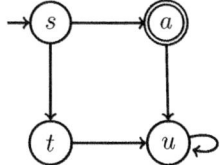

Fig. 8. Exploration order can influence r_N

We also observed that the speedup S_N is dependent on the fraction of red states r_N, as can be expected from the fact that r_N is the fraction of work that can be parallelized: $S_N \approx \frac{T_{seq}}{T_{seq} \times (1-r_N) + T_{seq} \times r_N / N} = \frac{1}{1-(1-1/N)r_N}$, where $T_{seq} \times (1 - r_N)$ is duplicated work. This shows us that the algorithm barely waits for a long time at 1.22, which is also confirmed by direct measurements.

6 Conclusions

In this paper, we introduced a multi-core NDFS algorithm, starting from a multi-core SV version, and proved its correctness. Its time complexity is linear in the size of the input graph, and it acts on-the-fly, addressing an open question put forward by Holzmann et al. and Barnat et al. [4, 12]. However, in the worst case, each worker might still traverse the whole graph. We showed empirically that the algorithm scales well on many inputs. The on-the-fly property of MC-NNDFS, combined with the speedups on cycle-free models, makes MC-NNDFS highly competitive to OTF_OWCTY.

The experiments were needed because MC-NNDFS is a heuristic algorithm: in the worst case (no accepting states, hence no red states) no work is shared between workers and the performance reduces to the SV version. However, in these cases no other known linear-time parallel algorithm obtains any speedup (including dual-core NDFS [11]).

The space complexity of MC-NNDFS remains decent: per state $2 \times N$ local color bits, $\log_2(N)$ bits for the *count* variable, and one global red color bit, with N the number of workers. The *count* variable could be omitted, at the expense of inspecting the pink flags of all other workers. However, this would lead to a significant memory contention. The overhead of $\log_2(N)$ bits per state is insignificant next to the space required by the local colors.

Recent development. After preparing this final version, we noticed that another approach on parallelizing NDFS appears in this same volume [7]. Their approach seems complementary, since they share the blue color, where we share red. Instead of our synchronization, they speculatively continue parallel execution and call a sequential repair procedure in the case of dangerous situations.

Future work. We have strong indications that MC-NNDFS can be improved. The previous section showed that a heuristic for exploration order might be of great benefit for the scalability. Furthermore, we think that early cycle detection and work sharing can be improved with SCC-like techniques.

Acknowledgements. We thank Elwin Pater for providing feedback on our algorithms and proofs.

References

1. Baier, C., Katoen, J.P.: Principles of Model Checking. The MIT Press, Cambridge (2008)
2. Barnat, J., Brim, L., Ročkai, P.: Scalable Shared Memory LTL Model Checking. STTT 12(2), 139–153 (2010)
3. Barnat, J., Brim, L., Češka, M., Ročkai, P.: DiVinE: Parallel Distributed Model Checker (Tool paper). In: Parallel and Distributed Methods in Verification and High Performance Computational Systems Biology (HiBi/PDMC 2010), pp. 4–7. IEEE, Los Alamitos (2010)
4. Barnat, J., Brim, L., Ročkai, P.: A Time-Optimal On-The-Fly Parallel Algorithm for Model Checking of Weak LTL Properties. In: Breitman, K., Cavalcanti, A. (eds.) ICFEM 2009. LNCS, vol. 5885, pp. 407–425. Springer, Heidelberg (2009)
5. Courcoubetis, C., Vardi, M.Y., Wolper, P., Yannakakis, M.: Memory-Efficient Algorithms for the Verification of Temporal Properties. Formal Methods in System Design 1(2/3), 275–288 (1992)

6. Dwyer, M.B., Elbaum, S.G., Person, S., Purandare, R.: Parallel Randomized State-Space Search. In: Proc. ICSE 2007, pp. 3–12. IEEE Computer Society Press, Los Alamitos (2007)

7. Evangelista, S., Petrucci, L., Youcef, S.: Parallel nested depth-first searches for LTL model checking. In: Bultan, T., Hsiung, P.-A. (eds.) ATVA 2011. LNCS, vol. 6996, pp. 381–396. Springer, Heidelberg (2011)

8. Foster, I.: Designing and Building Parallel Programs. Addison-Wesley, Reading (1995)

9. Gaiser, A., Schwoon, S.: Comparison of Algorithms for Checking Emptiness on Büchi Automata. CoRR, abs/0910.3766 (2009)

10. Geldenhuys, J., Valmari, A.: Tarjan's Algorithm Makes On-the-Fly LTL Verification More Efficient. In: Jensen, K., Podelski, A. (eds.) TACAS 2004. LNCS, vol. 2988, pp. 205–219. Springer, Heidelberg (2004)

11. Holzmann, G.J., Bošnački, D.: The Design of a Multicore Extension of the SPIN Model Checker. IEEE Trans. On Software Engineering 33(10), 659–674 (2007)

12. Holzmann, G.J., Bošnački, D.: The Design of a Multicore Extension of the SPIN Model Checker. IEEE Transactions on Software Engineering 33(10), 659–674 (2007)

13. Holzmann, G.J., Joshi, R., Groce, A.: Swarm Verification. In: Proc. ASE 2008, pp. 1–6. IEEE Computer Society Press, Los Alamitos (2008)

14. Holzmann, G.J., Joshi, R., Groce, A.: Tackling Large Verification Problems with the Swarm Tool. In: Havelund, K., Majumdar, R. (eds.) SPIN 2008. LNCS, vol. 5156, pp. 134–143. Springer, Heidelberg (2008)

15. Holzmann, G.J., Peled, D., Yannakakis, M.: On Nested Depth First Search. In: The Spin Verification System, pp. 23–32. American Mathematical Society, Providence (1996)

16. Laarman, A.W., van de Pol, J.C., Weber, M.: Boosting Multi-Core Reachability Performance with Shared Hash Tables. In: Sharygina, N., Bloem, R. (eds.) Proceedings of the 10th International Conference on Formal Methods in Computer-Aided Design, Lugano, Swiss, USA. IEEE Computer Society, Los Alamitos (2010)

17. Laarman, A.W., van de Pol, J.C., Weber, M.: Multi-core LTSmin: Marrying modularity and scalability. In: Bobaru, M., Havelund, K., Holzmann, G., Joshi, R. (eds.) NFM 2011. LNCS, vol. 6617, pp. 506–511. Springer, Heidelberg (2011)

18. Moore, G.E.: Cramming more Components onto Integrated Circuits. Electronics 38(10), 114–117 (1965)

19. Pelánek, R.: BEEM: Benchmarks for Explicit Model Checkers. In: Bošnački, D., Edelkamp, S. (eds.) SPIN 2007. LNCS, vol. 4595, pp. 263–267. Springer, Heidelberg (2007)

20. Reif, J.H.: Depth-first Search is Inherently Sequential. Information Processing Letters 20(5), 229–234 (1985)

21. Schwoon, S., Esparza, J.: A Note on On-the-Fly Verification Algorithms. In: Halbwachs, N., Zuck, L.D. (eds.) TACAS 2005. LNCS, vol. 3440, pp. 174–190. Springer, Heidelberg (2005)

22. Sivaraj, H., Gopalakrishnan, G.: Random Walk Based Heuristic Algorithms for Distributed Memory Model Checking. Electronic Notes in Theoretical Computer Science 89(1), 51–67 (2003)

23. Vardi, M.Y., Wolper, P.: An automata-theoretic approach to automatic program verification. In: Proc. 1st Symp. on Logic in Computer Science, Cambridge, pp. 332–344 (June 1986)

Self-Loop Aggregation Product — A New Hybrid Approach to On-the-Fly LTL Model Checking

Alexandre Duret-Lutz[1], Kais Klai[2], Denis Poitrenaud[3], and Yann Thierry-Mieg[3]

[1] LRDE, EPITA, Kremlin-Bicêtre, France
[2] LIPN, Université Paris-Nord, Villetaneuse, France
[3] LIP6/MoVe, Université Pierre & Marie Curie, Paris, France

Abstract. We present the *Self-Loop Aggregation Product* (SLAP), a new hybrid technique that replaces the synchronized product used in the automata-theoretic approach for LTL model checking. The proposed product is an explicit graph of aggregates (symbolic sets of states) that can be interpreted as a Büchi automaton. The criterion used by SLAP to aggregate states from the Kripke structure is based on the analysis of self-loops that occur in the Büchi automaton expressing the property to verify. Our hybrid approach allows on the one hand to use classical emptiness-check algorithms and build the graph on-the-fly, and on the other hand, to have a compact encoding of the state space thanks to the symbolic representation of the aggregates. Our experiments show that this technique often outperforms other existing (hybrid or fully symbolic) approaches.

1 Introduction

Model checking for Linear-time Temporal Logic (LTL) is usually based on converting the property into a Büchi automaton, composing the automaton and the model (given as a Kripke structure), and finally checking the language emptiness of the composed system [20]. This verification process suffers from a well known state explosion problem. Among the various techniques that have been suggested as improvement, we can distinguish two large families: explicit and symbolic approaches.

Explicit model checking approaches explore an explicit representation of the product graph. A common optimization builds the graph on-the-fly as required by the emptiness check algorithm: the construction stops as soon as a counterexample is found [4].

Another source of optimization is to take advantage of stuttering equivalence between paths in the Kripke structure when verifying a stuttering-invariant property [8]: this has been done either by ignoring some paths in the Kripke structure [13], or by representing the property using a *testing automaton* [12]. To our knowledge, all these solutions require dedicated algorithms to check the emptiness of the product graph.

Symbolic model checking tackles the state-explosion problem by representing the product automaton symbolically, usually by means of decision diagrams (a concise way to represent large sets or relations). Various symbolic algorithms exist to verify LTL using fix-point computations (see [9,18] for comparisons and [14] for the clarity of the presentation). As-is, these approaches do not mix well with stuttering-invariant reductions or on-the-fly emptiness checks.

T. Bultan and P.-A. Hsiung (Eds.): ATVA 2011, LNCS 6996, pp. 336–350, 2011.

However explicit and symbolic approaches are not exclusive, some combinations have already been studied [2,10,17,15] to get the best of both worlds. They are referred to as **hybrid approaches**. Most of these approaches consist in replacing the Kripke structure by an explicit graph where each node contains sets of states (called aggregates throughout this paper), that is an abstraction preserving properties of the original structure. For instance in Biere et al.'s approach [2], each aggregate contains states that share their atomic proposition values, and the successor aggregates contain direct successors of the previous aggregate, thus preserving LTL but not branching temporal properties. The Symbolic Observation Graph [10] takes this idea one step further in the context of stuttering invariant properties: each aggregate contains sets of consecutive states that share their atomic proposition values. In both of these approaches, an explicit product with the formula automaton is built and checked for emptiness, allowing to stop early (on-the-fly) if a witness trace is found.

Sebastiani et al.'s approach [17] is a bit different, as it builds one aggregate for each state of the Büchi automata (usually few in number), and uses a partitioned symbolic transition relation to check for emptiness of the product, thus resorting to a symbolic emptiness-check (based on a symbolic SCC hull computation).

The hybrid approach we define in this paper is based on explicit graphs of aggregates (symbolic sets of states) that can be interpreted as Büchi automata. With this combination, we can use classical emptiness-check algorithms and build the graph on-the-fly, moreover the symbolic representation of aggregates gives us a compact encoding of the state space along with efficient fixpoint algorithms.

The aggregation criterion is based on the study of the self-loops around the current state of the Büchi automaton. Roughly speaking, consecutive states of the system are aggregated when they are compatible with the labels of self-loops. We allow to stutter according to a boolean formula computed as the disjunction of the labels of self-loops of the automaton. This aggregation graph is called the *Self-Loop Aggregation Product* (SLAP) and preserves full Büchi expressible properties.

This paper is organized as follows. Section 2 introduces our notations and presents the basic automata-theoretic approach. Section 3 defines our new hybrid construction SLAP. We explain how we implemented this approach and how it compares to others in Section 4.

2   Preliminaries

2.1   Boolean Formulas

Let AP be a set of (atomic) propositions, and let $\mathbb{B} = \{\bot, \top\}$ represent Boolean values. We denote $\mathbb{B}(AP)$ the set of all Boolean formulas over AP, i.e., formulas built inductively from the propositions AP, $\mathbb{B}$, and the connectives $\wedge$, $\vee$, and $\neg$.

An assignment is a function $\rho : AP \rightarrow \mathbb{B}$ that assigns a truth value to each proposition. We denote $\mathbb{B}^{AP}$ the set of all assignments of AP. Given a formula $f \in \mathbb{B}(AP)$ and an assignment $\rho \in \mathbb{B}^{AP}$, we denote $\rho(f)$ the evaluation of f under ρ[1]. In particular, we will

---

[1] This can be defined straightforwardly as $\rho(f \wedge g) = \rho(f) \wedge \rho(g)$, $\rho(\neg f) = \neg \rho(f)$, etc.

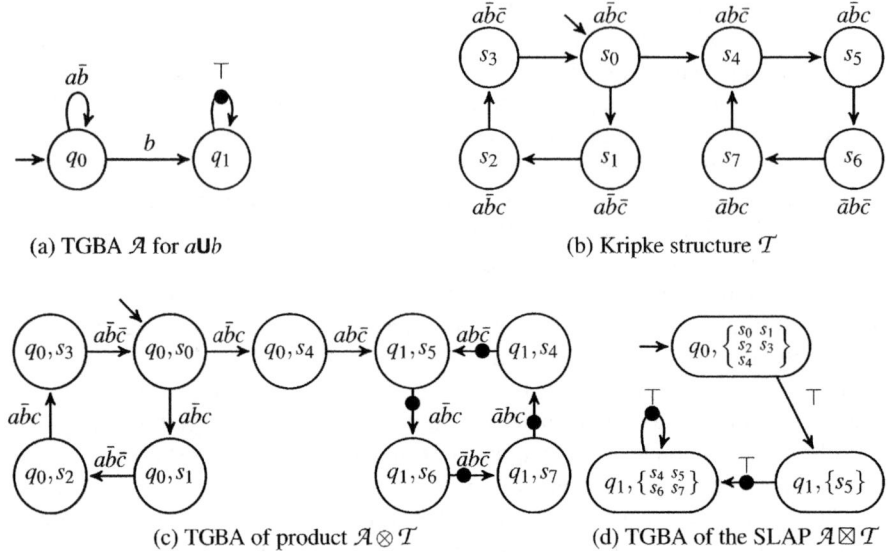

(a) TGBA $\mathcal{A}$ for $a \mathsf{U} b$ 　　　　　　　(b) Kripke structure $\mathcal{T}$

(c) TGBA of product $\mathcal{A} \otimes \mathcal{T}$ 　　　　(d) TGBA of the SLAP $\mathcal{A} \boxtimes \mathcal{T}$

Fig. 1. Examples

write $\rho \models f$ iff ρ is a satisfying assignment for f, i.e., $\rho \models f \iff \rho(f) = \top$. The set $\mathbb{B}^\star(\mathrm{AP}) = \{f \in \mathbb{B}(\mathrm{AP}) \mid \exists \rho \in \mathbb{B}^{\mathrm{AP}}, \rho \models f\}$ contains all satisfiable formulas.

We will use assignments to label the states of the model we want to verify, and the propositional functions will be used as labels in the automaton representing the property to check. The intuition is that a behavior of the model (a sequence of assignments) will match the property if we can find a sequence of formulas in the automaton that are satisfied by the sequence of assignments.

It is sometimes convenient to interpret an assignment ρ as a formula that is only true for this assignment. For instance the assignment $\{a \mapsto \top, b \mapsto \top, c \mapsto \bot\}$ can be interpreted as the formula $a \wedge b \wedge \neg c$. So we may use an assignment where a formula is expected, as if we were abusively assuming that $\mathbb{B}^{\mathrm{AP}} \subset \mathbb{B}(\mathrm{AP})$.

2.2　TGBA

A *Transition-based Generalized Büchi Automaton* (TGBA) is a Büchi automaton in which generalized acceptance conditions are expressed in term of transitions that must be visited infinitely often. The reason we use these automata is that they allow a more compact representation of properties than traditional Büchi automata (even generalized Büchi automata) [7] without making the emptiness check harder [5].

Definition 1 (TGBA). *A Transition-based Generalized Büchi Automata is a tuple* $A = \langle \mathrm{AP}, Q, \mathcal{F}, \delta, q^0 \rangle$ *where*
- AP *is a finite set of atomic propositions,*
- Q *is a finite set of states,*
- $\mathcal{F} \neq \emptyset$ *is a finite and non-empty set of acceptance conditions,*

- $\delta \subseteq Q \times \mathbb{B}^{\star}(\mathrm{AP}) \times 2^{\mathcal{F}} \times Q$ *is a transition relation. We will commonly denote*
$q_1 \xrightarrow{f,ac} q_2$ *an element* $(q_1, f, ac, q_2) \in \delta,$
- $q^0 \in Q$ *is the initial state.*

An execution (or a run) of A is an infinite sequence of transitions $\pi = (s_1, f_1, ac_1, d_1) \cdots$ $(s_i, f_i, ac_i, d_i) \cdots \in \delta^{\omega}$ with $s_1 = q^0$ and $\forall i, d_i = s_{i+1}$. We shall simply denote it as $\pi = s_1 \xrightarrow{f_1, ac_1} s_2 \xrightarrow{f_2, ac_2} s_3 \cdots$. Such an execution is *accepting* iff it visits each acceptance condition infinitely often, i.e., if $\forall a \in \mathcal{F}, \forall i > 0, \exists j \geq i, a \in ac_j$. We denote $\mathrm{Acc}(A) \subseteq \delta^{\omega}$ the set of accepting executions of A.

A behavior of the model is an infinite sequence of assignments: $\rho_1 \rho_2 \rho_3 \cdots \in (\mathbb{B}^{\mathrm{AP}})^{\omega}$, while an execution of the automaton A is an infinite sequence of transitions labeled by Boolean formulas. The language of A, denoted $\mathcal{L}(A)$, is the set of behaviors compatible with an accepting execution of A: $\mathcal{L}(A) = \{\rho_1 \rho_2 \cdots \in (\mathbb{B}^{\mathrm{AP}})^{\omega} \mid \exists s_1 \xrightarrow{f_1, ac_1} s_2 \xrightarrow{f_2, ac_2} \cdots \in \mathrm{Acc}(A)$ and $\forall i \geq 1, \rho_i \models f_i\}$

The non-emptiness constraint on $\mathcal{F}$ was introduced into definition 1 to avoid considering $\mathcal{F} = \emptyset$ as a separate case. If no acceptance conditions exist, one can be artificially added to some edges, ensuring that every cycle of the TGBA bears one on at least an edge. Simply adding this artificial acceptance condition to all edges might seriously hurt subsequent verification performance, as some emptiness-check algorithms are sensitive to the position of acceptance conditions.

Fig. 1a represents a TGBA for the LTL formula $a\mathsf{U}b$. The black dot on the self-loop $q_1 \xrightarrow{\top, \{\bullet\}} q_1$ denotes an acceptance conditions from $\mathcal{F} = \{\bullet\}$. The labels on edges ($a\bar{b}, b$ and $\top$) represent the Boolean expressions over $\mathrm{AP} = \{a, b\}$. There are many other TGBA in Fig. 1, that represent product constructions of this TGBA and the Kripke Structure of Fig. 1b.

2.3 Kripke Structure

For the sake of generality, we use *Kripke Structures* (KS for short) as a framework, since the formalism is well adapted to state-based semantics.

Definition 2 (Kripke structure). *A Kripke structure is a 4-tuple* $\mathcal{T} = \langle \mathrm{AP}, \Gamma, \lambda, \Delta, s_0 \rangle$ *where:*

- AP *is a finite set of atomic propositions,*
- Γ *is a finite set of* states,
- $\lambda : \Gamma \to \mathbb{B}^{\mathrm{AP}}$ *is a state labeling function,*
- $\Delta \subseteq \Gamma \times \Gamma$ *is a transition relation. We will commonly denote* $s_1 \to s_2$ *the element* $(s_1, s_2) \in \Delta.$
- $s_0 \in \Gamma$ *is the* initial state.

Fig. 1b represents a Kripke structure over $\mathrm{AP} = \{a, b, c\}$. The state graph of a system is typically represented by a KS, where state labels in the KS give the atomic proposition truth values in a given state of the system.

We now define a synchronized product for a TGBA and a KS, such that the language of the resulting TGBA is the intersection of the languages of the two automata.

Definition 3 (Synchronized product of a TGBA and a Kripke structure). *Let* $\mathcal{A} = \langle AP', Q, \mathcal{F}, \delta, q^0 \rangle$ *be a TGBA and* $\mathcal{T} = \langle AP, \Gamma, \lambda, \Delta, s_0 \rangle$ *be a Kripke structure over* $AP \supseteq AP'$.

The synchronized product *of* $\mathcal{A}$ *and* $\mathcal{T}$ *is the TGBA denoted by* $\mathcal{A} \otimes \mathcal{T} = \langle AP, Q_\times, \mathcal{F}, \delta_\times, q^0_\times \rangle$ *defined as:*

- $Q_\times = Q \times \Gamma$,
- $\delta_\times \subseteq Q_\times \times \mathbb{B}^\star(AP) \times 2^{\mathcal{F}} \times Q_\times$ *where*

$$\delta_\times = \left\{ (q_1, s_1) \xrightarrow{f, ac} (q_2, s_2) \left| \begin{array}{l} s_1 \to s_2 \in \Delta, \lambda(s_1) = f \text{ and} \\ \exists g \in \mathbb{B}^\star(AP) \text{ s.t. } q_1 \xrightarrow{g, ac} q_2 \in \delta \text{ and } \lambda(s_1) \models g \end{array} \right. \right\}$$

- $q^0_\times = (q^0, s_0)$.

Fig. 1c represents such a product of the TGBA $a\mathsf{U}b$ of Fig. 1a and the Kripke structure of Fig. 1b. State (s_0, q_0) is the initial state of the product. Since $\lambda(s_0) = a\bar{b}c$ we have $\lambda(s_0) \models a\bar{b}$, successors $\{s_1, s_4\}$ of s_0 in the KS will be synchronized through the edge $q_0 \xrightarrow{a\bar{b}, \emptyset} q_0$ of the TGBA with q_0. In state (q_0, s_4) the product can progress through the $q_0 \xrightarrow{b, \emptyset} q_1$ edge of the TGBA, since $\lambda(s_4) = ab\bar{c} \models b$. Successor s_5 of s_4 in the KS is thus synchronized with q_1. The TGBA state q_1 now only requires states to verify $\top$ to validate the acceptance condition $\bullet$, so any cycle in the *KS* from s_5 will be accepted by the product. The resulting edge of the product bears the acceptance conditions contributed by the TGBA edge, and the atomic proposition Boolean formula label that comes from the KS. The size of the product in both nodes and edges is bounded by the product of the sizes of the TGBA and the KS.

3 Self-Loop Aggregation Product (SLAP)

This section presents a specialized synchronized product that aggregates states of the KS as long as the TGBA state does not change, and no *new* acceptance conditions are visited.

3.1 Definition

The notion of self-loop aggregation is captured by $SF(q, ac)$, the Self-loop Formulas (labeling edges $q \to q$) that are weaker in terms of visited acceptance conditions than ac.

When synchronizing with an edge of the property TGBA bearing ac leading to q, successive states of the Kripke will be aggregated as long as they model $SF(q, ac)$. More formally, for a TGBA state q and a set of accepting condition $ac \subseteq \mathcal{F}$, let us define

$$SF(q, ac) = \bigvee_{q \xrightarrow{f, ac'} q \in \delta \text{ s.t. } ac' \subseteq ac} f$$

Moreover, for $a \subseteq \Gamma$ and $f \in \mathbb{B}(AP)$, we define $FSucc(a, f) = \{s' \in \Gamma \mid \exists s \in a, s \to s' \in \Delta \wedge \lambda(s) \models f\}$. That is, first **Filter** a to only keep states satisfying f, then produce their **Succ**essors. We denote by $FReach(a, f)$ the least subset of Γ satisfying both $a \subseteq FReach(a, f)$ and $FSucc(FReach(a, f), f) \subseteq FReach(a, f)$.

Definition 4 (SLAP of a TGBA and a KS). *Given a TGBA* $\mathcal{A} = \langle AP', Q, \mathcal{F}, \delta, q^0 \rangle$ *and a Kripke structure* $\mathcal{T} = \langle AP, \Gamma, \lambda, \Delta, s_0 \rangle$ *over* $AP \supseteq AP'$, *the Self-Loop Aggregation Product of* $\mathcal{A}$ *and* $\mathcal{T}$ *is the TGBA denoted* $\mathcal{A} \boxtimes \mathcal{T} = \langle \emptyset, Q_{\boxtimes}, \mathcal{F}, \delta_{\boxtimes}, q^0_{\boxtimes} \rangle$ *where:*

- $Q_{\boxtimes} = Q \times (2^{\Gamma} \setminus \{\emptyset\})$

- $\delta_{\boxtimes} = \left\{ (q_1, a_1) \xrightarrow{\top, ac} (q_2, a_2) \,\middle|\, \begin{array}{l} \exists f \in \mathbb{B}(AP') \text{ s.t. } q_1 \xrightarrow{f, ac} q_2 \in \delta, \\ q_1 = q_2 \Rightarrow ac \neq \emptyset, \text{ and} \\ a_2 = \mathrm{FReach}(\mathrm{FSucc}(a_1, f), \mathrm{SF}(q_2, ac)) \end{array} \right\}$

- $q^0_{\boxtimes} = (q^0, \mathrm{FReach}(\{s_0\}, \mathrm{SF}(q^0, \emptyset)))$

Note that because of the way the product is built, it is not obvious what Boolean formula should label the edges of the SLAP product. Since in fact this label is irrelevant when checking language emptiness, we label all arcs of the SLAP with $\top$ and simply denote $(q_1, a_1) \xrightarrow{ac} (q_2, a_2)$ any transition $(q_1, a_1) \xrightarrow{\top, ac} (q_2, a_2)$.

$Q \times 2^{\Gamma}$ might seem very large but, as we will see in section 4.2 in practice the reachable states of the SLAP is a much smaller set than that of the product $Q \times \Gamma$. Furthermore the FReach operation can be efficiently implemented as a symbolic least fix point.

Fig. 1d represents the SLAP built from our example KS, and the TGBA of $a\mathbf{U}b$. The initial state of the SLAP iteratively aggregates successors of states verifying $\mathrm{SF}(q^0, \emptyset) = a\bar{b}$. Then following the edge $q^0 \xrightarrow{b, \emptyset} q_1$, states are aggregated with condition $\mathrm{SF}(q_1, \emptyset) = \bot$. Hence q_1 is synchronized with successors of states in $\{s_0, s_1, s_2, s_3, s_4\}$ satisfying b (i.e., successors of $\{s_4\}$). Because $\mathrm{SF}(q_1, \emptyset) = \bot$ the successors of $\{s_5\}$ are not gathered when building $(q_1, \{s_5\})$. Finally, when synchronizing with edge $q_1 \xrightarrow{\top, \bullet} q_1$, we have $\mathrm{SF}(q_1, \{\bullet\}) = \top$, hence all states of the cycle $\{s_4, s_5, s_6, s_7\}$ are added.

3.2 Proof of Correctness

Our ultimate goal is to establish that, given a KS and a TGBA, the emptiness of the language of the corresponding SLAP is equivalent to the emptiness of the language of the original synchronized product (see Theorem 1). This result is progressively demonstrated in the following. We proceed by construction, i.e., if there exists an accepting run of the SLAP then we build an accepting run of the original product and vice versa. In order to ease the proof, we introduce some intermediate lemmas.

Lemma 1. *Let* $\mathcal{A}$ *and* $\mathcal{T}$ *be defined as in Definition 4. Let* $(q_1, a_1) \xrightarrow{ac} (q_2, a_2) \in \delta_{\boxtimes}$ *be a transition of the SLAP* $\mathcal{A} \boxtimes \mathcal{T}$. *For any state* $s_2 \in a_2$ *there exists at least one (possibly indirect) ancestor* $s_1 \in a_1$ *such that* $(q_1, s_1) \xrightarrow{ac} (q_2, t_1) \xrightarrow{\alpha_1} (q_2, t_2) \xrightarrow{\alpha_2} \cdots (q_2, t_n) \xrightarrow{\alpha_n} (q_2, s_2)$ *is a sequence of the synchronized product* $\mathcal{A} \otimes \mathcal{T}$ *with* $\forall i, t_i \in a_2$, *and* $\forall i, \alpha_i \subseteq ac$.

For example consider transition $(q_1, a_1) \xrightarrow{ac} (q_2, a_2)$ on Fig. 2, and some state in a_2, say s_2. Then $s_1 \in a_1$ is an indirect ancestor of s_2 s.t. $(q_1, s_1) \xrightarrow{ac} (q_2, x_2) \xrightarrow{\alpha_2} (q_2, s_2)$.

Proof. Let us define the set of input states of the aggregate a_2 as $In(a_2) = \{s' \in a_2 \mid \exists s \in a_1, s \to s' \in \Delta\}$. This set cannot be empty since $(q_1, a_1) \xrightarrow{ac} (q_2, a_2)$.

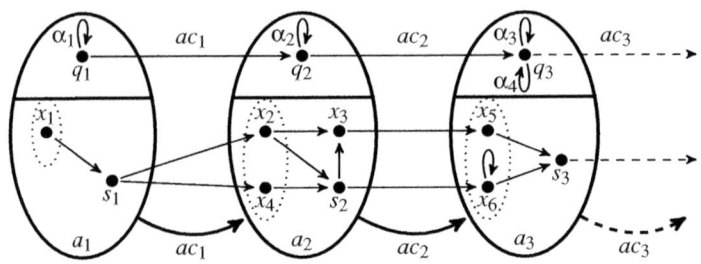

Fig. 2. A prefix $(q_1,a_1) \xrightarrow{ac_1} (q_2,a_2) \xrightarrow{ac_2} (q_2,a_2)$ of a run of some SLAP $\mathcal{A} \boxtimes \mathcal{T}$ (with *different* $\mathcal{A}$ and $\mathcal{T}$ from Fig. 1) is shown using big ellipses and bended arrows. The straight lines also shows the underlying connections between the states $\{q_1,q_2,q_3,\dots\}$ of the automaton $\mathcal{A}$ and between the states $\{s_1,s_2,\dots,x_1,x_2\dots\}$ of the Kripke structure $\mathcal{T}$ that have been aggregated as $a_1,a_2,a_3\dots$ The acceptance conditions have been depicted as ac_i or α_i and the labels of the transitions have been omitted for clarity. The dotted ellipses show the set of input states ($In(a_1)$, $In(a_2)$, $In(a_3)$) as used in the proof of Lemma 1.

Consider a state $s_2 \in a_2$. By construction of a_2, s_2 is reachable from some state in $t_1 \in In(a_2)$, so there exists a path $t_1 \to t_2 \to \cdots \to s_2$ in the Kripke structure.

By definition of $\delta_\boxtimes$, if $t_1,t_2,\dots,s_2$ belong to a_2, the transitions between these states of $\mathcal{T}$ have been synchronized with self-loops $q_2 \xrightarrow{\alpha_i} q_2$ of $\mathcal{A}$ with $\alpha_i \subseteq ac$. Therefore the sequence $(q_2,t_1) \xrightarrow{\alpha_1} (q_2,t_2) \xrightarrow{\alpha_2} \cdots (q_2,t_n) \xrightarrow{\alpha_n} (q_2,s_2)$ is a sequence of the synchronized product $\mathcal{A} \otimes \mathcal{T}$.

Moreover, since $t_1 \in In(a_2)$, there exists a state s_1 in a_1 such that $(q_1,s_1) \xrightarrow{ac} (q_2,t_1)$.

Consequently, the path $(q_1,s_1) \xrightarrow{ac} (q_2,t_1) \xrightarrow{\alpha_1} (q_2,t_2) \xrightarrow{\alpha_2} \cdots (q_2,t_n) \xrightarrow{\alpha_n} (q_2,s_2)$ satisfies the lemma. $\qquad\square$

Lemma 2. *If there exists $\sigma \in \mathrm{Acc}(\mathcal{A} \boxtimes \mathcal{T})$ an infinite run accepted by the SLAP, then there exists an accepting run $\pi \in \mathrm{Acc}(\mathcal{A} \otimes \mathcal{T})$ in the classical product.*

Proof. Let us denote $\sigma = (q_1,a_1) \xrightarrow{ac_1} (q_2,a_2) \xrightarrow{ac_2} (q_3,a_3) \xrightarrow{ac_3} \cdots$ an accepting run of $\mathcal{A} \boxtimes \mathcal{T}$. Let us build an infinite tree in which all nodes (except the root) are states of $\mathcal{A} \otimes \mathcal{T}$. Let us call $\top$ the root, at depth 0. The set of nodes at depth $n > 0$ is exactly the finite set of pairs $\{(q_n,s) \mid s \in a_n\} \subseteq Q \times \Gamma$.

The parent of any node at level 1 is $\top$. For any $i > 0$, the parent of a node (q_{i+1},s') with $s' \in a_{i+1}$ is the node (q_i,s) for is any state $s \in a_i$ such that (q_i,s) is a (possibly indirect) ancestor of (q_{i+1},s') such that we observe ac_i on the path between these two states. We know such a state (q_i,s) exists because of Lemma 1. As a consequence of this parenting relation, every edge in this tree, except those leaving the root, correspond to a path between two states of $\mathcal{A} \otimes \mathcal{T}$.

Because the set of nodes at depth $n > 0$ is finite, this infinite tree has finite branching. By König's Lemma it therefore contains an infinite branch. By following this branch and ignoring the first edge, we can construct a path of $\mathcal{A} \otimes \mathcal{T}$ that starts in (q_1,s_1) for some $s_1 \in a_1$, and that visits at least all the acceptance conditions ac_i of σ in the same order (and maybe more). To prove that this accepting path we have constructed actually occurs in a run of $\mathcal{A} \otimes \mathcal{T}$, it remains to show that (q_1, s_1) is a state that is accessible from the initial state of $\mathcal{A} \otimes \mathcal{T}$.

Obviously $q_1 = q^0$ because $(q_1, a_1) = q^0_{\boxtimes}$ is the initial state of $\mathcal{A} \boxtimes \mathcal{T}$. Furthermore we have $s_1 \in a_1$, so by definition of $q^0_{\boxtimes}$, (q^0, s_1) must be reachable from (or equal to) (q^0, s_0) in $\mathcal{A} \otimes \mathcal{T}$. $\qquad \square$

Lemma 3. *For a given n and a finite path $\pi_n = (q_0, s_0) \xrightarrow{f_0, ac_0} (q_1, s_1) \cdots \xrightarrow{f_{n-1}, ac_{n-1}}$ (q_n, s_n) of $\mathcal{A} \otimes \mathcal{T}$, there exists a finite path $\sigma_n = (q'_0, a_0) \xrightarrow{ac_{\varphi(0)}} (q'_1, a_1) \cdots \xrightarrow{ac_{\varphi(m-1)}}$ (q'_m, a_m) of $\mathcal{A} \boxtimes \mathcal{T}$, with $m \leq n$, $q_n = q'_m$, $s_n \in a_m$ and $\varphi_n : \{0, \ldots, m-1\} \to \{0, \ldots, n-1\}$ is a strictly increasing function such that $\forall j (\exists i, \varphi_n(i) = j \iff ac_i \neq \emptyset)$.*

Proof. Let us prove this lemma by induction on n. It is true if $n = 0$: Given $\pi_0 = (q_0, s_0)$, the path $\sigma_0 = (q'0, a_0) = q^0_{\boxtimes} = (q_0, \mathrm{FReach}(\{s_0\}, \{\lambda(s_0)\} \cap \lambda(q_0, \emptyset))$ satisfies the conditions (with φ being a null function).

Let us now demonstrate that the lemma is true for $n + 1$ assuming it is true for n. Given a path $\pi_{n+1} = \pi_n \xrightarrow{f_n, ac_n} (q_{n+1}, s_{n+1})$, we know by hypothesis that we have a matching σ_n for π_n. Let us consider how to extend σ_n into σ_{n+1} to handle the new transition $(q_n, s_n) \xrightarrow{f_n, ac_n} (q_{n+1}, s_{n+1})$ of π_{n+1}.

There are two cases to consider:

1. If $q_n = q_{n+1}$ and $acc_n = \emptyset$ and $\lambda(s_{n+1}) \models SF(q_n, ac)$, then by definition of FSucc and SF the last state of σ_n, (q'_m, a_m) is such that $s_{n+1} \in a_m$ and $q'_m = q_n = q_{n+1}$. In that case $\sigma_{n+1} = \sigma_n$, and $\varphi_{n+1} = \varphi_n$.
2. If $q_n \neq q_{n+1}$ or $acc_n \neq \emptyset$ or $\lambda(s_{n+1}) \not\models SF(q_n, ac)$, then because $\lambda(s_n) \models f_n$ and $s_n \to s_{n+1}$, by definition of $\delta_{\boxtimes}$ there exists $(q'_m, a_m) \xrightarrow{acc_n} (q'_{m+1}, a_{m+1})$ such that $s_{n+1} \in a_{m+1}$ and $q'_{m+1} = q_{n+1}$. In this case, we can define $\sigma_{n+1} = \sigma_n \xrightarrow{acc_n} (q'_{m+1}, a_{m+1})$ with $\forall i < n$, $\varphi_{n+1}(i) = \varphi_n(i)$ and $\varphi_{n+1}(n) = n$.

So by induction this lemma is true for all $n \in \mathbb{N}$. $\qquad \square$

Lemma 4. *If there exists an infinite path $\pi \in \mathrm{Acc}(\mathcal{A} \otimes \mathcal{T})$ accepting in $\mathcal{A} \otimes \mathcal{T}$. Then there exists an accepting path in $\mathcal{A} \boxtimes \mathcal{T}$ as well.*

Proof. $\mathcal{A} \otimes \mathcal{T}$ has a finite number of states, so if $\mathrm{Acc}(\mathcal{A} \otimes \mathcal{T}) \neq \emptyset$ then it contains at least one infinite path $\pi \in \mathrm{Acc}(\mathcal{A} \otimes \mathcal{T})$ that can be represented as a finite prefix followed by a finite cycle that is repeated infinitely often.

Lemma 3 tells us that any prefix π_n of π corresponds to some prefix σ_n of a path in $\mathcal{A} \boxtimes \mathcal{T}$ in which the acceptance conditions of π_n occur in the same order. We have $|\sigma_n| \leq |\pi_n| = n$ but because π will visit all acceptance conditions infinitely often, and these transitions will all appear in σ_n (only transition without acceptance conditions can be omitted from $\delta_{\boxtimes}$), we can find some value of n for which $|\sigma_n|$ is arbitrary large. Because $|\sigma_n|$ can be made larger than the size of the SLAP, at some point this finite sequence will have to loop in a way that visits the acceptance conditions exactly in the same order as they appear in the cycle part of π. By repeating this cycle part of σ_n we can therefore construct an infinite path σ that is accepted by $\mathcal{A} \boxtimes \mathcal{T}$. $\qquad \square$

Theorem 1. *Let $\mathcal{A}$ be a TGBA, and $\mathcal{T}$ be a Kripke structure. We have*

$$\mathrm{Acc}(\mathcal{A} \otimes \mathcal{T}) \neq \emptyset \iff \mathrm{Acc}(\mathcal{A} \boxtimes \mathcal{T}) \neq \emptyset$$

In other words, the SLAP of $\mathcal{A}$ and $\mathcal{T}$ accepts a run if and only if the synchronized product of these two structures accepts a run.

Proof. $\Longleftarrow$ follows from Lemma 2; $\Longrightarrow$ follows from Lemma 4. $\square$

3.3   Mixing SLAP and Fully Symbolic Approaches

This section informally presents a variation on the SLAP algorithm, to use a fully symbolic algorithm in cases where the automaton state will no longer evolve.

The principle is the following: when the product has reached a state where the TGBA state is terminal (i.e., it has itself as only successor), we proceed to use a fully symbolic search for an accepted path in the states of the current aggregate. This variant is called SLAP-FST, standing for Fully Symbolic search in Terminal states. Note that we suppose here that such a terminal state allows accepting runs, otherwise semantic simplifications would have removed the state from the TGBA.

In this variant, if q_1 is a terminal state, i.e., $\nexists q_1 \xrightarrow{f,ac} q_2 \in \delta$, with $q_1 \neq q_2$, a state (q_1, a_1) of the product has itself as sole successor through an arc labeled $(\top, \mathcal{F})$ if and only if a_1 admits a solution computed using a fully symbolic algorithm, or has no successors otherwise.

The fully symbolic search uses the self-loop arcs on the formula TGBA state to compute the appropriate transition relation(s), and takes into account possibly multiple acceptance conditions.

The rationale is that discovering this behavior when the aggregate is large, and particularly if there are long prefixes before reaching the SCC that bears all acceptance conditions, tends to create large SLAP structures in explicit size. The counterpart is that when no such solution exists, the fully symbolic SCC hull search may be quite costly.

In practice this variation on the SLAP was proposed after manually examining cases where SLAP performance was disappointing. As discussed in the performance section, this variation is on average more effective than the basic SLAP algorithm.

4   Experimentations

4.1   Implementation

We have implemented several hybrid or fully symbolic algorithms within our framework to allow fair algorithmic comparisons. The software, available from ddd.lip6.fr, builds upon two existing components: Spot and SDD/ITS.

Spot (http://spot.lip6.fr) is a model checking library [7]: it provides bricks to build your own model checker based on the automata-theoretic approach using TGBAs. It has been evaluated as "the best explicit LTL model-checker" [16]. Spot provides translation algorithms from LTL to TGBA, an implementation of a product between a Kripke structure and a TGBA (def. 3), and various emptiness-check algorithms to decide if the language of a TGBA is empty (among other things). The library uses abstract interfaces, so any object that can be wrapped to conform to the Kripke or TGBA interfaces can interoperate with the algorithms supplied by Spot.

SDD/ITS (http://ddd.lip6.fr) is a library representing Instantiable Transition Systems efficiently using Hierarchical Set Decision Diagrams [19]. ITS are essentially an abstract interface for (a variant of) labeled transition systems, and several input formalisms are supported (discrete time Petri nets, automata, and compositions thereof). SDD are a particular type of decision diagram that a) allow hierarchy in the state encoding, yielding smaller representations, b) support rewriting rules that allow the library to automatically [11] apply the symbolic saturation algorithm [3]. These features allow the SDD/ITS package to offer very competitive performance.

The fully symbolic OWCTY (One-Way Catch Them Young) and EL (Emerson-Lei) algorithms [9,18] were implemented directly on top of the ITS interface; they use an ITS representing the TGBA derived from the LTL formula by Spot composed (at the ITS formalism level) with the ITS representing the system. The resulting ITS is then analyzed using OWCTY or EL with the forward transition relation.

The SOG [10] (Symbolic Observation Graph) and BCZ [2] (Biere-Clarke-Zhu) are implemented as objects conforming to Spot's Kripke interface. They load an ITS model, then build the SOG or BCZ on the fly, as required by the emptiness check of the product with the formula automaton.

The SLAP is implemented as an object conforming to Spot's product interface. The SLAP class takes an ITS model and a TGBA (the formula automaton) as input parameters, and builds its specialized product on the fly, driven by the emptiness-check algorithm.

4.2 Benchmark

We use here classic scalable Petri net examples taken from Ciardo's benchmark set [3]: slotted ring, Kanban, flexible manufacturing system, and dining philosophers. The model occurences we used had from a few million to 10^{66} reachable states. More details are available in our technical report [6].

The formulas considered include a selection of random LTL formulas, which were filtered to have a (basic TGBA/Kripke) product size of at least 1000 states. We also chose to have as many verified formulas (empty products) as violated formulas (nonempty products) to avoid favoring on-the-fly algorithms too much. To produce TGBA with several acceptance conditions, this benchmark includes 200 formulas for each model built from fairness assumptions of the form: $(\mathbf{GF}p_1 \wedge \mathbf{GF}p_2 \ldots) \implies \varphi$.

We also used 100 random formulas that use the next operator, and hence are not stuttering invariant (these were not used for SOG that does not support them).

We killed any process that exceeded 120 seconds of runtime, and set the garbage collection threshold at 1.3GB. Cases where all considered methods performed under 0.1s were filtered out from the results presented here: these trivial cases represent only 4.2% of the entire benchmark, and were too fast to allow any pertinent comparison.

Table 1 gives a synthetic overview of the results presented hereafter. SLAP or SLAP-FST are the fastest methods in over half of all cases, and they are rarely the slowest. Furthermore, they have the least failure rate. This table also shows that BCZ has the highest failure rate and that the fully symbolic algorithms (OWCTY, EL) have trouble with non-empty products.

Table 1. On all experiments (grouped with respect to the existence of a counterexample), we count the number of cases a specific method has (Fast) the best time or (Slow) it has either run out of time or it has the worst time amongst successful methods. The Fail line shows how much of the Lost cases were timeouts. The sum of a line may exceed 100% if several methods are equally placed.

		OWCTY	EL	BCZ	SOG	SLAP	SLAP-FST
empty	Fast	118 (3%)	189 (5%)	53 (1%)	595 (18%)	1359 (42%)	1811 (56%)
(3227 cases)	Slow	259 (8%)	271 (8%)	2909 (90%)	509 (15%)	245 (7%)	93 (2%)
	Fail	220 (6%)	252 (7%)	1785 (55%)	301 (9%)	212 (6%)	86 (2%)
non empty	Fast	3 (0%)	10 (0%)	209 (5%)	782 (19%)	2510 (62%)	1406 (34%)
(4046 cases)	Slow	1869 (46%)	1390 (34%)	1940 (47%)	315 (7%)	70 (1%)	40 (0%)
	Fail	803 (19%)	817 (20%)	1069 (26%)	262 (6%)	69 (1%)	33 (0%)

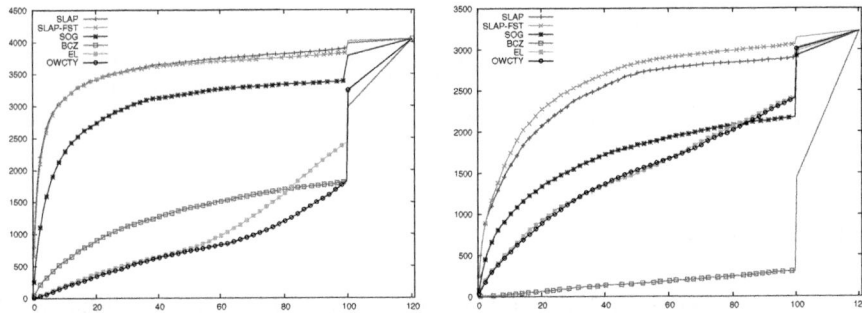

Fig. 3. Cumulative plots comparing the time of all methods. Non-empty products are shown on the left, and empty products on the right.

Table 1 presents only the best and the worst methods. While Fig. 3 allows to compare the different methods in a finer manner.

For each experiment (model/formula pair) we first collect the maximum time reached by a technique that did not fail, then compute for the other approaches what percentage of this maximum was used. The vertical segments visible at 100% thus show the number of runs for which this technique was the worst of those that did not fail. Any failures are plotted arbitrarily at 120%. This gives us a set of values between 0% and 120% for which we plot the cumulative distribution function. For instance, if a curve goes through the (20%,2000) point, it means that for this technique, 2000 experiments took at most 20% of the time taken by the worst technique for the same experiments.

The behavior at 120% represents the "Fail" line of previous table, while the behavior at 100% represents the difference between the "Slow" and "Fail" lines ("Slow" methods include methods that failed).

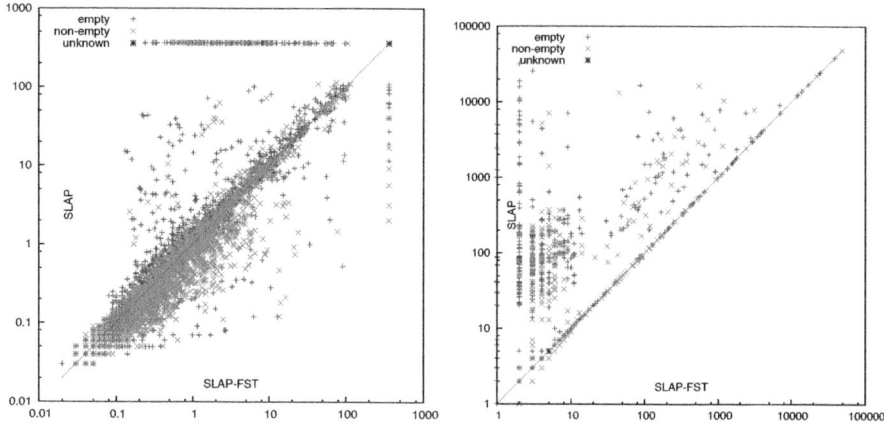

Fig. 4. Comparison of SLAP-FST against SLAP. Left: time; Right: product size.

The left plot for the non-empty cases shows that the on-the-fly mechanism allows all hybrid algorithms (SLAP, SLAP-FST, SOG, BCZ) to outperform the symbolic ones (OWCTY, EL). However as seen previously, BCZ still fails more often than other methods. The SLAP and SLAP-FST method take less than 10% of the time of the slowest method in 80% of the cases.

The right plot for the empty cases shows that fully symbolic algorithm behave relatively far better (all methods have to explore the full product anyway). BCZ spends too much time exploring enormous products, and timeouts.

SLAP-FST and SLAP have similar performance, with a slight edge for SLAP-FST when the product is empty.

EL appears slightly superior to OWCTY in the non-empty case, while they have similar performances in the empty case.

SOG shows good results when there is a counterexample, and it performs better than BCZ in most cases. However SOG only supports stuttering-invariant properties.

To study the differences between SLAP and SLAP-FST consider the scatter plots from Fig. 4. The performances are presented using a logarithmic scale. Each point represents an experiment, i.e., a model and formula pair. We plot experiments that failed (due to timeout) as if they had taken 360 seconds, so they are clearly separated from experiments that didn't fail (by the wide white band).

SLAP is on the average faster (and consume less memory [6]) than SLAP-FST, but fails more often. Indeed the explicit product size of SLAP-FST is always smaller than that of SLAP, and often by several orders of magnitude. In some cases the SLAP degenerates to a state-space proportional to size of the explicit product while the SLAP-FST is able to keep the symbolic advantage.

In Fig. 5 we compare SLAP-FST to the four other methods from the literature, using the same kind of logarithmic scatter plots in time. Unsurprisingly, the only method that appears competitive is SOG; but to our advantage, SOG is not able to handle non stuttering-invariant properties.

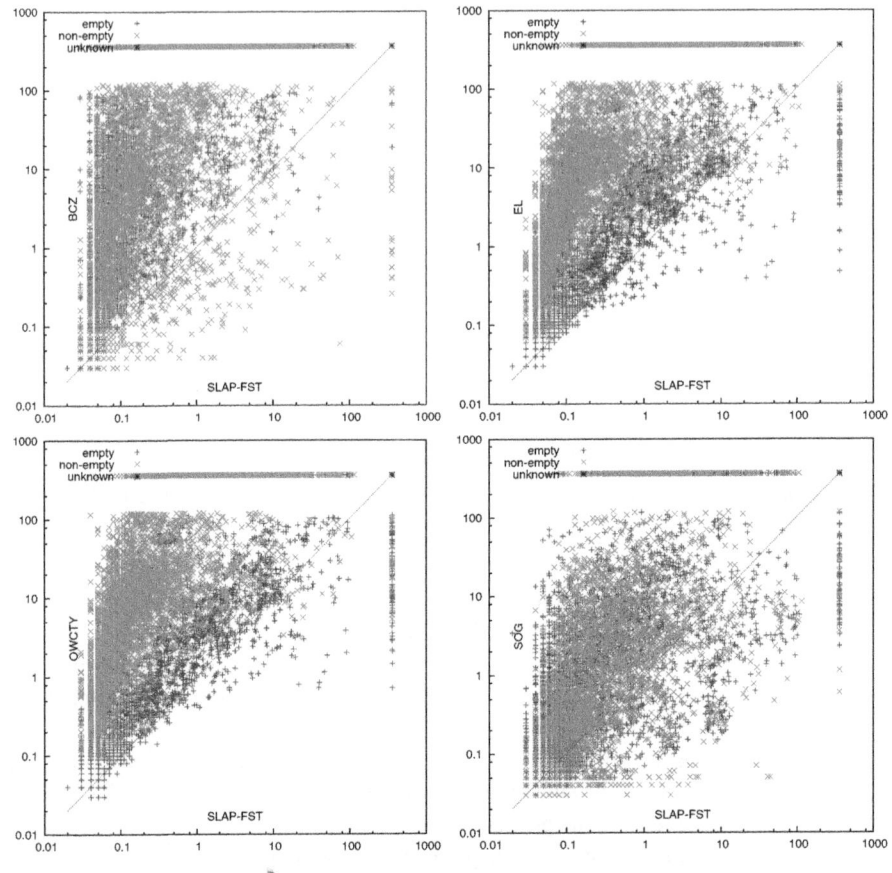

Fig. 5. Comparison of SLAP-FST against the four other methods

5 Conclusion and Perspectives

We have presented a new hybrid technique, the *Self-Loop Aggregation Product*, that exploits the self-loops of the property automaton even if it does not express a stuttering formula.

During our evaluation, we have found that SLAP (and especially its variant SLAP-FST) significantly outperforms the other hybrid and symbolic methods we implemented. In presence of a counterexample we can benefit from the on-the-fly mechanism, while purely symbolic methods like EL and OWCTY cannot. On empty products, the SLAP-FST has a small explicit size, allowing to outperform other hybrid algorithms.

This work opens several perspectives.

It would be interesting to compare our approach to the property-driven partitioning [17] even if this hybrid algorithm uses a fully symbolic emptiness check and is not based on an aggregation criterion.

Another class of methods we would like to compare against, are purely explicit ones, in particular those based on partial order reductions.

The SLAP technique replaces the product used in the traditional automata-theoretic approach to model-checking in order to reduce the product graph while preserving the result of the emptiness-check.

We also used this idea to improve the SOG, by working at the product-level and reducing the set of observed propositions according to the current state of the TGBA. This technique called Symbolic Observation Product (SOP) is described in our technical report [6].

Another idea would be to take advantage of the inclusion between the aggregates to detect cycles earlier. This would require a dedicated emptiness check such as those proposed by Baarir and Duret-Lutz [1].

Finally, since the SOG is a Kripke structure, and the SLAP is built upon a KS, it is possible to construct the SLAP of SOG. This is something we did not implement due to technical issues: in this case the aggregates are sets of sets of states.

References

1. Baarir, S., Duret-Lutz, A.: Emptiness check of powerset Büchi automata. In: Proc. of ACSD 2007, pp. 41–50. IEEE Computer Society, Los Alamitos (2007)
2. Biere, A., Clarke, E.M., Zhu, Y.: Multiple state and single state tableaux for combining local and global model checking. In: Olderog, E.-R., Steffen, B. (eds.) CSD 1999. LNCS, vol. 1710, pp. 163–179. Springer, Heidelberg (1999)
3. Ciardo, G., Marmorstein, R., Siminiceanu, R.: Saturation unbound. In: Garavel, H., Hatcliff, J. (eds.) TACAS 2003. LNCS, vol. 2619, pp. 379–393. Springer, Heidelberg (2003)
4. Courcoubetis, C., Vardi, M.Y., Wolper, P., Yannakakis, M.: Memory-efficient algorithm for the verification of temporal properties. In: Clarke, E., Kurshan, R.P. (eds.) CAV 1990. LNCS, vol. 531, pp. 233–242. Springer, Heidelberg (1991)
5. Couvreur, J.-M., Duret-Lutz, A., Poitrenaud, D.: On-the-fly emptiness checks for generalized büchi automata. In: Godefroid, P. (ed.) SPIN 2005. LNCS, vol. 3639, pp. 169–184. Springer, Heidelberg (2005)
6. Duret-Lutz, A., Klai, K., Poitrenaud, D., Thierry-Mieg, Y.: Combining explicit and symbolic approaches for better on-the-fly LTL model checking. Technical Report 1106.5700, arXiv (June 2011); Extended version of the present paper, presenting two new techniques instead of one, http://arxiv.org/abs/1106.5700
7. Duret-Lutz, A., Poitrenaud, D.: Spot: an extensible model checking library using transition-based generalized Büchi automata. In: Proc. of MASCOTS 2004, pp. 76–83. IEEE Computer Society Press, Los Alamitos (2004)
8. Etessami, K.: Stutter-invariant languages, ω-automata, and temporal logic. In: Halbwachs, N., Peled, D.A. (eds.) CAV 1999. LNCS, vol. 1633, pp. 236–248. Springer, Heidelberg (1999)
9. Fisler, K., Fraer, R., Kamhi, G., Vardi, M.Y., Yang, Z.: Is there a best symbolic cycle-detection algorithm? In: Margaria, T., Yi, W. (eds.) TACAS 2001. LNCS, vol. 2031, pp. 420–434. Springer, Heidelberg (2001)
10. Haddad, S., Ilié, J.-M., Klai, K.: Design and evaluation of a symbolic and abstraction-based model checker. In: Wang, F. (ed.) ATVA 2004. LNCS, vol. 3299, pp. 196–210. Springer, Heidelberg (2004)

11. Hamez, A., Thierry-Mieg, Y., Kordon, F.: Hierarchical set decision diagrams and automatic saturation. In: van Hee, K.M., Valk, R. (eds.) PETRI NETS 2008. LNCS, vol. 5062, pp. 211–230. Springer, Heidelberg (2008)

12. Hansen, H., Penczek, W., Valmari, A.: Stuttering-insensitive automata for on-the-fly detection of livelock properties. In: Proc. of FMICS 2002. Electronic Notes in Theoretical Computer Science, vol. 66(2). Elsevier, Amsterdam (2002)

13. Kaivola, R., Valmari, A.: The weakest compositional semantic equivalence preserving nexttime-less linear temporal logic. In: Cleaveland, W.R. (ed.) CONCUR 1992. LNCS, vol. 630, pp. 207–221. Springer, Heidelberg (1992)

14. Kesten, Y., Pnueli, A., Raviv, L.-o.: Algorithmic verification of linear temporal logic specifications. In: Larsen, K.G., Skyum, S., Winskel, G. (eds.) ICALP 1998. LNCS, vol. 1443, pp. 1–16. Springer, Heidelberg (1998)

15. Klai, K., Poitrenaud, D.: MC-SOG: An LTL model checker based on symbolic observation graphs. In: van Hee, K.M., Valk, R. (eds.) PETRI NETS 2008. LNCS, vol. 5062, pp. 288–306. Springer, Heidelberg (2008)

16. Rozier, K.Y., Vardi, M.Y.: LTL satisfiability checking. In: Bošnački, D., Edelkamp, S. (eds.) SPIN 2007. LNCS, vol. 4595, pp. 149–167. Springer, Heidelberg (2007)

17. Sebastiani, R., Tonetta, S., Vardi, M.Y.: Symbolic systems, explicit properties: On hybrid approaches for LTL symbolic model checking. In: Etessami, K., Rajamani, S.K. (eds.) CAV 2005. LNCS, vol. 3576, pp. 350–363. Springer, Heidelberg (2005)

18. Somenzi, F., Ravi, K., Bloem, R.: Analysis of symbolic SCC hull algorithms. In: Aagaard, M.D., O'Leary, J.W. (eds.) FMCAD 2002. LNCS, vol. 2517, pp. 88–105. Springer, Heidelberg (2002)

19. Thierry-Mieg, Y., Poitrenaud, D., Hamez, A., Kordon, F.: Hierarchical set decision diagrams and regular models. In: Kowalewski, S., Philippou, A. (eds.) TACAS 2009. LNCS, vol. 5505, pp. 1–15. Springer, Heidelberg (2009)

20. Vardi, M.Y.: An automata-theoretic approach to linear temporal logic. In: Moller, F., Birtwistle, G. (eds.) Logics for Concurrency. LNCS, vol. 1043, pp. 238–266. Springer, Heidelberg (1996)

A Lightweight Approach for Loop Summarization

Mohamed Nassim Seghir

University of Oxford, Computer Science Department

Abstract. A problem common to most of the tools based on the abstraction refinement paradigm is the divergence of the CEGAR process. In particular, infinitely many (spurious) counterexamples may arise from unfolding the same (while- or for-) loop in the given program again and again; this leads to an infinite or at least too large sequence of refinement steps. Loop summarization is an approach that permits to overcome this problem. It consists of abstracting not just states but also the state changes (transition relation) induced by structured program statements. The effectiveness of this approach depends on two factors: (*a*) the computation of loop summaries must not be the bottleneck of the verification algorithm (*b*) loop summaries must be precise enough to prove the property of interest. We present a technique that permits to achieve both goals. It uses inference rules to compute summaries. A lightweight test is performed to check whether a given loop matches the premise of a given rule. If so, a summary is automatically inferred by instantiating the rule. Despite its simplicity, our technique performs well in practice. We were able to verify safety properties for many examples which are out of the scope of several existing tools.

1 Introduction

Software model checking is a popular approach for program verification. Many tools based on this approach have been developed (e.g. SLAM [1], BLAST [12], MAGIC [2] and TERMINATOR [5]) and successfully applied to real world software. Abstraction is the key to the effectiveness of software model checking. All these tools combine the predicate abstraction technique [11] with the counterexample guided abstraction refinement paradigm [3], commonly known as CEGAR, to efficiently abstract programs. A problem common to most of the tools based on the abstraction refinement paradigm is the divergence of the CEGAR process. In particular, infinitely many (spurious) counterexamples may arise from unfolding the same (while- or for-) loop in the given program again and again; this leads to an infinite or at least too large sequence of refinement steps. The divergence of the abstraction refinement loop is not just a theoretical problem but one that hits us in our practical use of software model checking. We present a solution to this problem based on the idea of abstracting not just states but also the state changes induced by structured program statements, including for- and while-statements. We propose a lightweight mechanism, based

T. Bultan and P.-A. Hsiung (Eds.): ATVA 2011, LNCS 6996, pp. 351–365, 2011.

```
 1  main(){                          1  main(){
 2                                    2
 3    char x[101], y[101], z[201];    3    char x[101], y[101], z[201];
 4    int i,j;                        4    int i,j;
 5                                     5
 6    i = 0;                          6    i = 0;
 7    while(x[i] != 0){               7    while(x[i] != 0){
 8      z[i] = x[i];                  8      z[i] = x[i];
 9      i++;                          9      i++;
10    }                             10    }
11    /* length of x is less than 100 */   11    /* length of x is less than 100 */
12    assume(i < 100);              12    assume(i < 100);
13                                   13
14    j = 0;                        14    j = 0;
15    while(y[j] != 0){             15    if(y[j] != 0){
16      z[i] = y[j];                16      assume((j_1 − j)==(i_1 − i));
17      i++;                        17      i = i_1;
18      j++;                        18      j = j_1;
19    }                             19      z = z_1;
20    /* length of y is less than 100 */   20    }
21    assume(j < 100);              21    /* length of y is less than 100 */
22                                   22    assume(j < 100);
23    z[i] = 0;                     23
24    /* prove we don't overflow z */   24    z[i] = 0;
25    if(i >= 200)                  25    /* prove we don't overflow z */
26      {ERROR: goto ERROR;}        26    if(i >= 200)
27  }                               27      {ERROR: goto ERROR;}
                                    28  }

              (a)                                  (b)
```

Fig. 1. Example in C code before and after transformation

on a set of inference rules, for generating loop summaries. A correspondence test is performed to check whether a given loop matches the premise of a given rule. If so, a summary is automatically inferred by instantiating the rule without having to perform any fixpoint computation. Another advantage of our method is its generic implementation scheme which is based on a source-to-source transformation. Thus, our approach can be seamlessly integrated into other software verification tools as black-box.

Let us consider the program in Figure 1(a) which is taken from the list of benchmarks that were used by McMillan and Jhala in [14]. This program performs the concatenation of two strings. The key word assume is used to communicate additional assumptions to the model checker. When applied to the example of Figure 1(a), a classical refinement, based on weakest precondition, unrolls the loop (15, 16, 17, 18, 19, 15) as many times as the number of loop iterations in a real execution. This leads to the generation of predicates $i \geq 200, j < 100, i+1 \geq 200, j+1 < 100, i+2 \geq 200, j+2 < 100 \ldots i+99 \geq 200, j+99 < 100$. Moreover, if we want to verify a generic version of the example (with arbitrary string length), by substituting $size$ for 100 at lines 12 and 21, and $size * 2$ for

200 at line 25, the refinement process completely diverges. This problem is inherent to the CEGAR scheme in its present form (based on state abstraction), where each transition in the concrete system corresponds to one transition in the abstract system. As the refinement fails to find an adequate loop invariant, the execution of loop (15, 16, 17, 18, 19, 15) is simulated in the abstract system by unfolding it over and over again. For this example, neither the interpolation approach nor the split prover method seem to help [14][1]. As alternative to the iterative unfolding of loops, we propose an approach based on the abstraction of state changes (transition relation) induced by loop execution.

Cycle detection. The first step of our method is the extraction of transition constraints that form the cycle (15, 16, 17, 18, 19, 15). In our case, the cycle is constituted of one transition constraint which is[2]

$$pc = 15 \wedge y(j) \neq 0 \wedge z' = z[i := y(j)] \wedge i' = i + 1 \wedge j' = j + 1 \wedge pc' = 15. \quad (1)$$

Cycle abstraction. Constraints expressing relationships over program variables that are modified within the cycle are extracted. For example, the formula $i' - i = j' - j$ is extracted as both variables i and j increase by the same constant amount. Also, constraint $z' \neq z$ is introduced to express that array z is modified. We obtain transition constraint (1').

$$pc = 15 \wedge i' - i = j' - j \wedge z' \neq z \wedge pc' = 15. \quad (1')$$

Finally, transition constraint (1) in the program is replaced by its abstraction (1'). In the verification phase we monitor paths by disallowing transition (1') to be successively taken more than once as it already overapproximates the effect of unfolding cycle (15, 16, 17, 18, 19, 15) an arbitrary number of times.

Source-to-source transformation. To express the abstraction of a cycle in terms of source-to-source transformation, we write the transition constraint as a program expression (using an *uninitialized* auxiliary variable x_1 for the primed version of the variable x) and use the program expression in an assume statement and then add assignment statements of the form x = x_1, see Figure 1(b). The cycle (15, 16, 17, 18, 19, 15) is replaced by an 'if' block which models the unrolling of the cycle an arbitrary number of times. Our tool succeeds to prove that the code resulting from the transformation (Figure 1(b)) is safe.

The reminder of this paper is organized as follows: section 2 introduces inference rules for generating summaries. Section 3 presents our program transformation algorithm to integrate summaries into the target program. Section 4 illustrates our new CEGAR algorithm which is extended with the loop summarization phase. Section 5 presents results obtained with our implementation. Section 6 compares our technique with similar work in the literature. Finally, section 7 concludes the paper.

---

[1] According to experiments performed by author.

[2] In a transition constraint, an array a is represented by an uninterpreted function symbol. The notation $a[x := e]$ stands for a function update.

2   Inferring Summary Constraints

We consider three examples that illustrate divergence patterns observed in our experiments. Based on these observations, we specify function Infer which computes summaries. Function Infer is based on other functions: EXT, INT, QR and QW. We specify each of these functions along this section in terms of inference rules. With each function we associate an inference rule that describes the function outcome depending on the cycle $\mathcal{C}$ taken as argument by the function. Let us first introduce some preliminary material.

Program. For the purpose of the formal presentation, we assume that a program comes as a set $\mathcal{TC}$ of transition constraints. A transition constraint τ is a formula of the form

$$\tau \equiv g(X) \wedge x_1' = e_1(X) \wedge \ldots \wedge x_n' = e_n(X) \tag{1}$$

where $X = \langle x_1, \ldots, x_n \rangle$ is a tuple (vector) of program variables including the program counter pc. In (1) unprimed variables refer to the program state before performing the transition and primed ones represent the program state after performing the transition. Formula $g(X)$ is called the guard and the remaining part of τ is the update or assignment.

Composition of Transition Constraints. Given two transition constraints $\tau_1(X, X')$ and $\tau_2(X, X')$, their composition is defined as

$$\tau_1 \circ \tau_2 \equiv g_1(X) \wedge \tau_2[\langle e_1(X), \ldots, e_n(X) \rangle / X]. \tag{2}$$

Definition 1. *A cycle $\mathcal{C}$ is a sequence of transition constraints $\tau_1, \ldots, \tau_k$ such that $\forall i \in [1..k-1]$. $\tau_i.pc' = \tau_{i+1}.pc$[3] and $\tau_1.pc = \tau_k.pc'$. A program loop consists of at least one cycle.*

Definition 2. *Given a cycle $\mathcal{C} = \tau_1; \ldots; \tau_k$ ($\tau_1.pc = \tau_k.pc'$), we call* main location *of $\mathcal{C}$ the value of $\tau_1.pc$ ($\tau_k.pc'$) that we denote by $\mathcal{C}_m$. I.e., it represents the location where the cycle $\mathcal{C}$ begins and where it ends.*

2.1   Cycle Exit Information

If g is the condition of a given loop and $X := E$ corresponds to variable updates within the loop (X is the tuple of variables) then we have

- the negation of the loop condition holds after exiting the loop: $\neg g[X'/X]$.
- before the last iteration, the loop condition holds: $g[X''/X] \wedge X' = E[X''/X]$ (X'' is fresh)

---

[3] The notation '.' is used for field access, $\tau.pc$ refers to the value of the program counter at the pre-state of transition τ.

Function EXT infers such information, it is specified by rule EXIT below.

$$\frac{\mathcal{C} = (g(X) \wedge X' = E(X) \wedge pc = \mathcal{C}_m \wedge pc' = \mathcal{C}_m)}{\mathsf{EXT}(\mathcal{C}) \equiv (\neg g[X'/X] \wedge g[X''/X] \wedge X' = E[X''/X])} \; \Gamma \; (\text{EXIT})$$

$$\Gamma : X'' \text{is fresh}$$

In rule EXIT, Γ represents a side condition.

Remark 1. When we write cycle $\mathcal{C}$ in a logical formula as in the rule EXIT, we mean the transition resulting from the composition of transitions forming $\mathcal{C}$.

The intuition behind the application of rule EXIT is that in some cases information about the state following loop execution is sufficient to prove the specified assertion, without having to consider intermediary computations (states) leading to that state.

2.2 Inter Variable Relations

We want to keep track of relations correlating program variables. We restrict our study to relations over variables which are incremented (decremented) with constant numbers. I.e., assignments of the form $x := x + c$ (c is a constant). Function INT infers such formulas, it is specified below via rule INTER.

$$\frac{\mathcal{C} \Rightarrow (x_1' = x_1 + c_1 \wedge x_2' = x_2 + c_2 \wedge \dots \wedge x_k' = x_k + c_k)}{\mathsf{INT}(\mathcal{C}) \equiv ((x_1' - x_1) * c_2 = (x_2' - x_2) * c_1 \wedge \dots \wedge (x_1' - x_1) * c_k = (x_k' - x_k) * c_1)} \quad (\text{INTER})$$

As the rule INTER shows, we do not have to consider all combinations of two variables, it is sufficient to combine one variable (e.g., x_1) with all remaining variables. Although the relation between variables x_2 and x_k does not syntactically appear in the result, it is implicitly represented. One can easily check that the result of function INT implies $(x_2' - x_2) * c_k = (x_k' - x_k) * c_2$.

Applying rule INTER to the example of Figure 1(a), we infer formula $i' - i = j' - j$. In terms of source-to-source transformation, the computed summary is illustrated in Figure 1(b). Despite restrictions on the form of assignments, our method performs well in practice. In fact, loops are often composed of assignments of the form $x := x + c$. However, more general relationships over program variables can be inferred using sophisticated techniques such as Karr's analysis [15] [18] or template-based techniques [20].

2.3 Quantified Array Formulas

We noticed from our observations that aggregate data types such as arrays are often a cause for CEGAR divergence. Thus, we want summaries to carry information about collections of array elements.

Definition 3. *Given a counter i for a cycle $\mathcal{C}$, i.e., $\mathcal{C} \Rightarrow i' = i + 1$ ($i' = i - 1$), the parameterization of $\mathcal{C}$ through i that we denote $\mathcal{C}_i$ is the cycle obtained as follows:*

- *rewrite all integer variables appearing in guards in C in terms of i*
- *if the left side expression of an assignment (update) is an array expression then rewrite all integer variables in both the left and right side of the assignment in terms of i*

The parameterization of a formula (expression) φ is denoted by φ_i which contains i as unique integer variable. For the formula resulting from the substitution $\varphi_i[x/i]$ we simply write φ_x. For an array expression $a[i]$, i is called the index expression and a the array name. Given a formula (expression) φ, function $\mathsf{Array}(\varphi)$ returns the set of array names contained in φ, function $\mathsf{Index}(\varphi)$ returns the set of index expressions in φ and function $\mathsf{Ids}(\varphi)$ returns the set of identifiers (variable names not including arrays) in φ.

Proposition 1. *Given a cycle C and a counter i for C, if all updates in C are restricted to the form $x := x + c$ (c is a constant) then there exists a parameterization C_i for C, where each variable is represented by a linear expression that exclusively involves variable i.*

Proof. (Proposition 1) An extended version of the paper containing the proof is available from author upon request.

Read-once formulas. We propose function QR to infer universally quantified array formulas based on expressions that appear in the guard of cycle C. Function QR is specified by rule QUANT-READ below.

$$\frac{C_i \Rightarrow (\varphi_i \wedge i' = i + 1 \wedge (\bigwedge_{a \in \mathsf{Array}(\varphi_i)} a' = a))}{\mathsf{QR}(C) \equiv ((\forall x.\, i \le x < i' \Rightarrow \varphi_x) \wedge (\bigwedge_{a \in \mathsf{Array}(\varphi_i)} a' = a))} \; \Gamma \; \text{(QUANT-READ)}$$

$$\Gamma \equiv \exists e \in \mathsf{Index}(\varphi_i).\, i \in \mathsf{Ids}(e)$$

Rule QUANT-READ simply says: if φ_i holds at each loop (cycle) iteration, and all arrays appearing in φ_i are not affected by assignments in the cycle, then φ_i holds on the whole interval in which i ranges during cycle execution. The side condition Γ imposes that φ_i contains at least one index expression that refers to i, otherwise the rule does not make sense.

Write-once formulas. The rule QUANT-WRITE specifies the function QW which uses information regarding array updates in the cycle to infer quantified formulas.

$$\frac{C_i \Rightarrow ((i' = i + 1 \wedge b' = b[d_i := e_i] \wedge (\bigwedge_{a \in \mathsf{Array}(e_i)} a' = a))}{\begin{array}{c} \mathsf{QW}(C, b) \equiv ((\forall x.\, (x \in [i, i'[\Rightarrow (b'(d_x) = e_x)) \\ \wedge(x \notin [i, i'[\Rightarrow (b'(d_x) = b(d_x)))) \wedge (\bigwedge_{a \in \mathsf{Array}(e_i)} a' = a)) \end{array}} \; \Gamma \; \text{(QUANT-WRITE)}$$

$$\Gamma \equiv i \in \mathsf{Ids}(d_i)$$

As the rule QUANT-WRITE shows, function QW takes two arguments, the cycle $\mathcal{C}$ and an array b. The side condition Γ indicates that i must occur in the index expression d_i, otherwise the rule does not make sense. We can define another version of QW which only takes the cycle $\mathcal{C}$ as parameter as follows

$$\mathsf{QW}(\mathcal{C}) \equiv \bigwedge_{b \in \mathsf{Array}(\mathcal{C})} \mathsf{QW}(\mathcal{C}, b).$$

The rule QUANT-WRITE stipulates that having an assignment to an array element of the form $b[d_i] := e_i$, if b is exclusively modified through that assignment and if no array expression in e_i is modified then, after the loop execution, the equality $b[d_i] = e_i$ holds on the whole interval in which i ranges.

Proposition 2. *The transition resulting from unfolding a cycle $\mathcal{C}$ an arbitrary number n ($n > 0$) of times is overapproximated by $\mathsf{QR}(\mathcal{C})$ and $\mathsf{QW}(\mathcal{C}, b)$ (i.e., $\mathsf{QW}(\mathcal{C})$). Formally, we have*

$$\mathcal{C}^{\langle n \rangle} \Rightarrow \mathsf{QR}(\mathcal{C})$$

and

$$\mathcal{C}^{\langle n \rangle} \Rightarrow \mathsf{QW}(\mathcal{C}, b) \quad thus \quad \mathcal{C}^{\langle n \rangle} \Rightarrow \mathsf{QW}(\mathcal{C})$$

Proof. (Proposition 2) Available from author upon request.

2.4   Function Infer

Before defining function Infer let us mention that each of the functions EXT, INT, QR and QW returns true if the premise of the associated rule is not valid. Function Infer is simply defined as

$$\mathsf{Infer}(\mathcal{C}) \overset{\text{def}}{=} pc = \mathcal{C}_m \wedge \mathsf{EXT}(\mathcal{C}) \wedge \mathsf{INT}(\mathcal{C}) \wedge \mathsf{QR}(\mathcal{C}) \wedge \mathsf{QW}(\mathcal{C}) \wedge pc' = \mathcal{C}_m$$

From the definition, it is clear that Infer soundly overapproximates $\mathcal{C}^{\langle n \rangle}$ for an arbitrary n ($n > 0$) as each of its components (EXT, INT, QR and QW) is an overapproximation of $\mathcal{C}^{\langle n \rangle}$.

3   Cycle Elimination

To apply loop summarization (abstraction) on demand, we must be able to detect situations where the refinement process is diverging. Based on the observation that divergence of the refinement is due to the presence of a cycle which is unfolded again and again, we propose a simple heuristic to detect potential divergence situations.

3.1   Divergence (Cycle) Detection

Given a trace $\pi = \tau_1; \tau_2; \ldots; \tau_{k-1}; \tau_k$, the *location projection* π_ℓ corresponding to π is the sequence of program locations traversed by the trace, i.e., $\pi_\ell = \tau_1.pc, \tau_1.pc', \tau_2.pc', \ldots, \tau_{k-1}.pc', \tau_k.pc'$.

Our cycle detection approach works as follows: given a trace π, we check whether it contains a cycle which is repeated k times such that k is given as parameter. We are interested in simple cycles $\mathcal{C}$ that do not contain other cycles, i.e., if $\mathcal{C}'$ is a cycle included in $\mathcal{C}$ then $\mathcal{C} = \mathcal{C}'$. The cycle detection algorithm DetectCycle takes as argument a trace π and a natural number k. As output it returns a cycle $\mathcal{C}$ if $\mathcal{C}^{\langle k \rangle}$ is a subtrace of π, otherwise the empty trace is returned. The notation $\mathcal{C}^{\langle k \rangle}$ means k times unfolding of cycle $\mathcal{C}$.

3.2   Cycle Replacement

We propose a program transformation that replaces a cycle $\mathcal{C}$ with a set of transition constraints $S_{\mathcal{C}}$ namely the summary. In program $\mathcal{TC}$, the set of *entry transitions* with respect to a cycle $\mathcal{C}$, denoted by $\mathcal{C}_e$, is the set of transition constraints whose pre-state pc value does not belong to cycle $\mathcal{C}$ and whose post-state pc value belongs to $\mathcal{C}$. Formally, we have

$$\mathcal{C}_e = \{\tau \mid \tau \in \mathcal{TC} \wedge \tau \notin \mathcal{C} \wedge \exists \tau' \in \mathcal{C}. \, \tau.pc' = \tau'.pc\}.$$

Similarly, the set of *exit transitions* is denoted by $\mathcal{C}_x$ and defined as

$$\mathcal{C}_x = \{\tau \mid \tau \in \mathcal{TC} \wedge \tau \notin \mathcal{C} \wedge \exists \tau' \in \mathcal{C}. \, \tau.pc = \tau'.pc\}.$$

Algorithm ReplaceCycle (Algorithm 1) takes a cycle $\mathcal{C}$ and a program $\mathcal{TC}$ (set of transition constraints) as arguments and returns a program $\mathcal{TC}'$. The resulting program $\mathcal{TC}'$ is free of transitions forming the cycle $\mathcal{C}$; instead it contains the summary $S_{\mathcal{C}}$ of cycle $\mathcal{C}$. This program transformation is conservative with respect to reachability. Formally speaking

$$\forall \ell, \ell'. \, (REACH(\ell, \ell', \mathcal{TC}) \wedge \ell, \ell' \notin \mathcal{C}_\ell) \Rightarrow REACH(\ell, \ell', \mathcal{TC}') \qquad (3)$$

such that $REACH(\ell, \ell', \mathcal{TC})$ is a predicate expressing that location ℓ' is reachable from location ℓ in the program $\mathcal{TC}$. The symbol $\mathcal{C}_\ell$ denotes the projection of cycle $\mathcal{C}$ on locations that it traverses. A sketch for proving (3) is provided in an extended version of this papers which can be obtained from author upon request.

In our study, we focus on cycles having a single entry point ($\mathcal{C}_m$), this is expressed by the test at line 5 of Algorithm 1. In general, most of the loops encountered in practice have one entry point.

Algorithm 1 calls functions Compose and SubTrace. Function Compose takes a trace $\pi = \tau_1; \ldots; \tau_n$ as argument and returns the transition resulting from the composition of transitions forming π, i.e., $\text{Compose}(\tau_1; \ldots; \tau_n) = \tau_1 \circ \ldots \circ \tau_n$.

Procedure SubTrace takes as parameters a trace π and two transition constraints τ and τ'. It returns the subtrace of π that has τ as initial transition and τ' as final transition. If π does not contain such a trace then empty_trace is returned.

Algorithm 1. ReplaceCycle

Input: set of transition constraints (program) TC, cycle C
Output: set of transition constraints (program)

1 **Var** S: set of transition constraints;
2 **if** $C_e \cap C_x \neq \emptyset$ **then**
3 | **return** TC;
4 **end**
5 **if** $\exists. \tau \in C_e \wedge \tau.pc' \neq C_m$ **then**
6 | **return** TC;
7 **end**
8 **foreach** $\tau \in C_x$ **do**
9 | **if** $\tau.pc \neq C_m$ **then**
10 | | Let $\tau' \in C$ s.t. $\tau'.pc = C_m$;
11 | | Let $\tau'' \in C$ s.t. $\tau''.pc' = \tau.pc$;
12 | | $\pi := \mathsf{SubTrace}(C, \tau', \tau'')$;
13 | | $\tau' := \mathsf{Compose}(\pi)$;
14 | | $\tau' := \mathsf{Compose}(\tau', \tau)$;
15 | | $S := S \cup \{\tau'\}$;
16 | **end**
17 **end**
18 $S := S \cup \{\mathsf{Infer}(C)\}$;
19 Let $S' = \{\tau \mid \tau \in C\}$;
20 $S := (TC - S') \cup S$;
21 **return** S;

---

4   Extended CEGAR

First, we introduce the main ingredients and concepts on which the CEGAR algorithm is based, then we present the CEGAR algorithm extended with loop summarization.

State symbolic representation. A set of (or single) program states is symbolically represented by a formula φ over program variables.

State transformer. For a formula φ, the application of the operator pre with respect to the transition constraint τ returns a formula representing the set of all predecessor states of φ under the transition constraint τ, formally

$$\mathsf{pre}(\tau, \varphi(X)) \equiv g(X) \wedge \varphi[\langle e_1(X), \dots, e_n(X)\rangle / X].$$

The state transformer pre with respect to the whole program is given by

$$\mathsf{pre}(\varphi(X)) \equiv \bigvee_{\tau \in TC} \mathsf{pre}(\tau, \varphi(X)).$$

For a trace $\pi = \tau_1; \dots; \tau_n$ we have

$$\mathsf{pre}(\tau_1; \tau_2; \dots; \tau_n, \varphi) = \mathsf{pre}(\tau_1, \dots \mathsf{pre}(\tau_{n-1}, \mathsf{pre}(\tau_n, \varphi))).$$

If $\mathsf{pre}(\pi, \varphi)$ is not equal to false then the trace π is feasible and φ is satisfiable after the execution of π.

Program correctness. In order to specify correctness, we fix formulas nonInit and unsafe denoting the complement of the set of *initial* and *safe* states, respectively. We define the given program to be *correct* if no unsafe state is reachable from an initial state. This can be proven by showing the condition below. Here, lfp(pre, φ) stands for the least fixpoint of the operator pre above φ.

$$\mathsf{lfp}(\mathsf{pre}, \mathsf{unsafe}) \leq \mathsf{nonInit}$$

If the least fixpoint is disjoint from the set of initial states then it represents an *inductive backward safe invariant* that we denote by ψ. This is an invariant which is *inductive* under pre and implies nonInit, i.e.,

- unsafe $\leq \psi$ ($\varphi \leq \varphi'$ means $\varphi \Rightarrow \varphi'$),
- $\mathsf{pre}(\psi) \leq \psi$,
- $\psi \leq \mathsf{nonInit}$.

Predicate abstraction. As the domain of formulas is not finite, there is no guarantee for computing an inductive backward invariant. Predicate abstraction permits to approximate a state φ with a formula φ' built up from a finite set P of base predicates. As the set of predicates is finite we obtain a finite domain of formulas. Thus, if an inductive invariant is expressible via the set of base predicates, we can compute it. Given a formula φ, its abstraction is obtained via the function α as follows

$$\alpha(\varphi) \equiv \bigwedge p \quad | \quad p \in P \wedge \varphi \Rightarrow p.$$

The abstract domain of states (formulas) is not closed under the pre operator. Thus, we define $\mathsf{pre}^\sharp$ the abstract version of pre under which the domain is closed

$$\mathsf{pre}^\sharp(\tau, \varphi) = \alpha(\mathsf{pre}(\tau, \varphi)) = \bigwedge p \quad | \quad p \in P \wedge \mathsf{pre}(\tau, \varphi) \Rightarrow p.$$

Let ψ denotes the fix point $\mathsf{lfp}(\mathsf{pre}^\sharp, \mathsf{unsafe})$ for operator $\mathsf{pre}^\sharp$ above unsafe. If ψ is disjoint from the set of initial states then it is an inductive backward safe invariant, as we have

- unsafe $\leq \psi$,
- $\mathsf{pre}^\sharp(\psi) \leq \psi$ implies $\mathsf{pre}(\psi) \leq \psi$ as $\mathsf{pre}(\psi) \leq \mathsf{pre}^\sharp(\psi)$,
- $\psi \leq \mathsf{nonInit}$.

4.1 Integrating Loop Summarization into CEGAR

Algorithm ExtendedCEGAR (Algorithm 2) illustrates our counterexample guided abstraction refinement method. It proceeds by iteratively building abstractions of increasing precision. If it computes an inductive invariant which is disjoint from the set of initial states (line 5 in the algorithm) then the system is proven to be safe. Otherwise a trace (counterexample) leading from an initial state to an error state exists. If the trace is real, i.e., feasible (test at line 10), then it is returned and the algorithm terminates, otherwise the trace is spurious. In this case we need to make the abstraction more precise, this is carried out by adding predicates needed to eliminate the spurious trace (line 19). The notation $\text{pre}^\sharp_P$ indicates that $\text{pre}^\sharp$ is computed with respect to the set of predicates P. It is easy to see that by adding predicates we increase the precision of $\text{pre}^\sharp$ as we have $P \subseteq P' \Rightarrow \text{pre}^\sharp_{P'} \leq \text{pre}^\sharp_P$. Phases that we have described so far are common to most of CEGAR-based tools. The specific part of our algorithm is the code portion from line 15 to line 18. Function DetectCycle, presented previously, is called to check whether the spurious counterexample contains a cycle which is repeated k times (k is a parameter), if so, the cycle is summarized by calling function ReplaceCycle (Algorithm 1). Note the flexibility of the integration of our approach. By removing the code fragment between lines 15 and 18, we obtain the classical CEGAR algorithm, and no further modifications are required.

Algorithm 2. ExtendedCEGAR

Input: set of transition constraints (program) $\mathcal{TC}$
1 **Var** P: set of predicates, ψ: formula, k: natural;
2 $P := \emptyset$;
3 **while** true **do**
4      $\psi := \text{lfp}(\text{pre}^\sharp_P, \text{error})$;
5   **if** $\psi \wedge \text{init} \equiv \text{false}$ **then**
6   print("system is safe");
7   exit;
8   **end**
9   Let π be a trace such that $\text{pre}^\sharp_P(\pi, \text{error}) \not\equiv \text{false}$;
10   **if** $\text{pre}(\pi, \text{error}) \not\equiv \text{false}$ **then**
11   print("counterexample found");
12   print(π);
13   exit;
14   **end**
15     $\mathcal{C} := \text{DetectCycle}(\pi, k)$;
16   **if** $\mathcal{C} \neq \text{empty\_trace}$ **then**
17         $\mathcal{TC} := \text{ReplaceCycle}(\mathcal{TC}, \mathcal{C})$;
18   **else**
19   find a set of predicates P' s.t. $\text{pre}^\sharp_{P'}(\pi, \text{error}) \equiv \text{false}$;
20         $P := P \cup P'$;
21   **end**
22 **end**

Discussion. The proposal of the previously seen rules is based on the observation of different divergence patterns. However, triggering a particular rule is not just syntactically based. This is expressed by having a logical implication in the premise of rules (except rule EXIT) rather than an equality. Regarding the cycle detection algorithm, we have seen that it handles simple cycles, this does not mean that our approach is not able to handle nested loops. In fact, all depends on the state exploration strategy, if the inner loop is treated (unfolded) first then the summarization is applied. However, if the outer loop is treated first then the summarization is not applied as the unfolded cycle is not a simple one. In the former case, as transition τ corresponding to the computed summary is in a loop, it can be applied several times and thus have several occurrences within a same trace. Let us assume that x is a variable that appears in the summary. We have seen (Figure 1) how the after-value corresponding to x can be modeled via a fresh variable x_1. If τ occurs several times within a trace, we use a new fresh variable x_i in each occurrence of τ as we have no guarantee that the after-value corresponding to x is the same for each application of the summary τ.

5 Experimental Evaluation

We implemented our cycle abstraction approach in the ACSAR software model checker [21]. We performed tests using an X41 Thinkpad laptop with 1 GB of RAM and a 1.6 GHz CPU, running Linux. ACSAR uses Yices [7] and Simplify [6] for computing the abstraction and analyzing spurious counterexamples. The communication with Yices is performed through its API Lite and it is performed through pipes with Simplify. The input to ACSAR is a C program annotated with assertions to be verified. The output is either an invariant that implies the correctness of the annotated program or a counterexample trace. One can also obtain the transformed part of the code (abstracted loop) in terms of transition constraints.

Results of our experiments are illustrated in Table 1. Column "Time" represents the verification time in seconds, considering the whole verification process (parsing, transition constraint generation, theorem prover requests, etc.). The column "#LS" contains the number of loops which were summarized in order to

Table 1. Experimental results obtained with ACSAR for the benchmarks used in [14]

Program	Time (s)	#LS	Rule
anubhav	0.32	1	INTER
array_init	0.79	0	–
copy1	0.84	0	–
cousot	0.85	2	EXIT + INTER
loop1	0.76	1	QUANT-WRITE
loop1-fixed	0.54	1	QUANT-WRITE
scan	0.19	0	–
simple	0.80	1	QUANT-READ
string_concat1	0.34	1	INTER
string_concat	5.15	2	INTER + QUANT-READ + QUANT-WRITE
string_copy	0.28	0	–
substring1	1.49	1	QUANT-READ
substring	0.40	0	–

verify the specified assertion. Column "Rule" represents the rule whose application is relevant to the verification of the target assertion. For cycle detection, we have set the number of successive cycles to 2. It means that if a cycle is unfolded successively twice by the refinement process, the loop summary procedure is applied.

The 13 examples presented in Table 1 were used by Jhala and McMillan in [14]. According to their report, apart from string_concat1, they were able to handle the remaining 12 examples. In their experiments, they used a version of the model checker BLAST [9] which is augmented with a split prover [14]. The basic version of BLAST fails to handle 4 of the 12 examples which are handled by the split prover based method. They also conducted a comparative study involving other tools: MAGIC [8] and SATABS [4]. According to their experiments, neither MAGIC nor SATABS were able to verify any of the examples in Table 1. Using our cycle abstraction approach, we are able to handle all examples in a short time. Except for string_concat and substring1, the verification time for each of the remaining examples is less than one second.

6   Related Work

A variety of solutions have been proposed in the literature to cope with problems related to loops. Sharygina and Browne proposed a loop abstraction approach based on a syntactic transformation [22]. Their technique abstracts branches within the loop body such that the flow of operations in each path is preserved. This abstraction does not deliver the kind of information we are interested in. Moreover, their method is applied to a dialect of UML, our approach is applied to source code. Jhala and Majumdar presented an idea to deal with long traces based on path slicing [13]. Given a program trace, their technique computes relevant statements that show the (in)feasibility of that trace. Thus, irrelevant loops within the trace are ignored (abstracted away). An advantage of their approach is that, under the assumption of loop termination, it can abstract loops in real counterexamples. Hence, it provides a concise form of the counterexample. However, their method does not solve the divergence problem if the loop is relevant to the target property as in Figure 1(a). Kroening and Weissenbacher proposed an approach for treating traces that contain loops [17]. Their method is based on the parameterization of loops with their iteration counter n. First, they associate a recurrence equation to each variable. Next, they compute the closed form for each equation, a formula that expresses the actual value of each variable in terms of n the loop iteration counter. Finally, They compute the strongest post condition with respect to the loop body and obtain a formula parameterized with n as result. The existence of a value for n that satisfies the resulting formula decides about the feasibility of the counterexample that involves the loop. Their approach can be seen as complimentary to ours, we can use it to generate and represent real error traces which are long. The SMASH algorithm [10] is able to reason about long error traces using *must* summaries. It can also prove absence of bugs using *may* summaries. While our technique summarizes loops and

SMASH computes summaries for procedures, we think that a must analysis can also be combined with our method as well to compute summaries that show the absence of bugs. Closer to our approach is the technique proposed by Kroening *et al.* [16]. Their method is based on replacing code fragments, including loops, with the corresponding abstract transformers. Their approach is more general than ours as they treat nested loops. However, they assume that the invariant is provided, which is not the case for our method. Moreover, they summarize the whole code in advance before the verification phase. In our approach the summarization procedure is part of CEGAR and is applied on demand. In the context of proving termination of programs, Rybalchenko and Podelski proposed the concept of *transition invariants* [19] which allows to overapproximate the transition relation induced by pre- and post-state of program statements. Their approach provides information about variable progress but does not deliver information about the final state when loop terminates. Thus, alone their method can not reason precisely about (in)feasibility of traces.

7   Conclusion

We presented an approach to handle the divergence problem of CEGAR. In particular, the problem related to the infinitely many (spurious) counterexamples that may arise from unfolding the same (while- or for-) loop in the given program. Our solution consists of abstracting (summarizing) not just states but also the state changes induced by structured program statements, including for- and while-statements. A lightweight mechanism based on inference rules is used to generate summaries. If the premise of a given rule matches a loop a summary is automatically generated by just instantiating the rule with information from the loop. Thus, no fixpoint computation is required. We proposed a generic scheme for the implementation of our loop abstraction technique which is based on a source-to-source transformation. Hence, our approach can be seamlessly integrated into other software verification tools as black-box. Our loop summarization technique is applied on demand within CEGAR, i.e., whenever a potential divergence situation is detected. Despite restrictions on the form of loops that we handle, experimental results show that our method performs well in practice. We are able to verify all benchmarks used in [14]. Most of these benchmarks are not handled by several existing tools.

References

1. Ball, T., Rajamani, S.K.: The SLAM project: debugging system software via static analysis. In: POPL, pp. 1–3 (2002)
2. Chaki, S., Clarke, E.M., Groce, A., Jha, S., Veith, H.: Modular verification of software components in C. In: ICSE, pp. 385–395 (2003)
3. Clarke, E.M., Grumberg, O., Jha, S., Lu, Y., Veith, H.: Counterexample-guided abstraction refinement. In: Emerson, E.A., Sistla, A.P. (eds.) CAV 2000. LNCS, vol. 1855, pp. 154–169. Springer, Heidelberg (2000)

4. Clarke, E.M., Kroening, D., Sharygina, N., Yorav, K.: SATABS: SAT-based predicate abstraction for ANSI-C. In: Halbwachs, N., Zuck, L.D. (eds.) TACAS 2005. LNCS, vol. 3440, pp. 570–574. Springer, Heidelberg (2005)
5. Cook, B., Podelski, A., Rybalchenko, A.: Terminator: Beyond safety. In: Ball, T., Jones, R.B. (eds.) CAV 2006. LNCS, vol. 4144, pp. 415–418. Springer, Heidelberg (2006)
6. Detlefs, D., Nelson, G., Saxe, J.B.: Simplify: A theorem prover for program checking. Technical Report HPL-2003-148, HP Lab. (2003)
7. Dutertre, B., de Moura, L.M.: A fast linear-arithmetic solver for DPLL(T). In: Ball, T., Jones, R.B. (eds.) CAV 2006. LNCS, vol. 4144, pp. 81–94. Springer, Heidelberg (2006)
8. Chaki, S., et al.: Modular verification of software components in C. In: ICSE, pp. 385–395 (2003)
9. Henzinger, T.A., Jhala, R., Majumdar, R., Sutre, G.: Software verification with BLAST. In: Ball, T., Rajamani, S.K. (eds.) SPIN 2003. LNCS, vol. 2648, pp. 235–239. Springer, Heidelberg (2003)
10. Godefroid, P., Nori, A.V., Rajamani, S.K., Tetali, S.: Compositional may-must program analysis: unleashing the power of alternation. In: POPL, pp. 43–56 (2010)
11. Graf, S., Saïdi, H.: Construction of abstract state graphs with PVS. In: Grumberg, O. (ed.) CAV 1997. LNCS, vol. 1254, pp. 72–83. Springer, Heidelberg (1997)
12. Henzinger, T.A., Jhala, R., Majumdar, R., Sutre, G.: Lazy abstraction. In: POPL, pp. 58–70 (2002)
13. Jhala, R., Majumdar, R.: Path slicing. In: PLDI, pp. 38–47 (2005)
14. Jhala, R., McMillan, K.L.: A practical and complete approach to predicate refinement. In: Hermanns, H. (ed.) TACAS 2006. LNCS, vol. 3920, pp. 459–473. Springer, Heidelberg (2006)
15. Karr, M.: Affine relationships among variables of a program. Acta Inf. 6, 133–151 (1976)
16. Kroening, D., Sharygina, N., Tonetta, S., Tsitovich, A., Wintersteiger, C.M.: Loop summarization using abstract transformers. In: Cha, S(S.), Choi, J.-Y., Kim, M., Lee, I., Viswanathan, M. (eds.) ATVA 2008. LNCS, vol. 5311, pp. 111–125. Springer, Heidelberg (2008)
17. Kroening, D., Weissenbacher, G.: Counterexamples with loops for predicate abstraction. In: Ball, T., Jones, R.B. (eds.) CAV 2006. LNCS, vol. 4144, pp. 152–165. Springer, Heidelberg (2006)
18. Müller-Olm, M., Seidl, H.: A note on karr's algorithm. In: Díaz, J., Karhumäki, J., Lepistö, A., Sannella, D. (eds.) ICALP 2004. LNCS, vol. 3142, pp. 1016–1028. Springer, Heidelberg (2004)
19. Podelski, A., Rybalchenko, A.: Transition invariants. In: LICS, pp. 32–41 (2004)
20. Sankaranarayanan, S., Sipma, H.B., Manna, Z.: Scalable analysis of linear systems using mathematical programming. In: Cousot, R. (ed.) VMCAI 2005. LNCS, vol. 3385, pp. 25–41. Springer, Heidelberg (2005)
21. Seghir, M.N., Podelski, A.: ACSAR: Software model checking with transfinite refinement. In: Bošnački, D., Edelkamp, S. (eds.) SPIN 2007. LNCS, vol. 4595, pp. 274–278. Springer, Heidelberg (2007)
22. Sharygina, N., Browne, J.C.: Model checking software via abstraction of loop transitions. In: Pezzé, M. (ed.) FASE 2003. LNCS, vol. 2621, pp. 325–340. Springer, Heidelberg (2003)

A Succinct Canonical Register Automaton Model[*]

Sofia Cassel[1], Falk Howar[2], Bengt Jonsson[1], Maik Merten[2],
and Bernhard Steffen[2]

[1] Dept. of Information Technology, Uppsala University, Sweden
{sofia.cassel,bengt.jonsson}@it.uu.se
[2] Chair of Programming Systems, University of Dortmund, Germany
{falk.howar,maik.merten,steffen}@cs.tu-dortmund.de

Abstract. We present a novel canonical automaton model, based on register automata, that can easily be used to specify protocol or program behavior. More concretely, register automata are reminiscent of control flow graphs: they comprise a finite control structure, assignments, and conditionals, allowing to assign values of an infinite domain to registers (variables) and to compare them for equality. A major contribution is the definition of a canonical automaton representation of any language recognizable by a deterministic register automaton, by means of a Nerode congruence. Not only is this canonical form easier to comprehend than previous proposals, but it can also be exponentially more succinct than these. Key to the canonical form is the symbolic treatment of data languages, which overcomes the structural restrictions in previous formalisms, and opens the way to new practical applications.

1 Introduction

Automata models that process words or trees over infinite alphabets are becoming increasingly important in many areas, including specification, verification, and testing (e.g., [2,21]), databases [1], and user modeling [5]. A natural form for such models consists of a finite control structure, augmented by a finite set of registers (aka state variables), processing input symbols using a predefined set of operations (tests and updates) over input data and registers. Specialized classes, such as timed automata [2], counter automata, and data-independent transition systems [17] have long been used for specification and verification. From a language-theoretic perspective, decision problems and connections with logics have been studied (e.g., [10,8,7,23]).

Modeling and reasoning with automata models can be made much more efficient if it is possible to transform models into a canonical form. Transformation into a canonical form is heavily used in verification, equivalence checking, and refinement checking, e.g., using (bi)simulation based criteria [16,20]. While for finite automata, there are standard algorithms for determinization and minimization, based on the Myhill-Nerode theorem [13,19], it has proven difficult to

---

[*] Supported in part by the European FP7 project CONNECT (IST 231167).

T. Bultan and P.-A. Hsiung (Eds.): ATVA 2011, LNCS 6996, pp. 366–380, 2011.
© Springer-Verlag Berlin Heidelberg 2011

carry over such constructions and define canonical forms for automata models over infinite alphabets, including timed automata [24]. Often, canonical forms are obtained at the price of (re-)encoding extensive information about the relation between parameter values in the state space (e.g., [18,3]).

In this paper, we present a novel canonical automaton model, based on a form of register automata (RA). We define a form of RAs that are particularly suited to faithfully model a large class of systems that do not compute or manipulate data but manage their adequate distribution, e.g., protocols, as well as certain mediators and connectors. This class of systems is the backbone to support the large-scale, seamless integration and orchestration of, e.g., (Web) services to complex business applications running on the (Inter)net. One concrete current example for the application of such automata models is the CONNECT Project [14], which aims at dynamically synthesizing required connectors based on descriptions of component behavior in the form of automata.

RAs have a finite control structure. They process words over an infinite alphabet consisting of terms with parameters from an infinite domain. RAs can thus can be regarded as a simple programming language, with variables, parallel assignments, and conditions. In contrast to other types of automata that have been suggested for data languages [23,6], our form of RAs does not restrict the access to variables to a specific order or pattern, nor do they constrain the contents of the variables (e.g., by uniqueness). This supports a much more intuitive modeling of data languages, while leaving the expressiveness untouched.

We present a Nerode congruence for RAs that yields a canonical form. Key to this generalization of Nerode's right congruence ([13,19]) to RAs is the symbolic treatment of data languages in a way that abstracts from concrete data values and rather concentrates on the relations between parameter values. This allows for the required flexibility, and also leads to a more elegant canonical form, which may even be exponentially more succinct than other suggested canonical forms. This is very important in many applications. For instance, in automata learning, the complexity of the learning procedure directly depends on the size of the minimal canonical form of the automaton.

We could compare the difference between the automata of [11,3] and our canonical form to the difference between the region graph and zone graph constructions for timed automata. The region graph considers all possible combinations between constraints on clock values, be they relevant to acceptance of the input word or not, whereas the zone graph construction aims to consider only relevant constraints. Our form of RAs is, however, always more succinct than those of [11,3].

In summary, the contribution of this paper is a succinct and intuitive RA formalism that can easily be used to specify protocol or program behavior, with a canonical representation of any (deterministic) RA-recognizable data language by means of a Nerode congruence.

Related Work. Generalizations of regular languages to infinite alphabets have been studied previously. Kaminski and Francez [15] introduced finite memory automata (FMA) that recognize languages with infinite input alphabets. Since then, a number of formalisms have been suggested (pebble automata, data automata, ...) that accept different flavors of data languages (see [23,8,6,7] for an overview). Most of these formalisms recognize data languages that are invariant under permutations on the data domain. In [9] a logical characterization of data languages is given plus a transformation from logical descriptions to automata.

While most of the above mentioned work focuses on non-deterministic automata and are concerned with closedness properties and expressiveness results of data languages, we are interested in a framework for deterministic RAs that can be used to model the behavior of protocols or (restricted) programs. This includes in particular, the development of canonical models on the basis of a new Myhill Nerode-like theorem.

In [11,3], a Myhill-Nerode theorem for a form of register automata is presented. Canonicity is achieved by restricting how state variables are stored, which leads to complex and hardly comprehensible models, as argued in [12]. These complications are overcome in our structurally much easier RA-based approach.

Organization. In the next section we introduce the RA model as a basis for representing data languages. In Section 3, we introduce a succinct representation of data languages, which suppresses non-essential tests, in the form of a novel, decision tree-like structure called *constraint decision trees* (CDTs). Based on this representation, in Section 4 we define a Nerode congruence, and prove that it characterizes minimal canonical forms of deterministic RAs, called (right-invariant) DRAs. In Section 5 we relate our canonical form to previously suggested ones, and establish some exponential succinctness results before we conclude in Section 6.

2   Data Languages and Register Automata

In this section, we introduce formally the notions of data languages and register automata. While a very general definition of data languages would define them simply as sets of data words, for our modeling purposes, focus is on data languages that are closed under permutations on the data domain. Such languages are agnostic to the concrete identitiy of data values, which they all treat alike. With this restriction, data languages are ideal to describe the flow of data as required for an adequate modeling of systems, whose behavior does not depend on the data content they distribute.

We assume an unbounded domain D of data values and a set I of *actions*. Each action has a certain *arity* which determines how many parameters it takes from the domain D. A *data symbol* is a term of form $\alpha(d_1, \ldots, d_n)$, where α is an action with arity n, and $d_1, \ldots, d_n$ are data values in D. A *data word* is a (finite) sequence of data symbols. A *data language* is a set of data words, which is closed under permutations on D. We will often represent a data language as a mapping from the set of data words to $\{+, -\}$, e.g. accept and reject.

We will now present an automaton model that recognizes data languages. Assume a set of *formal parameters*, ranged over by $p_1, \ldots, p_n$, and a finite set of *variables* (or registers), ranged over by $x_1, \ldots, x_n$. A *parameterized symbol* is a term of form $\alpha(p_1, \ldots, p_n)$, consisting of an action α and formal parameters $p_1, \ldots, p_n$ (respecting the arity of α). A *guard* is a conjunction of equalities and inequalities (here, an inequality means a negated equality, e.g., $x_2 \neq p_3$) over formal parameters and variables. We write $\bar{p}$ for $p_1, \ldots, p_n$ and $\bar{d}$ for $d_1, \ldots, d_n$.

Definition 1. A *Register Automaton* (RA) is a tuple $\mathcal{A} = (L, l_0, X, T, \lambda)$, where

- L is a finite set of *locations*,
- $l_0 \in L$ is the *initial location*
- X maps each location $l \in L$ to a finite set $X(l)$ of variables, where $X(l_0)$ is the empty set,
- T is a finite set of *transitions*, each of which is of form $\langle l, \alpha(\bar{p}), g, \pi, l' \rangle$, where l is a *source location*, l' is a *target location*, $\alpha(\bar{p})$ is a parameterized symbol, g is a guard over $\bar{p}$ and $X(l)$, and π (the *assignment*) is a mapping from $X(l')$ to $X(l) \cup \bar{p}$ (intuitively, the value of $x \in X(l')$ is assigned to the value of $\pi(x)$), and
- $\lambda : L \mapsto \{+, -\}$ maps each location to either $+$ (accept) or $-$ (reject),

such that for any location l and action α, the disjunction of all guards g in transitions of form $\langle l, \alpha(\bar{p}), g, \pi, l' \rangle$ in T is equivalent to *true* (i.e., $\mathcal{A}$ should be *completely specified*).   □

Example: We model the behavior of a fragment of the XMPP protocol [22] as a running example (shown in Figure 1). XMPP is widely used in instant messaging. In our fragment of XMPP, a user can register an account (providing a username and a password), log in using this account, change the password, and delete the account. In the figure, arcs are labeled with actions, guards, and assignments. Actions and guards are written above the horizontal delimiter; assignments are written below it. Accepting locations (where the user is logged in) are denoted by two concentric circles. For example, the user Bob could register his account with the action register(Bob, secret) (providing his username and password), and then log in with the action login(Bob, secret). Once logged in, he could change his password to boblovesalice with the action pw(boblovesalice). (For reasons of brevity, several transitions are omitted.)   □

A register automaton $\mathcal{A}$ classifies data words as either accepted or rejected. One way to describe how this is done is to define a state of $\mathcal{A}$ as consisting of

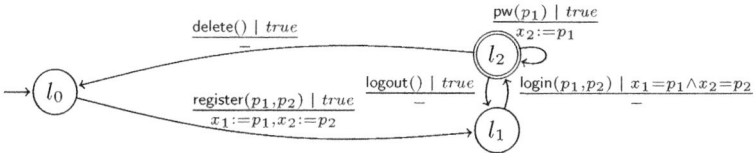

Fig. 1. Partial model for a fragment of XMPP

a location and an assignment to the variables of that location. Then, one can describe how $\mathcal{A}$ processes a data word symbol by symbol: on each symbol, $\mathcal{A}$ finds a transition with a guard that is satisfied by the parameters of the symbol and the current assignment to variables; this transition determines a next location and an assignment to the variables of the new location. For the purposes of this paper, it will be more convenient to use a different but equivalent definition. A *run* of $\mathcal{A}$ is defined as a pair consisting of a sequence of parameterized symbols and a guard over its formal parameters. Each run is extracted from some sequence of transitions, and is used to classify the data words that match its sequence of symbols and satisfy its guards. We will now discuss this in more detail.

A *parameterized word* w is a sequence of parameterized symbols in which all formal parameters are distinct; we assume a (re)naming scheme that avoids clashes. For a mapping π from a set X of variables, let $\tilde{\pi}$ denote the mapping obtained by extending the domain of X to include the set of formal parameters; these are all mapped to themselves (i.e., $\tilde{\pi}(x) = \pi(x)$ if x is a variable, and $\tilde{\pi}(p) = p$ if p is a formal parameter); we extend $\tilde{\pi}$ to expressions and guards in the natural way.

A sequence σ of transitions of $\mathcal{A}$ from l_0 to l_k is of form

$$\sigma = \langle l_0, \alpha_1(\bar{p}_1), g_1, \pi_1, l_1 \rangle \quad \langle l_1, \alpha_2(\bar{p}_2), g_2, \pi_2, l_2 \rangle \quad \cdots \quad \langle l_{k-1}, \alpha_k(\bar{p}_k), g_k, \pi_k, l_k \rangle \ ,$$

which starts in l_0 and ends in l_k. We define

- the *parameterized word* of σ as $\alpha_1(\bar{p}_1)\alpha_2(\bar{p}_2)\cdots\alpha_k(\bar{p}_k)$, and
- the *guard* of σ as $g = g_1 \wedge \tilde{\pi}_1(g_2 \wedge \tilde{\pi}_2(g_3 \wedge \tilde{\pi}_3(\cdots \wedge \tilde{\pi}_{k-1}(g_k))))$, i.e., essentially as the conjunction the guards $g_1, \ldots, g_k$ in σ, where the result of applying the mappings $\tilde{\pi}_1, \ldots, \tilde{\pi}_{k-1}$ is that each variable is replaced by the formal parameter from which it originally received its value.

A *run* of an RA $\mathcal{A}$ is a pair $\langle w, g \rangle$ such that w is the parameterized word and g is the guard of some sequence of transitions σ from the initial location l_0 to some l_k. A run is *accepting* if $\lambda(l_k) = +$. It is *rejecting* if $\lambda(l_k) = -$. (A run may be both accepting and rejecting if it can be extracted from two different sequences of transitions.)

A data word $\mathsf{w}_d = \alpha_1(\bar{d}_1)\cdots\alpha_k(\bar{d}_k)$ *satisfies* a run $\langle w, g \rangle$, denoted $\mathsf{w}_d \models \langle w, g \rangle$, if w_d has the same sequence of actions as w, and the parameters of w_d satisfy g in the obvious way (i.e., $d_{i_p} = d_{j_q}$ whenever $p_{i_p} = p_{j_q}$ is a conjunct in g, and $d_{i_p} \neq d_{j_q}$ whenever $p_{i_p} \neq p_{j_q}$ is a conjunct in g).

Example: The data word $\mathsf{register}(\mathsf{Bob}, \mathsf{secret})\mathsf{login}(\mathsf{Bob}, \mathsf{secret})$ takes the automaton in Figure 1 from l_0 to l_2. The sequence σ of transitions is of the form $\langle l_0, \mathsf{register}(p_1, p_2), true, \pi, l_1 \rangle\langle l_1, \mathsf{login}(p_3, p_4), (x_1 = p_3 \wedge x_2 = p_4), id, l_2 \rangle$, where π is $(x_1 := p_1, x_2 := p_2)$ (note that parameters have been renamed to avoid clashes). The guard of σ is $g = (true \wedge \tilde{\pi}(x_1 = p_3 \wedge x_2 = p_4))$, i.e., $g = (p_1 = p_3 \wedge p_2 = p_4)$. Then $\langle \mathsf{register}(p_1, p_2)\mathsf{login}(p_3, p_4), g \rangle$ is a run of $\mathcal{A}$. □

An RA is *determinate* (called a DRA) if no data word satisfies both accepting and rejecting runs. A data word is *accepted* (*rejected*) by a DRA $\mathcal{A}$ if all runs that it satisfies are accepting (rejecting). We define $\mathcal{A}(\mathsf{w}_d)$ to be $+$ $(-)$ if w_d is accepted (rejected) by $\mathcal{A}$. The language recognized by $\mathcal{A}$ is the set of data words that it accepts.

We have chosen to work with determinate, rather than deterministic, RAs, since a determinate RA can be easily transformed into a deterministic RA by strengthening its guards, and a deterministic RA, by definition, is also determinate. Our construction of canonical automata in Theorem 2 will generate determinate RAs which are not necessarily deterministic. They can easily be made deterministic, but this conversion can be done in several ways.

We call two variables $x_i, x_j \in X(l)$ in the same location of a DRA *independent* if the behavior of the DRA does not depend on the relation between the values of x_i and x_j. Technically, this means that (1) no guard of any transition may compare x_i and x_j when l is the source location, and (2) no combination of a guard and an assignment may imply the equality of x_i and x_j when l is the target location of a transition. If all variables of a DRA are pairwise independent, i.e., no relation between variables influences the DRA's branching behavior, we refer to it as a *right-invariant* DRA (in reminiscence of the right-congruence that is represented in the locations of the automaton).

For the remainder of this paper we will restrict our attention to right-invariant DRAs. Any DRA $\mathcal{A}$ can be transformed into an equivalent right-invariant DRA by expanding locations with dependent variables into sub-locations representing different valuations of the variables. This may, however, result in an exponential (in the number of variables) blow-up of the number of locations.

3   Symbolic Representation of Data Languages

A given data language may be accepted by many different DRAs. In order to obtain a succinct, canonical form of DRAs, we will in this section define a canonical representation of data languages; in the next section we will describe how to derive canonical DRAs from this representation.

Our plan for this section is to first introduce a canonical form for runs of a DRA, called *constrained words*, which can only contain equalities (no inequalities) between parameters. Since now constrained words are less expressive than runs, each data word typically satisfies several constrained words. We therefore define a new notion of satisfaction between sets of constrained words and data words, which intuitively selects a "best matching" constrained word for a given data word. We can then use sets of constrained words, together with a classification of these words as "accepted" or "rejected", as a representation of data languages. We establish, as a central result (in Theorem 1), that any data language can be represented by a *minimal* set of constrained words. This minimal set will correspond to the set of runs of our canonical automaton, and will serve several purposes during automata construction:

(1) it will allow us to keep only the essential relations between data values and filter out inessential ("accidental") relations between data values, (2) from it, we can derive the parameters an automaton must store in variables after processing

a data word, and (3) we can transform parts of it directly into transitions when constructing the canonical DRA.

Constrained Words. A *constraint* is a conjunction of equalities over formal parameters (i.e., without any inequalities). We always write constraints as ordered lists of equalities without parentheses (using associativity). We use *true* to denote the empty constraint. For a parameterized word w, let $p \sqsubset_w p'$ denote that p and p' are formal parameters in w such that p occurs before p'.

A *constrained word* is a pair $\langle w, \varphi \rangle$ consisting of a parameterized word w and a constraint φ of form $p_1 = p'_1 \wedge p_2 = p'_2 \wedge \cdots \wedge p_k = p'_k$ over the formal parameters of w, in which the constraint φ satisfies the following conditions:

- $p_i \sqsubset_w p'_i$ for each $i = 1, \ldots, k$,
- $p'_1 \sqsubset_w \cdots \sqsubset_w p'_k$, and
- all $p_1, \ldots, p_k$ are distinct.

In other words, in each equality the arguments are ordered, the right-hand sides of φ are ordered, and each parameter occurs at most once as a left-hand side. Constrained words that differ only by permutation of formal parameters are regarded as equivalent. We can easily see that for each pair $\langle w, \varphi \rangle$ of a parameterized word w and constraint φ, there is a unique equivalent constrained word.

Since a constrained word is a special case of a run, we directly inherit a definition of satisfaction between data words and constrained words. Let $cw[w_d]$ be the 'strongest' (w.r.t. number of equalities) constrained word that w_d satisfies, i.e., $cw[w_d]$ contains exactly the equalities that w_d satisfies, put on the special form of constrained words. For example, $cw[\text{register}(\text{Bob}, \text{secret})\text{login}(\text{Bob}, \text{secret})] =$ $= \langle \text{register}(p_1, p_2)\text{login}(p_3, p_4), p_1 = p_3 \wedge p_2 = p_4 \rangle$.

Constraint Decision Trees. We will now define how sets of constrained words can be used to classify data words as accepted or rejected. This view of a set of constrained words is called a *constraint decision tree* (CDT). A CDT consists of a set of constrained words together with a mapping from this set to $\{+, -\}$, and classifies a data word by finding a "best matching" constrained word.

A set Φ of constrained words is *prefix-closed* if $\langle wv, \varphi \wedge \psi \rangle \in \Phi$ implies $\langle w, \varphi \rangle \in \Phi$ whenever $\langle w, \varphi \rangle$ is a constrained word. (We recall that constraints are regarded as ordered lists of equalities, so that $\langle wv, \varphi \wedge \psi \rangle$ is a constrained word when equalities appear exactly in the order defined by φ and ψ.) It is *extension-closed* if $\langle w, \varphi \rangle \in \Phi$ implies $\langle wv, \varphi \rangle \in \Phi$ for any parameterized word v. It follows that any non-empty prefix-closed and extension-closed set of constrained words also contains $\langle w, true \rangle$ for each parameterized word w.

Definition 2. A *constraint decision tree* (CDT) $\mathcal{T}$ pair $\langle Dom(\mathcal{T}), \lambda_\mathcal{T} \rangle$ where $Dom(\mathcal{T})$ is a non-empty prefix-closed and extension-closed set of constrained words, and $\lambda_\mathcal{T} : Dom(\mathcal{T}) \mapsto \{+, -\}$ is a mapping from $Dom(\mathcal{T})$ to $\{+, -\}$. $\square$

For a constraint ψ, let $p \sqsubset_w \psi$ denote that $p \sqsubset_w p_j$ whenever $p_i = p_j$ is an equality in ψ (note that ψ may also be empty). We define a strict partial order

$<$ on constrained words by defining $\langle w, \varphi \rangle < \langle w', \varphi' \rangle$ if $w = w'$ and there are constraints φ'', ψ, and ψ', such that

- φ is of form $\varphi'' \wedge \psi$, and
- φ' is of form $\varphi'' \wedge p = p' \wedge \psi'$, with $p' \sqsubset_w \psi$.

Example: For $w = \text{register}(p_1, p_2)\text{login}(p_3, p_4)$ we have $\langle w, p_1 = p_3 \rangle < \langle w, p_1 = p_2 \rangle$ since $p_1 = p_2$ is not present in $\langle w, p_1 = p_3 \rangle$, and since $p_2 \sqsubset_w (p_1 = p_3)$. $\quad\square$

For a set Φ of constrained words, define a relation $\preceq_\Phi$ between constrained words in Φ and data words, by letting $\langle w, \varphi \rangle \preceq_\Phi w_d$ iff $\langle w, \varphi \rangle$ is a maximal (w.r.t. $<$) constrained word in Φ such that $w_d \models \langle w, \varphi \rangle$.

   Intuitively, if $\langle w, \varphi \rangle \preceq_\Phi w_d$, then $\langle w, \varphi \rangle$ can be viewed as a constrained word in Φ which "best matches" w_d, obtained by adding equalities in φ from left to right. More precisely, given w_d, we successively build $\langle w, \varphi \rangle$ as the limit of a sequence of constrained words in Φ. We start with $\langle w, true \rangle$, and whenever we have built $\langle w, \varphi \rangle$ we extend it to some $\langle w, \varphi \wedge p_i = p_j \rangle$, where $p_i = p_j$ is chosen such that w_d satisfies the equality $p_i = p_j$, and such that there is no other extension $\langle w, \varphi \wedge p_i' = p_j' \rangle$ with $p_j' \sqsubset_w p_j$, where w_d satisfies $p_i' = p_j'$. If there is no such extension (of form $\langle w, \varphi \wedge p_i = p_j \rangle$), we know that $\langle w, \varphi \rangle \preceq_\Phi w_d$.

   We call a CDT $\mathcal{T}$ *determinate* (a DCDT) if $\lambda_{\mathcal{T}}(\langle w, \varphi \rangle) = \lambda_{\mathcal{T}}(\langle w, \varphi' \rangle)$ whenever $\langle w, \varphi \rangle \preceq_{Dom(\mathcal{T})} w_d$ and $\langle w, \varphi' \rangle \preceq_{Dom(\mathcal{T})} w_d$ for some data word w_d.

Example: A partially specified prefix of a DCDT for our running example can be seen in Figure 2. Here, the root node is the leftmost one, and the ordering $<$ is from top to bottom in the figure (i.e., lower nodes are bigger w.r.t. $<$). Let us illustrate the process of finding the maximal (w.r.t. $<$) constrained word $\langle w, \varphi \rangle$ that $w_d = \text{register}(\text{Bob}, \text{secret})\text{login}(\text{Bob}, \text{secret})$ satisfies. The idea is to start from the root node and then successively add equalities to the constraint φ, until we have obtained the maximal one. We start with $\langle w, \varphi \rangle = \langle \text{register}(p_1, p_2)\text{login}(p_3, p_4), true \rangle$ and add the equality $p_1 = p_3$ which w_d satisfies. We can finally add the equality $p_2 = p_4$, and we see that $\langle w, p_1 = p_3 \wedge p_2 = p_4 \rangle \preceq_\Phi w_d$. (In fact, we also see that $\langle w, p_1 = p_3 \rangle < \langle w, p_1 = p_3 \wedge p_2 = p_4 \rangle$.) $\quad\square$

We can now define the data language represented by a DCDT, i.e., as a mapping from the set of data words to $\{+, -\}$.

Definition 3. For a DCDT $\mathcal{T}$, define $\lambda_{\mathcal{T}}(w_d) = \lambda_{\mathcal{T}}(\langle w, \varphi \rangle)$ whenever $\langle w, \varphi \rangle \preceq_{Dom(\mathcal{T})} w_d$. $\quad\square$

We now establish as a central result that for any data language λ there is a unique minimal DCDT that recognizes λ.

Theorem 1 (Minimal DCDT). For any data language λ, there is a unique minimal DCDT $\mathcal{T}$ such that $\lambda = \lambda_{\mathcal{T}}$. $\quad\square$

By minimal, we mean that if $\mathcal{T}'$ is any other DCDT with $\lambda = \lambda_{\mathcal{T}'}$, then $Dom(\mathcal{T}) \subseteq Dom(\mathcal{T}')$. We will sometimes use the term λ-*essential* (constrained) words for members of $Dom(\mathcal{T})$ where $\mathcal{T}$ is the minimal DCDT with $\lambda = \lambda_{\mathcal{T}}$.

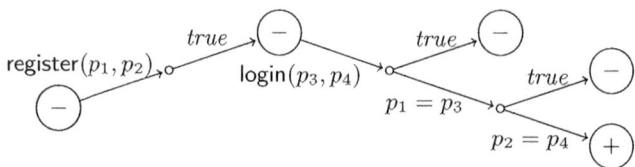

Fig. 2. Partially specified prefix of minimal DCDT for the XMPP language

Proof. (Sketch) We prove Theorem 1 by defining how a minimal set $Dom(\mathcal{T})$ of constrained words can be constructed incrementally for any data language λ. We first extend the ordering $<$ so that it relates constrained words of different lengths, by defining $\langle w, \varphi \rangle < \langle w', \varphi' \rangle$ if w is a prefix of w' or vice versa and $\langle w'', \varphi \rangle < \langle w'', \varphi' \rangle$, where w'' is the longest of the two words w and w'. We construct $Dom(\mathcal{T})$ incrementally, starting with the set of constrained words of form $\langle w, true \rangle$, and then considering constrained words in increasing $<$-order (using the extended definition of $<$). Each such constrained word is added to $Dom(\mathcal{T})$ if it is needed in order to classify some data word correctly.

More precisely, consider a constrained word $\langle w, \varphi \rangle$, and let φ' be such that $\langle w, \varphi \rangle$ is of form $\langle w, \varphi' \wedge p = p' \rangle$. Let $\Phi^{<\langle w, \varphi \rangle}$ be the set of λ-essential constrained words that are less than (w.r.t. $<$) $\langle w, \varphi \rangle$. Then $\langle w, \varphi' \wedge p = p' \rangle$ is λ-essential if $\langle w, \varphi' \rangle$ is λ-essential (by prefix-closure), and if there is a data word $\mathbf{w}_d$, a constraint ψ, and some extension $w' = wv$ of w such that

- $cw[\mathbf{w}_d] = \langle w', \varphi' \wedge p = p' \wedge \psi \rangle$,
- $\langle w', \varphi'' \rangle \preceq_{\Phi^{<\langle w, \varphi \rangle}} \mathbf{w}_d$ for some λ-essential constrained word $\langle w', \varphi'' \rangle \in \Phi^{<\langle w, \varphi \rangle}$,
- and $\lambda(\langle w', \varphi'' \rangle) \neq \lambda(\mathbf{w}_d)$.

The incremental construction works, because only the set $\Phi^{<\langle w, \varphi \rangle}$ of λ-essential constrained words is needed to determine whether $\langle w, \varphi \rangle$ is λ-essential.   □

Example: To illustrate the above procedure, we will partially sketch how to obtain the λ-essential constrained words of the form $\langle w_1, \varphi \rangle$ where $w_1 = \mathsf{register}(p_1, p_2)$, and of the form $\langle w_2, \varphi \rangle$ where $w_2 = \mathsf{register}(p_1, p_2)\mathsf{login}(p_3, p_4)$. Initially, the words $\langle w_1, true \rangle$ and $\langle w_2, true \rangle$ are λ-essential.

We then consider constrained words in increasing $<$-order, beginning with a smallest constrained word, say $\langle w_2, p_2 = p_4 \rangle$. We find a data word $\mathbf{w}_d = \mathsf{register}(\mathsf{Bob}, \mathsf{secret})\mathsf{login}(\mathsf{Alice}, \mathsf{secret})$ such that $cw[\mathbf{w}_d] = \langle w_2, p_2 = p_4 \rangle$. We also find a λ-essential word $\langle w_2, true \rangle$ such that $\langle w_2, true \rangle \preceq_{\Phi^{<\langle w_2, p_2 = p_4 \rangle}} \mathbf{w}_d$. Since $\lambda(\mathbf{w}_d) = -$ and $\lambda(w_2, true) = -$ we see that $\mathbf{w}_d$ is already correctly classified and thus $\langle w_2, p_2 = p_4 \rangle$ is not λ-essential.

Next, we pick the constrained word $\langle w_2, p_1 = p_3 \rangle$ which is larger than $\langle w_2, p_2 = p_4 \rangle$ w.r.t. $<$. Consider the data word $\mathbf{w}'_d = \mathsf{register}(\mathsf{Bob}, \mathsf{secret})\mathsf{login}(\mathsf{Bob}, \mathsf{secret})$ such that $cw[\mathbf{w}'_d] = \langle w_2, p_1 = p_3 \wedge p_2 = p_4 \rangle$. We find a λ-essential word $\langle w_2, true \rangle$ such that $\langle w_2, true \rangle \preceq_{\Phi^{<\langle w_2, p_1 = p_3 \rangle}} \mathbf{w}'_d$. Since $\lambda(\mathbf{w}'_d) = +$ but $\lambda(\langle w_2, true \rangle) = -$ we see that $\mathbf{w}'_d$ is incorrectly classified and thus $\langle w_2, p_1 = p_3 \rangle$ is λ-essential.

We now test the constrained word $\langle w_2, p_1 = p_3 \wedge p_2 = p_4 \rangle$ with $\mathbf{w}'_d$. However, since the set of λ-essential constrained words has increased, we get a different λ-essential word $\langle w_2, p_1 = p_3 \rangle$ such that $\langle w_2, p_1 = p_3 \rangle \preceq_{\Phi < \langle w_2, p_1 = p_3 \wedge p_2 = p_4 \rangle} \mathbf{w}'_d$. We see that $\lambda(\mathbf{w}'_d) = +$ but $\lambda(\langle w_2, p_1 = p_3 \rangle) = -$, so $\langle w_2, p_1 = p_3 \wedge p_2 = p_4 \rangle$ is also λ-essential.

The λ-essential constrained words are now $\langle w_2, p_1 = p_3 \wedge p_2 = p_4 \rangle$, $\langle w_2, p_1 = p_3 \rangle$, $\langle w_2, true \rangle$, and $\langle w_1, true \rangle$. Note that these (together with the empty word) are exactly the constrained words in the DCDT of Figure 2.   □

4   Nerode Congruence and Canonical Form

In this section, we define a Nerode-type congruence on the set of constrained words of some (minimal) DCDT, which is then used to construct a succinct DRA that recognizes a data language.

Following standard Nerode, we will define equivalence of words w.r.t. suffixes. When splitting a constrained word into a prefix and a suffix, however, the equalities between parameters in the prefix and parameters in the suffix are also split. In the resulting RA, the "loose" connections will be represented by variables. These will be derived from the concept of *memorable* parameters, which is the set of parameters that need to be remembered after processing a prefix. Based on the minimal DCDT representation, this will guarantee that the number of variables stored by a canonical DRA is minimal. Similar definitions of data values that need to be remembered after a sequence of input symbols are also found in [4,3].

In order for our canonical form to capture exactly the causal relations between parameters, we will allow memorable parameters to be re-shuffled when comparing words. Two words will be considered equivalent if they require equivalent parameters to be stored, independent of their ordering or their names.

Let us first see how a constrained word can be split into a prefix and a suffix. Consider a constrained word $\langle w, \varphi \rangle$, where w is a concatenation uv. We can make a corresponding split of φ as $\varphi' \wedge \psi$, where the right-hand sides of equalities in φ' are parameters of u and the right-hand sides of equalities in ψ are parameters of v. Then $\langle u, \varphi' \rangle$ (the prefix) is a constrained word, but $\langle v, \psi \rangle$ (the suffix) is in general not, since ψ refers to parameters that are not in v. We therefore define a $\langle w, \varphi \rangle$-*suffix* as a tuple $\langle v, \psi \rangle$, where ψ is a constraint in which right-hand sides of equalities are parameters of v, and such that $\langle uv, \varphi \wedge \psi \rangle$ (which we often denote $\langle u, \varphi' \rangle; \langle v, \psi \rangle$) is a constrained word.

We define the *potential* of a constrained word $\langle w, \varphi \rangle$, denoted $pot[\langle w, \varphi \rangle]$, as the set of formal parameters in w that do not occur as the left argument of any equality in φ; for example, $pot[\langle \alpha_1(p_1, p_2)\alpha_2(p_3, p_4), p_1 = p_2 \wedge p_2 = p_3 \rangle] = \{p_3, p_4\}$.

Definition 4 (Memorable). Let λ be a data language, and let $\mathcal{T}$ be the minimal DCDT recognizing λ. The λ-*memorable parameters* of a constrained word $\langle w, \varphi \rangle \in Dom(\mathcal{T})$, denoted $\text{mem}_\lambda(\langle w, \varphi \rangle)$, is the set of parameters in $pot[\langle w, \varphi \rangle]$ that occur in some $\langle w, \varphi \rangle$-suffix $\langle v, \psi \rangle$ such that $\langle w, \varphi \rangle; \langle v, \psi \rangle \in Dom(\mathcal{T})$.   □

We are now ready to define our Nerode congruence on constrained words.

Definition 5 (Nerode Congruence). Let λ be a data language, and let $\mathcal{T}$ be the minimal DCDT recognizing λ. We define the equivalence $\equiv_\lambda$ on constrained words by $\langle w, \varphi \rangle \equiv_\lambda \langle w', \varphi' \rangle$ if there is a bijection $\gamma : \text{mem}_\lambda(\langle w, \varphi \rangle) \mapsto \text{mem}_\lambda(\langle w', \varphi' \rangle)$ such that

- $\langle v, \psi \rangle$ is a $\langle w, \varphi \rangle$-suffix with $\langle w, \varphi \rangle$; $\langle v, \psi \rangle \in Dom(\mathcal{T})$ iff $\langle v, \gamma(\psi) \rangle$ is a $\langle w', \varphi' \rangle$-suffix with $\langle w', \varphi' \rangle$; $\langle v, \gamma(\psi) \rangle \in Dom(\mathcal{T})$, and then
- $\lambda(\langle w, \varphi \rangle; \langle v, \psi \rangle) = \lambda(\langle w', \varphi' \rangle; \langle v, \gamma(\psi) \rangle)$,

where $\gamma(\psi)$ is obtained from ψ by replacing all parameters in $\text{mem}_\lambda(\langle w, \varphi \rangle)$ by their image under γ.   □

Intuitively, two constrained words are equivalent if they induce the same residual languages modulo a remapping of their memorable parameters. The equivalence $\equiv_\lambda$ is also a congruence in the following sense. If $\langle w, \varphi \rangle \equiv_\lambda \langle w', \varphi' \rangle$ is established by the bijection $\gamma : \text{mem}_\lambda(\langle w, \varphi \rangle) \mapsto \text{mem}_\lambda(\langle w', \varphi' \rangle)$, then for any $\text{mem}_\lambda(\langle w, \varphi \rangle)$-suffix $\langle v, \psi \rangle$ we have $\langle w, \varphi \rangle$; $\langle v, \psi \rangle \equiv_\lambda \langle w', \varphi' \rangle$; $\langle v, \gamma(\psi) \rangle$.

Example: In the data language that is accepted by the DRA of Figure 3, the word $\langle \mathsf{register}(p_1, p_2)\mathsf{login}(p_3, p_4)\mathsf{pw}(p_5), p_1 = p_3 \wedge p_2 = p_4 \rangle$ and the word $\langle \mathsf{register}(p_1, p_2)\mathsf{login}(p_3, p_4), p_1 = p_3 \wedge p_2 = p_4 \rangle$ are equivalent w.r.t. $\equiv_\lambda$. For the remapping $\gamma(p_4) = p_5$, and $\gamma(p_3) = p_3$ the residuals become identical. E.g., the suffix $\langle \mathsf{logout}()\mathsf{login}(p_6, p_7), p_3 = p_6 \wedge p_4 = p_7 \rangle$, will become the suffix $\langle \mathsf{logout}()\mathsf{login}(p_6, p_7), p_3 = p_6 \wedge p_5 = p_7 \rangle$ under remapping. Concatenation with the original words will lead to accepted words in both cases.   □

Guard transformation. We will introduce a transformation from suffixes to guards, which will be needed in Theorem 2 when constructing DRAs from DCDTs.

Let Φ be a set of constrained words, with $\langle w, \varphi \rangle \in \Phi$. We say that $p_i \neq p_j$ is an *implicit inequality* of $\langle w, \varphi \rangle$ w.r.t. Φ if φ is of form $\varphi' \wedge \psi$ for some ψ with $p_j \sqsubseteq_w \psi$, and Φ contains a constrained word of form $\langle w, \varphi' \wedge p_i = p_j \wedge \psi' \rangle$. Let $ineqs_\Phi(\langle w, \varphi \rangle)$ be the conjunction of all implicit inequalities of $\langle w, \varphi \rangle$ w.r.t. Φ. Define the guard $g_\Phi^{\langle w, \varphi \rangle}$ as $g_\Phi^{\langle w, \varphi \rangle} \equiv \varphi \wedge ineqs_\Phi(\langle w, \varphi \rangle)$. Then, $g_\Phi^{\langle w, \varphi \rangle}$ has the property that $\mathsf{w}_d \models \langle w, g_\Phi^{\langle w, \varphi \rangle} \rangle$ iff $\langle w, \varphi \rangle \preceq_\Phi \mathsf{w}_d$

Example: Consider the DCDT from Figure 2. Let Φ contain $\langle w, true \rangle$, $\langle w, p_1 = p_3 \rangle$, and $\langle w, p_1 = p_3 \wedge p_2 = p_4 \rangle$, and let $w = \mathsf{register}(p_1, p_2)\mathsf{login}(p_3, p_4)$. Then $p_1 \neq p_3$ is an implicit inequality of $\langle w, true \rangle$, because $p_3 \sqsubseteq_w true$, and because $\langle w, p_1 = p_3 \rangle$ contains $p_1 = p_3$. Similarly, $p_2 \neq p_4$ is an implicit inequality of $\langle w, p_1 = p_3 \rangle$. We then obtain the guard $g_\Phi^{\langle w, true \rangle}$ as $p_1 \neq p_3$, the guard $g_\Phi^{\langle w, p_1 = p_3 \rangle}$ as $p_1 = p_3 \wedge p_2 \neq p_4$, and the guard $g_\Phi^{\langle w, p_1 = p_3 \wedge p_2 = p_4 \rangle}$ as $p_1 = p_3 \wedge p_2 = p_4$.   □

We now state the main result of our paper, which relates our Nerode congruence to DRAs.

Theorem 2 (Myhill-Nerode). A data language λ is recognizable by a DRA iff the equivalence $\equiv_\lambda$ on λ-essential words has finite index.

Proof. If: The if-direction follows by constructing a DRA from a given $\equiv_\lambda$, as the DRA $\mathcal{A} = (\; locs, l_0, X, T, \lambda)$, where

- L is given by the finitely many equivalence classes of the equivalence relation $\equiv_\lambda$ on λ-essential words. For each equivalence class, we choose a representative λ-essential constrained word.
- l_0 is $[\langle \epsilon, true \rangle]_{\equiv_\lambda}$, with the empty word as representative element.
- X maps each location $[\langle w, \varphi \rangle]_{\equiv_\lambda}$ with representative word $\langle w, \varphi \rangle$ to the set $X([\langle w, \varphi \rangle]_{\equiv_\lambda})$ of λ-memorable parameters of $\langle w, \varphi \rangle$. Note that we here use parameters as variables.
- T is constructed as follows. For each location $l = [\langle w, \varphi \rangle]_{\equiv_\lambda}$ in L with representative element $\langle w, \varphi \rangle$ and each λ-essential one-symbol extension of $\langle w, \varphi \rangle$ of form $\langle w, \varphi \rangle; \langle \alpha(\overline{p}), \psi \rangle$, there is a transition in T of form $\langle l, \alpha(\overline{p}), g, \gamma, l' \rangle$, where
  - $l' = [\langle w, \varphi \rangle; \langle \alpha(\overline{p}), \psi \rangle]_{\equiv_\lambda}$; let $\langle w', \varphi' \rangle$ be the representative element of the equivalence class $[\langle w, \varphi \rangle; \langle \alpha(\overline{p}), \psi \rangle]_{\equiv_\lambda}$,
  - γ is the bijection $\gamma : \text{mem}_\lambda(\langle w', \varphi' \rangle) \mapsto \text{mem}_\lambda(\langle w, \varphi \rangle; \langle \alpha(\overline{p}), \psi \rangle)$ which is used to establish $\langle w', \varphi' \rangle \equiv_\lambda \langle w, \varphi \rangle; \langle \alpha(\overline{p}), \psi \rangle$ in Definition 5,
  - g is obtained as g_Φ^ψ, where Φ is the set of all λ-essential extensions of $\langle w, \varphi \rangle$ by the action α, i.e., the set of λ-essential words of form $\langle w, \varphi \rangle; \langle \alpha(\overline{p}), \psi' \rangle$.
- $\lambda([\langle w, \varphi \rangle]_{\equiv_\lambda}) = \lambda(\mathbf{w}_d)$ whenever $\langle w, \varphi \rangle = \mathrm{cw}[\mathbf{w}_d]$.

The constructed DRA is well defined: it has finitely many locations since the index of $\equiv_\lambda$ is finite, the initial location is defined as the class of the empty word, and λ is defined from λ for the representative elements of the locations. The transition relation is total and determinate. This is guaranteed by construction of guards from DCDTs, and by construction of DCDTs.

To complete this direction of the proof, we need to show that the constructed automaton $\mathcal{A}$ indeed recognizes λ. Consider an arbitrary sequence of transitions of $\mathcal{A}$, of form

$$\langle l_0, \alpha_1(\overline{p}_1), g_1, \pi_1, l_1 \rangle \quad \cdots \quad \langle l_{k-1}, \alpha_k(\overline{p}_k), g_k, \pi_k, l_k \rangle \;,$$

which generates a run of form $\langle \alpha_1(\overline{p}_1) \cdots \alpha_k(\overline{p}_k) \;, g \rangle$, where g is $g_1 \wedge \tilde{\pi}_1(\cdots \wedge \tilde{\pi}_{k-1}(g_k)))$. Let $w = \alpha_1(\overline{p}_1) \cdots \alpha_k(\overline{p}_k)$, and let φ be the ordered sequence of equalities in g (i.e., omitting inequalities). By construction, $\langle w, \varphi \rangle$ is a λ-essential constrained word such that g is equivalent to $g_{Dom(T)}^{\langle w, \varphi \rangle}$, which implies that $\mathbf{w}_d \models \langle w, g \rangle$ iff $\langle w, \varphi \rangle \preceq_{Dom(T)} \mathbf{w}_d$ for any data word $\mathbf{w}_d$. In summary, this implies that $\mathcal{A}$ correctly classifies data words that satisfy any of its runs.

Only if: For the only-if direction, we assume any (right-invariant) DRA that accepts λ. The proof idea then is to show that two λ-essential constrained words corresponding to sequences of transitions that lead to the same location are also equivalent w.r.t. $\equiv_\lambda$, i.e., that one location of a DRA cannot represent more than one class of $\equiv_\lambda$. This can be shown straight-forwardly using right-invariance. $\quad \square$

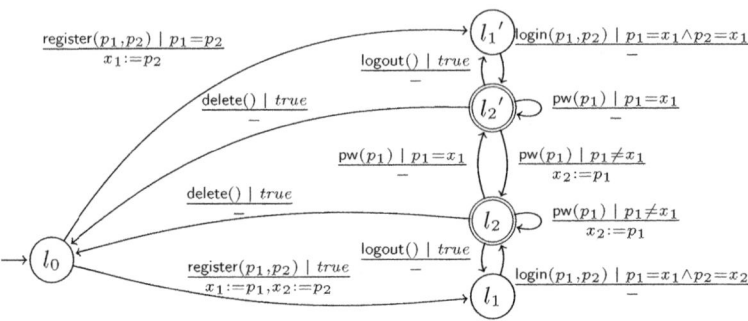

Fig. 3. Partial DURA model for a fragment of XMPP

We get as a corollary result from the only-if direction of the proof that the automaton generated in the first part of this proof is in fact a minimal (in the set of locations) right-invariant DRA recognizing λ. As stated already, minimality of the DCDT representation guarantees that the automaton will also use a minimal number of variables.

5   Comparison between Different Automata Models

In this section we will compare our register automata to previously proposed formalisms. We will show that our models can be exponentially more succinct.

There are already proposals for DRAs that accept data languages, which, however, fail to be simple and do not exactly match the flavor of data languages we are using [15,3]. For instance, in these automata, variables have to be unique, or can only be accessed in a queue-like fashion. A Myhill-Nerode-like theorem has been proposed for these data languages and automata [11,3]. It is, however, formulated on the level of concrete data words. This makes it difficult to identify essential relations between parameters in the corresponding canonical form.

Both the design of the DRAs and the Nerode congruence on the level of data words thus require encoding information about accidental relations between parameters into the set of locations. This makes the models harder to understand and work with. We will show that in the worst case the resulting canonical models can be exponentially bigger than our canonical models.

Let us define a class of RAs that resembles the automata of [3]. An RA is *unique-valued* (called a URA) if the valuation σ in any reachable state $\langle l, \sigma \rangle$ is injective, i.e., two variables can never store the same data value. An RA is *ordered* (called an ORA) if state variables are ordered (we will use $<$ to represent this ordering), and data values are stored only in order of appearance. That is if x_i and x_j are two state variables with $x_i < x_j$, then in any reachable state, either x_j is undefined, or the transition at which x_i was assigned a value must coincide with or precede the transition at which x_j was last assigned a value. We will also define an OURA, which is both *ordered* and *unique-valued*. We will refer to the automata resulting from our Nerode congruence as DRAs. The automata of [3] correspond to deterministic OURAs (DOURAs).

In the worst case, there are two exponential blow-ups: between DRAs and DURAs, and between DURAs and DOURAs. The first exponential blow-up between DRAs and DURAs can be shown by constructing a DRA that can store n independent variables, while the corresponding DURA has to maintain in the set of locations which of the n variables have the same value. The second exponential blow-up between DURAs and DOURAs can be shown by constructing a DURA that allows random (write) access to n variables. The corresponding DOURA has to maintain in the set of locations the order in which the variables are written.

These blow-ups will not always be exponential. We will illustrate the difference between DURAs and our canonical form using our running example. Figure 3 shows a partial DURA model for the DRA from Figure 1. The DURA has to maintain if provided username and password (p_1, p_2 from register(p_1, p_2)) accidentally coincide. In this case this leads to replication of each location from which these two data values can be accessed, namely l_1 and l_2. A DOURA in this case would look the same as the DURA. Adding a primitive to change the username, however, would lead to another blow-up in the DOURA: the order in which username and password have been set would have to be encoded in the set of locations.

6   Conclusions and Future Work

In this paper, we present a novel form of register automata, which also has an intuitive and succinct minimal canonical form, which can be derived from a Nerode-like right congruence.

Our immediate plans are to use these results to generalize Angluin-style active learning to data languages over infinite alphabets, which can be used to characterize protocols, services, and interfaces. Another obvious problem is to generalize the canonical model to more expressive signatures with other simple operations on data values, e.g., including comparisons of various forms.

References

1. Alon, N., Milo, T., Neven, F., Suciu, D., Vianu, V.: XML with data values: type-checking revisited. J. Comput. Syst. Sci. 66(4), 688–727 (2003)
2. Alur, R., Dill, D.: A theory of timed automata. Theoretical Computer Science 126, 183–235 (1994)
3. Benedikt, M., Ley, C., Puppis, G.: What you must remember when processing data words. In: Proc. 4th Alberto Mendelzon Int. Workshop on Foundations of Data Management, Buenos Aires, Argentina. CEUR Workshop Proceedings, vol. 619 (2010)
4. Berg, T., Jonsson, B., Raffelt, H.: Regular inference for state machines using domains with equality tests. In: Fiadeiro, J.L., Inverardi, P. (eds.) FASE 2008. LNCS, vol. 4961, pp. 317–331. Springer, Heidelberg (2008)

5. Bielecki, M., Hidders, J., Paredaens, J., Tyszkiewicz, J., den Bussche, J.V.: Navigating with a browser. In: Widmayer, P., Triguero, F., Morales, R., Hennessy, M., Eidenbenz, S., Conejo, R. (eds.) ICALP 2002. LNCS, vol. 2380, pp. 764–775. Springer, Heidelberg (2002)
6. Björklund, H., Schwentick, T.: On notions of regularity for data languages. Theoretical Computer Science 411, 702–715 (2010)
7. Bojanczyk, M.: Data monoids. In: STACS, pp. 105–116 (2011)
8. Bojanczyk, M., David, C., Muscholl, A., Schwentick, T., Segoufin, L.: Two-variable logic on data words. ACM Transactions on Computational Logic (to appear, 2011)
9. Bouyer, P.: A logical characterization of data languages. Information Processing Letters 84, 200–202 (2001)
10. Bouyer, P., Petit, A., Thérien, D.: An algebraic approach to data languages and timed languages. Information and Computation 182(2), 137–162 (2003)
11. Francez, N., Kaminski, M.: An algebraic characterization of deterministic regular languages over infinite alphabets. Theoretical Computer Science 306(1-3), 155–175 (2003)
12. Grumberg, O., Kupferman, O., Sheinvald, S.: Variable automata over infinite alphabets. In: Dediu, A.-H., Fernau, H., Martín-Vide, C. (eds.) LATA 2010. LNCS, vol. 6031, pp. 561–572. Springer, Heidelberg (2010)
13. Hopcroft, J., Ullman, J.: Introduction to Automata Theory, Languages, and Computation. Addison-Wesley, Reading (1979)
14. Issarny, V., Steffen, B., Jonsson, B., Blair, G.S., Grace, P., Kwiatkowska, M.Z., Calinescu, R., Inverardi, P., Tivoli, M., Bertolino, A., Sabetta, A.: CONNECT Challenges: Towards Emergent Connectors for Eternal Networked Systems. In: ICECCS, pp. 154–161 (2009)
15. Kaminski, M., Francez, N.: Finite-memory automata. Theoretical Computer Science 134(2), 329–363 (1994)
16. Kanellakis, P., Smolka, S.: CCS expressions, finite state processes, and three problems of equivalence. Information and Computation 86(1), 43–68 (1990)
17. Lazic, R., Nowak, D.: A unifying approach to data-independence. In: Palamidessi, C. (ed.) CONCUR 2000. LNCS, vol. 1877, pp. 581–595. Springer, Heidelberg (2000)
18. Maler, O., Pnueli, A.: On recognizable timed languages. In: Walukiewicz, I. (ed.) FOSSACS 2004. LNCS, vol. 2987, pp. 348–362. Springer, Heidelberg (2004)
19. Nerode, A.: Linear Automaton Transformations. Proceedings of the American Mathematical Society 9(4), 541–544 (1958)
20. Paige, R., Tarjan, R.: Three partition refinement algorithms. SIAM Journal of Computing 16(6), 973–989 (1987)
21. Petrenko, A., Boroday, S., Groz, R.: Confirming configurations in EFSM testing. IEEE Trans. on Software Engineering 30(1), 29–42 (2004)
22. Saint-Andre, P.: Extensible Messaging and Presence Protocol (XMPP): Instant Messaging and Presence. RFC 6121 (Proposed Standard) (March 2011)
23. Segoufin, L.: Automata and logics for words and trees over an infinite alphabet. In: Ésik, Z. (ed.) CSL 2006. LNCS, vol. 4207, pp. 41–57. Springer, Heidelberg (2006)
24. Wilke, T.: Specifying timed state sequences in powerful decidable logics and timed automata. In: Langmaack, H., de Roever, W.-P., Vytopil, J. (eds.) FTRTFT 1994 and ProCoS 1994. LNCS, vol. 863, pp. 694–715. Springer, Heidelberg (1994)

Parallel Nested Depth-First
Searches for LTL Model Checking

Sami Evangelista, Laure Petrucci, and Samir Youcef

LIPN, CNRS UMR 7030, Université Paris XIII
99, avenue Jean-Baptiste Clément
F-93430 Villetaneuse, France
firstname.lastname@lipn.univ-paris13.fr

Abstract. Even though the well-known nested-depth first search algorithm for LTL model checking provides good performance, it cannot benefit from the recent advent of multi-core computers. This paper proposes a new version of this algorithm, adapted to multi-core architectures with a shared memory. It can exhibit good speed-ups as supported by a series of experiments.

1 Introduction

The model checking problem aims at verifying whether a given hardware or software system meets its specification. For the analysis of properties expressed in the Linear-time Temporal Logic (LTL) this problem is often reduced to checking the emptiness of a Büchi automaton defined as the product of the system and an automaton negating the formula to check [26]. Thus, model checking boils down to find a cycle in a directed graph, and more precisely, to verify the existence of an *accepting cycle*. The latter is defined as a cycle (in the sense of graph theory) containing at least one accepting state.

This problem has been intensively explored because of its importance, using diverse techniques. In the context of *explicit-state* model checking, algorithms usually rely on depth-first-search (DFS) strategies allowing to check for Büchi emptiness in linear time. They are split in two main families: *Nested* DFS (ndfs), originally proposed by Courcoubetis et al [11], consist of two procedures where the first one allows to find and sort the accepting states while the second one, interleaved with the first one, searches for cycles containing these states ; SCC (*strongly-connected components*) based algorithms [12, 17] exploit the fact that a counter-example exists if and only if a strongly connected component containing an accepting state is reachable from the initial state.

Despite the existence of algorithms with linear complexity for this emptiness check, combinatorial aspects remain due to the state space size of real systems, their exact analysis often being intractable. However, recent hardware developments, such as 64-bits technologies, contribute to harnessing formal verification memory limitations. Hence, the problem we can now often face is a "time explosion" rather than a lack of memory. For instance, using aggressive memory reduction techniques [21] one can hope to analyse state space graphs with e.g. 10^{10}–10^{11} states. Even with the fastest tools available, such as SPIN [19], a full exploration of such a graph would require weeks.

T. Bultan and P.-A. Hsiung (Eds.): ATVA 2011, LNCS 6996, pp. 381–396, 2011.
© Springer-Verlag Berlin Heidelberg 2011

The use of parallel search algorithms can naturally leverage this time explosion. Most algorithms of this category were initially designed for distributed-memory architectures [1,5,7,8,9], fostered by easy access to networks of workstations. The availability of multi-core chips on desktop computers now offers opportunities to speed up tasks execution and also for the development of new approaches to model checking [3,22].

Our contribution is a parallel algorithm designed for shared memory and multi-core architectures: Multi-Core ndfs (mc-ndfs). It solves the Büchi emptiness problem by launching multiple instances of ndfs. The use of both randomisation and synchronisations allows, to some extent, to force processes to visit different parts of the graph and to avoid, as much as possible, multiple revisits of a same state. Thus, even if our algorithm is theoretically not scalable it provides significant speed-ups for many case studies as attested by a wide range of experiments.

The paper is organised as follows. Section 2 presents related works: the well-known ndfs algorithm is recalled and existing parallel algorithms for LTL model checking summarised after outlining the accepting cycle detection problem. Section 3 details the proposed algorithm and gives its formal proof. Section 4 presents experimental results. Our work is concluded by Section 5 that also gives some perspectives for future work.

2   Background

In order to facilitate the understanding of our algorithm and its comparison with algorithms from the literature, we begin with a brief state of the art: LTL model checking, some algorithms based on ndfs, and parallel algorithms for LTL model checking.

2.1   The LTL Model Checking Problem

This paper addresses LTL model checking of finite-state systems where both the systems and their properties are modelled as automata. Then, verification is often reduced to checking the emptiness of a Büchi automaton defined as the product of the system and the negated formula [26]. This problem can be stated in its basic form as follows:

Definition 1 (Synchronised graph). *A synchronised graph is a tuple $G = (S, T, \mathcal{A}, s_0)$, where S is a finite set of states; $T \subseteq S \times S$ is a set of transitions; $\mathcal{A} \subseteq S$ is the set of accepting states, and $s_0 \in S$ is an initial state.*

The set of *successors* of $s \in S$ is denoted by $succ(s) = \{s' | (s,s') \in S\}$. A *path* is a sequence of states $s_1 \ldots s_k$ with $(s_i, s_{i+1}) \in T$ for all $i \in \{1, \ldots, k-1\}$ denoted by $s_1 \rightsquigarrow s_k$. A *cycle* is a path with $s_1 = s_k$. An *accepting cycle* is a cycle that contains at least one state $a \in \mathcal{A}$. An *accepting run* is a path from s_0 to s_l through s_k where $s_k \ldots s_l$ form an accepting cycle. The *accepting cycle detection problem* aims at determining if a given graph G contains an accepting cycle. The major algorithms addressing this problem are based either on nested DFS (ndfs) or on SCCs (originating from Tarjan's algorithm for decomposing the graph into strongly connected components). Since the algorithm proposed in this paper is essentially based on ndfs, we shall focus on this one only. Details on SCC-based algorithms can be found elsewhere [12, 17].

2.2   Algorithms Based on Nested Depth-First Search

The well-known nested-depth first search algorithm for LTL model checking, was initially introduced in [11]. All algorithms belonging to this category still follow the same scheme. The ndfs algorithm (see Algorithm 1.1) is defined by two procedures called *dfsBlue* and *dfsRed*. The first one, which is the main loop, allows for marking each newly visited state as blue. The second one tries to find a loop back to a given accepting state *s*, and marks all encountered states as red. If a cycle is detected then a counterexample is reported, otherwise the first DFS continues and the red markings remain. Note that each DFS visits each state at most once and requires one bit per state. Procedure *dfsBlue* performs a depth-first search and sets the blue bits of all visited states. Procedure *dfsRed* is invoked when the search from an accepting state *s* finishes. Finally, if *dfsRed* finds that some accepting state *s* can be reached from itself, an accepting cycle is returned, otherwise the graph does not contain any cycle.

Since its introduction, several improvements have been proposed. Some aim at reporting accepting runs faster [13, 14, 15, 18] while others [16] focus on the length of counter-examples. Nested DFS is now implemented by a large range of explicit state model checkers among which SPIN [19] was historically the first.

2.3   Parallel Algorithms for LTL Model Checking

The best known enumerative *sequential* algorithms in the area of LTL model checking are Nested DFS and SCC-based algorithms. Adapting them to take advantage of parallel architectures is difficult since they rely on inherently sequential depth-first search postorder. Hence, it is necessary to propose new techniques and algorithms. Before getting into the details of the proposed algorithm, seven existing parallel algorithms are outlined: *Maximal Accepting Predecessor* (map), *One Way Catch Them Young* (owcty), *One Way Catch Them Young On-The-Fly* (owcty-otf), *Negative Cycle* (negc), *Back-Level Edges* (bledge), *Back-Level Edges On-The-Fly* (bledge-otf), and SPIN's double DFS (2-ndfs). All except the last one have been initially designed for distributed memory architectures, but it is well known that they can easily be transformed into shared memory algorithms. To compare the different complexities of these algorithms the following notations are used: $n = |S|$, $m = |T|$, $a = |A|$, $p =$ number of working processes and h (height) is the smallest integer s.t. s_0 can reach all states using at most h transitions.

Algorithm map [8] uses an order relation on states to compute the maximal accepting predecessor function *map* mapping each state *s* to the identity of the greatest accepting state that is backward reachable from *s*.

Algorithm 1.1. The ndfs algorithm adapted from [11]

1 **procedure** *ndfs(s)* **is**	*6* **procedure** *dfsBlue(s)* **is**	*14* **procedure** *dfsRed(s)* **is**
2 **initialise all flags to** *false*	*7* *s.blue* := *true*	*15* *s.red* := *true*
3 *dfsBlue(s_0)*	*8* **for** $s' \in succ(s)$ **do**	*16* **for** $s' \in succ(s)$ **do**
4 **if** ¬ **cycle** reported **then**	*9* **if** ¬s'.*blue* **then**	*17* **if** $s' = seed$ **then**
5 **report no-cycle**	*10* *dfsBlue(s')*	*18* **report cycle**
	11 **if** $s \in A$ **then**	*19* **else if** ¬s'.*red* **then**
	12 *seed* := *s*	*20* *dfsRed(s')*
	13 *dfsRed(s)*	

The key idea behind algorithm owcty is to repeatedly remove from the graph states that cannot lead to an accepting cycle [9], according to two rules: a state s can be removed if it has no successor in the graph and/or it cannot lead to an accepting state. An extension of owcty algorithm is presented in [2]. The owcty-otf algorithm employs back-level edges as computed by the breadth-first search.

An extension of the owcty algorithm is presented in [4]. The owcty-otf algorithm combines the basic owcty algorithm with a limited propagation of selected accepting states as performed within the map algorithm.

Algorithm negc [7] reduces the LTL model checking problem to a negative cycle detection problem. To do so, the initial graph is transformed: every edge exiting an accepting state is labeled with -1 while every edge exiting a non-accepting state is labeled with 0 (a counter-example exists iff the transformed graph contains a negative cycle).

Every accepting cycle contains at least one accepting state and one *back-level edge* (s, s') such that $d(s) \geq d(s')$, where $d(x)$ is the length of the shortest path from s_0 to x. Algorithm bledge [1] stems from this observation. It detects all back-level edges using a distributed BFS and then checks in parallel whether at least one back-level edge belongs to a cycle by using DFS. In [2], an extension of the bledge algorithm has been proposed (bledge-otf) that allows on-the-fly accepting cycle detection.

An extension of ndfs for a dual-core machine, called double-DFS (2-ndfs) hereafter, is presented in [22] and implemented in SPIN [19]. It is based on the observation that the blue and the red DFS can be performed independently. The linear complexity of ndfs is kept although the algorithm can only be applied to dual-core systems.

After preparing this final version, we noticed that another approach on parallelising Nested Depth First Search appears in this same volume [23]. Both approaches appear to be complementary, since the colours shared are not the same, thus affecting different parts of the program execution. Moreover, in the other approach, a synchronisation mechanism is required whereas we use randomised executions with a repair procedure.

Table 1 summarises explicit states algorithms designed for LTL model checking. It provides, for each algorithm, the reference introducing it, its time complexity, the number of core(s) it can be run on, the acceleration (experimentally observed) that can be provided and finally its "on-the-flyness" as defined in [4]:

level 0. The algorithm has to explore the whole graph before checking emptiness.

level 1. The algorithm can find an accepting run before building the whole synchronised graph but is not guaranteed to do so.

level 2. The algorithm works on-the-fly. There is always an exploration order of transitions guaranteeing an early termination in the presence of an accepting run.

Note that, with our new algorithm mc-ndfs, the aggregate work performed by all processes increases as more processes get involved in the verification. Hence mc-ndfs does not scale in theory and, in the worst case, does not offer any improvement with respect to a sequential ndfs. Our algorithm is therefore a heuristic algorithm: we can hope to reduce the exploration time through the mechanism it implements, but for some problems it may be equivalent to spawning multiple instances of ndfs. Nevertheless, even in this pathological situation, the use of randomisation can help to report counter-examples faster. This is one of the founding principles of the Swarm tool [20].

Table 1. Explicit state algorithms for Büchi emptiness check

Algorithm	Source	Time Complexity	Scalability	Acceleration	On-the-flyness
ndfs	[11]	$O(n+m)$	1 core	-	2
couv-tarjan	[12]	$O(n+m)$	1 core	-	2
GV-tarjan	[17]	$O(n+m)$	1 core	-	2
2-ndfs	[22]	$O(n+m)$	1–2 core(s)	average	2
map	[8]	$O(a^2 \cdot m)$	1–N core(s)	excellent	1
owcty	[9]	$O(h \cdot m)$	1–N core(s)	excellent	0
owcty-otf	[4]	$O((h \cdot (m+n)))$	1–N core(s)	excelent	1
negc	[7]	$O(n \cdot m)$	1–N core(s)	excellent	0
bledge	[1]	$O(m \cdot (n+m))$	1–N core(s)	excellent	0
bledge-otf	[2]	$O(m \cdot (n+m))$	1–N core(s)	excellent	2
mc-ndfs	this paper	$O(p \cdot (n+m))$	1–N core(s)	average-good	2

3   mc-ndfs, a Multi-core Algorithm for LTL Model Checking

This section introduces mc-ndfs, a new algorithm for LTL model checking, designed for multi-core, shared memory architectures. It first emphasises the difficulty of parallelising ndfs. The principle of mc-ndfs is then explained, the algorithm detailed and formally proven. Finally, its complexity is discussed and a possible extension introduced.

Throughout this section, we denote by $G = (S, T, A, s_0)$ a synchronised graph and by $P = \{1, \ldots, P\}$ a pool of running processes.

3.1   Difficulty of Parallelising ndfs

Fig. 1(a) describes a synchronised graph used as a running example throughout this section. Accepting states are drawn, as usual, using double circles. This graph contains a single accepting run $0{\rightarrow}1{\rightarrow}2{\rightarrow}1$ highlighted using thick arcs.

Let us consider a naive multi-core version of the ndfs algorithm: processes execute procedure ndfs and share all data (i.e. blue and red flags). Running this algorithm with two processes p_1 and p_2 on the graph of Fig. 1(a) will not necessarily report the accepting cycle, as shown by the execution in Fig. 1(b).

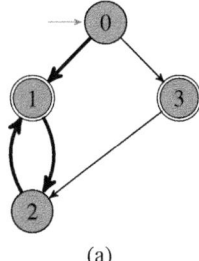

Process p_1	Process p_2	Blue states	Red States	Seed
dfsBlue(0)	dfsBlue(0)	0	-	-
dfsBlue(1)		0, 1	-	-
dfsBlue(2)		0, 1, 2	-	1
dfsRed(1)		0, 1, 2	1	1
	dfsBlue(3)	0, 1, 2, 3	1	3
	dfsRed(3)	0, 1, 2, 3	1, 3	3
	dfsRed(2)	0, 1, 2, 3	1, 2, 3	3

(a)   (b)

Fig. 1. A synchronised graph (1(a)) and a possible faulty execution with a naive parallel version of ndfs (1(b))

The blue DFS launched by p_1 starts exploring the left part of the graph and colours the states it meets in blue (i.e. 0, 1 and 2). When backtracking from 2 and then 1, process p_1 initiates a red DFS on state 1. Suppose that meanwhile the blue DFS launched by process p_2 visits the right part of the graph. It colours state 3 in blue and then reaches state 2 previously marked blue by p_1. Since all successors of state 3 are blue, p_2 can start a red DFS on this same state. If p_2 progresses faster than p_1, it will colour states 3 and 2 in red before terminating. Process p_1, when evaluating the successor of state 1, will only find state 2 (already red) and terminate without noticing the accepting cycle.

This small example highlights the key idea behind the correctness of ndfs: the red DFS being nested in the blue DFS guarantees that the invocation sequence of $dfsRed$ respects a DFS post-ordering of states. Hence, if two accepting states a_1 and a_2 are such that $a_1 \rightsquigarrow a_2 \wedge \neg(a_2 \rightsquigarrow a_1)$ (noted $a_1 > a_2$ in the sequel) then for all executions the red DFS on a_1 cannot start unless the red DFS on a_2 did terminate. Otherwise the red DFS started on a_1 would colour in red the states of the accepting cycle including a_2 (if any), which would then not be detected by the red DFS initiated on a_2. In all other cases, the invocation order is irrelevant: either the two red DFS cannot interfere ($\neg(a_1 \rightsquigarrow a_2) \wedge \neg(a_2 \rightsquigarrow a_1)$), or a_1 and a_2 belong to the same accepting cycle ($a_1 \rightsquigarrow a_2 \wedge a_2 \rightsquigarrow a_1$) and this cycle will be detected anyway. This naive parallel version of ndfs exhibits the first situation since the DFS post-order is not respected anymore (with $a_2 = 1$ and $a_1 = 3$ in our example).

Solving this kind of conflict constitutes the core difficulty when designing a multi-core version of ndfs.

3.2   Principle of the Algorithm

The previous problem has first been detailed in [5] that proposes an algorithm designed for distributed memory algorithms. Its underlying principle is to maintain a dependency graph that avoids these conflicts and ensures that the red DFS is initiated in the appropriate order: $a_1 > a_2 \Rightarrow dfsRed(a_2)$ terminates before $dfsRed(a_1)$ starts. The principle of mc-ndfs is instead to detect, on-the-fly, configurations in which the invocation order of the red DFS is broken. It is optimistic in the sense that processes evolve without preventing conflicts, and operations to fix problems are performed a posteriori. Thus, all synchronisations required in [5] are avoided, but states may be revisited if a conflict is detected. More precisely, a process notifies its peers by marking state a_2 as *dangerous*. It must then be treated differently as explained below. In our previous example, process p_2 would detect that the red DFS it initiated on state 3 interferes with the one on state 1 still handled by p_1. This conflict is detected by p_2 and reported to p_1 by marking state 1 as *dangerous*. In this situation, p_1 restarts a nested DFS using Algorithm 1.1 but exploits local data only. Hence, the red flag set to *true* by p_2 (i.e. 2.*red*) during the red DFS it performed on state 3 is ignored by p_1, which reports the cycle $1 \rightarrow 2 \rightarrow 1$.

Marking an accepting state a as *dangerous* is thus a means for a process to warn its peers that a red DFS it performed has potentially corrupted the outcome of a red DFS on a. The easiest way to proceed is then, after the red DFS on a has terminated, to reinitiate a nested depth-first search on a since an accepting state could have been missed. Hence, mc-ndfs can be viewed as a two levels algorithm: a *multi-core level* with inter-processes synchronisations to distribute work among processes; and an *emergency level* without any synchronisation and triggered in case of failure of the first level.

3.3 Details of the Algorithm

Algorithm 1.2 shows the pseudo-code of our new algorithm. States have several attributes. Some are local to a process p (attributes $s.blue_p$ and $s.red_p$ for $p \in \mathcal{P}$) while others are global and shared by all processes ($s.blue, s.dangerous, s.red$).

The main procedure (ll. 1–6) first initialises all boolean attributes of states to *false* and spawns P working processes that will start a blue DFS on the initial state. If they terminate without reporting any accepting cycle, the algorithm reports that none exists.

Roughly speaking, two modifications have been brought to the sequential algorithm. First, to ensure, as much as possible, that processes will engage in different parts of the graph, successor states are visited in a random order thanks to the *shuffle* function (l. 11 and l. 20). Second, inter-process synchronisations have been integrated to both DFSs — through the global attributes $s.blue$ and $s.red$ — in order to limit the visits of a same state by different processes (see l. 16 and l. 21).[1]

Modifications to the blue DFS. First, states visited by the red DFS are not directly marked as red but instead put in set $\mathcal{R}_p$ to be later marked by the blue DFS once the red search has terminated (ll. 28–30). Note that a dangerous state may not be marked as red, unless it is the state currently visited. Second, a state s, marked as dangerous by another process, is revisited with $ndfs_p$ (ll. 31–32). Red and blue attributes associated with each state s by $ndfs_p$ — the same as in Algorithm 1.1 except for the few minor changes listed below — are distinct from those used by mc-ndfs and local to each process so that data computed by another process may not corrupt the result that will come out from a call to procedure $ndfs_p$. Moreover, the computation result of an invocation of $ndfs_p$ can be used during subsequent calls to this same procedure. Therefore, a state cannot be visited more than once by a process p with procedure $ndfs_p$. Consequently, the initialisation step (l. 2 of Algorithm 1.1) is not performed during an invocation of $ndfs_p$ and local flags used in this procedure can be initialised at l. 1 of Algorithm 1.2.

Modifications to the red DFS. First, a successor state s' of s is marked as dangerous (ll. 14–15) when it is accepting but not red. In this situation, the red DFS on s' has not terminated (since $\neg s'.red$) although it may have started. The red flags of states reachable from s' that the current process p will set to *true* (at l. 30) must thus be ignored by any process $q \neq p$ that will later launch $ndfs_q(s')$ if $dfsRed_q(s')$ does not report a cycle. This situation corresponds to the kind of conflict exhibited by our previous example.

---

[1] Attribute *s.blue* is set to *true* as soon as s is backtracked from a process whereas it could instead be set before the exploration loop of ll. 20–22. This second alternative would have severely limited the degree of parallelism: as soon as a process p would push a state s on its blue DFS stack, it would prevent all other processes from visiting s and all its successors. For instance, if the initial state had a single successor mc-ndfs would then most likely degenerate into a sequential ndfs. However, by doing so, we leave the possibility to have different processes visiting the same state with the blue DFS: this is thus a tradeoff between the degree of parallelism and the amount of work performed.

Algorithm 1.2. The mc-ndfs algorithm for P working processes

1 **initialise all flags to** *false*	*18* **procedure** *dfsBlue$_p$(s)* **is**
2 **execute** *dfsBlue$_1$(s$_0$)* $\|$ ... $\|$ *dfsBlue$_P$(s$_0$)*	*19* *s.blue$_p$* := *true*
3 **wait for termination of**	*20* **for** *s′* $\in$ *shuffle(succ(s))* **do**
4 *dfsBlue$_1$*, ..., *dfsBlue$_P$*	*21* **if** $\neg s′.blue \wedge \neg s′.blue_p$ **then**
5 **if** $\neg$ **cycle** reported **then**	*22* *dfsBlue$_p$(s′)*
6 **report no-cycle**	*23* *s.blue* := *true*
7	*24* **if** $s \in \mathcal{A}$ **then**
8 **procedure** *dfsRed$_p$(s)* **is**	*25* *seed$_p$* := *s*
9 *s.red$_p$* := *true*	*26* $\mathcal{R}_p$:= $\emptyset$
10 $\mathcal{R}_p$:= $\mathcal{R}_p \cup \{s\}$	*27* *dfsRed$_p$(s)*
11 **for** *s′* $\in$ *shuffle(succ(s))* **do**	*28* **for** $r \in \mathcal{R}_p$ **do**
12 **if** *s′* = *seed$_p$* **then**	*29* **if** $\neg r.dangerous \vee s = r$ **then**
13 **report cycle**	*30* *r.red* := *true*
14 **if** $s′ \in \mathcal{A} \wedge \neg s′.red$ **then**	*31* **if** *s.dangerous* **then**
15 *s′.dangerous* := *true*	*32* *ndfs$_p$(s)*
16 **if** $\neg s′.red \wedge \neg s′.red_p$ **then**	
17 *dfsRed$_p$(s′)*	

Another major change with respect to ndfs is that mc-ndfs marks states as red when a red DFS terminates (ll. 28–30) by storing in $\mathcal{R}_p$ all states visited by the DFS. Indeed, as a red DFS terminates, all states it visited are guaranteed not to belong to an accepting cycle unless a state marked as red led to a non-red and accepting state (hence marked dangerous, as explained above). This information can also be used by other processes. The proof of the algorithm will clarify the motivation for marking states as red only when the red DFS terminates and not earlier.

3.4   Proof of the Algorithm

Intuitively, the correctness of our algorithm stems from the way states are marked red and dangerous. When a red DFS on an accepting state a_1 is triggered by process p before the red DFS has terminated on a state a_2 with $a_1 > a_2$, some states $s \in \mathcal{R}_p$ around a_2 will be marked red and a_2 dangerous. However, since a_2 is marked as dangerous before states of $\mathcal{R}_p$ become red (states are marked as dangerous during the red DFS while states become red once the red DFS has terminated), if an accepting cycle on state a_2 is not discovered, then it is due to the fact that the red DFS on a_2 reached a red state which in turn implies that a_2 has been marked as dangerous. Hence, $ndfs_p(a_2)$ will necessarily be triggered after the red DFS, and the cycle will be reported.

The proof proceeds in five steps. First, it is straightforward that all states will be visited by a blue DFS and thus all accepting states will be visited by a red DFS.

Proposition 1. *After the termination of algorithm* mc-ndfs, *either* an accepting cycle is reported *or* $\forall s \in \mathcal{S}, s.blue \wedge s \in \mathcal{A} \Rightarrow s.red$.

Second, it is an invariant property that an accepting state a can only be marked red after the termination of $dfsRed_p(a)$ (for a process $p \in \mathcal{P}$).

Proposition 2. *Let $a \in \mathcal{A}$. There exists $p \in \mathcal{P}$ such that $dfsRed_p(a)$ is initiated by mc-ndfs with $a.red = false$.*

Proof. Initially, $s.red = false, \forall s \in \mathcal{S}$. From the conditions at l. 29 and l. 14, it holds that $dfsBlue_p(s)$ changes $r.red$ from *false* to *true* (at l. 30) if and only if $r \notin \mathcal{A} \vee r = s$. Hence, if $a \in \mathcal{A}$, $a.red$ can be set to *true* by $p \in \mathcal{P}$ after the termination of $dfsRed_p(a)$. Since, from Prop. 1, $\forall a \in \mathcal{A}, a.red = true$ when mc-ndfs terminates, our claim is proven. □

Third, all accepting states reachable from a red state are either red or dangerous.

Proposition 3. *For any $(s,s') \in \mathcal{S} \times \mathcal{A}: s.red \wedge s \rightsquigarrow s' \Rightarrow s'.red \vee s'.dangerous$.*

Proof. The proof proceeds by induction on set $\mathcal{S}$. Initially, $s.red = false, \forall s \in \mathcal{S}$ and the proposition holds. Let $s \in \mathcal{S}$ be a state marked as red at l. 30 by $dfsBlue_p$. Now assume that the proposition does not hold for s: $\exists a \in \mathcal{A}$ with $s \rightsquigarrow a \wedge \neg a.red \wedge \neg a.dangerous$.

Necessarily, $dfsRed_p(s)$ has been initiated and terminated (since s has been put in $\mathcal{R}_p$). Let us consider a path $s = s_0 \rightarrow \ldots \rightarrow s_n \rightarrow a$. After the initiation of $dfsRed_p(s)$ we necessarily reached a configuration where $dfsRed_p(s_i)$ is initiated; and $s_j = s_{i+1}$ is not visited by the red DFS: $s_j.red \vee s_j.red_p$. Otherwise it would hold, from ll. 14–15, that $a.dangerous$. Now two possibilities arise:

$s_j.red$ — Using our induction hypothesis, $s_j.red \Rightarrow a.dangerous$ (since $s_j \rightsquigarrow a$) which leads to a contradiction.

$\neg s_j.red \wedge s_j.red_p$ — $s_j.red_p$ implies that $dfsRed_p(s_j)$ has been initiated. By recursively applying the same reasoning with path $s_j \rightarrow \ldots \rightarrow s_n \rightarrow a$ we will necessarily find $s_k \in \{s_j, \ldots s_n\}$ with $s_k.red$ which, again, leads to a contradiction.

Hence, if the proposition holds before the assignment at l. 30 then so does it after its execution. Using the induction hypothesis, the proposition holds. □

The fourth point is the key to ensure the correctness of our algorithm: for any accepting cycle going through accepting states $a_1 \ldots a_n$, at least one process p will, by executing $dfsRed_p(a_i)$ for some a_i, report the cycle or revisit a_i through the execution of $ndfs_p(a_i)$ because $a_i.dangerous$ has been set to *true* by another process before $dfsRed_p(a_i)$ terminates.

Proposition 4. *Let $a_1 \in \mathcal{A}, \ldots, a_n \in \mathcal{A}$ belong to the same accepting cycle. Then there exists $p \in \mathcal{P}, a_i \in \{a_1, \ldots, a_n\}$ such that either $dfsRed_p(a_i)$ reports the accepting cycle or $a_i.dangerous = true$ once $dfsRed_p(a_i)$ has terminated.*

Proof. Let us consider an accepting cycle $s_1 \ldots s_n$ with $s_1 = s_n \in \mathcal{A}$. In this proof we assume that $dfsRed_p(s_1)$ starts for some $p \in \mathcal{P}$ and that $s_1.red = false$. This will necessarily happen thanks to Prop. 2. If $dfsRed_p(s_1)$ does not report this accepting cycle we necessarily reach the following configuration:

1. States $s_1, \ldots, s_i$ (with $i < n$) are (in this order) on the red DFS stack of process p.
2. When visiting the successor(s) of s_i, $dfsRed_p(s_i)$ ignores state $s_j = s_{i+1}$ and does not launch $dfsRed_p(s_j)$.

This situation occurs since otherwise the cycle would be discovered by process p. From the condition at l. 16, there are two possibilities:

$s_j.red$ —— From Prop. 3, $s_1.dangerous = true$ since $s_j \rightsquigarrow s_1 \wedge s_j.red = true \wedge s_1.red = false$. Hence, since $s_1.dangerous = true$ when $dfsRed_p(s_1)$ terminates, our proposition holds.

$\neg s_j.red \wedge s_j.red_p$ —— $s_j.red_p$ has necessarily been set to $true$ during a previous invocation of $dfsRed_p$. Hence, s_j was previously added to $\mathcal{R}_p$ and it holds that either $s_j.red = true$ (which leads to a contradiction), or $s_j.dangerous$ and, again, our proposition holds since we had $s_j.dangerous$ when $dfsRed_p(s_j)$ terminated.   □

At last we can prove that the nested DFS initiated, at l. 32, on a dangerous state s will report any accepting cycle containing a or a' reachable from a.

Proposition 5. *For any $a \in \mathcal{A}$, $p \in \mathcal{P}$, $ndfs_p(a)$ reports an accepting cycle if and only if there is an accepting cycle around state $a' \in \mathcal{A}$ with $a \rightsquigarrow a'$.*

Proof. The correctness of Prop. 5 is a direct consequence of the correctness of algorithm ndfs (see [11]). If $ndfs_p(a)$ is initiated and if a cycle containing $a' \in \mathcal{A}$ (with $a \rightsquigarrow a'$) is not reported then $ndfs_p(a)$ necessarily reaches a state s belonging to the cycle and already visited by a previous invocation of $ndfs_p(a'')$. This is however impossible, since the cycle would have been visited during this previous search.   □

Theorem 1 establishes the correctness of mc-ndfs as a consequence of Prop. 2, 4 and 5.

Theorem 1. *Algorithm mc-ndfs reports an accepting cycle if and only if there is an accepting cycle in $\mathcal{G}$.*

Proof. Let us consider an accepting cycle containing $a \in \mathcal{A}$. From Prop. 2, there exists $p \in \mathcal{P}$ s.t. $dfsRed_p(a)$ will be invoked with $a.red = false$. From Prop. 4, it will report the accepting cycle, or $a.dangerous = true$ will hold after the termination of $dfsRed_p(a)$. In the latter case, $ndfs_p(a)$ will be initiated and the accepting cycle reported (from Prop. 5).
     □

3.5   Complexity of the Algorithm

It is straightforward to see that a state will be visited at most four times by each process: by the blue and red DFS of mc-ndfs and by the blue and red DFS of ndfs. Hence, following the notations of Section 2, the time complexity of mc-ndfs is $O(p \cdot (m + n))$.

To encode flags associated with a state $3 + 4 \cdot p$ bits are required: 3 bits for global attributes ($dangerous$, $blue$, and red); and 4 bits for local process attributes ($blue_p$, red_p for mc-ndfs and ndfs). This is negligible if we perform an exact exploration and store full state vectors, but a trade-off has to be made if we use e.g. bitstate hashing [21] that encodes the graph as a large bit vector where each bit represents a single state. For instance, with 8 cores and 16 GB, we can visit graphs with up to $3.8 \cdot 10^9$ states and may divide the execution time by 8. With the same amount of RAM and 16 cores, the execution time can drop by the same factor, but the graph size is limited to $2 \cdot 10^9$ states.

3.6 Using Tarjan's Algorithm in Nested Searches

Algorithm mc-ndfs waits for a red DFS to be completed before reporting new red states. However, one could proceed more efficiently. Indeed, the important property to be verified is that dangerous states are discovered and reported as such before states leading to them become red. Hence, we could easily replace the existing *dfsRed_p* procedure by Tarjan's algorithm for SCC decomposition and register red states as the search progresses. When Tarjan's algorithm pops states belonging to a same strongly connected component *scc*, we are sure that all states reachable from $s \in scc$ (and hence, all states potentially dangerous) have already been visited. Therefore all states of a same component can become red as the component is backtracked from. Although this extension is expected to improve the time performance of our algorithm, it also requires the use of extra memory (2 integers per state, see [25] for details on Tarjan's algorithm), which, once again, can be problematic if we combine mc-ndfs with bitstate hashing.

4 Experimental Results

We implemented a prototype of the mc-ndfs algorithm on top of the pthread library and experimented with it on a 16-core machine. Instead of selecting the execution time as a *performance* criterion, we consider the maximal number of visited states over all CPU cores. Several reasons motivated this choice. First the input graphs analysed were given implicitly as a disk file. Therefore, all time-consuming operations (e.g. successor computation, state comparison, insertion in hash table) were already performed and synchronisations dominate the whole execution times. This observation is not only valid for mc-ndfs but also with the map algorithm, that we also implemented in our prototype. Therefore using time as a performance criterion did give a good insight of their performances. Moreover this measure is more reliable than the execution time as it gives a very accurate idea on the "theoretical" scalability of an algorithm: it is independent of the implementation; and it focuses on the search algorithm by putting aside all other time consuming operations like, e.g. synchronisations or data structure initialisations. All measurements reported in this section are expressed this way. These results and the accompanying comments must therefore be taken with care: they do not show the exact acceleration of mc-ndfs but what can be achieved in the ideal situation. As explained in Section 5 our next goal is to provide a real implementation of algorithm mc-ndfs in a verification platform to evaluate its concrete performance.

Input models. All models are issued from the BEEM database [24] that includes more than 50 models of different categories, e.g. mutual exclusion algorithms, communication protocols. We deliberately removed instances of families *Puzzles* (9 models) and *Planning* (5 models) that contain mostly toy examples and only experimented with graphs containing more than 10^6 states. This finally represented a total of 163 input graphs out of which 44 do not have an accepting run while the other 119 do. The results shown below deal only with the former family. Indeed, in most cases, ndfs could easily report an accepting cycle by visiting only a few hundreds of states. Therefore, it did not make much sense to experiment with mc-ndfs on these instances. We found only very few graphs (6 out of 119) for which the use of mc-ndfs could significantly speed up the

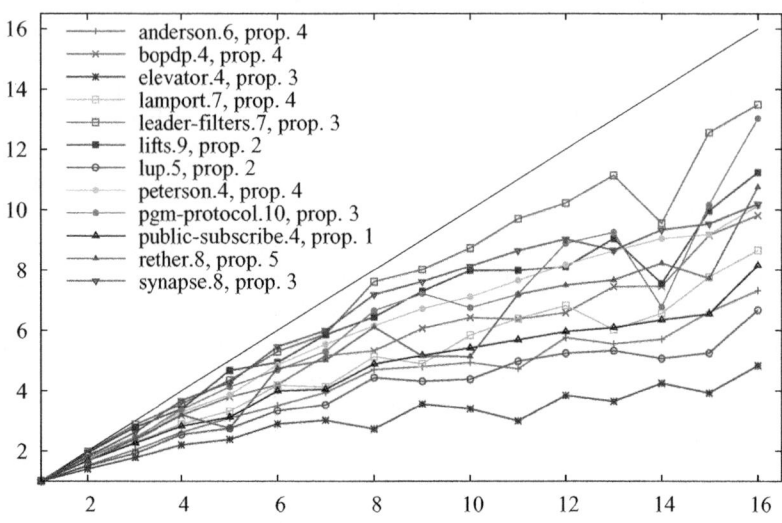

Fig. 2. Acceleration of mc-ndfs on some selected instances

reporting of an accepting run w.r.t. ndfs. Due to space constraints we have selected a few representative instances from our experiments to be presented in this section. The description of all models used can be found on the BEEM webpage [24].

Accelerations. We first analysed the acceleration of mc-ndfs, defined, for N cores, as the ratio of the performance (as defined above) with 1 core over the performance with N cores (using the same algorithm on the same model instance). Figure 2 shows the acceleration as a function of the number of processing cores used for some selected instances. We tried to select a representative set of instances according to different criteria: characteristics of the state graph (width, height, SCC graph structure, ...), type of system modeled (mutual exclusion algorithm, communication protocol, ...), complexity of the model (from simple models to industrial protocols).

The results observed are more or less in line with expectations. The performance of our algorithm is largely impacted by the graph structure. Indeed, for graphs composed of a single or few large SCCs (e.g. lup, public-subscribe) processes often visit the same part of the graph and the use of additional cores does not always bring significant improvements. In contrast, when the graph is clustered into unconnected parts (e.g. pgm-protocol) or acyclic (e.g. leader-filters) processes engage in different parts of the graph, thanks to the use of randomisation, and the acceleration observed is much better. An important parameter also seems to be the length of the longest elementary cycle (i.e. a cycle that does not contain two occurrences of the same state). Since, our algorithm proceeds in a depth-first manner, it is obvious that at least one of the blue DFSs performed concurrently will have, at some point, all the states of this cycle in its stack, and the acceleration will stay low. We also applied mc-ndfs on some graphs randomly generated with long such cycles and the acceleration observed was negligible. Fortunately, real-life systems usually do not exhibit this characteristic.

Table 2. Process workload of mc-ndfs for 16 cores on instances of Figure 2

Instance	Prop.	States	Min.	Max.	Avg.	Std. Dev.
anderson.6	4	36,119,671	5,894,164	7,396,706	6,617,656	12,956
bopdp.4	4	15,923,138	1,291,852	1,625,304	1,396,039	10,203
elevator.4	3	1,006,453	187,061	232,980	209,744	14,128
lamport.7	4	74,413,141	9,938,566	12,723,438	10,958,991	5,308
leader-filters.7	2	26,302,351	2,983,182	3,902,860	3,383,017	7,068
lifts.9	2	7,831,426	1,016,685	1,161,696	1,093,915	12,757
lup.5	2	34,425,340	4,797,633	6,107,470	5,453,463	13,906
peterson.4	4	2,239,039	247,738	332,069	279,644	8,841
pgm-protocol.10	3	7,233,361	458,128	618,476	509,445	5,808
public-subscribe.4	1	1,977,587	248,933	258,743	253,194	2,410
rether.8	5	25,405,545	3,252,470	3,541,148	3,397,022	11,524
synapse.8	3	19,045,831	1,079,676	1,871,015	1,362,764	15,684

Workload. Table 2 provides for instances of Figure 2: the number of states visited by the least and most loaded processes (columns Min. and Max.), the arithmetic average workload (column Avg.) and the standard deviation in the workload (column Std. Dev.) for 16 cores only. It appears the work is usually well balanced among processes although there can be some important variations between the most and least loaded processes. This is clear from the low standard deviation, even in these cases.

Comparison with the map algorithm. Algorithm map uses a modified parallel breadth-first search to compute maximal accepting predecessors. It is as such a very good candidate for parallelisation and, indeed, we observed that mc-ndfs can not compete with it if we compare them w.r.t. acceleration: map always provides a quasi-optimal acceleration

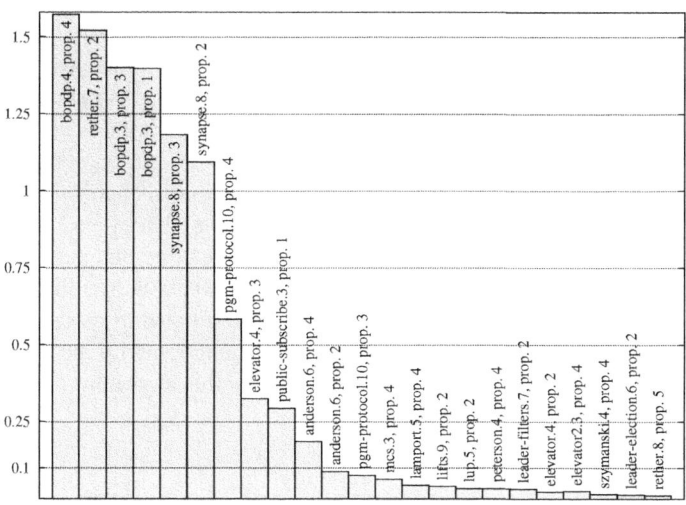

Fig. 3. Absolute performances of mc-ndfs and map on 23 instances for 16 cores

regardless of the model considered. Nevertheless, since map has a polynomial complexity, mc-ndfs often outperforms it when considering their absolute performances. For some selected model instances the ratio of the performance of mc-ndfs over the performance of map for 16 cores only is plotted on Figure 3. Hence, above 1 (resp. below 1), map behaves better (resp. worse) than mc-ndfs. Algorithm map provides better results for a few instances, but in most cases, mc-ndfs is faster, and sometimes significantly. Especially for graphs having a large proportion of accepting states (e.g. lifts.9 with property 2), mc-ndfs often outperforms map. In contrast, map is to be preferred for problems having few or no accepting states (e.g. bopdp.4 with property 4), in which case map reduces to a parallel BFS.

5   Conclusion and Perspectives

We have proposed in this paper a new parallel algorithm for the accepting cycle detection problem. It is a variation of the well-known nested depth-first search algorithm dedicated to multi-core and shared memory architectures. Although, it does not theoretically scale, our experiments revealed that it could provide good accelerations on a variety of interesting instances through the mechanisms it implements. Moreover, similar to the sequential algorithm it is built on, mc-ndfs can detect accepting cycles on-the-fly which few parallel algorithms designed so far are able to do.

We focus on several perspectives for this work. Our experiment only revealed the optimal acceleration that can possibly be achieved using mc-ndfs but the experimentation context can not lead to any conclusion concerning the effective speed-up of our algorithm. A first short term goal is thus to integrate our algorithm into a verification platform such as Divine [6] that also implements many other algorithms (e.g. map, owcty) and will allow a direct comparison of these. Second, we would like to study the combination of our algorithm with existing reduction techniques. Indeed, although mc-ndfs is intended to reduce search times its use can still face the state explosion problem that can only be tackled using dedicated techniques. If mc-ndfs can clearly be combined with some of these techniques, such as bitstate hashing [21] that is a state representation techniques independent of the search algorithm. This observation is not that trivial for some other algorithms such as *partial order reduction* [10]. An implementation of this technique is typically made of two components: a selection mechanism (independent of the search algorithm and, hence, compatible with mc-ndfs) that filters executable transitions of a given state and an *ignoring problem* solver ensuring that a transition will not always be forgotten by the selection function. This solver usually relies on the model checking algorithm. We therefore have to investigate if existing *provisos* used to prevent the ignoring problem can be safely used in conjunction with mc-ndfs and, if not, to devise another solution to this problem, tailored for this algorithm.

References

1. Barnat, J., Brim, L., Chaloupka, J.: Parallel Breadth-First Search LTL Model-Checking. In: ASE 2003, pp. 106–115. IEEE Computer Society, Los Alamitos (2003)
2. Barnat, J., Brim, L., Chaloupka, J.: From distributed memory cycle detection to parallel LTL model checking. ENTCS 133, 21–39 (2005)

3. Barnat, J., Brim, L., Ročkai, P.: Scalable Multi-core LTL Model-Checking. In: Bošnački, D., Edelkamp, S. (eds.) SPIN 2007. LNCS, vol. 4595, pp. 187–203. Springer, Heidelberg (2007)
4. Barnat, J., Brim, L., Ročkai, P.: A Time-Optimal On-the-Fly Parallel Algorithm for Model Checking of Weak LTL Properties. In: Breitman, K., Cavalcanti, A. (eds.) ICFEM 2009. LNCS, vol. 5885, pp. 407–425. Springer, Heidelberg (2009)
5. Barnat, J., Brim, L., Stríbrná, J.: Distributed LTL Model-Checking in SPIN. In: Dwyer, M.B. (ed.) SPIN 2001. LNCS, vol. 2057, pp. 200–216. Springer, Heidelberg (2001)
6. Barnat, J., Brim, L., Černá, I., Moravec, P., Ročkai, P., Šimeček, P.: DiVinE – A Tool for Distributed Verification. In: Ball, T., Jones, R.B. (eds.) CAV 2006. LNCS, vol. 4144, pp. 278–281. Springer, Heidelberg (2006)
7. Brim, L., Černá, I., Krčál, P., Pelánek, R.: Distributed LTL Model Checking Based on Negative Cycle Detection. In: Hariharan, R., Mukund, M., Vinay, V. (eds.) FSTTCS 2001. LNCS, vol. 2245, pp. 96–107. Springer, Heidelberg (2001)
8. Brim, L., Černá, I., Moravec, P., Šimša, J.: Accepting Predecessors Are Better than Back Edges in Distributed LTL Model-Checking. In: Hu, A.J., Martin, A.K. (eds.) FMCAD 2004. LNCS, vol. 3312, pp. 352–366. Springer, Heidelberg (2004)
9. Černá, I., Pelánek, R.: Distributed Explicit Fair Cycle Detection (Set Based Approach). In: Ball, T., Rajamani, S.K. (eds.) SPIN 2003. LNCS, vol. 2648, pp. 49–73. Springer, Heidelberg (2003)
10. Clarke, E.M., Grumberg, O., Minea, M., Peled, D.: State Space Reduction Using Partial Order Techniques. In: STTT, pp. 279–287 (1999)
11. Courcoubetis, C., Vardi, M.Y., Wolper, P., Yannakakis, M.: Memory Efficient Algorithms for the Verification of Temporal Properties. In: Clarke, E., Kurshan, R.P. (eds.) CAV 1990. LNCS, vol. 531, pp. 233–242. Springer, Heidelberg (1991)
12. Couvreur, J.-M.: On-the-Fly Verification of Linear Temporal Logic. In: Woodcock, J.C.P., Davies, J. (eds.) FM 1999. LNCS, vol. 1708, pp. 253–271. Springer, Heidelberg (1999)
13. Couvreur, J.-M., Duret-Lutz, A., Poitrenaud, D.: On-the-fly Emptiness Checks for Generalized Büchi Automata. In: Godefroid, P. (ed.) SPIN 2005. LNCS, vol. 3639, pp. 169–184. Springer, Heidelberg (2005)
14. Esparza, J., Schwoon, S.: A Note on On-the-Fly Verification Algorithms. In: Halbwachs, N., Zuck, L.D. (eds.) TACAS 2005. LNCS, vol. 3440, pp. 174–190. Springer, Heidelberg (2005)
15. Gaiser, A., Schwoon, S.: Comparison of Algorithms for Checking Emptiness on Büchi Automata. In: MEMICS 2009 (2009)
16. Gastin, P., Moro, P., Zeitoun, M.: Minimization of Counterexamples in SPIN. In: Graf, S., Mounier, L. (eds.) SPIN 2004. LNCS, vol. 2989, pp. 92–108. Springer, Heidelberg (2004)
17. Geldenhuys, J., Valmari, A.: Tarjan's Algorithm Makes On-the-Fly LTL Verification More Efficient. In: Jensen, K., Podelski, A. (eds.) TACAS 2004. LNCS, vol. 2988, pp. 205–219. Springer, Heidelberg (2004)
18. Godefroid, P., Holzmann, G.J.: On the Verification of Temporal Properties. In: PSTV 1993, pp. 109–124. North-Holland Publishing Co., Amsterdam (1993)
19. Holzmann, G.J.: The Model Checker SPIN. IEEE Transactions on Software Engineering 23(5), 279–295 (1997)
20. Holzmann, G.J., Joshi, R., Groce, A.: Swarm Verification Techniques. IEEE Transactions on Software Engineering (2010)
21. Holzmann, G.J.: An Analysis of Bistate Hashing. In: PSTV 1995, pp. 301–314 (1995)
22. Holzmann, G.J., Bosnacki, D.: The Design of a Multi-Core Extension of the Spin Model Checker. IEEE Trans. on Software Engineering 33(10), 659–674 (2007)

23. Laarman, A., Langerak, R., van de Pol, J., Weber, M., Wijs, A.: Multi-core nested depth-first search. In: Bultan, T., Hsiung, P.-A. (eds.) ATVA 2011, pp. 321–335. Springer, Heidelberg (2011)
24. Pelánek, R.: BEEM: Benchmarks for Explicit Model Checkers. In: Bošnački, D., Edelkamp, S. (eds.) SPIN 2007. LNCS, vol. 4595, pp. 263–267. Springer, Heidelberg (2007), http://anna.fi.muni.cz/models/
25. Tarjan, R.: Depth-First Search and Linear Graph Algorithms. SIAM Journal on Computing 1(2), 146–160 (1972)
26. Vardi, M.Y., Wolper, P.: An Automata-Theoretic Approach to Automatic Program Verification. In: LICS 1986, pp. 332–344. IEEE Computer Society, Los Alamitos (1986)

Evaluating LTL Satisfiability Solvers

Viktor Schuppan and Luthfi Darmawan

Viktor.Schuppan@gmx.de,
luthfi@alumni.itb.ac.id

Abstract. We perform a comprehensive experimental evaluation of off-the-shelf solvers for satisfiability of propositional LTL. We consider a wide range of solvers implementing three major classes of algorithms: reduction to model checking, tableau-based approaches, and temporal resolution. Our set of benchmark families is significantly more comprehensive than those in previous studies. It takes the benchmark families of previous studies, which only have a limited overlap, and adds benchmark families not used for that purpose before.

We find that no solver dominates or solves all instances. Solvers focused on finding models and solvers using temporal resolution or fixed point computation show complementary strengths and weaknesses. This motivates and guides estimation of the potential of a portfolio solver. It turns out that even combining two solvers in a simple fashion significantly increases the share of solved instances while reducing CPU time spent.

1 Introduction

More and more, system specifications are not only used for classical verification of the correctness of a given system, e.g., via model checking, but they themselves become the subject of investigation (e.g., [56, 33]). This is justified by observations in industry that many specifications contain errors (e.g., [16]) as well as by transition to property-based design (e.g., [57]). Propositional Linear Temporal Logic (LTL) [29] is a popular choice for system specifications and many checks on specifications reduce to determining (un)satisfiability (see, e.g., [56, 33, 60]). Hence, satisfiability of LTL is of considerable practical relevance.

A broad range of techniques for determining satisfiability of LTL has been developed: tableau-based methods (e.g., [68,48,63]), temporal resolution (e.g., [32]), and reduction to model checking (e.g., [60,69,25]). Despite the relevance of the problem and the range of techniques, we are not aware of a recent, comprehensive experimental comparison of solvers for satisfiability of propositional LTL on a broad set of benchmarks. In fact, the only line of work containing a representative from each of the above mentioned techniques that we know is the one by Hustadt et al. [45, 42, 46] (see below), which is somewhat dated.

In this paper we make the following contributions. 1. We perform an experimental evaluation of solvers for satisfiability of propositional LTL using ALASKA [1,69], LWB [2,41], NuSMV [3,26], pltl [4], TRP++ [5,44], and TSPASS [6,51]. Both the range of techniques in the solvers we use and the set of benchmarks we collected are significantly more comprehensive than in any previous study we know. We have made our data available for further analysis [7]. 2. We consider

T. Bultan and P.-A. Hsiung (Eds.): ATVA 2011, LNCS 6996, pp. 397–413, 2011.

number of solved instances, run time, memory usage, and model size. The analysis is greatly helped by using contour/discrete raw data plots, which complement the traditional cactus plots by preserving the relationship between benchmark instances. 3. The analysis shows complementary behavior between some solvers. This motivates estimating the potential of a portfolio solver. We consider portfolio solvers without communication between members of the portfolio for a best case scenario (which is unrealistic) and a reference case scenario (which any portfolio solver should aim to beat). Finally, we show that even a trivially implementable solver that sequentially executes one solver first for a short amount of time and, if necessary, then invokes another solver reduces the number of unsolved instances as well as the average run time.

Related Work. Rozier and Vardi compare several explicit state and symbolic BDD-based model checkers for LTL satisfiability checking [60]. They find the symbolic tools to be superior in terms of performance and, generally, also in terms of quality. They do not consider SAT-based bounded model checkers, tableau-based solvers, or temporal resolution. While they perform an in-depth comparison of solvers using very similar techniques, our focus is on comparing selected representatives of a broad variety of techniques. We also use more benchmark families and consider memory usage and model size. The same authors compare symbolic constructions of Büchi automata in [59] using the BDD-based engine of Cadence SMV as backend solver. They show that a portfolio approach to automata construction is advantageous. De Wulf et al. compare NuSMV and ALASKA [69]. For a detailed discussion see Sect. 6. Hustadt et al. perform several comparisons [45, 42, 46] of TRP, a version of LWB, and a version of SMV on the **trp** benchmark set (see Sect. 4). Goré and Widmann perform an experimental comparison of solvers for CTL [37]. Goranko et al. [35] compare an implementation of Wolper's tableau construction with pltl. For references on solver competitions and on their methodology see App. A of [62].

We are not aware of previous work on portfolio approaches to LTL satisfiability, except for [59]. We use entire solvers as members of a portfolio, while [59] uses different frontends for Büchi automata construction all relying on the same BDD-based backend solver. For other problem classes see, e.g., [43] (graph coloring, web browsing), [49] (winner determination problem), [34] (constraint satisfaction, mixed integer programming), [70] (SAT), or [58] (QBF).

Organization. In Sect. 2 we introduce notation. In Sect. 3, 4, and 5 we describe solvers, benchmarks, and methodology. Section 6 contains the results of our evaluation. An estimation of the potential of a portfolio solver follows in Sect. 7. Section 8 concludes. Due to space constraints the following parts are in appendices [62]: general concepts and terminology (App. A), details on our benchmark set (App. B), discussion (App. C), and some plots (App. D).

2   Preliminaries

We consider formulas in future time propositional LTL with temporal operators **F, G, R, U, X**. We assume familiarity with LTL; otherwise see [29].

The terminology we use is largely standard (e.g., [64, 19]); a reader unfamiliar with competition terminology is referred to App. A of [62]. A somewhat non-standard term we use is *configuration*, which denotes a tool (solver) with specific option values. A tool is a *state-of-the-art contributor* (sota) if an instance is solved only by configurations of that tool (see also [66]). Given a set of configurations C the *virtual best solver* (vbs) is the hypothetical solver using the best configuration in C on any given instance (e.g., [19]). We use **bold font** for sets of benchmark instances and `teletype` for configurations.

3   Solvers

Choice of Solvers. We consider tools to solve satisfiability of propositional LTL from 3 major classes of approaches: 1. reduction to model checking, 2. tableau-based algorithms, and 3. temporal resolution. Tools were chosen as detailed below. To the best of our knowledge this set of solvers is the most diverse considered in an evaluation of solvers for satisfiability of propositional LTL to date.

Reduction to Model Checking. We chose ALASKA [1, 69] and NuSMV [3, 26] using BDDs (NuSMV-BDD) and SAT (NuSMV-SBMC). We ruled out explicit state model checkers, as they did not scale as well as BDD-based symbolic model checkers for LTL satisfiability in [60]. The BDD-based engine of Cadence SMV [8] performed comparable to NuSMV-BDD in [60]. sal-smc [54] constructs explicit Büchi automata and was found not to scale [60]. The BDD-based variant of VIS [67] uses explicit construction of Büchi automata; initial experiments confirmed that this does not scale for satisfiability of LTL. sal-bmc [54] can only prove safety properties [53]. For an alternative using SAT-based symbolic model checking we contacted the VIS group for advice on recommended configurations (the space of configurations is quite large), but have not received an answer yet. Finally, we checked the publicly available versions of the participants of HWMCC'10 [20]; as far as we could see, the solvers that are not included in our study only handle safety properties.

Tableau-Based Algorithms. We chose LWB [2, 41] and pltl [4]. TWB [15] is superseded by pltl [36]. LTL Tableau turns out to be inferior to pltl [35].

Temporal Resolution. We chose TRP++ [5, 44] and TSPASS [6, 51]. An alternative tool is TeMP [47]. TeMP was shown to be inferior to TRP++ on propositional problems in [47] and comparable to TSPASS on monodic problems in [51]. Note, that TSPASS is fair, while TeMP is not [50].

Solver Descriptions. Below we briefly describe the tools we consider as well as the set of their options that we take into account. Note that not all combinations of options are valid. Due to space constraints the descriptions have to be kept short, and we refer the reader to the respective tool documentation.

ALASKA performs model checking and satisfiability checking of LTL via symbolic computation of fixed points using antichains [1, 69]. Relevant options are: noc/c dis-/enables model construction, nos/s uses a semisymbolic/fully symbolic algorithm, and nob/b switches between forward and backward image computation. We use version 0.4 with an additional patch by N. Maquet.

LWB   [2, 41] implements tableau-based algorithms for LTL by Janssen [48] (no model construction) in the function "satisfiable" and by Schwendimann [63] (model construction) in the function "model". Neither has relevant options. We designate the former by sat and the latter by mod. We use version 1.1.

NuSMV-BDD In this evaluation we treat NuSMV [3, 26] as two tools NuSMV-BDD and NuSMV-SBMC. NuSMV-BDD performs symbolic model checking of LTL using symbolic fixed point computation with BDDs [27]. Experience with NuSMV-BDD allows us to restrict experiments to the following options. nodcx/dcx en-/disables model construction, nofflt/fflt dis-/enables forward computation of reachable states in the model and tableau for the LTL formula, nodyn/dyn dis-/enables dynamic reordering, and elbwd/elfwd switches between backward and forward image computation in the Emerson-Lei algorithm [30, 40]. We use version 2.5.0.

NuSMV-SBMC performs incremental simple bounded model checking [39] of LTL using MiniSat [9]. Options considered are nodcx/dcx to en-/disable model construction and noc/c to dis-/enable checking completeness. With the latter disabled NuSMV-SBMC cannot solve *unsat* instances. We use version 2.5.0.

pltl   [4] implements tableau-based algorithms for LTL along the lines of [38] via the command line argument "graph" and by Schwendimann [63] via the command line argument "tree". Neither has model construction or relevant options. We designate the former by graph and the latter by tree. We use version r1424.

TRP++   [5, 44] uses temporal resolution for LTL [32]. Relevant options: nos/s to dis-/enable simplification, nor/r to dis-/enable rewriting, noal/al to ex-/include an order statement, dfs/bfs to choose dfs/bfs in loop search, nop/p to dis-/enable pre-test for sometime resolution, and nofsr/fsr to dis-/enable forward subsumption resolution. TRP++ cannot construct models. We use v. 2.x.

TSPASS   [6, 51] is a temporal resolution solver for monodic first-order temporal logic with model construction for propositional LTL [52]. We consider noext/ext to dis-/enable extended step clauses, nogrp/grp to dis-/enable regrouping of **X**, nosev/sev to dis-/enable transforming multiple eventualities into a single one, log/sub to select logical equivalence or subsumption in loop tests, nosls/sls to dis-/enable sequential loop search, norfmrr/rfmrr (resp. norbmrr/rbmrr) to dis-/enable forward (resp. backward) matching replacement resolution, nomod/mod to dis-/enable model construction, and mur/mor to select unordered or ordered resolution in model construction. We use version 0.94-0.16.

4   Benchmarks

In Tab. 1 we give an overview of the benchmark families we use. To our knowledge this set of benchmarks is the most comprehensive used for evaluating propositional LTL satisfiability solvers so far. [60] used **rozier_counter**, **rozier_pattern**, and **rozier_formulas**. [69] used **alaska_lift**, **alaska_szymanski**, and subsets of **rozier_counter** and **rozier_formulas**. [46] used **trp**. Note that there is little

Table 1. Overview of benchmark families, grouped by benchmark categories. The first column lists the name of the family. Columns 2 – 5 show the size (see App. A of [62]) of the largest instance and the number of *sat*, *unsat*, and *unknown* instances, respectively, in that family. The 6th column provides references to the source and the 7th column gives a brief description.

family	max. size	num. sat	num. unsat	num. unkn.	source	description
application						
acacia_demo-v22	76	10	–		[10, 31]	window screens
acacia_demo-v3	426	36	–		[10, 31]	arbiters (scaled up, added variants)
acacia_example	144	25	–		[10, 31]	mostly arbiters and traffic light controllers
alaska_lift	4450	102	34		[1, 69]	lifts (scaled up, added variants, added fixes [61])
alaska_szymanski	183	4	–		[1, 69]	mutual exclusion protocols
anzu_amba	6173	43	–	8	[11, 23]	microcontroller buses (scaled up, added variants)
anzu_genbuf	5805	48	–	12	[11, 24]	generalized buffers (scaled up, added variants)
forobots	636	14	25	–	[17]	foraging robots
crafted						
rozier_counter	751	78	–		[12, 60]	serial counters (long models)
rozier_pattern	7992	244	–		[12, 60]	patterns to test explicit state model checkers (scaled up)
schuppan_O1formula	4007	–	27		(new)	patterns that trigger exponential behavior in some
schuppan_O2formula	6001	–	15	12		solvers
schuppan_phltl	40501	–	10	8	(new)	temporal formulation of pigeonhole principle [22]
random						
rozier_formulas	185	1943	57		[12, 60]	random formulas as in [28] (subset of original family)
trp	1422	573	397		[13, 46]	random formulas from fixed conjunctive normal form templates (subset of original family)

overlap. [60, 69] and [46] represent separate communities. We added the following benchmark families that, to our knowledge, had not been used to evaluate solvers for propositional LTL satisfiability before: **acacia**, **anzu**, and **forobots**.[1] To provide more challenging instances we scaled up some families. Moreover, for the families **acacia_demo-v3**, **anzu_amba**, and **anzu_genbuf**, which consist of a set of assumptions and a set of guarantees, we not only used the form $(\bigwedge_i a_i) \rightarrow (\bigwedge_i g_i)$ but also $(\bigwedge_i a_i) \wedge (\bigwedge_i g_i)$ (marked by "c" in the family name). For **acacia_demo-v3**, **alaska_lift**, **anzu_amba**, and **anzu_genbuf** we added variants with liveness conditions to trigger nontrivial behavior (marked by "l" in the family name). For **alaska_lift** we also use a fixed [61] variant (marked by "f" in the family name). Finally, we added the families **schuppan_O1formula**, **schuppan_O2formula**, and **schuppan_phltl**. Our set of benchmarks contains 3723 instances. All benchmarks are available from [7].

5   Methodology

Hardware and Software. We used machines with Intel Xeon 3.0 GHz processors and 4 GB memory running Red Hat Linux 5.4 with 64 bit kernel 2.6.18-164.2.1.el5. Run time and memory usage were measured with run [21].

Input Format and No Shuffling. We converted all instances into NuSMV format and from there to the input formats of the other tools. We did not syntactically alter instances as there was no risk of cheating by syntactic recognition of benchmarks (e.g., [18]) and we, too, think that syntactic information should be preserved for the benefit of solvers (e.g., [64]).

---

[1] While the full version of [59] uses **acacia** and **anzu**, these were included based on a previous submission of this paper that we made available to the authors of [59].

Stages. The valid option combinations of the options in Sect. 3 yield the following number of configurations (model construction dis-/enabled): ALASKA 4/2, LWB 1/1, NuSMV-BDD 6/4, NuSMV-SBMC 2/2, pltl 2/-, TRP++ 64/-, TSPASS 128/128.

The number of configurations of TRP++ and TSPASS is too large to include all of them in the main stage of our evaluation. We therefore performed a preliminary stage with a time limit of 10 seconds and a memory limit of 2 GB on a representative subset of instances. In that stage we used all 64 combinations of TRP++. For TSPASS we considered the following subset of configurations: all options at their default value (sometimes implied by other options) as well as a single option switched to its non-default value. This resulted in 24/24 configurations. We then fixed options that either had a clear benefit one way or the other or clearly had little effect to the corresponding values and kept the remaining configurations for the main stage (see Sect. 6). In the main stage all configurations of ALASKA, LWB, NuSMV-BDD, NuSMV-SBMC, and pltl as well as the remaining configurations of TRP++ and TSPASS were run with a time limit of 60 seconds and a memory limit of 2 GB.

In each stage, each configuration was run only once on each instance. While performing more than one run would provide more accurate information about run time distributions [55] performing only a single run allows to use more configurations, more instances, or higher time bounds with equal resources.

Tracks. We have two tracks: one for configurations with model construction dis- or enabled (e.g., LWB using mod constructs models but is superior to sat that doesn't) and one for configurations with model construction enabled. The former considers all instances; the latter is restricted to *sat* instances.

Correctness of Solvers is a recurring issue in tool competitions and comparisons (e.g., [60]). Besides obvious cross checking of the *sat/unsat* results reported by different configurations for the same instance we used the fact that NuSMV-SBMC produces shortest (possibly plus one) models as an additional correctness check. We did not perform further validation of generated models.

Scoring. We essentially use scoring based on a higher number of solved instances and lower time taken on solved instances (see Sect. 2) as it preserves and clearly shows what we consider two important performance indicators.

However, there are fairly big differences in the number of instances in our benchmark families. Still, we would like to consider many benchmarks rather than only sampling the larger families. Hence, we modify the above scoring method as follows. We consider the benchmark families as a tree. We then compute the share of solved instances and the average run time on solved instances for each leaf (here all instances have equal weight). Then, for each non-leaf node, aggregate values are computed as averages with equal weights for all children of that node. For the tree of families see App. B.2 of [62].

6   Results

For more plots and data see App. D of the full version [62] and the website [7].

Table 2. Selecting a winning configuration per tool (separately for tracks). The left-most column lists the tool name. Next come 2 groups of 4 columns. The 1st group is for configurations with model construction dis- or enabled, the 2nd with model construction enabled. In each group the 1st column shows the winning configuration per tool. The 2nd column shows its score, the 3rd column shows the worst score, and the 4th column shows the score of the vbs of all configurations of that tool.

tool	model construction dis- or enabled (all instances)				model construction enabled (*sat* instances)			
	winning configuration	max	min	vbs	winning configuration	max	min	vbs
ALASKA	noc_nos_nob	0.581	0.322	0.595	c_nos_nob	0.595	0.318	0.595
LWB	mod	0.740	0.656	0.800	mod	0.795	0.795	0.795
NuSMV-BDD	dcx_fflt_dyn_elbwd	0.743	0.607	0.823	nodcx_fflt_dyn_elbwd	0.754	0.625	0.771
NuSMV-SBMC	nodcx_c	0.723	0.651	0.726	nodcx_noc	0.860	0.857	0.861
pltl	tree	0.694	0.687	0.702	—	—	—	—
TRP++	s_r_noal_bfs_nop_fsr	0.752	0.593	0.776	—	—	—	—
TSPASS	ext_nogrp_nosev_sub_nosls_rfmrr-_norbmrr_nomod_mor	0.667	0.479	0.670	ext_grp_sev_sub_nosls_rfmrr-_rbmrr_mod_mor	0.531	0.495	0.538

Preliminary Stage. For TRP++ configurations with s_nor proved inferior so that only s_r, nos_r, and nos_nor were kept. The effects of noal/al, dfs/bfs, and nofsr/fsr are unclear; hence all combinations were kept. nop/p had little effect so that we set it to its default nop. All in all this left us with 24 configurations.

For TSPASS ext, nosev, sub, and mor turned out to be advantageous. The effects of nogrp/grp, norfmrr/rfmrr, and norbmrr/rbmrr are unclear and we kept all. nosls/sls had little effect so that we disabled it as is default. This resulted in 8 configurations each with model construction disabled and enabled.

We now move to the main stage.

Correctness of Solvers. We found no bug in pltl but 1 or 2 bugs in each of NuSMV, ALASKA, TRP++, and TSPASS. All of them were kindly fixed by the respective tool authors. As of now we are not aware of wrong results or bugs triggered in the above tools by our benchmark set. In LWB we found several bugs. We emailed our findings to the developers but have not received a response. There are currently 187 out of 7446 (non-negated and negated) instances known to us that trigger bugs in LWB; 13 are wrong results. Hence, LWB is hors-concours. Some large instances failed in ALASKA and TSPASS due to certain built-in limits. These instances were rerun with increased limits.

Selecting Winning Configurations per Tool. To focus the subsequent comparison we select one winning configuration per tool to be used for the comparisons between tools in the remainder of this section. We choose the configuration with the highest weighted share of solved instances (see Sect. 5) for each tool. We distinguish between model construction dis- or enabled and model construction enabled as model construction is not available for some tools or options.

Table 2 provides a summary. For all tools except NuSMV-BDD and LWB the weighted share of instances solved by the winning configurations is close to that of the vbs of all configurations of that tool (Tab. 2). Below we mostly restrict the analysis to the winning configurations. We use the tool name to identify the respective winning configurations.

Track Model Construction Disabled. In Fig. 1 we show *contour/discrete raw data plots* of the run time for the winning configurations with model construction dis- or enabled. The name is taken from [65]. A somewhat related way to display results of a solver competition was used in Pseudo-Boolean Competitions [14].

Contrary to cactus plots contour/discrete raw data plots retain the relationship between instances (one x-coordinate corresponds to the same rather than different instances) but are more legible than line plots. They allow to see the performance of the solvers on benchmark families that are a subfamily of the one comprising a plot. A particular advantage is that they permit identification of similar and complementary behavior in performance. They also allow to see how difficult a particular instance or subfamily is. However, these plots make it harder to determine a ranking of solvers by higher number of solved instances with ties broken by lower average time taken on solved instances. Due to space constraints we cannot show both kinds of plots for the same data. We chose to use the contour/discrete raw data plots here to demonstrate their utility. For corresponding cactus plots see Fig. 10–13 in App. D.2 of [62].

Overall Picture. In this paragraph we refer to all configurations used in the main stage. No configuration solves all instances. 8–12 instances in **anzu_amba**, **anzu_genbuf**, **schuppan_O2formula**, and **schuppan_phltl** remain unsolved. The instances in the former two families are expected to be *sat*, in the latter *unsat*. The smallest unsolved instance is **O2formula50** (size 301). NuSMV-BDD is a sota on a number of (*unsat*) instances in **alaska_lift** and **schuppan_O2formula**; NuSMV-SBMC on instances in **alaska_lift**, **anzu_amba**, and **anzu_genbuf** (all *sat*); TRP++ on instances in **rozier_counter** (*sat*); LWB on instances in **schuppan_phltl** (*unsat*). See also Fig. 8 in App. D.1 of [62].

Families. The majority of benchmark families contain instances that are challenging for some solver. In category **application** the 3 families with larger instances, **alaska_lift**, **anzu_amba**, and **anzu_genbuf**, are the more difficult ones. Among them the variants that were modified to trigger meaningful behavior are the hardest. In category **crafted** the (*unsat*) families **schuppan_O2formula** and **schuppan_phltl** are the most difficult. **rozier_counter** is hard for most solvers, except for TRP++ and TSPASS (and NuSMV-BDD in a configuration using only backward fixed point computation). The two families in category **random** show very different pictures. Family **rozier_random** is solved well by non-resolution-based tools but somewhat more difficult for TRP++ and TSPASS; roles are reversed in family **trp**. Note that **trp** comes from the temporal resolution community, while **rozier_random** is taken from the model checking community.

Solvers: Similarities and Differences. Figure 1 shows that TRP++ and TSPASS, which both use temporal resolution, have similar strengths and weaknesses. TSPASS tends to improve over TRP++ on **trp**, while TRP++ tends to be faster on most of the remaining families. Between the two tools using symbolic fixed point computation NuSMV-BDD mostly dominates ALASKA; the latter has a higher start up time than the other tools. The strengths and weaknesses of NuSMV-BDD mostly

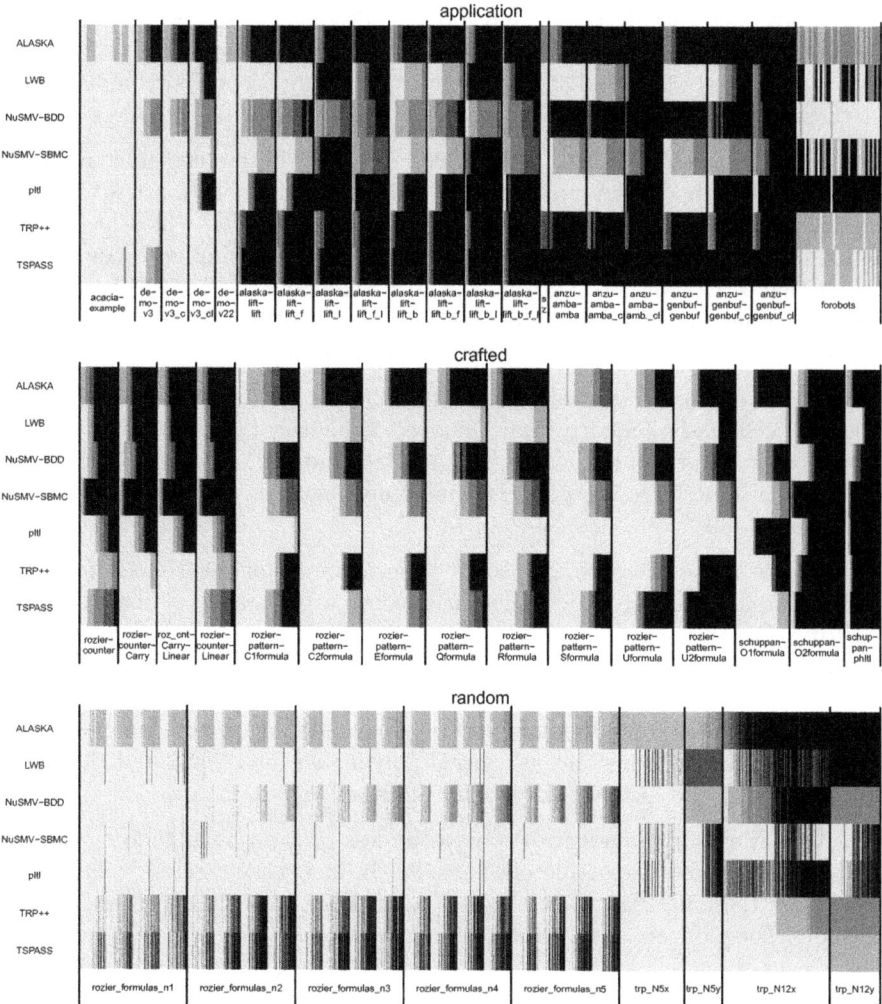

Fig. 1. Contour/discrete raw data plots of run time for winning configurations with model construction dis- or enabled (all instances). Instances are on the x-axes (only identified by their families), configurations on the y-axes. Each rectangle represents the run time of one configuration on one instance. **sz** abbreviates **alaska_szymanski**, **roz_cnt** abbreviates **rozier_counter**, and **demo** stands for **acacia_demo**. Run times are encoded using the following colors:
≤ 0.1 sec; > 0.1 sec, ≤ 1 sec; > 1 sec, ≤ 10 sec; > 10 sec, ≤ 60 sec; unsolved.

resemble those of TRP++ and TSPASS. Intuitively, symbolic fixed point computation [30] is closer in spirit to temporal resolution as performed in TRP++ [44] than to searching models (stating a more formal relationship is left as future work). LWB, NuSMV-SBMC, and pltl display similar characteristics. Note that these solvers essentially try to find models, although NuSMV-SBMC uses a fairly different technique than pltl and LWB. It is important to note that the strengths and weaknesses of NuSMV-BDD, TRP++, and TSPASS are somewhat complementary to those of LWB, NuSMV-SBMC, and pltl.

Sat versus Unsat Instances. NuSMV-SBMC exhibits the largest difference in its behavior between *sat* and *unsat* instances. NuSMV-SBMC solves most *sat* instances among the solvers. A notable exception is **rozier_counter**, which has shortest models of exponential size; few shortest models outside **rozier_counter** have size larger than 3 (see below). On the contrary, NuSMV-BDD and ALASKA, which are based on symbolic fixed computation, are hardly affected. For plots see Fig. 14–17 in App. D.3 of [62] and Fig. 18–21 in App. D.4 of [62].

Instance Size. The two tools based on symbolic fixed point computation, ALASKA and NuSMV-BDD, show a fairly clear influence of the size of an instance on their run time. At the other end of the spectrum are LWB and pltl, trying to find models. They solve some large instances in almost no time. For plots see Fig. 22–25 in App. D.5 of [62].

Non-negated versus Negated Instances. The relevance of negated versions of instances is questionable. We have not included negated versions of instances in any part of this paper, except where stated explicitly. However, we briefly comment on one aspect because of the size of the observed effect. On the **rozier_formulas** family — where negation should not change any relevant characteristic of the benchmark set — the variation in performance between the non-negated and the negated version of an instance is considerably higher for TSPASS and TRP++ than for NuSMV-BDD and ALASKA. For scatter plots see Fig. 26 in App. D.6 of [62].

Memory. Memory usage turned out to be less of a problem than time taken, therefore we do not report detailed results. In fact, very rarely a configuration used more than 300 MB when it solved an instance. ALASKA typically used most memory. For plots see App. D of [62].

VBS rather than Winning Configurations. While the findings above were mostly stated for the winning configurations of each tool, the picture does not change significantly when comparing the vbs of each tool (for plots see App. D of [62]). As suggested by Tab. 2 notable improvements only happen for NuSMV-BDD, LWB, and, to a lesser extent, TRP++.

Track Model Construction Enabled. We focus on model size. Figure 2 shows a cactus plot for the winning configurations with model construction enabled (*sat* instances). A vbs of all configurations with model construction enabled solves all but the largest instances of **anzu_amba**, **anzu_genbuf**, and **rozier_counter**. NuSMV-BDD is a sota based on instances in **rozier_counter**; NuSMV-SBMC on instances in **alaska_lift**, **anzu_amba**, **anzu_genbuf**, and **rozier_pattern**; LWB on instances in **rozier_pattern**.

95 % of the satisfiable instances have shortest models of size 3 or less. Instances with shortest models of size larger than 11 are either from **rozier_counter** or from the variants in **application** modified to trigger meaningful behavior.

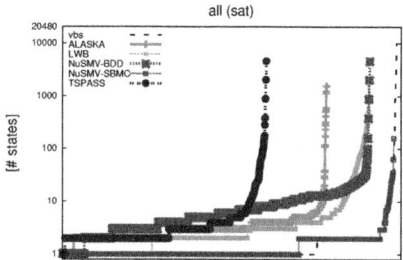

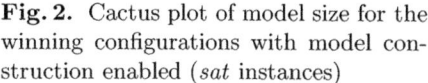

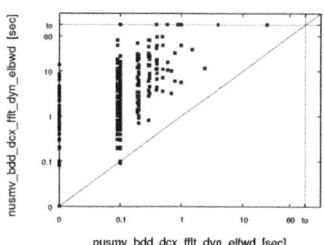

Fig. 2. Cactus plot of model size for the winning configurations with model construction enabled (*sat* instances)

Fig. 3. Scatter plot comparing run time for the forward and the backward version of the Emerson-Lei algorithm in NuSMV-BDD on the **rozier_formulas** family. "to" marks *time-out*

NuSMV-SBMC mostly produces shortest models, while NuSMV-BDD produces the longest ones. On the other hand, NuSMV-BDD solves more instances of the **rozier_counter** family (which has very long models) than the other tools.

A Performance Advantage of ALASKA over NuSMV-BDD? In [69] De Wulf et al. perform a comparison between ALASKA and NuSMV-BDD for satisfiability and model checking of LTL. For LTL satisfiability they find that ALASKA outperforms NuSMV-BDD on **alaska_lift**, **alaska_szymanski**, and a subfamily of **rozier_formulas**, while NuSMV-BDD performs better on **rozier_counter**.

A comparison of the antichain-based algorithm in ALASKA [69] and the Emerson-Lei algorithm [30] used in NuSMV-BDD shows that the algorithm in [69] computes fixed points using forward image computation, while NuSMV-BDD up to version 2.4.3 only uses (as is common) backward image computations for [30]. This triggered us to implement a forward version (e.g., [40]) of the Emerson-Lei algorithm in NuSMV-BDD. Figure 3 shows that the forward version performs considerably better than the backward version on the **rozier_formulas** family. Using forward image computation NuSMV-BDD outperforms ALASKA on **rozier_formulas**. Note also that ALASKA can be switched to perform backward image computation in which case its performance degrades considerably.

Our evaluation shows that NuSMV-BDD can solve the **alaska_lift** and **alaska_szymanski** families easily (and faster than ALASKA) by restricting computation to reachable states (**fflt**) and enabling dynamic reordering (**dyn**).

7   Potential of a Portfolio Solver

In the previous section we saw that some configurations behave complementarily. This motivates constructing *portfolio solvers* that consist of a set of configurations with the goal that the resulting solver performs better than any of its constituent configurations (e.g., [43]). Different modes of execution are considered for portfolio solvers in the literature (e.g., [43,49,34,70]).

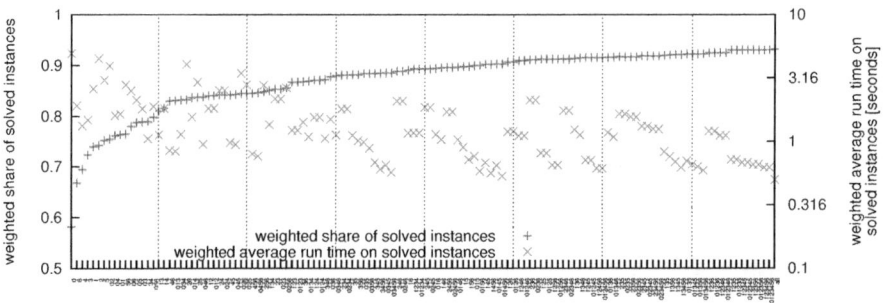

Fig. 4. Potential of a portfolio solver consisting of subsets of the winning configurations with model construction dis- or enabled using a perfect oracle. Portfolios are identified by their constituent configurations: 0: ALASKA; 1: LWB; 2: NuSMV-BDD; 3: NuSMV-SBMC; 4: pltl; 5: TRP++; 6: TSPASS. On the x-axis are the portfolios sorted in increasing order of weighted share of solved instances; ties are broken by decreasing order of weighted average run time on solved instances. For each portfolio the weighted share of solved instances is marked by a red vertical/horizontal cross (scale on the left y-axis); the corresponding weighted average run time on solved instances is marked by a green diagonal cross (scale on the right y-axis). "all" considers all configurations with model construction dis- or enabled rather than only the winning configurations. For an enlarged plot see App. D.8 of [62].

Perfect Oracle. We assume an oracle that for each instance predicts (using no time and memory) an optimal configuration in a portfolio and then executes that configuration on that instance (see, e.g., [49]). I.e., the performance of a portfolio solver on an instance is determined by the performance of an optimal configuration in a portfolio on that instance. If configurations do not collaborate (e.g., by exchanging partial results) that is a bound on the performance of a practical solver using that portfolio. An alternative view of this mode of execution is that each member of the portfolio is run on a separate processor in parallel until one configuration finishes while taking into account only the cost of one processor and disregarding the cost of other processors.

We estimate the potential of such a portfolio solver by considering all portfolios consisting of subsets of winning configurations with model construction dis- or enabled from Tab. 2. Figure 4 shows the result.

While individual configurations solve at most a weighted share of 0.752, using a portfolio helps to solve up to 0.931. All portfolios that solve a weighted share of 0.866 or more contain at least one of ALASKA, NuSMV-BDD, TRP++, and TSPASS and at least one of LWB, NuSMV-SBMC, and pltl. All that solve 0.9 or more contain at least one of LWB and NuSMV-SBMC and at least one of TRP++ and TSPASS. The 4 best portfolios with two configurations are (LWB, TRP++), (LWB, TSPASS), (NuSMV-SBMC, TRP++), and (NuSMV-SBMC, TSPASS). Adding ALASKA to a portfolio that contains NuSMV-BDD does not help in most cases.

Perfect Task Switcher. We now assume that all configurations of a portfolio are executed on a single processor in a time-sharing fashion with equal

Table 3. Performance of the 4 best 2-configuration portfolios in various execution modes. After the portfolio members in the 1st column there are 8 groups of 2 columns. In each group the 1st column shows the weighted share of solved instances, the 2nd column shows the weighted average run time on solved instances in seconds. The 1st and 2nd column groups are for the 1st and 2nd member of each portfolio in isolation. The 3rd and 4th groups are for perfect oracle and perfect task switcher modes. The 5th and 6th groups are for fast presolver mode with 1 and 2 seconds time limit when the 1st member of the portfolio is used as a fast presolver; the 7th and 8th groups are analogous for the 2nd member as a fast presolver. The time limits of 1 and 2 seconds were chosen among some that we tried as they represent a sweet spot that exhibits both an increase in weighted share of solved instances and a decrease in weighted average run time on solved instances.

	1st in isolation		2nd in isolation		perfect oracle		perf. task switcher		1st as fast presolver 1 second		2 seconds		2nd as fast presolver 1 second		2 seconds	
	share	time	share	time	share	time	share	time	share	time	share	time	share	time	share	time
(LWB, TRP++)	0.740	2.59	0.752	3.03	0.896	0.89	0.894	1.12	0.880	1.09	0.885	1.30	0.841	1.26	0.850	1.45
(LWB, TSPASS)	0.740	2.59	0.667	1.91	0.889	1.16	0.881	1.27	0.868	0.88	0.874	1.10	0.850	1.20	0.858	1.48
(NuSMV-SBMC, TRP++)	0.723	1.47	0.752	3.03	0.880	1.11	0.874	1.37	0.823	1.03	0.841	1.18	0.860	0.97	0.862	1.31
(NuSMV-SBMC, TSPASS)	0.723	1.47	0.667	1.91	0.867	1.41	0.853	1.60	0.813	1.00	0.831	1.21	0.837	1.17	0.840	1.42

and infinitely small time slices, no task switching overhead, and memory usage not an issue (e.g., [43]). I.e., rather than assuming a perfect oracle, we only assume a perfect task switcher. Now the performance of a portfolio solver with k configurations on an instance is determined by the performance of an optimal configuration in a portfolio on that instance multiplied by k (that might induce *time-out* even if some configuration solves the instance). If configurations do not collaborate this can be considered a portfolio solver that any practical portfolio solver using that portfolio should aim to beat. An alternative view is that each portfolio member runs on a separate processor in parallel until one member finishes and taking into account the cost for all processors.

For a plot analogous to Figure 4 see App. D.8 of [62]. Here the best portfolio considered is (LWB, NuSMV-BDD, NuSMV-SBMC, TRP++), which solves a weighted share of 0.922. Otherwise, similar remarks as for the case of a perfect oracle apply.

Fast Presolver. We now show that even a simplistic portfolio solver (implementable as shell script) can yield considerable benefits. We take the 4 best 2-configuration portfolios from above and use one of the two solvers as *fast presolver* [70] by executing it until it either solves an instance or reaches its (short) time limit. If the instance is not yet solved, then we execute the other solver for the remaining time (60 seconds minus the time limit of the presolver).

Results are shown in Tab. 3. In each case the portfolios using a fast presolver significantly increase the weighted share of solved instances while decreasing the weighted average run time over the respective portfolio members in isolation.

8   Conclusion

Benchmarks and data from our evaluation, available at [7], identify reference solvers with their command line options at the level of benchmark instances.

This helps to improve existing solvers, provides a point of reference in the evaluation of new techniques, and can serve as a basis for developing heuristics for portfolio solvers. Our evaluation shows that solvers have different, complementary strengths and weaknesses. We do not declare any solver to be the winner (those who disagree are referred to Tab. 2). Instead, for a solver aiming to be competitive on a broad range of benchmarks we advocate a portfolio approach.

Acknowledgements. J.-F. Raskin and N. Maquet for help with ALASKA and hosting the 1st author for 1 week. R. Goré and F. Widmann for help with pltl. B. Konev and M. Ludwig for help with TRP++ and TSPASS. C. Dixon for the **forobots** family. B. Jobstmann and G. Hofferek for help with the **amba** family. K. Rozier for feedback. A. Artale for supervising the 2nd author's MSc thesis. The ES group at FBK, esp. A. Cimatti, A. Mariotti, and M. Roveri, for discussion and support. The Provincia Autonoma di Trento (project EMTE-LOS) for financial support of the 1st author. The European Master's Program in Computational Logic for financial support of the 2nd author.

References

1. http://www.antichains.be/alaska/
2. http://www.lwb.unibe.ch/index.html
3. http://nusmv.fbk.eu/
4. http://users.cecs.anu.edu.au/~rpg/PLTLProvers/
5. http://www.csc.liv.ac.uk/~konev/software/trp++/
6. http://www.csc.liv.ac.uk/~michel/software/tspass/
7. http://www.schuppan.de/viktor/atva11/
8. http://www.kenmcmil.com/smv.html
9. http://minisat.se/
10. http://www.antichains.be/acacia/
11. http://www.iaik.tugraz.at/content/research/design_verification/anzu/
12. http://shemesh.larc.nasa.gov/people/kyr/benchmarking_scripts/benchmarking_scripts.html
13. http://www.csc.liv.ac.uk/~ullrich/TRP/
14. http://www.cril.univ-artois.fr/PB10/
15. Abate, P., Goré, R.: The Tableau Workbench. In: M4M (2007)
16. Beer, I., et al.: Efficient Detection of Vacuity in Temporal Model Checking. FMSD 18(2) (2001)
17. Behdenna, A., Dixon, C., Fisher, M.: Deductive Verification of Simple Foraging Robotic Behaviours. Int. J. of Intelligent Comput. and Cybernetics 2(4) (2009)
18. Le Berre, D., Simon, L.: The Essentials of the SAT 2003 Competition. In: Giunchiglia, E., Tacchella, A. (eds.) SAT 2003. LNCS, vol. 2919, pp. 452–467. Springer, Heidelberg (2004)
19. Le Berre, D., et al.: The SAT 2009 competition results: does theory meet practice (presentation). In: Kullmann, O. (ed.) SAT 2009. LNCS, vol. 5584. Springer, Heidelberg (2009)
20. Biere, A., Claessen, K.: Hardware Model Checking Competition (presentation). In: Hardware Verification Workshop 2010, Edinburgh, UK (2010)
21. Biere, A., Jussila, T.: Benchmark Tool Run, http://fmv.jku.at/run/

22. Biere, A., et al.: Handbook of Satisfiability. IOS Press, Amsterdam (2009)
23. Bloem, R., et al.: Automatic hardware synthesis from specifications: a case study. In: DATE (2007)
24. Bloem, R., et al.: Specify, Compile, Run: Hardware from PSL. In: COCV. ENTCS, vol. 190(4). Elsevier, Amsterdam (2007)
25. Cimatti, A., et al.: Boolean Abstraction for Temporal Logic Satisfiability. In: Damm, W., Hermanns, H. (eds.) CAV 2007. LNCS, vol. 4590, pp. 532–546. Springer, Heidelberg (2007)
26. Cimatti, A., et al.: NuSMV 2: An OpenSource Tool for Symbolic Model Checking. In: Brinksma, E., Larsen, K.G. (eds.) CAV 2002. LNCS, vol. 2404, pp. 359–364. Springer, Heidelberg (2002)
27. Clarke, E., Grumberg, O., Hamaguchi, K.: Another Look at LTL Model Checking. FMSD 10(1) (1997)
28. Daniele, M., Giunchiglia, F., Vardi, M.: Improved Automata Generation for Linear Temporal Logic. In: Halbwachs, N., Peled, D.A. (eds.) CAV 1999. LNCS, vol. 1633, pp. 249–260. Springer, Heidelberg (1999)
29. Emerson, E.: Temporal and Modal Logic. In: Handbook of Theoretical Computer Science, vol. B: Formal Models and Sematics (B) (1990)
30. Emerson, E., Lei, C.: Efficient Model Checking in Fragments of the Propositional Mu-Calculus (Extended Abstract). In: LICS (1986)
31. Filiot, E., Jin, N., Raskin, J.: An Antichain Algorithm for LTL Realizability. In: Bouajjani, A., Maler, O. (eds.) CAV 2009. LNCS, vol. 5643, pp. 263–277. Springer, Heidelberg (2009)
32. Fisher, M., Dixon, C., Peim, M.: Clausal temporal resolution. ACM Trans. Comput. Log. 2(1) (2001)
33. Fisman, D., et al.: A Framework for Inherent Vacuity. In: Chockler, H., Hu, A.J. (eds.) HVC 2008. LNCS, vol. 5394, pp. 7–22. Springer, Heidelberg (2009)
34. Gomes, C., Selman, B.: Algorithm portfolios. Artif. Intell. 126(1-2) (2001)
35. Goranko, V., Kyrilov, A., Shkatov, D.: Tableau Tool for Testing Satisfiability in LTL: Implementation and Experimental Analysis. In: M4M (2009)
36. Goré, R.: Personal Communication (2010)
37. Goré, R., Widmann, F.: An Experimental Comparison of Theorem Provers for CTL. In: CLoDeM (2010)
38. Goré, R., Widmann, F.: An Optimal On-the-Fly Tableau-Based Decision Procedure for PDL-Satisfiability. In: Schmidt, R.A. (ed.) CADE-22. LNCS, vol. 5663, pp. 437–452. Springer, Heidelberg (2009)
39. Heljanko, K., Junttila, T., Latvala, T.: Incremental and Complete Bounded Model Checking for Full PLTL. In: Etessami, K., Rajamani, S.K. (eds.) CAV 2005. LNCS, vol. 3576, pp. 98–111. Springer, Heidelberg (2005)
40. Henzinger, T., Kupferman, O., Qadeer, S.: From Pre-Historic to Post-Modern Symbolic Model Checking. FMSD 23(3) (2003)
41. Heuerding, A., et al.: Propositional Logics on the Computer. In: Baumgartner, P., Posegga, J., Hähnle, R. (eds.) TABLEAUX 1995. LNCS, vol. 918, pp. 310–323. Springer, Heidelberg (1995)
42. Hirsch, B., Hustadt, U.: Translating PLTL into WS1S: Application Description. In: M4M (2001)
43. Huberman, B., Lukose, R., Hogg, T.: An Economics Approach to Hard Computational Problems. Science 275(5296) (1997)
44. Hustadt, U., Konev, B.: TRP++: A temporal resolution prover. In: Collegium Logicum, vol. 8. Kurt Gödel Society (2004)

45. Hustadt, U., Schmidt, R.A.: Formulae which Highlight Differences between Temporal Logic and Dynamic Logic Provers. Issues in the Design and Experimental Evaluation of Systems for Modal and Temporal Logics. Dipartimento, di Ingegneria dell'Informazione, Unversitá degli Studi di Siena (2001)

46. Hustadt, U., Schmidt, R.A.: Scientific Benchmarking with Temporal Logic Decision Procedures. In: KR. Morgan Kaufmann, San Francisco (2002)

47. Hustadt, U., et al.: TeMP: A Temporal Monodic Prover. In: Basin, D., Rusinowitch, M. (eds.) IJCAR 2004. LNCS (LNAI), vol. 3097, pp. 326–330. Springer, Heidelberg (2004)

48. Janssen, G.: Logics for Digital Circuit Verification: Theory, Algorithms, and Applications. PhD thesis. Technische Universiteit Eindhoven (1999)

49. Leyton-Brown, K., et al.: A Portfolio Approach to Algorithm Selection. In: IJCAI. Morgan Kaufmann, San Francisco (2003)

50. Ludwig, M., Hustadt, U.: Fair Derivations in Monodic Temporal Reasoning. In: Schmidt, R.A. (ed.) CADE-22. LNCS, vol. 5663, pp. 261–276. Springer, Heidelberg (2009)

51. Ludwig, M., Hustadt, U.: Implementing a fair monodic temporal logic prover. AI Commun. 23(2-3) (2010)

52. Ludwig, M., Hustadt, U.: Resolution-Based Model Construction for PLTL. In: TIME (2009)

53. de Moura, L.: SAL: Tutorial (2004)

54. de Moura, L., et al.: SAL 2. In: Alur, R., Peled, D.A. (eds.) CAV 2004. LNCS, vol. 3114, pp. 496–500. Springer, Heidelberg (2004)

55. Nikolić, M.: Statistical Methodology for Comparison of SAT Solvers. In: Strichman, O., Szeider, S. (eds.) SAT 2010. LNCS, vol. 6175, pp. 209–222. Springer, Heidelberg (2010)

56. Pill, I., et al.: Formal analysis of hardware requirements. In: DAC (2006)

57. Prosyd, http://www.prosyd.org/

58. Pulina, L., Tacchella, A.: A self-adaptive multi-engine solver for quantified Boolean formulas. Constraints 14(1) (2009)

59. Rozier, K., Vardi, M.: A Multi-Encoding Approach for LTL Symbolic Satisfiability Checking. In: Butler, M., Schulte, W. (eds.) FM 2011. LNCS, vol. 6664, pp. 417–431. Springer, Heidelberg (2011)

60. Rozier, K., Vardi, M.: LTL Satisfiability Checking. STTT 12(2) (2010)

61. Schuppan, V.: Towards a notion of unsatisfiable and unrealizable cores for LTL. Sci. Comput. Program (2010) (in Press), doi:10.1016/j.scico.2010.11.004

62. Schuppan, V., Darmawan, L.: Evaluating LTL Satisfiability Solvers (full version) (2011),
http://www.schuppan.de/viktor/VSchuppanLDarmawan-ATVA-2011-full.pdf

63. Schwendimann, S.: A New One-Pass Tableau Calculus for PLTL. In: de Swart, H. (ed.) TABLEAUX 1998. LNCS (LNAI), vol. 1397, pp. 277–292. Springer, Heidelberg (1998)

64. Simon, L., Le Berre, D.: Some Results and Lessons from the SAT Competitions (invited talk, slides only). In: Second International Workshop on Constraint Propagation and Implementation, Sitges, Spain (October 1, 2005)

65. StatSoft, Inc. Electronic Statistics Textbook. StatSoft, Tulsa, OK, USA, http://www.statsoft.com/textbook/

66. Sutcliffe, G., Suttner, C.: Evaluating general purpose automated theorem proving systems. Artif. Intell. 131(1-2) (2001)

67. The VIS Group: VIS: A System for Verification and Synthesis. In: Alur, R., Henzinger, T.A. (eds.) CAV 1996. LNCS, vol. 1102, pp. 428–432. Springer, Heidelberg (1996)

68. Wolper, P.: The Tableau Method for Temporal Logic: An Overview. Logique et Analyse 28(110-111) (1985)

69. De Wulf, M., et al.: Antichains: Alternative Algorithms for LTL Satisfiability and Model-Checking. In: Ramakrishnan, C.R., Rehof, J. (eds.) TACAS 2008. LNCS, vol. 4963, pp. 63–77. Springer, Heidelberg (2008)

70. Xu, L., et al.: SATzilla: Portfolio-based Algorithm Selection for SAT. JAIR 32 (2008)

McAiT – A Timing Analyzer for Multicore Real-Time Software[*]

Mingsong Lv[1,**], Nan Guan[1,2], Qingxu Deng[1], Ge Yu[1], and Wang Yi[1,2,**]

[1] Northeastern University, Shenyang, China
lvmingsong@ise.neu.edu.cn
[2] Uppsala University, Uppsala, Sweden
yi@it.uu.se

Abstract. We present McAiT, a tool for estimating the Worst-Case Execution Times (WCET) of programs running on multicore processors. The highlight of McAiT is that it leverages timed automata to model both the timing behaviors of the programs' interaction with its environment (based on the results of local cache analysis by abstract interpretation) and a broad range of on-chip shared resources, such as shared buses and shared caches. McAiT also allows for modeling complex task models, such as synchronization, jitter, etc. High analysis precision is achieved by the McAiT approach, which is demonstrated by extensive experiments. The tool also supports the classical Implicit Path Enumeration Technique (IPET) combined with worst-case shared resource access delay for WCET estimation, to provide the users with the flexibility to trade analysis precision for efficiency.

1 Introduction

Multicores are predicted to be increasingly used in future real-time embedded systems, but the downside of this trend is that timing predictability of multicore software is serverly degraded due to inter-core conflicts when programs access shared resources concurrently. Estimating WCET becomes a key challenge on multicore architectures, since it is very difficult to tightly bound the time to access shared resources. Existing tools [1] cannot provide satisfactory results, in that they are either designed for single-core architectures or hard to produce precise bounds on the access delays in the presence of resource contention.

We present McAiT, a tool for WCET estimation of programs running on multicores with on-chip shared resources. McAiT exploits abstract interpretation (AI) for local cache analysis of each program on each core, and automatically generates a timed automaton (TA) to capture the precise timing behavior of the program's interaction with its environment, i.e., all the time sequences of the program for accessing the shared resources and complex task relations (such as synchronization) with programs on different cores. The generated

---

[*] This work was sponsored by NSF of China (60973017), and the Fundamental Research Funds for the Central Universities of China (N100304001).
[**] Corresponding authors.

T. Bultan and P.-A. Hsiung (Eds.): ATVA 2011, LNCS 6996, pp. 414–417, 2011.

automata are used for the WCET estimation of the programs using UPPAAL, based on the abstract behavior of the shared resources, modeled also as timed automata. High analysis precision is achieved by the McAiT approach, which is demonstrated by extensive experiments. The tool also supports the classical IPET technique [2] combined with worst-case resource access delay for WCET estimation, to provide the users with the flexibility to trade analysis precision for efficiency. Technical details on applying the McAiT approach in the analysis of shared buses was presented in [3]. This paper describes the complete tool features and the implementation details of McAiT developed jointly by Uppsala University (Sweden) and Northeastern University (China). McAiT is available at: `http://www.neu-rtes.org/mcait`

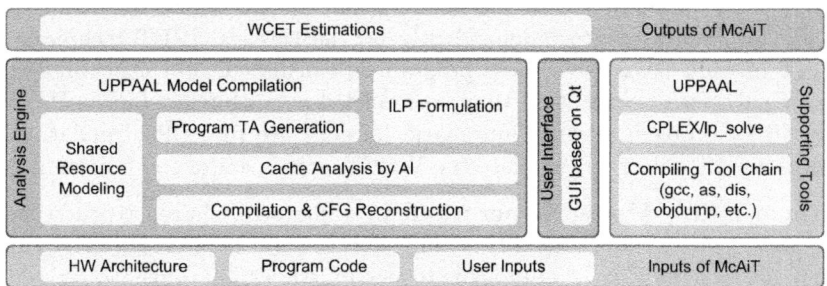

Fig. 1. The architecture of McAiT

2   Main Features and Implementation of McAiT

Fig.1 illustrates the architecture and the components of McAiT, the core features of which is detailed below.

The Graphical User Interface (GUI). The GUI of McAiT provides the users with functionalities to manage analysis projects (such as creating, copying and removing a project) and guide the analysis procedure (either "one-click" WCET estimation or step-by-step progressing). Users may start multiple analysis projects concurrently thanks to the multi-threaded architecture of McAiT. The GUI is designed using the Qt SDK[1], since Qt is portable to most popular platforms and has good performance due to the C++ implementation.

CFG Reconstruction from Program Binaries. McAiT works on program binaries instead of source files, since compiler optimization may produce an executable file with a control flow significantly different from that of the source file. In such cases, estimations based on source files may be very imprecise. However, McAiT allows source files of any procedural language as input, as long as they can be compiled to the target architecture, i.e., the PISA instruction set supported by McAiT. The program binaries are disassembled, from which the Control Flow Graph (CFG) of each program is reconstructed by identifying the jump instructions. This component is developed based on the Chronos tool [4].

---

[1] http://qt.nokia.com

AI-Based Cache Analysis. McAiT employs AI presented in [5] for local cache analysis. An abstract cache state (ACS) is maintained on each program point (basic block boundary) for each of the three independent analyses (MUST, MAY, PERSISTENCE). The results of these analyses are the cache hit/miss classifications for each program instruction. Currently, McAiT is able to handle multilevel private instruction caches with LRU replacement policy. But the analysis framework of McAiT allows for integration of analysis for any replacement policy other than LRU as long as it can be analyzed by AI.

WCET Estimation by IPET. If there is no effective technique to analyze inter-core conflicts, then one has to assume that each time a cache miss occurs, the accesses to shared resources take the longest possible delay. Based on the results of cache analysis and this assumption, McAiT allows to estimate the WCET for each program independently by the classical IPET technique: the WCET of each basic block of a program is calculated, and then finding the longest path (w.r.t. execution time) is modeled as an Integer Linear Programming (ILP) problem. McAiT automatically generate the ILP formulation and invokes an ILP solver to calculate the WCET estimation of the program.

Automatic TA Model Generation. In multicores, shared resource access time may be very unpredictable mainly due to inter-core conflicts. Assuming worst-case access delay usually leads to pessimistic estimations. To tighten the bounds, McAiT offers a novel approach which introduces model checking to precisely model and analyze the behaviors of shared resource accesses. The timing behavior of each program is modeled as a timed automaton, which carries information on when the program accesses shared resources based on the results of local cache analysis. When a program tries to access a shared resource, the program TA will communicate with the TA model for the resource access protocol via a standard interface, "*accessSR[pid]*", defined by McAiT (see Fig.2(a)). This standard interface detaches program modeling and shared resource modeling, so any new resource model can be integrated as long as it conforms to the interface. The WCET estimations are tight since by this technique the timing of shared resource accesses is precisely preserved.

McAiT allows for the modeling of other complex task models, e.g., synchronization and jitter. Once task synchronization is identified from the program code and marked within the CFG, a channel provided by UPPAAL is created in the program TA to accept signals which make the program TA to proceed execution. If different task phasing are modeled, some conflicts on the shared resources are safely excluded, which may further tighten the WCET bounds.

Modeling Shared Resources. For any shared resource, McAiT uses a timed automaton (or a set of timed automata) to model the resource access protocol (which could be arbitration policies for buses or replacement policies for caches). The TA for the shared resource receives access requests from the programs' TA via the standard interface and simulates the access protocol, exactly modeling how long each access may take. Fig.2(b) and Fig.2(c) show the TA models for a First-Come-First-Service shared bus and a shared L2 Cache, which are provided

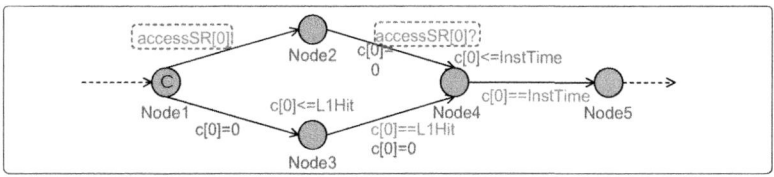

(a) A chunk of program TA

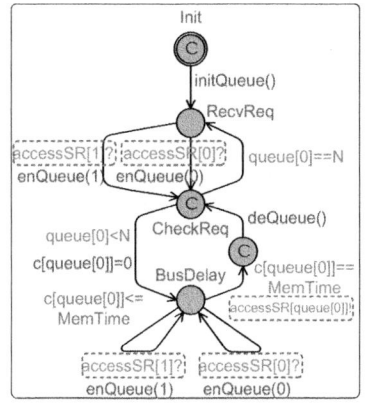

(b) The TA for a shared FCFS bus

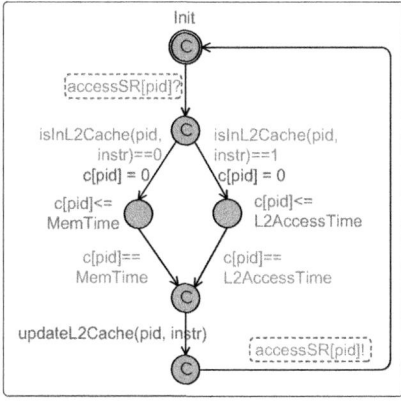

(c) The TA for a shared L2 Cache

Fig. 2. The TA models for programs, shared bus and shared cache

by McAiT. Other shared resources could also be modeled similarly and integrated into McAiT. To obtain the WCET bounds, McAiT invokes UPPAAL to explore the models for both the programs and the shared resources.

We refer interested readers to an appendix [6] for the results on the analysis precision and the analysis overhead for the case of shared buses. The McAiT User Manual [7] provides details on how to install the tool from scratch and an example showing the complete procedure of WCET estimation by McAiT.

References

1. Wilhelm, R., et al.: The Worst-Case Execution-Time Problem - Overview of Methods and Survey of Tools. ACM Trans. Embed. Comput. Syst. (2008)
2. Li, Y.-T.S., Malik, S.: Performance Analysis of Embedded Software Using Implicit Path Enumeration. In: DAC (1995)
3. Lv, M., Guan, N., Yi, W., Yu, G.: Combining Abstract Interpretation with Model Checking for Timing Analysis of Multicore Software. In: The 31st IEEE Real-Time Systems Symposium, RTSS (2010)
4. Li, X., Liang, Y., Mitra, T., Roychoudury, A.: Chronos: A Timing Analyzer for Embedded Software. Science of Computer Programming, 56–67 (2007)
5. Ferdinand, C.: Cache Behavior Prediction for Real-Time Systems. Ph.D. Thesis of Saarland University (1997)
6. http://www.neu-rtes.org/mcait/McAiT_APPENDIX.pdf
7. http://www.neu-rtes.org/mcait/McAiT_UM_1.0.pdf

MIO Workbench: A Tool for Compositional Design with Modal Input/Output Interfaces[*]

Sebastian S. Bauer[1], Philip Mayer[1], and Axel Legay[2]

[1] Ludwig-Maximilians-Universität München, Germany
[2] INRIA/IRISA Rennes, France

Abstract. Modal Input/Output interfaces (MIOs) is a new specification theory for systems communicating via inputs and outputs. The approach combines the advantages of both modal automata and interface automata, two dominant specification theories for component-based design. This paper presents the MIO Workbench that is the first complete implementation of the MIO theory.

1 Context

Evolution of computer science technology has permitted the development of large size systems that facilitate (if not govern) our daily life. Such systems, which have to interact with uncertain environments, are much too complex to be developed by a single team or unit. Rather, the current trend in software engineering suggests that huge systems shall result from the assembly of several subsystems called components, each of them being developed by a dedicated team. This component-based design view has the advantage of not only reducing complexity but also hiding code information/secrets of individual participants.

While this view offers flexibility in the design, there is still the need that all the participants agree on what the interface of each component shall be. Such an interface precises the behaviors expected from the component as well as the environment in where it can be used. According to state of practice, interfaces are typically described using Word/Excel text documents or modeling languages such as UML/XML. A series of recent works, now widely accepted by industrials [5,15], instead recommend relying most possibly on mathematically sound formalisms, thus best reducing ambiguities.

Existing interface models [13,9,4,2,8] are generally nothing more than transition systems whose transitions are equipped with labels on which a dedicated semantic can be built. Many of those powerful theories have recently been unified through the *Modal Input/Output interface* (MIO) theory. Like modal automata [8], the formalism allows to finitely model a possibly infinite set of systems (aka implementations) by distinguishing those behaviors (transitions) that *must* always be implemented from those that *may* not be implemented. Moreover, similarly to *I/O automata* [10], MIOs communicate via *input* and *output* actions and propose

---

[*] This work has been partially sponsored by the EU project ASCENS, 257414.

T. Bultan and P.-A. Hsiung (Eds.): ATVA 2011, LNCS 6996, pp. 418–421, 2011.
© Springer-Verlag Berlin Heidelberg 2011

the optimistic structural composition from interface automata [2]. This means that, contrary to I/O automata, MIOs are not input-enabled and a state in a composed system, where one component can perform an output that cannot be caught by a receiving component, is declared as an error state. However, reaching an error state does not necessarily mean that the two components cannot work properly together. Instead, two components can be composed if there exists an environment in where no such communication errors occur. As a summary, the MIO theory is equipped with *structural (optimistic and pessimistic) composition together with compatibility, refinement* (that allows to compare two sets of implementations), *satisfiability* (that allows to check whether an implementation matches the requirements of the specification), and a *logical composition* that allows to combine requirements represented by interfaces. In addition, there is a *quotient* operator that allows to synthesize missing interface requirements in a large size design. Finally the theory also permit independent implementability [3].

It is clear that interface theories can be used to facilitate the development of real-life applications. But, surprisingly, only a few tools exist for specific theories [6,1]. This paper introduces the MIO Workbench toolset, that is the very first complete implementation of the MIO theory. The paper presents the tool architecture and describes the basic creation and analysis facilities the MIO Workbench provides. Details about theory and tool can be found at [12].

2   Tool Architecture

The MIO Workbench is implemented in Java as a series of Eclipse plug-ins [7] which makes it easily extendable in case new operations are added to the MIO theory. We have used the Eclipse Modeling Framework (EMF) to define a meta-model for MIOs. This allowed us to generate code for creation and access of (objects representing) MIOs, thus code maintenance is much easier and flexible, particularly for later changes and extensions of the domain model. The architecture of the tool is briefly described hereafter. For details, see [11,12].

The graphical user interface of the tool consists of an *editor* for drawing MIOs, a *verification view* to execute operations on MIOs (composition, refinement, . . .), and finally, a *command-line shell* which is a powerful interface of computing complex tasks (e.g., combining operations and checks). An overview of the standard perspective of the tool can be seen in Fig. 1.

The MIO Editor displays MIOs as a graph in the classical way by using nodes as states and edges as transitions. May and must transitions are drawn with dashed and solid arrows, respectively. Furthermore, each transition is equipped with an internal action (black arrow), input action (suffixed with *?*, green arrow), or output action (suffixed with *!*, red arrow). The MIO editor offers all the usual operations such as adding new states and transitions, moving them around, changing labels, types, and manual layouting.

The MIO Workbench Verification View provides a way to visually execute individual operations and depict the results graphically. Two MIOs can be placed on the left hand and right hand side, by dragging .mio files from the project explorer and dropping them on one side of the verification view; then all the

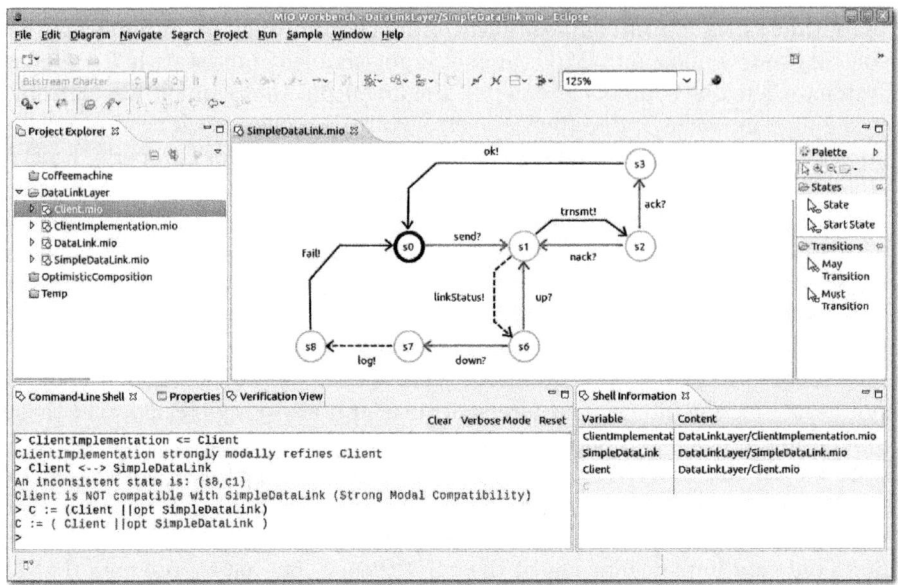

Fig. 1. MIO Workbench and its editor and views

MIO operations are available from the middle panel. The output of performing a refinement or compatibility check is a refinement relation or the matching states side-by-side between the two input MIOs in the positive case, or in the negative case the view graphically displays, side-by-side, the path which led to an erroneous state or the transition possible in one automaton, but not in the other. The output of composition, conjunction and quotient is a MIO which can be saved and reused.

The MIO Workbench Shell is a shell-like interpreter that facilitates combination of operations. MIOs from the project explorer can be made available in the shell by drag-and-drop. All the operations can be executed by entering simple commands. For instance, if S and T are variables, then the command S <= T performs a refinement check. To construct new MIOs, we can compose two MIOs S1 and S2 and store the result in a new variable by executing C := (S1 || S2). The main advantage is the possibility of performing complex verification tasks like (S && T && U) <= (A - B) (where && is conjunction and - is quotient). The complete input grammar as well as a tutorial can be found at [12].

3   Experiments and Future Work

As of yet, interface theories are not used on a large scale in industry. However, together with industrials, we believe that such theories can greatly facilitate the development of real-life applications, and that the major stumbling block to their deployment lies in the unavailability of tools, to which the MIO Workbench is a remedy. We have already applied the MIO Workbench and the implemented interface theories in the context of the EU project Sensoria [14], where we have worked with industry partners to model and verify service-based architectures (based on Web services) from the domains of Finance, Automotive, and Education. Using the UML profile UML4SOA [16,11] for modeling the system, we were able to automatically translate the models into MIOs and perform a rigorous analysis with the MIO Workbench, like compatibility and refinement checks, which was later re-annotated to the UML model. This analysis has proven helpful in finding the more subtle problems in the UML models.

For future work, we plan to integrate our recent work on extensions of modal interfaces to include data by an efficient BDD-based implementation. Also, code generation transforming MIOs to correct implementations is of interest.

References

1. Adler, B.T., de Alfaro, L., da Silva, L.D., Faella, M., Legay, A., Raman, V., Roy, P.: Ticc: A Tool for Interface Compatibility and Composition. In: Ball, T., Jones, R.B. (eds.) CAV 2006. LNCS, vol. 4144, pp. 59–62. Springer, Heidelberg (2006)
2. de Alfaro, L., Henzinger, T.A.: Interface Theories for Component-Based Design. In: Henzinger, T.A., Kirsch, C.M. (eds.) EMSOFT 2001. LNCS, vol. 2211, pp. 148–165. Springer, Heidelberg (2001)
3. de Alfaro, L., Henzinger, T.A.: Interface-based Design. In: Engineering Theories of Software-intensive Systems. NATO, vol. 195, pp. 83–104. Springer, Heidelberg (2005)
4. Bauer, S.S., Mayer, P., Schroeder, A., Hennicker, R.: On weak modal compatibility, refinement, and the MIO Workbench. In: Esparza, J., Majumdar, R. (eds.) TACAS 2010. LNCS, vol. 6015, pp. 175–189. Springer, Heidelberg (2010)
5. COMBEST, http://www.combest.eu/home/
6. David, A., Larsen, K.G., Legay, A., Nyman, U., Wąsowski, A.: ECDAR: An Environment for Compositional Design and Analysis of Real Time Systems. In: Bouajjani, A., Chin, W.-N. (eds.) ATVA 2010. LNCS, vol. 6252, pp. 365–370. Springer, Heidelberg (2010)
7. Eclipse, http://www.eclipse.org/
8. Hüttel, H., Larsen, K.G.: The Use of Static Constructs in A Modal Process Logic. In: Meyer, A.R., Taitslin, M.A. (eds.) Logic at Botik 1989. LNCS, vol. 363, pp. 163–180. Springer, Heidelberg (1989)
9. Larsen, K.G., Nyman, U., Wąsowski, A.: Modal I/O Automata for Interface and Product Line Theories. In: De Nicola, R. (ed.) ESOP 2007. LNCS, vol. 4421, pp. 64–79. Springer, Heidelberg (2007)
10. Lynch, N.A., Tuttle, M.R.: An introduction to input/output automata. CWI Quarterly 2, 219–246 (1989)
11. Mayer, P.: MDD4SOA: Model-Driven Development for Service-Oriented Architectures. Ph.D. thesis, LMU München (December 2010)
12. MIO Workbench, http://www.miowb.net/
13. Raclet, J.B., Badouel, E., Benveniste, A., Caillaud, B., Legay, A., Passerone, R.: Modal interfaces: unifying interface automata and modal specifications. In: EMSOFT 2009, pp. 87–96. ACM, New York (2009)
14. Sensoria, http://www.sensoria-ist.eu/
15. SPEEDS, http://www.speeds.eu.com/
16. UML4SOA – A profile for modeling service behaviour in UML, http://www.uml4soa.eu/

The Buck Stops Here: Order, Chance, and Coordination in Distributed Control[⋆]

Gal Katz[1], Doron Peled[1], and Sven Schewe[2]

[1] Department of Computer Science, Bar Ilan University, Ramat Gan 52900, Israel
[2] Department of Computer Science, University of Liverpool, Liverpool, UK

Abstract. Distributed control for enforcing a global invariant can be achieved based on calculating the knowledge of processes. When the local knowledge of individual processes is insufficient, processes can temporarily join their knowledge by means of synchronization. While synchronization can be used to guarantee progress, it is computationally expensive and should be used sparsely. In this paper, we introduce several solutions for minimizing the synchronization overhead. One possibility is to calculate the knowledge of a process of whether or not the system can progress without it. This knowledge can be used by the process to avoid unnecessary synchronization. Because of the distributed nature of the system, mutual passing of responsibility, based on such knowledge may result in deadlocks. We discuss three independent solutions to this problem. Our first solution breaks the symmetry between processes in order to avoid such situations, while our second solution is based on chance (coin tossing). Finally, we use automatically constructed stable properties to increase the joint knowledge of processes in order to minimize the number of processes that need to interact.

1 Introduction

While formal verification techniques allow for debugging existing systems, synthesis techniques are used to construct correct-by-design systems from their specification. Synthesis is highly intractable for sequential systems and undecidable for distributed systems [11], although there exist some cases and architectures where this is decidable [3,7,15]. Adding control to an existing distributed system in order to satisfy further properties, including invariants, turns out to be undecidable as well [4,16,17].

In a series of papers [1,2,4,5], we developed a synthesis method for controlling distributed systems to satisfy invariant properties based on knowledge. The problem becomes decidable when further temporary synchronization between processes is allowed for in order to obtain knowledge that may not be available locally. Unfortunately, the addition of temporary synchronization is rather expensive.

The mechanism for controlling the system to enforce a global invariant involves precalculating the local knowledge of processes. This knowledge can be used at runtime to support the firing of a transition, while guaranteeing that the imposed invariant is maintained. When such knowledge does not exist locally, processes can check their

⋆ This work was partly supported by the Israel Science Foundation Grant 1262/09 and by the Engineering and Physical Science Research Council Grant EP/H046623/1.

T. Bultan and P.-A. Hsiung (Eds.): ATVA 2011, LNCS 6996, pp. 422–431, 2011.

knowledge about other processes (knowledge of knowledge), or hang on a supervisor that collects the local information until enough joint knowledge is achieved [5]. A single supervisor can be responsible for multiple processes and may make different decisions according to the order in which processes hang on it. As these interactions between processes and their supervisor are expensive, our goal here is to minimize them without introducing new deadlocks to the system.

A major source of redundancy appears when processes do not have enough local knowledge, but other processes, teaming up together, are sufficient for achieving their goal (in our case, to decide on executing a transition). In fact, a process may calculate its knowledge regarding the joint knowledge of other processes. A naive approach would instruct this process to wait instead of hanging on a supervisor. However, carefully observing this solution reveals that the system may deadlock: it is possible that multiple processes know that other processes are sufficient for coordination, while not enough processes are volunteering to make the coordination themselves. If we want to take advantage of such knowledge of processes about other processes, we need to break the cycle of passing responsibility in order to make a correct decision when to avoid coordination.

The first solution we propose involves the breaking of symmetry. Processes are assigned indexes. A process of lower index can avoid coordination if it has the knowledge that processes of higher indexes have enough combined knowledge. This solution may create some imbalance in the system on both, coordination and progress, according to this prioritization. A second solution is probabilistic, tossing a coin when local knowledge is lacking, but knowledge about the coordination of other processes exists. A third solution is to improve the knowledge that a set of processes may have together. This is done by calculating stable properties that depend on the set of processes that are ready to coordinate. The calculation of such invariants use the constructions known in Petri Net theory as *traps* and *siphons* [10]. Increasing the knowledge available to the set of coordinating processes can reduce the number of processes needed for synchronization.

2   Knowledge Based Control in a Nutshell

The model used in this paper is Petri Nets. It was chosen due to its visual representation. The method and algorithms developed here can equally apply to other models, e.g., transition systems, communicating automata, etc. We use the same terminology as in [5]. Due to space restrictions, we only give a brief summary in this section.

A *(1-safe) Petri Net N* is a tuple (P, T, E, s_0) where P is a finite set of *places*, the *states* are defined as $S = 2^P$ where $s_0 \in S$ is the *initial state*, T is a finite set of *transitions*, and $E \subseteq (P \times T) \cup (T \times P)$ is a bipartite relation between the places and the transitions. For a transition $t \in T$, we define the set of *input places* $\bullet t$ as $\{p \in P \mid (p, t) \in E\}$, and *output places* $t^\bullet$ as $\{p \in P \mid (t, p) \in E\}$. Similarly, for a place $p \in P$, we denote by $p^\bullet$ the transitions $\{t \in T \mid (p, t) \in E\}$, and by $\bullet p$ the transitions $\{p \in P \mid (t, p) \in E\}$.

Figure 1 shows two Petri Nets. Transitions are visualized as lines, places as circles, and the relation E is represented using arrows. In Figure 1(a), there are places $p_1, p_2, \ldots, p_7$ and transitions a, b, c, d. We depict a state by putting full circles, called *tokens*, inside its places. In the example in Figure 1(a), the initial state s_0 is $\{p_1, p_2, p_7\}$.

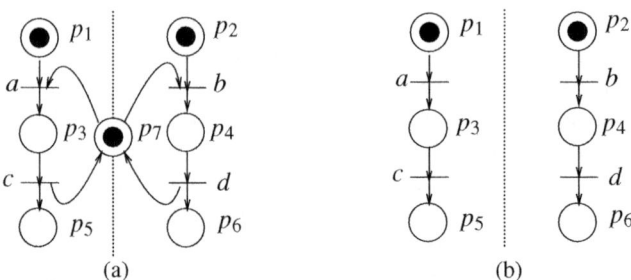

Fig. 1. Petri Nets: (a) without priorities and (b) with priorities $a \ll d$ and $b \ll c$

We extend the definitions of input and output to sets of places and transitions by means of union, e.g., for $L \subseteq P$, $^\bullet L = \cup_{p \in L} {}^\bullet p$. A transition t is *enabled* in a state s, denoted $s[t\rangle$, if $^\bullet t \subseteq s$ and $t^\bullet \cap s \subseteq {}^\bullet t$. A state s is in *deadlock* if there is no enabled transition from it. A transition t can be *fired* (or *executed*) from state s to state s', denoted by $s[t\rangle s'$, when t is enabled at s. Then, $s' = (s \setminus {}^\bullet t) \cup t^\bullet$. An *execution* of a Petri Net N is a maximal alternating sequence $s_0[t_1\rangle s_1[t_2\rangle s_2 \ldots$, where s_0 is the initial state of N. An execution is sometimes referred to by writing only the sequence of states or sequence of transition fired. Two transitions t_1 and t_2 are *dependent* if $(^\bullet t_1 \cup t_1^\bullet) \cap (^\bullet t_2 \cup t_2^\bullet) \neq \emptyset$. Let $D \subseteq T \times T$ be the *dependence* relation. Two transitions are *independent* if they are not dependent.

The transitions that are enabled from the initial state in the Petri Net of Figure 1(a) are a and b. If we fire a from the initial state, the tokens from p_1 and p_7 will be removed, and a token will be placed in p_3. In this Petri Net, all transitions are dependent on each other, since they all involve the place p_7. Removing p_7, see Figure 1(b), makes both a and c become independent from both b and d. A *process* π of a Petri Net N is a subset of the transitions T satisfying that, for each pair $t_1, t_2 \in \pi$ of independent (i.e., $(t_1, t_2) \notin D$) transitions in π, there is no reachable state s in which both t_1 and t_2 are enabled.

We will represent the separation of transitions of a Petri Net into processes using dotted lines. We assume a given set of processes C that *covers* all transitions of the net, i.e., $\cup_{\pi \in C} \pi = T$. A transition can belong to several processes, e.g., when it models a synchronization between processes. For the Petri Net in Figure 1(a), there are two executions: *acbd* and *bdac*. There are two processes: the *left* process $\pi_l = \{a, c\}$ and the *right* process $\pi_r = \{b, d\}$. We use the same partitioning of transitions to processes in Figure 1(b).

The *neighborhood* of a set of processes Π, denoted $ngb(\Pi)$, includes all places that are either inputs or outputs to transitions of Π. We say that a set of processes Π *owns* the places in their neighborhood that cannot gain or lose a token by a transition that is not exclusively in Π, and denote the places owned by a set of processes Π $own(\Pi) = ngb(\Pi) \setminus ngb(C \setminus \Pi)$.

When a notation refers to a set of processes Π, we will often replace writing the singleton process set $\{\pi\}$ by writing π, e.g., we write $own(\pi)$. Note that $ngb(\Pi_1) \cup ngb(\Pi_2) = ngb(\Pi_1 \cup \Pi_2)$, while $own(\Pi_1) \cup own(\Pi_2) \subseteq own(\Pi_1 \cup \Pi_2)$. The neighborhood of process π_l is $\{p_1, p_3, p_5, p_7\}$. Place p_7 in Figure 1(a) is neither owned by π_l, nor by π_r, but it is owned by $\{\pi_l, \pi_r\}$. It belongs to the neighborhood of both processes and acts as a semaphore. It can be captured by the execution of a or of b, guaranteeing that $\neg(p_3 \wedge p_4)$ is an invariant of the system.

We use weak and strong knowledge without recall [8]. For weak knowledge, $K_{\Pi}^{w}\varphi$ holds in a state s if for all the reachable states of the Petri Net that have the same full and empty places in the neighborhood of Π as in s, φ holds. Similarly, for strong knowledge, $K_{\Pi}^{s}\varphi$ is defined based on the places that the processes in Π *own* rather than their neighborhood.

In control theory, a transformation takes a system and allows blocking some transitions in order to impose some constraint on the system. This is done by adding a supervisor process [12,19,14], which is usually an automaton that runs synchronously with the controlled system. This (finite state) automaton observes the controlled system, progresses according to the transitions it observes, and blocks some of the enabled transitions, depending on its current state [19]. This is often insufficient for obtaining distributed control [13]. This section briefly summarizes results & constructions of [5].

Our control goal is to restrict the system such that each reachable state and subsequent transition t would belong to a given set $\Psi \subseteq S \times T$. As a preparatory stage, we calculate a predicate $\varphi_{good(t)}$ that encodes the states, where executing t according to Ψ is allowed (see [5]). In order to control the execution of the system, a transition can fire, when enabled, only if it is also *supported* by a process, or by a supervisor, as described below. A transition t is supported by a process π that contains t ($t \in \pi$) if π weakly knows that a transition t is good:

$$K_{\pi}^{w}\varphi_{good(t)},$$

Thus, a process π supports some transition, when

$$\kappa_{1}^{\pi} = \bigvee_{t \in \pi} K_{\pi}^{w}\varphi_{good(t)}.$$

A process knows that another process supports a transition, when

$$\kappa_{2}^{\pi} = K_{\pi}^{w} \bigvee_{\pi' \neq \pi} \kappa_{1}^{\pi'}.$$

In [5], we proposed a control mechanism with supervisors that run asynchronously with the controlled processes. The set C of processes is partitioned into a set $S = \{\Pi_i \mid i = 1,\ldots,k\}$ of *supervisors*. When a process does not have the local knowledge to support a transition or to trust another process to do so, it hangs on a supervisor.

The decision by a process π to either support a transition $t \in \pi$, wait, or hang on a supervisor such that $\pi \in \Pi_i$ is as follows:

1. If a process π knows that a transition is good, i.e., κ_{1}^{π} holds, then it supports it.
2. Otherwise, if a process π knows that, for some transition t, a different process knows that it is good, i.e., κ_{2}^{π} holds, then π idles (i.e., supports no transition).
3. Otherwise, π hangs on its supervisor.

A supervisor Π_i collects the local information of the processes that hang on it. The subtle distinction between local state and local information plays a major role here. While a process may base its (weak) knowledge on the local information, there is nothing to guarantee that the local information of the hung processes will not be changed by other processes. Thus, the supervisor collects their joint local state, which cannot change as long as these processes do not progress. The local information of a hung process may still be changed by another process. In this case, the process may unhang, and support a transition based on its local knowledge, after updating the supervisor.

A supervisor Π_i can support a transition t when a set of processes $\Pi \subseteq \Pi_i$ are hung on it such that $t \in \pi \in \Pi$ when $K_\Pi^s \varphi_{good(t)}$ holds. We define

$$\kappa^\Pi = \bigvee_{t \in \cup \Pi} K_\Pi^s \varphi_{good(t)}.$$

Theorem 1. *[5] If $\varphi_G \to (\bigvee_{\pi \in C} \kappa_1^\pi \vee \bigvee_{\Pi_i \in S} \kappa^{\Pi_i})$ holds, then the knowledge based control achieves the desired invariant without introducing new deadlocks.*

Theorem 1 provides a condition under which the supervised control does not lead to any new deadlocks. This is guaranteed when (there is a global solution and) there is just a single supervisor, containing all processes. The proof of Theorem 1 makes use of a translation to extended Petri Nets, where the extension is used for the communication between the supervisors and the processes they supervise.

3   Reducing Process Hanging and Passing Responsibility

In the proposed solution for controlling a distributed system to satisfy a global invariant, the process/supervisor interaction may be expensive. Hanging can be necessary for the accumulation of joint knowledge that helps the system to progress. But hanging is an expensive operation, and it can be the case that, if a process refrains from hanging, another process may change its local information and subsequently facilitate knowledge to support a transition. In this section, we suggest two techniques to reduce process hanging: the introduction of a (partial) order on the processes and the introduction of randomized actions.

Order.   The introduction of a partial order $\succ$ on the set of processes leads to a situation, where a smaller process w.r.t. $\succ$ can avoid hanging on its supervisor if the bigger processes together can progress. Besides the advantage of reducing the number of calls to supervisors, it also allows for providing a preference to important processes, giving them an advanced access to supervisor support while reducing supervisor interaction for lesser processes significantly.

This makes use of nested knowledge, a generalization of the property κ_2^π to a set of processes. The intuition is that a process can check whether it knows that the joint knowledge of the other processes, besides itself, is sufficient to support a transition:

$$K_\pi^w \bigvee_{t \in \cup C \setminus \{\pi\}} K_{C \setminus \{\pi\}}^s \varphi_{good(t)}.$$

In that case, a process may decide not to hang, but to rather let the others provide the joint local state needed for making the progress decision. However, this solution makes

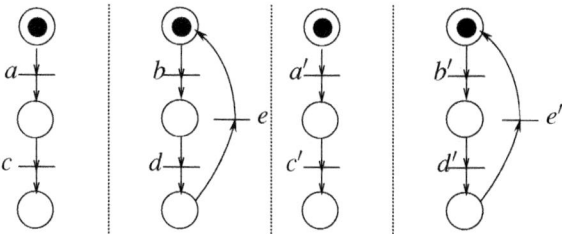

Fig. 2. Priorities: $a \ll d$, $b \ll c$, $a' \ll d'$, and $b' \ll c'$

it possible that too many processes will decide to delegate responsibility to others, without informing them. This can lead to the introduction of a deadlock.

As an example, consider the Petri Net with priorities from Figure 2. This net duplicates the net in Figure 1(b) and adds two new transitions. It consists of four processes: $\pi_1 = \{a,c\}$, $\pi_2 = \{b,d,e\}$, $\pi_3 = \{a',c'\}$ and $\pi_4 = \{b',d',e'\}$. In the initial state, each process does not have enough knowledge to support a transition. However, each process locally knows that the other processes together (in particular, two of the other processes) have enough knowledge to support a transition. For example, process π_1 knows that the joint knowledge of π_3 and π_4 together is sufficient to support one of the transitions of these processes, whatever their local state is. If, based on this knowledge about the other processes, each process will abstain from hanging, the supervisor will not be able to collect enough knowledge to support any move and the system will deadlock.

One way of dealing with the situation where too many processes independently 'pass the buck' to other processes to contribute to the joint knowledge, is to break symmetry in the decision to hang. For simplicity, assume first that we use a single supervisor. We number the processes in some way $\pi_1, \pi_2, \ldots, \pi_n$. Then the ith process also checks whether or not it (weakly) knows that the joint (strong) knowledge of the processes *with higher indexes* is sufficient to support a transition (see Theorem 2). That is,

$$\kappa_1^{\pi_i} \vee \kappa_2^{\pi_i} \vee K_{\pi_i}^w \kappa^{\{\pi_j | j > i\}}$$

becomes a sufficient condition for process π_i to avoid calling the supervisor. More generally, we can use any partial order $\succ$ on the processes and any set of distributed controllers, and change the control strategy as follows.

For a supervisor Π_i and a process π, we denote with $\Pi_i^{\succ \pi} = \{\pi' \in \Pi_i \mid \pi' \succ \pi\}$ the processes of Π_i that are strictly greater than π with respect to the partial order $\succ$. Naturally, a supervisor Π_i would support some transition based on the knowledge of the processes in $\Pi_i^{\succ \pi}$ if $\kappa^{\Pi_i^{\succ \pi}}$ holds. A process π can thus idle if it knows

$$\kappa_3^{\pi} = K_{\pi}^w \bigvee_{\Pi_i \in \mathcal{S}} \kappa^{\Pi_i^{\succ \pi}}.$$

This is used to reduce the states in which a process hangs on its supervisor.

The control strategy of the supervisors is not affected. The *ordered control strategy* is as follows:

1. If a process π knows that a transition is good, i.e., if κ_1^π holds, then it supports it.
2. Otherwise, if a process π knows that, for some transition $t \in \pi$, a different process knows that t is good, i.e., if κ_2^π holds, then π idles.
3. Otherwise, if a process π knows that, for some supervisor Π_i, the joint knowledge of $\Pi_i^{\succ\pi}$ is that some $t \in \Pi_i^{\succ\pi}$ is good, i.e., if κ_3^π holds, then π idles.
4. Otherwise, π hangs on its supervisor.

Ordered control does not introduce new deadlocks, and the sufficient condition for un-ordered control strategies also applies to ordered control strategies:

Theorem 2. *If* $\varphi_G \rightarrow (\bigvee_{\pi \in C} \kappa_1^\pi \vee \bigvee_{\Pi_i \in S} \kappa^{\Pi_i})$ *holds, then the ordered knowledge based control strategy introduces no deadlocks.*

Chance. An alternative solution is to allow processes to randomly hang on their super-visors if they do not know whether or not the system could progress without them. The advantage of hanging randomly rather than deterministically on a supervisor is a means to avoid, with high probability, a situation where a process hangs on its supervisor, while the system could progress. The solution based on breaking symmetry is biased towards processes with lower indexes: processes with low indexes would avoid hang-ing as soon as they know that the cooperation between processes with higher indexes suffices to prevent blocking. Our solution for regaining symmetry[1] is simple: when a process π has checked that neither κ_1^π nor κ_2^π hold, it makes a random choice either to wait or to hang.

Correctness of this algorithm is independent of the actual probability of each individ-ual probabilistic selection by a process. In a situation where no process knows locally how to proceed, the system will wait indefinitely with probability 0.

Using chance and order to reduce the situations in which processes hang on their supervisors are independent of each other. For generality, we discuss the extension of the technique proposed in the previous section, bearing in mind that the case where all processes are incomparable by $\succ$ reflects the unordered case. For the ordered case, however, we suggest that a process π should hang immediately if it knows that no supervisor Π_i has, based on the processes in $\Pi_i^{\succ\pi}$, sufficient knowledge to support a transition; that is, if

$$\kappa_4^\pi = K_\pi^w \neg \bigvee_{\Pi_i \in S} \kappa^{\Pi_i^{\succ\pi}}$$

holds. The local control strategy of the processes is to follow the *randomized control strategy* described below:

1. If a process π knows that a transition is good, i.e., if κ_1^π holds, then it supports it.
2. Otherwise, if a process π knows that, for some transition $t \in \pi$, a different process knows that t is good, i.e., if κ_2^π holds, then π idles.
3. Otherwise, if a process π knows that, for some supervisor Π_i, the joint knowledge of $\Pi_i^{\succ\pi}$ is that some $t \in \Pi_i^{\succ\pi}$ is good, i.e., if κ_3^π holds, then π idles.
4. Otherwise, if a process π knows that, for no supervisor Π_i, the joint knowledge of $\Pi_i^{\succ\pi}$ is that some $t \in \Pi_i^{\succ\pi}$ is good, i.e., if κ_4^π holds, then π hangs.

---

[1] Symmetry is not defined here in a strict manner as in [6], where processes are not aware of their index value. Our solution is symmetric in the sense of not giving an a priory advantage to hang according to their index.

5. Otherwise, π tosses a coin to decide whether to hang on its supervisor or to wait further and then repeat this strategy.

The only formal requirement that we put on the random choice is that, if the local knowledge of a process π eventually always never changes, then π will almost surely eventually always hang on its supervisor. For randomized control, a deadlock occurs in a state of a Petri Net unless the system will almost surely eventually progress from this state. The control strategy of the supervisors is again unaffected.

Randomized control does not introduce new deadlocks, and the sufficient condition for unordered control strategies also applies to randomized control strategies:

Theorem 3. *If* $\varphi_G \rightarrow (\bigvee_{\pi \in C} \kappa_1^\pi \vee \bigvee_{\Pi_i \in S} \kappa^{\Pi_i})$ *holds, then the randomized control strategy provides a deadlock free solution.*

4 Refinig Knowledge

In our synthesis approach, it is important to minimize the number of processes that are hung until enough knowledge is available for a supervisor to support some transition. Deepening the knowledge is one way of progressing towards this goal. One possibility is to use knowledge of perfect recall [8,1]; however, this is very costly. Another possibility is to use weak knowledge based on joint local information through a powerful (and very expensive) synchronization protocol like α-core [9,4].

We present a solution, which uses knowledge that is in between strong and weak knowledge. The idea is to exploit some conditionally stable properties, i.e., properties that, once started to hold under some condition, do not cease to hold while this condition lasts. As our approach does not allow us to freeze the joint local information, this will at least allow us to limit the number of possible states by exploiting the value of the entire local information of the process when it hangs.

Definition 1. *A conditionally stable property J_φ for a condition φ is a state predicate (over the places of the system) such that, while φ holds, if J_φ starts to hold then it continues to hold.*

In temporal logic, one can write $\square((\varphi \wedge J_\varphi) \rightarrow (J_\varphi \, \mathcal{W} \, \neg\varphi))$, where $\mathcal{W}$ is the temporal *weak until* operator. In order to calculate stable properties for a given Petri Net, we can use the concepts of *siphons* and *traps* [10] in Petri Nets.

Definition 2. *A set of places $L \subseteq P$ is a siphon if $^\bullet L \subseteq L^\bullet$ and a trap if $L^\bullet \subseteq ^\bullet L$.*

A siphon L induces the stable property $\sigma_L = \bigwedge_{p \in L} \neg p$ that there is no token in *any* of the places in L. A trap L induces the stable property $\sigma_L = \bigvee_{p \in L} p$ such that there is a token in *at least one* place in L [10].

We can strengthen weak or strong knowledge by taking into account only states, in which a given property η holds.

Definition 3. *Given a state property η, for $s \in G$, $s \models \eta$, the guarded (weak or strong) knowledge $K_{\eta,\Pi}$ operator satisfies that $s \models K_{\eta,\Pi}\varphi$ if, for each s' such that $s \equiv_\Pi s'$ and $s' \models \eta$, it holds that $s' \models \varphi$.*

Suppose that we are at a point where a new process π hangs. According to our approach, π communicates to its supervisor the value of the places that will complete a joint local state with the processes already hung. The guarded knowledge allows us to take advantage of stable properties that hold while these processes do not support a transition. (If one of them does, then the information on the supervisor may become stale and needs to be updated before the supervisor can support a transition.) Thus, we need to calculate traps and siphons that hold under the condition of a particular joint local state. Now, when a process π hangs and is added to the already hanging Π (then $\pi \in \Pi$), the information in $ngb(\pi) \setminus own(\Pi)$ can be used to check whether or not a conditionally stable property that is induced by a siphon or a trap L holds at the time of hanging. This is done using the following *exclusion procedure*:

1. Remove from the net all the transitions that belong *only* to the processes Π that are hung on a supervisor $\Pi_i \supseteq \Pi$, i.e., $t \in (\cup \Pi) \setminus \cup(C \setminus \Pi)$. These transitions will not fire while these processes are hung.
2. Remove all the places that are input or output only to the transitions removed in the previous step.
3. For the remaining Petri Net, calculate siphons $L \subseteq ngb(\pi) \setminus own(\Pi)$ whose places are all empty at the point when π is hanging, and traps L such that $L \cap (ngb(\pi) \setminus own(\Pi)) \neq \emptyset$ and have at least one nonempty place when π is hanging. These are the *active* siphons and traps (for current joint local state of Π and local information of π). Deadlocks and traps can be calculated, e.g, according to the algorithm [18].

Theorem 4. *Let φ_r be the characterizing formula[2] for the joint local state r of the processes Π when hung on Π_i. Then the active sipons and traps, calculated using the exclusion procedure for r, are the siphons and the traps, respectively, of the original Petri Net N, conditioned on φ_r.*

Consequently, while there is no change to the set of hung processes, the conjunction of the active conditionally stable properties that held on time of hanging, still holds. Let μ_r be the conjunction of the formulas σ_L, associated with active siphons or traps L calculated by the exclusion procedure for a given joint local state r. In this case, the guarded strong knowledge $K^s_{\mu_r, \Pi}$ can be used instead of the strong knowledge K^s_Π in the algorithms presented in the previous sections.

Note that traps and siphons are not the only possible stable properties. However, their calculation is well studied and quite efficient.

A special case of our construction are places p that belong to the local information of the hanging process π, but not to the joint local state of the hung processes Π (including π). In particular, such a place could have a token at the time of hanging that it cannot lose (or be empty and unable to obtain a token) by any transition of processes not in Π.

There is a tradeoff associated with the construction suggested in this section. On one hand, it can increase the joint knowledge of the hung processes, eliminating the need to wait for further processes to hang before a transition can be supported by the supervisor. On the other hand, it can enlarge the number of cases handled by the supervisor: a

---

[2] This formula is the conjunction of the places in $own(\Pi)$, negated when a place is empty and nonnegated when it has a token.

case of a joint local state may now be split according to the traps and siphons that are associated with different local information of the newly hung process.

References

1. Basu, A., Bensalem, S., Peled, D., Sifakis, J.: Priority Scheduling of distributed Systems Based on Model Checking. In: Bouajjani, A., Maler, O. (eds.) CAV 2009. LNCS, vol. 5643, pp. 79–93. Springer, Heidelberg (2009)
2. Bensalem, S., Bozga, M., Graf, S., Peled, D., Quinton, S.: Methods for Knowledge Based Controlling of Distributed Systems. In: Bouajjani, A., Chin, W.-N. (eds.) ATVA 2010. LNCS, vol. 6252, pp. 52–66. Springer, Heidelberg (2010)
3. Finkbeiner, B., Schewe, S.: Uniform distributed synthesis. In: LICS 2005, Chicago, IL, pp. 321–330 (2005)
4. Graf, S., Peled, D., Quinton, S.: Achieving Distributed Control Through Model Checking. In: Touili, T., Cook, B., Jackson, P. (eds.) CAV 2010. LNCS, vol. 6174, pp. 396–409. Springer, Heidelberg (2010)
5. Katz, G., Peled, D., Schewe, S.: Synthesis of Distribute Control through Knowledge Accumulation. In: Gopalakrishnan, G., Qadeer, S. (eds.) CAV 2011. LNCS, vol. 6806, pp. 510–525. Springer, Heidelberg (2011)
6. Lehman, D., Rabin, M.O.: On the Advantages of Free Choice: A symmetric and Fully Distributed Solution to the Dining Philosophers Problem. In: POPL 1981, Williamsburg, Virginia, pp. 133–138 (1981)
7. Madhusudan, P., Thiagarajan, P.S.: Distributed Controller Synthesis for Local Specifications. In: Yu, Y., Spirakis, P.G., van Leeuwen, J. (eds.) ICALP 2001. LNCS, vol. 2076, pp. 396–407. Springer, Heidelberg (2001)
8. van der Meyden, R.: Common Knowledge and Update in Finite Environment. Information and Computation 140, 115–157 (1980)
9. Pérez, J.A., Corchuelo, R., Toro, M.: An Order-based Algorithm for Implementing Multiparty Synchronization. Concurrency - Practice and Experience 16(12), 1173–1206 (2004)
10. Peterson, J.: Petri Net Theory and the Modeling of Systems. Prentice-Hall, Englewood Cliffs (1981)
11. Pnueli, A., Rosner, R.: Distributed Reactive Systems are Hard to Synthesize. In: FOCS 1990, St. Louis, Missouri, pp. 746–757 (1990)
12. Ramadge, P.J., Wonham, W.M.: Supervisory control of a class of discrete event processes. SIAM Journal on Control and Optimization 25(1), 206–230 (1987)
13. Rudie, K., Ricker, S.L.: Know means no: Incorporating knowledge into discrete-event control systems. IEEE Transactions on Automatic Control 45(9), 1656–1668 (2000)
14. Rudie, K., Wonham, W.M.: Think globally, act locally: decentralized supervisory control. IEEE Transactions on Automatic Control 37(11), 1692–1708 (1992)
15. Schewe, S., Finkbeiner, B.: Synthesis of Asynchronous Systems. In: Puebla, G. (ed.) LOPSTR 2006. LNCS, vol. 4407, pp. 127–142. Springer, Heidelberg (2007)
16. Thistle, J.G.: Undecidability in Decentralized Supervision. Systems and control letters 54, 503–509 (2005)
17. Tripakis, S.: Undecidable problems of decentralized observation and control on regular languages. Information Processing Letters 90(1), 21–28 (2004)
18. Wegrzyn, A., Karatekevich, A., Bieganowski, J.: Detection of Deadlocks and Traps in Petri Nets by Means of Thelen's Prime Implicant Method. International Journal of Applied Math and Computer Science 14, 113–121 (2004)
19. Yoo, T.S., Lafortune, S.: A general architecture for decentralized supervisory control of discrete-event systems. Discrete Event Dynamic Systems, Theory & Applications 12(3), 335–377 (2002)

Symbolic Verification and Test Generation for a Network of Communicating FSMs*

Xiaoqing Jin[1], Gianfranco Ciardo[1], Tae-Hyong Kim[2], and Yang Zhao[1]

[1] University of California, Riverside, USA
{jinx,ciardo,zhaoy}@cs.ucr.edu
[2] Kumoh National Institute of Technology, Gumi, Korea
taehyong@kumoh.ac.kr

Abstract. A network of communicating FSMs (NCFSMs) is a useful formalism to model complex concurrent systems, but its use demands efficient analysis algorithms. We propose a new symbolic framework for NCFMS verification and test generation. We explore the use of the breadth-first search (BFS) and saturation algorithms to compute the "unstable transitive closure" of transitions for the observable product machine of an NCFSM. Our framework can verify properties such as livelock freeness and includes a fully automatic test generation based on mutation analysis. Being symbolic, our framework can efficiently manage a large number of mutants with moderate resource consumption and derive a test suite to distinguish all non-equivalent first-order mutants.

1 Introduction

Concurrent systems, such as communication and multiprocessor systems, consist of several components connected via FIFO queues and can be naturally modeled as a network of communicating finite state machines (NCFSMs) where each component is a communicating finite state machine (CFSM). While the state space of an NCFSM with unbounded queues is infinite, the *slow environment assumption* [8] satisfied by most systems avoids the need to manage infinite state spaces. Our slow environment NCFSMs require a single global queue of size one.

Both structural and fault-based testing can be employed on NCFSMs. Approaches to structural testing either transform an NCFSM into a behaviorally equivalent FSM, the *observable product machine*, or try to restrict the model to allow only local transition tests, but suffer from state-space explosion [7] or require an exhaustive search to generate executable test cases [6,9]. Fault-based testing adopts mutation analysis, which scales well in web applications and other collaborative systems, but requires dealing with a large number of mutants and must generate a distinguishing sequence for each non-equivalent mutant [13].

The lack of an efficient and fully automated verification and test derivation framework for NCFSMs limits their applicability and results in large manual testing efforts. As symbolic methods such as binary decision diagrams (BDDs) [3]

* This work was supported in part by the National Science Foundation under Grant CCF-1018057 and by a UC MEXUS-CONACYT Collaborative Research Grant.

T. Bultan and P.-A. Hsiung (Eds.): ATVA 2011, LNCS 6996, pp. 432–442, 2011.

have had great success in verification, we propose a framework for critical property verification and test generation using a symbolic strategy and mutation analysis. We use multiway decision diagrams (MDDs) [10] to compute the unstable transitive closure of the transition relation for the observable product machine, then employ verification techniques to check critical properties and provide counter-examples. Finally, we generate first-order mutants through specification mutant operators and use edge-value decision diagrams [5] to symbolically obtain distinguishing sequences (a test suite) that "kill" all non-equivalent mutants.

The remainder of this paper is organized as follows. Sect. 2 provides some background. Sect. 3 elaborates our symbolic framework and preprocessing algorithms. Sect. 4 focuses on verification algorithms and Sect. 5 on automatic test derivation algorithms. Sect. 6 gives experimental results. We conclude in Sect. 7.

2   Preliminaries

A CFSM M_k is a tuple $(\mathcal{S}_k, \mathcal{X}_k, \mathcal{Y}_k, \delta_k, \lambda_k, s_k)$ where $\mathcal{S}_k$ is a finite set of local states, $\mathcal{X}_k$ is a finite set of input symbols generated from the environment or other CFSMs, $\mathcal{Y}_k$ is a finite set of output symbols absorbed by the environment or other CFSMs, $\delta_k : \mathcal{S}_k \times \mathcal{X}_k \to \mathcal{S}_k$ is the local state transition function, $\lambda_k : \mathcal{S}_k \times \mathcal{X}_k \to \mathcal{Y}_k$ is the output function, and $s_k \in \mathcal{S}_k$ is the initial state. If $\delta_k(i,a) = j$ and $\lambda_k(i,a) = b$, we let $i_{[M_k, a/b\rangle} j$ denote this *local* transition from state i to j caused by input a and output b in M_k.

An NCFSM M consists of K CFSMs $M_1, M_2, ..., M_K$ with pairwise disjoint sets of input symbols and a FIFO buffer β containing symbols in transit between CFSMs. The semantics of an NCFSM is defined by the *product* FSM $(\mathcal{S}, \mathcal{X}, \mathcal{Y}, \delta, \lambda, s_{init})$ where $\mathcal{X} = \bigcup_{1 \le k \le K} \mathcal{X}_k$, $\mathcal{Y} = \bigcup_{1 \le k \le K} \mathcal{Y}_k$, $\mathcal{S} = (\{\epsilon\} \cup \mathcal{Y} \cup \mathcal{X}) \times \mathcal{S}_1 \times ... \times \mathcal{S}_K$ is the set of global states, $\bar{\delta} : \mathcal{S} \times (\{\epsilon\} \cup \mathcal{X}) \to \mathcal{S}$ and $\lambda : \mathcal{S} \times (\{\epsilon\} \cup \mathcal{X}) \to \mathcal{Y}$ are the global state transition and output functions, respectively, which will be defined later, and $s_{init} = (\epsilon, s_1, ..., s_K) \in \mathcal{S}$ is the initial global state.

Let $\mathcal{Z}_{int} = \mathcal{X} \cap \mathcal{Y}$ be the set of *internal* symbols that can appear in buffer β (we underline these symbols, e.g., $\underline{a}$). Let $\mathcal{X} \setminus \mathcal{Y} \subseteq \mathcal{X}_{ext} \subseteq \mathcal{X}$ and $\mathcal{Y}_{ext} = \mathcal{Y} \setminus \mathcal{X}$ be the set of *external input* and *external output* symbols. $\mathcal{Y}_{ext}$ contains the output symbols observable outside the system. $\mathcal{X}_{ext}$ must contain all the symbols that only the environment can place into the buffer β, thus $\mathcal{X} \setminus \mathcal{Y}$, but it may include symbols in $\mathcal{Z}_{int}$. Given $\mathbf{i} = (i_1, ..., i_K)$, define $\mathbf{i}|_{k:j_k}$ to be the vector $(i_1, ..., j_k, ..., i_K)$ obtained by setting the kth component of $\mathbf{i}$ to j_k. A (global) state $(i_\beta, i_1, ..., i_K)$ is *stable* if $i_\beta = \epsilon$, we write it as $\mathbf{i}$, otherwise it is *unstable*, we write as $a.\mathbf{i}$, with $a \in \mathcal{Z}_{int}$. Let $\mathcal{S}_{st}$ and $\mathcal{S}_{unst}$ be the set of reachable stable and unstable states, respectively, and $\mathcal{S}_{rch} = \mathcal{S}_{st} \cup \mathcal{S}_{unst}$. If $i_k {}_{[M_k, a/x\rangle} j_k$, λ and δ satisfy:

- $\delta(\mathbf{i},a) = \mathbf{i}|_{k:j_k}$ and $\lambda(\mathbf{i},a) = x$, if $a \in \mathcal{X}_{ext}$, $x \in \mathcal{Y}_{ext}$, written as $\mathbf{i}_{[M, a/x\rangle} \mathbf{i}|_{k:j_k}$, or simply $\mathbf{i}_{[a/x\rangle} \mathbf{i}|_{k:j_k}$ if M is clear from the context.
- $\delta(\mathbf{i},a) = x.\mathbf{i}|_{k:j_k}$ and $\lambda(\mathbf{i},a) = \epsilon$, if $a \in \mathcal{X}_{ext}$, $x \in \mathcal{Z}_{int}$, written as $\mathbf{i}_{[a/\underline{x}\rangle} x.\mathbf{i}|_{k:j_k}$.
- $\delta(a.\mathbf{i},\epsilon) = \mathbf{i}|_{k:j_k}$ and $\lambda(a.\mathbf{i}, \epsilon) = x$, if $a \in \mathcal{Z}_{int}$, $x \in \mathcal{Y}_{ext}$, written as $a.\mathbf{i}_{[\underline{a}/x\rangle} \mathbf{i}|_{k:j_k}$.
- $\delta(a.\mathbf{i},\epsilon) = x.\mathbf{i}|_{k:j_k}$ and $\lambda(a.\mathbf{i},\epsilon) = \epsilon$, if $a \in \mathcal{Z}_{int}$, $x \in \mathcal{Z}_{int}$, written as $a.\mathbf{i}_{[\underline{a}/\underline{x}\rangle} x.\mathbf{i}|_{k:j_k}$.

The NCFSMs we study conform to the slow environment assumption [8]: if the output symbol a of a CFSM can be absorbed by another CFSM as an input symbol, then the system does not accept any other input symbol from the environment until a has been consumed. A buffer of size one is sufficient under this assumption, as β can only be empty or contain one symbol from $\mathcal{Z}_{int}$.

As neither unstable states nor the symbols in β are observable, we focus on stable state transitions: if $\mathbf{i}\,[a/\underline{a^{(1)}}\rangle\, a^{(1)}.\mathbf{i}^{(1)}{}_{[\underline{a^{(1)}}/\underline{a^{(2)}}\rangle}\cdots{}_{[\underline{a^{(n-1)}}/\underline{a^{(n)}}\rangle}\, a^{(n)}.\mathbf{i}^{(n)}{}_{[\underline{a^{(n)}}/b\rangle}\,\mathbf{j}$, where $n \geq 1$, $\mathbf{i},\mathbf{j} \in \mathcal{S}_{st}$, $a \in \mathcal{X}_{ext}$, $a^{(1)}\cdots a^{(n)} \in \mathcal{Z}_{int}$ and $b \in \mathcal{Y}_{ext}$, we merge this sequence into a *stable transition* $\mathbf{i}\,\llbracket a/b\rangle\!\rangle\,\mathbf{j}$. We define the observable transition function δ_{obs} and output function λ_{obs}, $\delta_{obs}(\mathbf{i}, a) = \mathbf{j}$ and $\lambda_{obs}(\mathbf{i}, a) = b$ if $\mathbf{i}\,\llbracket a/b\rangle\!\rangle\,\mathbf{j}$. Then, we define the *observable product machine* M_{obs} of an NCFSM as a six-tuple $(\mathcal{S}_{st},\mathcal{X}_{ext},\mathcal{Y}_{ext},\delta_{obs},\lambda_{obs},s_{init})$. Sect. 3 presents our symbolic algorithm to generate M_{obs}, needed to verify NCFSM equivalence and used in test derivation and test selection [12]. We let $a_1/b_1, ..., a_n/b_n \in (\mathcal{X}_{ext}\times\mathcal{Y}_{ext})^*$ be a *sequence* from state $\mathbf{i} \in \mathcal{S}_{st}$ if $\lambda_{obs}(\mathbf{i}, a_1 a_2 \cdots a_n) = \lambda_{obs}(\mathbf{i}, a_1)\lambda_{obs}(\delta_{obs}(\mathbf{i}, a_1), a_2 \cdots a_n) = b_1 b_2 \cdots b_n$.

2.1   Decision Diagrams

Symbolic encodings such as BDDs [3] and MDDs [10] work well for formal verification. We use MDDs to encode boolean functions for sets and EV$^+$MDDs [5] to encode partial integer functions, where ∞ means "undefined".

Given L *domain* variables v_l $(1 \leq l \leq L)$ having finite domain $\mathcal{V}_{v_l}$ and a boolean *range* variable v_0, ordered $v_L \succ \cdots \succ v_1 \succ v_0$, a *(quasi-reduced)* MDD is a directed acyclic edge-labeled graph where:

- Each node p is associated with a domain variable v_l. We write $p.v = v_l$.
- The *terminal* nodes are $\mathbf{0}$ and $\mathbf{1}$, and are the only nodes with $\mathbf{0}.v = \mathbf{1}.v = v_0$.
- A *nonterminal* node p with $p.v = v_l$ has, for each $i \in \mathcal{V}_{v_l}$, an edge pointing to node q, with $q.v = v_{l-1}$ or $q = \mathbf{0}$. We write $p[i] = q$. We must have at least one $p[i] \neq \mathbf{0}$.
- For canonicity, there are no *duplicates*: given two nonterminal nodes p and q with $p.v = q.v$, there must be at least one $i \in \mathcal{V}_{p.v}$ such that $p[i] \neq q[i]$.

A nonterminal MDD node p with $p.v = v_l$ encodes the set of tuples recursively defined by $\mathcal{B}_p = \bigcup_{i \in \mathcal{V}_{v_l}} \{i\} \cdot \mathcal{B}_{p[i]}$, with terminal cases $\mathcal{B}_{\mathbf{0}} = \emptyset$, the empty set, and $\mathcal{B}_{\mathbf{1}} = \{\epsilon\}$, the empty tuple, where "$\cdot$" indicates tuple concatenation.

To encode partial integer functions, we use a variant of the above. A normalized EV$^+$MDD [5] is a directed acyclic edge-labeled graph where:

- Ω is the only *terminal* node, with $\Omega.v = v_0$.
- A nonterminal node a with $a.v = v_l$ has, for each $i \in \mathcal{V}_{v_l}$, an edge labeled with $\rho \in \mathbb{N}\cup\{\infty\}$ pointing to node b. We write $a[i] = \langle\rho,b\rangle$, $b = a[i].node$, and $\rho = a[i].val$. We must have $b = \Omega$ if $\rho = \infty$, $b.v = v_{l-1}$ otherwise, and at least one $a[i].val = 0$.
- For canonicity, there are no *duplicates*: given two nonterminal nodes a and b with $a.v = b.v$, there must be at least one $i \in \mathcal{V}_{p.v}$ such that $a[i] \neq b[i]$, i.e., $a[i].node \neq b[i].node$, or $a[i].val \neq b[i].val$, or both.

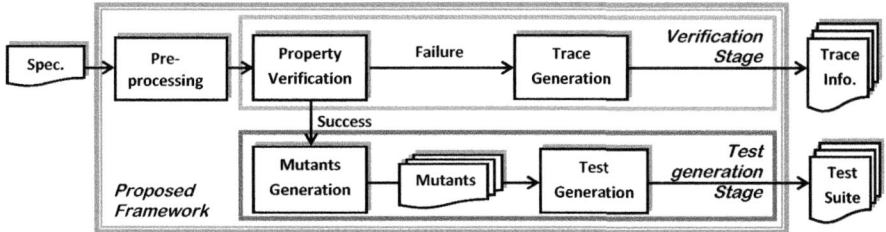

Fig. 1. System framework

Given EV$^+$MDD node a with $a.v = v_l$ and $\rho \in \mathbb{N}$, $\langle \rho, a \rangle$ encodes the function $f_{\langle \rho, a \rangle} : \mathcal{V}_{v_l} \times \cdots \times \mathcal{V}_{v_1} \to \mathbb{N} \cup \{\infty\}$ recursively defined by $f_{\langle \rho, a \rangle} = \rho + f_{a[v_l]}$, with base case $f_{\langle \rho, \Omega \rangle} = \rho$.

To make MDDs and EV$^+$MDDs more compact and their manipulation more efficient, edges can skip variables under various reduction rules [3,17]. These rules still ensure canonicity and implicitly define the meaning of these "long" edges, but we do not discuss them further in the interest of clarity and brevity.

$Or(a, b)$ and $And(a, b)$ are two operators used to compute the MDD encoding $\mathcal{B}_a \cup \mathcal{B}_b$ and $\mathcal{B}_a \cap \mathcal{B}_b$. Analogously, $Min(\langle \rho, a \rangle, \langle \sigma, b \rangle)$, returns the EV$^+$MDD encoding $\min(f_{\langle \rho, a \rangle}, f_{\langle \sigma, b \rangle})$, and *Normalize* puts an EV$^+$MDD in canonical form [5].

2.2 Previous Work

Structural test generation approaches for NCFSMs mostly fall into two classes. One transforms an NCFSM into its M_{obs} [12] which may encounter state-space explosion problem, then applies standard FSM test derivation techniques, such as the W-method, Wp-method, and UIO-method. However, a high complexity limits the applicability of these well-known approaches. More importantly, even if all CFSMs are deterministic, minimal, completely specified, and strongly connected, the resulting M_{obs} might not be. M_{obs} is deterministic and completely specified iff $\mathcal{M}$ is livelock-free while, if $\mathcal{Y}_{ext} \subset \mathcal{Y}$, minimal and strongly connected properties may be lost. In these cases, standard structural FSM-based test derivation algorithms are not directly applicable.

The other category of approaches [6,9,11] avoids building M_{obs} and uses instead branching coverage [11] or heuristic techniques [6]. These methods check local transitions instead of global transitions, and reduce testing efforts under the assumption that the system only has one fault. However, for some complex models, exhaustive searches or heuristic algorithms must be employed.

Our work falls into the first class. Our fully symbolic techniques copes with the large computational cost to generate M_{obs} for verification and test generation. Moreover, we adopt mutation analysis for test derivation, thus we do not require M_{obs} to be minimal, completely specified, or strongly connected.

3   System Framework and Symbolic Encoding

Both specification or implementation errors can cause system failures. Our symbolic framework takes in an NCFSM model described in XML as the system specification and aims at detecting both types of errors. It has two stages: verification and test derivation, as in Fig. 1. The verification stage checks three important properties of the specification: livelock freeness, strong connectedness, and absence of dead transitions. If a check fails, counter-examples are generated to help fixing the error. The test derivation stage generates a test suite using mutation analysis, to test the consistency between the *implementation under test* (IUT) and the specification.

Given an NCFSM with K component CFSMs and a system buffer, we use an MDD with variables $(w_K, ..., w_1, w_b)$ to encode sets of global states. The first K variables correspond to each CFSM local state, w_b corresponds to the current buffer content. A next-state function $T : \mathcal{S} \times (\mathcal{X} \cup \{\epsilon\}) \to \mathcal{S} \times (\mathcal{Y} \cup \{\epsilon\})$ encoded using MDDs on $2(K+1)$ variables $(w_K, w'_K, ..., w_1, w'_1, w_b, w'_b)$, captures the global state transition function δ and output function λ, so that $T(x, y) = (x', y')$ iff $\delta(x, y) = x'$ and $\lambda(x, y) = y'$, where x and x' are global states and $y, y' \in \mathcal{X} \cup \mathcal{Y} \cup \{\epsilon\}$. We define $\mathcal{T}_s = \bigcup_{1 \leq k \leq K} \mathcal{T}_k$, where $\mathcal{T}_k$ encodes the next-state function of M_k. Thus, $T = \mathcal{T}_s \cup \mathcal{T}_\beta$, where $\mathcal{T}_\beta$ encodes the interaction with the environment.

Generation of the state-space $\mathcal{S}_{rch} = \{\mathbf{s}_{init}\} \cup T(\mathbf{s}_{init}) \cup T^2(\mathbf{s}_{init}) \cup \cdots$ is often the first step in formal verification. $\mathcal{S}_{rch}$ can be built by standard symbolic state-space generation algorithms [4] and we can split it into $\mathcal{S}_{st}$ and $\mathcal{S}_{unst}$ based on the status of the system buffer w_b: if $w_b = \epsilon$, the state is stable, otherwise it is unstable.

To compute the stable next-state function $\mathcal{T}_{obs}$ encoding δ_{obs} and λ_{obs}, we first define the *unstable transitive closure* (*UTC*): given $\mathcal{T}_s$, *UTC* is the smallest relation containing $\mathcal{T}_s$ and satisfying

$$
\begin{aligned}
(c.\mathbf{j}, \epsilon) \in \mathcal{T}_s(b.\mathbf{i}, \epsilon) \wedge (b.\mathbf{i}, \epsilon) \in UTC(a.\mathbf{h}, \epsilon) &\Rightarrow (c.\mathbf{j}, \epsilon) \in UTC(a.\mathbf{h}, \epsilon), \\
(c.\mathbf{j}, \epsilon) \in \mathcal{T}_s(b.\mathbf{i}, \epsilon) \wedge (b.\mathbf{i}, \epsilon) \in UTC(\mathbf{h}, a) &\Rightarrow (c.\mathbf{j}, \epsilon) \in UTC(\mathbf{h}, a), \\
(\mathbf{j}, c) \in \mathcal{T}_s(b.\mathbf{i}, \epsilon) \wedge (b.\mathbf{i}, \epsilon) \in UTC(a.\mathbf{h}, \epsilon) &\Rightarrow (\mathbf{j}, c) \in UTC(a.\mathbf{h}, \epsilon), \\
(\mathbf{j}, c) \in \mathcal{T}_s(b.\mathbf{i}, \epsilon) \wedge (b.\mathbf{i}, \epsilon) \in UTC(\mathbf{h}, a) &\Rightarrow (\mathbf{j}, c) \in UTC(\mathbf{h}, a).
\end{aligned}
$$

UTC captures all transition sequences in M that do not pass through stable states. We use *UTC* to build $\mathcal{T}_{obs}$, by applying the *And* operator (Sect. 2) to select the elements with $w_b \in \mathcal{X}_{ext}$ and $w'_b \in \mathcal{Y}_{ext}$, corresponding to input and output symbols leading from stable to stable states. *UTC* is the most time and memory consuming step in our framework. First, we define a *ComRP* operator to calculate this composition effect of next-state functions, taking two $2(K+1)$-variable MDDs and returning the result composition $2(K+1)$-variable MDD. *UTC* can be obtained by repeatedly applying *ComRP* to $\mathcal{T}_s$: $UTC = \mathcal{T}_s \cup ComRP(\mathcal{T}_s) \cup ComRP^2(\mathcal{T}_s) \cup \cdots$. Thus, *UtcBfs* performs a global fixpoint in BFS style at Line 2-5 and uses *ComRP* with Line 26b in Fig. 2.

However, for asynchronous systems, saturation [4] is often orders of magnitude more efficient in memory and runtime than BFS algorithms, due to its effective

mdd ComRP(mdd p, mdd r)	mdd UtcSat(mdd p)

1 if $r = 1$ or $p = 1$ then   • *terminal*
2   return p;
3 endif
4 mdd $t \leftarrow \mathbf{0}, s \leftarrow \mathbf{0}$;
5 if $CHit_{ComRP}(p,r,t)$ then
6   return t;   • *cache hit*
7 endif
8 if $p.v = r.v$ then
9   for $i, i' \in \mathcal{V}_{p.v}$ s.t. $p[i][i'] \neq \mathbf{0}, r[i'] \neq \mathbf{0}$
    do
10   if $r.v = r[i'].v$ then
11   for $j \in \mathcal{V}_{r.v}$ do
12     $s \leftarrow ComRP(p[i][i'], r[i'][j])$;
13     $t[i][j] \leftarrow Or(t[i][j], s)$;
14   endfor
15   else • $r[i']$'s edge skips 1 variable
16    $s \leftarrow ComRP(p[i][i'], r[i'])$;
17    $t[i][i'] \leftarrow Or(t[i][i'], s)$;
18   endif
19 endfor
20 else   • r's edges skip 2 variables
21   for $i, i' \in \mathcal{V}_{p.v}$ s.t. $p[i][i'] \neq \mathbf{0}$ do
22    $s \leftarrow ComRP(p[i][i'], r)$;
23    $t[i][i'] \leftarrow Or(t[i][i'], s)$;
24   endfor
25 endif
	1 if $p.v = v_0$ then return z; • *terminal*
	2 mdd $t \leftarrow \mathbf{0}, s \leftarrow \mathbf{0}$;
	3 if $CHit_{UtcSat}(z,t)$ then return t;
	4 for $i, i' \in \mathcal{V}_{p.v}$ s.t. $p[i][i'] \neq \mathbf{0}$ do
	5 $t[i][i'] \leftarrow UtcSat(p[i][i'])$;
	6 endfor • *saturate all lower variables*
	7 repeat • *local fixpoint iteration*
	8 for $i, i' \in \mathcal{V}_{p.v}, r \in \mathcal{T}_s$ s.t. $t.v = r.v$,
	     $p[i][i'] \neq \mathbf{0}, r[i'] \neq \mathbf{0}$ do
	9 if $r.v = r[i'].v$ then
	10 for $j \in \mathcal{V}_{r.v}$ s.t. $r[i'][j] \neq \mathbf{0}$ do
	11 $s \leftarrow ComRP(p[i][i'], r[i'][j])$;
	12 $t[i][j] \leftarrow Or(t[i][j], s)$;
	13 endfor
	14 else • $r[i']$'s edge skips 1 variable
	15 $s \leftarrow ComRP(p[i][i'], r[i'])$; • *26s*
	16 $t[i][i'] \leftarrow Or(t[i][i'], s)$;
	17 endif
	18 endfor
	19 until t does not change;
	20 $t \leftarrow UniIns(t)$; • *for canonicity*
	21 $CAdd_{UtcSat}(z,t)$; • *store result in cache*
	22 return t;

26b $t \leftarrow UniIns(t)$; • *for UtcBfs* 26s $t \leftarrow UtcSat(UniIns(t))$; • *for UtcSat* 27 $CAdd_{ComRP}(p,r,t)$; • *store in cache* 28 return t;	mdd UtcBfs(mdd $\mathcal{T}_s$)
	1 mdd $z \leftarrow \mathcal{T}_s, s \leftarrow \mathbf{0}, z_p \leftarrow \mathbf{0}$; 2 repeat • *global fixpoint iteration* 3 $z_p \leftarrow z$; 4 $z \leftarrow Or(z_p, ComRP(z_p, \mathcal{T}_s))$; • *26b* 5 until $z = z_p$; return z;

Fig. 2. The *ComRP* operator, the *UtcBfs*, and the *UtcSat* algorithms.

utilization of *locality* (transitions in $\mathcal{T}_k$ only affecting i_k of M_k and β) through a series of light-weight recursions. Our saturation algorithm *UtcSat* chooses a different iteration strategy to approach the fixpoint with exhaustive utilization of locality. Thus, instead of taking $\mathcal{T}_s$ as one MDD, *UtcSat* uses its *disjunctive* form as K MDDs and divides the whole procedure into K phases. The kth phase starts when the lower $(k-1)^{th}$ phases end at Line 4-6 and extends the fixpoint using $\mathcal{T}_k$ until node p is "saturated" (no more new states can be found) at Line 7-19. If it finds new states during this phase, only these need to be resaturated by all previous $k-1$ phases by using *ComRP* with Line 26s. Saturation works bottom-up and the result of local fixpoint for the Kth phase converges to the same global fixpoint as BFS. An *operation cache* avoids wasteful recomputations (Procedures *CAdd* and *CHit* are used to insert and retrieve computed results). Newly created nodes are inserted in a *unique table* (Procedure *UniIns*) to ensure MDD canonicity by avoiding duplicates. Our experience shows that the larger K is, the greater improvement saturation achieves. After building UTC, we obtain its restriction to stable transitions as $\mathcal{T}_{obs} = \{(a.\mathbf{i}, b.\mathbf{j}) \in UTC : \mathbf{i}, \mathbf{j} \in \mathcal{S}_{st}, a \in \mathcal{X}_{ext}, b \in \mathcal{Y}_{ext}\}$.

4   Symbolic NCFSM Verification

Symbolic Livelock Check. An NCFSM does not terminate if it reaches a live-lock (a cycle of unstable transitions): $a^{(1)}.\mathbf{i}^{(1)}{}_{[a^{(1)}/a^{(2)}\rangle} \cdots a^{(n)}.\mathbf{i}^{(n)}{}_{[a^{(n)}/a^{(1)}\rangle}a^{(1)}.\mathbf{i}^{(1)}$. Since livelock is a fatal design error, we need to guarantee livelock-freeness before test generation. If an NCFSM contains livelocks, the MDD encoding UTC has transitions where the "from" global state is the same as the "to" global state, and the input symbol equals the output symbol and belongs to $\mathcal{Z}_{int}$. Thanks to our MDD encoding, we can find all reachable states originating a livelock by And-ing $\mathcal{S}_{rch}$ and the "from" global states of the UTC. We not only verify livelock free-ness, but also generate sequences from $\mathbf{s}_{init}$ to all livelocks, which is similar to distinguishing sequence generation, discussed in the next section.

Symbolic Strong Connectedness Check. Many traditional FSM-based test derivation algorithms require the FSM to be strongly connected. While our ap-proach does not require this property, strong connectedness can be checked in our framework. An NCFSM is *strongly connected* iff the initial state $\mathbf{s}_{init}$ is reachable from every reachable state $\mathbf{i} \in \mathcal{S}_{st}$. To check this property, we build the MDD for $\mathcal{T}^{-1}$, defined by $\mathbf{i}_{[a/x\rangle}\mathbf{j}\in\mathcal{T} \Leftrightarrow \mathbf{j}_{[x/a\rangle}\mathbf{i}\in\mathcal{T}^{-1}$, by switching the "from" and "to" variables. Then, we perform a backward state-space search from $\mathbf{s}_{init}$ along $\mathcal{T}^{-1}$ and build the set of reachable states $\mathcal{S}_{st}^{-1}$ using BFS or saturation. The global state space is strongly connected iff $\mathcal{S}_{st} = \mathcal{S}_{st}^{-1} \cap \mathcal{S}_{rch}$. Note that $\mathcal{T}^{-1}$ might be non-deterministic even if $\mathcal{T}$ is deterministic, but this does not hinder the applicability of symbolic state-space exploration.

Symbolic Dead Transition Check. Transition i_k $_{[M_k, a/b\rangle}$ j_k is *dead* if it does not contribute to building M_{obs}. Dead transitions reflect wasteful designs or useless functions, which should be reported to the designer. As $\mathcal{S}_{rch} = \mathcal{S}_{st} \cup \mathcal{S}_{unst}$ is available, dead transitions can be detected symbolically. For each i_k $_{[M_k, a/b\rangle}$ j_k, we can first check if $\mathcal{S}_{unst}$ contains an unstable state with $w_k = i_k$ and $w_b = a$; if it does, i_k $_{[M_k, a/b\rangle}$ j_k is not dead. Otherwise, if $a \in \mathcal{X}_{ext}$, we check if $\mathcal{S}_{rch}$ contains a stable state with $w_k = i_k$; if it does, i_k $_{[M_k, a/b\rangle}$ j_k is not dead, since a can be received from the environment in that state. Otherwise, i_k $_{[M_k, a/b\rangle}$ j_k is dead.

5   Symbolic NCFSM Test Derivation

Given specification NCFSM M, we apply the following mutant operators, cor-responding to possible error classes, to generate a set of first-order mutants $\mathcal{U}$.

- **Alter the initial state:** create a mutant by changing one of the local states in the initial state $\mathbf{s}_{init}$. This generates $\sum_{1\le k\le K}(|\mathcal{S}_k| - 1)$ mutants.
- **Alter the output of a local transition:** create a mutant by changing local transition $i_{[M_k, a/b\rangle} j$ to $i_{[M_k, a/b'\rangle} j$, for $b' \in \mathcal{Y}_k \setminus \{b\}$. This generates $\sum_{1\le k\le K} |\delta_k|(|\mathcal{Y}_k| - 1)$ mutants, where $|\delta_k|$ is the number of local transitions in M_k, thus $|\delta_k| = |\mathcal{X}_k|\cdot|\mathcal{S}_k|$ if the model is completely specified.
- **Alter the destination state of a local transition:** create a mutant by changing local transition $i_{[M_k, a/b\rangle} j$ to $i_{[M_k, a/b\rangle} j'$, where $j' \in \mathcal{S}_k \setminus \{j\}$. This generates $\sum_{1\le k\le K} |\delta_k|(|\mathcal{S}_k| - 1)$ mutants.

evmdd $PairRP(evmdd\ \langle\mu,p\rangle, mdd\ g_1, mdd\ g_2)$	seq $TCGen(evmdd\ r,$
1 if $g_1.v = w_b$ or $g_2.v = w_b$ then	$mdd\ \mathcal{G}, evmdd\ f_{dis}, seq\ a/x)$
2 return $\langle\mu, MDD2EV(g_1)\rangle$; $\bullet\ g_1 = g_2$	
3 if $CHit_{PairRP}(p, g_1, g_2, \langle\lambda, r\rangle)$ then return$\langle\lambda + \mu, r\rangle$;	1 $seq\ tr \leftarrow a/x$;
4 $node\ t \leftarrow \mathbf{0}$;	2 while $r.val > 0$ do
5 for $i, i' \in \mathcal{V}_{p.v}$, s.t. $p[i].val \neq \infty \wedge g_1[i][i'] \neq \mathbf{0}$ do	3 for $\mathcal{G}_{b/y} \in \mathcal{G}$ do
6 for $j, j' \in \mathcal{V}_{p.v}$ s.t. $g_2[j][j'] \neq \mathbf{0} \wedge p[i][j].val \neq \infty$ do	4 if $t \in f_{dis}^{-1}(f_{dis}(r)-1) \wedge$
7 evmdd $\langle\eta, u\rangle \leftarrow PairRP(p[i][j], g_1[i][i'], g_2[j][j'])$;	$r = \mathcal{G}_{b/y}(t)$ then
8 $t[i'][j'] \leftarrow Min(t[i'][j'], \langle\eta, u\rangle)$;	5 $r \leftarrow t$; $\bullet$ predecessor
9 endfor	6 $tr \leftarrow b/y \cdot tr$;
10 endfor	7 break;
11 $\langle\lambda, t\rangle \leftarrow Normalize(t)$;	8 endif
12 $UniIns(t)$; $\bullet$ For canonicity	9 endfor
13 $CAdd_{PairRP}(p, g_1, g_2, \langle\lambda, t\rangle)$;	10 endwhile
14 return $\langle\lambda + \mu, t\rangle$;	11 return tr

Fig. 3. Algorithms for the *PairRP* operator and test case generation.

Given a mutant $\overline{M}$ of specification M ("—" indicates quantities related to the mutant), we seek a sequence $a_1/b_1, \ldots, a_n/b_n$ that kills this mutant, if not equivalent to M, where each a_i/b_i pair corresponds to an input symbol and the corresponding expected output in M. Let $\alpha = a_1 a_2 \cdots a_{n-1}$ and $\beta = b_1 b_2 \cdots b_{n-1}$, then $\lambda_{obs}(s, \alpha) = \beta = \overline{\lambda}_{obs}(s, \alpha)$ and $\lambda_{obs}(\delta_{obs}(s, \alpha), a_n) = b_n \neq \overline{\lambda}_{obs}(\overline{\delta}_{obs}(s, \alpha), a_n)$.

If the *state pair* set is $\mathcal{P} = \mathcal{S}_{st} \times \overline{\mathcal{S}}_{st}$, define the *next-state-pair function* $\mathcal{G} = \{\mathcal{G}_{a/b} : a \in \mathcal{X}, b \in \mathcal{Y}\}$ and the *distinguishable-state-pairs* $\mathcal{D} = \{\mathcal{D}_{a/b} : a \in \mathcal{X}, b \in \mathcal{Y}\}$:

$$\mathcal{G}_{a/b} = \{((a.\mathbf{i}, b.\mathbf{j}), (a.\bar{\mathbf{i}}, b.\bar{\mathbf{j}})) : (a.\mathbf{i}, b.\mathbf{j}) \in \mathcal{T}_{obs} \wedge (a.\bar{\mathbf{i}}, b.\bar{\mathbf{j}}) \in \overline{\mathcal{T}}_{obs}\},$$
$$\mathcal{D}_{a/b} = \{(a.\mathbf{i}, b.\bar{\mathbf{i}}) : \exists (a.\mathbf{i}, b.\mathbf{j}) \in \mathcal{T}_{obs} \wedge \exists (a.\bar{\mathbf{i}}, b.\bar{\mathbf{j}}) \in \overline{\mathcal{T}}_{obs} \wedge b \neq \bar{b}\},$$

which can be built through symbolic operations on $\mathcal{S}_{st}$, $\mathcal{T}_{obs}$, and $\overline{\mathcal{T}}_{obs}$.

Our test derivation algorithm takes in input the set $\mathcal{U}$ of mutants, the stable next-state function $\mathcal{T}_{obs}$, and $\mathbf{p}_{init} = (\mathbf{i}_{init}, \overline{\mathbf{i}_{init}})$. For each mutant $\overline{M}$, we first run the current test suite to check whether an existing test kills $\overline{M}$. If not, we build $\overline{\mathcal{T}}_{obs}$ and encode the next-state-pair function $\mathcal{G}$ and the distinguishable-state-pairs $\mathcal{D}$. Fig. 3 shows the *PairRP* operator that is analogous to state-space exploration except that we explore pairs of states (one from M, one from $\overline{M}$), and keep track of the distance of each such pair from $\mathbf{p}_{init}$ by using a $2(K+1)$-variable EV$^+$MDD to encode the *distance function* $f_{dis} : \mathcal{P} \to \mathbb{N} \cup \{\infty\}$ s.t. $f_{dis}(\mathbf{p}) = \min\{d : \mathbf{p} \in \mathcal{G}^d(\mathbf{p}_{init})\}$. Thus, $f_{dis}(\mathbf{p}) = \infty$ iff $\mathbf{p}$ has not yet been reached in the exploration, initialized with $f_{dis}(\mathbf{p}_{init}) = 0$ and $f_{dis}(\mathbf{p}) = \infty$ for $\mathbf{p} \neq \mathbf{p}_{init}$. We also define the reverse function $f_{dis}^{-1}(d) = \{\mathbf{p} : f_{dis}(\mathbf{p}) = d\}$, where $d \in \mathbb{N}$.

The algorithm uses a BFS algorithm to generate the distance function for reachable state pairs until the search reaches a distinguishing state pair $\mathbf{p}_{err}$ in $\mathcal{D}$. $\mathbf{p}_{err}$ is used to generate a sequence as a new test case which is added to the test suite $\mathcal{C}$. Then, the algorithm *TCGen* in Fig. 3 use $f_{dis}^{-1}(d)$ to generate a sequence leading M and $\overline{M}$ from $\mathbf{p}_{init}$ to $\mathbf{p}_{err}$. This is the same approach proposed in [5] to generate the shortest path to a target state, except that now we target a *pair* of states $\mathbf{p}_{err}$. Starting from $\mathbf{p}$ at distance n, there must exist a predecessor $\mathbf{q}$, i.e., satisfying $\mathbf{p} = \mathcal{G}(\mathbf{q})$, at distance $n-1$, as Line 4. Thus, we keep reducing the distance value until reaching $\mathbf{p}_{init}$, at distance 0. If no such pair $\mathbf{p}_{err}$ is instead reachable, $\overline{M}$ is equivalent to M, and the algorithm builds a fixpoint $\mathcal{P}_{rch}$ containing all the pairs of states that can be reached from $\mathbf{p}_{init}$ by providing the same input sequence to both M and $\overline{M}$. Finally, the algorithm eliminates test cases subsumed by other test cases, to form a minimal test suite.

6   Experimental Results

We implemented the proposed framework using our MDD library [17], and report experimental results on an Intel Xeon 2.53GHz workstation with 36GB RAM running Linux. The main metrics of our comparison are runtime and peak memory. For BFS and saturation, we compare the cumulative time to compute the UTC on all mutants (UTC_{bfs} and UTC_{sat}), and the total runtime and peak memory (Tot_{bfs} and Tot_{sat}) using BFS and saturation respectively. For each model, we list the number of components (K), of mutants (Tot), of non-equivalent mutants (NE), of test cases (Num), and the average length of the tests in the suite (Avg). The total time includes preprocessing, livelock checking, and test suite generation.

Table 1 presents results for two sets of models. The first set, shown under "Ideal models", consists of M_{se} [8] and M_{hs} [9]. All components are completely specified, minimized, strongly connected, and deterministic. The second set contains control systems, communication protocols, and two corresponding incompletely specified models M'_{se} and M'_{hs} by eliminating some self-loops. Three control systems include a heating controller system [2] and a train gate controller [1] with two trains, M_{tr}, or three trains, M_{tr3}. Three communication

Table 1. Test derivation results (time in seconds or hours, memory in MB or GB)

Model		Mutants		Test Suite		UTC_{bfs}	UTC_{sat}	Tot_{bfs}		Tot_{sat}	
M	K	Tot	NE	Num	Avg	time	time	mem	time	mem	time
Ideal models											
M_{se}	3	96	96	27	3.19	0.053 s	0.021 s	3.63 M	0.427 s	3.42 M	0.235 s
M_{hs}	3	81	81	16	2.81	0.044 s	0.018 s	3.60 M	0.301 s	3.30 M	0.158 s
Not ideal and real models											
M'_{se}	3	90	90	23	3.30	0.039 s	0.014 s	3.28 M	0.245 s	3.10 M	0.192 s
M'_{hs}	3	77	77	13	3.08	0.041 s	0.012 s	3.24 M	0.252 s	3.00 M	0.126 s
M_{hcs}	4	179	157	12	11.17	0.17 s	0.03 s	7.01 M	1.00 s	6.54 M	0.48 s
M_{tr}	4	177	150	12	2.5	0.17 s	0.09 s	6.72 M	1.00 s	5.33 M	0.20 s
M_{tr3}	5	1024	849	43	3.14	4.69 s	3.35 s	69.75 M	9.25 s	50.72 M	7.74 s
ABP	2	96	81	12	3.83	0.005 s	0.004 s	2.90 M	0.49 s	2.90 M	0.32 s
BGP	4	4898	1613	79	5.16	344.26 s	24.1 s	96.48 M	1230.0 s	82.41 M	438.6 s
EGP	3	69066	27883	3501	9.24	11.14 h	5.28 h	6.78 G	21.58 h	4.51 G	14.03 h

protocols contain the alternating bit protocol (ABP) [16], the border gateway protocol (BGP) [15], and the exterior gateway protocol (EGP) [14].

Saturation works better in both time and memory, although only minor improvements are observable for some models. For communication protocols, BGP and EGP are two important TCP/IP exterior routing protocols. BGP is currently used on the Internet and other larger autonomous systems. For these two models, we only consider mandatory events. Thus, including the component for the environment, we encode the model with 5 variables. Saturation is clearly superior, 14 times faster than BFS when computing the UTC for all mutants. Similar trends can be observed for EGP with three peers: saturation saves almost 8 hours and over 2GB over BFS (there are about 1.2×10^5 global states, 6.7×10^5 local transitions, and 1.5×10^6 global transitions).

The benefit of symbolic encodings can be clearly seen in our results, as the memory consumption remains stable even if the number of generated mutants increases by an order of magnitude when growing the number of components. Also, we observe that the number of generated test cases and the average length of the test suite are stable even if the number of mutants increases dramatically. This is important for complex models in practice, as it reduces testing efforts.

7   Conclusion

We presented a new symbolic framework for NCFSM verification and test generation. We encode an NCFSM with MDDs and use the BFS and saturation algorithms to generate the unstable transitive closure of transitions. We symbolically check for livelocks, dead transitions, and strong connectedness. Then, we propose a symbolic mutation-based test generation algorithm. The experimental results demonstrate the effectiveness of this framework. A further advantage of our symbolic framework is that no constraints are required of IUTs. Some of those requirements by other test generation methods might not be met by many real models. Moreover, our framework guarantees a test suite with minimal-length tests to kill all non-equivalent mutants and it could be extended to non-deterministic NCFSMs by returning, instead of distinguishing sequences, pairs consisting of an input string and a set of all correct output strings.

References

1. BEEM models, http://anna.fi.muni.cz/models/cgi/models.cgi
2. Event-B examples, http://wiki.event-b.org/index.php/Event-B_Examples
3. Bryant, R.E.: Graph-based algorithms for boolean function manipulation. IEEE Transactions on Computers 35(8), 677–691 (1986)
4. Ciardo, G., Marmorstein, R., Siminiceanu, R.: The saturation algorithm for symbolic state space exploration. STTT 8(1), 4–25 (2006)
5. Ciardo, G., Siminiceanu, R.: Using edge-valued decision diagrams for symbolic generation of shortest paths. In: Aagaard, M.D., O'Leary, J.W. (eds.) FMCAD 2002. LNCS, vol. 2517, pp. 256–273. Springer, Heidelberg (2002)

6. Guo, Q., et al.: Computing unique input/output sequences using genetic algorithms. In: Proc. FATES, pp. 169–184 (2004)
7. Henniger, O.: On test case generation from asynchronously communicating state machines. In: Proc. TCS, pp. 255–271 (1997)
8. Hierons, R.: Testing from semi-independent communicating finite state machines with a slow environment. IEE Proc., Software Engineering 144(5), 291–295 (1997)
9. Hierons, R.: Checking states and transitions of a set of communicating finite state machines. Microprocessors and Microsystems 24, 443–452 (2000)
10. Kam, T., et al.: Multi-valued decision diagrams: theory and applications. Multiple-Valued Logic 4(1-2), 9–62 (1998)
11. Li, J., Wong, W.: Automatic test generation from communicating extended finite state machine (CEFSM)-based models. In: Proc. ISORC, pp. 181–185 (2002)
12. Luo, G., von Bochmann, G., Petrenko, A.: Test selection based on communicating nondeterministic finite-state machines using a generalized WP-method. IEEE Trans. Softw. Eng. 20, 149–162 (1994)
13. Mathur, A.P.: Foundations of Software Testing. Pearson Education, London (2008)
14. Mills, D.L.: Exterior gateway protocol formal specification (1984)
15. Rekhter, Y., Li, T.: A border gateway protocol 4 (BGP-4). RFC 4271 (2006)
16. Tanenbaum, A.: Computer Networks. Prentice Hall, Englewood Cliffs (2003)
17. Wan, M., Ciardo, G.: Symbolic state-space generation of asynchronous systems using extensible decision diagrams. In: Nielsen, M., Kučera, A., Miltersen, P.B., Palamidessi, C., Tůma, P., Valencia, F. (eds.) SOFSEM 2009. LNCS, vol. 5404, pp. 582–594. Springer, Heidelberg (2009)

Hierarchical Counterexamples for Discrete-Time Markov Chains[*]

Nils Jansen[1], Erika Ábrahám[1], Jens Katelaan[1], Ralf Wimmer[2],
Joost-Pieter Katoen[1], and Bernd Becker[2]

[1] RWTH Aachen University, Germany
[2] Albert-Ludwigs-University Freiburg, Germany

Abstract. This paper introduces a novel *counterexample generation* approach for the verification of discrete-time Markov chains (DTMCs) with two main advantages: (1) We generate *abstract* counterexamples which can be refined in a *hierarchical* manner. (2) We aim at minimizing the number of states involved in the counterexamples, and compute a *critical subsystem* of the DTMC whose paths form a counterexample. Experiments show that with our approach we can reduce the size of counterexamples and the number of computation steps by several orders of magnitude.

1 Introduction

Discrete-time Markov chains (DTMCs) are a well-known modeling formalism for probabilistic systems. The *probabilistic computation tree logic (PCTL)* [6] is suited to express bounds on the probability mass of all paths satisfying some properties. Efficient algorithms and tools are available to *verify* PCTL properties of DTMCs. Prominent model checkers like PRISM [9] and MRMC [8] offer methods based on the solution of linear equation systems [6].

If verification reveals that a system does not fulfill a required property, the ability to provide diagnostic information is crucial for bug fixing. A *counterexample* carries an explanation why the property is violated. E.g., for Kripke structures and linear temporal logic (LTL) formulae, a counterexample is a path that violates the property, which can be generated by LTL model checking as a *by-product* without additional overhead. State-of-the-art model checking algorithms for probabilistic systems do not exhibit this feature. After model checking, current techniques have to apply additional methods to *generate* probabilistic counterexamples.

Even for large state spaces, a counterexample consisting of a single path gives an intuitive explanation why the property is violated. In the probabilistic setting, instead of a *single path* we need a *set of paths* whose total probability mass violates the bound specified by the PCTL formula [5]. It is much harder

---

[*] This work was partly supported by the German Research Council (DFG) as part of the research project CEBug (AB 461/1-1), the Transregional Collaborative Research Center AVACS (SFB/TR 14) and the Research Training Group AlgoSyn (1298).

T. Bultan and P.-A. Hsiung (Eds.): ATVA 2011, LNCS 6996, pp. 443–452, 2011.

to understand the behavior represented by such a probabilistic counterexample as it may consist of a large or even infinite number of paths. To ease understanding, most approaches aim at finding counterexamples with a small number of paths having high probabilities. To generate more compact counterexamples, also the usage of regular expressions [5], the detection of loops [11], and the abstraction of strongly connected components (SCCs) [4] have been proposed, as well as diagnostic subgraphs [3], which is most related to our counterexample representation.

We suggested in [2] a model checking approach based on the hierarchical abstraction of SCCs. We abstract each SCC by a small loop-free graph in a recursive manner by the abstraction of sub-SCCs. The result is an abstract DTMC consisting of a single initial state and absorbing states, and transitions carrying the total probabilities of reaching target states. In [2] we also gave an idea of how to use the SCC-based model checking result for counterexample generation. In this paper we generalize this approach and suggest a novel method which computes a *critical subsystem* whose paths induce a counterexample. While other methods concentrate on minimizing the *number of paths*, our computation regards the system structure and aims at reducing the *number of involved states and transitions*.

Critical subsystems are computed *hierarchically*. We refine a critical subsystem by concretizing abstract states and reducing the concretized parts, such that the reduced subsystem still induces a counterexample. This hierarchical approach increases the usability of counterexamples for large state spaces. Concretization of only the user-relevant parts of the abstract critical subsystem allows for an intuitive approach for error correction.

The computation of critical subsystems is based on finding most probable paths or path fragments to be contained in the critical subsystem. We propose two approaches. The *global* method searches for paths through the entire system. Our main contribution is the *local* search which aims at connecting most probable *path fragments*. In contrast to most of the other approaches, our method is *complete*, i. e., termination is always guaranteed.

Experiments for two well-known case studies show that our approach reduces the size of counterexamples and the number of computation steps by several orders of magnitude.

The paper is structured as follows: Section 2 contains some preliminaries. We recall our model checking algorithm in Section 3. Section 4 describes our counterexample generation method, for which we give some experimental results in Section 5. A more detailed version of this paper, including examples and illustrations, can be found in [1].

2   Preliminaries

Definition 1. *Assume a set AP of atomic propositions. A* discrete-time Markov chain (DTMC) *is a tuple* $M = (S, I, P, L)$ *with a non-empty finite state set* S, *an initial discrete probability distribution* $I : S \rightarrow [0, 1]$ *with* $\sum_{s \in S} I(s) = 1$, *a* *transition probability matrix* $P : S \times S \to [0,1]$ *with* $\sum_{s' \in S} P(s,s') = 1$ *for all* $s \in S$, *and a labeling function* $L : S \to 2^{AP}$.

To reduce notation, we refer to the components of a DTMC M_l^u by S_l^u, I_l^u, P_l^u, and L_l^u. E.g., we use S' to denote the state set of the DTMC M'. Assume in the following a set AP of atomic propositions and a DTMC $M = (S, I, P, L)$.

We say that there is a *transition* from a state $s \in S$ to a state $s' \in S$ iff $P(s,s') > 0$. A *path* of M is a finite or infinite sequence $\pi = s_0 s_1 \ldots$ of states $s_i \in S$ such that $P(s_i, s_{i+1}) > 0$ for all i. We say that the transitions (s_i, s_{i+1}) are *contained* in the path π, written $(s_i, s_{i+1}) \in \pi$. We write $Paths_{inf}^M$ for the set of all infinite paths of M, and $Paths_{inf}^M(s)$ for those starting in $s \in S$. Analogously, $Paths_{fin}^M$ is the set of all finite paths of M, $Paths_{fin}^M(s)$ of those starting in s, and $Paths_{fin}^M(s,t)$ of those starting in s and ending in t. A state t is called *reachable* from another state s iff $Paths_{fin}^M(s,t) \neq \emptyset$.

A state set $S' \subseteq S$ is called *absorbing in* M iff there is a state in S' from which no state outside S' is reachable in M. We call S' *bottom in* M if this holds for all states in S'. States $s \in S$ with $P(s,s) = 1$ are also called *absorbing states*.

We call M *loop-free*, if all of its loops are self-loops on absorbing states. A set $S' \subseteq S$ is *strongly connected in* M iff for all $s, t \in S'$ there is a path from s to t visiting states from S' only. A *strongly connected component (SCC)* of M is a maximal strongly connected subset of S.

The probability measure for finite paths $\pi \in Paths_{fin}^M$ is defined by $Pr_{fin}^M(\pi) = \prod_{(s_i, s_{i+1}) \in \pi} P(s_i, s_{i+1})$. For a set $R \subseteq Paths_{fin}^M$ of paths we have $Pr_{fin}^M(R) = \sum_{\pi \in R'} Pr_{fin}^M(\pi)$ with $R' = \{\pi \in R \mid \forall \pi' \in R. \ \pi' \text{ is no prefix of } \pi\}$.

The syntax of *probabilistic computation tree logic (PCTL)* [6] is given by[1]

$$\varphi ::= p \mid \neg\varphi \mid \varphi \wedge \varphi \mid \mathbb{P}_{\sim\lambda}(\varphi \ U \ \varphi)$$

for (state) formulae with $p \in AP$, $\lambda \in [0,1] \subseteq \mathbb{R}$, and $\sim \, \in \{<, \leq, \geq, >\}$. We define $\Diamond$ and $\Box$ in the usual way.

For a property $\mathbb{P}_{\leq\lambda}(\varphi_1 \ U \ \varphi_2)$ refuted by M, a *counterexample* is a set $C \subseteq Paths_{fin}^M$, $Pr_{fin}^M(C) > \lambda$ of finite paths starting in an initial state and *satisfying* $\varphi_1 \ U \ \varphi_2$. For $\mathbb{P}_{<\lambda}(\varphi_1 \ U \ \varphi_2)$, the probability mass has to be at least λ. We consider upper probability bounds; see [5] for the reduction of lower bounds to this case.

Model checking of PCTL properties can be reduced to checking properties of the form $\mathbb{P}_{\sim\lambda}(\Diamond\varphi)$. The φ-states are also called *target* states. We concentrate on this case and assume DTMCs to have single initial and target states. Note that each DTMC can be equivalently transformed to satisfy these requirements.

3 SCC-Based Model Checking

Next we recall our model checking algorithm from [2]. Given a DTMC M, we are interested in the total probability of reaching its target state from its initial

---

[1] In this paper we only consider unbounded properties.

state. Each non-bottom SCC S' of M induces a DTMC M_{ind}: those states of the SCC through which paths may enter it are the initial states of M_{ind}; we call them *input states*. Those states outside the SCC to which paths may exit, the so-called *output states*, are absorbing states in M_{ind}. The remaining graph of M_{ind} is defined by the SCC's structure. We use $Inp^M(S') = \{t \in S' \mid I(t) > 0 \vee \exists s \in S \backslash S'. \ P(s,t) > 0\}$ and $Out^M(S') = \{t \in S \backslash S' \mid \exists s \in S'. \ P(s,t) > 0\}$ for the set of input respectively output states, and call states from S' *inner states*. Let in the following $M = (S, I, P, L)$ be a DTMC and $S' \subseteq S$ a not absorbing state set in M.

Definition 2. *The DTMC induced by S' in M, written $DTMC(S', M)$, is $M_{ind} = (S_{ind}, I_{ind}, P_{ind}, L_{ind})$ with*

1. $S_{ind} = S' \cup Out^M(S')$,
2. $\forall s \in S_{ind}. \ \big(I_{ind}(s) > 0 \leftrightarrow s \in Inp^M(S')\big)$,
3. $P_{ind}(s,t) = \begin{cases} P(s,t) & \text{for } s \in S' \text{ and } t \in S_{ind}, \\ 1 & \text{for } s = t \in Out^M(S'), \\ 0 & \text{else.} \end{cases}$
4. $\forall s \in S_{ind}. \ L_{ind}(s) = L(s)$.

We use the notation $Inp(M_{ind}) = \{s \in S_{ind} \mid I_{ind}(s) > 0\}$ and $Out(M_{ind}) = \{s \in S_{ind} \mid P_{ind}(s,s) = 1\}$.

The model checking procedure replaces inside M the subgraph M_{ind} by a smaller subgraph M_{abs} with the input and output states as state set and transitions from each input state s to each output state t carrying the total probability mass $Pr^{M_{ind}}\big(Paths_{fin}^{M_{ind}}(s,t)\big)$.

Definition 3. *Let $DTMC(S', M) = M_{ind} = (S_{ind}, I_{ind}, P_{ind}, L_{ind})$ and*

$$p_{s,t} = Pr_{fin}^{M_{ind}}\big(\{ss_1 \ldots s_n t \in Paths_{fin}^{M_{ind}} \mid \forall 1 \leq i \leq n. \ s_i \neq s \wedge s_i \neq t\}\big)$$

for all $s \in Inp(M_{ind})$ and $t \in Out(M_{ind})$. We define the abstraction of M_{ind}, written $Abs(M_{ind})$, to be the DTMC $M_{abs} = (S_{abs}, I_{abs}, P_{abs}, L_{abs})$ with

1. $S_{abs} = Inp(M_{ind}) \cup Out(M_{ind})$,
2. $I_{abs}(s) = I_{ind}(s)$ *for all $s \in S_{abs}$,*
3. $P_{abs}(s,t) = \begin{cases} p_{s,t}/\big(\sum_{t' \in Out(M_{ind})} p_{s,t'}\big) & \text{for } s \in Inp(M_{ind}), \ t \in Out(M_{ind}), \\ 1 & \text{for } s = t \in Out(M_{ind}), \\ 0 & \text{else.} \end{cases}$
4. $L_{abs}(s) = L_{ind}(s)$ *for all $s \in S_{abs}$.*

Next we formalize the abstraction and the concretization of an SCC.

Definition 4. *Let $DTMC(S', M) = M_1 = (S_1, I_1, P_1, L_1)$, and $M_2 = (S_2, I_2, P_2, L_2)$ a DTMC satisfying $S_2 \cap (S \backslash S_1) = \emptyset$ such that either $M_2 = Abs(M_1)$ or $M_1 = Abs(M_2)$. Then the result of the substitution of M_1 by M_2 in M, written $M[M_2/M_1]$, is the DTMC $M_{sub} = (S_{sub}, I_{sub}, P_{sub}, L_{sub})$ with*

Algorithm 1.

Model_check(DTMC $M = (S, I, P, L)$, PCTL-formula $\mathbb{P}_{\sim \lambda} (\Diamond p)$)
begin

$\quad (M, Sub) := \text{Abstract\_SCC}(M, \emptyset);$ \hfill (1)

$\quad result := \left(\sum_{s \in Inp(M)} \sum_{t \in Out(M)} (I(s) \cdot P(s,t)) \sim \lambda \right);$ \hfill (2)

$\quad \textbf{return } (result, M, Sub)$ \hfill (3)

end

Abstract_SCC(DTMC $M = (S, I, P, L)$, Abstractions Sub)
begin

$\quad \textbf{for all } \text{non-bottom SCCs } K \text{ in } DTMC(S \backslash Inp(M), M) \textbf{ do}$ \hfill (4)

$\quad\quad M_K := DTMC(K, M); \quad (M_K^{abs}, Sub) := \text{Abstract\_SCC}(M_K, Sub);$ \hfill (5)

$\quad\quad M := M[M_K^{abs}/M_K]$ \hfill (6)

$\quad \textbf{end for}$ \hfill (7)

$\quad M^{abs} := Abs(M); \; Sub := Sub \cup \{(M, M^{abs})\};$ \hfill (8)

$\quad \textbf{return } (M^{abs}, Sub)$ \hfill (9)

end

---

1. $S_{sub} = (S \backslash S_1) \cup S_2,$
2. $I_{sub}(s) = I(s)$ for $s \in S_{sub}$ and 0 otherwise,
3. $P_{sub}(s,t) = P_2(s,t)$ for $s \in (S_2 \backslash Out(M_2))$ and $t \in S_2$, and $P(s,t)$ otherwise,
4. $L_{sub}(s) = L_2(s)$ for $s \in S_2$ and $L(s)$ otherwise.

The replacement of an SCC by its abstraction and vice versa does not affect the total probabilities of reaching a target state from an initial state in M [1].

To compute the abstraction M_{abs} of an induced DTMC M_{ind}, we determine the probabilities $p_{s,t}$ recursively as follows. We detect all non-bottom SCCs in M_{ind} that do not contain any input states of M_{ind}, and replace them by their abstractions recursively. The result is a DTMC M'_{ind} which is loop-free in case M_{ind} has a single input state (multiple input states need a special treatment, see [2]), such that the probabilities $p_{s,t}$ can be computed easily.

The model checking algorithm is shown in Algorithm 1. We use a global variable Sub to store the pairs of abstracted DTMCs and their abstractions for the concretization during counterexample generation.[2]

4   Counterexample Generation

Our computation is based on the detection of single *paths*, which we use to determine a subgraph (*closure*) of the original system. We call the closure a *critical subsystem* if its paths form a counterexample for the violated property.

The closure is computed according to a *selection* $m \subseteq S \times S$. We use $extend^M$: $(2^{S \times S} \times Paths^M_{fin}) \to 2^{S \times S}$ defined by $extend(m, \pi) = \{(s, s') \in S \times S \mid (s, s') \in m \vee (s, s') \in \pi\}$ to extend a selection m with the transitions of a path π.

---

[2] Instead of copying, the implementation uses different markings to specify sub-graphs.

Algorithm 2.

SearchAbstractCex(DTMC M, PCTL-formula $\mathbb{P}_{\sim\lambda}(\Diamond p)$)
begin

    $(result, M_{ce}, Sub) := \text{ModelCheck}(M, \mathbb{P}_{\sim\lambda}(\Diamond p));$ (10)

    if result = true **then return** $\bot$ (11)

    else   (12)

        $m_{max} := \{(s_0, t)\};$ (13)

        while true **do**   (14)

            $m_{min} := m_{max};$ (15)

            $(ready, M_{ce}, m_{min}, m_{max}) := \text{Concretize}(M_{ce}, m_{min}, m_{max}, Sub);$ (16)

            if (ready = true) **then return** $closure^{M_{ce}}(m_{max})$ (17)

            else $m_{max} := \text{CriticalSubsystem}(M_{ce}, m_{min}, m_{max}, \mathbb{P}_{\sim\lambda}(\Diamond p));$ (18)

            end if   (19)

        end while   (20)

    end if   (21)

end

Definition 5 (Closure). *For a DTMC $M = (S, I, P, L)$, target state t, and a selection $m \subseteq S \times S$, the* closure $closure^M(m) = (S_{cl}, I_{cl}, P_{cl}, L_{cl})$ *of m in M is given by $S_{cl} = S \uplus \{s_\perp\}$, $I_{cl}(s) = I(s)$, $L_{cl}(s) = L(s)$ for $s \in S$ and $I_{cl}(s_\perp) = 0, L_{cl}(s_\perp) = \emptyset$ and*

$$
P_{cl}(s, s') = \begin{cases} P(s, s') & \text{for } (s, s') \in m, \\ 1 - \sum_{(s, s'') \in m} P(s, s'') & \text{for } s \in S \setminus \{t\} \text{ and } s' = s_\perp, \\ 1 & \text{for } s = s' = t \text{ or } s = s' = s_\perp, \\ 0 & \text{otherwise.} \end{cases}
$$

Given a PCTL property φ, we call a DTMC M' a critical subsystem *of M for φ if $M' = closure^M(m)$ for some selection m and M' violates φ.*

4.1 The Basic Hierarchical Algorithm

We compute counterexamples in a hierarchical manner (see Algorithm 2): Intuitively, at first we compute a critical subsystem for the resulting abstract DTMC of the model checking procedure. Then we refine the DTMC stepwise hand in hand with its critical subsystem. For each refinement step, the abstract and the refined critical subsystems differ only in states and transitions affected by the refinement step.

    The initial critical subsystem is given by the closure $closure^{M_{ce}}(m_{max})$ where the selection m_{max} contains the only transition from the initial state s_0 to the target state t of M_{ce} (line 13). Note that this initial subsystem represents *all* paths of M from its initial to its target state.

    The *Concretize* method (Algorithm 3) concretizes some heuristically determined abstract states in M_{ce}. Thereby we remove all transitions from m_{max} that were removed by the concretization and add all transitions added by the

---

Algorithm 3.

Concretize(DTMC M_{ce}, Selection m_{min}, Selection m_{max}, Abstractions Sub)
begin
    first = true;   (22)
    while true **do**   (23)
        $s_a :=$ ChooseAbstractState($closure^{M_{ce}}(m_{max})$);   (24)
        if $(s_a = \bot)$ **then return** (first, M_{ce}, m_{min}, m_{max})   (25)
        else   (26)
            first := false;   (27)
            Let $(M_{abs}, M_{con}) \in Sub$ s.t. $s_a \in Inp(M_{abs})$;   (28)
            $Tr_{abs} := \big\{(s, s') \in S_{abs} \times S_{abs} \mid s \notin Out(M_{abs}) \wedge P_{abs}(s, s') > 0\big\};$ (29)
            $Tr_{con} := \big\{(s, s') \in S_{con} \times S_{con} \mid s \notin Out(M_{con}) \wedge P_{con}(s, s') > 0\big\};$ (30)
            $m_{min} := m_{min} \backslash Tr_{abs};$ $m_{max} := \big(m_{max} \backslash Tr_{abs}\big) \cup Tr_{con};$ (31)
            $M_{ce} := M_{ce}[M_{con}/M_{abs}];$ (32)
        end if   (33)
    end while   (34)
end

Algorithm 4. Global Search

CriticalSubsystem(DTMC M_{ce}, Selection m_{min}, Selection m_{max}, Formula $\mathbb{P}_{\sim\lambda}(\Diamond p)$)
begin
    $k := 0;$ $M_{max} := closure^{M_{ce}}(m_{max});$ (35)
    Let s_0 be the initial and t the target state of M_{max};   (36)
    repeat   (37)
        $k := k + 1;$ $\pi :=$ FindNextPath(s_0, t, M_{max}, k); $m_{min} := extend(m_{min}, \pi);$ (38)
    until ModelCheck($closure^{M_{ce}}(m_{min})$, $\mathbb{P}_{\sim\lambda}(\Diamond p)$) reports violation; (39)
    return m_{min};   (40)
end

---

concretization (line 31). If the closure of m_{max} in M_{ce} represents a counterexample, then also the closure of the updated selection m_{max} in the concretization of M_{ce} represents a counterexample with the same probability. However, this counterexample may be unnecessarily large. *CriticalSubsystem* searches for a smaller selection included in m_{max} that still contains all transitions that were not affected by the concretization.

4.2 Search Algorithms

Global Search. An implementation for *CriticalSubsystem*, which we call the *global search* algorithm, is proposed in Algorithm 4. Similarly to [5], we search for most probable paths from the initial state to the target state in the subsystem $M_{max} = closure^{M_{ce}}(m_{max})$ (line 35). After a next most probable path has been found (line 38), the algorithm extends m_{min} with the found path (line 38). This procedure is repeated until the closure of m_{min} is large enough to represent a counterexample (line 39).

Algorithm 5. Local Search

CriticalSubsystem(DTMC M_{ce}, Selection m_{min}, Selection m_{max},
$\qquad\qquad\qquad$ PCTL-formula $\mathbb{P}_{\sim\lambda}(\lozenge p)$)
begin
$\qquad M_{cl} := closure^{M_{ce}}(m_{min});$ $\qquad\qquad\qquad\qquad\qquad\qquad\qquad\qquad\qquad$ (41)
$\qquad$**while** ModelCheck($M_{cl}, \mathbb{P}_{\sim\lambda}(\lozenge p)$) reports satisfaction **do** $\qquad$ (42)
$\qquad\qquad M_{search} := closure^{M_{ce}}(m_{max}\backslash m_{min});$ $\qquad\qquad\qquad\qquad\qquad$ (43)
$\qquad\qquad \Pi := \left\{\pi' \in Paths_{fin}^{M_{search}}(s,t) \mid s \in Inp(M_{search}) \wedge t \in Out(M_{search})\right\};$ (44)
$\qquad\qquad \pi := \arg\max_{\pi \in \Pi} Pr_{fin}(\pi);$ $\qquad\qquad\qquad\qquad\qquad\qquad\qquad\qquad$ (45)
$\qquad\qquad m_{min} := extend(m_{min}, \pi); \quad M_{cl} := closure^{M_{ce}}(m_{min});$ $\qquad$ (46)
$\qquad$**end while** $\qquad\qquad\qquad\qquad\qquad\qquad\qquad\qquad\qquad\qquad\qquad\qquad$ (47)
$\qquad$**return** m_{min} $\qquad\qquad\qquad\qquad\qquad\qquad\qquad\qquad\qquad\qquad\qquad\qquad$ (48)
end

Local Search. The global search is complete, but it may find most probable paths which do not extend the minimal selection m_{min}. This can be time-consuming, e.g., when many different traversals of loops are considered.

Our second implementation for *CriticalSubsystem* (Algorithm 5), which we call the *local search*, overcomes this problem and finds only paths that extend the minimal selection and increase the target reachability probability of its closure. Instead of searching for paths from the initial to the target state, it aims at finding most probable *path fragments* that connect fragments of already found paths to new paths. The path fragments should, as the paths for the global search, lie in the closure of m_{max}. But this time they should (1) start at states reachable from an initial state via transitions of m_{min}, (2) end in states from which the target state is reachable via transitions from m_{min}, and (3) contain transitions from $m_{max}\backslash m_{min}$ only. I. e., we only search for path fragments in the subgraphs inserted by the last concretization step, which connect path fragments in the closure of m_{min} to whole paths from the initial to the target state.

5   Experimental Results

We developed a C++ implementation with exact arithmetic for both search algorithms, and used it to run experiments on a 2.4 GHz dual core CPU with 4 GB RAM. We used PRISM [9] to generate models for different instances of the parametrized *synchronous leader election protocol* [?] and the *crowds protocol* [10].

The global and the local search work on hierarchical data types. However, they can also directly be applied to concrete models. We consider this non-hierarchical approach to obtain a fair comparison to [5]. Table 1 compares the global method with the k-shortest path search for the leader election protocol, where the probability of reaching a target state is always 1. Table 2 depicts results for the crowds benchmark additionally containing the local search. The global search finds paths in the same order as k-sp, but due to the closure computation *earlier termination*, a significantly *smaller number of needed paths*, and therefore

Table 1. Results for the leader benchmark on concrete models (TO > 1*h*)

states		3902			12302		
transitions		5197			16397		
prob. threshold	0.92	0.93	0.95	0.95	0.96	0.97	
k-sp	# paths	1193	8043	41636	3892	53728	-TO-
	# states	3593	3903	3903	11690	12302	12302
global	# paths	1193	1301	1850	3892	4360	5870
	# states	3593	3634	3676	11690	11815	11941
	prob.	0.9205	0.9302	0.9501	0.9502	0.9600	0.9700

Table 2. Results for the crowds benchmark on concrete models (TO > 1*h*)

states		396		3515					18817	
transitions		576		6035					32677	
total prob.		0.1891		0.2346					0.4270	
prob. threshold		0.12	0.15	0.1	0.12	0.15	0.21	0.23	0.2	0.25
k-sp	# paths	1301	26184	3974	26981	488644	-TO-	-TO-	-TO-	-TO-
	# states	133	133	671	831	1071	-TO-	-TO-	-TO-	-TO-
global	# paths	38	76	91	220	935	3478	151639	3007	56657
	# closures	24	29	58	73	181	364	623	302	767
	# states	89	93	143	169	631	671	1071	663	2047
	prob.	0.1339	0.1514	0.1014	0.1203	0.1501	0.2101	0.2300	0.2002	0.2500
local	# paths	26	32	60	68	98	326	665	202	798
	# states	55	67	99	104	171	670	900	326	1439
	prob.	0.1238	0.1509	0.1018	0.1211	0.1525	0.2101	0.2300	0.2001	0.2508

a smaller number of *computation steps* are achieved. For probability thresholds
near the total probability, the number of paths for *k*-sp is several orders of magnitude larger. The number of considered states can also be reduced significantly.
The local search not only leads to smaller critical subsystems in most cases, but
also needs a much smaller number of found path fragments in comparison to the
global search. The probability mass for all types of counterexamples is always
very close to the specified probability threshold. Note that for our methods we
model check only extended subsystems, while for the local search actually every
new path extends the system.

The search for hierarchical counterexamples is motivated by their usefulness
and understandability. The results in Table 3 show that the hierarchical search
leads to critical subsystems of comparable size (the third last column is the
hierarchical version of the global search in the second last column of Table 2).
The number of found paths is much larger in the hierarchical approach, because
we have to search at each abstraction level. However, due to abstraction, the
found paths are shorter, especially for the local search, and the concretization
up to the concrete level seems not necessary for many cases. We did experiments
using different heuristics for the number of abstract states that are concretized
in one step (e. g., either a single one or $\sqrt{n}$ with n the number of abstract

Table 3. Results for a crowds instance (18817 states, 32677 transitions, 0.2 probability threshold) on the hierarchical model

search type	global				local	
# abstract states to concretize in one step	$\sqrt{}$		single		$\sqrt{}$	single
heuristic to choose the next abstract state	prob	none	prob	none	prob	prob
# paths	13525	912455	38379	594881	496	545
# closures	728	730	728	729	496	545
# states	457	457	458	457	319	347
# refinements	13	10	37	37	9	28

states). We also tried two different heuristics for the choice of the next abstract state, either being just the next one found ("none"), or the one whose outgoing transitions have the maximal average probability ("prob").

References

1. Ábrahám, E., Jansen, N., Katelaan, J., Wimmer, R., Katoen, J.P., Becker, B.: Hierarchical counterexamples for discrete-time Markov chains. Tech. rep., RWTH Aachen University (2011), http://sunsite.informatik.rwth-aachen.de/Publications/AIB/2011/2011-11.pdf
2. Ábrahám, E., Jansen, N., Wimmer, R., Katoen, J.P., Becker, B.: DTMC model checking by SCC reduction. In: Proc. of QEST, pp. 37–46. IEEE CS, Los Alamitos (2010)
3. Aljazzar, H., Leue, S.: Directed explicit state-space search in the generation of counterexamples for stochastic model checking. IEEE Trans. on Software Engineering 36(1), 37–60 (2010)
4. Andrés, M.E., D'Argenio, P., van Rossum, P.: Significant diagnostic counterexamples in probabilistic model checking. In: Chockler, H., Hu, A.J. (eds.) HVC 2008. LNCS, vol. 5394, pp. 129–148. Springer, Heidelberg (2009)
5. Han, T., Katoen, J.P., Damman, B.: Counterexample generation in probabilistic model checking. IEEE Trans. on Software Engineering 35(2), 241–257 (2009)
6. Hansson, H., Jonsson, B.: A logic for reasoning about time and reliability. Formal Aspects of Computing 6(5), 512–535 (1994)
7. Itai, A., Rodeh, M.: Symmetry breaking in distributed networks. Information and Computation 88(1), 60–87 (1990)
8. Katoen, J.P., Zapreev, I.S., Hahn, E.M., Hermanns, H., Jansen, D.N.: The ins and outs of the probabilistic model checker MRMC. In: Proc. of QEST, pp. 167–176. IEEE CS, Los Alamitos (2009)
9. Kwiatkowska, M., Norman, G., Parker, D.: PRISM 4.0: Verification of probabilistic real-time systems. In: Gopalakrishnan, G., Qadeer, S. (eds.) CAV 2011. LNCS, vol. 6806, pp. 585–591. Springer, Heidelberg (2011)
10. Reiter, M.K., Rubin, A.D.: Crowds: Anonymity for web transactions. ACM Trans. on Information and System Security 1(1), 66–92 (1998)
11. Wimmer, R., Braitling, B., Becker, B.: Counterexample generation for discrete-time Markov chains using bounded model checking. In: Jones, N.D., Müller-Olm, M. (eds.) VMCAI 2009. LNCS, vol. 5403, pp. 366–380. Springer, Heidelberg (2009)

Efficient Loop Navigation for Symbolic Execution

Jan Obdržálek and Marek Trtík

Masaryk University, Brno, Czech Republic
{obdrzalek,trtik}@fi.muni.cz

Abstract. Symbolic execution is a successful technique used in software verification and testing. A key limitation of symbolic execution is in dealing with code containing loops. We introduce a technique which, given a start location above some loops and a target location anywhere below these loops, returns a feasible path between these two locations, if such a path exists. The technique infers a collection of constraint systems from the program and uses them to steer the symbolic execution towards the target. On reaching a loop it iteratively solves the appropriate constraint system to find out which path through this loop to take, or, alternatively, whether to continue below the loop. To construct the constraint systems we express the values of variables modified in a loop as functions of the number of times a given path through the loop was executed.

1 Introduction

Symbolic execution quickly reaches its limits when confronted with loops. As loops are widely used this is a significant problem. A typical situation is that reaching a particular location below a loop depends on the number of times this loop was iterated. Even worse, reaching that location may depend not only on the number of iterations, but also on what particular paths through the loop were chosen, and the order in which they were taken. Since in symbolic execution any iteration of a loop creates a new branch in the tree of symbolic executions, the size of the tree can become very large with even a single loop. Without deriving any information about the loop symbolic execution is forced to systematically explore all branches of this tree, running out of time even on small programs.

We aim to solve the following problem: Given a start location above a piece of code containing complicated loops, including loop sequences and loop nesting, and a target location anywhere in the code below, the goal is to find some feasible path between the start and target location, if such a path exists.

The idea behind our algorithm is relatively simple. On reaching a loop during symbolic execution we enquire an oracle which paths through this loop, and in which order, we should execute in order to reach the target location. Following the oracle's advice we get to our target, building path condition along the way. Only in our approach the oracle is replaced by a constraint system, which is less powerful. For each iteration it may suggest the next path to take, or to finish iterating this loop.

T. Bultan and P.-A. Hsiung (Eds.): ATVA 2011, LNCS 6996, pp. 453–462, 2011.

To build the constraint system we express the values of variables modified in a loop as functions of the number of times a given path through the loop was executed. This concept extends the simple one of counting loop iterations. Moreover, multiple counters for each path through the loop may be needed to correctly handle loop nesting. The expressed values are then 'merged' over all paths through a given loop. Constraint system is then created by taking branching conditions and replacing all variables with the corresponding functions of loop counters.

We suggest that our algorithm is most useful when integrated into existing tools based on symbolic execution. It would work as a specific search strategy, activated when a global search strategy needs to navigate to a specific program location below some complicated loop structure.

To evaluate our approach, we have built an experimental implementation of our technique – a tool called CBA. We tested CBA on nine benchmarks we designed to capture those loop structures which often appear in practice. We also compare the performance of CBA to successful symbolic execution tools PEX [16] and KLEE [3] and show that, on our set of benchmarks, CBA is several orders of magnitude faster than either of these tools.

Due to space restrictions many details have been left out. Interested reader is encouraged to read the full version [13].

2   Overview

Let us consider a program in Figure 1 (a). The goal is to find a feasible path to the assert statement on line 9 among the roughly 2^{30} possible execution paths. It took the symbolic execution tool PEX 99 seconds to find such a path. The problem here is that the condition on line 8 refers to the values of a and b, which depend on the input (the arrays A and B) only indirectly. Moreover when we substituted the predicate a>12 on line 8 with a>17 (thus line 9 becomes unreachable), PEX was not able to finish within 5 hours. Our technique works in three distinct phases:

```
1    int a=0, b=0;
2    for (int i=0; i<15; ++i)
3        if (A[i]==1)
4            ++a;
5    for (int j=0; j<15; ++j)
6        if (B[j]==2)
7            ++b;
8    if (a>12 && a+b==23)
9        assert(0);
```
(a)

c_0
```
a=0
b=0
i=0
i>=15 : {c_1, c_2}
j=0
j>=15 : {c_3, c_4}
a>12
a+b==23
```

c_1	c_3
i<15	j<15
A[i]==1	B[j]==2
++a	++b
++i	++j

c_2	c_4
i<15	j<15
A[i]!=1	B[j]!=2
++i	++j

(b)

Fig. 1. Example used throughout Section 2. **(a)** C program containing loops. **(b)** Its chain program form.

Phase 1: Conversion to chain normal form. To better facilitate reasoning about loops we represent the program using linear code fragments called *chains*. The decomposition of our program to chains (what we call *chain program form* later in the text) is shown in Figure 1 (b). Chain c_0 is the topmost chain (called *root chain* later in the paper), corresponding to a path through the code where we replace the outermost loops by constructs of the form $\varphi : \{c_1, c_2, \ldots\}$ with the following meaning: at this point chains $c_1, c_2, \ldots$ may be executed any number of times and in any order, but the condition φ must hold after we finish executing them. Note that the condition on line 8 was replaced by a pair of assertions.

As to the other chains, chain c_1 represents the path through the loop on lines 2-4 which goes through the positive branch of the if statement and c_2 the only other path through this loop. The same holds for the chains c_3 and c_4 and the loop at lines 5-7. One can easily see that there is a natural correspondence between the program (Figure 1 (a)) and its linear representation (Figure 1 (b)).

The task of finding some feasible path to the assert statement now depends on finding a proper interleaving of chains c_1 and c_2 for the first loop, and c_3 and c_4 for the second one.

$$
\begin{array}{cc}
\mathbf{c_1} & \mathbf{c_2} \\
i(\kappa_1) = \kappa_1 + \alpha_i & i(\kappa_2) = \kappa_2 + \alpha_i \\
a(\kappa_1) = \kappa_1 + \alpha_a & a(\kappa_2) = \alpha_a \\
\multicolumn{2}{c}{\{c_1, c_2\}} \\
\multicolumn{2}{c}{i(\kappa_1, \kappa_2) = \kappa_1 + \kappa_2 + \alpha_i} \\
\multicolumn{2}{c}{a(\kappa_1) = \kappa_1 + \alpha_a}
\end{array}
\qquad
\begin{array}{cc}
\mathbf{c_3} & \mathbf{c_4} \\
j(\kappa_3) = \kappa_3 + \alpha_j & j(\kappa_4) = \kappa_4 + \alpha_j \\
b(\kappa_3) = \kappa_3 + \alpha_b & b(\kappa_4) = \alpha_b \\
\multicolumn{2}{c}{\{c_3, c_4\}} \\
\multicolumn{2}{c}{j(\kappa_3, \kappa_4) = \kappa_3 + \kappa_4 + \alpha_j} \\
\multicolumn{2}{c}{b(\kappa_3) = \kappa_3 + \alpha_b}
\end{array}
$$

$$
\begin{array}{ll}
(1) \quad \kappa_1 + \kappa_2 \geq 15 & (4)\ \kappa_3 + \kappa_4 - 1 < 15 \ \text{if}\ \kappa_3 + \kappa_4 > 0 \\
(2)\ \kappa_1 + \kappa_2 - 1 < 15 \ \text{if}\ \kappa_1 + \kappa_2 > 0 & (5) \quad\quad \kappa_1 > 12 \\
(3) \quad\quad \kappa_3 + \kappa_4 \geq 15 & (6) \quad \kappa_1 + \kappa_3 = 23\ \kappa_1, \kappa_2, \kappa_3, \kappa_4 \in \mathbb{N}
\end{array}
$$

Fig. 2. Top: Recurrent variables expressed as functions of counters, including the functions after merging. **Bottom:** Constraint system $S(c_0)$ of the root chain $\mathbf{c_0}$.

Phase 2: Building a constraint system. We start by expressing the values of variables in each chain (except root chains) as functions of the number of times this chain was executed – κ_i. Each chain c_i is linked to *chain counter* κ_i, which takes values from $\mathbb{N}_0$. The link is given by the bottom index of the counter. We show how to compute the values of variables on chain c_1, using counter κ_1. Let α_i and α_a be the initial symbolic values of variables i and a, which are not known to this chain. Then $i(\kappa_1) = \kappa_1 + \alpha_i$ and $a(\kappa_1) = \kappa_1 + \alpha_a$ are the values of these variables expressed as functions of κ_1. The functions for the other chains are shown in Figure 2 (top). In terms of the original program we have introduced a counter for each unique path through each loop.

Now for any given variable i and each path through a given loop there may be different function expressing the value of i in terms of the relevant counter. In the second step we try to express the value of i by a single function of multiple counters. This abstracts from any concrete interleaving of the subchains, but the value of the variable is expressed precisely. So in the case of chains c_1 and c_2

the value of i can be expressed as $i(\kappa_1, \kappa_2) = \kappa_1 + \kappa_2 + \alpha_i$. The results for our example are presented in Figure 2 under the headings $\{c_1, c_2\}$ and $\{c_3, c_4\}$.

We can now build a constraint system for the topmost chain c_0. The constraints are obtained by processing all its assertions. There are four assertions in the chain c_0: i>=15, j>=15, a>12, and a+b==23. We replace the variables by their previously computed values (i.e. functions of counters), arriving the constraint system $\mathcal{S}(c_0)$ depicted at Figure 2 (bottom). The constraints (1), and (2) came from the assertion i>=15, (3), and (4) from the assertion j>=15, (5) from a>12, and finally (6) from a+b==23. The constraint (1) was computed as follows. First we substitute variables in the assertion by their values, obtaining $i(\kappa_1, \kappa_2) = \kappa_1 + \kappa_2 + \alpha_i \geq 15$. α_i represents the value of i on reaching the i>=15 : $\{c_1, c_2\}$ instruction. Here $\alpha_i = 0$, giving us the constraint (1), which speaks about the values of κ_1 and κ_2 just after the associated loop was executed for the last time. However, this also means that for all previous executions, where the values are $\kappa_1' \leq \kappa_1$ and $\kappa_2' \leq \kappa_2$ such that $\kappa_1' + \kappa_2' < \kappa_1 + \kappa_2$, the negated condition $i(\kappa_1', \kappa_2') < 15$ must hold – i.e. there is an additional constraint for each such choice of κ_1' and κ_2'. This can be rephrased as $\kappa_1 + \kappa_2 - a < 15$ for $a \in \{1, 2, \ldots, \kappa_1 + \kappa_2 - 1\}$. Our experimentation shows that it is sufficient to take only a single constraint for $a = 1$, giving us the constraint (2). Constraints (3), (5) and (6) are derived similarly to (1) and constraint (4) in the same way as (2). Note that we do not construct constraint systems for chains c_1, c_2, c_3, c_4 since they do not contain any subchains.

The point of the constructed constraint system $\mathcal{S}(c_0)$ is that only those executions which reach the assert statement satisfy $\mathcal{S}(c_0)$. Which in turn means that solving our constraint system will limit the space of paths we need to consider.

Phase 3: Navigating the symbolic execution. With the chains, counters and constraint systems in place we may proceed with the final stage of the algorithm – finding some feasible path to line 9. We do this by employing slightly modified symbolic execution. We initialize all counters to 0 and proceed down the chain c_0 in a standard way until we reach the line 4: i>=15: $\{c_1, c_2\}$ (i.e. the entry point of the first loop). There are two subchains c_1 and c_2 for this loop, linked to counters κ_1 and κ_2. Now we iteratively do the following:

- Check whether we can improve current solution of the system by incrementing κ_1 or κ_2. If we cannot, we stop iterating and continue down the chain c_0.
- Otherwise we call a decision procedure to tell us which counter to increment. This procedure will be described in more detail in Section 3.
- Lets assume κ_1 was chosen. In that case we symbolically execute the chain linked to κ_1, i.e. c_1. We also increment the counter κ_1.

Having solved the loop related to chains c_1 and c_2 we proceed with the execution, handling the loop related to chains c_3 and c_4 in the same way. Once we arrive at the end of c_0 we return the current path condition, which identifies a feasible path.

3   The Algorithm

Phase 1: Programs as Chains. We describe how to convert a program to chain program form. It may be helpful for the reader to follow the example in Fig. 1. We understand a program P to be expressed as a control flow graph. We write $u \to v$ ($u \to^* v$) if there is an edge (path) from u to v. We assume that there is a single start and a single terminal vertex (s_0 and t_0), and that P is in the static single assignment (SSA) form.

We define the *chain program form* $C(P)$ of P to be the set of all chains in P. A *chain* in P is a path in P which is of one of the two specific types: *Root chain* is a simple path (no vertex appear twice) $s_0 \to^* t_0$. *Subchain* is a simple path $v' \to^* v$ such that it is a suffix of some path $\pi : s_0 \to^* v \to v' \to^* v$ in P where v is the only vertex which appears twice in π. (If there are two different paths $s_0 \to^* v$, then the same path $v' \to^* v$ is treated as two different subchains.) In the rest of the paper we treat chains as linear sequences of vertices, and call their vertices *nodes*. In our example c_0 is the root chain, and $c_1 \ldots c_4$ are the subchains.

In chains there are three types of nodes – assume nodes, transform nodes and loop nodes. *Assume nodes*, e.g. a>12 in c_0, correspond to branching conditions. *Transform nodes*, e.g. j=0 in c_0, correspond to assignment statements which change the programs state. Finally *loop nodes*, e.g. i>=15 : $\{c_1, c_2\}$ in c_0, are those nodes, from which there is at least one edge in P to the first vertex of some subchain. We call such a subchain a chain *associated* to this node (c_1 and c_2 in this case). Note that each subchain corresponds to a unique path through a loop. In the following two phases of the algorithm we assume that there is only one root chain. If there are multiple root chains, we run the remaining two phases of the algorithm separately for each root chain. and the results are then combined in an obvious way.

Let $C(P)$ be the chain program form associated to a program P. Then an *execution path* in $C(P)$ is a sequence of nodes, which is created as follows: we take some root chain and take the nodes one by one. On reaching a loop node, we may either continue with the next node in the chain, or choose one of the subchains associated with this loop node. In that case we take this subchain and proceed recursively. On reaching the end in the subchain we go "one level up" to the associated loop node in the parent chain and repeat our choice to either take the next node of the parent chain or choose another associated subchain. We finish once we reach the terminal node for the root chain.

Theorem 1. *The algorithm described above converts each program P to chain normal form $C(P)$ such that for each path in P there is a corresponding execution path in $C(P)$ and vice versa. (By correspondence we mean that the sequences of instructions along these two paths are the same). Moreover if P is in SSA form, then so is each chain of $C(P)$.*

Phase 2: Building the Constraint Systems. Here we show how to build the constraint system $S(c)$ for each chain c. An important idea behind the construction is to express the values of variables used in loops as functions of counters for the subchains.

We proceed using modified symbolic execution. The modification is twofold: First, it works on chains, not programs. Second, the domain of symbolic values is extended to contain counters (and expressions using counters) and a special value $\star$ with the intended meaning "do not know". (Any expression containing $\star$ evaluates to $\star$.)

At the beginning each variable i has a symbolic value α_i and the constraint system $S(c)$ is empty. Next we symbolically execute the chain: Handling of the transform nodes is clear. Assume nodes are treated as sources of constraints for $S(c)$. Each assertion is first instantiated with the current values of variables, and then inserted to the constraint system only if it references some counter. On reaching a loop node n we first recursively build the constraint systems for all subchains associated to this node, obtaining symbolic values of variables (which can now depend on counters of some (possibly nested) subchains). For each variable we then merge the symbolic values obtained in the subchains (see the section *Merging values ...* below). The current symbolic state of c is then updated with the merged values. At this point we also detect the variables for which this chain is the reset chain (see the section *Expressing values ...* below). Since each loop node has an associated branching condition, we finish processing this condition as we would for the assume node. Finally, when we reach the end of the chain, we express the values of variables as functions of loop counters (and return these values). $S(c)$ now contains the complete constraint system for the chain c.

Expressing values using counters. The goal is for each variable to compute a function expressing its value in terms of counters. We focus on so called *recurrent variables*, which are the variables whose value 1) changes on the execution path corresponding to c and 2) their value is function of their initial value before executing c. An example of a recurrent variable is the variable i in the chain c_1, for which we get $i = \alpha_i + 1$. To detect recurrent variables for a given chain c we simply analyze symbolic state resulting from symbolic execution of this chain.

For each recurrent variable we express its value in terms of how many times the chain c was executed – using the counter κ_c associated with the chain c. In our example, $i(\kappa_1) = \alpha_i + \kappa_1$. We use a custom difference equation solver and only handle those recurrences which correspond to arithmetic (e.g. $i = \alpha_i + 7$) and geometric (e.g. $i = 3 \cdot \alpha_i$) progressions. In case we are not able to solve a recurrence, we use the "do not know" value $\star$.

An important point to make is that the initial value for i, α_i, can be set by some chain r, of which the current chain c is a subchain. Therefore the value of i does not depend only on the number of times c was executed, but, more specifically, on the number of times c was executed since last execution of r. Therefore the value of i in fact depends on a counter κ_c^r parametrized by two chains: the *update chain* c and the *reset chain* r – i.e. $i(\kappa_c^r) = \alpha_i + 2 \cdot \kappa_c^r$. This counter is incremented each time the chain c is executed, and set to zero each time the chain r executed. If there is no reset chain for a given variable, we use the plain counter κ_c, where c is the update chain and the root chain is used as the reset chain. Note that all counters used in our example in Figure 1 are of this type. The following statement is true for chain program forms, and follows from the fact all chains are in the SSA form:

Lemma 1. *Let v be a recurrent variable whose update chain is c. Then v is not reset in any subchain of c and there exists at most one superchain of c where v is reset.*

Merging values from subchains. We explain the merging process on the case of two subchains. The extension to multiple subchains is straightforward. Let us assume that a chain c has two subchains e, d with the associated counters being κ_e and κ_d (as the reset chains are not important here, we omit the upper indices) and there is a variable i value of which is expressed as $i = i_1(\kappa_e)$ in the first chain and $i = i_2(\kappa_d)$ in the second. We would like to "merge" the values of i – i.e. to find a function $i(\cdot, \cdot)$ such that $i = i(\kappa_e, \kappa_d)$. Let α_i be the symbolic value of i on entering the subchains. There are some simple cases: e.g. if $i_1(\kappa_e) = i_2(\kappa_d) = v$ for some constant v, then obviously also $i(\kappa_e, \kappa_d) = v$. Similarly if $i_1(\kappa_e) = i_2(\kappa_d) = \alpha_i$. On the other hand if $i_1(\kappa_e) = v_1 \neq v_2 = i_2(\kappa_d)$ then there is no such function $i(\kappa_e, \kappa_d)$. In that case we put $i(\kappa_e, \kappa_d) = \star$. The most interesting case is when both $i_1(\kappa_e)$ and $i_2(\kappa_d)$ depend on α_i – e.g. $i_1(\kappa_e) = v_1 \cdot \kappa_e + \alpha_i$ and $i_2(\kappa_d) = v_2 \cdot \kappa_d + \alpha_i$. This means that the value of i is updated in both subchains. In this case we can easily derive that $i(\kappa_e, \kappa_d) = v_1 \cdot \kappa_e + v_2 \cdot \kappa_d + \alpha_i$. In all other cases we put $i(\kappa_e, \kappa_d) = \star$.

Phase 3: Constraints-Driven Symbolic Execution. The last stage of our algorithm is to navigate (modified) symbolic execution in order to find a feasible path from s_0 to t_0. We modify the standard symbolic execution in order to run on the chain program form. To do so, we first extend the symbolic state by extra variables representing the values of counters. Second, on entering a chain, we instantiate all symbols α_v in the constraint system associated with the chain by their actual symbolic values.

The symbolic execution starts by setting all counters for which the current chain is the reset chain to zero and then proceeds on the root chain as normal until it reaches a loop node i. Let c be the currently executed chain, A its (instantiated) constraint system, i the processed loop node, and D be the subset of the set of subchains associated to i (containing those subchains which have not been yet explored during backtracking). If A has no solution, we immediately stop symbolic execution. Otherwise, if the current values of counters already form a solution of A, we continue executing c, as there is no reason to execute any of the subchains is D. Otherwise we need to choose a chain $d \in D$ which, hopefully, brings us closer to a solution of A. If there is such d, we continue with the symbolic execution of d. Finally if there is no such d, then we also continue executing c, hoping that we can closer to a solution of A at some loop node below.

Now we describe what we mean by "getting closer to a solution of A". Let w be a vector of current values of all the counters such that w is not a solution to A. We now ask whether there is a vector v on natural numbers such that 1) $v + w$ is a solution to A, and 2) there is a counter κ such that $d \in D$

(or some of its subchains) is the update chain for κ (reset chain for κ) and there is a positive (negative) number in the corresponding position in v. If yes, then executing the chain d gets us "closer to a solution of A".

Finally we have to say what happens when the symbolic execution reaches the terminal node of a chain c. We first increment all the associated counters κ_c^d (for all d). If c is a subchain we continue by (again) executing the associated loop node in the parent chain, otherwise c is a root chain and we reached the target node.

Theorem 2 (Soundness). *If the symbolic execution of $C(P)$ (as described in Section 3) terminates with success, then the returned path condition represents a feasible path from start to target instruction in the original program P. Moreover if the symbolic execution fails, then there is no feasible path in P to the target instruction.*

Theorem 3 (Incompleteness). *There exists a program P with reachable target instruction for which the symbolic execution of $C(P)$ never terminates.*

4   Experimental Results

To evaluate the effectiveness of our technique we implemented it in our tool CBA, and tested it on a set of nine benchmarks. We also compared the performance of CBA to that of two very successful tools PEX [16] and KLEE [3]. All the nine benchmarks share some common properties: 1. the code contains loops (so the benchmarks produce a huge symbolic execution tree), and 2. there is a unique location to be reached. In the first six benchmarks the goal is to find a feasible path to the target location, whereas in the last three there is no feasible path to the target location and the goal is to show that no feasible path exists.

The first three benchmarks **Hello/HW/HWM** are adapted from [1] (there is only verbal description, no code). The HWM benchmark accepts a C string as an input and scans the string for the presence of substrings `"Hello"`,`"World"`, `"At"` and `"Microsoft!"`. HW and Hello are simplified versions of the HWM benchmark, looking for the first two words (one word) only. In **DOIF** we model a typical piece of code which scans an input and, for each member of the input array, performs an action which depends on its value. This benchmark is supposed to exercise primarily the third stage of the algorithm. Branching inside the loops enormously expands the number of paths in the model. **DOIFex** is an extension of this benchmark, and tests behaviour on sequences of loops with internal branching. The **EQCNT** benchmark contains nested loops with branching, where a variable defined in the outermost scope is modified in the innermost loop. **EQCNTex** is a modified benchmark (in a sense two instances of EQCNT in sequence). The **OneLoop** benchmark consists of simple loop in which the variable i, with initial value 0, is increased by 4 in every iteration. Once the loop is finished we check whether i==15, which is false for any value of the input variable n. **TwoLoops** is a an extension of the previous benchmark by adding a second loop, whose loop condition depends on the value computed in the first loop.

We ran our benchmarks on an Intel i7/920 2.67GHz Windows machine with 6GB of RAM. The results are presented in Table 1. We measured the time required to reach the target location. Each benchmark has an associated timeout (column **t/o**), which was set according to the perceived difficulty of that particular benchmark. The success was defined as reaching the target location (or demonstrating it is not possible to reach this location) within the specified time limit. As we can see, CBA significantly outperforms both PEX and KLEE.

Table 1. Running times of PEX, KLEE and CBA

Test	t/o	PEX	KLEE	CBA
Hello	30m	3.234s	0.093s	0.026s
HW	1h	14.890s	37m 0s	0.175s
HWM	1h	**fail**	t/o	1.997s
DOIF	30m	t/o	t/o	0.388s
DOIFex	1h	t/o	t/o	1.745s
EQCNT	30m	1m 43s	t/o	0.191s

Test	t/o	PEX	KLEE	CBA
EQCNTex	1h	46m 12s	t/o	2.458s
OneLoop	30m	2m 14s	t/o	0.002s
TwoLoops	30m	1m 4s	t/o	0.003s

5 Related Work

Modern effective techniques based on symbolic execution are mostly hybrid, combining symbolic execution with other approaches. Firstly, there are the techniques based of combining (alternating) concrete and symbolic execution [6,15,16,7]. This approach primarily avoids the problems caused by limitations of SMT solvers. Although the practical usability is greatly improved, these techniques have no effect on the ability to handle loops. The second group of techniques combines symbolic execution with some validation method [8,12,9]. This approach is much more successful from the point of handling loops. Thanks to employing complementary techniques, many symbolic paths can be effectively pruned away when exploring the symbolic state space. This can often lead to effective navigation of symbolic execution in programs with loops. Finally there are also techniques which aim to make symbolic execution effective in the general case, not specifically focused on just programs with loops [2,5,1,3].

The idea of using constraint system for analyzing loops was considered before in different contexts. First approach, dating back to 70's, infers relations between program variables [11,4], while the more recent techniques are primarily focused on formal verification, and inductive invariant computation [10].

The technique of Loop-Extended Symbolic Execution [14] (LESE) is probably the one most closely related to our approach. The LESE approach introduces symbolic variables for the number of times each loop was executed, and links these with features of a known input grammar such as variable-length or repeating fields. This allows the symbolic constraints to cover a class of paths that includes different number of loop iterations, expressing loop-dependent program values in terms of properties of the input.

Acknowledgements. We would like to thank N. Tillmann for answering our questions about Pex. We also thank V. Brožek, V. Forejt, A. Kučera and J. Strejček for their helpful comments. The work has been supported by the Institute for Theoretical Computer Science, project No. 1M0545.

References

1. Anand, S., Godefroid, P., Tillmann, N.: Demand-driven compositional symbolic execution. In: Ramakrishnan, C.R., Rehof, J. (eds.) TACAS 2008. LNCS, vol. 4963, pp. 367–381. Springer, Heidelberg (2008)
2. Boonstoppel, P., Cadar, C., Engler, D.: RWset: Attacking path explosion in constraint-based test generation. In: Ramakrishnan, C.R., Rehof, J. (eds.) TACAS 2008. LNCS, vol. 4963, pp. 351–366. Springer, Heidelberg (2008)
3. Cadar, C., Dunbar, D., Engler, D.: KLEE: Unassisted and automatic generation of high-coverage tests for complex systems programs. In: OSDI 2008, pp. 209–224. USENIX Association (2008)
4. Cousot, P., Halbwachs, N.: Automatic discovery of linear restraints among variables of a program. In: POPL 1978, pp. 84–96. ACM, New York (1978)
5. Godefroid, P.: Compositional dynamic test generation. In: POPL 2007, pp. 47–54. ACM, New York (2007)
6. Godefroid, P., Klarlund, N., Sen, K.: DART: directed automated random testing. In: PLDI 2005, pp. 213–223. ACM, New York (2005)
7. Godefroid, P., Levin, M.Y., Molnar, D.A.: Automated whitebox fuzz testing. In: Network Distributed Security Symposium (NDSS), pp. 151–166 (2008)
8. Godefroid, P., Nori, A.V., Rajamani, S.K., Tetali, S.D.: Compositional must program analysis: unleashing the power of alternation. In: POPL 2010, pp. 43–56. ACM, New York (2010)
9. Gulavani, B.S., Henzinger, T.A., Kannan, Y., Nori, A.V., Rajamani, S.K.: SYNERGY: a new algorithm for property checking. In: SIGSOFT 2006/FSE-14, pp. 117–127. ACM, New York (2006)
10. Gulwani, S., Srivastava, S., Venkatesan, R.: Program analysis as constraint solving. In: PLDI 2008, pp. 281–292. ACM, New York (2008)
11. Karr, M.: Affine relationships among variables of a program. Acta Informatica 6, 133–151 (1976)
12. Nori, A.V., Rajamani, S.K., Tetali, S., Thakur, A.V.: The Yogi project: Software property checking via static analysis and testing. In: Kowalewski, S., Philippou, A. (eds.) TACAS 2009. LNCS, vol. 5505, pp. 178–181. Springer, Heidelberg (2009)
13. Obdržálek, J., Trtík, M.: Efficient loop navigation for symbolic execution. arXiv:1107.1398v1 [cs.PL] (2011)
14. Saxena, P., Poosankam, P., McCamant, S., Song, D.: Loop-extended symbolic execution on binary programs. In: ISSTA 2009, pp. 225–236. ACM, New York (2009)
15. Sen, K., Marinov, D., Agha, G.: CUTE: a concolic unit testing engine for C. In: ESEC/FSE-13, pp. 263–272. ACM, New York (2005)
16. Tillmann, N., de Halleux, J.: Pex – white box test generation for .NET. In: Beckert, B., Hähnle, R. (eds.) TAP 2008. LNCS, vol. 4966, pp. 134–153. Springer, Heidelberg (2008)

An Efficient Algorithm for Learning Event-Recording Automata[*]

Shang-Wei Lin[1], Étienne André[1], Jin Song Dong[1], Jun Sun[2], and Yang Liu[1]

[1] School of Computing, National University of Singapore
{linsw,andre,dongjs,liuyang}@comp.nus.edu.sg
[2] Singapore University of Technology and Design
{sunjun}@sutd.edu.sg

Abstract. In inference of untimed regular languages, given an unknown language to be inferred, an automaton is constructed to accept the unknown language from answers to a set of membership queries each of which asks whether a string is contained in the unknown language. One of the most well-known regular inference algorithms is the L^* algorithm, proposed by Angluin in 1987, which can learn a minimal deterministic finite automaton (DFA) to accept the unknown language. In this work, we propose an efficient polynomial time learning algorithm, TL^*, for timed regular language accepted by event-recording automata. Given an unknown timed regular language, TL^* first learns a DFA accepting the untimed version of the timed language, and then passively refines the DFA by adding time constraints. We prove the correctness, termination, and minimality of the proposed TL^* algorithm.

1 Introduction

In formal verification such as model checking [4,13], system models and properties are assumed to be a priori during the verification process. However, modeling a system appropriately is not an easy task because if the model is too abstract, it may not describe the exact behavior of the system; if the model is too detailed, it suffers from the state space explosion problem. Thus an automatic inference or construction of abstract model is very helpful for system development.

In 1987, Angluin [3] proposed the L^* learning algorithm for inference of regular languages. Given an unknown language U to be inferred, L^* learns a minimal deterministic finite automaton (DFA) to accept U from answers to a set of membership queries each of which asks whether a string is contained in U.

After the L^* algorithm was proposed, it is widely used in several research fields. The most impressive one is that Cobleigh et al. [5] used the L^* algorithm to automatically generate the assumptions needed in assume-guarantee reasoning (AGR), which can alleviate the state explosion problem of model checking. Another interesting work is that Lin and Hsiung proposed a compositional synthesis

---

[*] This research is supported by the research grant MOE2009-T2-1-072 (Advanced Model Checking Systems) in School of Computing, National University of Singapore.

T. Bultan and P.-A. Hsiung (Eds.): ATVA 2011, LNCS 6996, pp. 463–472, 2011.

framework, CAGS [10], based on the L* algorithm to automatically eliminate all behavior violating the user-given properties.

However, there were almost no extensions of the learning algorithm to inference timed regular languages until 2004, Grinchtein et al. [7,8] proposed a learning algorithm for event-recording automata [2] based on L*. Grinchtein's learning algorithm, TL^*_{sg}, uses region construction to actively guess all possible time constraints for each untimed word. That is, each original membership query of an untimed word in L* gives rise to several membership queries of timed words with possible time constraints, which increases the number of membership queries exponentially with the largest constant appearing in the time constraints.

In this work, we propose an efficient *polynomial time* learning algorithm TL^* for timed regular languages accepted by event-recording automata. *Event-recording automata* (ERA) [2] are a determinizable subclass of timed automata [1] such that a timed language accepted by an ERA can be classified into finite number of classes. Given a timed regular language U_T accepted by ERA, TL^* first learns a DFA M accepting U (the untimed version of U_T) and then passively refines M by adding time constraints. Thus the number of membership queries required by TL^* is much smaller than that of Grinchtein's algorithm. We prove that the TL^* algorithm will correctly learn an ERA accepting the unknown language U_T after a finite number of iterations. Further, we also prove the minimality of our TL^* algorithm, i.e., the number of locations of the ERA learned by TL^* is minimal.

This paper is organized as follows: Section 2 gives preliminary knowledge and introduces the L* algorithm. The proposed efficient learning algorithm, TL^*, is described in Section 3. The conclusion and future work are given in Section 4.

2   Preliminaries

We give some background knowledge about timed languages and event-recording automata in Section 2.1 and introduce the L* algorithm in Section 2.2.

2.1   Timed Languages and Event-Recording Automata

Let Σ be a finite alphabet. A *timed word* over Σ is a finite sequence $w_t = (a_1, t_1)(a_2, t_2) \ldots (a_n, t_n)$ of symbols $a_i \in \Sigma$ for $i \in \{1, 2, \ldots, n\}$ that are paired with nonnegative real numbers $t_i \in \mathbb{R}^+$ such that the sequence $\bar{t} = t_1 t_2 \ldots t_n$ of time-stamps is nondecreasing. For every symbol $a \in \Sigma$, we use x_a to denote the *event-recording clock* of a [2]. Intuitively, x_a records the time elapsed since the last occurrence of the symbol a. We use C_Σ to denote the set of event-recording clocks over Σ, i.e., $C_\Sigma = \{x_a \mid a \in \Sigma\}$. A *clock valuation* $\gamma : C_\Sigma \mapsto \mathbb{R}^+$ assigns a nonnegative real number to an event-recording clock.

A *clocked word* over Σ is a finite sequence $w_c = (a_1, \gamma_1)(a_2, \gamma_2) \ldots (a_n, \gamma_n)$ of symbols $a_i \in \Sigma$ for $i \in \{1, 2, \ldots, n\}$ that are paired with clock valuations γ_i such that $\gamma_1(x_a) = \gamma_1(x_b)$ for all $a, b \in \Sigma$ and $\gamma_i(x_a) = \gamma_{i-1}(x_a) + \gamma_i(x_{a_{i-1}})$ when $1 < i \leq n$ and $a \neq a_{i-1}$. Each timed word $w_t = (a_1, t_1)(a_2, t_2) \ldots (a_n, t_n)$ can be naturally transformed into a clocked word $cw(w_t) = (a_1, \gamma_1)(a_2, \gamma_2) \ldots (a_n, \gamma_n)$

where $\gamma_i(x_a) = t_i$ if $a_j \neq a$ for $1 \leq j < i$; $\gamma_i(x_a) = t_i - t_j$ if there exists a_j such that $a_j = a$ for $1 \leq j < i$ and $a_k \neq a$ for $j < k < i$.

A *clock guard* g is a conjunction of constraints of the form $x_a \sim n$ for $x_a \in C_\Sigma$, $n \in \mathbb{N}$, and $\sim \in \{<, \leq, >, \geq\}$. A clock guard g identifies a hypercube zone $[\![g]\!] \subseteq (\mathbb{R}^+)^{|\Sigma|}$. We use G_Σ to denote the set of clock guards over C_Σ. A *guarded word* is a sequence $w_g = (a_1, g_1)(a_2, g_2) \dots (a_n, g_n)$ where $a_i \in \Sigma$ for $i \in \{1, 2, \dots, n\}$ and $g_i \in G_\Sigma$ is a clock guard. For a clocked word $w_c = (a_1, \gamma_1)(a_2, \gamma_2) \dots (a_n, \gamma_n)$, we use $w_c \models w_g$ to denote $\gamma_i \models g_i$ for all $i \in \{1, 2, \dots, n\}$.

Definition 1. (Event-Recording Automata) *[2]. An* event-recording automaton *(ERA)* $D = (\Sigma, L, l_0, \delta, L^f)$ *consists of a finite input alphabet* Σ, *a finite set* L *of locations, an initial location* $l^0 \in L$, *a set* L^f *of accepting locations, and a transition function* $\delta : \subseteq L \times \Sigma \times G_\Sigma \mapsto 2^L$. *An ERA is deterministic if* $\delta(l, a, g)$ *is a singleton set when it is defined, and when both* $\delta(l, a, g_1)$ *and* $\delta(l, a, g_2)$ *are both defined then* $[\![g_1]\!] \cap [\![g_2]\!] = \emptyset$, *where* $l \in L$, $a \in \Sigma$, *and* $g_1, g_2 \in G_\Sigma$. *A deterministic ERA is* complete *if for all* $l \in L$ *and for all* $a \in \Sigma$, $\delta(l, a, g_i)$ *is defined for all* $i \in \{1, 2, \dots, n\}$ *such that* $[\![g_1]\!] \cup [\![g_2]\!] \cup \dots \cup [\![g_n]\!] = [\![true]\!]$. *A guarded word* $w_g = (a_1, g_1)(a_2, g_2) \dots (a_n, g_n)$ *is accepted by an ERA* $D = (\Sigma, L, l_0, \delta, L^f)$ *if* $l_i = \delta(l_{i-1}, a_i, g_i)$ *is defined for all* $i \in \{1, 2, \dots, n\}$ *and* $l_n \in L^f$. *The language accepted by* D, *denoted by* $\mathcal{L}(D)$, *is the set of guarded words accepted by* D.

Note that in an ERA, each event-recording clock $x_a \in C_\Sigma$ is implicitly and automatically reset when a transition with event a is taken, which gives a good characteristic that each non-deterministic ERA can be determinized by subset construction [2]. Fig. 1 (a) p. 467 gives a deterministic ERA $\mathcal{A}_1$ accepting the timed word $(a, t_1)(a, t_2)(a, t_3) \dots$, where $t_{2i} = t_{2i-1} + 3$ and $t_{2i+1} = t_{2i} + 1$ for $i \in \mathbb{N}$. We can also use a clocked word $(a, \gamma_1)(a, \gamma_2)(a, \gamma_3) \dots$ to represent the timed word such that $\gamma_{2i-1}(x_a) = 1$ and $\gamma_{2i}(x_a) = 3$ for $i \in \mathbb{N}$. Or we can use a guarded word $(a, g_1)(a, g_2)(a, g_3) \dots$ to represent the timed word such that $g_{2i-1} = (x_a = 1)$ and $g_{2i} = (x_a = 3)$ for $i \in \mathbb{N}$. Thus $\mathcal{A}_1$ accepts the timed language $\mathcal{L}(\mathcal{A}_1) = ((a, x_a = 1)(a, x_a = 3))^*$.

2.2   The L* Algorithm

The L* algorithm [3] is a formal method to learn a minimal DFA (with the minimal number of locations) that accepts an unknown language U over an alphabet Σ. During the learning process, L* interacts with a *Minimal Adequate Teacher* (Teacher for short) to ask *membership* and *candidate* queries. A *membership query* for a string σ is a function $\mathcal{Q}_m$ such that if $\sigma \in U$, then $\mathcal{Q}_m(\sigma) = 1$; otherwise, $\mathcal{Q}_m(\sigma) = 0$. A *candidate query* for a DFA M is a function $\mathcal{Q}_c$ such that if $\mathcal{L}(M) = U$, then $\mathcal{Q}_c(M) = 1$; otherwise, $\mathcal{Q}_c(M) = 0$. The results of membership queries are stored in an *observation table* (S, E, T) where $S \subseteq \Sigma^*$ is a set of prefixes, $E \subseteq \Sigma^*$ is a set of suffixes, and $T : (S \cup S \cdot \Sigma) \times E \mapsto \{0, 1\}$ is a mapping function such that if $s \cdot e \in U$, then $T(s, e) = 1$; otherwise, i.e., $s \cdot e \notin U$, then $T(s, e) = 0$, where $s \in (S \cup S \cdot \Sigma)$ and $e \in E$. The L* algorithm categorizes strings based on Myhill-Nerode Congruence [9].

Algorithm 1. L* Algorithm

---

input : Σ: alphabet
output: a DFA accepting the unknown language U

1 Let $S = E = \{\lambda\}$;
2 Update T by $\mathcal{Q}_m(\lambda)$ and $\mathcal{Q}_m(\lambda \cdot \alpha)$, for all $\alpha \in \Sigma$;
3 **while** *true* **do**
4   **while** *there exists* $(s \cdot \alpha)$ *such that* $(s \cdot \alpha) \not\equiv s'$ *for all* $s' \in S$ **do**
5         $S \longleftarrow S \cup \{s \cdot \alpha\}$;
6   Update T by $\mathcal{Q}_m((s \cdot \alpha) \cdot \beta)$, for all $\beta \in \Sigma$;
7   Construct candidate DFA M from (S, E, T) ;
8   **if** $\mathcal{Q}_c(M) = 1$ **then** **return** M ;
9   **else**
10        $\sigma_{ce} \longleftarrow$ the counterexample given by Teacher ;
11        $E \longleftarrow E \cup \{v\}$ where $v = WS(\sigma_{ce})$;
12   Update T by $\mathcal{Q}_m(s \cdot v)$ and $\mathcal{Q}_m(s \cdot \alpha \cdot v)$, for all $s \in S$ and $\alpha \in \Sigma$;

Definition 2. Myhill-Nerode Congruence. *For any two strings $\sigma, \sigma' \in \Sigma^*$, we say they are* equivalent, *denoted by $\sigma \equiv \sigma'$, if $\sigma \cdot \rho \in U \Leftrightarrow \sigma' \cdot \rho \in U$, for all $\rho \in \Sigma^*$. Under the equivalence relation, we can say σ and σ' are the representing strings of each other, denoted by $\sigma = [\sigma']_r$ and $\sigma' = [\sigma]_r$.*

L* will always keep the observation table *closed* and *consistent*. An observation table is *closed* if for all $s \in S$ and $\alpha \in \Sigma$, there always exists $s' \in S$ such that $s \cdot \alpha \equiv s'$. An observation table is *consistent* if for every two elements $s, s' \in S$ such that $s \equiv s'$, then $(s \cdot \alpha) \equiv (s' \cdot \alpha)$ for all $\alpha \in \Sigma$. Once the table (S, E, T) is closed and consistent, the L* algorithm will construct a corresponding candidate DFA $C = (\Sigma_C, L_C, l_C^0, \delta_C, L_C^f)$ such that $\Sigma_C = \Sigma$, $L_C = S$, $l_C^0 = \{\lambda\}$, $\delta_C(s, \alpha) = [s \cdot \alpha]_r$ for $s \in S$ and $\alpha \in \Sigma$, and $L_C^f = \{s \in S \mid T(s, \lambda) = 1\}$.

Subsequently, L* makes a candidate query for C. If $\mathcal{L}(C) \neq U$, Teacher gives a counterexample σ_{ce} such that σ_{ce} is *positive* if $\sigma_{ce} \in \mathcal{L}(U) \setminus \mathcal{L}(C)$; *negative* if $\sigma_{ce} \in \mathcal{L}(C) \setminus \mathcal{L}(U)$. L* analyzes the counterexample σ_{ce} to find the witness suffix. A *witness suffix* is a string that when appended to two strings provides enough evidence for the two strings to be classified into two different equivalence classes under the Myhill-Nerode Congruence. Given an observation table (S, E, T) and a counterexample σ_{ce}, we define an *i-decomposition query* of σ_{ce}, denoted by $\mathcal{Q}_m^i(\sigma_{ce})$, as follows: $\mathcal{Q}_m^i(\sigma_{ce}) = \mathcal{Q}_m([u_i]_r \cdot v_i)$ where $\sigma_{ce} = u_i \cdot v_i$ with $|u_i| = i$, and $[u_i]_r$ is the representing string of u_i in S. The *witness suffix* of σ_{ce}, denoted by $WS(\sigma_{ce})$, is the suffix v_i of σ_{ce} such that $\mathcal{Q}_m^i(\sigma_{ce}) \neq \mathcal{Q}_m^0(\sigma_{ce})$. Once the witness suffix $WS(\sigma_{ce})$ is obtained, L* uses it to refine the candidate C until $\mathcal{L}(C) = \mathcal{L}(U)$. The pseudo-code of the L* algorithm is given in Algorithm 1.

Assume Σ is the alphabet of the unknown regular language U and the number of locations of the minimal DFA is n. The L* algorithm needs $n - 1$ candidate queries and $O(|\Sigma|n^2 + n \log m)$ membership queries to learn the minimal DFA, where m is the length of the longest counterexample returned by Teacher.

3   An Efficient Algorithm for Learning ERA

The intuition behind the L* algorithm is to classify untimed words into the minimal finite number of classes by performing membership queries, and each class can be represented by a location of a DFA. Because event-recording automata (ERA) are determinizable, a timed language (guarded words) accepted by an ERA can also be classified into a finite number of classes. The TL* algorithm tries to find the finite and minimal number of classes (locations).

3.1   The TL* Algorithm

Given a timed language U_T, the proposed TL* algorithm interacts with a timed Teacher to make two types of queries: the *timed membership* and *timed candidate queries*. A *timed membership query* for a guarded word w_g is a function $\mathcal{Q}_{m^T}$ such that $\mathcal{Q}_{m^T}(w_g) = 1$ if $w_g \in U_T$; otherwise $\mathcal{Q}_{m^T}(w_g) = 0$. A *timed candidate query* for an ERA M is a function $\mathcal{Q}_{c^T}$ such that $\mathcal{Q}_{c^T}(M) = 1$ if $\mathcal{L}(M) = U_T$; otherwise, $\mathcal{Q}_{c^T}(M) = 0$. TL* assumes Teacher can answer membership queries for guarded words (instead of timed words) and give counterexamples in guarded words for candidate queries. This is not a strong assumption since there are data structures such as DBM [6] to represent time symbolically.

Algorithm 2 gives the pseudo-code of the TL* algorithm. The idea behind TL* is to first learn a DFA M accepting $Untime(U_T)$, the untimed language with respect to U_T, and then to refine the untimed language by adding time constraints. Therefore, TL* consists of two phases, namely the *untimed learning* phase (Lines 1-3) and the *timed refinement* phase (Lines 7-22). Note that the splitting of zones in Line 10 can be done by DBM subtraction [11].

We use an example to illustrate the TL* algorithm. Suppose the timed language U_T to be learned is accepted by the ERA $\mathcal{A}_1$ as shown in Fig. 1 (a). In the untimed learning phase, L* is used to learn the DFA M_1, as shown in Fig. 1 (c), accepting the untimed language a^*, and the observation table (S, E, T) obtained by L* is shown in Fig. 1 (b). At this time, $\Sigma = \{a\}$, $S = \{\lambda\}$, and $E = \{\lambda\}$.

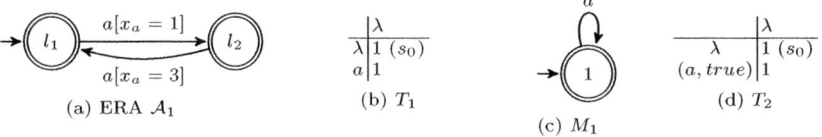

(a) ERA $\mathcal{A}_1$ (b) T_1 (c) M_1 (d) T_2

Fig. 1. Untimed Learning Phase

In the timed refinement phase, TL* first modifies the alphabet and the observation table into timed version, i.e., $\Sigma = \{(a, true)\}$, $S = \{(\lambda, true)\}$, and $E = \{(\lambda, true)\}$. The current timed observation table T_2 is shown in Fig. 1 (d). Then, TL* performs the timed candidate query for the first candidate ERA M_1. However, the answer to the candidate query is "no" with a negative counterexample $(a, x_a < 1) \in \mathcal{L}(M_1)\backslash\mathcal{L}(U_T)$. Because there is a prefix $(a, true)$ in the observation such that $[\![x_a < 1]\!] \subset [\![true]\!]$, the prefix $(a, true)$ is split into $(a, x_a < 1)$ and

---

Algorithm 2. TL* Algorithm

---

input : Σ: alphabet, C_Σ: the set of event-recording clocks

output: a deterministic ERA accepting the unknown timed language U_T

1 Use L^* to learn a DFA M accepting $Untime(U_T)$;
2 Let (S, E, T) be the observation table during the L* learning process ;
3 Replace α by $(\alpha, true)$, s by $(s, true)$, and e by $(e, true)$ for each $\alpha \in \Sigma$, $s \in S$ and $e \in E$;
4 **while** *true* **do**
5 $\quad$ **if** $Q_c^T(M) = 1$ **then** **return** M ;
6 $\quad$ **else**
7 $\qquad$ Let $(a_1, g_1)(a_2, g_2) \cdots (a_n, g_n)$ be the counterexample given by Teacher ;
8 $\qquad$ **foreach** (a_i, g_i), $i \in \{1, 2, \ldots, n\}$ **do**
9 $\qquad\quad$ **if** (a_i, g) *is a substring of* p *or* e *for some* $p \in S \cup (S \cdot \Sigma)$ *and* $e \in E$ *such that* $[\![g_i]\!] \subset [\![g]\!]$ **then**
10 $\qquad\qquad$ Let $G = \{\hat{g_1}, \hat{g_2}, \ldots, \hat{g_m}\}$ obtained by $[\![g]\!] - [\![g_i]\!]$;
11 $\qquad\qquad$ $\Sigma \longleftarrow \Sigma \setminus \{(a_i, g)\} \cup \{(a_i, g_i), (a_i, \hat{g_1}), (a_i, \hat{g_2}), \ldots, (a_i, \hat{g_m})\}$;
12 $\qquad\qquad$ Split p into $\{\hat{p_0}, \hat{p_1}, \hat{p_2}, \ldots, \hat{p_m}\}$ where (a_i, g_i) is a substring of $\hat{p_0}$ and $(a_i, \hat{g_j})$ is a substring of $\hat{p_j}$ for all $j \in \{1, 2, \ldots, m\}$;
13 $\qquad\qquad$ Split e into $\{\hat{e_0}, \hat{e_1}, \hat{e_2}, \ldots, \hat{e_m}\}$ where (a_i, g_i) is a substring of $\hat{e_0}$ and $(a_i, \hat{g_j})$ is a substring of $\hat{e_j}$ for all $j \in \{1, 2, \ldots, m\}$;
14 $\qquad\qquad$ Update T by $Q_{mT}(\hat{p_j} \cdot \hat{e_j})$ for all $j \in \{0, 1, 2, \ldots, m\}$;
15 $\qquad$ **while** *there exists* $(s \cdot \alpha)$ *such that* $s \cdot \alpha \not\equiv s'$ *for all* $s' \in S$ **do**
16 $\qquad\quad$ $S \longleftarrow S \cup \{s \cdot \alpha\}$;
17 $\qquad\quad$ Update T by $Q_{mT}((s \cdot \alpha) \cdot \beta)$ for all $\beta \in \Sigma$;
18 $\qquad$ $v \longleftarrow WS((a_1, g_1)(a_2, g_2) \cdots (a_n, g_n))$;
19 $\qquad$ **if** $|v| > 0$ **then**
20 $\qquad\quad$ $E \longleftarrow E \cup \{v\}$;
21 $\qquad\quad$ Update T by $Q_{mT}(s \cdot v)$ and $Q_{mT}(s \cdot \alpha \cdot v)$ for all $s \in S$ and $\alpha \in \Sigma$;
22 $\qquad$ Construct candidate M from (S, E, T) ;

$(a, x_a \geq 1)$, and the timed membership queries for $(a, x_a < 1)$ and $(a, x_a \geq 1)$ are performed, respectively. The current observation table T_3 is shown in Fig. 2 (a). However, T_3 is not closed because there is $(a, x_a < 1)$ with no $s \in S$ such that $s \equiv (a, x_a < 1)$, so $(a, x_a < 1)$ is added into S and the membership queries for $(a, x_a < 1)(a, x_a < 1)$ and $(a, x_a < 1)(a, x_a \geq 1)$ are performed, respectively. The closed observation table T_4 and its the corresponding ERA M_2 are shown in Fig. 2 (b) and (c), respectively. At this time, $\Sigma = \{(a, x_a < 1), (a, x_a \geq 1)\}$, $S = \{(\lambda, true), (a, x_a < 1)\}$, and $E = \{(\lambda, true)\}$.

In the second iteration of the timed refinement phase, TL* performs the timed candidate query for M_2. However, the answer is still "no" with a positive counterexample $(a, x_a = 1) \in \mathcal{L}(U_T) \setminus \mathcal{L}(M_2)$. Because there are two prefixes $(a, x_a \geq 1)$ and $(a, x_a < 1)(x_a \geq 1)$ in the observation table (S, E, T) such that $[\![x_a = 1]\!] \subset [\![x_a \geq 1]\!]$, the prefix $(a, x_a \geq 1)$ is split into $(a, x_a = 1)$ and $(a, x_a > 1)$, and the prefix $(a, x_a < 1)(x_a \geq 1)$ is split into $(a, x_a < 1)(x_a = 1)$ and $(a, x_a < 1)(x_a > 1)$, respectively. The timed membership queries for the

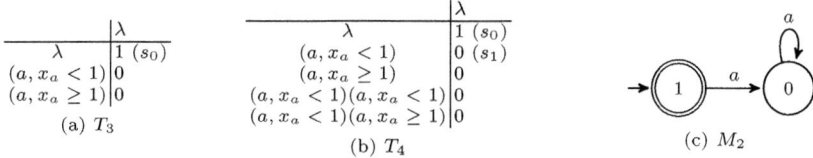

Fig. 2. Timed Refinement 1

new prefixes are performed. The current closed observation table T_5 and its corresponding ERA M_3 are shown in Fig. 3 (a) and (b), respectively. At this time, $\Sigma = \{(a, x_a < 1), (a, x_a = 1), (a, x_a > 1)\}$, $S = \{(\lambda, true), (a, x_a < 1)\}$, and $E = \{(\lambda, true)\}$.

Fig. 3. Timed Refinement 2

In the third iteration of the timed refinement phase, TL* performs the timed candidate query for the ERA M_3. However, the answers is still "no" with a negative counterexample $\pi = (a, x_a = 1)(a, x_a = 1) \in \mathcal{L}(M_3) \setminus \mathcal{L}(U_T)$. This time, no prefix or suffix in the observation table has to be split. TL* analyzes the counterexample as follows. $Q^0_{m^T}(\pi) = Q_{m^T}((a, x_a = 1)(a, x_a = 1)) = 0$. $Q^1_{m^T}(\pi) = Q^1_{m^T}([(a, x_a = 1)]_r(a, x_a = 1)) = Q_{m^T}((a, x_a = 1)) = 1 \neq Q^0_{m^T}(\pi)$. Thus, we have a witness suffix $v = (a, x_a = 1)$, and v is added into the set E. Then the membership queries for $s \cdot (a, x_a = 1)$ for all $s \in S$ are performed. The closed observation table T_7 and its corresponding ERA M_4 are shown in Fig. 4 (a) and (b), respectively. At this time, $\Sigma = \{(a, x_a < 1), (a, x_a = 1), (a, x_a > 1)\}$, $S = \{(\lambda, true), (a, x_a < 1), (a, x_a = 1)\}$, and $E = \{(\lambda, true), (a, x_a = 1)\}$.

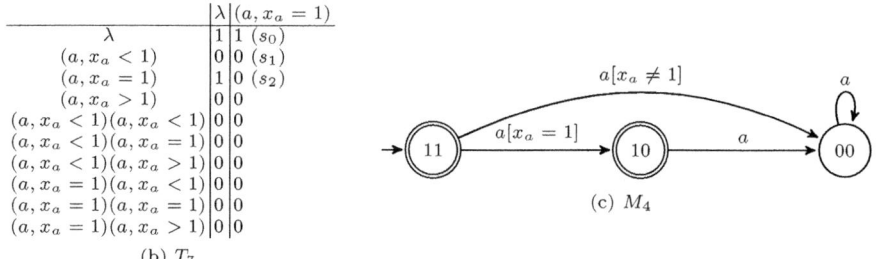

Fig. 4. Timed Refinement 3

In the fourth iteration of the timed refinement phase, TL* performs the timed candidate query for the ERA M_4 again. However, the answer is still "no" with a positive counterexample $\pi = (a, x_a = 1)(a, x_a = 3) \in \mathcal{L}(U_T) \setminus \mathcal{L}(M_4)$. Three prefixes $(a, x_a > 1)$, $(a, x_a < 1)(a, x_a > 1)$, and $(a, x_a = 1)(a, x_a > 1)$ in the observation table T_7 have to be split, and the new split prefixes are shown in Fig. 5 (a). The timed membership queries for the new split prefixes concatenated with e for all $e \in E$ are performed. Then the TL* algorithm analyzes the counterexample. Since $Q_{m^T}^0(\pi) = Q_{m^T}^1(\pi) = Q_{m^T}^2(\pi)$, therefore there is no witness suffix for π. The closed observation table T_8 is shown in Fig. 5 (a), and it corresponding ERA M_5 is constructed as shown in Fig. 5 (b). At this time, $\Sigma = \{(a, x_a < 1), (a, x_a = 1), (a, 1 < x_a < 3), (a, x_a = 3), (a, x_a > 3)\}$, $E = \{(\lambda, true), (a, x_a < 1), (a, x_a = 1)\}$, and $E = \{(\lambda, true), (a, x_a = 1)\}$.

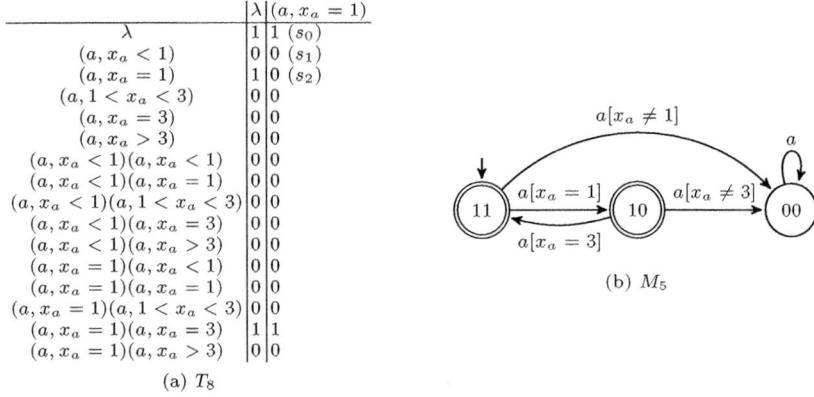

	λ	$(a, x_a = 1)$
λ	1	1 (s_0)
$(a, x_a < 1)$	0	0 (s_1)
$(a, x_a = 1)$	1	0 (s_2)
$(a, 1 < x_a < 3)$	0	0
$(a, x_a = 3)$	0	0
$(a, x_a > 3)$	0	0
$(a, x_a < 1)(a, x_a < 1)$	0	0
$(a, x_a < 1)(a, x_a = 1)$	0	0
$(a, x_a < 1)(a, 1 < x_a < 3)$	0	0
$(a, x_a < 1)(a, x_a = 3)$	0	0
$(a, x_a < 1)(a, x_a > 3)$	0	0
$(a, x_a = 1)(a, x_a < 1)$	0	0
$(a, x_a = 1)(a, x_a = 1)$	0	0
$(a, x_a = 1)(a, 1 < x_a < 3)$	0	0
$(a, x_a = 1)(a, x_a = 3)$	1	1
$(a, x_a = 1)(a, x_a > 3)$	0	0

(a) T_8

(b) M_5

Fig. 5. Timed Refinement 4

In the fifth iteration of the timed refinement, TL* performs the timed candidate query for M_5. This time, Teacher says that $\mathcal{L}(M_5) = U_T$, and the learning process of TL* is finished.

3.2 Analysis of the TL* Algorithm

Given a timed language U_T accepted by a deterministic ERA $\mathcal{A} = (\Sigma, L, l_0, \delta, L^f)$, TL* learns $Com(\mathcal{A})$ to accept U_T. In the learning process of TL*, each untimed word $(\alpha, true)$ for $\alpha \in \Sigma$ might be split into $|G_{\mathcal{A}}|$ timed words, where $G_{\mathcal{A}}$ is the set of clock zones partitioned by the clock guards appearing in $\mathcal{A}$. For example, the clock guards appearing in $\mathcal{A}_1$, as shown in Fig. 1 (a) p. 467, are $x_a = 1$ and $x_a = 3$, so $G_{\mathcal{A}} = \{x_a < 1, x_a = 1, 1 < x_a < 3, x_a = 3, x_a > 3\}$. Thus, each membership query of untimed word $(a, true)$ gives rise to $|G_{\mathcal{A}}|$ timed membership queries. Totally, TL* needs to perform $O(|\Sigma| \cdot |G_{\mathcal{A}}| \cdot |L|^2 + |L| \log |\pi|)$ membership queries to learn $Com(\mathcal{A})$, where π is the counterexample given by Teacher. By Theorem 1, TL* needs to perform $O(|L| + |\Sigma| \cdot |G_{\mathcal{A}}|)$ candidate queries.

Lemma 1. *Given a closed and consistent observation table (S, E, T), any deterministic ERA consistent with T must have at least $|S|$ locations.*

Proof. We first define a row in the observation table. If $p \in S \cup (S \cdot \Sigma)$ is a prefix (row) of the table, we use $row(p)$ to denote the function $f : E \mapsto \{0, 1\}$ defined by $f(e) = T(p \cdot e)$ for $e \in E$. Let $M = (\Sigma, L, l^0, \delta, L^f)$ be an ERA consistent with T. We then define $f'(s) = \delta(l^0, s)$ for every $s \in S$. For any two $s_1, s_2 \in S$, we have $row(s_1) \neq row(s_2)$ implying that there exists $e \in E$ such that $T(s_1 \cdot e) \neq T(s_2 \cdot e)$. Since M is consistent with T, exactly one of $\delta(l^0, s_1 \cdot e)$ and $\delta(l^0, s_2 \cdot e)$ is in L^f implying that $\delta(l^0, s_1)$ and $\delta(l^0, s_2)$ are distinct locations. Thus, $f'(s)$ takes on at least $|S|$ values implying that M has at lease $|S|$ locations.

Theorem 1. *TL* is correct and terminates in a finite number of iterations.*

Proof. The correctness is based on the fact that TL* returns an ERA only if it accepts the unknown timed language U_T. Let $\mathcal{A} = (\Sigma, L, l^0, \delta, L^f)$ be an ERA accepting U_T. In each iteration, TL* either adds a row into S in the observation table (S, E, T) or splits a clock guard of an event $\alpha \in \Sigma$ into at least two disjoint clock guards. Since the observation table should be consistent with $\mathcal{A}$ (otherwise, Teacher must have given wrong answers to membership queries), TL* adds at most $|L|$ rows into S. At last, each split clock guard will belong to $G_\mathcal{A}$. Thus, TL* terminates after $O(|L| + |\Sigma| \cdot |G_\mathcal{A}|)$ iterations.

Theorem 2. *The ERA learned by TL* has the minimal number of locations.*

Proof. Given a closed and consistent observation table (S, E, T), TL* constructs an ERA M exactly with $|S|$ locations. By Lemma 1, we can conclude that M has the minimal number of locations.

Comparison. Grinchtein et al.'s TL^*_{sg} uses region construction to actively guess all possible time constraints for an untimed word, so an original untimed membership query in L* gives rise to several membership queries of time words. The number of timed membership queries required by the TL^*_{sg} algorithm is $O(|\Sigma \times G_\Sigma| \cdot n^2 |\pi| \cdot |w| \binom{|\Sigma| + K}{|\Sigma|})$ where n is the number of locations of the learned ERA, π is the counterexample given by Teacher, w is the longest guarded word queried, and K is the largest constant appearing in the clock guards. We can observe that the number of timed membership queries required by TL^*_{sg} increases exponentially with the largest constant K and the size of the alphabet $|\Sigma|$. To learn the timed language accepted by $\mathcal{A}_1$, as shown in Fig. 1 (a) p. 467, TL^*_{sg} needs 34 timed membership queries, while our TL* only needs 16 timed membership queries. Note that our TL* algorithm is not affected by the largest constant K. If we change the guarded word $a[x_a = 3]$ in $\mathcal{A}_1$, as shown in Fig. 1 (a), into $a[x_a = 100]$, the number of membership queries required by our TL* algorithm is still 16, while that required by TL^*_{sg} increases exponentially.

4   Conclusion and Future Work

We proposed an efficient polynomial time algorithm, TL*, for learning ERAs. TL* can also be applied to other subclasses of timed automata, such as event-predicting automata [2], as they are determinizable. Our future work will implement TL* into the PAT model checker [12,14] such that PAT can automatically generate the assumptions for assume-guarantee reasoning for timed systems.

Acknowledgment. This work benefited from the discussions via e-mails with Olga Grinchtein, one of the authors of [7,8].

References

1. Alur, R., Dill, D.L.: A theory of timed automata. Theoretical Computer Science 126(2), 183–235 (1994)
2. Alur, R., Fix, L., Henzinger, T.A.: Event-clock automata: A determinizable class of timed automata. Theoretical Computer Science 211(1-2), 253–273 (1999)
3. Angluin, D.: Learning regular sets from queries and counterexamples. Information and Computation 75(2), 87–106 (1987)
4. Clarke, E.M., Emerson, E.A.: Design and sythesis of synchronization skeletons using branching time temporal logic. In: Proceedings of the Logics of Programs Workshop, vol. 131, pp. 52–71 (1981)
5. Cobleigh, J.M., Giannakopoulou, D., Păsăreanu, C.S.: Learning assumptions for compositional verification. In: Garavel, H., Hatcliff, J. (eds.) TACAS 2003. LNCS, vol. 2619, pp. 331–346. Springer, Heidelberg (2003)
6. Dill, D.L.: Timing assumptions and verification of finite-state concurrent systems. In: Sifakis, J. (ed.) CAV 1989. LNCS, vol. 407, pp. 197–212. Springer, Heidelberg (1990)
7. Grinchtein, O., Jonsson, B., Leucker, M.: Learning of event-recording automata. In: Lakhnech, Y., Yovine, S. (eds.) FORMATS 2004 and FTRTFT 2004. LNCS, vol. 3253, pp. 379–395. Springer, Heidelberg (2004)
8. Grinchtein, O., Jonsson, B., Leucker, M.: Learning of event-recording automata. Theorectical Computer Science 411(47), 4029–4054 (2010)
9. Hopcroft, J.E., Ullman, J.D.: Introduction to Automata Theory, Languages, and Computation. Addison-Wesley, Reading (1979)
10. Lin, S.W., Hsiung, P.A.: Counterexample-guided assume-guarantee synthesis through learning. IEEE Transactions on Computers 60(5), 734–750 (2011)
11. Lin, S.W., Hsiung, P.A., Huang, C.H., Chen, Y.R.: Model checking prioritized timed automata. In: Peled, D.A., Tsay, Y.-K. (eds.) ATVA 2005. LNCS, vol. 3707, pp. 370–384. Springer, Heidelberg (2005)
12. Liu, Y., Sun, J., Dong, J.S.: Analyzing hierarchical complex real-time systems. In: Proceedings of the 8th ACM SIGSOFT International Symposium on the Foundations of Software Engineering (FSE), pp. 365–366. ACM, New York (2010)
13. Queille, J.P., Sifakis, J.: Specification and verification of concurrent systems in CE-SAR. In: Dezani-Ciancaglini, M., Montanari, U. (eds.) Programming 1982. LNCS, vol. 137, pp. 337–351. Springer, Heidelberg (1982)
14. Sun, J., Liu, Y., Dong, J.S., Pang, J.: PAT: Towards flexible verification under fairness. In: Bouajjani, A., Maler, O. (eds.) CAV 2009. LNCS, vol. 5643, pp. 709–714. Springer, Heidelberg (2009)

Discretizing Affine Hybrid Automata with Uncertainty[*][**]

Thao Dang[1] and Thomas Martin Gawlitza[1]

VERIMAG
{Thao.Dang,Thomas.Gawlitza}@imag.fr

Abstract. Over-approximating the set of all reachable states of a given system is an important task for the verification of *safety properties*. Such an unbounded time verification is in particular challenging for *hybrid systems*. We recently developed an algorithm that over-approximates the set of all reachable states of a given *affine hybrid automata* by performing linear template-based abstract interpretation [4]. In this article we extend the previous results by adding *uncertainty* to the model of affine hybrid automata. Uncertainty can be used for abstracting the behavior of non-linear hybrid systems. We adapt our techniques to this model and show that, w.r.t. given linear templates, the abstract reachability problem is still in coNP by reducing abstract reachability for affine hybrid automata with uncertainty to abstract reachability for affine programs (affine hybrid automata where only discrete transitions are allowed). We thus provide a new connection between a continuous time model and a purely discrete model.

1 Introduction

Hybrid systems have been widely recognized as a mathematical model appropriate for describing and reasoning about the interactions of software, modeled by discrete systems such as automata, with the physical world, described by continuous systems such as differential equations. Cyber-physical systems are recent applications involving such interactions. In addition, many applications of cyber-physical systems must be reliable and safe, not only for economic reasons but also for human safety. Automated verification technologies are thus indispensable for the efficiency of their design. Uncertainty is an important feature of cyber-physical systems. Indeed, accurate models of some of their components may not be available or reliability of interoperation of their heterogeneous subsystems may not be guantanteed. Moreover, modelling complex cyber-physical systems with reasonable accuracy is a very challenging task; therefore uncertainty in their models is often unavoidable. While uncertainty can result from imprecision in modelling, it can also result from the abstraction and approximation procedures frequenty used in systems design. Indeed, the dynamics of real-life systems are often non-linear, for which most common analysis techniques involve some "linearization" step, since the resulting linear approximation can be treated using well-developed numerical and symbolic methods.

---

[*] This work was partially funded by the ANR project VEDECY.

[**] VERIMAG is a joint laboratory of CNRS, Université Joseph Fourier and Grenoble INP.

T. Bultan and P.-A. Hsiung (Eds.): ATVA 2011, LNCS 6996, pp. 473–481, 2011.
© Springer-Verlag Berlin Heidelberg 2011

In this article, we study affine hybrid automata with uncertainty and propose a method for computing invariants of such systems. Such an invariant, being a conservative approximation of the reachable set, can be used to verify safety proterties.

Hybrid automata with linear continuous dynamics have been a focus in hybrid systems verification, and a number of tools for verifying such systems have been developed [1, 2, 5, 8, 9]. The state-of-the-art reachability computation techniques can efficiently handle *continuous systems* described by linear differential equations with uncertain inputs of up to a few hundreds of variables [7]. However, their extension to handle *hybrid systems* is still limited. *Unbounded time* reachability analysis of hybrid systems with linear continuous dynamics remains a challenge.

The novelty of our approach lies in its ability to efficiently handle *unbounded time verification*. Indeed, by exporting abstract interpretation techniques in hybrid systems verification, we avoid the complexity of the step-by-step approximations of reachable sets in the continuous phase. Our work is close in spirit to the works on barrier certificates [10], polynomial invariants [14] and, in particular polyhedral invariants [12]. Computationally, an important advantage of our approach is the application of efficient techniques for computing invariants and abstract semantics, initially developed for program analysis, to verify hybrid systems.

2   Affine Hybrid Automata with Uncertainty

The set of real numbers is denoted by $\mathbb{R}$. The complete linearly ordered set $\mathbb{R} \cup \{-\infty, \infty\}$ is denoted by $\overline{\mathbb{R}}$. The transpose of a matrix A is denoted by $A^\top$. We denote the i-th row (resp. the j-th column) of a matrix A by $A_{i\cdot}$ (resp. $A_{\cdot j}$). Accordingly, $A_{i\cdot j}$ denotes the component in the i-th row and the j-th column. We also use this notation for vectors and functions $f : X \to Y^k$, i.e., $f_{i\cdot}(x) = (f(x))_{i\cdot}$ for all $x \in X$ and all $i \in \{1, \ldots, k\}$. For $x, y \in \overline{\mathbb{R}}^n$, we write $x \leq y$ iff $x_{i\cdot} \leq y_{i\cdot}$ for all $i \in \{1, \ldots, n\}$. The complete lattice $\overline{\mathbb{R}}^n$ is partially ordered by $\leq$. We write $x < y$ iff $x \leq y$ and $x \neq y$. The elements x and y are called *comparable* iff $x \leq y$ or $y \leq x$. Let $\mathbb{D}$ be a partially ordered set. We denote the *least upper bound* and the *greatest lower bound* of a set $X \subseteq \mathbb{D}$ by $\bigvee X$ and $\bigwedge X$, respectively, provided that they exist. Their existence is in particular guaranteed if $\mathbb{D}$ is a *complete lattice*. The least element $\bigvee \emptyset$ (resp. the greatest element $\bigwedge \emptyset$) is denoted by $\bot$ (resp. $\top$), provided that it exists. We define the binary operators $\vee$ and $\wedge$ by $x \vee y := \bigvee \{x, y\}$ and $x \wedge y := \bigwedge \{x, y\}$ for all $x, y \in \mathbb{D}$, respectively. If $\mathbb{D}$ is a *linearly ordered set* (for instance $\mathbb{R}$ or $\overline{\mathbb{R}}$), then $\vee$ is the *maximum* operator and $\wedge$ the *minimum* operator. A function $f : \mathbb{D}_1 \to \mathbb{D}_2$, where $\mathbb{D}_1$ and $\mathbb{D}_2$ are partially ordered sets, is called *monotone* iff $x \leq y$ implies $f(x) \leq f(y)$ for all $x, y \in \mathbb{D}_1$. The fixpoint theorem of Knaster/Tarski [13] states that any monotone self-map $f : \mathbb{D} \to \mathbb{D}$ on a complete lattice $\mathbb{D}$ has a least fixpoint $\mu f = \bigwedge \{x \in \mathbb{D} \mid x \geq f(x)\}$.

A mapping $V : \mathbb{R}^n \to 2^{\mathbb{R}^n}$ is called a *vector field with uncertainty over* $\mathbb{R}^n$. It assigns a set $V(x) \subseteq \mathbb{R}^n$ of vectors to each state $x \in \mathbb{R}^n$. We denote the set $\{x \in \mathbb{R}^n \mid V(x) \neq \emptyset\}$ by $\mathrm{dom}(V)$. A vector field with uncertainty over $\mathbb{R}^n$ is called *affine* iff there exists some convex polyhedron $P \subseteq \mathbb{R}^{2n}$ such that $V(x) = \{x' \in \mathbb{R}^n \mid (x, x') \in P\}$ for all $x \in \mathbb{R}^n$. The set $\mathrm{dom}(V)$ is a convex polyhedron, whenever V is affine. In the remainder of this article we assume w.l.o.g. that all affine vector fields with uncertainty are specified by existentially quantified conjunctions of non-strict inequalities and equalities with free variables x and x' that take values from $\mathbb{R}^n$. We say that a continuous differentiable time trajectory $\tau : [0, \delta] \rightarrow \mathbb{R}^n$ ($\delta \in \mathbb{R}_{\geq 0}$) *evolves from* $\tau(0)$ *to* $\tau(\delta)$ *according to the vector field with uncertainty* V iff $\dot{\tau}(t) \in V(\tau(t))$ for all $t \in [0, \delta)$.

An *affine hybrid automaton with uncertainty* differs from an affine hybrid automaton on the description of the continuous dynamics. They are now described by affine vector fields with uncertainty instead of ordinary affine vector fields: A *hybrid automaton with uncertainty* $\Psi = (n, \mathbf{L}, \mathcal{T}, \Theta, \mathbf{D}, l_0)$ consists of the following components: n is the number of *continuous variables*. $\mathbf{L}$ is a finite set of *locations*. $l_0 \in \mathbf{L}$ is the *initial location*. $\mathcal{T}$ is a finite set of *discrete transitions*. Each transition $(l_1, \Xi, l_2) \in \mathcal{T}$ consists of a move from the location $l_1 \in \mathbf{L}$ to the location $l_2 \in \mathbf{L}$, and an assertion $\Xi \subseteq (\mathbb{R}^n)^2$. $\Theta \subseteq \mathbb{R}^n$ is the set of possible *initial values* of the continuous variables at l_0. $\mathbf{D}$ is a mapping that maps each $l \in \mathbf{L}$ to a vector field with uncertainty $\mathbf{D}(l)$.

At each location $l \in \mathbf{L}$, the values of the continuous variables evolve according to $\mathbf{D}(l)$. A hybrid automaton with uncertainty $\Psi = (n, \mathbf{L}, \mathcal{T}, \Theta, \mathbf{D}, l_0)$ is called *affine* iff the following statements are fulfilled: (1) The initial condition Θ and all transition relations Ξ are convex polyhedra (we identify $(\mathbb{R}^n)^2$ with $\mathbb{R}^{2n}$). (2) The dynamics $\mathbf{D}(l)$ at each location $l \in \mathbf{L}$ is an affine vector field with uncertainty. In the following we will assume that all convex polyhedra are specified by existentially quantified conjunctions of linear equalities and non-strict linear inequalities.

A computation is a possibly infinite sequence $(l_0, x_0), (l_1, x_1), \ldots$, where $x_0 \in \Theta$ and, for all $i \in \mathbb{N}$, one of the following statements hold: *(Discrete Consecution)* There exists a discrete transition $(l_i, \Xi, l_{i+1}) \in \mathcal{T}$ such that $(x_i, x_{i+1}) \in \Xi$. *(Continuous Consecution)* $l_i = l_{i+1}$ and there exists a $\delta \in \mathbb{R}_{>0}$ and a continuous differentiable time trajectory $\tau : [0, \delta]$ that evolves from x_i to x_{i+1} according to $\mathbf{D}(l_i)$.

As an abstract domain [3] we use template polyhedra as introduced by Sankaranarayanan et al. [11]. For that we fix a *template constraint matrix* $T \in \mathbb{R}^{m \times n}$, where we w.l.o.g. assume that $T_i. \neq (0, \ldots, 0)$ for every $i \in \{1, \ldots, m\}$. Each row of T represents a linear template (a linear function). Each template relates n variables. The *concretization* $\gamma_T : \overline{\mathbb{R}}^m \rightarrow 2^{\mathbb{R}^n}$ and the *abstraction* $\alpha_T : 2^{\mathbb{R}^n} \rightarrow \overline{\mathbb{R}}^m$ are defined by $\gamma_T(d) := \{x \in \mathbb{R}^n \mid Tx \leq d\}$ for all $d \in \overline{\mathbb{R}}^m$, and $\alpha_T(X) := \min\{d \in \overline{\mathbb{R}}^m \mid \gamma_T(d) \supseteq X\}$ for all $X \subseteq \mathbb{R}^n$. We omit the subscripts T, whenever they are clear from the context. As shown by Sankaranarayanan et al. [11], α and γ form a Galois connection. Hence, $\alpha \circ \gamma$ is a downward closure operator, and $\gamma \circ \alpha$ is an upward closure operator. This in particular implies that $\alpha \circ \gamma$ and $\gamma \circ \alpha$ are monotone. In order to simplify notations, we denote $\alpha \circ \gamma$ by cl. The abstract elements from $\alpha(2^{\mathbb{R}^n}) = \mathbf{cl}(\overline{\mathbb{R}}^m)$ are called *closed*. The convex polyhedra from the set $\gamma(\overline{\mathbb{R}}^m) = \gamma(\alpha(2^{\mathbb{R}^n}))$ are called *template polyhedra*.

For all $X \subseteq \mathbb{R}^n$, we moreover define the operator $\mathbf{cl}^X$ on $\overline{\mathbb{R}}^m$ by $\mathbf{cl}^X(d) := \alpha(\gamma(d) \cap X)$ for all $d \in \overline{\mathbb{R}}^m$. The operator $\mathbf{cl}^X$ is a downward closure operator. Moreover, note that $\mathbf{cl}^{\mathbb{R}^n} = \mathbf{cl}$. Similar to Sankaranarayanan et al. [11] we get

$$\mathbf{cl}_i^X(d) = \sup\{T_i.x \mid x \in X \text{ and } Tx \leq d\} \quad \forall X \subseteq \mathbb{R}^n, i \in \{1, \ldots, m\}, d \in \overline{\mathbb{R}}^m. \quad (1)$$

Let V be a vector field with uncertainty over $\mathbb{R}^n$. A set $X \subseteq \mathbb{R}^n$ is called an *invariant* of V iff every trajectory that starts in X and evolves according to V stays in X. Before going further, we introduce the following notation: For all $d \in \overline{\mathbb{R}}^m$ and all

$R \subseteq \{1, \ldots, m\}$, we define $d|_R \in \overline{\mathbb{R}}^m$ by $(d|_R)_{i.} = d_{i.}$, if $i \in R$, and $(d|_R)_{i.} = \infty$, if $i \notin R$ (for all $i \in \{1, \ldots, m\}$).

Assume now that the vector field with uncertainty V is affine. A template polyhedron $P \in \gamma(\overline{\mathbb{R}}^m)$ is called a *positive invariant* of V iff there exists some $R \subseteq \{1, \ldots, m\}$ such that the following properties are fulfilled: (1) $T_i.v \leq 0$ for all $v \in V(x)$ and all $x \in P$ with $T_i.x = \alpha_{i.}(P)$ and all $i \in R$. (2) $P \supseteq \gamma(\alpha(P)|_R) \cap \mathrm{dom}(V)$.

Each $i \in \{1, \ldots, m\}$ stands for a face of the template polyhedron P. Condition 1 ensures that there is no point x on the face i such that some vector from $V(x)$ points to the outside. Condition 2 ensures that all faces i that are not from R are implied by the faces from R and the staying condition $\mathrm{dom}(V)$.

We emphasize that our definition of positive invariants differs from the ones we used in [4]. In [4], we assumed that the staying condition is a template polyhedron that is represented by a vector from $\overline{\mathbb{R}}^m$. Our new definition does not require this precondition to be fulfilled. We do so, because the staying condition $\mathrm{dom}(V)$ is obtained from V by projecting out variables. However, we want to avoid this, since it might be costly to compute the templates that are necessary to fulfill that precondition (polynomial-time algorithms for projecting out a set of variables are not known). Hence, we cannot w.l.o.g. assume that $\mathrm{dom}(V)$ is a template polyhedron. The advantage of our new definition is that it does not require such technical preconditions.

We emphasize that every template polyhedron that is positive invariant according to the definition in [4] is also a positive invariant according to the definition in this article, i.e., the above definition gives us additional precision. The two notions coincide, whenever $\mathrm{dom}(V)$ is a template polyhedron.

Our goal is to compute the abstract semantics for affine hybrid automata with uncertainty w.r.t. given linear templates. The *abstract semantics* for the affine hybrid automaton with uncertainty $\Psi = (n, \mathbf{L}, \mathcal{T}, \Theta, \mathbf{D}, l_0)$ (w.r.t. given linear templates that are specified by T) is the point-wise minimal mapping $V_\square^\sharp$ that maps every location $l \in \mathbf{L}$ to a template polyhedron $V_\square^\sharp[l] \in \gamma(\overline{\mathbb{R}}^m)$ and fulfills the following constraints: (1) $V_\square^\sharp[l_0] \supseteq \Theta$. (2) $V_\square^\sharp[l]$ is a positive invariant of $\mathbf{D}(l)$ for every location $l \in \mathbf{L}$. (3) $x' \in V_\square^\sharp[l']$ for all $(l, \Xi, l') \in \mathcal{T}$ and all $(x, x') \in \Xi$ with $x \in V_\square^\sharp[l]$. The existence of such a point-wise minimal mapping will be ensured by our findings.

In order to verify safety properties, a problem one is interested in is *abstract reachability*, which is the following decision problem: Decide whether or not, for a given template constraint matrix $T \in \mathbb{R}^{m \times n}$, a given affine hybrid automaton with uncertainty $\Psi = (n, \mathbf{L}, \mathcal{T}, \Theta, \mathbf{D}, l_0)$, and a given location $l \in L$, the statement $V_\square^\sharp[l] \neq \emptyset$ holds. The location l may represent an unsafe state. The decision problem then answers the question, whether or not the unsafe state can be reached within the abstraction. The system is safe, whenever this is not the case. If the unsafe state can be reached within the abstraction, then either the system is unsafe or the abstraction is too coarse.

It is important to note that most existing hybrid systems verification techniques were developed first for purely continuous systems (defined by ordinary differential equations) and were then adapted with some loss of precision to handle staying conditions in hybrid automata. Our approach, in contrast, can handle in a unified manner differential equations and differential algebraic inequalities (i.e. inequalities involving differential and algebraic variables).

3 From Affine Hybrid Automata to Affine Programs

The Time Elapse Operation We will firstly prepare our main result by studying the time elapse operation. We will basically extend the results of Dang and Gawlitza [4] by allowing *uncertainty*. Let V be an affine vector field with uncertainty. Firstly, we define the operator Δ^V on $\overline{\mathbb{R}}^m$ by $\Delta_{k.}^V(d) := \sup \{T_{k.}v \mid x \in \mathbb{R}^n,\ Tx \leq d,\ T_{k.}x \geq d_{k.},\ v \in V(x)\}$ for all $k \in \{1,\ldots,m\}$ and all $d \in \overline{\mathbb{R}}^m$ with $d_{k.} < \infty$. Note that $\Delta_{k.}^V(d) = -\infty$, whenever $\{v \in \mathbb{R}^n \mid x \in \mathbb{R}^n, Tx \leq d, T_{k.}x \geq d_{k.}, v \in V(x)\} = \emptyset$. This is in particular fulfilled, if there exists some $i \in \{1,\ldots,m\}$ with $d_{i.} = -\infty$. Moreover, we set $\Delta_{k.}^V(d) := 0$ for all $k \in \{1,\ldots,m\}$ and $d \in \overline{\mathbb{R}}^m$ with $d_{k.} = \infty$. Intuitively, $\Delta_{k.}^V(d) > 0$ iff there exists some point x on the face $\mathcal{F} := \{x \in \mathbb{R}^n \mid Tx \leq d, T_{k.}x \geq d_{k.}\}$ such that some vector $v \in V(x)$ points to the outside. For all $\epsilon \in \mathbb{R}_{>0}^m$, we define the operator $f^{V,\epsilon}$ on $\overline{\mathbb{R}}^m$ by $f^{V,\epsilon}(d) := d + \epsilon^{\top}\Delta^V(d)$ for all $d \in \overline{\mathbb{R}}^m$. An application of the operator $f^{V,\epsilon}$ corrects the bounds to the templates according to the vector field with uncertainty V. Note that the staying condition (a.k.a. location invariant) $\mathrm{dom}(V)$ is not completely taken into account so far. More precisely, we have not taken care of the second requirement of the definition of positive invariants. This will be done through the operator $\mathbf{cl}^{\mathrm{dom}(V)}$. Similarly to Dang and Gawlitza [4], we get:

Lemma 1. *Let $\epsilon \in \mathbb{R}_{>0}^m$ and $d \in \overline{\mathbb{R}}^m$. The template polyhedron $\gamma(d)$ is a positive invariant of V iff $d \geq \mathbf{cl}^{\mathrm{dom}(V)}(\mathbf{cl}(d) \vee f^{V,\epsilon}(\mathbf{cl}(d)))$.* □

In order to use the above lemma within a monotone framework, we have to ensure that $f^{V,\epsilon} \circ \mathbf{cl}$ is monotone. Then $f^{V,\epsilon} \circ \mathbf{cl}^{\mathrm{dom}(V)}$ and $\mathcal{F} := \mathbf{cl}^{\mathrm{dom}(V)} \circ (\mathbf{cl} \vee f^{V,\epsilon} \circ \mathbf{cl})$ are monotone, too, and the fixpoint theorem of Knaster/Tarski [13] can be applied.[1] The operator $f^{V,\epsilon} \circ \mathbf{cl}$ is monotone on $\overline{\mathbb{R}}^m$, whenever the operator $f^{V,\epsilon}$ is monotone on $\mathbf{cl}(\overline{\mathbb{R}}^m)$ (It is not always possible to choose an ϵ such that $f^{V,\epsilon}$ is monotone on $\overline{\mathbb{R}}^m$). Analogously to Dang and Gawlitza [4], we get:

Lemma 2 (Monotonicity of $f^{V,\epsilon}$). *In polynomial time we can compute an $\epsilon^{(0)} \in \mathbb{R}_{>0}^m$ such that $f^{V,\epsilon}$ is monotone on $\mathbf{cl}(\overline{\mathbb{R}}^m)$, whenever $\epsilon \leq \epsilon^{(0)}$.* □

Because of Lemma 2, we from now on assume that we have chosen an $\epsilon \in \mathbb{R}_{>0}^m$ such that $f^{V,\epsilon} \circ \mathbf{cl}$ and thus finally $\mathbf{cl}^{\mathrm{dom}(V)} \circ (\mathbf{cl} \vee f^{V,\epsilon} \circ \mathbf{cl}) = \mathbf{cl}^{\mathrm{dom}(V)} \circ (\mathrm{id} \vee f^{V,\epsilon}) \circ \mathbf{cl}$ is monotone. Therefore, for all sets $\Theta \subseteq \mathbb{R}^n$ of values, there exists a least positive invariant P of V which is a superset of Θ. It is given by $\gamma(\mu(\alpha(\Theta) \vee \mathbf{cl}^{\mathrm{dom}(V)} \circ (\mathbf{cl} \vee f^{V,\epsilon} \circ \mathbf{cl})))$. However, we want to have a simpler formulation that allows to perform time elapse operations in polynomial time. In order to obtain such a simpler formulation, we observe that $\mu(\theta \vee \mathbf{cl}^{\mathrm{dom}(V)} \circ (\mathbf{cl} \vee f^{V,\epsilon} \circ \mathbf{cl})) = \mathbf{cl}^{\mathrm{dom}(V)}(\mu(\theta \vee f^{V,\epsilon} \circ \mathbf{cl}^{\mathrm{dom}(V)}))$ for all $\theta \in \mathbf{cl}^{\mathrm{dom}(V)}(\overline{\mathbb{R}}^m)$. Here, θ denotes the function that returns θ for every argument. Putting everything together, we obtain our main result for the time elapse operation:

Theorem 1 (The Time Elapse Operation). *Let V be an affine vector field with uncertainty over $\mathbb{R}^n$, and $\Theta \subseteq \mathbb{R}^n$. Assume that $\epsilon \in \mathbb{R}_{>0}^m$ is chosen such that $f^{V,\epsilon} \circ \mathbf{cl}$ is monotone. The template polyhedron $\gamma(\alpha(\Theta \cup \gamma(\mu(\alpha(\Theta \cap \mathrm{dom}(V)) \vee f^{V,\epsilon} \circ \mathbf{cl}^{\mathrm{dom}(V)})))))$ is the least positive invariant of V which is a superset of Θ.* □

---

[1] For mappings $f, g : X \to \mathbb{D}$, $f \vee g$ is defined by $(f \vee g)(x) := f(x) \vee g(x)$ for all $x \in X$.

The Abstract Semantic Inequalities We will now set up a system of inequalities over $\overline{\mathbb{R}}^m$ whose least solution corresponds to the abstract semantics of the affine hybrid automaton with uncertainty Ψ. In the next subsection, we will construct an affine program whose abstract semantics gives us the solution of this system of inequalities.

So far, we have ignored the discrete transitions. In order to take them into account, we define an abstract semantics for discrete transitions $(l, \Xi, l') \in \mathcal{T}$. Recall that the assertion $\Xi \subseteq \mathbb{R}^{2n}$ is a convex polyhedron (represented by an existentially quantified conjunction of inequalities with free variables x and x' that take values from $\mathbb{R}^n$). The collecting semantics $[\![\Xi]\!]$ of Ξ is defined by $[\![\Xi]\!](X) := \{y \in \mathbb{R}^n \mid \exists x \in X . (x, y) \in \Xi\}$ for all $X \subseteq \mathbb{R}^n$. The abstract semantics $[\![\Xi]\!]^\sharp$ of Ξ is defined by $[\![\Xi]\!]^\sharp := \alpha \circ [\![\Xi]\!] \circ \gamma$. The abstract semantics $[\![\Xi]\!]^\sharp$ safely over-approximates the collecting semantics $[\![\Xi]\!]$ and the concrete semantics.

We are now going to define an abstract semantics $V^\sharp$ for an *affine* hybrid automaton $\Psi = (n, \mathbf{L}, \mathcal{T}, \Theta, \mathbf{D}, l_0)$ with uncertainty that corresponds to the abstract semantics $V^\sharp_\square$ of Ψ. The abstract semantics $V^\sharp$ of Ψ is the least solution to the following constraints:

$$\mathbf{A}^\sharp[l_0] \geq \alpha(\Theta) \qquad \mathbf{A}^\sharp[l'] \geq [\![\Xi]\!]^\sharp(\mathbf{V}^\sharp[l]) \qquad\qquad \forall(l, \Xi, l') \in \mathcal{T}$$
$$\mathbf{B}^\sharp[l] \geq \mathbf{cl}^{\mathrm{dom}(\mathbf{D}(l))}(\mathbf{A}^\sharp[l])) \qquad \mathbf{B}^\sharp[l] \geq f^{\mathbf{D}(l), \epsilon(l)}(\mathbf{cl}^{\mathrm{dom}(\mathbf{D}(l))}(\mathbf{B}^\sharp[l])) \quad \forall l \in \mathbf{L}$$
$$\mathbf{V}^\sharp[l] \geq \mathbf{A}^\sharp[l] \qquad\qquad \mathbf{V}^\sharp[l] \geq \mathbf{cl}^{\mathrm{dom}(\mathbf{D}(l))}(\mathbf{B}^\sharp[l])) \qquad\qquad \forall l \in \mathbf{L}$$

The variables $\mathbf{A}^\sharp[l]$, $\mathbf{B}^\sharp[l]$, and $\mathbf{V}^\sharp[l]$ (for $l \in \mathbf{L}$) take values from $\overline{\mathbb{R}}^m$. $\mathbf{A}^\sharp[l]$ and $\mathbf{B}^\sharp[l]$ are just auxiliary variables. The existence of the least solution is ensured by the fixpoint theorem of Knaster/Tarski, since we assume that, for all locations $l \in \mathbf{L}$, $\epsilon(l) \in \mathbb{R}^m_{>0}$ is chosen such that $f^{\mathbf{D}(l), \epsilon(l)} \circ \mathbf{cl}$ and thus $f^{\mathbf{D}(l), \epsilon(l)} \circ \mathbf{cl}^{\mathrm{dom}(\mathbf{D}(l))}$ are monotone. The existence of such an $\epsilon(l)$ is again ensured by Lemma 2.

The first constraint takes all possible initial values of the continuous variables at the initial location l_0 into account. The second constraint ensures that the template polyhedron $\gamma(\mathbf{V}^\sharp[l'])$ contains at least all values that can come through the discrete transition (l, Ξ, l'). The remaining constraint ensure that the template polyhedron $\gamma(\mathbf{V}^\sharp[l])$ is a positive invariant of $\mathbf{D}(l)$ (cf. Theorem 1). By construction, we get $V^\sharp_\square[l] = \gamma(\mathbf{V}^\sharp[l])$ for all locations $l \in \mathbf{L}$.

The Reduction. We are now going to reduce the problem of computing abstract semantics of affine hybrid automata w.r.t. template polyhedra to the problem of computing abstract semantics of affine programs w.r.t. template polyhedra. An *affine program* is an affine hybrid automaton with uncertainty $\Psi = (n, \mathbf{L}, \mathcal{T}, \Theta, \mathbf{D}, l_0)$, where $\mathbf{D}(l) = \emptyset$ for every location $l \in \mathbf{L}$. That is, only discrete transitions are allowed.

Abstract reachability for affine programs is in coNP (see e.g. Dang and Gawlitza [4]). Moreover, it is known to be at least as hard as computing the winning regions of mean-payoff games (cf. Gawlitza [6]). The latter problem is known to be in UP∩coUP, but not known to be in P. It is an open question whether or not abstract reachability for affine programs is coNP−hard. Hence, it makes sense to ask the question, whether or not abstract reachability for affine hybrid automata with uncertainty is more difficult than abstract reachability for affine programs. In this section, we show that this is not the case by providing a polynomial-time reduction from abstract reachability for affine hybrid automata with uncertainty to abstract reachability for affine programs. Hence, any efficient algorithm for affine programs gives us an efficient algorithm for affine hybrid automata with uncertainty.

Let $\Psi = (n, \mathbf{L}, \mathcal{T}, \Theta, \mathbf{D}, \mathrm{st})$ be an affine hybrid automaton with uncertainty and $T \in \mathbb{R}^{m \times n}$ be a template constraint matrix. We construct an affine program $\Psi' = (m, \mathbf{L}', \mathcal{T}', \Theta', \mathbf{D}', \mathrm{st}')$ such that we can read off the abstract semantics of Ψ from the abstract semantics of Ψ'. Here, we consider the abstract semantics of Ψ' w.r.t. the template constraint matrix T' that is simply the identity matrix of size m, i.e., we restrict our considerations to upper bounds. We set $\mathbf{L}' := \{l, l_\mathbf{A}, l_\mathbf{B} \mid l \in \mathbf{L}\}$, i.e., we replace each location of Ψ by three locations. We will use the location l for the variable $\mathbf{V}^\sharp[l]$, the location $l_\mathbf{A}$ for the variable $\mathbf{A}^\sharp[l]$, and the location $l_\mathbf{B}$ for the variable $\mathbf{B}^\sharp[l]$.

The initial location st' is the location $\mathrm{st}_\mathbf{A}$. The set Θ' of initial states of the affine program Ψ' is given by $\Theta' := \{x \in \mathbb{R}^m \mid x \leq \alpha_T(\Theta)\}$. Hence, $\alpha_{T'}(\Theta') = \alpha_T(\Theta)$. These definitions correspond to the first inequality.

Moreover, we set $\mathbf{D}'(l) := \emptyset$ for all locations $l \in \mathbf{L}$, i.e., we are actually constructing an affine program. The set $\mathcal{T}'$ of discrete transitions is the smallest set that fulfills the following constraints:

1. If $(l, \Xi, l') \in \mathcal{T}$, then $(l, \Xi', l'_\mathbf{A}) \in \mathcal{T}'$, where

$$\Xi' := \{(d, d') \in (\mathbb{R}^m)^2 \mid \exists x, x' \in \mathbb{R}^n \ .\ Tx \leq d, \ (x, x') \in \Xi, \ d' \leq Tx'\}$$

Recall that Ξ is a convex polyhedron. Therefore, Ξ' is a convex polyhedron. By the construction, we get $\alpha_T(\llbracket \Xi \rrbracket (\gamma_T(d))) = \alpha_{T'}(\llbracket \Xi' \rrbracket (\gamma_{T'}(d)))$ for all $d \in \overline{\mathbb{R}}^m$. This discrete transition corresponds to the second inequality.

2. For every location $l \in \mathbf{L}$, we have to add additional discrete transitions in order to deal with the time elapse operation. For simplicity, let $V := \mathbf{D}(l)$. Assume further that $\epsilon \in \mathbb{R}^m_{\geq 0}$ is chosen such that $f^{V,\epsilon} \circ \mathbf{cl}$ is monotone. In order to apply $\mathbf{cl}^{\mathrm{dom}(V)}$, we define the polyhedron $\Xi_{\mathbf{cl}} := \{(d, d') \in (\mathbb{R}^m)^2 \mid \exists x \in \mathrm{dom}(V) . d' \leq Tx, \ Tx \leq d\}$. By construction, we have $\alpha_{T'}(\llbracket \Xi_{\mathbf{cl}} \rrbracket (\gamma_{T'}(d))) = \mathbf{cl}^{\mathrm{dom}(V)}(d)$ for all $d \in \overline{\mathbb{R}}^m$ (see (1)). Hence, we add the discrete transitions $(l_\mathbf{A}, \Xi_{\mathbf{cl}}, l_\mathbf{B})$ and $(l_\mathbf{B}, \Xi_{\mathbf{cl}}, l)$ for the 3rd and the 6th inequality, respectively. For the 5th inequality, we add the discrete transition $(l_\mathbf{A}, \Xi_{\mathrm{id}}, l)$, where $\Xi_{\mathrm{id}} := \{(d, d') \in (\mathbb{R}^m)^2 \mid d' = d\}$. For the 4th inequality, we finally add the discrete transition $(l_\mathbf{B}, \Xi, l_\mathbf{B})$, where

$$\Xi := \left\{(d, d') \in (\mathbb{R}^m)^2 \mid d' \leq f^{V,\epsilon}(\mathbf{cl}^{\mathrm{dom}(V)}(d))\right\}$$
$$= \{(d, d') \in (\mathbb{R}^m)^2 \mid \forall k \in \{1, \ldots, m\} \ .$$
$$\exists x \in \mathbb{R}^n, \ v \in V(x) . d'_{k\cdot} \leq d_{k\cdot} + \epsilon_k . T_{k\cdot}v, \ Tx \leq d, \ T_{k\cdot}x \geq d_{k\cdot}\}$$
$$= \{(d, d') \in (\mathbb{R}^m)^2 \mid \exists x^{(1)}, \ldots, x^{(m)} \in \mathbb{R}^n, v^{(1)} \in V(x^{(1)}), \ldots, v^{(m)} \in V(x^{(m)}) .$$
$$\forall k \in \{1, \ldots, m\} . d'_{k\cdot} \leq d_{k\cdot} + \epsilon_k . T_{k\cdot}v^{(k)}, \ Tx^{(k)} \leq d, \ T_{k\cdot}x^{(k)} \geq d_{k\cdot}\}$$

Ξ is a convex polyhedron, and $\alpha_{T'}(\llbracket \Xi \rrbracket (\gamma_{T'}(d))) = f^{V,\epsilon}(\mathbf{cl}^{\mathrm{dom}(V)}(d)) \ \forall d \in \overline{\mathbb{R}}^m$.

We finally get: Let $V^\sharp_\square$ denote the abstract semantics of Ψ w.r.t. the template constraint matrix T, and $V^{\sharp'}_\square$ denote the abstract semantics of Ψ' w.r.t. the template constraint matrix T'. Then $\alpha_T(V^\sharp_\square[l]) = \alpha_{T'}(V^{\sharp'}_\square[l])$ for all locations $l \in \mathbf{L}$.

The construction contains existential quantifications. This does not cause any problems, since the existential quantifications can be eliminated by introducing at most polynomially many auxiliary program variables (We cannot simply project out the existentially quantified variables, since this could not be carried out in polynomial time). Since the above construction can be carried out in polynomial time, we obtain:

Theorem 2. *Abstract reachability w.r.t. template polyhedra for affine hybrid automata with uncertainty is polynomial-time equivalent to abstract reachability w.r.t. template polyhedra for affine programs.* □

4 Conclusion

In this article, we studied the problem of template-based unbounded time verification of safety properties for affine hybrid automata with uncertainty. This model is used to safely over-approximate non-linear behavior. We showed that, w.r.t. template polyhedra, abstract reachability for affine hybrid automata with uncertainty is polynomial-time reducible to abstract reachability for affine programs. That is, these problems are polynomial-time equivalent. The reduction replaces every time elapse operation by a bunch of discrete transitions forming a loop.

References

[1] Asarin, E., Bournez, O., Dang, T., Maler, O.: Approximate reachability analysis of piecewise linear dynamical systems. In: Lynch, N.A., Krogh, B.H. (eds.) HSCC 2000. LNCS, vol. 1790, pp. 20–31. Springer, Heidelberg (2000)
[2] Chutinan, A., Krogh, B.: Computational techniques for hybrid system verification. IEEE Trans. on Automatic Control (48), 64–75 (2003)
[3] Cousot, P., Cousot, R.: Abstract interpretation: A unified lattice model for static analysis of programs by construction or approximation of fixpoints. In: POPL (1977)
[4] Dang, T., Gawlitza, T.M.: Template-based unbounded time verification of affine hybrid automata. Technical report, VERIMAG (2011)
[5] Frehse, G., Guernic, C.L., Donzé, A., Cotton, S., Ray, R., Lebeltel, O., Ripado, R., Girard, A., Dang, T., Maler, O.: Spaceex: Scalable verification of hybrid systems. In: Gopalakrishnan, G., Qadeer, S. (eds.) CAV 2011. LNCS, vol. 6806, pp. 379–395. Springer, Heidelberg (2011)
[6] Gawlitza, T.M.: Strategieverbesserungsalgorithmen für exakte Programmanalysen, Ph.D. Thesis. Dr. Hut Verlag, München, Munich, Germany (October 2009)
[7] Girard, A., Guernic, C.L., Maler, O.: Efficient computation of reachable sets of linear time-invariant systems with inputs. In: Hespanha, J.P., Tiwari, A. (eds.) HSCC 2006. LNCS, vol. 3927, pp. 257–271. Springer, Heidelberg (2006)
[8] Kurzhanskiy, A., Varaiya, P.: Ellipsoidal techniques for reachability analysis of discrete-time linear systems. IEEE Trans. Automatic Control (52), 26–38 (2007)
[9] Kvasnica, M., Grieder, P., Baotić, M., Morari, M.: Multi-parametric toolbox (mpt). In: Alur, R., Pappas, G.J. (eds.) HSCC 2004. LNCS, vol. 2993, pp. 448–462. Springer, Heidelberg (2004)
[10] Prajna, S., Jadbabaie, A.: Safety verification of hybrid systems using barrier certificates. In: Alur, R., Pappas, G.J. (eds.) HSCC 2004. LNCS, vol. 2993, pp. 477–492. Springer, Heidelberg (2004)

[11] Sankaranarayanan, S., Sipma, H.B., Manna, Z.: Scalable analysis of linear systems using mathematical programming. In: Cousot, R. (ed.) VMCAI 2005. LNCS, vol. 3385, pp. 25–41. Springer, Heidelberg (2005)

[12] Sankaranarayanan, S., Dang, T., Ivančić, F.: A policy iteration technique for time elapse over template polyhedra. In: Egerstedt, M., Mishra, B. (eds.) HSCC 2008. LNCS, vol. 4981, pp. 654–657. Springer, Heidelberg (2008)

[13] Tarski, A.: A lattice-theoretical fixpoint theorem and its appications. Pac. J. Math. 5, 285–309 (1955)

[14] Tiwari, A., Khanna, G.: Nonlinear systems: Approximating reach sets. In: Alur, R., Pappas, G.J. (eds.) HSCC 2004. LNCS, vol. 2993, pp. 600–614. Springer, Heidelberg (2004)

What's Decidable about Weighted Automata?

Shaull Almagor[1], Udi Boker[1,2], and Orna Kupferman[1]

[1] Hebrew University, School of Engineering and Computer Science, Jerusalem, Israel
[2] IST, Austria

Abstract. *Weighted automata* map input words to numerical values. Applications of weighted automata include formal verification of quantitative properties, as well as text, speech, and image processing.

In the 90's, Krob studied the decidability of problems on rational series, which strongly relate to weighted automata. In particular, it follows from Krob's results that the universality problem (that is, deciding whether the values of all words are below some threshold) is decidable for weighted automata with weights in $\mathbb{N} \cup \{\infty\}$, and that the equality problem is undecidable when the weights are in $\mathbb{Z} \cup \{\infty\}$.

In this paper we continue the study of the borders of decidability in weighted automata, describe alternative and direct proofs of the above results, and tighten them further. Unlike the proofs of Krob, which are algebraic in their nature, our proofs stay in the terrain of state machines, and the reduction is from the halting problem of a two-counter machine. This enables us to significantly simplify Krob's reasoning and strengthen the results to apply already to a very simple class of automata: all the states are accepting, there are no initial nor final weights, and all the weights are from the set $\{-1, 0, 1\}$. The fact we work directly with automata enables us to tighten also the decidability results and to show that the universality problem for weighted automata with weights in $\mathbb{N} \cup \{\infty\}$, and in fact even with weights in $\mathbb{Q}^{\geq 0} \cup \{\infty\}$, is PSPACE-complete. Our results thus draw a sharper picture about the decidability of decision problems for weighted automata, in both the front of equality vs. universality and the front of the $\mathbb{N} \cup \{\infty\}$ vs. the $\mathbb{Z} \cup \{\infty\}$ domains.

1 Introduction

Traditional automata accept or reject their input, and are therefore Boolean. A *weighted finite automaton* (WFA, for short) has numeric weights on its transitions and maps each word to a numeric value. Applications of weighted automata include formal verification, where they are used for the verification of quantitative properties, for reasoning about probabilistic systems, and for reasoning about the competitive ratio of on-line algorithms, as well as text, speech, and image processing, where the weights of the automaton are used in order to account for the variability of the data and to rank alternative hypotheses [5].

The rich structure of weighted automata makes them intriguing mathematical objects. Fundamental problems that have been solved decades ago for Boolean automata are still open or known to be undecidable in the weighted setting. Two problems of great interest in the context of automata are the *universality* and

T. Bultan and P.-A. Hsiung (Eds.): ATVA 2011, LNCS 6996, pp. 482–491, 2011.

containment problems. In the Boolean setting, the universality problem asks, given a nondeterministic automaton (NFA) $\mathcal{A}$, whether all the words in Σ^* are accepted by $\mathcal{A}$. In the weighted setting, the "goal" of words is not just to get accepted, but also to do it with a minimal value. Accordingly, the universality problem for WFAs asks, given a WFA $\mathcal{A}$ and a threshold v, whether $\mathcal{A}$ assigns a value that is smaller than v to all words in Σ^*. Similarly, the containment problem in the weighted setting naturally extends the Boolean one by asking, given two WFAs $\mathcal{A}$ and $\mathcal{B}$, whether for all words $w \in \Sigma^*$, the value of w in $\mathcal{B}$ is less than or equal to its value in $\mathcal{A}$. In the Boolean setting, the complexity for the two problems coincide, and is PSPACE-complete [8]. As we shall see in this paper, in the weighted setting the picture is more involved.

Recall that weighted automata map words to numerical values. Technically, each weighted automaton is defined with respect to an algebraic semiring. For example, $\langle \mathbb{N} \cup \{\infty\}, \min, +, \infty, 0 \rangle$ is a semiring whose sum operator is min (with ∞ being the identity element) and whose product operator is $+$ (with 0 being the identity element). Such a min-sum semiring is called a *tropical semiring*. The value of a run is the semiring-product of the weights along the transitions traversed (and the initial and final weights). The value of a word is the semiring-sum of the values of the accepting runs on it. A formalism that is analogous to the one of weighted automata is the one of *rational series* [10]. There too, the series is defined with respect to a semiring, and maps words to values from the domain of the semiring.

In [6], Krob proved that the universality problem for rational series is undecidable for the tropical semiring with domain $\mathbb{Z} \cup \{\infty\}$, and that this implies undecidability of the containment problem for the tropical semiring with domain $\mathbb{N} \cup \{\infty\}$. Moreover, in [7], Krob proved that universality for rational series defined with respect to the tropical semiring with domain $\mathbb{N} \cup \{\infty\}$ is decidable. The analogy between rational series and weighted automata implies the same results for the universality and containment problems for weighted automata.

In this paper we describe alternative and direct proofs of the above results. Our clean reduction enables us to strengthen the result to a weaker model of automata, and to make the proof generalizable to automata over infinite words.

Our proofs offer the following advantages. First, unlike the undecidability proofs of Krob, which refer to rational series and are therefore algebraic in their nature, our proofs stay in the terrain of state machines: while Krob's reduction is from Hilbert's 10th problem (solving a Diophantine equation), ours is from the halting problem of a two-counter machine. This enables us to significantly simplify Krob's reasoning and make the undecidability result accessible to the automata-theoretic community.

Second, the clean reduction enables us to strengthen the result and show that undecidability applies already to a very simple class of automata: the weights of the automaton are in $\{-1, 0, 1\}$, it has no initial nor final weights, and all its states are accepting. We note that Krob's reduction does not capture this weaker class of automata.

Third, the pure algebraic view of rational series has the drawback that it cannot be generalized to some natural extensions of the weighted setting. For example, rational series cannot capture weighted automata on infinite words (where one cannot speak about final states or final weights), nor can it capture discounted-sum automata over finite and infinite words [2,1]. For these cases, the non-algebraic, automata-theoretic definition, is useful [2,4,3].

Our proof uses ideas similar to those presented in [4]. Given a two counter machine $\mathcal{M}$, we define a weighted automaton $\mathcal{A}$ whose alphabet is the set of $\mathcal{M}$'s operations. We show that $\mathcal{A}$ assigns a positive value to a word w if and only if w describes the actual run of $\mathcal{M}$ and this run is halting with both counters having value 0. Hence, we have that $\mathcal{M}$ halts iff $\mathcal{A}$ is not universal with respect to the threshold 1. A direct corollary is that the containment problem is also undecidable.

Recall that when rational series are defined with respect to the tropical semiring with domain $\mathbb{N} \cup \{\infty\}$, universality becomes decidable [7]. The fact that we work directly with the automata enables us to tighten this result too. By bounding the length of the shortest witness to non-universality we are able to show that the universality problem for weighted automata defined with respect to the tropical semiring with domain $\mathbb{N} \cup \{\infty\}$ is PSPACE-complete. We extend this good news also to weighted automata defined with respect to the tropical semiring with domain $\mathbb{Q}^{\geq 0} \cup \{\infty\}$. On the other hand, we show that restricting to the domain $\mathbb{N} \cup \{\infty\}$ is not helpful for the containment problem, which is undecidable. We conclude that, unlike the Boolean case, the universality and containment problems do not have the same complexity in the weighted setting, and are in fact on different sides of the border of decidability. Moreover, this border crucially depends on whether the weights of the weighted automaton are all of the same polarity (all in $\mathbb{N} \cup \{\infty\}$ or all in $-\mathbb{N} \cup \{-\infty\}$) or are mixed (as in $\mathbb{Z} \cup \{\infty\}$).

Due to the lack of space, full proofs and examples are omitted from this version. A full version can be found in the authors' home pages.

2   Preliminaries

A *weighted finite automaton* (WFA, for short) is $\mathcal{A} = \langle \Sigma, Q, \Delta, c, Q_0, F, i, f \rangle$, where Σ is a finite input alphabet, Q is a finite set of states, $\Delta \subseteq Q \times \Sigma \times Q$ is a transition relation, $c : \Delta \to \mathbb{Q}$ is a cost function, $Q_0 \subseteq Q$ is a set of initial states, $F \subseteq Q$ is a set of final states, $i : Q_0 \to \mathbb{Q} \cup \{\infty\}$ is an initial-weight function, and $f : F \to \mathbb{Q} \cup \{\infty\}$ is a final-weight function. A transition $d = \langle q, a, p \rangle \in \Delta$ (also written as $\Delta(q, a, p)$) can be taken by $\mathcal{A}$ when reading the input letter a in the state q, and it causes $\mathcal{A}$ to move to the state p with *cost* $c(d)$. Note that a WFA $\mathcal{A}$ may be nondeterministic in the sense that it may have many initial states, and that for some $q \in Q$ and $a \in \Sigma$, it may have $\Delta(q, a, p_1)$ and $\Delta(q, a, p_2)$, with $p_1 \neq p_2$. We say that $\mathcal{A}$ is *complete* if Δ is total; that is, for every state $q \in Q$ and letter $a \in \Sigma$, there is at least one state $p \in Q$ such that $\Delta(q, a, p)$.

For a word $w = w_1 \ldots w_n \in \Sigma^*$, and states $q, q' \in Q$, a *run* of $\mathcal{A}$ on w is a sequence $r = r_0 r_1 \ldots r_n \in Q^+$, where $r_0 \in Q_0, r_n \in F$, and for all $1 \leq i \leq n$, we have $d_i = \langle r_{i-1}, w_i, r_i \rangle \in \Delta$. The cost of the run r is $c(r) = i(r_0) + \sum_{i=1}^{n} c(d_i) + f(r_n)$. Note that if $\mathcal{A}$ is nondeterministic, it may have several runs on w. The *cost* of w in $\mathcal{A}$ is $L_{\mathcal{A}}(w) = \min \{ c(r) : r \text{ is a run of } \mathcal{A} \text{ on } w \}$. If the minimum is taken over an empty set, then w is not in the range of $L_{\mathcal{A}}$. [1] Recall that in the binary setting, the *universality* problem asks, given a nondeterministic automaton (NFA) $\mathcal{A}$, whether $L(\mathcal{A}) = \Sigma^*$. Thus, all the words in Σ^* have to be accepted by the automaton. In the weighted setting, the "goal" of words is not just to get accepted, but also to do it with a minimal value. Accordingly, the universality problem for WFAs asks, given a WFA $\mathcal{A}$ and a threshold $v \in \mathbb{Q}$ given in binary, whether $L_{\mathcal{A}}(w) < v$ for all $w \in \Sigma^*$. We denote the latter fact by $L_{\mathcal{A}} < v$. The *containment* and *equality* problems for NFAs are lifted to the weighted setting in a similar manner: Given two WFAs $\mathcal{A}$ and $\mathcal{B}$, the containment problem is to decide whether $L_{\mathcal{A}}(w) \geq L_{\mathcal{B}}(w)$ for all $w \in \Sigma^*$. We refer to $\perp$ as being greater than ∞, thus if $L_{\mathcal{B}}(w) = \perp$ then $L_{\mathcal{A}}(w) = \perp$ too. Thus, the domain of $\mathcal{A}$ has to be contained in the domain of $\mathcal{B}$. [2] Similarly, the equality problem is to decide whether $L_{\mathcal{A}}(w) = L_{\mathcal{B}}(w)$ for all $w \in \Sigma^*$. In particular, the domains of $L_{\mathcal{A}}$ and $L_{\mathcal{B}}$ coincide. It is easy to see that an upper bound on the containment problem implies upper bounds on the equality and the universality problems. Also, a lower bound on the universality problem implies a lower bound on the containment and the equality problems. In the Boolean setting, the complexity for the three problems coincide, and is PSPACE-complete [8]. As we shall see in this paper, in the weighted setting the picture is more involved, and depends on the domain of the weights in the WFA. Studying the universality problem, it is more convenient to consider its dual, namely the *non-universality* problem. There, given $\mathcal{A}$ and v, we ask whether there is a word $w \in \Sigma^*$ such that $L_{\mathcal{A}}(w) \geq v$. Thus, the non-universality problem asks whether there exists a word for which all the runs of $\mathcal{A}$ have value of at least v.

3 Weighted Automata with Integer Weights

In this section we show that the universality problem, and therefore also the containment problem, are undecidable for WFAs with weights in $\mathbb{Z}$. In fact, even when only considering complete automata where all states are final, and

---

[1] In general, a WFA may be defined with respect to a semiring $\langle \mathbb{K}, \oplus, \otimes, \mathbf{0}, \mathbf{1} \rangle$. The cost of a run is then the semiring product of the initial weight of the first state, the weights along the run, and the final weight of the last state. The cost of an accepted word is the semiring sum over the costs of all accepting runs on it. In this work, we focus on weighted automata defined with respect to the *min-sum semiring*, $\langle \mathbb{Q} \cup \{\infty\}, \min, +, \infty, 0 \rangle$, sometimes called the *tropical* semiring, as defined above.

[2] For our confused readers, the $\geq$ in the $L_{\mathcal{A}}(w) \geq L_{\mathcal{B}}(w)$ condition is not a typo: recall that the goal of words is to get accepted, and with a minimal value. When $\mathcal{A}$ is contained in $\mathcal{B}$, it is more challenging for words to satisfy their goal in $\mathcal{A}$ rather than in $\mathcal{B}$. In the Boolean setting, this amounts to $L(\mathcal{A})$ being a subset of $L(\mathcal{B})$. In the weighted setting, this amounts to the values that words are mapped to in $\mathcal{A}$ being greater than the values to which they are mapped in $\mathcal{B}$.

without initial or final weights, in which the weights are only in $\{-1, 0, 1\}$, the problems remain undecidable.

We show this by a reduction from the halting problem for two-counter (Minsky) machines. Our proof uses ideas similar to those presented in [4]. A two-counter machine $\mathcal{M}$ is a sequence $(l_1, \ldots, l_n)$ of commands involving two counters x and y. We refer to $\{1, \ldots, n\}$ as the *locations* of the machine. There are five possible forms of commands:

$$\text{INC}(c), \ \text{DEC}(c), \ \text{GOTO } l_i, \ \text{IF } c\!=\!0 \text{ GOTO } l_i \text{ ELSE GOTO } l_j, \ \text{HALT},$$

where $c \in \{x, y\}$ is a counter and $1 \leq i, j \leq n$ are locations. Since we can always check whether $c = 0$ before a $\text{DEC}(c)$ command, we assume that the machine never reaches $\text{DEC}(c)$ with $c = 0$. That is, the counters never have negative values. Given a counter machine $\mathcal{M}$, deciding whether $\mathcal{M}$ halts is known to be undecidable [9]. Given $\mathcal{M}$, deciding whether $\mathcal{M}$ halts with both counters having value 0 is also undecidable. Indeed, given a counter machine $\mathcal{M}$, we can replace every HALT command with code that clears the counters before halting. Thus, the halting problem can be reduced to the latter problem, termed the 0-*halting problem*.

We are going to reduce the 0-halting problem to the non-universality problem for complete WFAs with weights in $\{-1, 0, 1\}$, without initial weights or final weights, in which all the states are final.

Theorem 1. *The universality problem for complete WFAs over the semiring $\langle \mathbb{Z} \cup \{\infty\}, \min, +, \infty, 0 \rangle$ with weights in $\{-1, 0, 1\}$, without initial weights or final weights, in which all the states are final, is undecidable.*

Proof. We show a reduction from the 0-halting problem for two-counter machines to the non-universality problem. Let $\mathcal{M}$ be a two-counter machine with commands $(l_1, \ldots, l_n)$. A *halting run* of a two-counter machine with commands from the set $L = \{l_1, \ldots, l_n\}$ is a sequence $\rho = \rho_1, \ldots, \rho_m \in (L \times \mathbb{N} \times \mathbb{N})^*$ such that the following hold.

1. $\rho_1 = \langle l_1, 0, 0 \rangle$.
2. For all $1 < i \leq m$, let $\rho_{i-1} = (l_k, \alpha, \beta)$ and $\rho_i = (l', \alpha', \beta')$. Then, the following hold.
   - If l_k is a $\text{INC}(x)$ command (resp. $\text{INC}(y)$), then $\alpha' = \alpha + 1$, $\beta' = \beta$ (resp. $\beta = \beta + 1$, $\alpha' = \alpha$), and $l' = l_{k+1}$.
   - If l_k is a $\text{DEC}(x)$ command (resp. $\text{DEC}(y)$), then $\alpha' = \alpha - 1$, $\beta' = \beta$ (resp. $\beta = \beta - 1$, $\alpha' = \alpha$), and $l' = l_{k+1}$.
   - If l_k is a GOTO l_s command, then $\alpha' = \alpha$, $\beta' = \beta$, and $l' = l_s$.
   - If l_k is an IF $x\!=\!0$ GOTO l_s ELSE GOTO l_t command, then $\alpha' = \alpha$, $\beta' = \beta$, and $l' = l_s$ if $\alpha = 0$, and $l' = l_t$ otherwise.
   - If l_k is a IF $y\!=\!0$ GOTO l_s ELSE GOTO l_t command, then $\alpha' = \alpha$, $\beta' = \beta$, and $l' = l_s$ if $\beta = 0$, and $l' = l_t$ otherwise.
   - If l' is a HALT command, then $i = m$. That is, a run does not continue after HALT.
3. $\rho_m = \langle l_k, \alpha, \beta \rangle$ such that l_k is a HALT command.

Observe that the machine $\mathcal{M}$ is deterministic. We say that a machine $\mathcal{M}$ 0-halts if its run ends in $\langle l, 0, 0 \rangle$.

We say that a sequence of commands $\tau \in L^*$ *fits* a run ρ, if τ is the projection of ρ on its first component.

The *command trace* $\pi = \pi_1, \ldots, \pi_m$ of a run $\rho = \rho_1, \ldots, \rho_m$ is defined as follows. For every $1 \le i \le m$, if the command taken in ρ_i is not of the form IF $c=0$ GOTO l_k ELSE GOTO $l_{k'}$, then $\pi_i = l_i$. Otherwise, $\pi_i = $ GOTO l_s, where s is the location of the command in ρ_{i+1}.

We start by explaining the intuition behind the reduction. We construct a WFA $\mathcal{A}$ such that $\mathcal{M}$ 0-halts iff there exists $w \in \Sigma^*$ such that $L_\mathcal{A}(w) \ge 1$. The alphabet of $\mathcal{A}$ consists of the following $n + 5$ letters:

$$\Sigma = \{\text{INC}(x), \text{DEC}(x), \text{INC}(y), \text{DEC}(y), \text{HALT}\} \cup \{\text{GOTO } l_i : i \in \{1, \ldots, n\}\}.$$

When $\mathcal{A}$ reads a sequence of commands w, it tries to simulate the run of $\mathcal{M}$ that induces the command trace w. If the sequence of commands fits the actual run, and this run 0-halts, then all the runs of $\mathcal{A}$ cost at least 1. Thus, the word w is such that $L_\mathcal{A}(w) \ge 1$. If, however, the sequence of commands does not fit the actual run, then the violation is detected and $\mathcal{A}$ has a run on w with non-positive cost.

We now construct the WFA $\mathcal{A} = \langle \Sigma, Q, \Delta, c, Q_0 \rangle$. Observe that we omit F, i and f, as all the states are accepting, and there are no initial nor final weights. A detailed example can be found in the full version.

We designate a state q_{freeze} such that for all $\sigma \in \Sigma$, the WFA $\mathcal{A}$ has the transition $\Delta(q_{freeze}, \sigma, q_{freeze})$ with $c((q_{freeze}, \sigma, q_{freeze})) = 0$. There is also a state q_{halt} with the transition $\Delta(q_{halt}, \sigma, q_{freeze})$ and $c((q_{halt}, \sigma, q_{freeze})) = -1$ for all $\sigma \in \Sigma$ (see Figure 1).

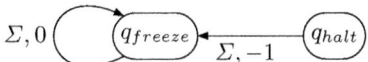

Fig. 1. q_{freeze} and q_{halt}

In order to define $\mathcal{A}$, we first define a "skeleton" ComCheck, which is an underspecified WFA. We then compose $\mathcal{A}$ from variants of ComCheck.

The skeleton ComCheck consists of states $q_1, \ldots, q_n$ that correspond to the commands $l_1, \ldots, l_n$. For two locations i and j, there is a transition from q_i to q_j iff l_j can *locally follow* l_i in a run of $\mathcal{M}$. That is, either $j = i + 1$ and l_i is an INC or DEC command, l_i is a GOTO l_j command, or l_i is an IF $c=0$ GOTO l_k ELSE GOTO $l_{k'}$ command, with $j \in \{k, k'\}$. The letters labeling the transition from q_i to q_j corresponds to the command trace. That is, the letter is l_i, except the case l_i is an IF $c=0$ GOTO l_k ELSE GOTO $l_{k'}$ command with $j \in \{k, k'\}$, in which case the letter is GOTO l_j. The weights on the transitions, as well as additional transitions, are specified below in every variant of ComCheck.

The WFA $\mathcal{A}$ is composed of 5 gadgets, each responsible for checking a certain type of violation in the description of a 0-halting run of $\mathcal{M}$. The gadgets are obtained from ComCheck as described below.

Command Checker. The first gadget we construct is the *command checker*. This gadget checks for local violations of succesive commands. That is, it makes sure that the letter w_i represents a command that can follow the command represented by w_{i-1} in $\mathcal{M}$. The test is local, as this gadget does not check for violations involving illegal jumps due to the value of the counters. The command checker consists of a ComCheck in which all the weights are 0. In addition, we add transitions labeled by HALT from every state q_i such that l_i = HALT to q_{halt}. These transitions cost 1. Every other transition that is not specified in ComCheck leads to q_{freeze} with weight 0. For example, reading a command that does not correspond to l_i in q_i leads to q_{freeze} with weight 0. Note that indeed, if a word represents the command trace of a halting run, it ends with a HALT letter from a state q_i such that l_i = HALT. Thus, the last transition has weight 1. Otherwise, the run of the command checker on w ends with a 0 weight transition.

Positive Jump Checker. The second gadget we need is the *positive jump checker*, which is defined for each counter $c \in \{x, y\}$. This gadget checks for violations in conditional jumps. In every IF $c=0$ GOTO l_j ELSE GOTO l_k command, it makes sure that if the jump GOTO l_k is taken, then the value of c is indeed greater than 0.

This gadget is a variant of ComCheck in which the weights are defined as follows. Every transition that is taken upon reading INC(c) has weight 1, and every transition that is taken upon reading DEC(c) has weight -1. In every state q_i such that l_i = IF $c=0$ GOTO l_j ELSE GOTO l_k, we add a transition $\langle q_i, \text{GOTO } l_k, q_{freeze}\rangle$ with weight -1. We add an initial state q_0 that, intuitively, has an ϵ transition with weight 1 to q_1 in ComCheck. Since we do not allow ϵ transitions, we remove the transition by connecting q_0 to the appropriate descendants of q_1. All the other transitions induced by ComCheck have weight 0. In addition, for every state q in ComCheck we add a transition $\langle q, \text{HALT}, q_{freeze}\rangle$ with weight 0 (See Figure 2).

The intuition behind this gadget is as follows. Along the run, the cost of the run reflects the value of the counter c plus 1. Whenever a conditional jump is taken, $\mathcal{A}$ nondeterministically moves to q_{freeze}, accumulating a weight of -1. If the jump is legal, then the value of the counter is at least 1, so the cost of the run so far is at least $1 + 1 = 2$. Thus, the nondeterministic run that follows this route has weight at least 1 when it reaches q_{freeze}. Otherwise, the value of the counter is 0, so the cost of the run is 1, and the nondeterministic move to q_{freeze} induces a run with cost 0, thus "detecting" the violation.

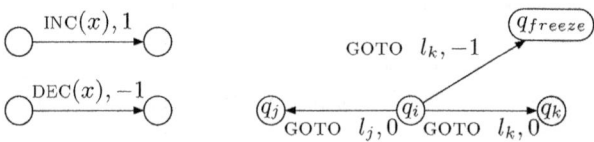

Fig. 2. Positive Jump Checker for x, where l_i : IF $x=0$ GOTO l_j ELSE GOTO l_k

Zero Jump Checker. Dually to the positive jump checker, we define the gadget *zero jump checker* for each counter $c \in \{x, y\}$.

This gadget checks for the dual violations in conditional jumps. Thus, in every command of the form IF $c=0$ GOTO l_j ELSE GOTO l_k, it makes sure that if the jump GOTO l_j is taken, then the value of c is indeed 0.

This gadget is a variant of ComCheck in which the weights are as follows. Every transition that is taken upon reading INC(c) has weight -1, and every transition that is taken upon reading DEC(c) has weight 1. In every state q_i such that l_i = IF $c=0$ GOTO l_j ELSE GOTO l_k, we add a transition $\langle q_i, \text{GOTO } l_j, q_{freeze}\rangle$ with weight 0. We add an initial state q_0 exactly as in the positive jump checker. All the other transitions in ComCheck have weight 0. In addition, for every state q in ComCheck we have a transition $\langle q, \text{HALT}, q_{freeze}\rangle$ with weight 0 (See Figure 3).

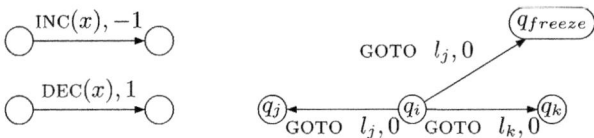

Fig. 3. Zero Jump Checker for x, where l_i : IF $x=0$ GOTO l_j ELSE GOTO l_k

To complete the definition of the automaton, we define Q_0 to include the states corresponding to l_1 in the command checker gadget and the q_0 states defined for the jump checkers for each counter $c \in \{x, y\}$.

We claim that $\mathcal{M}$ 0-halts iff there exists $w \in \Sigma^*$ such that $L_A(w) \geq 1$. Observe that the runs of $\mathcal{A}$ consist of all the runs in the underlying gadgets. Thus, it is enough to prove that $\mathcal{M}$ 0-halts iff there exists $w \in \Sigma^*$ such that all the runs of all the gadgets of $\mathcal{A}$ on w have cost of at least 1. A formal correctness proof can be found in the full version.   □

4   Weighted Automata with Positive Weights

In many models, the complexity of the universality problem and of the containment problem coincide. This is the case with Boolean automata, in which they are both PSPACE-complete [8], as well as with weighted automata over integer weights, for which the previous section shows undecidability. In this section we show that the model of weighted automata over positive integers is different: while the universality problem is PSPACE-complete, the containment problem is undecidable.

4.1   Universality Is PSPACE-Complete

In this section we prove that the universality problem for WFAs defined over the tropical semiring with domain $\mathbb{N} \cup \{\infty\}$, and in fact even $\mathbb{Q}^{\geq 0} \cup \{\infty\}$, is decidable, and is PSPACE-complete.

Theorem 2. *The universality problem for WFAs defined with respect to the semiring* $\langle \mathbb{N} \cup \{\infty\}, \min, +, \infty, 0 \rangle$ *is PSPACE-complete.*

The idea behind the proof is as follows. Consider a WFA $\mathcal{A}$ and a threshold $v \in \mathbb{N}$. The fact the weights are all positive enables us to bound the length of a shortest witness to non-universality by $(v + 2)^{|Q|}$. Intuitively, it follows from the fact that the relevant information about the runs of $\mathcal{A}$ after reading a prefix u can be summarized by a function from each state q to $\bot$, in case q is not reachable by reading u, or the minimum between v and the cost of reaching q by reading u; that is, a total of $v + 2$ values. Moreover, in a witness of a shortest length, such an information need not repeat. Consequently, it is possible to reason about a bounded unwinding (one of depth $(v + 2)^{|Q|}$) of $\mathcal{A}$ into a deterministic WFA, which can be done on-the-fly in PSPACE.

A careful anlysis of the proof of Theorem 2 shows that the result can be extended to the semiring $\langle \mathbb{Q}^{\geq 0} \cup \{\infty\}, \min, +, \infty, 0 \rangle$, by multiplying the weights by a common denominator. We can thus conclude with the following.

Theorem 3. *The universality problem for WFAs defined with respect to the semiring* $\langle \mathbb{Q}^{\geq 0} \cup \{\infty\}, \min, +, \infty, 0 \rangle$ *is PSPACE-complete.*

4.2   Containment Is Undecidable

We now show that the containment problem is undecidable for WFAs with weights in $\mathbb{N}$. In fact, the problem is undecidable already for complete WFAs with weights in $\{0,1,2\}$, without initial or final weights, in which all the states are final.

The decidability result for the universality problem used the monotonicity of weights accumulated in weighted automata with weights in $\mathbb{N}$. One may wonder why a similar approach cannot work for the containment problem. The reason is that the containment problem relates to the difference between two WFAs. Consequently, the underlying function, which is the difference in the weight accumulated in the two WFAs, is not monotonic even when the automata have only positive weights.

The undecidability proof is by a reduction from the containment problem for WFAs defined with respect to the domain $\mathbb{Z}$. It follows an analogous lemma in [6], according to which, two WFAs with domain $\mathbb{Z}$ are equal iff so are WFAs that they induce, and that are with domain $\mathbb{N}$. Intuitively, the induced WFAs are obtained by increasing all the weights in the original WFAs. Formally, we have the following.

Theorem 4. *The containment and equality problems for complete WFAs over the semiring* $\langle \mathbb{N} \cup \{\infty\}, \min, +, \infty, 0 \rangle$ *with weights in* $\{0,1,2\}$*, without initial or final weights, in which all the states are final, is undecidable.*

Proof. We start by defining a "weight-increase" operation on WFAs. Consider a number $k \in \mathbb{N}$ and a WFA $\mathcal{A}$ over $\mathbb{Z}$ with a cost function c. We define the k-*increase* of $\mathcal{A}$, denoted $\mathcal{A}^{+k}$, to be a WFA with a cost function c^{+k} that is equivalent to $\mathcal{A}$, except for having all weights increased by k; that is, for every transition d of $\mathcal{A}$, we have that $c^{+k}(d) = c(d) + k$.

We claim that for every word w, we have that $L_{\mathcal{A}+k}(w) = L_{\mathcal{A}}(w) + k|w|$. Indeed, consider a run r of $\mathcal{A}$ on w, such that $c(r) = L_{\mathcal{A}}(w)$. Since $\mathcal{A}^{+k}$ has the same transitions as $\mathcal{A}$, there is a run r' of $\mathcal{A}^{+k}$ on w that follows the same transitions as r. Thus, $c(r') = c(r) + k|w|$, and therefore $L_{\mathcal{A}+k}(w) \leq L_{\mathcal{A}}(w) + k|w|$. Analogously, we have that $L_{\mathcal{A}}(w) \leq L_{\mathcal{A}+k}(w) - k|w|$, choosing the same run for $\mathcal{A}$ as the one used for $\mathcal{A}^{+k}$. Hence, $L_{\mathcal{A}+k}(w) = L_{\mathcal{A}}(w) + k|w|$.

Now, consider two automata, $\mathcal{A}$ and $\mathcal{B}$, over $\mathbb{Z}$. Let k be the maximal absolute value of a weight in the transitions of $\mathcal{A}$ and $\mathcal{B}$. It is easy to see that all the weights in $\mathcal{A}^{+k}$ and $\mathcal{B}^{+k}$ are positive, thus they are defined with respect to the domain $\mathbb{N}$. We claim that $L_{\mathcal{A}} \leq L_{\mathcal{B}}$ iff $L_{\mathcal{A}+k} \leq L_{\mathcal{B}+k}$. Indeed, for every word w, $L_{\mathcal{A}+k}(w) \leq L_{\mathcal{B}+k}(w)$ iff $L_{\mathcal{A}+k}(w) + k|w| \leq L_{\mathcal{B}+k}(w) + k|w|$. Hence, the containment problem of WFAs over $\mathbb{Z}$ can be reduced to the containment problem of WFAs over $\mathbb{N}$, which is undecidable by Theorem 1. Furthermore, as the automata in Theorem 1 can be restricted to have weights in $\{-1, 0, 1\}$, their corresponding automata over $\mathbb{N}$ can be restricted to have weights in $\{0, 1, 2\}$.

We now reduce the containment problem to the equality problem, showing that the latter is undecidable as well. For WFAs $\mathcal{A}$ and $\mathcal{B}$, observe that $L_{\mathcal{A}} \leq L_{\mathcal{B}}$ iff $L_{\mathcal{A}} = min\{L_{\mathcal{A}}, L_{\mathcal{B}}\}$. Since we can easily construct a WFA for $min\{L_{\mathcal{A}}, L_{\mathcal{B}}\}$, then we can indeed reduce the containment problem to the equality problem.

$\square$

References

1. Boker, U., Henzinger, T.A.: Determinizing discounted-sum automata. In: Proc. 20th Annual Conf. for Computer Science Logic (2011)
2. Chatterjee, K., Doyen, L., Henzinger, T.: Quantative languages. In: Proc. 17th Annual Conf. for Computer Science Logic, pp. 385–400 (2008)
3. Chatterjee, K., Doyen, L., Henzinger, T.A.: Expressiveness and closure properties for quantitative languages. Logical Methods in Computer Science 6(3) (2010)
4. Degorre, A., Doyen, L., Gentilini, R., Raskin, J., Torunczyk, S.: Energy and mean-payoff games with imperfect information. In: Proc. 19th Annual Conf. for Computer Science Logic, pp. 260–274 (2010)
5. Droste, M., Kuich, W., Vogler, H. (eds.): Handbook of Weighted Automata. Springer, Heidelberg (2009)
6. Krob, D.: The equality problem for rational series with multiplicities in the tropical semiring is undecidable. Int. J. of Algebra and Computation 4(3), 405–425 (1994)
7. Krob, D.: Some consequences of a fatou property of the tropical semiring. Journal of Pure and Appllied Algebra 93(3), 231–249 (1994)
8. Meyer, A.R., Stockmeyer, L.J.: The equivalence problem for regular expressions with squaring requires exponential time. In: Proc. 13th IEEE Symp. on Switching and Automata Theory, pp. 125–129 (1972)
9. Minsky, M.L.: Computation: Finite and Infinite Machines, 1st edn. (1967)
10. Simon, I.: Recognizable sets with multiplicitives in the tropical semiring. In: Koubek, V., Janiga, L., Chytil, M.P. (eds.) MFCS 1988. LNCS, vol. 324, pp. 107–120. Springer, Heidelberg (1988)

Widening with Thresholds for Programs with Complex Control Graphs*

Lies Lakhdar-Chaouch, Bertrand Jeannet, and Alain Girault

INRIA

Abstract. The precision of an analysis based on abstract interpretation does not only depend on the abstract domain, but also on the solving method. The traditional solution is to solve iteratively abstract fixpoint equations, using extrapolation with a widening operator to make the iterations converge. Unfortunately, this extrapolation often loses crucial information for the analysis goal. A classical technique for improving the precision is "widening with thresholds", which bounds the extrapolation. Its benefit strongly depends on the choice of relevant thresholds. In this paper we propose a semantic-based technique for automatically inferring such thresholds, which applies to any control graph, be it intraprocedural, interprocedural or concurrent, without specific assumptions on the abstract domain. Despite its technical simplicity, our technique is able to infer the relevant thresholds in many practical cases.

1   Introduction and Related Work

Many static analysis problems boil down to the computation of the least solution of a fixpoint equation $X = F(X), X \in C$ where C is a domain of concrete properties, and F a function derived from the semantics of the analyzed program. Abstract Interpretation provides a framework for reducing this problem to the solving of a simpler equation in a domain A of *abstract properties*:

$$Y = G(Y), Y \in A \tag{1}$$

Having performed this *static approximation*, one is left with the problem of solving (1). The paper focuses on this problem. It considers the traditional iterative solving technique with widening and narrowing, and focuses more specifically on the widening with thresholds technique. We first review existing techniques before presenting our approach.

Exact equation solving. Some techniques solves directly (1) in the case where concrete properties are invariants on numerical variables. In [1,2] classes of equations on intervals are identified, for which the least solution can be computed exactly. *Policy iteration* methods solve (1) by solving a succession of simpler equations $Y = G_\pi(Y)$ indexed by a *policy* π [3,4]. However, such approaches are currently restricted to domains that infer bounds on a fixed set of numerical expressions, which excludes for instance the convex polyhedra abstract domain [5] and they do not make obsolete the classical iterative method described next.

---

* This work was supported by the OpenTLM project (pôle de compétitivité Minalogic).

T. Bultan and P.-A. Hsiung (Eds.): ATVA 2011, LNCS 6996, pp. 492–502, 2011.

Approximate equation solving by widening/narrowing. Under the classical hypothesis the sequence $Y_0 = \bot, Y_{n+1} = G(Y_n)$ converges to $lfp(G)$. However, if A contains infinite ascending sequences, which is the case of the abstract lattices mentioned above, the limit is extrapolated by using a *widening* operator $\nabla : A \times A \rightarrow A$. One computes the ascending sequence

$$Y_0 = \bot, \ Y_{n+1} = Y_n \nabla G(Y_n) \qquad (2)$$

which converges after a bounded number of iterations to a post-fixpoint $Y_\infty \sqsupseteq lfp(G)$, see Fig. 1. The approximations induced by widening can be partially recovered by performing a few descending iterations defined by the sequence

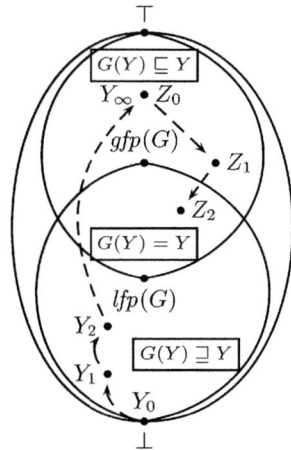

Fig. 1. Kleene iteration with widening and narrowing

$$Z_0 = Y_\infty, \ Z_{n+1} = G(Z_n) \qquad (3)$$

This is the most common instance of the concept of *narrowing* (see [6]). For many numerical abstract domains (like octagons [7] or convex polyhedra [5]) the "standard" widening consists in keeping in the result $R = P \nabla Q$ the numerical constraints of P that are still satisfied by Q.

The use of widening adds *dynamic approximations* to the *static approximations* induced by the choice of the abstract domain. Although it is shown in [6] that abstract domains with infinitely ascending sequences can discover properties that simpler abstract domains cannot infer, these dynamic approximations often raise accuracy issues. In particular no widening operator is monotonic. Moreover, as we show in §2, narrowing often fails to recover important information lost by widening, even on simple examples. In particular, if the function G is *extensive* (*i.e.,* $\forall Y \in A, Y \sqsubseteq G(Y)$), narrowing has no effect at all.

Techniques for controlling dynamic approximations. One approach is to improve the standard widening operators [8,9]. Other approaches are more global. For instance, *abstract acceleration* computes precisely with a single formula the effect of "accelerable" cycles in the CFG [10], and relies on widening for more complex cycles. *Guided static analysis* technique alternates ascending and descending sequences on an increasingly larger part of the system of equations [11]. This improves the accuracy of the analysis in many cases, but still it relies ultimately on the effectiveness of narrowing (see §2).

Widening with thresholds. Among local techniques, *widening up-to* or *widening with thresholds* attempts to bound the extrapolation performed by the standard widening ∇ operator [5,12]. The idea is to parameterize ∇ with a finite set C of *threshold constraints*, and to keep in the result $R = P \nabla_C Q$ those constraints $c \in C$ that are still satisfied by Q: $P \nabla_C Q = (P \nabla Q) \sqcap \{c \in C \mid Q \models c\}$. . Similarly to abstract acceleration techniques, widening with thresholds prevents from going too high in the lattice of properties (see Fig. 1) and from propagating inaccurate invariants in the CFG of the program, which cannot be strengthened later by narrowing. However, the benefit provided by widening with thresholds fully depends on the choice of the thresholds.

Our contribution: thresholds inference. This paper develops a semantic-based technique to infer automatically relevant thresholds, by propagating constraints in the CFG of the program in an adequate way. §2 illustrates on small examples the strengths and weaknesses of widening and narrowing, and gives the rationale for our technique for inferring relevant thresholds, which is formalized in §3. §4 evaluates it on a number of example programs and compares it to guided static analysis [11] and policy iteration [3]. A longer version of this paper is available as a research report [13].

2   The Widening/Narrowing Approach in Practice

We assume a static analysis problem formalized as an equation system

$$X^{(k)} = F^{(k)}(X) \qquad X = (X^{(1)}, \dots, X^{(K)}) \in C^K \tag{4}$$

where $X^{(k)} \in C$ is the concrete property associated with a node of the CFG of the program and $(C, \subseteq)$ is ordered by logical implication. Given an abstract domain $(A, \sqsubseteq)$ connected to C with a concretization function $\gamma : A \to C$, and a a *widening operator* $\nabla : A \times A \to A$ [6] we derive from (4) the system of equations

$$Y^{(k)} = G^{(k)}(Y) \qquad Y = (Y^{(1)}, \dots, Y^{(K)}) \in A^K \tag{5}$$

In order to solve (5), we use chaotic iterations with widening [14]: we follow the iteration order $1 \dots K$ and we apply widening as follows:

$$Y_0^{(k)} = \bot \qquad Y_{n+1}^{(k)} = \begin{cases} Y_n^{(k)} \nabla Y' & \text{if } k \in W \\ Y' & \text{otherwise} \end{cases} \tag{6}$$
$$\text{where } Y' = G^{(k)}(Y_{n+1}^{(0)} \dots Y_{n+1}^{(k-1)}, Y_n^{(k)} \dots Y_n^{(K)})$$

W is the subset of widening nodes: any dependency cycle in (5) contains a node in W. Narrowing by descending iteration is performed as in ((3)).

In all the examples of this paper, the static analysis problem is the computation of reachable values of the numerical variables of a program. A is the convex polyhedra domain, equipped with its standard widening operator [5].

Analysis of a simple loop program. Fig. 2 shows our first example. The double-line around a CFG node indicates a widening node in W. The table on the right details the Kleene iteration with widening and descending sequence, starting from $\bot$ at nodes ② and ③. In the steps 1 and 2, the widening operator has no effect. The row indexed by 3' corresponds to the computation of Y' in (6). In step 3, we have $Y_3^{(2)} = Y_2^{(2)} \nabla Y_{3'}^{(2)}$ and the effect of widening is to lose the upper bound on i. One descending step discovers the constraint $i \leq 26/3$, which comes from the postcondition of $Y_3^{(2)}$ by the loop:

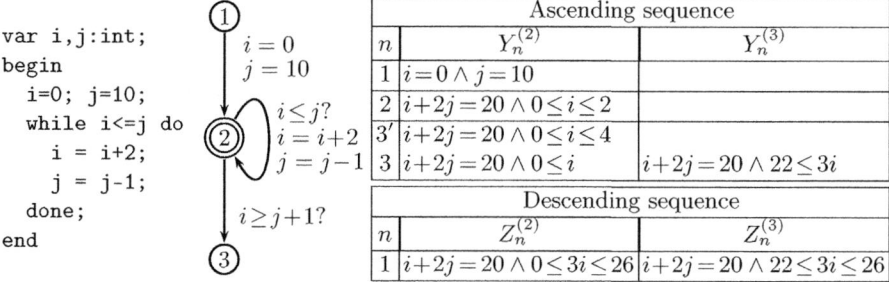

Fig. 2. Example: single loop

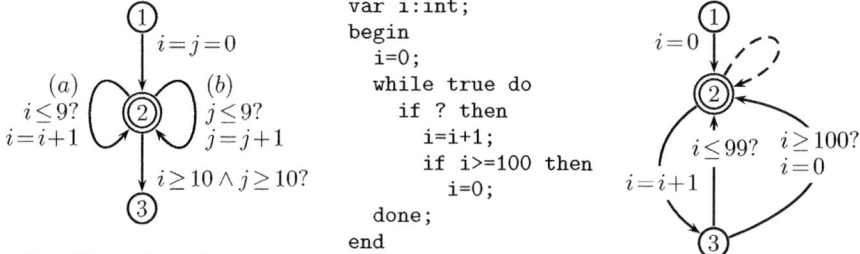

Fig. 3. Example: two non-deterministic loops

Fig. 4. Example: a single loop with break

$$\exists i,j : \left(\overbrace{i+2j=20}^{\text{implied by }Y_3^{(2)}} \wedge \overbrace{i\leq j \wedge i'=i+2 \wedge j'=j-1}^{\text{loop transition}}\right) = \left(i'=20-2j' \wedge \boxed{i'\leq j'+3}\right) \tag{7}$$
$$\Rightarrow \underline{i'\leq 20-2(i'-3)}$$
$$= 3i' \leq 26$$

We first observe that the invariant $Z^{(3)}$ at point ③ can be rewritten into $i+2j=20 \wedge 8-\frac{2}{3}\leq i\leq 8+\frac{2}{3}$, so $i\leq 26/3$ is the right bound for i at node ② Second, if one wants to use widening with thresholds, the guard of the loop $i\leq j$ is not a useful threshold constraint. The effect of using this threshold constraint allows us to keep the constraint $i\leq j$ at step 3, but this bound is violated at step 4' by the postcondition of the loop transition, hence this does not change the final result. We conclude that

(1) The important threshold constraint in a simple while loop is the postcondition of the guard of the loop by the loop body, here $i\leq j+3$, see Eqn. (7).

Two non-deterministic loops. The CFG of Fig. 3 is typically the result of the asynchronous parallel product of two threads with a simple loop. It shows the limitation of descending sequences. The ascending sequence converges to $Y^{(2)} = 0\leq i \wedge 0\leq j$. The descending sequence fails to improve it:

$$Z_1^{(2)} = G^{1\rightsquigarrow 2}(Y^{(1)}) \sqcup G^{2\rightsquigarrow 2(a)}(Y^{(2)}) \sqcup G^{2\rightsquigarrow 2(b)}(Y^{(2)})$$
$$= \{i=j=0\} \sqcup \{1\leq i\leq 10 \wedge 0\leq j\} \sqcup \{0\leq i \wedge 0\leq j\leq 10\}$$
$$= \{0\leq i \wedge 0\leq j\}$$

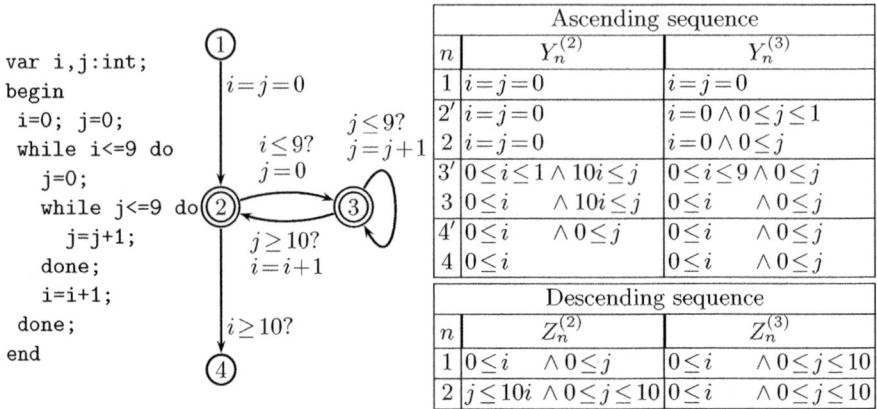

Fig. 5. Example: nested loop

The problem is that, for both variables i and j, there is always one incoming edge in node ② that propagates an invariant without an upper bound on it. As a result, no variable gets an upper bound in the result.

A single loop with break. Another example, inspired by a real controller, is depicted on Fig. 4. The dashed self-loop comes from the non-deterministic test "?" modeling an input from the environment. When the "then" branch is not taken, nothing happens in the loop body. It makes the transfer function on node ② extensive: $G^{(2)}(Y) \sqsupseteq Y^{(2)}$. Hence, the descending sequence will never improve the invariant $Y^{(2)} = i \geq 0$ found by the ascending sequence.

Nested loop. The nested loop program of Fig. 5 contains two widening nodes ② and ③ and raises some additional issues. The ascending sequence loses the two constraints $j \leq 10$ (step 2) and $i \leq 10$ (step 3) as expected (it even loses $0 \leq j$ at step 4). The descending sequence first recovers $j \leq 10$ at point ③, but then fails to recover $i \leq 10$ at point ②. The problem is similar to the problem with the non-deterministic loops of Fig. 3:

 – at point ②, the incoming edge ③ ↝ ② is not guarded by $i \leq 9$, and
 – at point ③ the self-loop ③ ↝ ③ is also not guarded by $i \leq 9$.

Hence, $i \leq 10$ is neither recovered at node ② nor ③. On this example, the guided static analysis of [11] also fails to discover this bound. We observe that

(3) Applying the heuristics sketched at the end of single loop example for generating the threshold constraint, *i.e.*, considering the postcondition of the guard $i \leq 9$ by the body of the outer loop on i, already implies a fixpoint computation because of the inner loop on j.

(4) Once an important fact is lost and the induced approximation is propagated, it is not always possible to recover it with narrowing.

A loop with conditional and guided analysis. The example of Fig. 6 is taken from [11]. The loop proceeds in two phases: in the first one, i and j are incremented together until $i = 51$; in the second one, i is incremented and j is decremented, and the loop exits with $i=102$ and $j=-1$. The standard approach finds, at node ④, $Y^{(4)} = j \leq -1 \wedge j \leq i+1$ and $Z_1^{(4)} = 51 \leq i \wedge j = -1$; it does not discover $i \leq 102$.

The intuition behind guided static analysis [11] is that widening implicitly assumes that the behavior of the program is "regular", which is not the case when a new behavior is activated in the program (in Fig. 6, such a new behavior is the activation of the "else" branch in the loop body). Hence its principle is (i) to discover the currently active part of the CFG (by a simple propagation); (ii) to perform a complete analysis with widening and narrowing on this part, starting from the invariants discovered so far; (iii) and to go back to step (i) to check whether new parts of the CFG may now be activated. The process is iterated up to convergence, which is guaranteed because the CFG is finite.

In this example, guided static analysis detects that only the "then" branch is initially activated. The ascending sequence on the active part of the CFG discovers $0 \leq i = j$ at node ② *followed by a descending sequence* that adds the bound $i \leq 51$. Only at this point does it take into account the activation of the "else" branch. The technique restarts a new analysis from the invariants inferred so far, and eventually obtains $Z_1^{(4)} = 51 \leq i \leq 102 \wedge j = -1$.

```
var i,j:int;
begin ①
  i=0; j=0; ②
  while true do
    if i<=50 then j=j+1;
              else j=j-1;
    if j<0 then goto ④
    i=i+1;
  done; ④
end
```

Fig. 6. Example: loop with conditional

In this example, widening with thresholds would behave like guided static analysis, *provided that the threshold constraint $i \leq 51$ is inferred.* Therefore,

(4) Thresholds are useful not only to bound $lfp(G)$, but also to *temporarily* bound the ascending iteration up to the activation of a new behavior.

Rationale for inferring thresholds. We made the following observations in the previous sections:

(1) For a while loop, the relevant threshold constraints are found in the post-condition of the guard of the loop by its body.
(2) Computing this postcondition may imply a fixpoint computation when the loop body itself contains loops; but then it implies widening.
(3) Threshold constraints inferred at a widening node should be propagated to the other widening nodes of the CFG.
(4) Thresholds are useful not only to bound the extrapolation, but also to detect the activation of new behaviors and to emulate guided analysis.

Because of observation (2), our solution propagates constraints without trying to converge to a fixpoint. Instead of the idea of propagating backward to the loop head the negation of the tests attached to transitions exiting a loop [15], our technique propagates forward the conditions for staying or exiting the loop body, which has a similar effect. In addition, *it also emulates guided analysis* by propagating tests attached to conditionals inside the loops.

3   Inferring Thresholds by Propagating Disjunctions

We assume the hypothesis of §2: we have to solve (4), which is abstracted in the abstract domain A into (5).

Definition 1 (Widening with thresholds). *Given two abstract values* $a_1, a_2 \in A$, *and a finite set* $T \subseteq A$ *of* threshold values, *we define*

$$a_1 \nabla_T a_2 = (a_1 \nabla a_2) \sqcap \bigsqcap \{a \in T \mid a_1 \sqsubseteq a \wedge a_2 \sqsubseteq a\}$$

Extracting thresholds from an abstract property. We assume that we have an *extraction function* $\pi : A \to \wp(Elt(A))$ that extracts, from any value $a \in A$, a set of "threshold" abstract values $\{a_1, \ldots, a_t\}$ that satisfies $\forall i : a \sqsubseteq a_i$. The definition of π depends on the domain A and possibly on the widening operator ∇. For *numerical domains*, π typically extracts the set of numerical constraints on which abstract values are built by conjunction. For the logico-numerical domain BDDAPRON [16], π also returns all the numerical constraints involved in the abstract property. π is extended to the disjunctive domain $\wp(A)$ with $\pi(X) = \bigcup_{a \in X} \pi(a)$.

Propagating thresholds in the system of equations. We now assume that (4) is abstracted into $\wp(A)$ rather than A. This can be done by replacing $\sqcup$ by $\cup$ inside the functions $G^{(k)}$ in (5). We thus have an equation system $T^{(k)} = G_d^{(k)}(T)$ with $T = (T^{(1)}, \ldots, T^{(K)}) \in (\wp(A))^K$. We also assume that, in the disjunctive domain $\wp(A)$, disjuncts are not simplified using the order $\sqsubseteq$ in A. We infer thresholds by considering the first steps of the following sequence:

$$\begin{aligned} T_0^{(k)} &= \top_{\wp(A)} = \{\top_A\} \\ T_{n+1}^{(k)} &= \pi \circ G_d^{(k)}(T_{n+1}^{(0)} \ldots T_{n+1}^{(k-1)}, T_n^{(k)} \ldots T_n^{(K)}) \end{aligned} \tag{8}$$

Given a number N of iterations, we define the set $T^{(k)}$ of threshold values attached to the node $k \in T$ as $T^{(k)} = T_N^{(k)}$. In practice, we take $N = 2$. This allows us to propagate conditions from loop heads to each node of their body (first iteration) but also to propagate conditions of possible inner loops back to the head of the outer loops (second iteration).

Applying widening with thresholds. Finally we solve (5) by computing the sequence (6) in which $\nabla_{T^{(k)}}$ replaces the standard widening operator ∇.

Application to the running examples. Figs 7 shows the application of our method to the examples described in §2. In each subfigure, the upper table shows the thresholds computed at each step while the lower table gives the result of the ascending sequence using thresholds. In all cases, the ascending sequence discovers the expected invariant. We do not break equality constraints $e = 0$ in $e \geq 0 \wedge e \leq$ during the inference of thresholds, but we do it at the end of the inference (in Fig. 7(d) the threshold $j \leq 10$ at node ② is extracted from the

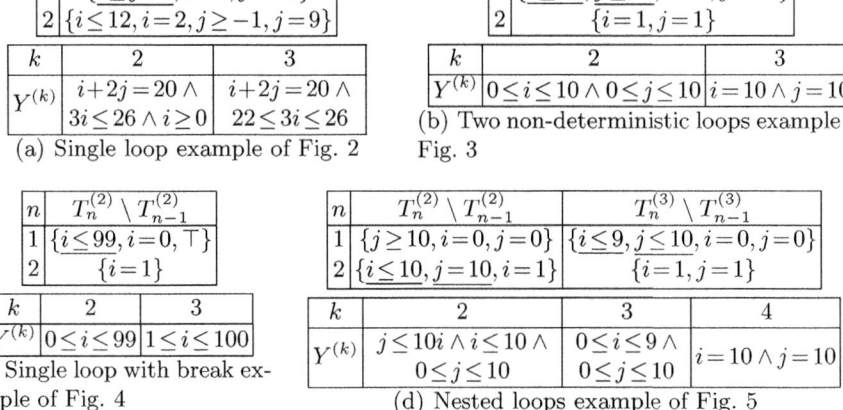

(a) Single loop example of Fig. 2

(b) Two non-deterministic loops example of Fig. 3

(c) Single loop with break example of Fig. 4

(d) Nested loops example of Fig. 5

Fig. 7. Inferring thresholds and widening with thresholds on running examples

Table 1. Comparison between standard, guided, policy iteration, and thresholds techniques using the box domain, on the examples of [3]

Program	guided vs standard	policy vs guided	thresholds vs policy
test5	$=$	4/0	$=$
test6	0/4	6/ $-$ 4	0/4
test7	$=$	9/0	$-4/0$
test8	$=$	4/0	$=$
test9	2/0	4/0	$=$
test1, test2, test3, test4: same results (simple examples)			

N1/N2 in column A vs B: number $N1$ of *additional* finite interval bounds and number $N2$ of *improved* finite interval bounds found by technique A compared to technique B, in all the program CFG; "$=$" indicates identical results.

value $j = 10$). Although our method infers many useless threshold constraints, it does infer all the required ones (which are underlined). It can be noticed that the second iteration step adds useful threshold constraints only in the nested loop example: this confirms observation (3) in §2.

4 Experiments and Conclusion

We implemented our inference technique for the BDDAPRON logico-numerical abstract domain used by the CONCURINTERPROC tool [16,17].[1] We first consider the box abstract domain, and three alternative methods: (1) the **standard**

---

[1] These experiments can be run with the online version of the analyzer, see [17].

Table 2. Comparison between standard, guided and our technique (inference+analysis), using the convex polyhedra domain

Program	CFG Size	Standard		Guided		Inf. of Thres.		Thresholds	
	#K/#F	Time	Prec.	Time	Prec.	Time	Av.nb.	Time	Prec.
Sequential, intraprocedural programs									
loop1	3/3	0.02	=	0.03	=	0.02	14	0.02	=
loop_nondet	3/4	0.03	B	0.03	B	0.02	12	0.04	A
loop_reset	4/6	0.01	B	0.01	B	0.01	6	0.02	A
loop2	4/5	0.06	B	0.09	B	0.02	12	0.08	A
gopanreps	4/6	0.06	B	0.09	A	0.04	16	0.08	A
loop2Bis	5/7	0.14	B	0.24	B	0.07	18	0.20	A
gopanrepsBis	5/8	0.29	B	0.49	B	0.28	39	0.85	A
nestedLoop	5/8	0.61	B	0.68	B	0.58	39	0.72	A
sipma91	7/11	0.35	B	0.42	B	0.57	33	0.37	A
car	3/4	0.06	=	0.07	=	0.01	14	0.06	=
Concurrent programs									
concurrent_loop	9/16	0.04	B	0.04	B	0.07	8	0.05	A
loop2_TLM	24/26	0.24	B	0.25	B	1.63	19	0.33	A^+
barrier_counter_2	61/108	1.71	B	1.91	B	2.09	18	4.90	A^+
barrier_counter_3	405/847	158.00	B	190.00	B	1553.00	78	1096.00	A^+
Programs with non-inlined procedure calls									
loop2_rec	15/18	0.25	B	0.42	B	1.88	28	0.47	A
gopanreps_rec	9/11	0.22	B	0.38	A	2.17	46	0.46	A
loop2Bis_rec	16/20	1.07	B	1.74	B	23.75	43	1.25	A
gopanrepsBis_rec	17/21	3.29	B'	9.23	A	651.00	82	9.86	B"
loop2_TLM_rec	34/38	0.86	B	0.86	B	17.76	20	1.97	A^+

#K/#F: size of the CFG, with #K the number of control nodes and #F the number of basic blocks; **Time:** running times in seconds, on a MacBook Air (Intel Core 2 Duo, 2.13 GHz); **Prec.:** relative precision: A is best, C is worse; A^+ indicates the proof of a specific property; **Av.nb.:** average number of inferred threshold constraints at each CFG node.

Kleene iteration with widening and descending sequence; (2) the **guided** static analysis technique of [11]; (3) and the **policy** iteration technique of [3] mentioned in the introduction, which is able to converge to the least fixpoint under some assumptions. Tab. 2 compares the results of the 4 methods on the examples of [3], which are purely numerical, by counting the total number of better bounds inferred by one technique over the other. On these tricky examples:

- **guided** is always better than **standard**;
- **policy** is better than **guided**, with the exception of **test6**, where it infers 6 additional finite bounds, but where 4 of the other inferred bounds are less accurate. **Thresholds** does strictly better than the other techniques here.
- **test7** is the only example for which widening with thresholds is less accurate than policy iteration, but still more accurate that guided analysis.

These experiments showed us the usefulness of considering also the constraint $x \geq 0$ when $x \leq 0$ is inferred. Typically, if we have a *inner* loop while (x>=1) do x-, the exit constraint $x \leq 0$ will be propagated to the *outer* loop head, whereas it is the constraint $x \geq 0$ which is relevant as a threshold at this point.

We then considered the convex polyhedra abstract domain combined in BDDAPRON with finite-state variables, Tab. 1. Policy iteration could not be experimented, because it is not defined on convex polyhedra. For all but 5 of these examples, widening with thresholds is strictly more precise than the standard or guided analyses, and it is less precise than guided analysis for a single example. W.r.t. efficiency, for the **sequential, simple examples**, the additional cost can be considered moderate, even when the number of inferred thresholds is not so small; for **concurrent programs**, the additional complexity is higher and may be dramatic in some cases, typically **barrier_counter_3** for which the number of thresholds have an impact of the analysis time (factor 6.0 w.r.t. standard analysis, besides the inference time). The performance problem here can be fixed by performing a thread-modular inference, which would infer the required thresholds on these examples (checked by manual inspection); for **relational interprocedural analysis**, we also have a performance problem, which results from the procedure return operation that implies a relation composition between abstract values. This problem desserves further investigations. Observe however that the technique infers the right thresholds, when for instance nested loops are implemented as tail recursive calls (**X_rec** versions of **X** examples).

To conclude, our technique is very successful w.r.t. precision, but needs efficiency improvements for concurrent and recursive programs. Abstract acceleration [10] might be better than our technique because it computes $\alpha \circ F^* \circ \gamma$ instead of the less precise $(\alpha \circ F \circ \gamma)^*$, but it does not solve the **nestedLoop** example with 3 nested loops, and is hardly applicable if loops are transformed in tail-recursive calls. It should combine efficiently with our technique. [18] describes the inference of thresholds in the ASTRÉE analyzer; it infers thresholds for single variables, and considers intraprocedural programs (procedures are inlined).

References

1. Su, Z., Wagner, D.: A class of polynomially solvable range constraints for interval analysis without widenings and narrowings. In: Jensen, K., Podelski, A. (eds.) TACAS 2004. LNCS, vol. 2988, pp. 280–295. Springer, Heidelberg (2004)
2. Gawlitza, T., Leroux, J., Reineke, J., Seidl, H., Sutre, G., Wilhelm, R.: Polynomial precise interval analysis revisited. In: Albers, S., Alt, H., Näher, S. (eds.) EA 2009. LNCS, vol. 5760, pp. 422–437. Springer, Heidelberg (2009)
3. Costan, A., Gaubert, S., Goubault, É., Martel, M., Putot, S.: A policy iteration algorithm for computing fixed points in static analysis of programs. In: Etessami, K., Rajamani, S.K. (eds.) CAV 2005. LNCS, vol. 3576, pp. 462–475. Springer, Heidelberg (2005)
4. Gawlitza, T., Seidl, H.: Precise relational invariants through strategy iteration. In: Duparc, J., Henzinger, T.A. (eds.) CSL 2007. LNCS, vol. 4646, pp. 23–40. Springer, Heidelberg (2007)

5. Halbwachs, N., Proy, Y., Roumanoff, P.: Verification of real-time systems using linear relation analysis. Formal Methods in System Design 11 (1997)
6. Cousot, P., Cousot, R.: Comparing the Galois connection and widening/narrowing approaches to abstract interpretation. In: Bruynooghe, M., Wirsing, M. (eds.) PLILP 1992. LNCS, vol. 631, pp. 269–295. Springer, Heidelberg (1992)
7. Miné, A.: The octagon abstract domain. In: Higher-Order and Symbolic Computation, vol. 19 (2006)
8. Bagnara, R., Hill, P.M., Ricci, E., Zafanella, E.: Precise widening operators for convex polyhedra. In: Science of Computer Programming (SCP), vol. 58 (2005)
9. Simon, A., Chen, L.: Simple and precise widenings for polyhedra. In: Ueda, K. (ed.) APLAS 2010. LNCS, vol. 6461, pp. 139–155. Springer, Heidelberg (2010)
10. Gonnord, L., Halbwachs, N.: Combining widening and acceleration in linear relation analysis. In: Yi, K. (ed.) SAS 2006. LNCS, vol. 4134, pp. 144–160. Springer, Heidelberg (2006)
11. Gopan, D., Reps, T.W.: Guided static analysis. In: Riis Nielson, H., Filé, G. (eds.) SAS 2007. LNCS, vol. 4634, pp. 349–365. Springer, Heidelberg (2007)
12. Cousot, P., Cousot, R., Feret, J., Mauborgne, L., Miné, A., Rival, X.: Why does astrée scale up? Formal Methods in System Design 35 (2009)
13. Lakhdar-Chaouch, L., Jeannet, B., Girault, A.: Widening with thresholds for programs with complex control graphs. Rapport de recherche RR-7673, INRIA (2011)
14. Bourdoncle, F.: Efficient chaotic iteration strategies with widenings. In: Pottosin, I.V., Bjorner, D., Broy, M. (eds.) FMP&TA 1993. LNCS, vol. 735, pp. 128–141. Springer, Heidelberg (1993)
15. Halbwachs, N.: A heuristics for inferring thresholds (personal communication)
16. Jeannet, B.: The BDDAPRON logico-numerical abstract domains library, http://www.inrialpes.fr/pop-art/people/bjeannet/bjeannet-forge/bddapron/
17. Jeannet, B.: The CONCURINTERPROC interprocedural analyzer for concurrent programs, http://pop-art.inrialpes.fr/interproc/concurinterprocweb.cgi
18. Cousot, P., Cousot, R., Feret, J., Mauborgne, L., Miné, A., Monniaux, D., Rival, X.: Combination of abstractions in the astrée static analyzer. In: Okada, M., Satoh, I. (eds.) ASIAN 2006. LNCS, vol. 4435, pp. 272–300. Springer, Heidelberg (2008)

Linear Hybrid System Falsification through Local Search*

Houssam Abbas and Georgios Fainekos

Arizona State University, Tempe, AZ, USA
{hyabbas,fainekos}@asu.edu

Abstract. In this paper, we address the problem of local search for the falsification of hybrid automata with affine dynamics. Namely, given a sequence of locations and a maximum simulation time, we return the trajectory that comes closest to the unsafe set. This problem is formulated as a differentiable optimization problem and solved. The purpose of developing such a local search method is to combine it with high level stochastic optimization algorithms in order to falsify hybrid systems with complex discrete dynamics and high dimensional continuous spaces. Experimental results indicate that the local search procedure improves upon the results of pure stochastic optimization algorithms.

Keywords: Model Validation and Analysis; Robustness; Simulation; Hybrid systems.

1 Introduction

Despite the recent advances in the computation of reachable sets in medium to large-sized linear systems (about 500 continuous variables) [1], the verification of hybrid systems through the computation of the reachable state space remains a challenging problem [2]. To overcome this difficult problem, many researchers have looked into testing methodologies as an alternative. Testing methodologies can be coarsely divided into two categories: robust testing (e.g. [3, 4] and systematic/randomized testing [5, 6].

Along the lines of randomized testing, we investigated the application of Monte Carlo techniques [7] to the temporal logic falsification problem of hybrid systems. In detail, utilizing the robustness of temporal logic specifications [8] as a cost function, we managed to convert a decision problem, i.e., does there exist a trajectory that falsifies the system, into an optimization problem, i.e., what is the trajectory with the minimum robustness value? The resulting optimization problem is highly nonlinear and, in general, without any obvious structure. Therefore, we treated the model of the hybrid system as a black box, and the cost function was minimized using Simulated Annealing (SA).

* This work was partially supported by a grant from the NSF Industry/University Cooperative Research Center (I/UCRC) on Embedded Systems at Arizona State University and NSF award CNS-1017074.

T. Bultan and P.-A. Hsiung (Eds.): ATVA 2011, LNCS 6996, pp. 503–510, 2011.

A stochastic optimization algorithm for the falsification problem picks a point in the set of initial conditions, simulates the system for a bounded duration, computes the distance to the unsafe set and, then, decides on the next point in the set of initial conditions to try. Our goal in this paper is to provide assistance at exactly this last step. Namely, how do we pick the next point in the set of initial conditions? Note that we are essentially looking for a descent direction for the cost function in the set of initial conditions.

Our main contribution, in this paper, is an algorithm that can propose such descent directions. Given a test trajectory $s_{x_0} : \mathbb{R}_+ \mapsto \mathbb{R}^n$ starting from a point x_0, the algorithm tries to find some vector d such that s_{x_0+d} gets closer to the unsafe set than s_{x_0}. We prove that it converges to a local minimum of the robustness function in the set of initial conditions, and demonstrate its advantages within a stochastic falsification algorithm. These results will enable local descent search for the satisfaction of arbitrary linear temporal logic specifications, not only safety specifications. The extended version of the paper appears in [9].

2   Problem Formulation

The results in this paper will focus on the model of hybrid automata with affine dynamics. A hybrid automaton is a mathematical model that captures systems that exhibit both discrete and continuous dynamics. In brief, a *hybrid automaton* is a tuple $\mathcal{H} = (X, L, E, Inv, Flow, Guard, Re)$ where $X \subseteq \mathbb{R}^n$ is the state space of the system, L is the set of control locations, $E \subseteq L \times L$ is the set of control switches, $Inv : L \to 2^X$ assigns an invariant set to each location, $Flow : L \times X \to \mathbb{R}^n$ defines the time derivative of the continuous part of the state, $Guard : E \to 2^X$ is the guard condition that enables a control switch e and, $Re : X \times E \to X \times L$ is a reset map. Finally, we let $H = L \times X$ to denote the state space of the hybrid automaton $\mathcal{H}$. For the purposes of this paper, we define a *trajectory* η_{h_0} starting from a point $h_0 \in H$ to be a function $\eta_{h_0} : \mathbb{R}_+ \to H$ defined by: $\eta_{h_0}(t) = (l(t), s_{x_0}(t))$, where $l(t)$ is the location at time t, and $s_{x_0}(t)$ is the continuous state at time t. We will denote by $\mathrm{loc}(\eta_{h_0})$ the sequence of control locations that the trajectory η_{h_0} visits (no repetitions).

The hybrid systems dealt with in this paper are deterministic and non-Zeno. In each location, the dynamics are affine, the guards are non-overlapping and the transitions are taken as soon as possible. This will permit us to use directly results from [4]. To avoid a digression into unnecessary technicalities, we will assume that the set of initial conditions $X_0 \subset \mathbb{R}^n$ and the unsafe set $\mathcal{U} \subset H$ are included in single control locations, l_0 and $l_{\mathcal{U}}$, respectively.

Let $D_{\mathcal{U}} : H \mapsto \mathbb{R}_+$ be the distance function to $\mathcal{U}$, defined by $D_{\mathcal{U}}(v, x) = \inf_{u \in \mathcal{U}} \|x - u\|$ if $v = l_{\mathcal{U}}$, and $D_{\mathcal{U}}(v, x) = +\infty$ otherwise. Given a compact time interval $[0, T]$, we define the *robustness* of a system trajectory η_h to be $f(h) \triangleq \min_{0 \leq t \leq T} D_{\mathcal{U}}(\eta_h(t))$. When l is clear from the context, we'll write $f(x)$. Trajectories of minimal robustness indicate potentially unsafe operation of the system. Finding such a trajectory can be seen as a 2-stage problem: first, decide on a sequence of locations to be followed by the trajectory. Second, out of all trajectories following this sequence of locations, find the trajectory of minimal robustness. This paper addresses the second stage. The central step is the solution the following problem:

Problem 1 *Given a hybrid automaton $\mathcal{H}$, a compact time interval $[0,T]$, a set of initial conditions $H_0 \subseteq H$ and a point $h_0 = (l_0, x_0) \in H_0$ such that $0 < f(h_0) < +\infty$, find a vector dx such that $h_0' = (l_0, x_0 + dx)$, $loc(\eta_{h_0}) = loc(\eta_{h_0'})$ and $f(h_0') \leq f(h_0)$.*

An efficient solution to Problem 1 may substantially increase the performance of the stochastic falsification algorithms by proposing search directions in which the robustness decreases. In summary, our contributions are: a) We formulate Problem 1 as a nonlinear optimization problem, which we prove to be differentiable w.r.t. the initial conditions. Thus it is solvable with standard optimizers. b) We developed an algorithm, Algorithm 1, to find local minima of the robustness function. c) We demonstrate the use of Algorithm 1 in a higher-level stochastic falsification algorithm, and present experimental results to analyze its competitiveness against existing methods. We now make some **assumptions**:

a. The continuous dynamics in each location are stable.[1]
b. The resets $Re(\cdot, e)$ are differentiable in their first argument.
c. Conditions 4 and 5 of Theorem III.2 in [12] are satisfied, namely: for all i, there exists a differentiable function $\sigma_i : \mathbb{R}^n \mapsto \mathbb{R}$ such that $Inv(l_i) = \{x \in \mathbb{R}^n | \sigma_i(x) \geq 0\}$; and, for all i, x such that $\sigma_i(x) = 0$, the Lie derivative $L_F\sigma_i(x) \neq 0$. This allows us to have *differentiable* transition times t_x of the trajectory starting at the initial point $x \in X_0$.
d. $l_\mathcal{U} \in loc(\eta_{h_0})$. This is required for our problem to be well-defined (specifically, for the objective function to have finite values). The task of finding such an h_0 is delegated to the higher-level stochastic search algorithm, within which our method is integrated. Due to space restrictions, all proofs are relegated to the technical report [9].

3   Descent in the Robustness Ellipsoid

Consider a trajectory η_{h_0} with positive robustness, with $loc(\eta_{h_0}) = l_0 l_1 \dots l_N$. This is provided by the simulation. We search for an initial point $h_0' \in H_0$ (actually $x_0' \in X_0$), whose trajectory gets closer to the unsafe set than the current trajectory η_{h_0}. In order to satisfy the constraints of Problem 1, we need to make sure that the new point h_0' generates a trajectory that follows the same sequence of locations as η_{h_0}. This constraint can be satisfied using the notion of robust neighborhoods introduced in [4]. In [4], it is shown that for stable systems and for a given safe initial point $h_0 = (l_0, x_0)$, there exists an 'ellipsoid of robustness' $E(x_0)$ centered on x_0, such that any trajectory starting in the ellipsoid follows the same sequence of locations as η_{h_0}. Therefore, we restrict the

---

[1] This is not a restrictive assumption since we can also consider incrementally stable systems [10], and even unstable linear systems [11].

choice of initial point to $X_0 \bigcap E(x_0)$, where $E(y) = \{x|(x-y)^T P_y^{-1}(x-y) \le 1\}$ is the ellipsoid of robustness centered on y, with shape matrix P_y.

We now proceed to pose our search problem as a feasibility problem. Let t_0 be the time at which s_{x_0} is closest to $\mathcal{U}$, and $\mathcal{W}$ be the set of all points which are closer to $\mathcal{U}$ than $s_{x_0}(t_0)$. $\mathcal{W}$ is represented as $\mathcal{W} = \{x \in \mathbb{R}^n : p_i(x) \le 0, i = 1 \ldots k\}$, where the p_i are suitably defined predicates, and $X_0 = \{x|C_0 x - g_0 \le 0\}$. If there exists $x^* \in X_0 \bigcap E(x_0)$ and $t^* \ge 0$ such that $s_{x^*}(t^*) \in \mathcal{W}$, it follows that $f(x^*) \le f(x_0)$. Our search problem then consists in finding such x^* and t^*. Therefore define the decision variable $z = (x, t, \nu) \in \mathbb{R}^n \times \mathbb{R}_+ \times \mathbb{R}$, the objective function $F(z) = \nu$, and the constraint functions: $G_0(z) = C_0 x - g_0$, $G_E(z) = (x-x_0)^T P_{x_0}^{-1}(x-x_0) - 1$, and $G_{\mathcal{W}}(z) = (p_1(s_x(t)), \ldots, p_k(s_x(t)))^T$. The search problem can now be cast as a feasibility problem over z:

$$\min_{z=(x,t,\nu)} F(z) \text{ s.t. } G_0(z) \le 0, G_E(z) \le \nu, G_{\mathcal{W}}(z) \le \nu \tag{1}$$

(In our implementation of Problem (1), the first constraint is specified as bounds to the optimization and so is always satisfied).

The objective function $F(z)$ measures the *slack* in satisfying the constraints: a negative ν means all constraints are satisfied, and in particular, $G_{\mathcal{W}}$. Thus, we have a trajectory that enters $\mathcal{W}$ and, hence, gets closer to $\mathcal{U}$. Formally:

Proposition 1. *Let $z^* = (x^*, t^*, \nu^*)$ be a minimum of $F(z)$ in program* (1). *Then $f(l_0, x^*) \le f(l_0, x_0)$.*

Functions F, G_0 and G_E are differentiable in z. The next proposition asserts differentiability of $G_{\mathcal{W}}$. Thus, standard gradient-based optimizers can be used to solve Problem (1). Let $E_0 \triangleq \text{int}(E(X_0) \bigcap X_0)$.

Proposition 2. *Fix $t \in (t_{N-1}, T]$, and consider the hybrid trajectory over $N \ge 1$ locations. Then $s_x(t)$ is differentiable at x_0 for all $x_0 \in E_0$. Moreover, for a fixed $x \in E_0$, $s_x(t)$ is differentiable in t over (t_{N-1}, T). If p_i is differentiable for all $i = 1, \ldots, k$, then $G_{\mathcal{W}}$ is differentiable in z.*

We choose Sequential Quadratic Programming (SQP), as a good general-purpose optimizer to solve Problem 1. SQP is a Q-quadratically convergent iterative algorithm. At each iterate, $G_{\mathcal{W}}(x_i, t_i, \nu_i)$ is computed by simulating the system at x_i. This is the main computational bottleneck of this method, and will be discussed in more detail in the Experiments section.

Solving Problem (1), for a given $\mathcal{W}$, produces a descent direction for the robustness function, but not necessarily a minimum. Algorithm 1 (RED) describes how to setup a *sequence* of optimization problems that leads to a local minimum of f (see [9] for proof): for $i = 0, 1, 2, \ldots$, let $x_i \in X_0 \bigcap E(x_{i-1})$, and let t_i be the time when s_{x_i} is closest to $\mathcal{U}$. Let $\mathcal{W}_i$ be the set of points closer to $\mathcal{U}$ than $s_{x_i}(t_i)$. For each $\mathcal{W}_i$, one can setup the optimization Problem (1) with $\mathcal{W} = \mathcal{W}_i$, and initial point $(x_i, t_i, 0)$; this problem is denoted by Prob1[$\mathcal{W}_i$].

Ellipsoid Descent with Stochastic Falsification: As outlined in the introduction, RED can be used as a sub-routine in a higher-level stochastic search

---

Algorithm 1. Robustness Ellipsoid Descent (RED)

Input: An initial point $x_0 \in X_0$, and corresponding t_0.

Output: z_Q.

1: Initialization: $i = 0$
2: Compute $z_i^* = (x_i^*, t_i^*, \nu_i^*) =$ minimum of Prob1$[\mathcal{W}_i]$.
3: **while** $\nu_i^* < 0$ **do**
4:     $x_{i+1} \leftarrow x_i^*$
5:     $t_{i+1} = \arg\min_t d_{\mathcal{U}}(s_{x_{i+1}}(t))$
6:     $\mathcal{W}_{i+1} = P(x_{i+1})$
7:     Compute $z_i^* = (x_i^*, t_i^*, \nu_i^*) =$ min of Prob1$[\mathcal{W}_{i+1}]$.
8:     $i = i + 1$
9: **end while**
10:
11: Return $z_Q \triangleq z_i^*$

Algorithm 2. Simulated Annealing with RED (SA+RED)

Input: An initial point $x \in X_0$.

Output: Samples $\Theta \subset X_0$.

Initialization: BestSoFar $= x$, $f_b = f(\text{BestSoFar})$

1: **while** $f(x) > 0$ **do**
2:     $x' = \text{ProposalScheme}(x)$
3:     $\alpha = \exp\left(-\beta(f(x') - f_b)\right)$
4:     **if** $UniformRandom(0, 1) \leq \alpha$ **then**
5:         $x = \text{RED}(x')$
6:     **else**// Use the usual acceptance criterion
7:         $\alpha = \exp\left(-\beta(f(x') - f(x))\right)$
8:         **if** $UniformRandom(0, 1) \leq \alpha$ **then** $x = x'$
9:     **end if**
10:    **end if**
11:    (BestSoFar,f_b) = BetterOf(x, BestSoFar)
12: **end while**

---

falsification algorithm. A stochastic search will have a ProposalScheme routine which, given a point x in the search space, will propose a new point x' as a falsification candidate. RED may then be used to further descend from some judiciously chosen proposals. Algorithm 2 illustrates the use of RED within the Simulated Annealing (SA) stochastic falsification algorithm of [7]. Given two samples x and y, BetterOf(x, y) returns the sample with smaller robustness, and its robustness.

For each proposed sample x', it is *attempted* with certainty if its robustness is less than the smallest robustness f_b found so far. Else, it is attempted with probability $e^{-\beta(f(x') - f_b)}$ (lines 3-4). If x' is attempted, RED is run with x' as starting point, and the found local minimum is used as final accepted sample (line 5). If the proposed sample is not attempted, then the usual acceptance-rejection criterion is used: accept x' with probability $\min\{1, e^{-\beta(f(x') - f(x))}\}$. As in the original SA method, ProposalScheme is implemented as a Hit-and-Run sampler (other choices can be made). The next section presents experimental results on three benchmarks.

3.1   Experiments

This section describes the experiments used to test the proposed algorithm SA+RED. The technical report [9] contains details of the benchmarks, methods, experiments and more results. We chose 3 navigation benchmarks from the literature: Nav0 (4-dimensional with 16 locations, unknown whether it is falsifiable or not), and Nav1 and Nav2 (4-dimensional with 3 locations, both falsifiable); and a filtered osciallator Fosc (32-dimensional with 4 locations). The methods compared are: SA+RED, pure Simulated Annealing (SA) [7], and the reachability analysis tool SpaceEx [13]. In a falsification framework, SpaceEx is used as follows: for a given bound j on the number of discrete jumps, SpaceEx computes an $over$-approximation $\overline{R(j)}$ of the set $R(j)$ reachable in j jumps: $R(j) \subset \overline{R(j)}$. If $\overline{R(j)} \cap \mathcal{U}$ is empty, then a $fortiori$ $R(j) \cap \mathcal{U}$ is empty, and the system is safe if trajectories are restricted to j jumps. When, however, $\overline{R(j)} \cap \mathcal{U} \neq \emptyset$, no conclusion can be drawn. Because SA and SA+RED are stochastic methods, their behavior will be studied by analyzing a number of runs. A $regression$ will mean a set of 20 runs, all executed with the same set of parameters, on the same benchmark. SpaceEx was run in deterministic mode on Nav0.

Parameter setting: We set the test duration $T = 12$sec for all benchmarks. For SA+RED, we chose to generate 10 samples ($|\Theta| = 10$). Even this small number is enough for the algorithm to be competitive. The SpaceEx parameters were varied in such a way that the approximation $\overline{R}$ of the reachable set R became increasingly precise. See [9].

The performance and cost metrics: Each run produces a minimum robustness. For a given regression, we measure: the smallest, the average, and the largest minimum robustness found by the regression (min, avg, max in Table 1). The standard deviation of minimum robustness is also reported (σ_f). For SpaceEx, we had to simply assess whether $\overline{R(j)}$ intersected $\mathcal{U}$ or not. SA and SA+RED each simulates trajectories of a fixed length T in the course of its operation, so their costs are compared by looking at the average Number of Trajectories ($\overline{NT}$) each simulates. The operations that SpaceEx does are radically different from those of the other methods compared here. The only way to compare performance is through the runtime.

Experiments: We impose an upper limit NT_{MAX} on NT: SA+RED is aborted when its NT reaches this maximum, and SA is made to generate NT_{MAX} samples. (Of course, SA+RED might converge before simulating all NT_{MAX} trajectories). 3 values were chosen for NT_{MAX}: 1000, 3000 and 5000. For each value, a regression is run and the results reported.

Table 1 compares SA+RED to SA: we start by noting that SA+RED falsified Nav2, whereas SA failed to so. On most regressions, SA+RED achieves better performance metrics than SA, for the same (or lower) computational cost. This is

Table 1. Comparison of SA and SA+RED. Robustness values are reported to the first differing decimal at least. σ_f is standard deviation of robustness for SA+RED.

System	NT_{MAX}	$\overline{NT}$ (σ_{NT})	σ_f	SA+RED Rob. min, avg, max	SA Rob. min, avg, max
Nav0	1000	1004 (1.4)	0.022	0.2852, 0.30,0.35	0.2853,0.33,0.33
	3000	2716 (651)	0.019	0.2852,0.29,0.32	0.2858,0.31,0.36
	5000	4220 (802)	0.009	0.285,0.28,0.32	0.286,0.32,0.35
Nav1	1000	662 (399)	0.21	0,0.43,0.65	0,0.96,1.88
	3000	1129 (1033)	0.23	0,0.39,0.65	0,0.99,1.80
	5000	1723 (1770)	0.23	0,0.38,0.68	0,0,0
Nav2	1000	902 (246)	0.32	0,0.54,0.78	0.3089,1.11,1.90
	3000	1720 (1032)	0.3	0,0.53,0.83	0.3305,1.29,1.95
	5000	1726 (1482)	0.27	0,0.62,0.79	0,0.002,0.01
Fosc	1000	1000 (9.3)	0.024	0.162,0.206,0.251	0.1666,0.216,0.271
	3000	3000 (8.7)	0.024	0.163,0.203,0.270	0.173,0.212,0.254
	5000	5000 (11)	0.028	0.167,0.193,0.258	0.185, 0.218, 0.245

consistent whether considering best case (min), average case (avg) or worst case (max). There are 2 exceptions: on Nav1 and Nav2, $NT_{MAX} = 5000$ produces better average and max results for SA than for SA+RED. When running realistic system models, trajectory simulation is the biggest time consumer, so effectively NT is the limiting factor. So we argue that these 2 exceptions don't invalidate the superiority of SA+RED as they occur for high values of NT that might not be practical with real-world models.

For SpaceEx running on Nav0, we observed that our initial parameter set produces an $\overline{R(j)}$ that intersects $\mathcal{U}$. Since this is inconclusive, we modified the parameters to get a better approximation, but SpaceEx runtimes far exceeded those of SA+RED (more than 1.5 hours). Moreover, SpaceEx did not reach a fixed point of its iterations. Thus, we can not be sure that all of the reachable space was covered. While this may be seen as an analogous problem to the choice of T in SA+RED, the computational cost of increasing j is much more prohibitive than that of increasing T. Thus we may conclude that stochastic falsification and reachability analysis can play complementary roles in good design practice: first, stochastic falsification computes the robustness of the system with respect to some unsafe set. Guided by this, the designer may make the system more robust, which effectively increases the distance between the (unknown) reachable set and the unsafe set. Then the designer can run a reachability analysis algorithm where coarse over-approximations can yield conclusive results.

4 Conclusions

The minimum robustness of a hybrid system is an important indicator of how safe it is. In this paper, we presented an algorithm for computing a local minimum of the robustness for a certain class of linear hybrid systems. When integrated with a higher-level stochastic search algorithm, the proposed algorithm has been shown to perform better than existing methods on literature benchmarks, and to complement reachability analysis in falsification. We will next deploy this capability to perform local descent search for the satisfaction of arbitrary linear temporal logic specifications, not only safety specifications. It will be important to reduce the required number of tests NT, and to determine an appropriate test duration T, rather than a fixed arbitrary value. Finally, it is important to get a theoretical understanding of the behavior of the two Markov chains iterated by SA+RED to further improve it.

References

1. Girard, A., LeGuernic, C.: Efficient reachability analysis for linear systems using support functions. In: IFAC World Congress, pp. 22–35 (2008)
2. Althoff, M., Stursberg, O., Buss, M.: Computing reachable sets of hybrid systems using a combination of zonotopes and polytopes. Nonlinear Analysis: Hybrid Systems 4(2), 233–249 (2010)
3. Girard, A., Pappas, G.J.: Verification using simulation. In: Hespanha, J.P., Tiwari, A. (eds.) HSCC 2006. LNCS, vol. 3927, pp. 272–286. Springer, Heidelberg (2006)
4. Julius, A.A., Fainekos, G., Anand, M., Lee, I., Pappas, G.: Robust test generation and coverage for hybrid systems. In: Bemporad, A., Bicchi, A., Buttazzo, G. (eds.) HSCC 2007. LNCS, vol. 4416, pp. 329–342. Springer, Heidelberg (2007)
5. Branicky, M., Curtiss, M., Levine, J., Morgan, S.: Sampling-based planning, control and verification of hybrid systems. IEE Proc.-Control Theory Appl. 153(5), 575–590 (2006)
6. Zuliani, P., Platzer, A., Clarke, E.M.: Bayesian statistical model checking with application to simulink/stateflow verification. In: Proceedings of the 13th ACM International Conference on Hybrid Systems: Computation and Control, pp. 243–252 (2010)
7. Nghiem, T., Sankaranarayanan, S., Fainekos, G., Ivancic, F., Gupta, A., Pappas, G.: Monte-carlo techniques for falsification of temporal properties of non-linear hybrid systems. In: Hybrid Systems: Computation and Control (2010)
8. Fainekos, G., Pappas, G.: Robustness of temporal logic specifications for continuous-time signals. Theoretical Computer Science 410(42), 4262–4291 (2009)
9. Abbas, H., Fainekos, G.: Linear hybrid system falsification through descent, technical Report arXiv:1105.1733 (2011)
10. Tabuada, P.: Verification and Control of Hybrid Systems: A Symbolic Approach. Springer, Heidelberg (2009)
11. Julius, A.A., Pappas, G.J.: Trajectory based verification using local finite-time invariance. In: Majumdar, R., Tabuada, P. (eds.) HSCC 2009. LNCS, vol. 5469, pp. 223–236. Springer, Heidelberg (2009)
12. Lygeros, J., Johansson, K.H., Simic, S.N., Zhang, J., Sastry, S.: Dynamical properties of hybrid automata. IEEE Transactions on Automatic Control 48, 2–17 (2003)
13. Frehse, G., Guernic, C.L., Donzé, A., Cotton, S., Ray, R., Lebeltel, O., Ripado, R., Girard, A., Dang, T., Maler, O.: Spaceex: Scalable verification of hybrid systems. In: Gopalakrishnan, G., Qadeer, S. (eds.) CAV 2011. LNCS, vol. 6806, pp. 379–395. Springer, Heidelberg (2011)

Learning-Based Compositional Verification
for Synchronous Probabilistic Systems

Lu Feng, Tingting Han, Marta Kwiatkowska, and David Parker

Department of Computer Science, University of Oxford, Oxford, OX1 3QD, UK

Abstract. We present novel techniques for automated compositional verification of synchronous probabilistic systems. First, we give an assume-guarantee framework for verifying probabilistic safety properties of systems modelled as discrete-time Markov chains. Assumptions about system components are represented as probabilistic finite automata (PFAs) and the relationship between components and assumptions is captured by weak language inclusion. In order to implement this framework, we develop a semi-algorithm to check language inclusion for PFAs and a new active learning method for PFAs. The latter is then used to automatically generate assumptions for compositional verification.

1 Introduction

Probabilistic model checking is a formal verification technique for analysing quantitative properties of systems that exhibit stochastic behaviour. A key challenge in this area is scalability, motivating the development of *compositional* verification methods that decompose the analysis of a large system model into smaller sub-tasks. We focus on the *assume-guarantee* paradigm, in which each system component is analysed under an *assumption* about the other component(s) it is composed with. After checking that the assumption is satisfied, proof rules are used to deduce properties of the overall system.

Several assume-guarantee frameworks for verifying probabilistic systems have been proposed, mainly for models with both probabilistic and nondeterministic behaviour [1,13,10]. The main difficulty when developing such a framework is formulating an appropriate notion of *assumptions* that can support compositional reasoning. Our goal is to develop assume-guarantee techniques for probabilistic model checking that are practical, efficient and fully-automated. This means that assumptions should ideally: (i) be expressive enough for practical applications; (ii) allow efficient, fully-automated verification; and (iii) be amenable to automatic generation.

One promising direction is the framework of [13] (and its extensions in [10,9]). In [13], assumptions are *probabilistic safety properties* (e.g. "event A always occurs before event B with probability at least 0.98") and [10] generalises this to boolean combinations of ω-regular and reward properties. In both cases, this yields efficiently checkable assumptions and the approaches were successfully implemented and applied to some large case studies. Furthermore, [9] shows how to *automatically* generate probabilistic safety property assumptions [13] using *learning* techniques based on L*.

In this work, we continue to develop probabilistic assume-guarantee techniques in which assumptions can be automatically generated via learning. In particular, our focus is on using a more expressive class of assumptions. Probabilistic safety property

T. Bultan and P.-A. Hsiung (Eds.): ATVA 2011, LNCS 6996, pp. 511–521, 2011.

assumptions [13] can only capture a limited amount of information about a component, restricting the cases where assume-guarantee reasoning can be applied. The framework of [13] is *incomplete* in the sense that, if the property being verified is true, there does not necessarily exists an assumption that can be used to verify it compositionally.

This paper proposes novel techniques for compositional probabilistic verification in which assumptions are *probabilistic finite automata* (PFAs) [15]. Unlike [13,10], our approach *is* complete. Furthermore, as in [10], we use learning to automatically generate assumptions. PFAs represent weighted languages, mapping finite words to probabilities. In our framework, an assumption about a system component M is represented by a PFA that gives upper bounds on the probabilities of traces being observed in M. This is an inherently *linear-time* relation, which is well-known to be difficult to adapt to compositional techniques for systems that exhibit both probabilistic and nondeterministic behaviour [16]. So, in the present work, we restrict our attention to *fully probabilistic* systems. To do so, we model components as *probabilistic I/O systems* (PIOSs), which, when combined through *synchronous* parallel composition, result in a (fully probabilistic) discrete-time Markov chain (DTMC). The relation between a PIOS M and a PFA A representing an assumption about M is captured by *weak language inclusion*. Based on this, we give an asymmetric proof rule for verifying probabilistic safety properties on a DTMC composed of two PIOSs.

In order to implement our framework, we give an algorithm to check weak language inclusion, reducing it to the existing notion of (strong) language inclusion for PFAs. Although checking PFA language *equivalence* (that each word maps to the same probability) is decidable in polynomial time [18,7], checking language *inclusion* is undecidable [5]. We propose a semi-algorithm, inspired by [18], to check language inclusion; in the case where the check fails, a minimal counterexample is produced.

We also develop a novel technique for *learning* PFAs, which we use to automatically generate assumptions for our framework. Our algorithm, like L*, is based on *active learning*, posing queries in an interactive fashion about the PFA to be generated. Several active PFA learning algorithms exist [12,17,4] but are not suitable for our needs: [12] applies to a restricted class of PFAs, [17] needs to know the size of the PFA in advance, and [4] actually learns multiplicity automata, which may contain negative values.

Full version: For an extended version of this paper, including additional details, explanations and running examples, experimental results and proofs, see [8].

2   Preliminaries

We first briefly describe *probabilistic finite automata* and *discrete-time Markov chains*. We use $SDist(S)$ to denote the set of probability *sub-distributions* over set S, η_s for the point distribution on $s \in S$, and $\mu_1 \times \mu_2$ for the product distribution of μ_1 and μ_2.

Definition 1 (PFA). *A probabilistic finite automaton (PFA) is a tuple* $A = (S, \overline{s}, \alpha, \mathbf{P})$, *where S is a finite set of states, $\overline{s} \in S$ is an initial state, α is an alphabet and $\mathbf{P} : \alpha \rightarrow (S \times S \rightarrow [0, 1])$ is a function mapping actions to transition probability matrices. For each $a \in \alpha$ and $s \in S$, $\sum_{s' \in S} \mathbf{P}(a)[s, s'] \in [0, 1]$.*

A PFA A defines a mapping $Pr^A : \alpha^* \rightarrow [0, 1]$ giving the probability of accepting each finite word $w \in \alpha^*$. Intuitively, the probability $Pr^A(w)$ for a word $w = a_1 \cdots a_n$ is determined by tracing paths through A that correspond to w, with $\mathbf{P}(a)[s, s']$ giving the probability to move from s to s' on reading a. More precisely, we let ι be an S-indexed 0-1 row vector with $\iota[s] = 1$ if and only if $s = \bar{s}$, κ be an S-indexed column vector of 1s and $\mathbf{P}(w) = \mathbf{P}(a_1)\cdots\mathbf{P}(a_n)$. Then, we define $Pr^A(w) = \iota\mathbf{P}(w)\kappa$.

Definition 2 (Language inclusion/equivalence). *Given two PFAs A_1 and A_2 with the same alphabet α, we say A_1 and A_2 are related by (strong) language inclusion (resp. language equivalence), denoted $A_1 \sqsubseteq A_2$ (resp. $A_1 \equiv A_2$), if for every word $w \in \alpha^*$, $Pr^{A_1}(w) \leqslant Pr^{A_2}(w)$ (resp. $Pr^{A_1}(w) = Pr^{A_2}(w)$).*

Definition 3 (DTMC). *A discrete-time Markov chain (DTMC) is a tuple $D=(S, \bar{s}, \alpha, \delta)$, where S is a finite set of states, $\bar{s} \in S$ is an initial state, α is an alphabet of action labels and $\delta : S \times (\alpha \cup \{\tau\}) \to SDist(S)$ is a (partial) probabilistic transition function, such that, for any s, $\delta(s, a)$ is defined for at most one $a \in \alpha \cup \{\tau\}$.*

If $\delta(s, a) = \mu$, the DTMC can make a transition, labelled with action a, and move to state s' with probability $\mu(s')$. We denote such transitions by $s \xrightarrow{a} \mu$ (or $s \xrightarrow{a} s'$). The DTMC deadlocks when $\delta(s, a)$ is not defined for any a, which we denote by $s \nrightarrow$. We use action label τ to denote a "silent" (or "internal") transition. A (finite or infinite) path through D is a sequence of transitions $\theta = s_0 \xrightarrow{a_0} s_1 \xrightarrow{a_1} \cdots$ with $s_0 = \bar{s}$.

In this paper, we consider *probabilistic safety properties* $\langle G \rangle_{\geqslant p}$, where G is a *regular safety property* [3], defining a set of "good" executions, and $p \in [0, 1]$ is a probability bound. Model checking $\langle G \rangle_{\geqslant p}$ reduces to solving a linear equation system [3].

3 Assume-Guarantee for Synchronous Probabilistic Systems

We now define a compositional verification framework for fully probabilistic systems. Components are modelled by *probabilistic I/O systems* (PIOSs). These exhibit (input) nondeterminism but, when composed *synchronously* in parallel, result in a DTMC.

Definition 4 (PIOS). *A probabilistic I/O system (PIOS) is a tuple $M = (S, \bar{s}, \alpha, \delta)$, where S and $\bar{s}$ are as for DTMCs, and the alphabet α and transition function $\delta : S \times (\alpha \cup \{\tau\}) \to SDist(S)$ satisfy the following two conditions: (i) α is partitioned into three disjoint sets of input, output and hidden actions, which we denote α^I, α^O and α^H, respectively; input actions α^I are further partitioned into m disjoint bundles $\alpha^{I,i}$ $(1 \leqslant i \leqslant m)$ for some m; (ii) the set $enab(s) \subseteq \alpha \cup \{\tau\}$ of enabled actions for each state s (i.e. the actions a for which $\delta(s, a)$ is defined) satisfies either $|enab(s)| = 1$ if $enab(s) \in \alpha^O \cup \alpha^H \cup \{\tau\}$ or $enab(s) = \alpha^{I,i}$ for some input action bundle $\alpha^{I,i}$.*

From any state s of a PIOS M, there is either a single transition with an output, hidden or τ action, or k transitions, each with one action from a particular bundle $\alpha^{I,i}$ comprising k input actions. Transitions and paths in PIOSs are defined as for DTMCs. The probability of a finite path $\theta = s_0 \xrightarrow{a_0} s_1 \cdots \xrightarrow{a_{n-1}} s_n$ in M is given by $Pr^M(\theta) = \prod_{i=0}^{n-1} \delta(s_i, a_i)(s_{i+1})$. Since PIOSs only have nondeterminism on input actions, the probability for a word $w \in (\alpha \cup \{\tau\})^*$ is well defined: letting $wd(\theta)$ denote the word $a_0 \ldots a_{n-1}$ of actions from path θ, we have $Pr^M(w) = \sum_{wd(\theta)=w} Pr^M(\theta)$. Then, letting $st : (\alpha \cup \{\tau\})^* \alpha \to \alpha^*$ be the function that removes all τs, we define the probability $Pr_\tau^M(w')$ for a τ-free word $w' \in \alpha^*$ as $Pr_\tau^M(w) = \sum_{w=st(w')} Pr^M(w')$.

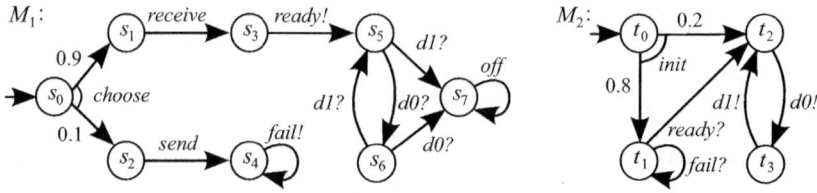

Fig. 1. Running example: two PIOSs M_1 and M_2

Example 1. Fig. 1 depicts two PIOSs M_1 and M_2. M_1 is a data communicator which chooses (probabilistically) to either send or receive data. This simple example only models receiving; choosing to send results in a failure. M_1 tells M_2, a data generator, that it is ready to receive using action *ready*. M_2 should then send a sequence of packets, modelled by the alternating actions *d0* and *d1*. If M_1 has failed, it sends a message *fail*. M_2 also has an initialisation step (*init*), which can fail. With probability 0.8, it is ready to receive signals from M_1; otherwise, it just tries to send packets anyway. Input/output actions for M_1, M_2 are labelled with ?/! in the figure; all other actions are hidden. Each PIOS has a single input action bundle: $\alpha_1^{I,1} = \{d0, d1\}$, $\alpha_2^{I,1} = \{ready, fail\}$.

Given PIOSs M_1, M_2 with alphabets α_1, α_2, we say M_1 and M_2 are *composable* if $\alpha_1^I = \alpha_2^O$, $\alpha_1^O = \alpha_2^I$ and $\alpha_1^H \cap \alpha_2^H = \varnothing$ and define their parallel composition as follows.

Definition 5 (Parallel composition). *The* parallel composition *of composable PIOSs* $M_i = (S_i, \bar{s}_i, \alpha_i, \delta_i)$ *for* $i=1,2$ *is given by the PIOS* $M_1 \| M_2 = (S_1 \times S_2, (\bar{s}_1, \bar{s}_2), \alpha, \delta)$, *where* $\alpha = \alpha^H = \alpha_1^I \cup \alpha_1^O \cup ((\alpha_1^H \cup \{\perp\}) * (\alpha_2^H \cup \{\perp\}))$ *and, for* $b_i \in \alpha_i^H \cup \tau$ *and* $a \in \alpha_1^I \cup \alpha_1^O$, δ *is defined such that* $(s_1, s_2) \xrightarrow{\gamma} \mu_1 \times \mu_2$ *iff one of the following holds:*
(i) $s_1 \xrightarrow{a} \mu_1$, $s_2 \xrightarrow{a} \mu_2$, $\gamma = a$; *(ii)* $s_1 \xrightarrow{b_1} \mu_1$, $s_2 \xrightarrow{b_2} \mu_2$, $\gamma = b_1 * b_2$; *(iii)* $s_1 \xrightarrow{b_1} \mu_1$, $s_2 \xrightarrow{a}$
(or $s_2 \nrightarrow$*)*, $\mu_2 = \eta_{s_2}$, $\gamma = b_1 * \perp$; *(iv)* $s_1 \xrightarrow{a}$ *(or* $s_1 \nrightarrow$*)*, $s_2 \xrightarrow{b_2} \mu_2$, $\mu_1 = \eta_{s_1}$, $\gamma = \perp * b_2$.

Notice PIOS $M_1 \| M_2$ has only τ or hidden actions and can thus be considered a DTMC.

We next introduce our notion of *assumptions* about PIOSs, for which we use a specific class of PFAs and *weak language inclusion*, which relaxes the definition of language inclusion for PFAs introduced earlier by ignoring τ actions.

Definition 6 (Assumption). *Let* M *be a PIOS with alphabet* $\alpha = \alpha^I \uplus \alpha^O \uplus \alpha^H$ *and input action bundles* $\alpha^I = \biguplus_{i=1}^m \alpha^{I,i}$. *An assumption* A *about* M *is a PFA* $A = (S, \bar{s}, \alpha, \mathbf{P})$ *satisfying, for each state* $s \in S$: *(i) either all or none of the actions in a bundle* $\alpha^{I,i}$ $(1 \leqslant i \leqslant m)$ *are enabled in* s; *(ii)* $p^{\max}(s) \in [0,1]$, *where:*

$$p^{\max}(s) \stackrel{\text{def}}{=} \sum_{a \in \alpha^O \cup \alpha^H} \sum_{s' \in S} \mathbf{P}(a)[s, s'] + \sum_{i=1}^m p_i^{\max}(s) \text{ and } p_i^{\max}(s) \stackrel{\text{def}}{=} \max_{a \in \alpha^{I,i}} \sum_{s' \in S} \mathbf{P}(a)[s, s']$$

Definition 7 (Weak language inclusion/equivalence). *For PIOS* M *with alphabet* α *and an assumption* A *about* M, *we say that* M *and* A *are related by* weak language inclusion *(resp. equivalence), denoted* $M \sqsubseteq_w A$ *(resp.* $M \equiv_w A$*), if for every word* $w \in \alpha^*$, $Pr_\tau^M(w) \leqslant Pr^A(w)$ *(resp.* $Pr_\tau^M(w) = Pr^A(w)$*).*

A *valid* assumption A for M is one that satisfies $M \sqsubseteq_w A$. We can reduce the problem of checking whether this is true to the problem of checking (strong) language inclusion between two PFAs (see Section 4) by the following proposition.

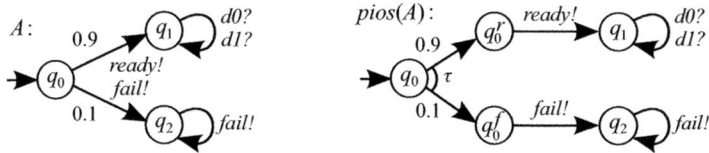

Fig. 2. Assumption A and its PIOS conversion $pios(A)$

Proposition 1. *Let* $M = (S, \bar{s}, \alpha, \delta)$ *be a PIOS and* A *be an assumption about* M. $pfa(M) = (S, \bar{s}, \alpha \cup \{\tau\}, \mathbf{P})$ *is the translation of* M *to a PFA, where* $\mathbf{P}(a)[s, s'] = \delta(s, a)(s')$ *for* $a \in \alpha \cup \{\tau\}$. *Letting* A^τ *be the PFA derived from* A *by adding* τ *to its alphabet and a probability 1* τ-*loop to every state, then:* $M \sqsubseteq_w A \Leftrightarrow pfa(M) \sqsubseteq A^\tau$.

We will also need to perform a conversion in the opposite direction, translating an assumption PFA A into a (weak language) equivalent PIOS, which we denote $pios(A)$.

Definition 8 (Assumption-to-PIOS conversion). *Given assumption* $A = (S, \bar{s}, \alpha, \mathbf{P})$, *and action partition* $\alpha = (\biguplus_{i=1}^{m} \alpha^{I,i}) \uplus \alpha^O \uplus \alpha^H$, *its conversion to a PIOS is defined as* $pios(A) = (S', \bar{s}, \alpha, \delta)$, *where* $S' = S \uplus \{s^a | s \in S, a \in \alpha^H \cup \alpha^O\} \uplus \{s^i | s \in S, 1 \leq i \leq m\}$ *and* δ *is constructed as follows. For any transition* $s \xrightarrow{a} s'$, *let* p *denote* $\mathbf{P}(a)[s, s']$ *and* $p^{\max}(s)$ *and* $p_i^{\max}(s)$ *be as defined in Definition 6. Then:*

- *if* $a \in \alpha^O \cup \alpha^H$, *then* $\delta(s, \tau)(s^a) = \frac{p}{p^{\max}(s)}$ *and* $\delta(s^a, a)(s') = p^{\max}(s)$;
- *if* $a \in \alpha^{I,i}$ *(for* $1 \leq i \leq m$*), then* $\delta(s, \tau)(s^i) = \frac{p_i^{\max}(s)}{p^{\max}(s)}$ *and* $\delta(s^i, a)(s') = p \cdot \frac{p^{\max}(s)}{p_i^{\max}(s)}$.

Example 2. Consider PIOS M_1 from Example 1. Fig. 2 shows a valid assumption A for M_1 (i.e. $M_1 \sqsubseteq_w A$) and the corresponding PIOS $pios(A)$. In A, state q_0 has two output actions leading to respective sub-distributions. Thus A is not a PIOS. In $pios(A)$, a τ transition and the states q_0^{ready} and q_0^{fail} (abbreviated to q_0^r and q_0^f) are added.

Now, we describe how to perform compositional verification using our framework. We focus on verifying $\langle G \rangle_{\geq p}$ on a DTMC $M_1 \| M_2$ where M_i are PIOSs. For simplicity, we will assume that the property refers only to input/output actions of M_1 and M_2 and assume that all hidden actions of M_1 and M_2 have been renamed as τ actions, which affects neither the parallel composition $M_1 \| M_2$ nor the probability of satisfying G.

An *assume-guarantee triple* $\langle A \rangle M \langle G \rangle_{\geq p}$ means "whenever component M is part of a system satisfying the assumption A, the system is guaranteed to satisfy $\langle G \rangle_{\geq p}$".

Definition 9 (Assume-guarantee triple). *If* M *is a PIOS with alphabet* α, A *is an assumption about* M *and* $\langle G \rangle_{\geq p}$ *is a probabilistic safety property, then* $\langle A \rangle M \langle G \rangle_{\geq p}$ *is an* assume-guarantee triple, *with the following meaning:*

$$\langle A \rangle M \langle G \rangle_{\geq p} \Leftrightarrow \forall M'. (M' \sqsubseteq_w A \implies M' \| M \models \langle G \rangle_{\geq p}).$$

Using the translation $pios(A)$ from PFA to PIOS described above, checking whether a triple is true reduces to standard probabilistic model checking (see Section 2).

Proposition 2. *For* A, M *and* $\langle G \rangle_{\geq p}$ *as given in Definition 9, the assume-guarantee triple* $\langle A \rangle M \langle G \rangle_{\geq p}$ *holds if and only if* $pios(A) \| M \models \langle G \rangle_{\geq p}$.

Finally, we give an asymmetric assume-guarantee proof rule (in the style of those from [14,13]) for verifying a system $M_1 \| M_2$ compositionally.

Theorem 1. *Let M_1, M_2 be PIOSs, A an assumption for M_1 and $\langle G \rangle_{\geq p}$ a probabilistic safety property for $M_1 \| M_2$. Then the following proof rule holds:*

$$\frac{M_1 \sqsubseteq_w A \quad and \quad \langle A \rangle \, M_2 \, \langle G \rangle_{\geq p}}{M_1 \| M_2 \models \langle G \rangle_{\geq p}} \quad \text{(ASYM-PIOS)}$$

Thus, given an appropriate assumption A about M_1, we can decompose the verification of $M_1 \| M_2$ into two sub-problems: checking weak language inclusion between M_1 and A; and checking that $\langle A \rangle \, M_2 \, \langle G \rangle_{\geq p}$. The former, as shown in Proposition 1, reduces to (strong) language inclusion on PFAs, which we discuss in the next section. The latter, as shown in Proposition 2, requires construction of the DTMC $pios(A) \| M_2$ and then application of standard probabilistic model checking techniques.

Example 3. Consider probabilistic safety property $\langle G \rangle_{\geq 0.9}$, where G means "*fail* never occurs". We can check this on running example $M_1 \| M_2$ using assumption A from Example 2. Since $M_1 \sqsubseteq_w A$, we just need to check that $pios(A) \| M_2 \models \langle G \rangle_{\geq 0.9}$. As $pios(A) \| M_2$ has a single path $(q_0 t_0) \xrightarrow{\tau * init, 0.08} (q_2 t_1) \xrightarrow{fail, 1} (q_4 t_1) \cdots$ containing *fail* with probability 0.08, $\langle G \rangle_{\geq 0.9}$ is satisfied (since $1 - 0.08 \geq 0.9$) and we are done.

Completeness. Our framework is *complete* in the sense that, if $M_1 \| M_2 \models \langle G \rangle_{\geq p}$, we can always find an assumption A to apply Theorem 1 by converting M_1 to a PFA.

4   Deciding Language Inclusion for PFAs

As discussed above, verifying whether a component satisfies an assumption in our framework reduces to checking language inclusion between PFAs, i.e. deciding whether two PFAs A_1 and A_2 over the same alphabet α satisfy $A_1 \sqsubseteq A_2$. In this section, we propose a *semi*-algorithm for performing this check. If $A_1 \sqsubseteq A_2$ does *not* hold, then the algorithm is guaranteed to terminate and return a lexicographically minimal word as a counterexample; but if $A_1 \sqsubseteq A_2$ *does* hold, then the algorithm may not terminate. The latter case is unavoidable since the problem is undecidable (see [8]).

Input: PFAs A_1 and A_2 over the same alphabet α.
Output: true if $A_1 \sqsubseteq A_2$; or **false** and a cex $w' \in \alpha^*$.
1: *queue* := $\{(\iota_1, \iota_2, \varepsilon)\}$, $V := \{(\iota_1, \iota_2, \varepsilon)\}$
2: **while** *queue* $\neq \varnothing$ **do**
3:    remove (v_1, v_2, w) from the head of *queue*
4:    **for all** $a \in \alpha$ **do**
5:       $v'_1 := v_1 P_1(a)$; $v'_2 := v_2 P_2(a)$; $w' := wa$
6:       **if** $v'_1 \kappa_1 > v'_2 \kappa_2$ **then return false** and cex w'
7:       **else if** (v'_1, v'_2, w') does not satisfy (C1), (C2) **then**
8:          add (v'_1, v'_2, w') to the tail of *queue*
9:          $V := V \cup \{(v'_1, v'_2, w')\}$
10: **return true**

Fig. 3. Semi-algorithm for deciding PFA language inclusion

Fig. 3 shows the semi-algorithm to decide if $A_1 \sqsubseteq A_2$, where $A_i = (S_i, \bar{s}_i, \alpha, \mathbf{P}_i)$ for $i = 1, 2$. We also define ι_i and κ_i as in Section 2. Inspired by the language equivalence decision algorithm in [18], our method proceeds by expanding a tree. Each node of the tree is of the form (v_1, v_2, w), where w is a word and $v_i = \iota_i \mathbf{P}_i(w)$ (for $i = 1, 2$) is the vector of probabilities of reaching each state via word w in A_i. Note that $\boldsymbol{v}_i\boldsymbol{\kappa}_i$ is the probability of PFA A_i accepting the word w. The root of the tree is $(\iota_1, \iota_2, \varepsilon)$, where ε is the empty word. As shown in Fig. 3, we use a *queue* of tree nodes, which expands the tree in breadth-first order. In addition, we maintain a set V of non-leaf nodes, which initially only contains the root. The main difference between our method and [18] is that we adopt different criteria to decide when to add a node to the non-leaf set V. In [18], the set V is maintained by calculating the span of vector space. However, for the language inclusion check, we cannot simply use the same criteria.

In each iteration, we remove a node $(\boldsymbol{v}_1, \boldsymbol{v}_2, w)$ from the head of *queue*. We then expand the tree by appending a set of its child nodes $(\boldsymbol{v}_1', \boldsymbol{v}_2', w')$, where $\boldsymbol{v}_1' := \boldsymbol{v}_1\mathbf{P}_1(a)$, $\boldsymbol{v}_2' := \boldsymbol{v}_2\mathbf{P}_2(a)$ and $w' := wa$ for all actions $a \in \alpha$. If there is a node $(\boldsymbol{v}_1', \boldsymbol{v}_2', w')$ such that $Pr_1(w') = \boldsymbol{v}_1'\boldsymbol{\kappa}_1 > \boldsymbol{v}_2'\boldsymbol{\kappa}_2 = Pr_2(w')$, then the algorithm terminates and returns w' as a counterexample for $A_1 \sqsubseteq A_2$. Otherwise, we check if we can *prune* each child node $(\boldsymbol{v}_1', \boldsymbol{v}_2', w')$ (i.e. make it a leaf node) by seeing if it satisfies either of the following two criteria: (C1) $\boldsymbol{v}_1'\boldsymbol{\kappa}_1 = 0$; (C2) There exist $|V|$ non-negative rational numbers ρ^i such that, for all $(\boldsymbol{v}_1^i, \boldsymbol{v}_2^i, w^i) \in V$, $\boldsymbol{v}_1' \leq \sum_{0 \leq i < |V|} \rho^i \boldsymbol{v}_1^i$ and $\boldsymbol{v}_2' \geq \sum_{0 \leq i < |V|} \rho^i \boldsymbol{v}_2^i$, where $\leq$ and $\geq$ denote pointwise comparisons between vectors.

Criterion (C1) is included because it is never possible to find a counterexample word with accepting probability less than $\boldsymbol{v}_1'\boldsymbol{\kappa}_1 = 0$. Criterion (C2) is included because any node satisfying it would guarantee $\boldsymbol{v}_1'\boldsymbol{\kappa}_1 \leq \boldsymbol{v}_2'\boldsymbol{\kappa}_2$; moreover, if the algorithm terminates and a node satisfies (C2), all of its descendants also satisfy (C2). We can thus make it a leaf node. In practice, (C2) can easily be checked using an SMT solver. If a node cannot be pruned, we add it to the tail of *queue* and to the non-leaf set V. The algorithm terminates if *queue* becomes empty, concluding that $A_1 \sqsubseteq A_2$.

Correctness and termination. The correctness of the semi-algorithm in Fig. 3 is shown formally in [8]. A guarantee of termination, on the other hand, cannot be expected due to the undecidability of the underlying problem.

5   L*-Style Learning for PFAs

In this section, we propose a novel method to learn a PFA for a target weighted language generated by an unknown PFA. It works in a similar style to the well-known L* algorithm [2] for learning regular languages: it constructs an *observation table* (of acceptance probabilities for each word) based on two types of *queries* posed to a *teacher*. *Membership queries* ask the probability of accepting a particular word in the target PFA; *equivalence queries* ask whether a hypothesised PFA yields exactly the target language.

Fig. 4 shows the learning algorithm. It builds an observation table (P, E, T), where P is a finite, non-empty, prefix-closed set of words, E is a finite, non-empty, suffix-closed set of words and $T : ((P \cup P\cdot\alpha) \cdot E) \to [0, 1]$ maps each word to its accepting probability in the target language ($\cdot$ denotes concatenation over sets). The rows of table (P, E, T) are labelled by elements in the prefix set $P \cup P\cdot\alpha$ and the columns are labelled by elements in the suffix set E. The value $T(u\cdot e)$ of the entry at row u and column e is the acceptance probability of the word $u\cdot e$. We use $row(u)$ to represent the $|E|$-dimensional row vector in the table labelled by the prefix $u \in (P \cup P\cdot\alpha)$.

Input: The alphabet α of a target weighted language generated by an unknown PFA.
Output: A PFA accepting the target language.
 1: initialise the observation table (P, E, T), letting $P = E = \{\varepsilon\}$, where ε is the empty word
 2: fill T by asking membership queries for ε and each action $a \in \alpha$
 3: **while** (P, E, T) is not *closed* or not *consistent* **do**
 4:     **if** (P, E, T) is not *closed* **then** find $u \in P, a \in \alpha$ that make (P, E, T) not closed
 5:         add $u \cdot a$ to P, and extend T to $(P \cup P \cdot \alpha) \cdot E$ using membership queries
 6:     **if** (P, E, T) is not *consistent* **then** find $a \in \alpha, e \in E$ that make (P, E, T) not consistent
 7:         add $a \cdot e$ to E, and extend T to $(P \cup P \cdot \alpha) \cdot E$ using membership queries
 8: construct a hypothesised PFA A and ask an equivalence query
 9: **if** answer = no, with a counterexample c **then** add c and all its prefixes to P
10:     extend T to $(P \cup P \cdot \alpha) \cdot E$ using membership queries, **goto** Line 4
11: **else return** PFA A

Fig. 4. L*-style learning algorithm for PFAs

Inspired by [4], which gives an L*-style algorithm for learning multiplicity automata, we define the notions of *closed* and *consistent* observation tables by establishing linear dependencies between row vectors. Observation table (P, E, T) is *closed* if, for all $u \in P$ and $a \in \alpha$, there exist non-negative rational coefficients ϕ_i such that $row(u \cdot a) = \sum_{u_i \in P} \phi_i row(u_i)$ and *consistent* if, for any rational coefficients ψ_i, $\forall e \in E. \sum_{u_i \in P} \psi_i T(u_i \cdot e) = 0$ implies $\forall a \in \alpha, e \in E. \sum_{u_i \in P} \psi_i T(u_i \cdot a \cdot e) = 0$. The need for coefficients to be non-negative (for *closed*) is a stronger condition than in [4].

As shown in Fig. 4, the observation table is filled with the results of membership queries until it is both closed and consistent. At each step, if (P, E, T) is not closed (resp. consistent), then the algorithm finds $u \in P, a \in \alpha$ (resp. $a \in \alpha, e \in E$) that make it not closed (resp. consistent), according to the definitions above, and adds $u.a$ (resp. $a.e$) to the table. When (P, E, T) is closed and consistent, the learning algorithm builds a hypothesis PFA A (see below) and poses an equivalence query. If the teacher answers "no" (that A does not yield the target language), a counterexample $c \in \alpha^*$ is given, for which $Pr^A(c)$ is incorrect. The algorithm adds c and all its prefixes to P, updates the observation table and continues to check if the table is closed and consistent. If the teacher answers "yes", the algorithm terminates and returns A.

Construction of a hypothesis PFA $A = (S, \bar{s}, \alpha, \mathbf{P})$, from a closed and consistent table (P, E, T), proceeds as follows. First, we find a subset of P, denoted $con(P)$, such that every element of $\{row(u)|u \in P\}$ can be represented as a *conical combination* of elements in $\{row(v)|v \in con(P)\}$, i.e. there are non-negative rational coefficients λ_i such that, for all $u \in P$, $row(u) = \sum_{v_i \in con(P)} \lambda_i row(v_i)$. The set of states in the PFA is then $S = \{s_0, \ldots, s_{n-1}\}$, where each state s_i corresponds to a row vector in $\{row(v)|v \in con(P)\}$ and the initial state $\bar{s}$ corresponds to $row(\varepsilon)$. To obtain $\mathbf{P}(a)$ for each $a \in \alpha$, we compute, for $s_i \in S$, rational coefficients γ_j such that $row(s_i \cdot a) = \sum_{s_j \in S} \gamma_j row(s_j)$ and then define $\mathbf{P}(a)[s_i, s_j] := \gamma_j \cdot (T(s_j \cdot \varepsilon)/T(s_i \cdot \varepsilon))$.

Correctness and termination. When the learning algorithm terminates, it returns a correct PFA, as guaranteed by the equivalence query check. Unfortunately, we cannot prove the termination of our method. For L*, the corresponding proof uses the existence

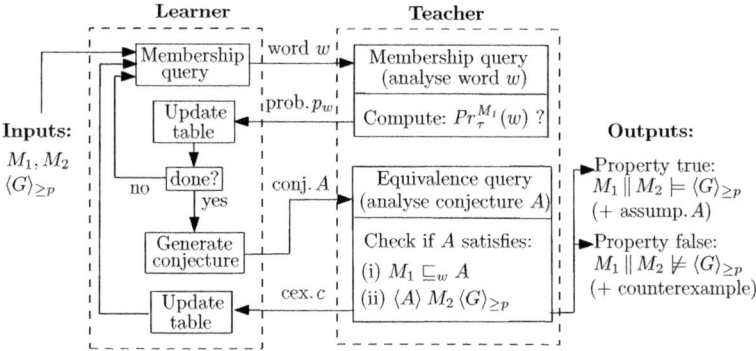

Fig. 5. L*-style PFA learning loop for probabilistic assumption generation

of a unique minimal DFA for a regular language. However, an analogous property does not exist for weighted languages and PFAs. According to [4], the smallest multiplicity automaton *can* be learnt given a weighted language. However, as shown in [6], converting a multiplicity automaton to a PFA (even for the subclass that define stochastic languages) is not always possible.

6   Learning Assumptions for Compositional Verification

Finally, we build upon the techniques introduced in Sections 4 and 5 to produce a fully-automated implementation of the assume-guarantee framework proposed in Section 3. In particular, we use PFA learning to automatically generate assumptions to perform compositional verification. Fig. 5 summarises the overall structure of our approach, which aims to verify (or refute) $M_1 \parallel M_2 \models \langle G \rangle_{\geqslant p}$ for two PIOSs M_1, M_2 and a probabilistic safety property $\langle G \rangle_{\geqslant p}$. This is done using proof rule (ASYM-PIOS) from Section 3, with the required assumption PFA A about component M_1 being generated through learning. The left-hand side of the figure shows the learning algorithm of Section 5, which drives the whole process; the right-hand side shows the teacher.

The teacher answers *membership queries* (about word w) by computing the probability $Pr_\tau^{M_1}(w)$ of word w in M_1. It answers *equivalence queries* (about conjectured PFA A) by checking if A satisfies both premises of rule (ASYM-PIOS): (i) $M_1 \sqsubseteq_w A$, and (ii) $\langle A \rangle M_2 \langle G \rangle_{\geqslant p}$. The first is done using Proposition 1 and the algorithm in Section 4. The second is done using Proposition 2, which reduces to probabilistic model checking of the DTMC $pios(A) \parallel M_2$.

If both premises are true, we can conclude that $M_1 \parallel M_2 \models \langle G \rangle_{\geqslant p}$ holds. Otherwise, the teacher needs to provide a counterexample c for the learning algorithm to update the observation table and proceed. If premise (i) failed, then c is taken as the word showing the violation of (weak) language inclusion. If premise (ii) failed, we try to extract c from the results of model checking. We extract a *probabilistic counterexample* [11] C: a set of paths showing $pios(A) \parallel M_2 \not\models \langle G \rangle_{\geqslant p}$. Following the same approach as [9], we transform C into a (small) fragment of M_1 (denoted M_1^C) and check whether $M_1^C \parallel M_2 \not\models \langle G \rangle_{\geqslant p}$. If so, we stop the learning loop, concluding that $M_1 \parallel M_2 \not\models \langle G \rangle_{\geqslant p}$. If, on the other hand, C is a *spurious counterexample*, we can always extract, from C

a counterexample (word) c such that the learning algorithm can update its observation table. Full details can be found in the extended version of this paper [8].

From the arguments above, we can show that, when the learning loop terminates, it always yields a correct result. It should be pointed out, though, that since the loop is driven by the learning algorithm of Section 5, whose termination we cannot prove, we are also unable to guarantee that the loop finishes. Furthermore, weak language inclusion checks use the semi-algorithm of Section 4, which is not guaranteed to terminate.

7   Implementation and Results

We have implemented the PFA language inclusion check from Section 4, the PFA learning algorithm from Section 5 and the assumption-generation loop described in Section 6. Based on these, we have built a prototype tool that performs fully-automated assume-guarantee verification, as described in Section 3. Due to space limitations, we refer the reader to [8] for further details of this implementation, as well as experimental results from its application to several benchmark case studies.

Acknowledgments. The authors are supported by ERC Advanced Grant VERIWARE, EU FP7 project CONNECT and EPSRC grant EP/F001096/1. We also thank Taolue Chen, Stefan Kiefer, Björn Wachter and James Worrell for insightful discussions.

References

1. de Alfaro, L., Henzinger, T., Jhala, R.: Compositional methods for probabilistic systems. In: Larsen, K.G., Nielsen, M. (eds.) CONCUR 2001. LNCS, vol. 2154, p. 351. Springer, Heidelberg (2001)
2. Angluin, D.: Learning regular sets from queries and counterexamples. Information and Computation 75(2), 87–106 (1987)
3. Baier, C., Katoen, J.P.: Principles of Model Checking. MIT Press, Cambridge (2008)
4. Bergadano, F., Varricchio, S.: Learning behaviors of automata from multiplicity and equivalence queries. SIAM J. Comput. 25(6), 1268–1280 (1996)
5. Blondel, V., Canterini, V.: Undecidable problems for probabilistic automata of fixed dimension. Theory of Computing Systems 36, 231–245 (2001)
6. Denis, F., Esposito, Y.: Learning classes of probabilistic automata. In: Shawe-Taylor, J., Singer, Y. (eds.) COLT 2004. LNCS (LNAI), vol. 3120, pp. 124–139. Springer, Heidelberg (2004)
7. Doyen, L., Henzinger, T.A., Raskin, J.F.: Equivalence of labeled Markov chains. Int. J. Found. Comput. Sci. 19(3), 549–563 (2008)
8. Feng, L., Han, T., Kwiatkowska, M., Parker, D.: Learning-based compositional verification for synchronous probabilistic systems. Tech. Rep. RR-11-05, Department of Computer Science, University of Oxford (2011)
9. Feng, L., Kwiatkowska, M., Parker, D.: Compositional verification of probabilistic systems using learning. In: Proc. QEST 2010, pp. 133–142. IEEE CS Press, Los Alamitos (2010)
10. Forejt, V., Kwiatkowska, M., Norman, G., Parker, D., Qu, H.: Quantitative multi-objective verification for probabilistic systems. In: Abdulla, P.A., Leino, K.R.M. (eds.) TACAS 2011. LNCS, vol. 6605, pp. 112–127. Springer, Heidelberg (2011)
11. Han, T., Katoen, J.P., Damman, B.: Counterexample generation in probabilistic model checking. IEEE Trans. Software Eng. 35(2), 241–257 (2009)

12. de la Higuera, C., Oncina, J.: Learning stochastic finite automata. In: Paliouras, G., Sakak-ibara, Y. (eds.) ICGI 2004. LNCS (LNAI), vol. 3264, pp. 175–186. Springer, Heidelberg (2004)
13. Kwiatkowska, M., Norman, G., Parker, D., Qu, H.: Assume-guarantee verification for probabilistic systems. In: Esparza, J., Majumdar, R. (eds.) TACAS 2010. LNCS, vol. 6015, pp. 23–37. Springer, Heidelberg (2010)
14. Pasareanu, C., Giannakopoulou, D., Bobaru, M., Cobleigh, J., Barringer, H.: Learning to divide and conquer: Applying the L* algorithm to automate assume-guarantee reasoning. Formal Methods in System Design 32(3), 175–205 (2008)
15. Rabin, M.: Probabilistic automata. Information and Control 6, 230–245 (1963)
16. Segala, R.: Modelling and Verification of Randomized Distributed Real Time Systems. Ph.D. thesis, Massachusetts Institute of Technology (1995)
17. Tzeng, W.G.: Learning probabilistic automata and Markov chains via queries. Mach. Learn. 8, 151–166 (1992)
18. Tzeng, W.G.: A polynomial-time algorithm for the equivalence of probabilistic automata. SIAM J. Comput. 21(2), 216–227 (1992)

An Algorithmic Framework for Synthesis of Concurrent Programs

E. Allen Emerson and Roopsha Samanta

Dept. of Computer Science and Computer Engineering Research Centre,
University of Texas, Austin, TX 78712, USA
{emerson,roopsha}@cs.utexas.edu

Abstract. We present a framework that takes unsynchronized sequential processes along with a temporal specification of their global concurrent behaviour, and automatically generates a concurrent program with synchronization code ensuring correct global behaviour. The synthesized synchronization code is based on monitors with `wait` and `notify` operations on condition variables, and mutual-exclusion locks. Novel aspects of our framework include realistic low-level synchronization implementations, synthesis of both simple coarse-grained synchronization and more complex fine-grained synchronization, and accommodation of both safety and liveness in global correctness properties. The method is fully automatic as well as sound and complete.

1 Introduction

We postulate design and employment of automated synthesis engines for the most precarious component of a concurrent program - the synchronization code. Given unsynchronized *skeletons* of sequential processes $P_1, \ldots, P_n$, and a temporal specification ϕ of their global concurrent behaviour, our framework *automatically* generates synchronized skeletons, $\overline{P}_1, \ldots, \overline{P}_n$, such that the resulting concurrent program $\overline{P}_1 \mathbin{/\mkern-5mu/} \ldots \mathbin{/\mkern-5mu/} \overline{P}_n$ is guaranteed to exhibit the desired behaviour. This is effected in two steps. The first step involves computer-aided construction of a model $\mathcal{M}$ for the specified behaviour of the concurrent program based on $P_1, \ldots, P_n$, and extraction of *synchronization skeletons* $P_1^s, \ldots, P_n^s$, with high-level synchronization actions (guarded commands), such that $P_1^s \mathbin{/\mkern-5mu/} \ldots \mathbin{/\mkern-5mu/} P_n^s \models \phi$. The second step comprises a correctness-preserving mechanical compilation of the high-level synchronization actions into synchronization code based on lower-level primitives such as monitors and mutual-exclusion (mutex) locks.

The first step in our framework could be completed by manually constructing a high-level solution, and then verifying its correctness using a model checker (cf. [15]). However, the lack of automation in constructing the high-level solution is a potentially serious drawback as it may necessitate multiple iterations of manual (re-)design, verification, and manual debugging and correction. We propose a substantial improvement to this approach that results in a fully algorithmic framework. By specifying the system temporally, we can apply the method of [7,6] to algorithmically synthesize the high-level solution guaranteed to meet the

T. Bultan and P.-A. Hsiung (Eds.): ATVA 2011, LNCS 6996, pp. 522–530, 2011.

temporal specification. We alleviate the user's burden of specification-writing by automatically inferring local temporal constraints, describing process behaviour, from a state-machine based representation of the unsynchronized processes.

We provide the ability to synthesize coarse-grained synchronization code with a single monitor (and no mutex locks), or fine-grained synchronization code with multiple monitors and mutex locks. It is up to the user to choose an appropriate granularity of atomicity that suitably balances the trade-off between concurrency and overhead for a particular application/system architecture. This is an important feature of our framework as programmers often restrict themselves to using coarse-grained synchronization for its inherent simplicity. In fact, manual implementations of synchronization code using `wait`/`notify` operations on condition variables are particularly hard to get right in the presence of multiple locks. We establish the correctness of both translations - guarded commands to coarse-grained synchronization and guarded commands to fine-grained synchronization - with respect to typical concurrency properties that include both safety properties (e.g., mutual exclusion) and liveness properties (e.g., starvation-freedom).

We further establish soundness and completeness of the overall proposed methodology. Thus, our generated concurrent programs are *correct-by-construction*, with no further verification effort required. Moreover, if the specification as a whole is consistent, a correct concurrent program will be generated. We have developed a tool for the compilation of synchronization skeletons into concurrent Java programs with both coarse-grained and fine-grained synchronization. We used the tool successfully to synthesize synchronization code for an airport ground traffic simulator program, and some well-known synchronization problems such as readers-writers and dining philosophers. We emphasize that the synchronization code generated by our framework can be translated into programs written using PThreads or in C# as well.

The most important contribution of our work is the combination of an algorithmic front end for synthesizing a high-level synchronization solution, with an algorithmic back end that yields a readily-implementable low-level synchronization solution. We use the CTL-based decision procedure from [7,6] because it is handy and available. But an algorithmic front end could be supplied in many alternative ways; for instance, any linear temporal logic (LTL) decision procedure could be used. Other novel ingredients of our fully algorithmic framework include provably correct translations of high-level to low-level synchronization, synthesis of both coarse-grained and fine-grained solutions, and accommodation of both safety and liveness in global correctness properties. Moreover, our method is sound and complete.

The paper is structured as follows. We explain our algorithmic framework using an example concurrent program in Sec. 2. We discuss extensions and experimental results in Sec. 3 and conclude with a review of related work in Sec. 4.

2 Algorithmic Framework

In this section, we present an overview of our approach for concurrent programs based on two processes, using a single-reader-single-writer (RW) example. We

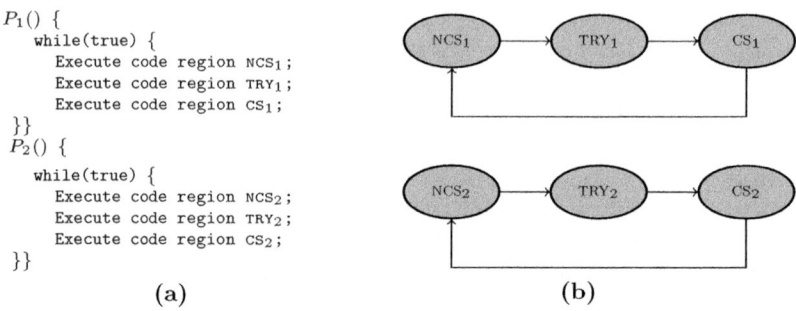

```
P₁() {
    while(true) {
        Execute code region NCS₁;
        Execute code region TRY₁;
        Execute code region CS₁;
}}
P₂() {
    while(true) {
        Execute code region NCS₂;
        Execute code region TRY₂;
        Execute code region CS₂;
}}
```

(a)   (b)

Fig. 1. Synchronization-free skeletons of two processes: reader P_1 and writer P_2

Table 1. Specification of synchronization for single-reader-single-writer problem

Mutual exclusion: $AG(\neg(CS_1 \wedge CS_2))$.
Absence of starvation for reader P_1, provided writer P_2 remains in its non-critical region: $AG(TRY_1 \Rightarrow AF(CS_1 \vee \neg NCS_2))$.
Absence of starvation for writer: $AG(TRY_2 \Rightarrow AF\, CS_2)$.
Priority of writer over reader for outstanding requests to enter the critical region: $AG((TRY_1 \wedge TRY_2) \Rightarrow A[TRY_1\ U\ CS_2])$.

refer the reader to [8] for a more detailed treatment of our formal framework and algorithms.

We assume that we are given the synchronization-free skeletons of sequential processes P_1 and P_2 and a temporal specification ϕ of their desired global behaviour. The synchronization-free skeletons of the reader process P_1 and the writer process P_2 are as shown in Fig. 1a. Both processes have three *code regions* - 'non-critical' (NCS), 'trying' (TRY) and 'critical' (CS); the control-flow between these code regions can be encoded as state-machines, as shown in Fig. 1b. Each code region may represent a *terminating* sequential block of code, which is irrelevant for the synthesis of synchronization, and hence suppressed within a single state. The set of properties that the concurrent program composed of P_1 and P_2 must guarantee are shown in Table 1. It is easy to see that in the absence of synchronization $P_1 \parallel P_2 \not\models \phi$, where ϕ represents the conjunction of the properties in Table 1. Our goal is to modify P_1 and P_2 by inserting synchronization code, to obtain $\overline{P}_1$ and $\overline{P}_2$, such that $\overline{P}_1 \parallel \overline{P}_2 \models \phi$.

We propose an automated framework to do this in two steps. The first step entails computer-aided construction of a high-level solution with synchronization actions based on guarded commands. The second step comprises a correctness-preserving, mechanical translation into a low-level solution based on monitors (along with `wait` and `notify` operations on condition variables) and mutex locks.

For the first step, we mechanically translate the state-machine representations of P_1 and P_2 into equivalent CTL formulae. We then use the methodology presented in [7] to: (1) synthesize a global model $\mathcal{M}$ for the specified behaviour of the concurrent program based on P_1 and P_2, such that $\mathcal{M} \models \phi$, and (2) derive

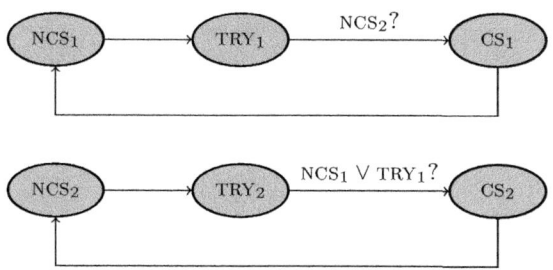

Fig. 2. Synchronization skeletons P_1^s and P_2^s for reader P_1 and writer P_2

the synchronization skeletons, P_1^s and P_2^s (see Fig. 2) from $\mathcal{M}$. We refer the interested reader to [8,7] for details about the synthesis of $\mathcal{M}$ and P_1^s, P_2^s. For our current purpose, it suffices to note that each transition between two sequential code regions in the synchronization skeleton of a process is labeled with a guarded command of the form $G? \rightarrow A$, consisting of an enabling condition G, evaluated atomically, and a corresponding set of actions A to be performed atomically if G evaluates to *true*. A guard is a predicate on the current state (code region) of all processes and the values of shared synchronization variables, $x_1, \ldots, x_m$ (this tuple is often denoted as $\bar{x}$), which may be introduced during the synthesis of $\mathcal{M}$. An action is a parallel assignment statement that updates the values of the $\bar{x}$ variables. All guards with the same action are merged into one transition label. An omitted guard is interpreted as *true* in general. In the RW example (Fig. 2), there are no actions as no $\bar{x}$ variables were introduced during the synthesis of $\mathcal{M}$.

In the second step of our approach, we mechanically compile the guarded commands of P_1^s and P_2^s into either coarse-grained or fine-grained synchronization code for P_1 and P_2, as desired. The resulting processes are denoted as P_1^c, P_2^c (coarse-grained) or P_1^f, P_2^f (fine-grained). In both cases, we introduce Boolean shared variables, ncs_1, try_2 etc., to represent the code regions NCS_1, TRY_2 etc., of each sequential process. We also introduce mutex locks and monitors along with conditions variables for synchronization. For the program $P_1^c \mathbin{/\!/} P_2^c$, which has a coarser level of lock granularity, we declare a single lock l for controlling access to shared variables and condition variables. For the program $P_1^f \mathbin{/\!/} P_2^f$ with a finer level of lock granularity, we allow more concurrency by declaring separate mutex locks l_{ncs_1}, l_{try_2} etc., for controlling access to each Boolean shared variable ncs_1, try_2 etc. (and each shared synchronization variable, when necessary). We further define separate monitor locks $l_{cv_{cs_1}}$, $l_{cv_{cs_2}}$ for the condition variables cv_{cs_1}, cv_{cs_2} to allow simultaneous processing of different condition variables.

The modifications to each process are restricted to insertion of *synchronization regions* between the sequential code regions of the process. We refer the reader to Fig. 3a for an example coarse-grained synchronization region (between code regions TRY_1 and CS_1 in P_1). Note that we find it convenient to express locks, as $\text{lock(1)}\{\ldots\}$ (in a manner similar to Java's synchronized keyword), wherein

```
Execute TRY₁;
/* Synch. region */
lock(l) {
   while (!ncs₂)
      wait(cv_cs₁,l);
   try₁,cs₁ := 0,1;
}
Execute CS₁;
```

(a) Coarse-grained

```
Execute TRY₁;
/* Synch. region */
lock(l_cv_cs₁) {
   while (!Guard_cs₁())
      wait(cv_cs₁,l_cv_cs₁);
}
Execute CS₁;
```

```
boolean Guard_cs₁() {
   lock((l_try₁,l_cs₁,l_ncs₂) {
      if (ncs₂) {
         try₁,cs₁ := 0,1;
         return(true);
      }
      else return(false);
}}
```

(b) Fine-grained

Fig. 3. Coarse and fine-grained synchronization regions between code regions TRY₁ and CS₁ of reader process P_1

l is a lock variable, '{' denotes *lock acquisition* and '}' denotes *lock release*. The implementation of a coarse-grained synchronization region for the RW example involves acquiring the monitor lock l and checking, within the monitor, if the guard G (ncs_2 in Fig. 3a) for entering the next code region is enabled. While the guard is *false*, P_1^c waits for P_2^c to be in an enabling code region. This is implemented by associating a condition variable cv (cv_{cs_1} in Fig. 3a) with the guard for the next code region. Thus while G is *false*, P_1^c *waits* till P_2^c *notifies* it that G could be *true*. If the guard G is *true*, P_1^c updates the values of (the $\bar{x}$ variables, when present, and) the shared Boolean variables in parallel to indicate that it is effectively in the next code region and releases the monitor lock. Before the lock release, P_1^c, in general, sends a notification signal corresponding to every guard (i.e. condition variable) of P_2^c which may be changed to *true* by P_1^c's shared variables update - there is no such notification in Fig. 3a as the update does not change any guard of P_2^c to *true*. If the guard for a code region is always *true*, e.g., code region TRY₁, then we do not need to check its guard, and hence, do not need a condition variable corresponding to the guard of the code region.

While fine-grained locking can typically be achieved by careful definition and nesting of multiple locks, one needs to be especially cautious in the presence of monitor locks for various reasons. For instance, upon execution of wait(cv,l) in a nested locking scheme, a process only releases the lock l before going to sleep, while still holding all outer locks. This can potentially lead to a deadlock. A fine-grained synchronization region synthesized in our approach (see Fig. 3b for an example fine-grained synchronization region preceding code region CS₁ in P_1), circumvents these issues by utilizing a separate subroutine to evaluate the guard G. In this subroutine, P_1^f first acquires all *necessary* mutex locks, corresponding to all shared variables accessed in the subroutine. These locks are acquired in a strictly nested fashion in a predecided fixed order to prevent deadlocks. We use lock($l_1, l_2, \ldots$){...} to denote the nested locks lock(l_1){ lock(l_2){ ...}}, with l_1 being the outermost lock variable. The subroutine then evaluates G and returns its value to the main body of P_1^f. If found *true*, the subroutine also performs an appropriate parallel update to the shared variables similar to the coarse-grained case. The synchronization region in the main body of P_1^f acquires the relevant monitor lock ($l_{cv_{cs_1}}$ in Fig. 3b) and calls its guard-computing subroutine within a `while` loop till it returns *true*, after which it releases the monitor lock. If the subroutine returns *false*, the process waits on the associated condition variable (cv_{cs_1} in Fig. 3b). Each notification signal for a condition variable, on which the other process may be waiting, is sent out by acquiring the corresponding monitor lock.

2.1   Correctness of Synthesis

Let $\mathcal{M}^c$ and $\mathcal{M}^f$, be the global models corresponding to $P_1^c \parallel P_2^c$ and $P_1^f \parallel P_2^f$, respectively. We have the following *Correspondence Lemmas*:

Lemma 1. *[Coarse-grained Correspondence] Given an $ACTL \setminus X$ formula ϕ, $\mathcal{M} \models \phi \Rightarrow \mathcal{M}^c \models \phi$.*

Lemma 2. *[Fine-grained Correspondence] Given an $ACTL \setminus X$ formula ϕ, $\mathcal{M} \models \phi \Rightarrow \mathcal{M}^f \models \phi$.*

The proofs are based on establishing *stuttering simulations* between the models (cf. [8][1]). Note that the models are not stuttering bisimilar, and hence our compilations do not preserve arbitrary $CTL \setminus X$ properties. This is not a problem, as most global concurrency properties of interest (see Table 1) are expressible in $ACTL \setminus X$.

Theorem 1. *[Soundness]: Given unsynchronized skeletons P_1, P_2, and an $ACTL \setminus X$ formula ϕ, if our method generates P_1^c, P_2^c (resp., P_1^f, P_2^f), then $P_1^c \parallel P_2^c \models \phi$ (resp., $P_1^f \parallel P_2^f \models \phi$).*

Theorem 2. *[Completeness]: Given unsynchronized skeletons P_1, P_2, and an $ACTL \setminus X$ formula ϕ, if the temporal specifications describing P_1, P_2 and their global behaviour ϕ are consistent as a whole, then our method constructs P_1^c, P_2^c (resp., P_1^f, P_2^f) such that $P_1^c \parallel P_2^c \models \phi$(resp., $P_1^f \parallel P_2^f \models \phi$).*

The soundness follows directly from the soundness of the synthesis of synchronization skeletons [7,6], and from the above Correspondence Lemmas. The completeness follows from the completeness of the synthesis of synchronization skeletons for overall consistent specifications and from the completeness of the compilation of guarded commands to coarse-grained and fine-grained synchronization.

3   Extensions and Experiments

The synthesis of synchronization skeletons in the first step in our framework can be extended directly to handle an arbitrary number n of sequential processes.

---

[1] While we choose to restrict our attention to the preservation of $ACTL \setminus X$ formulas here, we can show that the translations from $\mathcal{M}$ to $\mathcal{M}^c$ and $\mathcal{M}^f$ actually preserve all $ACTL^* \setminus X$ properties, as well as CTL^* properties of the form Ah or Eh, where h is an $LTL \setminus X$ formula.

While the direct extension based on [7] can be exponential in the length of ϕ and in n, the decision procedure in [6], corresponding to the subset of CTL used in this paper, is polynomial in the length of ϕ. Moreover, we can use the approaches of [2,1] which avoid building the entire global model (exponential in n), and instead compose interacting process pairs to synthesize the synchronization skeletons. The compilation of guarded commands into coarse-grained and fine-grained synchronization code can be extended in a straight-forward manner to $n > 2$ processes. We emphasize that this compilation acts on individual skeletons directly, without construction or manipulation of the global model, and hence circumvents the state-explosion problem for arbitrary n.

We have implemented a prototype synthesis tool [8] in Perl, which automatically compiles synchronization skeletons into concurrent Java programs based on both coarse-grained and fine-grained synchronization. We used the tool successfully to synthesize synchronization code for an example airport ground traffic simulator (AGTS) program (cf. [8]), and for several configurations of n-process mutual exclusion, readers-writers, dining philosophers, etc..

Table 2. Experimental Results

Program	Granularity	Norm. Run. Time
2-plane AGTS	Coarse	1
	Fine	0.92
1-Reader, 1-Writer	Coarse	1
	Fine	0.79
2-process Mutex	Coarse	1
	Fine	1.08
2-Readers, 3-Writers	Coarse	1
	Fine	1.14

Our experiments were run on a quad-core 3.4GHz machine with 4GB of RAM. The time taken by the tool to generate these small examples was a few milliseconds. We present the normalized running times of some of the generated examples in Table 2. As expected, the fine-grained synchronization version does not always outperform the coarse-grained synchronization version. In particular, it suffers in the 2-Readers, 3-Writers example due to excessive locking overhead.

4 Concluding Remarks

Our framework for concurrent program synthesis: (a) caters for both safety and liveness, (b) is fully algorithmic, (c) constructs a high-level synchronization solution, (c) yields a low level solution based on widely used synchronization primitives, (d) can generate both coarse-grained and fine-grained low-level solutions, and (e) is provably sound and complete.

Early work on synthesis of high-level concurrent programs from temporal specifications [7] utilized decision procedures but had little practical impact due to unrealistic synchronization primitives. Other work inferring high level synchronization using guarded commands [13] or atomic sections [14], is limited to safety specifications. Moreover, it can be shown that such synthesis methods that rely on pruning a global product graph [10,13,14] cannot work in general for liveness.

On the other end of the spectrum, the important papers [5,15] describe a needed mapping of a high-level system into a low-level, coarse-grained system, akin to ours. But these frameworks are less flexible. They do not yield low-level fine-grained solutions; they do not treat liveness properties; and, because they are not fully algorithmic, they fail to ensure correctness-by-design. Instead, these papers are verification-driven, and involve verifying either the synthesized implementation [5] or the manually-written high-level implementation [15]. In contrast, our approach is the first to provably translate a high-level system into correct low-level systems for both coarse- and fine-grained solutions, thereby eliminating the need for verification. The low-level global models are guaranteed correct by our Correspondence Lemmas.

Among papers that do address refinement of locking granularity, are [3], which translates guarded commands, into synchronization based on atomic reads and atomic writes, and papers on compiler-based lock inference for atomic sections ([9], [4] etc.). Unlike in [3], our framework does not manipulate or generate the global model corresponding to either the coarse-grained or fine-grained solutions. The lock-inference papers [9], [4] rely on the availability of high-level synchronization in the form of atomic sections, and do not, in general, support monitors and condition variables. Sketching [12], a search-based program synthesis technique, is also a verification-driven approach, which can be used to synthesize optimized implementations of synchronization primitives, e.g. barriers, from partial program sketches.

We remark that these approaches and ours are oriented towards closed systems[2], which include classical synchronization problems and have been used to capture many real-world software systems.

References

1. Attie, P.C.: Synthesis of Large Concurrent Programs via Pairwise Composition. In: Proceedings of Conference on Concurrency Theory (CONCUR), pp. 130–145. ACM, New York (1999)
2. Attie, P.C., Emerson, E.A.: Synthesis of Concurrent Systems with Many Similar Sequential Processes. In: Proceedings of Principles of Programming Languages (POPL), pp. 191–201. ACM, New York (1989)
3. Attie, P.C., Emerson, E.A.: Synthesis of Concurrent Systems for an Atomic Read/Atomic Write Model of Computation. In: Proceedings of Principles of Distributed Computing (PODC), pp. 111–120. ACM, New York (1996)
4. Cherem, S., Chilimbi, T., Gulwani, S.: Inferring Locks for Atomic Sections. In: Proceedings of Programming Language Design and Implementation (PLDI), pp. 304–315. ACM, New York (2008)
5. Deng, X., Dwyer, M.B., Hatcliff, J., Mizuno, M.: Invariant-based Specification, Synthesis, and Verification of Synchronization in Concurrent Programs. In: Proceedings of International Conference on Software Engineering (ICSE), pp. 442–452. ACM, New York (2001)
6. Emerson, E.A., Sadler, T., Srinivasan, J.: Effcient Temporal Reasoning. In: Proceedings of Principles of Programming Languages (POPL), pp. 166–178. ACM, New York (1989)

---

[2] In contrast, another active thread of foundational research [11] investigates synthesis of open systems.

7. Emerson, E.A., Clarke, E.M.: Using Branching Time Temporal Logic to Synthesize Synchronization Skeletons. Sci. Comput. Program. 2(3), 241–266 (1982)
8. Emerson, E.A., Samanta, R.: An Algorithmic Framework for Synthesis of Concurrent Programs, http://www.cerc.utexas.edu/~roopsha/synthsync.html
9. Emmi, M., Fishcher, J.S., Jhala, R., Majumdar, R.: Lock Allocation. In: Proceedings of Principles of Programming Languages (POPL), pp. 291–296 (2007)
10. Janjua, M.U., Mycroft, A.: Automatic Correction to Safety Violations in Programs. In: Proceedings of Thread Verification (2006)
11. Pnueli, A., Rosner, R.: On the Synthesis of a Reactive Module. In: Proceedings of Principles of Programming Languages (POPL), pp. 179–190. ACM, New York (1989)
12. Solar-Lezama, A., Rabbah, R., Bodik, R., Ebcioglu, K.: Programming by Sketching for Bit-streaming Programs. In: Proceedings of Programming Language Design and Implementation (PLDI), pp. 281–294. ACM, New York (2005)
13. Vechev, M.T., Yahav, E., Yorsh, G.: Inferring Synchronization under Limited Observability. In: Kowalewski, S., Philippou, A. (eds.) TACAS 2009. LNCS, vol. 5505, pp. 139–154. Springer, Heidelberg (2009)
14. Vechev, M.T., Yahav, E., Yorsh, G.: Abstraction-Guided Synthesis Of Synchronization. In: Proceedings of Principles of Programming Languages (POPL), pp. 327–388 (2010)
15. Yavuz-Kahveci, T., Bultan, T.: Specification, Verification, and Synthesis of Concurrency Control Components. In: Proceedings of International Symposium on Software Testing and Analysis (ISSTA), pp. 169–179. ACM, New York (2002)

Author Index